Table of Equations and Formulas (*continued*)

Volume and Surface Area of a Right Circular Cylinder

$$V = \pi r^2 h$$
$$SA = 2\pi r^2 + 2\pi rh$$

Volume and Surface Area of a Right Circular Cone

$$V = \frac{1}{3}\pi r^2 h$$
$$SA = \pi r^2 + \pi rl$$

Volume and Surface Area of a Sphere

$$V = \frac{4}{3}\pi r^3$$
$$SA = 4\pi r^2$$

Table of Measurement Abbreviations

U.S. Customary System

Length		Capacity		Weight		Area	
in.	inches	oz	fluid ounces	oz	ounces	in^2	square inches
ft	feet	c	cups	lb	pounds	ft^2	square feet
yd	yards	qt	quarts				
mi	miles	gal	gallons				

Metric System

Length		Capacity		Weight/Mass		Area	
mm	millimeters (0.001 m)	ml	milliliters (0.001 L)	mg	milligrams (0.001 g)	cm^2	square centimeters
cm	centimeters (0.01 m)	cl	centiliters (0.01 L)	cg	centigrams (0.01 g)		
dm	decimeters (0.1 m)	dl	deciliters (0.1 L)	dg	decigrams (0.1 g)	m^2	square meters
m	meters	L	liters	g	grams		
dam	decameters (10 m)	dal	decaliters (10 L)	dag	decagrams (10 g)		
hm	hectometers (100 m)	hl	hectoliters (100 L)	hg	hectograms (100 g)		
km	kilometers (1000 m)	kl	kiloliters (1000 L)	kg	kilograms (1000 g)		

Time

h	hours	min	minutes	s	seconds

INSTRUCTOR'S ANNOTATED EDITION

Beginning Algebra

with Applications

Fifth Edition

Richard N. Aufmann
Palomar College, California

Vernon C. Barker
Palomar College, California

Joanne S. Lockwood
Plymouth State College, New Hampshire

HOUGHTON MIFFLIN COMPANY   Boston   Toronto

Sponsoring Editor: Maureen O'Connor
Senior Associate Editor: Dawn M. Nuttall
Editorial Assistant: Amanda Bafaro
Senior Project Editor: Cathy Labresh Brooks
Senior Production/Design Coordinator: Carol Merrigan
Senior Manufacturing Coordinator: Sally Culler
Marketing Manager: Ros Kane

Cover design: Diana Coe/KO Design Studio
Cover photograph: © Shigeru Tanaka/Photonica

Photo Credits

Chapter 1: Peter Beck/The Stock Market; Chapter 2: Peter Cade/TSI; Chapter 3: Elena Rooraid/PhotoEdit; Chapter 4: Spencer Grant/PhotoEdit; Chapter 5: Jeff Zaruba/The Stock Market; Chapter 6: Roger Tully/TSI; Chapter 7: Tony Freeman/PhotoEdit; Chapter 8: Carol Lundeen; Chapter 9: Joseph Nettis/Stock Boston, Inc.; Chapter 10: Michael Newman/PhotoEdit; Chapter 11: Richard Hutchings/PhotoEdit.

Printed in the U.S.A.

Library of Congress Catalog Card Number: 99-072028

ISBNs:
Text: 0-395-96979-4
Instructor's Annotated Edition: 0-395-96980-8

123456789-WC-03 02 01 00 99

CONTENTS

PREFACE

The fifth edition of *Beginning Algebra with Applications* provides a mathematically sound and comprehensive coverage of the topics considered essential in a beginning algebra course. The text has been designed not only to meet the needs of the traditional college student but also to serve the needs of returning students whose mathematical proficiency may have declined during their years away from formal education.

In this new edition of *Beginning Algebra with Applications,* careful attention has been given to implementing the standards suggested by NCTM and AMATYC. Each chapter begins with a mathematical vignette consisting of an application, historical note, or curiosity related to mathematics, as well as a career note. At the end of each section there are Applying Concepts exercises that include writing, synthesis, critical thinking, and challenge problems. The chapter ends with Focus on Problem Solving and Projects and Group Activities. The Focus on Problem Solving feature demonstrates various proven problem-solving strategies and then asks the student to use the strategies to solve problems. The Projects and Group Activities feature extensions, or applications, of a concept that was covered in the chapter. These projects can be used for cooperative learning activities or extra credit.

Instructional Features

Interactive Approach

Beginning Algebra with Applications uses an interactive style that gives the student an opportunity to try a skill as it is presented. Each section is divided into objectives, and every objective contains one or more sets of matched-pair examples. The first example in each pair is worked out; the second example, labeled Problem, is for the student to work. By solving this problem, the student practices using concepts as they are presented in the text. There are *complete* worked-out solutions to these problems in a Solutions section at the end of the book. By comparing their solutions to model solutions, students can get immediate feedback on and reinforcement of the concepts.

Emphasis on Problem-Solving Strategies

Beginning Algebra with Applications features a carefully sequenced approach to application problems that emphasizes using proven strategies to solve problems. Students are encouraged to develop their own strategies, to draw diagrams, and to write their strategies as part of the solution to each application problem. In each case, model strategies are presented as guides for students to follow as they attempt the matched-pair Problem.

Emphasis on Applications

The traditional approach to teaching algebra covers only the straightforward manipulation of numbers and variables and thereby fails to teach students the practical value of algebra. By contrast, *Beginning Algebra with Applications* contains an extensive collection of contemporary application problems. Wherever appropriate, the last objective of a section presents applications that require the student to use the skills covered in that section to solve practical problems. This carefully integrated, applied approach generates awareness on the student's part of the value of algebra as a real-life tool.

Integrated Learning System Organized by Objectives

Each chapter begins with a list of the learning objectives included within that chapter. Each objective is then restated in the chapter to remind the student of the current topic of discussion. The same objectives that organize the text are reflected in the structure for exercises, for the testing programs, and for the HM³ Tutorial. Associated with every objective in the text is a corresponding computer tutorial and a corresponding set of test questions.

The Interactive Approach

Instructors have long recognized the need for a text that requires the student to use a skill as it is being taught. *Beginning Algebra with Applications* uses an interactive technique that meets this need. Every objective, including the one shown below, contains at least one pair of examples. One of the examples in the pair is worked. The second example in the pair (the Problem) is not worked so that the student may "interact" with the text by solving it. In order to provide immediate feedback, a complete solution to this Problem is provided in the Solutions section. The benefit of this interactive style is that students can check whether they have learned the new skill before they attempt a homework assignment.

Emphasis on Applications

The solution of an application problem in *Beginning Algebra with Applications* comprises two parts: **Strategy** and **Solution**. The strategy is a written description of the steps that are necessary to solve the problem; the solution is the implemen-

An explanatory passage begins each skill objective.

Paired examples follow the explanatory passage.

The Problem is the key to the interactive approach. It has not been worked so that the student may practice the skill, referring to the worked example above if necessary.

Reference to the page where the problem is solved in the Solutions section allows the student to check solutions immediately.

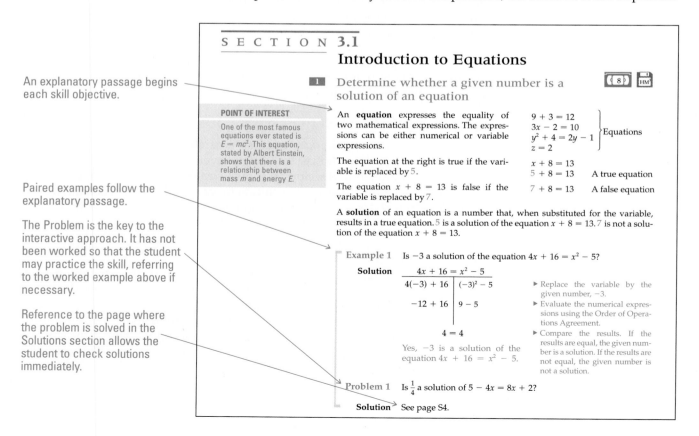

S E C T I O N **3.1**

Introduction to Equations

1 Determine whether a given number is a solution of an equation

POINT OF INTEREST

One of the most famous equations ever stated is $E = mc^2$. This equation, stated by Albert Einstein, shows that there is a relationship between mass m and energy E.

An **equation** expresses the equality of two mathematical expressions. The expressions can be either numerical or variable expressions.

$$\left. \begin{array}{l} 9 + 3 = 12 \\ 3x - 2 = 10 \\ y^2 + 4 = 2y - 1 \\ z = 2 \end{array} \right\} \text{Equations}$$

The equation at the right is true if the variable is replaced by 5.

$x + 8 = 13$
$5 + 8 = 13$ A true equation

The equation $x + 8 = 13$ is false if the variable is replaced by 7.

$7 + 8 = 13$ A false equation

A **solution** of an equation is a number that, when substituted for the variable, results in a true equation. 5 is a solution of the equation $x + 8 = 13$. 7 is not a solution of the equation $x + 8 = 13$.

Example 1 Is -3 a solution of the equation $4x + 16 = x^2 - 5$?

Solution $4x + 16 = x^2 - 5$

$$\begin{array}{c|c} 4(-3) + 16 & (-3)^2 - 5 \\ \hline -12 + 16 & 9 - 5 \\ 4 = 4 \end{array}$$

▸ Replace the variable by the given number, -3.
▸ Evaluate the numerical expressions using the Order of Operations Agreement.
▸ Compare the results. If the results are equal, the given number is a solution. If the results are not equal, the given number is not a solution.

Yes, -3 is a solution of the equation $4x + 16 = x^2 - 5$.

Problem 1 Is $\frac{1}{4}$ a solution of $5 - 4x = 8x + 2$?

Solution See page S4.

tation of the strategy. Using this format provides students with a structure for problem solving. It also encourages students to write strategies for solving problems, which in turn fosters their organizing problem-solving strategies in a logical way. Having students write strategies is a natural way to incorporate writing into the math curriculum.

A strategy that the student may use in solving an application problem is stated.

This strategy is used in the solution of the worked example.

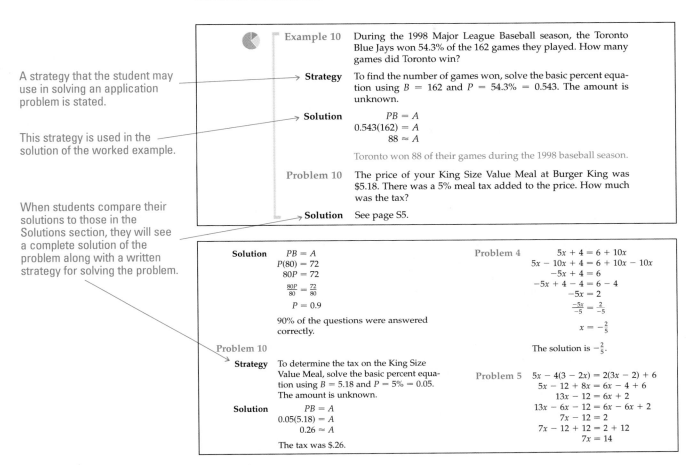

Example 10 During the 1998 Major League Baseball season, the Toronto Blue Jays won 54.3% of the 162 games they played. How many games did Toronto win?

Strategy To find the number of games won, solve the basic percent equation using $B = 162$ and $P = 54.3\% = 0.543$. The amount is unknown.

Solution
$$PB = A$$
$$0.543(162) = A$$
$$88 \approx A$$

Toronto won 88 of their games during the 1998 baseball season.

Problem 10 The price of your King Size Value Meal at Burger King was $5.18. There was a 5% meal tax added to the price. How much was the tax?

Solution See page S5.

When students compare their solutions to those in the Solutions section, they will see a complete solution of the problem along with a written strategy for solving the problem.

Solution
$$PB = A$$
$$P(80) = 72$$
$$80P = 72$$
$$\frac{80P}{80} = \frac{72}{80}$$
$$P = 0.9$$

90% of the questions were answered correctly.

Problem 10

Strategy To determine the tax on the King Size Value Meal, solve the basic percent equation using $B = 5.18$ and $P = 5\% = 0.05$. The amount is unknown.

Solution
$$PB = A$$
$$0.05(5.18) = A$$
$$0.26 \approx A$$

The tax was $.26.

Problem 4
$$5x + 4 = 6 + 10x$$
$$5x - 10x + 4 = 6 + 10x - 10x$$
$$-5x + 4 = 6$$
$$-5x + 4 - 4 = 6 - 4$$
$$-5x = 2$$
$$\frac{-5x}{-5} = \frac{2}{-5}$$
$$x = -\frac{2}{5}$$

The solution is $-\frac{2}{5}$.

Problem 5
$$5x - 4(3 - 2x) = 2(3x - 2) + 6$$
$$5x - 12 + 8x = 6x - 4 + 6$$
$$13x - 12 = 6x + 2$$
$$13x - 6x - 12 = 6x - 6x + 2$$
$$7x - 12 = 2$$
$$7x - 12 + 12 = 2 + 12$$
$$7x = 14$$

The Objective-Specific Approach

Many texts in mathematics are not organized in a manner that facilitates management of learning. Typically, students are left to wander through a maze of apparently unrelated lessons, exercise sets, and tests. *Beginning Algebra with Applications* solves this problem by organizing all lessons, exercise sets, computer tutorials, and tests around a carefully constructed hierarchy of objectives. The advantage of this objective-by-objective organization is that it enables the student who is uncertain at any step in the learning process to refer easily to the original presentation and review that material.

The objective-specific approach also gives the instructor greater control over the management of student progress. The computerized testing program and the printed testing program are organized in terms of the same objectives as the text. These references are provided with the answers to the test items. This allows the instructor to identify quickly those objectives for which a student may need additional instruction.

The HM³ Tutorial is also organized around the objectives of the text. As a result, supplemental instruction is available for any objectives that are troublesome for a student.

An objective statement names the topic of each lesson.

SECTION 3.1

Introduction to Equations

   1   Determine whether a given number is a solution of an equation

---

The exercise sets correspond to the objectives in the text.

EXERCISES 3.1

1   **1.**   What is the difference between an equation and an expression?

     2.   How can you determine whether a number is a solution of an equation?

     3.   Is 4 a solution of   **4.**   Is 3 a solution of   **5.**   Is -1 a solution of
$2x = 8$?   Yes $y + 4 = 7$?   Yes $2b - 1 = 3$?   No

The answers to the odd-numbered exercises are provided in the Answer section.

SECTION 3.1

3. Yes   **5.** No   **7.** No   **9.** Yes   **11.** Yes   **13.** Yes   **15.** No   **17.** No   **19.** No   **21.** Yes

---

The answers to the Chapter Review Exercises, the Chapter Test, and the Cumulative Review Exercises show the objective to study if the student incorrectly answers the exercise.

CHAPTER REVIEW EXERCISES

1. No (Obj. 3.1.1)   **2.** 20 (Obj. 3.1.2)   **3.** -7 (Obj. 3.1.3)   **4.** 7 (Obj. 3.2.1)   **5.** 4 (Obj. 3.2.2)

CHAPTER TEST

1. -12 (Obj. 3.1.3)   **2.** $-\frac{1}{2}$ (Obj. 3.2.2)   **3.** -3 (Obj. 3.2.1)   **4.** No (Obj. 3.1.1)   **5.** $\frac{1}{8}$ (Obj. 3.1.2)

CUMULATIVE REVIEW EXERCISES

1. 6 (Obj. 1.2.2)   **2.** -48 (Obj. 1.2.3)   **3.** $-\frac{19}{48}$ (Obj. 1.3.3)   **4.** -2 (Obj. 1.3.4)   **5.** 54 (Obj. 1.4.1)

Features of This Edition

Topical Coverage

Beginning Algebra with Applications carefully integrates a balance of applications and skill development to help students understand the connection between mathematics and its application.

The application problems in the text are diverse and contemporary. We have included applications from business, sports, economics, and medicine, to name but a few. Many of these applications are new and include topics not included in earlier editions. A complete list of the applications can be found in the Index of Applications.

Margin Notes

There are two types of margin notes in the student text. *Point of Interest* notes feature interesting sidelights of the topic being discussed. The *Look Closely* feature warns students that a procedure may be particularly involved or reminds students that there are certain checks of their work that should be performed. In addition, there are *Instructor Notes* that are printed only in the Instructor's Annotated Edition. These notes provide suggestions for presenting the material or related material that can be used in class.

Study Tips

Effective study skills are an important factor in achieving success in any discipline. This is especially true in mathematics. To help students acquire these skills, we offer Study Tips boxes throughout the first few chapters of the text. Each box contains a suggestion that will lead to improved study habits.

Focus on Problem Solving

Although successful problem solvers use a variety of techniques, it has been well established that there are basic recurring strategies. Among these are trying to solve a related problem, finding a counterexample, trying to solve an easier problem, working backwards, trial and error. The Focus on Problem Solving features present some of these methods in the context of a problem to be solved. Students are encouraged to apply these strategies in solving similar problems.

Projects and Group Activities

The Projects and Group Activities appear near the end of each chapter. These projects can be used for extra credit or as cooperative learning activities. Through these projects, some of the strategies suggested by AMATYC can be implemented. These projects offer an opportunity for students to explore topics relating to functions, geometry, statistics, science, and business.

HM³ Tutorial

This state-of-the-art tutorial software is a networkable, interactive, algorithmically-driven software package that supports *every* objective in the text. The HM³ Tutorial and the text are both written by the authors. Features include full-color graphics, a glossary, extensive hints, animated examples, and a comprehensive classroom-management system.

The algorithmic feature provides a virtually infinite number of practice problems for students to attempt. The algorithms have been carefully crafted to present a variety of problem types, from easy to difficult. Helpful hints and a complete worked-out solution are available for every problem. When students complete a problem, there is an option to repeat a similar problem or move on to another type of problem. A quiz feature is now also part of the package.

The interactive feature asks students to respond to questions about the topic in the current lesson. In this way, students can assess their understanding of concepts as these are presented. These interactive questions are also algorithmically driven and offer hints as well as a full solution.

The user-friendly classroom-management system allows instructors to create a syllabus, post notes to individual students or a class, enter their own assessment items (for example, homework, class participation, and so forth), and choose the mastery level. There are a variety of printable reports offered; these can be called up by student, by class, or by objective, and many reports tell at a glance those students who are not achieving the mastery level specified by the instructor.

Index of Applications

The Index of Applications that follows the Preface provides a quick reference for application problems from a wide variety of fields.

Graphing Calculators

Graphing calculators are incorporated as an optional feature at appropriate places throughout the text. Graphing calculator material is designated by the graphing calculator icon shown at the beginning of this paragraph. The graphing calculator may help some students as they struggle with new concepts. However, all graphing calculator material can be omitted without destroying the integrity of the course. Students can consult the Appendix, Guidelines for Using Graphing Calculators, for help with keystroking procedures to use for several models of graphing calculators.

Chapter Summaries

The Chapter Summaries have been written to be a useful guide to students as they review for a test. The Chapter Summary includes the Key Words and the Essential Rules and Procedures that were covered in the chapter. Each key word and essential rule is accompanied by an example of that concept.

Glossary

The Glossary at the back of the book includes definitions of terms used in the text.

Exercises

End-of-Section Exercises

Beginning Algebra with Applications contains more than 6000 exercises. At the end of each section there are exercise sets that are keyed to the corresponding learning objectives. The exercises have been carefully developed to ensure that students can apply the concepts in the section to a variety of problem situations.

Concept Review Exercises

These "Always true, Sometimes true, or Never true" exercises precede every exercise set and are designed to test a student's understanding of the material. Using Concept Review exercises as oral exercises at the end of a class session can lead to interesting class discussions.

Applying Concepts Exercises

The end-of-section exercises are followed by Applying Concepts exercises. These contain a variety of exercise types:

Challenge problems (designated by [C] in the Instructor's Annotated Edition only)

Problems that ask students to interpret and work with real-world data

Writing exercises

Problems that ask students to determine incorrect procedures

Problems that require a more in-depth analysis

Data Exercises

These exercises, designated by ⬤, ask students to analyze and solve problems taken from actual situations. Students are often required to work with tables, graphs, and charts drawn from a variety of disciplines.

Writing Exercises

Writing exercises, denoted by ✎ , occur at the beginning of many exercise sets and within Applying Concepts exercises. These exercises ask students to write about a topic in the section or to research and report on a related topic. There are also writing exercises in some of the application problems. These exercises ask students to write a sentence that describes the meaning of their answers in the context of the problem.

Chapter Review Exercises and Chapter Tests

Chapter Review exercises and a Chapter Test are found at the end of each chapter. These exercises are selected to help the student integrate all the topics presented in the chapter. The answers to all Chapter Review and Chapter Test exercises are given in the Answers section. Along with the answer, there is a reference to the objective that pertains to each exercise.

Cumulative Review Exercises and Final Exam

Cumulative Review exercises, which appear at the end of Chapters 2–11, help the student maintain skills learned in previous chapters. In addition, a Final Exam appears at the end of Chapter 11. The answers to all Cumulative Review and Final Exam exercises are given in the Answers section. Along with the answer, there is a reference to the objective that pertains to each exercise.

New to this Edition

Material on similar triangles has been added to Chapter 9, *Algebraic Fractions*.

Geometry material in Chapter 4, *Solving Equations and Inequalities: Applications*, has been expanded and new material on angles of intersecting lines has been added.

The calculator material within the exposition has been expanded. We have given more prominence to the in-text calculator commentary by boxing this material and identifying it with an icon.

We have more than doubled the number of projects found at the end of each chapter. In addition, those projects involving calculators and Internet sites have been easily identified with an appropriate icon. Graph interpretation exercises have also been added to the projects.

Career notes and photos have been added to the chapter openers to illustrate to students the diverse ways in which mathematics is used in the workplace.

In response to suggestions by users, the writing and data icons appear in the student text as well as the Instructor's Annotated Edition. We have also integrated writing exercises within the exercise sets rather than limit them to the Applying Concepts section of the exercises.

All the real-sourced data exercises and examples have been updated and many new data problems have been added. We have also titled application exercises to help motivate student interest.

To be consistent with our objective-specific approach, we have expanded the table of contents to include objective statements.

Supplements for the Instructor

Instructor's Annotated Edition

The Instructor's Annotated Edition is an exact replica of the student text except that answers to all exercises are given in the text. Also, there are Instructor Notes in the margins that offer suggestions for presenting the material in that objective.

Instructor's Resource Manual with Solutions Manual

The *Instructor's Resource Manual* includes suggestions for course sequencing and gives sample answers for the writing exercises. The *Solutions Manual* contains worked-out solutions for all end-of-section exercises, Concept Review exercises, Focus on Problem Solving exercises, Projects and Group Activities, Chapter Review exercises, Chapter Test exercises, Cumulative Review exercises, and Final Exam exercises.

Computerized Test Generator

The *Computerized Test Generator* is the first of three sources of testing material. The database contains more than 2000 test items. These questions are unique to the Test Generator. The Test Generator is designed to provide an unlimited number of chapter tests, cumulative chapter tests, and final exams. It is available for Microsoft Windows® and the Macintosh. Both versions provide **algorithms, gradebook** functions, and **on-line testing**.

Printed Test Bank with Chapter Tests

The printed *Test Bank*, the second component of the testing material, is a printout of all items in the Computerized Test Generator. Instructors who do not have access to a computer can use the test bank to select items to include on tests prepared by hand. The *Chapter Tests* comprise the printed testing program, which is the third source of testing material. Eight printed tests, four free-response and four multiple-choice, are provided for each chapter. In addition, there are cumulative tests for use after Chapters 4, 8, and 11, and a Final Exam.

Supplements for the Student

Student Solutions Manual

The *Student Solutions Manual* contains complete solutions to all odd-numbered exercises in the text.

HM^3 Tutorial

The content of this new interactive state-of-the-art tutorial software was written by the text authors. The *HM^3 Tutorial* supports every objective in the text. Problems are algorithmically generated, lessons provide animated examples, lessons and problems are presented in a colorful, lively manner, and an integrated classroom management system tracks and reports student performance. Features include:

- assessment
- free-response problems
- ability to repeat same problem type
- printing capability
- glossary
- resizable screen

- pedagogical animations
- interactivity within lessons
- algorithms
- extensive classroom management with syllabus customization and a variety of reports

The HM³ Tutorial can be used in several ways: (1) to cover material the student missed because of absence; (2) to reinforce instruction on a concept that the student has not yet mastered; (3) to review material in preparation for exams; (4) for self instruction.

This networkable HM³ Tutorial is available on CD-ROM for Windows. There is also an alternate version offered for the Macintosh, available only on floppy disk. The HM³ Tutorial is free to any school upon adoption of this text; however, students can purchase a non-networkable copy of the HM³ Tutorial for home use.

 Within each section of the book, a computer disk icon appears next to each objective. The icon serves as a reminder that there is an HM³ Tutorial lesson corresponding to that objective.

Videotapes

The videotape series contains lessons that accompany *Beginning Algebra with Applications*. These lessons follow the format and style of the text and are closely tied to specific sections of the text. Each videotape begins with an application, and then the mathematics needed to solve that application is presented. The tape closes with the solution of the application problem.

Within each section of the book, a videotape icon appears next to each objective that is covered by a videotape lesson. The icon contains the reference number of the appropriate video.

Acknowledgments

The authors would like to thank the people who have reviewed this manuscript and provided many valuable suggestions:

Maria Blon, *Orange County Community College, NY*
Beth Fraser, *Middlesex Community College, MA*
Michael A. Jones
Cheryl Keeton, *College of the Albemarle, NC*
Kim Lane, *University of New Orleans—Lakefront Campus*
Linda J. Murphy, *Northern Essex Community College, MA*
Nancy K. Nickerson, *Northern Essex Community College, MA*
C. Susan Riley, *University of Wisconsin—Stevens Point*
Lauri Semarne
William A. Steed, Jr., *Saddleback College, CA*
Harriet Thompson, *Albany State University, GA*
Patty Waltermire, *Ivy Tech State College, IN*

INDEX of Applications

1

Real Numbers

County agricultural agents work with farmers to help them produce better crops. Many agents are specialists in soils. They teach farmers about the physical and chemical characteristics of the soil, helping them to make the most productive use of their land. Agricultural agents must have a good understanding of percents in order to analyze the composition of nutrients in farmland. Their goal is to assist farmers in improving the quality and quantity of crop yields and in controlling diseases and pests.

Early Egyptian Fractions

One of the earliest written documents of mathematics is the Rhind Papyrus. This tablet was found in Egypt in 1858, but it is estimated that the writings date back to 1650 B.C.

The Rhind Papyrus contains over 80 problems. Studying these problems has enabled mathematicians and scientists to understand some of the methods by which the early Egyptians used mathematics.

Evidence gained from the Papyrus shows that the Egyptian method of calculating with fractions was much different from the methods used today. All fractions were represented in terms of what are called unit fractions. A **unit fraction** is a fraction in which the numerator is 1. This fraction was symbolized with a bar over the number. Examples (using modern numbers) include

$$\overline{3} = \frac{1}{3} \qquad \overline{15} = \frac{1}{15}$$

The early Egyptians also tended to deal with powers of two **(2, 4, 8, 16, …)**. As a result, representing fractions with a 2 in the numerator in terms of unit fractions was an important matter. The Rhind Papyrus has a table giving the equivalent unit fractions for all odd denominators from 5 to 101 with 2 as the numerator. Some of these are listed below.

$$\frac{2}{5} = \overline{3}\ \overline{15} \qquad\qquad \left(\frac{2}{5} = \frac{1}{3} + \frac{1}{15}\right)$$

$$\frac{2}{7} = \overline{4}\ \overline{28}$$

$$\frac{2}{11} = \overline{6}\ \overline{66}$$

$$\frac{2}{19} = \overline{12}\ \overline{76}\ \overline{114}$$

SECTION 1.1
Introduction to Integers

1 Order relations

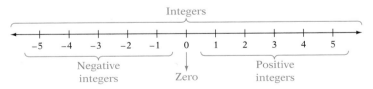

INSTRUCTOR NOTE

Margin notes entitled
Point of Interest or Look
Closely are printed in the
student text. The Point of
Interest feature provides a
historical note or mathematical
fact of interest. The Look
Closely feature flags important
information or provides
assistance in understanding a
concept. The margin notes
entitled Instructor Note are
printed only in the Instructor's
Annotated Edition.

It seems to be a human characteristic to group similar items. For instance, a botanist places plants with similar characteristics in groups called species. Nutritionists classify foods according to food groups; for example, pasta, crackers, and rice are among the foods in the bread group.

Mathematicians place objects with similar properties in groups called sets. A **set** is a collection of objects. The objects in a set are called the **elements** of the set.

The **roster method** of writing sets encloses a list of the elements in braces. The set of sections within an orchestra is written {brass, percussion, strings, woodwind}.

The numbers that we use to count objects, such as the number of students in a classroom or the number of people living in an apartment house, are the natural numbers.

$$\textbf{Natural numbers} = \{1, 2, 3, 4, 5, 6, 7, 8, 9, 10, \ldots\}$$

The three dots mean that the list of natural numbers continues on and on and that there is no largest natural number.

The natural numbers do not include zero. The number zero is used for describing data such as the number of people who have run a two-minute mile and the number of college students at Providence College who are under the age of 10. The set of whole numbers includes the natural numbers and zero.

$$\textbf{Whole numbers} = \{0, 1, 2, 3, 4, 5, 6, 7, \ldots\}$$

The whole numbers do not provide all the numbers that are useful in applications. For instance, a meteorologist also needs numbers below zero.

$$\textbf{Integers} = \{\ldots, -5, -4, -3, -2, -1, 0, 1, 2, 3, 4, 5, \ldots\}$$

POINT OF INTEREST

The Alexandrian astronomer Ptolemy began using *omicron*, *o*, the first letter of the Greek word that means "nothing," as the symbol for zero in A.D 150. It was not until the 13th century, however, that Fibonacci introduced 0 to the Western world as a placeholder so that we could distinguish, for example, 45 from 405.

Each integer can be shown on a number line. The integers to the left of zero on the number line are called **negative integers.** The integers to the right of zero are called **positive integers,** or natural numbers. Zero is neither a positive nor a negative integer.

The **graph** of an integer is shown by placing a heavy dot on the number line directly above the number. The graphs of -3 and 4 are shown on the number line below.

Consider the following sentences.

The quarterback threw the football, and the receiver caught *it*.

A student purchased a computer and used *it* to write English and history papers.

In the first sentence, *it* is used to mean the football; in the second sentence, *it* means the computer. In language, the word *it* can stand for many different objects. Similarly, in mathematics, a letter of the alphabet can be used to stand for a number. Such a letter is called a **variable.** Variables are used in the following definition of inequality symbols.

Definition of Inequality Symbols

If *a* and *b* are two numbers and *a* is to the left of *b* on the number line, then *a* **is less than** *b*. This is written *a* < *b*.

If *a* and *b* are two numbers and *a* is to the right of *b* on the number line, then *a* **is greater than** *b*. This is written *a* > *b*.

Negative 4 is less than negative 1.

$-4 < -1$

5 is greater than 0.

$5 > 0$

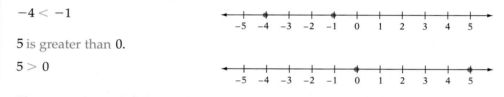

There are also inequality symbols for **is less than or equal to** ($\leq$) and **is greater than or equal to** ($\geq$).

$7 \leq 15$	7 is less than or equal to 15. This is true because $7 < 15$.	$6 \leq 6$ 6 is less than or equal to 6. This is true because $6 = 6$.

Example 1   Use the roster method to write the set of negative integers greater than or equal to -6.

   Solution $A = \{-6, -5, -4, -3, -2, -1\}$ ▶ A set is designated by a capital letter.

Problem 1   Use the roster method to write the set of positive integers less than 5.

   Solution   See page S1. $A = \{1, 2, 3, 4\}$

Example 2   Given $A = \{-6, -2, 0\}$, which elements of set A are less than or equal to -2?

Solution $-6 < -2$ ▶ Find the order relation between each element of set A and -2.

$-2 = -2$

$0 > -2$

The elements -6 and -2 are less than or equal to -2.

Problem 2   Given $B = \{-5, -1, 5\}$, which elements of set B are greater than -1?

Solution   See page S1.   5

2 Opposites and absolute value

Two numbers that are the same distance from zero on the number line but are on opposite sides of zero are **opposite numbers,** or **opposites.** The opposite of a number is also called its **additive inverse.**

The opposite of 5 is -5.

The opposite of -5 is 5.

The negative sign can be read "the opposite of."

$$-(2) = -2 \qquad \text{The opposite of 2 is } -2.$$

$$-(-2) = 2 \qquad \text{The opposite of } -2 \text{ is 2.}$$

Example 3   Find the opposite number.   A. 6   B. -51

Solution   A. -6 B. 51

Problem 3   Find the opposite number.   A. -9 B. 62

Solution   See page S1.   A. 9   B. -62

The **absolute value** of a number is its distance from zero on the number line. Therefore, the absolute value of a number is a positive number or zero. The symbol for absolute value is two vertical bars, $|\ |$.

The distance from 0 to 3 is 3. Therefore, the absolute value of 3 is 3.

$$|3| = 3$$

The distance from 0 to -3 is 3. Therefore, the absolute value of -3 is 3.

$$|-3| = 3$$

Absolute Value

The absolute value of a positive number is the number itself. The absolute value of zero is zero. The absolute value of a negative number is the opposite of the negative number.

Example 4   Evaluate.   A. $|-4|$ B. $-|-10|$

   Solution   A. $|-4| = 4$
              B. $-|-10| = -10$ ▸ The absolute value sign does not affect the negative sign in front of the absolute value sign. You can read $-|-10|$ as "the opposite of the absolute value of negative 10."

Problem 4   Evaluate.   A. $|-5|$ B. $-|-9|$

   Solution   See page S1.   A. 5   B. -9

STUDY TIPS

KNOW YOUR INSTRUCTOR'S REQUIREMENTS

To do your best in this course, you must know exactly what your instructor requires. If you don't, you probably will not meet his or her expectations and are not likely to earn a good grade in the course.
    Instructors ordinarily explain course requirements during the first few days of class. Course requirements may be stated in a *syllabus*, which is a printed outline of the main topics of the course, or they may be presented orally. When they are listed in a syllabus or on other printed pages, keep them in a safe place. When they are presented orally, be sure to take complete notes. In either case, understand them completely and follow them exactly.

INSTRUCTOR NOTE

The Concept Review feature of this text appears before every exercise set. After presenting the material in this section, you might elect to use these exercises as oral classroom exercises or as a basis for class discussion on the topics of the lesson.

CONCEPT REVIEW 1.1

Determine whether the statement is always true, sometimes true, or never true.

1. The absolute value of a number is positive.   Sometimes true

2. The absolute value of a number is negative.   Never true

3. If x is an integer, then $|x| < -3$.   Never true

4. If x is an integer, then $|x| > -2$.   Always true

5. The opposite of a number is a positive number.   Sometimes true

6. The set of positive integers is $\{0, 1, 2, 3, 4, \ldots\}$.   Never true

7. If a is an integer, then $a \leq a$.   Always true

8. If a and b are integers and $a > b$, then $a \geq b$.   Always true

9. If x is a negative integer, then $|x| = -x$.   Always true

10. Suppose a and b are integers and $a < b$. Then $|a| < |b|$.   Sometimes true

EXERCISES 1.1

1 **1.**   How do the whole numbers differ from the natural numbers?

    2.   Explain the difference between the symbols $<$ and $\leq$.

Place the correct symbol, $<$ or $>$, between the two numbers.

3. $-2 > -5$ **4.** $-6 < -1$ **5.** $-16 < 1$ **6.** $-2 < 13$

7. $3 > -7$ **8.** $5 > -6$ **9.** $0 > -3$ **10.** $8 > 0$

11. $-42 < 27$ **12.** $-36 < 49$ **13.** $21 > -34$ **14.** $53 > -46$

15. $-27 > -39$ **16.** $-51 < -20$ **17.** $-131 < 101$ **18.** $127 > -150$

Use the roster method to write the set.

19.   the natural numbers less than 9
     $\{1, 2, 3, 4, 5, 6, 7, 8\}$

20.   the natural numbers less than or equal to 6
     $\{1, 2, 3, 4, 5, 6\}$

21.   the positive integers less than or equal to 8
     $\{1, 2, 3, 4, 5, 6, 7, 8\}$

22.   the positive integers less than 4
     $\{1, 2, 3\}$

23.   the negative integers greater than -7
     $\{-6, -5, -4, -3, -2, -1\}$

24.   the negative integers greater than or equal to -5
     $\{-5, -4, -3, -2, -1\}$

Solve.

25.   Given $A = \{-7, 0, 2, 5\}$, which elements of set A are greater than 2?   5

26.   Given $B = \{-8, 0, 7, 15\}$, which elements of set B are greater than 7?   15

27.   Given $D = \{-23, -18, -8, 0\}$, which elements of set D are less than -8? $-23, -18$

28.   Given $C = \{-33, -24, -10, 0\}$, which elements of set C are less than -10? $-33, -24$

29.   Given $E = \{-35, -13, 21, 37\}$, which elements of set E are greater than -10?   21, 37

30.   Given $F = \{-27, -14, 14, 27\}$, which elements of set F are greater than -15? $-14, 14, 27$

31.   Given $B = \{-52, -46, 0, 39, 58\}$, which elements of set B are less than or equal to 0?
     $-52, -46, 0$

32.   Given $A = \{-12, -9, 0, 12, 34\}$, which elements of set A are greater than or equal to 0?
     0, 12, 34

33.   Given $C = \{-23, -17, 0, 4, 29\}$, which elements of set C are greater than or equal to -17?
     $-17, 0, 4, 29$

34.   Given $D = \{-31, -12, 0, 11, 45\}$, which elements of set D are less than or equal to -12?
     $-31, -12$

35.   Given that set A is the positive integers less than 10, which elements of set A are greater than or equal to 5?   5, 6, 7, 8, 9

36.   Given that set B is the positive integers less than or equal to 12, which elements of set B are greater than 6?   7, 8, 9, 10, 11, 12

37.   Given that set D is the negative integers greater than or equal to -10, which elements of set D are less than -4? $-10, -9, -8, -7, -6, -5$

38.   Given that set C is the negative integers greater than -8, which elements of set C are less than or equal to -3? $-7, -6, -5, -4, -3$

2 **39.** What is the additive inverse of a number?

40. What is the absolute value of a number?

Find the opposite number.

41. 22   −22
42. 45   −45
43. −31   31
44. −88   88

45. −168   168
46. −97   97
47. 630   −630
48. 450   −450

Evaluate.

49. −(−18)   18
50. −(−30)   30
51. −(49)   −49
52. −(67)   −67

53. |16| 16
54. |19| 19
55. |−12| 12
56. |−22| 22

57. −|29| −29
58. −|20| −20
59. −|−14| −14
60. −|−18| −18

61. −|0| 0
62. |−30| 30
63. −|34| −34
64. −|−45| −45

Solve.

65. Given $A = \{-8, -5, -2, 1, 3\}$, find
   a. the opposite of each element of set A.
   b. the absolute value of each element of set A.
   a. 8, 5, 2, −1, −3   **b.** 8, 5, 2, 1, 3

66. Given $B = \{-11, -7, -3, 1, 5\}$, find
   a. the opposite of each element of set B.
   b. the absolute value of each element of set B.
   a. 11, 7, 3, −1, −5   **b.** 11, 7, 3, 1, 5

Place the correct symbol, < or >, between the two numbers.

67. |−83| > |58|
68. |22| > |−19|
69. |43| < |−52|
70. |−71| < |−92|

71. |−68| > |−42|
72. |12| < |−31|
73. |−45| < |−61|
74. |−28| < |43|

APPLYING CONCEPTS 1.1

Write the given numbers in order from least to greatest.

75. |−5|, 6, −|−8|, −19   −19, −|−8|, |−5|, 6

76. −4, |−15|, −|−7|, 0   −|−7|, −4, 0, |−15|

77. −(−3), −22, |−25|, |−14|
   −22, −(−3), |−14|, |−25|

78. −|−26|, −(−8), |−17|, −(5)
   −|−26|, −(5), −(−8), |−17|

INSTRUCTOR NOTE
Each group of Applying Concepts exercises contains one or more challenge, data, or writing exercises, indicated by a [C], 🥧, or ✏ next to the exercise number. Sample answers for all writing exercises are given in the *Instructor's Resource Manual.*

A meteorologist may report a wind-chill temperature. This is the equivalent temperature, including the effects of wind and temperature, that a person would feel in calm air conditions. The table that follows gives the wind-chill temperature for various wind speeds and temperatures. For instance, when the temperature is 5°F and the wind is blowing at 15 mph, the wind-chill temperature is −25°F. Use this table for Exercises 79 and 80. (Source: *Information Please Almanac*)

Wind-Chill Factors

Wind Speed (in mph)	Thermometer Reading (in degrees Fahrenheit)																
	35	**30**	**25**	**20**	**15**	**10**	**5**	**0**	**−5**	**−10**	**−15**	**−20**	**−25**	**−30**	**−35**	**−40**	**−45**
5	33	27	21	19	12	7	0	−5	−10	−15	−21	−26	−31	−36	−42	−47	−52
10	22	16	10	3	−3	−9	−15	−22	−27	−34	−40	−46	−52	−58	−64	−71	−77
15	16	9	2	−5	−11	−18	−25	−31	−38	−45	−51	−58	−65	−72	−78	−85	−92
20	12	4	−3	−10	−17	−24	−31	−39	−46	−53	−60	−67	−74	−81	−88	−95	−103
25	8	1	−7	−15	−22	−29	−36	−44	−51	−59	−66	−74	−81	−88	−96	−103	−110
30	6	−2	−10	−18	−25	−33	−41	−49	−56	−64	−71	−79	−86	−93	−101	−109	−116
35	4	−4	−12	−20	−27	−35	−43	−52	−58	−67	−74	−82	−89	−97	−105	−113	−120
40	3	−5	−13	−21	−29	−37	−45	−53	−60	−69	−76	−84	−92	−100	−107	−115	−123
45	2	−6	−14	−22	−30	−38	−46	−54	−62	−70	−78	−85	−93	−102	−109	−117	−125

79.   *Meteorology*   Which of the following weather conditions feels colder?

a. a temperature of 5°F with a 20 mph wind or a temperature of 10°F with a 15 mph wind   5°F with a 20 mph wind

b. a temperature of −25°F with a 10 mph wind or a temperature of −15°F with a 20 mph wind   −15°F with a 20 mph wind

80.   *Meteorology*   Which of the following weather conditions feels warmer?

a. a temperature of 25°F with a 25 mph wind or a temperature of 10°F with a 10 mph wind   25°F with a 25 mph wind

b. a temperature of −5°F with a 10 mph wind or a temperature of −15°F with a 5 mph wind   −15°F with a 5 mph wind

Complete.

81. On the number line, the two points that are four units from 0 are __−4__ and __4__.

82. On the number line, the two points that are six units from 0 are __−6__ and __6__.

[C] **83.** On the number line, the two points that are seven units from 4 are __−3__ and __11__.

[C] **84.** On the number line, the two points that are five units from −3 are __−8__ and __2__.

[C] **85.** If a is a positive number, then $-a$ is a __negative__ number.

[C] **86.** If a is a negative number, then $-a$ is a __positive__ number.

[C] **87.** An integer that is its own opposite is __0__ .

88. True or False. If $a \geq 0$, then $|a| = a$.   True

89. True or False. If $a \leq 0$, then $|a| = -a$.   True

90. Give examples of some games that use negative integers in the scoring.   Golf, rummy, hearts

91. Give some examples of English words that are used as variables.

92. Write an essay describing your interpretation of the data presented in the table at the right.

The Twenty-First Century: An Easier Ladder to Climb Number of 30- to 34-year-olds competing for jobs			
	1992	**1999**	**2005**
Men	10.3 million	9.2 million	8.5 million
Women	8.3 million	7.9 million	7.8 million
Total	**18.6 million**	**17.1 million**	**16.3 million**

S E C T I O N **1.2**

Operations with Integers

1   Add integers

INSTRUCTOR NOTE

There are a number of models of the addition of integers. Using arrows on the number line is just one of them. Another suggestion is to use a checking account. If there is a balance of $25 in a checking account, and a check is written for $30, the account will be overdrawn by $5 ($-5$).

Another model uses two colors of plastic chips, say blue for positive and red for negative, and the idea that a blue/red pair is equal to zero. To add $-8 + 3$, place 8 red and 3 blue chips in a circle. Make as many blue/red pairs as possible and remove them from the region. There are 5 red chips remaining, or -5.

A number can be represented anywhere along the number line by an arrow. A positive number is represented by an arrow pointing to the right, and a negative number is represented by an arrow pointing to the left. The size of the number is represented by the length of the arrow.

Addition is the process of finding the total of two numbers. The numbers being added are called **addends.** The total is called the **sum.** Addition of integers can be shown on the number line. To add integers, find the point on the number line corresponding to the first addend. At that point, draw an arrow representing the second addend. The sum is the number directly below the tip of the arrow.

$4 + 2 = 6$

$-4 + (-2) = -6$

$-4 + 2 = -2$

$4 + (-2) = 2$

The pattern for addition shown on the preceding number lines is summarized in the following rules for adding integers.

Addition of Integers

Integers with the same sign
To add two numbers with the same sign, add the absolute values of the numbers. Then attach the sign of the addends.

$2 + 8 = 10$

$-2 + (-8) = -10$

Integers with different signs
To add two numbers with different signs, find the absolute value of each number. Then subtract the smaller of these absolute values from the larger one. Attach the sign of the number with the larger absolute value.

$-2 + 8 = 6$

$2 + (-8) = -6$

Example 1   Add.   A. $162 + (-247)$ B. $-14 + (-47)$
                       C. $-4 + (-6) + (-8) + 9$

Solution   A. $162 + (-247) = -85$ ▶ The signs are different. Subtract the absolute values of the numbers $(247 - 162)$. Attach the sign of the number with the larger absolute value.

B. $-14 + (-47) = -61$ ▶ The signs are the same. Add the absolute values of the numbers $(14 + 47)$. Attach the sign of the addends.

C. $-4 + (-6) + (-8) + 9$ ▶ To add more than two numbers, add the first two numbers. Then add the sum to the third number. Continue until all the numbers have been added.
$\quad = -10 + (-8) + 9$
$\quad = -18 + 9$
$\quad = -9$

Problem 1   Add.

A. $-162 + 98$ B. $-154 + (-37)$ C. $-36 + 17 + (-21)$

Solution   See page S1.   A. -64 B. -191 C. -40

2   Subtract integers

INSTRUCTOR NOTE
Sometimes students do not see the difference between a negative sign and a minus sign. Give examples such as $-4 - 6$, $-5 - (-3)$, and $8 - 12$, and ask students to read each expression.

Subtraction is the process of finding the difference between two numbers. Subtraction of an integer is defined as addition of the opposite integer.

Subtract $8 - 3$ by using addition of the opposite.

Subtraction ⟶ Addition of the Opposite

$8\ \ -\ \ (+3)\ \ =\ \ 8\ \ +\ \ (-3)\ \ =\ \ 5$

└── Opposites ──┘

To subtract one integer from another, add the opposite of the second integer to the first number.

first number	$-$	second number	$=$	first number	$+$	the opposite of the second number		

$$
\begin{array}{rcrcrcrcr}
40 & - & 60 & = & 40 & + & (-60) & = & -20 \\
-40 & - & 60 & = & -40 & + & (-60) & = & -100 \\
-40 & - & (-60) & = & -40 & + & 60 & = & 20 \\
40 & - & (-60) & = & 40 & + & 60 & = & 100 \\
\end{array}
$$

Example 2   Subtract: $-12 - 8$

   Solution $-12 - 8 = -12 + (-8)$ ▶ Rewrite subtraction as addition of the opposite.

$\qquad\qquad\qquad\quad = -20$ ▶ Add.

Problem 2   Subtract: $-8 - 14$

   Solution   See page S1. -22

When subtraction occurs several times in a problem, rewrite each subtraction as addition of the opposite. Then add.

Example 3   Subtract: $-8 - 30 - (-12) - 7 - (-14)$

   Solution $-8 - 30 - (-12) - 7 - (-14)$

$\qquad = -8 + (-30) + 12 + (-7) + 14$ ▶ Rewrite each subtraction as addition of the opposite.

$\qquad = -38 + 12 + (-7) + 14$ ▶ Add the first two numbers. Then add the sum to the third number. Continue until all the numbers have been added.
$\qquad = -26 + (-7) + 14$
$\qquad = -33 + 14$
$\qquad = -19$

Problem 3   Subtract: $4 - (-3) - 12 - (-7) - 20$

   Solution   See page S1. -18

3   ## Multiply integers

Multiplication is the process of finding the product of two numbers.

Several different symbols are used to indicate multiplication. The numbers being multiplied are called **factors;** for instance, 3 and 2 are factors in each of the examples at the right. The result is called the **product.** Note that when parentheses are used and there is no arithmetic operation symbol, the operation is multiplication.

$$
\begin{array}{r}
3 \times 2 = 6 \\
3 \cdot 2 = 6 \\
(3)(2) = 6 \\
3(2) = 6 \\
(3)2 = 6 \\
\end{array}
$$

When 5 is multiplied by a sequence of decreasing integers, each product decreases by 5.

$$(5)(3) = 15$$
$$(5)(2) = 10$$
$$(5)(1) = 5$$
$$(5)(0) = 0$$

The pattern developed can be continued so that 5 is multiplied by a sequence of negative numbers. The resulting products must be negative in order to maintain the pattern of decreasing by 5.

$$(5)(-1) = -5$$
$$(5)(-2) = -10$$
$$(5)(-3) = -15$$
$$(5)(-4) = -20$$

This illustrates that the product of a positive number and a negative number is negative.

When -5 is multiplied by a sequence of decreasing integers, each product increases by 5.

$$(-5)(3) = -15$$
$$(-5)(2) = -10$$
$$(-5)(1) = -5$$
$$(-5)(0) = 0$$

The pattern developed can be continued so that -5 is multiplied by a sequence of negative numbers. The resulting products must be positive in order to maintain the pattern of increasing by 5.

$$(-5)(-1) = 5$$
$$(-5)(-2) = 10$$
$$(-5)(-3) = 15$$
$$(-5)(-4) = 20$$

This illustrates that the product of two negative numbers is positive.

This pattern for multiplication is summarized in the following rules for multiplying integers.

Multiplication of Integers

Integers with the same sign
To multiply two numbers with the same sign, multiply the absolute values of the numbers. The product is positive.

$$4 \cdot 8 = 32$$

$$(-4)(-8) = 32$$

Integers with different signs
To multiply two numbers with different signs, multiply the absolute values of the numbers. The product is negative.

$$-4 \cdot 8 = -32$$

$$(4)(-8) = -32$$

Example 4   Multiply.   A. $-42 \cdot 62$ B. $2(-3)(-5)(-7)$

Solution   A. $-42 \cdot 62$
   $= -2604$

▸ The signs are different. The product is negative.

   B. $2(-3)(-5)(-7)$
   $= -6(-5)(-7)$
   $= 30(-7)$
   $= -210$

▸ To multiply more than two numbers, multiply the first two numbers. Then multiply the product by the third number. Continue until all the numbers have been multiplied.

Problem 4   Multiply.   A. $-38 \cdot 51$ B. $-7(-8)(9)(-2)$

Solution   See page S1.   A. -1938 B. -1008

4   Divide integers

For every division problem there is a related multiplication problem.

$$\text{Division: } \frac{8}{2} = 4 \qquad \text{Related multiplication: } 4 \cdot 2 = 8$$

This fact can be used to illustrate the rules for dividing signed numbers.

The quotient of two numbers with the same sign is positive.

$$\frac{12}{3} = 4 \text{ because } 4 \cdot 3 = 12.$$

$$\frac{-12}{-3} = 4 \text{ because } 4(-3) = -12.$$

The quotient of two numbers with different signs is negative.

$$\frac{12}{-3} = -4 \text{ because } -4(-3) = 12.$$

$$\frac{-12}{3} = -4 \text{ because } -4 \cdot 3 = -12.$$

Division of Integers

Integers with the same sign
To divide two numbers with the same sign, divide the absolute values of the numbers. The quotient is positive.

Integers with different signs
To divide two numbers with different signs, divide the absolute values of the numbers. The quotient is negative.

Note that $\frac{-12}{3} = -4$, $\frac{12}{-3} = -4$, and $-\frac{12}{3} = -4$. This suggests the following rule.

If a and b are two integers, and $b \neq 0$, then $\frac{a}{-b} = \frac{-a}{b} = -\frac{a}{b}$.

Read $b \neq 0$ as "b is not equal to 0." The reason why the denominator must not be equal to 0 is explained in the following discussion of zero and one in division.

Zero and One in Division

Zero divided by any number other than zero is zero.	$\frac{0}{a} = 0, a \neq 0$	because $0 \cdot a = 0$.
Division by zero is not defined.	$\frac{4}{0} = ?$	$? \times 0 = 4$ There is no number whose product with zero is 4.
Any number other than zero divided by itself is 1.	$\frac{a}{a} = 1, a \neq 0$	because $1 \cdot a = a$.
Any number divided by 1 is the number.	$\frac{a}{1} = a$	because $a \cdot 1 = a$.

Example 5 Divide.   A. $(-120) \div (-8)$ B. $\frac{95}{-5}$ C. $-\frac{-81}{3}$

Solution   A. $(-120) \div (-8) = 15$

   B. $\frac{95}{-5} = -19$

   C. $-\frac{-81}{3} = -(-27) = 27$

Problem 5 Divide.   A. $(-135) \div (-9)$ B. $\frac{84}{-6}$ C. $-\frac{36}{-12}$

Solution See page S1.   A. 15   B. −14   C. 3

5   Application problems

In many courses, your course grade depends on the *average* of all your test scores. You compute the average by calculating the sum of all your test scores and then dividing that result by the number of tests. Statisticians call this average an **arithmetic mean.** Besides its application to finding the average of your test scores, the arithmetic mean is used in many other situations.

Stock market analysts calculate the **moving average** of a stock. This is the arithmetic mean of the changes in the value of a stock for a given number of days. To illustrate the procedure, we will calculate the 5-day moving average of a stock. In actual practice, a stock market analyst may use 15 days, 30 days, or some other number.

The table below shows the amount of increase or decrease, in cents, in the closing price of a stock for a 10-day period.

Day 1	Day 2	Day 3	Day 4	Day 5	Day 6	Day 7	Day 8	Day 9	Day 10
+50	−175	+225	0	−275	−75	−50	+50	−475	−50

To calculate the 5-day moving average of this stock, determine the average of the stock for days 1 through 5, days 2 through 6, days 3 through 7, and so on.

Days 1–5	Days 2–6	Days 3–7	Days 4–8	Days 5–9	Days 6–10
+50	−175	+225	0	−275	−75
−175	+225	0	−275	−75	−50
+225	0	−275	−75	−50	+50
0	−275	−75	−50	+50	−475
−275	−75	−50	+50	−475	−50
Sum = −175	Sum = −300	Sum = −175	Sum = −350	Sum = −825	Sum = −600
$Av = \frac{-175}{5} = -35$	$Av = \frac{-300}{5} = -60$	$Av = \frac{-175}{5} = -35$	$Av = \frac{-350}{5} = -70$	$Av = \frac{-825}{5} = -165$	$Av = \frac{-600}{5} = -120$

The 5-day moving average is the list of means: $-35, -60, -35, -70, -165,$ and -120. If the numbers in the list tend to increase, the price of the stock is showing an upward trend; if they decrease, the price of the stock is showing a downward trend. For the stock shown here, the price of the stock is showing a downward trend. These trends help analysts determine whether to recommend a stock.

Example 6   The daily low temperatures, in degrees Celsius, during one week were recorded as follows: $-8°, 2°, 0°, -7°, 1°, 6°, -1°$. Find the average daily low temperature for the week.

Strategy   To find the average daily low temperature:
- Add the seven temperature readings.
- Divide the sum by 7.

Solution
$$
\begin{aligned}
-8 + 2 &+ 0 + (-7) + 1 + 6 + (-1) \\
&= -6 + 0 + (-7) + 1 + 6 + (-1) \\
&= -6 + (-7) + 1 + 6 + (-1) \\
&= -13 + 1 + 6 + (-1) \\
&= -12 + 6 + (-1) \\
&= -6 + (-1) \\
&= -7
\end{aligned}
$$

$$-7 \div 7 = -1$$

The average daily low temperature was $-1°C$.

Problem 6   The daily high temperatures, in degrees Celsius, during one week were recorded as follows: $-5°, -6°, 3°, 0°, -4°, -7°, -2°$. Find the average daily high temperature for the week.

Solution   See page S1. $-3°C$

INSTRUCTOR NOTE
Another of the major pedagogical features of this text is written *strategies* that accompany every application problem. For the paired Problem, we ask students to provide their own written strategy. A suggested strategy, along with a complete solution to the problem, can be found in the Solutions section.

STUDY TIPS

SURVEY THE CHAPTER

Before you begin reading a chapter, take a few minutes to survey it. Glancing through the chapter will give you an overview of its content and help you see how the pieces fit together as you read.

   Begin by reading the chapter title. The title summarizes what the chapter is about. Next read the section headings. The section headings summarize the major topics presented in the chapter. Then read the objectives under each section heading. The objective headings describe the learning goals for that section. Keep these headings in mind as you work through the material. They provide direction as you study.

CONCEPT REVIEW 1.2

Determine whether the statement is always true, sometimes true, or never true.

1. The sum of two integers is larger than either of the integers being added.   Sometimes true

2. The sum of two nonzero integers with the same sign is positive.   Sometimes true

3. The quotient of two integers with different signs is negative.   Always true

4. To find the opposite of a number, multiply the number by -1.   Always true

5. To find the opposite of an integer, divide the integer by -1.   Always true

6. To perform the subtraction $a - b$, add the opposite of a to b.   Never true

7. $4(-8) = -4$ Never true

8. If x and y are two integers and $y = 0$, then $\frac{x}{y} = 0$.   Never true

9. If x and y are two different integers, then $x - y = y - x$.   Never true

10. If x is an integer and $4x = 0$, then $x = 0$.   Always true

---

EXERCISES 1.2

1   **1.** ✍ Explain how to add two integers with the same sign.

    2. ✍ Explain how to add two integers with different signs.

Add.

3. $-3 + (-8)$ -11 **4.** $-12 + (-1)$ -13 **5.** $-4 + (-5)$ -9 **6.** $-12 + (-12)$
                                                                                           -24

7. $6 + (-9)$ -3 **8.** $4 + (-9)$ -5 **9.** $-6 + 7$ 1 **10.** $-12 + 6$ -6

11. $2 + (-3) + (-4)$ -5 **12.** $7 + (-2) + (-8)$ -3 **13.** $-3 + (-12) + (-15)$
                                                                                                      -30

14. $9 + (-6) + (-16)$ -13 **15.** $-17 + (-3) + 29$ 9 **16.** $13 + 62 + (-38)$ 37

17. $-3 + (-8) + 12$ 1 **18.** $-27 + (-42) + (-18)$ -87

19. $13 + (-22) + 4 + (-5)$ -10 **20.** $-14 + (-3) + 7 + (-6)$ -16

21. $-22 + 10 + 2 + (-18)$ -28 **22.** $-6 + (-8) + 13 + (-4)$ -5

23. $-126 + (-247) + (-358) + 339$ -392 **24.** $-651 + (-239) + 524 + 487$ 121

2   **25.** ✍ Explain the meaning of the words *minus* and *negative*.

    26. ✍ Explain how to rewrite $6 - (-9)$ as addition of the opposite.

Subtract.

27. $16 - 8$ 8 **28.** $12 - 3$ 9 **29.** $7 - 14$ -7

30. $7 - (-2)$ 9 **31.** $3 - (-4)$ 7 **32.** $-6 - (-3)$ -3

33. $-4 - (-2)$ -2 **34.** $6 - (-12)$ 18 **35.** $-12 - 16$ -28

36. $-4 - 3 - 2$ -9 **37.** $4 - 5 - 12$ -13 **38.** $12 - (-7) - 8$ 11

39. $-12 - (-3) - (-15)$ 6 **40.** $4 - 12 - (-8)$ 0 **41.** $13 - 7 - 15$ -9

42. $-6 + 19 - (-31)$ 44 **43.** $-30 - (-65) - 29 - 4$ 2 **44.** $42 - (-82) - 65 - 7$ 52

45. $-16 - 47 - 63 - 12$ -138 **46.** $42 - (-30) - 65 - (-11)$ 18

47. $-47 - (-67) - 13 - 15$ -8 **48.** $-18 - 49 - (-84) - 27$ -10

3 **49.** Explain how to multiply two integers with the same sign.

50. Explain how to multiply two integers with different signs.

Multiply.

51. $14 \cdot 3$ 42 **52.** $62 \cdot 9$ 558 **53.** $5(-4)$ -20

54. $4(-7)$ -28 **55.** $-8(2)$ -16 **56.** $-9(3)$ -27

57. $(-5)(-5)$ 25 **58.** $(-3)(-6)$ 18 **59.** $(-7)(0)$ 0

60. $-32 \cdot 4$ -128 **61.** $-24 \cdot 3$ -72 **62.** $19(-7)$ -133

63. $6(-17)$ -102 **64.** $-8(-26)$ 208 **65.** $-4(-35)$ 140

66. $-5(23)$ -115 **67.** $5 \cdot 7(-2)$ -70 **68.** $8(-6)(-1)$ 48

69. $(-9)(-9)(2)$ 162 **70.** $-8(-7)(-4)$ -224 **71.** $-5(8)(-3)$ 120

72. $(-6)(5)(7)$ -210 **73.** $-1(4)(-9)$ 36 **74.** $6(-3)(-2)$ 36

75. $4(-4) \cdot 6(-2)$ 192 **76.** $-5 \cdot 9(-7) \cdot 3$ 945 **77.** $-9(4) \cdot 3(1)$ -108

78. $8(8)(-5)(-4)$ 1280 **79.** $-6(-5)(12)(0)$ 0 **80.** $7(9) \cdot 10(-1)$ -630

4 Divide.

81. $12 \div (-6)$ -2 **82.** $18 \div (-3)$ -6 **83.** $(-72) \div (-9)$ 8

84. $(-64) \div (-8)$ 8 **85.** $0 \div (-6)$ 0 **86.** $-49 \div 0$ Undefined

87. $45 \div (-5)$ -9 **88.** $-24 \div 4$ -6 **89.** $-36 \div 4$ -9

90. $-56 \div 7$ -8 **91.** $-81 \div (-9)$ 9 **92.** $-40 \div (-5)$ 8

93. $72 \div (-3)$ -24 **94.** $44 \div (-4)$ -11 **95.** $-60 \div 5$ -12

96. $144 \div 9$ 16 **97.** $78 \div (-6)$ -13 **98.** $84 \div (-7)$ -12

99. $-72 \div 4$ -18 **100.** $-80 \div 5$ -16 **101.** $-114 \div (-6)$ 19

102. $-128 \div 4$ -32 **103.** $-130 \div (-5)$ 26 **104.** $(-280) \div 8$ -35

105. $-132 \div (-12)$ 11 **106.** $-156 \div (-13)$ 12 **107.** $-182 \div 14$ -13

108. $-144 \div 12$ -12 **109.** $143 \div 11$ 13 **110.** $168 \div 14$ 12

5 **111.** *Temperature*   Find the temperature after a rise of 9°C from −6°C.   3°C

112. *Temperature*   Find the temperature after a rise of 7°C from −18°C.   −11°C

113. *Temperature*   The high temperature for the day was 10°C. The low temperature was −4°C. Find the difference between the high and low temperatures for the day.   14°C

114. *Temperature*   The low temperature for the day was −2°C. The high temperature was 11°C. Find the difference between the high and low temperatures for the day.   13°C

115. *Chemistry*   The temperature at which mercury boils is 360°C. Mercury freezes at −39°C. Find the difference between the temperature at which mercury boils and the temperature at which it freezes.   399°C

116. *Chemistry*   The temperature at which radon boils is −62°C. Radon freezes at −71°C. Find the difference between the temperature at which radon boils and the temperature at which it freezes.   9°C

The elevation, or height, of places on Earth is measured in relation to sea level, or the average level of the ocean's surface. The following table shows height above sea level as a positive number and depth below sea level as a negative number. (Source: *Information Please Almanac*)

Continent	Highest Elevation (in meters)		Lowest Elevation (in meters)	
Africa	Mt. Kilimanjaro	5895	Qattara Depression	−133
Asia	Mt. Everest	8848	Dead Sea	−400
Europe	Mt. Elbrus	5634	Caspian Sea	−28
North America	Mt. McKinley	6194	Death Valley	−86
South America	Mt. Aconcagua	6960	Salinas Grandes	−40

117. *Geography*   Use the table to find the difference in elevation between Mt. Elbrus and the Caspian Sea.   5662 m

118. *Geography*   Use the table to find the difference in elevation between Mt. Aconcagua and Salinas Grandes.   7000 m

119. *Geography*   Use the table to find the difference in elevation between Mt. Kilimanjaro and the Qattara Depression.   6028 m

120. *Geography*   Use the table to find the difference in elevation between Mt. McKinley and Death Valley.   6280 m

121. *Geography*   Use the table to find the difference in elevation between Mt. Everest and the Dead Sea.   9248 m

122. *Temperature*   The daily low temperatures, in degrees Celsius, during one week were recorded as follows: 4°, −5°, 8°, 0°, −9°, −11°, −8°. Find the average daily low temperature for the week.   −3°C

123. *Temperature*   The daily high temperatures, in degrees Celsius, during one week were recorded as follows: −8°, −9°, 6°, 7°, −2°, −14°, −1°. Find the average daily high temperature for the week.   −3°C

124. *Temperature*   On January 22, 1943, the temperature at Spearfish, South Dakota, rose from −4°F to 45°F in two minutes. How many degrees did the temperature rise during those two minutes?   49°F

125. *Temperature*   In a 24-hour period in January of 1916, the temperature in Browning, Montana, dropped from 44°F to −56°F. How many degrees did the temperature drop during that time?   100°F

The bar graph at the right shows the net income or loss for US Airways for the years 1992 to 1997. Use this graph for Exercises 126 to 129.

US Airways' Net Income (Loss) in Millions of Dollars

Sources: Transportation Department; US Airways.

126. *Business*   What was the total net income or loss for the years shown in the graph?
−$900 million

127. *Business*   What was the difference between the net income or loss in 1993 and that in 1994?
$292 million

128. *Business*   What was the difference between the net income or loss in 1995 and that in 1994?
$804 million

129. *Business*   For what two years shown in the graph is the difference between the net income or loss greatest? What is that difference?
1997 and 1992; $2,254 million

130. *Education*   To discourage random guessing on a multiple-choice exam, a professor assigns 5 points for a correct answer, −2 points for an incorrect answer, and 0 points for leaving the question blank. What is the score for a student who had 20 correct answers, had 13 incorrect answers, and left 7 questions blank?   74

131. *Education*   To discourage random guessing on a multiple-choice exam, a professor assigns 7 points for a correct answer, −3 points for an incorrect answer, and −1 point for leaving the question blank. What is the score for a student who had 17 correct answers, had 8 incorrect answers, and left 2 questions blank?   93

132. *The Stock Market*   The value of a share of McDonald's stock on June 12, 1998, was $64.25. The table below shows the amount of increase or decrease, to the nearest 10 cents, from the June 12 closing price of the stock for a 10-day period. Calculate the 5-day moving average for this stock.

Day 1	Day 2	Day 3	Day 4	Day 5	Day 6	Day 7	Day 8	Day 9	Day 10
+40	−90	+40	+130	+240	+20	−10	−50	+10	+40

72, 68, 84, 66, 42, 2

133.   *The Stock Market*   The value of a share of Disney stock on June 12, 1998, was $116.1875. The table below shows the amount of increase or decrease, to the nearest 10 cents, from the June 12 closing price of the stock for a 10-day period. Calculate the 5-day moving average for this stock.

Day 1	Day 2	Day 3	Day 4	Day 5	Day 6	Day 7	Day 8	Day 9	Day 10
-110	-290	$+70$	$+140$	-230	-440	$+120$	$+100$	$+290$	-20

$-84, -150, -68, -62, -32, 10$

APPLYING CONCEPTS 1.2

Simplify.

134. $|-7 + 12|$ 5

135. $|13 - (-4)|$ 17

136. $|-13 - (-2)|$ 11

137. $|18 - 21|$ 3

Assuming the pattern is continued, find the next three numbers in the pattern.

138. $-7, -11, -15, -19, \ldots$ $-23, -27, -31$

139. $16, 11, 6, 1, \ldots$ $-4, -9, -14$

140. $7, -14, 28, -56, \ldots$ $112, -224, 448$

141. $1024, -256, 64, \ldots$ $-16, 4, -1$

Solve.

[C] **142.**   32,844 is divisible by 3. By rearranging the digits, find the largest possible number that is still divisible by 3.   84,432

[C] **143.**   4563 is not divisible by 4. By rearranging the digits, find the largest possible number that is divisible by 4.   5436

[C] **144.**   How many three-digit numbers of the form 8__4 are divisible by 3?
4 (804, 834, 864, 894)

In each exercise, determine which statement is false.

145. **a.** $|3 + 4| = |3| + |4|$ **b.** $|3 - 4| = |3| - |4|$ **c.** $|4 + 3| = |4| + |3|$ **d.** $|4 - 3| = |4| - |3|$ b

146. **a.** $|5 + 2| = |5| + |2|$ **b.** $|5 - 2| = |5| - |2|$ **c.** $|2 + 5| = |2| + |5|$ **d.** $|2 - 5| = |2| - |5|$ d

Determine which statement is true for all real numbers.

[C] **147.** **a.** $|x + y| \leq |x| + |y|$ **b.** $|x + y| = |x| + |y|$ **c.** $|x + y| \geq |x| + |y|$ a

[C] **148.** **a.** $||x| - |y|| \leq |x| - |y|$ **b.** $||x| - |y|| = |x| - |y|$ **c.** $||x| - |y|| \geq |x| - |y|$ c

149.   Is the difference between two integers always smaller than either one of the numbers in the difference? If not, give an example for which the difference between two integers is greater than either integer.   No. $10 - (-8) = 18$

150.   If $-4x$ equals a positive integer, is x a positive or a negative integer? Explain your answer.

151.   Explain why division by zero is not allowed.

SECTION 1.3
Rational Numbers

1 Write rational numbers as decimals

POINT OF INTEREST

As early as A.D. 630 the Hindu mathematician Brahmagupta wrote a fraction as one number over another separated by a space. The Arab mathematician al Hassar (around A.D. 1050) was the first to show a fraction with the horizontal bar separating the numerator and denominator.

A **rational number** is the quotient of two integers. Therefore, a rational number is a number that can be written in the form $\frac{a}{b}$, where a and b are integers, and b is not zero. A rational number written in this way is commonly called a **fraction**.

$\frac{a}{b}$ ← an integer
  ← a nonzero integer

$\left.\dfrac{2}{3}, \ \dfrac{-4}{9}, \ \dfrac{18}{-5}, \ \dfrac{4}{1}\right\}$ Rational numbers

Because an integer can be written as the quotient of the integer and 1, every integer is a rational number.

$$5 = \frac{5}{1} \qquad -3 = \frac{-3}{1}$$

A number written in **decimal notation** is also a rational number.

three-tenths $0.3 = \dfrac{3}{10}$

thirty-five hundredths $0.35 = \dfrac{35}{100}$

negative four-tenths $-0.4 = \dfrac{-4}{10}$

A rational number written as a fraction can be written in decimal notation.

LOOK CLOSELY

The fraction bar can be read "divided by."
$$\frac{5}{8} = 5 \div 8$$

Example 1 Write $\dfrac{5}{8}$ as a decimal.

Solution

$$\begin{array}{r} 0.625 \\ 8\overline{)5.000} \\ -4\,8 \\ \hline 20 \\ -16 \\ \hline 40 \\ -40 \\ \hline 0 \end{array}$$

← This is called a **terminating decimal.**

← The remainder is zero.

LOOK CLOSELY

Dividing the numerator by the denominator results in a remainder of 0. The decimal 0.625 is a terminating decimal.

$$\frac{5}{8} = 0.625$$

Problem 1 Write $\dfrac{4}{25}$ as a decimal.

Solution See page S1. 0.16

Example 2   Write $\frac{4}{11}$ as a decimal.

Solution

$$\begin{array}{r} 0.3636\ldots \\ 11\overline{)4.0000} \\ -3\,3 \\ \hline 70 \\ -66 \\ \hline 40 \\ -33 \\ \hline 70 \\ -66 \\ \hline 4 \end{array}$$

$\leftarrow$ This is called a **repeating decimal.**

$\leftarrow$ The remainder is never zero.

$\frac{4}{11} = 0.\overline{36}$ $\leftarrow$ The bar over the digits 3 and 6 is used to show that these digits repeat.

Problem 2   Write $\frac{4}{9}$ as a decimal. Place a bar over the repeating digits of the decimal.

Solution   See page S1. $0.\overline{4}$

Rational numbers can be written as fractions, such as $-\frac{6}{7}$ or $\frac{8}{3}$, where the numerator and denominator are integers. But every rational number also can be written as a repeating decimal (such as 0.25767676…) or a terminating decimal (such as 1.73). This was illustrated in Examples 1 and 2.

Some numbers cannot be written either as a repeating decimal or as a terminating decimal. These numbers are called **irrational numbers.** For example, 2.45445444544445… is an irrational number. Two other examples are $\sqrt{2}$ and π.

$$\sqrt{2} = 1.414213562\ldots \quad \pi = 3.141592654\ldots$$

The three dots mean that the digits continue on and on without ever repeating or terminating. Although we cannot write a decimal that is exactly equal to $\sqrt{2}$ or to π, we can give approximations of these numbers. The symbol $\approx$ is read "is approximately equal to." Shown below is $\sqrt{2}$ rounded to the nearest thousandth and π rounded to the nearest hundredth.

$$\sqrt{2} = 1.414 \quad \pi = 3.14$$

The rational numbers and the irrational numbers taken together are called the **real numbers.**

2   ## Convert among percents, fractions, and decimals

"A population growth rate of 3%," "a manufacturer's discount of 25%," and "an 8% increase in pay" are typical examples of the many ways in which percent is used in applied problems. **Percent** means "parts of 100." Thus 27% means 27 parts of 100.

In applied problems involving a percent, it is usually necessary either to rewrite the percent as a fraction or a decimal, or to rewrite a fraction or a decimal as a percent.

To write 27% as a fraction, remove the percent sign and multiply by $\frac{1}{100}$.

$$27\% = 27\left(\frac{1}{100}\right) = \frac{27}{100}$$

To write a percent as a decimal, remove the percent sign and multiply by 0.01.

To write 33% as a decimal, remove the percent sign and multiply by 0.01.

$$33\% = 33(0.01) = 0.33$$

Move the decimal point two places to the left. Then remove the percent sign.

➡ Write 100% as a decimal.

$$100\% = 100(0.01) = 1$$

⬅

Example 3   Write 130% as a fraction and as a decimal.

Solution $130\% = 130\left(\frac{1}{100}\right) = \frac{130}{100} = 1\frac{3}{10}$ ▶ To write a percent as a fraction, remove the percent sign and multiply by $\frac{1}{100}$.

$130\% = 130(0.01) = 1.30$ ▶ To write a percent as a decimal, remove the percent sign and multiply by 0.01.

Problem 3   Write 125% as a fraction and as a decimal.

Solution   See page S1. $1\frac{1}{4}$, 1.25

Example 4   Write $33\frac{1}{3}\%$ as a fraction.

Solution $33\frac{1}{3}\% = 33\frac{1}{3}\left(\frac{1}{100}\right) = \frac{100}{3}\left(\frac{1}{100}\right)$ ▶ Write the mixed number $33\frac{1}{3}$ as the improper fraction $\frac{100}{3}$.

$= \frac{1}{3}$

Problem 4   Write $16\frac{2}{3}\%$ as a fraction.

Solution   See page S1. $\frac{1}{6}$

Example 5   Write 0.25% as a decimal.

Solution $0.25\% = 0.25(0.01) = 0.0025$ ▶ Remove the percent sign and multiply by 0.01.

Problem 5   Write 6.08% as a decimal.

Solution   See page S1.   0.0608

A fraction or decimal can be written as a percent by multiplying by 100%. Recall that 100% = 1, and multiplying a number by 1 does not change the number.

To write $\frac{5}{8}$ as a percent, multiply by 100%.

$$\frac{5}{8} = \frac{5}{8}(100\%) = \frac{500}{8}\% = 62.5\% \text{ or } 62\frac{1}{2}\%$$

To write 0.82 as a percent, multiply by 100%.

$$0.82 \qquad = \qquad 0.82(100\%) \qquad = \qquad 82\%$$

Move the decimal point two places to the right. Then write the percent sign.

Example 6   Write as a percent.   A. 0.027   B. 1.34

Solution   A. 0.027 = 0.027(100%) = 2.7%   ▶ To write a decimal as a percent, multiply by 100%.

B. 1.34 = 1.34(100%) = 134%

Problem 6   Write as a percent.   A. 0.043   B. 2.57

Solution   See page S1.   A. 4.3%   B. 257%

Example 7   Write $\frac{5}{6}$ as a percent. Round to the nearest tenth of a percent.

Solution $\frac{5}{6} = \frac{5}{6}(100\%) = \frac{500}{6}\% \approx 83.3\%$ ▶ To write a fraction as a percent, multiply by 100%.

Problem 7   Write $\frac{5}{9}$ as a percent. Round to the nearest tenth of a percent.

Solution   See page S1.   55.6%

Example 8   Write $\frac{7}{16}$ as a percent. Write the remainder in fractional form.

Solution $\frac{7}{16} = \frac{7}{16}(100\%) = \frac{700}{16}\% = 43\frac{3}{4}\%$ ▶ Multiply the fraction by 100%.

Problem 8   Write $\frac{9}{16}$ as a percent. Write the remainder in fractional form.

Solution   See page S1. $56\frac{1}{4}\%$

---

3   ## Add and subtract rational numbers

To add or subtract fractions, first rewrite each fraction as an equivalent fraction with a common denominator, using the least common multiple (LCM) of the denominators as the common denominator. Then add the numerators, and place the sum over the common denominator. Write the answer in simplest form.

The sign rules for adding integers apply to addition of rational numbers.

Example 9   Add: $-\dfrac{5}{6} + \dfrac{3}{10}$

Solution   Prime factorization of 6 and 10:

$6 = 2 \cdot 3 \qquad 10 = 2 \cdot 5$

$\text{LCM} = 2 \cdot 3 \cdot 5 = 30$

▶ Find the LCM of the denominators 6 and 10. The LCM of denominators is sometimes called the **least common denominator** (LCD).

$$-\frac{5}{6} + \frac{3}{10} = -\frac{25}{30} + \frac{9}{30}$$

▶ Rewrite the fractions as equivalent fractions, using the LCM of the denominators as the common denominator.

$$= \frac{-25 + 9}{30}$$

▶ Add the numerators, and place the sum over the common denominator.

$$= \frac{-16}{30}$$

$$= -\frac{8}{15}$$

▶ Write the answer in simplest form.

Problem 9   Subtract: $\dfrac{5}{9} - \dfrac{11}{12}$

Solution   See page S1. $-\dfrac{13}{36}$

Example 10   Simplify: $-\dfrac{3}{4} + \dfrac{1}{6} - \dfrac{5}{8}$

Solution $-\dfrac{3}{4} + \dfrac{1}{6} - \dfrac{5}{8} = -\dfrac{18}{24} + \dfrac{4}{24} - \dfrac{15}{24}$

▶ The LCM of 4, 6, and 8 is 24.

$$= \frac{-18}{24} + \frac{4}{24} + \frac{-15}{24}$$

$$= \frac{-18 + 4 + (-15)}{24}$$

$$= \frac{-29}{24}$$

$$= -\frac{29}{24}$$

Problem 10   Simplify: $-\dfrac{7}{8} - \dfrac{5}{6} + \dfrac{1}{2}$

Solution   See page S2. $-\dfrac{29}{24}$

To add or subtract decimals, write the numbers so that the decimal points are in a vertical line. Then proceed as in the addition or subtraction of integers. Write the decimal point in the answer directly below the decimal points in the problem.

Example 11   Add: $14.02 + 137.6 + 9.852$

Solution
$$\begin{array}{r} 14.02 \\ 137.6 \\ +\ \ 9.852 \\ \hline 161.472 \end{array}$$

▶ Write the decimals so that the decimal points are in a vertical line.

▶ Write the decimal point in the sum directly below the decimal points in the problem.

Problem 11   Add: $3.097 + 4.9 + 3.09$

Solution   See page S2. 11.087

Example 12   Add: $-114.039 + 84.76$

Solution
$$\begin{array}{r} 114.039 \\ -\ \ 84.76 \\ \hline 29.279 \end{array}$$

▶ The signs are different. Subtract the absolute value of the number with the smaller absolute value from the absolute value of the number with the larger absolute value.

$$\begin{aligned} -114.039 + 84.76 \\ = -29.279 \end{aligned}$$

▶ Attach the sign of the number with the larger absolute value.

Problem 12   Subtract: $16.127 - 67.91$

Solution   See page S2. -51.783

4   Multiply and divide rational numbers

The sign rules for multiplying and dividing integers apply to multiplication and division of rational numbers. The product of two fractions is the product of the numerators divided by the product of the denominators.

Example 13   Multiply: $\dfrac{3}{8} \cdot \dfrac{12}{17}$

Solution
$$\dfrac{3}{8} \cdot \dfrac{12}{17} = \dfrac{3 \cdot 12}{8 \cdot 17}$$

▶ Multiply the numerators. Multiply the denominators.

$$= \dfrac{3 \cdot \overset{1}{\cancel{2}} \cdot \overset{1}{\cancel{2}} \cdot 3}{2 \cdot \underset{1}{\cancel{2}} \cdot \underset{1}{\cancel{2}} \cdot 17}$$

▶ Write the prime factorization of each factor. Divide by the common factors.

$$= \dfrac{9}{34}$$

▶ Multiply the numbers remaining in the numerator. Multiply the numbers remaining in the denominator.

Problem 13   Multiply: $-\dfrac{7}{12} \cdot \dfrac{9}{14}$

Solution   See page S2. $-\dfrac{3}{8}$

To divide fractions, invert the divisor. Then proceed as in the multiplication of fractions.

Example 14   Divide: $\dfrac{3}{10} \div \left(-\dfrac{18}{25}\right)$

Solution
$$\dfrac{3}{10} \div \left(-\dfrac{18}{25}\right) = -\left(\dfrac{3}{10} \div \dfrac{18}{25}\right)$$

▶ The signs are different. The quotient is negative.

$$= -\left(\dfrac{3}{10} \cdot \dfrac{25}{18}\right)$$

▶ Change division to multiplication. Invert the divisor.

$$= -\left(\dfrac{3 \cdot 25}{10 \cdot 18}\right)$$

▶ Multiply the numerators. Multiply the denominators.

$$= -\left(\dfrac{\overset{1}{\cancel{3}} \cdot \overset{1}{\cancel{5}} \cdot 5}{2 \cdot \underset{1}{\cancel{5}} \cdot 2 \cdot \underset{1}{\cancel{3}} \cdot 3}\right)$$

$$= -\dfrac{5}{12}$$

> **Problem 14**   Divide: $-\dfrac{3}{8} \div \left(-\dfrac{5}{12}\right)$
>
> **Solution**   See page S2. $\dfrac{9}{10}$

To multiply decimals, multiply as in the multiplication of whole numbers. Write the decimal point in the product so that the number of decimal places in the product equals the sum of the decimal places in the factors.

> **Example 15**   Multiply: $(-6.89)(0.00035)$
>
> **Solution**
>
> $$\begin{array}{r} 6.89 \\ \times\ 0.00035 \\ \hline 3445 \\ 2067\ \ \ \\ \hline 0.0024115 \end{array}$$
>
> 6.89 — 2 decimal places   ▶ Multiply the absolute values.
> × 0.00035 — 5 decimal places
> 0.0024115 — 7 decimal places
>
> $(-6.89)(0.00035) = -0.0024115$ ▶ The signs are different. The product is negative.

> **Problem 15**   Multiply: $(-5.44)(3.8)$
>
> **Solution**   See page S2. -20.672

To divide decimals, move the decimal point in the divisor to make it a whole number. Move the decimal point in the dividend the same number of places to the right. Place the decimal point in the quotient directly over the decimal point in the dividend. Then divide as in the division of whole numbers.

> **Example 16**   Divide: $1.32 \div 0.27$. Round to the nearest tenth.
>
> **Solution** $0.27.\overline{)1.32.}$ ▶ Move the decimal point two places to the right in the divisor and in the dividend. Place the decimal point in the quotient.
>
> $$\begin{array}{r} 4.88 \approx 4.9 \\ 27\overline{)132.00} \\ -108\ \ \ \ \\ \hline 24\,0\ \ \\ -21\,6\ \ \\ \hline 2\,40 \\ -2\,16 \\ \hline 24 \end{array}$$
>
> ▶ The symbol $\approx$ is used to indicate that the quotient is an approximate value that has been rounded off.

> **Problem 16**   Divide $-0.394 \div 1.7$. Round to the nearest hundredth.
>
> **Solution**   See page S2. -0.23

USE THE TEXTBOOK TO LEARN THE MATERIAL

For each objective studied, read very carefully all of the material from the objective statement to the examples provided for that objective. As you read, note carefully the formulas and words printed in **boldface** type. It is important for you to know these formulas and the definitions of these words.

You will note that each example is paired with a problem. The example is worked out for you; the problem is left for you to do. After studying the example, do the problem. Immediately look up the answer to this problem in the Solutions section at the back of the text. The page number on which the solution appears is printed on the solution line below the problem statement. If your answer is correct, continue. If your answer is incorrect, check your solution against the one given in the Solutions section. It may be helpful to review the worked-out example also. Determine where you made your mistakes.

Next, do the problems in the exercise set that correspond to the objective just studied. The answers to all the odd-numbered exercises appear in the Answers section in the back of the book. Check your answers to the exercises against these.

If you have difficulty solving problems in the exercise set, review the material in the text. Many examples are solved within the text material. Review the solutions to these problems. Reread the examples provided for the objective. If, after checking these sources and trying to find your mistakes, you are still unable to solve a problem correctly, make a note of the exercise number so that you can ask someone for help with that problem.

CONCEPT REVIEW 1.3

Determine whether the statement is always true, sometimes true, or never true.

1. To multiply two fractions, you must first rewrite the fractions as equivalent fractions with a common denominator.   Never true

2. The number $\frac{\pi}{3}$ is an example of a rational number.   Never true

3. A rational number can be written as a terminating decimal.   Sometimes true

4. The number 2.585585558 . . . is an example of a repeating decimal.   Never true

5. An irrational number is a real number.   Always true

6. 37%, 0.37, and $\frac{37}{100}$ are three numbers that have the same value.   Always true

7. To write a decimal as a percent, multiply the decimal by $\frac{1}{100}$.   Never true

8. If a, b, c, and d are natural numbers, then $\frac{a}{b} + \frac{c}{d} = \frac{a+c}{b+d}$.   Never true

9. -12 is an example of a number that is both an integer and a rational number.
   Always true

10. $\frac{7}{9}$ is an example of a number that is both a rational number and an irrational number.   Never true

EXERCISES 1.3

1 Write as a decimal. Place a bar over the repeating digits of a repeating decimal.

1. $\frac{1}{3}$ $0.\overline{3}$
2. $\frac{2}{3}$ $0.\overline{6}$
3. $\frac{1}{4}$ 0.25
4. $\frac{3}{4}$ 0.75
5. $\frac{2}{5}$ 0.4

6. $\frac{4}{5}$ 0.8
7. $\frac{1}{6}$ $0.1\overline{6}$
8. $\frac{5}{6}$ $0.8\overline{3}$
9. $\frac{1}{8}$ 0.125
10. $\frac{7}{8}$ 0.875

11. $\frac{2}{9}$ $0.\overline{2}$
12. $\frac{8}{9}$ $0.\overline{8}$
13. $\frac{5}{11}$ $0.\overline{45}$
14. $\frac{10}{11}$ $0.\overline{90}$
15. $\frac{7}{12}$ $0.58\overline{3}$

16. $\frac{11}{12}$ $0.91\overline{6}$
17. $\frac{4}{15}$ $0.2\overline{6}$
18. $\frac{8}{15}$ $0.5\overline{3}$
19. $\frac{9}{16}$ 0.5625
20. $\frac{15}{16}$ 0.9375

21. $\frac{6}{25}$ 0.24
22. $\frac{14}{25}$ 0.56
23. $\frac{9}{40}$ 0.225
24. $\frac{21}{40}$ 0.525
25. $\frac{15}{22}$ $0.68\overline{1}$

26. $\frac{19}{22}$ $0.86\overline{3}$
27. $\frac{11}{24}$ $0.458\overline{3}$
28. $\frac{19}{24}$ $0.791\overline{6}$
29. $\frac{5}{33}$ $0.\overline{15}$
30. $\frac{25}{33}$ $0.\overline{75}$

31. $\frac{3}{37}$ $0.\overline{081}$
32. $\frac{14}{37}$ $0.\overline{378}$

2 33. ✏ **a.** Explain how to convert a fraction to a percent.
   b. Explain how to convert a percent to a fraction.
   c. Explain how to convert a decimal to a percent.
   d. Explain how to convert a percent to a decimal.

34. ✏ Explain why multiplying a number by 100% does not change the value of the number.

Write as a fraction and as a decimal.

35. 75% $\frac{3}{4}$, 0.75
36. 40% $\frac{2}{5}$, 0.4
37. 50% $\frac{1}{2}$, 0.5
38. 10% $\frac{1}{10}$, 0.1

39. 64% $\frac{16}{25}$, 0.64
40. 88% $\frac{22}{25}$, 0.88
41. 175% $1\frac{3}{4}$, 1.75
42. 160% $1\frac{3}{5}$, 1.6

43. 19% $\frac{19}{100}$, 0.19
44. 87% $\frac{87}{100}$, 0.87
45. 5% $\frac{1}{20}$, 0.05
46. 2% $\frac{1}{50}$, 0.02

47. 450% $4\frac{1}{2}$, 4.5
48. 380% $3\frac{4}{5}$, 3.8
49. 8% $\frac{2}{25}$, 0.08
50. 4% $\frac{1}{25}$, 0.04

Write as a fraction.

51. $11\frac{1}{9}\%$ $\frac{1}{9}$
52. $37\frac{1}{2}\%$ $\frac{3}{8}$
53. $31\frac{1}{4}\%$ $\frac{5}{16}$
54. $66\frac{2}{3}\%$ $\frac{2}{3}$

55. $\frac{1}{2}\%$ $\frac{1}{200}$
56. $5\frac{3}{4}\%$ $\frac{23}{400}$
57. $6\frac{1}{4}\%$ $\frac{1}{16}$
58. $83\frac{1}{3}\%$ $\frac{5}{6}$

Write as a decimal.

59. 7.3%   0.073   **60.** 9.1%   0.091   **61.** 15.8%   0.158   **62.** 0.3%   0.003

63. 9.15%   0.0915   **64.** 121.2%   1.212   **65.** 18.23%   0.1823   **66.** 0.15%   0.0015

Write as a percent.

67. 0.15   15%   **68.** 0.37   37%   **69.** 0.05   5%   **70.** 0.02   2%

71. 0.175   17.5%   **72.** 0.125   12.5%   **73.** 1.15   115%   **74.** 2.142   214.2%

75. 0.008   0.8%   **76.** 0.004   0.4%   **77.** 0.065   6.5%   **78.** 0.083   8.3%

Write as a percent. Round to the nearest tenth of a percent.

79. $\frac{27}{50}$ 54%   **80.** $\frac{83}{100}$ 83%   **81.** $\frac{1}{3}$ 33.3%   **82.** $\frac{3}{8}$ 37.5%

83. $\frac{4}{9}$ 44.4%   **84.** $\frac{9}{20}$ 45%   **85.** $2\frac{1}{2}$ 250%   **86.** $1\frac{2}{7}$ 128.6%

Write as a percent. Write the remainder in fractional form.

87. $\frac{3}{8}$ $37\frac{1}{2}$%   **88.** $\frac{7}{16}$ $43\frac{3}{4}$%   **89.** $\frac{5}{14}$ $35\frac{5}{7}$%   **90.** $\frac{4}{7}$ $57\frac{1}{7}$%

91. $1\frac{1}{4}$ 125%   **92.** $2\frac{5}{8}$ $262\frac{1}{2}$%   **93.** $1\frac{5}{9}$ $155\frac{5}{9}$%   **94.** $1\frac{13}{16}$ $181\frac{1}{4}$%

3 Simplify.

95. $\frac{2}{3} + \frac{5}{12}$ $\frac{13}{12}$ **96.** $\frac{1}{2} + \frac{3}{8}$ $\frac{7}{8}$ **97.** $\frac{5}{8} - \frac{5}{6}$ $-\frac{5}{24}$ **98.** $\frac{1}{9} - \frac{5}{27}$ $-\frac{2}{27}$

99. $-\frac{5}{12} - \frac{3}{8}$ $-\frac{19}{24}$ **100.** $-\frac{5}{6} - \frac{5}{9}$ $-\frac{25}{18}$ **101.** $-\frac{6}{13} + \frac{17}{26}$ $\frac{5}{26}$ **102.** $-\frac{7}{12} + \frac{5}{8}$ $\frac{1}{24}$

103. $-\frac{5}{8} - \left(-\frac{11}{12}\right)$ $\frac{7}{24}$ **104.** $\frac{1}{3} + \frac{5}{6} - \frac{2}{9}$ $\frac{17}{18}$ **105.** $\frac{1}{2} - \frac{2}{3} + \frac{1}{6}$ 0   **106.** $-\frac{3}{8} - \frac{5}{12} - \frac{3}{16}$ $-\frac{47}{48}$

107. $-\frac{5}{16} + \frac{3}{4} - \frac{7}{8}$ $-\frac{7}{16}$ **108.** $\frac{1}{2} - \frac{3}{8} - \left(-\frac{1}{4}\right)$ $\frac{3}{8}$ **109.** $\frac{3}{4} - \left(-\frac{7}{12}\right) - \frac{7}{8}$ $\frac{11}{24}$ **110.** $\frac{1}{3} - \frac{1}{4} - \frac{1}{5}$ $-\frac{7}{60}$

111. $\frac{2}{3} - \frac{1}{2} + \frac{5}{6}$ 1   **112.** $\frac{5}{16} + \frac{1}{8} - \frac{1}{2}$ $-\frac{1}{16}$ **113.** $\frac{5}{8} - \left(-\frac{5}{12}\right) + \frac{1}{3}$ $\frac{11}{8}$ **114.** $\frac{1}{8} - \frac{11}{12} + \frac{1}{2}$ $-\frac{7}{24}$

115. $-\frac{7}{9} + \frac{14}{15} + \frac{8}{21}$ $\frac{169}{315}$ **116.** 1.09 + 6.2   7.29   **117.** $-32.1 - 6.7$ -38.8 **118.** 5.13 − 8.179   −3.049

119. $-13.092 + 6.9$ −6.192   **120.** 2.54 − 3.6   −1.06   **121.** 5.43 + 7.925   13.355   **122.** $-16.92 - 6.925$ −23.845

123. $-3.87 + 8.546$ 4.676   **124.** 6.9027 − 17.692 -10.7893

125. 2.09 − 6.72 − 5.4   −10.03   **126.** 16.4 + 3.09 − 7.93   11.56

127. $-18.39 + 4.9 - 23.7$ −37.19   **128.** 19 − (−3.72) − 82.75   −60.03

129. $-3.07 - (-2.97) - 17.4$ -17.5

130. $-3.09 - 4.6 - 27.3$ -34.99

131. $317.09 - 46.902 + 583.0714$ 853.2594

132. $71.0235 - 86.0974 + 254.309$ 239.2351

4 Simplify.

133. $\frac{1}{2}\left(-\frac{3}{4}\right)$ $-\frac{3}{8}$

134. $-\frac{2}{9}\left(-\frac{3}{14}\right)$ $\frac{1}{21}$

135. $\left(-\frac{3}{8}\right)\left(-\frac{4}{15}\right)$ $\frac{1}{10}$

136. $\frac{5}{8}\left(-\frac{7}{12}\right)\frac{16}{25}$ $-\frac{7}{30}$

137. $\left(\frac{1}{2}\right)\left(-\frac{3}{4}\right)\left(-\frac{5}{8}\right)$ $\frac{15}{64}$

138. $\left(\frac{5}{12}\right)\left(-\frac{8}{15}\right)\left(-\frac{1}{3}\right)$ $\frac{2}{27}$

139. $\frac{3}{8} \div \frac{1}{4}$ $\frac{3}{2}$

140. $\frac{5}{6} \div \left(-\frac{3}{4}\right)$ $-\frac{10}{9}$

141. $-\frac{5}{12} \div \frac{15}{32}$ $-\frac{8}{9}$

142. $\frac{1}{8} \div \left(-\frac{5}{12}\right)$ $-\frac{3}{10}$

143. $-\frac{4}{9} \div \left(-\frac{2}{3}\right)$ $\frac{2}{3}$

144. $-\frac{6}{11} \div \frac{4}{9}$ $-\frac{27}{22}$

145. $(1.2)(3.47)$ 4.164

146. $(-0.8)(6.2)$ -4.96

147. $(-1.89)(-2.3)$ 4.347

148. $(6.9)(-4.2)$ -28.98

149. $(1.06)(-3.8)$ -4.028

150. $(-2.7)(-3.5)$ 9.45

151. $(1.2)(-0.5)(3.7)$ -2.22

152. $(-2.4)(6.1)(0.9)$ -13.176

153. $(-0.8)(3.006)(-5.1)$
12.26448

Simplify. Round to the nearest hundredth.

154. $-24.7 \div 0.09$ -274.44

155. $-1.27 \div (-1.7)$ 0.75

156. $9.07 \div (-3.5)$ -2.59

157. $-354.2086 \div 0.1719$
-2060.55

158. $-2658.3109 \div (-0.0473)$
$56,201.08$

159. $(-3.92) \div (-45.008)$
0.09

APPLYING CONCEPTS 1.3

Classify each of the following numbers as a natural number, an integer, a positive integer, a negative integer, a rational number, an irrational number, and a real number. List all that apply.

160. -1 Integer, neg. integer, rational no., real no.

161. 28 Natural no., integer, pos. integer, rational no., real no.

162. $-\frac{9}{34}$ Rational no., real no.

163. -7.707 Rational no., real no.

164. $5.2\overline{6}$ Rational no., real no.

165. $0.171771777\ldots$ Irrational no., real no.

Solve.

166. Find the average of $\frac{5}{8}$ and $\frac{3}{4}$. $\frac{11}{16}$

167. *The Postal Service*   Postage for first-class mail is \$.33 for the first ounce or fraction of an ounce and \$.22 for each additional ounce or fraction of an ounce.

Find the cost of mailing, by first-class mail, a letter that weighs $4\frac{1}{2}$ oz.   \$1.21

The graph at the right shows the net earnings or loss for Chrysler Corporation for the years 1993 to 1997. Use this graph for Exercises 168 and 169.

168. *Business* What is the average annual net earnings or loss for the years shown in the graph?
$1.9042 billion

169. *Business* For what two years shown in the graph is the difference between the net earnings or loss greatest? What is that difference?
1993 and 1994; $6.264 billion

Chrysler Corporation's Net Earnings or Loss
Source: Chrysler Corporation financial statements.

170. Use a calculator to determine the decimal representations of $\frac{17}{99}$, $\frac{45}{99}$, and $\frac{73}{99}$. Make a conjecture as to the decimal representation of $\frac{83}{99}$. Does your conjecture work for $\frac{33}{99}$? What about $\frac{1}{99}$?
$\frac{17}{99} = 0.\overline{17}$; $\frac{45}{99} = 0.\overline{45}$; $\frac{73}{99} = 0.\overline{73}$; $\frac{83}{99} = 0.\overline{83}$; $\frac{33}{99} = 0.\overline{33} = 0.\overline{3}$, yes; $\frac{1}{99} = 0.\overline{01}$, yes

171. If the same positive integer is added to both the numerator and the denominator of $\frac{2}{5}$, is the new fraction less than, equal to, or greater than $\frac{2}{5}$?
Greater than

[C] 172. A magic square is one in which the numbers in every row, column, and diagonal sum to the same number. Complete the magic square at the right.

$\frac{2}{3}$	$-\frac{1}{6}$	0
$-\frac{1}{2}$	$\frac{1}{6}$	$\frac{5}{6}$
$\frac{1}{3}$	$\frac{1}{2}$	$-\frac{1}{3}$

173. Let x represent the price of a car. If the sales tax is 6% of the price, express the total of the price of the car and the sales tax in terms of x. $1.06x$

[C] 174. Let x represent the price of a suit. If the suit is on sale at a discount rate of 30%, express the price of the suit after the discount in terms of x. $0.70x$

[C] 175. The price of a pen was 60¢. During a storewide sale, the price was reduced to a different whole number of cents, and the entire stock was sold for $54.59. Find the price of the pen during the sale.   53¢

[C] 176. Find three natural numbers a, b, and c such that $\frac{1}{a} + \frac{1}{b} + \frac{1}{c}$ is a natural number.
$a = 2$; $b = 3$; $c = 6$

[C] 177. If a and b are rational numbers and $a < b$, is it always possible to find a rational number c such that $a < c < b$? If not, explain why. If so, show how to find one.   Yes; $c = \dfrac{a + b}{2}$

178. In your own words, define **a.** a rational number, **b.** an irrational number, and **c.** a real number.

179. Explain why you "invert and multiply" when dividing a fraction by a fraction.

180. Explain why you need a common denominator when adding two fractions and why you don't need a common denominator when multiplying two fractions.

181. 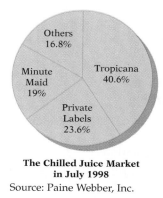 Write an essay describing your interpretation of the data presented in the chart shown below.

Others
16.8%

Tropicana
40.6%

**Minute
Maid**
19%

**Private
Labels**
23.6%

**The Chilled Juice Market
in July 1998**
Source: Paine Webber, Inc.

S E C T I O N 1.4

Exponents and the Order of Operations Agreement

1 **Exponential expressions**

POINT OF INTEREST

René Descartes (1596–1650) was the first mathematician to use exponential notation extensively as it is used today. However, for some unknown reason, he always used *xx* for *x²*.

Repeated multiplication of the same factor can be written using an exponent.

$$2 \cdot 2 \cdot 2 \cdot 2 \cdot 2 = 2^5 \leftarrow \text{exponent}$$
$$\underset{\text{base}}{\uparrow}$$

$$a \cdot a \cdot a \cdot a = a^4 \leftarrow \text{exponent}$$
$$\underset{\text{base}}{\uparrow}$$

The **exponent** indicates how many times the factor, called the **base,** occurs in the multiplication. The multiplication $2 \cdot 2 \cdot 2 \cdot 2 \cdot 2$ is in **factored form.** The exponential expression 2^5 is in **exponential form.**

2^1 is read "the first power of two" or just "two." ⟶ Usually the exponent 1 is not written.

2^2 is read "the second power of two" or "two squared."

2^3 is read "the third power of two" or "two cubed."

2^4 is read "the fourth power of two."

2^5 is read "the fifth power of two."

a^5 is read "the fifth power of a."

There is a geometric interpretation of the first three natural-number powers.

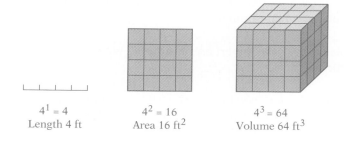

$4^1 = 4$
Length 4 ft

$4^2 = 16$
Area 16 ft^2

$4^3 = 64$
Volume 64 ft^3

To evaluate an exponential expression, write each factor as many times as indicated by the exponent. Then multiply.

$$3^5 = 3 \cdot 3 \cdot 3 \cdot 3 \cdot 3 = 243$$

$$2^3 \cdot 3^2 = (2 \cdot 2 \cdot 2) \cdot (3 \cdot 3) = 8 \cdot 9 = 72$$

LOOK CLOSELY

The -4 is squared only when the negative sign is *inside* the parentheses. In $(-4)^2$, we are squaring -4; in -4^2, we are finding the opposite of 4^2.

Example 1 Evaluate $(-4)^2$ and -4^2.

Solution $(-4)^2 = (-4)(-4) = 16$
$-4^2 = -(4 \cdot 4) = -16$

Problem 1 Evaluate $(-5)^3$ and -5^3.

Solution See page S2. -125 and -125

LOOK CLOSELY

The product of an even number of negative factors is positive. The product of an odd number of negative factors is negative.

Example 2 Evaluate $(-2)^4$ and $(-2)^5$.

Solution
$$\begin{aligned}(-2)^4 &= (-2)(-2)(-2)(-2) \\ &= 4(-2)(-2) \\ &= -8(-2) \\ &= 16\end{aligned}$$
$$\begin{aligned}(-2)^5 &= (-2)(-2)(-2)(-2)(-2) \\ &= 4(-2)(-2)(-2) \\ &= -8(-2)(-2) \\ &= 16(-2) \\ &= -32\end{aligned}$$

Problem 2 Evaluate $(-3)^3$ and $(-3)^4$.

Solution See page S2. -27 and 81

Example 3 Evaluate $(-3)^2 \cdot 2^3$ and $\left(-\dfrac{2}{3}\right)^3$.

Solution $(-3)^2 \cdot 2^3 = (-3)(-3) \cdot (2)(2)(2) = 9 \cdot 8 = 72$

$$\left(-\frac{2}{3}\right)^3 = \left(-\frac{2}{3}\right)\left(-\frac{2}{3}\right)\left(-\frac{2}{3}\right) = -\frac{2 \cdot 2 \cdot 2}{3 \cdot 3 \cdot 3} = -\frac{8}{27}$$

Problem 3 Evaluate $(3^3)(-2)^3$ and $\left(-\dfrac{2}{5}\right)^2$.

Solution See page S2. -216 and $\dfrac{4}{25}$

2 ## The Order of Operations Agreement

Evaluate $2 + 3 \cdot 5$.

There are two arithmetic operations, addition and multiplication, in this problem. The operations could be performed in different orders.

Add first. $2 + 3 \cdot 5$ Multiply first. $2 + \underline{3 \cdot 5}$

Then multiply. $\underline{5} \cdot 5$ Then add. $2 + \quad 15$

25 17

In order to prevent there being more than one answer to the same problem, an Order of Operations Agreement has been established.

The Order of Operations Agreement

> **Step 1** Perform operations inside grouping symbols. Grouping symbols include parentheses ( ), brackets [ ], absolute value symbols | |, and the fraction bar.
>
> **Step 2** Simplify exponential expressions.
>
> **Step 3** Do multiplication and division as they occur from left to right.
>
> **Step 4** Do addition and subtraction as they occur from left to right.

Example 4   Simplify: $12 - 24(8 - 5) \div 2^2$

Solution $12 - 24(8 - 5) \div 2^2$

$= 12 - 24(3) \div 2^2$ ▶ Perform operations inside grouping symbols.

$= 12 - 24(3) \div 4$ ▶ Simplify exponential expressions.

$= 12 - 72 \div 4$ ▶ Do multiplication and division as they occur

$= 12 - 18$ from left to right.

$= -6$ ▶ Do addition and subtraction as they occur from left to right.

Problem 4   Simplify: $36 \div (8 - 5)^2 - (-3)^2 \cdot 2$

Solution   See page S2. -14

One or more of the steps shown in Example 4 may not be needed to simplify an expression. In that case, proceed to the next step in the Order of Operations Agreement.

Example 5   Simplify: $\dfrac{4 + 8}{2 + 1} - |3 - 1| + 2$

Solution $\dfrac{4 + 8}{2 + 1} - |3 - 1| + 2$

$= \dfrac{12}{3} - |2| + 2$ ▶ Perform operations inside grouping symbols (above and below the fraction bar and inside the absolute value symbols).

$= \dfrac{12}{3} - 2 + 2$ ▶ Find the absolute value of 2.

$= 4 - 2 + 2$ ▶ Do multiplication and division as they occur from left to right.

$= 2 + 2$ ▶ Do addition and subtraction as they occur from left to right.

$= 4$

Problem 5   Simplify: $27 \div 3^2 + (-3)^2 \cdot 4$

Solution   See page S2.   39

When an expression has grouping symbols inside grouping symbols, first perform the operations inside the *inner* grouping symbols by following Steps 2, 3, and 4 of the Order of Operations Agreement. Then perform the operations inside the *outer* grouping symbols by following Steps 2, 3, and 4 in sequence.

Example 6   Simplify: $6 \div [4 - (6 - 8)] + 2^2$

Solution $6 \div [4 - (6 - 8)] + 2^2$
$= 6 \div [4 - (-2)] + 2^2$ ▸ Perform operations inside inner grouping symbols.

$= 6 \div 6 + 2^2$ ▸ Perform operations inside outer grouping symbols.

$= 6 \div 6 + 4$ ▸ Simplify exponential expressions.
$= 1 + 4$ ▸ Do multiplication and division.
$= 5$ ▸ Do addition and subtraction.

Problem 6   Simplify: $4 - 3[4 - 2(6 - 3)] \div 2$

Solution   See page S2.   7

STUDY TIPS

USE THE END-OF-CHAPTER MATERIAL

To help you review the material presented within a chapter, a Chapter Summary appears at the end of each chapter. In the Chapter Summary, definitions of the important terms and concepts introduced in the chapter are provided under "Key Words." Listed under "Essential Rules and Procedures" are the formulas and procedures presented in the chapter. After completing a chapter, be sure to read the Chapter Summary. Use it to check your understanding of the material presented and to determine what concepts you need to review.

   Each chapter ends with Chapter Review Exercises and a Chapter Test. The problems these contain summarize what you should have learned when you have finished the chapter. Do these exercises as you prepare for an examination. Check your answers against those in the back of the book. Answers to all Chapter Review and Chapter Test exercises are provided there. The objective being reviewed by any particular problem is written in parentheses following the answer. For any problem you answer incorrectly, review the material corresponding to that objective in the textbook. Determine *why* your answer was wrong.

CONCEPT REVIEW 1.4

Determine whether the statement is always true, sometimes true, or never true.

1. $(-5)^2$, -5^2, and $-(5)^2$ all represent the same number.   Never true

2. By the Order of Operations Agreement, addition is performed before division.   Never true

3. In the expression 3^8, 8 is the base.   Never true

4. The expression 9^4 is in exponential form.   Always true

5. To evaluate the expression $6 + 7 \cdot 10$ means to determine what one number it is equal to.   Always true

6. When using the Order of Operations Agreement, we consider the absolute value symbol a grouping symbol.   Always true

7. Using the Order of Operations Agreement, it is possible to get more than one correct answer to a problem.   Never true

8. The Order of Operations Agreement is used for natural numbers, integers, rational numbers, and real numbers.   Always true

9. The expression $(2^3)^2$ equals $2^{(3^2)}$.   Never true

10. Suppose a and b are positive integers. Then $a^b = b^a$.   Sometimes true

EXERCISES 1.4

1 Evaluate.

1. 6^2 36

2. 7^4 2401

3. -7^2 -49

4. -4^3 -64

5. $(-3)^2$ 9

6. $(-2)^3$ -8

7. $(-3)^4$ 81

8. $(-5)^3$ -125

9. $\left(\frac{1}{2}\right)^2$ $\frac{1}{4}$

10. $\left(-\frac{3}{4}\right)^3$ $-\frac{27}{64}$

11. $(0.3)^2$ 0.09

12. $(1.5)^3$ 3.375

13. $\left(\frac{2}{3}\right)^2 \cdot 3^3$ 12

14. $\left(-\frac{1}{2}\right)^3 \cdot 8$ -1

15. $(0.3)^3 \cdot 2^3$ 0.216

16. $(0.5)^2 \cdot 3^3$ 6.75

17. $(-3) \cdot 2^2$ -12

18. $(-5) \cdot 3^4$ -405

19. $(-2) \cdot (-2)^3$ 16

20. $(-2) \cdot (-2)^2$ -8

21. $2^3 \cdot 3^3 \cdot (-4)$ -864

22. $(-3)^3 \cdot 5^2 \cdot 10$ -6750

23. $(-7) \cdot 4^2 \cdot 3^2$ -1008

24. $(-2) \cdot 2^3 \cdot (-3)^2$ -144

25. $\left(\frac{2}{3}\right)^2 \cdot \frac{1}{4} \cdot 3^3$ 3

26. $\left(\frac{3}{4}\right)^2 \cdot (-4) \cdot 2^3$ -18

27. $8^2 \cdot (-3)^5 \cdot 5$ $-77,760$

2 28. Why do we need an Order of Operations Agreement?

29. Describe each step in the Order of Operations Agreement.

Simplify by using the Order of Operations Agreement.

30. $4 - 8 \div 2$ 0

31. $2^2 \cdot 3 - 3$ 9

32. $2(3 - 4) - (-3)^2$ -11

33. $16 - 32 \div 2^3$ 12

34. $24 - 18 \div 3 + 2$ 20

35. $8 - (-3)^2 - (-2)$ 1

36. $16 + 15 \div (-5) - 2$ 11

37. $14 - 2^2 - |4 - 7|$ 7

38. $3 - 2[8 - (3 - 2)]$ -11

39. $-2^2 + 4[16 \div (3 - 5)]$ -36

40. $6 + \dfrac{16 - 4}{2^2 + 2} - 2$ 6

41. $24 \div \dfrac{3^2}{8 - 5} - (-5)$ 13

42. $96 \div 2[12 + (6 - 2)] - 3^3$ 741

43. $4 \cdot [16 - (7 - 1)] \div 10$ 4

44. $16 \div 2 - 4^2 - (-3)^2$ -17

45. $18 \div |9 - 2^3| + (-3)$ 15

46. $16 - 3(8 - 3)^2 \div 5$ 1

47. $4(-8) \div [2(7 - 3)^2]$ -1

48. $\dfrac{(-10) + (-2)}{6^2 - 30} \div |2 - 4|$ -1

49. $16 - 4 \cdot \dfrac{3^3 - 7}{2^3 + 2} - (-2)^2$ 4

50. $(0.2)^2 \cdot (-0.5) + 1.72$ 1.7

51. $0.3(1.7 - 4.8) + (1.2)^2$ 0.51

52. $(1.8)^2 - 2.52 \div (1.8)$ 1.84

53. $(1.65 - 1.05)^2 \div 0.4 + 0.8$ 1.7

54. $\dfrac{3}{8} \div \left|\dfrac{5}{6} + \dfrac{2}{3}\right|$ $\dfrac{1}{4}$

55. $\left(\dfrac{3}{4}\right)^2 - \left(\dfrac{1}{2}\right)^3 \div \dfrac{3}{5}$ $\dfrac{17}{48}$

APPLYING CONCEPTS 1.4

56. Using the Order of Operations Agreement, describe how to simplify Exercise 46.

Place the correct symbol, $<$ or $>$, between the two numbers.

57. $(0.9)^3 < 1^5$

58. $(-3)^3 > (-2)^5$

59. $(-1.1)^2 > (0.9)^2$

Simplify.

60. $1^2 + 2^2 + 3^2 + 4^2$ 30

61. $1^3 + 2^3 + 3^3 + 4^3$ 100

62. $(-1)^3 + (-2)^3 + (-3)^3 + (-4)^3$ -100

63. $(-2)^2 + (-4)^2 + (-6)^2 + (-8)^2$ 120

Solve.

[C] **64.** Find a rational number, r, that satisfies the condition.
a. $r^2 < r$ **b.** $r^2 = r$ **c.** $r^2 > r$ Answers will vary. For example: a. $r = \dfrac{1}{2}$ b. $r = 0$ or $r = 1$ c. $r = 2$

65. *Computers*   A computer can do 6,000,000 additions in 1 s. To the nearest second, how many seconds will it take the computer to do 10^8 additions?   17 s

66. The sum of two natural numbers is 41. Each of the two numbers is the square of a natural number. Find the two numbers.   16, 25

Determine the ones digit when the expression is evaluated.

[C] **67.** 34^{202} 6

[C] **68.** 23^{502} 9

[C] **69.** 27^{622} 9

70. Prepare a report on the Kelvin scale. Include in your report an explanation of how to convert between the Kelvin scale and the Celsius scale.

Focus on Problem Solving

Inductive Reasoning

Suppose you take 9 credit hours each semester. The total number of credit hours you have taken at the end of each semester can be described in a list of numbers.

$$9, 18, 27, 36, 45, 54, 63, \ldots$$

The list of numbers that indicates the total credit hours is an ordered list of numbers, called a **sequence.** Each number in a sequence is called a **term** of the sequence. The list is ordered because the position of a number in the list indicates the semester in which that number of credit hours has been taken. For example, the 7th term of the sequence is 63, and a total of 63 credit hours have been taken after the 7th semester.

Assuming the pattern is continued, find the next three numbers in the pattern

$$-6, -10, -14, -18, \ldots$$

This list of numbers is a sequence. The first step in solving this problem is to observe the pattern in the list of numbers. In this case, each number in the list is 4 less than the previous number. The next three numbers are $-22, -26, -30$.

This process of discovering the pattern in a list of numbers is inductive reasoning. **Inductive reasoning** involves making generalizations from specific examples; in other words, we reach a conclusion by making observations about particular facts or cases.

Try the following exercises. Each exercise requires inductive reasoning.

Name the next two terms in the sequence.

1. $1, 3, 5, 7, 1, 3, 5, 7, 1, \ldots$ 	**2.** $1, 4, 2, 5, 3, 6, 4, \ldots$

3. $1, 2, 4, 7, 11, 16, \ldots$ 	**4.** A, B, C, G, H, I, M, …

Draw the next shape in the sequence.

5.

6. |• ||• ||•• 	|||•• 	|||•••

Solve.

7. Convert $\frac{1}{11}, \frac{2}{11}, \frac{3}{11}, \frac{4}{11}$, and $\frac{5}{11}$ to decimals. Then use the pattern you observe to convert $\frac{6}{11}, \frac{7}{11}$, and $\frac{9}{11}$ to decimals.

8. Convert $\frac{1}{33}, \frac{2}{33}, \frac{4}{33}, \frac{5}{33}$, and $\frac{7}{33}$ to decimals. Then use the pattern you observe to convert $\frac{8}{33}, \frac{13}{33}$, and $\frac{19}{33}$ to decimals.

Projects and Group Activities

Calculators

INSTRUCTOR NOTE

Projects and Group Activities appears at the end of each chapter in this text. The feature can be used for individual assignments, such as extra credit, or for cooperative learning exercises, such as small-group projects, or for class discussions.

Does your calculator use the Order of Operations Agreement? To find out, try this problem:

$$2 + 4 \cdot 7$$

If your answer is 30, then the calculator uses the Order of Operations Agreement. If your answer is 42, it does not use that agreement.

Even if your calculator does not use the Order of Operations Agreement, you can still correctly evaluate numerical expressions. The parentheses keys, (and) , are used for this purpose.

Remember that $2 + 4 \cdot 7$ means $2 + (4 \cdot 7)$ because the multiplication must be completed before the addition. To evaluate this expression, enter the following:

Enter: 2   +   (4   ×   7   )   =

Display: 2   2   (4   4   7   28   30

When using your calculator to evaluate numerical expressions, insert parentheses around multiplications or divisions. This has the effect of forcing the calculator to do the operations in the order you want rather than in the order the calculator wants.

Evaluate.

1. $3 \cdot (15 - 2 \cdot 3) - 36 \div 3$ **2.** $4 \cdot 2^2 - (12 + 24 \div 6) - 5$

3. $16 \div 4 \cdot 3 + (3 \cdot 4 - 5) + 2$ **4.** $15 \cdot 3 \div 9 + (2 \cdot 6 - 3) + 4$

Using your calculator to simplify numerical expressions sometimes requires use of the +/− key or, on some calculators, the negative key, which is frequently shown as (−) . These keys change the sign of the number currently in the display. To enter −4:

- For those calculators with +/− , press 4 and then +/− .
- For those calculators with (−) , press (−) and then 4.

Here are the keystrokes for evaluating the expression $3(-4) - (-5)$.

Calculators with +/− key: 3 × 4 +/− − 5 +/− =

Calculators with (−) key: 3 × (−) 4 − (−) 5 =

This example illustrates that calculators make a distinction between negative and minus. To perform the operation $3 - (-3)$, you cannot enter 3 − − 3. This would result in 0, which is not the correct answer. You must enter

3 − 3 +/− =   or   3 − (−) 3 =

Use a calculator to evaluate each of the following exercises.

1. $-16 \div 2$ **2.** $3(-8)$ **3.** $47 - (-9)$

4. $-50 - (-14)$ **5.** $4 - (-3)^2$ **6.** $-8 + (-6)^2 - 7$

Moving Averages

Stock	Div	PE	Sales 100s	High	Low	Close	Chg.
A							
AAR	.48	23	2495	$13^{1}4$	$117\!8$	$12^{1}4$	$-7\!8$
ACMin	.96		814	$111\!8$	11	11	$-1\!8$
ACM Op	.80a		324	$93\!4$	$93\!8$	$95\!8$	$+1\!4$
ACM Sc	.96a		1104	$113\!8$	$111\!4$	$113\!8$	
ACMSp	.80a		497	$91\!2$	$93\!8$	$91\!2$	
ACM MI	1.08a		678	$103\!4$	$105\!8$	$103\!4$	$+1\!8$
ACMMM	.78		156	$91\!4$	$91\!8$	$91\!8$	
ADT wt			742	$15\!8$	$13\!8$	$11\!2$	
ADT			4357	$91\!2$	9	$91\!8$	
AFLAC	.44	16	1355	$351\!2$	$343\!4$	$347\!8$	$-1\!2$
AL Lab	.18	168	911	$231\!2$	$221\!4$	$231\!2$	$+13\!8$
AM Intl			64	11-32	5-16	11-32	
AM In pf			2	$11\!8$	$11\!8$	$11\!8$	
AMR			3400	$603\!4$	$593\!4$	$597\!8$	-1
ANR pf	2.67		1	$271\!8$	$271\!8$	$271\!8$	$+3\!8$
ARCOCh	2.50	21	116	$431\!8$	43	$433\!8$	$+1\!2$
ARX		12	111	$17\!8$	$17\!8$	$17\!8$	$+1\!8$
ASA Ltd	2		483	$363\!4$	$361\!8$	$361\!8$	$-3\!8$
AbtLab s	68	18	20304	$261\!2$	$263\!8$	$263\!8$	$+11\!8$

Objective 1.2.5 describes how to find the moving average of a stock. Use this method to calculate the 5-day moving average for at least three different stocks. Discuss and compare the results for the different stocks.

For this project, you will need to use stock tables, which are printed in the business section of major newspapers. Your college library should have copies of these publications. In a stock table, the column headed "Chg." provides the change in the price of a share of the stock; that is, it gives the difference between the closing price for the day shown and the closing price for the previous day. The symbol $+$ indicates the change was an increase in price; the symbol $-$ indicates the change was a decrease in price.

You can also look up stock prices on the Internet by using a search engine and typing in "stocks."

www.fedstats.gov

Information regarding the history of the federal budget can be found on the World Wide Web. Go to the web site www.fedstats.gov. Click on "Fast Facts" and then on "Frequently Requested Tables." In the list of tables printed to the screen, find the table entitled "Federal Budget - Summary." Click on it. When the federal budget table appears on the screen, look for the column that lists each year's surplus or deficit. You will see that a negative sign $(-)$ is used to show a deficit. Note that it states near the top of the screen that the figures in the table are in millions of dollars.

1. During which years shown in the table was there a surplus?

2. During which year was the debt the greatest?

3. Find the difference between the surplus or debt this year and the surplus or debt 5 years ago.

4. What is the difference between the surplus or debt this year and the surplus or debt a decade ago?

5. Determine what two numbers in the table are being subtracted in each row in order to arrive at the number in the surplus or deficit column.

6. Describe the trend of the federal deficit over the last 10 years.

Chapter Summary

Key Words

A *set* is a collection of objects. The objects in the set are called the *elements* of the set. The *roster method* of writing sets encloses a list of the elements in braces. (Objective 1.1.1)

The set of *natural numbers* is {1, 2, 3, 4, 5, 6, 7,…}. The set of *integers* is {…, -4, -3, -2, -1, 0, 1, 2, 3, 4,…}. (Objective 1.1.1)

The set of even natural numbers less than 10 is written $A = \{2, 4, 6, 8\}$. The elements in this set are the numbers 2, 4, 6, and 8.

A number a *is less than* another number b, written $a < b$, if a is to the left of b on the number line. A number a *is greater than* another number b, written $a > b$, if a is to the right of b on the number line. The symbol $\leq$ means *is less than or equal to*. The symbol $\geq$ means *is greater than or equal to*.   (Objective 1.1.1)

$-9 < 7$
$4 > -5$

Two numbers that are the same distance from zero on the number line but on opposite sides of zero are *opposite numbers*, or *opposites*. The opposite of a number is also called its *additive inverse*.   (Objective 1.1.2)

5 and -5 are opposites.

The *absolute value* of a number is its distance from zero on the number line. The absolute value of a number is positive or zero.   (Objective 1.1.2)

$|-12| = 12$
$-|7| = -7$

A *rational number* is a number that can be written in the form $\frac{a}{b}$, where a and b are integers and $b \neq 0$. A rational number written in this form is commonly called a *fraction*. (Objective 1.3.1)

$\frac{3}{8}, \frac{-9}{11}$, and $\frac{4}{1}$ are rational numbers.

An *irrational number* is a number that has a decimal representation that never terminates or repeats.   (Objective 1.3.1)

π, $\sqrt{2}$, and 2.17117111711117. . . are irrational numbers.

The rational numbers and the irrational numbers taken together are called the *real numbers*.   (Objective 1.3.1)

$\frac{3}{8}, \frac{-9}{11}, \frac{4}{1}, \pi, \sqrt{2}$, and 2.17117111711117. . . are real numbers.

Percent means "parts of 100."   (Objective 1.3.2)

63% means 63 of 100 equal parts.

An expression of the form a^n is in *exponential form*, where a is the *base* and n is the *exponent*.   (Objective 1.4.1)

6^3 is an exponential expression in which 6 is the base and 3 is the exponent.

Essential Rules and Procedures

To add two integers with the same sign, add the absolute values of the numbers. Then attach the sign of the addends. (Objective 1.2.1)

$9 + 3 = 12$
$-9 + (-3) = -12$

To add two integers with different signs, find the absolute value of each number. Then subtract the smaller of these absolute values from the larger one. Attach the sign of the number with the greater absolute value.   (Objective 1.2.1)

$9 + (-3) = 6$
$-9 + 3 = -6$

To subtract one integer from another, add the opposite of the second integer to the first integer.   (Objective 1.2.2)

$6 - 11 = 6 + (-11) = -5$
$-2 - (-8) = -2 + 8 = 6$

To multiply two integers with the same sign, multiply the absolute values of the numbers. The product is positive. (Objective 1.2.3)

$3(5) = 15$
$(-3)(-5) = 15$

To multiply two integers with different signs, multiply the absolute values of the numbers. The product is negative. (Objective 1.2.3)

$-3(5) = -15$
$3(-5) = -15$

To divide two integers with the same sign, divide the absolute values of the numbers. The quotient is positive. (Objective 1.2.4)

$$14 \div 2 = 7$$
$$-14 \div (-2) = 7$$

To divide two integers with different signs, divide the absolute values of the numbers. The quotient is negative. (Objective 1.2.4)

$$14 \div (-2) = -7$$
$$-14 \div 2 = -7$$

Zero and One in Division (Objective 1.2.4)

$\dfrac{0}{a} = 0, a \neq 0$ $\dfrac{0}{3} = 0$

Division by zero is undefined. $\dfrac{9}{0}$ is undefined.

$\dfrac{a}{a} = 1, a \neq 0$ $\dfrac{-2}{-2} = 1$

$\dfrac{a}{1} = a$ $\dfrac{-6}{1} = -6$

To convert a percent to a decimal, remove the percent sign and multiply by 0.01. (Objective 1.3.2)

$$85\% = 85(0.01) = 0.85$$

To convert a percent to a fraction, remove the percent sign and multiply by $\dfrac{1}{100}$. (Objective 1.3.2)

$$25\% = 25 \cdot \dfrac{1}{100} = \dfrac{25}{100} = \dfrac{1}{4}$$

To convert a decimal or a fraction to a percent, multiply by 100%. (Objective 1.3.2)

$$0.5 = 0.5(100\%) = 50\%$$
$$\dfrac{3}{8} = \dfrac{3}{8} \cdot 100\% = \dfrac{300}{8}\% = 37.5\%$$

Order of Operations Agreement (Objective 1.4.2)

Step 1 Perform operations inside grouping symbols.
Step 2 Simplify exponential expressions.
Step 3 Do multiplication and division as they occur from left to right.
Step 4 Do addition and subtraction as they occur from left to right.

$$16 \div (-2)^3 + (7 - 12)$$
$$= 16 \div (-2)^3 + (-5)$$
$$= 16 \div (-8) + (-5)$$
$$= -2 + (-5)$$
$$= -7$$

Chapter Review Exercises

1. Use the roster method to write the set of natural numbers less than 7.   {1, 2, 3, 4, 5, 6}

2. Write $\dfrac{5}{8}$ as a percent.   62.5%

3. Evaluate: $-|-4|$ -4

4. Subtract: $16 - (-30) - 42$ 4

5. Divide: $-561 \div (-33)$ 17

6. Write $\dfrac{7}{9}$ as a decimal. Place a bar over the repeating digits of the decimal. $0.\overline{7}$

7. Simplify: $(6.02)(-0.89)$ -5.3578

8. Simplify: $\dfrac{-10 + 2}{2 + (-4)} \div 2 + 6$ 8

9. Find the opposite of -4. 4

10. Subtract: $16 - 30$ -14

11. Write 0.672 as a percent.   67.2%

12. Write $79\frac{1}{2}\%$ as a fraction. $\frac{159}{200}$

13. Divide: $-72 \div 8$ -9

14. Write $\frac{17}{20}$ as a decimal.   0.85

15. Divide: $\frac{5}{12} \div \left(-\frac{5}{6}\right)$ $-\frac{1}{2}$

16. Simplify: $3^2 - 4 + 20 \div 5$ 9

17. Place the correct symbol, $<$ or $>$, between the two numbers.
$$-1 \ < \ 0$$

18. Add: $-22 + 14 + (-8)$ -16

19. Multiply: $(-5)(-6)(3)$ 90

20. Subtract: $6.039 - 12.92$ -6.881

21. Given $A = \{-5, -3, 0\}$, which elements of set A are less than or equal to -3? $-5, \ -3$

22. Write 7% as a decimal.   0.07

23. Evaluate: $\frac{3}{4} \cdot (4)^2$ 12

24. Place the correct symbol, $<$ or $>$, between the two numbers.
$$-2 \ > \ -40$$

25. Add: $13 + (-16)$ -3

26. Multiply: $(-4)(12)$ -48

27. Add: $-\frac{2}{5} + \frac{7}{15}$ $\frac{1}{15}$

28. Evaluate: $(-3^3) \cdot 2^2$ -108

29. Write $2\frac{7}{9}$ as a percent. Round to the nearest tenth of a percent.   277.8%

30. Write 240% as a decimal.   2.4

31. Find the opposite of -2.   2

32. Subtract: $7 - 21$ -14

33. Divide: $96 \div (-12)$ -8

34. Write $\frac{7}{20}$ as a decimal.   0.35

35. Divide: $-\frac{7}{16} \div \frac{3}{8}$ $-\frac{7}{6}$

36. Simplify: $2^3 \div 4 - 2(2 - 7)$ 12

37. Evaluate: $|-3|$ 3

38. Subtract: $12 - (-10) - 4$ 18

39. Write $2\frac{8}{9}$ as a percent. Write the remainder in fractional form. $288\frac{8}{9}\%$

40. Given $C = \{-12, -8, -1, 7\}$, find
  a. the opposite of each element of set C.
  b. the absolute value of each element of set C.
  a. 12, 8, 1, -7 **b.** 12, 8, 1, 7

41. Divide: $(-204) \div (-17)$ 12

42. Write $\frac{7}{11}$ as a decimal. Place a bar over the repeating digits of the decimal. $0.\overline{63}$

43. Divide: $0.2654 \div (-0.023)$
Round to the nearest tenth. -11.5

44. Simplify: $(7 - 2)^2 - 5 - 3 \cdot 4$ 8

45. Place the correct symbol, $<$ or $>$, between the two numbers.
$$8 > -10$$

46. Add: $-12 + 8 + (-4)$ -8

47. Multiply: $2(-3)(-12)$ 72

48. Add: $-\frac{5}{8} + \frac{1}{6}$ $-\frac{11}{24}$

49. Given $D = \{-24, -17, -9, 0, 4\}$, which elements of set D are greater than -19?
$-17, -9, 0, 4$

50. Write 0.002 as a percent.   0.2%

51. Evaluate: $-4^2 \cdot \left(\frac{1}{2}\right)^2$ -4

52. Add: $-1.329 + 4.89$ 3.561

53. Evaluate: $-|17|$ -17

54. Subtract: $-5 - 22 - (-13) - 19 - (-6)$ -27

55. Multiply: $\left(\frac{1}{3}\right)\left(-\frac{4}{5}\right)\left(\frac{3}{8}\right)$ $-\frac{1}{10}$

56. Place the correct symbol, $<$ or $>$, between the two numbers.
$$-43 < -34$$

57. Write $\frac{18}{25}$ as a decimal.   0.72

58. Evaluate $(-2)^3 \cdot 4^2$. -128

59. Write 0.075 as a percent.   7.5%

60. Write $\frac{19}{35}$ as a percent. Write the remainder in fractional form. $54\frac{2}{7}\%$

61. Add: $14 + (-18) + 6 + (-20)$ -18

62. Multiply: $-4(-8)(12)(0)$ 0

63. Simplify: $2^3 - 7 + 16 \div (-3 + 5)$ 9

64. Simplify: $\frac{3}{4} + \frac{1}{2} - \frac{3}{8}$ $\frac{7}{8}$

65. Divide: $-128 \div (-8)$ 16

66. Place the correct symbol, $<$ or $>$, between the two numbers.
$$-57 < 28$$

67. Evaluate: $\left(-\frac{1}{3}\right)^3 \cdot 9^2$ -3

68. Add: $-7 + (-3) + (-12) + 16$ -6

69. Multiply: $5(-2)(10)(-3)$ 300

70. Use the roster method to write the set of negative integers greater than -4. $\{-3, -2, -1\}$

71. Find the temperature after a rise of 14°C from -6°C.   8°C

72. The daily low temperatures, in degrees Celsius, for a three-day period were recorded as follows: $-8°$, $7°$, $-5°$. Find the average low temperature for the three-day period. -2°C

73. The high temperature for the day was 8°C. The low temperature was −5°C. Find the difference between the high and low temperatures for the day. 13°C

74. Find the temperature after a rise of 7°C from −13°C.   −6°C

75. The temperature on the surface of the planet Venus is 480°C. The temperature on the surface of the planet Pluto is −234°C. Find the difference between the surface temperatures on Venus and Pluto.   714°C

Chapter Test

1. Write 55% as a fraction. $\frac{11}{20}$

2. Given $B = \{-8, -6, -4, -2\}$, which elements of set B are less than −5?   −6, −8

3. Subtract: −9 − (−6)   −3

4. Write $\frac{17}{20}$ as a decimal.   0.85

5. Multiply: $\frac{3}{4}\left(-\frac{2}{21}\right)$ $-\frac{1}{14}$

6. Divide: −75 ÷ 5   −15

7. Evaluate: $\left(-\frac{2}{3}\right)^3 \cdot 3^2$ $-\frac{8}{3}$

8. Add: −7 + (−3) + 12   2

9. Use the roster method to write the set of positive integers less than or equal to 6. {1, 2, 3, 4, 5, 6}

10. Write 1.59 as a percent.   159%

11. Evaluate: |−29| 29

12. Place the correct symbol, < or >, between the two numbers.

$$-47 > -68$$

13. Subtract: $-\frac{4}{9} - \frac{5}{6}$ $-\frac{23}{18}$

14. Multiply: −6(−43)   258

15. Simplify: $8 + \frac{12 - 4}{3^2 - 1} - 6$ 3

16. Divide: $-\frac{5}{8} \div \left(-\frac{3}{4}\right)$ $\frac{5}{6}$

17. Write $\frac{3}{13}$ as a percent. Round to the nearest tenth of a percent.   23.1%

18. Write 6.2% as a decimal.   0.062

19. Subtract: 13 − (−5) − 4   14

20. Write $\frac{13}{30}$ as a decimal. Place a bar over the repeating digits of the decimal. $0.4\bar{3}$

21. Multiply: (−0.9)(2.7)   −2.43

22. Divide: −180 ÷ (−12)   15

23. Evaluate: $2^2 \cdot (-4)^2 \cdot 10$ 640

24. Add: 15 + (−8) + (−19)   −12

25.   Evaluate: $-|-34|$ -34

26.   Place the correct symbol, $<$ or $>$, between the two numbers.

$$53 > -92$$

27.   Given $A = \{-17, -6, 5, 9\}$, find
   a. the opposite of each element of set A.
   b. the absolute value of each element of set A.
   a. $17, 6, -5, -9$ **b.** $17, 6, 5, 9$

28.   Write $\frac{16}{23}$ as a percent. Write the remainder in fractional form. $69\frac{13}{23}\%$

29.   Add: $-18.354 + 6.97$ -11.384

30.   Multiply: $-4(8)(-5)$ 160

31.   Simplify: $9(-4) \div [2(8-5)^2]$ -2

32.   Find the temperature after a rise of $12°C$ from $-8°C$. $4°C$

33.   The daily high temperatures, in degrees Celsius, for a four-day period were recorded as follows: $-8°, -6°, 3°, -5°$. Find the average high temperature for the four-day period. $-4°C$

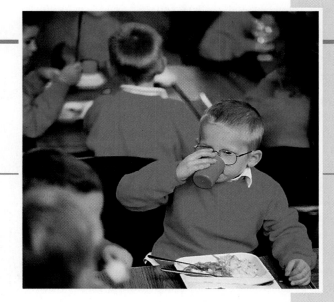

2

Variable Expressions

Nutritionists are hired by schools, hospitals, and other institutions to plan appealing meals that supply the nutrition needed to maintain good health. To plan a balanced diet, they need to know the recommended daily requirements of vitamins and minerals and the vitamin and mineral content of different foods. As meal planning requires dealing with so many "variables," a knowledge of variable expressions is very helpful in this career.

OBJECTIVES

History of Variables

Before the 16th century, unknown quantities were represented by words. In Latin, the language in which most scholarly works were written, the word *res*, meaning "thing," was used. In Germany the word *zahl*, meaning "number," was used. In Italy the word *cosa*, also meaning "thing," was used.

Then in 1637, René Descartes, a French mathematician, began using the letters x, y, and z to represent variables. It is interesting to note, upon examining Descartes's work, that toward the end of the book the letters y and z were no longer used and x became the choice for a variable.

One explanation of why the letters y and z appeared less frequently has to do with the nature of printing presses during Descartes's time. A printer had a large tray that contained all the letters of the alphabet. There were many copies of each letter, especially those letters that are used frequently. For example, there were more e's than q's. Because the letters y and z do not occur frequently in French, a printer would have few of these letters on hand. Consequently, when Descartes started using these letters as variables, it quickly depleted the printer's supply and x's had to be used instead.

Today, most nations use x as the standard letter for a single unknown. In fact, x-rays were so named because the scientists who discovered them did not know what they were and thus labeled them the "unknown rays" or x-rays.

SECTION 2.1
Evaluating Variable Expressions

1   Evaluate variable expressions

Often we discuss a quantity without knowing its exact value, such as the price of gold next month, the cost of a new automobile next year, or the tuition for next semester. In algebra, a letter of the alphabet is used to stand for a quantity that is unknown or one that can change, or *vary*. The letter is called a **variable.** An expression that contains one or more variables is called a **variable expression.**

A variable expression is shown at the right. The expression can be rewritten by writing subtraction as the addition of the opposite.

$$3x^2 - 5y + 2xy - x - 7$$

$$3x^2 + (-5y) + 2xy + (-x) + (-7)$$

Note that the expression has five addends. The **terms** of a variable expression are the addends of the expression. The expression has five terms.

The terms $3x^2, -5y, 2xy,$ and $-x$ are **variable terms.**

The term -7 is a **constant term,** or simply a **constant.**

Each variable term is composed of a **numerical coefficient** and a **variable part** (the variable or variables and their exponents).

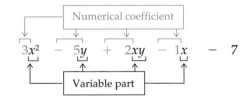

When the numerical coefficient is 1 or -1, the 1 is usually not written ($x = 1x$ and $-x = -1x$).

> **Example 1**   Name the variable terms of the expression $2a^2 - 5a + 7$.
>
> **Solution** $2a^2, -5a$
>
> **Problem 1**   Name the constant term of the expression $6n^2 + 3n - 4$.
>
> **Solution**   See page S2. -4

Variable expressions occur naturally in science. In a physics lab, a student may discover that a weight of 1 pound will stretch a spring $\frac{1}{2}$ inch. A weight of 2 pounds will stretch the spring 1 inch. By experimenting, the student can discover that the distance the spring will stretch is found by multiplying the weight, in pounds, by $\frac{1}{2}$. By letting W represent the number of pounds attached to the spring, the distance, in inches, the spring stretches can be represented by the variable expression $\frac{1}{2}W$.

With a weight of W pounds, the spring will stretch $\frac{1}{2} \cdot W = \frac{1}{2}W$ inches.

With a weight of 10 pounds, the spring will stretch $\frac{1}{2} \cdot 10 = 5$ inches.

With a weight of 3 pounds, the spring will stretch $\frac{1}{2} \cdot 3 = 1\frac{1}{2}$ inches.

Replacing the variable or variables in a variable expression with numbers and then simplifying the resulting numerical expression is called **evaluating the variable expression.**

Example 2   Evaluate $ab - b^2$ when $a = 2$ and $b = -3$.

Solution $ab - b^2$
$2(-3) - (-3)^2$ ▸ Replace each variable in the expression with the number it represents.
$= 2(-3) - 9$ ▸ Use the Order of Operations Agreement to simplify the resulting numerical expression.
$= -6 - 9$
$= -15$

Problem 2   Evaluate $2xy + y^2$ when $x = -4$ and $y = 2$.

Solution   See page S2. -12

Example 3   Evaluate $\dfrac{a^2 - b^2}{a - b}$ when $a = 3$ and $b = -4$.

Solution $\dfrac{a^2 - b^2}{a - b}$

$\dfrac{(3)^2 - (-4)^2}{3 - (-4)}$ ▸ Replace each variable in the expression with the number it represents.

$= \dfrac{9 - 16}{3 - (-4)}$ ▸ Use the Order of Operations Agreement to simplify the resulting numerical expression.

$= \dfrac{-7}{7}$

$= -1$

Problem 3   Evaluate $\dfrac{a^2 + b^2}{a + b}$ when $a = 5$ and $b = -3$.

Solution   See page S3. 17

Example 4   Evaluate $x^2 - 3(x - y) - z^2$ when $x = 2$, $y = -1$, and $z = 3$.

Solution $x^2 - 3(x - y) - z^2$
$(2)^2 - 3[2 - (-1)] - (3)^2$ ▶ Replace each variable in the expression with the number it represents.

$= (2)^2 - 3(3) - (3)^2$ ▶ Use the Order of Operations Agreement to simplify the resulting numerical expression.
$= 4 - 3(3) - 9$
$= 4 - 9 - 9$
$= -5 - 9$
$= -14$

Problem 4   Evaluate $x^3 - 2(x + y) + z^2$ when $x = 2$, $y = -4$, and $z = -3$.

Solution   See page S3.   21

Example 5   The diameter of the base of a right circular cylinder is 5 cm. The height of the cylinder is 8.5 cm. Find the volume of the cylinder. Round to the nearest tenth.

8.5 cm

5 cm

Solution $V = \pi r^2 h$ ▶ Use the formula for the volume of a right circular cylinder.

$V = \pi(2.5)^2(8.5)$ ▶ $r = \frac{1}{2}d = \frac{1}{2}(5) = 2.5$

$V = \pi(6.25)(8.5)$ ▶ Use the π key on your calculator to enter the
$V \approx 166.9$ value of π.

The volume is approximately 166.9 cm^3.

Problem 5   The diameter of the base of a right circular cone is 9 cm. The height of the cone is 9.5 cm. Find the volume of the cone. Round to the nearest tenth.

9.5 cm

9 cm

Solution   See page S3.   201.5 cm^3

 A graphing calculator can be used to evaluate variable expressions. When the value of each variable is stored in the calculator's memory and a variable expression is then entered on the calculator, the calculator evaluates that variable expression for the values of the variables stored in its memory. See the Appendix for a description of keystroking procedures for different models of graphing calculators.

STUDY TIPS

ATTENDANCE

Attending class is vital if you are to succeed in your algebra course. Your instructor will provide not only information but also practice in the skills you are learning. Be sure to arrive on time. You are responsible for *everything* that happens in class, even if you are absent. If you must be absent from a class session:

1. Deliver due assignments to the instructor as soon as possible.

2. Contact a classmate to learn about assignments or tests announced in your absence.

3. Hand copy or photocopy notes taken by a classmate while you were absent.

CONCEPT REVIEW 2.1

Determine whether the statement is always true, sometimes true, or never true.

1. The expression $3x^2$ is a variable expression.   Always true

2. In the expression $8y^3 - 4y$, the terms are $8y^3$ and $4y$.   Never true

3. For the expression x^5, the value of x is 1.   Sometimes true

4. For the expression $6a + 7b$, 7 is a constant term.   Never true

5. The Order of Operations Agreement is used in evaluating a variable expression.
   Always true

6. The result of evaluating a variable expression is a single number.   Always true

---

EXERCISES 2.1

1 Name the terms of the variable expression. Then underline the constant term.

1. $2x^2 + 5x - 8$
   $2x^2, 5x, \underline{-8}$

2. $-3n^2 - 4n + 7$
   $-3n^2, -4n, \underline{7}$

3. $6 - a^4$
   $-a^4, \underline{6}$

Name the variable terms of the expression. Then underline the variable part of each term.

4. $9b^2 - 4ab + a^2$
   $9\underline{b^2}, -4\underline{ab}, \underline{a^2}$

5. $7x^2y + 6xy^2 + 10$
   $7\underline{x^2y}, 6\underline{xy^2}$

6. $5 - 8n - 3n^2$
   $-8\underline{n}, -3\underline{n^2}$

Name the coefficients of the variable terms.

7. $x^2 - 9x + 2$
   $1, -9$

8. $12a^2 - 8ab - b^2$
   $12, -8, -1$

9. $n^3 - 4n^2 - n + 9$
   $1, -4, -1$

10. 🖋 What is the meaning of the phrase "evaluate a variable expression"?

11. 🖋 What is the difference between the meaning of "the value of the variable" and the meaning of "the value of the variable expression"?

Evaluate the variable expression when $a = 2$, $b = 3$, and $c = -4$.

12. $3a + 2b$ 12

13. $a - 2c$ 10

14. $-a^2$ -4

15. $2c^2$ 32

16. $-3a + 4b$ 6

17. $3b - 3c$ 21

18. $b^2 - 3$ 6

19. $-3c + 4$ 16

20. $16 \div (2c)$ -2

21. $6b \div (-a)$ -9

22. $bc \div (2a)$ -3

23. $-2ab \div c$ 3

24. $a^2 - b^2$ -5

25. $b^2 - c^2$ -7

26. $(a + b)^2$ 25

27. $a^2 + b^2$ 13

28. $2a - (c + a)^2$ 0

29. $(b - a)^2 + 4c$ -15

30. $b^2 - \dfrac{ac}{8}$ 10

31. $\dfrac{5ab}{6} - 3cb$ 41

32. $(b - 2a)^2 + bc$ -11

Evaluate the variable expression when $a = -2$, $b = 4$, $c = -1$, and $d = 3$.

33. $\dfrac{b + c}{d}$ 1

34. $\dfrac{d - b}{c}$ 1

35. $\dfrac{2d + b}{-a}$ 5

36. $\dfrac{b + 2d}{b}$ $\dfrac{5}{2}$

37. $\dfrac{b - d}{c - a}$ 1

38. $\dfrac{2c - d}{-ad}$ $-\dfrac{5}{6}$

39. $(b + d)^2 - 4a$ 57

40. $(d - a)^2 - 3c$ 28

41. $(d - a)^2 \div 5$ 5

42. $(b - c)^2 \div 5$ 5

43. $b^2 - 2b + 4$ 12

44. $a^2 - 5a - 6$ 8

45. $\dfrac{bd}{a} \div c$ 6

46. $\dfrac{2ac}{b} \div (-c)$ 1

47. $2(b + c) - 2a$ 10

48. $3(b - a) - bc$ 22

49. $\dfrac{b - 2a}{bc^2 - d}$ 8

50. $\dfrac{b^2 - a}{ad + 3c}$ -2

51. $\dfrac{1}{3}d^2 - \dfrac{3}{8}b^2$ -3

52. $\dfrac{5}{8}a^4 - c^2$ 9

53. $\dfrac{-4bc}{2a - b}$ -2

54. $\dfrac{abc}{b - d}$ 8

55. $a^3 - 3a^2 + a$ -22

56. $d^3 - 3d - 9$ 9

57. $-\dfrac{3}{4}b + \dfrac{1}{2}(ac + bd)$ 4

58. $-\dfrac{2}{3}d - \dfrac{1}{5}(bd - ac)$ -4

59. $(b - a)^2 - (d - c)^2$ 20

60. $(b + c)^2 + (a + d)^2$ 10

61. $4ac + (2a)^2$ 24

62. $3dc - (4c)^2$ -25

Evaluate the variable expression when $a = 2.7$, $b = -1.6$, and $c = -0.8$.

63. $c^2 - ab$ 4.96

64. $(a + b)^2 - c$ 2.01

65. $\dfrac{b^3}{c} - 4a$ -5.68

Solve. Round to the nearest tenth.

66. *Geometry*   Find the volume of a sphere that has a radius of 8.5 cm.
2572.4 cm³

67. *Geometry*   Find the volume of a right circular cylinder that has a radius
of 1.25 in. and a height of 5.25 in.   25.8 in³

8.5 cm

68. *Geometry*   The radius of the base of a right circular cylinder is 3.75 ft. The
height of the cylinder is 9.5 ft. Find the surface area of the cylinder.
312.2 ft²

69. *Geometry*   The length of one base of a trapezoid is 17.5 cm, and the length
of the other base is 10.25 cm. The height is 6.75 cm. What is the area of the
trapezoid?   93.7 cm²

10.25 cm

6.75 cm

17.5 cm

70. *Geometry*   A right circular cone has a height of 2.75 in. The diameter of
the base is 1 in. Find the volume of the cone.   0.7 in³

71. *Geometry*   A right circular cylinder has a height of 12.6 m. The diameter
of the base is 7 m. Find the volume of the cylinder.   484.9 m³

12.6 m

7 m

APPLYING CONCEPTS 2.1

Evaluate the variable expression when $a = -2$ and $b = -3$.

72. $|2a + 3b|$ 13

73. $|-4ab|$ 24

74. $|5a - b|$ 7

Evaluate the variable expression when $a = \frac{2}{3}$ and $b = -\frac{3}{2}$.

[C] **75.** $\frac{1}{3}a^5b^6$ $\frac{1}{2}$

[C] **76.** $\frac{(2ab)^3}{2a^3b^3}$ 4

[C] **77.** $|5ab - 8a^2b^2|$ 13

Evaluate the following expressions for $x = 2$, $y = 3$, and $z = -2$.

78. $3^x - x^3$ 1

79. $2^y - y^2$ -1

80. z^y -8

81. z^x 4

82. $x^x - y^y$ -23

83. $y^{(x^2)}$ 81

[C] **84.**   For each of the following, determine the first natural number x, greater than
2, for which the second expression is larger than the first. On the basis of
your answers, make a conjecture that appears to be true about the expressions x^n and n^x, where $n = 3, 4, 5, 6, 7, \ldots$ and x is a natural number greater
than 2.

  a. $x^3, 3^x$
  4

  b. $x^4, 4^x$
  5

  c. $x^5, 5^x$
  6

  d. $x^6, 6^x$
  7     $n^x > x^n$ if $x \geq n + 1$

S E C T I O N **2.2**

Simplifying Variable Expressions

1   The Properties of the Real Numbers

The Properties of the Real Numbers describe the way operations on numbers can be performed. Here are some of the Properties of the Real Numbers and an example of each.

The Commutative Property of Addition

If a and b are real numbers, then $a + b = b + a$.

Two terms can be added in either order; the sum is the same.

$$4 + 3 = 7 \quad \text{and} \quad 3 + 4 = 7$$

The Commutative Property of Multiplication

If a and b are real numbers, then $a \cdot b = b \cdot a$.

Two factors can be multiplied in either order; the product is the same.

$$(5)(-2) = -10 \quad \text{and} \quad (-2)(5) = -10$$

The Associative Property of Addition

If a, b, and c are real numbers, then $(a + b) + c = a + (b + c)$.

When three or more terms are added, the terms can be grouped (with parentheses, for example) in any order; the sum is the same.

$$2 + (3 + 4) = 2 + 7 = 9 \quad \text{and} \quad (2 + 3) + 4 = 5 + 4 = 9$$

The Associative Property of Multiplication

If a, b, and c are real numbers, then $(a \cdot b) \cdot c = a \cdot (b \cdot c)$.

When three or more factors are multiplied, the factors can be grouped in any order; the product is the same.

$$(2 \cdot 3) \cdot 4 = 6 \cdot 4 = 24 \quad \text{and} \quad 2 \cdot (3 \cdot 4) = 2 \cdot 12 = 24$$

The Addition Property of Zero

If a is a real number, then $a + 0 = 0 + a = a$.

The sum of a term and zero is the term.

$$4 + 0 = 4 \qquad 0 + 4 = 4$$

The Multiplication Property of Zero

If a is a real number, then $a \cdot 0 = 0 \cdot a = 0$.

The product of a term and zero is zero.

$$(5)(0) = 0 \qquad (0)(5) = 0$$

The Multiplication Property of One

If a is a real number, then $a \cdot 1 = 1 \cdot a = a$.

The product of a term and 1 is the term.

$$6 \cdot 1 = 6 \qquad 1 \cdot 6 = 6$$

The Inverse Property of Addition

If a is a real number, then $a + (-a) = (-a) + a = 0$.

The sum of a number and its opposite is zero.
The opposite of a number is called its **additive inverse.**

$$8 + (-8) = 0 \qquad (-8) + 8 = 0$$

The Inverse Property of Multiplication

If a is a real number, and $a \neq 0$, then $a \cdot \dfrac{1}{a} = \dfrac{1}{a} \cdot a = 1$.

The product of a number and its reciprocal is 1.
$\dfrac{1}{a}$ is the **reciprocal** of a. $\dfrac{1}{a}$ is also called the **multiplicative inverse** of a.

$$7 \cdot \frac{1}{7} = 1 \qquad \frac{1}{7} \cdot 7 = 1$$

The Distributive Property

If a, b, and c are real numbers, then $a(b + c) = ab + ac$ or $(b + c)a = ba + ca$.

By the Distributive Property, the term outside the parentheses is multiplied by each term inside the parentheses.

$$2(3 + 4) = 2 \cdot 3 + 2 \cdot 4 \qquad\qquad (4 + 5)2 = 4 \cdot 2 + 5 \cdot 2$$
$$2 \cdot 7 = 6 + 8 \qquad\qquad\qquad 9 \cdot 2 = 8 + 10$$
$$14 = 14 \qquad\qquad\qquad\qquad 18 = 18$$

Example 1   Complete the statement by using the Commutative Property of Multiplication.

$(6)(5) = (?)(6)$

Solution $(6)(5) = (5)(6)$ ▶ The Commutative Property of Multiplication states that $a \cdot b = b \cdot a$.

Problem 1   Complete the statement by using the Inverse Property of Addition.

$7 + ? = 0$

Solution   See page S3. -7

Example 2   Identify the property that justifies the statement.

$2(8 + 5) = 16 + 10$

Solution   The Distributive Property   ▶ The Distributive Property states that $a(b + c) = ab + ac$.

Problem 2   Identify the property that justifies the statement.

$5 + (13 + 7) = (5 + 13) + 7$

Solution   See page S3.   The Associative Property of Addition

2 ## Simplify variable expressions using the Properties of Addition

Like terms of a variable expression are terms with the same variable part. (Because $x^2 = x \cdot x$, x^2 and x are not like terms.)

Constant terms are like terms. 4 and 9 are like terms.

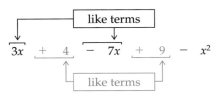

To **combine** like terms, use the Distributive Property $ba + ca = (b + c)a$ to add the coefficients.

$$2x + 3x = (2 + 3)x$$
$$= 5x$$

Example 3   Simplify.   A. $-2y + 3y$ B. $5x - 11x$

Solution   A. $-2y + 3y$

$= (-2 + 3)y$ ▶ Use the Distributive Property $ba + ca = (b + c)a$.

$= 1y$ ▶ Add the coefficients.

$= y$ ▶ Use the Multiplication Property of One.

B. $5x - 11x$

$= [5 + (-11)]x$ ▶ Use the Distributive Property $ba + ca = (b + c)a$.

$= -6x$ ▶ Add the coefficients.

Problem 3   Simplify.   A. $9x + 6x$ B. $-4y - 7y$

Solution   See page S3.   A. $15x$ B. $-11y$

In simplifying more complicated expressions, use the Properties of Addition.

The Commutative Property of Addition can be used when adding two like terms. The terms can be added in either order. The sum is the same.

$$2x + (-4x) = -4x + 2x$$
$$[2 + (-4)]x = (-4 + 2)x$$
$$-2x = -2x$$

The Associative Property of Addition is used when adding three or more terms. The terms can be grouped in any order. The sum is the same.

$$3x + 5x + 9x = (3x + 5x) + 9x = 3x + (5x + 9x)$$
$$8x + 9x = 3x + 14x$$
$$17x = 17x$$

By the Addition Property of Zero, the sum of a term and zero is the term.

$$5x + 0 = 0 + 5x = 5x$$

By the Inverse Property of Addition, the sum of a term and its additive inverse is zero.

$$7x + (-7x) = -7x + 7x = 0$$

Example 4   Simplify.   A. $8x + 3y - 8x$ B. $4x^2 + 5x - 6x^2 - 2x$

Solution   A. $8x + 3y - 8x$

$= 3y + 8x - 8x$ ▶ Use the Commutative Property of Addition to rearrange the terms.

$= 3y + (8x - 8x)$ ▶ Use the Associative Property of Addition to group like terms.

$= 3y + 0$ ▶ Use the Inverse Property of Addition.

$= 3y$ ▶ Use the Addition Property of Zero.

B. $4x^2 + 5x - 6x^2 - 2x$

$\quad = 4x^2 - 6x^2 + 5x - 2x$ ▶ Use the Commutative Property of Addition to rearrange the terms.

$\quad = (4x^2 - 6x^2) + (5x - 2x)$ ▶ Use the Associative Property of Addition to group like terms.

$\quad = -2x^2 + 3x$ ▶ Combine like terms.

Problem 4   Simplify.   A. $3a - 2b + 5a$ B. $x^2 - 7 + 9x^2 - 14$

Solution   See page S3.   A. $8a - 2b$ B. $10x^2 - 21$

3   **Simplify variable expressions using the Properties of Multiplication**

The Properties of Multiplication are used in simplifying variable expressions.

The Associative Property is used when multiplying three or more factors. $2(3x) = (2 \cdot 3)x = 6x$

The Commutative Property can be used to change the order in which factors are multiplied. $(3x) \cdot 2 = 2 \cdot (3x) = 6x$

By the Multiplication Property of One, the product of a term and 1 is the term. $(8x)(1) = (1)(8x) = 8x$

By the Inverse Property of Multiplication, the product of a term and its reciprocal is 1. $5x \cdot \dfrac{1}{5x} = \dfrac{1}{5x} \cdot 5x = 1,\ x \neq 0$

Example 5   Simplify.   A. $2(-x)$ B. $\dfrac{3}{2}\left(\dfrac{2x}{3}\right)$ C. $(16x)2$

Solution   A. $2(-x) = 2(-1 \cdot x)$ ▶ $-x = -1x = -1 \cdot x$

$\quad\quad\quad\quad\quad\quad = [2 \cdot (-1)]x$ ▶ Use the Associative Property of Multiplication to group factors.

$\quad\quad\quad\quad\quad\quad = -2x$ ▶ Multiply.

B. $\dfrac{3}{2}\left(\dfrac{2x}{3}\right) = \dfrac{3}{2}\left(\dfrac{2}{3}x\right)$ ▶ Note that $\dfrac{2x}{3} = \dfrac{2}{3} \cdot \dfrac{x}{1} = \dfrac{2}{3}x$.

$\quad\quad\quad\quad = \left(\dfrac{3}{2} \cdot \dfrac{2}{3}\right)x$ ▶ Use the Associative Property of Multiplication to group factors.

$\quad\quad\quad\quad = 1x$ ▶ Use the Inverse Property of Multiplication.

$\quad\quad\quad\quad = x$ ▶ Use the Multiplication Property of One.

C. $(16x)2 = 2(16x)$ ▶ Use the Commutative Property of Multiplication to rearrange factors.

$\quad\quad\quad\quad = (2 \cdot 16)x$ ▶ Use the Associative Property of Multiplication to group factors.

$\quad\quad\quad\quad = 32x$ ▶ Multiply.

Problem 5   Simplify.   A. $-7(-2a)$ B. $-\dfrac{5}{6}(-30y^2)$ C. $(-5x)(-2)$

Solution   See page S3.   A. $14a$ B. $25y^2$ C. $10x$

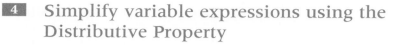

4 Simplify variable expressions using the Distributive Property

The Distributive Property is used to remove parentheses from a variable expression.

$3(2x - 5)$
$= 3(2x) - 3(5)$
$= 6x - 15$

An extension of the Distributive Property is used when an expression contains more than two terms.

$4(x^2 + 6x - 1)$
$= 4(x^2) + 4(6x) - 4(1)$
$= 4x^2 + 24x - 4$

Example 6 Simplify.   A. $-3(5 + x)$ B. $-(2x - 4)$
C. $(2y - 6)2$ D. $5(3x + 7y - z)$

Solution A. $-3(5 + x)$
$= -3(5) + (-3)x$ ▶ Use the Distributive Property.
$= -15 - 3x$ ▶ Multiply.

B. $-(2x - 4)$
$= -1(2x - 4)$ ▶ Just as $-x = -1x$,
$-(2x - 4) = -1(2x - 4)$.

$= -1(2x) - (-1)(4)$ ▶ Use the Distributive Property.
$= -2x + 4$ ▶ Note: When a negative sign immediately precedes the parentheses, remove the parentheses and change the sign of *each* term inside the parentheses.

C. $(2y - 6)2$
$= (2y)(2) - (6)(2)$ ▶ Use the Distributive Property
$= 4y - 12$ $(b + c)a = ba + ca$.

D. $5(3x + 7y - z)$
$= 5(3x) + 5(7y) - 5(z)$ ▶ Use the Distributive Property.
$= 15x + 35y - 5z$

Problem 6 Simplify.   A. $7(4 + 2y)$ B. $-(5x - 12)$
C. $(3a - 1)5$ D. $-3(6a^2 - 8a + 9)$

Solution See page S3.
A. $28 + 14y$ B. $-5x + 12$ C. $15a - 5$ D. $-18a^2 + 24a - 27$

5 Simplify general variable expressions

When simplifying variable expressions, use the Distributive Property to remove parentheses and brackets used as grouping symbols.

Example 7 Simplify: $4(x - y) - 2(-3x + 6y)$

Solution $4(x - y) - 2(-3x + 6y)$
$= 4x - 4y + 6x - 12y$ ▶ Use the Distributive Property to remove parentheses.

$= 10x - 16y$ ▶ Combine like terms.

Problem 7   Simplify: $7(x - 2y) - 3(-x - 2y)$

   Solution   See page S3. $10x - 8y$

Example 8   Simplify: $2x - 3[2x - 3(x + 7)]$

   Solution $2x - 3[2x - 3(x + 7)]$

$= 2x - 3[2x - 3x - 21]$ ▸ Use the Distributive Property to remove the inner grouping symbols.

$= 2x - 3[-x - 21]$ ▸ Combine like terms inside the grouping symbols.

$= 2x + 3x + 63$ ▸ Use the Distributive Property to remove the brackets.

$= 5x + 63$ ▸ Combine like terms.

Problem 8   Simplify: $3y - 2[x - 4(2 - 3y)]$

   Solution   See page S3. $-2x - 21y + 16$

STUDY TIPS

KEEP UP TO DATE WITH COURSE WORK

College terms start out slowly. Then they gradually get busier and busier, reaching a peak of activity at final examination time. If you fall behind in the work for a course, you will find yourself trying to catch up at a time when you are very busy with all of your other courses. Don't fall behind—keep up to date with course work.

   Keeping up with course work is doubly important for a course in which information and skills learned early in the course are needed to learn information and skills later in the course. Skills must be learned immediately and reviewed often.

   Your instructor gives assignments to help you acquire a skill or understand a concept. Do each assignment as it is assigned or you may well fall behind and have great difficulty catching up. Keeping up with course work also makes it easier to prepare for each exam.

CONCEPT REVIEW 2.2

Determine whether the statement is always true, sometimes true, or never true.

1. The Associative Property of Addition states that two terms can be added in either order and the sum will be the same.   Never true

2. When three numbers are multiplied, the numbers can be grouped in any order and the product will be the same.   Always true

3. The Multiplication Property of One states that multiplying a number by one does not change the number.   Always true

4. The sum of a number and its additive inverse is zero.   Always true

5. The product of a number and its multiplicative inverse is one.   Always true

6. The terms x and x^2 are like terms because both have a coefficient of 1.   Never true

7. $3(x + 4) = 3x + 4$ is an example of the correct application of the Distributive Property.   Never true

8. To add like terms, add the coefficients; the variable part remains unchanged.   Always true

---

EXERCISES 2.2

1 Use the given property to complete the statement.

1. The Commutative Property of Multiplication
   $2 \cdot 5 = 5 \cdot ?$ 2

2. The Commutative Property of Addition
   $9 + 17 = ? + 9$ 17

3. The Associative Property of Multiplication
   $(4 \cdot 5) \cdot 6 = 4 \cdot (? \cdot 6)$ 5

4. The Associative Property of Addition
   $(4 + 5) + 6 = ? + (5 + 6)$ 4

5. The Distributive Property
   $2(4 + 3) = 8 + ?$ 6

6. The Addition Property of Zero
   $? + 0 = -7$ -7

7. The Inverse Property of Addition
   $8 + ? = 0$ -8

8. The Inverse Property of Multiplication
   $\frac{1}{-5}(-5) = ?$ 1

9. The Multiplication Property of One
   $? \cdot 1 = -4$ -4

10. The Multiplication Property of Zero
    $12 \cdot ? = 0$ 0

Identify the property that justifies the statement.

11. $-7 + 7 = 0$
    The Inverse Property of Addition

12. $(-8)\left(-\frac{1}{8}\right) = 1$
    The Inverse Property of Multiplication

13. $23 + 19 = 19 + 23$
    The Commutative Property of Addition

14. $-21 + 0 = -21$
    The Addition Property of Zero

15. $2 + (6 + 14) = (2 + 6) + 14$
    The Associative Property of Addition

16. $(-3 + 9)8 = -24 + 72$
    The Distributive Property

17. $3 \cdot 5 = 5 \cdot 3$
    The Commutative Property of Multiplication

18. $-32(0) = 0$ The Multiplication Property of Zero

19. $(4 \cdot 3) \cdot 5 = 4 \cdot (3 \cdot 5)$
    The Associative Property of Multiplication

20. $\frac{1}{4}(1) = \frac{1}{4}$ The Multiplication Property of One

2 Simplify.

21. $6x + 8x$ $14x$

22. $12x + 13x$ $25x$

23. $9a - 4a$ $5a$

24. $12a - 3a$ $9a$

25. $4y - 10y$ $-6y$

26. $8y - 6y$ $2y$

27. $-3b - 7$ $-3b - 7$

28. $-12y - 3$
    $-12y - 3$

29. $-12a + 17a$ $5a$

30. $-3a + 12a$ $9a$

31. $5ab - 7ab$ $-2ab$

32. $9ab - 3ab$ $6ab$

33. $-12xy + 17xy$ $5xy$

34. $-15xy + 3xy$
    $-12xy$

35. $-3ab + 3ab$ 0

36. $-7ab + 7ab$ 0

37. $-\dfrac{1}{2}x - \dfrac{1}{3}x$ $\quad -\dfrac{5}{6}x$ **38.** $-\dfrac{2}{5}y + \dfrac{3}{10}y$ $\quad -\dfrac{1}{10}y$ **39.** $\dfrac{3}{8}x^2 - \dfrac{5}{12}x^2$ $\quad -\dfrac{1}{24}x^2$ **40.** $\dfrac{2}{3}y^2 - \dfrac{4}{9}y^2$ $\quad \dfrac{2}{9}y^2$

41. $3x + 5x + 3x$ $\quad 11x$ **42.** $8x + 5x + 7x$ $\quad 20x$ **43.** $5a - 3a + 5a$ $\quad 7a$ **44.** $10a - 17a + 3a$ $\quad -4a$

45. $-5x^2 - 12x^2 + 3x^2$ $\quad -14x^2$ **46.** $-y^2 - 8y^2 + 7y^2$ $\quad -2y^2$ **47.** $7x - 8x + 3y$ $\quad -x + 3y$

48. $8y - 10x + 8x$ $\quad -2x + 8y$ **49.** $7x - 3y + 10x$ $\quad 17x - 3y$ **50.** $8y + 8x - 8y$ $\quad 8x$

51. $3a - 7b - 5a + b$ $\quad -2a - 6b$ **52.** $-5b + 7a - 7b + 12a$ $\quad 19a - 12b$ **53.** $3x - 8y - 10x + 4x$ $\quad -3x - 8y$

54. $3y - 12x - 7y + 2y$ $\quad -12x - 2y$ **55.** $x^2 - 7x - 5x^2 + 5x$ $\quad -4x^2 - 2x$ **56.** $3x^2 + 5x - 10x^2 - 10x$ $\quad -7x^2 - 5x$

3 Simplify.

57. $4(3x)$ $\quad 12x$ **58.** $12(5x)$ $\quad 60x$ **59.** $-3(7a)$ $\quad -21a$ **60.** $-2(5a)$ $\quad -10a$

61. $-2(-3y)$ $\quad 6y$ **62.** $-5(-6y)$ $\quad 30y$ **63.** $(4x)2$ $\quad 8x$ **64.** $(6x)12$ $\quad 72x$

65. $(3a)(-2)$ $\quad -6a$ **66.** $(7a)(-4)$ $\quad -28a$ **67.** $(-3b)(-4)$ $\quad 12b$ **68.** $(-12b)(-9)$ $\quad 108b$

69. $-5(3x^2)$ $\quad -15x^2$ **70.** $-8(7x^2)$ $\quad -56x^2$ **71.** $\dfrac{1}{3}(3x^2)$ $\quad x^2$ **72.** $\dfrac{1}{5}(5a)$ $\quad a$

73. $\dfrac{1}{8}(8x)$ $\quad x$ **74.** $-\dfrac{1}{4}(-4a)$ $\quad a$ **75.** $-\dfrac{1}{7}(-7n)$ $\quad n$ **76.** $\left(\dfrac{3x}{4}\right)\left(\dfrac{4}{3}\right)$ $\quad x$

77. $\dfrac{12x}{5}\left(\dfrac{5}{12}\right)$ $\quad x$ **78.** $(-6y)\left(-\dfrac{1}{6}\right)$ $\quad y$ **79.** $(-10n)\left(-\dfrac{1}{10}\right)$ $\quad n$ **80.** $\dfrac{1}{3}(9x)$ $\quad 3x$

81. $\dfrac{1}{7}(14x)$ $\quad 2x$ **82.** $-\dfrac{1}{5}(10x)$ $\quad -2x$ **83.** $-\dfrac{1}{8}(16x)$ $\quad -2x$ **84.** $-\dfrac{2}{3}(12a^2)$ $\quad -8a^2$

85. $-\dfrac{5}{8}(24a^2)$ $\quad -15a^2$ **86.** $-\dfrac{1}{2}(-16y)$ $\quad 8y$ **87.** $-\dfrac{3}{4}(-8y)$ $\quad 6y$ **88.** $(16y)\left(\dfrac{1}{4}\right)$ $\quad 4y$

89. $(33y)\left(\dfrac{1}{11}\right)$ $\quad 3y$ **90.** $(-6x)\left(\dfrac{1}{3}\right)$ $\quad -2x$ **91.** $(-10x)\left(\dfrac{1}{5}\right)$ $\quad -2x$ **92.** $(-8a)\left(-\dfrac{3}{4}\right)$ $\quad 6a$

4 Simplify.

93. $-(x + 2)$ $\quad -x - 2$ **94.** $-(x + 7)$ $\quad -x - 7$ **95.** $2(4x - 3)$ $\quad 8x - 6$ **96.** $5(2x - 7)$ $\quad 10x - 35$

97. $-2(a + 7)$ $\quad -2a - 14$ **98.** $-5(a + 16)$ $\quad -5a - 80$ **99.** $-3(2y - 8)$ $\quad -6y + 24$ **100.** $-5(3y - 7)$ $\quad -15y + 35$

101. $(5 - 3b)7$ $\quad 35 - 21b$ **102.** $(10 - 7b)2$ $\quad 20 - 14b$ **103.** $-3(3 - 5x)$ $\quad -9 + 15x$ **104.** $-5(7 - 10x)$ $\quad -35 + 50x$

105. $3(5x^2 + 2x)$ $\quad 15x^2 + 6x$ **106.** $6(3x^2 + 2x)$ $\quad 18x^2 + 12x$ **107.** $-2(-y + 9)$ $\quad 2y - 18$ **108.** $-5(-2x + 7)$ $\quad 10x - 35$

109. $(-3x - 6)5$ $\quad -15x - 30$ **110.** $(-2x + 7)7$ $\quad -14x + 49$ **111.** $2(-3x^2 - 14)$ $\quad -6x^2 - 28$ **112.** $5(-6x^2 - 3)$ $\quad -30x^2 - 15$

113. $-3(2y^2 - 7)$ $-6y^2 + 21$ **114.** $-8(3y^2 - 12)$ $-24y^2 + 96$ **115.** $-(6a^2 - 7b^2)$ $-6a^2 + 7b^2$

116. $3(x^2 + 2x - 6)$
$3x^2 + 6x - 18$

117. $4(x^2 - 3x + 5)$
$4x^2 - 12x + 20$

118. $-2(y^2 - 2y + 4)$
$-2y^2 + 4y - 8$

119. $-3(y^2 - 3y - 7)$
$-3y^2 + 9y + 21$

120. $2(-a^2 - 2a + 3)$
$-2a^2 - 4a + 6$

121. $4(-3a^2 - 5a + 7)$
$-12a^2 - 20a + 28$

122. $-5(-2x^2 - 3x + 7)$
$10x^2 + 15x - 35$

123. $-3(-4x^2 + 3x - 4)$
$12x^2 - 9x + 12$

124. $3(2x^2 + xy - 3y^2)$
$6x^2 + 3xy - 9y^2$

125. $5(2x^2 - 4xy - y^2)$
$10x^2 - 20xy - 5y^2$

126. $-(3a^2 + 5a - 4)$
$-3a^2 - 5a + 4$

127. $-(8b^2 - 6b + 9)$
$-8b^2 + 6b - 9$

5 Simplify.

128. $4x - 2(3x + 8)$ $-2x - 16$ **129.** $6a - (5a + 7)$ $a - 7$ **130.** $9 - 3(4y + 6)$ $-12y - 9$

131. $10 - (11x - 3)$ $-11x + 13$ **132.** $5n - (7 - 2n)$ $7n - 7$ **133.** $8 - (12 + 4y)$ $-4y - 4$

134. $3(x + 2) - 5(x - 7)$
$-2x + 41$

135. $2(x - 4) - 4(x + 2)$
$-2x - 16$

136. $12(y - 2) + 3(7 - 3y)$
$3y - 3$

137. $6(2y - 7) - 3(3 - 2y)$
$18y - 51$

138. $3(a - b) - 4(a + b)$
$-a - 7b$

139. $2(a + 2b) - (a - 3b)$
$a + 7b$

140. $4[x - 2(x - 3)]$
$-4x + 24$

141. $2[x + 2(x + 7)]$
$6x + 28$

142. $-2[3x + 2(4 - x)]$
$-2x - 16$

143. $-5[2x + 3(5 - x)]$
$5x - 75$

144. $-3[2x - (x + 7)]$
$-3x + 21$

145. $-2[3x - (5x - 2)]$
$4x - 4$

146. $2x - 3[x - 2(4 - x)]$
$-7x + 24$

147. $-7x + 3[x - 7(3 - 2x)]$
$38x - 63$

148. $-5x - 2[2x - 4(x + 7)] - 6$
$-x + 50$

149. $4a - 2[2b - (b - 2a)] + 3b$
b

150. $2x + 3(x - 2y) + 5(3x - 7y)$
$20x - 41y$

151. $5y - 2(y - 3x) + 2(7x - y)$
$20x + y$

APPLYING CONCEPTS 2.2

Simplify.

152. $C - 0.7C$ $0.3C$

153. $\frac{1}{3}(3x + y) - \frac{2}{3}(6x - y)$
$-3x + y$

154. $-\frac{1}{4}[2x + 2(y - 6y)]$
$-\frac{1}{2}x + \frac{5}{2}y$

Complete.

155. A number that has no reciprocal is ____0____.

156. A number that is its own reciprocal is __1, -1__.

157. The additive inverse of $a - b$ is __$-a + b$__.

158. Determine whether the statement is true or false. If the statement is false, give an example that illustrates that it is false.

    a. Division is a commutative operation.   False; $8 \div 4 \neq 4 \div 8$

    b. Division is an associative operation.   False; $(8 \div 4) \div 2 \neq 8 \div (4 \div 2)$

    c. Subtraction is an associative operation.   False; $(7 - 5) - 1 \neq 7 - (5 - 1)$

    d. Subtraction is a commutative operation.   False; $6 - 3 \neq 3 - 6$

    e. Addition is a commutative operation.   True

[C] **159.** Define an operation $\otimes$ as $a \otimes b = (a \cdot b) - (a + b)$.
For example, $7 \otimes 5 = (7 \cdot 5) - (7 + 5) = 35 - 12 = 23$.

    a. Is $\otimes$ a commutative operation? Support your answer.   Yes

    b. Is $\otimes$ an associative operation? Support your answer.   No

160. Give examples of two operations that occur in everyday experience that are not commutative (for example, putting on socks and then shoes).

161. In your own words, explain the Distributive Property.

S E C T I O N **2.3**

Translating Verbal Expressions into Variable Expressions

1 Translate a verbal expression into a variable expression given the variable

One of the major skills required in applied mathematics is the ability to translate a verbal expression into a variable expression. This requires recognizing the verbal phrases that translate into mathematical operations. Here is a partial list of the phrases used to indicate the different mathematical operations.

Addition	added to	6 added to y	$y + 6$
	more than	8 more than x	$x + 8$
	the sum of	the sum of x and z	$x + z$
	increased by	t increased by 9	$t + 9$
	the total of	the total of 5 and y	$5 + y$
	plus	b plus 17	$b + 17$
Subtraction	minus	x minus 2	$x - 2$
	less than	7 less than t	$t - 7$
	less	7 less t	$7 - t$
	subtracted from	5 subtracted from d	$d - 5$
	decreased by	m decreased by 3	$m - 3$
	the difference between	the difference between y and 4	$y - 4$

Multiplication	times	10 times t	$10t$
	of	one half of x	$\frac{1}{2}x$
	the product of	the product of y and z	yz
	multiplied by	y multiplied by 11	$11y$
	twice	twice n	$2n$
Division	divided by	x divided by 12	$\frac{x}{12}$
	the quotient of	the quotient of y and z	$\frac{y}{z}$
	the ratio of	the ratio of t to 9	$\frac{t}{9}$
Power	the square of	the square of x	x^2
	the cube of	the cube of a	a^3

Translating a phrase that contains the word *sum, difference, product,* or *quotient* can sometimes cause a problem. In the examples at the right, note where the operation symbol is placed.

the *sum* of x and y $x + y$

the *difference* between x and y $x - y$

the *product* of x and y $x \cdot y$

the *quotient* of x and y $\frac{x}{y}$

Example 1   Translate into a variable expression.
A. the total of five times b and c
B. the quotient of eight less than n and fourteen
C. thirteen more than the sum of seven and the square of x

Solution   A. the total of five times b and c

$5b + c$

▶ Identify words that indicate mathematical operations.
▶ Use the operations to write the variable expression.

B. the quotient of eight less than n and fourteen

$\frac{n - 8}{14}$

▶ Identify words that indicate mathematical operations.
▶ Use the operations to write the variable expression.

C. thirteen more than the sum of seven and the square of x
$(7 + x^2) + 13$

Problem 1   Translate into a variable expression.
A. eighteen less than the cube of x
B. y decreased by the sum of z and nine
C. the difference between the square of q and the sum of r and t

Solution   See page S3.   A. $x^3 - 18$ B. $y - (z + 9)$ C. $q^2 - (r + t)$

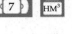

2 Translate a verbal expression into a variable expression by assigning the variable

In most applications that involve translating phrases into variable expressions, the variable to be used is not given. To translate these phrases, a variable must be assigned to an unknown quantity before the variable expression can be written.

LOOK CLOSELY

The expression $n(6 + n^3)$ must have parentheses. If we write $n \cdot 6 + n^3$, then by the Order of Operations Agreement, only the 6 is multiplied by n, but we want n to be multiplied by the *total* of 6 and n^3.

Example 2   Translate "a number multiplied by the total of six and the cube of the number" into a variable expression.

Solution   the unknown number: n ▶ Assign a variable to one of the unknown quantities.

the cube of the number: n^3 ▶ Use the assigned variable to write
the total of six and the   an expression for any other
   cube of the number: $6 + n^3$ unknown quantity.

$n(6 + n^3)$ ▶ Use the assigned variable to write
                                the variable expression.

Problem 2   Translate "a number added to the product of five and the square of the number" into a variable expression.

Solution   See page S3. $5n^2 + n$

Example 3   Translate "the quotient of twice a number and the difference between the number and twenty" into a variable expression.

Solution   the unknown number: n
twice the number: $2n$
the difference between the number and twenty: $n - 20$

$$\frac{2n}{n - 20}$$

Problem 3   Translate "the product of three and the sum of seven and twice a number" into a variable expression.

Solution   See page S3. $3(7 + 2n)$

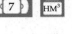

3 Translate a verbal expression into a variable expression and then simplify the resulting expression

After translating a verbal expression into a variable expression, simplify the variable expression by using the Properties of the Real Numbers.

Example 4   Translate and simplify "the total of four times an unknown number and twice the difference between the number and eight."

Solution   the unknown number: n ▸ Assign a variable to one of the unknown quantities.

four times the unknown number: $4n$ ▸ Use the assigned variable to write an expression for any other unknown quantity.
twice the difference between the number and eight: $2(n - 8)$

$4n + 2(n - 8)$ ▸ Use the assigned variable to write the variable expression.

$= 4n + 2n - 16$ ▸ Simplify the variable expression.
$= 6n - 16$

Problem 4   Translate and simplify "a number minus the difference between twice the number and seventeen."

Solution   See page S3. $n - (2n - 17); \ -n + 17$

Example 5   Translate and simplify "the difference between five-eighths of a number and two-thirds of the same number."

Solution   the unknown number: n ▸ Assign a variable to one of the unknown quantities.

five-eighths of the number: $\frac{5}{8}n$ ▸ Use the assigned variable to write an expression for any other unknown quantity.
two-thirds of the number: $\frac{2}{3}n$

$\frac{5}{8}n - \frac{2}{3}n$ ▸ Use the assigned variable to write the variable expression.
$= \frac{15}{24}n - \frac{16}{24}n$ ▸ Simplify the variable expression.
$= -\frac{1}{24}n$

Problem 5   Translate and simplify "the sum of three-fourths of a number and one-fifth of the same number."

Solution   See page S4. $\frac{3}{4}n + \frac{1}{5}n; \ \frac{19}{20}n$

4   Translate application problems

Many of the applications of mathematics require that you identify an unknown quantity, assign a variable to that quantity, and then attempt to express another unknown quantity in terms of that variable.

Suppose we know that the sum of two numbers is 10 and that one of the two numbers is 4. We can find the other number by subtracting 4 from 10.

one number: 4
other number: $10 - 4 = 6$
The two numbers are 4 and 6.

INSTRUCTOR NOTE

In Chapter 4, investment problems and coin problems are solved. In these applications it is useful to express *two* integers with a known sum in terms of *one* variable.

Now suppose we know that the sum of two numbers is 10, we don't know either number, and we want to express *both* numbers in terms of the *same* variable.

Let one number be x. Again, we can find the other number by subtracting x from 10.

one number: x
other number: $10 - x$
The two numbers are x and $10 - x$.

Note that the sum of x and $10 - x$ is 10. $x + (10 - x) = x + 10 - x = 10$

LOOK CLOSELY

Any variable can be used. For example, if the width is y, then the length is $y + 20$.

Example 6   The length of a swimming pool is 20 ft longer than the width. Express the length of the pool in terms of the width.

    Solution   the width of the pool: W ▸ Assign a variable to the width of the pool.

        the length is 20 more than the width: $W + 20$ ▸ Express the length of the pool in terms of W.

Problem 6   An older computer takes twice as long to process a set of data as does a newer model. Express the amount of time it takes the older computer to process the data in terms of the amount of time it takes the newer model.

    Solution   See page S4. $2t$

LOOK CLOSELY

It is also correct to assign the variable to the amount in the money market fund. Then the amount in the mutual fund is $5000 - x$.

Example 7   An investor divided $5000 between two accounts, one a mutual fund and the other a money market fund. Use one variable to express the amounts invested in each account.

    Solution   the amount invested in the mutual fund: x ▸ Assign a variable to the amount invested in one account.

        the amount invested in the money market fund: $5000 - x$ ▸ Express the amount invested in the other account in terms of x.

Problem 7   A guitar string 6 ft long was cut into two pieces. Use one variable to express the lengths of the two pieces.

    Solution   See page S4. L and $6 - L$

STUDY TIPS

TAKE CAREFUL NOTES IN CLASS

You need a notebook in which to keep class notes and records about assignments and tests. Make sure to take complete and well-organized notes. Your instructor will explain text material that may be difficult for you to understand on your own and may offer important information that is not provided in the textbook. Be sure to include in your notes everything that is written on the chalkboard.

Information recorded in your notes about assignments should explain exactly what they are, how they are to be done, and when they are due. Information about tests should include exactly what text material and topics will be covered on each test and the dates on which the tests will be given.

CONCEPT REVIEW 2.3

Determine whether the statement is always true, sometimes true, or never true.

1. "Five less than n" can be translated as "$5 - n$."   Never true

2. A variable expression contains an equals sign.   Never true

3. If the sum of two numbers is 12 and one of the two numbers is x, then the other number can be expressed as $x - 12$.   Never true

4. The words *total* and *times* both indicate multiplication.   Never true

5. The words *quotient* and *ratio* both indicate division.   Always true

6. The expressions $7y - 8$ and $(7y) - 8$ are equivalent.   Always true

7. The phrase "five times the sum of x and y" and the phrase "the sum of five times x and y" yield the same variable expression.   Never true

EXERCISES 2.3

1 Translate into a variable expression.

1. d less than nineteen $19 - d$

2. the sum of six and c $6 + c$

3. r decreased by twelve $r - 12$

4. w increased by fifty-five $w + 55$

5. a multiplied by twenty-eight $28a$

6. y added to sixteen $16 + y$

7. five times the difference between n and seven $5(n - 7)$

8. thirty less than the square of b $b^2 - 30$

9. y less the product of three and y $y - 3y$

10. the sum of four-fifths of m and eighteen $\frac{4}{5}m + 18$

11. the product of negative six and b $-6b$

12. nine increased by the quotient of t and five $9 + \frac{t}{5}$

13. four divided by the difference between p and six $\frac{4}{p - 6}$

14. the product of seven and the total of r and eight $7(r + 8)$

15. the quotient of nine less than x and twice x $\frac{x - 9}{2x}$

16. the product of a and the sum of a and thirteen $a(a + 13)$

17. twenty-one less than the product of s and negative four $-4s - 21$

18. fourteen more than one-half of the square of z $\frac{1}{2}z^2 + 14$

19. the ratio of eight more than d to d $\frac{d + 8}{d}$

20. the total of nine times the cube of m and the square of m $9m^3 + m^2$

21. three-eighths of the sum of t and fifteen
$\frac{3}{8}(t + 15)$

22. s decreased by the quotient of s and two
$s - \frac{s}{2}$

23. w increased by the quotient of seven and w
$w + \frac{7}{w}$

24. the difference between the square of c and the total of c and fourteen
$c^2 - (c + 14)$

25. d increased by the difference between sixteen times d and three $d + (16d - 3)$

26. the product of eight and the total of b and five
$8(b + 5)$

2 Translate into a variable expression.

27. a number divided by nineteen $\frac{n}{19}$

28. thirteen less a number $13 - n$

29. forty more than a number $n + 40$

30. three-sevenths of a number $\frac{3}{7}n$

31. the square of the difference between a number and ninety $(n - 90)^2$

32. the quotient of twice a number and five $\frac{2n}{5}$

33. the sum of four-ninths of a number and twenty
$\frac{4}{9}n + 20$

34. eight subtracted from the product of fifteen and a number $15n - 8$

35. the product of a number and ten more than the number $n(n + 10)$

36. six less than the total of a number and the cube of the number $(n + n^3) - 6$

37. fourteen added to the product of seven and a number $7n + 14$

38. the quotient of three and the total of four and a number $\frac{3}{4 + n}$

39. the quotient of twelve and the sum of a number and two $\frac{12}{n + 2}$

40. eleven plus one-half of a number $11 + \frac{1}{2}n$

41. the ratio of two and the sum of a number and one $\frac{2}{n + 1}$

42. a number multiplied by the difference between twice the number and nine $n(2n - 9)$

43. the difference between sixty and the quotient of a number and fifty $60 - \frac{n}{50}$

44. the product of nine less than a number and the number $(n - 9)n$

45. the sum of the square of a number and three times the number $n^2 + 3n$

46. the quotient of seven more than twice a number and the number $\frac{2n + 7}{n}$

47. the sum of three more than a number and the cube of the number $(n + 3) + n^3$

48. a number decreased by the difference between the cube of the number and ten $n - (n^3 - 10)$

49. the square of a number decreased by one-fourth of the number $n^2 - \frac{1}{4}n$

50. four less than seven times the square of a number $7n^2 - 4$

51. twice a number decreased by the quotient of seven and the number $2n - \dfrac{7}{n}$

52. eighty decreased by the product of thirteen and a number $80 - 13n$

53. the cube of a number decreased by the product of twelve and the number $n^3 - 12n$

54. the quotient of five and the sum of a number and nineteen $\dfrac{5}{n + 19}$

3   Translate into a variable expression. Then simplify the expression.

55. a number increased by the total of the number and ten $n + (n + 10)$; $2n + 10$

56. a number added to the product of five and the number $5n + n$; $6n$

57. a number decreased by the difference between nine and the number $n - (9 - n)$; $2n - 9$

58. eight more than the sum of a number and eleven $(n + 11) + 8$; $n + 19$

59. the difference between one-fifth of a number and three-eighths of the number $\dfrac{1}{5}n - \dfrac{3}{8}n$; $-\dfrac{7}{40}n$

60. a number minus the sum of the number and fourteen $n - (n + 14)$; -14

61. four more than the total of a number and nine $(n + 9) + 4$; $n + 13$

62. the sum of one-eighth of a number and one-twelfth of the number $\dfrac{1}{8}n + \dfrac{1}{12}n$; $\dfrac{5}{24}n$

63. twice the sum of three times a number and forty $2(3n + 40)$; $6n + 80$

64. the sum of a number divided by two and the number $\dfrac{n}{2} + n$; $\dfrac{3n}{2}$

65. seven times the product of five and a number $7(5n)$; $35n$

66. sixteen multiplied by one-fourth of a number $16\left(\dfrac{1}{4}n\right)$; $4n$

67. the total of seventeen times a number and twice the number $17n + 2n$; $19n$

68. the difference between nine times a number and twice the number $9n - 2n$; $7n$

69. a number plus the product of the number and twelve $n + 12n$; $13n$

70. nineteen more than the difference between a number and five $(n - 5) + 19$; $n + 14$

71. three times the sum of the square of a number and four $3(n^2 + 4)$; $3n^2 + 12$

72. a number subtracted from the product of the number and seven $7n - n$; $6n$

73. three-fourths of the sum of sixteen times a number and four $\dfrac{3}{4}(16n + 4)$; $12n + 3$

74. the difference between fourteen times a number and the product of the number and seven $14n - 7n$; $7n$

75. sixteen decreased by the sum of a number and nine $16 - (n + 9)$; $-n + 7$

76. eleven subtracted from the difference between eight and a number $(8 - n) - 11$; $-n - 3$

77. five more than the quotient of four times a number and two $\dfrac{4n}{2} + 5$; $2n + 5$

78. twenty minus the sum of four-ninths of a number and three $20 - \left(\dfrac{4}{9}n + 3\right)$; $-\dfrac{4}{9}n + 17$

79. six times the total of a number and eight
    $6(n + 8)$; $6n + 48$

80. four times the sum of a number and twenty
    $4(n + 20)$; $4n + 80$

81. seven minus the sum of a number and two
    $7 - (n + 2)$; $-n + 5$

82. three less than the sum of a number and ten
    $(n + 10) - 3$; $n + 7$

83. one-third of the sum of a number and six times the number $\dfrac{1}{3}(n + 6n)$; $\dfrac{7n}{3}$

84. twice the quotient of four times a number and eight $2\left(\dfrac{4n}{8}\right)$; n

85. the total of eight increased by the cube of a number and twice the cube of the number
    $(8 + n^3) + 2n^3$; $3n^3 + 8$

86. the sum of five more than the square of a number and twice the square of the number
    $(n^2 + 5) + 2n^2$; $3n^2 + 5$

87. twelve more than a number added to the difference between the number and six
    $(n + 12) + (n - 6)$; $2n + 6$

88. a number plus four added to the difference between three and twice the number
    $(n + 4) + (3 - 2n)$; $-n + 7$

89. the sum of a number and nine added to the difference between the number and twenty
    $(n + 9) + (n - 20)$; $2n - 11$

90. seven increased by a number added to twice the difference between the number and two
    $(7 + n) + 2(n - 2)$; $3n + 3$

91. fourteen plus the product of three less than a number and ten $14 + (n - 3)10$; $10n - 16$

92. a number plus the product of the number minus five and seven $n + (n - 5)7$; $8n - 35$

4 Write a variable expression.

93. *The Economy* The per capita income in New Jersey in 1997 was $7506 more than the per capita income in the United States in that year. Express the per capita income in New Jersey in 1997 in terms of the per capita income in the United States. $P + 7506$

94. *Literacy* According to *USA Today*, annual spending per person for books is $40 more in Norway than it is in the United States. Express the annual spending per person for books in Norway in terms of the annual spending per person for books in the United States. $B + 40$

95. *Sports* In football, the number of points awarded for a touchdown is three times the number of points awarded for a safety. Express the number of points awarded for a touchdown in terms of the number of points awarded for a safety. $3s$

96. *Sports* The diameter of a basketball is approximately four times the diameter of a baseball. Express the diameter of a basketball in terms of the diameter of a baseball. $4d$

97. *Business* According to the *Wall Street Journal*, in a recent year, retail sales in Boston were one-half the retail sales in Los Angeles. Express the retail sales in Boston in terms of the retail sales in Los Angeles. $\dfrac{1}{2}L$

98.   *The IRS*   According to the IRS, it should take about one-fourth as much time to prepare Schedule A as to prepare Form 1040. Express the time it should take to prepare Schedule A in terms of the time it should take to prepare Form 1040. $\frac{1}{4}t$

99.   *Demographics*   The world population in the year 2050 is expected to be twice the world population in 1990. Express the world population in 2050 in terms of the world population in 1990. $2p$

100.   *Geometry*   The length of a rectangle is 5 m more than twice the width. Express the length of the rectangle in terms of the width. $2W + 5$

101.   *Geometry*   In a triangle, the measure of the smallest angle is three degrees less than one-half the measure of the largest angle. Express the measure of the smallest angle in terms of the measure of the largest angle. $\frac{1}{2}L - 3$

102.   *Consumerism*   The cost of renting a car for a day is $39.95 plus 15¢ per mile driven. Express the cost of a one-day rental in terms of the number of miles driven. Use decimals for constants and coefficients. $39.95 + 0.15m$

103.   *The Postal Service*   In 1999, first-class mail cost 33¢ for the first ounce and 22¢ for each additional ounce. Express the cost of mailing a package first class in terms of the weight of the package. Use decimals for constants and coefficients. $0.33 + 0.22(w - 1), w \geq 1$

104.   *Sports*   A halyard 12 ft long was cut into two pieces. Use one variable to express the lengths of the two pieces. S and $12 - S$

105.   *Coins*   A coin purse contains thirty-five coins in nickels and dimes. Use one variable to express the number of nickels and the number of dimes in the coin purse. n and $35 - n$

106.   *Commodities*   Twenty gallons of oil were poured into two containers of different sizes. Use one variable to express the amount of oil poured into each container. g and $20 - g$

107.   *Travel*   Two cars are traveling in opposite directions and at different rates. Two hours later the cars are 200 mi apart. Express the distance traveled by the faster car in terms of the distance traveled by the slower car. $200 - x$

108.   *Wages*   An employee is paid $640 per week plus $24 for each hour of overtime worked. Express the employee's weekly pay in terms of the number of hours of overtime worked. $640 + 24h$

109.   *Billing*   An auto repair bill is $92 for parts and $25 for each hour of labor. Express the amount of the repair bill in terms of the number of hours of labor. $92 + 25h$

APPLYING CONCEPTS 2.3

[C] **110.** *Chemistry*   The chemical formula for glucose (sugar) is $C_6H_{12}O_6$. This formula means that there are twelve hydrogen atoms, six carbon atoms, and six oxygen atoms in each molecule of glucose. If x represents the number of atoms of oxygen in a pound of sugar, express the number of hydrogen atoms in the pound of sugar in terms of x. $2x$

111. *Metalwork*   A wire whose length is given as x inches is bent into a square. Express the length of a side of the square in terms of x. $\frac{1}{4}x$

[C] **112.** *Pulleys*   A block-and-tackle system is designed so that pulling one end of a rope five feet will move a weight on the other end a distance of three feet. If x represents the distance the rope is pulled, express the distance the weight moves in terms of x. $\frac{3}{5}x$

113. Translate the expressions $5x + 8$ and $5(x + 8)$ into phrases.

114. In your own words, explain how variables are used.

115. Explain the similarities and the differences between the expressions "the difference between x and 5" and "5 less than x."

Focus on Problem Solving

From Concrete to Abstract

In your study of algebra, you will find that the problems are less concrete than those you studied in arithmetic. Problems that are concrete provide information pertaining to a specific instance. Algebra is more abstract. Abstract problems are theoretical; they are stated without reference to a specific instance. Let's look at an example of an abstract problem.

How many minutes are there in h hours?

A strategy that can be used to solve this problem is to solve the same problem after substituting a number for the variable.

How many minutes are there in 5 hours?

You know that there are 60 minutes in 1 hour. To find the number of minutes in 5 hours, multiply 5 by 60.

$$60 \cdot 5 = 300$$ There are 300 minutes in 5 hours.

Use the same procedure to find the number of minutes in h hours: multiply h by 60.

$$60 \cdot h = 60h \qquad \text{There are } 60h \text{ minutes in } h \text{ hours.}$$

This problem might be taken a step further:

If you walk one mile in x minutes, how far can you walk in h hours?

Consider the same problem using numbers in place of the variables.

If you walk one mile in 20 minutes, how far can you walk in 3 hours?

To solve this problem, you need to calculate the number of minutes in 3 hours (multiply 3 by 60), and divide the result by the number of minutes it takes to walk one mile (20 minutes).

$$\frac{60 \cdot 3}{20} = \frac{180}{20} = 9 \qquad \text{If you walk one mile in 20 minutes, you can walk 9 miles in 3 hours.}$$

Use the same procedure to solve the related abstract problem. Calculate the number of minutes in h hours (multiply h by 60), and divide the result by the number of minutes it takes to walk one mile (x minutes).

$$\frac{60 \cdot h}{x} = \frac{60h}{x} \qquad \text{If you walk one mile in } x \text{ minutes, you can walk } \frac{60h}{x} \text{ miles in } h \text{ hours.}$$

At the heart of the study of algebra is the use of variables. It is the variables in the problems above that make them abstract. But it is variables that allow us to generalize situations and state rules about mathematics.

Try each of the following problems.

1. How many hours are there in d days?

2. You earn d dollars an hour. What are your wages for working h hours?

3. If p is the price of one share of stock, how many shares can you purchase with d dollars?

4. A company pays a television station d dollars to air a commercial lasting s seconds. What is the cost per second?

5. After every v video tape rentals, you are entitled to one free rental. You have rented t tapes, where $t < v$. How many more do you need to rent before you are entitled to a free rental?

6. Your car gets g miles per gallon. How many gallons of gasoline does your car consume traveling t miles?

7. If you drink j ounces of juice each day, how many days will q quarts of the juice last?

8. A TV station has m minutes of commercials each hour. How many ads lasting s seconds each can be sold for each hour of programming?

9. A factory worker can assemble p products in m minutes. How many products can the factory worker assemble in h hours?

10. If one candy bar costs n nickels, how many candy bars can be purchased with q quarters?

Projects and Group Activities

Investigation into Operations with Even and Odd Integers

Complete each statement with the word *even* or *odd*.

1.   If k is an odd integer, then $k + 1$ is an _____ integer.

2.   If k is an odd integer, then $k - 2$ is an _____ integer.

3.   If n is an integer, then $2n$ is an _____ integer.

4.   If m and n are even integers, then $m - n$ is an _____ integer.

5.   If m and n are even integers, then mn is an _____ integer.

6.   If m and n are odd integers, then $m + n$ is an _____ integer.

7.   If m and n are odd integers, then $m - n$ is an _____ integer.

8.   If m and n are odd integers, then mn is an _____ integer.

9.   If m is an even integer and n is an odd integer, then $m - n$ is an _____ integer.

10. If m is an even integer and n is an odd integer, then $m + n$ is an _____ integer.

Applications of Patterns in Mathematics

For the circle shown at the left, use a straight line to connect each dot on the circle with every other dot on the circle. How many different straight lines are there?

Follow the same procedure for each of the circles shown below. How many different straight lines are there in each?

1.   Find a pattern to describe the number of dots on a circle and the corresponding number of different lines drawn.

2.   Use the pattern from Exercise 1 to determine the number of different lines that would be drawn in a circle with 7 dots and in a circle with 8 dots.

3.   You are arranging a tennis tournament with nine players. How many singles matches will be played among the nine players if each player plays each of the other players once?

Now consider **triangular numbers,** which were studied by ancient Greek mathematicians. The numbers 1, 3, 6, 10, 15, 21 are the first six triangular numbers. Note in the following diagram that a triangle can be formed using the number of dots that correspond to a triangular number.

Observe that the number of dots in a row is one more than the number in the row above. The total number of dots can be found by addition.

$$1 = 1 \qquad\qquad\qquad 1 + 2 = 3$$
$$1 + 2 + 3 = 6 \qquad\qquad 1 + 2 + 3 + 4 = 10$$
$$1 + 2 + 3 + 4 + 5 = 15 \qquad 1 + 2 + 3 + 4 + 5 + 6 = 21$$

4. Use this pattern to find the seventh triangular number and the eighth triangular number. Check your answers by drawing the corresponding triangles of dots.

5. Discuss the relationship between triangular numbers and the pattern describing the correspondence between the number of dots on a circle and the number of different lines drawn (see Exercise 1).

6. Suppose you are in charge of scheduling softball games for a league. There are 10 teams in the league. Use the pattern of triangular numbers to determine the number of games that must be scheduled.

Chapter Summary

Key Words

A *variable* is a letter that is used to stand for a quantity that is unknown or that can change. A *variable expression* is an expression that contains one or more variables.   (Objective 2.1.1)

$5x - 4y + 7z$ is a variable expression. It contains the variables x, y, and z.

The *terms of a variable expression* are the addends of the expression. Each term is a *variable term* or a *constant term*. (Objective 2.1.1)

The expression $4a^2 - 6b^3 + 7$ has three terms: $4a^2$, $-6b^3$, and 7. $4a^2$ and $-6b^3$ are variable terms. 7 is a constant term.

A variable term is composed of a *numerical coefficient* and a *variable part*.   (Objective 2.1.1)

For the expression $8p^4r$, 8 is the coefficient and p^4r is the variable part.

Replacing the variables in a variable expression with numbers and then simplifying the numerical expression is called *evaluating the variable expression*.   (Objective 2.1.1)

To evaluate $a^2 - 2b$ when $a = -3$ and $b = -5$, simplify the expression $(-3)^2 - 2(-5)$.

Like terms of a variable expression are the terms with the same variable part.   (Objective 2.2.2)

For the expression $2st - 3t + 9s - 11st$, the terms $2st$ and $-11st$ are like terms.

The *additive inverse* of a number is the opposite of the number. (Objective 2.2.1)

The additive inverse of 8 is -8.
The additive inverse of -15 is 15.

The *multiplicative inverse* of a number is the reciprocal of the number.   (Objective 2.2.1)

The multiplicative inverse of $\frac{3}{8}$ is $\frac{8}{3}$.

Essential Rules and Procedures

The Commutative Property of Addition
If a and b are real numbers, then $a + b = b + a$.
(Objective 2.2.1)

$5 + 2 = 7$ and $2 + 5 = 7$

The Commutative Property of Multiplication
If a and b are real numbers, then $ab = ba$. (Objective 2.2.1)

$6(-3) = -18$ and $-3(6) = -18$

The Associative Property of Addition
If a, b, and c are real numbers, then $(a + b) + c = a + (b + c)$.
(Objective 2.2.1)

$-1 + (4 + 7) = -1 + 11 = 10$
$(-1 + 4) + 7 = 3 + 7 = 10$

The Associative Property of Multiplication
If a, b, and c are real numbers, then $(ab)c = a(bc)$.
(Objective 2.2.1)

$(-2 \cdot 5) \cdot 3 = -10 \cdot 3 = -30$
$-2 \cdot (5 \cdot 3) = -2 \cdot 15 = -30$

The Addition Property of Zero
If a is a real number, then $a + 0 = 0 + a = a$. (Objective 2.2.1)

$9 + 0 = 9$ $0 + 9 = 9$

The Multiplication Property of Zero
If a is a real number, then $a \cdot 0 = 0 \cdot a = 0$. (Objective 2.2.1)

$-8(0) = 0$ $0(-8) = 0$

The Multiplication Property of One
If a is a real number, then $1 \cdot a = a \cdot 1 = a$. (Objective 2.2.1)

$7 \cdot 1 = 7$ $1 \cdot 7 = 7$

The Inverse Property of Addition
If a is a real number, then $a + (-a) = (-a) + a = 0$.
(Objective 2.2.1)

$4 + (-4) = 0$ $-4 + 4 = 0$

The Inverse Property of Multiplication
If a is a real number and $a \neq 0$, then $a \cdot \dfrac{1}{a} = \dfrac{1}{a} \cdot a = 1$.
(Objective 2.2.1)

$6 \cdot \dfrac{1}{6} = 1$ $\dfrac{1}{6} \cdot 6 = 1$

The Distributive Property
If a, b, and c are real numbers, then $a(b + c) = ab + ac$.
(Objective 2.2.1)

$5(2 + 3) = 5 \cdot 2 + 5 \cdot 3$
$\qquad = 10 + 15$
$\qquad = 25$

Chapter Review Exercises

1. Simplify: $-7y^2 + 6y^2 - (-2y^2)$ y^2

2. Simplify: $(12x)\left(\dfrac{1}{4}\right)$ $3x$

3. Simplify: $\dfrac{2}{3}(-15a)$ $-10a$

4. Simplify: $-2(2x - 4)$ $-4x + 8$

5. Simplify: $5(2x + 4) - 3(x - 6)$ $7x + 38$

6. Evaluate $a^2 - 3b$ when $a = 2$ and $b = -4$.   16

7. Complete the statement by using the Inverse Property of Addition.
   $-9 + ? = 0$ 9

8. Simplify: $-4(-9y)$ $36y$

9. Simplify: $-2(-3y + 9)$ $6y - 18$

10. Simplify: $3[2x - 3(x - 2y)] + 3y$ $-3x + 21y$

11. Simplify: $-4(2x^2 - 3y^2)$ $-8x^2 + 12y^2$

12. Simplify: $3x - 5x + 7x$ $5x$

13. Evaluate $b^2 - 3ab$ when $a = 3$ and $b = -2$.
    22

14. Simplify: $\frac{1}{5}(10x)$ $2x$

15. Simplify: $5(3 - 7b)$ $15 - 35b$

16. Simplify: $2x + 3[4 - (3x - 7)]$ $-7x + 33$

17. Identify the property that justifies the statement.
    $-4(3) = 3(-4)$
    The Commutative Property of Multiplication

18. Simplify: $3(8 - 2x)$ $24 - 6x$

19. Simplify: $-2x^2 - (-3x^2) + 4x^2$ $5x^2$

20. Simplify: $-3x - 2(2x - 7)$ $-7x + 14$

21. Simplify: $-3(3y^2 - 3y - 7)$ $-9y^2 + 9y + 21$

22. Simplify: $-2[x - 2(x - y)] + 5y$ $2x + y$

23. Evaluate $\frac{-2ab}{2b - a}$ when $a = -4$ and $b = 6$.   3

24. Simplify: $(-3)(-12y)$ $36y$

25. Simplify: $4(3x - 2) - 7(x + 5)$ $5x - 43$

26. Simplify: $(16x)\left(\frac{1}{8}\right)$ $2x$

27. Simplify: $-3(2x^2 - 7y^2)$ $-6x^2 + 21y^2$

28. Evaluate $3(a - c) - 2ab$ when $a = 2$, $b = 3$, and $c = -4$.   6

29. Simplify: $2x - 3(x - 2)$ $-x + 6$

30. Simplify: $2a - (-3b) - 7a - 5b$ $-5a - 2b$

31. Simplify: $-5(2x^2 - 3x + 6)$ $-10x^2 + 15x - 30$

32. Simplify: $3x - 7y - 12x$ $-9x - 7y$

33. Simplify: $\frac{1}{2}(12a)$ $6a$

34. Simplify: $2x + 3[x - 2(4 - 2x)]$ $17x - 24$

35. Simplify: $3x + (-12y) - 5x - (-7y)$
    $-2x - 5y$

36. Simplify: $\left(-\frac{5}{6}\right)(-36b)$ $30b$

37. Complete the statement by using the Distributive Property.
    $(6 + 3)7 = 42 + ?$ 21

38. Simplify: $4x^2 + 9x - 6x^2 - 5x$ $-2x^2 + 4x$

39. Simplify: $-\frac{3}{8}(16x^2)$ $-6x^2$

40. Simplify: $-3[2x - (7x - 9)]$ $15x - 27$

41. Simplify: $-(8a^2 - 3b^2)$ $-8a^2 + 3b^2$

42. Identify the property that justifies the statement.
    $-32(0) = 0$ The Multiplication Property of Zero

43. Translate "b decreased by the product of seven and b" into a variable expression. $b - 7b$

44. Translate "the sum of a number and twice the square of the number" into a variable expression. $n + 2n^2$

45. Translate "three less than the quotient of six and a number" into a variable expression. $\frac{6}{n} - 3$

46. Translate "ten divided by the difference between y and two" into a variable expression. $\frac{10}{y - 2}$

47. Translate and simplify "eight times the quotient of twice a number and sixteen." $8\left(\frac{2n}{16}\right)$; n

48. Translate and simplify "the product of four and the sum of two and five times a number." $4(2 + 5n)$; $8 + 20n$

49. One car was driven 15 mph faster than a second car. Express the speed of the first car in terms of the speed of the second car. $s + 15$

50. A coffee merchant made 20 lb of a blend of coffee using only mocha java beans and espresso beans. Use one variable to express the amounts of mocha java beans and espresso beans in the coffee blend. b and $20 - b$

Chapter Test

1. Simplify: $(9y)4$ $36y$

2. Simplify: $7x + 5y - 3x - 8y$ $4x - 3y$

3. Simplify: $8n - (6 - 2n)$ $10n - 6$

4. Evaluate $3ab - (2a)^2$ when $a = -2$ and $b = -3$.   2

5. Identify the property that justifies the statement. $\frac{3}{8}(1) = \frac{3}{8}$ The Multiplication Property of One

6. Simplify: $-4(-x + 10)$ $4x - 40$

7. Simplify: $\frac{2}{3}x^2 - \frac{7}{12}x^2$ $\frac{1}{12}x^2$

8. Simplify: $(-10x)\left(-\frac{2}{5}\right)$ $4x$

9. Simplify: $(-4y^2 + 8)6$ $-24y^2 + 48$

10. Complete the statement by using the Inverse Property of Addition. $-19 + ? = 0$ 19

11. Evaluate $\frac{-3ab}{2a + b}$ when $a = -1$ and $b = 4$.   6

12. Simplify: $5(x + y) - 8(x - y)$ $-3x + 13y$

13. Simplify: $6b - 9b + 4b$ b

14. Simplify: $13(6a)$ $78a$

15. Simplify: $3(x^2 - 5x + 4)$ $3x^2 - 15x + 12$

16. Evaluate $4(b - a) + bc$ when $a = 2$, $b = -3$, and $c = 4$. -32

17. Simplify: $6x - 3(y - 7x) + 2(5x - y)$ $37x - 5y$

18. Translate "the quotient of eight more than n and seventeen" into a variable expression. $\frac{n + 8}{17}$

19. Translate "the difference between the sum of a and b and the square of b" into a variable expression. $(a + b) - b^2$

20. Translate "the sum of the square of a number and the product of the number and eleven" into a variable expression. $n^2 + 11n$

21. Translate and simplify "twenty times the sum of a number and nine." $20(n + 9)$; $20n + 180$

22. Translate and simplify "two more than a number added to the difference between the number and three." $(n + 2) + (n - 3)$; $2n - 1$

23. Translate and simplify "a number minus the product of one-fourth and twice the number." $n - \frac{1}{4}(2n)$; $\frac{1}{2}n$

24. The distance from Neptune to the Sun is thirty times the distance from Earth to the Sun. Express the distance from Neptune to the Sun in terms of the distance from Earth to the Sun. $30d$

25. A nine-foot board is cut into two pieces of different lengths. Use one variable to express the lengths of the two pieces. L and $9 - L$

Cumulative Review Exercises

1. Add: $-4 + 7 + (-10)$ -7

2. Subtract: $-16 - (-25) - 4$ 5

3. Multiply: $(-2)(3)(-4)$ 24

4. Divide: $(-60) \div 12$ -5

5. Write $1\frac{1}{4}$ as a decimal. 1.25

6. Write 60% as a fraction and as a decimal. $\frac{3}{5}$, 0.60

7. Use the roster method to write the set of negative integers greater than or equal to -4. $\{-4, -3, -2, -1\}$

8. Write $\frac{2}{25}$ as a percent. 8%

9. Subtract: $\frac{7}{12} - \frac{11}{16} - \left(-\frac{1}{3}\right)$ $\frac{11}{48}$

10. Divide: $\frac{5}{12} \div \left(\frac{3}{2}\right)$ $\frac{5}{18}$

11. Multiply: $\left(-\frac{9}{16}\right)\left(\frac{8}{27}\right)\left(-\frac{3}{2}\right)$ $\frac{1}{4}$

12. Simplify: $-3^2 \cdot \left(-\frac{2}{3}\right)^3$ $\frac{8}{3}$

13. Simplify: $-2^5 \div (3-5)^2 - (-3)$ -5

14. Simplify: $\left(-\frac{3}{4}\right)^2 - \left(\frac{3}{8} - \frac{11}{12}\right)$ $\frac{53}{48}$

15. Evaluate $a - 3b^2$ when $a = 4$ and $b = -2$. -8

16. Simplify: $-2x^2 - (-3x^2) + 4x^2$ $5x^2$

17. Simplify: $8a - 12b - 9a$ $-a - 12b$

18. Simplify: $\frac{1}{3}(9a)$ $3a$

19. Simplify: $\left(-\frac{5}{8}\right)(-32b)$ $20b$

20. Simplify: $5(4 - 2x)$ $20 - 10x$

21. Simplify: $-3(-2y + 7)$ $6y - 21$

22. Simplify: $-2(3x^2 - 4y^2)$ $-6x^2 + 8y^2$

23. Simplify: $-4(2y^2 - 5y - 8)$ $-8y^2 + 20y + 32$

24. Simplify: $-4x - 3(2x - 5)$ $-10x + 15$

25. Simplify: $3(4x - 1) - 7(x + 2)$ $5x - 17$

26. Simplify: $3x + 2[x - 4(2 - x)]$ $13x - 16$

27. Simplify: $3[4x - 2(x - 4y)] + 5y$ $6x + 29y$

28. Translate "the difference between six and the product of a number and twelve" into a variable expression. $6 - 12n$

29. Translate and simplify "the total of five and the difference between a number and seven." $5 + (n - 7)$; $n - 2$

30. A turboprop plane can fly at one-half the speed of sound. Express the speed of the turboprop plane in terms of the speed of sound. $\frac{1}{2}s$

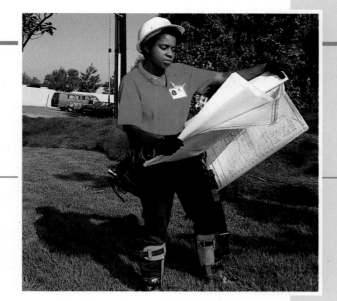

3

Solving Equations and Inequalities

It is the job of construction electricians to install heating, lighting, air conditioning, controls, communications, and other types of electrical equipment. Electricians follow specifications such as blueprints to connect equipment to power sources and circuit breakers. In their work, they must apply various algebraic and scientific formulas. One equation in Ohm's Law is IR = V, where I is current, R is resistance, and V is voltage. For example, if I = 10 amps and R = 12 ohms, then V = 120 volts.

OBJECTIVES

3.1.1   Determine whether a given number is a solution of an equation

3.1.2   Solve equations of the form $x + a = b$

3.1.3   Solve equations of the form $ax = b$

3.1.4   Application problems: the basic percent equation

3.2.1   Solve equations of the form $ax + b = c$

3.2.2   Solve equations of the form $ax + b = cx + d$

3.2.3   Solve equations containing parentheses

3.2.4   Application problems

3.3.1   Solve inequalities using the Addition Property of Inequalities

3.3.2   Solve inequalities using the Multiplication Property of Inequalities

3.3.3   Solve general inequalities

Mersenne Primes

A prime number that can be written in the form $2^n - 1$, where n is also prime, is called a **Mersenne prime.** The table at the right shows some Mersenne primes.

$$3 = 2^2 - 1$$
$$7 = 2^3 - 1$$
$$31 = 2^5 - 1$$
$$127 = 2^7 - 1$$

Not every prime number is a Mersenne prime. For example, 5 is a prime number but not a Mersenne prime. Also, not all numbers in the form $2^n - 1$, where n is prime, yield a prime number. For example, $2^{11} - 1 = 2047$, which is not a prime number.

The search for Mersenne primes has been quite extensive, especially since the advent of the computer. One reason for the extensive research into large prime numbers (not only Mersenne primes) involves cryptology.

Cryptology is the study of making or breaking secret codes. One method of making a code that is difficult to break is called public-key cryptology. For this method to work, it is necessary to use very large prime numbers. To keep anyone from breaking the code, each prime should have at least 200 digits.

Today, the largest known Mersenne prime is $2^{216091} - 1$. This number has 65,050 digits in its representation.

Another Mersenne prime got special recognition in a postage-meter stamp. It is the number $2^{11213} - 1$. This number has 3276 digits in its representation.

SECTION **3.1**

Introduction to Equations

1   Determine whether a given number is a solution of an equation

An **equation** expresses the equality of two mathematical expressions. The expressions can be either numerical or variable expressions.

$$\left. \begin{array}{l} 9 + 3 = 12 \\ 3x - 2 = 10 \\ y^2 + 4 = 2y - 1 \\ z = 2 \end{array} \right\} \text{Equations}$$

The equation at the right is true if the variable is replaced by 5.

$x + 8 = 13$
$5 + 8 = 13$ A true equation

The equation $x + 8 = 13$ is false if the variable is replaced by 7.

$7 + 8 = 13$ A false equation

A **solution** of an equation is a number that, when substituted for the variable, results in a true equation. 5 is a solution of the equation $x + 8 = 13$. 7 is not a solution of the equation $x + 8 = 13$.

Example 1   Is -3 a solution of the equation $4x + 16 = x^2 - 5$?

Solution

$$4x + 16 = x^2 - 5$$

$4(-3) + 16$	$(-3)^2 - 5$
$-12 + 16$	$9 - 5$

$$4 = 4$$

Yes, -3 is a solution of the equation $4x + 16 = x^2 - 5$.

▶ Replace the variable by the given number, -3.
▶ Evaluate the numerical expressions using the Order of Operations Agreement.
▶ Compare the results. If the results are equal, the given number is a solution. If the results are not equal, the given number is not a solution.

Problem 1   Is $\frac{1}{4}$ a solution of $5 - 4x = 8x + 2$?

Solution   See page S4.   Yes

Example 2   Is -4 a solution of $4 + 5x = x^2 - 2x$?

Solution

$$4 + 5x = x^2 - 2x$$

$4 + 5(-4)$	$(-4)^2 - 2(-4)$
$4 + (-20)$	$16 - (-8)$

$$-16 \neq 24$$

No, -4 is not a solution of the equation $4 + 5x = x^2 - 2x$.

▶ Replace the variable by the given number, -4.
▶ Evaluate the numerical expressions using the Order of Operations Agreement.
▶ Compare the results. If the results are equal, the given number is a solution. If the results are not equal, the given number is not a solution.

> **Problem 2**   Is 5 a solution of $10x - x^2 = 3x - 10$?
>
>   **Solution**   See page S4.   No

2   ## Solve equations of the form $x + a = b$

To **solve** an equation means to find a solution of the equation. The simplest equation to solve is an equation of the form **variable = constant**, because the constant is the solution.

If $x = 5$, then 5 is the solution of the equation because $5 = 5$ is a true equation.

INSTRUCTOR NOTE

The model of an equation as a balance scale will appeal to some students. If the same weight is not added to each side of the equation, the pans no longer balance.

The solution of the equation shown at the right is 7.

$$x + 2 = 9 \qquad 7 + 2 = 9$$

Note that if 4 is added to each side of the equation, the solution is still 7.

$$x + 2 + 4 = 9 + 4$$
$$x + 6 = 13 \qquad 7 + 6 = 13$$

If -5 is added to each side of the equation, the solution is still 7.

$$x + 2 + (-5) = 9 + (-5)$$
$$x - 3 = 4 \qquad 7 - 3 = 4$$

This illustrates the Addition Property of Equations.

Addition Property of Equations

The same number or variable term can be added to each side of an equation without changing the solution of the equation.

This property is used in solving equations. Note the effect of adding, to each side of the equation $x + 2 = 9$, the opposite of the constant term 2. After each side of the equation is simplified, the equation is in the form variable = constant. The solution is the constant.

$$x + 2 = 9$$
$$x + 2 + (-2) = 9 + (-2)$$
$$x + 0 = 7$$
$$x = 7$$

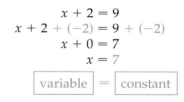

The solution is 7.

In solving an equation, the goal is to rewrite the given equation in the form variable = constant. The Addition Property of Equations can be used to rewrite an equation in this form. The Addition Property of Equations is used to **remove a term** from one side of an equation **by adding the opposite of that term** to each side of the equation.

> **Example 3**   Solve and check: $y - 6 = 9$
>
>   **Solution** $y - 6 = 9$ ▶ The goal is to rewrite the equation in the form
>   *variable = constant.*

$$y - 6 + 6 = 9 + 6$$

▶ Add the opposite of the constant term -6 to each side of the equation (the Addition Property of Equations).

$$y + 0 = 15$$

▶ Simplify using the Inverse Property of Addition.

$$y = 15$$

▶ Simplify using the Addition Property of Zero. Now the equation is in the form *variable = constant*.

Check

$$y - 6 = 9$$
$$\overline{15 - 6 \mid 9}$$
$$9 = 9$$

▶ This is a true equation. The solution checks.

The solution is 15. ▶ Write the solution.

Problem 3 Solve and check: $x - \dfrac{1}{3} = -\dfrac{3}{4}$

Solution See page S4. $-\dfrac{5}{12}$

Because subtraction is defined in terms of addition, the Addition Property of Equations makes it possible to subtract the same number from each side of an equation without changing the solution of the equation.

➡ Solve: $y + \dfrac{1}{2} = \dfrac{5}{4}$

The goal is to rewrite the equation in the form *variable = constant*.

$$y + \frac{1}{2} = \frac{5}{4}$$

Add the opposite of the constant term $\dfrac{1}{2}$ to each side of the equation. This is equivalent to subtracting $\dfrac{1}{2}$ from each side of the equation.

$$y + \frac{1}{2} - \frac{1}{2} = \frac{5}{4} - \frac{1}{2}$$
$$y + 0 = \frac{5}{4} - \frac{2}{4}$$
$$y = \frac{3}{4}$$

The solution $\dfrac{3}{4}$ checks.

The solution is $\dfrac{3}{4}$. ◀

Example 4 Solve: $\dfrac{1}{2} = x + \dfrac{2}{3}$

Solution

$$\frac{1}{2} = x + \frac{2}{3}$$

$$\frac{1}{2} - \frac{2}{3} = x + \frac{2}{3} - \frac{2}{3}$$ ▶ Subtract $\dfrac{2}{3}$ from each side of the equation.

$$-\frac{1}{6} = x$$ ▶ Simplify each side of the equation.

The solution is $-\dfrac{1}{6}$.

Problem 4 Solve: $-8 = 5 + x$

Solution See page S4. -13

Note from the solution to Example 4 that an equation can be rewritten in the form *constant* = *variable*. Whether the equation is written in the form *variable* = *constant* or in the form *constant* = *variable*, the solution is the constant.

3 | ## Solve equations of the form $ax = b$

The solution of the equation shown at the right is 3.

$$2x = 6 \qquad 2 \cdot 3 = 6$$

Note that if each side of the equation is multiplied by 5, the solution is still 3.

$$5 \cdot 2x = 5 \cdot 6$$
$$10x = 30 \qquad 10 \cdot 3 = 30$$

If each side is multiplied by -4, the solution is still 3.

$$(-4) \cdot 2x = (-4) \cdot 6$$
$$-8x = -24 \qquad -8 \cdot 3 = -24$$

This illustrates the Multiplication Property of Equations.

Multiplication Property of Equations

Each side of an equation can be multiplied by the same nonzero number without changing the solution of the equation.

This property is used in solving equations. Note the effect of multiplying each side of the equation $2x = 6$ by the reciprocal of the coefficient 2. After each side of the equation is simplified, the equation is in the form *variable* = *constant*. The solution is the constant.

$$2x = 6$$
$$\frac{1}{2} \cdot 2x = \frac{1}{2} \cdot 6$$
$$1x = 3$$
$$x = 3$$

| variable | = | constant |

The solution is 3.

In solving an equation, the goal is to rewrite the given equation in the form *variable* = *constant*. The Multiplication Property of Equations can be used to rewrite an equation in this form. The Multiplication Property of Equations is used to **remove a coefficient** from a variable term in an equation **by multiplying each side of the equation by the reciprocal of the coefficient.**

Example 5   Solve: $\dfrac{3x}{4} = -9$

Solution $\dfrac{3x}{4} = -9$ ▸ $\dfrac{3x}{4} = \dfrac{3}{4}x$

$\dfrac{4}{3} \cdot \dfrac{3}{4}x = \dfrac{4}{3}(-9)$ ▸ Multiply each side of the equation by the reciprocal of the coefficient $\dfrac{3}{4}$ (the Multiplication Property of Equations).

$1x = -12$ ▸ Simplify using the Inverse Property of Multiplication.

$$x = -12$$

▶ Simplify using the Multiplication Property of One. Now the equation is in the form *variable = constant*.

The solution is -12. ▶ Write the solution.

Problem 5 Solve: $-\dfrac{2x}{5} = 6$

Solution See page S4. -15

Because division is defined in terms of multiplication, the Multiplication Property of Equations makes it possible to divide each side of an equation by the same number without changing the solution of the equation.

▶ Solve: $8x = 16$

The goal is to rewrite the equation in the form *variable = constant*.	$8x = 16$
Multiply each side of the equation by the reciprocal of 8. This is equivalent to dividing each side by 8.	$\dfrac{8x}{8} = \dfrac{16}{8}$ $x = 2$
The solution 2 checks.	The solution is 2. ◀

When using the Multiplication Property of Equations to solve an equation, multiply each side of the equation by the reciprocal of the coefficient when the coefficient is a fraction. Divide each side of the equation by the coefficient when the coefficient is an integer or a decimal.

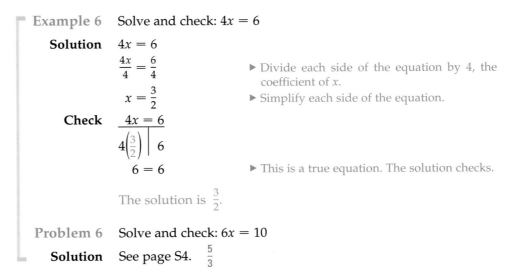

Example 6 Solve and check: $4x = 6$

Solution $4x = 6$

$\dfrac{4x}{4} = \dfrac{6}{4}$ ▶ Divide each side of the equation by 4, the coefficient of x.

$x = \dfrac{3}{2}$ ▶ Simplify each side of the equation.

Check $4x = 6$

$4\left(\dfrac{3}{2}\right) \Big| 6$

$6 = 6$ ▶ This is a true equation. The solution checks.

The solution is $\dfrac{3}{2}$.

Problem 6 Solve and check: $6x = 10$

Solution See page S4. $\dfrac{5}{3}$

Before using one of the Properties of Equations, check to see whether one or both sides of the equation can be simplified. In Example 7, like terms appear on the left side of the equation. The first step in solving this equation is to combine the like terms so that there is only one variable term on the left side of the equation.

Example 7 Solve: $5x - 9x = 12$

Solution
$$5x - 9x = 12$$
$$-4x = 12 \quad \blacktriangleright \text{ Combine like terms.}$$
$$\frac{-4x}{-4} = \frac{12}{-4} \quad \blacktriangleright \text{ Divide each side of the equation by } -4.$$
$$x = -3$$

The solution is -3.

Problem 7 Solve: $4x - 8x = 16$

Solution See page S4. -4

---

4 ## Application problems: the basic percent equation

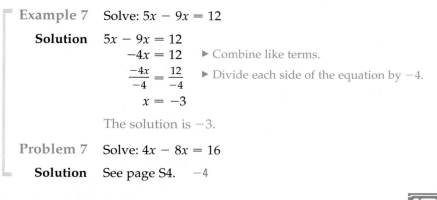

The solution of a problem that involves a percent requires solving the basic percent equation.

The Basic Percent Equation

$$\text{Percent} \cdot \text{Base} = \text{Amount}$$
$$P \quad \cdot \quad B \quad = \quad A$$

To translate a problem involving a percent into an equation, remember that the word *of* translates into "multiply" and the word *is* translates into "=". The base usually follows the word *of*.

➡ 20% of what number is 30?

Given: $P = 20\% = 0.20$
$\qquad A = 30$
Unknown: Base

$$PB = A$$
$$(0.20)B = 30$$
$$\frac{0.20B}{0.20} = \frac{30}{0.20}$$
$$B = 150$$

The number is 150. ◄

➡ What percent of 40 is 30?

Given: $B = 40$
$\qquad A = 30$
Unknown: Percent

$$PB = A$$
$$P(40) = 30$$
$$40P = 30$$
$$\frac{40P}{40} = \frac{30}{40}$$

We must write the fraction as a percent in order to answer the question.

$$P = \frac{3}{4}$$
$$P = 75\%$$

30 is 75% of 40. ◄

⮕ Find 25% of 200.

Given: $P = 25\% = 0.25$ $PB = A$
          $B = 200$ $0.25(200) = A$
Unknown: Amount $50 = A$

25% of 200 is 50. ⬅

In most cases, we write a percent as a decimal before solving the basic percent equation. However, some percents are more easily written as a fraction. For example,

$$33\tfrac{1}{3}\% = \tfrac{1}{3} \qquad 66\tfrac{2}{3}\% = \tfrac{2}{3} \qquad 16\tfrac{2}{3}\% = \tfrac{1}{6} \qquad 83\tfrac{1}{3}\% = \tfrac{5}{6}$$

Example 8   12 is $33\tfrac{1}{3}\%$ of what number?

Solution $PB = A$ ▸ $33\tfrac{1}{3}\% = \tfrac{1}{3}$

$$\tfrac{1}{3}B = 12$$

$$3 \cdot \tfrac{1}{3}B = 3 \cdot 12$$

$$B = 36$$

The number is 36.

Problem 8   27 is what percent of 60?

Solution   See page S4.   45%

Example 9   A Gateway 2000 computer is selling for $1500. If you have saved $840 toward the purchase, what percent of the price have you saved?

Strategy   To find the percent of the price, solve the basic percent equation using $B = 1500$ and $A = 840$. The percent is unknown.

Solution $PB = A$

$$P(1500) = 840$$

$$\frac{1500P}{1500} = \frac{840}{1500}$$

$$P = 0.56$$
$$P = 56\%$$

You have saved 56% of the price.

Problem 9   A student correctly answered 72 of the 80 questions on an exam. What percent of the questions were answered correctly?

Solution   See page S4.   90%

Example 10   During the 1998 Major League Baseball season, the Toronto Blue Jays won 54.3% of the 162 games they played. How many games did Toronto win?

Strategy   To find the number of games won, solve the basic percent equation using $B = 162$ and $P = 54.3\% = 0.543$. The amount is unknown.

Solution
$$PB = A$$
$$0.543(162) = A$$
$$88 \approx A$$

Toronto won 88 of their games during the 1998 baseball season.

Problem 10   The price of your King Size Value Meal at Burger King was $5.18. There was a 5% meal tax added to the price. How much was the tax?

Solution   See page S5. $.26

STUDY TIPS

GET HELP FOR ACADEMIC DIFFICULTIES

If you do have trouble in this course, teachers, counselors, and advisers can help. They usually know of study groups, tutors, or other sources of help that are available. They may suggest visiting an office of academic skills, a learning center, a tutorial service, or some other department or service on campus.

Students who have already taken the course and who have done well in it may be a source of assistance. If they have a good understanding of the material, they may be able to help by explaining it to you.

CONCEPT REVIEW 3.1

Determine whether the statement is always true, sometimes true, or never true.

1. Both sides of an equation can be multiplied by the same number without changing the solution of the equation.   Sometimes true

2. Both sides of an equation can be divided by the same number without changing the solution of the equation.   Sometimes true

3. For an equation of the form $ax = b$, $a \neq 0$, multiplying both sides of the equation by the reciprocal of a will result in an equation of the form $x = constant$.   Always true

4. Use the Multiplication Property of Equations to remove a term from one side of an equation.   Never true

5. Adding a negative 3 to each side of an equation yields the same result as subtracting 3 from each side of the equation.   Always true

6. In the basic percent equation, the amount follows the word *of*.   Never true

7. An equation contains an equals sign.   Always true

EXERCISES 3.1

1 1. What is the difference between an equation and an expression?

2. How can you determine whether a number is a solution of an equation?

3. Is 4 a solution of
$2x = 8$?   Yes

4. Is 3 a solution of
$y + 4 = 7$?   Yes

5. Is −1 a solution of
$2b − 1 = 3$?   No

6. Is −2 a solution of
$3a − 4 = 10$?   No

7. Is 1 a solution of
$4 − 2m = 3$?   No

8. Is 2 a solution of
$7 − 3n = 2$?   No

9. Is 5 a solution of
$2x + 5 = 3x$?   Yes

10. Is 4 a solution of
$3y − 4 = 2y$?   Yes

11. Is 0 a solution of
$4a + 5 = 3a + 5$?   Yes

12. Is 0 a solution of
$4 − 3b = 4 − 5b$?   Yes

13. Is −2 a solution of
$4 − 2n = n + 10$?   Yes

14. Is −3 a solution of
$5 − m = 2 − 2m$?   Yes

15. Is 3 a solution of
$z^2 + 1 = 4 + 3z$?   No

16. Is 2 a solution of
$2x^2 − 1 = 4x − 1$?   Yes

17. Is −1 a solution of
$y^2 − 1 = 4y + 3$?   No

18. Is −2 a solution of
$m^2 − 4 = m + 3$?   No

19. Is 4 a solution of
$x(x + 1) = x^2 + 5$?   No

20. Is 3 a solution of
$2a(a − 1) = 3a + 3$?   Yes

21. Is $−\frac{1}{4}$ a solution of
$8t + 1 = −1$?   Yes

22. Is $\frac{1}{2}$ a solution of
$4y + 1 = 3$?   Yes

23. Is $\frac{2}{5}$ a solution of
$5m + 1 = 10m − 3$?   No

24. Is $\frac{3}{4}$ a solution of
$8x − 1 = 12x + 3$?   No

25. Is 2.1 a solution of
$x^2 − 4x = x + 1.89$?   No

26. Is 1.5 a solution of
$c^2 − 3c = 4c − 8.25$?   Yes

2 27. How is the Addition Property of Equations used to solve an equation?

28. Explain why the goal in solving an equation is to write the equation in the form *variable* $=$ *constant*.

Solve and check.

29. $x + 5 = 7$ 2

30. $y + 3 = 9$ 6

31. $b - 4 = 11$ 15

32. $z - 6 = 10$ 16

33. $2 + a = 8$ 6

34. $5 + x = 12$ 7

35. $m + 9 = 3$ -6

36. $t + 12 = 10$ -2

37. $n - 5 = -2$ 3

38. $x - 6 = -5$ 1

39. $b + 7 = 7$ 0

40. $y - 5 = -5$ 0

41. $a - 3 = -5$ -2

42. $x - 6 = -3$ 3

43. $z + 9 = 2$ -7

44. $n + 11 = 1$ -10

45. $10 + m = 3$ -7

46. $8 + x = 5$ -3

47. $9 + x = -3$ -12

48. $10 + y = -4$ -14

49. $b - 5 = -3$ 2

50. $t - 6 = -4$ 2

51. $2 = x + 7$ -5

52. $-8 = n + 1$ -9

53. $4 = m - 11$ 15

54. $-6 = y - 5$ -1

55. $12 = 3 + w$ 9

56. $-9 = 5 + x$ -14

57. $4 = -10 + b$ 14

58. $-7 = -2 + x$ -5

59. $m + \frac{2}{3} = -\frac{1}{3}$ -1

60. $c + \frac{3}{4} = -\frac{1}{4}$ -1

61. $x - \frac{1}{2} = \frac{1}{2}$ 1

62. $x - \frac{2}{5} = \frac{3}{5}$ 1

63. $\frac{5}{8} + y = \frac{1}{8}$ $-\frac{1}{2}$

64. $\frac{4}{9} + a = -\frac{2}{9}$ $-\frac{2}{3}$

65. $m + \frac{1}{2} = -\frac{1}{4}$ $-\frac{3}{4}$

66. $b + \frac{1}{6} = -\frac{1}{3}$ $-\frac{1}{2}$

67. $x + \frac{2}{3} = \frac{3}{4}$ $\frac{1}{12}$

68. $n + \frac{2}{5} = \frac{2}{3}$ $\frac{4}{15}$

69. $-\frac{5}{6} = x - \frac{1}{4}$ $-\frac{7}{12}$

70. $-\frac{1}{4} = c - \frac{2}{3}$ $\frac{5}{12}$

71. $-\frac{1}{21} = m + \frac{2}{3}$ $-\frac{5}{7}$

72. $\frac{5}{9} = b - \frac{1}{3}$ $\frac{8}{9}$

73. $\frac{5}{12} = n + \frac{3}{4}$ $-\frac{1}{3}$

74. $d + 1.3619 = 2.0148$ 0.6529

75. $w + 2.932 = 4.801$ 1.869

76. $-0.813 + x = -1.096$ -0.283

77. $-1.926 + t = -1.042$ 0.884

3 **78.** How is the Multiplication Property of Equations used to solve an equation?

79. Why, when the Multiplication Property of Equations is used, must the number that multiplies each side of the equation not be zero?

Solve and check.

80. $5x = 15$ 3

81. $4y = 28$ 7

82. $3b = -12$ -4

83. $2a = -14$ -7

84. $-3x = 6$ -2

85. $-5m = 20$ -4

86. $-3x = -27$ 9

87. $-6n = -30$ 5

88. $20 = 4c$ 5

89. $18 = 2t$ 9

90. $-32 = 8w$ -4

91. $-56 = 7x$ -8

92. $8d = 0$ 0

93. $-5x = 0$ 0

94. $36 = 9z$ 4

95. $35 = -5x$ -7

96. $-64 = 8a$ -8

97. $-32 = -4y$ 8

98. $-42 = 6t$ -7

99. $-12m = -144$ 12

100. $\frac{x}{3} = 2$ 6

101. $\frac{x}{4} = 3$ 12

102. $-\frac{y}{2} = 5$ -10

103. $-\frac{b}{3} = 6$ -18

104. $\frac{n}{7} = -4$ -28

105. $\frac{t}{6} = -3$ -18

106. $\frac{2}{5}x = 12$ 30

107. $-\frac{4}{3}c = -8$ 6

108. $\frac{5}{6}y = -20$ -24

109. $-\frac{2}{3}d = 8$ -12

110. $-\frac{3}{5}m = 12$ -20

111. $\frac{2n}{3} = 2$ 3

112. $\frac{5x}{6} = -10$ -12

113. $\frac{-3z}{8} = 9$ -24

114. $\frac{-4x}{5} = -12$ 15

115. $-6 = -\frac{2}{3}y$ 9

116. $-15 = -\frac{3}{5}x$ 25

117. $\frac{2}{9} = \frac{2}{3}y$ $\frac{1}{3}$

118. $-\frac{6}{7} = -\frac{3}{4}b$ $\frac{8}{7}$

119. $-\frac{2}{5}m = -\frac{6}{7}$ $\frac{15}{7}$

120. $5x + 2x = 14$ 2

121. $3n + 2n = 20$ 4

122. $7d - 4d = 9$ 3

123. $10y - 3y = 21$ 3

124. $2x - 5x = 9$ -3

125. $\frac{x}{1.4} = 3.2$ 4.48

126. $\frac{z}{2.9} = -7.8$ -22.62

127. $3.4a = 7.004$ 2.06

128. $2.3m = 2.415$ 1.05

129. $-3.7x = 7.77$ -2.1

130. $-1.6m = 5.44$ -3.4

4 **131.** Employee A had an annual salary of $22,000, Employee B had an annual salary of $28,000, and Employee C had an annual salary of $26,000 before each employee was given a 5% raise. Which of the three employees now has the highest annual salary? Explain how you arrived at your answer.

132. Each of three employees earned an annual salary of $25,000 before Employee A was given a 3% raise, Employee B was given a 6% raise, and Employee C was given a 4.5% raise. Which of the three employees now has the highest annual salary? Explain how you arrived at your answer.

Solve.

133. 12 is what percent of 50?   24%

134. What percent of 125 is 50?   40%

135. Find 18% of 40.   7.2

136. What is 25% of 60?   15

137. 12% of what is 48?   400

138. 45% of what is 9?   20

139. What is $33\frac{1}{3}$% of 27?   9

140. Find $16\frac{2}{3}$% of 30.   5

141. What percent of 12 is 3?   25%

142. 10 is what percent of 15?
$66\frac{2}{3}$%

143. 60% of what is 3?   5

144. 75% of what is 6?   8

145. 12 is what percent of 6?
200%

146. 20 is what percent of 16?
125%

147. $5\frac{1}{4}$% of what is 21?   400

148. $37\frac{1}{2}$% of what is 15?   40

149. Find 15.4% of 50.   7.7

150. What is 18.5% of 46?   8.51

151. 1 is 0.5% of what?   200

152. 3 is 1.5% of what?   200

153. $\frac{3}{4}$% of what is 3?   400

154. $\frac{1}{2}$% of what is 3?   600

155. Find 125% of 16.   20

156. What is 250% of 12?   30

157. 16.4 is what percent of 20.4? Round to the nearest percent.   80%

158. Find 18.3% of 625. Round to the nearest tenth.   114.4

159. *Construction*   The Arthur Ashe Tennis Stadium in New York has a seating capacity of 22,500 people. Of these seats, 1.11% are wheelchair-accessible seats. How many seats in the stadium are reserved for wheelchair accessibility? Round to the nearest whole number.
250 seats

160. *Sports*   In a survey on the World Wide Web, people were asked to name their favorite football team. Forty-nine people named the Miami Dolphins, 56 chose the Denver Broncos, 68 named the Dallas Cowboys, and 130 chose the Green Bay Packers. What percent of the people surveyed chose the Dallas Cowboys? Round to the nearest percent.   22%

161. *Entertainment*   In an Internet survey, people were asked to name their favorite male stand-up comedian. 15.3% responded that Robin Williams was their favorite. 12.2% responded that Jerry Seinfeld was their favorite. If 4523 people were surveyed, how many more people voted for Robin Williams than for Jerry Seinfeld? Round to the nearest whole number.   140 more people

162. *Research and Development*   The circle graph at the right represents funding for research and development of $215.4 billion in 1998. What percent of the total was funded by industry? Round to the nearest tenth of a percent.   66.1%

163. *Travel*   According to the Travel Industry Association of America, a typical traveler's total vacation bill is $1442. Of that amount, $735 is paid in cash. To the nearest percent, what percent of a typical traveler's vacation bill is paid in cash?   51%

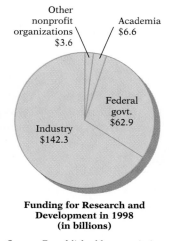

Other nonprofit organizations $3.6

Academia $6.6

Federal govt. $62.9

Industry $142.3

Funding for Research and Development in 1998 (in billions)

Source: Republished by permission of Dow Jones, Inc. via Copyright Clearance Center, Inc. © 1997 Dow Jones and Company, Inc. All rights reserved worldwide.

164. *Taxes*   In a recent year, 238 U.S. airports collected $1.1 billion in passenger taxes. Of this amount, $88 million was spent on noise reduction. What percent of the passenger taxes collected was spent on noise reduction?   8%

165. *Education*   To receive a B grade in a history course, a student must correctly answer 75 of the 90 questions on an exam. What percent of the questions must a student answer correctly to receive a B grade? $83\frac{1}{3}$%

166. *Politics*   In a recent city election, 16,400 out of 80,000 registered voters voted. What percent of the people voted in the election?   20.5%

167. *Safety*   Recently the National Safety Council collected data on the leading causes of accidental death. The findings revealed that for people age 20, 30 died from a fall, 47 from fire, 200 from drowning, and 1950 from motor vehicle accidents. What percent of the accidental deaths were not attributed to motor vehicle accidents? Round to the nearest percent.   12%

168. *Health*   According to *Health* magazine, the average American has increased his or her daily consumption of calories from 18 years ago by 11.6%. If the average daily consumption was 1970 calories 18 years ago, what is the average daily consumption today? Round to the nearest whole number.   2199 calories

169. *The Labor Force*   In 1950, 12% of mothers with children under age 6 worked outside the home. By 1995, that percent had increased to 64%. How many more mothers with children under age 6 worked outside the home in 1995 than in 1950?   Insufficient information

170. *Energy*   The Energy Information Administration reports that if every U.S. household switched 4 h of lighting per day from incandescent bulbs to compact fluorescent bulbs, we would save 31.7 billion kilowatt-hours of electricity a year, or 33% of the total electricity used for home lighting. What is the total electricity used for home lighting in this country? Round to the nearest tenth of a billion.
96.1 billion kilowatt-hours

171. *The Federal Government*   To override a presidential veto, at least $66\frac{2}{3}$% of the Senate must vote to override the veto. There are 100 senators in the Senate. What is the minimum number of votes needed to override a veto?   67 votes

172. *Agriculture*   A Holstein cow in Wisconsin recently set a milk production record. She averaged 174 lb of milk per day for 365 days. What percent of the average daily milk production in 1996 was the production by this Wisconsin Holstein? See the graph at the right. Round to the nearest percent.   385%

173. *Consumerism*   A 16-horsepower lawn tractor with automatic transmission sells for $1579.99. This is 11% more than the price of the same lawn tractor with a standard transmission. What is the price of the less expensive model? Round to the nearest cent.
$1423.41

Average Milk Production by U.S. Dairy Cows

Source: Department of Agriculture

APPLYING CONCEPTS 3.1

Solve.

174. $\dfrac{2m + m}{5} = -9$ -15

175. $\dfrac{3y - 8y}{7} = 15$ -21

[C] **176.** $\dfrac{1}{\frac{1}{x}} = 5$ 5

[C] **177.** $\dfrac{1}{\frac{1}{x}} + 8 = -19$ -27

[C] **178.** $\dfrac{4}{\frac{3}{b}} = 8$ 6

[C] **179.** $\dfrac{5}{\frac{7}{a}} - \dfrac{3}{\frac{7}{a}} = 6$ 21

[C] **180.** Solve for x: $x \div 28 = 1481$ remainder 25   41,493

181. *Geometry*   Find the value of x in the diagram shown at the right.   22°

[C] **182.** *Consumerism*   Your bill for dinner, including a 7.25% sales tax, was $62.74. You want to leave a 15% tip on the cost of the dinner before the sales tax. Find the amount of the tip to the nearest dollar. $9

[C] **183.** *Consumerism*   The total cost for a dinner was $54.86. This included a 15% tip calculated on the cost of the dinner after a 6% sales tax. Find the cost of dinner before the tip and tax. $45

184. *Business*   A retailer decides to increase the original price of each item in the store by 10%. After the price increase, the retailer notices a significant drop in sales and so decides to reduce the current price of each item in the store by 10%. Are the prices back to the original prices? If not, are the prices lower or higher than the original prices?   No, lower.

185. If a quantity increases by 100%, how many times its original value is the new value?   2

186. Make up an equation of the form $x + a = b$ that has 2 as a solution.
One possible answer is $x + 7 = 9$.

187. Make up an equation of the form $ax = b$ that has -2 as a solution.
One possible answer is $5x = -10$.

[C]**188.** Suppose you have a $100,000 30-year mortgage. What is the difference between the monthly payment if the interest rate on your loan is 7.75% and the monthly payment if the interest rate is 7.25%? (*Hint:* You will need to discuss the question with an agent at a bank that provides mortgage services, discuss the question with a real estate agent, or find and use the formula for determining the monthly payment on a mortgage.)
$36.48

189. The following problem does not contain enough information: "How many hours does it take to fly from Los Angeles to New York?" What additional information do we need in order to answer the question?

190. Write an explanation of how to use the tax rate schedule shown below. Provide an example of calculating the income tax on a single taxpayer's taxable income of any amount between $30,000 and $75,000.

1997 Tax Rate Schedule			
For single taxpayers			
If taxable income is more than	but not more than	Tax is	of the amount over
0	$24,650	15%	0
$24,650	$59,750	$3,697.50 plus 28%	$24,650
$59,750	$124,650	$13,525. 50 plus 31%	$59,750
$124,650	$271,050	$33,644.50 plus 36%	$124,650
$271,050	—	$86,348.50 plus 39.6%	$271,050
For married taxpayers, filing jointly			
0	$41,200	15%	0
$41,200	$99,600	$6,180 plus 28%	$41,200
$99,600	$151,750	$22,532 plus 31%	$99,600
$151,750	$271,050	$38,698.50 plus 36%	$151,750
$271,050	—	$81,646.50 plus 39.6%	$271,050

S E C T I O N **3.2**

General Equations

1 Solve equations of the form $ax + b = c$

In solving an equation of the form $ax + b = c$, the goal is to rewrite the equation in the form *variable* = *constant*. This requires applying both the Addition and the Multiplication Properties of Equations.

➡ Solve: $\frac{2}{5}x - 3 = -7$

Add 3 to each side of the equation.

$$\frac{2}{5}x - 3 = -7$$

$$\frac{2}{5}x - 3 + 3 = -7 + 3$$

Simplify.

$$\frac{2}{5}x = -4$$

Multiply each side of the equation by the reciprocal of the coefficient $\frac{2}{5}$.

$$\frac{5}{2} \cdot \frac{2}{5}x = \frac{5}{2}(-4)$$

Simplify. Now the equation is in the form *variable* = *constant*.

$$x = -10$$

Check: $\frac{2}{5}x - 3 = -7$

$$\frac{2}{5}(-10) - 3 \,\big|\, -7$$
$$-4 - 3 \,\big|\, -7$$
$$-7 = -7$$

Write the solution.

The solution is -10. ⬅

Example 1 Solve: $3x - 7 = -5$

Solution

$$3x - 7 = -5$$
$$3x - 7 + 7 = -5 + 7 \qquad \blacktriangleright \text{Add 7 to each side of the equation.}$$
$$3x = 2 \qquad \blacktriangleright \text{Simplify.}$$
$$\frac{3x}{3} = \frac{2}{3} \qquad \blacktriangleright \text{Divide each side of the equation by 3.}$$
$$x = \frac{2}{3} \qquad \blacktriangleright \text{Simplify. Now the equation is in the form } variable = constant.$$

The solution is $\frac{2}{3}$. ▶ Write the solution.

Problem 1 Solve: $5x + 7 = 10$

Solution See page S5. $\frac{3}{5}$

Example 2 Solve: $5 = 9 - 2x$

Solution

$$5 = 9 - 2x$$
$$5 - 9 = 9 - 9 - 2x \qquad \blacktriangleright \text{Subtract 9 from each side of the equation.}$$
$$-4 = -2x \qquad \blacktriangleright \text{Simplify.}$$
$$\frac{-4}{-2} = \frac{-2x}{-2} \qquad \blacktriangleright \text{Divide each side of the equation by } -2.$$
$$2 = x \qquad \blacktriangleright \text{Simplify.}$$

The solution is 2. ▶ Write the solution.

Problem 2 Solve: $11 = 11 + 3x$

Solution See page S5. 0

Note in Example 4 in the Introduction to Equations section, that the original equation, $\frac{1}{2} = x + \frac{2}{3}$, contained fractions with denominators of 2 and 3. The least common multiple of 2 and 3 is 6. The least common multiple has the property that both 2 and 3 will divide evenly into it. Therefore, if both sides of the equation are multiplied by 6, both of the denominators will divide evenly into 6. The result is an equation that does not contain any fractions. Multiplying an equation that contains fractions by the LCM of the denominators is called **clearing denominators.** It is an alternative method of solving an equation that contains fractions.

Solve: $\frac{1}{2} = x + \frac{2}{3}$

$$\frac{1}{2} = x + \frac{2}{3}$$

Multiply both sides of the equation by 6, the LCM of the denominators.

$$6\left(\frac{1}{2}\right) = 6\left(x + \frac{2}{3}\right)$$

Simplify each side of the equation. Use the Distributive Property on the right side of the equation.

$$3 = 6(x) + 6\left(\frac{2}{3}\right)$$

Note that multiplying both sides of the equation by the LCM of the denominators eliminated the fractions.

$$3 = 6x + 4$$

Solve the resulting equation.

$$3 - 4 = 6x + 4 - 4$$
$$-1 = 6x$$
$$\frac{-1}{6} = \frac{6x}{6}$$
$$-\frac{1}{6} = x$$

The solution is $-\frac{1}{6}$.

Example 3   Solve: $\frac{2}{3} + \frac{1}{4}x = -\frac{1}{3}$

Solution

$$\frac{2}{3} + \frac{1}{4}x = -\frac{1}{3}$$

▶ The equation contains fractions. Find the LCM of the denominators.

$$12\left(\frac{2}{3} + \frac{1}{4}x\right) = 12\left(-\frac{1}{3}\right)$$

▶ The LCM of 3 and 4 is 12. Multiply each side of the equation by 12.

$$12\left(\frac{2}{3}\right) + 12\left(\frac{1}{4}x\right) = -4$$

▶ Use the Distributive Property to multiply the left side of the equation by 12.

$$8 + 3x = -4$$
$$8 - 8 + 3x = -4 - 8$$
$$3x = -12$$
$$\frac{3x}{3} = \frac{-12}{3}$$
$$x = -4$$

▶ The equation now contains no fractions.

The solution is -4.

Problem 3   Solve: $\frac{5}{2} - \frac{2}{3}x = \frac{1}{2}$

Solution   See page S5.   3

2   Solve equations of the form
$ax + b = cx + d$

In solving an equation of the form $ax + b = cx + d$, the goal is to rewrite the equation in the form *variable = constant*. Begin by rewriting the equation so that there is only one variable term in the equation. Then rewrite the equation so that there is only one constant term.

➡ Solve: $4x - 5 = 6x + 11$

$$4x - 5 = 6x + 11$$

Subtract $6x$ from each side of the equation. $4x - 6x - 5 = 6x - 6x + 11$

Simplify. Now there is only one variable term in the equation. $-2x - 5 = 11$

Add 5 to each side of the equation. $-2x - 5 + 5 = 11 + 5$

Simplify. Now there is only one constant term in the equation. $-2x = 16$

Divide each side of the equation by -2. $\dfrac{-2x}{-2} = \dfrac{16}{-2}$

Simplify. Now the equation is in the form *variable = constant*. $x = -8$

Check:

$4x - 5$	$= 6x + 11$
$4(-8) - 5$	$6(-8) + 11$
$-32 - 5$	$-48 + 11$
$-37 =$	-37

Write the solution.   The solution is -8.

Example 4   Solve: $4x - 3 = 8x - 7$

Solution $4x - 3 = 8x - 7$

$4x - 8x - 3 = 8x - 8x - 7$ ▶ Subtract $8x$ from each side of the equation.

$-4x - 3 = -7$ ▶ Simplify. Now there is only one variable term in the equation.

$-4x - 3 + 3 = -7 + 3$ ▶ Add 3 to each side of the equation.

$-4x = -4$ ▶ Simplify. Now there is only one constant term in the equation.

$\dfrac{-4x}{-4} = \dfrac{-4}{-4}$ ▶ Divide each side of the equation by -4.

$x = 1$ ▶ Simplify. Now the equation is in the form *variable = constant*.

The solution is 1.   ▶ Write the solution.

Problem 4   Solve: $5x + 4 = 6 + 10x$

Solution   See page S5. $-\dfrac{2}{5}$

3 Solve equations containing parentheses

INSTRUCTOR NOTE

Remind students that the goal is still *variable = constant*.

When an equation contains parentheses, one of the steps in solving the equation requires the use of the Distributive Property. The Distributive Property is used to remove parentheses from a variable expression.

$$a(b + c) = ab + ac$$

Solve: $4 + 5(2x - 3) = 3(4x - 1)$

$$4 + 5(2x - 3) = 3(4x - 1)$$

Use the Distributive Property to remove parentheses.

$$4 + 10x - 15 = 12x - 3$$

Simplify.

$$10x - 11 = 12x - 3$$

Subtract $12x$ from each side of the equation.

$$10x - 12x - 11 = 12x - 12x - 3$$

Simplify. Now there is only one variable term in the equation.

$$-2x - 11 = -3$$

Add 11 to each side of the equation.

$$-2x - 11 + 11 = -3 + 11$$

Simplify. Now there is only one constant term in the equation.

$$-2x = 8$$

Divide each side of the equation by -2.

$$\frac{-2x}{-2} = \frac{8}{-2}$$

Simplify. Now the equation is in the form *variable = constant*.

$$x = -4$$

Check:

$$4 + 5(2x - 3) = 3(4x - 1)$$

$4 + 5[2(-4) - 3]$	$3[4(-4) - 1]$
$4 + 5(-8 - 3)$	$3(-16 - 1)$
$4 + 5(-11)$	$3(-17)$
$4 - 55$	-51
$-51 = -51$	

Write the solution.

The solution is -4.

 In Chapter 2, we discussed the use of a graphing calculator to evaluate variable expressions. The same procedure can be used to check the solution of an equation. Consider the example above. After we divide both sides of the equation by -2, the solution appears to be -4. To check this solution, store the value of x, -4, in the calculator. Evaluate the expression on the left side of the original equation: $4 + 5(2x - 3)$. The result is -51. Now evaluate the expression on the right side of the original equation: $3(4x - 1)$. The result is -51. Because the results are equal, the solution -4 checks. See the Appendix for a description of keystroking procedures for different models of graphing calculators.

Example 5 Solve: $3x - 4(2 - x) = 3(x - 2) - 4$

Solution
$$3x - 4(2 - x) = 3(x - 2) - 4$$
$$3x - 8 + 4x = 3x - 6 - 4$$ ▸ Use the Distributive Property to remove parentheses.

$$7x - 8 = 3x - 10$$ ▸ Simplify.
$$7x - 3x - 8 = 3x - 3x - 10$$ ▸ Subtract $3x$ from each side of the equation.
$$4x - 8 = -10$$
$$4x - 8 + 8 = -10 + 8$$ ▸ Add 8 to each side of the equation.
$$4x = -2$$
$$\frac{4x}{4} = \frac{-2}{4}$$ ▸ Divide each side of the equation by 4.

$$x = -\frac{1}{2}$$ ▸ The equation is in the form *variable = constant*.

The solution is $-\frac{1}{2}$.

Problem 5 Solve: $5x - 4(3 - 2x) = 2(3x - 2) + 6$

Solution See page S5. 2

Example 6 Solve: $3[2 - 4(2x - 1)] = 4x - 10$

Solution
$$3[2 - 4(2x - 1)] = 4x - 10$$
$$3[2 - 8x + 4] = 4x - 10$$ ▸ Use the Distributive Property to remove the parentheses.

$$3[6 - 8x] = 4x - 10$$ ▸ Simplify inside the brackets.
$$18 - 24x = 4x - 10$$ ▸ Use the Distributive Property to remove the brackets.

$$18 - 24x - 4x = 4x - 4x - 10$$ ▸ Subtract $4x$ from each side of the equation.
$$18 - 28x = -10$$
$$18 - 18 - 28x = -10 - 18$$ ▸ Subtract 18 from each side of the equation.
$$-28x = -28$$
$$\frac{-28x}{-28} = \frac{-28}{-28}$$ ▸ Divide each side of the equation by -28.

$$x = 1$$

The solution is 1.

Problem 6 Solve: $-2[3x - 5(2x - 3)] = 3x - 8$

Solution See page S5. 2

4 Application problems

Example 7 A company uses the equation $V = C - 6000t$ to determine the depreciated value V, after t years, of a milling machine that originally cost C dollars. If a milling machine originally cost $50,000, in how many years will the depreciated value of the machine be $38,000?

Strategy To find the number of years, replace C with 50,000 and V with 38,000 in the given equation, and solve for t.

Solution

$$V = C - 6000t$$
$$38{,}000 = 50{,}000 - 6000t$$
$$38{,}000 - 50{,}000 = 50{,}000 - 50{,}000 - 6000t$$
$$-12{,}000 = -6000t$$
$$\frac{-12{,}000}{-6000} = \frac{-6000t}{-6000}$$
$$2 = t$$

The depreciated value of the machine will be $38,000 in 2 years.

Problem 7   The value V of an investment of $7500 at an annual simple interest rate of 6% is given by the equation $V = 450t + 7500$, where t is the amount of time, in years, that the money is invested. In how many years will the value of a $7500 investment be $10,200?

Solution   See page S5.   6 years

A lever system is shown below. It consists of a lever, or bar; a fulcrum; and two forces, F_1 and F_2. The distance d represents the length of the lever, x represents the distance from F_1 to the fulcrum, and $d - x$ represents the distance from F_2 to the fulcrum.

LOOK CLOSELY

This system balances because

$$F_1 x = F_2(d - x)$$
$$60(6) = 90(10 - 6)$$
$$60(6) = 90(4)$$
$$360 = 360$$

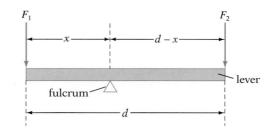

A principle of physics states that when the lever system balances,

$$F_1 x = F_2(d - x)$$

Example 8   A lever is 10 ft long. A force of 100 lb is applied to one end of the lever, and a force of 400 lb is applied to the other end. When the system balances, how far is the fulcrum from the 100-pound force?

Strategy   Draw a diagram of the situation.

The lever is 10 ft long, so $d = 10$. One force is 100 lb, so $F_1 = 100$. The other force is 400 lb, so $F_2 = 400$. To find the distance of the fulcrum from the 100-pound force, replace the variables F_1, F_2, and d in the lever system equation with the given values, and solve for x.

Solution

$$F_1 x = F_2(d - x)$$
$$100x = 400(10 - x)$$
$$100x = 4000 - 400x$$
$$100x + 400x = 4000 - 400x + 400x$$
$$500x = 4000$$
$$\frac{500x}{500} = \frac{4000}{500}$$
$$x = 8$$

The fulcrum is 8 ft from the 100-pound force.

Problem 8   A lever is 14 ft long. At a distance of 6 ft from the fulcrum, a force of 40 lb is applied. How large a force must be applied to the other end of the lever so that the system will balance?

Solution   See page S6.   30 lb

STUDY TIPS

REVIEWING MATERIAL

Reviewing material is the repetition that is essential for learning. Much of what we learn is soon forgotten unless we review it. If you find that you do not remember information that you studied previously, you probably have not reviewed it enough. *You will remember best what you review most.*

   One method of reviewing material is to begin a study session by reviewing a concept you have studied previously. For example, before trying to solve a new type of problem, spend a few minutes solving a kind of problem you already know how to solve. Not only will you provide yourself with the review practice you need, but you are also likely to put yourself in the right frame of mind for learning how to solve the new type of problem.

CONCEPT REVIEW 3.2

Determine whether the statement is always true, sometimes true, or never true.

1. The same variable term can be added to both sides of an equation without changing the solution of the equation.   Always true

2. The same variable term can be subtracted from both sides of an equation without changing the solution of the equation.   Always true

3. An equation of the form $ax + b = c$ cannot be solved if a is a negative number.   Never true

4. The solution of the equation $\frac{x}{3} = 0$ is 0.   Always true

5. The solution of the equation $\frac{x}{0} = 3$ is 0.   Never true

6. In solving an equation of the form $ax + b = cx + d$, the goal is to rewrite the equation in the form *variable* = *constant*.   Always true

7. In solving an equation of the form $ax + b = cx + d$, subtracting cx from each side of the equation results in an equation with only one variable term in it.   Always true

---

EXERCISES 3.2

1 Solve and check.

1. $3x + 1 = 10$ 3
2. $4y + 3 = 11$ 2
3. $2a - 5 = 7$ 6
4. $5m - 6 = 9$ 3

5. $5 = 4x + 9$ -1
6. $2 = 5b + 12$ -2
7. $13 = 9 + 4z$ 1
8. $7 - c = 9$ -2

9. $2 - x = 11$ -9
10. $4 - 3w = -2$ 2
11. $5 - 6x = -13$ 3
12. $8 - 3t = 2$ 2

13. $-5d + 3 = -12$ 3
14. $-8x - 3 = -19$ 2
15. $-7n - 4 = -25$ 3
16. $-12x + 30 = -6$ 3

17. $-13 = -11y + 9$ 2
18. $2 = 7 - 5a$ 1
19. $3 = 11 - 4n$ 2
20. $-35 = -6b + 1$ 6

21. $-8x + 3 = -29$ 4
22. $-3m - 21 = 0$ -7
23. $7x - 3 = 3$ $\frac{6}{7}$
24. $8y + 3 = 7$ $\frac{1}{2}$

25. $6a + 5 = 9$ $\frac{2}{3}$
26. $3m + 4 = 11$ $\frac{7}{3}$
27. $11 = 15 + 4n$ -1
28. $4 = 2 - 3c$ $-\frac{2}{3}$

29. $9 - 4x = 6$ $\frac{3}{4}$
30. $7 - 8z = 0$ $\frac{7}{8}$
31. $1 - 3x = 0$ $\frac{1}{3}$
32. $6y - 5 = -7$ $-\frac{1}{3}$

33. $8b - 3 = -9$ $-\frac{3}{4}$
34. $5 - 6m = 2$ $\frac{1}{2}$
35. $7 - 9a = 4$ $\frac{1}{3}$
36. $9 = -12c + 5$ $-\frac{1}{3}$

37. $10 = -18x + 7$ $-\frac{1}{6}$
38. $2y + \frac{1}{3} = \frac{7}{3}$ 1
39. $3x - \frac{5}{6} = \frac{13}{6}$ 1
40. $5y + \frac{3}{7} = \frac{3}{7}$ 0

41. $9x + \frac{4}{5} = \frac{4}{5}$ 0
42. $4 = 7 - 2w$ $\frac{3}{2}$
43. $7 = 9 - 5a$ $\frac{2}{5}$
44. $-6y + 5 = 13$ $-\frac{4}{3}$

45. $-4x + 3 = 9$ $-\frac{3}{2}$
46. $\frac{1}{2}a - 3 = 1$ 8
47. $\frac{1}{3}m - 1 = 5$ 18
48. $\frac{2}{5}y + 4 = 6$ 5

49. $\frac{3}{4}n + 7 = 13$ 8
50. $-\frac{2}{3}x + 1 = 7$ -9
51. $-\frac{3}{8}b + 4 = 10$ -16
52. $\frac{x}{4} - 6 = 1$ 28

53. $\frac{y}{5} - 2 = 3$ 25
54. $\frac{2x}{3} - 1 = 5$ 9
55. $\frac{3c}{7} - 1 = 8$ 21
56. $4 - \frac{3}{4}z = -2$ 8

57. $3 - \frac{4}{5}w = -9$ 15
58. $5 + \frac{2}{3}y = 3$ -3
59. $17 + \frac{5}{8}x = 7$ -16
60. $17 = 7 - \frac{5}{6}t$ -12

61. $\frac{2}{3} = y - \frac{1}{2}$ $\frac{7}{6}$
62. $\frac{3}{4} = \frac{1}{12}x + 2$ -15
63. $\frac{3}{8} = \frac{5}{12} - \frac{1}{3}b$ $\frac{1}{8}$
64. $\frac{2}{3} = \frac{3}{4} - \frac{1}{2}y$ $\frac{1}{6}$

65. $7 = \dfrac{2x}{5} + 4$ $\dfrac{15}{2}$

66. $5 - \dfrac{4c}{7} = 8$ $-\dfrac{21}{4}$

67. $7 - \dfrac{5}{9}y = 9$ $-\dfrac{18}{5}$

68. $6a + 3 + 2a = 11$ 1

69. $5y + 9 + 2y = 23$ 2

70. $7x - 4 - 2x = 6$ 2

71. $11z - 3 - 7z = 9$ 3

72. $2x - 6x + 1 = 9$ -2

73. $b - 8b + 1 = -6$ 1

74. $-1 = 5m + 7 - m$ -2

75. $8 = 4n - 6 + 3n$ 2

76. $0.15y + 0.025 = -0.074$ -0.66

77. $1.2x - 3.44 = 1.3$ 3.95

78. $3.5 = 3.5 + 0.076x$ 0

79. $-6.5 = 4.3y - 3.06$ -0.8

Solve.

80. If $2x - 3 = 7$, evaluate $3x + 4$.   19

81. If $3x + 5 = -4$, evaluate $2x - 5$. -11

82. If $4 - 5x = -1$, evaluate $x^2 - 3x + 1$. -1

83. If $2 - 3x = 11$, evaluate $x^2 + 2x - 3$.   0

2 Solve and check.

84. $8x + 5 = 4x + 13$ 2

85. $6y + 2 = y + 17$ 3

86. $7m + 4 = 6m + 7$ 3

87. $11n + 3 = 10n + 11$ 8

88. $5x - 4 = 2x + 5$ 3

89. $9a - 10 = 3a + 2$ 2

90. $12y - 4 = 9y - 7$ -1

91. $13b - 1 = 4b - 19$ -2

92. $15x - 2 = 4x - 13$ -1

93. $7a - 5 = 2a - 20$ -3

94. $3x + 1 = 11 - 2x$ 2

95. $n - 2 = 6 - 3n$ 2

96. $2x - 3 = -11 - 2x$ -2

97. $4y - 2 = -16 - 3y$ -2

98. $2b + 3 = 5b + 12$ -3

99. $m + 4 = 3m + 8$ -2

100. $4x - 7 = 5x + 1$ -8

101. $6d - 2 = 7d + 5$ -7

102. $4y - 8 = y - 8$ 0

103. $5a + 7 = 2a + 7$ 0

104. $6 - 5x = 8 - 3x$ -1

105. $10 - 4n = 16 - n$ -2

106. $2x - 4 = 6x$ -1

107. $2b - 10 = 7b$ -2

108. $8m = 3m + 20$ 4

109. $9y = 5y + 16$ 4

110. $-x - 4 = -3x - 16$ -6

111. $8 - 4x = 18 - 5x$ 10

112. $6 - 10a = 8 - 9a$ -2

113. $5 - 7m = 2 - 6m$ 3

114. $8b + 5 = 5b + 7$ $\dfrac{2}{3}$

115. $6y - 1 = 2y + 2$ $\dfrac{3}{4}$

116. $7x - 8 = x - 3$ $\dfrac{5}{6}$

117. $10x - 3 = 3x - 1$ $\dfrac{2}{7}$

118. $5n + 3 = 2n + 1$ $-\dfrac{2}{3}$

119. $8a - 2 = 4a - 5$ $-\dfrac{3}{4}$

120. $\dfrac{1}{5}d = \dfrac{1}{2}d + 3$ -10

121. $\dfrac{3}{4}x = \dfrac{1}{12}x + 2$ 3

122. $\dfrac{2}{3}a = \dfrac{1}{5}a + 7$ 15

123. $\dfrac{4}{5}c - 7 = \dfrac{1}{10}c$ 10

124. $\dfrac{1}{2}y = 10 - \dfrac{1}{3}y$ 12

125. $\dfrac{2}{3}b = 2 - \dfrac{5}{6}b$ $\dfrac{4}{3}$

126. $8.7y = 3.9y + 9.6$ 2

127. $4.5x - 5.4 = 2.7x$ 3

128. $5.6x = 7.2x - 6.4$ 4

Solve.

129. If $5x = 3x - 8$, evaluate $4x + 2$. -14

130. If $7x + 3 = 5x - 7$, evaluate $3x - 2$. -17

131. If $2 - 6a = 5 - 3a$, evaluate $4a^2 - 2a + 1$. 7

132. If $1 - 5c = 4 - 4c$, evaluate $3c^2 - 4c + 2$. 41

3 Solve and check.

133. $5x + 2(x + 1) = 23$ 3

134. $6y + 2(2y + 3) = 16$ 1

135. $9n - 3(2n - 1) = 15$ 4

136. $12x - 2(4x - 6) = 28$ 4

137. $7a - (3a - 4) = 12$ 2

138. $9m - 4(2m - 3) = 11$ -1

139. $5(3 - 2y) + 4y = 3$ 2

140. $4(1 - 3x) + 7x = 9$ -1

141. $10x + 1 = 2(3x + 5) - 1$ 2

142. $5y - 3 = 7 + 4(y - 2)$ 2

143. $4 - 3a = 7 - 2(2a + 5)$ -7

144. $9 - 5x = 12 - (6x + 7)$ -4

145. $3y - 7 = 5(2y - 3) + 4$ $\frac{4}{7}$

146. $2a - 5 = 4(3a + 1) - 2$ $-\frac{7}{10}$

147. $5 - (9 - 6x) = 2x - 2$ $\frac{1}{2}$

148. $7 - (5 - 8x) = 4x + 3$ $\frac{1}{4}$

149. $3[2 - 4(y - 1)] = 3(2y + 8)$ $-\frac{1}{3}$

150. $5[2 - (2x - 4)] = 2(5 - 3x)$ 5

151. $3a + 2[2 + 3(a - 1)] = 2(3a + 4)$ $\frac{10}{3}$

152. $5 + 3[1 + 2(2x - 3)] = 6(x + 5)$ $\frac{20}{3}$

153. $-2[4 - (3b + 2)] = 5 - 2(3b + 6)$ $-\frac{1}{4}$

154. $-4[x - 2(2x - 3)] + 1 = 2x - 3$ 2

155. $0.3x - 2(1.6x) - 8 = 3(1.9x - 4.1)$ 0.5

156. $0.56 - 0.4(2.1y + 3) = 0.2(2y + 6.1)$ -1.5

Solve.

157. If $4 - 3a = 7 - 2(2a + 5)$, evaluate $a^2 + 7a$. 0

158. If $9 - 5x = 12 - (6x + 7)$, evaluate $x^2 - 3x - 2$. 26

159. If $2z - 5 = 3(4z + 5)$, evaluate $\dfrac{z^2}{z - 2}$. -1

160. If $3n - 7 = 5(2n + 7)$, evaluate $\dfrac{n^2}{2n - 6}$. -2

4 The distance s, in feet, that an object will fall in t seconds is given by $s = 16t^2 + vt$, where v is the initial velocity of the object in feet per second.

161. *Physics*   Find the initial velocity of an object that falls 80 ft in 2 s. 8 ft/s

162. *Physics*   Find the initial velocity of an object that falls 144 ft in 3 s. 0 ft/s

The pressure at a certain depth in the ocean can be approximated by the equation $P = \frac{1}{2}D + 15$, where P is the pressure in pounds per square inch, and D is the depth in feet.

163. *Physics*   Find the depth of a diver when the pressure on the diver is 35 lb/in^2. 40 ft

164. *Physics*   Find the depth of a diver when the pressure on the diver is 45 lb/in². 60 ft

Black ice is an ice covering on roads that is especially difficult to see and therefore extremely dangerous for motorists. The distance that a car traveling 30 mph will slide after its brakes are applied is related to the outside temperature by the formula $C = \frac{1}{4}D - 45$, where C is the Celsius temperature and D is the distance in feet that the car will slide.

165. *Physics*   Determine the distance a car will slide on black ice when the outside temperature is −3°C. 168 ft

166. *Physics*   Determine the distance a car will slide on black ice when the outside temperature is −11°C. 136 ft

Anthropologists can approximate the height of a primate from the size of its humerus (the bone extending from the shoulder to the elbow) by using the equation $H = 1.2L + 27.8$, where L is the length of the humerus and H is the height of the primate in inches.

167. *Anthropology*   An anthropologist estimates the height of a primate to be 66 in. What is the approximate length of the humerus of this primate? Round to the nearest tenth. 31.8 in.

168. *Anthropology*   The height of a primate is estimated to be 62 in. Find the approximate length of the humerus of this primate. 28.5 in.

The fare, F, to be charged a customer by a taxi company is calculated using the formula $F = 1.50 + 0.95(m - 1)$, where m is the number of miles traveled.

169. *Business*   A customer is charged $6.25. How many miles was the passenger driven? 6 mi

170. *Business*   A passenger is charged $9.10. Find the number of miles the customer was driven. 9 mi

A person's accurate typing speed can be approximated by the equation $S = \frac{W - 5e}{10}$, where S is the accurate typing speed in words per minute, W is the number of words typed in ten minutes, and e is the number of errors made.

171. *Employment*   After taking a 10-minute typing test, a job candidate was told that he had an accurate speed of 35 words per minute. He had typed a total of 390 words. How many errors did he make? 8 errors

172. *Employment*   A job applicant took a 10-minute typing test and was told that she had an accurate speed of 37 words per minute. If she had typed a total of 400 words, how many errors did she make? 6 errors

A telephone company estimates that the number N of phone calls made per day between two cities of population P_1 and P_2 that are d miles apart is given by the equation $N = \dfrac{2.51P_1P_2}{d^2}$.

173. *Business*   Estimate the population P_2, given that P_1 is 48,000, the number of phone calls is 1,100,000 and the distance between the cities is 75 mi. Round to the nearest thousand.   51,000 people

174. *Business*   Estimate the population P_1, given that P_2 is 125,000, the number of phone calls is 2,500,000, and the distance between the cities is 50 mi. Round to the nearest thousand.   20,000 people

To determine the break-even point, or the number of units that must be sold so that no profit or loss occurs, an economist uses the equation $Px = Cx + F$, where P is the selling price per unit, x is the number of units sold, C is the cost to make each unit, and F is the fixed cost.

175. *Business*   An economist has determined that the selling price per unit for a television is $250. The cost to make one television is $165, and the fixed cost is $29,750. Find the break-even point.   350 television sets

176. *Business*   A manufacturing engineer determines that the cost per unit for a compact disc is $3.35 and that the fixed cost is $6180. The selling price for the compact disc is $8.50. Find the break-even point.   1200 compact discs

Use the lever-system equation $F_1x = F_2(d - x)$.

177. In the lever-system equation $F_1x = F_2(d - x)$, what does x represent? What does d represent? What does $d - x$ represent?

178. Suppose an 80-pound child is sitting at one end of a 7-foot see-saw, and a 60-pound child is sitting at the other end. The 80-pound child is 3 ft from the fulcrum. Use the lever system equation to explain why the see-saw balances.

179. *Lever Systems*   Two children are sitting 8 ft apart on a see-saw. One child weighs 60 lb and the second child weighs 50 lb. The fulcrum is 3.5 ft from the child weighing 60 lb. Is the see-saw balanced?   No

50 lb   60 lb
          3.5 ft
        8 ft

180. *Lever Systems*   An adult and a child are on a see-saw 14 ft long. The adult weighs 175 lb and the child weighs 70 lb. How many feet from the child must the fulcrum be placed so that the see-saw balances?   10 ft

F_2
                    100 lb
                 2 ft

181. *Lever Systems*   A lever 10 ft long is used to balance a 100-pound rock. The fulcrum is placed 2 ft from the rock. What force must be applied to the other end of the lever to balance the rock?   25 lb

182. *Lever Systems*   A 50-pound weight is applied to the left end of a see-saw 10 ft long. The fulcrum is 4 ft from the 50-pound weight. A weight of 30 lb is applied to the right end of the see-saw. Is the 30-pound weight adequate to balance the see-saw?   No

183. *Lever Systems*   In preparation for a stunt, two acrobats are standing on a plank 18 ft long. One acrobat weighs 128 lb and the second acrobat weighs 160 lb. How far from the 128-pound acrobat must the fulcrum be placed so that the acrobats are balanced on the plank?   10 ft

184. *Lever Systems*   A screwdriver 9 in. long is used as a lever to open a can of paint. The tip of the screwdriver is placed under the lip of the lid with the fulcrum 0.15 in. from the lip. A force of 30 lb is applied to the other end of the screwdriver. Find the force on the lip of the lid.   1770 lb

APPLYING CONCEPTS 3.2

Solve. If the equation has no solution, write "No solution."

185. $3(2x - 1) - (6x - 4) = -9$ No solution

186. $\frac{1}{5}(25 - 10b) + 4 = \frac{1}{3}(9b - 15) - 6$ 4

187. $3[4(w + 2) - (w + 1)] = 5(2 + w)$ $-\frac{11}{4}$

188. $\frac{2(5x - 6) - 3(x - 4)}{7} = x + 2$ No solution

[C] **189.** Solve for x: $32{,}166 \div x = 518$ remainder 50   62

190. One-half of a certain number equals two-thirds of the same number. Find the number.   0

191. Write an equation of the form $ax + b = cx + d$ that has 4 as a solution.
One possible answer is $3x - 6 = 2x - 2$.

192. If a, b, and c are real numbers, is it always possible to solve the equation $ax + b = c$? If not, what values of a, b, and/or c must be excluded?
No. $a \neq 0$.

193. Does the sentence "Solve $3x - 4(x - 1)$" make sense? Why or why not?

194. The equation $x = x + 1$ has no solution, whereas the solution of the equation $2x + 1 = 1$ is zero. Is there a difference between no solution and a solution of zero? Explain your answer.

195. Explain in your own words the steps you would take to solve the equation $\frac{3}{4}x - 7 = 2$. State the Property of Real Numbers or the Property of Equations that you used at each step.

196. Explain what is wrong with the following demonstration, which suggests that $2 = 3$.

$$2x + 5 = 3x + 5$$
$$2x + 5 - 5 = 3x + 5 - 5 \quad \blacktriangleright \text{Subtract 5 from each side of the equation.}$$
$$2x = 3x$$
$$\frac{2x}{x} = \frac{3x}{x} \quad \blacktriangleright \text{Divide each side of the equation by } x.$$
$$2 = 3$$

197. Archimedes supposedly said, "Give me a long enough lever and I can move the world." Explain what Archimedes meant by this statement.

S E C T I O N   3.3

Inequalities

1 **Solve inequalities using the Addition Property of Inequalities**

INSTRUCTOR NOTE

Students need to distinguish between $>$ and $\geq$ and between $<$ and $\leq$. Some oral exercises may help. For instance, give students $x > 2$ and ask if 3, 2.5, and 2 satisfy the inequality. Now try $x \leq 3$ and ask if 2, 2.5, and 3 satisfy the inequality.

An expression that contains the symbol $>$, $<$, $\geq$, or $\leq$ is called an **inequality.** An inequality expresses the relative order of two mathematical expressions. The expressions can be either numerical or variable expressions.

$$\left.\begin{array}{c} 4 > 2 \\ 3x \leq 7 \\ x^2 - 2x > y + 4 \end{array}\right\} \text{Inequalities}$$

The **solution set of an inequality** is a set of numbers, each element of which, when substituted for the variable, results in a true inequality. The solution set of an inequality can be graphed on the number line.

The graph of the solution set of $x > 1$ is shown at the right. The solution set is the real numbers greater than 1. The parenthesis on the graph indicates that 1 is not included in the solution set.

The graph of the solution set of $x \geq 1$ is shown at the right. The bracket at 1 indicates that 1 is included in the solution set.

The graph of the solution set of $x < -1$ is shown at the right. The numbers less than -1 are to the left of -1 on the number line.

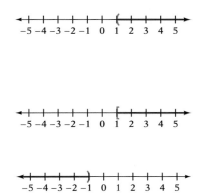

Example 1   Graph: $x < 3$

Solution   ▸ The solution set is the numbers less than 3.

Problem 1   Graph: $x > -2$

Solution   See page S6.

The inequality at the right is true if the variable is replaced by $7, 9.3,$ or $\frac{15}{2}$.

$$x + 3 > 8$$

$$\left.\begin{array}{l} 7 + 3 > 8 \\ 9.3 + 3 > 8 \\ \frac{15}{2} + 3 > 8 \end{array}\right\} \text{True inequalities}$$

The inequality $x + 3 > 8$ is false if the variable is replaced by $4, 1.5,$ or $-\frac{1}{2}$.

$$\left.\begin{array}{l} 4 + 3 > 8 \\ 1.5 + 3 > 8 \\ -\frac{1}{2} + 3 > 8 \end{array}\right\} \text{False inequalities}$$

There are many values of the variable x that will make the inequality $x + 3 > 8$ true. The solution set of $x + 3 > 8$ is any number greater than 5.

The graph of the solution set of $x + 3 > 8$ is shown at the right.

In solving an inequality, the goal is to rewrite the given inequality in the form *variable > constant* or *variable < constant*. The Addition Property of Inequalities is used to rewrite an inequality in this form.

Addition Property of Inequalities

The same number can be added to each side of an inequality without changing the solution set of the inequality.

If $a > b$, then $a + c > b + c$.
If $a < b$, then $a + c < b + c$.

The Addition Property of Inequalities also holds true for an inequality containing the symbol $\geq$ or $\leq$.

The Addition Property of Inequalities is used when, in order to rewrite an inequality in the form *variable > constant* or *variable < constant*, a term must be removed from one side of the inequality. Add the opposite of the term to each side of the inequality.

Because subtraction is defined in terms of addition, the Addition Property of Inequalities makes it possible to subtract the same number from each side of an inequality without changing the solution set of the inequality.

⇒ Solve: $x + 4 < 5$

Subtract 4 from each side of the inequality.

$$x + 4 < 5$$
$$x + 4 - 4 < 5 - 4$$

Simplify.

$$x < 1$$

The graph of the solution set of $x + 4 < 5$ is shown at the right.

⇒ Solve: $5x - 6 \le 4x - 4$

Subtract 4x from each side of the inequality.

$$5x - 6 \le 4x - 4$$
$$5x - 4x - 6 \le 4x - 4x - 4$$

Simplify.

$$x - 6 \le -4$$

Add 6 to each side of the inequality.

$$x - 6 + 6 \le -4 + 6$$

Simplify.

$$x \le 2$$

Example 2   Solve and graph the solution set of $x + 5 > 3$.

Solution
$$x + 5 > 3$$
$$x + 5 - 5 > 3 - 5 \quad \blacktriangleright \text{Subtract 5 from each side of the inequality.}$$
$$x > -2$$

Problem 2   Solve and graph the solution set of $x + 2 < -2$.

Solution   See page S6. $x < -4$

Example 3   Solve: $7x - 14 \le 6x - 16$

Solution
$$7x - 14 \le 6x - 16$$
$$7x - 6x - 14 \le 6x - 6x - 16 \quad \blacktriangleright \text{Subtract } 6x \text{ from each side of the}$$
$$x - 14 \le -16 \qquad\qquad \text{inequality.}$$
$$x - 14 + 14 \le -16 + 14 \quad \blacktriangleright \text{Add 14 to each side of the}$$
$$x \le -2 \qquad\qquad\qquad \text{inequality.}$$

Problem 3   Solve: $5x + 3 > 4x + 5$

Solution   See page S6. $x > 2$

2   Solve inequalities using the Multiplication Property of Inequalities

In solving an inequality, the goal is to rewrite the given inequality in the form *variable > constant* or *variable < constant*. The Multiplication Property of Inequalities is used when, in order to rewrite an inequality in this form, a coefficient must be removed from one side of the inequality.

Multiplication Property of Inequalities—Rule 1

Each side of an inequality can be multiplied by the same positive number without changing the solution set of the inequality.

If $a > b$ and $c > 0$, then $ac > bc$.   If $a < b$ and $c > 0$, then $ac < bc$.

$$5 > 4 \qquad\qquad\qquad\qquad 6 < 9$$
$$5(2) > 4(2) \qquad\qquad\qquad 6(3) < 9(3)$$
$$10 > 8 \quad \text{A true inequality} \qquad 18 < 27 \quad \text{A true inequality}$$

Multiplication Property of Inequalities—Rule 2

If each side of an inequality is multiplied by the same negative number and the inequality symbol is reversed, then the solution set of the inequality is not changed.

If $a > b$ and $c < 0$, then $ac < bc$.   If $a < b$ and $c < 0$, then $ac > bc$.

$$5 > 4 \qquad\qquad\qquad\qquad 6 < 9$$
$$5(-2) < 4(-2) \qquad\qquad\qquad 6(-3) > 9(-3)$$
$$-10 < -8 \quad \text{A true inequality} \qquad -18 > -27 \quad \text{A true inequality}$$

The Multiplication Property of Inequalities also holds true for an inequality containing the symbol $\geq$ or $\leq$.

➡ Solve: $-\dfrac{3}{2}x \leq 6$

Multiply each side of the inequality by the reciprocal of the coefficient $-\dfrac{3}{2}$. Because $-\dfrac{2}{3}$ is a negative number, the inequality symbol must be reversed.

$$-\frac{3}{2}x \leq 6$$
$$-\frac{2}{3}\left(-\frac{3}{2}x\right) \geq -\frac{2}{3}(6)$$

Simplify.

The graph of the solution set of $-\dfrac{3}{2}x \leq 6$ is shown at the right.

$$x \geq -4$$

Recall that division is defined in terms of multiplication. Therefore, the Multiplication Property of Inequalities allows each side of an inequality to be divided by the same number. When each side of an inequality is divided by a positive number, the inequality symbol remains the same. When each side of an inequality is divided by a negative number, the inequality symbol must be reversed.

➡ Solve: $-5x > 8$

Divide each side of the inequality by -5. Because -5 is a negative number, the inequality symbol must be reversed.

Simplify.

$$-5x > 8$$
$$\frac{-5x}{-5} < \frac{8}{-5}$$
$$x < -\frac{8}{5}$$

Example 4   Solve and graph the solution set of $7x < -14$.

Solution $7x < -14$

$\dfrac{7x}{7} < \dfrac{-14}{7}$ ▶ Divide each side of the inequality by 7. Because 7 is a *positive* number, do not change the inequality symbol.

$x < -2$

Problem 4   Solve and graph the solution set of $3x < 9$.

Solution   See page S6. $x < 3$

Example 5   Solve: $-\dfrac{5}{8}x \le \dfrac{5}{12}$

Solution $-\dfrac{5}{8}x \le \dfrac{5}{12}$

$-\dfrac{8}{5}\left(-\dfrac{5}{8}x\right) \ge -\dfrac{8}{5}\left(\dfrac{5}{12}\right)$ ▶ Multiply each side of the inequality by the reciprocal of $-\dfrac{5}{8}$. $-\dfrac{8}{5}$ is a negative number. Reverse the inequality symbol.

$x \ge -\dfrac{2}{3}$

Problem 5   Solve: $-\dfrac{3}{4}x \ge 18$

Solution   See page S6. $x \le -24$

[3] Solve general inequalities

In solving an inequality, it is often necessary to apply both the Addition and the Multiplication Properties of Inequalities.

➡ Solve: $3x - 2 < 5x + 4$

$$3x - 2 < 5x + 4$$

Subtract $5x$ from each side of the inequality. Simplify.

$$3x - 5x - 2 < 5x - 5x + 4$$
$$-2x - 2 < 4$$

Add 2 to each side of the inequality. Simplify.

$$-2x - 2 + 2 < 4 + 2$$
$$-2x < 6$$

Divide each side of the inequality by -2. Because -2 is a negative number, the inequality symbol must be reversed. Simplify.

$$\dfrac{-2x}{-2} > \dfrac{6}{-2}$$

$$x > -3$$ ◀

Example 6   Solve: $7x - 3 \le 3x + 17$

Solution $7x - 3 \le 3x + 17$

$7x - 3x - 3 \le 3x - 3x + 17$ ▶ Subtract $3x$ from each side of the inequality.

$4x - 3 \le 17$

$$4x - 3 + 3 \leq 17 + 3$$
$$4x \leq 20$$
$$\frac{4x}{4} \leq \frac{20}{4}$$
$$x \leq 5$$

▶ Add 3 to each side of the inequality.

▶ Divide each side of the inequality by 4.

Problem 6   Solve: $5 - 4x > 9 - 8x$

Solution   See page S6. $x > 1$

When an inequality contains parentheses, one of the steps in solving the inequality requires the use of the Distributive Property.

➡ Solve: $-2(x - 7) > 3 - 4(2x - 3)$

$$-2(x - 7) > 3 - 4(2x - 3)$$

Use the Distributive Property to remove parentheses. Simplify.

$$-2x + 14 > 3 - 8x + 12$$
$$-2x + 14 > 15 - 8x$$

Add $8x$ to each side of the inequality. Simplify.

$$-2x + 8x + 14 > 15 - 8x + 8x$$
$$6x + 14 > 15$$

Subtract 14 from each side of the inequality. Simplify.

$$6x + 14 - 14 > 15 - 14$$
$$6x > 1$$

Divide each side of the inequality by 6.

$$\frac{6x}{6} > \frac{1}{6}$$

Simplify.

$$x > \frac{1}{6}$$ ⬅

Example 7   Solve: $3(3 - 2x) \geq -5x - 2(3 - x)$

Solution

$$3(3 - 2x) \geq -5x - 2(3 - x)$$
$$9 - 6x \geq -5x - 6 + 2x$$
$$9 - 6x \geq -3x - 6$$
$$9 - 6x + 3x \geq -3x + 3x - 6$$
$$9 - 3x \geq -6$$
$$9 - 9 - 3x \geq -6 - 9$$
$$-3x \geq -15$$
$$\frac{-3x}{-3} \leq \frac{-15}{-3}$$
$$x \leq 5$$

▶ Use the Distributive Property.

▶ Add $3x$ to each side of the inequality.

▶ Subtract 9 from each side of the inequality.

▶ Divide each side of the inequality by -3. Reverse the inequality symbol.

Problem 7   Solve: $8 - 4(3x + 5) \leq 6(x - 8)$

Solution   See page S6. $x \geq 2$

STUDY TIPS

BE PREPARED FOR TESTS

The Chapter Test at the end of a chapter should be used to prepare for an examination. We suggest that you try the Chapter Test a few days before your actual exam. Do these exercises in a quiet place and try to complete the exercises in the same amount of time as you will be allowed for your exam. When completing the exercises, practice the strategies of successful test takers:

1. Look over the entire test before you begin to solve any problem.
2. Write down any rules or formulas you may need so they are readily available.
3. Read the directions carefully.
4. Work the problems that are easiest for you first.
5. Check your work, looking particularly for careless errors.

When you have completed the exercises in the Chapter Test, check your answers. If you missed a question, review the material in that objective and rework some of the exercises from that objective. This will strengthen your ability to perform the skills in that objective.

CONCEPT REVIEW 3.3

Determine whether the statement is always true, sometimes true, or never true.

1. The same variable term can be added to both sides of an inequality without changing the solution set of the inequality.   Always true

2. The same variable term can be subtracted from both sides of an inequality without changing the solution set of the inequality.   Always true

3. Both sides of an inequality can be multiplied by the same number without changing the solution set of the inequality.   Sometimes true

4. Both sides of an inequality can be divided by the same number without changing the solution set of the inequality.   Sometimes true

5. Suppose $a > 0$ and $b < 0$. Then $ab > 0$.   Never true

6. Suppose $a < 0$. Then $a^2 > 0$.   Always true

7. Suppose $a > 0$ and $b < 0$. Then $a^2 > b$.   Always true

8. Suppose $a > b$. Then $-a > -b$.   Never true

122 Chapter 3 / Solving Equations and Inequalities

9. Suppose $a < b$. Then $ac < bc$.   Sometimes true

10. Suppose $a \neq 0$, $b \neq 0$, and $a > b$. Then $\dfrac{1}{a} > \dfrac{1}{b}$.   Sometimes true

---

EXERCISES 3.3

1 Graph.

1. $x > 2$

2. $x \geq -1$

3. $x \leq 0$

4. $x < 4$

Solve and graph the solution set.

5. $x + 1 < 3$ $x < 2$

6. $y + 2 < 2$ $y < 0$

7. $x - 5 > -2$ $x > 3$

8. $x - 3 > -2$ $x > 1$

9. $n + 4 \geq 7$ $n \geq 3$

10. $x + 5 \geq 3$ $x \geq -2$

11. $x - 6 \leq -10$ $x \leq -4$

12. $y - 8 \leq -11$ $y \leq -3$

13. $5 + x \geq 4$ $x \geq -1$

14. $-2 + n \geq 0$ $n \geq 2$

Solve.

15. $y - 3 \geq -12$ $y \geq -9$

16. $x + 8 \geq -14$ $x \geq -22$

17. $3x - 5 < 2x + 7$ $x < 12$

18. $5x + 4 < 4x - 10$ $x < -14$

19. $8x - 7 \geq 7x - 2$ $x \geq 5$

20. $3n - 9 \geq 2n - 8$ $n \geq 1$

21. $2x + 4 < x - 7$ $x < -11$

22. $9x + 7 < 8x - 7$ $x < -14$

23. $4x - 8 \leq 2 + 3x$ $x \leq 10$

24. $5b - 9 < 3 + 4b$ $b < 12$

25. $6x + 4 \geq 5x - 2$ $x \geq -6$

26. $7x - 3 \geq 6x - 2$ $x \geq 1$

27. $2x - 12 > x - 10$ $x > 2$

28. $3x + 9 > 2x + 7$ $x > -2$

29. $d + \dfrac{1}{2} < \dfrac{1}{3}$ $d < -\dfrac{1}{6}$

30. $x - \dfrac{3}{8} < \dfrac{5}{6}$ $x < \dfrac{29}{24}$

31. $x + \dfrac{5}{8} \geq -\dfrac{2}{3}$ $x \geq -\dfrac{31}{24}$

32. $y + \dfrac{5}{12} \geq -\dfrac{3}{4}$ $y \geq -\dfrac{7}{6}$

33. $2x - \dfrac{1}{2} < x + \dfrac{3}{4}$ $x < \dfrac{5}{4}$

34. $6x - \dfrac{1}{3} \leq 5x - \dfrac{1}{2}$ $x \leq -\dfrac{1}{6}$

35. $3x + \dfrac{5}{8} > 2x + \dfrac{5}{6}$ $x > \dfrac{5}{24}$

36. $4b - \dfrac{7}{12} \geq 3b - \dfrac{9}{16}$ $b \geq \dfrac{1}{48}$

37. $x + 5.8 \leq 4.6$ $x \leq -1.2$

38. $n - 3.82 \leq 3.95$ $n \leq 7.77$

39. $x - 0.23 \leq 0.47$ $x \leq 0.70$

40. $3.8x < 2.8x - 3.8$ $x < -3.8$

41. $1.2x < 0.2x - 7.3$ $x < -7.3$

2 Solve and graph the solution set.

42. $3x < 12$ $x < 4$

43. $8x \leq -24$ $x \leq -3$

44. $5y \geq 15$ $y \geq 3$

45. $24x > -48$ $x > -2$

46. $16x \le 16$ $x \le 1$

47. $3x > 0$ $x > 0$

48. $-8x > 8$ $x < -1$

49. $-2n \le -8$ $n \ge 4$

50. $-6b > 24$ $b < -4$

51. $-4x < 8$ $x > -2$

Solve.

52. $-5y \ge 20$ $y \le -4$

53. $3x < 5$ $x < \dfrac{5}{3}$

54. $7x > 2$ $x > \dfrac{2}{7}$

55. $-8x \le -40$ $x \ge 5$

56. $-6x \le -40$ $x \ge \dfrac{20}{3}$

57. $10x > -25$ $x > -\dfrac{5}{2}$

58. $-3x \ge \dfrac{6}{7}$ $x \le -\dfrac{2}{7}$

59. $-5x \ge \dfrac{10}{3}$ $x \le -\dfrac{2}{3}$

60. $\dfrac{5}{6}n < 15$ $n < 18$

61. $\dfrac{2}{3}x < -12$ $x < -18$

62. $\dfrac{5}{6}x < -20$ $x < -24$

63. $-\dfrac{3}{8}x < 6$ $x > -16$

64. $\dfrac{3}{4}x < 12$ $x < 16$

65. $\dfrac{2}{3}y \ge 4$ $y \ge 6$

66. $\dfrac{5}{8}x \ge 10$ $x \ge 16$

67. $-\dfrac{2}{3}x \le 4$ $x \ge -6$

68. $-\dfrac{3}{7}x \le 6$ $x \ge -14$

69. $-\dfrac{2}{11}b \ge -6$ $b \le 33$

70. $-\dfrac{4}{7}x \ge -12$ $x \le 21$

71. $\dfrac{2}{3}n < \dfrac{1}{2}$ $n < \dfrac{3}{4}$

72. $\dfrac{3}{5}x > \dfrac{7}{10}$ $x > \dfrac{7}{6}$

73. $-\dfrac{2}{3}x \ge \dfrac{4}{7}$ $x \le -\dfrac{6}{7}$

74. $-\dfrac{3}{8}x \ge \dfrac{9}{14}$ $x \le -\dfrac{12}{7}$

75. $-\dfrac{3}{4}y \ge -\dfrac{5}{8}$ $y \le \dfrac{5}{6}$

76. $-\dfrac{8}{9}x \ge -\dfrac{16}{27}$ $x \le \dfrac{2}{3}$

77. $\dfrac{2}{3}x \le \dfrac{9}{14}$ $x \le \dfrac{27}{28}$

78. $\dfrac{7}{12}x \le \dfrac{9}{14}$ $x \le \dfrac{54}{49}$

79. $-\dfrac{3}{5}y < \dfrac{9}{10}$ $y > -\dfrac{3}{2}$

80. $-\dfrac{5}{12}y < \dfrac{1}{6}$ $y > -\dfrac{2}{5}$

81. $-0.27x < 0.135$ $x > -0.5$

82. $-0.63x < 4.41$ $x > -7$

83. $8.4y \ge -6.72$ $y \ge -0.8$

84. $3.7y \ge -1.48$ $y \ge -0.4$

85. $1.5x \le 6.30$ $x \le 4.2$

86. $2.3x \le 5.29$ $x \le 2.3$

87. $-3.9x \ge -19.5$ $x \le 5$

88. $0.035x < -0.0735$ $x < -2.1$

89. $0.07x < -0.378$ $x < -5.4$

90. $-11.7x \le 4.68$ $x \ge -0.4$

3 **91.** ✏ In your own words, state the Addition Property of Inequalities and the Multiplication Property of Inequalities.

92. ✏ What differentiates solving linear equations from solving linear inequalities?

Solve.

93. $4x - 8 < 2x$ $x < 4$

94. $7x - 4 < 3x$ $x < 1$

95. $2x - 8 > 4x$ $x < -4$

96. $3y + 2 > 7y$ $y < \dfrac{1}{2}$

97. $8 - 3x \le 5x$ $x \ge 1$

98. $10 - 3x \le 7x$ $x \ge 1$

99. $3x + 2 \ge 5x - 8$ $x \le 5$

100. $2n - 9 \ge 5n + 4$ $n \le -\dfrac{13}{3}$

101. $5x - 2 < 3x - 2$ $x < 0$

102. $8x - 9 > 3x - 9$ $x > 0$

103. $0.1(180 + x) > x$ $x < 20$

104. $x > 0.2(50 + x)$ $x > 12.5$

105. $0.15x + 55 > 0.10x + 80$
$x > 500$

106. $-3.6b + 16 < 2.8b + 25.6$
$b > -1.5$

107. $2(3x - 1) > 3x + 4$ $x > 2$

108. $5(2x + 7) > -4x - 7$
$x > -3$

109. $3(2x - 5) \geq 8x - 5$
$x \leq -5$

110. $5x - 8 \geq 7x - 9$ $x \leq \frac{1}{2}$

111. $2(2y - 5) \leq 3(5 - 2y)$ $y \leq \frac{5}{2}$

112. $2(5x - 8) \leq 7(x - 3)$ $x \leq -\frac{5}{3}$

113. $5(2 - x) > 3(2x - 5)$ $x < \frac{25}{11}$

114. $4(3d - 1) > 3(2 - 5d)$ $d > \frac{10}{27}$

115. $5(x - 2) > 9x - 3(2x - 4)$ $x > 11$

116. $3x - 2(3x - 5) > 4(2x - 1)$ $x < \frac{14}{11}$

117. $4 - 3(3 - n) \leq 3(2 - 5n)$ $n \leq \frac{11}{18}$

118. $15 - 5(3 - 2x) \leq 4(x - 3)$ $x \leq -2$

119. $2x - 3(x - 4) \geq 4 - 2(x - 7)$ $x \geq 6$

120. $4 + 2(3 - 2y) \leq 4(3y - 5) - 6y$ $y \geq 3$

121. $\frac{1}{2}(9x - 10) \leq -\frac{1}{3}(12 - 6x)$ $x \leq \frac{2}{5}$

122. $\frac{1}{4}(8 - 12d) < \frac{2}{5}(10d + 15)$ $d > -\frac{4}{7}$

123. $\frac{2}{3}(9t - 15) + 4 < 6 + \frac{3}{4}(4 - 12t)$ $t < 1$

124. $\frac{3}{8}(16 - 8c) - 9 \geq \frac{3}{5}(10c - 15) + 7$ $c \leq -\frac{1}{9}$

125. $3[4(n - 2) - (1 - n)] > 5(n - 4)$ $n > \frac{7}{10}$

126. $2(m + 7) \leq 4[3(m - 2) - 5(1 + m)]$ $m \leq -\frac{29}{5}$

APPLYING CONCEPTS 3.3

Use the roster method to list the set of positive integers that are solutions of the inequality.

127. $7 - 2b \leq 15 - 5b$ {1, 2}

128. $13 - 8a \geq 2 - 6a$ {1, 2, 3, 4, 5}

129. $2(2c - 3) < 5(6 - c)$ {1, 2, 3}

130. $-6(2 - d) \geq 4(4d - 9)$ {1, 2}

Use the roster method to list the set of integers that are common to the solution sets of the two inequalities.

[C] **131.** $5x - 12 \leq x + 8$
$3x - 4 \geq 2 + x$ {3, 4, 5}

[C] **132.** $6x - 5 > 9x - 2$
$5x - 6 < 8x + 9$ {−4, −3, −2}

[C] **133.** $4(x - 2) \leq 3x + 5$
$7(x - 3) \geq 5x - 1$ {10, 11, 12, 13}

[C] **134.** $3(x + 2) < 2(x + 4)$
$4(x + 5) > 3(x + 6)$ {−1, 0, 1}

Graph.

[C] **135.** $|x| < 3$

[C] **136.** $|x| < 4$

[C] **137.** $|x| > 2$

[C] **138.** $|x| > 1$

Focus on Problem Solving

Graphing Data

Graphs are very useful in displaying data. Highs and lows can be shown and trends observed from the graph. Predictions can then be made for a future time by assuming that these trends will continue.

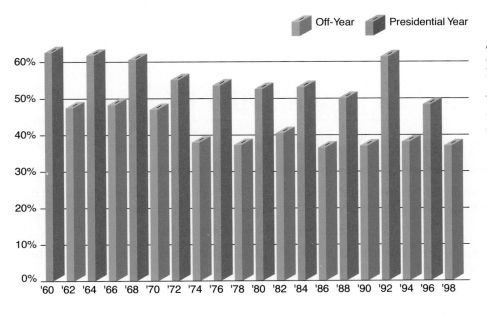

Off-Year   Presidential Year

The bar graph at the left depicts U.S. voter turnout during presidential election years and during off-year elections.

The heights of the bars indicate the percents of eligible voters who cast ballots.

1. During which presidential election years was voter turnout greater than 60%?

2. During which off-year elections was voter turnout less than 40%?

3. During which presidential election years was voter turnout less than 50%?

4. Write a paragraph describing any pattern you see in the graph.

5. Using any patterns that you may have observed, make a prediction about voter turnout in 2000 and 2002.

The table at the right shows the number of mobile phone users (in millions) for the years 1988 to 1996.

Year	Number (in millions)	Year	Number (in millions)
'88	2.1	'93	16.0
'89	3.5	'94	24.1
'90	5.3	'95	33.8
'91	7.6	'96	44.0
'92	11.0		

6. Make a bar graph of the number of mobile phone users.

7. Note the trend that this bar graph indicates. Do you expect the number of mobile phone users to be closer to 48 million, 55 million, or 80 million in 1997?

The federal budget deficit (in billions of dollars) since 1980 is shown below. The deficits for the years 1997, 1998, and 1999 are estimates made by the Office of Management and Budget.

Year	Deficit	Year	Deficit	Year	Deficit	Year	Deficit	Year	Deficit
'80	73.8	'84	185.3	'88	155.2	'92	290.4	'96	107.3
'81	78.9	'85	212.3	'89	152.5	'93	255.0	'97	67.0
'82	127.9	'86	221.2	'90	221.2	'94	203.1	'98	90.0
'83	207.8	'87	149.8	'91	269.4	'95	163.9	'99	90.0

8. Make a bar graph showing the federal budget deficits.

9. During which consecutive 3-year period was the deficit the greatest?

10. Write a paragraph describing any pattern you see in the graph.

Projects and Group Activities

Measurements as Approximations

From arithmetic, you know the rules for rounding decimals.

If the digit to the right of the given place value is less than 5, that digit and all digits to the right are dropped.

6.31 rounded to the nearest tenth is 6.3.

If the digit to the right of the given place value is greater than or equal to 5, increase the given place value by one and drop all digits to its right.

6.28 rounded to the nearest tenth is 6.3.

Given the rules for rounding numbers, what range of values can the number 6.3 represent? The smallest possible number that would be rounded to 6.3 is 6.25; any number smaller than that would not be rounded up to 6.3.

What about the largest possible number that would be rounded to 6.3? The number 6.34 would be rounded down to 6.3. So would the numbers 6.349, 6.3499, 6.349999, and so on. Therefore, we cannot name the largest possible value of 6.3. We can say that the number must be less than 6.35. Any number less than 6.35 would be rounded down to 6.3.

The exact value of 6.3 is greater than or equal to 6.25 and less than 6.35.

4.3 cm
3.2 cm

The dimensions of a rectangle are given as 4.3 cm by 3.2 cm. Using the smallest and the largest possible values of the length and of the width, we can represent the possible values of the area, A, of the rectangle as follows:

$$4.25(3.15) \leq A < 4.35(3.25)$$
$$13.3875 \leq A < 14.1375$$

The area is greater than or equal to 13.3875 cm^2 and less than 14.1375 cm^2.

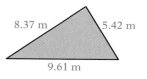
8.37 m   5.42 m
9.61 m

Solve.

1. The measurements of the three sides of a triangle are given as 8.37 m, 5.42 m, and 9.61 m. Find the possible lengths of the perimeter of the triangle.

2. The length of a side of a square is given as 4.7 cm. Find the possible values for the area of the square.

3. What are the possible values for the area of a rectangle whose dimensions are 6.5 cm by 7.8 cm?

4. The length of a box is 40 cm, the width is 25 cm, and the height is 8 cm. What are the possible values of the volume of the box?

Chapter Summary

Key Words

An *equation* expresses the equality of two mathematical expressions.   (Objective 3.1.1)

$5(3x - 2) = 4x + 7$ is an equation.

A *solution of an equation* is a number that, when substituted for the variable, results in a true equation.   (Objective 3.1.1)

1 is the solution of the equation $6x - 4 = 2$ because $6(1) - 4 = 2$ is a true equation.

To *solve* an equation means to find a solution of the equation. The goal is to rewrite the equation in the form *variable = constant*, because the constant is the solution.   (Objective 3.1.2)

The equation $x = -9$ is in the form *variable = constant*. The constant, -9, is the solution of the equation.

An *inequality* is an expression that contains the symbol, $<$, $>$, $\leq$, or $\geq$.   (Objective 3.3.1)

$8x - 1 \geq 5x + 23$ is an inequality.

The *solution set of an inequality* is a set of numbers, each element of which, when substituted for the variable, results in a true inequality.   (Objective 3.3.1)

The solution set of $8x - 1 \geq 5x + 23$ is $x \geq 8$ because every number greater than or equal to 8, when substituted for the variable, results in a true inequality.

Essential Rules and Procedures

The Addition Property of Equations
The same number or variable term can be added to each side of an equation without changing the solution of the equation. (Objective 3.1.2)

$$x + 12 = -19$$
$$x + 12 - 12 = -19 - 12$$
$$x = -31$$

The Multiplication Property of Equations
Each side of an equation can be multiplied by the same nonzero number without changing the solution of the equation.   (Objective 3.1.3)

$$-6x = 24$$
$$\frac{-6x}{-6} = \frac{24}{-6}$$
$$x = -4$$

To solve an equation of the form $ax + b = c$ or an equation of the form $ax + b = cx + d$, use both the Addition and the Multiplication Properties of Equations.   (Objectives 3.2.1 and 3.2.2)

$$7x - 4 = 3x + 16$$
$$7x - 3x - 4 = 3x - 3x + 16$$
$$4x - 4 = 16$$
$$4x - 4 + 4 = 16 + 4$$
$$4x = 20$$
$$\frac{4x}{4} = \frac{20}{4}$$
$$x = 5$$

To solve an equation containing parentheses, use the Distributive Property to remove parentheses.   (Objective 3.2.3)

$$3(2x - 1) = 15$$
$$6x - 3 = 15$$
$$6x - 3 + 3 = 15 + 3$$
$$6x = 18$$
$$\frac{6x}{6} = \frac{18}{6}$$
$$x = 3$$

The Addition Property of Inequalities
The same number or variable term can be added to each side of an inequality without changing the solution set of the inequality.

$$x - 9 \le 14$$
$$x - 9 + 9 \le 14 + 9$$
$$x \le 23$$

If $a > b$, then $a + c > b + c$.
If $a < b$, then $a + c < b + c$.   (Objective 3.3.1)

The Multiplication Property of Inequalities
(Objective 3.3.2)

Rule 1 Each side of an inequality can be multiplied by the same **positive number** without changing the solution set of the inequality.

$$7x < -21$$
$$\frac{7x}{7} < \frac{-21}{7}$$
$$x < -3$$

If $a > b$ and $c > 0$, then $ac > bc$.
If $a < b$ and $c > 0$, then $ac < bc$.

Rule 2 If each side of an inequality is multiplied by the same **negative number** and the inequality symbol is reversed, then the solution set of the inequality is not changed.

$$-7x \ge 21$$
$$\frac{-7x}{-7} \le \frac{21}{-7}$$
$$x \le -3$$

If $a > b$ and $c < 0$, then $ac < bc$.
If $a < b$ and $c < 0$, then $ac > bc$.

The Basic Percent Equation
Percent · Base = Amount
$$P \cdot B = A$$
(Objective 3.1.4)

40% of what number is 16?

$$PB = A$$
$$0.40B = 16$$
$$\frac{0.40B}{0.40} = \frac{16}{0.40}$$
$$B = 40$$

The number is 40.

Chapter Review Exercises

1.   Is 3 a solution of $5x - 2 = 4x + 5$?   No

2.   Solve: $x - 4 = 16$ 20

3.   Solve: $8x = -56$ -7

4.   Solve: $5x - 6 = 29$ 7

5.   Solve: $5x + 3 = 10x - 17$ 4

6.   Solve: $3(5x + 2) + 2 = 10x + 5[x - (3x - 1)]$
$$-\frac{1}{5}$$

7. What is 81% of 500?   405

8. 18 is 72% of what number?   25

9. 27 is what percent of 40?   67.5%

10. Graph: $x \le -2$

11. Solve and graph the solution set of $x - 3 > -1$. $x > 2$

12. Solve and graph the solution set of $3x > -12$. $x > -4$

13. Solve: $3x + 4 \ge -8$ $x \ge -4$

14. Solve: $7x - 2(x + 3) \ge x + 10$ $x \ge 4$

15. Is 2 a solution of $x^2 + 4x + 1 = 3x + 7$?   Yes

16. Solve: $4.6 = 2.1 + x$ 2.5

17. Solve: $\frac{x}{7} = -7$ -49

18. Solve: $14 + 6x = 17$ $\frac{1}{2}$

19. Solve: $12y - 1 = 3y + 2$ $\frac{1}{3}$

20. Solve: $x + 5(3x - 20) = 10(x - 4)$ 10

21. What is $66\frac{2}{3}\%$ of 24?   16

22. 60 is 48% of what number?   125

23. 0.5 is what percent of 3? $16\frac{2}{3}\%$

24. Solve and graph the solution set of $2 + x < -2$. $x < -4$

25. Solve and graph the solution set of $5x \le -10$. $x \le -2$

26. Solve: $6x + 3(2x - 1) = -27$ -2

27. Solve: $a - \frac{1}{6} = \frac{2}{3}$ $\frac{5}{6}$

28. Solve: $\frac{3}{5}a = 12$ 20

29. Solve: $32 = 9x - 4 - 3x$ 6

30. Solve: $-4[x + 3(x - 5)] = 3(8x + 20)$ 0

31. Solve: $4x - 12 < x + 24$ $x < 12$

32. What is $\frac{1}{2}\%$ of 3000?   15

33. Solve: $3x + 7 + 4x = 42$ 5

34. Solve: $5x - 6 > 19$ $x > 5$

35. 8 is what percent of 200?   4%

36. Solve: $6x - 9 < 4x + 3(x + 3)$ $x > -18$

37. Solve: $5 - 4(x + 9) > 11(12x - 9)$ $x < \frac{1}{2}$

38. Find the measure of the third angle of a triangle if the first angle is 20° and the second angle is 50°. Use the equation $A + B + C = 180°$, where A, B, and C are the measures of the angles of a triangle.   110°

39. A lever is 12 ft long. At a distance of 2 ft from the fulcrum, a force of 120 lb is applied. How large a force must be applied to the other end of the lever so that the system will balance? Use the lever system equation $F_1 x = F_2(d - x)$.
24 lb

40. Use the equation $P = 2L + 2W$, where P is the perimeter of a rectangle, L is its length, and W is its width, to find the width of a rectangle that has a perimeter of 49 ft and a length of 18.5 ft.   6 ft

41. Find the discount on a 26-inch, 21-speed dual-index grip-shifting bicycle if the sale price is $128 and the regular price is $159.99. Use the equation $S = R - D$, where S is the sale price, R is the regular price, and D is the discount. $31.99

42. The number of personal bankruptcy filings in the United States has been increasing, as illustrated in the table at the right. Find the percent increase in the number of personal bankruptcy filings from 1996 to 1997. Round to the nearest percent.   19%

Personal Bankruptcy Filings	
1995	926,601
1996	1,178,555
1997	1,404,145

Source: Administrative Office of the U.S. Courts

43. The pressure at a certain depth in the ocean can be approximated by the equation $P = 15 + \frac{1}{2}D$, where P is the pressure in pounds per square inch and D is the depth in feet. Use this equation to find the depth when the pressure is 55 lb/in^2.   80 ft

44. A lever is 8 ft long. A force of 25 lb is applied to one end of the lever, and a force of 15 lb is applied to the other end. Find the location of the fulcrum when the system balances. Use the lever system equation $F_1 x = F_2(d - x)$.
3 ft from the 25 lb force

45. Find the length of a rectangle when the perimeter is 84 ft and the width is 18 ft. Use the equation $P = 2L + 2W$, where P is the perimeter of a rectangle, L is the length, and W is the width.   24 ft

Chapter Test

1. Solve: $\frac{3}{4}x = -9$ -12

2. Solve: $6 - 5x = 5x + 11$ $-\frac{1}{2}$

3. Solve: $3x - 5 = -14$ -3

4. Is -2 a solution of $x^2 - 3x = 2x - 6$?   No

5. Solve: $x + \frac{1}{2} = \frac{5}{8}$ $\frac{1}{8}$

6. Solve: $5x - 2(4x - 3) = 6x + 9$ $-\frac{1}{3}$

7. Solve: $7 - 4x = -13$ 5

8. Solve: $11 - 4x = 2x + 8$ $\frac{1}{2}$

9. Solve: $x - 3 = -8$ -5

10. Solve: $3x - 2 = 5x + 8$ -5

11. Solve: $-\frac{3}{8}x = 5$ $-\frac{40}{3}$

12. Solve: $6x - 3(2 - 3x) = 4(2x - 7)$ $-\frac{22}{7}$

13. Solve: $6 - 2(5x - 8) = 3x - 4$ 2

14. Solve: $9 - 3(2x - 5) = 12 + 5x$ $\frac{12}{11}$

15. Solve: $3(2x - 5) = 8x - 9$ -3

16. 20 is what percent of 16?   125%

17. 30% of what is 12?   40

18. Graph: $x > -2$

19. Solve and graph the solution set of $-2 + x \le -3$. $x \le -1$

20. Solve and graph the solution set of $\frac{3}{8}x > -\frac{3}{4}$. $x > -2$

21. Solve: $x + \frac{1}{3} > \frac{5}{6}$ $x > \frac{1}{2}$

22. Solve: $3(x - 7) \geq 5x - 12$ $x \leq -\frac{9}{2}$

23. Solve: $-\frac{3}{8}x \leq 6$ $x \geq -16$

24. Solve: $4x - 2(3 - 5x) \leq 6x + 10$ $x \leq 2$

25. Solve: $3(2x - 5) \geq 8x - 9$ $x \leq -3$

26. Solve: $15 - 3(5x - 7) < 2(7 - 2x)$ $x > 2$

27. Solve: $-6x + 16 = -2x$ 4

28. 20 is $83\frac{1}{3}\%$ of what number? 24

29. Solve and graph the solution set of $\frac{2}{3}x \geq 2$.

$x \geq 3$

30. Is 5 a solution of $x^2 + 2x + 1 = (x + 1)^2$?   Yes

31. A person's weight on the moon is $16\frac{2}{3}\%$ of the person's weight on Earth. If an astronaut weighs 180 lb on Earth, how much would the astronaut weigh on the moon?   30 lb

32. A chemist mixes 100 g of water at 80°C with 50 g of water at 20°C. Use the equation $m_1 \cdot (T_1 - T) = m_2 \cdot (T - T_2)$ to find the final temperature of the water after mixing. In this equation, m_1 is the quantity of water at the hotter temperature, T_1 is the temperature of the hotter water, m_2 is the quantity of water at the cooler temperature, T_2 is the temperature of the cooler water, and T is the final temperature of the water after mixing.   60°C

33. A financial manager has determined that the cost per unit for a calculator is $15 and that the fixed costs per month are $2000. Find the number of calculators produced during a month in which the total cost was $5000. Use the equation $T = U \cdot N + F$, where T is the total cost, U is the cost per unit, N is the number of units produced, and F is the fixed cost.   200 calculators

Cumulative Review Exercises

1. Subtract: $-6 - (-20) - 8$ 6

2. Multiply: $(-2)(-6)(-4)$ -48

3. Subtract: $-\frac{5}{6} - \left(-\frac{7}{16}\right)$ $-\frac{19}{48}$

4. Divide: $-2\frac{1}{3} \div 1\frac{1}{6}$ -2

5. Simplify: $-4^2 \cdot \left(-\frac{3}{2}\right)^3$ 54

6. Simplify: $25 - 3 \cdot \frac{(5 - 2)^2}{2^3 + 1} - (-2)$ 24

7. Evaluate $3(a - c) - 2ab$, when $a = 2$, $b = 3$, and $c = -4$. 6

8. Simplify: $3x - 8x + (-12x)$ $-17x$

9. Simplify: $2a - (-3b) - 7a - 5b$ $-5a - 2b$

10. Simplify: $(16x)\left(\frac{1}{8}\right)$ $2x$

11. Simplify: $-4(-9y)$ $36y$

12. Simplify: $-2(-x^2 - 3x + 2)$ $2x^2 + 6x - 4$

13. Simplify: $-2(x - 3) + 2(4 - x)$ $-4x + 14$

14. Simplify: $-3[2x - 4(x - 3)] + 2$ $6x - 34$

15. Use the roster method to write the set of negative integers greater than -8.
    $\{-7, -6, -5, -4, -3, -2, -1\}$

16. Write $\frac{7}{8}$ as a percent. Write the remainder in fractional form. $87\frac{1}{2}\%$

17. Write 342% as a decimal.   3.42

18. Write $62\frac{1}{2}\%$ as a fraction. $\frac{5}{8}$

19. Is -3 a solution of $x^2 + 6x + 9 = x + 3$?   Yes

20. Solve: $x - 4 = -9$ -5

21. Solve: $\frac{3}{5}x = -15$ -25

22. Solve: $13 - 9x = -14$ 3

23. Solve: $5x - 8 = 12x + 13$ -3

24. Solve: $8x - 3(4x - 5) = -2x - 11$ 13

25. Solve: $-\frac{3}{4}x > \frac{2}{3}$ $x < -\frac{8}{9}$

26. Solve: $5x - 4 \geq 4x + 8$ $x \geq 12$

27. Solve: $3x + 17 < 5x - 1$ $x > 9$

28. Translate "the difference between eight and the quotient of a number and twelve" into a variable expression. $8 - \frac{n}{12}$

29. Translate and simplify "the sum of a number and two more than the number." $n + (n + 2); 2n + 2$

30. A club treasurer has some five-dollar bills and some ten-dollar bills. The treasurer has a total of 35 bills. Use one variable to express the number of each denomination of bill. b and $35 - b$

31. A wire is cut into two pieces. The length of the longer piece is four inches less than three times the length of the shorter piece. Express the length of the longer piece in terms of the length of the shorter piece. $3s - 4$

32. A computer programmer receives a weekly wage of $650, and $110.50 is deducted for income tax. Find the percent of the computer programmer's salary deducted for income tax.   17%

33. The world record time for a 1-mile race can be approximated by the equation $t = 17.08 - 0.0067y$, where t is the time in minutes and y is the year of the race. Use this equation to predict the year in which the first "4-minute mile" was run. (The actual year was 1954.) Round to the nearest whole number.   1952

34. A chemist mixes 300 g of water at 75°C with 100 g of water at 15°C. Use the equation $m_1 \cdot (T_1 - T) = m_2 \cdot (T - T_2)$ to find the final temperature of the water. In this equation, m_1 is the quantity of water at the hotter temperature, T_1 is the temperature of the hotter water, m_2 is the quantity of water at the cooler temperature, T_2 is the temperature of the cooler water, and T is the final temperature of the water after mixing.   60°C

35. A lever is 25 ft long. At a distance of 12 ft from the fulcrum, a force of 26 lb is applied. How large a force must be applied to the other end of the lever so that the system will balance?   24 lb

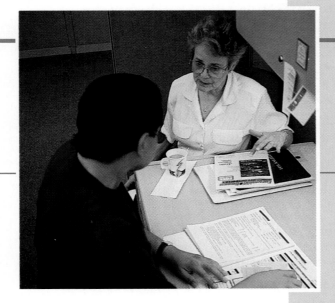

4

Solving Equations and Inequalities: Applications

The human resources department of a company is involved in all areas of a company's dealings and relationships with its employees. One member of this department is the employee benefits manager, who is responsible for the selection and administration of such company programs as retirement packages, profit-sharing plans, and group medical insurance. Because a benefits officer must compare benefits packages, an understanding of inequalities is important.

OBJECTIVES

4.1.1   Translate a sentence into an equation and solve
4.1.2   Application problems
4.2.1   Consecutive integer problems
4.2.2   Coin and stamp problems
4.3.1   Perimeter problems
4.3.2   Problems involving angles formed by intersecting lines
4.3.3   Problems involving the angles of a triangle
4.4.1   Markup problems
4.4.2   Discount problems
4.5.1   Investment problems
4.6.1   Value mixture problems
4.6.2   Percent mixture problems
4.7.1   Uniform motion problems
4.8.1   Applications of inequalities

Word Problems

Word problems have been challenging students of mathematics for a long time. Here are two types of problems you may have seen before.

A number added to $\frac{1}{7}$ of the number is 19. What is the number?

A dog is chasing a rabbit that has a head start of 150 feet. The dog jumps 9 feet every time the rabbit jumps 7 feet. In how many jumps will the dog catch up with the rabbit?

What is unusual about these problems is their age. The first one is about 4000 years old and occurred as Problem 1 in the Rhind Papyrus. The second problem is about 1550 years old and comes from a Latin algebra book written in 450 A.D.

These examples illustrate that word problems have been around for a long time. The long history of word problems also reflects the importance that each generation has placed on solving these problems. It is through word problems that the initial steps of applying mathematics are taken.

The answer to the first problem is $16\frac{5}{8}$.

The answer to the second problem is 75 jumps.

SECTION 4.1

Translating Sentences into Equations

1 Translate a sentence into an equation and solve

An equation states that two mathematical expressions are equal. Therefore, to translate a sentence into an equation requires recognizing the words or phrases that mean "equals." Besides "equals," some of these phrases are "is," "is equal to," "amounts to," and "represents."

Once the sentence is translated into an equation, the equation can be solved by rewriting the equation in the form *variable* = *constant*.

Example 1 Translate "two times the sum of a number and eight equals the sum of four times the number and six" into an equation and solve.

Solution the unknown number: n

▶ Assign a variable to the unknown quantity.

| two times the sum of a number and eight | equals | the sum of four times the number and six |

▶ Find two verbal expressions for the same value.

$$2(n + 8) = 4n + 6$$

▶ Write a mathematical expression for each verbal expression. Write the equals sign.

$$2n + 16 = 4n + 6$$
$$2n - 4n + 16 = 4n - 4n + 6$$
$$-2n + 16 = 6$$
$$-2n + 16 - 16 = 6 - 16$$
$$-2n = -10$$
$$\frac{-2n}{-2} = \frac{-10}{-2}$$
$$n = 5$$

▶ Solve the equation.

The number is 5.

Problem 1 Translate "nine less than twice a number is five times the sum of the number and twelve" into an equation and solve.

Solution See page S6. -23

2 Application problems

Example 2 The temperature of the sun on the Kelvin scale is 6500 K. This is 4740° less than the temperature on the Fahrenheit scale. Find the Fahrenheit temperature.

Strategy   To find the Fahrenheit temperature, write and solve an equation using F to represent the Fahrenheit temperature.

Solution

$$\boxed{6500} \;\text{is}\; \boxed{\begin{array}{l}4740° \text{ less than} \\ \text{the Fahrenheit} \\ \text{temperature}\end{array}}$$

$$6500 = F - 4740$$
$$6500 + 4740 = F - 4740 + 4740$$
$$11{,}240 = F$$

The temperature of the sun is 11,240°F.

Problem 2   A molecule of octane gas has eight carbon atoms. This represents twice the number of carbon atoms in a butane gas molecule. Find the number of carbon atoms in a butane molecule.

Solution   See page S7.   4 carbon atoms

Example 3   A board 10 ft long is cut into two pieces. Three times the length of the shorter piece is twice the length of the longer piece. Find the length of each piece.

Strategy   Draw a diagram. To find the length of each piece, write and solve an equation using x to represent the length of the shorter piece and $10 - x$ to represent the length of the longer piece.

Solution

$$\boxed{\begin{array}{l}\text{three times the} \\ \text{shorter piece}\end{array}} \;\text{is}\; \boxed{\begin{array}{l}\text{twice the} \\ \text{longer piece}\end{array}}$$

$$3x = 2(10 - x)$$
$$3x = 20 - 2x$$
$$3x + 2x = 20 - 2x + 2x$$
$$5x = 20$$
$$\frac{5x}{5} = \frac{20}{5}$$
$$x = 4 \qquad \blacktriangleright \text{ The length of the shorter piece is 4 ft.}$$
$$10 - x = 10 - 4 = 6 \qquad \blacktriangleright \text{ Substitute the value of } x \text{ into the variable expression for the longer piece and evaluate.}$$

The length of the shorter piece is 4 ft. The length of the longer piece is 6 ft.

Problem 3   A company manufactures 160 bicycles per day. Four times the number of 3-speed bicycles made equals 30 less than the number of 10-speed bicycles made. Find the number of 10-speed bicycles manufactured each day.

Solution   See page S7.   134 10-speed bicycles

INSTRUCTOR NOTE

Emphasize the fact that answers to application problems must have units, such as degrees, feet, dollars, or hours.

LOOK CLOSELY

We could also let x represent the length of the longer piece and $10 - x$ represent the length of the shorter piece. Then our equation would be

$$3(10 - x) = 2x$$

Show that this equation results in the same solutions.

STUDY TIPS

FIND GOOD STUDY AREAS

Find a place to study where you are comfortable and can concentrate well. Many students find the campus library to be a good place. You might select two or three places at the college library where you like to study. Or there may be a small, quiet lounge on the third floor of a building where you find you can study well. Take the time to find places that promote good study habits.

CONCEPT REVIEW 4.1

Determine whether the statement is always true, sometimes true, or never true.

1. When two expressions represent the same value, we say that the expressions are equal to each other.   Always true

2. Both "four less than a number" and "the difference between four and a number" are translated as "$4 - n$."   Never true

3. When translating a sentence into an equation, we can use any variable to represent an unknown number.   Always true

4. When translating a sentence into an equation, translate the word "is" as "$=$."
   Always true

5. If a rope 19 in. long is cut into two pieces and one of the pieces has length x in., then the length of the other piece can be expressed as $(x - 19)$ in.
   Never true

6. In addition to a number, the answer to an application problem must have units, such as meters, dollars, minutes, or miles per hour.   Always true

EXERCISES 4.1

1 Translate into an equation and solve.

1. The difference between a number and fifteen is seven. Find the number.
   $$n - 15 = 7; n = 22$$

2. The sum of five and a number is three. Find the number.
   $$5 + n = 3; n = -2$$

3. The product of seven and a number is negative twenty-one. Find the number.
   $$7n = -21; n = -3$$

4. The quotient of a number and four is two. Find the number. $\frac{n}{4} = 2; n = 8$

5. Four less than three times a number is five. Find the number.
   $$3n - 4 = 5; n = 3$$

6. The difference between five and twice a number is one. Find the number.
    $$5 - 2n = 1; \ n = 2$$

7. Four times the sum of twice a number and three is twelve. Find the number.
    $$4(2n + 3) = 12; \ n = 0$$

8. Twenty-one is three times the difference between four times a number and five. Find the number. $21 = 3(4n - 5); \ n = 3$

9. Twelve is six times the difference between a number and three. Find the number. $12 = 6(n - 3); \ n = 5$

10. The difference between six times a number and four times the number is negative fourteen. Find the number. $6n - 4n = -14; \ n = -7$

11. Twenty-two is two less than six times a number. Find the number.
    $22 = 6n - 2; \ n = 4$

12. Negative fifteen is three more than twice a number. Find the number.
    $-15 = 2n + 3; \ n = -9$

13. Seven more than four times a number is three more than two times the number. Find the number. $4n + 7 = 2n + 3; \ n = -2$

14. The difference between three times a number and four is five times the number. Find the number. $3n - 4 = 5n; \ n = -2$

15. Eight less than five times a number is four more than eight times the number. Find the number. $5n - 8 = 8n + 4; \ n = -4$

16. The sum of a number and six is four less than six times the number. Find the number. $n + 6 = 6n - 4; \ n = 2$

17. Twice the difference between a number and twenty-five is three times the number. Find the number. $2(n - 25) = 3n; \ n = -50$

18. Four times a number is three times the difference between thirty-five and the number. Find the number. $4n = 3(35 - n); \ n = 15$

19. The sum of two numbers is twenty. Three times the smaller is equal to two times the larger. Find the two numbers. $3n = 2(20 - n); \ 8 \text{ and } 12$

20. The sum of two numbers is fifteen. One less than three times the smaller is equal to the larger. Find the two numbers. $3n - 1 = 15 - n; \ 4 \text{ and } 11$

21. The sum of two numbers is eighteen. The total of three times the smaller and twice the larger is forty-four. Find the two numbers.
    $$3n + 2(18 - n) = 44; \ 8 \text{ and } 10$$

22. The sum of two numbers is two. The difference between eight and twice the smaller number is two less than four times the larger. Find the two numbers.
    $$8 - 2n = 4(2 - n) - 2; \ -1 \text{ and } 3$$

2 Write an equation and solve.

23. *Depreciation*   As a result of depreciation, the value of a car is now $9600. This is three-fifths of its original value. Find the original value of the car.
$16,000

24. *Computers*   The operating speed of a personal computer is 80 megahertz. This is one-third the speed of a newer model. Find the speed of the newer personal computer.   240 megahertz

25. *Computers*   The storage capacity of a hard-disk drive is 0.5 gigabyte. This is one-fourth of the storage capacity of a second hard-disk drive. Find the storage capacity of the second hard-disk drive.   2 gigabytes

26. *Nutrition*   One slice of cheese pizza contains 290 calories. A medium-size orange has one-fifth that number of calories. How many calories are in a medium-size orange?   58 calories

27. *Safety*   Loudness, or the intensity of sound, is measured in decibels. The sound level of a television is about 70 decibels, which is considered a safe hearing level. A food blender runs at 20 decibels higher than a TV, and a jet engine's decibel reading is 40 less than twice that of a blender. At this level, exposure can cause hearing loss. Find the intensity of the sound of a jet engine.   140 decibels

28. *Education*   A university employs a total of 600 teaching assistants and research assistants. There are three times as many teaching assistants as research assistants. Find the number of research assistants employed by the university.   150 research assistants

29. *Agriculture*   A soil supplement that weighs 24 lb contains iron, potassium, and a mulch. There is five times as much mulch as iron and twice as much potassium as iron. Find the amount of mulch in the soil supplement.
15 lb

30. *Commissions*   A real estate agent sold two homes and received commissions totaling $6000. The agent's commission on one home was one and one-half times the commission on the second home. Find the agent's commission on each home. $2400 and $3600

31. *Consumerism*   The purchase price of a new big-screen TV, including finance charges, was $3276. A down payment of $450 was made. The remainder was paid in 24 equal monthly installments. Find the monthly payment.
$117.75

32. *Consumerism*   The purchase price of a new computer system, including finance charges, was $6350. A down payment of $350 was made. The remainder was paid in 24 equal monthly installments. Find the monthly payment.
$250

33. *Consumerism*   The cost to replace a water pump in a sports car was $600. This included $375 for the water pump and $45 per hour for labor. How many hours of labor were required to replace the water pump?   5 h

34. *Utilities*   The cost of electricity in a certain city is $.08 for each of the first 300 kWh (kilowatt-hours) and $.13 for each kWh over 300 kWh. Find the number of kilowatt-hours used by a family that receives a $51.95 electric bill.

515 kWh

35. *Consumerism*   The fee charged by a ticketing agency for a concert is $3.50 plus $17.50 for each ticket purchased. If your total charge for tickets is $161, how many tickets are you purchasing?   9 tickets

36. *Construction*   The length of a rectangular cement patio is 3 ft less than three times the width. The sum of the length and width of the patio is 21 ft. Find the length of the patio.   15 ft

37. *Geometry*   Greek architects considered a rectangle whose length was approximately 1.6 times its width to be the most visually appealing. Find the length and width of a rectangle constructed in this manner if the sum of the length and width is 130 ft.   Length: 80 ft; width: 50 ft

38. *Computers*   A computer screen consists of tiny dots of light called pixels. In a certain graphics mode, there are 640 horizontal pixels. This is 40 more than three times the number of vertical pixels. Find the number of vertical pixels.

200 pixels

39. *Labor Unions*   A union charges monthly dues of $4.00 plus $.15 for each hour worked during the month. A union member's dues for March were $29.20. How many hours did the union member work during the month of March?   168 h

40. *Business*   The cellular phone service for a business executive is $35 per month plus $.40 per minute of phone use. In a month when the executive's cellular phone bill was $99.80, how many minutes did the executive use the phone?   162 min

41. *Business*   A technical information hotline charges a customer $9.00 plus $.50 per minute to answer questions about software. How many minutes did a customer who received a bill for $14.50 use this service?   11 min

42. *Metalwork*   A wire 12 ft long is cut into two pieces. Each piece is bent into the shape of a square. The perimeter of the larger square is twice the perimeter of the smaller square. Find the perimeter of the larger square.   8 ft

43. *Carpentry*   A carpenter is building a wood door frame. The height of the frame is 1 ft less than three times the width. What is the width of the largest door frame that can be constructed from a board 19 ft long? (*Hint:* A door frame consists of only three sides; there is no frame below a door.)   3 ft

44. *Carpentry*   A 20-foot board is cut into two pieces. Twice the length of the shorter piece is 4 ft more than the length of the longer piece. Find the length of the shorter piece.   8 ft

APPLYING CONCEPTS 4.1

45. The amount of liquid in a container triples every minute. The container becomes completely filled at 3:40 P.M. What fractional part of the container is filled at 3:39 P.M.? $\frac{1}{3}$

46. *Travel* A cyclist traveling at a constant speed completes $\frac{3}{5}$ of a trip in $1\frac{1}{2}$ h. In how many additional hours will the cyclist complete the entire trip?
1 h

47. *Consumerism* The charges for a long-distance telephone call are $1.21 for the first 3 minutes and $.42 for each additional minute or fraction of a minute. If the charges for a call were $6.25, how many minutes did the phone call last? Round up to the nearest whole number. 15 min

48. *Wages* Four employees are paid at four consecutive levels on a wage scale. The difference between any two consecutive levels is $320 per month. The average of the four employees' monthly wages is $2880. What is the monthly wage of the highest-paid employee? $3360

[C] **49.** *Coins* A coin bank contains nickels, dimes, and quarters. There are 14 nickels in the bank, $\frac{1}{6}$ of the coins are dimes, and $\frac{3}{5}$ of the coins are quarters. How many coins are in the coin bank? 60 coins

[C] **50.** *Business* During one day at an office, one-half of the amount of money in the petty cash drawer was used in the morning, and one-third of the remaining money was used in the afternoon, leaving $5 in the petty cash drawer at the end of the day. How much money was in the petty cash drawer at the start of the day? $15

51. A formula is an equation that relates variables in a known way. Find two examples of formulas that are used in your college major. Explain what each of the variables represents.

SECTION 4.2

Integer, Coin, and Stamp Problems

1 Consecutive integer problems

Recall that the integers are the numbers . . . , −3, −2, −1, 0, 1, 2, 3, 4, ...

An **even integer** is an integer that is divisible by 2. Examples of even integers are −8, 0, and 22.

An **odd integer** is an integer that is not divisible by 2. Examples of odd integers are −17, 1, and 39.

Consecutive integers are integers that follow one another in order. Examples of consecutive integers are shown at the right. (Assume the variable n represents an integer.)

11, 12, 13
$-8, -7, -6$
$n, n + 1, n + 2$

Examples of **consecutive even integers** are shown at the right. (Assume the variable n represents an even integer.)

24, 26, 28
$-10, -8, -6$
$n, n + 2, n + 4$

Examples of **consecutive odd integers** are shown at the right. (Assume the variable n represents an odd integer.)

19, 21, 23
$-1, 1, 3$
$n, n + 2, n + 4$

Solve: The sum of three consecutive odd integers is 51. Find the integers.

STRATEGY for solving a consecutive integer problem

■ Let a variable represent one of the integers. Express each of the other integers in terms of that variable. Remember that consecutive integers differ by 1. Consecutive even or consecutive odd integers differ by 2.

First odd integer: n
Second odd integer: $n + 2$
Third odd integer: $n + 4$

■ Determine the relationship among the integers.

The sum of the three odd integers is 51.

$$n + (n + 2) + (n + 4) = 51$$
$$3n + 6 = 51$$
$$3n = 45$$
$$n = 15$$

$n + 2 = 15 + 2 = 17$ ▶ Substitute the value of n into the variable expressions for the
$n + 4 = 15 + 4 = 19$ second and third integers.

The three consecutive odd integers are 15, 17, and 19.

Example 1   Find three consecutive even integers such that three times the second is six more than the sum of the first and third.

Strategy   ■ First even integer: n
Second even integer: $n + 2$
Third even integer: $n + 4$
■ Three times the second equals six more than the sum of the first and third.

Solution　$3(n + 2) = n + (n + 4) + 6$
$3n + 6 = 2n + 10$
$n + 6 = 10$
$n = 4$　　▶ The first even integer is 4.

$n + 2 = 4 + 2 = 6$　　▶ Substitute the value of n into the
$n + 4 = 4 + 4 = 8$　　variable expressions for the second
and third integers.

The three consecutive even integers are 4, 6, and 8.

Problem 1　Find three consecutive integers whose sum is -12.

Solution　See page S7.　$-5, -4, -3$

2　Coin and stamp problems

In solving problems that deal with coins or stamps of different values, it is necessary to represent the value of the coins or stamps in the same unit of money. Frequently, the unit of money is cents.

The value of 3 quarters in cents is $3 \cdot 25$ or 75 cents.
The value of 4 nickels in cents is $4 \cdot 5$ or 20 cents.
The value of d dimes in cents is $d \cdot 10$ or $10d$ cents.

Solve:　A coin bank contains $1.20 in dimes and quarters. In all, there are nine coins in the bank. Find the number of quarters in the bank.

STRATEGY for solving a coin problem

■ For each denomination of coin, write a numerical or variable expression for the number of coins, the value of the coin in cents, and the total value of the coins in cents. The results can be recorded in a table.

The total number of coins is 9.

Number of quarters: x
Number of dimes: $9 - x$

LOOK CLOSELY

Use the information given in the problem to fill in the number and value columns of the table. Fill in the total value column by multiplying the two expressions you wrote in each row.

Coin	Number of coins	·	Value of coin in cents	=	Total value in cents
Quarter	x	·	25	=	$25x$
Dime	$9 - x$	·	10	=	$10(9 - x)$

■ Determine the relationship between the total values of the different coins. Use the fact that the sum of the total values of the different denominations of coins is equal to the total value of all the coins.

The sum of the total values of the different denominations of coins is equal to the total value of all the coins (120 cents).

$$25x + 10(9 - x) = 120$$
$$25x + 90 - 10x = 120$$
$$15x + 90 = 120$$
$$15x = 30$$
$$x = 2$$

▶ The total value of the quarters plus the total value of the dimes equals the amount of money in the bank.

There are 2 quarters in the bank.

Example 2   A collection of stamps consists of 3¢ stamps and 8¢ stamps. The number of 8¢ stamps is five more than three times the number of 3¢ stamps. The total value of all the stamps is $1.75. Find the number of each type of stamp in the collection.

Strategy   ■ Number of 3¢ stamps: x
Number of 8¢ stamps: $3x + 5$

Stamp	Number	Value	Total value
3¢	x	3	$3x$
8¢	$3x + 5$	8	$8(3x + 5)$

■ The sum of the total values of the different types of stamps equals the total value of all the stamps (175 cents).

Solution
$$3x + 8(3x + 5) = 175$$
$$3x + 24x + 40 = 175$$
$$27x + 40 = 175$$
$$27x = 135$$
$$x = 5$$

▶ The total value of the 3¢ stamps plus the total value of the 8¢ stamps equals the total value of all the stamps.

$$3x + 5 = 3(5) + 5$$
$$= 15 + 5 = 20$$

▶ Find the number of 8¢ stamps.

There are five 3¢ stamps and twenty 8¢ stamps in the collection.

Problem 2   A coin bank contains nickels, dimes, and quarters. There are five times as many nickels as dimes and six more quarters than dimes. The total value of all the coins is $6.30. Find the number of each kind of coin in the bank.

Solution   See page S7.   40 nickels, 8 dimes, 14 quarters

CONCEPT REVIEW 4.2

Determine whether the statement is always true, sometimes true, or never true.

1. An even integer is a multiple of 2.   Always true

2. When $10d$ is used to represent the value of d dimes, 10 is written as the coefficient of d because it is the number of cents in one dime.   Always true

3. Given the consecutive odd integers -5 and -3, the next consecutive odd integer is -1.   Always true

4. If the first of three consecutive odd integers is n, then the second and third consecutive odd integers are represented as $n + 1$ and $n + 3$.   Never true

5. You have a total of 20 coins in nickels and dimes. If n represents the number of nickels you have, then $n - 20$ represents the number of dimes you have.   Never true

6. You have a total of 7 coins in dimes and quarters. The total value of the coins is $1.15. If d represents the number of dimes you have, then $10d + 25(7 - d) = 1.15$.   Never true

EXERCISES 4.2

1 Consecutive Integer Problems

1. Explain how to represent three consecutive integers using only one variable.

2. Explain why both consecutive even integers and consecutive odd integers are represented algebraically as $n, n + 2, n + 4, \dots$.

3. The sum of three consecutive integers is 54. Find the integers.   17, 18, 19

4. The sum of three consecutive integers is 75. Find the integers.   24, 25, 26

5. The sum of three consecutive even integers is 84. Find the integers.   26, 28, 30

6. The sum of three consecutive even integers is 48. Find the integers.   14, 16, 18

7. The sum of three consecutive odd integers is 57. Find the integers.   17, 19, 21

8. The sum of three consecutive odd integers is 81. Find the integers.   25, 27, 29

9. Find two consecutive even integers such that five times the first is equal to four times the second.   8, 10

10. Find two consecutive even integers such that six times the first equals three times the second.   2, 4

11. Nine times the first of two consecutive odd integers equals seven times the second. Find the integers.   7, 9

12. Five times the first of two consecutive odd integers is three times the second. Find the integers.   3, 5

13. Find three consecutive integers whose sum is negative twenty-four.
    −9, −8, −7

14. Find three consecutive even integers whose sum is negative twelve.
    −6, −4, −2

15. Three times the smallest of three consecutive even integers is two more than twice the largest. Find the integers.   10, 12, 14

16. Twice the smallest of three consecutive odd integers is five more than the largest. Find the integers.   9, 11, 13

17. Find three consecutive odd integers such that three times the middle integer is six more than the sum of the first and third.   No solution

18. Find three consecutive odd integers such that four times the middle integer is equal to two less than the sum of the first and third.   −3, −1, 1

2 Coin and Stamp Problems

19. Explain how to represent the total value of x nickels using the equation

Number of coins · Value of the coin in cents = Total value in cents.

20. Suppose a coin purse contains only dimes and quarters. In the context of this situation, explain the meaning of the statement "The sum of the total values of the different denominations of coins is equal to the total value of all the coins."

21. A bank contains 27 coins in dimes and quarters. The coins have a total value of $4.95. Find the number of dimes and quarters in the bank.
12 dimes, 15 quarters

22. A coin purse contains 18 coins in nickels and dimes. The coins have a total value of $1.15. Find the number of nickels and dimes in the coin purse.
13 nickels, 5 dimes

23. A business executive bought 40 stamps for $12.40. The purchase included 33¢ stamps and 23¢ stamps. How many of each type of stamp were bought?
23¢ stamps: 8; 33¢ stamps: 32

24. A postal clerk sold some 33¢ stamps and some 23¢ stamps. Altogether, 15 stamps were sold for a total cost of $4.35. How many of each type of stamp were sold?   23¢ stamps: 6; 33¢ stamps: 9

25. A drawer contains 29¢ stamps and 3¢ stamps. The number of 29¢ stamps is four less than three times the number of 3¢ stamps. The total value of all the stamps is $1.54. How many 29¢ stamps are in the drawer?   5 stamps

26. The total value of the dimes and quarters in a bank is $6.05. There are six more quarters than dimes. Find the number of each type of coin in the bank.
13 dimes, 19 quarters

27. A child's piggy bank contains 44 coins in quarters and dimes. The coins have a total value of $8.60. Find the number of quarters in the bank.   28 quarters

28. A coin bank contains nickels and dimes. The number of dimes is 10 less than twice the number of nickels. The total value of all the coins is $2.75. Find the number of each type of coin in the bank.   15 nickels, 20 dimes

29. A total of 26 bills are in a cash box. Some of the bills are one-dollar bills, and the rest are five-dollar bills. The total amount of cash in the box is $50. Find the number of each type of bill in the cash box.
20 one-dollar bills, 6 five-dollar bills

30. A bank teller cashed a check for $200 using twenty-dollar bills and ten-dollar bills. In all, twelve bills were handed to the customer. Find the number of twenty-dollar bills and the number of ten-dollar bills.
8 twenty-dollar bills, 4 ten-dollar bills

31. A coin bank contains pennies, nickels, and dimes. There are six times as many nickels as pennies and four times as many dimes as pennies. The total amount of money in the bank is $7.81. Find the number of pennies in the bank.   11 pennies

32. A coin bank contains pennies, nickels, and quarters. There are seven times as many nickels as pennies and three times as many quarters as pennies. The total amount of money in the bank is $5.55. Find the number of pennies in the bank.   5 pennies

33. A collection of stamps consists of 22¢ stamps and 40¢ stamps. The number of 22¢ stamps is three more than four times the number of 40¢ stamps. The total value of the stamps is $8.34. Find the number of 22¢ stamps in the collection.
27 stamps

34. A collection of stamps consists of 2¢ stamps, 8¢ stamps, and 14¢ stamps. The number of 2¢ stamps is five more than twice the number of 8¢ stamps. The number of 14¢ stamps is three times the number of 8¢ stamps. The total value of the stamps is $2.26. Find the number of each type of stamp in the collection.   2¢ stamps: 13; 8¢ stamps: 4; 14¢ stamps: 12

35. A collection of stamps consists of 3¢ stamps, 7¢ stamps, and 12¢ stamps. The number of 3¢ stamps is five less than the number of 7¢ stamps. The number of 12¢ stamps is one-half the number of 7¢ stamps. The total value of all the stamps is $2.73. Find the number of each type of stamp in the collection.
3¢ stamps: 13; 7¢ stamps: 18; 12¢ stamps: 9

36. A collection of stamps consists of 2¢ stamps, 5¢ stamps, and 7¢ stamps. There are nine more 2¢ stamps than 5¢ stamps and twice as many 7¢ stamps as 5¢ stamps. The total value of the stamps is $1.44. Find the number of each type of stamp in the collection.   2¢ stamps: 15; 5¢ stamps: 6; 7¢ stamps: 12

37. A collection of stamps consists of 6¢ stamps, 8¢ stamps, and 15¢ stamps. The number of 6¢ stamps is three times the number of 8¢ stamps. There are six more 15¢ stamps than there are 6¢ stamps. The total value of all the stamps is $5.16. Find the number of each type of stamp.
6¢ stamps: 18; 8¢ stamps: 6; 15¢ stamps: 24

38. A child's piggy bank contains nickels, dimes, and quarters. There are twice as many nickels as dimes and four more quarters than nickels. The total value of all the coins is $9.40. Find the number of each type of coin.
24 nickels, 12 dimes, 28 quarters

APPLYING CONCEPTS 4.2

39. Find four consecutive even integers whose sum is −36.   −12, −10, −8, −6

40. Find four consecutive odd integers whose sum is −48.   −15, −13, −11, −9

41. A coin bank contains only dimes and quarters. The number of quarters in the bank is two less than twice the number of dimes. There are 34 coins in the bank. How much money is in the bank? $6.70

42. A postal clerk sold twenty stamps to a customer. The number of 33¢ stamps purchased was two more than twice the number of 23¢ stamps purchased. If the customer bought only 33¢ stamps and 23¢ stamps, how much money did the clerk collect from the customer? $6.00

[C] **43.** Find three consecutive odd integers such that the sum of the first and third is twice the second.   Any three consecutive odd integers

[C] **44.** Find four consecutive integers such that the sum of the first and fourth equals the sum of the second and third.   Any four consecutive integers

S E C T I O N **4.3**

Geometry Problems

1 Perimeter problems

INSTRUCTOR NOTE

The problems in this section are only some of the geometry problems that can be found throughout the text.

The **perimeter** of a plane geometric figure is a measure of the distance around the figure. Perimeter is used, for example, in buying fencing for a lawn and in determining how much baseboard is needed for a room.

The perimeter of a triangle is the sum of the lengths of the three sides. Therefore, if a, b, and c represent the lengths of the sides of a triangle, the perimeter, P, of the triangle is given by $P = a + b + c$.

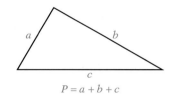

$$P = a + b + c$$

Two special types of triangles are shown below. An **isoceles triangle** has two sides of equal length. The three sides of an **equilateral triangle** are of equal length.

Isosceles triangle
$AC = BC$

Equilateral triangle
$AB = AC = BC$

The perimeter of a rectangle is the sum of the lengths of the four sides. Let L represent the length and W represent the width of a rectangle. Then the perimeter, P, of the rectangle is given by $P = L + W + L + W$. Combine like terms and the formula is $P = 2L + 2W$.

$$P = 2L + 2W$$

A square is a rectangle in which each side has the same length. Let s represent the length of each side of a square. Then the perimeter, P, of the square is given by $P = s + s + s + s$. Combine like terms and the formula is $P = 4s$.

$$P = 4s$$

Formulas for Perimeters of Geometric Figures

Perimeter of a triangle	$P = a + b + c$
Perimeter of a rectangle	$P = 2L + 2W$
Perimeter of a square	$P = 4s$

➡ The perimeter of a rectangle is 26 ft. The length of the rectangle is 1 ft more than twice the width. Find the width and length of the rectangle.

Strategy

Let a variable represent the width.   Width: W
Represent the length in terms of that variable.   Length: $2W + 1$
Use the formula for the perimeter of a rectangle.

Solution

$$P = 2L + 2W$$

$P = 26$. Substitute $2W + 1$ for L. $26 = 2(2W + 1) + 2W$

Use the Distributive Property. $26 = 4W + 2 + 2W$

Combine like terms. $26 = 6W + 2$

Subtract 2 from each side of the equation. $24 = 6W$

Divide each side of the equation by 6. $4 = W$

Find the length of the rectangle by substituting 4 $L = 2W + 1$
for W in $2W + 1$. $\quad = 2(4) + 1 = 8 + 1 = 9$

The width is 4 ft. The length is 9 ft.   ⬅

Example 1   The perimeter of an isosceles triangle is 25 ft. The length of the third side is 2 ft less than the length of one of the equal sides. Find the measures of the three sides of the triangle.

Strategy   ▪ Each equal side: x
The third side: $x - 2$
▪ Use the equation for the perime-
ter of a triangle.

Solution $P = a + b + c$
$25 = x + x + (x - 2)$
$25 = 3x - 2$
$27 = 3x$
$\ 9 = x$

$x - 2 = 9 - 2 = 7$ ▶ Substitute the value of x into the variable expression for the length of the third side.

Each of the equal sides measures 9 ft.
The third side measures 7 ft.

Problem 1   A carpenter is designing a square patio with a perimeter of 52 ft. What is the length of each side?

Solution   See page S7.   13 ft

2 ## Problems involving angles formed by intersecting lines

A unit used to measure angles is the **degree**. The symbol for degree is °. ∠ is the symbol for angle.

One complete revolution is 360°. It is probable that the Babylonians chose 360° for a circle because they knew that there are 365 days in one year, and 360 is the closest number to 365 that is divisible by many numbers.

A 90° angle is called a **right angle.** The symbol ∟ represents a right angle. Angle C (∠C) is a right angle.

A 180° angle is called a **straight angle.** The angle at the right is a straight angle.

An **acute angle** is an angle whose measure is between 0° and 90°. ∠A at the right is an acute angle.

An **obtuse angle** is an angle whose measure is between 90° and 180°. ∠B at the right is an obtuse angle.

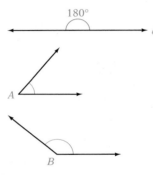

➡ Given the diagram at the left, find x.

> **Strategy**   The sum of the measures of the three angles is 360°. To find x, write an equation and solve for x.
>
> **Solution** $3x + 4x + 5x = 360°$
> $12x = 360°$
> $x = 30°$
>
> The measure of x is 30°.

Complementary angles are two angles whose measures have the sum 90°.

$∠D + ∠E = 70° + 20° = 90°$

∠D and ∠E are complementary angles.

Supplementary angles are two angles whose measures have the sum 180°.

$∠F + ∠G = 130° + 50° = 180°$

∠F and ∠G are supplementary angles.

┌ **Example 2**   Find the complement of a 39° angle.

> **Strategy**   To find the complement, let x represent the complement of a 39° angle. Use the fact that complementary angles are two angles whose sum is 90° to write an equation. Solve for x.

Solution $39° + x = 90°$

$x = 51°$ ▶ Subtract 39 from each side of the equation.

The complement of a 39° angle is a 51° angle.

Problem 2   Find the supplement of a 107° angle.

Solution   See page S8.   73°

Parallel lines never meet. The distance between them is always the same. The symbol ∥ means "is parallel to." In the figure at the right, $\ell_1 \parallel \ell_2$.

Perpendicular lines are intersecting lines that form right angles. The symbol ⊥ means "is perpendicular to." In the figure at the right, $p \perp q$.

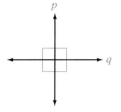

Four angles are formed by the intersection of two lines. If the two lines are perpendicular, then each of the four angles is a right angle. If the two lines are not perpendicular, then two of the angles formed are acute angles and two of the angles are obtuse angles. The two acute angles are always opposite each other, and the two obtuse angles are always opposite each other.

In the figure at the right, ∠w and ∠y are acute angles, and ∠x and ∠z are obtuse angles.

Two angles that are on opposite sides of the intersection of two lines are called **vertical angles.** Vertical angles have the same measure. ∠w and ∠y are vertical angles. ∠x and ∠z are vertical angles.

Vertical angles have the same measure.

$$\angle w = \angle y$$
$$\angle x = \angle z$$

Two angles that share a common side are called **adjacent angles.** For the figure shown above, ∠x and ∠y are adjacent angles, as are ∠y and ∠z, ∠z and ∠w, and ∠w and ∠x. Adjacent angles of intersecting lines are supplementary angles.

Adjacent angles of intersecting lines are supplementary angles.

$$\angle x + \angle y = 180°$$
$$\angle y + \angle z = 180°$$
$$\angle z + \angle w = 180°$$
$$\angle w + \angle x = 180°$$

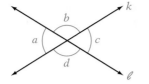

➡ In the diagram at the left, $\angle b = 115°$. Find the measures of angles a, c, and d.

$\angle a$ is supplementary to $\angle b$ because $\angle a$ and $\angle b$ are adjacent angles of intersecting lines.

$$\angle a + \angle b = 180°$$
$$\angle a + 115° = 180°$$
$$\angle a = 65°$$

$\angle c = \angle a$ because $\angle c$ and $\angle a$ are vertical angles.
$\angle d = \angle b$ because $\angle d$ and $\angle b$ are vertical angles.

$$\angle c = 65°$$
$$\angle d = 115°$$ ⬅

Example 3 Find x.

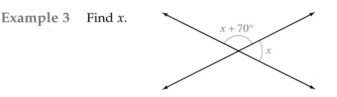

Strategy The angles labeled are adjacent angles of intersecting lines and are therefore supplementary angles. To find x, write an equation and solve for x.

Solution
$$x + (x + 70°) = 180°$$
$$2x + 70° = 180°$$
$$2x = 110°$$
$$x = 55°$$

Problem 3 Find x.

Solution See page S8. $40°$

A line that intersects two other lines at different points is called a **transversal**. If the lines cut by a transversal t are parallel lines and the transversal is not perpendicular to the parallel lines, all four acute angles have the same measure and all four obtuse angles have the same measure. In the figure at the right,

$$\angle b = \angle d = \angle x = \angle z$$
$$\angle a = \angle c = \angle w = \angle y$$

Alternate interior angles are two angles that are on opposite sides of the transversal and between the lines. In the figure above, $\angle c$ and $\angle w$ are alternate interior angles, and $\angle d$ and $\angle x$ are alternate interior angles. Alternate interior angles have the same measure.

Alternate interior angles have the same measure.

$$\angle c = \angle w$$
$$\angle d = \angle x$$

Alternate exterior angles are two angles that are on opposite sides of the transversal and outside the parallel lines. In the figure at the left, $\angle a$ and $\angle y$ are alternate exterior angles, and $\angle b$ and $\angle z$ are alternate exterior angles. Alternate exterior angles have the same measure.

Alternate exterior angles have the same measure.

$$\angle a = \angle y$$
$$\angle b = \angle z$$

INSTRUCTOR NOTE

These concepts will be used in the discussion of similar triangles presented in the section Equations Containing Fractions in the Algebraic Fractions chapter.

Corresponding angles are two angles that are on the same side of the transversal and are both acute angles or are both obtuse angles. In the figure above, the following pairs of angles are corresponding angles: $\angle a$ and $\angle w$, $\angle d$ and $\angle z$, $\angle b$ and $\angle x$, and $\angle c$ and $\angle y$. Corresponding angles have the same measure.

Corresponding angles have the same measure.

$$\angle a = \angle w$$
$$\angle d = \angle z$$
$$\angle b = \angle x$$
$$\angle c = \angle y$$

➡ In the diagram at the left, $\ell_1 \parallel \ell_2$ and $\angle f = 58°$. Find the measures of $\angle a$, $\angle c$, and $\angle d$.

$\angle a$ and $\angle f$ are corresponding angles. $\angle a = \angle f = 58°$

$\angle c$ and $\angle f$ are alternate interior angles. $\angle c = \angle f = 58°$

$\angle d$ is supplementary to $\angle a$. $\angle d + \angle a = 180°$
$$\angle d + 58° = 180°$$
$$\angle d = 122°$$

Example 4   Given $l_1 \parallel l_2$, find x.

Strategy $3x = y$ because corresponding angles have the same measure.
$y + (x + 40°) = 180°$ because adjacent angles of intersecting lines are supplementary angles.

Substitute $3x$ for y and solve for x.

Solution $$y + (x + 40°) = 180°$$
$$3x + (x + 40°) = 180°$$
$$4x + 40° = 180°$$
$$4x = 140°$$
$$x = 35°$$

Problem 4   Given $l_1 \parallel l_2$, find x.

Solution   See page S8.   55°

3 Problems involving the angles of a triangle

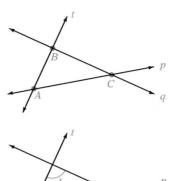

If the lines cut by a transversal are not parallel lines, the three lines will intersect at three points. In the figure at the right, the transversal t intersects lines p and q. The three lines intersect at points A, B, and C. The geometric figure formed by AB, BC, and AC is a **triangle**.

The angles within the region enclosed by the triangle are called **interior angles.** In the figure at the right, angles a, b, and c are interior angles. The sum of the measures of the interior angles is 180°.

$$\angle a + \angle b + \angle c = 180°$$

The Sum of the Measures of the Interior Angles of a Triangle

> The sum of the measures of the interior angles of a triangle is 180°.

An angle adjacent to an interior angle is an **exterior angle.** In the figure at the right, angles m and n are exterior angles for angle a. The sum of the measures of an interior and an exterior angle is 180°.

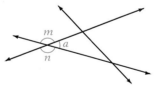

$$\angle a + \angle m = 180°$$
$$\angle a + \angle n = 180°$$

➡ Given that $\angle c = 40°$ and $\angle e = 60°$, find the measure of $\angle d$.

$\angle a$ and $\angle e$ are vertical angles.

The sum of the interior angles is 180°.

$$\angle a = \angle e = 60°$$
$$\angle c + \angle a + \angle b = 180°$$
$$40° + 60° + \angle b = 180°$$
$$100° + \angle b = 180°$$
$$\angle b = 80°$$

$\angle b$ and $\angle d$ are supplementary angles.

$$\angle b + \angle d = 180°$$
$$80° + \angle d = 180°$$
$$\angle d = 100°$$

Example 5   Given that $\angle a = 45°$ and $\angle x = 100°$, find the measures of angles b, c, and y.

Strategy   ▪ To find the measure of $\angle b$, use the fact that $\angle b$ and $\angle x$ are supplementary angles.
▪ To find the measure of $\angle c$, use the fact that the sum of the measures of the interior angles of a triangle is 180°.
▪ To find the measure of $\angle y$, use the fact that $\angle c$ and $\angle y$ are vertical angles.

Solution $$\angle b + \angle x = 180°$$
$$\angle b + 100° = 180°$$
$$\angle b = 80°$$

$$\angle a + \angle b + \angle c = 180°$$
$$45° + 80° + \angle c = 180°$$
$$125° + \angle c = 180°$$
$$\angle c = 55°$$

$$\angle y = \angle c = 55°$$

Problem 5   Given that $\angle y = 55°$, find the measures of angles a, b, and d.

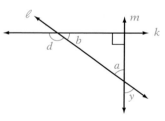

Solution   See page S8. $\angle a = 55°$, $\angle b = 35°$, $\angle d = 145°$

Example 6   Two angles of a triangle measure 43° and 86°. Find the measure of the third angle.

Strategy   To find the measure of the third angle, use the fact that the sum of the measures of the interior angles of a triangle is 180°. Write an equation using x to represent the measure of the third angle. Solve the equation for x.

Solution $$x + 43° + 86° = 180°$$
$$x + 129° = 180°$$
$$x = 51°$$

The measure of the third angle is 51°.

Problem 6   One angle of a triangle is a right angle, and one angle measures 27°. Find the measure of the third angle.

Solution   See page S8.   63°

CONCEPT REVIEW 4.3

Determine whether the statement is always true, sometimes true, or never true.

1. The formula for the perimeter of a rectangle is $P = 2L + 2W$, where L represents the length and W represents the width of a rectangle.   Always true

2. In the formula for the perimeter of a triangle, $P = a + b + c$, the variables a, b, and c represent the measures of the three angles of a triangle.   Never true

3. If two angles of a triangle measure 52° and 73°, then the third angle of the triangle measures 55°.   Always true

4. An isosceles triangle has two sides of equal measure and two angles of equal measure.   Always true

5. The perimeter of a geometric figure is a measure of the area of the figure.   Never true

6. In a right triangle, the sum of the measures of the two acute angles is 90°.   Always true

EXERCISES 4.3

1 Geometry Problems

1. In an isosceles triangle, the third side is 50% of the length of one of the equal sides. Find the length of each side when the perimeter is 125 ft.   50 ft, 50 ft, 25 ft

2. In an isosceles triangle, the length of one of the equal sides is 3 times the length of the third side. The perimeter is 21 m. Find the length of each side.   9 m, 9 m, 3 m

3. The perimeter of a rectangle is 42 m. The length of the rectangle is 3 m less than twice the width. Find the length and width of the rectangle.   length: 13 m; width: 8 m

4. The width of a rectangle is 25% of the length. The perimeter is 250 cm. Find the length and width of the rectangle.   length: 100 cm; width: 25 cm

5. The perimeter of a rectangle is 120 ft. The length of the rectangle is twice the width. Find the length and width of the rectangle.   length: 40 ft; width: 20 ft

6. The perimeter of a rectangle is 50 m. The width of the rectangle is 5 m less than the length. Find the length and width of the rectangle.

    length: 15 m; width: 10 m

7. The perimeter of a triangle is 110 cm. One side is twice the second side. The third side is 30 cm more than the second side. Find the length of each side.

    40 cm, 20 cm, 50 cm

8. The perimeter of a triangle is 33 ft. One side of the triangle is 1 ft longer than the second side. The third side is 2 ft longer than the second side. Find the length of each side.   11 ft, 10 ft, 12 ft

9. The width of the rectangular foundation of a building is 30% of the length. The perimeter of the foundation is 338 ft. Find the length and width of the foundation.   length: 130 ft; width: 39 ft

10. The perimeter of a rectangular playground is 440 ft. If the width is 100 ft, what is the length of the playground?   120 ft

11. A rectangular vegetable garden has a perimeter of 64 ft. The length of the garden is 20 ft. What is the width of the garden?   12 ft

12. Each of two sides of a triangular banner measures 18 in. If the perimeter of the banner is 46 in., what is the length of the third side of the banner?   10 in.

13. The perimeter of a square picture frame is 48 in. Find the length of each side of the frame.   12 in.

14. A square rug has a perimeter of 32 ft. Find the length of each side of the rug.   8 ft

2 Geometry Problems

15. Find the complement of a 28° angle.   62°

16. Find the complement of a 46° angle.   44°

17. Find the supplement of a 73° angle.   107°

18. Find the supplement of a 119° angle.   61°

Find the measure of $\angle x$.

19. $x + 20°$ x 35°

20. x $2x - 18°$ 36°

21. x $3x + 10°$ 20°

Find the measure of ∠*a*.

22.

127°

23.

53°

24.

116°

25.

121°

Find *x*.

26.

20°

27.

15°

28.

20°

29.

18°

30.

20°

31.

45°

Find the measure of ∠*x*.

32.

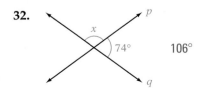

106°

33.

49°

Find x.

34.

11°

35.
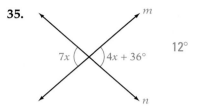

12°

Given that $\ell_1 \parallel \ell_2$, find the measures of angles a and b.

36.

$\angle a = 38°$,
$\angle b = 142°$

37.

$\angle a = 122°$,
$\angle b = 58°$

38.
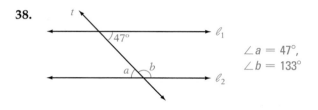

$\angle a = 47°$,
$\angle b = 133°$

39.

$\angle a = 44°$,
$\angle b = 136°$

Given that $\ell_1 \parallel \ell_2$, find x.

40.

20°

41.

20°

42.

47°

43.
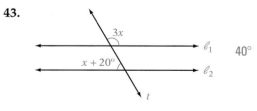

40°

44.   Given that $\angle a = 51°$, find the measure of $\angle b$.

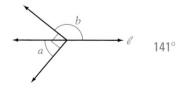

141°

45. Given that $\angle a = 38°$, find the measure of $\angle b$.

128°

3 Geometry Problems

46. Given that $\angle a = 95°$ and $\angle b = 70°$, find the measures of angles x and y.
$\angle x = 155°, \angle y = 70°$

47. Given that $\angle a = 35°$ and $\angle b = 55°$, find the measures of angles x and y.
$\angle x = 160°, \angle y = 145°$

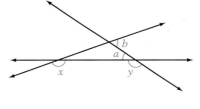

48. Given that $\angle y = 45°$, find the measures of angles a and b.
$\angle a = 45°, \angle b = 135°$

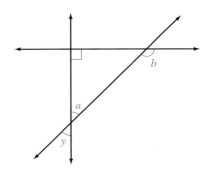

49. Given that $\angle y = 130°$, find the measures of angles a and b.
$\angle a = 40°, \angle b = 140°$

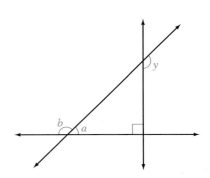

50. Given that $AO \perp OB$, express in terms of x the number of degrees in $\angle BOC$.
        $90° - x$

51. Given that $AO \perp OB$, express in terms of x the number of degrees in $\angle AOC$.
        $75° - x$

52. One angle in a triangle is a right angle, and one angle measures 30°. What is the measure of the third angle?   60°

53. A triangle has a 45° angle and a right angle. Find the measure of the third angle.   45°

54. Two angles of a triangle measure 42° and 103°. Find the measure of the third angle.   35°

55. Two angles of a triangle measure 62° and 45°. Find the measure of the third angle.   73°

56. A triangle has a 13° angle and a 65° angle. What is the measure of the third angle?   102°

57. A triangle has a 105° angle and a 32° angle. What is the measure of the third angle?   43°

58. In an isosceles triangle, one angle is three times the measure of one of the equal angles. Find the measure of each angle.   36°, 36°, and 108°

59. In an isosceles triangle, one angle is 10° less than three times the measure of one of the equal angles. Find the measure of each angle.   38°, 38°, and 104°

60. In an isosceles triangle, one angle is 16° more than twice the measure of one of the equal angles. Find the measure of each angle.   41°, 41°, and 98°

61. In a triangle, one angle is twice the measure of the second angle. The third angle is three times the measure of the second angle. Find the measure of each angle.   60°, 30°, and 90°

APPLYING CONCEPTS 4.3

62. A rectangle and an equilateral triangle have the same perimeter. The length of the rectangle is three times the width. Each side of the triangle is 8 cm. Find the length and width of the rectangle.   length: 9 cm; width: 3 cm

63. The length of a rectangle is 1 cm more than twice the width. If the length of the rectangle is decreased by 2 cm and the width is decreased by 1 cm, the perimeter is 20 cm. Find the length and width of the original rectangle.
length: 9 cm; width: 4 cm

64. For the figure at the right, find the sum of the measures of angles x, y, and z.
360°

65. ✒ For the figure at the right, explain why $\angle a + \angle b = \angle x$. Write a rule that describes the relationship between an exterior angle of a triangle and the opposite interior angles. Use the rule to write an equation involving angles a, c, and z.

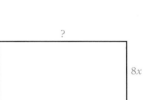

[C] 66. The width of a rectangle is $8x$. The perimeter is $48x$. Find the length of the rectangle in terms of the variable x. $16x$

67. ✒ Discuss the concepts of accuracy and precision.

68. ✒ Write a report stating the arguments of the proponents of changing to the metric system in the United States or a report stating the arguments of those opposed to switching from the U.S. Customary System of measurement to the metric system.

69. ✒ Prepare a report on the use of geometric form in architecture.

S E C T I O N 4.4
Markup and Discount Problems

1 Markup problems

Cost is the price that a business pays for a product. **Selling price** is the price for which a business sells a product to a customer. The difference between selling price and cost is called **markup**. Markup is added to a retailer's cost to cover the expenses of operating a business. Markup is usually expressed as a percent of the retailer's cost. This percent is called the **markup rate.**

The basic markup equations used by a business are

$$\text{Selling price} = \text{Cost} + \text{Markup}$$
$$S \quad = \quad C \; + \quad M$$
$$\text{Markup} = \text{Markup rate} \cdot \text{Cost}$$
$$M \quad = \quad r \quad \cdot \quad C$$

By substituting $r \cdot C$ for M in the first equation, we can also write selling price as

$$S = C + M$$
$$S = C + (r \cdot C)$$
$$S = C + rC$$

The equation $S = C + rC$ is the equation used to solve the markup problems in this section.

Example 1   The manager of a clothing store buys a suit for $90 and sells the suit for $126. Find the markup rate.

Strategy   Given: $C = \$90$
$ S = \$126$
Unknown markup rate: r
Use the equation $S = C + rC$.

Solution

$$S = C + rC$$
$$126 = 90 + 90r \quad \blacktriangleright \text{ Substitute the values of } C \text{ and } S \text{ into the equation.}$$

$$126 - 90 = 90 - 90 + 90r \quad \blacktriangleright \text{ Subtract 90 from each side of the equation.}$$
$$36 = 90r$$

$$\frac{36}{90} = \frac{90r}{90} \quad \blacktriangleright \text{ Divide each side of the equation by 90.}$$

$$0.4 = r \quad \blacktriangleright \text{ The decimal must be changed to a percent.}$$

The markup rate is 40%.

Problem 1   The cost to the manager of a sporting goods store for a tennis racket is $60. The selling price of the racket is $90. Find the markup rate.

Solution   See page S8.   50%

Example 2   The manager of a furniture store uses a markup rate of 45% on all items. The selling price of a chair is $232. Find the cost of the chair.

Strategy   Given: $r = 45\% = 0.45$
$ S = \$232$

Unknown cost: C
Use the equation $S = C + rC$.

Solution $S = C + rC$
$232 = C + 0.45C$
$232 = 1.45C \quad \blacktriangleright C + 0.45C = 1C + 0.45C = (1 + 0.45)C$
$160 = C$

The cost of the chair is $160.

Problem 2   A hardware store employee uses a markup rate of 40% on all items. The selling price of a lawnmower is $133. Find the cost.

Solution   See page S8. $95

2   Discount problems

Discount is the amount by which a retailer reduces the regular price of a product for a promotional sale. Discount is usually expressed as a percent of the regular price. This percent is called the **discount rate.**

The basic discount equations used by a business are

$$\text{Sale price} = \text{Regular price} - \text{Discount}$$
$$S = R - D$$

$$\text{Discount} = \text{Discount rate} \cdot \text{Regular price}$$
$$D = r \cdot R$$

By substituting $r \cdot R$ for D in the first equation, we can also write sale price as

$$S = R - D$$
$$S = R - (r \cdot R)$$
$$S = R - rR$$

The equation $S = R - rR$ is the equation used to solve the discount problems in this section.

Example 3   In a garden supply store, the regular price of a 100-foot garden hose is $48. During an "after-summer sale," the hose is being sold for $36. Find the discount rate.

Strategy   Given: $R = \$48$
$S = \$36$
Unknown discount rate: r
Use the equation $S = R - rR$.

Solution

$$S = R - rR$$
$$36 = 48 - 48r$$ ▶ Substitute the values of R and S into the equation.

$$36 - 48 = 48 - 48 - 48r$$ ▶ Subtract 48 from each side of the equation.
$$-12 = -48r$$

$$\frac{-12}{-48} = \frac{-48r}{-48}$$ ▶ Divide each side of the equation by -48.

$$0.25 = r$$ ▶ The decimal must be changed to a percent.

The discount rate is 25%.

Problem 3   A case of motor oil that regularly sells for $29.80 is on sale for $22.35. What is the discount rate?

Solution   See page S8.   25%

Example 4 The sale price for a chemical sprayer is $27.30. This price is 35% off the regular price. Find the regular price.

Strategy Given: $S = \$27.30$
$$r = 35\% = 0.35$$
Unknown regular price: R
Use the equation $S = R - rR$.

Solution $S = R - rR$
$27.30 = R - 0.35R$
$27.30 = 0.65R$ ▶ $R - 0.35R = 1R - 0.35R = (1 - 0.35)R$
$42 = R$

The regular price is $42.00.

Problem 4 The sale price for a telephone is $43.50. This price is 25% off the regular price. Find the regular price.

Solution See page S9. $58

CONCEPT REVIEW 4.4

Determine whether the statement is always true, sometimes true, or never true.

1. In the markup equation $S = C + rC$, the variable r represents the markup rate.
    Always true
2. Markup is an amount of money, whereas markup rate is a percent.
    Always true
3. In the discount equation $S = R - rR$, the variable R represents the discount rate.   Never true

4. In the markup equation, S represents sale price, and in the discount equation, S represents selling price.   Never true

5. $R - 0.45R = 1R - 0.45R = (1 - 0.45)R = 0.55R$ is an example of the application of the Distributive Property.   Always true

---

EXERCISES 4.4

1 Markup Problems

1. ⫽ Explain the difference between the cost and the selling price of a product.

2. ⫽ What is the difference between markup and markup rate?

3. A computer software retailer uses a markup rate of 40%. Find the selling price of a computer game that costs the retailer $40. $56

4. A car dealer advertises a 5% markup over cost. Find the selling price of a car that costs the dealer $16,000. $16,800

5. An electronics store uses a markup rate of 58%. Find the selling price of a camcorder that costs the store owner $358. $565.64

6. The cost to a landscape architect for a 25-gallon tree is $65. Find the selling price of the tree if the markup rate used by the architect is 30%. $84.50

7. A set of golf clubs costing $360 is sold for $630. Find the markup rate on the set of golf clubs.   75%

8. A jeweler purchases a diamond ring for $2399.50. The selling price is $4799. Find the markup rate.   100%

9. A freezer costing $360 is sold for $520. Find the markup rate. Round to the nearest tenth of a percent.   44.4%

10. A grocer purchases a can of fruit juice for $.92. The selling price of the fruit juice is $1.15. Find the markup rate.   25%

11. A watch costing $98 is sold for $156.80. Find the markup rate on the watch.   60%

12. A sofa costing $320 is sold for $479. Find the markup rate. Round to the nearest tenth of a percent.   49.7%

13. The selling price for a compact disc player is $168. The markup rate used by the seller is 40%. Find the cost of the compact disc player. $120

14. A manufacturer of exercise equipment uses a markup rate of 45%. One of the manufacturer's treadmills has a selling price of $580. Find the cost of the treadmill. $400

15. A markup rate of 40% was used on a basketball with a selling price of $82.60. Find the cost of the basketball. $59

16. A digitally recorded compact disc has a selling price of $11.90. The markup rate is 40%. Find the cost of the CD. $8.50

17. A markup rate of 25% is used on a computer that has a selling price of $2187.50. Find the cost of the computer. $1750

18. The selling price of a portable CD player is $132. The markup rate used by the retailer is 60%. Find the cost to the retailer. $82.50

2 Discount Problems

19. Explain the meaning of sale price and discount.

20. Explain the difference between discount and discount rate.

21. A tennis racket that regularly sells for $95 is on sale for 25% off the regular price. Find the sale price. $71.25

22. A fax machine that regularly sells for $219.99 is on sale for $33\frac{1}{3}$% off the regular price. Find the sale price. $146.66

23. A supplier of electrical equipment offers a 5% discount for a purchase that is paid for within 30 days. A transformer regularly sells for $230. Find the discount price of a transformer that is paid for 10 days after the purchase. $218.50

24. A clothing wholesaler offers a discount of 10% per shirt when 10 to 20 shirts are purchased and a discount of 15% per shirt when 21 to 50 shirts are purchased. A shirt regularly sells for $27. Find the sale price per shirt when 35 shirts are purchased. $22.95

25. A car stereo system that regularly sells for $425 is on sale for $318.75. Find the discount rate.   25%

26. A pair of roller blades that regularly sells for $99.99 is on sale for $79.99. Find the discount rate. Round to the nearest percent.   20%

27. An oak bedroom set with a regular price of $1295 is on sale for $995. Find the discount rate. Round to the nearest tenth of a percent.   23.2%

28. A stereo set with a regular price of $495 is on sale for $395. Find the markdown rate. Round to the nearest tenth of a percent.   20.2%

29. A compact disc player with a regular price of $325 is on sale for $201.50. Find the markdown rate.   38%

30. A luggage set with a regular price of $178 is on sale for $103.24. Find the discount rate.   42%

31. The sale price of a free-weight home gym is $248, which is 20% off the regular price. Find the regular price. $310

32. The sale price of a toboggan is $77, which is 30% off the regular price. Find the regular price. $110

33. A mechanic's tool set is on sale for $180 after a markdown of 40% off the regular price. Find the regular price. $300

34. The sale price of a 56K modem is $126, which is 30% off the regular price. Find the regular price. $180

35. A telescope is on sale for $165 after a markdown of 40% off the regular price. Find the regular price. $275

36. An exercise bike is on sale for $390, having been marked down 25% of the regular price. Find the regular price. $520

APPLYING CONCEPTS 4.4

37. A pair of shoes that now sells for $63 has been marked up 40%. Find the markup on the pair of shoes. $18

38. The sale price of a typewriter is 25% off the regular price. The discount is $70. Find the sale price. $210

39. A refrigerator selling for $770 has a markup of $220. Find the markup rate. 40%

40. The sale price of a word processor is $765 after a discount of $135. Find the discount rate.   15%

41. The manager of a camera store uses a markup rate of 30%. Find the cost of a camera selling for $299. $230

[C] **42.** The sale price of a television was $180. Find the regular price if the sale price was computed by taking $\frac{1}{3}$ off the regular price followed by an additional 25% discount on the reduced price. $360

[C] **43.** A customer buys four tires, three at the regular price and one for 20% off the regular price. The four tires cost $304. What was the regular price of a tire? $80

[C] **44.** A lamp, originally priced at under $100, was on sale for 25% off the regular price. When the regular price, a whole number of dollars, was discounted, the discounted price was also a whole number of dollars. Find the largest possible number of dollars in the regular price of the lamp. $96

[C] **45.** A used car is on sale for a discount of 20% off the regular price of $5500. An additional 10% discount on the sale price was offered. Is the result a 30% discount? What is the single discount that would give the same sale price? No; 28%

46. Write a report on series trade discounts. Explain how to convert a series discount to a single-discount equivalent.

S E C T I O N **4.5**

Investment Problems

1 Investment problems

The annual simple interest that an investment earns is given by the equation $I = Pr$, where I is the simple interest, P is the principal, or the amount invested, and r is the simple interest rate.

The annual simple interest rate on a $4500 investment is 8%. Find the annual simple interest earned on the investment.

Given: $P = \$4500$ $I = Pr$
        $r = 8\% = 0.08$ $I = 4500(0.08)$
Unknown interest: I $I = 360$

The annual simple interest is $360.

Solve: An investor has a total of $10,000 to deposit into two simple interest accounts. On one account, the annual simple interest rate is 7%. On the second account, the annual simple interest rate is 8%. How much should be invested in each account so that the total annual interest earned is $785?

***STRATEGY** for solving a problem involving money deposited in two simple interest accounts*

■ For each amount invested, use the equation $Pr = I$. Write a numerical or variable expression for the principal, the interest rate, and the interest earned. The results can be recorded in a table.

The sum of the amounts invested is $10,000.

Amount invested at 7%: x
Amount invested at 8%: $\$10,000 - x$

	Principal, P	·	Interest rate, r	=	Interest earned, I
Amount at 7%	x	·	0.07	=	$0.07x$
Amount at 8%	$10,000 - x$	·	0.08	=	$0.08(10,000 - x)$

■ Determine how the amounts of interest earned on the individual investments are related. For example, the total interest earned by both accounts may be known, or it may be known that the interest earned on one account is equal to the interest earned on the other account.

The sum of the interest earned by the two investments equals the total annual interest earned ($785).

$0.07x + 0.08(10,000 - x) = 785$ ▶ The interest earned on the 7% account plus
$0.07x + 800 - 0.08x = 785$ the interest earned on the 8% account equals
$-0.01x + 800 = 785$ the total annual interest earned.
$-0.01x = -15$
$x = 1500$

$10,000 - x = 10,000 - 1500 = 8500$ ▶ Substitute the value of x into the variable expression for the amount invested at 8%.

The amount invested at 7% is $1500.
The amount invested at 8% is $8500.

Example 1   An investment counselor invested 75% of a client's money into a 9% annual simple interest money market fund. The remainder was invested in 6% annual simple interest government securities. Find the amount invested in each if the total annual interest earned is $3300.

Strategy   ▪ Amount invested: x
Amount invested at 9%: $0.75x$
Amount invested at 6%: $0.25x$

	Principal	·	Rate	=	Interest
Amount at 9%	0.75x	·	0.09	=	0.09(0.75x)
Amount at 6%	0.25x	·	0.06	=	0.06(0.25x)

▪ The sum of the interest earned by the two investments equals the total annual interest earned ($3300).

Solution $0.09(0.75x) + 0.06(0.25x) = 3300$ ▸ The interest earned on the
$0.0675x + 0.015x = 3300$ 9% account plus the interest
$0.0825x = 3300$ earned on the 6% account
equals the total annual inter-
est earned.

$x = 40,000$ ▸ The amount invested is
$40,000.

$0.75x = 0.75(40,000) = 30,000$ ▸ Find the amount invested
at 9%.

$0.25x = 0.25(40,000) = 10,000$ ▸ Find the amount invested
at 6%.

The amount invested at 9% is $30,000.
The amount invested at 6% is $10,000.

Problem 1   An investment of $2500 is made at an annual simple interest rate of 7%. How much additional money must be invested at 10% so that the total interest earned will be 9% of the total investment?

Solution   See page S9. $5000

CONCEPT REVIEW 4.5

Determine whether the statement is always true, sometimes true, or never true.

1. In the simple interest formula $I = Pr$, the variable I represents the simple interest earned.   Always true

2. For one year, you have $1000 deposited in an account that pays 5% annual simple interest. You will earn exactly $5 in simple interest on this account.   Never true

3. For one year, you have x dollars deposited in an account that pays 7% annual simple interest. You will earn $0.07x$ in simple interest on this account.   Always true

4. If you have a total of $8000 deposited in two accounts and you represent the amount you have in the first account as x, then the amount in the second account is represented as $8000 - x$.   Always true

5. The amount of interest earned on one account is $0.05x$ and the amount of interest earned on a second account is $0.08(9000 - x)$. If the two accounts earn the same amount of interest, then we can write the equation $0.05x + 0.08(9000 - x)$.   Never true

6. If the amount of interest earned on one account is $0.06x$ and the amount of interest earned on a second account is $0.09(4000 - x)$, then the total interest earned on the two accounts can be represented as $0.06x + 0.09(4000 - x)$.
   Always true

EXERCISES 4.5

1 Investment Problems

1. A dentist invested a portion of $15,000 in a 7% annual simple interest account and the remainder in a 6.5% annual simple interest government bond. The two investments earn $1020 in interest annually. How much was invested in each account? $9000 at 7%; $6000 at 6.5%

2. A university alumni association invested part of $20,000 in preferred stock that earns 8% annual simple interest and the remainder in a municipal bond that earns 7% annual simple interest. The amount of interest earned each year is $1520. How much was invested in each account?
   $12,000 at 8%; $8000 at 7%

3. A professional athlete deposited an amount of money into a high-yield mutual fund that earns 13% annual simple interest. A second deposit, $2500 more than the first, was placed in a certificate of deposit earning 7% annual simple interest. In one year, the total interest earned on both investments was $475. How much money was invested in the mutual fund? $1500

4. Jan Moser made a deposit into a 7% annual simple interest account. She made another deposit, $1500 less than the first, in a certificate of deposit earning 9% annual simple interest. The total interest earned on both investments for one year was $505. How much money was deposited in the certificate of deposit? $2500

5. A team of cancer research specialists received a grant of $300,000 to be used for cancer research. They deposited some of the money in a 10% simple interest account and the remainder in an 8.5% annual simple interest account. How much was deposited in each account if the annual interest is $28,500?
   $200,000 at 10%; $100,000 at 8.5%

6. Reggie Means invested part of $30,000 in municipal bonds that earn 6.5% annual simple interest and the remainder of the money in 8.5% corporate bonds. How much is invested in each account if the total annual interest earned is $2190? $18,000 at 6.5%; $12,000 at 8.5%

7. To provide for retirement income, Teresa Puelo purchases a $5000 bond that earns 7.5% annual simple interest. How much money does Teresa have invested in bonds that earn 8% annual simple interest if the total annual interest earned from the two investments is $615? $3000

8. After the sale of some income property, Jeremy Littlefield invested $40,000 in a certificate of deposit that earns 7.25% annual simple interest. How much money does he have invested in certificates that earn an annual simple interest rate of 8.5% if the total annual interest earned from the two investments is $5025? $25,000

9. Suki Hiroshi has made an investment of $2500 at an annual simple interest rate of 7%. How much money does she have invested at an annual simple interest rate of 11% if the total interest earned is 9% of the total investment?
    $2500

10. Mae Jackson has a total of $6000 invested into two simple interest accounts. The annual simple interest rate on one account is 9%. The annual simple interest rate on the second account is 6%. How much is invested in each account if both accounts earn the same amount of interest?
    $3600 at 6%; $2400 at 9%

11. A charity deposited a total of $54,000 into two simple interest accounts. The annual simple interest rate on one account is 8%. The annual simple interest rate on the second account is 12%. How much was invested in each account if the total annual interest earned is 9% of the total investment?
    $40,500 at 8%; $13,500 at 12%

12. A sports foundation deposited a total of $24,000 into two simple interest accounts. The annual simple interest rate on one account is 7%. The annual simple interest rate on the second account is 11%. How much is invested in each account if the total annual interest earned is 10% of the total investment? $6000 at 7%; $18,000 at 11%

13. Wayne Miller, an investment banker, invested 55% of the bank's available cash in an account that earns 8.25% annual simple interest. The remainder of the cash was placed in an account that earns 10% annual simple interest. The interest earned in one year was $58,743.75. Find the total amount invested.
    $650,000

14. Mohammad Aran, a financial planner, recommended that 40% of a client's cash account be invested in preferred stock earning 9% annual simple interest. The remainder of the client's cash was placed in Treasury bonds earning 7% annual simple interest. The total annual interest earned from the two investments was $2496. Find the total amount invested. $32,000

15. Sarah Ontkean is the manager of a mutual fund. She placed 30% of the fund's available cash in a 6% annual simple interest account, 25% in 8% corporate bonds, and the remainder in a money market fund earning 7.5% annual simple interest. The total annual interest earned from the investments was $35,875. Find the total amount invested. $500,000

16. Joseph Abruzzio is the manager of a trust. He invested 30% of a client's cash in government bonds that earn 6.5% annual simple interest, 30% in utility stocks that earn 7% annual simple interest, and the remainder in an account that earns 8% annual simple interest. The total annual interest earned from the investments was $5437.50. Find the total amount invested. $75,000

APPLYING CONCEPTS 4.5

17. A sales representative invests in a stock paying 9% dividends. A research consultant invests $5000 more than the sales representative in bonds paying 8% annual simple interest. The research consultant's income from the investment is equal to the sales representative's. Find the amount of the research consultant's investment. $45,000

18. A financial manager invested 20% of a client's money in bonds paying 9% annual simple interest, 35% in an 8% simple interest account, and the remainder in 9.5% corporate bonds. Find the amount invested in each if the total annual interest earned is $5325. $12,000 at 9%; $21,000 at 8%; $27,000 at 9.5%

19. A plant manager invested $3000 more in stocks than in bonds. The stocks paid 8% annual simple interest, and the bonds paid 9.5% annual simple interest. Both investments yielded the same income. Find the total annual interest received on both investments. $3040

[C] **20.** A bank offers a customer a 2-year certificate of deposit (CD) that earns 8% compound annual interest. This means that the interest earned each year is added to the principal before the interest for the next year is calculated. Find the value in 2 years of a nurse's investment of $2500 in this CD. $2916

[C] **21.** A bank offers a customer a 3-year certificate of deposit (CD) that earns 8.5% compound annual interest. This means that the interest earned each year is added to the principal before the interest for the next year is calculated. Find the value in 3 years of an accountant's investment of $3000 in this CD.

$3831.87

22.   Write an essay on the topic of annual percentage rates.

23.   Financial advisors may predict how much money we should have saved for retirement by the ages of 35, 45, 55, and 65. One such prediction is included in the table below.

   a. According to the estimates in the table, how much should a couple who have earnings of $75,000 have saved for retirement by age 55? $170,000

   b. Write an explanation of how interest and interest rates affect the level of savings required at any given age. What effect do inflation rates have on savings?

Minimum Levels of Savings Required for Married Couples to Be Prepared for Retirement			
Savings Accumulation by Age			
35	45	55	65
Earnings = $50,000			
8,000	23,000	90,000	170,000
Earnings = $75,000			
17,000	60,000	170,000	310,000
Earnings = $100,000			
34,000	110,000	280,000	480,000
Earnings = $150,000			
67,000	210,000	490,000	840,000

SECTION **4.6**

Mixture Problems

1   Value mixture problems   [12] HM³

A value mixture problem involves combining two ingredients that have different prices into a single blend. For example, a coffee merchant may blend two types of coffee into a single blend, or a candy manufacturer may combine two types of candy to sell as a "variety pack."

The solution of a value mixture problem is based on the equation $V = AC$, where V is the value of an ingredient, A is the amount of the ingredient, and C is the cost per unit of the ingredient.

➡ Find the value of 5 oz of a gold alloy that costs $185 per ounce.

Given: $A = 5$ oz	$V = AC$
$C = \$185$	$V = 5(185)$
Unknown value: V	$V = 925$

The value of the 5 oz of gold alloy is $925.

Solve: A coffee merchant wants to make 9 lb of a blend of coffee costing $6 per pound. The blend is made using a $7 grade and a $4 grade of coffee. How many pounds of each of these grades should be used?

STRATEGY *for solving a value mixture problem*

▪ For each ingredient in the mixture, write a numerical or variable expression for the amount of the ingredient used, the unit cost of the ingredient, and the value of the amount used. For the blend, write a numerical or variable expression for the amount, the unit cost of the blend, and the value of the amount. The results can be recorded in a table.

The sum of the amounts is 9 lb.

Amount of $7 coffee: x

Amount of $4 coffee: $9 - x$

	Amount, A	·	Unit cost, C	=	Value, V
$7 grade	x	·	$7	=	$7x$
$4 grade	$9 - x$	·	$4	=	$4(9 - x)$
$6 blend	9	·	$6	=	$6(9)$

LOOK CLOSELY

Use the information given in the problem to fill in the amount and unit cost columns of the table. Fill in the value column by multiplying the two expressions you wrote in each row. Use the expressions in the last column to write the equation.

■ Determine how the values of the individual ingredients are related. Use the fact that the sum of the values of these ingredients is equal to the value of the blend.

The sum of the values of the $7 grade and the $4 grade is equal to the value of the $6 blend.

$7x + 4(9 - x) = 6(9)$ ▶ The value of the $7 grade plus the value of the $4 grade equals the value of the blend.
$7x + 36 - 4x = 54$
$3x + 36 = 54$
$3x = 18$
$x = 6$

$9 - x = 9 - 6 = 3$ ▶ Substitute the value of x into the variable expression for the amount of the $4 grade.

The merchant must use 6 lb of the $7 coffee and 3 lb of the $4 coffee.

Example 1   How many ounces of a silver alloy that costs $6 an ounce must be mixed with 10 oz of a silver alloy that costs $8 an ounce to make a mixture that costs $6.50 an ounce?

Strategy   ■ Ounces of $6 alloy: x

	Amount	Cost	Value
$6 alloy	x	$6	$6x$
$8 alloy	10	$8	8(10)
$6.50 mixture	$10 + x$	$6.50	$6.50(10 + x)$

■ The sum of the values before mixing equals the value after mixing.

Solution $6x + 8(10) = 6.50(10 + x)$ ▶ The value of the $6 alloy plus the value of the $8 alloy equals the value of the mixture.
$6x + 80 = 65 + 6.5x$
$-0.5x + 80 = 65$
$-0.5x = -15$
$x = 30$

30 oz of the $6 silver alloy must be used.

Problem 1   A gardener has 20 lb of a lawn fertilizer that costs $.90 per pound. How many pounds of a fertilizer that costs $.75 per pound should be mixed with this 20 lb of lawn fertilizer to produce a mixture that costs $.85 per pound?

Solution   See page S9.   10 lb

2 Percent mixture problems

The amount of a substance in a solution can be given as a percent of the total solution. For example, in a 5% saltwater solution, 5% of the total solution is salt. The remaining 95% is water.

The solution of a percent mixture problem is based on the equation $Q = Ar$, where Q is the quantity of a substance in the solution, r is the percent of concentration, and A is the amount of solution.

➡ A 500-milliliter bottle contains a 3% solution of hydrogen peroxide. Find the amount of hydrogen peroxide in the solution.

Given: $A = 500$ $Q = Ar$

          $r = 3\% = 0.03$ $Q = 500(0.03)$

Unknown amount: Q $Q = 15$

The bottle contains 15 ml of hydrogen peroxide.   ⬅

Solve: How many gallons of a 15% salt solution must be mixed with 4 gal of a 20% salt solution to make a 17% salt solution?

STRATEGY for solving a percent mixture problem

■ For each solution, use the equation $Ar = Q$. Write a numerical or variable expression for the amount of solution, the percent of concentration, and the quantity of the substance in the solution. The results can be recorded in a table.

The unknown quantity of 15% solution: x

	Amount of solution, A	·	Percent of concentration, r	=	Quantity of substance, Q
15% solution	x	·	0.15	=	$0.15x$
20% solution	4	·	0.20	=	$0.20(4)$
17% solution	$x + 4$	·	0.17	=	$0.17(x + 4)$

■ Determine how the quantities of the substance in the individual solutions are related. Use the fact that the sum of the quantities of the substances being mixed is equal to the quantity of the substance after mixing.

INSTRUCTOR NOTE

This is similar to the value mixture problems. The sum of the quantities being mixed equals the desired quantity.

The sum of the quantities of salt in the 15% solution and the 20% solution is equal to the quantity of salt in the 17% solution.

$$0.15x + 0.20(4) = 0.17(x + 4)$$
$$0.15x + 0.8 = 0.17x + 0.68$$
$$-0.02x + 0.8 = 0.68$$
$$-0.02x = -0.12$$
$$x = 6$$

▶ The amount of salt in the 15% solution plus the amount of salt in the 20% solution equals the amount of salt in the 17% solution.

6 gal of the 15% solution are required.

Example 2   A chemist wishes to make 3 L of a 7% acid solution by mixing a 9% acid solution and a 4% acid solution. How many liters of each solution should the chemist use?

Strategy   ▪ Liters of 9% solution: x
Liters of 4% solution: $3 - x$

	Amount	Percent	Quantity
9%	x	0.09	$0.09x$
4%	$3 - x$	0.04	$0.04(3 - x)$
7%	3	0.07	$0.07(3)$

▪ The sum of the quantities before mixing is equal to the quantity after mixing.

Solution $$0.09x + 0.04(3 - x) = 0.07(3)$$
$$0.09x + 0.12 - 0.04x = 0.21$$
$$0.05x + 0.12 = 0.21$$
$$0.05x = 0.09$$
$$x = 1.8$$

▶ The amount of acid in the 9% solution plus the amount of acid in the 4% solution equals the amount of acid in the 7% solution.

▶ 1.8 L of the 9% solution are needed.

$$3 - x = 3 - 1.8 = 1.2$$

▶ Find the amount of the 4% solution needed.

The chemist needs 1.8 L of the 9% solution and 1.2 L of the 4% solution.

Problem 2   How many quarts of pure orange juice are added to 5 qt of fruit drink that is 10% orange juice to make an orange drink that is 25% orange juice?

Solution   See page S9.   1 qt

CONCEPT REVIEW 4.6

Determine whether the statement is always true, sometimes true, or never true.

1. Both value mixture and percent mixture problems involve combining two or more ingredients into a single substance.   Always true

2. In the value mixture equation $V = AC$, the variable A represents the quantity of an ingredient.   Always true

3. Suppose we are mixing two salt solutions. Then the variable Q in the percent mixture equation $Q = Ar$ represents the amount of salt in a solution.

    Always true

4. If we combine an alloy that costs $8 an ounce with an alloy that costs $5 an ounce, the cost of the resulting mixture will be greater than $8 an ounce.

    Never true

5. If we combine a 9% acid solution with a solution that is 4% acid, the resulting solution will be less than 4% acid.   Never true

6. If 8 L of a solvent costs $75 per liter, then the value of the 8 L of solvent is $600.   Always true

7. If 100 oz of a silver alloy is 25% silver, then the alloy contains 25 oz of silver.

    Always true

EXERCISES 4.6

1 Value Mixture Problems

1. Explain the meaning of each variable in the equation $V = AC$. Give an example of how this equation is used.

2. Suppose you are mixing peanuts that cost $4 per pound with raisins that cost $2 per pound. In the context of this situation, explain the meaning of the statement "The sum of the values of these ingredients is equal to the value of the blend."

3. At a veterinary clinic, a special high-protein dog food that costs $6.75 per pound is mixed with a vitamin supplement that costs $3.25 per pound. How many pounds of each should be used to make 5 lb of a mixture that costs $4.65 per pound?   2 lb of dog food; 3 lb of vitamin supplement

4. A wild bird seed mix is made by combining 100 lb of millet seed costing $.60 per pound with sunflower seeds costing $1.10 per pound. How many pounds of sunflower seeds are needed to make a mixture that costs $.70 per pound?   25 lb

5. Find the cost per pound of a coffee mixture made from 8 lb of coffee that costs $9.20 per pound and 12 lb of coffee that costs $5.50 per pound. $6.98

6. How many pounds of chamomile tea that cost $4.20 per pound must be mixed with 12 lb of orange tea that cost $2.25 per pound to make a mixture that costs $3.40 per pound?   17.25 lb

7. A goldsmith combined an alloy that costs $4.30 per ounce with an alloy that costs $1.80 per ounce. How many ounces of each were used to make a mixture of 200 oz costing $2.50 per ounce? $4.30 alloy: 56 oz; $1.80 alloy: 144 oz

8. An herbalist has 30 oz of herbs costing $2 per ounce. How many ounces of herbs costing $1 per ounce should be mixed with these 30 oz of herbs to produce a mixture costing $1.60 per ounce?   20 oz

9. A health food store has a section in which you can create your own chocolate-covered fruit mixes. You choose 2 lb of the cherries that cost $3.50 per pound and blueberries that cost $2.75 per pound. How many pounds of blueberries can you add to create a mixture that costs $3.25 per pound?   1 lb

10. Find the cost per ounce of a mixture of 200 oz of a cologne that costs $5.50 per ounce and 500 oz of a cologne that costs $2.00 per ounce. $3.00

11. How many kilograms of hard candy that cost $7.50 per kilogram must be mixed with 24 kg of jelly beans that cost $3.25 per kilogram to make a mixture that costs $4.50 per kilogram?   10 kg

12. A grocery store offers a cheese sampler that includes a pepper cheddar cheese that costs $8 per kilogram and Pennsylvania Jack that costs $3 per kilogram. How many kilograms of each were used to make a 5-kilogram mixture that costs $4.50 per kilogram?

1.5 kg of pepper cheese; 3.5 kg of Pennsylvania Jack

13. A snack food is made by mixing 5 lb of popcorn that costs $.80 per pound with caramel that costs $2.40 per pound. How much caramel is needed to make a mixture that costs $1.40 per pound?   3 lb

14. A lumber company combined oak wood chips that cost $3.10 per pound with pine wood chips that cost $2.50 per pound. How many pounds of each were used to make an 80-pound mixture costing $2.65 per pound?

20 lb of oak chips; 60 lb of pine chips

15. The manager of a farmer's market has 500 lb of grain that costs $1.20 per pound. How many pounds of meal costing $.80 per pound should be mixed with the 500 lb of grain to produce a mixture that costs $1.05 per pound?

300 lb

16. A caterer made an ice cream punch by combining fruit juice that costs $2.25 per gallon with ice cream that costs $3.25 per gallon. How many gallons of each were used to make 100 gal of punch costing $2.50 per gallon?

Fruit juice: 75 gal; ice cream: 25 gal

17. The manager of a specialty food store combined almonds that cost $4.50 per pound with walnuts that cost $2.50 per pound. How many pounds of each were used to make a 100-pound mixture that costs $3.24 per pound?

Almonds: 37 lb; walnuts: 63 lb

18. Find the cost per pound of a "house blend" of coffee that is made from 12 lb of Central American coffee that costs $4 per pound and 30 lb of South American coffee that costs $2.25 per pound. $2.75

19. Find the cost per pound of a sugar-coated breakfast cereal made from 40 lb of sugar that cost $1.00 per pound and 120 lb of corn flakes that cost $.60 per pound. $.70

20. Find the cost per ounce of a gold alloy made from 25 oz of pure gold that costs $482 per ounce and 40 oz of an alloy that costs $300 per ounce. $370

21. Find the cost per ounce of a sun screen made from 100 oz of a lotion that costs $2.50 per ounce and 50 oz of a lotion that costs $4.00 per ounce. $3

22. How many liters of a blue dye that costs $1.60 per liter must be mixed with 18 L of anil that costs $2.50 per liter to make a mixture that costs $1.90 per liter?   36 L

2 Percent Mixture Problems

23. Explain the meaning of each variable in the equation $Q = Ar$. Give an example of how this equation is used.

24.   ✏ Suppose you are mixing a 5% acid solution with a 10% acid solution. In the context of this situation, explain the meaning of the statement "The sum of the quantities of the substances being mixed is equal to the quantity of the substance after mixing."

25.   Forty ounces of a 30% gold alloy are mixed with 60 oz of a 20% gold alloy. Find the percent concentration of the resulting gold alloy.   24%

26.   One hundred ounces of juice that is 50% tomato juice are added to 200 oz of a vegetable juice that is 25% tomato juice. What is the percent concentration of tomato juice in the resulting mixture? $33\frac{1}{3}\%$

27.   How many gallons of a 15% acid solution must be mixed with 5 gal of a 20% acid solution to make a 16% acid solution?   20 gal

28.   How many pounds of a chicken feed that is 50% corn must be mixed with 400 lb of a feed that is 80% corn to make a chicken feed that is 75% corn?
        80 lb

29.   A rug is made by weaving 20 lb of yarn that is 50% wool with a yarn that is 25% wool. How many pounds of the yarn that is 25% wool must be used if the finished rug is to be 35% wool?   30 lb

30.   Five gallons of a dark green latex paint that is 20% yellow paint are combined with a lighter green latex paint that is 40% yellow paint. How many gallons of the lighter green paint must be used to create a green paint that is 25% yellow paint? $1\frac{2}{3}$ gal

31.   How many gallons of a plant food that is 9% nitrogen must be combined with another plant food that is 25% nitrogen to make 10 gal of a solution that is 15% nitrogen?   6.25 gal

32.   A chemist wants to make 50 ml of a 16% acid solution by mixing a 13% acid solution and an 18% acid solution. How many milliliters of each solution should the chemist use?
        13% solution: 20 ml; 18% solution: 30 ml

33.   Five grams of sugar are added to a 45-gram serving of a breakfast cereal that is 10% sugar. What is the percent concentration of sugar in the resulting mixture?   19%

x ml of 13% acid + $(50 - x)$ ml of 18% acid = 50 ml of 16% acid

34.   Thirty ounces of pure silver are added to 50 oz of a silver alloy that is 20% silver. What is the percent concentration of the resulting alloy?   50%

35.   To make the potpourri mixture sold at a florist shop, 70 oz of a potpourri that is 80% lavender are combined with a potpourri that is 60% lavender. The resulting potpourri is 74% lavender. How much of the potpourri that is 60% lavender is used?   30 oz

36.   The manager of a garden shop mixes grass seed that is 60% rye grass with 70 lb of grass seed that is 80% rye grass to make a mixture that is 74% rye grass. How much of the 60% rye grass is used?   30 lb

37. A hair dye is made by blending a 7% hydrogen peroxide solution and a 4% hydrogen peroxide solution. How many milliliters of each are used to make a 300-milliliter solution that is 5% hydrogen peroxide?
     7% solution: 100 ml; 4% solution: 200 ml

38. At a cosmetics company, 40 L of pure aloe cream are mixed with 50 L of a moisturizer that is 64% aloe. What is the percent concentration of aloe in the resulting mixture?   80%

39. How many ounces of pure chocolate must be added to 150 oz of chocolate topping that is 50% chocolate to make a topping that is 75% chocolate?
     150 oz

40. How many ounces of pure bran flakes must be added to 50 oz of cereal that is 40% bran flakes to produce a mixture that is 50% bran flakes?   10 oz

41. A hair stylist combines 12 oz of shampoo that is 20% conditioner with an 8-ounce bottle of pure shampoo. What is the percent concentration of conditioner in the 20-ounce mixture?   12%

42. A clothing manufacturer has some pure silk thread and some thread that is 85% silk. How many kilograms of each must be woven together to make 75 kg of cloth that is 96% silk?   pure silk: 55 kg; 85% silk: 20 kg

43. How many ounces of dried apricots must be added to 18 oz of a snack mix that contains 20% dried apricots to make a mixture that is 25% dried apricots?
     1.2 oz

44. A recipe for a rice dish calls for 12 oz of a rice mixture that is 20% wild rice and 8 oz of pure wild rice. What is the percent concentration of wild rice in the 20-ounce mixture?   52%

APPLYING CONCEPTS 4.6

45. Find the cost per ounce of a mixture of 30 oz of an alloy that costs $4.50 per ounce, 40 oz of an alloy that costs $3.50 per ounce, and 30 oz of an alloy that costs $3.00 per ounce. $3.65

46. A grocer combined walnuts that cost $2.60 per pound and cashews that cost $3.50 per pound with 20 lb of peanuts that cost $2.00 per pound. Find the amount of walnuts and the amount of cashews used to make the 50 lb mixture costing $2.72 per pound.   Walnuts: 10 lb; cashews: 20 lb

[C] 47. How many ounces of water evaporated from 50 oz of a 12% salt solution to produce a 15% salt solution?   10 oz

[C] 48. A chemist mixed pure acid with water to make 10 L of a 30% acid solution. How much pure acid and how much water did the chemist use?
     Pure acid: 3 L; water: 7 L

[C] 49. How many grams of pure water must be added to 50 g of pure acid to make a solution that is 40% acid?   75 g

[C] **50.** A radiator contains 15 gal of a 20% antifreeze solution. How many gallons must be drained from the radiator and replaced by pure antifreeze so that the radiator will contain 15 gal of a 40% antifreeze solution?   3.75 gal

51. Tickets to a performance by the community theater cost $5.50 for adults and $2.75 for children. A total of 120 tickets were sold for $563.75. How many adults and how many children attended the performance?

85 adults, 35 children

52. Explain why we look for patterns and relationships in mathematics. Include a discussion of the relationship between value mixture problems and percent mixture problems and how understanding one of these can make it easier to understand the other. Also discuss why understanding how to solve the value mixture problems in this section can be helpful in solving Exercise 51.

S E C T I O N   **4.7**

Uniform Motion Problems

1 Uniform motion problems

A train that travels constantly in a straight line at 50 mph is in *uniform motion*. **Uniform motion** means the speed of an object does not change.

The solution of a uniform motion problem is based on the equation $d = rt$, where d is the distance traveled, r is the rate of travel, and t is the time spent traveling.

A car travels 50 mph for 3 h.

$$d = rt$$
$$d = 50(3)$$
$$d = 150$$

The car travels a distance of 150 mi.

Solve: A car leaves a town traveling at 35 mph. Two hours later, a second car leaves the same town, on the same road, traveling at 55 mph. In how many hours after the second car leaves will the second car be passing the first car?

STRATEGY for solving a uniform motion problem

■ For each object, use the equation $d = rt$. Write a numerical or variable expression for the distance, rate, and time. The results can be recorded in a table.

The first car traveled 2 h longer than the second car.

First car 🚗 $d = 35(t + 2)$

Unknown time for the second car: t
Time for the first car: $t + 2$

Second car 🚗 $d = 55t$

	Rate, r	$\cdot$	Time, t	$=$	Distance, d
First car	35	$\cdot$	$t + 2$	$=$	$35(t + 2)$
Second car	55	$\cdot$	t	$=$	$55t$

■ Determine how the distances traveled by the individual objects are related. For example, the total distance traveled by both objects may be known, or it may be known that the two objects traveled the same distance.

The two cars travel the same distance.

$35(t + 2) = 55t$ ▶ The distance traveled by the first car equals the distance traveled by
$35t + 70 = 55t$ the second car.
$70 = 20t$
$3.5 = t$

The second car will be passing the first car in 3.5 h.

Example 1   Two cars, one traveling 10 mph faster than the second car, start at the same time from the same point and travel in opposite directions. In 3 h, they are 288 mi apart. Find the rate of the second car.

Strategy   ■ Rate of second car: r
Rate of first car: $r + 10$

	Rate	Time	Distance
First car	$r + 10$	3	$3(r + 10)$
Second car	r	3	$3r$

■ The total distance traveled by the two cars is 288 mi.

$d = 3(r + 10)$ $d = 3r$
First car |◄———— 288 mi ————►| Second car

Solution $3(r + 10) + 3r = 288$ ▶ The distance traveled by the first car plus
$3r + 30 + 3r = 288$ the distance traveled by the second car is
$6r + 30 = 288$ 288 mi.
$6r = 258$
$r = 43$

The second car is traveling 43 mph.

Problem 1   Two trains, one traveling at twice the speed of the other, start at the same time from stations that are 306 mi apart and travel toward each other. In 3 h, the trains pass each other. Find the rate of each train.

Solution   See page S9.   34 mph and 68 mph

Example 2   A bicycling club rides out into the country at a speed of 16 mph and returns over the same road at 12 mph. How far does the club ride out into the country if it travels a total of 7 h?

Strategy   ▪ Time spent riding out: t
Time spent riding back: $7 - t$

	Rate	Time	Distance
Out	16	t	$16t$
Back	12	$7 - t$	$12(7 - t)$

▪ The distance out equals the distance back.

Solution $16t = 12(7 - t)$
$16t = 84 - 12t$
$28t = 84$
$t = 3$ ▶ The time is 3 h. Find the distance.

The distance out $= 16t = 16(3) = 48$.

The club rides 48 mi into the country.

Problem 2   On a survey mission, a pilot flew out to a parcel of land and back in 7 h. The rate out was 120 mph. The rate back was 90 mph. How far away was the parcel of land?

Solution   See page S9.   360 mi

CONCEPT REVIEW 4.7

Determine whether the statement is always true, sometimes true, or never true.

1. The solution of a uniform motion problem is based on the equation $d = rt$, where r is a percent.   Never true

2. If you drive at a constant speed of 60 mph for 4 h, you will travel a total distance of 240 mi.   Always true

3. It takes a student a total of 5 h to drive to a friend's house and back. If the variable t is used to represent the time it took to drive to the friend's house, then the expression $t - 5$ is used to represent the time spent on the return trip.   Never true

4. If the speed of one train is 20 mph slower than that of a second train, then the speeds of the two trains can be represented as r and $20 - r$.   Never true

5. A car and a bus both travel from city A to city B. The car leaves city A 1 h later than the bus, but both vehicles arrive in city B at the same time. If t represents the time the car was traveling, then $t + 1$ represents the time the bus was traveling. If t represents the time the bus was traveling, then $t - 1$ represents the time the car was traveling.   Always true

6. Two cars travel the same distance. If the distance traveled by the first car is represented by the expression $35t$, and the distance traveled by the second car is represented by the expression $45(t + 1)$, then we can write the equation $35t = 45(t + 1)$.   Always true

EXERCISES 4.7

1 Uniform Motion Problems

1. Two planes start from the same point and fly in opposite directions. The first plane is flying 25 mph slower than the second plane. In 2 h, the planes are 470 mi apart. Find the rate of each plane.   105 mph; 130 mph

470 mi

2. Two cyclists start from the same point and ride in opposite directions. One cyclist rides twice as fast as the other. In 3 h, they are 81 mi apart. Find the rate of each cyclist.   9 mph; 18 mph

3. Two planes leave an airport at 8 A.M., one flying north at 480 km/h and the other flying south at 520 km/h. At what time will they be 3000 km apart?   11 A.M.

4. A long-distance runner started on a course running at an average speed of 6 mph. Half an hour later, a second runner began the same course at an average speed of 7 mph. How long after the second runner started will the second runner overtake the first runner?   3 h

5. Michael Chan leaves a dock in his motorboat and travels at an average speed of 9 mph toward the Isle of Shoals, a small island off the coast of Massachusetts. Two hours later a tour boat leaves the same dock and travels at an average speed of 18 mph toward the same island. How many hours after the tour boat leaves will Michael's boat be alongside the tour boat?   2 h

6. A 555-mile, 5-hour plane trip was flown at two speeds. For the first part of the trip, the average speed was 105 mph. For the remainder of the trip, the average speed was 115 mph. How long did the plane fly at each speed?   2 h at 105 mph; 3 h at 115 mph

105 mph → ← 115 mph →
555 mi

7. An executive drove from home at an average speed of 30 mph to an airport where a helicopter was waiting. The executive boarded the helicopter and flew to the corporate offices at an average speed of 60 mph. The entire distance was 150 mi. The entire trip took 3 h. Find the distance from the airport to the corporate offices.   120 mi

8. Tim and Helena are at opposite ends of a 12-mile country road with plans to meet for a picnic lunch. Tim starts out jogging at the rate of 5 mph, while Helena roller blades at the rate of 7 mph. How long after they begin will they meet?   1 h

9. After a sailboat had been on the water for 3 h, a change in the wind direction reduced the average speed of the boat by 5 mph. The entire distance sailed was 57 mi. The total time spent sailing was 6 h. How far did the sailboat travel in the first 3 h?   36 mi

10. A car and a bus set out at 3 P.M. from the same point headed in the same direction. The average speed of the car is twice the average speed of the bus. In 2 h, the car is 68 mi ahead of the bus. Find the rate of the car.   68 mph

11. A passenger train leaves a train depot 2 h after a freight train leaves the same depot. The freight train is traveling 20 mph slower than the passenger train. Find the rate of each train if the passenger train overtakes the freight train in 3 h.   passenger train: 50 mph; freight train: 30 mph

12. A stunt driver was needed at the production site of a Hollywood movie. The average speed of the stunt driver's flight to the site was 150 mph, and the average speed of the return trip was 100 mph. Find the distance of the round trip if the total flying time was 5 h.   600 mi

13. A ship traveling east at 25 mph is 10 mi from a harbor when another ship leaves the harbor traveling east at 35 mph. How long does it take the second ship to catch up to the first ship?   1 h

14. At 10 A.M. a plane leaves Boston, Massachusetts, for Seattle, Washington, a distance of 3000 mi. One hour later a plane leaves Seattle for Boston. Both planes are traveling at a speed of 500 mph. How many hours after the plane leaves Seattle will the planes pass each other?   2.5 h

15. At noon a train leaves Washington, D.C., headed for Charleston, South Carolina, a distance of 500 mi. The train travels at a speed of 60 mph. At 1 P.M. a second train leaves Charleston headed for Washington, D.C., traveling at 50 mph. How long after the train leaves Charleston will the two trains pass each other?   4 h

16. Two cyclists start at the same time from opposite ends of a course that is 51 mi long. One cyclist is riding at a rate of 16 mph, and the second cyclist is riding at a rate of 18 mph. How long after they begin will they meet?   1.5 h

17. A bus traveled on a straight road for 2 h at an average speed that was 20 mph faster than its average speed on a winding road. The time spent on the winding road was 3 h. Find the average speed on the winding road if the total trip was 210 mi.   34 mph

18. A bus traveling at a rate of 60 mph overtakes a car traveling at a rate of 45 mph. If the car had a 1-hour head start, how far from the starting point does the bus overtake the car?   180 mi

19. A car traveling at 48 mph overtakes a cyclist who, riding at 12 mph, had a 3-hour head start. How far from the starting point does the car overtake the cyclist?   48 mi

20. A plane left Kennedy Airport Tuesday morning for a 605-mile, 5-hour trip. For the first part of the trip, the average speed was 115 mph. For the remainder of the trip, the average speed was 125 mph. How long did the plane fly at each speed?   2 h at 115 mph; 3 h at 125 mph

APPLYING CONCEPTS 4.7

21. A car and a cyclist start at 10 A.M. from the same point, headed in the same direction. The average speed of the car is 5 mph more than three times the average speed of the cyclist. In 1.5 h, the car is 46.5 mi ahead of the cyclist. Find the rate of the cyclist.   13 mph

22. A cyclist and a jogger set out at 11 A.M. from the same point, headed in the same direction. The average speed of the cyclist is twice the average speed of the jogger. In 1 h, the cyclist is 7 mi ahead of the jogger. Find the rate of the cyclist.   14 mph

23. A car and a bus set out at 2 P.M. from the same point, headed in the same direction. The average speed of the car is 30 mph slower than twice the average speed of the bus. In 2 h, the car is 30 mi ahead of the bus. Find the rate of the car.   60 mph

24. At 10 A.M., two campers left their campsite by canoe and paddled downstream at an average speed of 12 mph. They then turned around and paddled back upstream at an average rate of 4 mph. The total trip took 1 h. At what time did the campers turn around downstream?   10:15 A.M.

25. At 7 A.M., two joggers start from opposite ends of an 8-mile course. One jogger is running at a rate of 4 mph, and the other is running at a rate of 6 mph. At what time will the joggers meet?   7:48 A.M.

26. A truck leaves a depot at 11 A.M. and travels at a speed of 45 mph. At noon, a van leaves the same place and travels the same route at a speed of 65 mph. At what time does the van overtake the truck?   2:15 P.M.

[C] **27.** A bicyclist rides for 2 h at a speed of 10 mph and then returns at a speed of 20 mph. Find the cyclist's average speed for the trip. $13\frac{1}{3}$ mph

[C] **28.** A car travels a 1-mile track at an average speed of 30 mph. At what average speed must the car travel the next mile so that the average speed for the 2 mi is 60 mph?   It is impossible to average 60 mph.

29. Explain why the motion problems in this section are restricted to *uniform* motion.

30. Explain why 60 mph is the same as 88 ft/s.

S E C T I O N **4.8**

Inequalities

1 Applications of inequalities

Solving application problems requires recognition of the verbal phrases that translate into mathematical symbols. Here is a partial list of the phrases used to indicate each of the four inequality symbols.

$<$ is less than	$>$ is greater than
	is more than
	exceeds
$\leq$ is less than or equal to	$\geq$ is greater than or equal to
maximum	minimum
at most	at least
or less	or more

Example 1   A student must have at least 450 points out of 500 points on five tests to receive an A in a course. One student's results on the first four tests were 93, 79, 87, and 94. What scores on the last test will enable this student to receive an A in the course?

Strategy   To find the scores, write and solve an inequality using N to represent the score on the last test.

Solution

total number of points on the five tests	is greater than or equal to	450

$$93 + 79 + 87 + 94 + N \geq 450$$
$$353 + N \geq 450$$
$$353 - 353 + N \geq 450 - 353$$
$$N \geq 97$$

The student's score on the last test must be equal to or greater than 97.

Problem 1   An appliance dealer will make a profit on the sale of a television set if the cost of the new set is less than 70% of the selling price. What minimum selling price will enable the dealer to make a profit on a television set that costs the dealer $340?

Solution   See page S10. $485.72

Example 2   The base of a triangle is 8 in., and the height is $(3x - 5)$ in. Express as an integer the maximum height of the triangle when the area is less than 112 in^2.

Strategy   To find the maximum height:
- Replace the variables in the area formula by the given values and solve for x.
- Replace the variable in the expression $3x - 5$ with the value found for x.

Solution

| one-half the base times the height | is less than | 112 in^2 |

$$\frac{1}{2}(8)(3x - 5) < 112$$

$$4(3x - 5) < 112$$

$$12x - 20 < 112$$

$$12x - 20 + 20 < 112 + 20$$

$$12x < 132$$

$$\frac{12x}{12} < \frac{132}{12}$$

$$x < 11$$

$$3x - 5 = 3(11) - 5 = 28$$ ▶ Substitute the value of x into the variable expression for the height. Note that the height <u>is less than</u> 28 because $x < 11$.

The maximum height of the triangle is 27 in.

Problem 2   Company A rents cars for $9 per day and 10¢ per mile driven. Company B rents cars for $12 per day and 8¢ per mile driven. You want to rent a car for one week. What is the maximum number of miles you can drive a Company A car if it is to cost you less than a Company B car?

Solution   See page S10.   1049 mi

CONCEPT REVIEW 4.8

Determine whether the statement is always true, sometimes true, or never true.

1. Both "is greater than" and "is more than" indicate the inequality symbol $\geq$.
   Never true

2. A minimum refers to a lower limit, whereas a maximum refers to an upper limit.   Always true

3. Given that $x > \frac{32}{6}$, the minimum integer that satisfies the inequality is 6.

Always true

4. Given that $x < \frac{25}{4}$, the maximum integer that satisfies the inequality is 7.

Never true

5. A rental car costs $15 per day and 20¢ per mile driven. If m represents the number of miles the rental car is driven, then the expression $15 + 0.20m$ represents the cost to rent the car for one week.   Never true

6. A patient's physician recommends a maximum cholesterol level of 205 units. The patient's cholesterol level is 199 units and therefore must be lowered 6 units in order to meet the physician's recommended level.   Never true

---

EXERCISES 4.8

1 **1.** *Integer Problems*   Three-fifths of a number is greater than two-thirds. Find the smallest integer that satisfies the inequality.   2

2. *Sports*   To be eligible for a basketball tournament, a basketball team must win at least 60% of its remaining games. If the team has 17 games remaining, how many games must the team win to qualify for the tournament?

11 or more games

3. *Income Taxes*   To avoid a tax penalty, at least 90% of a self-employed person's total annual income tax liability must be paid by April 15. What amount of income tax must be paid by April 15 by a person with an annual income tax liability of $3500? $3150 or more

4. *Health*   A health official recommends a maximum cholesterol level of 220 units. A patient has a cholesterol level of 275. By how many units must this patient's cholesterol level be reduced to satisfy the recommended maximum level?   55 or more units

5. *Recycling*   A service organization will receive a bonus of $200 for collecting more than 1850 lb of aluminum cans during its four collection drives. On the first three drives, the organization collected 505 lb, 493 lb, and 412 lb. How many pounds of cans must the organization collect on the fourth drive to receive the bonus?   More than 440 lb

6. *Education*   A professor scores all tests with a maximum of 100 points. To earn an A in this course, a student must have an average of at least 92 on four tests. One student's grades on the first three tests were 89, 86, and 90. Can this student earn an A grade?   No

7. *Education*   A student must have an average of at least 80 points on five tests to receive a B in a course. The student's grades on the first four tests were 75, 83, 86, and 78. What scores on the last test will enable this student to receive a B in the course?   78 or better

8. *Compensation*   A car sales representative receives a commission that is the greater of $250 or 8% of the selling price of a car. What dollar amounts in the sale price of a car will make the commission offer more attractive than the $250 fee?   More than $3125

9. *Compensation*   A sales representative for a stereo store has the option of a monthly salary of $2000 or a 35% commission on the selling price of each item sold by the representative. What dollar amounts in sales will make the commission more attractive than the monthly salary?   More than $5714

10. *Integer Problem*   Four times the sum of a number and five is less than six times the number. Find the smallest integer that satisfies the inequality.   11

11. *Compensation*   The sales agent for a jewelry company is offered a flat monthly salary of $3200 or a salary of $1000 plus an 11% commission on the selling price of each item sold by the agent. If the agent chooses the $3200 salary, what dollar amount does the agent expect to sell in one month?
   $20,000 or less

12. *Compensation*   A baseball player is offered an annual salary of $200,000 or a base salary of $100,000 plus a bonus of $1000 for each hit over 100 hits. How many hits must the baseball player make to earn more than $200,000?
   201 or more hits

13. *Consumerism*   A computer bulletin board service charges a flat fee of $10 per month or $4 per month plus $.10 for each minute the service is used. For how many minutes must a person use this service for the cost to exceed $10?
   More than 60 min

14. *Business*   A site licensing fee for a computer program is $1500. The fee allows a company to use the program at any computer terminal within the company. Alternatively, a company can choose to pay $200 for each computer terminal it has. How many computer terminals must a company have for the site licensing fee to be the more economical plan?   8 or more terminals

15. *Nutrition*   For a product to be labeled orange juice, a state agency requires that at least 80% of the drink be real orange juice. How many ounces of artificial flavors can be added to 32 oz of real orange juice if the drink is to be labeled orange juice?   8 ounces or less

16. *Nutrition*   Grade A hamburger cannot contain more than 20% fat. How much fat can a butcher mix with 300 lb of lean meat to meet the 20% requirement?   75 pounds or less

17. *Consumerism*   A shuttle service taking skiers to a ski area charges $8 per person each way. Four skiers are debating whether to take the shuttle bus or rent a car for $45 plus $.25 per mile. Assuming that the skiers will share the cost of the car and that they want the least expensive method of transportation, how far away is the ski area if they choose to take the shuttle service?
   More than 38 mi

18. *Utilities*   A residential water bill is based on a flat fee of $10 plus a charge of $.75 for each 1000 gal of water used. Find the number of gallons of water a family can use and have a monthly water bill that is less than $55.

Less than 60,000 gal

19. *Consumerism*   Company A rents cars for $25 per day and 8¢ per mile driven. Company B rents cars for $15 per day and 14¢ per mile driven. You want to rent a car for one day. Find the maximum number of miles you can drive a Company B car if it is to cost you less than a Company A car.   166 mi

20.   *Geometry*   A rectangle is 8 ft wide and $(2x + 7)$ ft long. Express as an integer the maximum length of the rectangle when the area is less than 152 ft^2.

18 ft

$2x + 7$

8

APPLYING CONCEPTS 4.8

21. *Integer Problems*   Find three positive consecutive odd integers such that three times the sum of the first two integers is less than four times the third integer. (*Hint:* There is more than one solution.)   1, 3, and 5; 3, 5, and 7

22. *Integer Problems*   Find three positive consecutive even integers such that four times the sum of the first two integers is less than or equal to five times the third integer. (*Hint:* There is more than one solution.)   2, 4, and 6; 4, 6, and 8

23. *Aviation*   A maintenance crew requires between 30 min and 45 min to prepare an aircraft for its next flight. How many aircraft can this crew prepare for flight in a 6-hour period of time?   Between 8 and 12 aircraft

[C] 24. *Consumerism*   The charges for a long-distance telephone call are $1.21 for the first 3 min and $.42 for each additional minute or fraction of a minute. What is the largest whole number of minutes a call could last if it is to cost you less than $6?   14 min

[C] 25. *Fund Raising*   Your class decides to publish a calendar to raise money. The initial cost, regardless of the number of calendars printed, is $900. After the initial cost, each calendar costs $1.50 to produce. What is the minimum number of calendars your class must sell at $6 per calendar to make a profit of at least $1200?   467 calendars

26. *Health Care Plans*   The graph at the top of the next page depicts the enrollment of American employees in managed care vs. traditional insurance.

   a. During which years was enrollment in traditional insurance plans less than 25%?   1996, 1997

   b. During which years was enrollment in managed care programs greater than 75%?   1996, 1997

   c. During which years was enrollment in traditional insurance plans greater than 50%?   None

d. During which years was enrollment in traditional insurance programs greater than enrollment in managed care programs?   None

e. Write a paragraph describing any pattern you see in the graph.

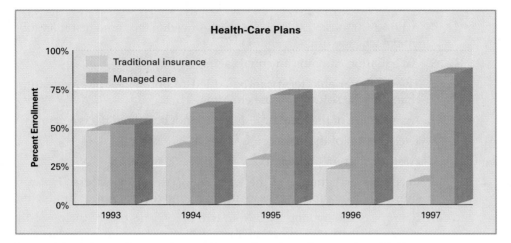

Source: Mercer/Foster Higgins National Survey of Employer-Sponsored Health Plans, 1998

Focus on Problem Solving

Trial-and-Error Approach to Problem Solving

The questions below require an answer of always true, sometimes true, or never true. These problems are best solved by the trial-and-error method. The trial-and-error method of arriving at a solution to a problem involves repeated tests or experiments.

For example, consider the statement

> Both sides of an equation can be divided by the same number without changing the solution of the equation.

The solution of the equation $6x = 18$ is 3. If we divide both sides of the equation by 2, the result is $3x = 9$ and the solution is still 3. Thus the answer "never true" has been eliminated. We still need to determine whether there is a case for which it is not true. Is there a number that we could divide both sides of the equation by and the result would be an equation for which the solution is not 3? If we divide both sides of the equation by 0, the result is $\frac{6x}{0} = \frac{18}{0}$; the solution of this equation is not 3 because the expressions on either side of the equals sign are undefined. Thus the statement is true for some numbers and not true for 0. The statement is sometimes true.

Determine whether the statement is always true, sometimes true, or never true.

1. Both sides of an equation can be multiplied by the same number without changing the solution of the equation.

2. For an equation of the form $ax = b, a \neq 0$, multiplying both sides of the equation by the reciprocal of a will result in an equation of the form $x = constant$.

3. The Multiplication Property of Equations is used to remove a term from one side of an equation.

4. Adding -3 to each side of an equation yields the same result as subtracting 3 from each side of the equation.

5. An equation contains an equals sign.

6. The same variable term can be added to both sides of an equation without changing the solution of the equation.

7. An equation of the form $ax + b = c$ cannot be solved if a is a negative number.

8. The solution of the equation $\frac{x}{0} = 0$ is 0.

9. For the diagram at the left, $\angle b = \angle d = \angle e = \angle g$.

10. In solving an equation of the form $ax + b = cx + d$, subtracting cx from each side of the equation results in an equation with only one variable term in it.

11. If a rope 8 meters long is cut into two pieces and one of the pieces has length x meters, then the length of the other piece can be represented as $(x - 8)$ meters.

12. An even integer is a multiple of 2.

13. If the first of three consecutive odd integers is n, then the second and third consecutive odd integers are represented as $n + 1$ and $n + 3$.

14. Suppose we are mixing two salt solutions. Then the variable Q in the percent mixture equation $Q = Ar$ represents the amount of salt in a solution.

15. If 100 oz of a silver alloy is 25% silver, then the alloy contains 25 oz of silver.

16. If we combine an alloy that costs $8 an ounce with an alloy that costs $5 an ounce, the cost of the resulting mixture will be greater than $8 an ounce.

17. If we combine a 9% acid solution with a solution that is 4% acid, the resulting solution will be less than 4% acid.

18. If the speed of one train is 20 mph slower than that of a second train, then the speeds of the two trains can be represented as r and $20 - r$.

Diagramming Problems

How do you best remember something? Do you remember best what you hear? The word *aural* means "pertaining to the ear"; people with a strong aural memory remember best those things that they hear. The word *visual* means "pertaining to the sense of sight"; people with a strong visual memory remember best that which they see written down. Some people claim their memory is in their writing hand—they remember something only if they write it down! The method by which you best remember something is probably also the method by which you can best learn something new.

In problem-solving situations, try to capitalize on your strengths. If you tend to understand material better when you hear it spoken, read application problems aloud or have someone else read them to you. If writing helps you to organize ideas, rewrite application problems in your own words.

No matter what your main strength, visualizing a problem can be a valuable aid in problem solving. A drawing, sketch, diagram, or chart can be a useful tool in problem solving, just as calculators and computers are tools. Making a diagram can help you gain an understanding of the relationships inherent in a problem-solving situation. A sketch will help you to organize the given information and devise or discover a method by which the solution can be determined.

A tour bus drives 5 mi south, then 4 mi west, then 3 mi north, and then 4 mi east. How far is the tour bus from the starting point?

Draw a diagram of the given information.

From the diagram, we can see that the solution can be determined by subtracting 3 from 5: $5 - 3 = 2$.

The bus is 2 mi from the starting point.

If you roll two ordinary six-sided dice and multiply the two numbers that appear on top, how many different products are there?

Make a chart of the possible products. In the chart below, repeated products are marked with an asterisk.

$1 \cdot 1 = 1$	$2 \cdot 1 = 2$ *	$3 \cdot 1 = 3$ *	$4 \cdot 1 = 4$ *	$5 \cdot 1 = 5$ *	$6 \cdot 1 = 6$ *
$1 \cdot 2 = 2$	$2 \cdot 2 = 4$ *	$3 \cdot 2 = 6$ *	$4 \cdot 2 = 8$ *	$5 \cdot 2 = 10$ *	$6 \cdot 2 = 12$ *
$1 \cdot 3 = 3$	$2 \cdot 3 = 6$ *	$3 \cdot 3 = 9$	$4 \cdot 3 = 12$ *	$5 \cdot 3 = 15$ *	$6 \cdot 3 = 18$ *
$1 \cdot 4 = 4$	$2 \cdot 4 = 8$	$3 \cdot 4 = 12$ *	$4 \cdot 4 = 16$	$5 \cdot 4 = 20$ *	$6 \cdot 4 = 24$ *
$1 \cdot 5 = 5$	$2 \cdot 5 = 10$	$3 \cdot 5 = 15$	$4 \cdot 5 = 20$	$5 \cdot 5 = 25$	$6 \cdot 5 = 30$ *
$1 \cdot 6 = 6$	$2 \cdot 6 = 12$	$3 \cdot 6 = 18$	$4 \cdot 6 = 24$	$5 \cdot 6 = 30$	$6 \cdot 6 = 36$

By counting the products that are not repeats, we can see that there are 18 different products.

In this chapter, you may have noticed that a drawing accompanies the strategy step of many application problems. We encourage you to draw a diagram when solving the application problems in these sections, as well as in any other situation where it can prove helpful. Doing so will undoubtedly improve your problem-solving skills.

Projects and Group Activities

Nielsen Ratings

Nielsen Media Research surveys television viewers to determine the number of people watching particular shows. There are an estimated 97 million television households in the United States. Each **rating point** represents 1% of that number, or 970,000 households. Therefore, for example, if *60 Minutes* receives a rating of 10 points, then 10%, or $(0.10)(97,000,000) = 9,700,000$ households, watched that program.

A rating point does not mean that 970,000 people are watching a program. A rating point refers to the number of TV sets tuned to that program; there may be more than one person watching a television set in a household.

The Nielsen Company also describes a program's share of the market. **Share** is the percentage of television sets in use that are tuned to a program. Suppose the same week that *60 Minutes* received 10 rating points, the show received a share of 20%. This would mean that 20% of all households with a television *turned on* were tuned to *60 Minutes*, while 10% of all households with a television were tuned to the program.

1. If *20/20-Wednesday* received a Nielsen rating of 11.2 and a share of 23, how many TV households watched the program that week? How many TV households were watching television during that hour?

2. Suppose that *X-Files* received a rating of 9.6 and a share of 18. How many TV households were watching television during that hour? How many TV households watched the program that week?

3. Suppose *Frasier* received a rating of 12.3 during a week that 17,100,000 people were watching the show. Find the average number of people per TV household who watched the program. Round to the nearest tenth.

The cost to advertise on a program is related to its Nielsen rating. The sponsor (the company paying for the advertisement) pays a certain number of dollars for each rating point a show receives.

4. Suppose a television network charges $25,000 per rating point for a 30-second commercial on a daytime talk show. Determine the cost for three 30-second commercials if the Nielsen rating of the show is 11.5.

Nielsen Media Research also tracks the exposure of advertisements. For example, it might be reported that commercials for McDonald's had 500,000,000 household exposures during a week when their advertisement was aired 90 times.

5. Information regarding household exposure of advertisements can be found in *USA Today* each Monday. For a recent week, find the information for the top four advertised brands. For each brand, calculate the average household exposure for each time the ad was aired.

 Nielsen Media Research has a web site on the Internet. You can locate the site under entertainment and television using a search engine. You will find the rating points and market share for the networks and cable stations, as well as rating points, share, and audience size for categories such as prime time and sports programming.

6. Find the top two prime-time television shows for last week. Calculate the number of TV households that watched each program. Compare these figures with the top two sports programs for last week.

Changes in Percent Concentration

Suppose you begin with a 30-milliliter solution that is 10% hydrochloric acid.

7. If 10 milliliters of a 30% solution of hydrochloric acid solution are added to this solution, what is the percent concentration of the resulting solution?

8. If x milliliters of a 30% hydrochloric acid solution are added to the original solution, what is the percent concentration of the resulting solution?

9. Let y represent the percent concentration and x the number of milliliters of the 30% hydrochloric acid solution that are being added. Use a graphing calculator to graph the equation. Use a viewing window of Xmin = 0, Xmax = 50, Ymin = 0, and Ymax = 0.3. Use the graph to determine whether the change in percent concentration from X = 10 to X = 20 is the same as the change in percent concentration from X = 20 to X = 30.

10. If more and more of the 30% hydrochloric acid solution is added to the original mixture, will the percent concentration of the resulting solution ever exceed 30%? Explain your answer.

Chapter Summary

Key Words

Consecutive integers follow one another in order. (Objective 4.2.1)

11, 12, 13 are consecutive integers.
−9, −8, −7 are consecutive integers.

The *perimeter* of a geometric figure is a measure of the distance around the figure.   (Objective 4.3.1)

The perimeter of a triangle is the sum of the lengths of the three sides.
The perimeter of a rectangle is the sum of the lengths of the four sides.

An angle is measured in *degrees*. A 90° angle is a *right angle*. A 180° angle is a *straight angle*. One complete revolution is 360°. An *acute angle* is an angle whose measure is between 0° and 90°. An *obtuse angle* is an angle whose measure is between 90° and 180°. An *isosceles triangle* has two sides of equal measure. The three sides of an *equilateral triangle* are of equal measure. *Complementary angles* are two angles whose measures have the sum 90°. *Supplementary angles* are two angles whose measures have the sum 180°.   (Objective 4.3.2)

Parallel lines never meet; the distance between them is always the same. *Perpendicular lines* are intersecting lines that form right angles. Two angles that are on opposite sides of the intersection of two lines are *vertical angles;* vertical angles have the same measure. Two angles that share a common side are *adjacent angles;* adjacent angles of intersecting lines are supplementary angles.   (Objective 4.3.2)

A line that intersects two other lines at two different points is a *transversal.* If the lines cut by a transversal are parallel lines, then pairs of equal angles are formed: *alternate interior angles, alternate exterior angles,* and *corresponding angles.* (Objective 4.3.2)

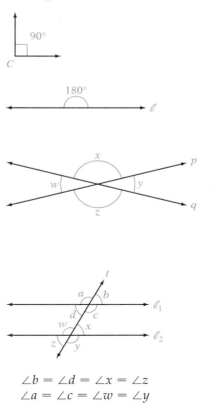

$\angle b = \angle d = \angle x = \angle z$
$\angle a = \angle c = \angle w = \angle y$

Cost is the price that a business pays for a product. *Selling price* is the price for which a business sells a product to a customer. *Markup* is the difference between selling price and cost. *Markup rate* is the markup expressed as a percent of the retailer's cost. (Objective 4.4.1)

If a business pays $100 for a product and sells that product for $140, then the cost of the product is $100, the selling price is $140, and the markup is $140 − $100 = $40.

Discount is the amount by which a retailer reduces the regular price of a product. *Discount rate* is the discount expressed as a percent of the regular price.   (Objective 4.4.2)

The regular price of a product is $100. The product is now on sale for $75. The discount on the product is $100 − $75 = $25.

Essential Rules and Procedures

Consecutive Integers
$n, n + 1, n + 2, \ldots$ (Objective 4.2.1)

The sum of three consecutive integers is 135.

$$n + (n + 1) + (n + 2) = 135$$

Consecutive Even or Consecutive Odd Integers
$n, n + 2, n + 4, \ldots$ (Objective 4.2.1)

The sum of three consecutive odd integers is 135.

$$n + (n + 2) + (n + 4) = 135$$

Coin and Stamp Equation
$$\frac{\text{Number}}{\text{of coins}} \cdot \frac{\text{Value of}}{\text{coin in cents}} = \frac{\text{Total value}}{\text{in cents}}$$ (Objective 4.2.2)

A coin bank contains $1.80 in dimes and quarters. In all, there are twelve coins in the bank. How many dimes are in the bank?

$$10d + 25(12 - d) = 180$$

Formulas for Perimeter
Triangle: $P = a + b + c$
Rectangle: $P = 2L + 2W$
Square: $P = 4s$
(Objective 4.3.1)

The perimeter of a rectangle is 108 m. The length is 6 m more than three times the width. Find the width of the rectangle.

$$108 = 2(3W + 6) + 2W$$

The perimeter of an isosceles triangle is 34 ft. The length of the third side is 5 ft less than the length of one of the equal sides. Find the length of one of the equal sides.

$$34 = x + x + (x - 5)$$

Sum of the Angles of a Triangle
The sum of the measures of the interior angles of a triangle is 180°.
$\angle A + \angle B + \angle C = 180°$
The sum of an interior and corresponding exterior angle is 180°.
(Objective 4.3.3)

In a right triangle, the measure of one acute angle is 12° more than the measure of the smallest angle. Find the measure of the smallest angle.

$$x + (x + 12) + 90 = 180$$

Basic Markup Equation
$S = C + rC$ (Objective 4.4.1)

The manager of a department buys a pasta maker machine for $70 and sells the machine for $98. Find the markup rate.

$$98 = 70 + 70r$$

Basic Discount Equation

$S = R - rR$ (Objective 4.4.2)

The sale price for a leather bomber jacket is $95. This price is 24% off the regular price. Find the regular price.

$$95 = R - 0.24R$$

Annual Simple Interest Equation

$I = Pr$ (Objective 4.5.1)

You invest a portion of $10,000 in a 7% annual simple interest account and the remainder in a 6% annual simple interest bond. The two investments earn total annual interest of $680. How much is invested in the 7% account?

$$0.07x + 0.06(10,000 - x) = 680$$

Value Mixture Equation

$V = AC$ (Objective 4.6.1)

An herbalist has 30 oz of herbs costing $2 per ounce. How many ounces of herbs costing $1 per ounce should be mixed with the 30 oz to produce a mixture costing $1.60 per ounce?

$$30(2) + 1x = 1.60(30 + x)$$

Percent Mixture Equation

$Q = Ar$ (Objective 4.6.2)

Forty ounces of a 30% gold alloy are mixed with 60 oz of a 20% gold alloy. Find the percent concentration of the resulting gold alloy.

$$0.30(40) + 0.20(60) = x(100)$$

Uniform Motion Equation

$d = rt$ (Objective 4.7.1)

A boat traveled from a harbor to an island at an average speed of 20 mph. The average speed on the return trip was 15 mph. The total trip took 3.5 h. How long did it take to travel to the island?

$$20t = 15(3.5 - t)$$

Chapter Review Exercises

1. Translate "seven less than twice a number is equal to the number" into an equation and solve. $2x - 7 = x$; 7

2. A piano wire is 35 in. long. A note can be produced by dividing this wire into two parts so that three times the length of the shorter piece is twice the length of the longer piece. Find the length of the shorter piece.   14 in.

3. The sum of two numbers is twenty-one. Three times the smaller number is two less than twice the larger number. Find the two numbers.   8 and 13

4. Translate "the sum of twice a number and six equals four times the difference between a number and two" into an equation and solve. $2x + 6 = 4(x - 2)$; 7

5. A ceiling fan that regularly sells for $60 is on sale for $40. Find the discount rate. $33\frac{1}{3}\%$

6. A total of $15,000 is deposited into two simple interest accounts. The annual simple interest rate on one account is 6%. The annual simple interest rate on the second account is 7%. How much should be invested in each account so that the total interest earned is $970? $8000 at 6%; $7000 at 7%

7. In an isosceles triangle, the measure of one of the two equal angles is 15° more than the measure of the third angle. Find the measure of each angle.
   65°, 65°, 50°

8. A motorcyclist and a bicyclist set out at 8 A.M. from the same point, headed in the same direction. The speed of the motorcyclist is three times the speed of the bicyclist. In 2 h, the motorcyclist is 60 mi ahead of the bicyclist. Find the rate of the motorcyclist.   45 mph

9. In an isosceles triangle, the measure of one angle is 25° less than half the measure of one of the equal angles. Find the measure of each angle.
   16°, 82°, and 82°

10. The manager of a sporting goods store buys packages of cleats for $5.25 each and sells them for $9.45 each. Find the markup rate.   80%

11. A dairy owner mixes 5 gal of cream that is 30% butterfat with 8 gal of milk that is 4% butterfat. Find the percent concentration of butterfat in the resulting mixture.   14%

12. The length of a rectangle is four times the width. The perimeter is 200 ft. Find the length and width of the rectangle.   Length: 80 ft; width: 20 ft

13. The manager of an accounting firm is investigating contracts whereby large quantities of material can be photocopied at minimum cost. The contract from the Copy Center offers a fee of $50 per year and $.03 per page. The Prints 4 U Company offers a fee of $27 per year and $.05 per page. What is the minimum number of copies per year that could be ordered from the Copy Center if these copies are to cost less than copies from Prints 4 U?
   1150 copies

14. The sale price for a carpet sweeper is $26.56, which is 17% off the regular price. Find the regular price. $32

15. The owner of a health food store combined cranberry juice that cost $1.79 per quart with apple juice that cost $1.19 per quart. How many quarts of each were used to make 10 qt of a cranapple juice mixture costing $1.61 per quart?
   Cranberry: 7 qt; apple: 3 qt

16. A famous mystery writer is contracted to autograph copies of her new book at a bookstore. As a special promotion that day, the book is selling for $15.95, which is only 30% above the cost of the book. Find the cost of the book.
   $12.27

17. The sum of two numbers is thirty-six. The difference between the larger number and eight equals the total of four and three times the smaller number. Find the two numbers.   6 and 30

18. An engineering consultant invested $14,000 in an individual retirement account paying 8.15% annual simple interest. How much money does the consultant have deposited in an account paying 12% annual simple interest if the total interest earned is 9.25% of the total investment? $5600

19. You have removed all the hearts from a standard deck of playing cards and have arranged them in numerical order. Suppose I pick two consecutive cards and tell you their sum is 15. Name the two cards I picked.
7 and 8 of hearts

20. A pharmacist has 15 L of an 80% alcohol solution. How many liters of pure water should be added to the alcohol solution to make an alcohol solution that is 75% alcohol?   1 L

21. A student's grades on five sociology exams were 68, 82, 90, 73, and 95. What is the lowest score this student can receive on the sixth exam and still have earned a total of at least 480 points?   72

22. Translate "the opposite of seven is equal to one-half a number less ten" into an equation and solve. $-7 = \frac{1}{2}x - 10$; 6

23. The Empire State Building is 1472 ft tall. This is 514 ft less than twice the height of the Eiffel Tower. Find the height of the Eiffel Tower.   993 ft

24. One angle of a triangle is 15° more than the measure of the second angle. The third angle is 15° less than the measure of the second angle. Find the measure of each angle.   75°, 60°, and 45°

25. The manager of a refreshment stand at a local stadium tallied the receipts for one evening. There was a total of $263 in one-dollar bills and five-dollar bills. In all, there were 155 bills. Find the number of one-dollar bills.
128 one-dollar bills

26. A board 10 ft long is cut into two pieces. Four times the length of the shorter piece is 2 ft less than two times the length of the longer piece. Find the length of the longer piece.   7 ft

27. An optical engineer's consulting fee was $600. This included $80 for supplies and $65 for each hour of consultation. Find the number of hours of consultation.
8 h

28. A stamp collector has 12¢ stamps and 17¢ stamps with a total face value of $15.53. The number of 12¢ stamps is three more than twice the number of 17¢ stamps. How many of each type are in the collection?
12¢ stamps: 77; 17¢ stamps: 37

29. A furniture store uses a markup rate of 60%. The store sells a solid oak curio cabinet for $1074. Find the cost of the curio cabinet. $671.25

30. The largest swimming pool in the world is located in Casablanca, Morocco, and is 480 m long. Two swimmers start at the same time from opposite ends of the pool and start swimming toward each other. One swimmer's rate is 65 m/min. The other swimmer's rate is 55 m/min. In how many minutes after they begin will they meet?   4 min

31. The perimeter of a triangle is 35 in. The second side is 4 in. longer than the first side. The third side is 1 in. shorter than twice the first side. Find the measure of each side.   8 in., 12 in., and 15 in.

32. The sum of three consecutive odd integers is −45. Find the integers.
     −17, −15, −13

33. A rectangle is 15 ft long and $(2x - 4)$ ft wide. Express as an integer the maximum width of the rectangle when the area is less than 180 ft².   11 ft

34. Given that $\ell_1 \parallel \ell_2$, find the measures of angles a and b. $\angle a = 138°, \angle b = 42°$

Chapter Test

1. Translate "the sum of six times a number and thirteen is five less than the product of three and the number" into an equation and solve.
    $$6n + 13 = 3n - 5; n = -6$$

2. Translate "the difference between three times a number and fifteen is twenty-seven" into an equation and solve. $3n - 15 = 27; n = 14$

3. The sum of two numbers is 18. The difference between four times the smaller number and seven is equal to the sum of two times the larger number and five. Find the two numbers.   8 and 10

4. A board 18 ft long is cut into two pieces. Two feet less than the product of five and the length of the shorter piece is equal to the difference between three times the length of the longer piece and eight. Find the length of each piece.
    6 ft and 12 ft

5. The manager of a sports shop uses a markup rate of 50%. The selling price for a set of golf clubs is $300. Find the cost of the golf clubs. $200

6. A portable typewriter that regularly sells for $100 is on sale for $80. Find the discount rate.   20%

7. How many gallons of a 15% acid solution must be mixed with 5 gal of a 20% acid solution to make a 16% acid solution?   20 gal

8. The perimeter of a rectangle is 38 m. The length of the rectangle is 1 m less than three times the width. Find the length and width of the rectangle.
    Length: 14 m; width: 5 m

9. Find three consecutive odd integers such that three times the first integer is one less than the sum of the second and third integers.   5, 7, 9

10. Florist A charges a $3 delivery fee plus $21 per bouquet delivered. Florist B charges a $15 delivery fee plus $18 per bouquet delivered. An organization wants to send each resident of a small nursing home a bouquet for Valentine's Day. How many residents are in the nursing home if it is more economical for the organization to use Florist B?   5 or more residents

11. A total of $7000 is deposited into two simple interest accounts. On one account, the annual simple interest rate is 10%, and on the second account, the annual simple interest rate is 15%. How much should be invested in each account so that the total annual interest earned is $800?
$5000 at 10%; $2000 at 15%

12. A coffee merchant wants to make 12 lb of a blend of coffee costing $6 per pound. The blend is made using a $7 grade and a $4 grade of coffee. How many pounds of each of these grades should be used? $7 coffee: 8 lb; $4 coffee: 4 lb

13. Two planes start at the same time from the same point and fly in opposite directions. The first plane is flying 100 mph faster than the second plane. In 3 h, the two planes are 1050 mi apart. Find the rate of each plane.
1st plane: 225 mph; 2nd plane: 125 mph

14. In a triangle, the first angle is 15° more than the second angle. The third angle is three times the second angle. Find the measure of each angle.
48°, 33°, and 99°

15. A coin bank contains 50 coins in nickels and quarters. The total amount of money in the bank is $9.50. Find the number of nickels and the number of quarters in the bank.   15 nickels, 35 quarters

16. A club treasurer deposited $2400 in two simple interest accounts. The annual simple interest rate on one account is 6.75%. The annual simple interest rate on the other account is 9.45%. How much should be deposited in each account so that the same interest is earned on each account?
$1400 at 6.75%; $1000 at 9.45%

17. The width of a rectangle is 12 ft. The length is $(3x + 5)$ ft. Express as an integer the minimum length of the rectangle if the area is greater than 276 ft^2.
24 ft

18. A file cabinet that normally sells for $99 is on sale for 20% off. Find the sale price. $79.20

Cumulative Review Exercises

1. Given $B = \{-12, -6, -3, -1\}$, which elements of set B are less than -4? $-12, -6$

2. Simplify: $-2 + (-8) - (-16)$ 6

3. Simplify: $\left(-\frac{2}{3}\right)^3\left(-\frac{3}{4}\right)^2$ $-\frac{1}{6}$

4. Simplify: $\frac{5}{6} - \left(\frac{2}{3}\right)^2 \div \left(\frac{1}{2} - \frac{1}{3}\right)$ $-\frac{11}{6}$

5. Evaluate $-|-18|$. -18

6. Evaluate $b^2 - (a - b)^2$ when $a = 4$ and $b = -1$. -24

7. Simplify: $5x - 3y - (-4x) + 7y$ $9x + 4y$

8. Simplify: $-4(3 - 2x - 5x^3)$ $-12 + 8x + 20x^3$

9. Simplify: $-2[x - 3(x - 1) - 5]$ $4x + 4$

10. Simplify: $-3x^2 - (-5x^2) + 4x^2$ $6x^2$

11. Is 2 a solution of $4 - 2x - x^2 = 2 - 4x$?   No

12. Solve: $9 - x = 12$ -3

13. Solve: $-\frac{4}{5}x = 12$ -15

14. Solve: $8 - 5x = -7$ 3

15. Solve: $-6x - 4(3 - 2x) = 4x + 8$ -10

16. Write 40% as a fraction. $\frac{2}{5}$

17. Solve and graph the solution set of $4x \geq 16$.
     $x \geq 4$![number line from -5 to 5 with arrow starting at 4 going right]
     $\begin{array}{ccccccccccc} & & & & & & & & & & \\ -5 & -4 & -3 & -2 & -1 & 0 & 1 & 2 & 3 & 4 & 5 \end{array}$

18. Solve: $-15x \leq 45$ $x \geq -3$

19. Solve: $2x - 3 > x + 15$ $x > 18$

20. Solve: $12 - 4(x - 1) \leq 5(x - 4)$ $x \geq 4$

21. Write 0.025 as a percent.   2.5%

22. Write $\frac{3}{25}$ as a percent.   12%

23. Find $16\frac{2}{3}\%$ of 18.   3

24. 40% of what is 18?   45

25. Translate "the sum of eight times a number and twelve is equal to the product of four and the number" into an equation and solve.
     $$8n + 12 = 4n;\ n = -3$$

26. The area of the cement foundation of a house is 2000 ft². This is 200 ft² more than three times the area of the garage. Find the area of the garage.   600 ft²

27. An auto repair bill was $213. This includes $88 for parts and $25 for each hour of labor. Find the number of hours of labor.   5 h

28. A survey of 250 librarians showed that 50 of the libraries had a particular reference book on their shelves. What percent of the libraries had the reference book?   20%

29. A deposit of $4000 is made into an account that earns 11% annual simple interest. How much money is also deposited in an account that pays 14% annual simple interest if the total annual interest earned is 12% of the total investment? $2000

30. The manager of a department store buys a chain necklace for $8 and sells it for $14. Find the markup rate.   75%

31. How many grams of a gold alloy that costs $4 a gram must be mixed with 30 g of a gold alloy that costs $7 a gram to make an alloy costing $5 a gram?   60 g

32. How many ounces of pure water must be added to 70 oz of a 10% salt solution to make a 7% salt solution?   30 oz

33. In an isosceles triangle, the third angle is 8° less than twice the measure of one of the equal angles. Find the measure of one of the equal angles.   47°

34. Three times the second of three consecutive even integers is 14 more than the sum of the first and third integers. Find the middle even integer.   14

35. A coin bank contains dimes and quarters. The number of quarters is five less than four times the number of dimes. The total amount in the bank is $6.45. Find the number of dimes in the bank.   7 dimes

5

Linear Equations and Inequalities

Broadcast technicians operate the electronic equipment used to record and transmit radio and television programs, and they help prepare movie soundtracks for production studios. They work with television cameras, microphones, tape recorders, light and sound effects, transmitters, antennas, and other equipment. These technicians must be able to read and interpret graphs such as those discussed in this chapter.

OBJECTIVES

5.1.1   Graph points in a rectangular coordinate system

5.1.2   Scatter diagrams

5.2.1   Determine solutions of linear equations in two variables

5.2.2   Graph equations of the form $y = mx + b$

5.2.3   Graph equations of the form $Ax + By = C$

5.3.1   Find the slope of a straight line

5.3.2   Graph a line using the slope and y-intercept

5.4.1   Find the equation of a line using the equation $y = mx + b$

5.4.2   Find the equation of a line using the point-slope formula

5.5.1   Introduction to functions

5.5.2   Graphs of linear functions

5.6.1   Graph inequalities in two variables

Magic Squares

A magic square is a square array of distinct integers so arranged that the numbers along any row, column, or main diagonal have the same sum. An example of a magic square is shown at the right.

8	3	4
1	5	9
6	7	2

The oldest known example of a magic square comes from China. Estimates are that this magic square is over 4000 years old. It is shown at the left.

There is a simple way to produce a magic square with an odd number of cells. Start by writing a 1 in the top middle cell. The rule then is to proceed diagonally upward to the right with the successive integers. See Figure A.

When the rule takes you outside the square, write the number by shifting either across the square from right to left or down the square from top to bottom, as the case may be. For example, in Figure B, the second number (2) is outside the square above a column. Because the 2 is above a column, it should be shifted down to the bottom cell in that column. In Figure C, the 3 is outside the square to the right of a column and should therefore be shifted all the way to the left.

If the rule takes you to a square that is already filled (as shown in Figure C), then write the number in the cell directly below the last number written. See Figure D. Continue until the entire square is filled.

It is possible to begin a magic square with any integer and proceed by using the above rule and consecutive integers.

For an odd magic square beginning with 1, the sum of a row, column, or diagonal is $\frac{n(n^2 + 1)}{2}$, where n is the number of rows.

Figure A

Figure B

Figure C

Figure D

Figure E

Figure F

Figure G

Figure H

SECTION 5.1

The Rectangular Coordinate System

1 Graph points in a rectangular coordinate system

Before the 15th century, geometry and algebra were considered separate branches of mathematics. That all changed when René Descartes, a French mathematician who lived from 1596 to 1650, founded **analytic geometry.** In this geometry, a *coordinate system* is used to study the relationships between variables.

A **rectangular coordinate system** is formed by two number lines, one horizontal and one vertical, that intersect at the zero point of each line. The point of intersection is called the **origin.** The two axes are called the **coordinate axes,** or simply the **axes.** Generally, the horizontal axis is labeled the **x-axis,** and the vertical axis is labeled the **y-axis.**

The axes determine a **plane,** which can be thought of as a large, flat sheet of paper. The two axes divide the plane into four regions called **quadrants,** which are numbered counterclockwise from I to IV starting at the upper right.

Each point in the plane can be identified by a pair of numbers called an **ordered pair.** The first number of the ordered pair measures a horizontal distance and is called the **abscissa,** or **x-coordinate.** The second number of the pair measures a vertical distance and is called the **ordinate,** or **y-coordinate.** The ordered pair (x, y) associated with a point is also called the **coordinates** of the point.

To **graph,** or **plot, a point in the plane,** place a dot at the location given by the ordered pair. For example, to graph the point $(4, 1)$, start at the origin. Move 4 units to the right and then 1 unit up. Draw a dot. To graph $(-3, -2)$, start at the origin. Move 3 units left and then 2 units down. Draw a dot.

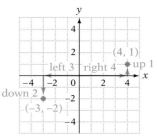

The **graph of an ordered pair** is the dot drawn at the coordinates of the point in the plane. The graphs of the ordered pairs $(4, 1)$ and $(-3, -2)$ are shown at the right.

The graphs of the points whose coordinates are $(2, 3)$ and $(3, 2)$ are shown at the right. Note that they are different points. The order in which the numbers in an ordered pair appear *is* important.

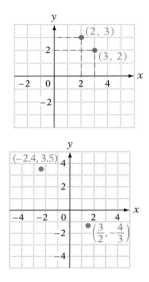

Each point in the plane is associated with an ordered pair, and each ordered pair is associated with a point in the plane. Although only integers are labeled on the coordinate grid, any ordered pair can be graphed by approximating its location. The graphs of the ordered pairs $\left(\frac{3}{2}, -\frac{4}{3}\right)$ and $(-2.4, 3.5)$ are shown at the right.

Example 1   Graph the ordered pairs $(-2, -3)$, $(3, -2)$, $(1, 3)$, and $(4, 1)$.

Solution

Problem 1   Graph the ordered pairs $(-1, 3)$, $(1, 4)$, $(-4, 0)$, and $(-2, -1)$.

Solution   See page S10.

Example 2   Find the coordinates of each of the points.

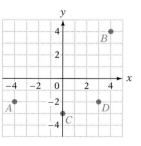

Solution $A(-4, -2)$, $B(4, 4)$, $C(0, -3)$, $D(3, -2)$

Problem 2   Find the coordinates of each of the points.

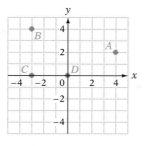

Solution   See page S10. $A(4, 2)$, $B(-3, 4)$, $C(-3, 0)$, $D(0, 0)$

2   Scatter diagrams

There are many situations in which the relationship between two variables may be of interest. For example, a college admissions director wants to know the relationship between SAT scores (one variable) and success in college (the second variable). An employer is interested in the relationship between scores on a pre-employment test and ability to perform a job.

A researcher can investigate the relationship between two variables by means of regression analysis, which is a branch of statistics. The study of the relationship between two variables may begin with a **scatter diagram,** which is a graph of some of the known data.

The following table gives the record times for events of different lengths at a track meet. Record times are rounded to the nearest second. Lengths are given in meters.

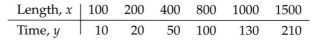

Length, x	100	200	400	800	1000	1500
Time, y	10	20	50	100	130	210

The scatter diagram for these data is shown at the right. Each ordered pair represents the length of the race and the record time. For example, the ordered pair $(400, 50)$ indicates that the record for the 400 m race is 50 s.

Length of race (in meters)

Example 3   To test a heart medicine, a doctor measures the heart rate, in beats per minute, of five patients before and after they take the medication. The results are recorded in the table on the next page. Graph the scatter diagram for these data.

Before medicine, x	85	80	85	75	90
After medicine, y	75	70	70	80	80

Strategy   Graph the ordered pairs on a rectangular coordinate system where the reading on the horizontal axis represents the heart rate before taking the medication and the vertical axis represents the heart rate after taking the medication.

Solution

The jags indicate that a portion of the axis has been omitted.

Heart rate before medicine (in beats per minute)

Problem 3   In March of 1998, the American Council for an Energy-Efficient Economy released its ranking of environmentally friendly and unfriendly cars and trucks sold in the United States. The following table shows the fuel use, in miles per gallon of gasoline, both in the city and on the highway, for six of the vehicles ranked worst for the environment. Graph the scatter diagram for these data.

Fuel use in the city, x	12	9	10	12	13	12
Fuel use on the highway, y	16	15	13	16	17	17

Solution   See page S10.

Fuel use in the city (in miles per gallon)

CONCEPT REVIEW 5.1

Determine whether the statement is always true, sometimes true, or never true.

1. The point $(0, 0)$ on a rectangular coordinate system is at the origin.   Always true

2. When a point is plotted in the rectangular coordinate system, the first number in an ordered pair indicates a movement up or down from the origin. The second number in the ordered pair indicates a movement left or right.
    Never true

3. In an xy-coordinate system, the first number is the y-coordinate and the second number is the x-coordinate.   Never true

4. When a point is plotted in the rectangular coordinate system, a negative x value indicates a movement to the left. A negative y value indicates a movement down.   Always true

5. Any point plotted in quadrant III has a positive y value.   Never true

6. In the figure at the right, point C is the graph of the point whose coordinates are $(-4, -2)$.   Always true

7. Any point on the x-axis has y-coordinate 0.   Always true

8. Any point on the y-axis has x-coordinate 0.   Always true

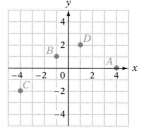

EXERCISES 5.1

1. Describe the signs of the coordinates of a point in **a.** quadrant I, **b.** quadrant II, **c.** quadrant III, and **d.** quadrant IV.
a. x and y both positive   **b.** x negative, y positive
c. x and y both negative   **d.** x positive, y negative

2. In which quadrant is the point located?
a. $(2, -4)$ **b.** $(-3, 2)$ **c.** $(-1, -6)$
a. IV   **b.** II   **c.** III

3. Graph the ordered pairs $(-2, 1)$, $(3, -5)$, $(-2, 4)$, and $(0, 3)$.

4. Graph the ordered pairs $(5, -1)$, $(-3, -3)$, $(-1, 0)$, and $(1, -1)$.

5. Graph the ordered pairs $(0, 0)$, $(0, -5)$, $(-3, 0)$, and $(0, 2)$.

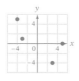

6. Graph the ordered pairs $(-4, 5)$, $(-3, 1)$, $(3, -4)$, and $(5, 0)$.

7. Graph the ordered pairs $(-1, 4)$, $(-2, -3)$, $(0, 2)$, and $(4, 0)$.

8. Graph the ordered pairs $(5, 2)$, $(-4, -1)$, $(0, 0)$, and $(0, 3)$.

9. Find the coordinates of each of the points.

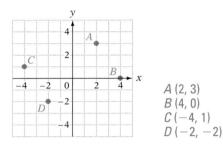

A (2, 3)
B (4, 0)
C (−4, 1)
D (−2, −2)

10. Find the coordinates of each of the points.

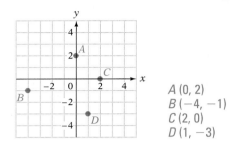

A (0, 2)
B (−4, −1)
C (2, 0)
D (1, −3)

11. Find the coordinates of each of the points.

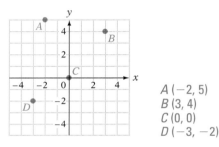

A (−2, 5)
B (3, 4)
C (0, 0)
D (−3, −2)

12. Find the coordinates of each of the points.

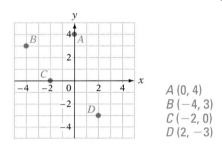

A (0, 4)
B (−4, 3)
C (−2, 0)
D (2, −3)

13. **a.** Name the abscissas of points A and C.
b. Name the ordinates of points B and D.

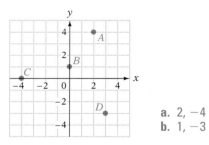

a. 2, −4
b. 1, −3

14. **a.** Name the abscissas of points A and C.
b. Name the ordinates of points B and D.

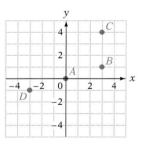

a. 0, 3
b. 1, −1

☑ 15. *Sports* The numbers of offensive and defensive players picked in the first round of the NFL draft for the years 1993 through 1998 are given in the following table. Graph the scatter diagram for these data.

Number of offensive players picked, x	15	13	18	17	14	14
Number of defensive players picked, y	14	16	14	13	16	16

16. 🥧 *Education* The number of students per computer in our schools and the number of computers in the schools for the school years 1991–1992 through 1996–1997 are given in the following table. The number of students has been rounded to the nearest whole number. The number of computers has been rounded to the nearest million. (Source: CEO Forum on Education and Technology.) Graph the scatter diagram for these data.

Number of students per computer, x	19	12	11	9	19	7
Number of computers, y	2	4	4	5	5	6

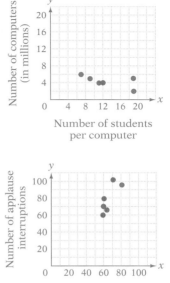

17. 🥧 *Presidential Addresses* The length of each president's State of the Union address and the number of interruptions by applause for the years 1993 through 1998 are given in the table below. (Source: USA TODAY research.) Graph the scatter diagram for these data.

Length, in minutes, x	59	64	81	61	60	71
Number of applause interruptions, y	60	66	96	79	70	102

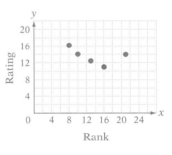

18. 🥧 *Television* The rank and the rating of the TV show *NYPD Blue* for each of the seasons from 1993–1994 through 1997–1998 are given in the table below. (Source: Nielsen Media Research.) Graph the scatter diagram for these data.

Rank, x	21	8	10	13	16
Rating, y	13.9	16.2	14.1	12.5	10.9

19. 🥧 *Airports* The table below records the number of public bathrooms and the number of stalls at each of the following airports: Miami International, Chicago O'Hare, Orlando International, Dallas/Fort Worth, and Seattle/Tacoma. (Source: USA TODAY research; Airports Council International.) Graph the scatter diagram of these data.

Number of public bathrooms, x	161	125	120	106	68
Number of stalls, y	721	605	600	439	500

20. 🥧 *Entertainment* The table below shows the price, in dollars, for a one-day admission ticket at Disney World for both an adult and a child for the years 1993 through 1998. (Source: Amusement Business.) Graph the scatter diagram for these data.

Adult's ticket, x	34.00	36.00	37.00	40.81	42.14	44.52
Child's ticket, y	27.00	29.00	30.00	32.86	33.92	36.04

APPLYING CONCEPTS 5.1

What is the distance from the given point to the horizontal axis?

21. $(-5, 1)$ 1 unit

22. $(3, -4)$ 4 units

23. $(-6, 0)$ 0 units

What is the distance from the given point to the vertical axis?

24. $(-2, 4)$ 2 units

25. $(1, -3)$ 1 unit

26. $(5, 0)$ 5 units

27. Name the coordinates of a point plotted at the origin of the rectangular coordinate system.   (0, 0)

28. A computer screen has a coordinate system that is different from the xy-coordinate system we have discussed. In one mode, the origin of the coordinate system is the top left point of the screen, as shown at the right. Plot the points whose coordinates are (200, 400), (0, 100), and (100, 300).

29. Write a paragraph explaining how to plot points in a rectangular coordinate system.

30. Decide on two quantities that may be related, and collect at least ten pairs of values. Here are some examples: height and weight, time studying for a test and the test grade, age of a car and its cost. Draw a scatter diagram for the data. Is there any trend? That is, as the values on the horizontal axis increase, do the values on the vertical axis increase or decrease?

31. There is a coordinate system on Earth that consists of *longitude* and *latitude*. Write a report on how location is determined on the surface of Earth.

S E C T I O N **5.2**

Graphs of Straight Lines

1 Determine solutions of linear equations in two variables

An equation of the form $y = mx + b$, where m is the coefficient of x and b is a constant, is a **linear equation in two variables.** Examples of linear equations follow.

$$y = 3x + 4 \qquad (m = 3, b = 4)$$
$$y = 2x - 3 \qquad (m = 2, b = -3)$$
$$y = -\frac{2}{3}x + 1 \qquad \left(m = -\frac{2}{3}, b = 1\right)$$
$$y = -2x \qquad (m = -2, b = 0)$$
$$y = x + 2 \qquad (m = 1, b = 2)$$

In a linear equation, the exponent of each variable is 1. The equations $y = 2x^2 - 1$ and $y = \frac{1}{x}$ are not linear equations.

A **solution of a linear equation in two variables** is an ordered pair of numbers (x, y) that makes the equation a true statement.

➡ Is $(1, -2)$ a solution of $y = 3x - 5$?

Replace x with 1. Replace y with -2.

$$\begin{array}{c|c} y = & 3x - 5 \\ \hline -2 & 3(1) - 5 \\ & 3 - 5 \end{array}$$

Compare the results. If the results are equal, the given ordered pair is a solution. If the results are not equal, the given ordered pair is not a solution.

$-2 = -2$

Yes, $(1, -2)$ is a solution of the equation $y = 3x - 5$. ◄

Besides the ordered pair $(1, -2)$, there are many other ordered-pair solutions of the equation $y = 3x - 5$. For example, the method used above can be used to show that $(2, 1)$, $(-1, -8)$, $\left(\frac{2}{3}, -3\right)$, and $(0, -5)$ are also solutions.

Example 1   Is $(-3, 2)$ a solution of $y = 2x + 2$?

Solution
$$\begin{array}{c|c} y = & 2x + 2 \\ \hline 2 & 2(-3) + 2 \\ & -6 + 2 \\ & -4 \end{array}$$
▸ Replace x with -3 and y with 2.

$2 \neq -4$

No, $(-3, 2)$ is not a solution of $y = 2x + 2$.

Problem 1   Is $(2, -4)$ a solution of $y = -\frac{1}{2}x - 3$?

Solution   See page S10.   Yes

In general, a linear equation in two variables has an infinite number of ordered-pair solutions. By choosing any value for x and substituting that value into the linear equation, we can find a corresponding value of y.

➡ Find the ordered-pair solution of $y = 2x - 5$ that corresponds to $x = 1$.

Substitute 1 for x.
Solve for y.

$$y = 2x - 5$$
$$y = 2 \cdot 1 - 5$$
$$y = 2 - 5$$
$$y = -3$$

The ordered-pair solution is $(1, -3)$. ◄

Example 2   Find the ordered-pair solution of $y = \frac{2}{3}x - 1$ that corresponds to $x = 3$.

Solution $y = \frac{2}{3}x - 1$

$y = \frac{2}{3}(3) - 1$ ▸ Substitute 3 for x.

$y = 2 - 1$ ▸ Solve for y.
$y = 1$ ▸ When $x = 3$, $y = 1$.

The ordered-pair solution is $(3, 1)$.

Problem 2   Find the ordered-pair solution of $y = -\frac{1}{4}x + 1$ that corresponds to $x = 4$.

Solution   See page S10. $(4, 0)$

2   ## Graph equations of the form $y = mx + b$

⟨13⟩ ⟨14⟩ HM³

The **graph of an equation in two variables** is a drawing of the ordered-pair solutions of the equation. For a linear equation in two variables, the graph is a straight line.

To graph a linear equation, find ordered-pair solutions of the equation. Do this by choosing any value of x and finding the corresponding value of y. Repeat this procedure, choosing different values for x, until you have found the number of solutions desired.

Because the graph of a linear equation in two variables is a straight line, and a straight line is determined by two points, it is necessary to find only two solutions. However, finding at least three points will ensure accuracy.

⇒ Graph $y = 2x + 1$.

Choose any values of x, and then find the corresponding values of y. The numbers 0, 2, and -1 were chosen arbitrarily for x. It is convenient to record these solutions in a table.

x	$y = 2x + 1$	y
0	$2(0) + 1$	1
2	$2(2) + 1$	5
-1	$2(-1) + 1$	-1

Graph the ordered-pair solutions $(0, 1)$, $(2, 5)$, and $(-1, -1)$. Draw a line through the ordered-pair solutions.

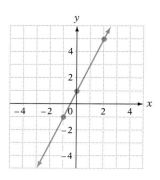

Note that the points whose coordinates are $(-2, -3)$ and $(1, 3)$ are on the graph and that these ordered pairs are solutions of the equation $y = 2x + 1$.

Remember that a graph is a drawing of the ordered-pair solutions of the equation. Therefore, every point on the graph is a solution of the equation, and every solution of the equation is a point on the graph.

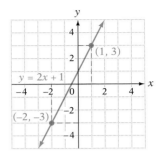

Example 3   Graph: $y = 3x - 2$

Solution

x	y
0	-2
2	4
-1	-5

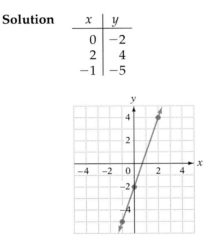

Problem 3   Graph: $y = 3x + 1$

Solution   See page S10.

 Graphing utilities create graphs by plotting points and then connecting the points to form a curve. Using a graphing utility, enter the equation $y = 3x - 2$ and verify the graph drawn in Example 3. (Refer to the Appendix for instructions on using a graphing calculator to graph a linear equation.) Trace along the graph and verify that $(0, -2)$, $(2, 4)$, and $(-1, -5)$ are coordinates of points on the graph. Now enter the equation $y = 3x + 1$ given in Problem 3. Verify that the ordered pairs you found for this equation are the coordinates of points on the graph.

When m is a fraction in the equation $y = mx + b$, choose values of x that will simplify the evaluation. For example, to graph $y = \frac{1}{3}x - 1$, we might choose the numbers 0, 3, and -3 for x. Note that these numbers are multiples of the denominator of $\frac{1}{3}$, the coefficient of x.

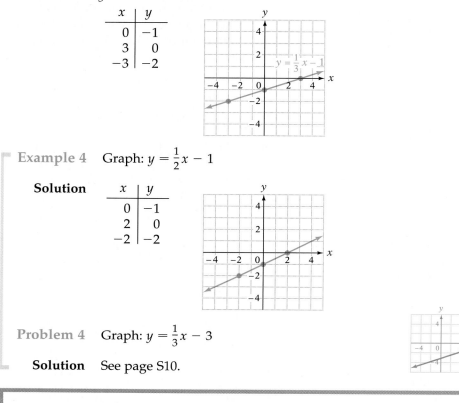

x	y
0	-1
3	0
-3	-2

$y = \frac{1}{3}x - 1$

Example 4   Graph: $y = \frac{1}{2}x - 1$

Solution

x	y
0	-1
2	0
-2	-2

Problem 4   Graph: $y = \frac{1}{3}x - 3$

Solution   See page S10.

Using a graphing utility, enter the equation $y = \frac{1}{2}x - 1$ and verify the graph drawn in Example 4. Trace along the graph and verify that $(0, -1)$, $(2, 0)$, $(-2, -2)$ are the coordinates of points on the graph. Follow the same procedure for Problem 4. (See the Appendix for instructions on entering a fractional coefficient of x.)

---

3   Graph equations of the form
$Ax + By = C$

$\langle 13 \rangle$ $\langle 14 \rangle$ HM³

An equation in the form $Ax + By = C$, where A and B are coefficients and C is a constant, is also a linear equation. Examples of these equations are shown below.

$$2x + 3y = 6 \qquad (A = 2, B = 3, C = 6)$$
$$x - 2y = -4 \qquad (A = 1, B = -2, C = -4)$$
$$2x + y = 0 \qquad (A = 2, B = 1, C = 0)$$
$$4x - 5y = 2 \qquad (A = 4, B = -5, C = 2)$$

One method of graphing an equation of the form $Ax + By = C$ involves first solving the equation for y and then following the same procedure used for graphing an equation of the form $y = mx + b$. To solve the equation for y means to rewrite the equation so that y is alone on one side of the equation and the term containing x and the constant are on the other side of the equation. The Addition and Multiplication Properties of Equations are used to rewrite an equation of the form $Ax + By = C$ in the form $y = mx + b$.

Solve the equation $3x + 2y = 4$ for y.

The equation is in the form $Ax + By = C$.

$$3x + 2y = 4$$

Use the Addition Property of Equations to subtract the term $3x$ from each side of the equation.

$$3x - 3x + 2y = -3x + 4$$

Simplify. Note that on the right side of the equation, the term containing x is first, followed by the constant.

$$2y = -3x + 4$$

Use the Multiplication Property of Equations to multiply each side of the equation by the reciprocal of the coefficient of y. (The coefficient of y is 2; the reciprocal of 2 is $\frac{1}{2}$.)

$$\frac{1}{2} \cdot 2y = \frac{1}{2}(-3x + 4)$$

Simplify. Use the Distributive Property on the right side of the equation.

$$y = \frac{1}{2}(-3x) + \frac{1}{2}(4)$$

The equation is now in the form

$y = mx + b$, with $m = -\frac{3}{2}$ and $b = 2$.

$$y = -\frac{3}{2}x + 2$$

In solving the equation $3x + 2y = 4$ for y, where we multiplied both sides of the equation by $\frac{1}{2}$, we could have divided both sides of the equation by 2, as shown at the right. In simplifying the right side after dividing both sides by 2, be sure to divide *each term* by 2.

$$2y = -3x + 4$$

$$\frac{2y}{2} = \frac{-3x + 4}{2}$$

$$y = \frac{-3x}{2} + \frac{4}{2}$$

$$y = -\frac{3}{2}x + 2$$

Being able to solve an equation of the form $Ax + By = C$ for y is important because most graphing utilities require that an equation be in the form $y = mx + b$ when the equation of the line is entered for graphing.

Example 5   Write $3x - 4y = 12$ in the form $y = mx + b$.

Solution
$$3x - 4y = 12$$
$$3x - 3x - 4y = -3x + 12 \qquad \blacktriangleright \text{Subtract } 3x \text{ from each side of the equation.}$$
$$-4y = -3x + 12 \qquad \blacktriangleright \text{Simplify.}$$
$$\frac{-4y}{-4} = \frac{-3x + 12}{-4} \qquad \blacktriangleright \text{Divide each side of the equation by } -4.$$
$$y = \frac{-3x}{-4} + \frac{12}{-4}$$
$$y = \frac{3}{4}x - 3$$

Problem 5   Write $5x - 2y = 10$ in the form $y = mx + b$.

Solution   See page S10. $y = \dfrac{5}{2}x - 5$

To graph an equation of the form $Ax + By = C$, we can first solve the equation for y and then follow the same procedure used for graphing an equation of the form $y = mx + b$. An example follows.

Graph: $3x + 4y = 12$

Write the equation in the form $y = mx + b$.

$$3x + 4y = 12$$
$$4y = -3x + 12$$
$$y = -\frac{3}{4}x + 3$$

Find at least three solutions.
Display the ordered pairs in a table.

x	y
0	3
4	0
-4	6

Graph the ordered pairs on a rectangular coordinate system, and draw a straight line through the points.

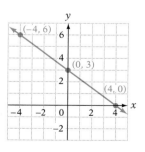

Example 6   Graph.   A. $2x - 5y = 10$ B. $x + 2y = 6$

Solution   A. $2x - 5y = 10$ B. $x + 2y = 6$

$-5y = -2x + 10$ $2y = -x + 6$

$y = \dfrac{2}{5}x - 2$ $y = -\dfrac{1}{2}x + 3$

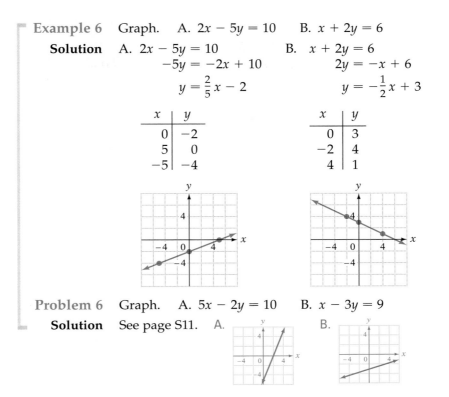

x	y
0	-2
5	0
-5	-4

x	y
0	3
-2	4
4	1

Problem 6   Graph.   A. $5x - 2y = 10$ B. $x - 3y = 9$

Solution   See page S11.   A.   B.

The graph of the equation $2x + 3y = 6$ is shown at the right. The graph crosses the x-axis at $(3, 0)$. This point is called the **x-intercept**. The graph also crosses the y-axis at $(0, 2)$. This point is called the **y-intercept**.

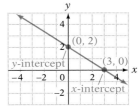

➡ Find the x-intercept and the y-intercept of the graph of the equation $2x + 3y = 6$ algebraically.

To find the x-intercept, let $y = 0$.
(Any point on the x-axis has y-coordinate 0.)

$2x + 3y = 6$
$2x + 3(0) = 6$
$2x = 6$
$x = 3$

LOOK CLOSELY

To find the x-intercept, let $y = 0$. To find the y-intercept, let $x = 0$.

The x-intercept is $(3, 0)$.

To find the y-intercept, let $x = 0$.
(Any point on the y-axis has x-coordinate 0.)

$2x + 3y = 6$
$2(0) + 3y = 6$
$3y = 6$
$y = 2$

The y-intercept is $(0, 2)$. ◀

Another method of graphing some equations of the form $Ax + By = C$ is to find the x- and y-intercepts, plot both intercepts, and then draw a line through the two points.

Example 7 Find the x- and y-intercepts for $x - 2y = 4$. Graph the line.

Solution x-intercept: $x - 2y = 4$
$\qquad\qquad\qquad\qquad x - 2(0) = 4$ ▶ To find the x-intercept, let $y = 0$.
$\qquad\qquad\qquad\qquad\qquad x = 4$

The x-intercept is $(4, 0)$.

y-intercept: $x - 2y = 4$
$\qquad\qquad\qquad\qquad 0 - 2y = 4$ ▶ To find the y-intercept, let $x = 0$.
$\qquad\qquad\qquad\qquad\quad -2y = 4$
$\qquad\qquad\qquad\qquad\qquad\quad y = -2$

The y-intercept is $(0, -2)$.

▶ Graph the ordered pairs $(4, 0)$ and $(0, -2)$. Draw a straight line through the points.

Problem 7 Find the x- and y-intercepts for $4x - y = 4$. Graph the line.

Solution See page S11. $(1, 0)$ and $(0, -4)$

The graph of an equation in which one of the variables is missing is either a horizontal line or a vertical line.

The equation $y = 2$ could be written $0 \cdot x + y = 2$. No matter what value of x is chosen, y is always 2. Some solutions to the equation are $(3, 2)$, $(-1, 2)$ $(0, 2)$, and $(-4, 2)$. The graph is shown at the right.

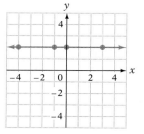

The **graph of $y = b$** is a horizontal line passing through the point whose coordinates are $(0, b)$.

Note that $(0, b)$ is the y-intercept of the graph of $y = b$. An equation of the form $y = b$ does not have an x-intercept.

The equation $x = -2$ could be written $x + 0 \cdot y = -2$. No matter what value of y is chosen, x is always -2. Some solutions to the equation are $(-2, 3)$, $(-2, -2)$, $(-2, 0)$, and $(-2, 2)$. The graph is shown at the right.

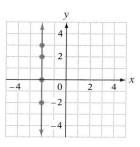

The **graph of $x = a$** is a vertical line passing through the point whose coordinates are $(a, 0)$.

Note that $(a, 0)$ is the x-intercept of the graph of $x = a$. An equation of the form $x = a$ does not have a y-intercept.

Example 8   Graph.   A. $y = -2$ B. $x = 3$

Solution   A. The graph of an equation of the form $y = b$ is a horizontal line with y-intercept $(0, b)$.

B. The graph of an equation of the form $x = a$ is a vertical line with x-intercept $(a, 0)$.

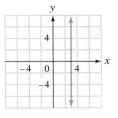

Problem 8   Graph.   A. $y = 3$ B. $x = -4$

Solution   See page S11.   A.

B.

CONCEPT REVIEW 5.2

Determine whether the statement is always true, sometimes true, or never true.

1. The equation $y = 3x^2 - 6$ is an example of a linear equation in two variables.   Never true

2. The value of m in the equation $y = 4x + 9$ is 9.   Never true

3. $(3, 5)$ is a solution of the equation $y = x + 2$.   Always true

4. The graph of a linear equation in two variables is a straight line.   Always true

5. To find the x-intercept of the graph of a linear equation, let $x = 0$.   Never true

6. The graph of an equation of the form $y = b$ is a horizontal line.   Always true

7. The graph of the equation $x = -4$ has an x-intercept of $(0, -4)$.   Never true

8. The graph shown at the right has a y-intercept of $(0, 3)$.   Always true

9. The graph of the equation $x = 2$ is a line that goes through every point that has an x-coordinate of 2.   Always true

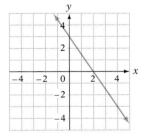

EXERCISES 5.2

1 For the given linear equation, find the value of m and the value of b.

1. $y = 4x + 1$ $m = 4, b = 1$

2. $y = -3x - 2$ $m = -3, b = -2$

3. $y = \dfrac{5}{6}x + \dfrac{1}{6}$ $m = \dfrac{5}{6}, b = \dfrac{1}{6}$

4. $y = -x$ $m = -1, b = 0$

5.   Is $(3, 4)$ a solution of $y = -x + 7$?   Yes

6.   Is $(2, -3)$ a solution of $y = x + 5$?   No

7.   Is $(-1, 2)$ a solution of $y = \frac{1}{2}x - 1$?   No

8.   Is $(1, -3)$ a solution of $y = -2x - 1$?   Yes

9.   Is $(4, 1)$ a solution of $y = \frac{1}{4}x + 1$?   No

10.   Is $(-5, 3)$ a solution of $y = -\frac{2}{5}x + 1$?   Yes

11.   Is $(0, 4)$ a solution of $y = \frac{3}{4}x + 4$?   Yes

12.   Is $(-2, 0)$ a solution of $y = -\frac{1}{2}x - 1$?   Yes

13.   Is $(0, 0)$ a solution of $y = 3x + 2$?   No

14.   Is $(0, 0)$ a solution of $y = -\frac{3}{4}x$?   Yes

15.   Find the ordered-pair solution of $y = 3x - 2$ that corresponds to $x = 3$. $(3, 7)$

16.   Find the ordered-pair solution of $y = 4x + 1$ that corresponds to $x = -1$. $(-1, -3)$

17.   Find the ordered-pair solution of $y = \frac{2}{3}x - 1$ that corresponds to $x = 6$. $(6, 3)$

18.   Find the ordered-pair solution of $y = \frac{3}{4}x - 2$ that corresponds to $x = 4$. $(4, 1)$

19.   Find the ordered-pair solution of $y = -3x + 1$ that corresponds to $x = 0$. $(0, 1)$

20.   Find the ordered-pair solution of $y = \frac{2}{5}x - 5$ that corresponds to $x = 0$. $(0, -5)$

21.   Find the ordered-pair solution of $y = \frac{2}{5}x + 2$ that corresponds to $x = -5$. $(-5, 0)$

22.   Find the ordered-pair solution of $y = -\frac{1}{6}x - 2$ that corresponds to $x = 12$. $(12, -4)$

2 Graph.

23. $y = 2x - 3$

24. $y = -2x + 2$

25. $y = \frac{1}{3}x$

26. $y = -3x$

27. $y = \frac{2}{3}x - 1$

28. $y = \frac{3}{4}x + 2$

29. $y = -\frac{1}{4}x + 2$

30. $y = -\frac{1}{3}x + 1$

31. $y = -\frac{2}{5}x + 1$

32. $y = -\frac{1}{2}x + 3$

33. $y = 2x - 4$

34. $y = 3x - 4$

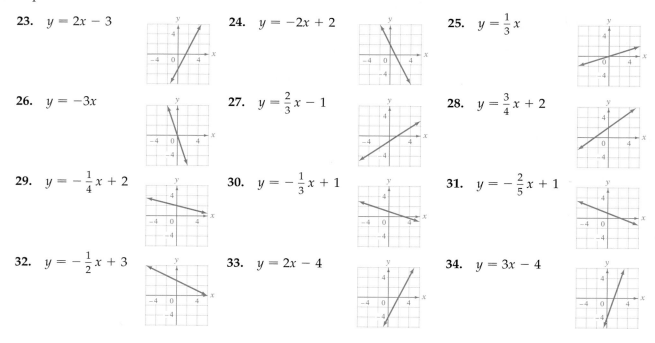

35. $y = -x + 2$

36. $y = -x - 1$

37. $y = -\dfrac{2}{3}x + 1$

38. $y = 5x - 4$

39. $y = -3x + 2$

40. $y = -x + 3$

Graph using a graphing utility.

41. $y = 3x - 4$

42. $y = -2x + 3$

43. $y = 2x - 3$

44. $y = -2x - 3$

45. $y = -\dfrac{2}{3}x$

46. $y = \dfrac{3}{2}x$

47. $y = \dfrac{3}{4}x + 2$

48. $y = -\dfrac{1}{3}x + 2$

49. $y = -\dfrac{3}{2}x - 3$

50. $y = -\dfrac{2}{5}x + 2$

51. $y = \dfrac{1}{4}x - 2$

52. $y = \dfrac{2}{3}x - 4$

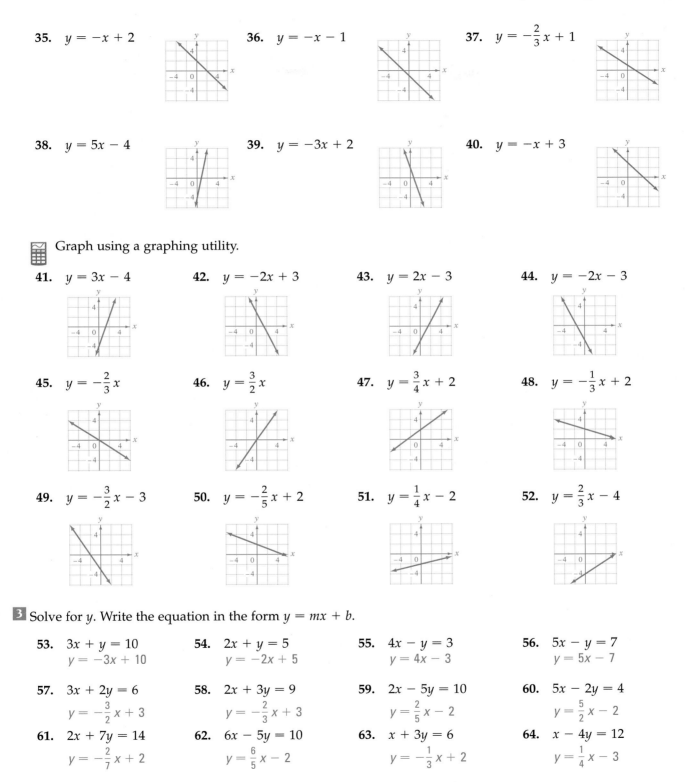

3 Solve for y. Write the equation in the form $y = mx + b$.

53. $3x + y = 10$
$y = -3x + 10$

54. $2x + y = 5$
$y = -2x + 5$

55. $4x - y = 3$
$y = 4x - 3$

56. $5x - y = 7$
$y = 5x - 7$

57. $3x + 2y = 6$
$y = -\dfrac{3}{2}x + 3$

58. $2x + 3y = 9$
$y = -\dfrac{2}{3}x + 3$

59. $2x - 5y = 10$
$y = \dfrac{2}{5}x - 2$

60. $5x - 2y = 4$
$y = \dfrac{5}{2}x - 2$

61. $2x + 7y = 14$
$y = -\dfrac{2}{7}x + 2$

62. $6x - 5y = 10$
$y = \dfrac{6}{5}x - 2$

63. $x + 3y = 6$
$y = -\dfrac{1}{3}x + 2$

64. $x - 4y = 12$
$y = \dfrac{1}{4}x - 3$

Graph.

65. $3x + y = 3$

66. $2x + y = 4$

67. $2x + 3y = 6$

68. $3x + 2y = 4$

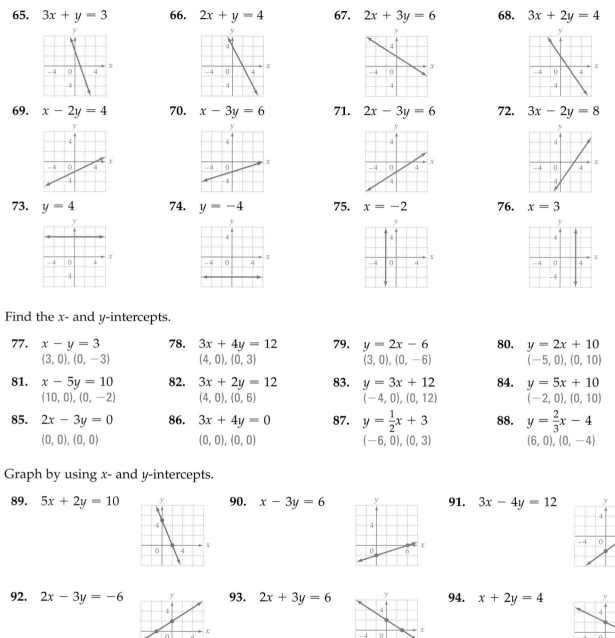

69. $x - 2y = 4$

70. $x - 3y = 6$

71. $2x - 3y = 6$

72. $3x - 2y = 8$

73. $y = 4$

74. $y = -4$

75. $x = -2$

76. $x = 3$

Find the x- and y-intercepts.

77. $x - y = 3$
$(3, 0), (0, -3)$

78. $3x + 4y = 12$
$(4, 0), (0, 3)$

79. $y = 2x - 6$
$(3, 0), (0, -6)$

80. $y = 2x + 10$
$(-5, 0), (0, 10)$

81. $x - 5y = 10$
$(10, 0), (0, -2)$

82. $3x + 2y = 12$
$(4, 0), (0, 6)$

83. $y = 3x + 12$
$(-4, 0), (0, 12)$

84. $y = 5x + 10$
$(-2, 0), (0, 10)$

85. $2x - 3y = 0$
$(0, 0), (0, 0)$

86. $3x + 4y = 0$
$(0, 0), (0, 0)$

87. $y = \frac{1}{2}x + 3$
$(-6, 0), (0, 3)$

88. $y = \frac{2}{3}x - 4$
$(6, 0), (0, -4)$

Graph by using x- and y-intercepts.

89. $5x + 2y = 10$

90. $x - 3y = 6$

91. $3x - 4y = 12$

92. $2x - 3y = -6$

93. $2x + 3y = 6$

94. $x + 2y = 4$

95. $2x + 5y = 10$

96. $3x + 4y = 12$

97. $x - 3y = 6$

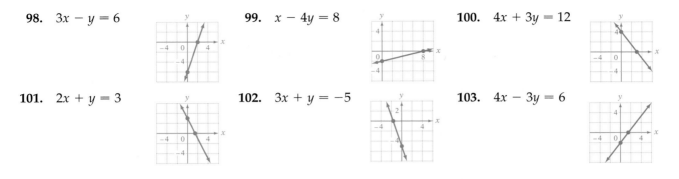

98. $3x - y = 6$

99. $x - 4y = 8$

100. $4x + 3y = 12$

101. $2x + y = 3$

102. $3x + y = -5$

103. $4x - 3y = 6$

Graph using a graphing utility. Verify that the graph has the correct x- and y-intercepts.

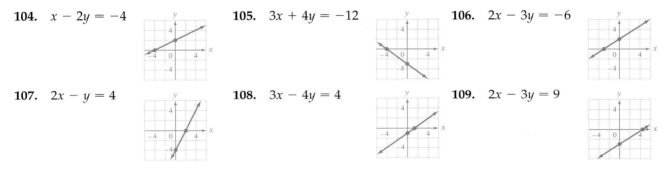

104. $x - 2y = -4$

105. $3x + 4y = -12$

106. $2x - 3y = -6$

107. $2x - y = 4$

108. $3x - 4y = 4$

109. $2x - 3y = 9$

APPLYING CONCEPTS 5.2

110. **a.** Show that the equation $y + 3 = 2(x + 4)$ is a linear equation by writing it in the form $y = mx + b$. $y = 2x + 5$

b. Find the ordered-pair solution that corresponds to $x = -4$. $(-4, -3)$

111. **a.** Show that the equation $y + 4 = -\dfrac{1}{2}(x + 2)$ is a linear equation by writing it in the form $y = mx + b$. $y = -\dfrac{1}{2}x - 5$

b. Find the ordered-pair solution that corresponds to $x = -2$. $(-2, -4)$

[C] **112.** For the linear equation $y = 2x - 3$, what is the increase in y that results when x is increased by 1?   2 units

[C] **113.** For the linear equation $y = -x - 4$, what is the decrease in y that results when x is increased by 1?   1 unit

[C] **114.** Write the equation of a line that has $(0, 0)$ as both the x-intercept and the y-intercept.   For example, $y = 2x$.

115. Explain **a.** why the y-coordinate of any point on the x-axis is 0 and **b.** why the x-coordinate of any point on the y-axis is 0.

S E C T I O N   **5.3**

Slopes of Straight Lines

1   Find the slope of a straight line

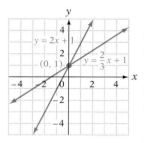

The graphs of $y = \frac{2}{3}x + 1$ and $y = 2x + 1$ are shown at the left. Each graph crosses the y-axis at $(0, 1)$, but the graphs have different slants. The **slope** of a line is a measure of the slant of the line. The symbol for slope is m.

The slope of a line is the ratio of the change in the y-coordinates between any two points on the line to the change in the x-coordinates.

The line containing the points whose coordinates are $(-2, -3)$ and $(6, 1)$ is graphed at the right. The change in y is the difference between the two y-coordinates.

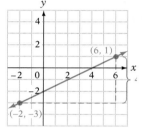

Change in $y = 1 - (-3) = 4$

The change in x is the difference between the two x-coordinates.

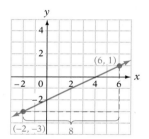

Change in $x = 6 - (-2) = 8$

For the line containing the points whose coordinates are $(-2, -3)$ and $(6, 1)$,

$$\text{Slope} = m = \frac{\text{change in } y}{\text{change in } x} = \frac{4}{8} = \frac{1}{2}$$

The slope of the line can also be described as the ratio of the vertical change (4 units) to the horizontal change (8 units) from the point whose coordinates are $(-2, -3)$ to the point whose coordinates are $(6, 1)$.

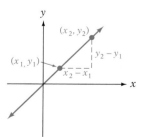

Slope Formula

The slope of a line containing two points P_1 and P_2, whose coordinates are (x_1, y_1) and (x_2, y_2), is given by

$$\text{Slope} = m = \frac{y_2 - y_1}{x_2 - x_1}, x_1 \neq x_2$$

In the slope formula, the points P_1 and P_2 are any two points on the line. The slope of a line is constant; therefore, the slope calculated using any two points on the line will be the same.

⟹ Find the slope of the line containing the points whose coordinates are $(-1, 1)$ and $(2, 3)$.

Let $P_1 = (-1, 1)$ and $P_2 = (2, 3)$. Then $x_1 = -1$, $y_1 = 1$, $x_2 = 2$, and $y_2 = 3$.

$$m = \frac{y_2 - y_1}{x_2 - x_1} = \frac{3 - 1}{2 - (-1)} = \frac{2}{3}$$

It does not matter which point is named P_1 and which P_2; the slope of the line will be the same. If the points are reversed, then $P_1 = (2, 3)$ and $P_2 = (-1, 1)$.

$$m = \frac{y_2 - y_1}{x_2 - x_1} = \frac{1 - 3}{-1 - 2} = \frac{-2}{-3} = \frac{2}{3}$$

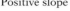

Positive slope

This is the same result. Here the slope is a positive number. A line that slants upward to the right has a **positive slope.**

LOOK CLOSELY

Positive slope means that the value of *y* increases as the value of *x* increases.

LOOK CLOSELY

Negative slope means that the value of *y* decreases as the value of *x* increases. Compare this to positive slope.

⟹ Find the slope of the line containing the points whose coordinates are $(-3, 4)$ and $(2, -2)$.

Let $P_1 = (-3, 4)$ and $P_2 = (2, -2)$.

$$m = \frac{y_2 - y_1}{x_2 - x_1} = \frac{-2 - 4}{2 - (-3)} = \frac{-6}{5} = -\frac{6}{5}$$

Here the slope is a negative number. A line that slants downward to the right has a **negative slope.**

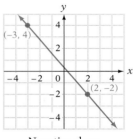

Negative slope

⟹ Find the slope of the line containing the points whose coordinates are $(-1, 3)$ and $(4, 3)$.

Let $P_1 = (-1, 3)$ and $P_2 = (4, 3)$.

$$m = \frac{y_2 - y_1}{x_2 - x_1} = \frac{3 - 3}{4 - (-1)} = \frac{0}{5} = 0$$

When $y_1 = y_2$, the graph is a horizontal line.

A horizontal line has **zero slope.**

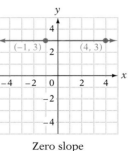

Zero slope

INSTRUCTOR NOTE

After completing the discussion of the different possibilities for slope, draw several lines with different slopes and ask students to identify the line as having positive, negative, zero, or undefined slope.

  Another possible activity is to draw a point in a coordinate grid and then ask students to draw a line with a specified slope through the point.

⟹ Find the slope of the line containing the points whose coordinates are $(2, -2)$ and $(2, 4)$.

Let $P_1 = (2, -2)$ and $P_2 = (2, 4)$.

$$m = \frac{y_2 - y_1}{x_2 - x_1} = \frac{4 - (-2)}{2 - 2} = \frac{6}{0} \leftarrow \text{Not a real number}$$

When $x_1 = x_2$, the denominator of $\frac{y_2 - y_1}{x_2 - x_1}$ is 0 and the

graph is a vertical line. Because division by zero is not defined, the slope of the line is not defined.

The slope of a vertical line is **undefined.**

Undefined slope

Remember that zero slope and undefined slope are different. The graph of a line with zero slope is horizontal. The graph of a line with undefined slope is vertical.

Example 1   Find the slope of the line containing the points P_1 and P_2.
A. $P_1(-2, -1), P_2(3, 4)$ B. $P_1(-3, 1), P_2(2, -2)$
C. $P_1(-1, 4), P_2(-1, 0)$ D. $P_1(-1, 2), P_2(4, 2)$

Solution   A. $m = \dfrac{y_2 - y_1}{x_2 - x_1} = \dfrac{4 - (-1)}{3 - (-2)} = \dfrac{5}{5} = 1$

The slope is 1.

B. $m = \dfrac{y_2 - y_1}{x_2 - x_1} = \dfrac{-2 - 1}{2 - (-3)} = \dfrac{-3}{5}$

The slope is $-\dfrac{3}{5}$.

C. $m = \dfrac{y_2 - y_1}{x_2 - x_1} = \dfrac{0 - 4}{-1 - (-1)} = \dfrac{-4}{0}$

The slope is undefined.

D. $m = \dfrac{y_2 - y_1}{x_2 - x_1} = \dfrac{2 - 2}{4 - (-1)} = \dfrac{0}{5} = 0$

The slope is 0.

Problem 1   Find the slope of the line containing the points P_1 and P_2.
A. $P_1(-1, 2), P_2(1, 3)$ B. $P_1(1, 2), P_2(4, -5)$
C. $P_1(2, 3), P_2(2, 7)$ D. $P_1(1, -3), P_2(-5, -3)$

Solution   See page S11.   A. $\dfrac{1}{2}$ B. $-\dfrac{7}{3}$ C. Undefined   D. 0

There are many applications of the concept of slope. Here are two possibilities.

In 1988, when Florence Griffith-Joyner set the world record for the 100-meter dash, her average rate of speed was approximately 9.5 m/s. The graph at the right shows the distance she ran during her record-setting run. From the graph, note that after 4 s she had traveled 38 m and that after 6 s she had traveled 57 m. The slope of the line between these two points is

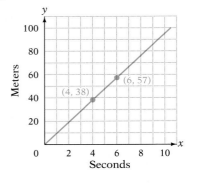

$$m = \frac{57 - 38}{6 - 4} = \frac{19}{2} = 9.5$$

Note that the slope of the line is the same as the rate she was running, 9.5 m/s. The average speed of an object is related to slope.

Here is an example taken from education. According to the U.S. Department of Education, from 1987 to 1997, the per-pupil spending on public education increased at a rate of approximately $259.40 per year. The graph at the right shows the per-pupil spending from 1987 to 1997. From the graph, we learn that in 1987 the per-pupil spending was $3970 and that in 1997 the per-pupil spending was $6564. The slope of the line between these two points is

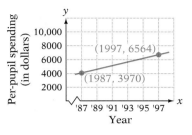

$$m = \frac{6564 - 3970}{1997 - 1987} = \frac{2594}{10} = 259.4$$

Observe that the slope of the line is the same as the rate at which per-pupil spending was increasing, $259.40 per year.

In general, any quantity that is expressed by using the word *per* is represented mathematically as slope. In the first example above, slope was 9.5 meters *per* second; in the second example, slope was $259.40 *per* year.

Example 2   The graph at the right shows the number of banks in the United States from 1990 to 1997. Numbers have been rounded to the nearest hundred. Find the slope of the line. Write a sentence that states the meaning of the slope.

Solution $m = \dfrac{11,000 - 15,200}{1997 - 1990} = -600$

The slope -600 means that from 1990 to 1997, the number of banks in the United States was *decreasing* at a rate of 600 per year.

Problem 2   The graph at the right shows the approximate decline in the value of a used car over a five-year period. Find the slope of the line. Write a sentence that states the meaning of the slope.

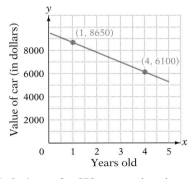

Solution   See page S11.   The slope is -850. A slope of -850 means that the value of the car was decreasing at a rate of $850 per year.

2 ## Graph a line using the slope and y-intercept

Recall that we can find the y-intercept of a linear equation by letting $x = 0$.

To find the y-intercept of $y = 3x + 4$, let $x = 0$.

$$y = 3x + 4$$
$$y = 3(0) + 4$$
$$y = 4$$

The y-intercept is $(0, 4)$.

The constant term of $y = 3x + 4$ is the y-coordinate of the y-intercept.

In general, for any equation of the form $y = mx + b$, the y-intercept is $(0, b)$.

The graph of the equation $y = \frac{2}{3}x + 1$ is shown at the right. The points whose coordinates are $(-3, -1)$ and $(3, 3)$ are on the graph. The slope of the line is

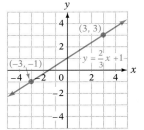

$$m = \frac{3 - (-1)}{3 - (-3)} = \frac{4}{6} = \frac{2}{3}$$

Note that the slope of the line has the same value as the coefficient of x.

Slope-Intercept Form of a Straight Line

For any equation of the form $y = mx + b$, the slope of the line is m, the coefficient of x. The y-intercept is $(0, b)$. The equation

$$y = mx + b$$

is called the **slope-intercept form of a straight line.**

The slope of the graph of $y = -\frac{3}{4}x + 1$ is $-\frac{3}{4}$. The y-intercept is $(0, 1)$.

$$y = \boxed{m}\,x + \boxed{b}$$
$$y = \boxed{-\frac{3}{4}}\,x + \boxed{1}$$

$\text{Slope} = m = -\frac{3}{4}$ — $y\text{-intercept} = (0, b) = (0, 1)$

➡ Find the slope and y-intercept of the graph of $y = \frac{5}{2}x - 6$.

$$\text{Slope} = m = \frac{5}{2} \qquad b = -6$$

The slope is $\frac{5}{2}$.　　　The y-intercept is $(0, -6)$.

When the equation of a straight line is in the form $y = mx + b$, the graph can be drawn using the slope and y-intercept. First locate the y-intercept. Use the slope to find a second point on the line. Then draw a line through the two points.

⇨ Graph $y = 2x - 3$ by using the slope and y-intercept.

y-intercept $= (0, b) = (0, -3)$

$m = 2 = \dfrac{2}{1} = \dfrac{\text{change in } y}{\text{change in } x}$

Beginning at the y-intercept, move right 1 unit (change in x) and then up 2 units (change in y).

(1, −1) are the coordinates of a second point on the graph.

Draw a line through (0, −3) and (1, −1).

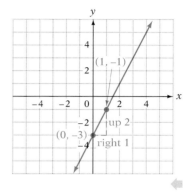

Using a graphing utility, enter the equation $y = 2x - 3$ and verify the graph shown above. Trace along the graph and verify that (0, −3) is the y-intercept and that the point whose coordinates are (1, −1) is on the graph.

Example 3   Graph $y = -\dfrac{2}{3}x + 1$ by using the slope and y-intercept.

Solution y-intercept $= (0, b) = (0, 1)$

$m = -\dfrac{2}{3} = \dfrac{-2}{3}$

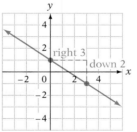

▶ A slope of $\dfrac{-2}{3}$ means to move right 3 units and then down 2 units.

Problem 3   Graph $y = -\dfrac{1}{4}x - 1$ by using the slope and y-intercept.

Solution   See page S11.

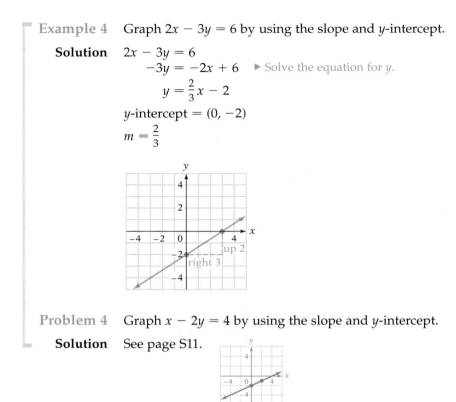

Example 4   Graph $2x - 3y = 6$ by using the slope and y-intercept.

Solution $2x - 3y = 6$
$$-3y = -2x + 6 \quad \blacktriangleright \text{ Solve the equation for } y.$$
$$y = \frac{2}{3}x - 2$$
$$y\text{-intercept} = (0, -2)$$
$$m = \frac{2}{3}$$

Problem 4   Graph $x - 2y = 4$ by using the slope and y-intercept.

Solution   See page S11.

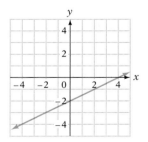

CONCEPT REVIEW 5.3

Determine whether the statement is always true, sometimes true, or never true.

1.   In the equation $y = mx + b$, m is the symbol for slope.   Always true

2.   The formula for slope is $m = \frac{y_2 - y_1}{x_2 - x_1}$.   Always true

3.   A vertical line has zero slope, and the slope of a horizontal line is undefined.
         Never true

4.   Any two points on a line can be used to find the slope of the line.   Always true

5.   Shown at the right is the graph of a line with negative slope.   Never true

6.   The y-intercept of the graph of the equation $y = -2x + 5$ is $(5, 0)$.   Never true

EXERCISES 5.3

1.   Explain how to find the slope of a line when you know two points on the line.

2.   What is the difference between a line that has zero slope and a line whose slope is undefined?

Find the slope of the line containing the points P_1 and P_2.

3. $P_1(4, 2), P_2(3, 4)$ -2 **4.** $P_1(2, 1), P_2(3, 4)$ 3 **5.** $P_1(-1, 3), P_2(2, 4)$ $\frac{1}{3}$

6. $P_1(-2, 1), P_2(2, 2)$ $\frac{1}{4}$ **7.** $P_1(2, 4), P_2(4, -1)$ $-\frac{5}{2}$ **8.** $P_1(1, 3), P_2(5, -3)$ $-\frac{3}{2}$

9. $P_1(-2, 3), P_2(2, 1)$ $-\frac{1}{2}$ **10.** $P_1(5, -2), P_2(1, 0)$ $-\frac{1}{2}$ **11.** $P_1(8, -3), P_2(4, 1)$ -1

12. $P_1(0, 3), P_2(2, -1)$ -2 **13.** $P_1(3, -4), P_2(3, 5)$ Undefined   **14.** $P_1(-1, 2), P_2(-1, 3)$ Undefined

15. $P_1(4, -2), P_2(3, -2)$ 0 **16.** $P_1(5, 1), P_2(-2, 1)$ 0 **17.** $P_1(0, -1), P_2(3, -2)$ $-\frac{1}{3}$

18. $P_1(3, 0), P_2(2, -1)$ 1 **19.** $P_1(-2, 3), P_2(1, 3)$ 0 **20.** $P_1(4, -1), P_2(-3, -1)$ 0

21. $P_1(-2, 4), P_2(-1, -1)$ -5 **22.** $P_1(6, -4), P_2(4, -2)$ -1 **23.** $P_1(-2, -3), P_2(-2, 1)$ Undefined

24. $P_1(5, 1), P_2(5, -2)$ Undefined   **25.** $P_1(-1, 5), P_2(5, 1)$ $-\frac{2}{3}$ **26.** $P_1(-1, 5), P_2(7, 1)$ $-\frac{1}{2}$

27.   **Business**   The graph at the right shows the sales of sunglasses during the years 1991 through 1997. Find the slope of the line. Write a sentence that explains the meaning of the slope.
$m = 200{,}000{,}000$
A slope of 200,000,000 means that sales of sunglasses have been increasing at a rate of 200,000,000 per year.

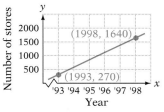

28.   **Business**   The graph at the right shows the number of Starbucks stores each year from 1993 to 1998. Numbers have been rounded to the nearest ten. (The 1998 figure is through March of that year.) Find the slope of the line. Write a sentence that explains the meaning of the slope.
$m = 274$
A slope of 274 means that the number of Starbucks stores has been increasing at a rate of 274 per year.

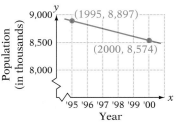

29.   **Demographics**   The graph at the right shows the population of London, England, in 1995 and the projected population of that city in the year 2000. Find the slope of the line. Write a sentence that explains the meaning of the slope.
$m = -64{,}600$
A slope of −64,600 means that the population of London is decreasing at a rate of 64,600 people per year.

30.   **Aviation**   The graph at the right shows the height of a plane above an airport during its 30-minute descent from cruising altitude to landing. Find the slope of the line. Write a sentence that explains the meaning of the slope.
$m = -1000$
A slope of −1000 means that the height of the plane is decreasing at a rate of 1000 feet per minute.

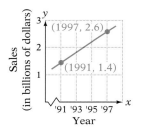

2 **31.** Why is an equation of the form $y = mx + b$ said to be in slope-intercept form?

32. Explain how to graph the equation $y = \frac{2}{3}x + 4$ by using the slope and the y-intercept.

Graph by using the slope and y-intercept.

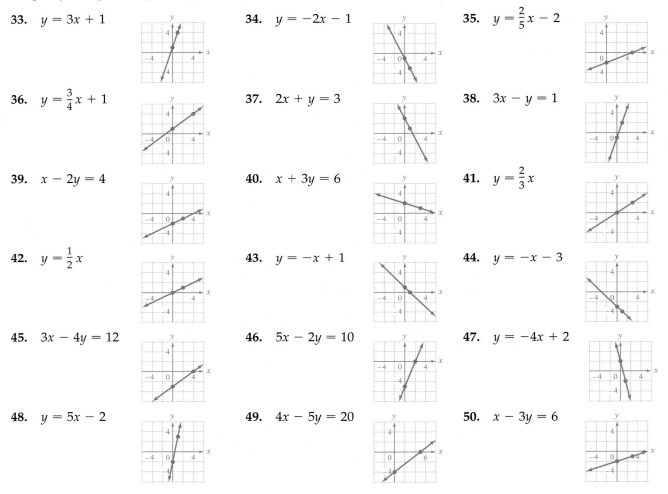

33. $y = 3x + 1$

34. $y = -2x - 1$

35. $y = \frac{2}{5}x - 2$

36. $y = \frac{3}{4}x + 1$

37. $2x + y = 3$

38. $3x - y = 1$

39. $x - 2y = 4$

40. $x + 3y = 6$

41. $y = \frac{2}{3}x$

42. $y = \frac{1}{2}x$

43. $y = -x + 1$

44. $y = -x - 3$

45. $3x - 4y = 12$

46. $5x - 2y = 10$

47. $y = -4x + 2$

48. $y = 5x - 2$

49. $4x - 5y = 20$

50. $x - 3y = 6$

APPLYING CONCEPTS 5.3

[C] **51.** What effect does increasing the coefficient of x have on the graph of $y = mx + b$?   Increases the slope

[C] **52.** What effect does decreasing the coefficient of x have on the graph of $y = mx + b$?   Decreases the slope

[C] **53.** What effect does increasing the constant term have on the graph of $y = mx + b$?   Increases the y-intercept

[C] **54.** What effect does decreasing the constant term have on the graph of $y = mx + b$?   Decreases the y-intercept

55. Do the graphs of all straight lines have a y-intercept? If not, give an example of one that does not.   No; for example, $x = 2$.

56. If two lines have the same slope and the same y-intercept, must the graphs of the lines be the same? If not, give an example.   Yes

57. What does the highway sign shown at the right have to do with slope?

Grade
6%

S E C T I O N **5.4**

Equations of Straight Lines

1 Find the equation of a line using the equation $y = mx + b$

When the slope of a line and a point on the line are known, the equation of the line can be written using the slope-intercept form, $y = mx + b$. In the first example shown below, the known point is the y-intercept. In the second example, the known point is a point other than the y-intercept.

▶ Find the equation of the line that has slope 3 and y-intercept $(0, 2)$.

The given slope, 3, is m.	$y = mx + b$
Replace m with 3.	$y = 3x + b$
The given point, $(0, 2)$, is the y-intercept. Replace b with 2.	$y = 3x + 2$

The equation of the line that has slope 3 and y-intercept 2 is $y = 3x + 2$. ◀

▶ Find the equation of the line that has slope $\frac{1}{2}$ and contains the point whose coordinates are $(-2, 4)$.

The given slope, $\frac{1}{2}$, is m.	$y = mx + b$
Replace m with $\frac{1}{2}$.	$y = \frac{1}{2}x + b$
The given point, $(-2, 4)$, is a solution of the equation of the line. Replace x and y in the equation with the coordinates of the point.	$4 = \frac{1}{2}(-2) + b$
Solve for b, the y-intercept.	$4 = -1 + b$ $5 = b$
Write the equation of the line by replacing m and b in the equation by their values.	$y = mx + b$ $y = \frac{1}{2}x + 5$

LOOK CLOSELY

Every ordered pair is of the form (x, y). For the point $(-2, 4)$, -2 is the x value and 4 is the y value. Substitute -2 for x and 4 for y.

The equation of the line that has slope $\frac{1}{2}$ and contains the point whose coordinates are $(-2, 4)$ is $y = \frac{1}{2}x + 5$. ◀

Example 1   Find the equation of the line that contains the point whose coordinates are $(3, -3)$ and has slope $\frac{2}{3}$.

Solution $y = mx + b$

$y = \frac{2}{3}x + b$ ▶ Replace m with the given slope.

$-3 = \frac{2}{3}(3) + b$ ▶ Replace x and y in the equation with the coordinates of the given point.

$-3 = 2 + b$ ▶ Solve for b.
$-5 = b$

$y = \frac{2}{3}x - 5$ ▶ Write the equation of the line by replacing m and b in $y = mx + b$ by their values.

Problem 1   Find the equation of the line that contains the point whose coordinates are $(4, -2)$ and has slope $\frac{3}{2}$.

Solution   See page S11. $y = \frac{3}{2}x - 8$

2   Find the equation of a line using the point-slope formula

An alternative method for finding the equation of a line, given the slope and the coordinates of a point on the line, involves use of the point-slope formula. The point-slope formula is derived from the formula for slope.

Let (x_1, y_1) be the coordinates of the given point on the line, and let (x, y) be the coordinates of any other point on the line.

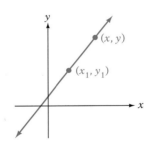

Use the formula for slope. $\dfrac{y - y_1}{x - x_1} = m$

Multiply both sides of the equation by $(x - x_1)$. $\dfrac{y - y_1}{x - x_1}(x - x_1) = m(x - x_1)$

Simplify. $y - y_1 = m(x - x_1)$

Point-Slope Formula

The equation of the line that has slope m and contains the point whose coordinates are (x_1, y_1) can be found by the point-slope formula:

$$y - y_1 = m(x - x_1)$$

INSTRUCTOR NOTE

A model of the point-slope formula with open parentheses may help students substitute correctly.

$y - y_1 = m(x - x_1)$
$\quad\downarrow\qquad\downarrow\qquad\quad\downarrow$
$y - (\ ) = (\ )[x - (\ )]$

Example 2   Use the point-slope formula to find the equation of a line that passes through the point whose coordinates are $(-2, -1)$ and has slope $\frac{3}{2}$.

Solution $(x_1, y_1) = (-2, -1)$ ▶ Let (x_1, y_1) be the given point.

$$m = \frac{3}{2}$$ ▶ m is the given slope.

$$y - y_1 = m(x - x_1)$$ ▶ This is the point-slope formula.

$$y - (-1) = \frac{3}{2}[x - (-2)]$$ ▶ Substitute -2 for x_1, -1 for y_1, and $\frac{3}{2}$ for m.

$$y + 1 = \frac{3}{2}(x + 2)$$ ▶ Rewrite the equation in the form $y = mx + b$.

$$y + 1 = \frac{3}{2}x + 3$$

$$y = \frac{3}{2}x + 2$$

Problem 2   Use the point-slope formula to find the equation of a line that passes through the point whose coordinates are $(5, 4)$ and has slope $\frac{2}{5}$.

Solution   See page S11. $y = \frac{2}{5}x + 2$

CONCEPT REVIEW 5.4

Determine whether the statement is always true, sometimes true, or never true.

1. The graph of the equation $y = 5x + 7$ has slope 5 and y-intercept $(0, 7)$.
Always true

2. If the equation of a line has y-intercept $(0, 4)$, then 4 can be substituted for b in the equation $y = mx + b$.   Always true

3. Suppose the equation of a line contains the point $(-3, 1)$. Then when y is -3, x is 1.   Sometimes true

4. The point-slope formula is $y - y_1 = mx - x_1$.   Never true

5. The point-slope formula can be used to find the equation of a line with zero slope.   Always true

6. If it is stated that the y-intercept is 2, then the y-intercept is the point $(2, 0)$.
Never true

EXERCISES 5.4

1 Use the slope-intercept form.

1. Find the equation of the line that contains the point whose coordinates are $(0, 2)$ and has slope 2. $y = 2x + 2$

2. Find the equation of the line that contains the point whose coordinates are $(0, -1)$ and has slope -2. $y = -2x - 1$

3. Find the equation of the line that contains the point whose coordinates are $(-1, 2)$ and has slope -3. $y = -3x - 1$

4. Find the equation of the line that contains the point whose coordinates are $(2, -3)$ and has slope 3. $y = 3x - 9$

5. Find the equation of the line that contains the point whose coordinates are $(3, 1)$ and has slope $\frac{1}{3}$. $y = \frac{1}{3}x$

6. Find the equation of the line that contains the point whose coordinates are $(-2, 3)$ and has slope $\frac{1}{2}$. $y = \frac{1}{2}x + 4$

7. Find the equation of the line that contains the point whose coordinates are $(4, -2)$ and has slope $\frac{3}{4}$. $y = \frac{3}{4}x - 5$

8. Find the equation of the line that contains the point whose coordinates are $(2, 3)$ and has slope $-\frac{1}{2}$. $y = -\frac{1}{2}x + 4$

9. Find the equation of the line that contains the point whose coordinates are $(5, -3)$ and has slope $-\frac{3}{5}$. $y = -\frac{3}{5}x$

10. Find the equation of the line that contains the point whose coordinates are $(5, -1)$ and has slope $\frac{1}{5}$. $y = \frac{1}{5}x - 2$

11. Find the equation of the line that contains the point whose coordinates are $(2, 3)$ and has slope $\frac{1}{4}$. $y = \frac{1}{4}x + \frac{5}{2}$

12. Find the equation of the line that contains the point whose coordinates are $(-1, 2)$ and has slope $-\frac{1}{2}$. $y = -\frac{1}{2}x + \frac{3}{2}$

13. Find the equation of the line that contains the point whose coordinates are $(-3, -5)$ and has slope $-\frac{2}{3}$. $y = -\frac{2}{3}x - 7$

14. Find the equation of the line that contains the point whose coordinates are $(-4, 0)$ and has slope $\frac{5}{2}$. $y = \frac{5}{2}x + 10$

2 15.   When is the point-slope formula used?

16.   Explain the meaning of each variable in the point-slope formula.

Use the point-slope formula.

17. Find the equation of the line that passes through the point whose coordinates are $(1, -1)$ and has slope 2. $y = 2x - 3$

18. Find the equation of the line that passes through the point whose coordinates are (2, 3) and has slope -1. $y = -x + 5$

19. Find the equation of the line that passes through the point whose coordinates are $(-2, 1)$ and has slope -2. $y = -2x - 3$

20. Find the equation of the line that passes through the point whose coordinates are $(-1, -3)$ and has slope -3. $y = -3x - 6$

21. Find the equation of the line that passes through the point whose coordinates are (0, 0) and has slope $\frac{2}{3}$. $y = \frac{2}{3}x$

22. Find the equation of the line that passes through the point whose coordinates are (0, 0) and has slope $-\frac{1}{5}$. $y = -\frac{1}{5}x$

23. Find the equation of the line that passes through the point whose coordinates are (2, 3) and has slope $\frac{1}{2}$. $y = \frac{1}{2}x + 2$

24. Find the equation of the line that passes through the point whose coordinates are $(3, -1)$ and has slope $\frac{2}{3}$. $y = \frac{2}{3}x - 3$

25. Find the equation of the line that passes through the point whose coordinates are $(-4, 1)$ and has slope $-\frac{3}{4}$. $y = -\frac{3}{4}x - 2$

26. Find the equation of the line that passes through the point whose coordinates are $(-5, 0)$ and has slope $-\frac{1}{5}$. $y = -\frac{1}{5}x - 1$

27. Find the equation of the line that passes through the point whose coordinates are $(-2, 1)$ and has slope $\frac{3}{4}$. $y = \frac{3}{4}x + \frac{5}{2}$

28. Find the equation of the line that passes through the point whose coordinates are $(3, -2)$ and has slope $\frac{1}{6}$. $y = \frac{1}{6}x - \frac{5}{2}$

29. Find the equation of the line that passes through the point whose coordinates are $(-3, -5)$ and has slope $-\frac{4}{3}$. $y = -\frac{4}{3}x - 9$

30. Find the equation of the line that passes through the point whose coordinates are $(3, -1)$ and has slope $\frac{3}{5}$. $y = \frac{3}{5}x - \frac{14}{5}$

APPLYING CONCEPTS 5.4

Is there a linear equation that contains all the given ordered pairs? If there is, find the equation.

31. (5, 1), (4, 2), (0, 6)   Yes; $y = -x + 6$

32. (−2, −4), (0, −3), (4, −1)   Yes; $y = \dfrac{1}{2}x - 3$

33. (−1, −5), (2, 4), (0, 2)   No

34. (3, −1), (12, −4), (−6, 2)   Yes; $y = -\dfrac{1}{3}x$

The given ordered pairs are solutions to the same linear equation. Find n.

35. (0, 1), (4, 9), (3, n)   7

36. (2, 2), (−1, 5), (3, n)   1

37. (2, −2), (−2, −4), (4, n)   −1

38. (1, −2), (−2, 4), (4, n)   −8

The relationship between Celsius and Fahrenheit temperature can be given by a linear equation. Water freezes at 0°C or at 32°F. Water boils at 100°C or at 212°F.

[C] **39.** Write a linear equation expressing Fahrenheit temperature in terms of Celsius temperature. $F = \dfrac{9}{5}C + 32$

[C] **40.** Graph the equation found in Exercise 39.

The formula $y - y_1 = \dfrac{y_2 - y_1}{x_2 - x_1}(x - x_1)$, where $x_1 \neq x_2$, is called the **two-point formula** for a straight line. This formula can be used to find the equation of a line given two points. Use this formula for Exercises 41 and 42.

41. Find the equation of the line that passes through (−2, 3) and (4, −1). $y = -\dfrac{2}{3}x + \dfrac{5}{3}$

42. Find the equation of the line that passes through the points (3, −1) and (4, −3). $y = -2x + 5$

43. Explain why the condition $x_1 \neq x_2$ is placed on the two-point formula given above.

44. Explain how the two-point formula given above can be derived from the point-slope formula.

S E C T I O N 5.5

Functions

1 ## Introduction to functions   ⟨16⟩ HM³

The definition of set given in the chapter on "Real Numbers" was that a set is a collection of objects. Recall that the objects in a set are called the elements of the set. The elements in a set can be anything.

The set of planets in our solar system is

{Mercury, Venus, Earth, Mars, Jupiter, Saturn, Uranus, Neptune, Pluto}

The set of colors in a rainbow is

{red, orange, yellow, green, blue, indigo, violet}

The objects in a set can be ordered pairs. When the elements in a set are ordered pairs, the set is called a relation. A **relation** is any set of ordered pairs.

The set {(1, 1), (2, 4), (3, 9), (4, 16), (5, 25)} is a relation. There are five elements in the set. The elements are the ordered pairs (1, 1), (2, 4), (3, 9), (4, 16), and (5, 25).

The following table shows the number of hours that each of eight students spent in the math lab during the week of the math midterm exam and the score that each of these students received on the math midterm.

Hours	2	3	4	4	5	6	6	7
Score	60	70	70	80	85	85	95	90

This information can be written as the relation

{(2, 60), (3, 70), (4, 70), (4, 80), (5, 85), (6, 85), (6, 95), (7, 90)}

where the first coordinate of each ordered pair is the hours spent in the math lab and the second coordinate is the score on the midterm exam.

The **domain** of a relation is the set of first coordinates of the ordered pairs. The **range** is the set of second coordinates of the ordered pairs. For the relation above,

Domain = {2, 3, 4, 5, 6, 7}   Range = {60, 70, 80, 85, 90, 95}

The **graph of a relation** is the graph of the ordered pairs that belong to the relation. The graph of the relation given above is shown at the left. The horizontal axis represents the domain (the hours spent in the math lab) and the vertical axis represents the range (the exam score).

A **function** is a special type of relation in which no two ordered pairs have the same first coordinate and different second coordinates. The relation above is not a function because the ordered pairs (4, 70) and (4, 80) have the same first coordinate and different second coordinates. The ordered pairs (6, 85) and (6, 95) also have the same first coordinate and different second coordinates.

The table at the right describes a grading scale that defines a relationship between a test score and a letter grade. Some of the ordered pairs in this relation are (38, F), (73, C), and (94, A).

Score	Letter Grade
90–100	A
80–89	B
70–79	C
60–69	D
0–59	F

This relation defines a function because no two ordered pairs can have the *same* first coordinate and *different* second coordinates. For instance, it is not possible to have an average of 73 paired with any grade other than C. Both (73, C) and (73, A) cannot be ordered pairs belonging to the function, or two students with the same score would receive different grades. Note that (81, B) and (88, B) are ordered pairs of this function. Ordered pairs of a function may have the same *second* coordinate paired with different *first* coordinates.

The domain of this function is $\{0, 1, 2, 3, \ldots, 98, 99, 100\}$.

The range of this function is $\{A, B, C, D, F\}$.

> **Example 1**   Find the domain and range of the relation
> $\{(-5, 1), (-3, 3), (-1, 5)\}$. Is the relation a function?
>
> **Solution**   The domain is $\{-5, -3, -1\}$.   ▶ The domain of the relation is the set of the first components of the ordered pairs.
>
> The range is $\{1, 3, 5\}$.   ▶ The range of the relation is the set of the second components of the ordered pairs.
>
> No two ordered pairs have the same first coordinate.
> The relation is a function.
>
> **Problem 1**   Find the domain and range of the relation
> $\{(1, 0), (1, 1), (1, 2), (1, 3), (1, 4)\}$. Is the relation a function?
>
> **Solution**   See page S12.   D: {1}, R: {0, 1, 2, 3, 4}; no

Although a function can be described in terms of ordered pairs or in a table, functions are often described by an equation. The letter f is commonly used to represent a function, but any letter can be used.

The "square" function assigns to each real number its square. The square function is described by the equation

$$f(x) = x^2 \qquad \text{read } f(x) \text{ as "} f \text{ of } x \text{" or "the value of } f \text{ at } x."$$

$f(x)$ is the symbol for the number that is paired with x. In terms of ordered pairs, this is written $(x, f(x))$. $f(x)$ is the **value of the function** at x because it is the result of evaluating the variable expression. For example, $f(4)$ means to replace x by 4 and then simplify the resulting numerical expression. This process is called **evaluating the function.**

INSTRUCTOR NOTE

One way to assist students with evaluating a function is to use open parentheses. For example,

$$f(x) = x^2$$
$$f(\ ) = (\ )^2$$
$$\downarrow \qquad \downarrow$$
$$f(4) = (4)^2$$

The notation $f(4)$ is used to indicate the number that is paired with 4. To evaluate $f(x) = x^2$ at 4, replace x with 4 and simplify.

$$f(x) = x^2$$
$$f(4) = 4^2$$
$$f(4) = 16$$

The square function squares a number, and when 4 is squared, the result is 16. For the square function, the number 4 is paired with 16. In other words, when x is 4, $f(x)$ is 16. The ordered pair $(4, 16)$ is an element of the function.

It is important to remember that $f(x)$ does not mean f times x. The letter f stands for the function, and $f(x)$ is the number that is paired with x.

> **Example 2**   Evaluate $f(x) = 2x - 4$ at $x = 3$. Write an ordered pair that is an element of the function.
>
> **Solution** $f(x) = 2x - 4$
> $f(3) = 2(3) - 4$ ▶ $f(3)$ is the number that is paired with 3. Replace x by 3 and evaluate.
> $f(3) = 6 - 4$
> $f(3) = 2$
>
> The ordered pair $(3, 2)$ is an element of the function.

Problem 2   Evaluate $f(x) = -5x + 1$ at $x = 2$. Write an ordered pair that is an element of the function.

Solution   See page S12. $-9; (2, -9)$

When a function is described by an equation and the domain is specified, the range of the function can be found by evaluating the function at each point of the domain.

Example 3   Find the range of the function given by the equation $f(x) = -3x + 2$ if the domain is $\{-4, -2, 0, 2, 4\}$. Write five ordered pairs that belong to the function.

Solution $f(x) = -3x + 2$
$f(-4) = -3(-4) + 2 = 12 + 2 = 14$ ▶ Replace x by each mem-
$f(-2) = -3(-2) + 2 = 6 + 2 = 8$ ber of the domain.
$f(0) = -3(0) + 2 = 0 + 2 = 2$
$f(2) = -3(2) + 2 = -6 + 2 = -4$
$f(4) = -3(4) + 2 = -12 + 2 = -10$

The range is $\{-10, -4, 2, 8, 14\}$.

The ordered pairs $(-4, 14)$, $(-2, 8)$, $(0, 2)$, $(2, -4)$, and $(4, -10)$ belong to the function.

Problem 3   Find the range of the function given by the equation $f(x) = 4x - 3$ if the domain is $\{-5, -3, -1, 1\}$. Write four ordered pairs that belong to the function.

Solution   See page S12.   R: $\{-23, -15, -7, 1\}$
$(-5, -23), (-3, -15), (-1, -7), (1, 1)$

2   Graphs of linear functions

The solutions of the equation

$$y = 7x - 3$$

are ordered pairs (x, y). For example, the ordered pairs $(-1, -10)$, $(0, -3)$, and $(1, 4)$ are solutions of the equation. Therefore, this equation defines a relation.

It is not possible to substitute one value of x into the equation $y = 7x - 3$ and get two different values of y. For example, the number 1 in the domain cannot be paired with any number other than 4 in the range. (*Remember:* A function cannot have ordered pairs in which the same first coordinate is paired with different second coordinates.) Therefore, the equation defines a function.

The equation $y = 7x - 3$ is an equation of the form $y = mx + b$. In general, any equation of the form $y = mx + b$ is a function.

In the equation $y = 7x - 3$, the variable y is called the **dependent variable** because its value *depends* on the value of x. The variable x is called the **independent variable**. We choose a value for x and substitute that value into the equation to determine the value of y. We say that y is a function of x.

INSTRUCTOR NOTE

The concept of a function was beginning to form with the work of Fermat and Descartes. However, it was Euler who gave us the word and its first definition. "A function of a variable quantity is an analytic expression composed in any way whatsoever of the variable quantity and numbers or constant quantities." The sense of function in Euler's definition is that of "y is a function of x," but it does not encompass the more general notion of a function as a certain set of ordered pairs.

When an equation defines y as a function of x, functional notation is frequently used to emphasize that the relation is a function. In this case, it is common to use the notation $f(x)$. Therefore, we can write the equation

$$y = 7x - 3$$

in functional notation as

$$f(x) = 7x - 3$$

The **graph of a function** is a graph of the ordered pairs (x, y) of the function. Because the graph of the equation $y = mx + b$ is a straight line, a function of the form $f(x) = mx + b$ is a **linear function.**

➡ Graph: $f(x) = \dfrac{2}{3}x - 1$

Think of the function as the equation $y = \dfrac{2}{3}x - 1$.

This is the equation of a straight line.

The y-intercept is $(0, -1)$. The slope is $\dfrac{2}{3}$.

Graph the point $(0, -1)$. From the y-intercept, go right 3 units and then up 2 units. Graph the point $(3, 1)$.

Draw a line through the two points.

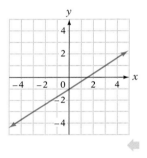

Example 4   Graph: $f(x) = \dfrac{3}{4}x + 2$

Solution $f(x) = \dfrac{3}{4}x + 2$

$$y = \dfrac{3}{4}x + 2$$

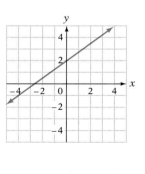

▶ Think of the function as the equation $y = \dfrac{3}{4}x + 2$.

▶ The graph is a straight line with y-intercept $(0, 2)$ and slope $\dfrac{3}{4}$.

Problem 4   Graph: $f(x) = -\dfrac{1}{2}x - 3$

Solution   See page S12.

Graphing utilities are used to graph functions. Using a graphing utility, enter the equation $y = \frac{3}{4}x + 2$ and verify the graph drawn in Example 4. Trace along the graph and verify that $(-4, -1)$, $(0, 2)$, and $(4, 5)$ are coordinates of points on the graph. Now enter the equation given in Problem 4 and verify the graph you drew.

There are a variety of applications of linear functions. For example, suppose an installer of marble kitchen countertops charges $250 plus $180 per foot of countertop. The equation that describes the total cost, C (in dollars), for having x ft of countertop installed is $C = 180x + 250$. In this situation, C is a function of x; the total cost depends on how many feet of countertop are installed. Therefore, we could rewrite the equation

$$C = 180x + 250$$

as the function

$$f(x) = 180x + 250$$

To graph this equation, we first choose a reasonable domain—for example, values of x between 0 and 25. It would not be reasonable to have $x \leq 0$, because no one would order the installation of 0 ft of countertop, and any amount less than 0 would be a negative amount of countertop. The upper limit of 25 is chosen because most kitchens have less than 25 ft of countertop.

Choosing $x = 5$, 10, and 20 results in the ordered pairs $(5, 1150)$, $(10, 2050)$, and $(20, 3850)$. Graph these points and draw a line through them. The graph is shown at the left.

The point whose coordinates are $(8, 1690)$ is on the graph. This ordered pair can be interpreted to mean that 8 ft of countertop costs $1690 to install.

Example 5 The value, V, of an investment of $2500 at an annual simple interest rate of 6% is given by the equation $V = 150t + 2500$, where t is the amount of time, in years, that the money is invested.

A. Write the equation in functional notation.

B. Graph the equation for values of t between 0 and 10.

C. The point whose coordinates are $(5, 3250)$ is on the graph. Write a sentence that explains the meaning of this ordered pair.

Solution A. $V = 150t + 2500$ ▸ The value V of the investment depends on the amount of time t it is invested.
$f(t) = 150t + 2500$ The value V is a function of the time t.

B.

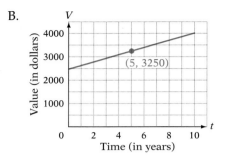

▶ Some ordered pairs of the function are (2, 2800), (4, 3100), and (6, 3400).

C. The ordered pair (5, 3250) means that in 5 years the value of the investment will be $3250.

Problem 5 A car is traveling at a uniform speed of 40 mph. The distance, d (in miles), the car travels in t hours is given by the equation $d = 40t$.

A. Write the equation in functional notation.

B. Use the coordinate axes at the right to graph this equation for values of t between 0 and 5.

C. The point whose coordinates are (3, 120) is on the graph. Write a sentence that explains the meaning of this ordered pair.

Solution See page S12.

A. $f(t) = 40t$ B.   C. In 3 h, the car travels a distance of 120 mi.

CONCEPT REVIEW 5.5

Determine whether the statement is always true, sometimes true, or never true.

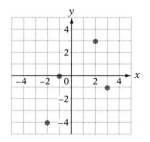

1. The graph shown at the right is the graph of a function.   Always true

2. For the relation graphed at the right, the domain is {−2, −1, 2, 3}.   Always true

3. The graph of the function $f(x) = -\frac{2}{3}x + 5$ has a positive slope.   Never true

4. The graphs of $y = \frac{1}{4}x - 6$ and $f(x) = \frac{1}{4}x - 6$ are identical.   Always true

5. The value of the function {(−3, 3), (−2, 2), (−1, 1), (0, 0)} at −2 is 2.   Always true

6. A function can be represented in a table, by an equation, by a graph, or in a chart.   Always true

7. The graph of a function of the form $f(x) = mx + b$ is a straight line.   Always true

8. The equation $y = 7x - 1$ defines a function.   Always true

EXERCISES 5.5

1. How are relations and functions similar? How are they different?

2. What is the domain of a function? What is the range?

3. *The Olympics* The numbers of gold medals earned by several countries during the 1992 and 1996 Olympic summer games are recorded in the table at the right. Write a relation wherein the first coordinate is the number of gold medals earned in 1992 and the second coordinate is the number earned in 1996. Is the relation a function? {(37, 44), (6, 3), (16, 16), (6, 13), (8, 15), (33, 20)}; no

Country	1992	1996
United States	37	44
Canada	6	3
China	16	16
Italy	6	13
France	8	15
Germany	33	20

4. *Health* The life expectancy in five countries and the prevalence of smoking, as a percent of the inhabitants, are recorded in the table at the right. Write a relation in which the first coordinate is the life expectancy and the second coordinate is the prevalence of smoking, as a percent. Is the relation a function? {(76.6, 31), (76.5, 59), (75.9, 35), (75.9, 45), (75.5, 22)}; no

Country	Life Expectancy	Percent of Smokers
Iceland	76.6	31
Japan	76.5	59
Costa Rica	75.9	35
Israel	75.9	45
Sweden	75.5	22

5. *Housing* The number of sunny days in a year in five different cities and the average cost of a four-bedroom house (in thousands of dollars) in those cities are given in the table at the right. Write a relation in which the first component is the number of sunny days annually and the second component is the cost of a four-bedroom house. Is the relation a function? {(197, 125), (205, 122), (257, 498), (226, 108), (205, 150)}; no

City	Sunny Days Annually	4-Bedroom House Cost (in thousands of dollars)
Nashua, NH	197	125
Portsmouth, NH	205	122
San Jose, CA	257	498
Jacksonville, FL	226	108
Manchester, NH	205	150

Source: *Money Magazine*, July 1997.

6. *Business* The budgets (in millions of dollars) for several movies and the gross ticket sales (in millions of dollars) are recorded in the table at the right. Write a relation in which the first component is the budget and the second component is the gross sales. Is the relation a function? {(30, 93), (62, 172), (30, 15), (50, 200), (100, 184)}; no

Movie	Budget	Gross Sales
Seven	30	93
Apollo 13	62	172
Nixon	30	15
Toy Story	50	200
Batman Forever	100	184

7. ◖◗ *Physics* The speeds of a car in miles per hour and the distance, in feet, needed to stop at those speeds are recorded in the table at the right. (Source: AAA Foundation for Traffic Safety.) Write a relation in which the first coordinate is the speed in miles per hour and the second coordinate is the distance needed to stop. Is the relation a function?   {(55, 273), (65, 355), (75, 447), (85, 549)}; yes

Speed (in miles per hour)	Distance Needed to Stop (in feet)
55	273
65	355
75	447
85	549

8. ◖◗ *Sports* The numbers of runs scored by the American League and by the National League in each of the Major League Baseball All-Star Games from 1990 to 1997 are recorded in the table at the right. Write a relation in which the first coordinate is the number of runs scored by the American League and the second coordinate is the number of runs scored by the National League. Is the relation a function? {(0, 2), (4, 2), (13, 6), (9, 3), (7, 8), (2, 3), (0, 6), (3, 1)}; no

Year	American League	National League
1990	0	2
1991	4	2
1992	13	6
1993	9	3
1994	7	8
1995	2	3
1996	0	6
1997	3	1

Find the domain and range of the relation. State whether or not the relation is a function.

9. {(0, 0), (2, 0), (4, 0), (6, 0)}
    D: {0, 2, 4, 6}; R: {0}; yes

10. {(−2, 2), (0, 2), (1, 2), (2, 2)}
    D: {−2, 0, 1, 2}; R: {2}; yes

11. {(2, 2), (2, 4), (2, 6), (2, 8)}
    D: {2}; R: {2, 4, 6, 8}; no

12. {(−4, 4), (−2, 2), (0, 0), (−2, −2)}
    D: {−4, −2, 0}; R: {−2, 0, 2, 4}; no

13. {(0, 0), (1, 1), (2, 2), (3, 3)}
    D: {0, 1, 2, 3}; R: {0, 1, 2, 3}; yes

14. {(0, 5), (1, 4), (2, 3), (3, 2), (4, 1), (5, 0)}
    D: {0, 1, 2, 3, 4, 5}; R: {0, 1, 2, 3, 4, 5}; yes

15. {(−2, −3), (2, 3), (−1, 2), (1, 2), (−3, 4), (3, 4)}
    D: {−3, −2, −1, 1, 2, 3}; R: {−3, 2, 3, 4}; yes

16. {(−1, 0), (0, −1), (1, 0), (2, 3), (3, 5)}
    D: {−1, 0, 1, 2, 3}; R: {−1, 0, 3, 5}; yes

Evaluate the function at the given value of x. Write an ordered pair that is an element of the function.

17. $f(x) = 4x; x = 10$
    40; (10, 40)

18. $f(x) = 8x; x = 11$
    88; (11, 88)

19. $f(x) = x − 5; x = −6$
    −11; (−6, −11)

20. $f(x) = x + 7; x = −9$
    −2; (−9, −2)

21. $f(x) = 3x^2; x = −2$
    12; (−2, 12)

22. $f(x) = x^2 − 1; x = −8$
    63; (−8, 63)

23. $f(x) = 5x + 1; x = \dfrac{1}{2}$
    $\dfrac{7}{2}; \left(\dfrac{1}{2}, \dfrac{7}{2}\right)$

24. $f(x) = 2x − 6; x = \dfrac{3}{4}$
    $−\dfrac{9}{2}; \left(\dfrac{3}{4}, −\dfrac{9}{2}\right)$

25. $f(x) = \dfrac{2}{5}x + 4; x = −5$
    2; (−5, 2)

26. $f(x) = \dfrac{3}{2}x − 5; x = 2$
    −2; (2, −2)

27. $f(x) = 2x^2; x = −4$
    32; (−4, 32)

28. $f(x) = 4x^2 + 2; x = −3$
    38; (−3, 28)

Find the range of the function defined by the given equation. Write five ordered pairs that belong to the function.

29. $f(x) = 3x - 4$; domain = $\{-5, -3, -1, 1, 3\}$
R: $\{-19, -13, -7, -1, 5\}$;
$(-5, -19), (-3, -13), (-1, -7), (1, -1), (3, 5)$

30. $f(x) = 2x + 5$; domain = $\{-10, -5, 0, 5, 10\}$
R: $\{-15, -5, 5, 15, 25\}$;
$(-10, -15), (-5, -5), (0, 5), (5, 15), (10, 25)$

31. $f(x) = \frac{1}{2}x + 3$; domain = $\{-4, -2, 0, 2, 4\}$
R: $\{1, 2, 3, 4, 5\}$; $(-4, 1), (-2, 2), (0, 3), (2, 4), (4, 5)$

32. $f(x) = \frac{3}{4}x - 1$; domain = $\{-8, -4, 0, 4, 8\}$
R: $\{-7, -4, -1, 2, 5\}$;
$(-8, -7), (-4, -4), (0, -1), (4, 2), (8, 5)$

33. $f(x) = x^2 + 6$; domain = $\{-3, -1, 0, 1, 3\}$
R: $\{6, 7, 15\}$; $(-3, 15), (-1, 7), (0, 6), (1, 7), (3, 15)$

34. $f(x) = 3x^2 + 6$; domain = $\{-2, -1, 0, 1, 2\}$
R: $\{6, 9, 18\}$; $(-2, 18), (-1, 9), (0, 6), (1, 9), (2, 18)$

2 Graph.

35. $f(x) = 5x$

36. $f(x) = -4x$

37. $f(x) = x + 2$

38. $f(x) = x - 3$

39. $f(x) = 6x - 1$

40. $f(x) = 3x + 4$

41. $f(x) = -2x + 3$

42. $f(x) = -5x - 2$

43. $f(x) = \frac{1}{3}x - 4$

44. $f(x) = \frac{3}{5}x + 1$

45. $f(x) = 4$

46. $f(x) = -3$

Graph using a graphing utility.

47. $f(x) = 2x - 1$

48. $f(x) = -3x - 1$

49. $f(x) = -\frac{1}{2}x + 1$

50. $f(x) = \frac{2}{3}x + 4$

51. $f(x) = \frac{3}{4}x + 1$

52. $f(x) = -\frac{1}{2}x - 2$

53. $f(x) = -\frac{4}{3}x + 5$

54. $f(x) = \frac{5}{2}x$

55. $f(x) = -1$

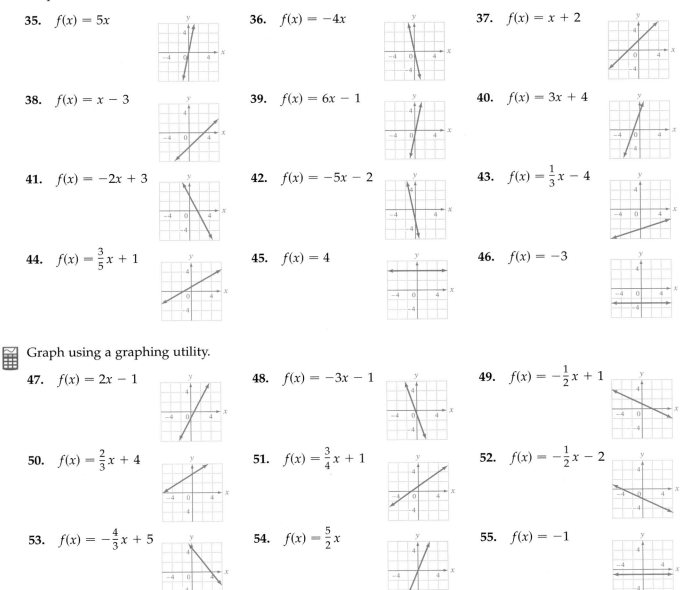

56. *Depreciation*   Depreciation is the declining value of an asset. For instance, a company that purchases a truck for $20,000 has an asset worth $20,000. In 5 years, however, the value of the truck will have declined and it may be worth only $4000. An equation that represents this decline is $V = 20,000 - 3200x$, where V is the value, in dollars, of the truck after x years.

    a. Write the equation in functional notation.

    b. Use the coordinate axes at the right to graph the equation for values of x between 0 and 5.

    c. The point (4, 7200) is on the graph. Write a sentence that explains the meaning of this ordered pair.

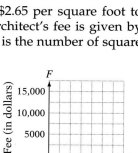

a. $f(x) = 20,000 - 3200x$

b.
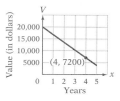

c. The value of the truck after 4 years is $7200.

57.   *Depreciation*   A company uses the equation $V = 30,000 - 5000x$ to estimate the depreciated value, in dollars, of a computer. (See Exercise 56.)

    a. Write the equation in functional notation.

    b. Use the coordinate axes at the right to graph the equation for values of x between 0 and 5.

    c. The point (1, 25,000) is on the graph. Write a sentence that explains the meaning of this ordered pair.

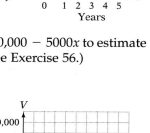

a. $f(x) = 30,000 - 5000x$

b.
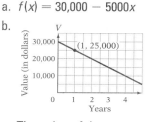

c. The value of the computer after 1 year is $25,000.

58.   *Business*   An architect charges a fee of $500 plus $2.65 per square foot to design a house. The equation that represents the architect's fee is given by $F = 2.65s + 500$, where F is the fee, in dollars, and s is the number of square feet in the house.

    a. Write the equation in functional notation.

    b. Use the coordinate axes at the right to graph the equation for values of s between 0 and 5000.

    c. The point (3500, 9775) is on the graph. Write a sentence that explains the meaning of this ordered pair.

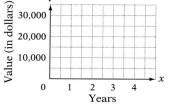

a. $f(s) = 2.65s + 500$

b.

c. The architect's fee for designing a house of 3500 ft² is $9775.

59.   *Business*   A rental car company charges a "drop-off" fee of $50 to return a car to a location different from that from which it was rented. In addition, it charges a fee of $.18 per mile the car is driven. An equation that represents the total cost to rent a car from this company is $C = 0.18m + 50$, where C is the total cost, in dollars, and m is the number of miles the car is driven.

    a. Write the equation in functional notation.

    b. Use the coordinate axes at the right to graph the equation for values of m between 0 and 1000.

    c. The point (500, 140) is on the graph. Write a sentence that explains the meaning of this ordered pair.

a. $f(m) = 0.18m + 50$

b.

c. The cost to drive this car 500 mi is $140.

APPLYING CONCEPTS 5.5

60. a. A function f consists of the ordered pairs {(−4, −6), (−2, −2), (0, 2), (2, 6), (4, 10)}. Find $f(2)$.   6

b. A function f consists of the ordered pairs {(0, 9), (1, 8), (2, 7), (3, 6), (4, 5)}. Find $f(1)$.   8

61. *Safety*   According to the AAA Foundation for Traffic Safety, the incidence of major "road rage" traffic violence has been increasing, as shown in the table at the right.

Year	Number of Incidents
1990	1129
1991	1297
1992	1478
1993	1555
1994	1669
1995	1708
1996	1800

a. Do these data represent a function? Why or why not?

b. If the data represent a function, do they represent a linear function? Why or why not?

c. If the data represent a function, is the year a function of the number of incidents, or is the number of incidents a function of the year?

d. If you had to predict the number of incidents of "road rage" traffic violence in 1997 on the basis of the information in the table, would you predict that it would be more or less than 1800? Explain your answer.

62. *Height-Time Graphs*   A child's height is a function of the child's age. The graph of this function is not linear, because children go through growth spurts as they develop. However, for the graph to be reasonable, the function must be an increasing function (that is, as the age increases, the height increases), because children do not get shorter as they grow older. Match each function described below with a reasonable graph of the function.

a. The height of a plane above the ground during take-off depends on how long it has been since the plane left the gate.

b. The height of a football above the ground is related to the number of seconds that have passed since it was punted.

c. A basketball player is dribbling a basketball. The basketball's distance from the floor is related to the number of seconds that have passed since the player began dribbling the ball.

d. Two children are seated together on a roller coaster. The height of the children above the ground depends on how long they have been on the ride.

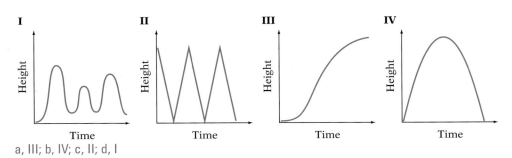

a, III; b, IV; c, II; d, I

63. Write a few sentences describing the similarities and differences between relations and functions.

64. Investigating a relationship between two variables is an important task in the application of mathematics. For example, botanists study the relationship between the number of bushels of wheat yielded per acre and the amount of watering per acre. Environmental scientists study the relationship between the incidence of skin cancer and the amount of ozone in the atmosphere. Business analysts study the relationship between the price of a product and the number of products that are sold at that price. Describe a relationship that is important to your major field of study.

65. Functions are a part of our everyday lives. For example, the cost to mail a package via first-class mail is a function of the weight of the package. The tuition paid by a part-time student is a function of the number of credit hours the student registers for. Provide other examples of functions.

S E C T I O N **5.6**

Graphing Linear Inequalities

1 Graph inequalities in two variables

POINT OF INTEREST

Linear inequalities play an important role in applied mathematics. They are used in a branch of mathematics called *linear programming,* which was developed during World War II to solve problems in supplying the Air Force with the machine parts necessary to keep planes flying. Today its applications have been broadened to many other disciplines.

The graph of the linear equation $y = x - 2$ separates a plane into three sets:

the set of points on the line

the set of points above the line

the set of points below the line

The point whose coordinates are (3, 1) is a solution of $y = x - 2$.

$$\frac{y = x - 2}{1 \mid 3 - 2}$$
$$1 = 1$$

The point whose coordinates are (3, 3) is a solution of $y > x - 2$.

$$\frac{y > x - 2}{3 \mid 3 - 2}$$
$$3 > 1$$

Any point above the line is a solution of $y > x - 2$.

The point whose coordinates are (3, −1) is a solution of $y < x - 2$.

$$\frac{y < x - 2}{-1 \mid 3 - 2}$$
$$-1 < 1$$

Any point below the line is a solution of $y < x - 2$.

The solution set of $y = x - 2$ is all points on the line. The solution set of $y > x - 2$ is all points above the line. The solution set of $y < x - 2$ is all points below the line. The solution set of an inequality in two variables is a **half-plane.**

The following illustrates the procedure for graphing a linear inequality.

➡️ Graph the solution set of $2x + 3y \leq 6$.

Solve the inequality for y.

$$2x + 3y \leq 6$$
$$2x - 2x + 3y \leq -2x + 6$$
$$3y \leq -2x + 6$$
$$\frac{3y}{3} \leq \frac{-2x + 6}{3}$$
$$y \leq -\frac{2}{3}x + 2$$

Change the inequality to an equality and graph the line. If the inequality is $\geq$ or $\leq$, the line is in the solution set and is shown by a **solid line.** If the inequality is $>$ or $<$, the line is not a part of the solution set and is shown by a **dashed line.**

$$y = -\frac{2}{3}x + 2$$

If the inequality is in the form $y > mx + b$ or $y \geq mx + b$, shade the **upper half-plane.** If the inequality is in the form $y < mx + b$ or $y \leq mx + b$, shade the **lower half-plane.**

The equation $y \leq -\frac{2}{3}x + 2$ is in the form $y \leq mx + b$. Draw a solid line and shade the lower half-plane.

The inequality $2x + 3y \leq 6$ can also be graphed as shown below.

➡️ Graph the solution set of $2x + 3y \leq 6$.

Change the inequality to an equality.

$$2x + 3y = 6$$

Find the x- and y-intercepts of the equation. To find the x-intercept, let $y = 0$.

$$2x + 3(0) = 6$$
$$2x = 6$$
$$x = 3$$

The x-intercept is $(3, 0)$.

To find the y-intercept, let $x = 0$.

$$2(0) + 3y = 6$$
$$3y = 6$$
$$y = 2$$

The y-intercept is $(0, 2)$.

Graph the ordered pairs $(3, 0)$ and $(0, 2)$. Draw a solid line through the points because the inequality is $\leq$. (See the following graph.)

The point $(0, 0)$ can be used to determine which region to shade. If $(0, 0)$ is a solution of the inequality, then shade the region that includes the point $(0, 0)$. If $(0, 0)$ is not a solution of the inequality, then shade the region that does not include the point $(0, 0)$. For this example, $(0, 0)$ is a solution of the inequality. The region that contains the point $(0, 0)$ is shaded.

If the line passes through the point $(0, 0)$, another point must be used to determine which region to shade. For example, use the point $(1, 0)$.

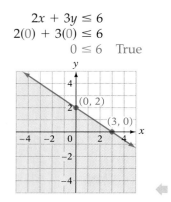

$$2x + 3y \leq 6$$
$$2(0) + 3(0) \leq 6$$
$$0 \leq 6 \quad \text{True}$$

It is important to note that every point in the shaded region is a solution of the inequality and that every solution of the inequality is a point in the shaded region. No point outside of the shaded region is a solution of the inequality.

Example 1   Graph the solution set of $3x + y > -2$.

   Solution
$$3x + y > -2$$
$$3x - 3x + y > -3x - 2 \quad \blacktriangleright \text{ Solve the inequality for } y.$$
$$y > -3x - 2$$

▶ Graph $y = -3x - 2$ as a dashed line. Shade the upper half-plane.

Problem 1   Graph the solution set of $x - 3y < 2$.

   Solution   See page S12.

Example 2   Graph the solution set of $y > 3$.

   Solution   ▶ The inequality is solved for y. Graph $y = 3$ as a dashed line. Shade the upper half-plane.

Problem 2   Graph the solution set of $x < 3$.

   Solution   See page S12.

CONCEPT REVIEW 5.6

Determine whether the statement is always true, sometimes true, or never true.

1. $y \geq \frac{1}{2}x - 5$ is an example of a linear equation in two variables.   Never true

2. $(-2, 4)$ is a solution of $y > x + 2$.   Always true

3. (3, 0) is a solution of $y \leq x - 1$.   Always true

4. Every point above the line $y = x - 3$ is a solution of $y < x - 3$.   Never true

5. (0, 0) is not a solution of $y > x + 4$. Therefore, the point (0, 0) should not be in the shaded region that indicates the solution set of the inequality.   Always true

6. In the graph of an inequality in two variables, any point in the shaded region is a solution of the inequality, and any point not in the shaded region is not a solution of the inequality.   Always true

---

EXERCISES 5.6

1   **1.**   In the graph of a linear inequality, what does a solid line represent? What does a dashed line represent?

2.   In the graph of a linear inequality, what does the shaded portion of the graph represent?

Graph the solution set.

3. $y > 2x + 3$ **4.** $y > 3x - 9$ **5.** $y > \frac{3}{2}x - 4$ **6.** $y > -\frac{5}{4}x + 1$

7. $y \leq -\frac{3}{4}x - 1$ **8.** $y \leq -\frac{5}{2}x - 4$ **9.** $y \leq -\frac{6}{5}x - 2$ **10.** $y < \frac{4}{5}x + 3$

11. $x + y > 4$ **12.** $x - y > -3$ **13.** $2x + y \geq 4$ **14.** $3x + y \geq 6$

15. $y \leq -2$ **16.** $y > 3$ **17.** $2x + 2y \leq -4$ **18.** $-4x + 3y < -12$

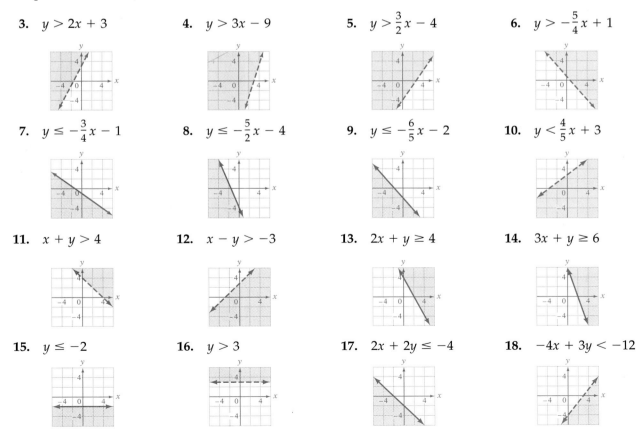

APPLYING CONCEPTS 5.6

Write the inequality given its graph.

19.

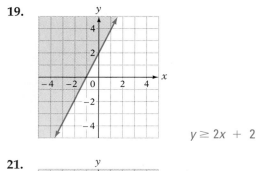

$y \geq 2x + 2$

20.

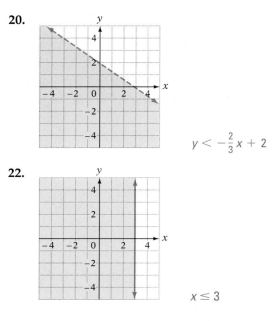

$y < -\dfrac{2}{3}x + 2$

21.

$y > 2$

22.

$x \leq 3$

Graph the solution set.

23. $y - 5 < 4(x - 2)$

24. $y + 3 < 6(x + 1)$

[C] **25.** $3x - 2(y + 1) \leq y - (5 - x)$

[C] **26.** $2x - 3(y + 1) \geq y - (4 - x)$

27. Does an inequality in two variables define a relation? Why or why not?
Does an inequality in two variables define a function? Why or why not?

Focus on Problem Solving

Counterexamples

Some of the exercises in this text ask you to determine whether a statement is true or false. For instance, the statement "Every real number has a reciprocal" is false because 0 is a real number and 0 does not have a reciprocal.

Finding an example, such as 0 has no reciprocal, to show that a statement is not always true is called "finding a counterexample." A counterexample is an example that shows that a statement is not always true.

Consider the statement "The product of two numbers is greater than either factor." A counterexample to this statement is the factors $\frac{2}{3}$ and $\frac{3}{4}$. The product of these numbers is $\frac{1}{2}$, and $\frac{1}{2}$ is smaller than $\frac{2}{3}$ or $\frac{3}{4}$. There are many other counterexamples to the given statement.

Here are some counterexamples to the statement "The square of a number is always larger than the number."

$$\left(\frac{1}{2}\right)^2 = \frac{1}{4} \quad \text{but} \quad \frac{1}{4} < \frac{1}{2} \qquad 1^2 = 1 \quad \text{but} \quad 1 = 1$$

For each of the next five statements, find at least one counterexample to show that the statement, or conjecture, is false.

1. The product of two integers is always a positive number.
2. The sum of two prime numbers is never a prime number.
3. For all real numbers, $|x + y| = |x| + |y|$.
4. If x and y are nonzero real numbers and $x > y$, then $x^2 > y^2$.
5. The quotient of any two nonzero real numbers is less than either one of the numbers.

When a problem is posed, it may not be known whether the statement is true or false. For instance, Christian Goldbach (1690–1764) stated that every even integer greater than 2 can be written as the sum of two prime numbers. No one has ever been able to find a counterexample to this statement, but neither has anyone been able to prove that it is always true.

In the next five exercises, answer true if the statement is always true. If there is an instance when the statement is false, give a counterexample.

6. The reciprocal of a positive number is always smaller than the number.
7. If $x < 0$, then $|x| = -x$.
8. For any two real numbers x and y, $x + y > x - y$.
9. For any positive integer n, $n^2 + n + 17$ is a prime number.
10. The list of numbers 1, 11, 111, 1111, 11111, . . . contains infinitely many composite numbers. (*Hint:* A number is divisible by 3 if the sum of the digits of the number is divisible by 3.)

Projects and Group Activities

 Graphing Linear Equations with a Graphing Utility

A computer or graphing calculator screen is divided into *pixels.* There are approximately 6000 to 790,000 pixels available on the screen (depending on the computer or calculator). The greater the number of pixels, the smoother a graph will appear. A portion of a screen is shown at the left. Each little rectangle represents one pixel.

The graphing utilities that are used by computers or calculators to graph an equation do basically what we have shown in the text: They choose values of x and, for each, calculate the corresponding value of y. The pixel corresponding to the ordered pair is then turned on. The graph is jagged because pixels are much larger than the dots we draw on paper.

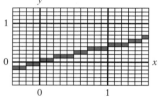

The graph of $y = 0.45x$ is shown at the left as the calculator drew it (jagged). The x- and y-axes have been chosen so that each pixel represents $\frac{1}{10}$ of a unit. Consider the region of the graph where $x = 1, 1.1,$ and 1.2.

The corresponding values of y are 0.45, 0.495, and 0.54. Because the y-axis is in tenths, the numbers 0.45, 0.495, and 0.54 are rounded to the nearest tenth before plotting. Rounding 0.45, 0.495, and 0.54 to the nearest tenth results in 0.5 for each number. Thus the ordered pairs (1, 0.45), (1.1, 0.495), and (1.2, 0.54) are graphed as (1, 0.5), (1.1, 0.5), and (1.2, 0.5). These points appear as three illuminated horizontal pixels. The graph of the line appears horizontal. However, if you use the TRACE feature of the calculator (see the appendix), the actual y-coordinate for each value of x is displayed.

LOOK CLOSELY

Xmin and Xmax are the smallest and largest values of x that will be shown on the screen. Ymin and Ymax are the smallest and largest values of y that will be shown on the screen.

Here are the keystrokes to graph $y = \frac{2}{3}x + 1$. First the equation is entered. Then the domain (Xmin to Xmax) and the range (Ymin to Ymax) are entered. This is called the **viewing window.** By changing the keystrokes 2 $\boxed{\text{X,T,θ,}n}$ $\boxed{÷}$ 3 $\boxed{+}$ 1 (use $\boxed{\text{X/θ/T/}n}$ for the Sharp EL-9600 or use $\boxed{\text{X,θ,T}}$ for the Casio CFX-9850), you can graph different equations.

TI-83	*SHARP EL-9600*	*CASIO CFX-9850*
$\boxed{\text{Y=}}$ $\boxed{\text{CLEAR}}$ 2 $\boxed{\text{X,T,θ,}n}$ $\boxed{÷}$ 3	$\boxed{\text{Y=}}$ $\boxed{\text{CL}}$ 2 $\boxed{\text{X/θ/T/}n}$ $\boxed{÷}$ 3 $\boxed{+}$	$\boxed{\text{MENU}}$ 5 $\boxed{\text{F2}}$ $\boxed{\text{F1}}$ 2 $\boxed{\text{X,θ,T}}$
$\boxed{+}$ 1 $\boxed{\text{WINDOW}}$ $\boxed{(-)}$ 10	1 $\boxed{\text{WINDOW}}$ $\boxed{(-)}$ 10 $\boxed{\text{ENTER}}$ 10	$\boxed{÷}$ 3 $\boxed{+}$ 1 $\boxed{\text{EXE}}$ $\boxed{\text{SHIFT}}$ F3
$\boxed{\text{ENTER}}$ 10 $\boxed{\text{ENTER}}$ 1 $\boxed{\text{ENTER}}$	$\boxed{\text{ENTER}}$ 1 $\boxed{\text{ENTER}}$ $\boxed{(-)}$ 10	$\boxed{(-)}$ 10 $\boxed{\text{EXE}}$ 10 $\boxed{\text{EXE}}$ 1 $\boxed{\text{EXE}}$
$\boxed{(-)}$ 10 $\boxed{\text{ENTER}}$ 10 $\boxed{\text{ENTER}}$ 1	$\boxed{\text{ENTER}}$ 10 $\boxed{\text{ENTER}}$ 1 $\boxed{\text{ENTER}}$	$\boxed{(-)}$ 10 $\boxed{\text{EXE}}$ 10 $\boxed{\text{EXE}}$ 1 $\boxed{\text{EXE}}$
$\boxed{\text{ENTER}}$ $\boxed{\text{GRAPH}}$	$\boxed{\text{GRAPH}}$	$\boxed{\text{EXIT}}$ $\boxed{\text{F6}}$

1. $y = 2x + 1$ For *2x,* you may enter 2 × *x* or just 2*x*. The times sign × is not necessary on many graphing calculators.

2. $y = -\frac{1}{2}x - 2$ Use the $\boxed{(-)}$ key to enter a negative sign.

3. $3x + 2y = 6$ Solve for *y.* Then enter the equation.

4. $4x + 3y = 75$ You must adjust the viewing window. *Suggestion:* Xmin = −25, Xmax = 25, Xscl = 5, Ymin = −35, Ymax = 35, Yscl = 5. See the Appendix for assistance.

Graphs of Motion

A graph can be useful in analyzing the motion of a body. For example, consider an airplane in uniform motion traveling at 100 m\s. The table at the right shows the distance, in meters, traveled by the plane at the end of each of five 1 second intervals.

Time (in seconds)	Distance (in meters)
0	0
1	100
2	200
3	300
4	400
5	500

These data can be graphed on a rectangular coordinate system and a straight line drawn through the points plotted. The travel time is shown along the horizontal axis, and the distance traveled by the plane is shown along the vertical axis. (Note that the units along the two axes are not the same length.)

To write the equation for the line just graphed, use the coordinates of any two points on the line to find the slope. The y-intercept is $(0, 0)$.

Let $(x_1, y_1) = (1, 100)$ and $(x_2, y_2) = (2, 200)$.

$$m = \frac{y_2 - y_1}{x_2 - x_1} = \frac{200 - 100}{2 - 1} = 100$$

$$y = mx + b$$
$$y = 100x + 0$$
$$y = 100x$$

Note that the slope of the line, 100, is equal to the speed, 100 m/s. *The slope of a distance-time graph represents the speed of the object.*

The distance-time graphs for two planes are shown at the left. One plane is traveling at 100 m/s, and the other is traveling at 200 m/s. The slope of the line representing the faster plane is greater than the slope of the line representing the slower plane.

In the speed-time graph at the left, the time a plane has been flying at 100 m/s is shown along the horizontal axis, and its speed is shown along the vertical axis. Because the speed is constant, the graph is a horizontal line.

The area between the horizontal line graphed and the horizontal axis is equal to the distance traveled by the plane up to that time. For example, the area of the shaded region on the graph is

$$\text{Length} \cdot \text{width} = (3 \text{ s})(100 \text{ m/s}) = 300 \text{ m}$$

The distance traveled by the plane in 3 s is equal to 300 m.

1. A car in uniform motion is traveling at 20 m/s.
   a. Prepare a distance-time graph for the car for 0 s to 5 s.
   b. Find the slope of the line.
   c. Find the equation of the line.
   d. Prepare a speed-time graph for the car for 0 s to 5 s.
   e. Find the distance traveled by the car after 3 s.

2. One car in uniform motion is traveling at 10 m/s. A second car in uniform motion is traveling at 15 m/s.
   a. Prepare one distance-time graph for both cars for 0 s to 5 s.

      b. Find the slope of each line.

      c. Find the equation of each line graphed.

      d. Assuming that the cars started at the same point at 0 s, find the distance between the cars at the end of 5 s.

  3. a. In a distance-time graph, is it possible for the graph to be a horizontal line?

      b. What does a horizontal line reveal about the motion of the object during that time period?

Chapter Summary

Key Words

A *rectangular coordinate system* is formed by two number lines, one horizontal and one vertical, that intersect at the zero point of each line. The number lines that make up a rectangular coordinate system are called the *coordinate axes,* or simply the *axes.* The *origin* is the point of intersection of the two coordinate axes. Generally, the horizontal axis is labeled the *x-axis,* and the vertical axis is labeled the *y-axis.* A rectangular coordinate system divides the plane determined by the axes into four regions called *quadrants.*   (Objective 5.1.1)

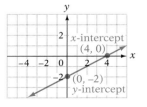

The coordinate axes determine a *plane.* Every point in the plane can be identified by an *ordered pair* (x, y). The first number in an ordered pair is called the *x-coordinate* or the *abscissa.* The second number is called the *y-coordinate* or the *ordinate.* The *coordinates* of a point are the numbers in the ordered pair associated with the point.   (Objective 5.1.1)

The ordered pair $(4, -9)$ has *x*-coordinate 4 and *y*-coordinate -9.

An equation of the form $y = mx + b$, where m is the coefficient of x and b is a constant, is a *linear equation in two variables.* A *solution of a linear equation in two variables* is an ordered pair (x, y) that makes the equation a true statement.   (Objective 5.2.1)

$y = 2x + 3$ is an example of a linear equation in two variables. The ordered pair $(1, 5)$ is a solution of this equation because when 1 is substituted for x and 5 is substituted for y, the result is a true statement.

The point at which a graph crosses the *x*-axis is called the *x-intercept.* At the *x*-intercept, the *y*-coordinate is 0. The point at which a graph crosses the *y*-axis is called the *y-intercept.* At the *y*-intercept, the *x*-coordinate is 0.   (Objective 5.2.3)

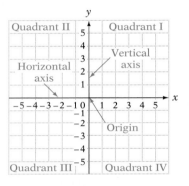

An equation of the form $Ax + By = C$ is also a *linear equation in two variables.*   (Objective 5.2.3)

$5x - 2y = 10$ is an example of an equation in $Ax + By = C$ form.

The *graph of* $y = b$ is a horizontal line with y-intercept $(0, b)$. The *graph of* $x = a$ is a vertical line with x-intercept $(a, 0)$. (Objective 5.2.3)

The graph of $y = -3$ is a horizontal line with y-intercept $(0, -3)$. The graph of $x = 2$ is a vertical line with x-intercept $(2, 0)$.

The *slope* of a line is a measure of the slant of the line. The symbol for slope is m. A line that slants upward to the right has a *positive slope*. A line that slants downward to the right has a *negative slope*. A horizontal line has *zero slope*. The slope of a vertical line is *undefined*.   (Objective 5.3.1)

For the graph of $y = 4x - 3$, $m = 4$; the slope is positive.

For the graph of $y = -6x + 1$, $m = -6$; the slope is negative.

For the graph of $y = -7$, $m = 0$; the slope is 0.

For the graph of $x = 8$, the slope is undefined.

A *relation* is any set of ordered pairs. The *domain* of a relation is the set of first coordinates of the ordered pairs. The *range* is the set of second coordinates of the ordered pairs. (Objective 5.5.1)

For the relation $\{(-2, -5), (0, -3), (4, -1)\}$, the domain is $\{-2, 0, 4\}$ and the range is $\{-5, -3, -1\}$.

A *function* is a relation in which no two ordered pairs have the same first coordinate and different second coordinates. (Objective 5.5.1)

$\{(-2, -5), (0, -3), (4, -1)\}$ is a function. $\{(-2, -5), (-2, -3), (4, -1)\}$ is not a function because two ordered pairs have x-coordinate -2 and different y-coordinates.

A function of the form $f(x) = mx + b$ is a *linear function*. Its graph is a straight line.   (Objective 5.5.2)

$f(x) = -3x + 8$ is an example of a linear function.

The solution set of an inequality in two variables is a *half-plane*. (Objective 5.6.1)

The solution set of $y > x - 2$ is all points above the line $y = x - 2$. The solution set of $y < x - 2$ is all points below the line $y = x - 2$.

Essential Rules and Procedures

To find the x-intercept, let $y = 0$.
To find the y-intercept, let $x = 0$.   (Objective 5.2.3)

To find the x-intercept of $4x - 3y = 12$, let $y = 0$. To find the y-intercept, let $x = 0$.

$$
\begin{array}{ll}
4x - 3y = 12 & \qquad 4x - 3y = 12 \\
4x - 3(0) = 12 & \qquad 4(0) - 3y = 12 \\
4x - 0 = 12 & \qquad 0 - 3y = 12 \\
4x = 12 & \qquad -3y = 12 \\
x = 3 & \qquad y = -4
\end{array}
$$

The x-intercept is $(3, 0)$.

The y-intercept is $(0, -4)$.

Slope of a Linear Equation

Slope $= m = \dfrac{y_2 - y_1}{x_2 - x_1}$, $x_2 \neq x_1$ (Objective 5.3.1)

To find the slope of the line between the points $(2, -3)$ and $(-1, 6)$, let $P_1 = (2, -3)$ and $P_2 = (-1, 6)$. Then $(x_1, y_1) = (2, -3)$ and $(x_2, y_2) = (-1, 6)$.

$$
m = \frac{y_2 - y_1}{x_2 - x_1} = \frac{6 - (-3)}{-1 - 2} = \frac{9}{-3} = -3
$$

Slope-Intercept Form of a Linear Equation

$y = mx + b$ (Objective 5.3.2)

For the equation $y = -4x + 7$,
the slope $= m = -4$ and
the y-intercept $= (0, b) = (0, 7)$.

Point-Slope Formula

$y - y_1 = m(x - x_1)$ (Objective 5.4.2)

To find the equation of the line that contains the point $(6, -1)$ and has slope 2, let $(x_1, y_1) = (6, -1)$ and $m = 2$.

$$y - y_1 = m(x - x_1)$$
$$y - (-1) = 2(x - 6)$$
$$y + 1 = 2x - 12$$
$$y = 2x - 13$$

Chapter Review Exercises

1. Find the ordered-pair solution of $y = -\frac{2}{3}x + 2$ that corresponds to $x = 3$. $(3, 0)$

2. Find the equation of the line that contains the point whose coordinates are $(0, -1)$ and has slope 3. $y = 3x - 1$

3. Graph: $x = -3$

4. Graph the ordered pairs $(-3, 1)$ and $(0, 2)$.

5. Evaluate $f(x) = 3x^2 + 4$ at $x = -5$.   79

6. Find the slope of the line that contains the points whose coordinates are $(3, -4)$ and $(1, -4)$.   0

7. Graph: $y = 3x + 1$

8. Graph: $3x - 2y = 6$

9. Find the equation of the line that contains the point whose coordinates are $(-1, 2)$ and has slope $-\frac{2}{3}$. $y = -\frac{2}{3}x + \frac{4}{3}$

10. Find the x- and y-intercepts for $6x - 4y = 12$. $(2, 0), (0, -3)$

11. Graph the line that has slope $\frac{1}{2}$ and y-intercept $(0, -1)$.

12. Graph: $f(x) = -\frac{2}{3}x + 4$

13. Find the equation of the line that contains the point whose coordinates are $(-3, 1)$ and has slope $\frac{2}{3}$. $y = \frac{2}{3}x + 3$

14. Find the slope of the line that contains the points whose coordinates are $(2, -3)$ and $(4, 1)$.
    2

15. Evaluate $f(x) = \frac{3}{5}x + 2$ at $x = -10$. -4

16. Find the domain and range of the relation $\{(-20, -10), (-10, -5), (0, 0), (10, 5)\}$. Is the relation a function?
    D: $\{-20, -10, 0, 10\}$; R: $\{-10, -5, 0, 5\}$; yes

17. Graph: $y = -\frac{3}{4}x + 3$

18. Graph the line that has slope 2 and y-intercept -2.

19. Graph the ordered pairs $(-2, -3)$ and $(2, 4)$.

20. Graph: $f(x) = 5x + 1$

21. Find the x- and y-intercepts for $2x - 3y = 12$. $(6, 0), (0, -4)$

22. Find the equation of the line that contains the point whose coordinates are $(-1, 0)$ and has slope 2. $y = 2x + 2$

23. Graph: $y = 3$

24. Graph the solution set of $3x + 2y \le 12$.

25. Find the slope of the line that contains the points whose coordinates are $(2, -3)$ and $(-3, 4)$.
    $-\frac{7}{5}$

26. Find the equation of the line that contains the point whose coordinates are $(2, 3)$ and has slope $\frac{1}{2}$. $y = \frac{1}{2}x + 2$

27. Graph the line that has slope -1 and y-intercept $(0, 2)$.

28. Graph: $2x - 3y = 6$

29. Find the ordered-pair solution of $y = 2x - 1$ that corresponds to $x = -2$. $(-2, -5)$

30. Find the equation of the line that contains the point $(0, 2)$ and has slope -3. $y = -3x + 2$

31. Graph: $f(x) = 2x$

32. Evaluate $f(x) = 3x - 5$ at $x = \frac{5}{3}$.   0

33. Find the slope of the line that contains the points whose coordinates are $(3, -2)$ and $(3, 5)$.
Undefined

34. Find the equation of the line that contains the point whose coordinates are $(2, -1)$ and has slope $\frac{1}{2}$. $y = \frac{1}{2}x - 2$

35. Is $(-10, 0)$ a solution of $y = \frac{1}{5}x + 2$?   Yes

36. Find the ordered-pair solution of $y = 4x - 9$ that corresponds to $x = 2$. $(2, -1)$

37. Find the x- and y-intercepts for $4x - 3y = 0$.
$(0, 0); (0, 0)$

38. Find the equation of the line that contains the point whose coordinates are $(-2, 3)$ and has zero slope. $y = 3$

39. Graph the solution set of $6x - y > 6$.

40. Graph the line that has slope -3 and y-intercept $(0, 1)$.

41. Find the equation of the line that contains the point whose coordinates are $(0, -4)$ and has slope 3. $y = 3x - 4$

42. Graph: $x + 2y = -4$

43. Find the domain and range of the relation $\{(-10, -5), (-5, 0), (5, 0), (-10, 0)\}$. Is the relation a function?   D: $\{-10, -5, 5\}$; R: $\{-5, 0\}$; no

44. Find the range of the function given by the equation $f(x) = 3x + 7$ if the domain is $\{-20, -10, 0, 10, 20\}$. $\{-53, -23, 7, 37, 67\}$

45. Find the range of the function given by the equation $f(x) = \frac{1}{3}x + 4$ if the domain is $\{-6, -3, 0, 3, 6\}$. $\{2, 3, 4, 5, 6\}$

46. According to the National Association of Chain Drug Stores, the largest drugstore chains are Walgreen, Rite-Aid, CVS, Eckerd, and American Drug. The revenue, to the nearest billion, for the 12 months ending October 30, 1997, and the number of stores in each chain, to the nearest hundred, are recorded in the table below. Graph the scatter diagram for these data.

Revenue (in billions of dollars)

Revenue, in billions of dollars, x	13	12	11	9	5
Number of stores, y	2300	3900	4000	2800	1000

47.   The major airlines routinely overbook flights, but generally passengers voluntarily give up their seats when offered free airline tickets as compensation. The table below gives the number of passengers who voluntarily gave up their seats and the number who involuntarily gave up their seats during the years 1993 through 1997. Numbers are rounded to the nearest ten thousand. (Source: USA TODAY analysis of Department of Transportation data.) Graph the scatter diagram for these data.

Number of volunteers, in ten thousands, x	60	77	79	90	102
Number involuntarily bumped, in ten thousands, y	4	5	5	6	5

48.   The table below shows the tread depth, in millimeters, of a tire and the number of miles, in thousands, that have been driven on that tire.

Miles driven	25	35	40	20	45
Tread depth	4.8	3.5	2.1	5.5	1.0

Write a relation in which the first coordinate is the number of miles driven and the second coordinate is the tread depth. Is the relation a function?   {(25, 4.8), (35, 3.5), (40, 2.1), (20, 5.5), (45, 1.0)}; yes

49.   A contractor uses the equation $C = 70s + 40,000$ to estimate the cost of building a new house. In this equation, C is the total cost, in dollars, and s is the number of square feet in the home.

   a. Write the equation in functional notation.

   b. Use the coordinate axes at the right to graph the equation for values of s between 0 and 5000.

   c. The point (1500, 145,000) is on the graph. Write a sentence that explains the meaning of this ordered pair.

a. $f(s) = 70s + 40,000$

b.

c. The contractor's cost to build a house of 1500 ft² is $145,000.

50.   The graph at the right shows the number of heart surgeries performed over a 10-year period. Find the slope of the line. Write a sentence that states the meaning of the slope.   The slope is 58.5. The number of heart surgeries performed is increasing at a rate of 58.5 per year.

Chapter Test

1.   Find the equation of the line that contains the point whose coordinates are (9, −3) and has slope $-\frac{1}{3}$. $y = -\frac{1}{3}x$

2.   Find the slope of the line that contains the points whose coordinates are (9, 8) and (−2, 1). $\frac{7}{11}$

3. Find the x- and y-intercepts for $3x - 2y = 24$.
$(8, 0); (0, -12)$

4. Find the ordered-pair solution of $y = -\frac{4}{3}x - 1$ that corresponds to $x = 9$. $(9, -13)$

5. Graph: $5x + 3y = 15$

6. Graph: $y = \frac{1}{4}x + 3$

7. Evaluate $f(x) = 4x + 7$ at $x = \frac{3}{4}$.   10

8. Is $(6, 3)$ a solution of $y = \frac{2}{3}x + 1$?   No

9. Graph the line that has slope $-\frac{2}{3}$ and y-intercept $(0, 4)$.

10. Graph the solution set of $2x - y \geq 2$.

11. Graph the ordered pairs $(3, -2)$ and $(0, 4)$.

12. Graph the line that has slope 2 and y-intercept $(0, -4)$.

13. Find the slope of the line that contains the points whose coordinates are $(4, -3)$ and $(-2, -3)$.   0

14. Find the equation of the line that contains the point whose coordinates are $(0, 7)$ and has slope $-\frac{2}{5}$. $y = -\frac{2}{5}x + 7$

15. Find the equation of the line that contains the point whose coordinates are $(2, 1)$ and has slope 4. $y = 4x - 7$

16. Evaluate $f(x) = 4x^2 - 3$ at $x = -2$.   13

17. Graph: $y = -2x - 1$

18. Graph the solution set of $y > 2$.

19. Graph: $x = -3$

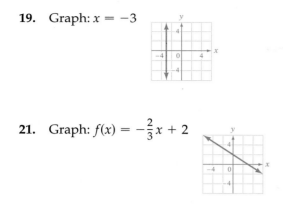

20. Graph the line that has slope $\frac{1}{2}$ and y-intercept $(0, -3)$.

21. Graph: $f(x) = -\frac{2}{3}x + 2$

22. Graph: $f(x) = -5x$

23. Evaluate $f(x) = -3x + 7$ at $x = -6$.   25

24. Find the domain and range of the relation $\{(8, 8), (8, 4), (8, 2), (8, 0)\}$. Is the relation a function?
D: {8}; R: {0, 2, 4, 8}; no

25. Find the equation of the line that contains the point whose coordinates are $(5, 0)$ and has slope $\frac{3}{5}$. $y = \frac{3}{5}x - 3$

26. Find the range of the function given by the equation $f(x) = -3x + 5$ if the domain is $\{-7, -2, 0, 4, 9\}$. $\{-22, -7, 5, 11, 26\}$

27. The distance, in miles, a house is from a fire station and the amount, in thousands of dollars, of fire damage that house sustained in a fire are given in the following table. Graph the scatter diagram for these data.

Distance (in miles), x	3.5	4.0	5.5	6.0
Damage (in thousands of dollars), y	25	30	40	35

28. A company that manufactures toasters has fixed costs of $1000 each month. The manufacturing cost per toaster is $8. An equation that represents the total cost to manufacture the toasters is $C = 8t + 1000$, where C is the total cost, in dollars, and t is the number of toasters manufactured each month.

a. Write the equation in functional notation.

b. Use the coordinate axes at the right to graph the equation for values of t between 0 and 500.

Toasters manufactured

a. $f(t) = 8t + 1000$

b.

c. The point $(340, 3720)$ is on the graph. Write a sentence that explains the meaning of this ordered pair.

c. The cost to manufacture 340 toasters is $3720.

29. The data in the following table show a reading test grade and the final exam grade in a history class.

Reading test grade	8.5	9.4	10.1	11.4	12.0
History exam	64	68	76	87	92

Write a relation in which the first coordinate is the reading test grade and the second coordinate is the score on the history final exam. Is the relation a function?   {(8.5, 64), (9.4, 68), (10.1, 76), (11.4, 87), (12.0, 92)}; yes

30. The graph at the right shows the cost, in dollars, per 1000 board feet of lumber over a six-month period. Find the slope of the line. Write a sentence that states the meaning of the slope.   The slope is 36. The cost of lumber has been increasing by $36 per month.

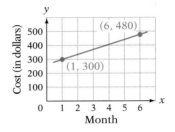

Cumulative Review Exercises

1. Simplify: $12 - 18 \div 3 \cdot (-2)^2$ -12

2. Evaluate $\dfrac{a-b}{a^2-c}$ when $a = -2, b = 3$, and $c = -4$. $-\dfrac{5}{8}$

3. Simplify: $4(2 - 3x) - 5(x - 4)$ $-17x + 28$

4. Solve: $2x - \dfrac{2}{3} = \dfrac{7}{3}$ $\dfrac{3}{2}$

5. Solve: $3x - 2[x - 3(2 - 3x)] = x - 6$ 1

6. Write $6\dfrac{2}{3}\%$ as a fraction. $\dfrac{1}{15}$

7. Use the roster method to write the set of natural numbers less than 9.   {1, 2, 3, 4, 5, 6, 7, 8}

8. Given $D = \{-23, -18, -4, 0, 5\}$, which elements of set D are greater than -16? $-4, 0, 5$

9. Solve: $8a - 3 \geq 5a - 6$ $a \geq -1$

10. Solve $4x - 5y = 15$ for y. $y = \frac{4}{5}x - 3$

11. Find the ordered-pair solution of $y = 3x - 1$ that corresponds to $x = -2$. $(-2, -7)$

12. Find the slope of the line that contains the points whose coordinates are $(2, 3)$ and $(-2, 3)$.
    0

13. Find the x- and y-intercepts for $5x + 2y = 20$.
$(4, 0)$, $(0, 10)$

14. Find the equation of the line that contains the point whose coordinates are $(3, 2)$ and has slope -1. $y = -x + 5$

15. Graph: $y = \frac{1}{2}x + 2$

16. Graph: $3x + y = 2$

17. Graph: $f(x) = -4x - 1$

18. Graph the solution set of $x - y \leq 5$.

19. Find the domain and range of the relation $\{(0, 4), (1, 3), (2, 2), (3, 1), (4, 0)\}$. Is the relation a function?   D: $\{0, 1, 2, 3, 4\}$; R: $\{0, 1, 2, 3, 4\}$; yes

20. Evaluate $f(x) = -4x + 9$ at $x = 5$. -11

21. Find the range of the function given by the equation $f(x) = -\frac{5}{3}x + 3$ if the domain is $\{-9, -6, -3, 0, 3, 6\}$. $\{-7, -2, 3, 8, 13, 18\}$

22. The sum of two numbers is 24. Twice the smaller number is three less than the larger number. Find the two numbers.   7 and 17

23. A lever is 8 ft long. A force of 80 lb is applied to one end of the lever, and a force of 560 lb is applied to the other end. Where is the fulcrum located when the system balances?   7 ft from the 80-pound force

24. The perimeter of a triangle is 49 ft. The length of the first side is twice the length of the third side, and the length of the second side is 5 ft more than the length of the third side. Find the length of the first side.   22 ft

25. A suit that regularly sells for $89 is on sale for 30% off the regular price. Find the sale price. $62.30

6

Systems of Linear Equations

A mechanical engineer designs engines and motors. It is part of the mechanical engineer's job to determine the size and the layout of pipes that are needed to transport water or air or any other material from one place to another within a motor. In these designs, the temperatures and pressures of the materials being transported must be taken into consideration. Therefore, calculations performed by a mechanical engineer normally require equations that have more than one variable.

OBJECTIVES

6.1.1 Solve systems of linear equations by graphing

6.2.1 Solve systems of linear equations by the substitution method

6.3.1 Solve systems of linear equations by the addition method

6.4.1 Rate-of-wind and water-current problems

6.4.2 Application problems

Input-Output Analysis

The economies of the industrial nations are very complex; they comprise hundreds of different industries, and each industry supplies other industries with goods and services needed in the production process. For example, the steel industry requires coal to produce steel, and the coal industry requires steel (in the form of machinery) to mine and transport coal.

Wassily Leontief, a Russian-born economist, developed a method of describing mathematically the interactions of an economic system. His technique was to examine various sectors of an economy (steel industry, oil, farms, autos, and so on) and determine how each sector interacted with the others. More than five hundred sectors of the economy were studied.

The interaction of each sector with the others was written as a series of equations. This series of equations is called a *system of equations*. Using a computer, economists searched for a solution to the system of equations that would determine the output levels various sectors would have to meet to satisfy the requests from other sectors. The method is called input-output analysis.

Input-output analysis has many applications. For example, it is used today to predict the production needs of large corporations and to determine the effect of price changes on the economy. In recognition of the importance of his ideas, Leontief was awarded the Nobel Prize in Economics in 1973.

This chapter begins the study of systems of equations.

SECTION **6.1**

Solving Systems of Linear Equations by Graphing

 Solve systems of linear equations by graphing

INSTRUCTOR NOTE

One way to introduce the study of systems of equations is through an example. Ask students, "Find two numbers whose sum is 5." There are obviously an infinite number of possible ordered pairs.

Now ask, "Find two numbers whose sum is 5 and whose difference is 3." Now there is only one ordered pair that satisfies both conditions.

Equations considered together are called a **system of equations.** A system of equations is shown at the right.

$$2x + y = 3$$
$$x + y = 1$$

A **solution of a system of equations in two variables** is an ordered pair that is a solution of each equation of the system.

For example, $(2, -1)$ is a solution of the system of equations given above because it is a solution of each equation in the system.

$2x + y = 3$		$x + y = 1$	
$2(2) + (-1)$	3	$2 + (-1)$	1
$4 + (-1)$	3		$1 = 1$
	$3 = 3$		

However, $(3, -3)$ is not a solution of this system because it is not a solution of each equation in the system.

$2x + y = 3$		$x + y = 1$	
$2(3) + (-3)$	3	$3 + (-3)$	1
$6 + (-3)$	3		$0 \neq 1$
	$3 = 3$		

Example 1 Is $(1, -3)$ a solution of the system $3x + 2y = -3$
$$x - 3y = 6?$$

Solution

$3x + 2y = -3$		$x - 3y = 6$	
$3 \cdot 1 + 2(-3)$	-3	$1 - 3(-3)$	6
$3 + (-6)$	-3	$1 - (-9)$	6
	$-3 = -3$		$10 \neq 6$

No, $(1, -3)$ is not a solution of the system of equations.

Problem 1 Is $(-1, -2)$ a solution of the system $2x - 5y = 8$
$$-x + 3y = -5?$$

Solution See page S12.   Yes

The solution of a system of linear equations in two variables can be found by graphing the two equations on the same coordinate system. Three possible conditions result.

1. The lines graphed can intersect at one point. The point of intersection of the lines is the ordered pair that is a solution of each equation of the system. It is the solution of the system of equations. The system of equations is **independent**.

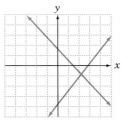

INSTRUCTOR NOTE

Inconsistent and dependent systems of equations can also be illustrated through examples. Here is one for an inconsistent system of equations.

"Find two numbers whose sum is 5 and whose sum is 7."

2. The lines graphed can be parallel and not intersect at all. The system of equations is **inconsistent** and has no solution.

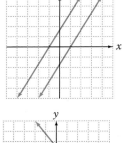

3. The lines graphed can represent the same line. The lines intersect at infinitely many points; therefore, there are infinitely many solutions. The system of equations is **dependent**. The solutions are the ordered pairs that are solutions of either one of the two equations in the system.

➡ Solve by graphing: $2x + 3y = 6$
$$2x + y = -2$$

Graph each line.

The graphs of the equations intersect at one point.
The system of equations is independent.

Find the point of intersection.

The solution is $(-3, 4)$.

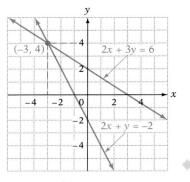

📟 The INTERSECT feature on a graphing calculator can be used to find the solution of the system of equations given above. However, if the ZOOM feature is used to estimate the solution, the estimated solution might be $(-3.03, 4.05)$, or some other ordered pair that contains decimals. When these values are rounded to the nearest integer, the ordered pair becomes $(-3, 4)$, which is the solution of the system. This solution can be verified by replacing x by -3 and y by 4 in the system of equations.

INSTRUCTOR NOTE

You might solve each equation in this system for y in order to show that the two equations have the same slope but different y-intercepts. (One equation is $y = 2x - 1$. The other is $y = 2x - 4$.)

Do the same for the dependent system that follows. Show the students that the equation of both lines is

$$y = -\frac{2}{3}x + 2.$$

➡ Solve by graphing: $2x - y = 1$
$$6x - 3y = 12$$

Graph each line.

The lines are parallel and therefore do not intersect.

The system of equations is inconsistent and has no solution.

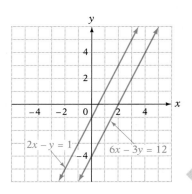

→ Solve by graphing: $2x + 3y = 6$
$\qquad\qquad\qquad 6x + 9y = 18$

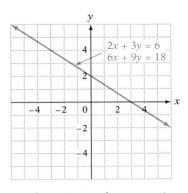

Graph each line.

The two equations represent the same line. The system of equations is dependent and, therefore, has an infinite number of solutions.

The solutions are the ordered pairs that are solutions of the equation $2x + 3y = 6$.

By choosing values for x, substituting these values into the equation $2x + 3y = 6$, and finding the corresponding values for y, we can find some specific ordered-pair solutions. For example, $(3, 0)$, $(0, 2)$, and $(6, -2)$ are solutions of this system of equations.

Example 2 Solve by graphing. A. $x - 2y = 2$ B. $4x - 2y = 6$
$\qquad\qquad\qquad\qquad\qquad\qquad\quad x + y = 5$ $\qquad\quad y = 2x - 3$

Solution A.   B.

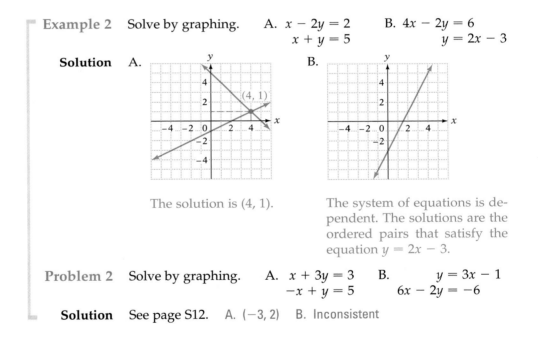

The solution is $(4, 1)$.

The system of equations is dependent. The solutions are the ordered pairs that satisfy the equation $y = 2x - 3$.

Problem 2 Solve by graphing. A. $x + 3y = 3$ B. $\qquad y = 3x - 1$
$\qquad\qquad\qquad\qquad\qquad\qquad -x + y = 5$ $6x - 2y = -6$

Solution See page S12.   A. $(-3, 2)$ B. Inconsistent

CONCEPT REVIEW 6.1

Determine whether the statement is always true, sometimes true, or never true.

1. A solution of a system of linear equations in two variables is an ordered pair (x, y).   Always true

2. Graphically, the solution of an independent system of linear equations in two variables is the point of intersection of the graphs of the two equations. Always true

3. Suppose an ordered pair is a solution of one equation in a system of linear equations and not of the other equation. Then the system has no solution. Sometimes true

4. Either a system of linear equations has one solution, represented graphically by two lines intersecting at exactly one point, or no solutions, represented graphically by two parallel lines.   Never true

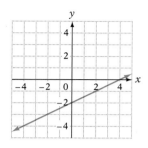

5. The graph at the right is the graph of a system of two linear equations. Sometimes true

6. An independent system of equations has no solution.   Never true

EXERCISES 6.1

1 1. 🖊 What is a system of equations?

2. 🖊 How can you determine whether an ordered pair is a solution of a system of equations in two variables?

3. Is (2, 3) a solution of the system $3x + 4y = 18$
$2x - y = 1$?
Yes

4. Is (2, −1) a solution of the system $x - 2y = 4$
$2x + y = 3$?
Yes

5. Is (1, −2) a solution of the system
$3x - y = 5$
$2x + 5y = -8$?   Yes

6. Is (−1, −1) a solution of the system
$x - 4y = 3$
$3x + y = 2$?   No

7. Is (4, 3) a solution of the system $5x - 2y = 14$
$x + y = 8$?
No

8. Is (2, 5) a solution of the system $3x + 2y = 16$
$2x - 3y = 4$?
No

9. Is (−1, 3) a solution of the system $4x - y = -5$
$2x + 5y = 13$?
No

10. Is (4, −1) a solution of the system
$x - 4y = 9$
$2x - 3y = 11$?   No

11. Is (0, 0) a solution of the system $4x + 3y = 0$
$2x - y = 1$?
No

12. Is (2, 0) a solution of the system $3x - y = 6$
$x + 3y = 2$?
Yes

13. Is (2, −3) a solution of the system
$y = 2x - 7$
$3x - y = 9$?   Yes

14. Is (−1, −2) a solution of the system
$3x - 4y = 5$
$y = x - 1$?   Yes

15. Is (5, 2) a solution of the system $y = 2x - 8$
$y = 3x - 13$?
Yes

16. Is (−4, 3) a solution of the system
$y = 2x + 11$
$y = 5x - 19$?   No

17. 🖊 Explain how to solve a system of two equations in two variables by graphing.

18. 🖊 Explain each of the following in terms of a system of linear equations in two variables: an independent system, an inconsistent system, a dependent system.

Solve by graphing.

19. $x - y = 3$
$x + y = 5$ (4, 1)

20. $2x - y = 4$
$x + y = 5$ (3, 2)

21. $x + 2y = 6$
$x - y = 3$ (4, 1)

22. $3x - y = 3$
$2x + y = 2$ (1, 0)

23. $3x - 2y = 6$
$y = 3$ (4, 3)

24. $x = 2$
$3x + 2y = 4$ (2, −1)

25. $x = 3$
$y = -2$ (3, −2)

26. $x + 1 = 0$
$y - 3 = 0$ (−1, 3)

27. $y = 2x - 6$
$x + y = 0$ (2, −2)

28. $5x - 2y = 11$
$y = 2x - 5$ (1, −3)

29. $2x + y = -2$
$6x + 3y = 6$ Inconsistent

30. $x + y = 5$
$3x + 3y = 6$ Inconsistent

31. $4x - 2y = 4$
$y = 2x - 2$ Dependent

32. $2x + 6y = 6$
$y = -\frac{1}{3}x + 1$ Dependent

33. $x - y = 5$
$2x - y = 6$ (1, −4)

34. $5x - 2y = 10$
$3x + 2y = 6$ (2, 0)

35. $3x + 4y = 0$
$2x - 5y = 0$ (0, 0)

36. $2x - 3y = 0$
$y = -\frac{1}{3}x$ (0, 0)

37. $x - 3y = 3$
$2x - 6y = 12$ Inconsistent

38. $4x + 6y = 12$
$6x + 9y = 18$ Dependent

39. $3x + 2y = -4$
$x = 2y + 4$ (0, −2)

40. $5x + 2y = -14$
$3x - 4y = 2$ (−2, −2)

41. $4x - y = 5$
$3x - 2y = 5$ (1, −1)

42. $2x - 3y = 9$
$4x + 3y = -9$ (0, −3)

Solve by graphing. Then use a graphing utility to verify your solution.

43. $5x - 2y = 10$
$3x + 2y = 6$ (2, 0)

44. $x - y = 5$
$2x + y = 4$ (3, −2)

45. $2x - 5y = 4$
$x - y = -1$ (−3, −2)

46. $x - 2y = -5$
$3x + 4y = -15$ (−5, 0)

47. $2x + 3y = 6$
$y = -\frac{2}{3}x + 1$ Inconsistent

48. $2x - 5y = 10$
$y = \frac{2}{5}x - 2$
Dependent

APPLYING CONCEPTS 6.1

Write a system of equations given the graph.

[C] **49.**

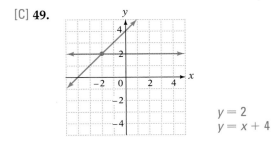

$y = 2$
$y = x + 4$

[C] **50.**

$x = 3$
$y = x - 1$

[C] **51.**

$y = x$
$y = -x + 2$

[C] **52.**

$y = 2x - 2$
$y = \dfrac{2}{3}x + \dfrac{2}{3}$

[C] **53.** Determine whether the statement is always true, sometimes true, or never true.

     a. Two parallel lines have the same slope.   Always true

     b. Two different lines with the same y-intercept are parallel.   Never true

     c. Two different lines with the same slope are parallel.   Always true

[C] **54.** Write three different systems of equations: **a.** one that has $(-3, 5)$ as its only solution, **b.** one for which there is no solution, and **c.** one that is a dependent system of equations.   For example: a. $y = x + 8$ b. $y = 2x - 3$ c. $y = 3x - 5$

                                                                $y = -x + 2$ $y = 2x + 4$ $3x - y = 5$

55.   Explain how you can determine from the graph of a system of two equations in two variables whether it is an independent system of equations. Explain how you can determine whether it is an inconsistent system of equations.

56.   The following graph shows the life expectancy at birth for males and females. Write an essay describing your interpretation of the data presented. Be sure to include in your discussion an interpretation of the point at which the two lines intersect.

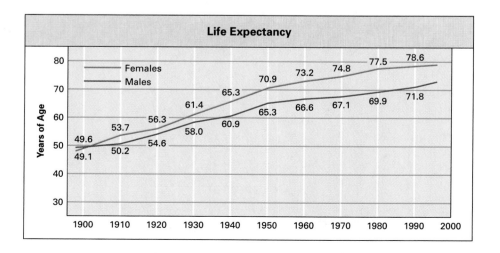

SECTION 6.2

Solving Systems of Linear Equations by the Substitution Method

1 Solve systems of linear equations by the substitution method

A graphical solution of a system of equations may give only an approximate solution of the system. For example, the point whose coordinates are $\left(\frac{1}{4}, \frac{1}{2}\right)$ would be difficult to read from the graph. An algebraic method called the **substitution method** can be used to find an exact solution of a system.

INSTRUCTOR NOTE

When students evaluate a variable expression, they replace a variable with a constant. Here the student is replacing a variable with a variable expression. Mentioning this connection will help some students master the substitution method of solving a system of equations.

▶ Solve by substitution: $2x + 5y = -11$ (1)
$\qquad\qquad\qquad\qquad\qquad\quad y = 3x - 9$ (2)

Equation (2) states that $y = 3x - 9$.

Substitute $3x - 9$ for y in equation (1).
$$2x + 5(3x - 9) = -11$$

Solve for x.
$$2x + 15x - 45 = -11$$
$$17x - 45 = -11$$
$$17x = 34$$
$$x = 2$$

Substitute the value of x into equation (2)   (2)
and solve for y.
$$y = 3x - 9$$
$$y = 3 \cdot 2 - 9$$
$$y = 6 - 9$$
$$y = -3$$

The solution is $(2, -3)$. ◀

The graph of the system of equations given above is shown at the right. Note that the lines intersect at the point whose coordinates are $(2, -3)$, which is the algebraic solution we determined by the substitution method.

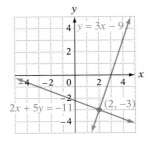

▶ Solve by substitution: $5x + y = 4$ (1)
$\qquad\qquad\qquad\qquad\quad 2x - 3y = 5$ (2)

Equation (1) is the easier equation to solve for one variable in terms of the other.

Solve equation (1) for y.
$$5x + y = 4$$
$$y = -5x + 4$$

Substitute $-5x + 4$ for y in equation (2). Solve for x.

$$2x - 3(-5x + 4) = 5$$
$$2x + 15x - 12 = 5$$
$$17x - 12 = 5$$
$$17x = 17$$
$$x = 1$$

Substitute the value of x in equation (1) and solve for y.

(1)

$$5x + y = 4$$
$$5(1) + y = 4$$
$$5 + y = 4$$
$$y = -1$$

The solution is $(1, -1)$.

➡ Solve by substitution: $y = 3x - 1$ (1)
$\qquad\qquad\qquad\qquad\quad y = -2x - 6$ (2)

Substitute $-2x - 6$ for y in equation (1).

Solve for x.

$$y = 3x - 1$$
$$-2x - 6 = 3x - 1$$
$$-5x - 6 = -1$$
$$-5x = 5$$
$$x = -1$$

Substitute the value of x into either equation and solve for y. Equation (1) is used here.

$$y = 3x - 1$$
$$y = 3(-1) - 1$$
$$y = -3 - 1$$
$$y = -4$$

The solution is $(-1, -4)$. ⬅

Example 1   Solve by substitution: $3x + 4y = -2$ (1)
$\qquad\qquad\qquad\qquad\qquad\qquad\quad -x + 2y = 4$ (2)

Solution
$$-x + 2y = 4$$
$$-x = -2y + 4$$
$$x = 2y - 4$$
▶ Solve equation (2) for x.

$$3x + 4y = -2$$
$$3(2y - 4) + 4y = -2$$
$$6y - 12 + 4y = -2$$
$$10y - 12 = -2$$
$$10y = 10$$
$$y = 1$$
▶ Substitute $2y - 4$ for x in equation (1).
▶ Solve for y.

$$-x + 2y = 4$$
$$-x + 2(1) = 4$$
$$-x + 2 = 4$$
$$-x = 2$$
$$x = -2$$
▶ Substitute the value of y into equation (2).
▶ Solve for x.

The solution is $(-2, 1)$.

Problem 1   Solve by substitution: $7x - y = 4$
$\qquad\qquad\qquad\qquad\qquad\qquad\quad 3x + 2y = 9$

Solution   See page S13. $(1, 3)$

Example 2   Solve by substitution: $4x + 2y = 5$ (1)
$ y = -2x + 1$ (2)

Solution $4x + 2y = 5$ ▶ Substitute $-2x + 1$ for y in equation (1).
$ 4x + 2(-2x + 1) = 5$
$ 4x - 4x + 2 = 5$
$ 2 = 5$

$2 = 5$ is not a true equation. The system of equations is inconsistent. The system does not have a solution.

Problem 2   Solve by substitution: $3x - y = 4$
$ y = 3x + 2$

Solution   See page S13.   Inconsistent

Example 3   Solve by substitution: $6x - 2y = 4$ (1)
$ y = 3x - 2$ (2)

Solution $6x - 2y = 4$ ▶ Substitute $3x - 2$ for y in equation (1).
$ 6x - 2(3x - 2) = 4$
$ 6x - 6x + 4 = 4$
$ 4 = 4$

$4 = 4$ is a true equation. The system of equations is dependent. The solutions are the ordered pairs that satisfy the equation $y = 3x - 2$.

Problem 3   Solve by substitution: $y = -2x + 1$
$ 6x + 3y = 3$

Solution   See page S13.   Dependent

Note from Examples 2 and 3 above: If, when you are solving a system of equations, the variable is eliminated and the result is a false equation, such as $2 = 5$, the system is inconsistent and does not have a solution. If the result is a true equation, such as $4 = 4$, the system is dependent and has an infinite number of solutions.

CONCEPT REVIEW 6.2

Determine whether the statement is always true, sometimes true, or never true.

1. If one of the equations in a system of two linear equations is $y = x + 2$, then $x + 2$ can be substituted for y in the other equation in the system.   Always true

2. If a system of equations contains the equations $y = 2x + 1$ and $x + y = 5$, then $x + 2x + 1 = 5$.   Always true

3. If the equation $x = 4$ results from solving a system of equations by the substitution method, then the solution of the system of equations is 4.   Never true

4. If the true equation $6 = 6$ results from solving a system of equations by the substitution method, then the system of equations has an infinite number of solutions.   Always true

5. If the false equation $0 = 7$ results from solving a system of equations by the substitution method, then the system of equations is independent.   Never true

6. The ordered pair $(0, 0)$ is a solution of a system of linear equations.   Sometimes true

---

EXERCISES 6.2

1 Solve by substitution.

1. $2x + 3y = 7$
    $x = 2$ $(2, 1)$

2. $y = 3$
    $3x - 2y = 6$ $(4, 3)$

3. $y = x - 3$
    $x + y = 5$ $(4, 1)$

4. $y = x + 2$
    $x + y = 6$ $(2, 4)$

5. $x = y - 2$
    $x + 3y = 2$ $(-1, 1)$

6. $x = y + 1$
    $x + 2y = 7$ $(3, 2)$

7. $2x + 3y = 9$
    $y = x - 2$ $(3, 1)$

8. $3x + 2y = 11$
    $y = x + 3$ $(1, 4)$

9. $3x - y = 2$
    $y = 2x - 1$ $(1, 1)$

10. $2x - y = -5$
    $y = x + 4$ $(-1, 3)$

11. $x = 2y - 3$
    $2x - 3y = -5$ $(-1, 1)$

12. $x = 3y - 1$
    $3x + 4y = 10$ $(2, 1)$

13. $y = 4 - 3x$
    $3x + y = 5$ Inconsistent

14. $y = 2 - 3x$
    $6x + 2y = 7$ Inconsistent

15. $x = 3y + 3$
    $2x - 6y = 12$ Inconsistent

16. $x = 2 - y$
    $3x + 3y = 6$ Dependent

17. $3x + 5y = -6$
    $x = 5y + 3$ $\left(-\frac{3}{4}, -\frac{3}{4}\right)$

18. $y = 2x + 3$
    $4x - 3y = 1$ $(-5, -7)$

19. $x = 4y - 3$
    $2x - 3y = 0$ $\left(\frac{9}{5}, \frac{6}{5}\right)$

20. $x = 2y$
    $-2x + 4y = 6$ Inconsistent

21. $y = 2x - 9$
    $3x - y = 2$ $(-7, -23)$

22. $y = x + 4$
    $2x - y = 6$ $(10, 14)$

23. $3x + 4y = 7$
    $x = 3 - 2y$ $(1, 1)$

24. $3x - 5y = 1$
    $y = 4x - 2$ $\left(\frac{9}{17}, \frac{2}{17}\right)$

25. $2x - y = 4$
    $3x + 2y = 6$ $(2, 0)$

26. $x + y = 12$
    $3x - 2y = 6$ $(6, 6)$

27. $4x - 3y = 5$
    $x + 2y = 4$ $(2, 1)$

28. $3x - 5y = 2$
    $2x - y = 4$ $\left(\frac{18}{7}, \frac{8}{7}\right)$

29. $7x - y = 4$
    $5x + 2y = 1$ $\left(\frac{9}{19}, -\frac{13}{19}\right)$

30. $x - 7y = 4$
    $-3x + 2y = 6$ $\left(-\frac{50}{19}, -\frac{18}{19}\right)$

31. $4x - 3y = -1$
    $y = 2x - 3$ $(5, 7)$

32. $3x - 7y = 28$
    $x = 3 - 4y$ $(7, -1)$

33. $7x + y = 14$
    $2x - 5y = -33$ $(1, 7)$

34. $3x + y = 4$
    $4x - 3y = 1$ $(1, 1)$

35. $x - 4y = 9$
    $2x - 3y = 11$ $\left(\frac{17}{5}, -\frac{7}{5}\right)$

36. $3x - y = 6$
    $x + 3y = 2$ $(2, 0)$

37. $4x - y = -5$
    $2x + 5y = 13$ $\left(-\frac{6}{11}, \frac{31}{11}\right)$

38. $3x - y = 5$
    $2x + 5y = -8$ $(1, -2)$

39. $3x + 4y = 18$
    $2x - y = 1$ $(2, 3)$

40. $4x + 3y = 0$
    $2x - y = 0$ $(0, 0)$

41. $5x + 2y = 0$
    $x - 3y = 0$ $(0, 0)$

42. $6x - 3y = 6$
    $2x - y = 2$ Dependent

43. $3x + y = 4$
$9x + 3y = 12$ Dependent

44. $x - 5y = 6$
$2x - 7y = 9$ $(1, -1)$

45. $x + 7y = -5$
$2x - 3y = 5$ $\left(\frac{20}{17}, -\frac{15}{17}\right)$

46. $y = 2x + 11$
$y = 5x - 19$ $(10, 31)$

47. $y = 2x - 8$
$y = 3x - 13$ $(5, 2)$

48. $y = -4x + 2$
$y = -3x - 1$ $(3, -10)$

49. $x = 3y + 7$
$x = 2y - 1$ $(-17, -8)$

50. $x = 4y - 2$
$x = 6y + 8$ $(-22, -5)$

51. $x = 3 - 2y$
$x = 5y - 10$ $\left(-\frac{5}{7}, \frac{13}{7}\right)$

52. $y = 2x - 7$
$y = 4x + 5$ $(-6, -19)$

53. $3x - y = 11$
$2x + 5y = -4$ $(3, -2)$

54. $-x + 6y = 8$
$2x + 5y = 1$ $(-2, 1)$

APPLYING CONCEPTS 6.2

Rewrite each equation so that the coefficients and constant are integers. Then solve the system of equations.

55. $0.1x - 0.6y = -0.4$
$-0.7x + 0.2y = 0.5$ $\left(-\frac{11}{20}, \frac{23}{40}\right)$

56. $0.8x - 0.1y = 0.3$
$0.5x - 0.2y = -0.5$ $(1, 5)$

57. $0.4x + 0.5y = 0.2$
$0.3x - 0.1y = 1.1$ $(3, -2)$

58. $-0.1x + 0.3y = 1.1$
$0.4x - 0.1y = -2.2$ $(-5, 2)$

59. $1.2x + 0.1y = 1.9$
$0.1x + 0.3y = 2.2$ $(1, 7)$

60. $1.25x - 0.01y = 1.5$
$0.24x - 0.02y = -1.52$

$(2, 100)$

For what value of k does the system of equations have no solution?

[C] **61.** $2x - 3y = 7$
$kx - 3y = 4$ 2

[C] **62.** $8x - 4y = 1$
$2x - ky = 3$ 1

[C] **63.** $x = 4y + 4$
$kx - 8y = 4$ 2

64. The following was offered as a solution to the system of equations shown at the right.

(1) $y = \frac{1}{2}x + 2$
(2) $2x + 5y = 10$

$2x + 5y = 10$ ▶ Equation (2)

$2x + 5\left(\frac{1}{2}x + 2\right) = 10$ ▶ Substitute $\frac{1}{2}x + 2$ for y.

$2x + \frac{5}{2}x + 10 = 10$ ▶ Solve for x.

$\frac{9}{2}x = 0$

$x = 0$

At this point the student stated that because $x = 0$, the system of equations has no solution. If this assertion is correct, is the system of equations independent, dependent, or inconsistent? If the assertion is not correct, what is the correct solution?   The assertion is not correct. The solution is $(0, 2)$.

65.   Describe in your own words the process of solving a system of equations by the substitution method.

66.   When you solve a system of equations by the substitution method, how do you determine whether the system of equations is dependent? How do you determine whether the system of equations is inconsistent?

Solving Systems of Linear Equations by the Addition Method

1   Solve systems of linear equations by the addition method

INSTRUCTOR NOTE

Although somewhat difficult for students, the explanation below of the addition method as it applies to the equations at the right may help some students.

Starting with $3x + 2y = 4$, add 10 to each side of the equation (10 is the constant term for the second equation). We now have

$$3x + 2y + 10 = 4 + 10$$

Now substitute $4x - 2y$ for 10 on the left side of the equation. After simplifying, we have

$$7x = 14$$

Another algebraic method for solving a system of equations is called the **addition method.** It is based on the Addition Property of Equations.

In the system of equations at the right, note the effect of adding equation (2) to equation (1). Because $2y$ and $-2y$ are opposites, adding the equations results in an equation with only one variable.

(1) $3x + 2y = 4$
(2) $4x - 2y = 10$
     $7x + 0y = 14$
       $7x = 14$

The solution of the resulting equation is the first coordinate of the ordered-pair solution of the system.

$$7x = 14$$
$$x = 2$$

The second coordinate is found by substituting the value of x into equation (1) or (2) and then solving for y. Equation (1) is used here.

(1) $3x + 2y = 4$
$3 \cdot 2 + 2y = 4$
$6 + 2y = 4$
$2y = -2$
$y = -1$

The solution is $(2, -1)$.

Sometimes adding the two equations does not eliminate one of the variables. In this case, use the Multiplication Property of Equations to rewrite one or both of the equations so that when the equations are added, one of the variables is eliminated.

To do this, first choose which variable to eliminate. The coefficients of that variable must be opposites. Multiply each equation by a constant that will produce coefficients that are opposites.

➡ Solve by the addition method: $3x + 2y = 7$ (1)
                             $5x - 4y = 19$ (2)

To eliminate y, multiply each side of equation (1) by 2.

$2(3x + 2y) = 2 \cdot 7$
$5x - 4y = 19$

Now the coefficients of the y terms are opposites.

$6x + 4y = 14$
$5x - 4y = 19$

Add the equations.
Solve for x.

$11x + 0y = 33$
$11x = 33$
$x = 3$

Substitute the value of x into one of the equations and solve for y. Equation (2) is used here.

(2) $5x - 4y = 19$
$5 \cdot 3 - 4y = 19$
$15 - 4y = 19$
$-4y = 4$
$y = -1$

The solution is $(3, -1)$. ◀

➡ Solve by the addition method: $5x + 6y = 3$ (1)
$2x - 5y = 16$ (2)

To eliminate x, multiply each side of equation (1) by 2 and each side of equation (2) by -5. Note how the constants are selected. The negative sign is used so that the coefficients will be opposites.

$2 \diagup (5x + 6y) = 2 \cdot 3$
$-5 \diagdown (2x - 5y) = -5 \cdot 16$

Now the coefficients of the x terms are opposites.

$10x + 12y = 6$
$-10x + 25y = -80$

Add the equations.
Solve for y.

$0x + 37y = -74$
$37y = -74$
$y = -2$

Substitute the value of y into one of the equations and solve for x. Equation (1) is used here.

(1) $5x + 6y = 3$
$5x + 6(-2) = 3$
$5x - 12 = 3$
$5x = 15$
$x = 3$

The solution is $(3, -2)$. ⬅

➡ Solve by the addition method: $5x = 2y - 7$ (1)
$3x + 4y = 1$ (2)

Write equation (1) in the form $Ax + By = C$.

$5x - 2y = -7$
$3x + 4y = 1$

Eliminate y. Multiply each side of equation (1) by 2.

$2(5x - 2y) = 2(-7)$
$3x + 4y = 1$

Now the coefficients of the y terms are opposites.

$10x - 4y = -14$
$3x + 4y = 1$

Add the equations.
Solve for x.

$13x + 0y = -13$
$13x = -13$
$x = -1$

Substitute the value of x into one of the equations and solve for y. Equation (1) is used here.

$5x = 2y - 7$
$5(-1) = 2y - 7$
$-5 = 2y - 7$
$2 = 2y$
$1 = y$

The solution is $(-1, 1)$. ⬅

➡ Solve by the addition method: $2x + y = 2$ (1)
$4x + 2y = -5$ (2)

To eliminate y, multiply each side of equation (1) by -2.

$-4x - 2y = -4$
$4x + 2y = -5$

Add the equations.
This is not a true equation.

$0x + 0y = -9$
$0 = -9$

The system of equations is inconsistent. The system does not have a solution. ⬅

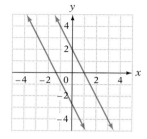

The graphs of the two equations in the system of equations above are shown at the left. Note that the graphs are parallel and therefore do not intersect. Thus the system of equations has no solutions.

Example 1   Solve by the addition method: $2x + 4y = 7$ (1)
$5x - 3y = -2$ (2)

Solution

$5(2x + 4y) = 5 \cdot 7$ ▶ Eliminate x. Multiply each side of
$-2(5x - 3y) = -2 \cdot (-2)$ equation (1) by 5 and each side of
equation (2) by -2.

$10x + 20y = 35$
$-10x + 6y = 4$
$26y = 39$ ▶ Add the equations.

$y = \dfrac{39}{26} = \dfrac{3}{2}$ ▶ Solve for y.

$2x + 4\left(\dfrac{3}{2}\right) = 7$ ▶ Substitute the value of y in equation (1).
$2x + 6 = 7$ ▶ Solve for x.
$2x = 1$
$x = \dfrac{1}{2}$

The solution is $\left(\dfrac{1}{2}, \dfrac{3}{2}\right)$.

Problem 1   Solve by the addition method: $x - 2y = 1$
$2x + 4y = 0$

Solution   See page S13. $\left(\dfrac{1}{2}, -\dfrac{1}{4}\right)$

Example 2   Solve by the addition method: $6x + 9y = 15$ (1)
$4x + 6y = 10$ (2)

Solution

$4(6x + 9y) = 4 \cdot 15$ ▶ Eliminate x. Multiply each side of equation (1) by 4 and each side of equation (2)
$-6(4x + 6y) = -6 \cdot 10$ by -6.

$24x + 36y = 60$
$-24x - 36y = -60$
$0 = 0$ ▶ Add the equations.

$0 = 0$ is a true equation. The system of equations is dependent. The solutions are ordered pairs that satisfy the equation $6x + 9y = 15$.

Problem 2   Solve by the addition method: $2x - 3y = 4$
$-4x + 6y = -8$

Solution   See page S14.   Dependent

CONCEPT REVIEW 6.3

Determine whether the statement is always true, sometimes true, or never true.

1. When using the addition method of solving a system of linear equations, if you multiply one side of an equation by a number, then you must multiply the other side of the equation by the same number.   Always true

2. When a system of linear equations is being solved by the addition method, in order for one of the variables to be eliminated, the coefficients of one of the variables must be opposites.   Always true

3. If the two equations in a system of equations have the same slope and different y-intercepts, then the system of equations has an infinite number of solutions.   Never true

4. You are using the addition method to solve the system of equations shown at the right. The first step you will perform is to add the two equations.   Never true
$$3x + 2y = 6$$
$$2x + 3y = -6$$

5. If the equation $y = -2$ results from solving a system of equations by the addition method, then the solution of the system of equations is -2.   Never true

6. If the true equation $-3 = -3$ results from solving a system of equations by the addition method, then the system of equations is dependent.   Always true

_____

EXERCISES 6.3

1 Solve by the addition method.

1. $x + y = 4$
   $x - y = 6$
   $(5, -1)$

2. $2x + y = 3$
   $x - y = 3$
   $(2, -1)$

3. $x + y = 4$
   $2x + y = 5$
   $(1, 3)$

4. $x - 3y = 2$
   $x + 2y = -3$
   $(-1, -1)$

5. $2x - y = 1$
   $x + 3y = 4$
   $(1, 1)$

6. $x - 2y = 4$
   $3x + 4y = 2$
   $(2, -1)$

7. $4x - 5y = 22$
   $x + 2y = -1$
   $(3, -2)$

8. $3x - y = 11$
   $2x + 5y = 13$
   $(4, 1)$

9. $2x - y = 1$
   $4x - 2y = 2$
   Dependent

10. $x + 3y = 2$
   $3x + 9y = 6$
   Dependent

11. $4x + 3y = 15$
   $2x - 5y = 1$
   $(3, 1)$

12. $3x - 7y = 13$
   $6x + 5y = 7$
   $(2, -1)$

13. $2x - 3y = 5$
   $4x - 6y = 3$
   Inconsistent

14. $2x + 4y = 3$
   $3x + 6y = 8$
   Inconsistent

15. $5x - 2y = -1$
   $x + 3y = -5$
   $\left(-\dfrac{13}{17}, -\dfrac{24}{17}\right)$

16. $4x - 3y = 1$
   $8x + 5y = 13$
   $(1, 1)$

17. $5x + 7y = 10$
   $3x - 14y = 6$
   $(2, 0)$

18. $7x + 10y = 13$
   $4x + 5y = 6$
   $(-1, 2)$

19. $3x - 2y = 0$
   $6x + 5y = 0$
   $(0, 0)$

20. $5x + 2y = 0$
   $3x + 5y = 0$
   $(0, 0)$

21. $2x - 3y = 16$
   $3x + 4y = 7$
   $(5, -2)$

22. $3x + 4y = 10$
   $4x + 3y = 11$
   $(2, 1)$

23. $5x + 3y = 7$
   $2x + 5y = 1$
   $\left(\dfrac{32}{19}, -\dfrac{9}{19}\right)$

24. $-2x + 7y = 9$
   $3x + 2y = -1$
   $(-1, 1)$

25. $7x - 2y = 13$
   $5x + 3y = 27$
   $(3, 4)$

26. $12x + 5y = 23$
   $2x - 7y = 39$
   $\left(\dfrac{178}{47}, -\dfrac{211}{47}\right)$

27. $8x - 3y = 11$
   $6x - 5y = 11$
   $(1, -1)$

28. $4x - 8y = 36$
   $3x - 6y = 27$
   Dependent

29. $5x + 15y = 20$
$2x + 6y = 8$

Dependent

30. $y = 2x - 3$
$4x + 4y = -1$

$\left(\dfrac{11}{12}, -\dfrac{7}{6}\right)$

31. $3x = 2y + 7$
$5x - 2y = 13$

$(3, 1)$

32. $2y = 4 - 9x$
$9x - y = 25$

$(2, -7)$

33. $2x + 9y = 16$
$5x = 1 - 3y$

$(-1, 2)$

34. $3x - 4 = y + 18$
$4x + 5y = -21$

$\left(\dfrac{89}{19}, -\dfrac{151}{19}\right)$

35. $2x + 3y = 7 - 2x$
$7x + 2y = 9$

$(1, 1)$

36. $5x - 3y = 3y + 4$
$4x + 3y = 11$

$(2, 1)$

37. $3x + y = 1$
$5x + y = 2$

$\left(\dfrac{1}{2}, -\dfrac{1}{2}\right)$

38. $2x - y = 1$
$2x - 5y = -1$

$\left(\dfrac{3}{4}, \dfrac{1}{2}\right)$

39. $4x + 3y = 3$
$x + 3y = 1$

$\left(\dfrac{2}{3}, \dfrac{1}{9}\right)$

40. $2x - 5y = 4$
$x + 5y = 1$

$\left(\dfrac{5}{3}, -\dfrac{2}{15}\right)$

41. $3x - 4y = 1$
$4x + 3y = 1$

$\left(\dfrac{7}{25}, -\dfrac{1}{25}\right)$

42. $2x - 7y = -17$
$3x + 5y = 17$

$\left(\dfrac{34}{31}, \dfrac{85}{31}\right)$

43. $2x - 3y = 4$
$-x + 4y = 3$

$(5, 2)$

44. $4x - 2y = 5$
$2x + 3y = 4$

$\left(\dfrac{23}{16}, \dfrac{3}{8}\right)$

APPLYING CONCEPTS 6.3

Solve.

45. $x - 0.2y = 0.2$
$0.2x + 0.5y = 2.2$ $(1, 4)$

46. $0.5x - 1.2y = 0.3$
$0.2x + y = 1.6$ $(3, 1)$

47. $1.25x - 1.5y = -1.75$
$2.5x - 1.75y = -1$ $(1, 2)$

48. The point of intersection of the graphs of the equations $Ax + 2y = 2$ and $2x + By = 10$ is $(2, -2)$. Find A and B. $A = 3, B = -3$

49. The point of intersection of the graphs of the equations $Ax - 4y = 9$ and $4x + By = -1$ is $(-1, -3)$. Find A and B. $A = 3, B = -1$

[C] **50.** Given that the graphs of the equations $2x - y = 6$, $3x - 4y = 4$, and $Ax - 2y = 0$ all intersect at the same point, find A. $A = 1$

[C] **51.** Given that the graphs of the equations $3x - 2y = -2$, $2x - y = 0$, and $Ax + y = 8$ all intersect at the same point, find A. $A = 2$

[C] **52.** For what value of k is the system of equations dependent?

a. $2x + 3y = 7$
$4x + 6y = k$ 14

b. $y = \dfrac{2}{3}x - 3$
$y = kx - 3$ $\dfrac{2}{3}$

c. $x = ky - 1$
$y = 2x + 2$ $\dfrac{1}{2}$

[C] **53.** For what values of k is the system of equations independent?

a. $x + y = 7$
$kx + y = 3$ $k \neq 1$

b. $x + 2y = 4$
$kx + 3y = 2$ $k \neq \dfrac{3}{2}$

c. $2x + ky = 1$
$x + 2y = 2$ $k \neq 4$

54. ✎ Describe in your own words the process of solving a system of equations by the addition method.

SECTION 6.4

Application Problems in Two Variables

1   Rate-of-wind and water-current problems

Solving motion problems that involve an object moving with or against a wind or current normally requires two variables. One variable represents the speed of the moving object in calm air or still water, and a second variable represents the rate of the wind or current.

A plane flying with the wind will travel a greater distance per hour than it would travel without the wind. The resulting rate of the plane is represented by the sum of the plane's speed and the rate of the wind.

A plane traveling against the wind, on the other hand, will travel a shorter distance per hour than it would travel without the wind. The resulting rate of the plane is represented by the difference between the plane's speed and the rate of the wind.

The same principle is used to describe the rate of a boat traveling with or against a water current.

Solve: Flying with the wind, a small plane can fly 750 mi in 3 h. Against the wind, the plane can fly the same distance in 5 h. Find the rate of the plane in calm air and the rate of the wind.

STRATEGY for solving rate-of-wind and water-current problems

> ■ Choose one variable to represent the rate of the object in calm conditions and a second variable to represent the rate of the wind or current. Use these variables to express the rate of the object with and against the wind or current. Then use these expressions for the rate, as well as the time traveled with and against the wind or current and the fact that $rt = d$, to write expressions for the distance traveled by the object. The results can be recorded in a table.

Rate of plane in calm air: p
Rate of wind: w

With wind: 750 mi in 3 h

Against wind: 750 mi in 5 h

	Rate	·	Time	=	Distance
With the wind	$p + w$	·	3	=	$3(p + w)$
Against the wind	$p - w$	·	5	=	$5(p - w)$

■ Determine how the expressions for distance are related.

The distance traveled with the wind is 750 mi. $3(p + w) = 750$
The distance traveled against the wind is 750 mi. $5(p - w) = 750$

Solve the system of equations.

$3(p + w) = 750$ $\qquad$ $\dfrac{3(p + w)}{3} = \dfrac{750}{3}$ $\qquad$ $p + w = 250$

$5(p - w) = 750$ $\qquad$ $\dfrac{5(p - w)}{5} = \dfrac{750}{5}$ $\qquad$ $p - w = 150$

$$2p = 400$$
$$p = 200$$

Substitute the value of p in the equation $p + w = 250$. $\qquad$ $p + w = 250$
Solve for w. $\qquad$ $200 + w = 250$
$\qquad$ $w = 50$

The rate of the plane in calm air is 200 mph.
The rate of the wind is 50 mph.

Example 1 A 600-mile trip from one city to another takes 4 h when a plane is flying with the wind. The return trip against the wind takes 5 h. Find the rate of the plane in still air and the rate of the wind.

Strategy

With wind: 600 mi in 4 h

Against wind: 600 mi in 5 h

■ Rate of the plane in still air: p
  Rate of the wind: w

	Rate	Time	Distance
With wind	$p + w$	4	$4(p + w)$
Against wind	$p - w$	5	$5(p - w)$

■ The distance traveled with the wind is 600 mi.
  The distance traveled against the wind is 600 mi.

Solution $4(p + w) = 600$ (1)
$5(p - w) = 600$ (2)

$\dfrac{4(p + w)}{4} = \dfrac{600}{4}$ ▶ Simplify equation (1) by dividing each side of the equation by 4.

$\dfrac{5(p - w)}{5} = \dfrac{600}{5}$ ▶ Simplify equation (2) by dividing each side of the equation by 5.

$p + w = 150$
$p - w = 120$
$2p = 270$ ▶ Add the two equations.
$p = 135$ ▶ Solve for p, the rate of the plane in still air.

$$p + w = 150$$
$$135 + w = 150$$
$$w = 15$$

▶ Substitute the value of p into one of the equations.

▶ Solve for w, the rate of the wind.

The rate of the plane in still air is 135 mph.
The rate of the wind is 15 mph.

Problem 1   A canoeist paddling with the current can travel 24 mi in 3 h. Against the current, it takes 4 h to travel the same distance. Find the rate of the current and the rate of the canoeist in calm water.

Solution   See page S14.   Rate of current: 1 mph; rate of canoeist in calm water: 7 mph

2 ◾ Application problems

The application problems in this section are varieties of those problems solved earlier in the text. Each of the strategies for the problems in this section will result in a system of equations.

Solve: A jeweler purchased 5 oz of a gold alloy and 20 oz of a silver alloy for a total cost of $700. The next day, at the same prices per ounce, the jeweler purchased 4 oz of the gold alloy and 30 oz of the silver alloy for a total cost of $630. Find the cost per ounce of the silver alloy.

STRATEGY *for solving an application problem in two variables*

◾ Choose one variable to represent one of the unknown quantities and a second variable to represent the other unknown quantity. Write numerical or variable expressions for all the remaining quantities. These results can be recorded in two tables, one for each of the conditions.

Cost per ounce of gold: g
Cost per ounce of silver: s

First day

	Amount	·	Unit cost	=	Value
Gold	5	·	g	=	$5g$
Silver	20	·	s	=	$20s$

Second day

	Amount	·	Unit cost	=	Value
Gold	4	·	g	=	$4g$
Silver	30	·	s	=	$30s$

◾ Determine a system of equations. The strategies presented in the chapter on "Solving Equations and Inequalities: Applications" can be used to determine the relationships between the expressions in the tables. Each table will give one equation of the system.

The total value of the purchase on the first day was \$700. $5g + 20s = 700$
The total value of the purchase on the second day was \$630. $4g + 30s = 630$

Solve the system of equations.

$$5g + 20s = 700$$
$$4g + 30s = 630$$
$\longrightarrow$
$$4(5g + 20s) = 4 \cdot 700$$
$$-5(4g + 30s) = -5 \cdot 630$$
$\longrightarrow$
$$20g + 80s = 2800$$
$$-20g - 150s = -3150$$
$$-70s = -350$$
$$s = 5$$

The cost per ounce of the silver alloy was \$5.

Example 2   A store owner purchased 20 incandescent light bulbs and 30 fluorescent bulbs for a total cost of \$40. A second purchase, at the same prices, included 30 incandescent bulbs and 10 fluorescent bulbs for a total cost of \$25. Find the cost of an incandescent bulb and of a fluorescent bulb.

Strategy   ▪ Cost of an incandescent bulb: I
Cost of a fluorescent bulb: F

First
purchase

	Amount	Unit cost	Value
Incandescent	20	I	$20I$
Fluorescent	30	F	$30F$

Second
purchase

	Amount	Unit cost	Value
Incandescent	30	I	$30I$
Fluorescent	10	F	$10F$

▪ The total of the first purchase was \$40.
The total of the second purchase was \$25.

Solution
$$20I + 30F = 40 \quad (1)$$
$$30I + 10F = 25 \quad (2)$$

$$3(20I + 30F) = 3(40)$$
$$-2(30I + 10F) = -2(25)$$
▸ Eliminate I. Multiply each side of equation (1) by 3 and each side of equation (2) by -2.

$$60I + 90F = 120$$
$$-60I - 20F = -50$$
$$70F = 70$$ ▸ Add the two equations.
$$F = 1$$ ▸ Solve for F, the cost of a fluorescent bulb.

$$20I + 30F = 40$$ ▸ Substitute the value of F into one of the equations.
$$20I + 30(1) = 40$$
$$20I = 10$$ ▸ Solve for I.
$$I = \frac{1}{2}$$

The cost of an incandescent bulb was \$.50.
The cost of a fluorescent bulb was \$1.00.

Problem 2   Two coin banks contain only dimes and quarters. In the first bank, the total value of the coins is $3.90. In the second bank, there are twice as many dimes as in the first bank and one-half the number of quarters. The total value of the coins in the second bank is $3.30. Find the number of dimes and the number of quarters in the first bank.

Solution   See page S14.   9 dimes; 12 quarters

CONCEPT REVIEW 6.4

Determine whether the statement is always true, sometimes true, or never true.

1. A plane flying with the wind is traveling faster than it would be traveling without the wind.   Always true

2. The uniform motion equation $r = dt$ is used to solve rate-of-wind and water-current problems.   Never true

3. If b represents the rate of a boat in calm water and c represents the rate of the water current, then $b + c$ represents the rate of the boat while it is traveling against the current.   Never true

4. Both sides of an equation can be divided by the same number without changing the solution of the equation.   Sometimes true

5. If, in a system of equations, p represents the rate of a plane in calm air and w represents the rate of the wind, and the solution of the system is $p = 100$, this means that the rate of the wind is 100.   Never true

6. The system of equations at the right represents the following problem:

    $$2(p + w) = 600$$
    $$3(p - w) = 600$$

    A plane flying with the wind flew 600 mi in 2 h. Flying against the wind, the plane could fly the same distance in 3 h. Find the rate of the plane in calm air.
    Always true

EXERCISES 6.4

1 Rate-of-Wind and Water-Current Problems

1. A whale swimming against an ocean current traveled 60 mi in 2 h. Swimming in the opposite direction, with the current, the whale was able to travel the same distance in 1.5 h. Find the speed of the whale in calm water and the rate of the ocean current.   Whale: 35 mph; current: 5 mph

2. A plane flying with the jet stream flew from Los Angeles to Chicago, a distance of 2250 mi, in 5 h. Flying against the jet stream, the plane could fly only 1750 mi in the same amount of time. Find the rate of the plane in calm air and the rate of the wind.   Plane: 400 mph; wind: 50 mph

3. A rowing team rowing with the current traveled 40 km in 2 h. Rowing against the current, the team could travel only 16 km in 2 h. Find the team's rowing rate in calm water and the rate of the current.
    Rowing team: 14 km/h; current: 6 km/h

4. The bird capable of the fastest flying speed is the swift. A swift flying with the wind to a favorite feeding spot traveled 26 mi in 0.2 h. On the return trip, against the wind, the swift was able to travel only 16 mi in the same amount of time. Find the rate of the swift in calm air and the rate of the wind.
    Swift: 105 mph; wind: 25 mph

5. A motorboat traveling with the current went 35 mi in 3.5 h. Traveling against the current, the boat went 12 mi in 3 h. Find the rate of the boat in calm water and the rate of the current.   Boat: 7 mph; current: 3 mph

6. A small plane, flying into a headwind, flew 270 mi in 3 h. Flying with the wind, the plane traveled 260 mi in 2 h. Find the rate of the plane in calm air and the rate of the wind.   Plane: 110 mph; wind: 20 mph

7. A private Learjet 31A transporting passengers was flying with a tailwind and traveled 1120 mi in 2 h. Flying against the wind on the return trip, the jet was able to travel only 980 mi in 2 h. Find the speed of the jet in calm air and the rate of the wind.   Jet: 525 mph; wind: 35 mph

8. A rowing team rowing with the current traveled 18 mi in 2 h. Against the current, the team rowed a distance of 8 mi in the same amount of time. Find the rate of the rowing team in calm water and the rate of the current.
    Rowing team: 6.5 mph; current: 2.5 mph

9. A seaplane flying with the wind flew from an ocean port to a lake, a distance of 240 mi, in 2 h. Flying against the wind, it made the trip from the lake to the ocean port in 3 h. Find the rate of the plane in calm air and the rate of the wind.   Plane: 100 mph; wind: 20 mph

10. Rowing with the current, a canoeist paddled 14 mi in 2 h. Against the current, the canoeist could paddle only 10 mi in the same amount of time. Find the rate of the canoeist in calm water and the rate of the current.
    Canoeist: 6 mph; current: 1 mph

11. A Boeing Apache Longbow military helicopter traveling directly into a strong headwind was able to travel 450 mi in 2.5 h. The return trip, now with a tailwind, took 1 h 40 min. Find the speed of the helicopter in calm air and the rate of the wind.   Helicopter: 225 mph; wind: 45 mph

12. With the wind, a quarterback passes a football 140 ft in 2 s. Against the wind, the same pass would have traveled 80 ft in 2 s. Find the rate of the pass and the rate of the wind.   Pass: 55 ft/s; wind: 15 ft/s

2 13. *Business*   The manager of a computer software store received two shipments of software. The cost of the first shipment, which contained 12 identical word processing programs and 10 identical spreadsheet programs, was $6190. The second shipment, at the same prices, contained 5 copies of the word processing program and 8 copies of the spreadsheet program. The cost of the second shipment was $3825. Find the cost for one copy of the word processing program. $245

14. *Business*   The manager of a discount clothing store received two shipments of fall clothing. The cost of the first shipment, which contained 10 identical sweaters and 20 identical jackets, was $800. The second shipment, at the same prices, contained 5 of the same sweaters and 15 of the same jackets. The cost of the second shipment was $550. Find the cost of one jacket. $30

15. *Business*   A baker purchased 12 lb of wheat flour and 15 lb of rye flour for a total cost of $18.30. A second purchase, at the same prices, included 15 lb of wheat flour and 10 lb of rye flour. The cost of the second purchase was $16.75. Find the cost per pound of the wheat and rye flours.   Wheat: $.65; rye: $.70

16. *Consumerism*   A computer on-line service charges one hourly price for regular use but a higher hourly rate for designated "premium" areas. One customer was charged $28 after spending 2 h in premium areas and 9 regular hours. Another customer spent 3 h in premium areas and 6 regular hours and was charged $27. What is the service charge per hour for regular and premium services?   Regular: $2; premium: $5

17. *Wages*   Shelly Egan works as a stocker at a grocery store during her summer vacation. She gets paid a standard hourly rate for her day hours but a higher hourly rate for any hours she works during the night shift. One week she worked 17 daylight hours and 8 nighttime hours and earned $191. The next week she earned $219 for a total of 12 daytime and 15 nighttime hours. What is the rate she is being paid for daytime hours and what is the rate for nighttime hours?   Daytime: $7; nighttime: $9

18. *Consumerism*   For using a computerized financial news network for 25 min during prime time and 35 min during non-prime time, a customer was charged $10.75. A second customer was charged $13.35 for using the network for 30 min of prime time and 45 min of non-prime time. Find the cost per minute for using the financial news network during prime time. $.22

19. *Sports*   A basketball team scored 87 points in two-point baskets and three-point baskets. If the two-point baskets had been three-point baskets and the three-point baskets had been two-point baskets, the team would have scored 93 points. Find how many two-point baskets and how many three-point baskets the team scored.   21 two-point baskets; 15 three-point baskets

20. *Consumerism*   The employees of a hardware store ordered lunch from a local delicatessen. The lunch consisted of 4 turkey sandwiches and 7 orders of french fries, for a total cost of $23.30. The next day, the employees ordered 5 turkey sandwiches and 5 orders of french fries totaling $25.75. What does the delicatessen charge for a turkey sandwich? What is the charge for an order of french fries?   Turkey sandwich: $4.25; order of french fries: $.90

21. *Coin Problems*   Two coin banks contain only nickels and quarters. The total value of the coins in the first bank is $2.90. In the second bank, there are two more quarters than in the first bank and twice as many nickels. The total value of the coins in the second bank is $3.80. Find the number of nickels and the number of quarters in the first bank.   8 nickels; 10 quarters

22. *Coin Problems*   Two coin banks contain only nickels and dimes. The total value of the coins in the first bank is $3. In the second bank, there are 4 more nickels than in the first bank and one-half as many dimes. The total value of the coins in the second bank is $2. Find the number of nickels and the number of dimes in the first bank.   12 nickels; 24 dimes

23. *Coin Problems*   The total value of the dimes and quarters in a coin bank is $3.30. If the quarters were dimes and the dimes were quarters, the total value of the coins would be $3. Find the number of dimes and the number of quarters in the bank.   8 dimes; 10 quarters

24. *Coin Problems*   The total value of the nickels and dimes in a coin bank is $3. If the nickels were dimes and the dimes were nickels, the total value of the coins would be $3.75. Find the number of nickels and the number of dimes in the bank.   30 nickels; 15 dimes

APPLYING CONCEPTS 6.4

25. *Geometry*   Two angles are supplementary. The larger angle is 15° more than twice the measure of the smaller angle. Find the measure of the two angles. (Supplementary angles are two angles whose sum is 180°.)   55°, 125°

26. *Geometry*   Two angles are complementary. The larger angle is four times the measure of the smaller angle. Find the measure of the two angles. (Complementary angles are two angles whose sum is 90°.)   18°, 72°

27. *Investments*   An investment club placed a portion of its funds in a 9% annual simple interest account and the remainder in an 8% annual simple interest account. The amount of interest earned for one year was $860. If the amounts placed in each account had been reversed, the interest earned would have been $840. How much was invested in each account? $6000 at 9%; $4000 at 8%

[C] 28. *Investments*   An investor has $5000 to invest in two accounts. The first account earns 8% annual simple interest, and the second account earns 10% annual simple interest. How much money should be invested in each account so that the annual interest earned is $600?   Impossible

[C] 29. *Coin Problems*   The value of the nickels and dimes in a coin bank is $.25. If the number of nickels and the number of dimes were doubled, the value of the coins would be $.50. How many nickels and how many dimes are in the bank?   0 dimes, 5 nickels; 1 dime, 3 nickels; or 2 dimes, 1 nickel

[C] 30. *Coin Problems*   A coin bank contains nickels and dimes, but there are no more than 27 coins. The value of the coins is $2.10. How many different combinations of nickels and/or dimes could be in the bank?   7

31.   The coin and stamp problems in the chapter on "Solving Equations and Inequalities: Applications" can be solved using a system of equations. For example, look at the first problem in the section on coin and stamp problems in the chapter. Let q represent the number of quarters in the bank, and let d represent the number of dimes. There is a total of 9 coins, so $q + d = 9$. The total value of the money in the bank is $1.20, so we can write the equation $25q + 10d = 120$. The solution of the system of equations

$$q + d = 9$$
$$25q + 10d = 120$$

is (2, 7), so there are 2 quarters and 7 dimes in the bank. Explain how to use a system of equations to solve the investment problems in the chapter on "Solving Equations and Inequalities: Applications." You might use the first problem in the section on investment problems in that chapter as a basis for your explanation.

Focus on Problem Solving

Using a Table and Searching for a Pattern

Consider the numbers 10, 12, and 28 and the sum of the proper factors (the natural-number factors less than the number) of those numbers.

10: $1 + 2 + 5 = 8$ 12: $1 + 2 + 3 + 4 + 6 = 16$ 28: $1 + 2 + 4 + 7 + 14 = 28$

10 is called a *deficient number* because the sum of its proper factors is less than the number ($8 < 10$). 12 is called an *abundant number* because the sum of its proper factors is greater than the number ($16 > 12$), and 28 is called a *perfect number* because the sum of its proper divisors equals the number ($28 = 28$).

Our goal for this "Focus on Problem Solving" is to try to find a method that will determine whether a number is deficient, abundant, or perfect without having to first find all the factors and then add them up. We will use a table and search for a pattern.

Before we begin, recall that a prime number is a number greater than 1 whose only factors are itself and 1 and that each natural number greater than 1 has a unique prime factorization. For instance, the prime factorization of 36 is given by $36 = 2^2 \cdot 3^2$. Note that the proper factors of 36 (1, 2, 3, 4, 6, 9, 12, 18) can be represented in terms of the same prime numbers.

$1 = 2^0, \quad 2 = 2^1, \quad 3 = 3^1, \quad 4 = 2^2, \quad 6 = 2 \cdot 3, \quad 9 = 3^2, \quad 12 = 2^2 \cdot 3, \quad 18 = 2 \cdot 3^2$

Now let us consider a trial problem of determining whether 432 is deficient, abundant, or perfect.

LOOK CLOSELY

This table contains the factor $432 = 2^4 \cdot 3^3$, which is not a proper factor.

We write the prime factorization of 432 as $2^4 \cdot 3^3$ and place the factors of 432 in a table as shown at the right. This table contains *all* the factors of 432 represented in terms of the prime number factors. The sum of each column is shown at the bottom.

	1	1·3	1·3²	1·3³
	2	2·3	2·3²	2·3³
	2²	2²·3	2²·3²	2²·3³
	2³	2³·3	2³·3²	2³·3³
	2⁴	2⁴·3	2⁴·3²	2⁴·3³
Sum	31	31·3	31·3²	31·3³

Here is the calculation of the sum for the column headed by $1 \cdot 3$.

$$1 \cdot 3 + 2 \cdot 3 + 2^2 \cdot 3 + 2^3 \cdot 3 + 2^4 \cdot 3 = (1 + 2 + 2^2 + 2^3 + 2^4)3 = 31(3)$$

For the column headed by $1 \cdot 3^2$ there is a similar situation.

$$1 \cdot 3^2 + 2 \cdot 3^2 + 2^2 \cdot 3^2 + 2^3 \cdot 3^2 + 2^4 \cdot 3^2 = (1 + 2 + 2^2 + 2^3 + 2^4)3^2 = 31(3^2)$$

The sum of *all* the factors (including 432) is the sum of the last row.

$$\underset{\text{all factors}}{\text{Sum of}} = 31 + 31 \cdot 3 + 31 \cdot 3^2 + 31 \cdot 3^3 = 31(1 + 3 + 3^2 + 3^3) = 31(40) = 1240$$

To find the sum of the *proper* factors, we must subtract 432 from 1240; we get 808 (see "Look Closely" on the previous page). Thus 432 is abundant.

We now look for some pattern for the sum of all the factors. Note that

$$\underset{\text{column}}{\text{Sum of left}} \quad 1 + 2 + 2^2 + 2^3 + 2^4 = \quad \rule{2cm}{0.4pt} \quad = 1 + 3 + 3^2 + 3^3 \quad \underset{\text{top row}}{\text{Sum of}}$$

$$31(40) = 1240$$

This suggests that the sum of the proper factors can be found by finding the sum of all the prime power factors for each prime, multiplying those numbers, and then subtracting the original number. Although we have not proved this for all cases, it is a true statement.

For instance, to find the sum of the proper factors of 3240, first find the prime factorization.

$$3240 = 2^3 \cdot 3^4 \cdot 5$$

Now find the following sums:

$$1 + 2 + 2^2 + 2^3 = 15 \qquad 1 + 3 + 3^2 + 3^3 + 3^4 = 121 \qquad 1 + 5 = 6$$

The sum of the proper factors $= (15)(121)6 - 3240 = 7650$. 3240 is abundant.

Determine whether the number is deficient, abundant, or perfect.

1. 200   **2.** 3125   **3.** 8128   **4.** 10,000

5. Is a prime number deficient, abundant, or perfect?

Projects and Group Activities

Find a Pattern

The "Focus on Problem Solving" involved finding the sum of $1 + 3 + 3^2$ and $1 + 2 + 2^2 + 2^3$. For sums that contain a larger number of terms, it may be difficult or time-consuming to try to evaluate the sum. Perhaps there is a pattern for these sums that can be used to calculate them without having to evaluate each exponential expression and then add the results.

Look at the following from the calculation of the sum of the factors of 3240.

$$1 + 2 + 2^2 + 2^3 = 1 + 2 + 4 + 8 = 15$$

$$\frac{2^{3+1} - 1}{2 - 1} = \frac{2^4 - 1}{1} = 16 - 1 = 15$$

$$1 + 3 + 3^2 + 3^3 + 3^4 = 1 + 3 + 9 + 27 + 81 = 121$$

$$\frac{3^{4+1} - 1}{3 - 1} = \frac{3^5 - 1}{2} = \frac{243 - 1}{2} = \frac{242}{2} = 121$$

Consider another sum of this type.

$$1 + 7 + 7^2 + 7^3 + 7^4 + 7^5 = 1 + 7 + 49 + 343 + 2401 + 16{,}807 = 19{,}608$$

$$\frac{7^{5+1} - 1}{7 - 1} = \frac{7^6 - 1}{6} = \frac{117{,}649 - 1}{6} = \frac{117{,}648}{6} = 19{,}608$$

On the basis of the examples shown above, make a conjecture as to the value of $1 + n + n^2 + n^3 + n^4 + \cdots + n^k$, where n and k are natural numbers greater than 1.

Solving a System of Equations with a Scientific Calculator

By using the addition method, it is possible to solve the system of equations

$$ax + by = c$$
$$dx + ey = f$$

The solution is

$$x = \frac{ce - bf}{ae - bd} \quad \text{and} \quad y = \frac{af - cd}{ae - bd} \quad \text{where } ae - bd \neq 0$$

Using this solution, a system of two equations in two variables can be solved with a calculator. It is helpful to observe that the denominators of both expressions are identical. The calculation for the denominator is done first and then stored in the calculator's memory. If the value of the denominator is zero, the system of equations is dependent or inconsistent, and this calculator method cannot be used.

Solve: $2x - 5y = 9$
　　　 $4x + 3y = 2$

Make a list of the values of a, b, c, d, e, and f.

$$a = 2 \qquad b = -5 \qquad c = 9$$
$$d = 4 \qquad e = 3 \qquad f = 2$$

Calculate the denominator $D = ae - bd$.

$2\ \boxed{\times}\ 3\ \boxed{-}\ 5\ \boxed{+/-}\ \boxed{\times}\ 4\ \boxed{=}\ \boxed{\text{M+}}^{[1]}$

Find x. Replace the variables in $x = \dfrac{ce - bf}{ae - bd}$ by their values.

$\boxed{(}\ 9\ \boxed{\times}\ 3\ \boxed{-}\ 5\ \boxed{+/-}\ \boxed{\times}\ 2\ \boxed{)}\ \boxed{\div}\ \boxed{\text{MR}}\ \boxed{=}$

The result should be approximately 1.423077.

Find y. Replace the variables in $y = \dfrac{af - cd}{ae - bd}$ by their values.

$\boxed{(}\ 2\ \boxed{\times}\ 2\ \boxed{-}\ 9\ \boxed{\times}\ 4\ \boxed{)}\ \boxed{\div}\ \boxed{\text{MR}}\ \boxed{=}$

The result should be approximately -1.230769.

The approximate solution is the ordered pair $(1.423077, -1.230769)$. The result is an approximation because the calculator display is an approximation to the exact result.

---

[1]Some calculators use STO to store a result and use RCL to recall the result.

Solve by using a scientific calculator.

1. $3.29x + 4.17y = -2.34$
$0.34x - 0.17y = 0.1$

2. $27x + 17y = 50$
$4.5x - 9.2y = 18.3$

3. $y = \dfrac{2}{3}x - 4$

$2x + y = 5$

4. $y = \dfrac{7}{4}x + 2$

$y = \dfrac{2}{3}x - 3$

5. Use the addition method to show that the solution of the system of equations $\begin{aligned} ax + by &= c \\ dx + ey &= f \end{aligned}$ is given by $x = \dfrac{ce - bf}{ae - bd}$ and $y = \dfrac{af - cd}{ae - bd}$, where $ae - bd \neq 0$.

Solving a System of Equations with a Graphing Calculator

A graphing calculator can also be used to approximate the solution of a system of equations in two variables. Graph each equation of the system of equations, and then approximate the coordinates of the point of intersection. The process by which you approximate the solution depends on the model of calculator you have. In all cases, however, you must first solve each equation in the system of equations for y.

➡ Solve: $2x - 5y = 9$
$\qquad\quad 4x + 3y = 2$

Solve each equation for y.

$$2x - 5y = 9 \qquad\qquad 4x + 3y = 2$$
$$-5y = -2x + 9 \qquad\quad 3y = -4x + 2$$
$$y = \dfrac{2}{5}x - \dfrac{9}{5} \qquad\quad y = -\dfrac{4}{3}x + \dfrac{2}{3}$$

TI-83 Press $\boxed{\text{Y=}}$. Enter one equation as Y1 and the other equation as Y2. Press $\boxed{\text{GRAPH}}$. The intersection point must be shown in the viewing window. If it is not shown, adjust the viewing window. Press $\boxed{\text{2nd}}$ CALC 5 $\boxed{\text{ENTER}}$ $\boxed{\text{ENTER}}$ $\boxed{\text{ENTER}}$.

The point of intersection will show on the bottom of the screen as $X = 1.4230769$ $Y = -1.230769$.

Sharp EL-9600 Press $\boxed{\text{Y=}}$. Enter one equation as Y1 and the other equation as Y2. Press $\boxed{\text{GRAPH}}$. The point of intersection must be shown on the display. If it is not shown, adjust the viewing window. Press $\boxed{\text{2ndF}}$ CALC 2.

The point of intersection will show on the bottom of the screen as $X = 1.4230769$ $Y = -1.230769$.

Casio CFX 9850 Press $\boxed{\text{MENU}}$ 5. Enter one equation as Y1 and the other equation as Y2. Press $\boxed{\text{F6}}$. The intersection point must be shown in the viewing window. If it is not shown, adjust the viewing window. Press $\boxed{\text{SHIFT}}$ G-SOLV $\boxed{\text{F5}}$.

The point of intersection will show on the bottom of the screen as X = 1.4230769   Y = −1.230769.

Each of these calculators has a built-in method of solving a system of equations. For calculators without those methods, use the ZOOM and TRACE features of the calculator. Graph the two equations and then use the arrow keys to place the cursor near the intersection point. Then ZOOM in on the point of intersection, and use TRACE to determine the approximate coordinates. Each time you ZOOM in on the point of intersection, the solution of the system of equations becomes more accurate (up to the limits of the calculator).

Solve by using a graphing calculator.

1. $4x − 5y = 8$
   $5x + 7y = 7$

2. $3x + 2y = 11$
   $7x − 6y = 13$

3. $x = 3y + 2$
   $y = 4x − 2$

4. $x = 2y − 5$
   $x = 3y + 2$

Chapter Summary

Key Words

Equations considered together are called a *system of equations*. (Objective 6.1.1)

An example of a system of equations is

$$4x + y = 6$$
$$3x + 2y = 7$$

A *solution of a system of equations in two variables* is an ordered pair that is a solution of each equation of the system. (Objective 6.1.1)

The solution of the system of equations shown above is the ordered pair (1, 2) because it is a solution of each equation in the system.

An *independent system of equations* has one solution. The graphs of the equations in an independent system of linear equations intersect at one point.   (Objective 6.1.1)

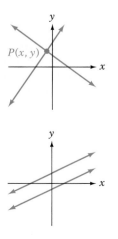

An *inconsistent system of equations* has no solution. The graphs of the equations in an inconsistent system of linear equations are parallel lines. If, when you are solving a system of equations algebraically, the variable is eliminated and the result is a false equation, such as $−3 = 8$, the system is inconsistent. (Objective 6.1.1/6.2.1/6.3.1)

A *dependent system of equations* has an infinite number of solutions. The graphs of the equations in a dependent system of linear equations represent the same line. If, when you are solving a system of equations algebraically, the variable is eliminated and the result is a true equation, such as $1 = 1$, the system is dependent.   (Objective 6.1.1/6.2.1/6.3.1)

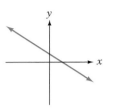

Essential Rules and Procedures

To solve a system of linear equations in two variables by graphing, graph each equation on the same coordinate system. If the lines graphed intersect at one point, the point of intersection is the ordered pair that is a solution of the system. If the lines graphed are parallel, the system is inconsistent. If the lines represent the same line, the system is dependent. (Objective 6.1.1)

Solve by graphing: $x + 2y = 4$
$$2x + y = -1$$

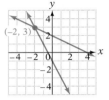

The solution is $(-2, 3)$.

To solve a system of linear equations by the substitution method, one variable must be written in terms of the other variable.   (Objective 6.2.1)

Solve by substitution: $2x - y = 5$ (1)
$$3x + y = 5 \quad (2)$$

$3x + y = 5$ ▶ Solve equation (2)
$\quad y = -3x + 5$ for y.

$\qquad\qquad 2x - y = 5$ ▶ Substitute for y in
$2x - (-3x + 5) = 5$ equation (1).
$\quad 2x + 3x - 5 = 5$
$\qquad\qquad\quad 5x = 10$
$\qquad\qquad\quad\; x = 2$

$y = -3x + 5$ ▶ Substitute the value
$y = -3(2) + 5$ of x to find y.
$y = -1$

The solution is $(2, -1)$.

To solve a system of linear equations by the addition method, use the Multiplication Property of Equations to rewrite one or both of the equations so that the coefficients of one variable are opposites. Then add the two equations and solve for the variables.   (Objective 6.3.1)

Solve by the addition method:
$3x + y = 4$ (1)
$\;x + y = 6$ (2)

$3x + y = 4$
$-x - y = -6$ ▶ Multiply both sides of
              equation (2) by -1.

$\quad\; 2x = -2$ ▶ Add the two equations.
$\qquad x = -1$ ▶ Solve for x.

$\;x + y = 6$ ▶ Substitute the value of x
$-1 + y = 6$ to find y.
$\qquad y = 7$

The solution is $(-1, 7)$.

Chapter Review Exercises

1. Solve by substitution: $4x + 7y = 3$
   (−1, 1) $x = y − 2$

2. Solve by graphing: $3x + y = 3$
   (2, −3) $x = 2$

3. Solve by the addition method: $3x + 8y = −1$
   (−3, 1) $x − 2y = −5$

4. Solve by substitution: $8x − y = 2$
   (1, 6) $y = 5x + 1$

5. Solve by graphing: $x + y = 2$
   (1, 1) $x − y = 0$

6. Solve by the addition method: $4x − y = 9$
   (1, −5) $2x + 3y = −13$

7. Solve by substitution: $−2x + y = −4$
   (3, 2) $x = y + 1$

8. Solve by the addition method:
   $8x − y = 25$
   $32x − 4y = 100$ Dependent

9. Solve by the addition method: $5x − 15y = 30$
   (3, −1) $2x + 6y = 0$

10. Solve by graphing: $3x − y = 6$
    (1, −3) $y = −3$

11. Solve by the addition method: $7x − 2y = 0$
    (−2, −7) $2x + y = −11$

12. Solve by substitution: $x − 5y = 4$
    (4, 0) $y = x − 4$

13. Is $(−1, −3)$ a solution of the system
    $5x + 4y = −17$
    $2x − y = 1?$ Yes

14. Solve by the addition method:
    $6x + 4y = −3$ $\left(-\frac{5}{6}, \frac{1}{2}\right)$
    $12x − 10y = −15$

15. Solve by the addition method: $5x + 2y = −9$
    (−1, −2) $12x − 7y = 2$

16. Solve by graphing: $x − 3y = 12$
    (3, −3) $y = x − 6$

17. Solve by the addition method:
    $5x + 7y = 21$
    $20x + 28y = 63$ Inconsistent

18. Solve by substitution: $9x + 12y = −1$
    $\left(-\frac{1}{3}, \frac{1}{6}\right)$ $x − 4y = −1$

19. Solve by graphing: $4x − 2y = 8$
    Dependent $y = 2x − 4$

20. Solve by the addition method:
    $3x + y = −2$
    $−9x − 3y = 6$ Dependent

21. Solve by the addition method: $11x − 2y = 4$
    (−2, −13) $25x − 4y = 2$

22. Solve by substitution: $4x + 3y = 12$
    Dependent
                        $y = −\frac{4}{3}x + 4$

23. Solve by graphing: $y = −\frac{1}{4}x + 3$
    (4, 2) $2x − y = 6$

24. Solve by the addition method: $2x − y = 5$
    Inconsistent $10x − 5y = 20$

25. Solve by substitution: $6x + 5y = −2$
    $\left(\frac{1}{2}, −1\right)$ $y = 2x − 2$

26. Is $(−2, 0)$ a solution of the system
    $−x + 9y = 2$
    $6x − 4y = 12?$ No

27. Solve by the addition method: $6x − 18y = 7$
    $\left(\frac{2}{3}, −\frac{1}{6}\right)$ $9x + 24y = 2$

28. Solve by substitution: $12x − 9y = 18$
    Inconsistent $y = \frac{4}{3}x − 3$

29. Solve by substitution: $9x - y = -3$
$\left(\frac{1}{3}, 6\right)$ $18x - y = 0$

30. Solve by graphing: $x + 2y = 3$
    Inconsistent $y = -\frac{1}{2}x + 1$

31. Solve by the addition method: $7x - 9y = 9$
$(0, -1)$ $3x - y = 1$

32. Solve by substitution: $7x + 3y = -16$
$(-1, -3)$ $x - 2y = 5$

33. Solve by substitution: $5x - 3y = 6$
$(0, -2)$ $x - y = 2$

34. Solve by the addition method: $6x + y = 12$
$(2, 0)$ $9x + 2y = 18$

35. Solve by the addition method: $5x + 12y = 4$
$(-4, 2)$ $x + 6y = 8$

36. Solve by substitution: $6x - y = 0$
$(1, 6)$ $7x - y = 1$

37. Flying with the wind, a plane can travel 800 mi in 4 h. Against the wind, the plane requires 5 h to fly the same distance. Find the rate of the plane in calm air and the rate of the wind.   Plane: 180 mph; wind: 20 mph

38. Admission to a movie theater is $7 for adults and $5 for children. If the receipts from 200 tickets were $1120, how many adults' tickets and how many children's tickets were sold?   Adults: 60; children: 140

39. A canoeist traveling with the current traveled the 30 mi between two riverside campsites in 3 h. The return trip took 5 h. Find the rate of the canoeist in still water and the rate of the current.   Canoeist: 8 mph; current: 2 mph

40. A small wood carving company mailed 190 advertisements, some requiring 33¢ in postage and others requiring 55¢ in postage. If the total cost for the mailings was $75.90, how many mailings that required 33¢ were sent?   130 mailings

41. A boat traveling with the current went 48 km in 3 h. Against the current, the boat traveled 24 km in 2 h. Find the rate of the boat in calm water and the rate of the current.   Boat: 14 km/h; current: 2 km/h

42. A music shop sells some compact discs for $15 and some for $10. A customer spent $120 on 10 compact discs. How many at each price did the customer purchase?   4 at $15; 6 at $10

43. With a tailwind, a flight crew flew 420 km in 3 h. Flying against the tailwind, the crew flew 440 km in 4 h. Find the rate of the plane in calm air and the rate of the wind.   Plane: 125 km/h; wind: 15 km/h

44. A paddle boat can travel 4 mi downstream in 1 h. Paddling upstream, against the current, the paddle boat traveled 2 mi in 1 h. Find the rate of the boat in calm water and the rate of the current.   Boat: 3 mph; current: 1 mph

45. A silo contains a mixture of lentils and corn. If 50 bushels of lentils were added to this mixture, there would be twice as many bushels of lentils as corn. If 150 bushels of corn were added to the original mixture, there would be the same amount of corn as lentils. How many bushels of each are in the silo?   Lentils: 350 bushels; corn: 200 bushels

46. Flying with the wind, a small plane flew 360 mi in 3 h. Against the wind, the plane took 4 h to fly the same distance. Find the rate of the plane in calm air and the rate of the wind.   Plane: 105 mph; wind: 15 mph

47. A coin purse contains 80¢ in nickels and dimes. If there are 12 coins in all, how many dimes are in the coin purse?   4 dimes

48. A pilot flying with the wind flew 2100 mi from one city to another in 6 h. The return trip against the wind took 7 h. Find the rate of the plane in calm air and the rate of the wind.   Plane: 325 mph; wind: 25 mph

49. An investor buys 1500 shares of stock, some costing $6 per share and the rest costing $25 per share. If the total cost of the stock is $12,800, how many shares of each did the investor buy? $6 shares: 1300; $25 shares: 200

50. Rowing with the wind, a sculling team went 24 mi in 2 h. Rowing against the current, the team went 18 mi in 3 h. Find the rate of the sculling team in calm water and the rate of the current.   Sculling team: 9 mph; current: 3 mph

Chapter Test

1. Solve by substitution: $4x - y = 11$
   (3, 1) $y = 2x - 5$

2. Solve by the addition method: $4x + 3y = 11$
   (2, 1) $5x - 3y = 7$

3. Is $(-2, 3)$ a solution of the system
   $2x + 5y = 11$
   $x + 3y = 7$?   Yes

4. Solve by substitution: $x = 2y + 3$
   (1, −1) $3x - 2y = 5$

5. Solve by the addition method: $2x - 5y = 6$
   $\left(\frac{1}{2}, -1\right)$ $4x + 3y = -1$

6. Solve by graphing: $3x + 2y = 6$
   (−2, 6) $5x + 2y = 2$

7. Solve by substitution: $4x + 2y = 3$
   Inconsistent $y = -2x + 1$

8. Solve by substitution: $3x + 5y = 1$
   (2, −1) $2x - y = 5$

9. Solve by the addition method: $7x + 3y = 11$
   (2, −1) $2x - 5y = 9$

10. Solve by substitution: $3x - 5y = 13$
    $\left(\frac{22}{7}, -\frac{5}{7}\right)$ $x + 3y = 1$

11. Solve by the addition method: $5x + 6y = -7$
    (1, −2) $3x + 4y = -5$

12. Is (2, 1) a solution of the system $3x - 2y = 8$
    No $4x + 5y = 3$?

13. Solve by substitution: $3x - y = 5$
    (2, 1) $y = 2x - 3$

14. Solve by the addition method: $3x + 2y = 2$
    (2, −2) $5x - 2y = 14$

15. Solve by graphing: $3x + 2y = 6$
    (2, 0) $3x - 2y = 6$

16. Solve by substitution: $x = 3y + 1$
    (4, 1) $2x + 5y = 13$

17. Solve by the addition method: $5x + 4y = 7$
$(3, -2)$ $3x - 2y = 13$

18. Solve by graphing: $3x + 6y = 2$
Dependent $y = -\frac{1}{2}x + \frac{1}{3}$

19. Solve by substitution: $4x - 3y = 1$
$(1, 1)$ $2x + y = 3$

20. Solve by the addition method: $5x - 3y = 29$
$(4, -3)$ $4x + 7y = -5$

21. Solve by substitution: $3x - 5y = -23$
$(-6, 1)$ $x + 2y = -4$

22. Solve by the addition method: $9x - 2y = 17$
$(1, -4)$ $5x + 3y = -7$

23. With the wind, a plane flies 240 mi in 2 h. Against the wind, the plane requires 3 h to fly the same distance. Find the rate of the plane in calm air and the rate of the wind.   Plane: 100 mph; wind: 20 mph

24. With the current, a motorboat can travel 48 mi in 3 h. Against the current, the boat requires 4 h to travel the same distance. Find the rate of the boat in calm water and the rate of the current.   Boat: 14 mph; current: 2 mph

25. Two coin banks contain only dimes and nickels. In the first bank, the total value of the coins is $5.50. In the second bank, there are one-half as many dimes as in the first bank and 10 fewer nickels. The total value of the coins in the second bank is $3. Find the number of dimes and the number of nickels in the first bank.   40 dimes; 30 nickels

Cumulative Review Exercises

1. Given $A = \{-8, -4, 0\}$, which elements of set A are less than or equal to -4? $-8, -4$

2. Use the roster method to write the set of positive integers less than or equal to 10.
$\{1, 2, 3, 4, 5, 6, 7, 8, 9, 10\}$

3. Simplify: $12 - 2(7 - 5)^2 \div 4$ 10

4. Simplify: $2[5a - 3(2 - 5a) - 8]$ $40a - 28$

5. Evaluate $\dfrac{a^2 - b^2}{2a}$ when $a = 4$ and $b = -2$. $\dfrac{3}{2}$

6. Solve: $-\dfrac{3}{4}x = \dfrac{9}{8}$ $-\dfrac{3}{2}$

7. Solve: $4 - 3(2 - 3x) = 7x - 9$ $-\dfrac{7}{2}$

8. Solve: $3[2 - 4(x + 1)] = 6x - 2$ $-\dfrac{2}{9}$

9. Solve: $-7x - 5 > 4x + 50$ $x < -5$

10. Solve: $5 + 2(x + 1) \le 13$ $x \le 3$

11. What percent of 50 is 12?   24%

12. Find the x- and y-intercepts of $3x - 6y = 12$.
$(4, 0), (0, -2)$

13. Find the slope of the line that contains the points whose coordinates are $(2, -3)$ and $(-3, 4)$. $-\dfrac{7}{5}$

14. Find the equation of the line that contains the point whose coordinates are $(-2, 3)$ and has slope $-\dfrac{3}{2}$. $y = -\dfrac{3}{2}x$

15. Graph: $3x - 2y = 6$

16. Graph: $y = -\dfrac{1}{3}x + 3$

17. Graph the solution set of $y > -3x + 4$.

18. Graph: $f(x) = \dfrac{3}{4}x + 2$

19. Find the domain and range of the relation $\{(-5, 5), (0, 5), (1, 5), (5, 5)\}$. Is the relation a function?   D: $\{-5, 0, 1, 5\}$; R: $\{5\}$; yes

20. Evaluate $f(x) = -2x - 5$ at $x = -4$.   3

21. Is $(2, 0)$ a solution of the system $5x - 3y = 10$
$4x + 7y = 8$?
Yes

22. Solve by substitution: $2x - 3y = -7$
$x + 4y = 2$ $(-2, 1)$

23. Solve by graphing: $2x + 3y = 6$
$3x + y = 2$ $(0, 2)$

24. Solve by the addition method: $5x - 2y = 8$
$4x + 3y = 11$
$(2, 1)$

25. Find the range of the function given by the equation $f(x) = 5x - 2$ if the domain is $\{-4, -2, 0, 2, 4\}$. $\{-22, -12, -2, 8, 18\}$

26. A business manager has determined that the cost per unit for a camera is $90 and that the fixed costs per month are $3500. Find the number of cameras produced during a month in which the total cost was $21,500. Use the equation $T = U \cdot N + F$, where T is the total cost, U is the cost per unit, N is the number of units produced, and F is the fixed cost.   200 cameras

27. A total of $8750 is invested in two simple interest accounts. On one account, the annual simple interest rate is 9.6%. On the second account, the annual simple interest rate is 7.2%. How much should be invested in each account so that both accounts earn the same amount of interest?
$3750 at 9.6%; $5000 at 7.2%

28. Flying with the wind, a plane can fly 570 mi in 3 h. Flying against the wind, it takes the same amount of time to fly 390 mi. Find the rate of the plane in calm air and the rate of the wind.   Plane: 160 mph; wind: 30 mph

29. With the current, a motorboat can travel 24 mi in 2 h. Against the current, the boat requires 3 h to travel the same distance. Find the rate of the boat in calm water.   10 mph

30. Two coin banks contain only dimes and nickels. In the first bank, the total value of the coins is $5.25. In the second bank, there are one-half as many dimes as in the first bank and 15 fewer nickels. The total value of the coins in the second bank is $2.50. Find the number of dimes in the first bank. 40 dimes

7

Polynomials

Astronomers use mathematics and physics to explore the nature of our universe. Theories pertaining to the universe are represented as mathematical equations. Astronomers analyze these theories using computers and data collected from observations of objects in space. Among the mathematical concepts that an astronomer must know is scientific notation, which is presented in Section 4 of this chapter.

Early Egyptian Arithmetic Operations

The early Egyptian arithmetic processes are recorded on the Rhind Papyrus, but the underlying principles are not included. Scholars of today can only guess how these early developments were discovered.

Egyptian hieroglyphics used a base-10 system of numbers in which a vertical line represented 1; a heel bone, ∩, represented 10; and a scroll, ☌, represented 100.

The symbols shown below represent the number 237. There are 7 vertical lines, 3 heel bones, and 2 scrolls. Thus the symbols represent $7 + 30 + 200$, or 237.

$$\underset{|||}{||||}\ \cap\cap\cap\ ☌☌$$

Addition in hieroglyphic notation does not require memorization of addition facts. Addition is done just by counting symbols.

The top example shown at the left shows that addition is a simple grouping operation. Write down the total of each kind of symbol. Then group 10 straight lines into one heel bone.

Subtraction in the hieroglyphic system is similar to making change. For example, what change do you get from a $1.00 bill when buying a $.55 item?

In the bottom example shown at the left, 5 cannot be subtracted from 3, so a 10 is "borrowed," and 10 ones are added.

Note that no zero is provided in this number system. That place value symbol is just not used. As shown at the left, the heel bone is not used when writing 208 because there are no 10's necessary in 208.

HIEROGLYPHIC NOTATION	MODERN NOTATION
$\quad||||\quad\cap\cap\quad ☌☌☌$	324
$+\ ||||\quad\cap\cap\cap\ ☌$	$+138$
$\underset{||||}{\overset{||||}{||||}}\ \cap\cap\cap\cap\ ☌☌☌☌$ $\cap$	
$12 + 50 + 400 = 462$	
$\underset{\cap\cap}{||}\ \cap\cap\cap\cap\ ☌☌☌☌$	
$\quad|||\quad\cap\cap\cap\ ☌☌☌☌$	433
$-\ ||||\quad\cap\cap\quad ☌☌$	-225
$\underset{|}{\overset{||||}{||||}}\ \cap\cap\quad ☌☌☌☌$	$4\overset{2\ 13}{\cancel{3}}\cancel{3}$
$-\ ||||\quad\cap\cap\quad ☌☌$	-225
$\underset{||||}{||||}\qquad\quad ☌☌$	208
$8\ +\quad 200\ =\ 208$	208

S E C T I O N **7.1**

Addition and Subtraction of Polynomials

1 ## Add polynomials

INSTRUCTOR NOTE

An analogy may help students understand these terms. *Polynomial* is similar to the word *car*. Chevrolet and Ford are types of cars. Monomials and binomials are types of polynomials.

As a class exercise, ask students to identify monomials. For instance, ask students to identify which of $\frac{1}{2}$, $\frac{2}{3}y$, $6x$,

$6 + x$, *abxy*, and $\frac{3}{z}$ are

monomials. Then ask them to identify polynomials. Here are some possible choices: $x + 7$, $\frac{x^2}{5} + \frac{x}{2} - 1$, $\frac{5}{x^2} + \frac{2}{x} - 1$, $\frac{x + 1}{x}$, and $\sqrt{2}x^4 - \pi x^2 - 7$.

A **monomial** is a number, a variable, or a product of numbers and variables. For instance,

7	b	$\frac{2}{3}a$	$12xy^2$
A number	A variable	A product of a number and a variable	A product of a number and variables

The expression $3\sqrt{x}$ is not a monomial because $\sqrt{x}$ cannot be written as a product of variables. The expression $\frac{2x}{y^2}$ is not a monomial because it is a *quotient* of variables.

A **polynomial** is a variable expression in which the terms are monomials.

A polynomial of *one* term is a **monomial**. $-7x^2$ is a monomial.

A polynomial of *two* terms is a **binomial**. $4x + 2$ is a binomial.

A polynomial of *three* terms is a **trinomial**. $7x^2 + 5x - 7$ is a trinomial.

The terms of a polynomial in one variable are usually arranged so that the exponents of the variable decrease from left to right. This is called **descending order**.

$$4x^3 - 3x^2 + 6x - 1$$
$$5y^4 - 2y^3 + y^2 - 7y + 8$$

The **degree of a polynomial in one variable** is its largest exponent. The degree of $4x^3 - 3x^2 + 6x - 1$ is 3. The degree of $5y^4 - 2y^3 + y^2 - 7y + 8$ is 4.

Polynomials can be added, using either a vertical or a horizontal format, by combining like terms.

INSTRUCTOR NOTE

Vertical addition is used in Section 3 of this chapter in multiplying polynomials.

Example 1   Add: $(2x^2 + x - 1) + (3x^3 + 4x^2 - 5)$
Use a vertical format.

Solution
$$\begin{array}{r} 2x^2 + x - 1 \\ 3x^3 + 4x^2 \quad\;\; - 5 \\ \hline \end{array}$$
▶ Arrange the terms of each polynomial in descending order with like terms in the same column.

$$3x^3 + 6x^2 + x - 6$$
▶ Combine the terms in each column.

Problem 1   Add: $(2x^2 + 4x - 3) + (5x^2 - 6x)$
Use a vertical format.

Solution   See page S15. $7x^2 - 2x - 3$

Example 2   Add: $(3x^3 - 7x + 2) + (7x^2 + 2x - 7)$
Use a horizontal format.

Solution $(3x^3 - 7x + 2) + (7x^2 + 2x - 7)$
$= 3x^3 + 7x^2 + (-7x + 2x) + (2 - 7)$ ▶ Use the Commutative and Associative Properties of Addition to rearrange and group like terms.

$= 3x^3 + 7x^2 - 5x - 5$ ▶ Combine like terms, and write the polynomial in descending order.

Problem 2   Add: $(-4x^2 - 3xy + 2y^2) + (3x^2 - 4y^2)$
Use a horizontal format.

Solution   See page S15. $-x^2 - 3xy - 2y^2$

2   ## Subtract polynomials

The **opposite** of the polynomial $x^2 - 2x + 3$ is $-(x^2 - 2x + 3)$.

To simplify the opposite of a polynomial, remove the parentheses and change the sign of every term inside the parentheses. $-(x^2 - 2x + 3) = -x^2 + 2x - 3$

Polynomials can be subtracted using either a vertical or a horizontal format. To subtract, add the opposite of the second polynomial to the first.

Example 3   Subtract: $(-3x^2 - 7) - (-8x^2 + 3x - 4)$
Use a vertical format.

Solution   The opposite of $-8x^2 + 3x - 4$ is $8x^2 - 3x + 4$.

$$
\begin{array}{l}
-3x^2 \quad\quad - 7 \\
\underline{8x^2 - 3x + 4} \\
5x^2 - 3x - 3
\end{array}
$$
▶ Write the terms of each polynomial in descending order with like terms in the same column.
▶ Combine the terms in each column.

Problem 3   Subtract: $(8y^2 - 4xy + x^2) - (2y^2 - xy + 5x^2)$
Use a vertical format.

Solution   See page S15. $6y^2 - 3xy - 4x^2$

Example 4   Subtract: $(5x^2 - 3x + 4) - (-3x^3 - 2x + 8)$
Use a horizontal format.

Solution $(5x^2 - 3x + 4) - (-3x^3 - 2x + 8)$
$= (5x^2 - 3x + 4) + (3x^3 + 2x - 8)$ ▶ Rewrite subtraction as addition of the opposite.
$= 3x^3 + 5x^2 + (-3x + 2x) + (4 - 8)$
$= 3x^3 + 5x^2 - x - 4$ ▶ Combine like terms. Write the polynomial in descending order.

Problem 4   Subtract: $(-3a^2 - 4a + 2) - (5a^3 + 2a - 6)$
Use a horizontal format.

Solution   See page S15. $-5a^3 - 3a^2 - 6a + 8$

CONCEPT REVIEW 7.1

Determine whether the statement is always true, sometimes true, or never true.

1. The terms of a polynomial are monomials.   Always true

2. The polynomial $5x^3 + 4x^6 + 3x + 2$ is written in descending order.   Never true

3. The degree of the polynomial $7x^2 - 8x + 1$ is 3.   Never true

4. Like terms have the same coefficient and the same variable part.   Sometimes true

5. The opposite of the polynomial $ax^3 - bx^2 + cx + d$ is $-ax^3 + bx^2 - cx - d$.   Always true

6. Subtraction is addition of the opposite.   Always true

EXERCISES 7.1

1 State whether the polynomial is a monomial, a binomial, or a trinomial.

1. $8x^4 - 6x^2$ Binomial

2. $4a^2b^2 + 9ab + 10$ Trinomial

3. $7x^3y^4$ Monomial

State whether or not the expression is a monomial.

4. $3\sqrt{x}$ No

5. $\dfrac{4}{x}$ No

6. x^2y^2 Yes

State whether or not the expression is a polynomial.

7. $\dfrac{1}{5}x^3 + \dfrac{1}{2}x$ Yes

8. $\dfrac{1}{5x^2} + \dfrac{1}{2x}$ No

9. $x + \sqrt{5}$ Yes

10. ✎ In your own words, explain the terms *monomial, binomial, trinomial,* and *polynomial.* Give an example of each.

Add. Use a vertical format.

11. $(x^2 + 7x) + (-3x^2 - 4x)$ $-2x^2 + 3x$

12. $(3y^2 - 2y) + (5y^2 + 6y)$ $8y^2 + 4y$

13. $(y^2 + 4y) + (-4y - 8)$ $y^2 - 8$

14. $(3x^2 + 9x) + (6x - 24)$ $3x^2 + 15x - 24$

15. $(2x^2 + 6x + 12) + (3x^2 + x + 8)$ $5x^2 + 7x + 20$

16. $(x^2 + x + 5) + (3x^2 - 10x + 4)$ $4x^2 - 9x + 9$

17. $(x^3 - 7x + 4) + (2x^2 + x - 10)$
    $x^3 + 2x^2 - 6x - 6$

18. $(3y^3 + y^2 + 1) + (-4y^3 - 6y - 3)$
    $-y^3 + y^2 - 6y - 2$

19. $(2a^3 - 7a + 1) + (-3a^2 - 4a + 1)$
    $2a^3 - 3a^2 - 11a + 2$

20. $(5r^3 - 6r^2 + 3r) + (r^2 - 2r - 3)$
    $5r^3 - 5r^2 + r - 3$

Add. Use a horizontal format.

21. $(4x^2 + 2x) + (x^2 + 6x)$ $5x^2 + 8x$

22. $(-3y^2 + y) + (4y^2 + 6y)$ $y^2 + 7y$

23. $(4x^2 - 5xy) + (3x^2 + 6xy - 4y^2)$ $7x^2 + xy - 4y^2$

24. $(2x^2 - 4y^2) + (6x^2 - 2xy + 4y^2)$ $8x^2 - 2xy$

25. $(2a^2 - 7a + 10) + (a^2 + 4a + 7)$ $3a^2 - 3a + 17$

26. $(-6x^2 + 7x + 3) + (3x^2 + x + 3)$ $-3x^2 + 8x + 6$

27. $(5x^3 + 7x - 7) + (10x^2 - 8x + 3)$
$5x^3 + 10x^2 - x - 4$

28. $(3y^3 + 4y + 9) + (2y^2 + 4y - 21)$
$3y^3 + 2y^2 + 8y - 12$

29. $(2r^2 - 5r + 7) + (3r^3 - 6r)$
$3r^3 + 2r^2 - 11r + 7$

30. $(3y^3 + 4y + 14) + (-4y^2 + 21)$
$3y^3 - 4y^2 + 4y + 35$

31. $(3x^2 + 7x + 10) + (-2x^3 + 3x + 1)$
$-2x^3 + 3x^2 + 10x + 11$

32. $(7x^3 + 4x - 1) + (2x^2 - 6x + 2)$
$7x^3 + 2x^2 - 2x + 1$

2 Subtract. Use a vertical format.

33. $(x^2 - 6x) - (x^2 - 10x)$ $4x$

34. $(y^2 + 4y) - (y^2 + 10y)$ $-6y$

35. $(2y^2 - 4y) - (-y^2 + 2)$ $3y^2 - 4y - 2$

36. $(-3a^2 - 2a) - (4a^2 - 4)$ $-7a^2 - 2a + 4$

37. $(x^2 - 2x + 1) - (x^2 + 5x + 8)$ $-7x - 7$

38. $(3x^2 + 2x - 2) - (5x^2 - 5x + 6)$ $-2x^2 + 7x - 8$

39. $(4x^3 + 5x + 2) - (-3x^2 + 2x + 1)$
$4x^3 + 3x^2 + 3x + 1$

40. $(5y^2 - y + 2) - (-2y^3 + 3y - 3)$
$2y^3 + 5y^2 - 4y + 5$

41. $(2y^3 + 6y - 2) - (y^3 + y^2 + 4)$
$y^3 - y^2 + 6y - 6$

42. $(-2x^2 - x + 4) - (-x^3 + 3x - 2)$
$x^3 - 2x^2 - 4x + 6$

Subtract. Use a horizontal format.

43. $(y^2 - 10xy) - (2y^2 + 3xy)$ $-y^2 - 13xy$

44. $(x^2 - 3xy) - (-2x^2 + xy)$ $3x^2 - 4xy$

45. $(3x^2 + x - 3) - (x^2 + 4x - 2)$ $2x^2 - 3x - 1$

46. $(5y^2 - 2y + 1) - (-3y^2 - y - 2)$ $8y^2 - y + 3$

47. $(-2x^3 + x - 1) - (-x^2 + x - 3)$
$-2x^3 + x^2 + 2$

48. $(2x^2 + 5x - 3) - (3x^3 + 2x - 5)$
$-3x^3 + 2x^2 + 3x + 2$

49. $(4a^3 - 2a + 1) - (a^3 - 2a + 3)$
$3a^3 - 2$

50. $(b^2 - 8b + 7) - (4b^3 - 7b - 8)$
$-4b^3 + b^2 - b + 15$

51. $(4y^3 - y - 1) - (2y^2 - 3y + 3)$
$4y^3 - 2y^2 + 2y - 4$

52. $(3x^2 - 2x - 3) - (2x^3 - 2x^2 + 4)$
$-2x^3 + 5x^2 - 2x - 7$

APPLYING CONCEPTS 7.1

Simplify.

53. $\left(\dfrac{2}{3}a^2 + \dfrac{1}{2}a - \dfrac{3}{4}\right) - \left(\dfrac{5}{3}a^2 + \dfrac{1}{2}a + \dfrac{1}{4}\right)$
$-a^2 - 1$

54. $\left(\dfrac{3}{5}x^2 + \dfrac{1}{6}x - \dfrac{5}{8}\right) + \left(\dfrac{2}{5}x^2 + \dfrac{5}{6}x - \dfrac{3}{8}\right)$
$x^2 + x - 1$

Solve.

[C] **55.** What polynomial must be added to $3x^2 - 4x - 2$ so that the sum is $-x^2 + 2x + 1$? $-4x^2 + 6x + 3$

[C] **56.** What polynomial must be added to $-2x^3 + 4x - 7$ so that the sum is $x^2 - x - 1$? $2x^3 + x^2 - 5x + 6$

[C] **57.** What polynomial must be subtracted from $6x^2 - 4x - 2$ so that the difference is $2x^2 + 2x - 5$? $4x^2 - 6x + 3$

[C] **58.** What polynomial must be subtracted from $2x^3 - x^2 + 4x - 2$ so that the difference is $x^3 + 2x - 8$? $x^3 - x^2 + 2x + 6$

[C] **59.** Is it possible to subtract two polynomials, each of degree 3, and have the difference be a polynomial of degree 2? If so, give an example. If not, explain why not.   Yes; $(3x^3 - 2x^2 + 3x - 4) - (3x^3 + 4x^2 - 6x + 5) = -6x^2 + 9x - 9$

[C] **60.** Is it possible to add two polynomials, each of degree 3, and have the sum be a polynomial of degree 2? If so, give an example. If not, explain why not.   Yes; $(2x^3 + 3x - 4) + (-2x^3 + 5x^2 - 6) = 5x^2 + 3x - 10$

S E C T I O N 7.2
Multiplication of Monomials

1 Multiply monomials

Recall that in the exponential expression x^5, x is the base and 5 is the exponent. The exponent indicates the number of times the base occurs as a factor.

The product of exponential expressions with the *same* base can be simplified by writing each expression in factored form and writing the result with an exponent.

$$x^3 \cdot x^2 = \overbrace{(x \cdot x \cdot x)}^{\text{3 factors}} \cdot \overbrace{(x \cdot x)}^{\text{2 factors}}$$
$$\underbrace{}_{\text{5 factors}}$$
$$= x \cdot x \cdot x \cdot x \cdot x$$
$$= x^5$$

Adding the exponents results in the same product.

$$x^3 \cdot x^2 = x^{3+2} = x^5$$

Rule for Multiplying Exponential Expressions

If m and n are integers, then $x^m \cdot x^n = x^{m+n}$.

For example, in the expression $a^2 \cdot a^6 \cdot a$, the bases are the same. The expression can be simplified by adding the exponents. Recall that $a = a^1$.

$$a^2 \cdot a^6 \cdot a = a^{2+6+1} = a^9$$

Example 1 Multiply: $(2xy)(3x^2y)$

Solution $(2xy)(3x^2y)$
$= (2 \cdot 3)(x \cdot x^2)(y \cdot y)$ ▶ Use the Commutative and Associative Properties of Multiplication to rearrange and group factors.

$= 6x^{1+2}y^{1+1}$ ▶ Multiply variables with the same base by adding the exponents.

$= 6x^3y^2$

Problem 1 Multiply: $(3x^2)(6x^3)$

Solution See page S15. $18x^5$

Example 2 Multiply: $(2x^2y)(-5xy^4)$

Solution $(2x^2y)(-5xy^4)$
$= [2(-5)](x^2 \cdot x)(y \cdot y^4)$ ▶ Use the Properties of Multiplication to rearrange and group factors.

$= -10x^3y^5$ ▶ Multiply variables with the same base by adding the exponents.

Problem 2 Multiply: $(-3xy^2)(-4x^2y^3)$

Solution See page S15. $12x^3y^5$

2 ## Simplify powers of monomials

A power of a monomial can be simplified by rewriting the expression in factored form and then using the Rule for Multiplying Exponential Expressions.

$(x^2)^3 = x^2 \cdot x^2 \cdot x^2$
$= x^{2+2+2}$
$= x^6$

$(x^4y^3)^2 = (x^4y^3)(x^4y^3)$
$= x^4 \cdot y^3 \cdot x^4 \cdot y^3$
$= (x^4 \cdot x^4)(y^3 \cdot y^3)$
$= x^{4+4}y^{3+3}$
$= x^8y^6$

Note that multiplying each exponent inside the parentheses by the exponent outside the parentheses gives the same result.

$(x^2)^3 = x^{2\cdot3} = x^6$

$(x^4y^3)^2 = x^{4\cdot2}y^{3\cdot2} = x^8y^6$

Rule for Simplifying Powers of Exponential Expressions

If m and n are integers, then $(x^m)^n = x^{mn}$.

Rule for Simplifying Powers of Products

If m, n, and p are integers, then $(x^my^n)^p = x^{mp}y^{np}$.

⮕ Simplify: $(x^5)^2$

Multiply the exponents.

$(x^5)^2 = x^{5 \cdot 2} = x^{10}$ ⬅

⮕ Simplify: $(3a^2b)^3$

Multiply each exponent inside the parentheses by the exponent outside the parentheses.

$$(3a^2b)^3 = 3^{1 \cdot 3}a^{2 \cdot 3}b^{1 \cdot 3}$$
$$= 3^3a^6b^3$$
$$= 27a^6b^3$$ ⬅

Example 3   Simplify: $(-2x)(-3xy^2)^3$

Solution $(-2x)(-3xy^2)^3$
$= (-2x)(-3)^3x^3y^6$ ▸ Multiply each exponent in $-3xy^2$ by the exponent outside the parentheses.
$= (-2x)(-27)x^3y^6$ ▸ Simplify $(-3)^3$.
$= [-2(-27)](x \cdot x^3)y^6$ ▸ Use the Properties of Multiplication to rearrange and group factors.
$= 54x^4y^6$ ▸ Multiply variables with the same base by adding the exponents.

Problem 3   Simplify: $(3x)(2x^2y)^3$

Solution   See page S15. $24x^7y^3$

CONCEPT REVIEW 7.2

Determine whether the statement is always true, sometimes true, or never true.

1. In the expression $(6x)^4$, x is the base and 4 is the exponent.   Never true

2. To multiply $x^m \cdot x^n$, multiply the exponents.   Never true

3. The expression "a power of a monomial" means the monomial is the base of an exponential expression.   Always true

4. $x^6 \cdot x \cdot x^8 = x^{14}$ Never true

5. $(4x^3y^5)^2 = 4x^6y^{10}$ Never true

6. $a^2 \cdot b^7 = ab^9$ Never true

EXERCISES 7.2

1. ✎ Explain how to multiply two exponential expressions with the same base. Provide an example.

2. ✎ Explain how to simplify the power of an exponential expression. Provide an example.

Multiply.

3. $(x)(2x)$ $2x^2$

4. $(-3y)(y)$ $-3y^2$

5. $(3x)(4x)$ $12x^2$

6. $(7y^3)(7y^2)$ $49y^5$

7. $(-2a^3)(-3a^4)$ $6a^7$

8. $(5a^6)(-2a^5)$ $-10a^{11}$

9. $(x^2y)(xy^4)$ x^3y^5

10. $(x^2y^4)(xy^7)$ x^3y^{11}

11. $(-2x^4)(5x^5y)$ $-10x^9y$

12. $(-3a^3)(2a^2b^4)$ $-6a^5b^4$

13. $(x^2y^4)(x^5y^4)$ x^7y^8

14. $(a^2b^4)(ab^3)$ a^3b^7

15. $(2xy)(-3x^2y^4)$ $-6x^3y^5$

16. $(-3a^2b)(-2ab^3)$ $6a^3b^4$

17. $(x^2yz)(x^2y^4)$ x^4y^5z

18. $(-ab^2c)(a^2b^5)$ $-a^3b^7c$

19. $(a^2b^3)(ab^2c^4)$ $a^3b^5c^4$

20. $(x^2y^3z)(x^3y^4)$ x^5y^7z

21. $(-a^2b^2)(a^3b^6)$ $-a^5b^8$

22. $(xy^4)(-xy^3)$ $-x^2y^7$

23. $(-6a^3)(a^2b)$ $-6a^5b$

24. $(2a^2b^3)(-4ab^2)$ $-8a^3b^5$

25. $(-5y^4z)(-8y^6z^5)$ $40y^{10}z^6$

26. $(3x^2y)(-4xy^2)$ $-12x^3y^3$

27. $(10ab^2)(-2ab)$ $-20a^2b^3$

28. $(x^2y)(yz)(xyz)$ $x^3y^3z^2$

29. $(xy^2z)(x^2y)(z^2y^2)$ $x^3y^5z^3$

30. $(-2x^2y^3)(3xy)(-5x^3y^4)$ $30x^6y^8$

31. $(4a^2b)(-3a^3b^4)(a^5b^2)$ $-12a^{10}b^7$

32. $(3ab^2)(-2abc)(4ac^2)$ $-24a^3b^3c^3$

2 Simplify.

33. $(2^2)^3$ 64

34. $(3^2)^2$ 81

35. $(-2)^2$ 4

36. $(-3)^3$ -27

37. $(-2^2)^3$ -64

38. $(-2^3)^3$ -512

39. $(x^3)^3$ x^9

40. $(y^4)^2$ y^8

41. $(x^7)^2$ x^{14}

42. $(y^5)^3$ y^{15}

43. $(-x^2)^2$ x^4

44. $(-x^2)^3$ $-x^6$

45. $(2x)^2$ $4x^2$

46. $(3y)^3$ $27y^3$

47. $(-2x^2)^3$ $-8x^6$

48. $(-3y^3)^2$ $9y^6$

49. $(x^2y^3)^2$ x^4y^6

50. $(x^3y^4)^5$ $x^{15}y^{20}$

51. $(3x^2y)^2$ $9x^4y^2$

52. $(-2ab^3)^4$ $16a^4b^{12}$

53. $(a^2)(3a^2)^3$ $27a^8$

54. $(b^2)(2a^3)^4$ $16a^{12}b^2$

55. $(-2x)(2x^3)^2$ $-8x^7$

56. $(2y)(-3y^4)^3$ $-54y^{13}$

57. $(x^2y)(x^2y)^3$ x^8y^4

58. $(a^3b)(ab)^3$ a^6b^4

59. $(ab^2)^2(ab)^2$ a^4b^6

60. $(x^2y)^2(x^3y)^3$ $x^{13}y^5$

61. $(-2x)(-2x^3y)^3$ $16x^{10}y^3$

62. $(-3y)(-4x^2y^3)^3$ $192x^6y^{10}$

63. $(-2x)(-3xy^2)^2$ $-18x^3y^4$

64. $(-3y)(-2x^2y)^3$ $24x^6y^4$

65. $(ab^2)(-2a^2b)^3$ $-8a^7b^5$

66. $(a^2b^2)(-3ab^4)^2$ $9a^4b^{10}$

67. $(-2a^3)(3a^2b)^3$ $-54a^9b^3$

68. $(-3b^2)(2ab^2)^3$ $-24a^3b^8$

69. $(-3ab)^2(-2ab)^3$ $-72a^5b^5$

70. $(-3a^2b)^3(-3ab)^3$ $729a^9b^6$

APPLYING CONCEPTS 7.2

Simplify.

71. $(6x)(2x^2) + (4x^2)(5x)$ $32x^3$

72. $(2a^7)(7a^2) - (6a^3)(5a^6)$ $-16a^9$

73. $(3a^2b^2)(2ab) - (9ab^2)(a^2b)$ $-3a^3b^3$

74. $(3x^2y^2)^2 - (2xy)^4$ $-7x^4y^4$

75. $(5xy^3)(3x^4y^2) - (2x^3y)(x^2y^4)$ $13x^5y^5$

76. $a^2(ab^2)^3 - a^3(ab^3)^2$ 0

77. $4a^2(2ab)^3 - 5b^2(a^5b)$ $27a^5b^3$

78. $9x^3(3x^2y)^2 - x(x^3y)^2$ $80x^7y^2$

79. $-2xy(x^2y)^3 - 3x^5(xy^2)^2$ $\quad -5x^7y^4$

80. $5a^2b(ab^2)^2 + b^3(2a^2b)^2$ $\quad 9a^4b^5$

[C] **81.** $a^n \cdot a^n$ $\quad a^{2n}$

[C] **82.** $(a^n)^2$ $\quad a^{2n}$

[C] **83.** $(a^2)^n$ $\quad a^{2n}$

[C] **84.** $a^2 \cdot a^n$ $\quad a^{n+2}$

For Exercises 85–88, answer true or false. If the answer is false, correct the right side of the equation.

85. $(-a)^5 = -a^5$ $\quad$ True

86. $(-b)^8 = b^8$ $\quad$ True

87. $(x^2)^5 = x^{2+5} = x^7$ $\quad$ False; $x^{2\cdot5} = x^{10}$

88. $x^3 + x^3 = 2x^{3+3} = 2x^6$ $\quad$ False; $x^3 + x^3 = 2x^3$

89. Evaluate $(2^3)^2$ and $2^{(3^2)}$. Are the results the same? If not, which expression has the larger value? No; $2^{(3^2)}$ is larger. $(2^3)^2 = 8^2 = 64$, $2^{(3^2)} = 2^9 = 512$

[C] **90.** What is the Order of Operations for the expression x^{m^n}? The Order of Operations is $x^{(m^n)}$.

[C] **91.** If n is a positive integer and $x^n = y^n$, when is $x = y$? $x = y$ when n is odd.

92. *Geometry* The length of a rectangle is $4ab$. The width is $2ab$. Find the perimeter of the rectangle in terms of ab. $12ab$

$4ab$

$2ab$

93. The distance a rock will fall in t seconds is $16t^2$ ft (neglecting air resistance). Find other examples of quantities that can be expressed in terms of an exponential expression, and explain where the expression is used.

SECTION 7.3
Multiplication of Polynomials

1 Multiply a polynomial by a monomial

To multiply a polynomial by a monomial, use the Distributive Property and the Rule for Multiplying Exponential Expressions.

➡ Simplify: $-2x(x^2 - 4x - 3)$

Use the Distributive Property and the Rule for Multiplying Exponential Expressions.

$$-2x(x^2 - 4x - 3) = -2x(x^2) - (-2x)(4x) - (-2x)(3)$$
$$= -2x^3 + 8x^2 + 6x$$

Example 1 Multiply. $\quad$ A. $(5x + 4)(-2x)$ $\quad$ B. $x^3(2x^2 - 3x + 2)$

Solution A. $(5x + 4)(-2x)$
$= 5x(-2x) + 4(-2x)$ $\quad$ ▶ Use the Distributive Property.
$= -10x^2 - 8x$ $\quad$ ▶ Use the Rule for Multiplying Exponential Expressions.

B. $x^3(2x^2 - 3x + 2)$
$= 2x^5 - 3x^4 + 2x^3$

Problem 1 Multiply. $\quad$ A. $(-2y + 3)(-4y)$ $\quad$ B. $-a^2(3a^2 + 2a - 7)$

Solution See page S15. $\quad$ A. $8y^2 - 12y$ $\quad$ B. $-3a^4 - 2a^3 + 7a^2$

2   Multiply two polynomials

Multiplication of two polynomials requires the repeated application of the Distributive Property.

$$(y - 2)(y^2 + 3y + 1) = (y - 2)(y^2) + (y - 2)(3y) + (y - 2)(1)$$
$$= y^3 - 2y^2 + 3y^2 - 6y + y - 2$$
$$= y^3 + y^2 - 5y - 2$$

INSTRUCTOR NOTE

Before doing an example similar to the one at the right, show students that the procedure for multiplication of polynomials can be related to multiplying whole numbers such as 473×28.

A convenient method of multiplying two polynomials is to use a vertical format similar to that used for multiplication of whole numbers.

$$
\begin{array}{r}
y^2 + 3y + 1 \\
y - 2 \\
\hline
-2y^2 - 6y - 2 \\
y^3 + 3y^2 + \ y \\
\hline
y^3 + \ y^2 - 5y - 2
\end{array}
$$

Multiply each term in the trinomial by -2.

Multiply each term in the trinomial by y.
Like terms must be in the same column.

Add the terms in each column.

Example 2   Multiply: $(2b^3 - b + 1)(2b + 3)$

Solution

$$
\begin{array}{r}
2b^3 - \ b + 1 \\
2b + 3 \\
\hline
6b^3 \qquad - 3b + 3 \\
4b^4 \qquad - 2b^2 + 2b \\
\hline
4b^4 + 6b^3 - 2b^2 - \ b + 3
\end{array}
$$

▸ Multiply $2b^3 - b + 1$ by 3.

▸ Multiply $2b^3 - b + 1$ by $2b$. Arrange the terms in descending order.

▸ Add the terms in each column.

Problem 2   Multiply: $(2y^3 + 2y^2 - 3)(3y - 1)$

Solution   See page S15. $6y^4 + 4y^3 - 2y^2 - 9y + 3$

Example 3   Multiply: $(4a^3 - 5a - 2)(3a - 2)$

Solution

$$
\begin{array}{r}
4a^3 - \ 5a - 2 \\
3a - 2 \\
\hline
-8a^3 \qquad + 10a + 4 \\
12a^4 \qquad - 15a^2 - \ 6a \\
\hline
12a^4 - 8a^3 - 15a^2 + \ 4a + 4
\end{array}
$$

▸ Multiply $4a^3 - 5a - 2$ by -2.

▸ Multiply $4a^3 - 5a - 2$ by $3a$.

▸ Add the terms in each column.

Problem 3   Multiply: $(3x^3 - 2x^2 + x - 3)(2x + 5)$

Solution   See page S15. $6x^4 + 11x^3 - 8x^2 - x - 15$

3   Multiply two binomials

It is often necessary to find the product of two binomials. The product can be found using a method called **FOIL**, which is based on the Distributive Property. The letters of FOIL stand for **F**irst, **O**uter, **I**nner, and **L**ast.

➡ Multiply: $(2x + 3)(x + 5)$

LOOK CLOSELY

FOIL is not really a different way of multiplying. It is based on the Distributive Property.

$(2x + 3)(x + 5)$
$= 2x(x + 5) + 3(x + 5)$
  F   O   I   L
$= 2x^2 + 10x + 3x + 15$
$= 2x^2 + 13x + 15$

Multiply the First terms.	$(2x + 3)(x + 5)$	$2x \cdot x = 2x^2$
Multiply the Outer terms.	$(2x + 3)(x + 5)$	$2x \cdot 5 = 10x$
Multiply the Inner terms.	$(2x + 3)(x + 5)$	$3 \cdot x = 3x$
Multiply the Last terms.	$(2x + 3)(x + 5)$	$3 \cdot 5 = 15$

Add the products. $(2x + 3)(x + 5)$
Combine like terms.

$$\begin{array}{cccc} \textbf{F} & \textbf{O} & \textbf{I} & \textbf{L} \\ \end{array}$$
$$= 2x^2 + 10x + 3x + 15$$
$$= 2x^2 + 13x + 15$$ ⬅

Example 4   Multiply: $(4x - 3)(3x - 2)$

Solution $(4x - 3)(3x - 2)$
$= 4x(3x) + 4x(-2) + (-3)(3x) + (-3)(-2)$ ▶ Use the FOIL method.
$= 12x^2 - 8x - 9x + 6$
$= 12x^2 - 17x + 6$ ▶ Combine like terms.

Problem 4   Multiply: $(4y - 5)(3y - 3)$

Solution   See page S15. $12y^2 - 27y + 15$

Example 5   Multiply: $(3x - 2y)(x + 4y)$

Solution $(3x - 2y)(x + 4y)$
$= 3x(x) + 3x(4y) + (-2y)(x) + (-2y)(4y)$ ▶ Use the FOIL method.
$= 3x^2 + 12xy - 2xy - 8y^2$
$= 3x^2 + 10xy - 8y^2$ ▶ Combine like terms.

Problem 5   Multiply: $(3a + 2b)(3a - 5b)$

Solution   See page S15. $9a^2 - 9ab - 10b^2$

---

4   ## Multiply binomials that have special products

The expression $(a + b)(a - b)$ is the product of the sum and difference of two terms. The first binomial in the expression is a sum; the second is a difference. The two terms are a and b. The first term in each binomial is a. The second term in each binomial is b.

The expression $(a + b)^2$ is the square of a binomial. The first term in the binomial is a. The second term in the binomial is b.

Using FOIL, it is possible to find a pattern for the product of the sum and difference of two terms and for the square of a binomial.

The Sum and Difference of Two Terms

$$(a + b)(a - b) = a^2 - ab + ab - b^2$$
$$= a^2 - b^2$$

Square of first term ─────────────────→

Square of second term ─────────────────→

The Square of a Binomial

$$(a + b)^2 = (a + b)(a + b) = a^2 + ab + ab + b^2$$
$$= a^2 + 2ab + b^2$$

Square of first term ─────────────────→

Twice the product of the two terms ─────────────────→

Square of last term ─────────────────→

$$(a - b)^2 = (a - b)(a - b) = a^2 - ab - ab + b^2$$
$$= a^2 - 2ab + b^2$$

Square of first term ─────────────────→

Twice the product of the two terms ─────────────────→

Square of last term ─────────────────→

Example 6   Multiply: $(2x + 3)(2x - 3)$

Solution $(2x + 3)(2x - 3)$ ▸ $(2x + 3)(2x - 3)$ is the product of the sum and difference of two terms.

$= (2x)^2 - 3^2$ ▸ Square the first term. Square the second term.
$= 4x^2 - 9$ ▸ Simplify.

Problem 6   Multiply: $(2a + 5c)(2a - 5c)$

Solution   See page S15. $4a^2 - 25c^2$

Example 7   Multiply: $(4c + 5d)^2$

Solution $(4c + 5d)^2$ ▸ $(4c + 5d)^2$ is the square of a binomial.

$= (4c)^2 + 2(4c)(5d) + (5d)^2$ ▸ Square the first term. Find twice the product of the two terms. Square the second term.

$= 16c^2 + 40cd + 25d^2$ ▸ Simplify.

Problem 7   Multiply: $(3x + 2y)^2$

Solution   See page S15. $9x^2 + 12xy + 4y^2$

Example 8   Multiply: $(3x - 2)^2$

Solution $(3x - 2)^2$ ▶ $(3x - 2)^2$ is the square of a binomial.

$$= (3x)^2 + 2(3x)(-2) + (-2)^2$$ ▶ Square the first term. Find twice the product of the two terms. Square the last term.

$$= 9x^2 - 12x + 4$$ ▶ Simplify.

Problem 8   Multiply: $(6x - y)^2$

Solution   See page S15. $36x^2 - 12xy + y^2$

5 Application problems

Example 9   The radius of a circle is $(x - 4)$ ft. Find the area of the circle in terms of the variable x. Leave the answer in terms of π.

Strategy   To find the area, replace the variable r in the formula $A = \pi r^2$ with the given value, and solve for A.

Solution $A = \pi r^2$
$A = \pi(x - 4)^2$ ▶ This is the square of a binomial.
$A = \pi(x^2 - 8x + 16)$
$A = \pi x^2 - 8\pi x + 16\pi$

The area is $(\pi x^2 - 8\pi x + 16\pi)$ ft^2.

Problem 9   The length of a rectangle is $(x + 7)$ m. The width is $(x - 4)$ m. Find the area of the rectangle in terms of the variable x.

Solution   See page S15. $(x^2 + 3x - 28)$ m^2

Example 10   The length of a side of a square is $(3x + 5)$ in. Find the area of the square in terms of the variable x.

Strategy   To find the area of the square, replace the variable s in the formula $A = s^2$ with the given value and simplify.

Solution $A = s^2$
$A = (3x + 5)^2$ ▶ This is the square of a binomial.
$A = 9x^2 + 30x + 25$

The area is $(9x^2 + 30x + 25)$ in^2.

Problem 10 The base of a triangle is $(x + 3)$ cm and the height is $(4x - 6)$ cm. Find the area of the triangle in terms of the variable x.

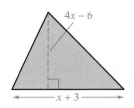

Solution See page S16. $(2x^2 + 3x - 9)$ cm²

CONCEPT REVIEW 7.3

Determine whether the statement is always true, sometimes true, or never true.

1. To multiply a monomial times a polynomial, use the Distributive Property to multiply each term of the polynomial by the monomial. Always true

2. To multiply two polynomials, multiply each term of one polynomial by the other polynomial. Always true

3. A binomial is a polynomial of degree 2. Sometimes true

4. $(x + 7)(x - 7)$ is the product of the sum and difference of the same two terms. Always true

5. To square a binomial means to multiply it times itself. Always true

6. The square of a binomial is a trinomial. Always true

7. The FOIL method is used to multiply two polynomials. Sometimes true

8. Using the FOIL method, the terms $3x$ and 5 are the "First" terms in $(3x + 5)(2x + 7)$. Never true

---

EXERCISES 7.3

1 Multiply.

1. $x(x - 2)$ $x^2 - 2x$

2. $y(3 - y)$ $-y^2 + 3y$

3. $-x(x + 7)$ $-x^2 - 7x$

4. $-y(7 - y)$ $y^2 - 7y$

5. $3a^2(a - 2)$ $3a^3 - 6a^2$

6. $4b^2(b + 8)$ $4b^3 + 32b^2$

7. $-5x^2(x^2 - x)$ $-5x^4 + 5x^3$

8. $-6y^2(y + 2y^2)$ $-12y^4 - 6y^3$

9. $-x^3(3x^2 - 7)$ $-3x^5 + 7x^3$

10. $-y^4(2y^2 - y^6)$ $y^{10} - 2y^6$

11. $2x(6x^2 - 3x)$ $12x^3 - 6x^2$

12. $3y(4y - y^2)$ $-3y^3 + 12y^2$

13. $(2x - 4)3x$ $6x^2 - 12x$

14. $(2x + 1)2x$ $4x^2 + 2x$

15. $-xy(x^2 - y^2)$ $-x^3y + xy^3$

16. $-x^2y(2xy - y^2)$
    $-2x^3y^2 + x^2y^3$

17. $x(2x^3 - 3x + 2)$
    $2x^4 - 3x^2 + 2x$

18. $y(-3y^2 - 2y + 6)$
    $-3y^3 - 2y^2 + 6y$

19. $-a(-2a^2 - 3a - 2)$
    $2a^3 + 3a^2 + 2a$

20. $-b(5b^2 + 7b - 35)$
    $-5b^3 - 7b^2 + 35b$

21. $x^2(3x^4 - 3x^2 - 2)$
    $3x^6 - 3x^4 - 2x^2$

22. $y^3(-4y^3 - 6y + 7)$
$-4y^6 - 6y^4 + 7y^3$

23. $2y^2(-3y^2 - 6y + 7)$
$-6y^4 - 12y^3 + 14y^2$

24. $4x^2(3x^2 - 2x + 6)$
$12x^4 - 8x^3 + 24x^2$

25. $(a^2 + 3a - 4)(-2a)$
$-2a^3 - 6a^2 + 8a$

26. $(b^3 - 2b + 2)(-5b)$
$-5b^4 + 10b^2 - 10b$

27. $-3y^2(-2y^2 + y - 2)$
$6y^4 - 3y^3 + 6y^2$

28. $-5x^2(3x^2 - 3x - 7)$
$-15x^4 + 15x^3 + 35x^2$

29. $xy(x^2 - 3xy + y^2)$
$x^3y - 3x^2y^2 + xy^3$

30. $ab(2a^2 - 4ab - 6b^2)$
$2a^3b - 4a^2b^2 - 6ab^3$

2 Multiply.

31. $(x^2 + 3x + 2)(x + 1)$ $x^3 + 4x^2 + 5x + 2$

32. $(x^2 - 2x + 7)(x - 2)$ $x^3 - 4x^2 + 11x - 14$

33. $(a - 3)(a^2 - 3a + 4)$ $a^3 - 6a^2 + 13a - 12$

34. $(2x - 3)(x^2 - 3x + 5)$ $2x^3 - 9x^2 + 19x - 15$

35. $(-2b^2 - 3b + 4)(b - 5)$ $-2b^3 + 7b^2 + 19b - 20$

36. $(-a^2 + 3a - 2)(2a - 1)$ $-2a^3 + 7a^2 - 7a + 2$

37. $(3x - 5)(-2x^2 + 7x - 2)$ $-6x^3 + 31x^2 - 41x + 10$

38. $(2a - 1)(-a^2 - 2a + 3)$ $-2a^3 - 3a^2 + 8a - 3$

39. $(x^3 - 3x + 2)(x - 4)$ $x^4 - 4x^3 - 3x^2 + 14x - 8$

40. $(y^3 + 4y^2 - 8)(2y - 1)$
$2y^4 + 7y^3 - 4y^2 - 16y + 8$

41. $(3y - 8)(5y^2 + 8y - 2)$ $15y^3 - 16y^2 - 70y + 16$

42. $(4y - 3)(3y^2 + 3y - 5)$ $12y^3 + 3y^2 - 29y + 15$

43. $(5a^3 - 15a + 2)(a - 4)$
$5a^4 - 20a^3 - 15a^2 + 62a - 8$

44. $(3b^3 - 5b^2 + 7)(6b - 1)$
$18b^4 - 33b^3 + 5b^2 + 42b - 7$

45. $(y + 2)(y^3 + 2y^2 - 3y + 1)$
$y^4 + 4y^3 + y^2 - 5y + 2$

46. $(2a - 3)(2a^3 - 3a^2 + 2a - 1)$
$4a^4 - 12a^3 + 13a^2 - 8a + 3$

3 Multiply.

47. $(x + 1)(x + 3)$
$x^2 + 4x + 3$

48. $(y + 2)(y + 5)$
$y^2 + 7y + 10$

49. $(a - 3)(a + 4)$
$a^2 + a - 12$

50. $(b - 6)(b + 3)$
$b^2 - 3b - 18$

51. $(y + 3)(y - 8)$
$y^2 - 5y - 24$

52. $(x + 10)(x - 5)$
$x^2 + 5x - 50$

53. $(y - 7)(y - 3)$
$y^2 - 10y + 21$

54. $(a - 8)(a - 9)$
$a^2 - 17a + 72$

55. $(2x + 1)(x + 7)$
$2x^2 + 15x + 7$

56. $(y + 2)(5y + 1)$
$5y^2 + 11y + 2$

57. $(3x - 1)(x + 4)$
$3x^2 + 11x - 4$

58. $(7x - 2)(x + 4)$
$7x^2 + 26x - 8$

59. $(4x - 3)(x - 7)$
$4x^2 - 31x + 21$

60. $(2x - 3)(4x - 7)$
$8x^2 - 26x + 21$

61. $(3x - 8)(y + 2)$
$3y^2 - 2y - 16$

62. $(5y - 9)(y + 5)$
$5y^2 + 16y - 45$

63. $(3x + 7)(3x + 11)$
$9x^2 + 54x + 77$

64. $(5a + 6)(6a + 5)$
$30a^2 + 61a + 30$

65. $(7a - 16)(3a - 5)$
$21a^2 - 83a + 80$

66. $(5a - 12)(3a - 7)$
$15a^2 - 71a + 84$

67. $(3b + 13)(5b - 6)$
$15b^2 + 47b - 78$

68. $(x + y)(2x + y)$
$2x^2 + 3xy + y^2$

69. $(2a + b)(a + 3b)$
$2a^2 + 7ab + 3b^2$

70. $(3x - 4y)(x - 2y)$
$3x^2 - 10xy + 8y^2$

71. $(2a - b)(3a + 2b)$
$6a^2 + ab - 2b^2$

72. $(5a - 3b)(2a + 4b)$
$10a^2 + 14ab - 12b^2$

73. $(2x + y)(x - 2y)$
$2x^2 - 3xy - 2y^2$

74. $(3x - 7y)(3x + 5y)$
$9x^2 - 6xy - 35y^2$

75. $(2x + 3y)(5x + 7y)$
$10x^2 + 29xy + 21y^2$

76. $(5x + 3y)(7x + 2y)$
$35x^2 + 31xy + 6y^2$

77. $(3a - 2b)(2a - 7b)$
$6a^2 - 25ab + 14b^2$

78. $(5a - b)(7a - b)$
$35a^2 - 12ab + b^2$

79. $(a - 9b)(2a + 7b)$
$2a^2 - 11ab - 63b^2$

80. $(2a + 5b)(7a - 2b)$
$14a^2 + 31ab - 10b^2$

81. $(10a - 3b)(10a - 7b)$
$100a^2 - 100ab + 21b^2$

82. $(12a - 5b)(3a - 4b)$
$36a^2 - 63ab + 20b^2$

83. $(5x + 12y)(3x + 4y)$
$15x^2 + 56xy + 48y^2$

84. $(11x + 2y)(3x + 7y)$
$33x^2 + 83xy + 14y^2$

85. $(2x - 15y)(7x + 4y)$
$14x^2 - 97xy - 60y^2$

86. $(5x + 2y)(2x - 5y)$
$10x^2 - 21xy - 10y^2$

87. $(8x - 3y)(7x - 5y)$
$56x^2 - 61xy + 15y^2$

88. $(2x - 9y)(8x - 3y)$
$16x^2 - 78xy + 27y^2$

4 Multiply.

89. $(y - 5)(y + 5)$ $y^2 - 25$

90. $(y + 6)(y - 6)$ $y^2 - 36$

91. $(2x + 3)(2x - 3)$ $4x^2 - 9$

92. $(4x - 7)(4x + 7)$ $16x^2 - 49$

93. $(x + 1)^2$ $x^2 + 2x + 1$

94. $(y - 3)^2$ $y^2 - 6y + 9$

95. $(3a - 5)^2$ $9a^2 - 30a + 25$

96. $(6x - 5)^2$ $36x^2 - 60x + 25$

97. $(3x - 7)(3x + 7)$ $9x^2 - 49$

98. $(9x - 2)(9x + 2)$ $81x^2 - 4$

99. $(2a + b)^2$ $4a^2 + 4ab + b^2$

100. $(x + 3y)^2$ $x^2 + 6xy + 9y^2$

101. $(x - 2y)^2$ $x^2 - 4xy + 4y^2$

102. $(2x - 3y)^2$ $4x^2 - 12xy + 9y^2$

103. $(4 - 3y)(4 + 3y)$ $16 - 9y^2$

104. $(4x - 9y)(4x + 9y)$
$16x^2 - 81y^2$

105. $(5x + 2y)^2$ $25x^2 + 20xy + 4y^2$

106. $(2a - 9b)^2$
$4a^2 - 36ab + 81b^2$

5 Geometry Problems

107. The length of a rectangle is $5x$ ft. The width is $(2x - 7)$ ft. Find the area of the rectangle in terms of the variable x.

$(10x^2 - 35x)$ ft^2

108. The width of a rectangle is $(x - 6)$ m. The length is $(2x + 3)$ m. Find the area of the rectangle in terms of the variable x.

$(2x^2 - 9x - 18)$ m^2

109. The width of a rectangle is $(3x + 1)$ in. The length of the rectangle is twice the width. Find the area of the rectangle in terms of the variable x.
$(18x^2 + 12x + 2)$ in^2

110. The width of a rectangle is $(4x - 3)$ cm. The length of the rectangle is twice the width. Find the area of the rectangle in terms of the variable x.
$(32x^2 - 48x + 18)$ cm^2

111. The length of a side of a square is $(2x + 1)$ km. Find the area of the square in terms of the variable x.

$(4x^2 + 4x + 1)$ km^2

112. The length of a side of a square is $(2x - 3)$ yd. Find the area of the square in terms of the variable x.

$(4x^2 - 12x + 9)$ yd^2

113. The base of a triangle is $4x$ m and the height is $(2x + 5)$ m. Find the area of the triangle in terms of the variable x.

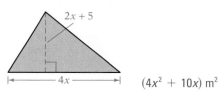

$(4x^2 + 10x)$ m^2

114. The base of a triangle is $(2x + 6)$ in. and the height is $(x - 8)$ in. Find the area of the triangle in terms of the variable x.

$(x^2 - 5x - 24)$ in^2

115. The radius of a circle is $(x + 4)$ cm. Find the area of the circle in terms of the variable x. Leave the answer in terms of π.

$(\pi x^2 + 8\pi x + 16\pi)$ cm²

116. The radius of a circle is $(x - 3)$ ft. Find the area of the circle in terms of the variable x. Leave the answer in terms of π.

$(\pi x^2 - 6\pi x + 9\pi)$ ft²

117. A softball diamond has dimensions 45 ft by 45 ft. A base path border x ft wide lies on both the first-base side and the third-base side of the diamond. Express the total area of the softball diamond and the base path in terms of the variable x. $(90x + 2025)$ ft²

118. An athletic field has dimensions 30 yd by 100 yd. An end zone that is w yards wide borders each end of the field. Express the total area of the field and the end zones in terms of the variable w. $(60w + 3000)$ yd²

APPLYING CONCEPTS 7.3

Simplify.

119. $(a + b)^2 - (a - b)^2$ $4ab$

120. $(x + 3y)^2 + (x + 3y)(x - 3y)$ $2x^2 + 6xy$

121. $(3a^2 - 4a + 2)^2$ $9a^4 - 24a^3 + 28a^2 - 16a + 4$

122. $(x + 4)^3$ $x^3 + 12x^2 + 48x + 64$

123. $3x^2(2x^3 + 4x - 1) - 6x^3(x^2 - 2)$ $24x^3 - 3x^2$

124. $(3b + 2)(b - 6) + (4 + 2b)(3 - b)$ $b^2 - 14b$

[C] **125.** $x^n(x^n + 1)$ $x^{2n} + x^n$

[C] **126.** $(x^n + 1)(x^n - 1)$ $x^{2n} - 1$

[C] **127.** $(x^n + 1)(x^n + 1)$ $x^{2n} + 2x^n + 1$

[C] **128.** $(x^n - 1)^2$ $x^{2n} - 2x^n + 1$

129. $(x + 1)(x - 1)$ $x^2 - 1$

130. $(x + 1)(-x^2 + x - 1)$ $-x^3 - 1$

131. $(x + 1)(x^3 - x^2 + x - 1)$ $x^4 - 1$

132. $(x + 1)(-x^4 + x^3 - x^2 + x - 1)$ $-x^5 - 1$

Use the pattern of the answers to Exercises 129–132 to write the product.

133. $(x + 1)(x^5 - x^4 + x^3 - x^2 + x - 1)$
$x^6 - 1$

134. $(x + 1)(-x^6 + x^5 - x^4 + x^3 - x^2 + x - 1)$
$-x^7 - 1$

Solve.

135. Find $(4n^3)^2$ if $2n - 3 = 4n - 7$. 1024

[C] **136.** What polynomial has quotient $x^2 + 2x - 1$ when divided by $x + 3$? $x^3 + 5x^2 + 5x - 3$

[C] **137.** What polynomial has quotient $3x - 4$ when divided by $4x + 5$? $12x^2 - x - 20$

[C] **138.**   Subtract $4x^2 - x - 5$ from the product of $x^2 + x + 3$ and $x - 4$. $x^3 - 7x^2 - 7$

[C] **139.**   Add $x^2 + 2x - 3$ to the product of $2x - 5$ and $3x + 1$. $7x^2 - 11x - 8$

140.   If a polynomial of degree 3 is multiplied by a polynomial of degree 2, what is the degree of the resulting polynomial?   5

141.   Is it possible to multiply a polynomial of degree 2 by a polynomial of degree 2 and have the product be a polynomial of degree 3? If so, give an example. If not, explain why not.

S E C T I O N   7.4
Division of Polynomials

1   Integer exponents

The quotient of two exponential expressions with the *same* base can be simplified by writing each expression in factored form, dividing by the common factors, and then writing the result with an exponent.

$$\frac{x^5}{x^2} = \frac{\overset{1}{\cancel{x}} \cdot \overset{1}{\cancel{x}} \cdot x \cdot x \cdot x}{\underset{1}{\cancel{x}} \cdot \underset{1}{\cancel{x}}} = x^3$$

Note that subtracting the exponents results in the same quotient.

$$\frac{x^5}{x^2} = x^{5-2} = x^3$$

INSTRUCTOR NOTE

Here we are just verbalizing the rule for division of monomials. The formal definition comes after we define negative exponents.
   Have students copy this rule onto a piece of paper and then practice a few exercises such as $\frac{a^5}{a^2}$ and $\frac{y^8}{y}$. It may also help to give them $\frac{a^9}{b^5}$ to emphasize that the bases must be the same.

To divide two monomials with the same base, subtract the exponents of the like bases.

➡ Simplify: $\frac{a^7}{a^3}$

The bases are the same. Subtract the exponent in the denominator from the exponent in the numerator.

$$\frac{a^7}{a^3} = a^{7-3} = a^4$$ ◀

➡ Simplify: $\frac{r^8 s^6}{r^7 s}$

Subtract the exponents of the like bases.

$$\frac{r^8 s^6}{r^7 s} = r^{8-7} s^{6-1} = r s^5$$

◀

Recall that for any number a, $a \neq 0$, $\frac{a}{a} = 1$. This property is true for exponential expressions as well. For example, for $x \neq 0$, $\frac{x^4}{x^4} = 1$.

This expression also can be simplified using the rule for dividing exponential expressions with the same base.

$$\frac{x^4}{x^4} = x^{4-4} = x^0$$

Because $\frac{x^4}{x^4} = 1$ and $\frac{x^4}{x^4} = x^{4-4} = x^0$, the following definition of zero as an exponent is used.

Zero as an Exponent

If $x \neq 0$, then $x^0 = 1$. The expression 0^0 is not defined.

⇒ Simplify: $(12a^3)^0$, $a \neq 0$

Any nonzero expression to the zero power is 1. $(12a^3)^0 = 1$ ⇐

⇒ Simplify: $-(xy^4)^0$, $x \neq 0$, $y \neq 0$

Any nonzero expression to the zero power is 1. Because the negative sign is outside the parentheses, the answer is -1. $-(xy^4)^0 = -(1) = -1$ ⇐

The meaning of a negative exponent can be developed by examining the quotient $\frac{x^4}{x^6}$.

The expression can be simplified by writing the numerator and denominator in factored form, dividing by the common factors, and then writing the result with an exponent.

$$\frac{x^4}{x^6} = \frac{\cancel{x} \cdot \cancel{x} \cdot \cancel{x} \cdot \cancel{x}}{\cancel{x} \cdot \cancel{x} \cdot \cancel{x} \cdot \cancel{x} \cdot x \cdot x} = \frac{1}{x^2}$$

Now simplify the same expression by subtracting the exponents of the like bases.

$$\frac{x^4}{x^6} = x^{4-6} = x^{-2}$$

Because $\frac{x^4}{x^6} = \frac{1}{x^2}$ and $\frac{x^4}{x^6} = x^{-2}$, the expressions $\frac{1}{x^2}$ and x^{-2} must be equal. The following definition of a negative exponent is used.

Definition of Negative Exponents

If n is a positive integer and $x \neq 0$, then $x^{-n} = \frac{1}{x^n}$ and $\frac{1}{x^{-n}} = x^n$.

⇒ Evaluate 2^{-4}.

Write the expression with a positive exponent. Then simplify. $2^{-4} = \frac{1}{2^4} = \frac{1}{16}$ ⇐

Now that negative exponents have been defined, the Rule for Dividing Exponential Expressions can be stated.

Rule for Dividing Exponential Expressions

If m and n are integers and $x \neq 0$, then $\frac{x^m}{x^n} = x^{m-n}$.

Example 1   Write $\dfrac{3^{-3}}{3^2}$ with a positive exponent. Then evaluate.

Solution $\dfrac{3^{-3}}{3^2} = 3^{-3-2}$ ▸ 3^{-3} and 3^2 have the same base. Subtract the exponents.

$= 3^{-5}$

$= \dfrac{1}{3^5}$ ▸ Use the Definition of Negative Exponents to write the expression with a positive exponent.

$= \dfrac{1}{243}$ ▸ Evaluate.

Problem 1   Write $\dfrac{2^{-2}}{2^3}$ with a positive exponent. Then evaluate.

Solution   See page S16. $\dfrac{1}{2^5} = \dfrac{1}{32}$

The rules for simplifying exponential expressions and powers of exponential expressions are true for all integers. These rules are restated here.

Rules of Exponents

If m, n, and p are integers, then

$$x^m \cdot x^n = x^{m+n} \qquad (x^m)^n = x^{mn} \qquad (x^m y^n)^p = x^{mp} y^{np}$$

$$\dfrac{x^m}{x^n} = x^{m-n}, x \neq 0 \qquad x^{-n} = \dfrac{1}{x^n}, x \neq 0 \qquad x^0 = 1, x \neq 0$$

An exponential expression is in simplest form when it is written with only positive exponents.

➡ Simplify: $a^{-7}b^3$.

Rewrite a^{-7} with a positive exponent. $a^{-7}b^3 = \dfrac{b^3}{a^7}$ ◀

Example 2   Simplify: $\dfrac{x^{-4}y^6}{xy^2}$

Solution $\dfrac{x^{-4}y^6}{xy^2} = x^{-4-1}y^{6-2}$ ▸ Divide variables with the same base by subtracting the exponents.

$= x^{-5}y^4$

$= \dfrac{y^4}{x^5}$ ▸ Write the expression with only positive exponents.

Problem 2   Simplify: $\dfrac{b^8}{a^{-5}b^6}$

Solution   See page S16. a^5b^2

Example 3   Simplify.   A. $\dfrac{-35a^6b^{-2}}{25a^{-2}b^5}$ B. $(-2x)(3x^{-2})^{-3}$

Solution   A. $\dfrac{-35a^6b^{-2}}{25a^{-2}b^5} = -\dfrac{35a^6b^{-2}}{25a^{-2}b^5}$ ▶ A negative sign is placed in front of a fraction.

$$= -\dfrac{\overset{1}{\cancel{5}} \cdot 7a^{6-(-2)}b^{-2-5}}{\underset{1}{\cancel{5}} \cdot 5}$$ ▶ Factor the coefficients. Divide by the common factors. Divide variables with the same base by subtracting the exponents.

$$= -\dfrac{7a^8b^{-7}}{5}$$

$$= -\dfrac{7a^8}{5b^7}$$ ▶ Write the expression with only positive exponents.

B. $(-2x)(3x^{-2})^{-3} = (-2x)(3^{-3}x^6)$ ▶ Use the Rule for Simplifying Powers of Products.

$$= \dfrac{-2x \cdot x^6}{3^3}$$ ▶ Write the expression with positive exponents.

$$= -\dfrac{2x^7}{27}$$ ▶ Use the Rule for Multiplying Exponential Expressions, and simplify the numerical exponential expression.

Problem 3   Simplify.   A. $\dfrac{12x^{-8}y^4}{-16xy^{-3}}$ B. $(-3ab)(2a^3b^{-2})^{-3}$

Solution   See page S16.   A. $-\dfrac{3y^7}{4x^9}$ B. $-\dfrac{3b^7}{8a^8}$

2   Scientific notation

Very large and very small numbers are encountered in the fields of science and engineering. For example, the charge of an electron is 0.00000000000000000000160 coulomb. These numbers can be written more easily in scientific notation. In **scientific notation,** a number is expressed as a product of two factors, one a number between 1 and 10 and the other a power of 10.

To change a number written in decimal notation to scientific notation, write it in the form $a \cdot 10^n$, where a is a number between 1 and 10 and n is an integer.

For numbers greater than 10, move the decimal point to the right of the first digit. The exponent n is positive and equal to the number of places the decimal point has been moved.

$240,000 = 2.4 \cdot 10^5$

$93,000,000 = 9.3 \cdot 10^7$

For numbers less than 1, move the decimal point to the right of the first nonzero digit. The exponent n is negative. The absolute value of the exponent is equal to the number of places the decimal point has been moved.

$0.00030 = 3.0 \cdot 10^{-4}$

$0.0000832 = 8.32 \cdot 10^{-5}$

Look at the last example above: $0.0000832 = 8.32 \cdot 10^{-5}$. Using the Definition of Negative Exponents,

$$10^{-5} = \dfrac{1}{10^5} = \dfrac{1}{100,000} = 0.00001$$

Because $10^{-5} = 0.00001$, we can write

$$8.32 \cdot 10^{-5} = 8.32 \cdot 0.00001 = 0.0000832$$

which is the number we started with. We have not changed the value of the number; we have just written it in another form.

Example 4   Write the number in scientific notation.
A. 824,300,000,000   B. 0.000000961

Solution   A. $824,300,000,000 = 8.243 \cdot 10^{11}$ ▶ Move the decimal point 11 places to the left. The exponent on 10 is 11.

B. $0.000000961 = 9.61 \cdot 10^{-7}$ ▶ Move the decimal point 7 places to the right. The exponent on 10 is -7.

Problem 4   Write the number in scientific notation.
A. 57,000,000,000   B. 0.000000017

Solution   See page S16.   A. $5.7 \cdot 10^{10}$ B. $1.7 \cdot 10^{-8}$

Changing a number written in scientific notation to decimal notation also requires moving the decimal point.

When the exponent on 10 is positive, move the decimal point to the right the same number of places as the exponent.

$3.45 \cdot 10^{9} = 3,450,000,000$

$2.3 \cdot 10^{8} = 230,000,000$

When the exponent on 10 is negative, move the decimal point to the left the same number of places as the absolute value of the exponent.

$8.1 \cdot 10^{-3} = 0.0081$

$6.34 \cdot 10^{-6} = 0.00000634$

Example 5   Write the number in decimal notation.
A. $7.329 \cdot 10^{6}$ B. $6.8 \cdot 10^{-10}$

Solution   A. $7.329 \cdot 10^{6} = 7,329,000$ ▶ The exponent on 10 is positive. Move the decimal point 6 places to the right.

B. $6.8 \cdot 10^{-10} = 0.00000000068$ ▶ The exponent on 10 is negative. Move the decimal point 10 places to the left.

Problem 5   Write the number in scientific notation.
A. $5 \cdot 10^{12}$ B. $4.0162 \cdot 10^{-9}$

Solution   See page S16.   A. 5,000,000,000,000   B. 0.0000000040162

The rules for multiplying and dividing with numbers in scientific notation are the same as those for calculating with algebraic expressions. The power of 10 corresponds to the variable, and the number between 1 and 10 corresponds to the coefficient of the variable.

	Algebraic Expressions	**Scientific Notation**
Multiplication	$(4x^{-3})(2x^5) = 8x^2$	$(4 \cdot 10^{-3})(2 \cdot 10^5) = 8 \cdot 10^2$
Division	$\dfrac{6x^5}{3x^{-2}} = 2x^{5-(-2)} = 2x^7$	$\dfrac{6 \cdot 10^5}{3 \cdot 10^{-2}} = 2 \cdot 10^{5-(-2)} = 2 \cdot 10^7$

Example 6   Multiply or divide.   A. $(3.0 \cdot 10^5)(1.1 \cdot 10^{-8})$ B. $\dfrac{7.2 \cdot 10^{13}}{2.4 \cdot 10^{-3}}$

Solution   A. $(3.0 \cdot 10^5)(1.1 \cdot 10^{-8}) = 3.3 \cdot 10^{-3}$ ▸ Multiply 3.0 and 1.1. Add the exponents on 10.

B. $\dfrac{7.2 \cdot 10^{13}}{2.4 \cdot 10^{-3}} = 3 \cdot 10^{16}$ ▸ Divide 7.2 by 2.4. Subtract the exponents on 10.

Problem 6   Multiply or divide.   A. $(2.4 \cdot 10^{-9})(1.6 \cdot 10^3)$ B. $\dfrac{5.4 \cdot 10^{-2}}{1.8 \cdot 10^{-4}}$

Solution   See page S16.   A. $3.84 \cdot 10^{-6}$ B. $3 \cdot 10^2$

3 ## Divide a polynomial by a monomial   [20] HM³

Note that $\dfrac{8 + 4}{2}$ can be simplified by first adding the terms in the numerator and then dividing the result. It can also be simplified by first dividing each term in the numerator by the denominator and then adding the result.

$\dfrac{8 + 4}{2} = \dfrac{12}{2} = 6$

$\dfrac{8 + 4}{2} = \dfrac{8}{2} + \dfrac{4}{2} = 4 + 2 = 6$

To divide a polynomial by a monomial, divide each term in the numerator by the denominator, and write the sum of the quotients.

$\dfrac{a + b}{c} = \dfrac{a}{c} + \dfrac{b}{c}$

▸ Divide: $\dfrac{6x^2 + 4x}{2x}$

Divide each term of the polynomial $6x^2 + 4x$ by the monomial $2x$. Simplify.

$\dfrac{6x^2 + 4x}{2x} = \dfrac{6x^2}{2x} + \dfrac{4x}{2x}$

$= 3x + 2$ ◂

Example 7   Divide: $\dfrac{6x^3 - 3x^2 + 9x}{3x}$

Solution $\dfrac{6x^3 - 3x^2 + 9x}{3x} = \dfrac{6x^3}{3x} - \dfrac{3x^2}{3x} + \dfrac{9x}{3x}$ ▸ Divide each term of the polynomial by the monomial $3x$.

$= 2x^2 - x + 3$ ▸ Simplify each expression.

Problem 7   Divide: $\dfrac{4x^3y + 8x^2y^2 - 4xy^3}{2xy}$

Solution   See page S16. $2x^2 + 4xy - 2y^2$

Example 8 Divide: $\dfrac{12x^2y - 6xy + 4x^2}{2xy}$

Solution

$\dfrac{12x^2y - 6xy + 4x^2}{2xy}$

$= \dfrac{12x^2y}{2xy} - \dfrac{6xy}{2xy} + \dfrac{4x^2}{2xy}$ ▶ Divide each term of the polynomial by the monomial $2xy$.

$= 6x - 3 + \dfrac{2x}{y}$ ▶ Simplify each expression.

Problem 8 Divide: $\dfrac{24x^2y^2 - 18xy + 6y}{6xy}$

Solution See page S16. $4xy - 3 + \dfrac{1}{x}$

---

4 **Divide polynomials** ⟨20⟩ HM³

INSTRUCTOR NOTE
It may help some students if you start with the division algorithm for whole numbers and show them that a similar procedure is used to divide polynomials.

To divide polynomials, use a method similar to that used for division of whole numbers. The same equation used to check division of whole numbers is used to check polynomial division.

$$\textbf{(Quotient} \times \textbf{Divisor)} + \textbf{Remainder} = \textbf{Dividend}$$

For example:

$$\begin{array}{r} 3 \\ 5\overline{)17} \\ -15 \\ \hline 2 \end{array}$$

$$\begin{array}{ccccc} \textbf{(Quotient} \times \textbf{Divisor)} & + & \textbf{Remainder} & = & \textbf{Dividend} \\ (3 \times 5) & + & 2 & = & 17 \end{array}$$

➡ Divide: $(x^2 - 5x + 8) \div (x - 3)$

Step 1

$$\begin{array}{r} x \\ x - 3\overline{)x^2 - 5x + 8} \\ \underline{x^2 - 3x} \\ -2x + 8 \end{array}$$

Think: $x\overline{)x^2} = \dfrac{x^2}{x} = x$

Multiply: $x(x - 3) = x^2 - 3x$

Subtract: $(x^2 - 5x) - (x^2 - 3x) = -2x$
Bring down $+ 8$.

Step 2

$$\begin{array}{r} x - 2 \\ x - 3\overline{)x^2 - 5x + 8} \\ \underline{x^2 - 3x} \\ -2x + 8 \\ \underline{-2x + 6} \\ 2 \end{array}$$

Think: $x\overline{)-2x} = \dfrac{-2x}{x} = -2$

Multiply: $-2(x - 3) = -2x + 6$

Subtract: $(-2x + 8) - (-2x + 6) = 2$
The remainder is 2.

INSTRUCTOR NOTE
Students are comfortable writing the answer to $15 \div 4$ as $3\frac{3}{4}$, which is $3 + \frac{3}{4}$. Tell students that this is the form in which a remainder for a quotient of polynomials is written.

Check:

$$\text{Quotient} \times \text{Divisor} + \text{Remainder} = \qquad \text{Dividend}$$

$$(x - 2)(x - 3) + 2 = x^2 - 3x - 2x + 6 + 2 = x^2 - 5x + 8$$

$$(x^2 - 5x + 8) \div (x - 3) = x - 2 + \dfrac{2}{x - 3}$$

If a term is missing in the dividend, insert the term with zero as its coefficient. This helps keep like terms in the same column. This is illustrated in Example 9.

Example 9   Divide: $(6x + 2x^3 + 26) \div (x + 2)$

Solution

$$\begin{array}{r} 2x^2 - 4x + 14 \\ x + 2\overline{)2x^3 + 0x^2 + 6x + 26} \\ \underline{2x^3 + 4x^2} \\ -4x^2 + 6x \\ \underline{-4x^2 - 8x} \\ 14x + 26 \\ \underline{14x + 28} \\ -2 \end{array}$$

▶ Arrange the terms in descending order. There is no term of x^2 in $2x^3 + 6x + 26$. Insert $0x^2$ for the missing term so that like terms will be in columns.

$$(6x + 2x^3 + 26) \div (x + 2) = 2x^2 - 4x + 14 - \frac{2}{x + 2}$$

Problem 9   Divide: $(x^3 - 2x - 4) \div (x - 2)$

Solution: See page S16. $x^2 + 2x + 2$

CONCEPT REVIEW 7.4

Determine whether the statement is always true, sometimes true, or never true.

1. The expression $\dfrac{x^5}{y^3}$ can be simplified by subtracting the exponents.   Never true

2. The rules of exponents can be applied to expressions that contain an exponent of zero or contain negative exponents.   Always true

3. The expression 3^{-2} represents the reciprocal of 3^2.   Always true

4. $5x^0 = 0$ Never true

5. The expression 4^{-3} represents a negative number.   Never true

6. To be in simplest form, an exponential expression cannot contain any negative exponents.   Always true

7. $2x^{-5} = \dfrac{1}{2x^5}$ Never true

8. $x^4 y^{-6} = \dfrac{1}{x^4 y^6}$ Never true

EXERCISES 7.4

1 Write with a positive or zero exponent. Then evaluate.

1. 5^{-2} $\dfrac{1}{25}$

2. 3^{-3} $\dfrac{1}{27}$

3. $\dfrac{1}{8^{-2}}$ 64

4. $\dfrac{1}{12^{-1}}$ 12

5. $\dfrac{3^{-2}}{3}$ $\dfrac{1}{27}$

6. $\dfrac{5^{-3}}{5}$ $\dfrac{1}{625}$

7. $\dfrac{2^3}{2^3}$ 1

8. $\dfrac{3^{-2}}{3^{-2}}$ 1

9. ✏️ Explain how to rewrite a variable that has a negative exponent as an expression with a positive exponent.

10. ✏️ Explain how to divide two exponential expressions with the same base. Provide an example.

Simplify.

11. $\dfrac{y^7}{y^3}$ y^4

12. $\dfrac{z^9}{z^2}$ z^7

13. $\dfrac{a^8}{a^5}$ a^3

14. $\dfrac{c^{12}}{c^5}$ c^7

15. $\dfrac{p^5}{p}$ p^4

16. $\dfrac{w^9}{w}$ w^8

17. $\dfrac{4x^8}{2x^5}$ $2x^3$

18. $\dfrac{12z^7}{4z^3}$ $3z^4$

19. $\dfrac{22k^5}{11k^4}$ $2k$

20. $\dfrac{14m^{11}}{7m^{10}}$ $2m$

21. $\dfrac{m^9n^7}{m^4n^5}$ m^5n^2

22. $\dfrac{y^5z^6}{yz^3}$ y^4z^3

23. $\dfrac{6r^4}{4r^2}$ $\dfrac{3r^2}{2}$

24. $\dfrac{8x^9}{12x^6}$ $\dfrac{2x^3}{3}$

25. $\dfrac{-16a^7}{24a^6}$ $-\dfrac{2a}{3}$

26. $\dfrac{-18b^5}{27b^4}$ $-\dfrac{2b}{3}$

27. x^{-2} $\dfrac{1}{x^2}$

28. y^{-10} $\dfrac{1}{y^{10}}$

29. $\dfrac{1}{a^{-6}}$ a^6

30. $\dfrac{1}{b^{-4}}$ b^4

31. $4x^{-7}$ $\dfrac{4}{x^7}$

32. $-6y^{-1}$ $-\dfrac{6}{y}$

33. $\dfrac{5}{b^{-8}}$ $5b^8$

34. $\dfrac{-3}{v^{-3}}$ $-3v^3$

35. $\dfrac{1}{3x^{-2}}$ $\dfrac{x^2}{3}$

36. $\dfrac{2}{5c^{-6}}$ $\dfrac{2c^6}{5}$

37. $(ab^5)^0$ 1

38. $(32x^3y^4)^0$ 1

39. $\dfrac{y^3}{y^8}$ $\dfrac{1}{y^5}$

40. $\dfrac{z^4}{z^6}$ $\dfrac{1}{z^2}$

41. $\dfrac{a^5}{a^{11}}$ $\dfrac{1}{a^6}$

42. $\dfrac{m}{m^7}$ $\dfrac{1}{m^6}$

43. $\dfrac{4x^2}{12x^5}$ $\dfrac{1}{3x^3}$

44. $\dfrac{6y^8}{8y^9}$ $\dfrac{3}{4y}$

45. $\dfrac{-12x}{-18x^6}$ $\dfrac{2}{3x^5}$

46. $\dfrac{-24c^2}{-36c^{11}}$ $\dfrac{2}{3c^9}$

47. $\dfrac{x^6y^5}{x^8y}$ $\dfrac{y^4}{x^2}$

48. $\dfrac{a^3b^2}{a^2b^3}$ $\dfrac{a}{b}$

49. $\dfrac{2m^6n^2}{5m^9n^{10}}$ $\dfrac{2}{5m^3n^8}$

50. $\dfrac{5r^3t^7}{6r^5t^7}$ $\dfrac{5}{6r^2}$

51. $\dfrac{pq^3}{p^4q^4}$ $\dfrac{1}{p^3q}$

52. $\dfrac{a^4b^5}{a^5b^6}$ $\dfrac{1}{ab}$

53. $\dfrac{3x^4y^5}{6x^4y^8}$ $\dfrac{1}{2y^3}$

54. $\dfrac{14a^3b^6}{21a^5b^6}$ $\dfrac{2}{3a^2}$

55. $\dfrac{14x^4y^6z^2}{16x^3y^9z}$ $\dfrac{7xz}{8y^3}$

56. $\dfrac{24a^2b^7c^9}{36a^7b^5c}$ $\dfrac{2b^2c^8}{3a^5}$

57. $\dfrac{15mn^9p^3}{30m^4n^9p}$ $\dfrac{p^2}{2m^3}$

58. $\dfrac{25x^4y^7z^2}{20x^5y^9z^{11}}$ $\dfrac{5}{4xy^2z^9}$

59. $(-2xy^{-2})^3$ $-\dfrac{8x^3}{y^6}$

60. $(-3x^{-1}y^2)^2$ $\dfrac{9y^4}{x^2}$

61. $(3x^{-1}y^{-2})^2$ $\dfrac{9}{x^2y^4}$

62. $(5xy^{-3})^{-2}$ $\dfrac{y^6}{25x^2}$

63. $(2x^{-1})(x^{-3})$ $\dfrac{2}{x^4}$

64. $(-2x^{-5})x^7$ $-2x^2$

65. $(-5a^2)(a^{-5})^2$ $-\dfrac{5}{a^8}$

66. $(2a^{-3})(a^7b^{-1})^3$ $\dfrac{2a^{18}}{b^3}$

67. $(-2ab^{-2})(4a^{-2}b)^{-2}$ $-\dfrac{a^5}{8b^4}$

68. $(3ab^{-2})(2a^{-1}b)^{-3}$ $\dfrac{3a^4}{8b^5}$

69. $(-5x^{-2}y)(-2x^{-2}y^2)$ $\dfrac{10y^3}{x^4}$

70. $\dfrac{a^{-3}b^{-4}}{a^2b^2}$ $\dfrac{1}{a^5b^6}$

71. $\dfrac{3x^{-2}y^2}{6xy^2}$ $\dfrac{1}{2x^3}$

72. $\dfrac{2x^{-2}y}{8xy}$ $\dfrac{1}{4x^3}$

73. $\dfrac{3x^{-2}y}{xy}$ $\dfrac{3}{x^3}$

74. $\dfrac{2x^{-1}y^4}{x^2y^3}$ $\dfrac{2y}{x^3}$

75. $\dfrac{2x^{-1}y^{-4}}{4xy^2}$ $\dfrac{1}{2x^2y^6}$

76. $\dfrac{12a^2b^3}{-27a^2b^2}$ $-\dfrac{4b}{9}$

77. $\dfrac{-16xy^4}{96x^4y^4}$ $-\dfrac{1}{6x^3}$

78. $\dfrac{-8x^2y^4}{44y^2z^5}$ $-\dfrac{2x^2y^2}{11z^5}$

2 **79.** Why might a number be written in scientific notation instead of decimal notation?

80. Explain how you can tell whether a number is in scientific notation.

Write the number in scientific notation.

81. 2,370,000 $2.37 \cdot 10^6$ **82.** 75,000 $7.5 \cdot 10^4$ **83.** 0.00045 $4.5 \cdot 10^{-4}$ **84.** 0.000076
$$7.6 \cdot 10^{-5}$$

85. 309,000 $3.09 \cdot 10^5$ **86.** 819,000,000   **87.** 0.000000601   **88.** 0.00000000096
$$8.19 \cdot 10^8 \qquad\qquad 6.01 \cdot 10^{-7} \qquad\qquad 9.6 \cdot 10^{-10}$$

Write the number in decimal notation.

89. $7.1 \cdot 10^5$ 710,000   **90.** $2.3 \cdot 10^7$ 23,000,000   **91.** $4.3 \cdot 10^{-5}$ 0.000043   **92.** $9.21 \cdot 10^{-7}$
$$0.000000921$$

93. $6.71 \cdot 10^8$ **94.** $5.75 \cdot 10^9$ **95.** $7.13 \cdot 10^{-6}$ **96.** $3.54 \cdot 10^{-8}$
671,000,000   5,750,000,000   0.00000713   0.0000000354

97. *Physics*   Light travels approximately 16,000,000,000 mi in one day. Write this number in scientific notation. $1.6 \cdot 10^{10}$

98. *Chemistry*   Avogadro's number is used in chemistry. Its value is approximately 602,300,000,000,000,000,000,000. Write this number in scientific notation. $6.023 \cdot 10^{23}$

99. *Geology*   The mass of Earth is 5,980,000,000,000,000,000,000,000 kg. Write this number in scientific notation. $5.98 \cdot 10^{24}$

100. *Astronomy*   A parsec is a distance measurement that is used by astronomers. One parsec is 3,086,000,000,000,000,000 cm. Write this number in scientific notation. $3.086 \cdot 10^{18}$

101. *Electricity*   The electric charge on an electron is approximately 0.00000000000000000016 coulomb. Write this number in scientific notation. $1.6 \cdot 10^{-19}$

102. *Light*   The length of an infrared light wave is approximately 0.0000037 m. Write this number in scientific notation. $3.7 \cdot 10^{-6}$

103. *Computers*   One unit used to measure the speed of a computer is the picosecond. One picosecond is 0.000000000001 second. Write this number in scientific notation. $1 \cdot 10^{-12}$

104. *Astronomy*   One light-year is the distance traveled by light in one year. One light-year is 5,880,000,000,000 mi. Write this number in scientific notation. $5.88 \cdot 10^{12}$

Simplify.

105. $(1.9 \cdot 10^{12})(3.5 \cdot 10^7)$ $6.65 \cdot 10^{19}$ **106.** $(4.2 \cdot 10^7)(1.8 \cdot 10^{-5})$ $7.56 \cdot 10^2$

107. $(2.3 \cdot 10^{-8})(1.4 \cdot 10^{-6})$ $3.22 \cdot 10^{-14}$ **108.** $(3 \cdot 10^{-20})(2.4 \cdot 10^9)$ $7.2 \cdot 10^{-11}$

109. $\dfrac{6.12 \cdot 10^{14}}{1.7 \cdot 10^{9}}$ $3.6 \cdot 10^{5}$ **110.** $\dfrac{6 \cdot 10^{-8}}{2.5 \cdot 10^{-2}}$ $2.4 \cdot 10^{-6}$

111. $\dfrac{5.58 \cdot 10^{-7}}{3.1 \cdot 10^{11}}$ $1.8 \cdot 10^{-18}$ **112.** $\dfrac{9.03 \cdot 10^{6}}{4.3 \cdot 10^{-5}}$ $2.1 \cdot 10^{11}$

3 Divide.

113. $\dfrac{2x + 2}{2}$ $x + 1$ **114.** $\dfrac{5y + 5}{5}$ $y + 1$ **115.** $\dfrac{10a - 25}{5}$ $2a - 5$

116. $\dfrac{16b - 40}{8}$ $2b - 5$ **117.** $\dfrac{3a^2 + 2a}{a}$ $3a + 2$ **118.** $\dfrac{6y^2 + 4y}{y}$ $6y + 4$

119. $\dfrac{4b^3 - 3b}{b}$ $4b^2 - 3$ **120.** $\dfrac{12x^2 - 7x}{x}$ $12x - 7$ **121.** $\dfrac{3x^2 - 6x}{3x}$ $x - 2$

122. $\dfrac{10y^2 - 6y}{2y}$ $5y - 3$ **123.** $\dfrac{5x^2 - 10x}{-5x}$ $-x + 2$ **124.** $\dfrac{3y^2 - 27y}{-3y}$ $-y + 9$

125. $\dfrac{x^3 + 3x^2 - 5x}{x}$ $x^2 + 3x - 5$ **126.** $\dfrac{a^3 - 5a^2 + 7a}{a}$ $a^2 - 5a + 7$ **127.** $\dfrac{x^6 - 3x^4 - x^2}{x^2}$ $x^4 - 3x^2 - 1$

128. $\dfrac{a^8 - 5a^5 - 3a^3}{a^2}$ $a^6 - 5a^3 - 3a$ **129.** $\dfrac{5x^2y^2 + 10xy}{5xy}$ $xy + 2$ **130.** $\dfrac{8x^2y^2 - 24xy}{8xy}$ $xy - 3$

131. $\dfrac{9y^6 - 15y^3}{-3y^3}$ $-3y^3 + 5$ **132.** $\dfrac{4x^4 - 6x^2}{-2x^2}$ $-2x^2 + 3$ **133.** $\dfrac{3x^2 - 2x + 1}{x}$ $3x - 2 + \dfrac{1}{x}$

134. $\dfrac{8y^2 + 2y - 3}{y}$ $8y + 2 - \dfrac{3}{y}$ **135.** $\dfrac{-3x^2 + 7x - 6}{x}$ $-3x + 7 - \dfrac{6}{x}$ **136.** $\dfrac{2y^2 - 6y + 9}{y}$ $2y - 6 + \dfrac{9}{y}$

137. $\dfrac{16a^2b - 20ab + 24ab^2}{4ab}$
$4a - 5 + 6b$

138. $\dfrac{22a^2b + 11ab - 33ab^2}{11ab}$
$2a + 1 - 3b$

139. $\dfrac{9x^2y + 6xy - 3xy^2}{xy}$
$9x + 6 - 3y$

4 Divide.

140. $(b^2 - 14b + 49) \div (b - 7)$
$b - 7$

141. $(x^2 - x - 6) \div (x - 3)$
$x + 2$

142. $(y^2 + 2y - 35) \div (y + 7)$
$y - 5$

143. $(2x^2 + 5x + 2) \div (x + 2)$
$2x + 1$

144. $(2y^2 - 13y + 21) \div (y - 3)$
$2y - 7$

145. $(4x^2 - 16) \div (2x + 4)$
$2x - 4$

146. $(2y^2 + 7) \div (y - 3)$
$2y + 6 + \dfrac{25}{y - 3}$

147. $(x^2 + 1) \div (x - 1)$
$x + 1 + \dfrac{2}{x - 1}$

148. $(x^2 + 4) \div (x + 2)$
$x - 2 + \dfrac{8}{x + 2}$

149. $(6x^2 - 7x) \div (3x - 2)$
$2x - 1 - \dfrac{2}{3x - 2}$

150. $(6y^2 + 2y) \div (2y + 4)$
$3y - 5 + \dfrac{20}{2y + 4}$

151. $(5x^2 + 7x) \div (x - 1)$
$5x + 12 + \dfrac{12}{x - 1}$

152. $(6x^2 - 5) \div (x + 2)$
$6x - 12 + \dfrac{19}{x + 2}$

153. $(a^2 + 5a + 10) \div (a + 2)$
$a + 3 + \dfrac{4}{a + 2}$

154. $(b^2 - 8b - 9) \div (b - 3)$
$b - 5 - \dfrac{24}{b - 3}$

155. $(2y^2 - 9y + 8) \div (2y + 3)$
$y - 6 + \dfrac{26}{2y + 3}$

156. $(3x^2 + 5x - 4) \div (x - 4)$
$3x + 17 + \dfrac{64}{x - 4}$

157. $(8x + 3 + 4x^2) \div (2x - 1)$
$2x + 5 + \dfrac{8}{2x - 1}$

158. $(10 + 21y + 10y^2) \div (2y + 3)$
$5y + 3 + \dfrac{1}{2y + 3}$

159. $(15a^2 - 8a - 8) \div (3a + 2)$
$5a - 6 + \dfrac{4}{3a + 2}$

160. $(12a^2 - 25a - 7) \div (3a - 7)$
$4a + 1$

161. $(5 - 23x + 12x^2) \div (4x - 1)$ $3x - 5$

162. $(24 + 6a^2 + 25a) \div (3a - 1)$ $2a + 9 + \dfrac{33}{3a - 1}$

163. $(x^3 + 3x^2 + 5x + 3) \div (x + 1)$ $x^2 + 2x + 3$

164. $(x^3 - 6x^2 + 7x - 2) \div (x - 1)$ $x^2 - 5x + 2$

165. $(x^4 - x^2 - 6) \div (x^2 + 2)$ $x^2 - 3$

166. $(x^4 + 3x^2 - 10) \div (x^2 - 2)$ $x^2 + 5$

APPLYING CONCEPTS 7.4

Evaluate.

167. $8^{-2} + 2^{-5}$ $\dfrac{3}{64}$

168. $9^{-2} + 3^{-3}$ $\dfrac{4}{81}$

169. Evaluate 2^x and 2^{-x} when $x = -2, -1, 0, 1,$ and 2. $\dfrac{1}{4}, \dfrac{1}{2}, 1, 2, 4; 4, 2, 1, \dfrac{1}{2}, \dfrac{1}{4}$

170. Evaluate 3^x and 3^{-x} when $x = -2, -1, 0, 1,$ and 2. $\dfrac{1}{9}, \dfrac{1}{3}, 1, 3, 9; 9, 3, 1, \dfrac{1}{3}, \dfrac{1}{9}$

Write in decimal notation.

171. 2^{-4} 0.0625

172. 25^{-2} 0.0016

Simplify.

173. $\left(\dfrac{9x^2y^4}{3xy^2}\right) - \left(\dfrac{12x^5y^6}{6x^4y^4}\right)$ xy^2

174. $\left(\dfrac{6x^2 + 9x}{3x}\right) + \left(\dfrac{8xy^2 + 4y^2}{4y^2}\right)$ $4x + 4$

175. $\left(\dfrac{6x^4yz^3}{2x^2y^3}\right)\left(\dfrac{2x^2z^3}{4y^2z}\right) \div \left(\dfrac{6x^2y^3}{x^4y^2z}\right)$ $\dfrac{x^6z^6}{4y^5}$

176. $\left(\dfrac{5x^2yz^3}{3x^4yz^3}\right) \div \left(\dfrac{10x^2y^5z^4}{2y^3z}\right) \div \left(\dfrac{5y^4z^2}{x^2y^6z}\right)$ $\dfrac{1}{15x^2z^4}$

Complete.

177. If $m = n$ and $a \neq 0$, then $\dfrac{a^m}{a^n} = $ _____ .   1

178. If $m = n + 1$ and $a \neq 0$, then $\dfrac{a^m}{a^n} = $ _____ .   a

Solve.

[C] **179.** $(-4.8)^x = 1$ 0

180. $-6.3^x = -1$ 0

Determine whether each equation is true or false. If the equation is false, change the right side of the equation to make a true equation.

181. $(2a)^{-3} = \dfrac{2}{a^3}$ False; $(2a)^{-3} = \dfrac{1}{8a^3}$

182. $((a^{-1})^{-1})^{-1} = \dfrac{1}{a}$ True

183. $(2 + 3)^{-1} = 2^{-1} + 3^{-1}$ False; $(2 + 3)^{-1} = 5^{-1} = \dfrac{1}{5}$

184. If $x \neq \dfrac{1}{3}$, then $(3x - 1)^0 = (1 - 3x)^0$.   True

Solve.

[C] **185.** The product of a monomial and $4b$ is $12a^2b$. Find the monomial. $3a^2$

[C] **186.** The product of a monomial and $6x$ is $24xy^2$. Find the monomial. $4y^2$

[C] **187.** The quotient of a polynomial and $2x + 1$ is $2x - 4 + \dfrac{7}{2x + 1}$. Find the polynomial. $4x^2 - 6x + 3$

[C] **188.** The quotient of a polynomial and $x - 3$ is $x^2 - x + 8 + \dfrac{22}{x - 3}$. Find the polynomial. $x^3 - 4x^2 + 11x - 2$

[C] **189.** Why is the condition $x \neq \dfrac{1}{3}$ given in Exercise 184?

190. If x is a nonzero real number, is x^{-2} always positive, always negative, or positive or negative depending on whether x is positive or negative? Explain your answer.

191. If x is a nonzero real number, is x^{-3} always positive, always negative, or positive or negative depending on whether x is positive or negative? Explain your answer.

Focus on Problem Solving

Dimensional Analysis

In solving application problems, it may be useful to include the units in order to organize the problem so that the answer is in the proper units. Using units to organize and check the correctness of an application is called **dimensional analysis.** We use the operations of multiplying units and dividing units in applying dimensional analysis to application problems.

The Rule for Multiplying Exponential Expressions states that we multiply two expressions with the same base by adding the exponents.

$$x^4 \cdot x^6 = x^{4+6} = x^{10}$$

In calculations that involve quantities, the units are operated on algebraically.

➡ A rectangle measures 3 m by 5 m. Find the area of the rectangle.

$$A = LW = (3 \text{ m})(5 \text{ m}) = (3 \cdot 5)(\text{m} \cdot \text{m}) = 15 \text{ m}^2$$

The area of the rectangle is 15 m^2 (**square meters**).

➡ A box measures 10 cm by 5 cm by 3 cm. Find the volume of the box.

$$V = LWH = (10 \text{ cm})(5 \text{ cm})(3 \text{ cm}) = (10 \cdot 5 \cdot 3)(\text{cm} \cdot \text{cm} \cdot \text{cm}) = 150 \text{ cm}^3$$

The volume of the box is 150 cm^3 (**cubic centimeters**).

➡ Find the area of a square whose side measures $(3x + 5)$ in.

$$A = s^2 = [(3x + 5) \text{ in.}]^2 = (3x + 5)^2 \text{ in}^2 = (9x^2 + 30x + 25) \text{ in}^2$$

The area of the square is $(9x^2 + 30x + 25)$ in^2 (**square inches**).

Dimensional analysis is used in the conversion of units.

The following example converts the unit miles to feet. The equivalent measures 1 mi and 5280 ft are used to form the following rates, which are called conversion

1 mi
|——|
5280 ft

factors: $\dfrac{1 \text{ mi}}{5280 \text{ ft}}$ and $\dfrac{5280 \text{ ft}}{1 \text{ mi}}$. Because 1 mi = 5280 ft, both of the conversion factors

$\dfrac{1 \text{ mi}}{5280 \text{ ft}}$ and $\dfrac{5280 \text{ ft}}{1 \text{ mi}}$ are equal to 1.

To convert 3 mi to feet, multiply 3 mi by the conversion factor $\dfrac{5280 \text{ ft}}{1 \text{ mi}}$.

3 mi
|←————————→|
15,840 ft

$$3 \text{ mi} = 3 \text{ mi} \cdot 1 = \frac{3 \text{ mi}}{1} \cdot \boxed{\frac{5280 \text{ ft}}{1 \text{ mi}}} = \frac{3 \text{ mi} \cdot 5280 \text{ ft}}{1 \text{ mi}} = 3 \cdot 5280 \text{ ft} = 15{,}840 \text{ ft}$$

There are two important points in the above illustration. First, you can think of dividing the numerator and denominator by the common unit "mile" just as you would divide the numerator and denominator of a fraction by a common factor.

Second, the conversion factor $\dfrac{5280 \text{ ft}}{1 \text{ mi}}$ is equal to 1, and multiplying an expression by 1 does not change the value of the expression.

In the application problem that follows, the units are kept in the problem while the problem is worked.

In the 1998 Kentucky Derby, a horse named Real Quiet ran the 1.25-mile race in 2.0367 min. Find Real Quiet's average speed for that race in miles per hour. Round to the nearest tenth.

Strategy   To find the average speed, use the formula $r = \dfrac{d}{t}$, where r is the speed, d is the distance, and t is the time. Use the conversion factor $\dfrac{60 \text{ min}}{1 \text{ h}}$.

Solution $r = \dfrac{d}{t} = \dfrac{1.25 \text{ mi}}{2.0367 \text{ min}} = \dfrac{1.25 \text{ mi}}{2.0367 \text{ min}} \cdot \dfrac{60 \text{ min}}{1 \text{ h}}$

$= \dfrac{75 \text{ mi}}{2.0367 \text{ h}} \approx 36.8 \text{ mph}$

Real Quiet's average speed was 36.8 mph.

Try each of the following problems. Round to the nearest tenth.

1. Convert 88 ft/s to miles per hour.

2. Convert 8 m/s to kilometers per hour (1 km = 1000 m).

3. A carpet is to be placed in a meeting hall that is 36 ft wide and 80 ft long. At $21.50 per square yard, how much will it cost to carpet the meeting hall?

4. A carpet is to be placed in a room that is 20 ft wide and 30 ft long. At $22.25 per square yard, how much will it cost to carpet the area?

5. Find the number of gallons of water in a fish tank that is 36 in. long and 24 in. wide and is filled to a depth of 16 in. (1 gal = 231 in³).

6. Find the number of gallons of water in a fish tank that is 24 in. long and 18 in. wide and is filled to a depth of 12 in. (1 gal = 231 in³).

7. A $\frac{1}{4}$-acre commercial lot is on sale for $2.15 per square foot. Find the sale price of the commercial lot (1 acre = 43,560 ft²).

8. A 0.75-acre industrial parcel was sold for $98,010. Find the parcel's price per square foot (1 acre = 43,560 ft²).

9. A new driveway will require 800 ft³ of concrete. Concrete is ordered by the cubic yard. How much concrete should be ordered?

10. ◐ A piston-engined dragster traveled 440 yd in 4.936 s at Ennis, Texas, on October 9, 1988. Find the average speed of the dragster in miles per hour.

11. ◐ The Marianas Trench in the Pacific Ocean is the deepest part of the ocean. The depth is 6.85 mi. The speed of sound under water is 4700 ft/s. Find the time it takes sound to travel from the surface to the bottom of the Marianas Trench and back.

Projects and Group Activities

Pascal's Triangle

Simplifying the power of a binomial is called *expanding the binomial*. The expansion of the first three powers of a binomial is shown below.

$$(a + b)^1 = a + b$$

$$(a + b)^2 = (a + b)(a + b) = a^2 + 2ab + b^2$$

$$(a + b)^3 = (a + b)^2(a + b) = (a^2 + 2ab + b^2)(a + b) = a^3 + 3a^2b + 3ab^2 + b^3$$

Find $(a + b)^4$. [*Hint:* $(a + b)^4 = (a + b)^3(a + b)$]

Find $(a + b)^5$. [*Hint:* $(a + b)^5 = (a + b)^4(a + b)$]

If we continue in this way, the results for $(a + b)^6$ are

$$(a + b)^6 = a^6 + 6a^5b + 15a^4b^2 + 20a^3b^3 + 15a^2b^4 + 6ab^5 + b^6$$

Now expand $(a + b)^8$. Before you begin, see if you can find a pattern that will help you write the expansion of $(a + b)^8$ without having to multiply it out. Here are some hints.

1. Write out the variable terms of each binomial expansion from $(a + b)^1$ through $(a + b)^6$. Observe how the exponents on the variables change.

2. Write out the coefficients of all the terms without the variable parts. It will be helpful to make a triangular arrangement as shown at the left. Note that each row begins and ends with a 1. Also note in the two shaded regions that any number in a row is the sum of the two closest numbers above it. For instance, $1 + 5 = 6$ and $6 + 4 = 10$.

```
        1   1
      1   2   1
    1   3   3   1
  1   4   6   4   1
1   5   10   10   5   1
1   6   15   20   15   6   1
```

The triangle of numbers shown at the left is called Pascal's Triangle. To find the expansion of $(a + b)^8$, you need to find the eighth row of Pascal's Triangle. First find row seven. Then find row eight and use the patterns you have observed to write the expansion $(a + b)^8$.

Pascal's Triangle has been the subject of extensive analysis, and many patterns have been found. See if you can find some of them. You might check the Internet, where you will find some web sites with information on Pascal's Triangle.

Properties of Polynomials

The graph of a fifth-degree polynomial with 4 *turning points* is shown at the right. In this project you will graph various polynomials and try to make a conjecture as to the relationship between the degree of a polynomial and the number of turning points in its graph. For each of the following, graph the equation. Record the degree of the equation and the number of turning points.

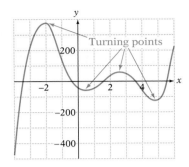

1. Graph: $y = x^3 + 1$
2. Graph $y = x^3 + 2x^2 - 5x - 6$
3. Graph: $y = x^4 - x^3 - 11x^2 - x - 12$
4. Graph: $y = x^4 - 2x^3 - 13x^2 + 14x + 24$
5. Graph: $y = x^5 - 2$
6. Graph: $y = x^5 - 3x^4 - 11x^3 + 27x^2 + 10x - 24$
7. Graph: $y = x^5 - 2x^4 - 10x^3 + 10x^2 - 11x + 12$

Make a conjecture as to a relationship between the degree of a polynomial and the number of turning points in its graph. Graph a few more polynomials of your choosing and see whether your conjecture is valid for those graphs. If not, refine your conjecture and test it again.

Chapter Summary

Key Words

A *monomial* is a number, a variable, or a product of numbers and variables.   (Objective 7.1.1)

5 is a number. y is a variable. $8a^2b^3$ is a product of numbers and variables. 5, y, and $8a^2b^3$ are monomials.

A *polynomial* is a variable expression in which the terms are monomials.   (Objective 7.1.1)

As shown above, 5, y, and $8a^2b^3$ are monomials. Therefore, $5 + y + 8a^2b^3$ is a polynomial.

A polynomial of one term is a *monomial*.   (Objective 7.1.1)

5, y, and $8a^2b^3$ are monomials.

A polynomial of two terms is a *binomial*.   (Objective 7.1.1)

$x + 9$, $y^2 - 3$, and $6a + 7b$ are binomials.

A polynomial of three terms is a *trinomial*.   (Objective 7.1.1)

$x^2 + 2x - 1$ is a trinomial.

The *degree of a polynomial in one variable* is the largest exponent on a variable.   (Objective 7.1.1)

The degree of $8x^3 - 5x^2 + 4x - 12$ is 3.

Essential Rules and Procedures

Rules for Multiplying Exponential Expressions
If m and n are integers, then $x^m \cdot x^n = x^{m+n}$.   (Objective 7.2.1)

$b^5 \cdot b^4 = b^{5+4} = b^9$

Rule for Simplifying Powers of Exponential Expressions
If m and n are integers, then $(x^m)^n = x^{mn}$.   (Objective 7.2.2)

$$(y^3)^7 = y^{3(7)} = y^{21}$$

Rule for Simplifying Powers of Products
If m, n, and p are integers, then $(x^m y^n)^p = x^{mp} y^{np}$.
(Objective 7.2.2)

$$(a^6 b^2)^3 = a^{6(3)} b^{2(3)} = a^{18} b^6$$

FOIL Method
To find the product of two binomials, add the products of the
First terms, the **O**uter terms, the **I**nner terms, and the **L**ast
terms.   (Objective 7.3.3)

$$(4x + 3)(2x - 1)$$
$$= (4x)(2x) + (4x)(-1) + (3)(2x) + (3)(-1)$$
$$= 8x^2 - 4x + 6x - 3 = 8x^2 + 2x - 3$$

The Sum and Difference of Two Terms
$(a + b)(a - b) = a^2 - b^2$ (Objective 7.3.4)

$$(3x + 4)(3x - 4) = (3x)^2 - 4^2 = 9x^2 - 16$$

The Square of a Binomial
$(a + b)^2 = a^2 + 2ab + b^2$

$$(2x + 5)^2$$
$$= (2x)^2 + 2(2x)(5) + 5^2 = 4x^2 + 20x + 25$$

$(a - b)^2 = a^2 - 2ab + b^2$
(Objective 7.3.4)

$$(2x - 5)^2$$
$$= (2x)^2 - 2(2x)(5) + 5^2 = 4x^2 - 20x + 25$$

Zero as an Exponent
Any nonzero expression to the zero power equals 1.
(Objective 7.4.1)

$$17^0 = 1 \qquad (5y)^0 = 1, y \neq 0$$

Definition of Negative Exponents
If n is a positive integer and $x \neq 0$, then $x^{-n} = \frac{1}{x^n}$ and $\frac{1}{x^{-n}} = x^n$.
(Objective 7.4.1)

$$x^{-6} = \frac{1}{x^6} \quad \text{and} \quad \frac{1}{x^{-6}} = x^6$$

Rule for Dividing Exponential Expressions
If m and n are integers and $x \neq 0$, then $\frac{x^m}{x^n} = x^{m-n}$.
(Objective 7.4.1)

$$\frac{y^8}{y^3} = y^{8-3} = y^5$$

Scientific Notation
To express a number in scientific notation, write it in the form
$a \cdot 10^n$, where a is a number between 1 and 10 and n is an integer. If the number is greater than 1, the exponent on 10 will be
positive. If the number is less than 1, the exponent on 10 will
be negative.

$$367,000,000 = 3.67 \cdot 10^8$$

$$0.0000059 = 5.9 \cdot 10^{-6}$$

To change a number written in scientific notation to decimal
notation, move the decimal point to the right if the exponent
on 10 is positive and to the left if the exponent on 10 is negative. Move the decimal point the same number of places as the
absolute value of the exponent on 10.   (Objective 7.4.2)

$$2.418 \cdot 10^7 = 24,180,000$$

$$9.06 \cdot 10^{-5} = 0.0000906$$

Chapter Review Exercises

1. Add: $(12y^2 + 17y - 4) + (9y^2 - 13y + 3)$
   $21y^2 + 4y - 1$

2. Multiply: $(5xy^2)(-4x^2y^3)$ $-20x^3y^5$

3. Multiply: $-2x(4x^2 + 7x - 9)$ $-8x^3 - 14x^2 + 18x$

4. Multiply: $(5a - 7)(2a + 9)$ $10a^2 + 31a - 63$

5. Divide: $\dfrac{36x^2 - 42x + 60}{6}$ $6x^2 - 7x + 10$

6. Subtract: $(5x^2 - 2x - 1) - (3x^2 - 5x + 7)$
   $2x^2 + 3x - 8$

7. Simplify: $(-3^2)^3$ -729

8. Multiply: $(x^2 - 5x + 2)(x - 1)$
   $x^3 - 6x^2 + 7x - 2$

9. Multiply: $(a + 7)(a - 7)$ $a^2 - 49$

10. Evaluate: $\dfrac{6^2}{6^{-2}}$ 1296

11. Divide: $(x^2 + x - 42) \div (x + 7)$ $x - 6$

12. Add: $(2x^3 + 7x^2 + x) + (2x^2 - 4x - 12)$
    $2x^3 + 9x^2 - 3x - 12$

13. Multiply: $(6a^2b^5)(3a^6b)$ $18a^8b^6$

14. Multiply: $x^2y(3x^2 - 2x + 12)$
    $3x^4y - 2x^3y + 12x^2y$

15. Multiply: $(2b - 3)(4b + 5)$ $8b^2 - 2b - 15$

16. Divide: $\dfrac{16y^2 - 32y}{-4y}$ $-4y + 8$

17. Subtract: $(13y^3 - 7y - 2) - (12y^2 - 2y - 1)$
    $13y^3 - 12y^2 - 5y - 1$

18. Simplify: $(2^3)^2$ 64

19. Multiply: $(3y^2 + 4y - 7)(2y + 3)$
    $6y^3 + 17y^2 - 2y - 21$

20. Multiply: $(2b - 9)(2b + 9)$ $4b^2 - 81$

21. Simplify: $(a^{-2}b^3c)^2$ $\dfrac{b^6c^2}{a^4}$

22. Divide: $(6y^2 - 35y + 36) \div (3y - 4)$ $2y - 9$

23. Write 0.00000397 in scientific notation.
    $3.97 \cdot 10^{-6}$

24. Multiply: $(xy^5z^3)(x^3y^3z)$ $x^4y^8z^4$

25. Multiply: $(6y^2 - 2y + 9)(-2y^3)$
    $-12y^5 + 4y^4 - 18y^3$

26. Multiply: $(6x - 12)(3x - 2)$ $18x^2 - 48x + 24$

27. Write $6.23 \cdot 10^{-5}$ in decimal notation.   0.0000623

28. Subtract: $(8a^2 - a) - (15a^2 - 4)$ $-7a^2 - a + 4$

29. Simplify: $(-3x^2y^3)^2$ $9x^4y^6$

30. Multiply: $(4a^2 - 3)(3a - 2)$
    $12a^3 - 8a^2 - 9a + 6$

31. Simplify: $(5y - 7)^2$ $25y^2 - 70y + 49$

32. Simplify: $(-3x^{-2}y^{-3})^{-2}$ $\dfrac{x^4y^6}{9}$

33. Divide: $(x^2 + 17x + 64) \div (x + 12)$
    $x + 5 + \dfrac{4}{x + 12}$

34. Write $2.4 \cdot 10^5$ in decimal notation.   240,000

35. Multiply: $(a^2b^7c^6)(ab^3c)(a^3bc^2)$ $a^6b^{11}c^9$

36. Multiply: $2ab^3(4a^2 - 2ab + 3b^2)$
    $8a^3b^3 - 4a^2b^4 + 6ab^5$

37. Multiply: $(3x + 4y)(2x - 5y)$ $6x^2 - 7xy - 20y^2$

38. Divide: $\dfrac{12b^7 + 36b^5 - 3b^3}{3b^3}$ $4b^4 + 12b^2 - 1$

39. Subtract: $(b^2 - 11b + 19) - (5b^2 + 2b - 9)$
    $-4b^2 - 13b + 28$

40. Simplify: $(5a^7b^6)^2(4ab)$ $100a^{15}b^{13}$

41. Multiply: $(6b^3 - 2b^2 - 5)(2b^2 - 1)$
    $12b^5 - 4b^4 - 6b^3 - 8b^2 + 5$

42. Multiply: $(6 - 5x)(6 + 5x)$ $36 - 25x^2$

43. Simplify: $\dfrac{6x^{-2}y^4}{3xy}$ $\dfrac{2y^3}{x^3}$

44. Divide: $(a^3 + a^2 + 18) \div (a + 3)$ $a^2 - 2a + 6$

45. Add: $(4b^3 - 7b^2 + 10) + (2b^2 - 9b - 3)$
    $4b^3 - 5b^2 - 9b + 7$

46. Multiply: $(2a^{12}b^3)(-9b^2c^6)(3ac)$ $-54a^{13}b^5c^7$

47. Multiply: $-9x^2(2x^2 + 3x - 7)$
    $-18x^4 - 27x^3 + 63x^2$

48. Multiply: $(10y - 3)(3y - 10)$
    $30y^2 - 109y + 30$

49. Write 9,176,000,000,000 in scientific notation.
$9.176 \cdot 10^{12}$

50. Subtract: $(6y^2 + 2y + 7) - (8y^2 + y + 12)$
$-2y^2 + y - 5$

51. Simplify: $(6x^4y^7z^2)^2(-2x^3y^2z^6)^2$ $144x^{14}y^{18}z^{16}$

52. Multiply: $(-3x^3 - 2x^2 + x - 9)(4x + 3)$
$-12x^4 - 17x^3 - 2x^2 - 33x - 27$

53. Simplify: $(8a + 1)^2$ $64a^2 + 16a + 1$

54. Simplify: $\dfrac{4a^{-2}b^{-8}}{2a^{-1}b^{-2}}$ $\dfrac{2}{ab^6}$

55. Divide: $(b^3 - 2b^2 - 33b - 7) \div (b - 7)$ $b^2 + 5b + 2 + \dfrac{7}{b-7}$

56. The length of a rectangle is $5x$ m. The width is $(4x - 7)$ m. Find the area of the rectangle in terms of the variable x. $(20x^2 - 35x)$ m^2

57. The length of a side of a square is $(5x + 4)$ in. Find the area of the square in terms of the variable x. $(25x^2 + 40x + 16)$ in^2

58. The base of a triangle is $(3x - 2)$ ft and the height is $(6x + 4)$ ft. Find the area of the triangle in terms of the variable x. $(9x^2 - 4)$ ft^2

59. The radius of a circle is $(x - 6)$ cm. Find the area of the circle in terms of the variable x. Leave the answer in terms of π. $(\pi x^2 - 12\pi x + 36\pi)$ cm^2

60. The width of a rectangle is $(3x - 8)$ mi. The length is $(5x + 4)$ mi. Find the area of the rectangle in terms of the variable x. $(15x^2 - 28x - 32)$ mi^2

Chapter Test

1. Add: $(3x^3 - 2x^2 - 4) + (8x^2 - 8x + 7)$
$3x^3 + 6x^2 - 8x + 3$

2. Multiply: $(-2x^3 + x^2 - 7)(2x - 3)$
$-4x^4 + 8x^3 - 3x^2 - 14x + 21$

3. Multiply: $2x(2x^2 - 3x)$ $4x^3 - 6x^2$

4. Simplify: $(-2a^2b)^3$ $-8a^6b^3$

5. Simplify: $\dfrac{12x^2}{-3x^{-4}}$ $-4x^6$

6. Simplify: $(2ab^{-3})(3a^{-2}b^4)$ $\dfrac{6b}{a}$

7. Subtract: $(3a^2 - 2a - 7) - (5a^3 + 2a - 10)$
$-5a^3 + 3a^2 - 4a + 3$

8. Multiply: $(a - 2b)(a + 5b)$ $a^2 + 3ab - 10b^2$

9. Divide: $\dfrac{16x^5 - 8x^3 + 20x}{4x}$ $4x^4 - 2x^2 + 5$

10. Divide: $(4x^2 - 7) \div (2x - 3)$ $2x + 3 + \dfrac{2}{2x-3}$

11. Multiply: $(-2xy^2)(3x^2y^4)$ $-6x^3y^6$

12. Multiply: $-3y^2(-2y^2 + 3y - 6)$
$6y^4 - 9y^3 + 18y^2$

13. Simplify: $\dfrac{27xy^3}{3x^4y^3}$ $\dfrac{9}{x^3}$

14. Simplify: $(2x - 5)^2$ $4x^2 - 20x + 25$

15. Multiply: $(2x - 7y)(5x - 4y)$
$10x^2 - 43xy + 28y^2$

16. Multiply: $(x - 3)(x^2 - 4x + 5)$
$x^3 - 7x^2 + 17x - 15$

17. Simplify: $(a^2b^{-3})^2$ $\dfrac{a^4}{b^6}$

18. Write 0.000029 in scientific notation. $2.9 \cdot 10^{-5}$

19. Multiply: $(4y - 3)(4y + 3)$ $16y^2 - 9$

20. Subtract: $(3y^3 - 5y + 8) - (-2y^2 + 5y + 8)$
$3y^3 + 2y^2 - 10y$

21. Simplify: $(-3a^3b^2)^2$ $9a^6b^4$

22. Multiply: $(2a - 7)(5a^2 - 2a + 3)$
$10a^3 - 39a^2 + 20a - 21$

23. Simplify: $(3b + 2)^2$ $9b^2 + 12b + 4$

24. Simplify: $\dfrac{-2a^2b^3}{8a^4b^8}$ $-\dfrac{1}{4a^2b^5}$

25. Divide: $(8x^2 + 4x - 3) \div (2x - 3)$
$4x + 8 + \dfrac{21}{2x - 3}$

26. Multiply: $(a^2b^5)(ab^2)$ a^3b^7

27. Multiply: $(a - 3b)(a + 4b)$ $a^2 + ab - 12b^2$

28. Write $3.5 \cdot 10^{-8}$ in decimal notation.
0.000000035

29. The length of a side of a square is $(2x + 3)$ m. Find the area of the square in terms of the variable x. $(4x^2 + 12x + 9)$ m^2

30. The radius of a circle is $(x - 5)$ in. Find the area of the circle in terms of the variable x. Leave the answer in terms of π. $(\pi x^2 - 10\pi x + 25\pi)$ in^2

Cumulative Review Exercises

1. Simplify: $\dfrac{3}{16} - \left(-\dfrac{3}{8}\right) - \dfrac{5}{9}$ $\dfrac{1}{144}$

2. Simplify: $-5^2 \cdot \left(\dfrac{2}{3}\right)^3 \cdot \left(-\dfrac{3}{8}\right)$ $\dfrac{25}{9}$

3. Simplify: $\left(-\dfrac{1}{2}\right)^2 \div \left(\dfrac{5}{8} - \dfrac{5}{6}\right) + 2$ $\dfrac{4}{5}$

4. Find the opposite of -87.   87

5. Write $\dfrac{31}{40}$ as a decimal.   0.775

6. Evaluate $\dfrac{b - (a - b)^2}{b^2}$ when $a = 3$ and $b = -2$. $-\dfrac{27}{4}$

7. Simplify: $-3x - (-xy) + 2x - 5xy$ $-x - 4xy$

8. Simplify: $(16x)\left(-\dfrac{3}{4}\right)$ $-12x$

9. Simplify: $-2[3x - 4(3 - 2x) + 2]$ $-22x + 20$

10. Complete the statement by using the Inverse Property of Addition.
$-8 + ? = 0$ 8

11. Solve: $12 = -\dfrac{2}{3}x$ -18

12. Solve: $3x - 7 = 2x + 9$ 16

13. Solve: $3 - 4(2 - x) = 3x + 7$ 12

14. Solve: $-\dfrac{4}{5}x = 16 - x$ 80

15. 38.4 is what percent of 160?   24%

16. Solve: $7x - 8 \geq -29$ $x \geq -3$

17. Find the slope of the line that contains the points whose coordinates are $(3, -4)$ and $(-2, 5)$. $-\dfrac{9}{5}$

18. Find the equation of the line that contains the point whose coordinates are $(1, -3)$ and has slope $-\dfrac{3}{2}$. $y = -\dfrac{3}{2}x - \dfrac{3}{2}$

19. Graph: $3x - 2y = -6$

20. Graph the solution set of

$$y \le \frac{4}{5}x - 3.$$

21. Find the domain and range of the relation $\{(-8, -7), (-6, -5), (-4, -2), (-2, 0)\}$. Is the relation a function?

D: $\{-8, -6, -4, -2\}$; R: $\{-7, -5, -2, 0\}$; yes

22. Evaluate $f(x) = -2x + 10$ at $x = 6$. -2

23. Solve by substitution: $x = 3y + 1$
(4, 1) $2x + 5y = 13$

24. Solve by the addition method: $9x - 2y = 17$
(1, −4) $5x + 3y = -7$

25. Subtract: $(5b^3 - 4b^2 - 7) - (3b^2 - 8b + 3)$
$5b^3 - 7b^2 + 8b - 10$

26. Multiply: $(3x - 4)(5x^2 - 2x + 1)$
$15x^3 - 26x^2 + 11x - 4$

27. Multiply: $(4b - 3)(5b - 8)$ $20b^2 - 47b + 24$

28. Simplify: $(5b + 3)^2$ $25b^2 + 30b + 9$

29. Simplify: $\dfrac{-3a^3b^2}{12a^4b^{-2}}$ $-\dfrac{b^4}{4a}$

30. Divide: $\dfrac{-15y^2 + 12y - 3}{-3y}$ $5y - 4 + \dfrac{1}{y}$

31. Divide: $(a^2 - 3a - 28) \div (a + 4)$ $a - 7$

32. Simplify: $(-3x^{-4}y)(-3x^{-2}y)$ $\dfrac{9y^2}{x^6}$

33. Find the range of the function given by the equation $f(x) = -\dfrac{4}{3}x + 9$ if the domain is $\{-12, -9, -6, 0, 6\}$. $\{1, 9, 17, 21, 25\}$

34. Translate and simplify "the product of five and the difference between a number and twelve." $5(n - 12); 5n - 60$

35. Translate "the difference between eight times a number and twice the number is eighteen" into an equation and solve. $8n - 2n = 18; n = 3$

36. The width of a rectangle is 40% of the length. The perimeter of the rectangle is 42 m. Find the length and width of the rectangle.   Length: 15 m; width: 6 m

37. A calculator costs a retailer $24. Find the selling price when the markup rate is 80%. $43.20

38. Fifty ounces of pure orange juice are added to 200 oz of a fruit punch that is 10% orange juice. What is the percent concentration of orange juice in the resulting mixture?   28%

39. A car traveling at 50 mph overtakes a cyclist who, riding at 10 mph, has had a 2-hour head start. How far from the starting point does the car overtake the cyclist?   25 mi

40. The length of a side of a square is $(3x + 2)$ ft. Find the area of the square in terms of the variable x. $(9x^2 + 12x + 4)$ ft²

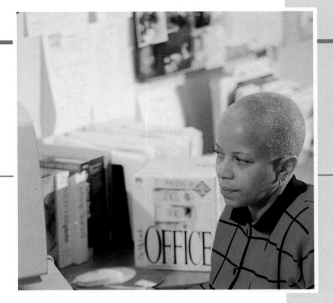

8

Factoring

Technical writers translate technological information into easily understood language for use in training manuals, public relations brochures, and the like. The computer industry uses software technical writers to explain the programs that computers run. Generally these technical writers need to learn from programmers how things work before they write the descriptions. It is common for software technical writers to have a liberal arts degree with some courses in mathematics and science, which help them understand technical instructions.

Algebra from Geometry

The early Babylonians made substantial progress in both algebra and geometry. Often the progress they made in algebra was based on geometric concepts.

Some geometric proofs of algebraic identities are shown below.

$$(a - b)^2 = a^2 - 2ab + b^2$$

$$(a + b)^2 = a^2 + 2ab + b^2$$

$$(a - b)(a + b) = a^2 - b^2$$

S E C T I O N **8.1**

Common Factors

1 Factor a monomial from a polynomial

The **greatest common factor (GCF)** of two or more integers is the greatest integer that is a factor of all the integers.

$24 = 2 \cdot 2 \cdot 2 \cdot 3$
$60 = 2 \cdot 2 \cdot 3 \cdot 5$
$\text{GCF} = 2 \cdot 2 \cdot 3 = 12$

The GCF of two or more monomials is the product of the GCF of the coefficients and the common variable factors.

$6x^3y = 2 \cdot 3 \cdot x \cdot x \cdot x \cdot y$
$8x^2y^2 = 2 \cdot 2 \cdot 2 \cdot x \cdot x \cdot y \cdot y$
$\text{GCF} = 2 \cdot x \cdot x \cdot y = 2x^2y$

Note that the exponent of each variable in the GCF is the same as the *smallest* exponent of that variable in either of the monomials.

The GCF of $6x^3y$ and $8x^2y^2$ is $2x^2y$.

Example 1 Find the GCF of $12a^4b$ and $18a^2b^2c$.

Solution $12a^4b = 2 \cdot 2 \cdot 3 \cdot a^4 \cdot b$ ▶ Factor each monomial.
$18a^2b^2c = 2 \cdot 3 \cdot 3 \cdot a^2 \cdot b^2 \cdot c$

$\text{GCF} = 2 \cdot 3 \cdot a^2 \cdot b = 6a^2b$ ▶ The common variable factors are a^2 and b. c is not a common factor.

Problem 1 Find the GCF of $4x^6y$ and $18x^2y^6$.

Solution See page S16. $2x^2y$

The Distributive Property is used to multiply factors of a polynomial. To **factor a polynomial** means to write the polynomial as a product of other polynomials.

```
                  ┌──── Multiply ────┐
                  │                  ↓
     Factors                    Polynomial
     2x(x + 5)        =          2x² + 10x
                  ↑                  │
                  └──── Factor ──────┘
```

In the example above, $2x$ is the GCF of the terms $2x^2$ and $10x$. It is a **common monomial factor** of the terms. $x + 5$ is a **binomial factor** of $2x^2 + 10x$.

Example 2 Factor.   A. $5x^3 - 35x^2 + 10x$ B. $16x^2y + 8x^4y^2 - 12x^4y^5$

Solution A. The GCF is $5x$. ▶ Find the GCF of the terms of the polynomial.

$\dfrac{5x^3}{5x} = x^2, \dfrac{-35x^2}{5x} = -7x, \dfrac{10x}{5x} = 2$ ▶ Divide each term of the polynomial by the GCF.

$5x^3 - 35x^2 + 10x$ ▶ Use the quotients to rewrite the polynomial, expressing each term as a product with the GCF as one of the factors.
$= 5x(x^2) + 5x(-7x) + 5x(2)$

$= 5x(x^2 - 7x + 2)$ ▶ Use the Distributive Property to write the polynomial as a product of factors.

B. $16x^2y = 2 \cdot 2 \cdot 2 \cdot 2 \cdot x^2 \cdot y$
$8x^4y^2 = 2 \cdot 2 \cdot 2 \cdot x^4 \cdot y^2$
$12x^4y^5 = 2 \cdot 2 \cdot 3 \cdot x^4 \cdot y^5$
The GCF is $4x^2y$.

$16x^2y + 8x^4y^2 - 12x^4y^5$
$= 4x^2y(4) + 4x^2y(2x^2y) + 4x^2y(-3x^2y^4)$
$= 4x^2y(4 + 2x^2y - 3x^2y^4)$

Problem 2 Factor.   A. $14a^2 - 21a^4b$ B. $6x^4y^2 - 9x^3y^2 + 12x^2y^4$

Solution See page S16.   A. $7a^2(2 - 3a^2b)$ B. $3x^2y^2(2x^2 - 3x + 4y^2)$

2 Factor by grouping

In the examples below, the binomials in parentheses are called **binomial factors**.

$$2a(a + b)$$
$$3xy(x - y)$$

The Distributive Property is used to factor a common binomial factor from an expression.

In the expression at the right, the common binomial factor is $y - 3$. The Distributive Property is used to write the expression as a product of factors.

$x(y - 3) + 4(y - 3)$
$= (y - 3)(x + 4)$

Example 3 Factor: $y(x + 2) + 3(x + 2)$

Solution $y(x + 2) + 3(x + 2)$ ▶ The common binomial factor is $x + 2$.
$= (x + 2)(y + 3)$

Problem 3 Factor: $a(b - 7) + b(b - 7)$

Solution See page S16. $(b - 7)(a + b)$

INSTRUCTOR NOTE
It will help students to give them examples of inserting parentheses into expressions before they try the examples that follow. Here are some suggestions.

$-a + 2b = -(a - 2b)$
$3x - 2y = -(-3x + 2y)$
$-4a - 3b = -(4a + 3b)$

Sometimes a binomial factor must be rewritten before a common binomial factor can be found.

▶ Factor: $a(a - b) + 5(b - a)$

$a - b$ and $b - a$ are different binomials.

Note that $(b - a) = (-a + b) = -(a - b)$.

Rewrite $(b - a)$ as $-(a - b)$ so that there is a common factor.

$$a(a - b) + 5(b - a) = a(a - b) + 5[-(a - b)]$$
$$= a(a - b) - 5(a - b)$$
$$= (a - b)(a - 5)$$

Example 4   Factor: $2x(x - 5) + y(5 - x)$

Solution $2x(x - 5) + y(5 - x)$
$= 2x(x - 5) - y(x - 5)$ ▶ Rewrite $5 - x$ as $-(x - 5)$ so that there is a common factor.

$= (x - 5)(2x - y)$ ▶ Write the expression as a product of factors.

Problem 4   Factor: $3y(5x - 2) - 4(2 - 5x)$

Solution   See page S16. $(5x - 2)(3y + 4)$

Some polynomials can be factored by grouping the terms so that a common binomial factor is found.

▶ Factor: $2x^3 - 3x^2 + 4x - 6$

Group the first two terms and the last two terms.

Factor out the GCF from each group.

Write the expression as a product of factors.

$2x^3 - 3x^2 + 4x - 6$
$= (2x^3 - 3x^2) + (4x - 6)$

$= x^2(2x - 3) + 2(2x - 3)$

$= (2x - 3)(x^2 + 2)$ ◀

Example 5   Factor: $3y^3 - 4y^2 - 6y + 8$

Solution $3y^3 - 4y^2 - 6y + 8$
$= (3y^3 - 4y^2) - (6y - 8)$ ▶ Group the first two terms and the last two terms. Note that $-6y + 8 = -(6y - 8)$.

$= y^2(3y - 4) - 2(3y - 4)$ ▶ Factor out the GCF from each group.
$= (3y - 4)(y^2 - 2)$ ▶ Write the expression as a product of factors.

Problem 5   Factor: $y^5 - 5y^3 + 4y^2 - 20$

Solution   See page S16. $(y^2 - 5)(y^3 + 4)$

CONCEPT REVIEW 8.1

Determine whether the statement is always true, sometimes true, or never true.

1. To factor a polynomial means to rewrite it as multiplication.   Always true

2. The expression $3x(x + 5)$ is a sum, and the expression $3x^2 + 15x$ is a product.
   Never true

3. The greatest common factor of two numbers is the largest number that divides evenly into both numbers.   Always true

4. x is a monomial factor of $x(2x - 1)$. $2x - 1$ is a binomial factor of $x(2x - 1)$.
   Always true

5. $y(y + 4) + 6$ is in factored form.   Never true

6. A common monomial factor is a factor of every term of a polynomial.
Always true

7. $a^2 - 8a - ab + 8b = a(a - 8) - b(a + 8)$ Never true

8. The binomial $d + 9$ is a common binomial factor in $2c(d + 9) - 7(d + 9)$.
Always true

EXERCISES 8.1

1   1.   ✍   Explain the meaning of "a factor" and the meaning of "to factor."

2.   ✍   Explain why the statement is true.
   a. The terms of the binomial $3x - 6$ have a common factor.
   b. The expression $3x^2 + 15$ is not in factored form.
   c. $5y - 7$ is a factor of $y(5y - 7)$.

Find the greatest common factor.

3. x^7, x^3 x^3

4. y^6, y^{12} y^6

5. x^2y^4, xy^6 xy^4

6. a^5b^3, a^3b^8 a^3b^3

7. $x^2y^4z^6, xy^8z^2$ xy^4z^2

8. ab^2c^3, a^3b^2c ab^2c

9. $14a^3, 49a^7$ $7a^3$

10. $12y^2, 27y^4$ $3y^2$

11. $3x^2y^2, 5ab^2$ 1

12. $8x^2y^3, 7ab^4$ 1

13. $9a^2b^4, 24a^4b^2$ $3a^2b^2$

14. $15a^4b^2, 9ab^5$ $3ab^2$

15. $ab^3, 4a^2b, 12a^2b^3$ ab

16. $12x^2y, x^4y, 16x$ x

17. $2x^2y, 4xy, 8x$ $2x$

18. $16x^2, 8x^4y^2, 12xy$ $4x$

19. $3x^2y^2, 6x, 9x^3y^3$ $3x$

20. $4a^2b^3, 8a^3, 12ab^4$ $4a$

Factor.

21. $5a + 5$
$5(a + 1)$

22. $7b - 7$
$7(b - 1)$

23. $16 - 8a^2$
$8(2 - a^2)$

24. $12 + 12y^2$
$12(1 + y^2)$

25. $8x + 12$
$4(2x + 3)$

26. $16a - 24$
$8(2a - 3)$

27. $30a - 6$
$6(5a - 1)$

28. $20b + 5$
$5(4b + 1)$

29. $7x^2 - 3x$
$x(7x - 3)$

30. $12y^2 - 5y$
$y(12y - 5)$

31. $3a^2 + 5a^5$
$a^2(3 + 5a^3)$

32. $9x - 5x^2$
$x(9 - 5x)$

33. $14y^2 + 11y$
$y(14y + 11)$

34. $6b^3 - 5b^2$
$b^2(6b - 5)$

35. $2x^4 - 4x$
$2x(x^3 - 2)$

36. $3y^4 - 9y$
$3y(y^3 - 3)$

37. $10x^4 - 12x^2$
$2x^2(5x^2 - 6)$

38. $12a^5 - 32a^2$
$4a^2(3a^3 - 8)$

39. $x^2y - xy^3$
$xy(x - y^2)$

40. $a^2b + a^4b^2$
$a^2b(1 + a^2b)$

41. $2a^5b + 3xy^3$
$2a^5b + 3xy^3$

42. $5x^2y - 7ab^3$
$5x^2y - 7ab^3$

43. $6a^2b^3 - 12b^2$
$6b^2(a^2b - 2)$

44. $8x^2y^3 - 4x^2$
$4x^2(2y^3 - 1)$

45. $6a^2bc + 4ab^2c$
$2abc(3a + 2b)$

46. $10x^2yz^2 + 15xy^3z$
$5xyz(2xz + 3y^2)$

47. $18x^2y^2 - 9a^2b^2$
$9(2x^2y^2 - a^2b^2)$

48. $9a^2x - 27a^3x^3$
$9a^2x(1 - 3ax^2)$

49. $6x^3y^3 - 12x^6y^6$
$6x^3y^3(1 - 2x^3y^3)$

50. $3a^2b^2 - 12a^5b^5$
$3a^2b^2(1 - 4a^3b^3)$

51. $x^3 - 3x^2 - x$
$x(x^2 - 3x - 1)$

52. $a^3 + 4a^2 + 8a$
$a(a^2 + 4a + 8)$

53. $2x^2 + 8x - 12$
$2(x^2 + 4x - 6)$

54. $a^3 - 3a^2 + 5a$
$a(a^2 - 3a + 5)$

55. $b^3 - 5b^2 - 7b$
$b(b^2 - 5b - 7)$

56. $5x^2 - 15x + 35$
$5(x^2 - 3x + 7)$

57. $8y^2 - 12y + 32$
$4(2y^2 - 3y + 8)$

58. $3x^3 + 6x^2 + 9x$
$3x(x^2 + 2x + 3)$

59. $5y^3 - 20y^2 + 10y$
$5y(y^2 - 4y + 2)$

60. $2x^4 - 4x^3 + 6x^2$
$2x^2(x^2 - 2x + 3)$

61. $3y^4 - 9y^3 - 6y^2$
$3y^2(y^2 - 3y - 2)$

62. $2x^3 + 6x^2 - 14x$
$2x(x^2 + 3x - 7)$

63. $3y^3 - 9y^2 + 24y$
$3y(y^2 - 3y + 8)$

64. $2y^5 - 3y^4 + 7y^3$
$y^3(2y^2 - 3y + 7)$

65. $6a^5 - 3a^3 - 2a^2$
$a^2(6a^3 - 3a - 2)$

66. $x^3y - 3x^2y^2 + 7xy^3$
$xy(x^2 - 3xy + 7y^2)$

67. $8x^2y^2 - 4x^2y + x^2$
$x^2(8y^2 - 4y + 1)$

68. $x^4y^4 - 3x^3y^3 + 6x^2y^2$
$x^2y^2(x^2y^2 - 3xy + 6)$

69. $4x^5y^5 - 8x^4y^4 + x^3y^3$
$x^3y^3(4x^2y^2 - 8xy + 1)$

70. $16x^2y - 8x^3y^4 - 48x^2y^2$
$8x^2y(2 - xy^3 - 6y)$

 Factor.

71. $x(a + b) + 2(a + b)$
$(a + b)(x + 2)$

72. $a(x + y) + 4(x + y)$
$(x + y)(a + 4)$

73. $x(b + 2) - y(b + 2)$
$(b + 2)(x - y)$

74. $a(y - 4) - b(y - 4)$
$(y - 4)(a - b)$

75. $a(x - 2) + 5(2 - x)$
$(x - 2)(a - 5)$

76. $a(x - 7) + b(7 - x)$
$(x - 7)(a - b)$

77. $b(y - 3) + 3(3 - y)$
$(y - 3)(b - 3)$

78. $c(a - 2) - b(2 - a)$
$(a - 2)(c + b)$

79. $a(x - y) - 2(y - x)$
$(x - y)(a + 2)$

80. $3(a - b) - x(b - a)$
$(a - b)(3 + x)$

81. $x^3 + 4x^2 + 3x + 12$
$(x + 4)(x^2 + 3)$

82. $x^3 - 4x^2 - 3x + 12$
$(x - 4)(x^2 - 3)$

83. $2y^3 + 4y^2 + 3y + 6$
$(y + 2)(2y^2 + 3)$

84. $3y^3 - 12y^2 + y - 4$
$(y - 4)(3y^2 + 1)$

85. $ab + 3b - 2a - 6$
$(a + 3)(b - 2)$

86. $yz + 6z - 3y - 18$
$(y + 6)(z - 3)$

87. $x^2a - 2x^2 - 3a + 6$
$(a - 2)(x^2 - 3)$

88. $x^2y + 4x^2 + 3y + 12$
$(y + 4)(x^2 + 3)$

89. $3ax - 3bx - 2ay + 2by$
$(a - b)(3x - 2y)$

90. $8 + 2c + 4a^2 + a^2c$
$(4 + c)(2 + a^2)$

91. $x^2 - 3x + 4ax - 12a$
$(x - 3)(x + 4a)$

92. $t^2 + 4t - st - 4s$
$(t + 4)(t - s)$

93. $xy - 5y - 2x + 10$
$(x - 5)(y - 2)$

94. $2y^2 - 10y + 7xy - 35x$
$(y - 5)(2y + 7x)$

95. $21x^2 + 6xy - 49x - 14y$ $(7x + 2y)(3x - 7)$

96. $4a^2 + 5ab - 10b - 8a$ $(4a + 5b)(a - 2)$

97. $2ra + a^2 - 2r - a$ $(2r + a)(a - 1)$

98. $2ab - 3b^2 - 3b + 2a$ $(2a - 3b)(b + 1)$

99. $4x^2 + 3xy - 12y - 16x$ $(4x + 3y)(x - 4)$

100. $8s + 12r - 6s^2 - 9rs$ $(2s + 3r)(4 - 3s)$

101. $10xy^2 - 15xy + 6y - 9$ $(2y - 3)(5xy + 3)$

102. $10a^2b - 15ab - 4a + 6$ $(2a - 3)(5ab - 2)$

APPLYING CONCEPTS 8.1

Factor by grouping.

103. **a.** $2x^2 + 6x + 5x + 15$ $(x + 3)(2x + 5)$ **b.** $2x^2 + 5x + 6x + 15$ $(2x + 5)(x + 3)$

104. **a.** $3x^2 + 3xy - xy - y^2$ $(x + y)(3x - y)$ **b.** $3x^2 - xy + 3xy - y^2$ $(3x - y)(x + y)$

105. **a.** $2a^2 - 2ab - 3ab + 3b^2$ $(a - b)(2a - 3b)$ **b.** $2a^2 - 3ab - 2ab + 3b^2$ $(2a - 3b)(a - b)$

Compare your answers to parts (a) and (b) of Exercises 103–105 in order to answer Exercise 106.

106. Do different groupings of the terms in a polynomial affect the binomial factoring?   No

A whole number is a perfect number if it is the sum of all of its factors that are less than itself. For example, 6 is a perfect number because all the factors of 6 that are less than 6 are 1, 2, and 3, and $1 + 2 + 3 = 6$.

[C] **107.** Find a perfect number between 20 and 30.   [C] **108.** Find a perfect number between 490 and 500.
28   496

Solve.

[C] **109.** In the equation $P = 2L + 2W$, what is the effect on P when the quantity $L + W$ doubles? P doubles

[C] **110.** Write an expression in factored form for the shaded portion in the diagram.

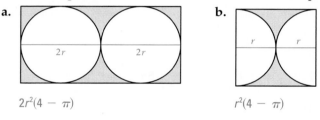

a.

2r   2r

$2r^2(4 - \pi)$

b.

r   r

$r^2(4 - \pi)$

S E C T I O N **8.2**

Factoring Polynomials of the Form $x^2 + bx + c$

1   Factor trinomials of the form $x^2 + bx + c$

Trinomials of the form $x^2 + bx + c$, where b and c are integers, are shown at the right.

$x^2 + 9x + 14$, $b = 9$, $c = 14$
$x^2 - x - 12$, $b = -1$, $c = -12$
$x^2 - 2x - 15$, $b = -2$, $c = -15$

To factor a trinomial of this form means to express the trinomial as the product of two binomials. Some trinomials expressed as the product of binomials (factored form) are shown at the right.

Trinomial	Factored Form
$x^2 + 9x + 14$	$= (x + 2)(x + 7)$
$x^2 - x - 12$	$= (x + 3)(x - 4)$
$x^2 - 2x - 15$	$= (x + 3)(x - 5)$

The method by which the factors of a trinomial are found is based on FOIL. Consider the following binomial products, noting the relationship between the constant terms of the binomials and the terms of the trinomials.

INSTRUCTOR NOTE

Students sometimes see factoring as unrelated to multiplication. Remind students that the relationships between the binomial factors and the terms of the polynomial are based on multiplying binomials.

Signs in the binomials are the same

$$(x + 6)(x + 2) = x^2 + 2x + 6x + (6)(2) = x^2 + 8x + 12$$

Sum of 6 and 2

Product of 6 and 2

$$(x - 3)(x - 4) = x^2 - 4x - 3x + (-3)(-4) = x^2 - 7x + 12$$

Sum of -3 and -4

Product of -3 and -4

Signs in the binomials are opposite

$$(x + 3)(x - 5) = x^2 - 5x + 3x + (3)(-5) = x^2 - 2x - 15$$

Sum of 3 and -5

Product of 3 and -5

$$(x - 4)(x + 6) = x^2 + 6x - 4x + (-4)(6) = x^2 + 2x - 24$$

Sum of -4 and 6

Product of -4 and 6

Points to Remember in Factoring $x^2 + bx + c$

1. In the trinomial, the coefficient of x is the sum of the constant terms of the binomials.
2. In the trinomial, the constant term is the product of the constant terms of the binomials.
3. When the constant term of the trinomial is positive, the constant terms of the binomials have the same sign as the coefficient of x in the trinomial.
4. When the constant term of the trinomial is negative, the constant terms of the binomials have opposite signs.

Success at factoring a trinomial depends on remembering these four points. For example, to factor

$$x^2 - 2x - 24$$

find two numbers whose sum is -2 and whose product is -24 [Points 1 and 2]. Because the constant term of the trinomial is negative (-24), the numbers will have opposite signs [Point 4].

A systematic method of finding these numbers involves listing the factors of the constant term of the trinomial and the sum of those factors.

Factors of -24	Sum of the Factors
1, -24	$1 + (-24) = -23$
-1, 24	$-1 + 24 = 23$
2, -12	$2 + (-12) = -10$
-2, 12	$-2 + 12 = 10$
3, -8	$3 + (-8) = -5$
-3, 8	$-3 + 8 = 5$
4, -6	$4 + (-6) = -2$
-4, 6	$-4 + 6 = 2$

LOOK CLOSELY

Always check your proposed factorization to ensure accuracy.

4 and -6 are two numbers whose sum is -2 and whose product is -24. Write the binomial factors of the trinomial.

$$x^2 - 2x - 24 = (x + 4)(x - 6)$$

Check: $(x + 4)(x - 6) = x^2 - 6x + 4x - 24 = x^2 - 2x - 24$

By the Commutative Property of Multiplication, the binomial factors can also be written as

$$x^2 - 2x - 24 = (x - 6)(x + 4)$$

Example 1   Factor: $x^2 + 18x + 32$

Solution

Factors of 32	Sum
1, 32	33
2, 16	**18**
4, 8	12

▶ Try only positive factors of 32 [Point 3].

▶ Once the correct pair is found, the other factors need not be tried.

$$x^2 + 18x + 32 = (x + 2)(x + 16)$$

▶ Write the factors of the trinomial.

Check $(x + 2)(x + 16) = x^2 + 16x + 2x + 32$
$= x^2 + 18x + 32$

Problem 1   Factor: $x^2 - 8x + 15$

Solution   See page S16. $(x - 3)(x - 5)$

Example 2   Factor: $x^2 - 6x - 16$

Solution

Factors of -16	Sum
1, -16	-15
$-1,\ \ 16$	15
2, -8	**-6**
$-2,\ \ \ 8$	6
4, -4	0

▶ The factors must be of opposite signs [Point 4].

$$x^2 - 6x - 16 = (x + 2)(x - 8)$$

▶ Write the factors of the trinomial.

Check $(x + 2)(x - 8) = x^2 - 8x + 2x - 16$
$= x^2 - 6x - 16$

Problem 2   Factor: $x^2 + 3x - 18$

Solution   See page S17. $(x + 6)(x - 3)$

INSTRUCTOR NOTE

The phrase *nonfactorable over the integers* may require additional examples. Explain that it does not mean the polynomial does not factor; it just does not factor if integers are used. An analogy to numbers may help. For instance, the only ways to write 7 as a product *involving integers* are $1 \cdot 7$ and $(-1)(-7)$. However, $\frac{21}{5} \cdot \frac{5}{3} = 7$. The ability to factor depends on the numbers that can be used.

Not all trinomials can be factored when using only integers. Consider the trinomial $x^2 - 6x - 8$.

Factors of -8	Sum
1, -8	-7
$-1,\ \ 8$	7
2, -4	-2
$-2,\ \ 4$	2

Because none of the pairs of factors of -8 have a sum of -6, the trinomial is not factorable using integers. The trinomial is said to be **nonfactorable over the integers**.

2   Factor completely

A polynomial is factored completely when it is written as a product of factors that are nonfactorable over the integers.

Example 3   Factor: $3x^3 + 15x^2 + 18x$

Solution   The GCF of $3x^3$, $15x^2$, and $18x$ is $3x$.   ▶ Find the GCF of the terms of the polynomial.

$3x^3 + 15x^2 + 18x$
$= 3x(x^2) + 3x(5x) + 3x(6)$ ▶ Factor out the GCF.
$= 3x(x^2 + 5x + 6)$ ▶ Write the polynomial as a product of factors.

Factors of 6	Sum
1, 6	7
2, 3	5

▶ Factor the trinomial $x^2 + 5x + 6$. Try only positive factors of 6.

$3x^3 + 15x^2 + 18x = 3x(x + 2)(x + 3)$

Check $3x(x + 2)(x + 3) = 3x(x^2 + 3x + 2x + 6)$
$= 3x(x^2 + 5x + 6)$
$= 3x^3 + 15x^2 + 18x$

Problem 3   Factor: $3a^2b - 18ab - 81b$

Solution   See page S17. $3b(a + 3)(a - 9)$

Example 4   Factor: $x^2 + 9xy + 20y^2$

Solution   There is no common factor.

Factors of 20	Sum
1, 20	21
2, 10	12
4, 5	9

▶ Try only positive factors of 20.

$x^2 + 9xy + 20y^2 = (x + 4y)(x + 5y)$

Check $(x + 4y)(x + 5y) = x^2 + 5xy + 4xy + 20y^2$
$= x^2 + 9xy + 20y^2$

Problem 4   Factor: $4x^2 - 40xy + 84y^2$

Solution   See page S17. $4(x - 3y)(x - 7y)$

CONCEPT REVIEW 8.2

Determine whether the statement is always true, sometimes true, or never true.

1.   The value of b in the trinomial $x^2 - 8x + 7$ is 8.   Never true

2.   The factored form of $x^2 - 5x - 14$ is $(x - 7)(x + 2)$.   Always true

3. To factor a trinomial of the form $x^2 + bx + c$ means to rewrite the polynomial as a product of two binomials.   Always true

4. In the factoring of a trinomial, if the constant term is positive, then the signs in both binomial factors will be the same.   Always true

5. In the factoring of a trinomial, if the constant term is negative, then the signs in both binomial factors will be negative.   Never true

6. The first step in factoring a trinomial is to determine whether the terms of the trinomial have a common factor.   Always true

EXERCISES 8.2

1 Factor.

1. $x^2 + 3x + 2$
    $(x + 1)(x + 2)$
2. $x^2 + 5x + 6$
    $(x + 2)(x + 3)$
3. $x^2 - x - 2$
    $(x + 1)(x - 2)$
4. $x^2 + x - 6$
    $(x + 3)(x - 2)$
5. $a^2 + a - 12$
    $(a + 4)(a - 3)$
6. $a^2 - 2a - 35$
    $(a + 5)(a - 7)$
7. $a^2 - 3a + 2$
    $(a - 1)(a - 2)$
8. $a^2 - 5a + 4$
    $(a - 1)(a - 4)$
9. $a^2 + a - 2$
    $(a + 2)(a - 1)$
10. $a^2 - 2a - 3$
    $(a + 1)(a - 3)$
11. $b^2 - 6b + 9$
    $(b - 3)(b - 3)$
12. $b^2 + 8b + 16$
    $(b + 4)(b + 4)$
13. $b^2 + 7b - 8$
    $(b + 8)(b - 1)$
14. $y^2 - y - 6$
    $(y + 2)(y - 3)$
15. $y^2 + 6y - 55$
    $(y + 11)(y - 5)$
16. $z^2 - 4z - 45$
    $(z + 5)(z - 9)$
17. $y^2 - 5y + 6$
    $(y - 2)(y - 3)$
18. $y^2 - 8y + 15$
    $(y - 3)(y - 5)$
19. $z^2 - 14z + 45$
    $(z - 5)(z - 9)$
20. $z^2 - 14z + 49$
    $(z - 7)(z - 7)$
21. $z^2 - 12z - 160$
    $(z + 8)(z - 20)$
22. $p^2 + 2p - 35$
    $(p + 7)(p - 5)$
23. $p^2 + 12p + 27$
    $(p + 3)(p + 9)$
24. $p^2 - 6p + 8$
    $(p - 2)(p - 4)$
25. $x^2 + 20x + 100$
    $(x + 10)(x + 10)$
26. $x^2 + 18x + 81$
    $(x + 9)(x + 9)$
27. $b^2 + 9b + 20$
    $(b + 4)(b + 5)$
28. $b^2 + 13b + 40$
    $(b + 5)(b + 8)$
29. $x^2 - 11x - 42$
    $(x + 3)(x - 14)$
30. $x^2 + 9x - 70$
    $(x + 14)(x - 5)$
31. $b^2 - b - 20$
    $(b + 4)(b - 5)$
32. $b^2 + 3b - 40$
    $(b + 8)(b - 5)$
33. $y^2 - 14y - 51$
    $(y + 3)(y - 17)$
34. $y^2 - y - 72$
    $(y + 8)(y - 9)$
35. $p^2 - 4p - 21$
    $(p + 3)(p - 7)$
36. $p^2 + 16p + 39$
    $(p + 3)(p + 13)$
37. $y^2 - 8y + 32$
    Nonfactorable
38. $y^2 - 9y + 81$
    Nonfactorable
39. $x^2 - 20x + 75$
    $(x - 5)(x - 15)$
40. $p^2 + 24p + 63$
    $(p + 3)(p + 21)$
41. $x^2 - 15x + 56$
    $(x - 7)(x - 8)$
42. $x^2 + 21x + 38$
    $(x + 2)(x + 19)$
43. $x^2 + x - 56$
    $(x + 8)(x - 7)$
44. $x^2 + 5x - 36$
    $(x + 9)(x - 4)$
45. $a^2 - 21a - 72$
    $(a + 3)(a - 24)$
46. $a^2 - 7a - 44$
    $(a + 4)(a - 11)$
47. $a^2 - 15a + 36$
    $(a - 3)(a - 12)$
48. $a^2 - 21a + 54$
    $(a - 3)(a - 18)$
49. $z^2 - 9z - 136$
    $(z + 8)(z - 17)$
50. $z^2 + 14z - 147$
    $(z + 21)(z - 7)$
51. $c^2 - c - 90$
    $(c + 9)(c - 10)$
52. $c^2 - 3c - 180$
    $(c + 12)(c - 15)$

2 Factor.

53. $2x^2 + 6x + 4$
    $2(x + 1)(x + 2)$
54. $3x^2 + 15x + 18$
    $3(x + 2)(x + 3)$
55. $3a^2 + 3a - 18$
    $3(a + 3)(a - 2)$
56. $4x^2 - 4x - 8$
    $4(x + 1)(x - 2)$
57. $ab^2 + 2ab - 15a$
    $a(b + 5)(b - 3)$
58. $ab^2 + 7ab - 8a$
    $a(b + 8)(b - 1)$

59. $xy^2 - 5xy + 6x$
$x(y - 2)(y - 3)$

60. $xy^2 + 8xy + 15x$
$x(y + 3)(y + 5)$

61. $z^3 - 7z^2 + 12z$
$z(z - 3)(z - 4)$

62. $2a^3 + 6a^2 + 4a$
$2a(a + 1)(a + 2)$

63. $3y^3 - 15y^2 + 18y$
$3y(y - 2)(y - 3)$

64. $4y^3 + 12y^2 - 72y$
$4y(y + 6)(y - 3)$

65. $3x^2 + 3x - 36$
$3(x + 4)(x - 3)$

66. $2x^3 - 2x^2 - 4x$
$2x(x + 1)(x - 2)$

67. $5z^2 - 15z - 140$
$5(z + 4)(z - 7)$

68. $6z^2 + 12z - 90$
$6(z + 5)(z - 3)$

69. $2a^3 + 8a^2 - 64a$
$2a(a + 8)(a - 4)$

70. $3a^3 - 9a^2 - 54a$
$3a(a + 3)(a - 6)$

71. $x^2 - 5xy + 6y^2$
$(x - 2y)(x - 3y)$

72. $x^2 + 4xy - 21y^2$
$(x + 7y)(x - 3y)$

73. $a^2 - 9ab + 20b^2$
$(a - 4b)(a - 5b)$

74. $a^2 - 15ab + 50b^2$
$(a - 5b)(a - 10b)$

75. $x^2 - 3xy - 28y^2$
$(x + 4y)(x - 7y)$

76. $s^2 + 2st - 48t^2$
$(s + 8t)(s - 6t)$

77. $y^2 - 15yz - 41z^2$
Nonfactorable

78. $y^2 + 85yz + 36z^2$
Nonfactorable

79. $z^4 - 12z^3 + 35z^2$
$z^2(z - 5)(z - 7)$

80. $z^4 + 2z^3 - 80z^2$
$z^2(z + 10)(z - 8)$

81. $b^4 - 22b^3 + 120b^2$
$b^2(b - 10)(b - 12)$

82. $b^4 - 3b^3 - 10b^2$
$b^2(b + 2)(b - 5)$

83. $2y^4 - 26y^3 - 96y^2$
$2y^2(y + 3)(y - 16)$

84. $3y^4 + 54y^3 + 135y^2$
$3y^2(y + 3)(y + 15)$

85. $x^4 + 7x^3 - 8x^2$
$x^2(x + 8)(x - 1)$

86. $x^4 - 11x^3 - 12x^2$
$x^2(x + 1)(x - 12)$

87. $4x^2y + 20xy - 56y$
$4y(x + 7)(x - 2)$

88. $3x^2y - 6xy - 45y$
$3y(x + 3)(x - 5)$

89. $8y^2 - 32y + 24$
$8(y - 1)(y - 3)$

90. $10y^2 - 100y + 90$
$10(y - 1)(y - 9)$

91. $c^3 + 13c^2 + 30c$
$c(c + 3)(c + 10)$

92. $c^3 + 18c^2 - 40c$
$c(c + 20)(c - 2)$

93. $3x^3 - 36x^2 + 81x$
$3x(x - 3)(x - 9)$

94. $4x^3 + 4x^2 - 24x$
$4x(x + 3)(x - 2)$

95. $x^2 - 8xy + 15y^2$
$(x - 3y)(x - 5y)$

96. $y^2 - 7xy - 8x^2$
$(y + x)(y - 8x)$

97. $a^2 - 13ab + 42b^2$
$(a - 6b)(a - 7b)$

98. $y^2 + 4yz - 21z^2$
$(y + 7z)(y - 3z)$

99. $y^2 + 8yz + 7z^2$
$(y + z)(y + 7z)$

100. $y^2 - 16yz + 15z^2$
$(y - z)(y - 15z)$

101. $3x^2y + 60xy - 63y$
$3y(x + 21)(x - 1)$

102. $4x^2y - 68xy - 72y$
$4y(x + 1)(x - 18)$

103. $3x^3 + 3x^2 - 36x$
$3x(x + 4)(x - 3)$

104. $4x^3 + 12x^2 - 160x$
$4x(x + 8)(x - 5)$

105. $4z^3 + 32z^2 - 132z$
$4z(z + 11)(z - 3)$

106. $5z^3 - 50z^2 - 120z$
$5z(z + 2)(z - 12)$

APPLYING CONCEPTS 8.2

Factor.

107. $20 + c^2 + 9c$ $(c + 4)(c + 5)$

108. $x^2y - 54y - 3xy$ $y(x + 6)(x - 9)$

109. $45a^2 + a^2b^2 - 14a^2b$ $a^2(b - 5)(b - 9)$

110. $12p^2 - 96p + 3p^3$ $3p(p + 8)(p - 4)$

Find all integers k such that the trinomial can be factored over the integers.

[C] **111.** $x^2 + kx + 35$ $36, 12, -12, -36$

[C] **112.** $x^2 + kx + 18$ $19, 11, 9, -9, -11, -19$

[C] **113.** $x^2 - kx + 21$ $22, 10, -10, -22$

[C] **114.** $x^2 - kx + 14$ $15, 9, -9, -15$

Determine the positive integer values of k for which the following polynomials are factorable over the integers.

[C] **115.** $y^2 + 4y + k$ 3, 4   [C] **116.** $z^2 + 7z + k$ 6, 10, 12   [C] **117.** $a^2 - 6a + k$ 5, 8, 9

[C] **118.** $c^2 - 7c + k$ 6, 10, 12   [C] **119.** $x^2 - 3x + k$ 2   [C] **120.** $y^2 + 5y + k$ 4, 6

121.   ✏️   Exercises 115–120 included the requirement that $k > 0$. If k is allowed to be any integer, how many different values of k are possible for each polynomial? Explain your answer.

S E C T I O N **8.3**

Factoring Polynomials of the Form $ax^2 + bx + c$

1   Factor trinomials of the form $ax^2 + bx + c$ using trial factors

Trinomials of the form $ax^2 + bx + c$, where a, b, and c are integers and $a \neq 0$, are shown at the right.

$3x^2 - x + 4, \quad a = 3, b = -1, c = 4$
$4x^2 + 5x - 8, a = 4, b = 5, \quad c = -8$

These trinomials differ from those in the previous section in that the coefficient of x^2 is not 1. There are various methods of factoring these trinomials. The method described in this objective is factoring trinomials using trial factors.

To **factor a trinomial of the form** $ax^2 + bx + c$ means to express the polynomial as the product of two binomials. Factoring such polynomials by trial and error may require testing many trial factors. To reduce the number of trial factors, remember the following points.

Points to Remember in Factoring $ax^2 + bx + c$

1. If the terms of the trinomial do not have a common factor, then the terms of a binomial factor cannot have a common factor.
2. When the constant term of the trinomial is positive, the constant terms of the binomials have the same sign as the coefficient of x in the trinomial.
3. When the constant term of the trinomial is negative, the constant terms of the binomials have opposite signs.

⇒ Factor: $10x^2 - x - 3$

The terms of the trinomial do not have a common factor; therefore, a binomial factor will not have a common factor.

Because the constant term, c, of the trinomial is negative (-3), the constant terms of the binomial factors will have opposite signs [Point 3].

Find the factors of a (10) and the factors of c (-3).

Factors of 10	Factors of -3
1, 10	1, -3
2, 5	-1, 3

Using these factors, write trial factors, and use the Outer and Inner products of FOIL to check the middle term.

Trial Factors	Middle Term
$(x + 1)(10x - 3)$	$-3x + 10x = 7x$
$(x - 1)(10x + 3)$	$3x - 10x = -7x$
$\mathbf{(2x + 1)(5x - 3)}$	$\mathbf{-6x + 5x = -x}$
$(2x - 1)(5x + 3)$	$6x - 5x = x$
$(10x + 1)(x - 3)$	$-30x + x = -29x$
$(10x - 1)(x + 3)$	$30x - x = 29x$
$(5x + 1)(2x - 3)$	$-15x + 2x = -13x$
$(5x - 1)(2x + 3)$	$15x - 2x = 13x$

From the list of trial factors, $10x^2 - x - 3 = (2x + 1)(5x - 3)$.

Check: $(2x + 1)(5x - 3) = 10x^2 - 6x + 5x - 3$
$\qquad\qquad\qquad\qquad = 10x^2 - x - 3$

All the trial factors for this trinomial were listed in this example. However, once the correct binomial factors are found, it is not necessary to continue checking the remaining trial factors.

⇨ Factor: $4x^2 - 27x + 18$

The terms of the trinomial do not have a common factor; therefore, a binomial factor will not have a common factor.

Because the constant term, c, of the trinomial is positive (18), the constant terms of the binomial factors will have the same sign as the coefficient of x. Because the coefficient of x is -27, both signs will be negative [Point 2].

Find the factors of a (4) and the negative factors of c (18).

Factors of 4	Factors of 18
1, 4	$-1, -18$
2, 2	$-2, -9$
	$-3, -6$

INSTRUCTOR NOTE

Remind students that eliminating the trial factors that have a common factor requires that the terms of the polynomial do not have a common factor.

Using these factors, write trial factors, and use the Outer and Inner products of FOIL to check the middle term.

Trial Factors	Middle Term
$(x - 1)(4x - 18)$	Common factor
$(x - 2)(4x - 9)$	$-9x - 8x = -17x$
$(x - 3)(4x - 6)$	Common factor
$(2x - 1)(2x - 18)$	Common factor
$(2x - 2)(2x - 9)$	Common factor
$(2x - 3)(2x - 6)$	Common factor
$(4x - 1)(x - 18)$	$-72x - x = -73x$
$(4x - 2)(x - 9)$	Common factor
$\mathbf{(4x - 3)(x - 6)}$	$\mathbf{-24x - 3x = -27x}$

The correct factors have been found. The remaining trial factors need not be checked.

$$4x^2 - 27x + 18 = (4x - 3)(x - 6)$$

This last example illustrates that many of the trial factors may have common factors and thus need not be tried. For the remainder of this chapter, the trial factors with a common factor will not be listed.

Example 1 Factor: $3x^2 + 20x + 12$

Solution

Factors of 3	Factors of 12
1, 3	1, 12
	2, 6
	3, 4

▶ Because 20 is positive, only the positive factors of 12 need be tried.

Trial Factors	Middle Term
$(x + 3)(3x + 4)$	$4x + 9x = 13x$
$(3x + 1)(x + 12)$	$36x + x = 37x$
$(3x + 2)(x + 6)$	$18x + 2x = 20x$

▶ Write the trial factors. Use FOIL to check the middle term.

$$3x^2 + 20x + 12 = (3x + 2)(x + 6)$$

Check $(3x + 2)(x + 6) = 3x^2 + 18x + 2x + 12$
$$= 3x^2 + 20x + 12$$

Problem 1 Factor: $6x^2 - 11x + 5$

Solution See page S17. $(x - 1)(6x - 5)$

Example 2 Factor: $6x^2 - 5x - 6$

Solution

Factors of 6	Factors of −6
1, 6	1, −6
2, 3	−1, 6
	2, −3
	−2, 3

▶ Find the factors of a (6) and the factors of c (−6).

Trial Factors	Middle Term
$(x - 6)(6x + 1)$	$x - 36x = -35x$
$(x + 6)(6x - 1)$	$-x + 36x = 35x$
$(2x - 3)(3x + 2)$	$4x - 9x = -5x$

▶ Write the trial factors. Use FOIL to check the middle term.

$$6x^2 - 5x - 6 = (2x - 3)(3x + 2)$$

Check $(2x - 3)(3x + 2) = 6x^2 + 4x - 9x - 6$
$$= 6x^2 - 5x - 6$$

Problem 2 Factor: $8x^2 + 14x - 15$

Solution See page S17. $(4x - 3)(2x + 5)$

Example 3   Factor: $15 - 2x - x^2$

Solution

Factors of 15	Factors of -1
1, 15	1, -1
3, 5	

▶ The terms have no common factors. The coefficient of x^2 is -1.

Trial Factors	Middle Term
$(1 + x)(15 - x)$	$-x + 15x = 14x$
$(1 - x)(15 + x)$	$x - 15x = -14x$
$(3 + x)(5 - x)$	$-3x + 5x = 2x$
$(3 - x)(5 + x)$	$3x - 5x = -2x$

▶ Write the trial factors. Use FOIL to check the middle term.

$$15 - 2x - x^2 = (3 - x)(5 + x)$$

Check $(3 - x)(5 + x) = 15 + 3x - 5x - x^2$
$$= 15 - 2x - x^2$$

Problem 3   Factor: $24 - 2y - y^2$

Solution   See page S17. $(4 - y)(6 + y)$

The first step in factoring a trinomial is to determine whether there is a common factor. If there is a common factor, factor out the GCF of the terms.

Example 4   Factor: $3x^3 - 23x^2 + 14x$

Solution   The GCF of $3x^3$, $23x^2$, and $14x$ is x.

▶ Find the GCF of the terms of the polynomial.

$$3x^3 - 23x^2 + 14x = x(3x^2 - 23x + 14)$$

▶ Factor out the GCF.

Factors of 3	Factors of 14
1, 3	$-1, -14$
	$-2, -7$

▶ Factor the trinomial $3x^2 - 23x + 14$.

Trial Factors	Middle Term
$(x - 1)(3x - 14)$	$-14x - 3x = -17x$
$(x - 14)(3x - 1)$	$-x - 42x = -43x$
$(x - 2)(3x - 7)$	$-7x - 6x = -13x$
$(x - 7)(3x - 2)$	$-2x - 21x = -23x$

$$3x^3 - 23x^2 + 14x = x(x - 7)(3x - 2)$$

Check $x(x - 7)(3x - 2) = x(3x^2 - 2x - 21x + 14)$
$$= x(3x^2 - 23x + 14)$$
$$= 3x^3 - 23x^2 + 14x$$

Problem 4   Factor: $4a^2b^2 - 30a^2b + 14a^2$

Solution   See page S17. $2a^2(b - 7)(2b - 1)$

2 Factor trinomials of the form $ax^2 + bx + c$ by grouping

In the previous objective, trinomials of the form $ax^2 + bx + c$ were factored using trial factors. In this objective, factoring by grouping is used.

To factor $ax^2 + bx + c$, first find two factors of $a \cdot c$ whose sum is b. Use the two factors to rewrite the middle term of the trinomial as the sum of two terms. Then use factoring by grouping to write the factorization of the trinomial.

Factor: $2x^2 + 13x + 15$

$a = 2, c = 15, a \cdot c = 2 \cdot 15 = 30$

Find two positive factors of 30 whose sum is 13.

Positive Factors of 30	Sum
1, 30	31
2, 15	17
3, 10	13
5, 6	11

The factors are 3 and 10.

Use the factors 3 and 10 to rewrite $13x$ as $3x + 10x$.

$$2x^2 + \quad 13x \quad + 15$$
$$= 2x^2 + 3x + 10x + 15$$

Factor by grouping.

$$= (2x^2 + 3x) + (10x + 15)$$
$$= x(2x + 3) + 5(2x + 3)$$
$$= (2x + 3)(x + 5)$$

Check: $(2x + 3)(x + 5) = 2x^2 + 10x + 3x + 15$
$$= 2x^2 + 13x + 15$$

Factor: $6x^2 - 11x - 10$

$a = 6, c = -10, a \cdot c = 6(-10) = -60$

Find two factors of -60 whose sum is -11.

Factors of -60	Sum
1, -60	-59
-1, 60	59
2, -30	-28
-2, 30	28
3, -20	-17
-3, 20	17
4, -15	-11

The required sum has been found. The remaining factors need not be checked. The factors are 4 and -15.

Use the factors 4 and -15 to rewrite $-11x$ as $4x - 15x$.

$$6x^2 - \quad 11x \quad - 10$$
$$= 6x^2 + 4x - 15x - 10$$

Factor by grouping.
Note: $-15x - 10 = -(15x + 10)$

$$= (6x^2 + 4x) - (15x + 10)$$
$$= 2x(3x + 2) - 5(3x + 2)$$
$$= (3x + 2)(2x - 5)$$

Check: $(3x + 2)(2x - 5) = 6x^2 - 15x + 4x - 10$
$$= 6x^2 - 11x - 10$$

⇒ Factor: $3x^2 - 2x - 4$

$a = 3, c = -4, a \cdot c = 3(-4) = -12$

Find two factors of -12 whose sum is -2.

Factors of -12	Sum
1, -12	-11
-1, 12	11
2, -6	-4
-2, 6	4
3, -4	-1
-3, 4	1

No integer factors of -12 have a sum of -2. Therefore, $3x^2 - 2x - 4$ is nonfactorable over the integers.

Example 5   Factor: $2x^2 + 19x - 10$

Solution $a \cdot c = 2(-10) = -20$ ▶ Find $a \cdot c$.

$-1(20) = -20$ ▶ Find two numbers whose product is
$-1 + 20 = 19$ -20 and whose sum is 19.

$2x^2 + 19x - 10$
$= 2x^2 - x + 20x - 10$ ▶ Rewrite $19x$ as $-x + 20x$.
$= (2x^2 - x) + (20x - 10)$ ▶ Factor by grouping.
$= x(2x - 1) + 10(2x - 1)$
$= (2x - 1)(x + 10)$

Problem 5   Factor: $2a^2 + 13a - 7$

Solution   See page S18. $(2a - 1)(a + 7)$

Example 6   Factor: $8y^2 - 10y - 3$

Solution $a \cdot c = 8(-3) = -24$ ▶ Find $a \cdot c$.

$2(-12) = -24$ ▶ Find two numbers whose product is
$2 + (-12) = -10$ -24 and whose sum is -10.

$8y^2 - 10y - 3$
$= 8y^2 + 2y - 12y - 3$ ▶ Rewrite $-10y$ as $2y - 12y$.
$= (8y^2 + 2y) - (12y + 3)$ ▶ Factor by grouping.
$= 2y(4y + 1) - 3(4y + 1)$
$= (4y + 1)(2y - 3)$

Problem 6   Factor: $4a^2 - 11a - 3$

Solution   See page S18. $(4a + 1)(a - 3)$

Remember that the first step in factoring a trinomial is to determine whether there is a common factor. If there is a common factor, factor out the GCF of the terms.

Example 7   Factor: $24x^2y - 76xy + 40y$

Solution $24x^2y - 76xy + 40y$
$= 4y(6x^2 - 19x + 10)$
▶ The terms of the polynomial have a common factor, $4y$. Factor out the GCF.

$a \cdot c = 6(10) = 60$
▶ To factor $6x^2 - 19x + 10$, first find $a \cdot c$.

$-4(-15) = 60$
$-4 + (-15) = -19$
▶ Find two numbers whose product is 60 and whose sum is -19.

$6x^2 - 19x + 10$
$= 6x^2 - 4x - 15x + 10$
$= (6x^2 - 4x) - (15x - 10)$
$= 2x(3x - 2) - 5(3x - 2)$
$= (3x - 2)(2x - 5)$
▶ Rewrite $-19x$ as $-4x - 15x$.
▶ Factor by grouping.

$24x^2y - 76xy + 40y$
$= 4y(6x^2 - 19x + 10)$
$= 4y(3x - 2)(2x - 5)$
▶ Write the complete factorization of the given polynomial.

Problem 7   Factor: $15x^3 + 40x^2 - 80x$

Solution   See page S18. $5x(3x - 4)(x + 4)$

CONCEPT REVIEW 8.3

Determine whether the statement is always true, sometimes true, or never true.

1. The value of a in the trinomial $3x^2 + 8x - 7$ is -7.   Never true

2. The factored form of $2x^2 - 7x - 15$ is $(2x + 3)(x - 5)$.   Always true

3. To check the factorization of a trinomial of the form $ax^2 + bx + c$, multiply the two binomial factors.   Sometimes true

4. The terms of the binomial $3x - 9$ have a common factor.   Always true

5. If the terms of a trinomial of the form $ax^2 + bx + c$ do not have a common factor, then one of its binomial factors cannot have a common factor.
    Always true

6. To factor a trinomial of the form $ax^2 + bx + c$ by grouping, first find two numbers whose product is ac and whose sum is b.   Always true

---

EXERCISES 8.3

1 Factor by the method of using trial factors.

1. $2x^2 + 3x + 1$
    $(x + 1)(2x + 1)$
2. $5x^2 + 6x + 1$
    $(x + 1)(5x + 1)$
3. $2y^2 + 7y + 3$
    $(y + 3)(2y + 1)$
4. $3y^2 + 7y + 2$
    $(y + 2)(3y + 1)$
5. $2a^2 - 3a + 1$
    $(a - 1)(2a - 1)$
6. $3a^2 - 4a + 1$
    $(a - 1)(3a - 1)$
7. $2b^2 - 11b + 5$
    $(b - 5)(2b - 1)$
8. $3b^2 - 13b + 4$
    $(b - 4)(3b - 1)$

9. $2x^2 + x - 1$
$(x + 1)(2x - 1)$

10. $4x^2 - 3x - 1$
$(x - 1)(4x + 1)$

11. $2x^2 - 5x - 3$
$(x - 3)(2x + 1)$

12. $3x^2 + 5x - 2$
$(x + 2)(3x - 1)$

13. $6z^2 - 7z + 3$
Nonfactorable

14. $9z^2 + 3z + 2$
Nonfactorable

15. $6t^2 - 11t + 4$
$(2t - 1)(3t - 4)$

16. $10t^2 + 11t + 3$
$(2t + 1)(5t + 3)$

17. $8x^2 + 33x + 4$
$(x + 4)(8x + 1)$

18. $7x^2 + 50x + 7$
$(x + 7)(7x + 1)$

19. $3b^2 - 16b + 16$
$(b - 4)(3b - 4)$

20. $6b^2 - 19b + 15$
$(2b - 3)(3b - 5)$

21. $2z^2 - 27z - 14$
$(z - 14)(2z + 1)$

22. $4z^2 + 5z - 6$
$(z + 2)(4z - 3)$

23. $3p^2 + 22p - 16$
$(p + 8)(3p - 2)$

24. $7p^2 + 19p + 10$
$(p + 2)(7p + 5)$

25. $6x^2 - 17x + 12$
$(2x - 3)(3x - 4)$

26. $15x^2 - 19x + 6$
$(3x - 2)(5x - 3)$

27. $5b^2 + 33b - 14$
$(b + 7)(5b - 2)$

28. $8x^2 - 30x + 25$
$(2x - 5)(4x - 5)$

29. $6a^2 + 7a - 24$
$(2a - 3)(3a + 8)$

30. $14a^2 + 15a - 9$
$(2a + 3)(7a - 3)$

31. $18t^2 - 9t - 5$
$(3t + 1)(6t - 5)$

32. $12t^2 + 28t - 5$
$(2t + 5)(6t - 1)$

33. $15a^2 + 26a - 21$
$(3a + 7)(5a - 3)$

34. $6a^2 + 23a + 21$
$(2a + 3)(3a + 7)$

35. $8y^2 - 26y + 15$
$(2y - 5)(4y - 3)$

36. $18y^2 - 27y + 4$
$(3y - 4)(6y - 1)$

37. $8z^2 + 2z - 15$
$(2z + 3)(4z - 5)$

38. $10z^2 + 3z - 4$
$(2z - 1)(5z + 4)$

39. $3x^2 + 14x - 5$
$(x + 5)(3x - 1)$

40. $15a^2 - 22a + 8$
$(3a - 2)(5a - 4)$

41. $12x^2 + 25x + 12$
$(3x + 4)(4x + 3)$

42. $10b^2 + 43b - 9$
$(2b + 9)(5b - 1)$

43. $3z^2 + 95z + 10$
Nonfactorable

44. $8z^2 - 36z + 1$
Nonfactorable

45. $3x^2 + xy - 2y^2$
$(x + y)(3x - 2y)$

46. $6x^2 + 10xy + 4y^2$
$2(x + y)(3x + 2y)$

47. $28 + 3z - z^2$
$(4 + z)(7 - z)$

48. $15 - 2z - z^2$
$(3 - z)(5 + z)$

49. $8 - 7x - x^2$
$(1 - x)(8 + x)$

50. $12 + 11x - x^2$
$(1 + x)(12 - x)$

51. $9x^2 + 33x - 60$
$3(x + 5)(3x - 4)$

52. $16x^2 - 16x - 12$
$4(2x + 1)(2x - 3)$

53. $24x^2 - 52x + 24$
$4(2x - 3)(3x - 2)$

54. $60x^2 + 95x + 20$
$5(3x + 4)(4x + 1)$

55. $35a^4 + 9a^3 - 2a^2$
$a^2(5a + 2)(7a - 1)$

56. $15a^4 + 26a^3 + 7a^2$
$a^2(3a + 1)(5a + 7)$

57. $15b^2 - 115b + 70$
$5(b - 7)(3b - 2)$

58. $25b^2 + 35b - 30$
$5(b + 2)(5b - 3)$

59. $10x^3 + 12x^2 + 2x$
$2x(x + 1)(5x + 1)$

60. $9x^3 - 39x^2 + 12x$
$3x(x - 4)(3x - 1)$

61. $10y^3 - 44y^2 + 16y$
$2y(y - 4)(5y - 2)$

62. $14y^3 + 94y^2 - 28y$
$2y(y + 7)(7y - 2)$

63. $4yz^3 + 5yz^2 - 6yz$
$yz(z + 2)(4z - 3)$

64. $2yz^3 - 17yz^2 + 8yz$
$yz(z - 8)(2z - 1)$

65. $20b^4 + 41b^3 + 20b^2$
$b^2(4b + 5)(5b + 4)$

66. $6b^4 - 13b^3 + 6b^2$
$b^2(2b - 3)(3b - 2)$

67. $9x^3y + 12x^2y + 4xy$
$xy(3x + 2)(3x + 2)$

68. $9a^3b - 9a^2b^2 - 10ab^3$
$ab(3a + 2b)(3a - 5b)$

2 Factor by grouping.

69. $2t^2 - t - 10$
$(t + 2)(2t - 5)$

70. $2t^2 + 5t - 12$
$(t + 4)(2t - 3)$

71. $3p^2 - 16p + 5$
$(p - 5)(3p - 1)$

72. $6p^2 + 5p + 1$
$(2p + 1)(3p + 1)$

73. $12y^2 - 7y + 1$
$(3y - 1)(4y - 1)$

74. $6y^2 - 5y + 1$
$(2y - 1)(3y - 1)$

75. $5x^2 - 62x - 7$
Nonfactorable

76. $9x^2 - 13x - 4$
Nonfactorable

77. $12y^2 + 19y + 5$
$(3y + 1)(4y + 5)$

78. $5y^2 - 22y + 8$
$(y - 4)(5y - 2)$

79. $7a^2 + 47a - 14$
$(a + 7)(7a - 2)$

80. $11a^2 - 54a - 5$
$(a - 5)(11a + 1)$

81. $4z^2 + 11z + 6$
$(z + 2)(4z + 3)$

82. $6z^2 - 25z + 14$
$(2z - 7)(3z - 2)$

83. $22p^2 + 51p - 10$
$(2p + 5)(11p - 2)$

84. $14p^2 - 41p + 15$
$(2p - 5)(7p - 3)$

85. $8y^2 + 17y + 9$
$(y + 1)(8y + 9)$

86. $12y^2 - 145y + 12$
$(y - 12)(12y - 1)$

87. $6b^2 - 13b + 6$
$(2b - 3)(3b - 2)$

88. $20b^2 + 37b + 15$
$(4b + 5)(5b + 3)$

89. $33b^2 + 34b - 35$
$(3b + 5)(11b - 7)$

90. $15b^2 - 43b + 22$
$(3b - 2)(5b - 11)$

91. $18y^2 - 39y + 20$
$(3y - 4)(6y - 5)$

92. $24y^2 + 41y + 12$
$(3y + 4)(8y + 3)$

93. $15x^2 - 82x + 24$
Nonfactorable

94. $13z^2 + 49z - 8$
Nonfactorable

95. $10z^2 - 29z + 10$
$(2z - 5)(5z - 2)$

96. $15z^2 - 44z + 32$
$(3z - 4)(5z - 8)$

97. $36z^2 + 72z + 35$
     $(6z + 5)(6z + 7)$

98. $16z^2 + 8z - 35$
     $(4z - 5)(4z + 7)$

99. $14y^2 - 29y + 12$
     $(2y - 3)(7y - 4)$

100. $8y^2 + 30y + 25$
     $(2y + 5)(4y + 5)$

101. $6x^2 + 35x - 6$
     $(x + 6)(6x - 1)$

102. $4x^2 + 6x + 2$
     $2(x + 1)(2x + 1)$

103. $12x^2 + 33x - 9$
     $3(x + 3)(4x - 1)$

104. $15y^2 - 50y + 35$
     $5(y - 1)(3y - 7)$

105. $30y^2 + 10y - 20$
     $10(y + 1)(3y - 2)$

106. $2x^3 - 11x^2 + 5x$
     $x(x - 5)(2x - 1)$

107. $2x^3 - 3x^2 - 5x$
     $x(x + 1)(2x - 5)$

108. $3a^2 + 5ab - 2b^2$
     $(a + 2b)(3a - b)$

109. $2a^2 - 9ab + 9b^2$
     $(a - 3b)(2a - 3b)$

110. $4y^2 - 11yz + 6z^2$
     $(y - 2z)(4y - 3z)$

111. $2y^2 + 7yz + 5z^2$
     $(y + z)(2y + 5z)$

112. $12 - x - x^2$
     $(3 - x)(4 + x)$

113. $18 + 17x - x^2$
     $(1 + x)(18 - x)$

114. $21 - 20x - x^2$
     $(1 - x)(21 + x)$

115. $360y^2 + 4y - 4$
     $4(9y + 1)(10y - 1)$

116. $10t^2 - 5t - 50$
     $5(t + 2)(2t - 5)$

117. $16t^2 + 40t - 96$
     $8(t + 4)(2t - 3)$

118. $3p^3 - 16p^2 + 5p$
     $p(p - 5)(3p - 1)$

119. $6p^3 + 5p^2 + p$
     $p(2p + 1)(3p + 1)$

120. $26z^2 + 98z - 24$
     $2(z + 4)(13z - 3)$

121. $30z^2 - 87z + 30$
     $3(2z - 5)(5z - 2)$

122. $12a^3 + 14a^2 - 48a$
     $2a(2a - 3)(3a + 8)$

123. $42a^3 + 45a^2 - 27a$
     $3a(2a + 3)(7a - 3)$

124. $36p^2 - 9p^3 - p^4$
     $p^2(3 - p)(12 + p)$

125. $9x^2y - 30xy^2 + 25y^3$ $y(3x - 5y)(3x - 5y)$

126. $8x^2y - 38xy^2 + 35y^3$ $y(2x - 7y)(4x - 5y)$

127. $9x^3y - 24x^2y^2 + 16xy^3$ $xy(3x - 4y)(3x - 4y)$

128. $45a^3b - 78a^2b^2 + 24ab^3$ $3ab(3a - 4b)(5a - 2b)$

APPLYING CONCEPTS 8.3

Factor.

129. $6y + 8y^3 - 26y^2$
     $2y(y - 3)(4y - 1)$

130. $22p^2 - 3p^3 + 16p$
     $p(2 + 3p)(8 - p)$

131. $a^3b - 24ab - 2a^2b$
     $ab(a + 4)(a - 6)$

132. $3xy^2 - 14xy + 2xy^3$
     $xy(y - 2)(2y + 7)$

133. $25t^2 + 60t - 10t^3$
     $5t(3 + 2t)(4 - t)$

134. $3xy^3 + 2x^3y - 7x^2y^2$
     $xy(y - 2x)(3y - x)$

Factor.

135. $2(y + 2)^2 - (y + 2) - 3$ $(y + 3)(2y + 1)$

136. $3(a + 2)^2 - (a + 2) - 4$ $(a + 3)(3a + 2)$

137. $10(x + 1)^2 - 11(x + 1) - 6$ $(2x - 1)(5x + 7)$

138. $4(y - 1)^2 - 7(y - 1) - 2$ $(y - 3)(4y - 3)$

Find all integers k such that the trinomial can be factored over the integers.

[C] 139. $2x^2 + kx + 3$ $7, 5, -7, -5$

[C] 140. $2x^2 + kx - 3$ $-1, 1, 5, -5$

[C] 141. $3x^2 + kx + 2$ $7, -7, 5, -5$

[C] 142. $3x^2 + kx - 2$ $-5, 5, -1, 1$

[C] 143. $2x^2 + kx + 5$ $11, -11, 7, -7$

[C] 144. $2x^2 + kx - 5$ $9, -9, -3, 3$

[C] 145. Given that $x + 2$ is a factor of $x^3 - 2x^2 - 5x + 6$, factor $x^3 - 2x^2 - 5x + 6$ completely. $(x + 2)(x - 3)(x - 1)$

146. In your own words, explain how the signs of the last terms of the two binomial factors of a trinomial are determined.

147. *Geometry*   The area of a rectangle is $(3x^2 + x - 2)$ ft². Find the dimensions of the rectangle in terms of the variable x. Given that $x > 0$, specify the dimension that is the length and the dimension that is the width. Can $x < 0$? Can $x = 0$? Explain your answers.

$A = 3x^2 + x - 2$

Special Factoring

1   Factor the difference of two squares and perfect-square trinomials

---

POINT OF INTEREST

For some geometric proofs for factoring the difference of two squares and perfect-square trinomials, see the feature on Algebra from Geometry at the beginning of the chapter.

Recall from Objective 4 in Section 3 of the chapter on Polynomials that the product of the sum and difference of the same two terms equals the square of the first term minus the square of the second term.

$$(a + b)(a - b) = a^2 - b^2$$

The expression $a^2 - b^2$ is the difference of two squares. The pattern above suggests the following rule for factoring the difference of two squares.

Rule for Factoring the Difference of Two Squares

Difference of Two Squares		Sum and Difference of Two Terms
$a^2 - b^2$	$=$	$(a + b)(a - b)$

LOOK CLOSELY

Convince yourself that the sum of two squares is nonfactorable over the integers by trying to factor $x^2 + 4$.

$a^2 + b^2$ is the *sum* of two squares. It is nonfactorable over the integers.

Example 1   Factor.   A. $x^2 - 16$ B. $x^2 - 10$ C. $z^6 - 25$

Solution   A. $x^2 - 16 = x^2 - 4^2$ ▶ Write $x^2 - 16$ as the difference of two squares.

$\qquad\qquad = (x + 4)(x - 4)$ ▶ The factors are the sum and difference of the terms x and 4.

B. $x^2 - 10$ is nonfactorable over the integers.   ▶ Because 10 is not the square of an integer, $x^2 - 10$ cannot be written as the difference of two squares.

C. $z^6 - 25 = (z^3)^2 - 5^2$ ▶ Write $z^6 - 25$ as the difference of two squares.

$\qquad\qquad = (z^3 + 5)(z^3 - 5)$ ▶ The factors are the sum and difference of the terms z^3 and 5.

Problem 1   Factor.   A. $25a^2 - b^2$ B. $6x^2 - 1$ C. $n^8 - 36$

Solution   See page S18.

A. $(5a + b)(5a - b)$ B. Nonfactorable   C. $(n^4 + 6)(n^4 - 6)$

Example 2   Factor: $z^4 - 16$

Solution $z^4 - 16 = (z^2)^2 - (4)^2$ ▶ This is the difference of two squares.

$= (z^2 + 4)(z^2 - 4)$ ▶ The factors are the sum and difference of the terms z^2 and 4.

$= (z^2 + 4)(z + 2)(z - 2)$ ▶ Factor $z^2 - 4$, which is the difference of two squares. $z^2 + 4$ is nonfactorable over the integers.

Problem 2   Factor: $n^4 - 81$

Solution   See page S18. $(n^2 + 9)(n + 3)(n - 3)$

Recall from Objective 4 in Section 3 in the chapter on Polynomials the pattern for finding the square of a binomial.

$$(\boldsymbol{a} + \boldsymbol{b})^2 = (a + b)(a + b) = a^2 + ab + ab + b^2$$

$$= \boldsymbol{a}^2 + \boldsymbol{2ab} + \boldsymbol{b}^2$$

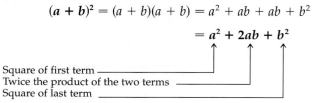

Square of first term
Twice the product of the two terms
Square of last term

The square of a binomial is a perfect-square trinomial. The pattern above suggests the following rule for factoring a perfect-square trinomial.

Rule for Factoring a Perfect-Square Trinomial

Perfect-Square Trinomial				**Square of a Binomial**
$a^2 + 2ab + b^2$	=	$(a + b)(a + b)$	=	$(a + b)^2$
$a^2 - 2ab + b^2$	=	$(a - b)(a - b)$	=	$(a - b)^2$

Note in these patterns that the sign in the binomial is the sign of the middle term of the trinomial.

➡ Factor: $4x^2 - 20x + 25$

Check that the first term and the last term are squares. $4x^2 = (2x)^2, 25 = 5^2$

Use the squared terms to factor the trinomial as the square of a binomial. The sign of the binomial is the sign of the middle term of the trinomial. $(2x - 5)^2$

Check the factorization. $(2x - 5)^2$
$= (2x)^2 + 2(2x)(-5) + (-5)^2$
$= 4x^2 - 20x + 25$

The factorization is correct. $4x^2 - 20x + 25 = (2x - 5)^2$ ◀

➡ Factor: $9x^2 + 30x + 16$

Check that the first term and the last term are squares.

$9x^2 = (3x)^2$, $16 = 4^2$

Use the squared terms to factor the trinomial as the square of a binomial. The sign of the binomial is the sign of the middle term in the trinomial.

$(3x + 4)^2$

Check the factorization.

$(3x + 4)^2$
$= (3x)^2 + 2(3x)(4) + 4^2$
$= 9x^2 + 24x + 16$

$9x^2 + 24x + 16 \neq 9x^2 + 30x + 16$
The proposed factorization is not correct.

In this case, the polynomial is not a perfect-square trinomial. It may, however, still factor. In fact, $9x^2 + 30x + 16 = (3x + 2)(3x + 8)$. If the trinomial does not check as a perfect-square trinomial, try to factor it by another method. ◀

A perfect-square trinomial can always be factored using either of the methods presented in Section 3 in this chapter. However, noticing that a trinomial is a perfect-square trinomial can save you a considerable amount of time.

Example 3 Factor.   A. $9x^2 - 30x + 25$ B. $4x^2 + 37x + 9$

Solution A. $9x^2 = (3x)^2$, $25 = 5^2$
▶ Check that the first and last terms are squares.

$(3x - 5)^2$
▶ Use the squared terms to factor the trinomial as the square of a binomial.

$(3x - 5)^2$
$= (3x)^2 + 2(3x)(-5) + (-5)^2$
$= 9x^2 - 30x + 25$
▶ Check the factorization.

▶ The factorization checks.

$9x^2 - 30x + 25 = (3x - 5)^2$

B. $4x^2 = (2x)^2$, $9 = 3^2$
▶ Check that the first and last terms are squares.

$(2x + 3)^2$
▶ Use the squared terms to factor the trinomial as the square of a binomial.

$(2x + 3)^2$
$= (2x)^2 + 2(2x)(3) + 3^2$
$= 4x^2 + 12x + 9$
▶ Check the factorization.

▶ The factorization does not check.

$4x^2 + 37x + 9$
$= (4x + 1)(x + 9)$
▶ Use another method to factor the trinomial.

Problem 3 Factor.   A. $16y^2 + 8y + 1$ B. $x^2 + 14x + 36$

Solution See page S18.   A. $(4y + 1)^2$ B. Nonfactorable

2   Factor completely

When factoring a polynomial completely, ask yourself the following questions about the polynomial.

1. Is there a common factor? If so, factor out the common factor.
2. Is the polynomial the difference of two squares? If so, factor.
3. Is the polynomial a perfect-square trinomial? If so, factor.
4. Is the polynomial a trinomial that is the product of two binomials? If so, factor.
5. Does the polynomial contain four terms? If so, try factoring by grouping.
6. Is each binomial factor nonfactorable over the integers? If not, factor.

Example 4   Factor.   A. $3x^2 - 48$ B. $x^3 - 3x^2 - 4x + 12$
C. $4x^2y^2 + 12xy^2 + 9y^2$

Solution   A. $3x^2 - 48$ ▶ The GCF of the terms is 3.
$= 3(x^2 - 16)$ Factor out the common factor.
$= 3(x + 4)(x - 4)$ ▶ Factor the difference of two squares.

B. $x^3 - 3x^2 - 4x + 12$ ▶ The polynomial contains four
$= (x^3 - 3x^2) - (4x - 12)$ terms. Factor by grouping.
$= x^2(x - 3) - 4(x - 3)$
$= (x - 3)(x^2 - 4)$
$= (x - 3)(x + 2)(x - 2)$ ▶ Factor the difference of two squares.

C. $4x^2y^2 + 12xy^2 + 9y^2$ ▶ The GCF of the terms is y^2.
$= y^2(4x^2 + 12x + 9)$ Factor out the common factor.
$= y^2(2x + 3)^2$ ▶ Factor the perfect-square trinomial.

Problem 4   Factor.   A. $12x^3 - 75x$ B. $a^2b - 7a^2 - b + 7$
C. $4x^3 + 28x^2 - 120x$

Solution   See page S18.
A. $3x(2x + 5)(2x - 5)$ B. $(b - 7)(a + 1)(a - 1)$
C. $4x(x + 10)(x - 3)$

CONCEPT REVIEW 8.4

Determine whether the statement is always true, sometimes true, or never true.

1. The expression $x^2 - 12$ is an example of the difference of two squares.
   Never true
2. The expression $(y + 8)(y - 8)$ is the product of the sum and difference of the same two terms. The two terms are y and 8.   Always true

3. A binomial is factorable.   Sometimes true

4. A trinomial is factorable.   Sometimes true

5. If a binomial is multiplied times itself, the result is a perfect-square trinomial.   Always true

6. In a perfect-square trinomial, the first and last terms are perfect squares. Always true

7. If a polynomial contains four terms, try to factor it as a perfect-square trinomial.   Never true

8. The expression $x^2 + 9$ is the sum of two squares. It factors as $(x + 3)(x + 3)$. Never true

---

EXERCISES 8.4

1 **1.** Provide an example of each of the following.
  a. the difference of two squares
  b. the product of the sum and difference of two terms
  c. a perfect-square trinomial
  d. the square of a binomial
  e. the sum of two squares

2. Explain the rule for factoring
  a. the difference of two squares
  b. a perfect-square trinomial

Factor.

3. $x^2 - 4$
$(x + 2)(x - 2)$

4. $x^2 - 9$
$(x + 3)(x - 3)$

5. $a^2 - 81$
$(a + 9)(a - 9)$

6. $a^2 - 49$
$(a + 7)(a - 7)$

7. $4x^2 - 1$
$(2x + 1)(2x - 1)$

8. $9x^2 - 16$
$(3x + 4)(3x - 4)$

9. $y^2 + 2y + 1$
$(y + 1)^2$

10. $y^2 + 14y + 49$
$(y + 7)^2$

11. $a^2 - 2a + 1$
$(a - 1)^2$

12. $x^2 + 8x - 16$
Nonfactorable

13. $z^2 - 18z - 81$
Nonfactorable

14. $x^2 - 12x + 36$
$(x - 6)^2$

15. $x^6 - 9$
$(x^3 + 3)(x^3 - 3)$

16. $y^{12} - 121$
$(y^6 + 11)(y^6 - 11)$

17. $25x^2 - 1$
$(5x + 1)(5x - 1)$

18. $9x^2 - 1$
$(3x + 1)(3x - 1)$

19. $1 - 49x^2$
$(1 + 7x)(1 - 7x)$

20. $1 - 64x^2$
$(1 + 8x)(1 - 8x)$

21. $x^2 + 2xy + y^2$
$(x + y)^2$

22. $x^2 + 6xy + 9y^2$
$(x + 3y)^2$

23. $4a^2 + 4a + 1$
$(2a + 1)^2$

24. $25x^2 + 10x + 1$
$(5x + 1)^2$

25. $64a^2 - 16a + 1$
$(8a - 1)^2$

26. $9a^2 + 6a + 1$
$(3a + 1)^2$

27. $t^2 + 36$
Nonfactorable

28. $x^2 + 64$
Nonfactorable

29. $x^4 - y^2$
$(x^2 + y)(x^2 - y)$

30. $b^4 - 16a^2$
$(b^2 + 4a)(b^2 - 4a)$

31. $9x^2 - 16y^2$
$(3x + 4y)(3x - 4y)$

32. $25z^2 - y^2$
$(5z + y)(5z - y)$

33. $16b^2 + 8b + 1$
$(4b + 1)^2$

34. $4a^2 - 20a + 25$
$(2a - 5)^2$

35. $4b^2 + 28b + 49$
$(2b + 7)^2$

36. $9a^2 - 42a + 49$
$(3a - 7)^2$

37. $25a^2 + 30ab + 9b^2$
$(5a + 3b)^2$

38. $4a^2 - 12ab + 9b^2$
$(2a - 3b)^2$

39. $x^2y^2 - 4$
$(xy + 2)(xy - 2)$

40. $a^2b^2 - 25$
$(ab + 5)(ab - 5)$

41. $16 - x^2y^2$
$(4 + xy)(4 - xy)$

42. $49x^2 + 28xy + 4y^2$
$(7x + 2y)^2$

43. $4y^2 - 36yz + 81z^2$
$(2y - 9z)^2$

44. $64y^2 - 48yz + 9z^2$
$(8y - 3z)^2$

45. $9a^2b^2 - 6ab + 1$
$(3ab - 1)^2$

46. $16x^2y^2 - 24xy + 9$
$(4xy - 3)^2$

47. $m^4 - 256$
$(m^2 + 16)(m + 4)(m - 4)$

48. $81 - t^4$
$(9 + t^2)(3 + t)(3 - t)$

49. $9x^2 + 13x + 4$
$(x + 1)(9x + 4)$

50. $x^2 + 10x + 16$
$(x + 2)(x + 8)$

51. $y^8 - 81$
$(y^4 + 9)(y^2 + 3)(y^2 - 3)$

52. $9 + 24a + 16a^2$
$(3 + 4a)^2$

2 Factor.

53. $2x^2 - 18$
$2(x + 3)(x - 3)$

54. $y^3 - 10y^2 + 25y$
$y(y - 5)^2$

55. $x^4 + 2x^3 - 35x^2$
$x^2(x + 7)(x - 5)$

56. $a^4 - 11a^3 + 24a^2$
$a^2(a - 8)(a - 3)$

57. $5b^2 + 75b + 180$
$5(b + 3)(b + 12)$

58. $6y^2 - 48y + 72$
$6(y - 2)(y - 6)$

59. $3a^2 + 36a + 10$
Nonfactorable

60. $5a^2 - 30a + 4$
Nonfactorable

61. $2x^2y + 16xy - 66y$
$2y(x + 11)(x - 3)$

62. $3a^2b + 21ab - 54b$
$3b(a + 9)(a - 2)$

63. $x^3 - 6x^2 - 5x$
$x(x^2 - 6x - 5)$

64. $b^3 - 8b^2 - 7b$
$b(b^2 - 8b - 7)$

65. $3y^2 - 36$
$3(y^2 - 12)$

66. $3y^2 - 147$
$3(y + 7)(y - 7)$

67. $20a^2 + 12a + 1$
$(2a + 1)(10a + 1)$

68. $12a^2 - 36a + 27$
$3(2a - 3)^2$

69. $x^2y^2 - 7xy^2 - 8y^2$
$y^2(x + 1)(x - 8)$

70. $a^2b^2 + 3a^2b - 88a^2$
$a^2(b + 11)(b - 8)$

71. $10a^2 - 5ab - 15b^2$
$5(a + b)(2a - 3b)$

72. $16x^2 - 32xy + 12y^2$
$4(2x - y)(2x - 3y)$

73. $50 - 2x^2$
$2(5 + x)(5 - x)$

74. $72 - 2x^2$
$2(6 + x)(6 - x)$

75. $12a^3b - a^2b^2 - ab^3$
$ab(3a - b)(4a + b)$

76. $2x^3y - 7x^2y^2 + 6xy^3$
$xy(x - 2y)(2x - 3y)$

77. $2ax - 2a + 2bx - 2b$
$2(x - 1)(a + b)$

78. $4ax - 12a - 2bx + 6b$
$2(x - 3)(2a - b)$

79. $12a^3 - 12a^2 + 3a$
$3a(2a - 1)^2$

80. $18a^3 + 24a^2 + 8a$
$2a(3a + 2)^2$

81. $243 + 3a^2$
$3(81 + a^2)$

82. $75 + 27y^2$
$3(25 + 9y^2)$

83. $12a^3 - 46a^2 + 40a$
$2a(2a - 5)(3a - 4)$

84. $24x^3 - 66x^2 + 15x$
$3x(2x - 5)(4x - 1)$

85. $x^3 - 2x^2 - x + 2$
$(x - 2)(x + 1)(x - 1)$

86. $ay^2 - by^2 - a + b$
$(a - b)(y + 1)(y - 1)$

87. $4a^3 + 20a^2 + 25a$
$a(2a + 5)^2$

88. $2a^3 - 8a^2b + 8ab^2$
$2a(a - 2b)^2$

89. $27a^2b - 18ab + 3b$
$3b(3a - 1)^2$

90. $a^2b^2 - 6ab^2 + 9b^2$
$b^2(a - 3)^2$

91. $48 - 12x - 6x^2$
$6(4 + x)(2 - x)$

92. $21x^2 - 11x^3 - 2x^4$
$x^2(3 - 2x)(7 + x)$

93. $ax^2 - 4a + bx^2 - 4b$
$(x + 2)(x - 2)(a + b)$

94. $a^2x - b^2x - a^2y + b^2y$
$(a + b)(a - b)(x - y)$

95. $x^4 - x^2y^2$
$x^2(x + y)(x - y)$

96. $b^4 - a^2b^2$
$b^2(b + a)(b - a)$

97. $18a^3 + 24a^2 + 8a$
$2a(3a + 2)^2$

98. $32xy^2 - 48xy + 18x$
$2x(4y - 3)^2$

99. $2b + ab - 6a^2b$
$b(2 - 3a)(1 + 2a)$

100. $20x - 11xy - 3xy^2$
$x(5 + y)(4 - 3y)$

101. $4x - 20 - x^3 + 5x^2$
$(x - 5)(2 + x)(2 - x)$

102. $ay^2 - by^2 - 9a + 9b$
$(a - b)(y + 3)(y - 3)$

103. $72xy^2 + 48xy + 8x$
$8x(3y + 1)^2$

104. $4x^2y + 8xy + 4y$
$4y(x + 1)^2$

105. $15y^2 - 2xy^2 - x^2y^2$
$y^2(5 + x)(3 - x)$

106. $4x^4 - 38x^3 + 48x^2$
$2x^2(2x - 3)(x - 8)$

107. $y^3 - 9y$
$y(y + 3)(y - 3)$

108. $a^4 - 16$
$(a^2 + 4)(a + 2)(a - 2)$

109. $2x^4y^2 - 2x^2y^2$
$2x^2y^2(x + 1)(x - 1)$

110. $6x^5y - 6xy^5$
$6xy(x^2 + y^2)(x + y)(x - y)$

111. $x^9 - x^5$
$x^5(x^2 + 1)(x + 1)(x - 1)$

112. $8b^5 - 2b^3$
$2b^3(2b + 1)(2b - 1)$

113. $24x^3y + 14x^2y - 20xy$
$2xy(3x - 2)(4x + 5)$

114. $12x^3y - 60x^2y + 63xy$
$3xy(2x - 3)(2x - 7)$

115. $4x^4y^2 - 20x^3y^2 + 25x^2y^2$
$x^2y^2(2x - 5)^2$

116. $9x^4y^2 + 24x^3y^2 + 16x^2y^2$
$x^2y^2(3x + 4)^2$

117. $x^3 - 2x^2 - 4x + 8$
$(x - 2)^2(x + 2)$

118. $24x^2y + 6x^3y - 45x^4y$
$3x^2y(2 + 3x)(4 - 5x)$

119. $8xy^2 - 20x^2y^2 + 12x^3y^2$
$4xy^2(1 - x)(2 - 3x)$

120. $45y^2 - 42y^3 - 24y^4$
$3y^2(5 + 2y)(3 - 4y)$

121. $36a^3b - 62a^2b^2 + 12ab^3$
$2ab(2a - 3b)(9a - 2b)$

122. $18a^3b + 57a^2b^2 + 30ab^3$
$3ab(2a + 5b)(3a + 2b)$

123. $5x^2y^2 - 11x^3y^2 - 12x^4y^2$
$x^2y^2(1 - 3x)(5 + 4x)$

124. $24x^2y^2 - 32x^3y^2 + 10x^4y^2$
$2x^2y^2(2 - x)(6 - 5x)$

125. $(4x - 3)^2 - y^2$
$(4x - 3 + y)(4x - 3 - y)$

126. $(2a + 3)^2 - 25b^2$
$(2a + 3 + 5b)(2a + 3 - 5b)$

127. $(x^2 - 4x + 4) - y^2$
$(x - 2 + y)(x - 2 - y)$

128. $(4x^2 + 12x + 9) - 4y^2$
$(2x + 3 + 2y)(2x + 3 - 2y)$

APPLYING CONCEPTS 8.4

Find all integers k such that the trinomial is a perfect-square trinomial.

129. $4x^2 - kx + 9$
$12, -12$

130. $25x^2 - kx + 1$
$10, -10$

131. $36x^2 + kxy + y^2$
$12, -12$

132. $64x^2 + kxy + y^2$
$16, -16$

133. $x^2 + 6x + k$ 9

134. $x^2 - 4x + k$ 4

135. $x^2 - 2x + k$ 1

136. $x^2 + 10x + k$ 25

137. The prime factorization of a number is $2^3 \cdot 3^2$. How many of its whole-number factors are perfect squares?   4

138. The product of two numbers is 48. One of the two numbers is a perfect square. The other is a prime number. Find the sum of the two numbers.   19

139. What is the smallest whole number by which 300 can be multiplied so that the product will be a perfect square?   3

140. *Geometry*   The area of a square is $(16x^2 + 24x + 9)$ ft^2. Find the dimensions of the square in terms of the variable x. Can $x = 0$? What are the possible values of x? $(4x + 3)$ ft by $(4x + 3)$ ft; yes; $x > -\dfrac{3}{4}$

$A = 16x^2 + 24x + 9$

The cube of an integer is a **perfect cube**. Because $2^3 = 8$, 8 is a perfect cube. Because $4^3 = 64$, 64 is a perfect cube. A variable expression can be a perfect cube; the exponents on variables of perfect cubes are multiples of 3. Therefore, x^3, x^6, and x^9 are perfect cubes. The sum and the difference of two perfect cubes are factorable. They can be written as the product of a binomial and a trinomial. Their factoring patterns are shown below.

$a^3 + b^3$ is the sum of two cubes.

$a^3 - b^3$ is the difference of two cubes.

$a^3 + b^3 = (a + b)(a^2 - ab + b^2)$

$a^3 - b^3 = (a - b)(a^2 + ab + b^2)$

To factor $x^3 - 8$, write the binomial as the difference of two perfect cubes. Use the factoring pattern shown above. Replace a with x and b with 2.

$x^3 - 8 = (x)^3 - (2)^3$
$= (x - 2)(x^2 + 2x + 4)$

Factor.

[C] **141.** $x^3 + 8$
$(x + 2)(x^2 - 2x + 4)$

[C] **142.** $y^3 + 27$
$(y + 3)(y^2 - 3y + 9)$

[C] **143.** $y^3 - 27$
$(y - 3)(y^2 + 3y + 9)$

[C] **144.** $x^3 - 1$
$(x - 1)(x^2 + x + 1)$

[C] **145.** $y^3 + 64$
$(y + 4)(y^2 - 4y + 16)$

[C] **146.** $x^3 - 125$
$(x - 5)(x^2 + 5x + 25)$

[C] **147.** $8x^3 - 1$
$(2x - 1)(4x^2 + 2x + 1)$

[C] **148.** $27y^3 + 1$
$(3y + 1)(9y^2 - 3y + 1)$

149. Select any odd integer greater than 1, square it, and then subtract 1. Is the result evenly divisible by 8? Prove that this procedure always produces a number divisible by 8. (*Suggestion:* Any odd integer greater than 1 can be expressed as $2n + 1$, where n is a natural number.)

SECTION 8.5
Solving Equations

1 Solve equations by factoring

Recall that the Multiplication Property of Zero states that the product of a number and zero is zero.

If a is a real number, then $a \cdot 0 = 0$.

Consider the equation $a \cdot b = 0$. If this is a true equation, then either $a = 0$ or $b = 0$.

Principle of Zero Products

> If the product of two factors is zero, then at least one of the factors must be zero.
>
> $$\text{If } a \cdot b = 0, \text{ then } a = 0 \text{ or } b = 0.$$

The Principle of Zero Products is used in solving equations.

LOOK CLOSELY

$x - 2$ is equal to a number. $x - 3$ is equal to a number. In $(x - 2)(x - 3)$, two numbers are being multiplied. Since their product is 0, one of the numbers must be equal to 0. The number $x - 2 = 0$ or the number $x - 3 = 0$.

➡ Solve: $(x - 2)(x - 3) = 0$

If $(x - 2)(x - 3) = 0$, then $(x - 2) = 0$ or $(x - 3) = 0$.

$$(x - 2)(x - 3) = 0$$

Solve each equation for x.

$$x - 2 = 0 \qquad\qquad x - 3 = 0$$
$$x = 2 \qquad\qquad x = 3$$

Check:

$$
\begin{array}{c|c}
(x - 2)(x - 3) = 0 & (x - 2)(x - 3) = 0 \\
\hline
(2 - 2)(2 - 3) \mid 0 & (3 - 2)(3 - 3) \mid 0 \\
0(-1) \mid 0 & 1(0) \mid 0 \\
0 = 0 & 0 = 0
\end{array}
$$

A true equation   A true equation

Write the solutions.   The solutions are 2 and 3. ◀

An equation of the form $ax^2 + bx + c = 0$, $a \neq 0$, is a **quadratic equation**. A quadratic equation is in **standard form** when the polynomial is in descending order and equal to zero.

$$3x^2 + 2x + 1 = 0$$

$$4x^2 - 3x + 2 = 0$$

A quadratic equation can be solved by using the Principle of Zero Products when the polynomial $ax^2 + bx + c$ is factorable.

Example 1 Solve: $2x^2 + x = 6$

Solution

$$2x^2 + x = 6$$
$$2x^2 + x - 6 = 0$$ ▶ Write the equation in standard form.

$$(2x - 3)(x + 2) = 0$$ ▶ Factor the trinomial.

$$2x - 3 = 0 \qquad x + 2 = 0$$ ▶ Set each factor equal to zero (the Principle of Zero Products).

$$2x = 3 \qquad\qquad x = -2$$ ▶ Solve each equation for x.

$$x = \frac{3}{2}$$

Check

$$
\begin{array}{c|c}
2x^2 + x = 6 & 2x^2 + x = 6 \\ \hline
2\left(\frac{3}{2}\right)^2 + \frac{3}{2} \quad\bigg|\quad 6 & 2(-2)^2 + (-2) \quad\bigg|\quad 6 \\
2\left(\frac{9}{4}\right) + \frac{3}{2} \quad\bigg|\quad 6 & 2 \cdot 4 - 2 \quad\bigg|\quad 6 \\
\frac{9}{2} + \frac{3}{2} \quad\bigg|\quad 6 & 8 - 2 \quad\bigg|\quad 6 \\
6 = 6 & 6 = 6
\end{array}
$$

The solutions are $\frac{3}{2}$ and -2. ▶ Write the solutions.

Problem 1 Solve: $2x^2 - 50 = 0$

Solution See page S18. -5 and 5

Example 2 Solve: $(x - 3)(x - 10) = -10$

Solution

$$(x - 3)(x - 10) = -10$$
$$x^2 - 13x + 30 = -10$$ ▶ Multiply $(x - 3)(x - 10)$.
$$x^2 - 13x + 40 = 0$$ ▶ Write the equation in standard form.

$$(x - 8)(x - 5) = 0$$ ▶ Factor.

$$x - 8 = 0 \qquad x - 5 = 0$$ ▶ Set each factor equal to zero.
$$x = 8 \qquad\qquad x = 5$$ ▶ Solve each equation for x.

The solutions are 8 and 5. ▶ Write the solutions.

Problem 2 Solve: $(x + 2)(x - 7) = 52$

Solution See page S18. -6 and 11

LOOK CLOSELY

The Principle of Zero Products cannot be used unless 0 is on one side of the equation.

2 Application problems

Example 3 The sum of the squares of two consecutive positive odd integers is equal to 130. Find the two integers.

Strategy ▪ First positive odd integer: n
Second positive odd integer: $n + 2$
Square of the first positive odd integer: n^2
Square of the second positive odd integer: $(n + 2)^2$

■ The sum of the square of the first positive odd integer and the square of the second positive odd integer is 130.

Solution

$$n^2 + (n + 2)^2 = 130$$
$$n^2 + n^2 + 4n + 4 = 130$$
$$2n^2 + 4n - 126 = 0$$
$$2(n^2 + 2n - 63) = 0$$
$$n^2 + 2n - 63 = 0$$
$$(n - 7)(n + 9) = 0$$

▶ Divide each side of the equation by 2.

$$n - 7 = 0 \qquad n + 9 = 0$$
$$n = 7 \qquad n = -9$$

▶ Because −9 is not a positive odd integer, it is not a solution.

$$n = 7$$

▶ The first positive odd integer is 7.

$$n + 2 = 7 + 2 = 9$$

▶ Substitute the value of n into the variable expression for the second positive odd integer and evaluate.

The two integers are 7 and 9.

Problem 3 The sum of the squares of two consecutive positive integers is 85. Find the two integers.

Solution See page S18.   6 and 7

Example 4 A stone is thrown into a well with an initial velocity of 8 ft/s. The well is 440 ft deep. How many seconds later will the stone hit the bottom of the well? Use the equation $d = vt + 16t^2$, where d is the distance in feet, v is the initial velocity in feet per second, and t is the time in seconds.

Strategy To find the time for the stone to drop to the bottom of the well, replace the variables d and v by their given values and solve for t.

Solution

$$d = vt + 16t^2$$
$$440 = 8t + 16t^2$$
$$0 = 16t^2 + 8t - 440$$
$$0 = 8(2t^2 + t - 55)$$
$$0 = 2t^2 + t - 55$$
$$0 = (2t + 11)(t - 5)$$

▶ Write the equation in standard form.

▶ Divide each side of the equation by 8.

$$2t + 11 = 0 \qquad t - 5 = 0$$
$$2t = -11 \qquad t = 5$$
$$t = -\frac{11}{2}$$

The time is 5 s.

▶ Because the time cannot be a negative number, $-\frac{11}{2}$ is not a solution.

Problem 4 The length of a rectangle is 3 m more than twice the width. The area of the rectangle is 90 m². Find the length and width of the rectangle.

Solution See page S19.   Length: 15 m; width: 6 m

CONCEPT REVIEW 8.5

Determine whether the statement is always true, sometimes true, or never true.

1. If you multiply two numbers and the product is zero, then either one or both of the numbers must be zero.   Always true

2. The equation $2x^2 + 5x - 7$ is a quadratic equation.   Never true

3. The equation $4x^2 - 9 = 0$ is a quadratic equation.   Always true

4. The equation $3x + 1 = 0$ is a quadratic equation in standard form.   Never true

5. If $(x - 8)(x + 6) = 0$, then $x = -8$ or $x = 6$.   Never true

6. If a quadratic equation is not in standard form, the first step in solving the equation by factoring is to write it in standard form.   Always true

---

EXERCISES 8.5

1 1. What does the Principle of Zero Products state?

2. Why is it possible to solve some quadratic equations by using the Principle of Zero Products?

Solve.

3. $(y + 3)(y + 2) = 0$ $-3, -2$
4. $(y - 3)(y - 5) = 0$ $3, 5$
5. $(z - 7)(z - 3) = 0$ $7, 3$

6. $(z + 8)(z - 9) = 0$ $-8, 9$
7. $x(x - 5) = 0$ $0, 5$
8. $x(x + 2) = 0$ $0, -2$

9. $a(a - 9) = 0$ $0, 9$
10. $a(a + 12) = 0$ $0, -12$
11. $y(2y + 3) = 0$ $0, -\frac{3}{2}$

12. $t(4t - 7) = 0$ $0, \frac{7}{4}$
13. $2a(3a - 2) = 0$ $0, \frac{2}{3}$
14. $4b(2b + 5) = 0$ $0, -\frac{5}{2}$

15. $(b + 2)(b - 5) = 0$ $-2, 5$
16. $(b - 8)(b + 3) = 0$ $8, -3$
17. $x^2 - 81 = 0$ $9, -9$

18. $9x^2 - 1 = 0$ $\frac{1}{3}, -\frac{1}{3}$
19. $16x^2 - 49 = 0$ $\frac{7}{4}, -\frac{7}{4}$
20. $x^2 + 6x + 8 = 0$ $-4, -2$

21. $x^2 - 8x + 15 = 0$ $3, 5$
22. $z^2 + 5z - 14 = 0$ $-7, 2$
23. $z^2 + z - 72 = 0$ $8, -9$

24. $x^2 - 5x + 6 = 0$ $3, 2$
25. $2y^2 - y - 1 = 0$ $-\frac{1}{2}, 1$
26. $2a^2 - 9a - 5 = 0$ $-\frac{1}{2}, 5$

27. $3a^2 + 14a + 8 = 0$ $-\frac{2}{3}, -4$
28. $2x^2 - 6x - 20 = 0$ $-2, 5$
29. $3y^2 + 12y - 63 = 0$ $-7, 3$

30. $a^2 - 5a = 0$ $0, 5$
31. $x^2 - 7x = 0$ $0, 7$
32. $2a^2 - 8a = 0$ $0, 4$

33. $a^2 + 5a = -4$ $-1, -4$
34. $a^2 - 5a = 24$ $8, -3$
35. $y^2 - 5y = -6$ $2, 3$

36. $y^2 - 7y = 8$ 8, −1

37. $2t^2 + 7t = 4$ $\frac{1}{2}$, −4

38. $3t^2 + t = 10$ −2, $\frac{5}{3}$

39. $3t^2 - 13t = -4$ $\frac{1}{3}$, 4

40. $5t^2 - 16t = -12$ $\frac{6}{5}$, 2

41. $x(x - 12) = -27$ 3, 9

42. $x(x - 11) = 12$ 12, −1

43. $y(y - 7) = 18$ 9, −2

44. $y(y + 8) = -15$ −5, −3

45. $p(p + 3) = -2$ −1, −2

46. $p(p - 1) = 20$ 5, −4

47. $y(y + 4) = 45$ 5, −9

48. $y(y - 8) = -15$ 3, 5

49. $x(x + 3) = 28$ 4, −7

50. $p(p - 14) = 15$ 15, −1

51. $(x + 8)(x - 3) = -30$
−2, −3

52. $(x + 4)(x - 1) = 14$ −6, 3

53. $(y + 3)(y + 10) = -10$
−8, −5

54. $(z - 5)(z + 4) = 52$ 9, −8

55. $(z - 8)(z + 4) = -35$ 1, 3

56. $(z - 6)(z + 1) = -10$ 1, 4

57. $(a + 3)(a + 4) = 72$ −12, 5

58. $(a - 4)(a + 7) = -18$ −5, 2

59. $(z + 3)(z - 10) = -42$ 3, 4

60. $(2x + 5)(x + 1) = -1$ $-\frac{3}{2}$, −2

61. $(y + 3)(2y + 3) = 5$ $-\frac{1}{2}$, −4

62. $(y + 5)(3y - 2) = -14$
$-\frac{1}{3}$, −4

2 **63.** *Integer Problems*   The square of a positive number is six more than five times the positive number. Find the number.   6

64. *Integer Problems*   The square of a negative number is fifteen more than twice the negative number. Find the number.   −3

65. *Integer Problems*   The sum of two numbers is six. The sum of the squares of the two numbers is twenty. Find the two numbers.   2, 4

66. *Integer Problems*   The sum of two numbers is eight. The sum of the squares of the two numbers is thirty-four. Find the two numbers.   3, 5

67. *Integer Problems*   The sum of the squares of two consecutive positive integers is forty-one. Find the two integers.   4, 5

68. *Integer Problems*   The sum of the squares of two consecutive positive even integers is one hundred. Find the two integers.   6, 8

69. *Integer Problems*   The product of two consecutive positive integers is two hundred forty. Find the two integers.   15, 16

70. *Integer Problems*   The product of two consecutive positive even integers is one hundred sixty-eight. Find the two integers.   12, 14

71. *Geometry*   The length of the base of a triangle is three times the height. The area of the triangle is 54 ft^2. Find the base and height of the triangle.
Base: 18 ft; height: 6 ft

72. *Geometry*   The height of a triangle is 4 m more than twice the length of the base. The area of the triangle is 35 m^2. Find the height of the triangle.   14 m

73. *Geometry* The length of a rectangle is two feet more than twice the width. The area is 144 ft². Find the length and width of the rectangle.
Length: 18 ft; width: 8 ft

74. *Geometry* The width of a rectangle is 5 ft less than the length. The area of the rectangle is 176 ft². Find the length and width of the rectangle.
Length: 16 ft; width: 11 ft

75. *Geometry* The length of each side of a square is extended 4 m. The area of the resulting square is 64 m². Find the length of a side of the original square.
4 m

76. *Geometry* The length of each side of a square is extended 2 cm. The area of the resulting square is 64 cm². Find the length of a side of the original square.   6 cm

77. *Geometry* The radius of a circle is increased by 3 in., which increases the area by 100 in². Find the radius of the original circle. Round to the nearest hundredth.   3.81 in.

78. *Geometry* A circle has a radius of 10 in. Find the increase in area that occurs when the radius is increased by 2 in. Round to the nearest hundredth.   138.23 in²

79. *Geometry* The page of a book measures 6 in. by 9 in. A uniform border around the page leaves 28 in² for type. What are the dimensions of the type area?   4 in. by 7 in.

80. *Geometry* A small garden measures 8 ft by 10 ft. A uniform border around the garden increases the total area to 143 ft². What is the width of the border?
1.5 ft

Use the formula $d = vt + 16t^2$, where d is the distance in feet, v is the initial velocity in feet per second, and t is the time in seconds.

81. *Physics* An object is released from a plane at an altitude of 1600 ft. The initial velocity is 0 ft/s. How many seconds later will the object hit the ground?
10 s

82. *Physics* An object is released from the top of a building 320 ft high. The initial velocity is 16 ft/s. How many seconds later will the object hit the ground?
4 s

Use the formula $S = \dfrac{n^2 + n}{2}$, where S is the sum of the first n natural numbers.

83. *Number Problems* How many consecutive natural numbers beginning with 1 will give a sum of 78?   12

84. *Number Problems* How many consecutive natural numbers beginning with 1 will give a sum of 120?   15

Use the formula $N = \dfrac{t^2 - t}{2}$, where N is the number of football games that must be scheduled in a league with t teams if each team is to play every other team once.

85. *Sports* A league has 28 games scheduled. How many teams are in the league if each team plays every other team once?   8 teams

86. *Sports* A league has 45 games scheduled. How many teams are in the league if each team plays every other team once?   10 teams

Use the formula $h = vt - 16t^2$, where h is the height in feet an object will attain (neglecting air resistance) in t seconds and v is the initial velocity in feet per second.

87. *Sports* A baseball player hits a "Baltimore chop," meaning the ball bounces off home plate after the batter hits it. The ball leaves home plate with an initial upward velocity of 64 ft/s. How many seconds after the ball hits home plate will the ball be 64 ft above the ground?   2 s

88. *Sports* A golf ball is thrown onto a cement surface and rebounds straight up. The initial velocity of the rebound is 96 ft/s. How many seconds later will the golf ball return to the ground?   6 s

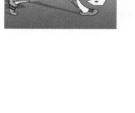

APPLYING CONCEPTS 8.5

Solve.

89. $2y(y + 4) = -5(y + 3)$ $-\frac{3}{2}, -5$

90. $2y(y + 4) = 3(y + 4)$ $\frac{3}{2}, -4$

91. $(a - 3)^2 = 36$ $9, -3$

92. $(b + 5)^2 = 16$ $-1, -9$

93. $p^3 = 9p^2$ $0, 9$

94. $p^3 = 7p^2$ $0, 7$

95. $(2z - 3)(z + 5) = (z + 1)(z + 3)$ $-6, 3$

96. $(x + 3)(2x - 1) = (3 - x)(5 - 3x)$ 18, 1

[C] 97. Find $3n^2$ if $n(n + 5) = -4$.   48 or 3

[C] 98. Find $2n^3$ if $n(n + 3) = 4$.   2 or -128

[C] 99. *Geometry* The length of a rectangle is 7 cm, and the width is 4 cm. If both the length and the width are increased by equal amounts, the area of the rectangle is increased by 42 cm². Find the length and width of the larger rectangle.   Length: 10 cm; width: 7 cm

[C] 100. *Geometry* A rectangular piece of cardboard is 10 in. longer than it is wide. Squares 2 in. on a side are to be cut from each corner, and then the sides will be folded up to make an open box with a volume of 192 in³. Find the length and width of the piece of cardboard.   Length: 20 in.; width: 10 in.

101. ✏ Explain the error made in solving the equation at the right. Solve the equation correctly.

$(x + 2)(x - 3) = 6$
$x + 2 = 6$ $x - 3 = 6$
$x = 4$ $x = 9$

102. ✏ Explain the error made in solving the equation at the right. Solve the equation correctly.

$x^2 = x$
$\dfrac{x^2}{x} = \dfrac{x}{x}$
$x = 1$

F ocus on Problem Solving

Making a Table

Sometimes a table can be used to organize information so that it is in a useful form. In the chapter "Solving Equations and Inequalities," we used tables in the applications to organize the data. Tables are also useful in applications that require us to find all possible combinations in a given situation.

> A basketball player scored 11 points in a game. The player can score 1 point for making a free throw, 2 points for making a field goal within the three-point line, and 3 points for making a field goal outside the three-point line. Find the possible combinations in which the player can score the 11 points.

The following table lists all the combinations of shots with which it is possible to score 11 points.

Free throws	0	2	1	3	5	0	2	4	6	8	1	3	5	7	9	11
2-point field goals	1	0	2	1	0	4	3	2	1	0	5	4	3	2	1	0
3-point field goals	3	3	2	2	2	1	1	1	1	1	0	0	0	0	0	0
Total points	11	11	11	11	11	11	11	11	11	11	11	11	11	11	11	11

There are 16 possible ways in which the basketball player could have scored 11 points.

1. A football team scores 17 points. A touchdown counts 6 points, an extra point scores 1 point, a field goal scores 3 points, and a safety scores 2 points. Find the possible combinations with which the team can score 17 points. Remember that the number of extra points cannot exceed the number of touchdowns scored.

2. Repeat Exercise 1. Assume that no safety was scored.

3. Repeat Exercise 1. Assume that no safety was scored and that the team scored two field goals.

4. Find the number of possible combinations of nickels, dimes, and quarters that one can get when receiving $.85 in change.

5. Repeat Exercise 4. Assume no combination contains coins that could be exchanged for a larger coin. That is, the combination of three quarters and two nickels would not be allowed, because the two nickels could be exchanged for a dime.

6. Find the number of possible combinations of $1, $5, $10, and $20 bills that one can get when receiving $33 in change.

The Trial-and-Error Method

A topic in Section 3 of this chapter is factoring trinomials using trial factors. This method involves writing trial factors and then using the FOIL method to determine which pair of factors is the correct one. The **trial-and-error method** of arriving at a solution to a problem involves performing repeated tests or experiments until a satisfactory conclusion is reached. However, not all problems solved using the trial-and-error method have a strategy by which to determine the answer. Here is an example:

Explain how you could cut through a cube so that the face of the resulting solid is **a.** a square, **b.** an equilateral triangle, **c.** a trapezoid, and **d.** a hexagon.

There is no formula to apply to this problem; there is no computation to perform. This problem requires picturing a cube and the results after cutting through it at different places on its surface and at different angles. For part (a), cutting perpendicular to the top and bottom of the cube and parallel to two of its sides will result in a square. The other shapes may prove more difficult.

When solving problems of this type, keep an open mind. Sometimes when using the trial-and-error method, we are hampered by narrowness of vision; we cannot expand our thinking to include other possibilities. Then when we see someone else's solution, it appears so obvious! For example, for the question above, it is necessary to conceive of cutting through the cube at places other than the top surface; we need to be open to the idea of beginning the cut at one of the corner points of the cube.

Look at the letter A printed at the left. If the letter were folded along line ℓ, the two sides of the letter would match exactly. This letter has **symmetry** with respect to line ℓ. Line ℓ is called the **axis of symmetry.** Now consider the letter H printed below at the left. Both line ℓ_1 and ℓ_2 are axes of symmetry for this letter; the letter could be folded along either line and the two sides would match exactly. Does the letter A have more than one axis of symmetry? Find axes of symmetry for other capital letters of the alphabet. Which lower-case letters have one axis of symmetry? Do any of the lower-case letters have more than one axis of symmetry?

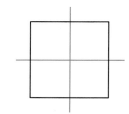

How many axes of symmetry does a square have? In determining lines of symmetry for a square, begin by drawing a square as shown at the right. The horizontal line of symmetry and the vertical line of symmetry may be immediately obvious to you. But there are two others. Do you see that a line drawn through opposite corners of the square is also a line of symmetry?

Find the number of axes of symmetry for each of the following figures: equilateral triangle, rectangle, regular pentagon, regular hexagon, and circle.

Many of the questions in this text that require an answer of "always true, sometimes true, or never true" are best solved by the trial-and-error method. For example, consider the following statement:

If two rectangles have the same area, then they have the same perimeter.

Try some numbers. Each of two rectangles, one measuring 6 units by 2 units and another measuring 4 units by 3 units, has an area of 12 square units, but the perimeter of the first is 16 units and the perimeter of the second is 14 units. Thus the answer "always true" has been eliminated. We still need to determine whether there is a case when it is true. After experimenting with a lot of numbers, you may come to realize that we are trying to determine whether it is possible for two different pairs of factors of a number to have the same sum. Is it?

Don't be afraid to make many experiments, and remember that *errors*, or tests that "don't work," are a part of the trial-and-*error* process.

Projects and Group Activities

Prime and Composite Numbers

A **prime number** is a natural number greater than 1 whose only natural number factors are itself and 1. The number 11 is a prime number because the only natural number factors of 11 are 11 and 1.

Eratosthenes, a Greek philosopher and astronomer who lived from 270 to 190 B.C., devised a method of identifying prime numbers. It is called the **Sieve of Eratosthenes.** The procedure is illustrated in the following paragraphs.

1	(2)	(3)	4	(5)	6	(7)	8	9	10
(11)	12	(13)	14	15	16	(17)	18	(19)	20
21	22	(23)	24	25	26	27	28	(29)	30
(31)	32	33	34	35	36	(37)	38	39	40
(41)	42	(43)	44	45	46	(47)	48	49	50
51	52	(53)	54	55	56	57	58	(59)	60
(61)	62	63	64	65	66	(67)	68	69	70
(71)	72	(73)	74	75	76	77	78	(79)	80
81	82	(83)	84	85	86	87	88	(89)	90
91	92	93	94	95	96	(97)	98	99	100

List all the natural numbers from 1 to 100. Cross out the number 1, because it is not a prime number. The number 2 is prime; circle it. Cross out all the other multiples of 2 (4, 6, 8, . . .), because they are not prime. The number 3 is prime; circle it. Cross out all the other multiples of 3 (6, 9, 12, . . .) that are not already crossed out. The number 4, the next consecutive number in the list, has already been crossed out. The number 5 is prime; circle it. Cross out all the other multiples of 5 that are not already crossed out. Continue in this manner until all the prime numbers less than 100 are circled.

A **composite number** is a natural number greater than 1 that has a natural-number factor other than itself and 1. The number 21 is a composite number because it has factors of 3 and 7. All the numbers crossed out in the table above, except the number 1, are composite numbers.

Solve.

1. Use the Sieve of Eratosthenes to find the prime numbers between 100 and 200.

2. How many prime numbers are even numbers?

3. Find the "twin primes" between 1 and 200. Twin primes are two prime numbers whose difference is 2. For instance, 3 and 5 are twin primes; 5 and 7 are also twin primes.

4. **a.** List two prime numbers that are consecutive natural numbers.

    b. Can there be any other pairs of prime numbers that are consecutive natural numbers?

5. Some primes are the sum of a square and 1. For example, $5 = 2^2 + 1$. Find another prime p such that $p = n^2 + 1$, where n is a natural number.

6. Find a prime p such that $p = n^2 - 1$, where n is a natural number.

7. **a.** 4! (which is read "4 factorial") is equal to $4 \cdot 3 \cdot 2 \cdot 1$. Show that $4! + 2$, $4! + 3$, and $4! + 4$ are all composite numbers.

    b. 5! (which is read "5 factorial") is equal to $5 \cdot 4 \cdot 3 \cdot 2 \cdot 1$. Will $5! + 2$, $5! + 3$, $5! + 4$, and $5! + 5$ generate four consecutive composite numbers?

    c. Use the notation 6! to represent a list of five consecutive composite numbers.

Search the World Wide Web

At the address http://www.utm.edu/research/primes/mersenne.shtml#hist, you can find the history, theorems, and lists of Mersenne Primes. A prime number that can be written in the form $2^n - 1$, where n is also prime, is said to be a Mersenne Prime. An interesting note is that the 25th and 26th Mersenne Primes were found by high school students Laura Nickel and Curt Noll.

Would you like to find the answer to questions such as these?

1. What good are perfect numbers?
2. Is zero prime, composite, or neither?
3. What is the difference between zero and nothing?
4. When something is divided by zero, why is the answer undefined?
5. What is infinity plus one?
6. Is infinity positive or negative?

These and many other questions are answered at the address

    http://www.forum.swarthmore.edu/dr.math/problems/purpose_zero.html

The answers to these questions are presented in a clever and interesting fashion. The answer to the question "What is the purpose of the number zero?" is given below.

> The invention of zero was one of the most important breakthroughs in the history of civilization. More important, in my opinion, than the invention of the wheel. I think that it's a fairly deep concept.
>
> One crucial purpose that zero holds is as a placeholder in our system of notation. When we write the number 408, we're really using a shorthand notation. What we really mean by 408 is "4 times 100, plus 0 times 10, plus 8 times 1." Without the number zero, we wouldn't be able to tell the numbers 408, 48, 480, 408,000, and 4800 apart. So yes, zero is important.
>
> Another crucial role that zero plays in mathematics is that of an "additive identity element." What this means is that when you add zero to any number, you get the number

that you started with. For instance, $5 + 0 = 5$. That may seem obvious and trivial, but it's actually quite important to have such a number. For instance, when you're manipulating some numerical quantity and you want to change its form but not its value, you might add some fancy version of zero to it, like this:

$$x^2 + y^2 = x^2 + y^2 + 2xy - 2xy$$
$$= x^2 + 2xy + y^2 - 2xy$$
$$= (x + y)^2 - 2xy$$

Now if we wanted to, we could use this as a proof that $(x + y)^2$ is always greater than $2xy$; the expression we started with was positive, so the one we ended up with must be positive, too. Therefore, subtracting $2xy$ from $(x + y)^2$ must leave us with a positive number. Neat stuff.*

The Internet is a good source for the history of, and interesting facts about, mathematical concepts. You can use the address

http://www-groups.dcs.st-and.ac.uk/~history/HistTopics/Prime_numbers.html

to find the history of prime numbers. This Web address also contains a list of unsolved problems that involve prime numbers.

Chapter Summary

Key Words

The *greatest common factor* (GCF) of two or more integers is the greatest integer that is a factor of all the integers. (Objective 8.1.1)

The greatest common factor of 12 and 18 is 6 because 6 is the greatest integer that divides evenly into both 12 and 18.

To *factor a polynomial* means to write the polynomial as a product of other polynomials.   (Objective 8.1.1)

To factor $8x + 12$ means to write it as the product $4(2x + 3)$. The expression $8x + 12$ is a sum. The expression $4(2x + 3)$ is a product (the polynomial $2x + 3$ is multiplied by 4).

To *factor a trinomial of the form* $ax^2 + bx + c$ means to express the trinomial as the product of two binomials. (Objective 8.3.1)

To factor $3x^2 + 7x + 2$ means to write it as the product $(3x + 1)(x + 2)$.

A polynomial that does not factor using only integers is *nonfactorable over the integers.*   (Objective 8.2.1)

The trinomial $x^2 + x + 2$ is nonfactorable over the integers. There are no two integers whose product is 2 and whose sum is 1.

An equation of the form $ax^2 + bx + c = 0$, $a \neq 0$, is a *quadratic equation.* A quadratic equation is in *standard form* when the polynomial is in descending order and equal to zero. (Objective 8.5.1)

The equation $2x^2 + 7x + 3 = 0$ is a quadratic equation in standard form.

Essential Rules and Procedures

Factoring the Difference of Two Squares
The difference of two squares is the product of the sum and difference of two terms.

$a^2 - b^2 = (a + b)(a - b)$ (Objective 8.4.1)

$y^2 - 81 = (y + 9)(y - 9)$

Factoring a Perfect-Square Trinomial
A perfect-square trinomial is the square of a binomial.

$a^2 + 2ab + b^2 = (a + b)^2$

$a^2 - 2ab + b^2 = (a - b)^2$ (Objective 8.4.1)

$x^2 + 10x + 25 = (x + 5)^2$

$x^2 - 10x + 25 = (x - 5)^2$

General Factoring Strategy   (Objective 8.4.2)

1. Is there a common factor? If so, factor out the common factor.

2. Is the polynomial the difference of two squares? If so, factor.

3. Is the polynomial a perfect-square trinomial? If so, factor.

4. Is the polynomial a trinomial that is the product of two binomials? If so, factor.

5. Does the polynomial contain four terms? If so, try factoring by grouping.

6. Is each binomial factor nonfactorable over the integers? If not, factor.

$24x + 6 = 6(4x + 1)$

$2x^2y + 6xy + 8y = 2y(x^2 + 3x + 4)$

$4x^2 - 49 = (2x + 7)(2x - 7)$

$9x^2 + 6x + 1 = (3x + 1)^2$

$2x^2 + 7x + 5 = (2x + 5)(x + 1)$

$x^3 - 3x^2 + 2x - 6 = (x^3 - 3x^2) + (2x - 6)$
$= x^2(x - 3) + 2(x - 3)$
$= (x - 3)(x^2 + 2)$

$x^4 - 16 = (x^2 + 4)(x^2 - 4)$
$= (x^2 + 4)(x + 2)(x - 2)$

The Principle of Zero Products
If the product of two factors is zero, then at least one of the factors must be zero.

If $a \cdot b = 0$, then $a = 0$ or $b = 0$.

The Principle of Zero Products is used to solve a quadratic equation by factoring.   (Objective 8.5.1)

$x^2 + x = 12$

$x^2 + x - 12 = 0$

$(x + 4)(x - 3) = 0$

$x + 4 = 0 \qquad x - 3 = 0$
$x = -4 \qquad\quad x = 3$

Chapter Review Exercises

1. Factor: $14y^9 - 49y^6 + 7y^3$ $7y^3(2y^6 - 7y^3 + 1)$

2. Factor: $3a^2 - 12a + ab - 4b$ $(a - 4)(3a + b)$

3. Factor: $c^2 + 8c + 12$ $(c + 2)(c + 6)$

4. Factor: $a^3 - 5a^2 + 6a$ $a(a - 2)(a - 3)$

5. Factor: $6x^2 - 29x + 28$ $(2x - 7)(3x - 4)$

6. Factor: $3y^2 + 16y - 12$ $(y + 6)(3y - 2)$

7. Factor: $18a^2 - 3a - 10$ $(3a + 2)(6a - 5)$

8. Factor: $a^2b^2 - 1$ $(ab + 1)(ab - 1)$

9. Factor: $4y^2 - 16y + 16$ $4(y - 2)^2$

10. Solve: $a(5a + 1) = 0$ $0, -\dfrac{1}{5}$

11. Factor: $12a^2b + 3ab^2$ $3ab(4a + b)$

12. Factor: $b^2 - 13b + 30$ $(b - 3)(b - 10)$

13. Factor: $10x^2 + 25x + 4xy + 10y$ $(2x + 5)(5x + 2y)$

14. Factor: $3a^2 - 15a - 42$ $3(a + 2)(a - 7)$

15. Factor: $n^4 - 2n^3 - 3n^2$ $n^2(n + 1)(n - 3)$

16. Factor: $2x^2 - 5x + 6$ Nonfactorable

17. Factor: $6x^2 - 7x + 2$ $(2x - 1)(3x - 2)$

18. Factor: $16x^2 + 49$ Nonfactorable

19. Solve: $(x - 2)(2x - 3) = 0$ $2, \frac{3}{2}$

20. Factor: $7x^2 - 7$ $7(x + 1)(x - 1)$

21. Factor: $3x^5 - 9x^4 - 4x^3$ $x^3(3x^2 - 9x - 4)$

22. Factor: $4x(x - 3) - 5(3 - x)$ $(x - 3)(4x + 5)$

23. Factor: $a^2 + 5a - 14$ $(a + 7)(a - 2)$

24. Factor: $y^2 + 5y - 36$ $(y + 9)(y - 4)$

25. Factor: $5x^2 - 50x - 120$ $5(x - 12)(x + 2)$

26. Solve: $(x + 1)(x - 5) = 16$ $-3, 7$

27. Factor: $7a^2 + 17a + 6$ $(a + 2)(7a + 3)$

28. Factor: $4x^2 + 83x + 60$ $(x + 20)(4x + 3)$

29. Factor: $9y^4 - 25z^2$ $(3y^2 + 5z)(3y^2 - 5z)$

30. Factor: $5x^2 - 5x - 30$ $5(x + 2)(x - 3)$

31. Solve: $6 - 6y^2 = 5y$ $-\frac{3}{2}, \frac{2}{3}$

32. Factor: $12b^3 - 58b^2 + 56b$ $2b(2b - 7)(3b - 4)$

33. Factor: $5x^3 + 10x^2 + 35x$ $5x(x^2 + 2x + 7)$

34. Factor: $x^2 - 23x + 42$ $(x - 2)(x - 21)$

35. Factor: $a(3a + 2) - 7(3a + 2)$ $(3a + 2)(a - 7)$

36. Factor: $8x^2 - 38x + 45$ $(2x - 5)(4x - 9)$

37. Factor: $10a^2x - 130ax + 360x$ $10x(a - 4)(a - 9)$

38. Factor: $2a^2 - 19a - 60$ $(a - 12)(2a + 5)$

39. Factor: $21ax - 35bx - 10by + 6ay$
$(3a - 5b)(7x + 2y)$

40. Factor: $a^6 - 100$ $(a^3 + 10)(a^3 - 10)$

41. Factor: $16a^2 + 8a + 1$ $(4a + 1)^2$

42. Solve: $4x^2 + 27x = 7$ $\frac{1}{4}, -7$

43. Factor: $20a^2 + 10a - 280$ $10(a + 4)(2a - 7)$

44. Factor: $6x - 18$ $6(x - 3)$

45. Factor: $3x^4y + 2x^3y + 6x^2y$ $x^2y(3x^2 + 2x + 6)$

46. Factor: $d^2 + 3d - 40$ $(d - 5)(d + 8)$

47. Factor: $24x^2 - 12xy + 10y - 20x$
$2(2x - y)(6x - 5)$

48. Factor: $4x^3 - 20x^2 - 24x$ $4x(x + 1)(x - 6)$

49. Solve: $x^2 - 8x - 20 = 0$ $-2, 10$

50. Factor: $3x^2 - 17x + 10$ $(x - 5)(3x - 2)$

51. Factor: $16x^2 - 94x + 33$ $(2x - 11)(8x - 3)$

52. Factor: $9x^2 - 30x + 25$ $(3x - 5)^2$

53. Factor: $12y^2 + 16y - 3$ $(2y + 3)(6y - 1)$

54. Factor: $3x^2 + 36x + 108$ $3(x + 6)^2$

55. The length of a playing field is twice the width. The area is 5000 yd². Find the length and width of the playing field.   Length: 100 yd; width: 50 yd

56. The length of a hockey field is 20 yd less than twice the width. The area of the field is 6000 yd². Find the length and width of the hockey field.
Length: 100 yd; width: 60 yd

57. The sum of the squares of two consecutive positive integers is forty-one. Find the two integers.   4 and 5

58. The size of a motion picture on the screen is given by the equation $S = d^2$, where d is the distance between the projector and the screen. Find the distance between the projector and the screen when the size of the picture is 400 ft². 20 ft

59. A rectangular garden plot has dimensions 15 ft by 12 ft. A uniform path around the garden increases the total area to 270 ft². What is the width of the larger rectangle?   15 ft

60. The length of each side of a square is extended 4 ft. The area of the resulting square is 576 ft². Find the length of a side of the original square.   20 ft

Chapter Test

1. Factor: $6x^2y^2 + 9xy^2 + 12y^2$ $3y^2(2x^2 + 3x + 4)$

2. Factor: $6x^3 - 8x^2 + 10x$ $2x(3x^2 - 4x + 5)$

3. Factor: $p^2 + 5p + 6$ $(p + 2)(p + 3)$

4. Factor: $a(x - 2) + b(2 - x)$ $(x - 2)(a - b)$

5. Solve: $(2a - 3)(a + 7) = 0$ $\frac{3}{2}, -7$

6. Factor: $a^2 - 19a + 48$ $(a - 3)(a - 16)$

7. Factor: $x^3 + 2x^2 - 15x$ $x(x + 5)(x - 3)$

8. Factor: $8x^2 + 20x - 48$ $4(x + 4)(2x - 3)$

9. Factor: $ab + 6a - 3b - 18$ $(b + 6)(a - 3)$

10. Solve: $4x^2 - 1 = 0$ $\frac{1}{2}, -\frac{1}{2}$

11. Factor: $6x^2 + 19x + 8$ $(2x + 1)(3x + 8)$

12. Factor: $x^2 - 9x - 36$ $(x + 3)(x - 12)$

13. Factor: $2b^2 - 32$ $2(b + 4)(b - 4)$

14. Factor: $4a^2 - 12ab + 9b^2$ $(2a - 3b)^2$

15. Factor: $px + x - p - 1$ $(p + 1)(x - 1)$

16. Factor: $5x^2 - 45x - 15$ $5(x^2 - 9x - 3)$

17. Factor: $2x^2 + 4x - 5$ Nonfactorable

18. Factor: $4x^2 - 49y^2$ $(2x + 7y)(2x - 7y)$

19. Solve: $x(x - 8) = -15$ 3, 5

20. Factor: $p^2 + 12p + 36$ $(p + 6)^2$

21. Factor: $18x^2 - 48xy + 32y^2$ $2(3x - 4y)^2$

22. Factor: $2y^4 - 14y^3 - 16y^2$ $2y^2(y + 1)(y - 8)$

23. The length of a rectangle is 3 cm more than twice the width. The area of the rectangle is 90 cm². Find the length and width of the rectangle.
Length: 15 cm; width: 6 cm

24. The length of the base of a triangle is three times the height. The area of the triangle is 24 in². Find the length of the base of the triangle.   12 in.

25. The product of two consecutive negative integers is one hundred fifty-six. Find the two integers.   −13, −12

Cumulative Review Exercises

1. Subtract: $4 - (-5) - 6 - 11$ -8

2. Divide: $0.372 \div (-0.046)$
Round to the nearest tenth. -8.1

3. Simplify: $(3 - 7)^2 \div (-2) - 3 \cdot (-4)$ 4

4. Evaluate $-2a^2 \div (2b) - c$ when $a = -4$, $b = 2$, and $c = -1$. -7

5. Identify the property that justifies the statement.
$(3 + 8) + 7 = 3 + (8 + 7)$
The Associative Property of Addition

6. Multiply: $-\frac{3}{4}(-24x^2)$ $18x^2$

7. Simplify: $-2[3x - 4(3 - 2x) - 8x]$ $-6x + 24$

8. Solve: $-\frac{5}{7}x = -\frac{10}{21}$ $\frac{2}{3}$

9. Solve: $4 + 3(x - 2) = 13$ 5

10. Solve: $3x - 2 = 12 - 5x$ $\frac{7}{4}$

11. Solve: $-2 + 4[3x - 2(4 - x) - 3] = 4x + 2$ 3

12. 120% of what number is 42? 35

13. Solve: $-4x - 2 \geq 10$ $x \leq -3$

14. Solve: $9 - 2(4x - 5) < 3(7 - 6x)$ $x < \frac{1}{5}$

15. Graph: $y = \frac{3}{4}x - 2$

16. Graph: $f(x) = -3x - 3$

17. Find the domain and range of the relation $\{(-5, -4), (-3, -2), (-1, 0), (1, 2), (3, 4)\}$. Is the relation a function?
D: $\{-5, -3, -1, 1, 3\}$; R: $\{-4, -2, 0, 2, 4\}$; yes

18. Evaluate $f(x) = 6x - 5$ at $x = 11$.   61

19. Graph the solution set of $x + 3y > 2$.

20. Solve by substitution: $6x + y = 7$
$x - 3y = 17$ $(2, -5)$

21. Solve by the addition method: $2x - 3y = -4$
$(1, 2)$ $5x + y = 7$

22. Add: $(3y^3 - 5y^2 - 6) + (2y^2 - 8y + 1)$
$3y^3 - 3y^2 - 8y - 5$

23. Simplify: $(-3a^4b^2)^3$ $-27a^{12}b^6$

24. Multiply: $(x + 2)(x^2 - 5x + 4)$
$x^3 - 3x^2 - 6x + 8$

25. Divide: $(8x^2 + 4x - 3) \div (2x - 3)$
$4x + 8 + \dfrac{21}{2x - 3}$

26. Simplify: $(x^{-4}y^2)^3$ $\dfrac{y^6}{x^{12}}$

27. Factor: $3a - 3b - ax + bx$ $(a - b)(3 - x)$

28. Factor: $x^2 + 3xy - 10y^2$ $(x + 5y)(x - 2y)$

29. Factor: $6a^4 + 22a^3 + 12a^2$ $2a^2(3a + 2)(a + 3)$

30. Factor: $25a^2 - 36b^2$ $(5a + 6b)(5a - 6b)$

31. Factor: $12x^2 - 36xy + 27y^2$ $3(2x - 3y)^2$

32. Solve: $3x^2 + 11x - 20 = 0$ $\dfrac{4}{3}, -5$

33. Find the range of the function given by the equation $f(x) = \frac{4}{5}x - 3$ if the domain is $\{-10, -5, 0, 5, 10\}$. $\{-11, -7, -3, 1, 5\}$

34. The daily high temperatures, in degrees Celsius, during one week were recorded as follows: $-4°, -7°, 2°, 0°, -1°, -6°, -5°$. Find the average daily high temperature for the week. $-3°C$

35. The width of a rectangle is 40% of the length. The perimeter of the rectangle is 42 cm. Find the length and width of the rectangle.
Length: 15 cm; width: 6 cm

36. A board 10 ft long is cut into two pieces. Four times the length of the shorter piece is 2 ft less than three times the length of the longer piece. Find the length of each piece.   4 ft and 6 ft

37. Company A rents cars for $6 a day and 25¢ for every mile driven. Company B rents cars for $15 a day and 10¢ per mile. You want to rent a car for 6 days. What is the maximum number of miles you can drive a Company A car if it is to cost you less than a Company B car?   359 mi

38. An investment of $4000 is made at an annual simple interest rate of 8%. How much additional money must be invested at an annual simple interest rate of 11% so that the total interest earned is $1035? $6500

39. A stereo that regularly sells for $165 is on sale for $99. Find the discount rate.
40%

40. Find three consecutive even integers such that five times the middle integer is twelve more than twice the sum of the first and third.   10, 12, 14

9

Algebraic Fractions

Carpentry requires the application of geometric concepts. A cabinet, for instance, has sides that must lie in parallel planes and doors that are in the shape of rectangles. A carpenter also applies the geometric principles of congruence and similarity; for example, the drawers in a dresser may be the same size and shape, or they may be the same shape but different sizes. Similar objects are a topic in Section 5 of this chapter.

OBJECTIVES

Measurement of the Circumference of Earth

Distances on Earth, the circumference of Earth, and the distance to the moon and stars are known to great precision. Eratosthenes, the fifth librarian of Alexandria (230 B.C.), laid the foundation of scientific geography with his determination of the circumference of Earth.

Eratosthenes was familiar with certain astronomical data that enabled him to calculate the circumference of Earth by using a proportion statement.

Eratosthenes knew that on a mid-summer day, the sun was directly overhead at Syrene, as shown in the diagram. At the same time, at Alexandria the sun was at a $7\frac{1}{2}°$ angle from the zenith. The distance from Syrene to Alexandria was 5000 stadia (about 520 mi).

Knowing that the ratio of the $7\frac{1}{2}°$ angle to one revolution (360°) is equal to the ratio of the arc length (520 mi) to the circumference, Eratosthenes was able to write and solve a proportion.

This result, calculated over 2000 years ago, is very close to the accepted value of 24,800 miles.

Syrene

Alexandria

520 mi

$7\frac{1}{2}°$

$$\frac{7\frac{1}{2}°}{360°} = \frac{520 \text{ mi}}{C}$$

$C = 24{,}960$ miles

SECTION **9.1**

Multiplication and Division of Algebraic Fractions

1   Simplify algebraic fractions

A fraction in which the numerator and denominator are polynomials is called an **algebraic fraction.** Examples of algebraic fractions are shown at the right.

$$\frac{5}{z} \qquad \frac{x^2 + 1}{2x - 1} \qquad \frac{y^2 - 3}{3xy + 1}$$

Care must be exercised with algebraic fractions to ensure that when the variables are replaced with numbers, the resulting denominator is not zero.

Consider the algebraic fraction at the right. The value of x cannot be 2 because the denominator would then be zero.

$$\frac{3x + 1}{2x - 4}$$

$$\frac{3 \cdot 2 + 1}{2 \cdot 2 - 4} = \frac{7}{0} \leftarrow \text{Not a real number}$$

A fraction is in simplest form when the numerator and denominator have no common factors other than 1. The Multiplication Property of One is used to write an algebraic fraction in simplest form.

INSTRUCTOR NOTE

Simplifying an algebraic fraction is closely related to simplifying a rational number—the common factors are removed. Making this connection will help some students.

As a classroom exercise, have students evaluate

$$\frac{x^2 - 4}{x^2 - 2x - 8} \quad \text{and} \quad \frac{x - 2}{x - 4}$$

for various values of x and determine that, except for -2 and 4, the expressions are equal.

➡ Simplify: $\dfrac{x^2 - 4}{x^2 - 2x - 8}$

Factor the numerator and denominator.

$$\frac{x^2 - 4}{x^2 - 2x - 8} = \frac{(x - 2)(x + 2)}{(x - 4)(x + 2)}$$

$$= \frac{x - 2}{x - 4} \cdot \boxed{\frac{x + 2}{x + 2}}$$

$$= \frac{x - 2}{x - 4} \cdot 1$$

The restrictions $x \neq -2$ and $x \neq 4$ are necessary to prevent division by zero.

$$= \frac{x - 2}{x - 4}, \ x \neq -2, 4$$

This simplification is usually shown with slashes through the common factors. The last simplification would be shown as follows.

$$\frac{x^2 - 4}{x^2 - 2x - 8} = \frac{(x - 2)\overset{1}{\cancel{(x + 2)}}}{(x - 4)\underset{1}{\cancel{(x + 2)}}} = \frac{x - 2}{x - 4}, \ x \neq -2, 4$$

In this problem, it is stated that $x \neq -2, 4$. Look at the factored form of the original algebraic fraction.

$$\frac{(x - 2)(x + 2)}{(x - 4)(x + 2)}$$

If either of the factors in the denominator is zero, then the denominator is zero.

$$x + 2 = 0 \qquad x - 4 = 0$$
$$x = -2 \qquad x = 4$$

When x is -2 or 4, the denominator is 0. Therefore, for this fraction, $x \neq -2, 4$.

For the remaining examples, we will omit the restrictions on the variables that prevent division by zero and assume the values of the variables are such that division by zero is not possible.

➡ Simplify: $\dfrac{10 + 3x - x^2}{x^2 - 4x - 5}$

Factor the numerator and denominator.

$$\dfrac{10 + 3x - x^2}{x^2 - 4x - 5} = \dfrac{(5 - x)(2 + x)}{(x - 5)(x + 1)}$$

Divide by the common factors. Remember that $5 - x = -(x - 5)$. Therefore,

$$\dfrac{5 - x}{x - 5} = \dfrac{-(x - 5)}{x - 5} = \dfrac{-1}{1} = -1$$

$$= \dfrac{\overset{-1}{\cancel{(5 - x)}}(2 + x)}{\underset{1}{\cancel{(x - 5)}}(x + 1)}$$

Write the answer in simplest form.

$$= -\dfrac{x + 2}{x + 1} \quad ⬅$$

Example 1   Simplify.   A. $\dfrac{4x^3 y^4}{6x^4 y}$ B. $\dfrac{9 - x^2}{x^2 + x - 12}$

Solution   A. $\dfrac{4x^3 y^4}{6x^4 y} = \dfrac{\overset{1}{\cancel{2}} \cdot 2x^3 y^4}{\underset{1}{\cancel{2}} \cdot 3x^4 y} = \dfrac{2y^3}{3x}$ ▸ Simplify using the rules of exponents.

B. $\dfrac{9 - x^2}{x^2 + x - 12} = \dfrac{\overset{-1}{\cancel{(3 - x)}}(3 + x)}{\underset{1}{\cancel{(x - 3)}}(x + 4)} = -\dfrac{x + 3}{x + 4}$

Problem 1   Simplify.   A. $\dfrac{6x^5 y}{12x^2 y^3}$ B. $\dfrac{x^2 + 2x - 24}{16 - x^2}$

Solution   See page S19.   A. $\dfrac{x^3}{2y^2}$ B. $-\dfrac{x + 6}{x + 4}$

---

2   ## Multiply algebraic fractions

The product of two fractions is a fraction whose numerator is the product of the numerators of the two fractions and whose denominator is the product of the denominators of the two fractions.

$$\dfrac{a}{b} \cdot \dfrac{c}{d} = \dfrac{ac}{bd}$$

$$\dfrac{2}{3} \cdot \dfrac{4}{5} = \dfrac{8}{15}$$

$$\dfrac{3x}{y} \cdot \dfrac{2}{z} = \dfrac{6x}{yz}$$

$$\dfrac{x + 2}{x} \cdot \dfrac{3}{x - 2} = \dfrac{3(x + 2)}{x(x - 2)}$$

➡ Multiply: $\dfrac{x^2 + 3x}{x^2 - 3x - 4} \cdot \dfrac{x^2 - 5x + 4}{x^2 + 2x - 3}$

$$\dfrac{x^2 + 3x}{x^2 - 3x - 4} \cdot \dfrac{x^2 - 5x + 4}{x^2 + 2x - 3}$$

Factor the numerator and denominator of each fraction.

$$= \dfrac{x(x + 3)}{(x - 4)(x + 1)} \cdot \dfrac{(x - 4)(x - 1)}{(x + 3)(x - 1)}$$

Multiply. Divide by the common factors.

$$= \dfrac{x\cancel{(x + 3)}\cancel{(x - 4)}\cancel{(x - 1)}}{\cancel{(x - 4)}(x + 1)\cancel{(x + 3)}\cancel{(x - 1)}}$$

Write the answer in simplest form.

$$= \dfrac{x}{x + 1}$$

⬅

Example 2   Multiply.

A. $\dfrac{10x^2 - 15x}{12x - 8} \cdot \dfrac{3x - 2}{20x - 25}$ B. $\dfrac{x^2 + x - 6}{x^2 + 7x + 12} \cdot \dfrac{x^2 + 3x - 4}{4 - x^2}$

Solution   A. $\dfrac{10x^2 - 15x}{12x - 8} \cdot \dfrac{3x - 2}{20x - 25}$

$$= \dfrac{5x(2x - 3)}{4(3x - 2)} \cdot \dfrac{(3x - 2)}{5(4x - 5)}$$ ▶ Factor the numerator and denominator of each fraction.

$$= \dfrac{\cancel{5}x(2x - 3)\cancel{(3x - 2)}}{2 \cdot 2\cancel{(3x - 2)}\cancel{5}(4x - 5)}$$ ▶ Multiply. Divide by the common factors.

$$= \dfrac{x(2x - 3)}{4(4x - 5)}$$ ▶ Write the answer in simplest form.

B. $\dfrac{x^2 + x - 6}{x^2 + 7x + 12} \cdot \dfrac{x^2 + 3x - 4}{4 - x^2}$

$$= \dfrac{(x + 3)(x - 2)}{(x + 3)(x + 4)} \cdot \dfrac{(x + 4)(x - 1)}{(2 - x)(2 + x)}$$

$$= \dfrac{\cancel{(x + 3)}\overset{-1}{\cancel{(x - 2)}}\cancel{(x + 4)}(x - 1)}{\cancel{(x + 3)}\cancel{(x + 4)}\cancel{(2 - x)}(2 + x)}$$

$$= -\dfrac{x - 1}{x + 2}$$

Problem 2   Multiply.

A. $\dfrac{12x^2 + 3x}{10x - 15} \cdot \dfrac{8x - 12}{9x + 18}$ B. $\dfrac{x^2 + 2x - 15}{9 - x^2} \cdot \dfrac{x^2 - 3x - 18}{x^2 - 7x + 6}$

Solution   See page S19.   A. $\dfrac{4x(4x + 1)}{15(x + 2)}$ B. $-\dfrac{x + 5}{x - 1}$

3 Divide algebraic fractions

The **reciprocal** of a fraction is a fraction with the numerator and denominator interchanged.

Fraction $\left\{\begin{array}{l}\dfrac{a}{b}\\[6pt] x^2 = \dfrac{x^2}{1}\\[6pt] \dfrac{x+2}{x}\end{array}\right.$ $\left.\begin{array}{l}\dfrac{b}{a}\\[6pt] \dfrac{1}{x^2}\\[6pt] \dfrac{x}{x+2}\end{array}\right\}$ Reciprocal

To divide two fractions, multiply by the reciprocal of the divisor.

$$\frac{a}{b} \div \frac{c}{d} = \frac{a}{b} \cdot \frac{d}{c} = \frac{ad}{bc}$$

$$\frac{4}{x} \div \frac{y}{5} = \frac{4}{x} \cdot \frac{5}{y} = \frac{20}{xy}$$

$$\frac{x+4}{x} \div \frac{x-2}{4} = \frac{x+4}{x} \cdot \frac{4}{x-2} = \frac{4(x+4)}{x(x-2)}$$

The basis for the division rule is shown below.

$$\underbrace{\frac{a}{b} \div \frac{c}{d}}_{} = \frac{\dfrac{a}{b}}{\dfrac{c}{d}} = \frac{\dfrac{a}{b} \cdot \dfrac{d}{c}}{\dfrac{c}{d} \cdot \dfrac{d}{c}} = \frac{\dfrac{a}{b} \cdot \dfrac{d}{c}}{1} = \underbrace{\frac{a}{b} \cdot \frac{d}{c}}_{}$$

Example 3 Divide.

A. $\dfrac{xy^2 - 3x^2y}{z^2} \div \dfrac{6x^2 - 2xy}{z^3}$ B. $\dfrac{2x^2 + 5x + 2}{2x^2 + 3x - 2} \div \dfrac{3x^2 + 13x + 4}{2x^2 + 7x - 4}$

Solution A. $\dfrac{xy^2 - 3x^2y}{z^2} \div \dfrac{6x^2 - 2xy}{z^3} = \dfrac{xy^2 - 3x^2y}{z^2} \cdot \dfrac{z^3}{6x^2 - 2xy}$

$$= \frac{xy\overset{-1}{\cancel{(y - 3x)}} \cdot z^3}{z^2 \cdot 2x\underset{1}{\cancel{(3x - y)}}}$$

$$= -\frac{yz}{2}$$

B. $\dfrac{2x^2 + 5x + 2}{2x^2 + 3x - 2} \div \dfrac{3x^2 + 13x + 4}{2x^2 + 7x - 4} = \dfrac{2x^2 + 5x + 2}{2x^2 + 3x - 2} \cdot \dfrac{2x^2 + 7x - 4}{3x^2 + 13x + 4}$

$$= \frac{(2x + 1)\overset{1}{\cancel{(x + 2)}}}{\underset{1}{\cancel{(2x - 1)}}\overset{1}{\cancel{(x + 2)}}} \cdot \frac{\underset{1}{\cancel{(2x - 1)}}\overset{1}{\cancel{(x + 4)}}}{(3x + 1)\underset{1}{\cancel{(x + 4)}}}$$

$$= \frac{2x + 1}{3x + 1}$$

Problem 3 Divide.

A. $\dfrac{a^2}{4bc^2 - 2b^2c} \div \dfrac{a}{6bc - 3b^2}$ B. $\dfrac{3x^2 + 26x + 16}{3x^2 - 7x - 6} \div \dfrac{2x^2 + 9x - 5}{x^2 + 2x - 15}$

Solution See page S19. A. $\dfrac{3a}{2c}$ B. $\dfrac{x+8}{2x-1}$

CONCEPT REVIEW 9.1

Determine whether the statement is always true, sometimes true, or never true.

1. Algebraic fractions are rational expressions.   Always true

2. A fraction is in simplest form when the only factor common to both the numerator and the denominator is 1.   Always true

3. Before multiplying two algebraic fractions, we must write the fractions in terms of a common denominator.   Never true

4. The expression $\dfrac{x}{x + 2}$ is not a real number if $x = 0$.   Never true

5. The procedure for multiplying algebraic fractions is the same as that for multiplying arithmetic fractions.   Always true

6. When an algebraic fraction is rewritten in simplest form, its value is less than it was before it was rewritten in simplest form.   Never true

7. To divide two algebraic fractions, multiply the reciprocal of the first fraction by the second fraction.   Never true

EXERCISES 9.1

I 1. What is an algebraic fraction? Provide an example.

2. When is an algebraic fraction in simplest form?

3. For the algebraic fraction $\dfrac{x + 7}{x - 4}$, explain why the value of x cannot be 4.

4. Explain why the following simplification is incorrect.

$$\frac{x + 3}{x} = \frac{\overset{1}{\cancel{x}} + 3}{\underset{1}{\cancel{x}}} = 4$$

Simplify.

5. $\dfrac{9x^3}{12x^4}$ $\quad \dfrac{3}{4x}$

6. $\dfrac{16x^2y}{24xy^3}$ $\quad \dfrac{2x}{3y^2}$

7. $\dfrac{(x + 3)^2}{(x + 3)^3}$ $\quad \dfrac{1}{x + 3}$

8. $\dfrac{(2x - 1)^5}{(2x - 1)^4}$ $\quad 2x - 1$

9. $\dfrac{3n - 4}{4 - 3n}$ $\quad -1$

10. $\dfrac{5 - 2x}{2x - 5}$ $\quad -1$

11. $\dfrac{6y(y + 2)}{9y^2(y + 2)}$ $\quad \dfrac{2}{3y}$

12. $\dfrac{12x^2(3 - x)}{18x(3 - x)}$ $\quad \dfrac{2x}{3}$

13. $\dfrac{6x(x - 5)}{8x^2(5 - x)}$ $\quad -\dfrac{3}{4x}$

14. $\dfrac{14x^3(7 - 3x)}{21x(3x - 7)}$ $\quad -\dfrac{2x^2}{3}$

15. $\dfrac{a^2 + 4a}{ab + 4b}$ $\quad \dfrac{a}{b}$

16. $\dfrac{x^2 - 3x}{2x - 6}$ $\quad \dfrac{x}{2}$

17. $\dfrac{4-6x}{3x^2-2x}$ $\quad -\dfrac{2}{x}$

18. $\dfrac{5xy-3y}{9-15x}$ $\quad -\dfrac{y}{3}$

19. $\dfrac{y^2-3y+2}{y^2-4y+3}$ $\quad \dfrac{y-2}{y-3}$

20. $\dfrac{x^2+5x+6}{x^2+8x+15}$ $\quad \dfrac{x+2}{x+5}$

21. $\dfrac{x^2+3x-10}{x^2+2x-8}$ $\quad \dfrac{x+5}{x+4}$

22. $\dfrac{a^2+7a-8}{a^2+6a-7}$ $\quad \dfrac{a+8}{a+7}$

23. $\dfrac{x^2+x-12}{x^2-6x+9}$ $\quad \dfrac{x+4}{x-3}$

24. $\dfrac{x^2+8x+16}{x^2-2x-24}$ $\quad \dfrac{x+4}{x-6}$

25. $\dfrac{x^2-3x-10}{25-x^2}$ $\quad -\dfrac{x+2}{x+5}$

26. $\dfrac{4-y^2}{y^2-3y-10}$ $\quad \dfrac{2-y}{y-5}$

27. $\dfrac{2x^3+2x^2-4x}{x^3+2x^2-3x}$ $\quad \dfrac{2(x+2)}{x+3}$

28. $\dfrac{3x^3-12x}{6x^3-24x^2+24x}$ $\quad \dfrac{x+2}{2(x-2)}$

29. $\dfrac{6x^2-7x+2}{6x^2+5x-6}$ $\quad \dfrac{2x-1}{2x+3}$

30. $\dfrac{2n^2-9n+4}{2n^2-5n-12}$ $\quad \dfrac{2n-1}{2n+3}$

2 Multiply.

31. $\dfrac{8x^2}{9y^3}\cdot\dfrac{3y^2}{4x^3}$ $\quad \dfrac{2}{3xy}$

32. $\dfrac{4a^2b^3}{15x^5y^2}\cdot\dfrac{25x^3y}{16ab}$ $\quad \dfrac{5ab^2}{12x^2y}$

33. $\dfrac{12x^3y^4}{7a^2b^3}\cdot\dfrac{14a^3b^4}{9x^2y^2}$ $\quad \dfrac{8xy^2ab}{3}$

34. $\dfrac{18a^4b^2}{25x^2y^3}\cdot\dfrac{50x^5y^6}{27a^6b^2}$ $\quad \dfrac{4x^3y^3}{3a^2}$

35. $\dfrac{3x-6}{5x-20}\cdot\dfrac{10x-40}{27x-54}$ $\quad \dfrac{2}{9}$

36. $\dfrac{8x-12}{14x+7}\cdot\dfrac{42x+21}{32x-48}$ $\quad \dfrac{3}{4}$

37. $\dfrac{3x^2+2x}{2xy-3y}\cdot\dfrac{2xy^3-3y^3}{3x^3+2x^2}$ $\quad \dfrac{y^2}{x}$

38. $\dfrac{4a^2x-3a^2}{2by+5b}\cdot\dfrac{2b^3y+5b^3}{4ax-3a}$ $\quad ab^2$

39. $\dfrac{x^2+5x+4}{x^3y^2}\cdot\dfrac{x^2y^3}{x^2+2x+1}$ $\quad \dfrac{y(x+4)}{x(x+1)}$

40. $\dfrac{x^2+x-2}{xy^2}\cdot\dfrac{x^3y}{x^2+5x+6}$ $\quad \dfrac{x^2(x-1)}{y(x+3)}$

41. $\dfrac{x^4y^2}{x^2+3x-28}\cdot\dfrac{x^2-49}{xy^4}$ $\quad \dfrac{x^3(x-7)}{y^2(x-4)}$

42. $\dfrac{x^5y^3}{x^2+13x+30}\cdot\dfrac{x^2+2x-3}{x^7y^2}$ $\quad \dfrac{y(x-1)}{x^2(x+10)}$

43. $\dfrac{2x^2-5x}{2xy+y}\cdot\dfrac{2xy^2+y^2}{5x^2-2x^3}$ $\quad -\dfrac{y}{x}$

44. $\dfrac{3a^3+4a^2}{5ab-3b}\cdot\dfrac{3b^3-5ab^3}{3a^2+4a}$ $\quad -ab^2$

45. $\dfrac{x^2-2x-24}{x^2-5x-6}\cdot\dfrac{x^2+5x+6}{x^2+6x+8}$ $\quad \dfrac{x+3}{x+1}$

46. $\dfrac{x^2-8x+7}{x^2+3x-4}\cdot\dfrac{x^2+3x-10}{x^2-9x+14}$ $\quad \dfrac{x+5}{x+4}$

47. $\dfrac{x^2+2x-35}{x^2+4x-21}\cdot\dfrac{x^2+3x-18}{x^2+9x+18}$ $\quad \dfrac{x-5}{x+3}$

48. $\dfrac{y^2+y-20}{y^2+2y-15}\cdot\dfrac{y^2+4y-21}{y^2+3y-28}$ $\quad 1$

49. $\dfrac{x^2-3x-4}{x^2+6x+5}\cdot\dfrac{x^2+5x+6}{8+2x-x^2}$ $\quad -\dfrac{x+3}{x+5}$

50. $\dfrac{25-n^2}{n^2-2n-35}\cdot\dfrac{n^2-8n-20}{n^2-3n-10}$ $\quad -\dfrac{n-10}{n-7}$

51. $\dfrac{12x^2-6x}{x^2+6x+5}\cdot\dfrac{2x^4+10x^3}{4x^2-1}$ $\quad \dfrac{12x^4}{(x+1)(2x+1)}$

52. $\dfrac{8x^3+4x^2}{x^2-3x+2}\cdot\dfrac{x^2-4}{16x^2+8x}$ $\quad \dfrac{x(x+2)}{2(x-1)}$

53. $\dfrac{16+6x-x^2}{x^2-10x-24}\cdot\dfrac{x^2-6x-27}{x^2-17x+72}$ $\quad -\dfrac{x+3}{x-12}$

54. $\dfrac{x^2-11x+28}{x^2-13x+42}\cdot\dfrac{x^2+7x+10}{20-x-x^2}$ $\quad -\dfrac{x+2}{x-6}$

55. $\dfrac{2x^2+5x+2}{2x^2+7x+3}\cdot\dfrac{x^2-7x-30}{x^2-6x-40}$ $\quad \dfrac{x+2}{x+4}$

56. $\dfrac{x^2-4x-32}{x^2-8x-48}\cdot\dfrac{3x^2+17x+10}{3x^2-22x-16}$ $\quad \dfrac{x+5}{x-12}$

57. $\dfrac{2x^2+x-3}{2x^2-x-6}\cdot\dfrac{2x^2-9x+10}{2x^2-3x+1}$ $\quad \dfrac{2x-5}{2x-1}$

58. $\dfrac{3y^2+14y+8}{2y^2+7y-4}\cdot\dfrac{2y^2+9y-5}{3y^2+16y+5}$ $\quad \dfrac{3y+2}{3y+1}$

59. $\dfrac{6x^2-11x+4}{6x^2+x-2}\cdot\dfrac{12x^2+11x+2}{8x^2+14x+3}$ $\quad \dfrac{3x-4}{2x+3}$

60. $\dfrac{6-x-2x^2}{4x^2+3x-10}\cdot\dfrac{3x^2+7x-20}{2x^2+5x-12}$ $\quad -\dfrac{3x-5}{4x-5}$

3 61. ✎ What is the reciprocal of a fraction?

62. ✎ Explain how to divide two fractions.

Divide.

63. $\dfrac{4x^2y^3}{15a^2b^3} \div \dfrac{6xy}{5a^3b^5}$ $\dfrac{2xy^2ab^2}{9}$

64. $\dfrac{9x^3y^4}{16a^4b^2} \div \dfrac{45x^4y^2}{14a^7b}$ $\dfrac{7a^3y^2}{40bx}$

65. $\dfrac{6x-12}{8x+32} \div \dfrac{18x-36}{10x+40}$ $\dfrac{5}{12}$

66. $\dfrac{28x+14}{45x-30} \div \dfrac{14x+7}{30x-20}$ $\dfrac{4}{3}$

67. $\dfrac{6x^3+7x^2}{12x-3} \div \dfrac{6x^2+7x}{36x-9}$ $3x$

68. $\dfrac{5a^2y+3a^2}{2x^3+5x^2} \div \dfrac{10ay+6a}{6x^3+15x^2}$ $\dfrac{3a}{2}$

69. $\dfrac{x^2+4x+3}{x^2y} \div \dfrac{x^2+2x+1}{xy^2}$
$\dfrac{y(x+3)}{x(x+1)}$

70. $\dfrac{x^3y^2}{x^2-3x-10} \div \dfrac{xy^4}{x^2-x-20}$
$\dfrac{x^2(x+4)}{y^2(x+2)}$

71. $\dfrac{x^2-49}{x^4y^3} \div \dfrac{x^2-14x+49}{x^4y^3}$ $\dfrac{x+7}{x-7}$

72. $\dfrac{x^2y^5}{x^2-11x+30} \div \dfrac{xy^6}{x^2-7x+10}$
$\dfrac{x(x-2)}{y(x-6)}$

73. $\dfrac{4ax-8a}{c^2} \div \dfrac{2y-xy}{c^3}$ $-\dfrac{4ac}{y}$

74. $\dfrac{3x^2y-9xy}{a^2b} \div \dfrac{3x^2-x^3}{ab^2}$ $-\dfrac{3by}{ax}$

75. $\dfrac{x^2-5x+6}{x^2-9x+18} \div \dfrac{x^2-6x+8}{x^2-9x+20}$
$\dfrac{x-5}{x-6}$

76. $\dfrac{x^2+3x-40}{x^2+2x-35} \div \dfrac{x^2+2x-48}{x^2+3x-18}$
$\dfrac{(x+6)(x-3)}{(x+7)(x-6)}$

77. $\dfrac{x^2+2x-15}{x^2-4x-45} \div \dfrac{x^2+x-12}{x^2-5x-36}$ 1

78. $\dfrac{y^2-y-56}{y^2+8y+7} \div \dfrac{y^2-13y+40}{y^2-4y-5}$ 1

79. $\dfrac{8+2x-x^2}{x^2+7x+10} \div \dfrac{x^2-11x+28}{x^2-x-42}$
$-\dfrac{x+6}{x+5}$

80. $\dfrac{x^2-x-2}{x^2-7x+10} \div \dfrac{x^2-3x-4}{40-3x-x^2}$
$-\dfrac{x+8}{x-4}$

81. $\dfrac{2x^2-3x-20}{2x^2-7x-30} \div \dfrac{2x^2-5x-12}{4x^2+12x+9}$
$\dfrac{2x+3}{x-6}$

82. $\dfrac{6n^2+13n+6}{4n^2-9} \div \dfrac{6n^2+n-2}{4n^2-1}$
$\dfrac{2n+1}{2n-3}$

83. $\dfrac{9x^2-16}{6x^2-11x+4} \div \dfrac{6x^2+11x+4}{8x^2+10x+3}$
$\dfrac{4x+3}{2x-1}$

84. $\dfrac{15-14x-8x^2}{4x^2+4x-15} \div \dfrac{4x^2+13x-12}{3x^2+13x+4}$
$-\dfrac{3x+1}{2x-3}$

85. $\dfrac{8x^2+18x-5}{10x^2-9x+2} \div \dfrac{8x^2+22x+15}{10x^2+11x-6}$
$\dfrac{(2x+5)(4x-1)}{(2x-1)(4x+5)}$

86. $\dfrac{10+7x-12x^2}{8x^2-2x-15} \div \dfrac{6x^2-13x+5}{10x^2-13x+4}$
$\dfrac{(5-4x)(2+3x)(5x-4)}{(4x+5)(2x-3)(3x-5)}$

APPLYING CONCEPTS 9.1

For what values of x is the algebraic fraction undefined? (*Hint:* Set the denominator equal to zero and solve for x.)

87. $\dfrac{x}{(x+6)(x-1)}$ $-6, 1$

88. $\dfrac{x}{(x-2)(x+5)}$ $2, -5$

89. $\dfrac{8}{x^2-1}$ $1, -1$

90. $\dfrac{7}{x^2-16}$ $4, -4$

91. $\dfrac{x-4}{x^2-x-6}$ $3, -2$

92. $\dfrac{x+5}{x^2-4x-5}$ $5, -1$

93. $\dfrac{3x}{x^2+6x+9}$ -3

94. $\dfrac{3x-8}{3x^2-10x-8}$ $-\dfrac{2}{3}, 4$

95. $\dfrac{4x+7}{6x^2-5x-4}$ $\dfrac{4}{3}, -\dfrac{1}{2}$

Simplify.

96. $\dfrac{y^2}{x} \cdot \dfrac{x}{2} \div \dfrac{y}{x}$ $\dfrac{xy}{2}$

97. $\dfrac{ab}{3} \cdot \dfrac{a}{b^2} \div \dfrac{a}{4}$ $\dfrac{4a}{3b}$

98. $\left(\dfrac{2x}{y}\right)^3 \div \left(\dfrac{x}{3y}\right)^2$ $\dfrac{72x}{y}$

99. $\left(\dfrac{c}{3}\right)^2 \div \left(\dfrac{c}{2} \cdot \dfrac{c}{4}\right)$ $\dfrac{8}{9}$

100. $\left(\dfrac{a-3}{b}\right)^2 \left(\dfrac{b}{3-a}\right)^3$ $-\dfrac{b}{a-3}$

101. $\left(\dfrac{x-4}{y^2}\right)^3 \cdot \left(\dfrac{y}{4-x}\right)^2$ $\dfrac{x-4}{y^4}$

[C] 102. $\dfrac{x^2+3x-40}{x^2+2x-35} \div \dfrac{x^2+2x-48}{x^2+3x-18} \cdot \dfrac{x^2-36}{x^2-9}$
$\dfrac{(x+6)(x+6)}{(x+7)(x+3)}$

[C] 103. $\dfrac{x^2+x-6}{x^2+7x+12} \cdot \dfrac{x^2+3x-4}{x^2+x-2} \div \dfrac{x^2-16}{x^2-4}$
$\dfrac{(x-2)(x-2)}{(x-4)(x+4)}$

104. Given the expression $\dfrac{9}{x^2+1}$, choose some values of x and evaluate the expression for those values. Is it possible to choose a value of x for which the value of the expression is greater than 10? If so, what is that value of x? If not, explain why it is not possible.

105. Given the expression $\dfrac{1}{y-3}$, choose some values of y and evaluate the expression for those values. Is it possible to choose a value of y for which the value of the expression is greater than 10,000,000? If so, what is that value of y? Explain your answer.

S E C T I O N **9.2**

Expressing Fractions in Terms of the Least Common Multiple (LCM)

1 Find the least common multiple (LCM) of two or more polynomials

The **least common multiple (LCM)** of two or more numbers is the smallest number that contains the prime factorization of each number.

The LCM of 12 and 18 is 36. 36 contains the prime factors of 12 and the prime factors of 18.

$$12 = 2 \cdot 2 \cdot 3$$
$$18 = 2 \cdot 3 \cdot 3$$

$$\overbrace{\text{Factors of 12}}$$
$$\text{LCM} = 36 = 2 \cdot 2 \cdot 3 \cdot 3$$
$$\underbrace{\text{Factors of 18}}$$

The least common multiple of two or more polynomials is the simplest polynomial that contains the factors of each polynomial.

To find the LCM of two or more polynomials, first factor each polynomial completely. The LCM is the product of each factor the greatest number of times it occurs in any one factorization.

⇒ Find the LCM of $4x^2 + 4x$ and $x^2 + 2x + 1$.

The LCM of $4x^2 + 4x$ and $x^2 + 2x + 1$ is the product of the LCM of the numerical coefficients and each variable factor the greatest number of times it occurs in any one factorization.

$4x^2 + 4x = 4x(x + 1) = 2 \cdot 2 \cdot x(x + 1)$
$x^2 + 2x + 1 = (x + 1)(x + 1)$

$$\overbrace{}^{\text{Factors of } 4x^2 + 4x}$$
$$\text{LCM} = 2 \cdot 2 \cdot \underbrace{x(x + 1)(x + 1)}_{\text{Factors of } x^2 + 2x + 1} = 4x(x + 1)(x + 1)$$

Example 1   Find the LCM of $4x^2y$ and $6xy^2$.

Solution $4x^2y = 2 \cdot 2 \cdot x \cdot x \cdot y$ ▸ Factor each polynomial com-
            $6xy^2 = 2 \cdot 3 \cdot x \cdot y \cdot y$ pletely.

            $\text{LCM} = 2 \cdot 2 \cdot 3 \cdot x \cdot x \cdot y \cdot y$ ▸ Write the product of the LCM of
                $= 12x^2y^2$ the numerical coefficients and
                                    each variable factor the greatest
                                    number of times it occurs in any
                                    one factorization.

Problem 1   Find the LCM of $8uv^2$ and $12uw$.

Solution   See page S19. $24uv^2w$

Example 2   Find the LCM of $x^2 - x - 6$ and $9 - x^2$.

Solution $x^2 - x - 6 = (x - 3)(x + 2)$
        $9 - x^2 = -(x^2 - 9) = -(x + 3)(x - 3)$

        $\text{LCM} = (x - 3)(x + 2)(x + 3)$

Problem 2   Find the LCM of $m^2 - 6m + 9$ and $m^2 - 2m - 3$.

Solution   See page S19. $(m - 3)(m - 3)(m + 1)$

2   ## Express two fractions in terms of the LCM of their denominators

When adding and subtracting fractions, it is often necessary to express two or more fractions in terms of a common denominator. This common denominator is the LCM of the denominators of the fractions.

⇒ Write the fractions $\dfrac{x + 1}{4x^2}$ and $\dfrac{x - 3}{6x^2 - 12x}$ in terms of the LCM of the denominators.

Find the LCM of the de-nominators.

The LCM is $12x^2(x - 2)$.

For each fraction, multiply the numerator and denom-inator by the factors whose product with the denomi-nator is the LCM.

$$\dfrac{x + 1}{4x^2} = \dfrac{x + 1}{4x^2} \cdot \dfrac{3(x - 2)}{3(x - 2)} = \dfrac{3x^2 - 3x - 6}{12x^2(x - 2)}$$

$$\dfrac{x - 3}{6x^2 - 12x} = \dfrac{x - 3}{6x(x - 2)} \cdot \dfrac{2x}{2x} = \dfrac{2x^2 - 6x}{12x^2(x - 2)}$$

LCM

Example 3 Write the fractions $\frac{x+2}{3x^2}$ and $\frac{x-1}{8xy}$ in terms of the LCM of the denominators.

Solution The LCM is $24x^2y$.

$$\frac{x+2}{3x^2} = \frac{x+2}{3x^2} \cdot \frac{8y}{8y} = \frac{8xy+16y}{24x^2y}$$ ▶ The product of $3x^2$ and $8y$ is the LCM.

$$\frac{x-1}{8xy} = \frac{x-1}{8xy} \cdot \frac{3x}{3x} = \frac{3x^2-3x}{24x^2y}$$ ▶ The product of $8xy$ and $3x$ is the LCM.

Problem 3 Write the fractions $\frac{x-3}{4xy^2}$ and $\frac{2x+1}{9y^2z}$ in terms of the LCM of the denominators.

Solution See page S19. $\quad \frac{9xz-27z}{36xy^2z}, \frac{8x^2+4x}{36xy^2z}$

Example 4 Write the fractions $\frac{2x-1}{2x-x^2}$ and $\frac{x}{x^2+x-6}$ in terms of the LCM of the denominators.

Solution $\frac{2x-1}{2x-x^2} = \frac{2x-1}{-(x^2-2x)} = -\frac{2x-1}{x^2-2x}$ ▶ Rewrite $\frac{2x-1}{2x-x^2}$ with a denominator of x^2-2x.

The LCM is $x(x-2)(x+3)$.

$$\frac{2x-1}{2x-x^2} = -\frac{2x-1}{x(x-2)} \cdot \frac{x+3}{x+3} = -\frac{2x^2+5x-3}{x(x-2)(x+3)}$$

$$\frac{x}{x^2+x-6} = \frac{x}{(x-2)(x+3)} \cdot \frac{x}{x} = \frac{x^2}{x(x-2)(x+3)}$$

Problem 4 Write the fractions $\frac{x+4}{x^2-3x-10}$ and $\frac{2x}{25-x^2}$ in terms of the LCM of the denominators.

Solution See page S19. $\quad \frac{x^2+9x+20}{(x+2)(x-5)(x+5)}, -\frac{2x^2+4x}{(x+2)(x-5)(x+5)}$

CONCEPT REVIEW 9.2

Determine whether the statement is always true, sometimes true, or never true.

1. The least common multiple of two numbers is the smallest number that contains all the prime factors of both numbers.   Always true

2. The LCD is the least common multiple of the denominators of two or more fractions.   Always true

3. The LCM of x^2, x^5, and x^8 is x^2.   Never true

4. We can rewrite $\frac{x}{y}$ as $\frac{4x}{4y}$ by using the Multiplication Property of One.   Always true

5. Rewriting two fractions in terms of the LCM of their denominators is the reverse process of simplifying the fractions.   Always true

6. To rewrite an algebraic fraction in terms of a common denominator, determine what factor you must multiply the denominator by so that the denominator will be the common denominator. Then multiply the numerator and denominator of the fraction by that factor.   Always true

EXERCISES 9.2

1 Find the LCM of the expressions.

1. $8x^3y$
    $12xy^2$
    $24x^3y^2$

2. $6ab^2$
    $18ab^3$
    $18ab^3$

3. $10x^4y^2$
    $15x^3y$
    $30x^4y^2$

4. $12a^2b$
    $18ab^3$
    $36a^2b^3$

5. $8x^2$
    $4x^2 + 8x$
    $8x^2(x + 2)$

6. $6y^2$
    $4y + 12$
    $12y^2(y + 3)$

7. $2x^2y$
    $3x^2 + 12x$
    $6x^2y(x + 4)$

8. $4xy^2$
    $6xy^2 + 12y^2$
    $12xy^2(x + 2)$

9. $8x^2(x - 1)^2$
    $10x^3(x - 1)$
    $40x^3(x - 1)^2$

10. $3x + 3$
    $2x^2 + 4x + 2$
    $6(x + 1)^2$

11. $4x - 12$
    $2x^2 - 12x + 18$
    $4(x - 3)^2$

12. $(x - 1)(x + 2)$
    $(x - 1)(x + 3)$
    $(x - 1)(x + 2)(x + 3)$

13. $(2x - 1)(x + 4)$
    $(2x + 1)(x + 4)$
    $(2x - 1)(2x + 1)(x + 4)$

14. $(2x + 3)^2$
    $(2x + 3)(x - 5)$
    $(2x + 3)^2(x - 5)$

15. $(x - 7)(x + 2)$
    $(x - 7)^2$
    $(x - 7)^2(x + 2)$

16. $x - 1$
    $x - 2$
    $(x - 1)(x - 2)$
    $(x - 1)(x - 2)$

17. $(x + 4)(x - 3)$
    $x + 4$
    $x - 3$
    $(x + 4)(x - 3)$

18. $x^2 - x - 6$
    $x^2 + x - 12$
    $(x + 2)(x - 3)(x + 4)$

19. $x^2 + 3x - 10$
    $x^2 + 5x - 14$
    $(x + 5)(x - 2)(x + 7)$

20. $x^2 + 5x + 4$
    $x^2 - 3x - 28$
    $(x + 1)(x + 4)(x - 7)$

21. $x^2 - 10x + 21$
    $x^2 - 8x + 15$
    $(x - 7)(x - 3)(x - 5)$

22. $x^2 - 2x - 24$
    $x^2 - 36$
    $(x + 6)(x - 6)(x + 4)$

23. $x^2 + 7x + 10$
    $x^2 - 25$
    $(x + 2)(x + 5)(x - 5)$

24. $x^2 - 7x - 30$
    $x^2 - 5x - 24$
    $(x - 10)(x + 3)(x - 8)$

25. $2x^2 - 7x + 3$
    $2x^2 + x - 1$
    $(2x - 1)(x - 3)(x + 1)$

26. $3x^2 - 11x + 6$
    $3x^2 + 4x - 4$
    $(x - 3)(3x - 2)(x + 2)$

27. $2x^2 - 9x + 10$
    $2x^2 + x - 15$
    $(2x - 5)(x - 2)(x + 3)$

28. $6 + x - x^2$
    $x + 2$
    $x - 3$
    $(x + 2)(x - 3)$

29. $15 + 2x - x^2$
    $x - 5$
    $x + 3$
    $(x + 3)(x - 5)$

30. $5 + 4x - x^2$
    $x - 5$
    $x + 1$
    $(x - 5)(x + 1)$

31. $x^2 + 3x - 18$
    $3 - x$
    $x + 6$
    $(x + 6)(x - 3)$

32. $x^2 - 5x + 6$
    $1 - x$
    $x - 6$
    $(x - 3)(x - 2)(x - 6)(x - 1)$

2 Write each fraction in terms of the LCM of the denominators.

33. $\dfrac{4}{x}; \dfrac{3}{x^2}$ $\dfrac{4x}{x^2}; \dfrac{3}{x^2}$

34. $\dfrac{5}{ab^2}; \dfrac{6}{ab}$ $\dfrac{5}{ab^2}; \dfrac{6b}{ab^2}$

35. $\dfrac{x}{3y^2}; \dfrac{z}{4y}$ $\dfrac{4x}{12y^2}; \dfrac{3yz}{12y^2}$

36. $\dfrac{5y}{6x^2}; \dfrac{7}{9xy}$ $\dfrac{15y^2}{18x^2y}; \dfrac{14x}{18x^2y}$

37. $\dfrac{y}{x(x - 3)}; \dfrac{6}{x^2}$ $\dfrac{xy}{x^2(x - 3)}; \dfrac{6x - 18}{x^2(x - 3)}$

38. $\dfrac{a}{y^2}; \dfrac{6}{y(y + 5)}$ $\dfrac{ay + 5a}{y^2(y + 5)}; \dfrac{6y}{y^2(y + 5)}$

39. $\dfrac{9}{(x - 1)^2}; \dfrac{6}{x(x - 1)}$ $\dfrac{9x}{x(x - 1)^2}; \dfrac{6x - 6}{x(x - 1)^2}$

40. $\dfrac{a^2}{y(y + 7)}; \dfrac{a}{(y + 7)^2}$ $\dfrac{a^2y + 7a^2}{y(y + 7)^2}; \dfrac{ay}{y(y + 7)^2}$

41. $\dfrac{3}{x - 3}; -\dfrac{5}{x(3 - x)}$ $\dfrac{3x}{x(x - 3)}; \dfrac{5}{x(x - 3)}$

42. $\dfrac{b}{y(y-4)}; \dfrac{b^2}{4-y}$

$\dfrac{b}{y(y-4)}; -\dfrac{b^2 y}{y(y-4)}$

43. $\dfrac{3}{(x-5)^2}; \dfrac{2}{5-x}$

$\dfrac{3}{(x-5)^2}; -\dfrac{2x-10}{(x-5)^2}$

44. $\dfrac{3}{7-y}; \dfrac{2}{(y-7)^2}$

$-\dfrac{3y-21}{(y-7)^2}; \dfrac{2}{(y-7)^2}$

45. $\dfrac{3}{x^2+2x}; \dfrac{4}{x^2}$

$\dfrac{3x}{x^2(x+2)}; \dfrac{4x+8}{x^2(x+2)}$

46. $\dfrac{2}{y-3}; \dfrac{3}{y^3-3y^2}$

$\dfrac{2y^2}{y^2(y-3)}; \dfrac{3}{y^2(y-3)}$

47. $\dfrac{x-2}{x+3}; \dfrac{x}{x-4}$

$\dfrac{x^2-6x+8}{(x+3)(x-4)}; \dfrac{x^2+3x}{(x+3)(x-4)}$

48. $\dfrac{x^2}{2x-1}; \dfrac{x+1}{x+4}$

$\dfrac{x^3+4x^2}{(2x-1)(x+4)}; \dfrac{2x^2+x-1}{(2x-1)(x+4)}$

49. $\dfrac{3}{x^2+x-2}; \dfrac{x}{x+2}$

$\dfrac{3}{(x+2)(x-1)}; \dfrac{x^2-x}{(x+2)(x-1)}$

50. $\dfrac{3x}{x-5}; \dfrac{4}{x^2-25}$

$\dfrac{3x^2+15x}{(x+5)(x-5)}; \dfrac{4}{(x+5)(x-5)}$

51. $\dfrac{5}{2x^2-9x+10}; \dfrac{x-1}{2x-5}$

$\dfrac{5}{(2x-5)(x-2)}; \dfrac{x^2-3x+2}{(2x-5)(x-2)}$

52. $\dfrac{x-3}{3x^2+4x-4}; \dfrac{2}{x+2}$

$\dfrac{x-3}{(3x-2)(x+2)}; \dfrac{6x-4}{(3x-2)(x+2)}$

53. $\dfrac{x}{x^2+x-6}; \dfrac{2x}{x^2-9}$

$\dfrac{x^2-3x}{(x+3)(x-3)(x-2)}; \dfrac{2x^2-4x}{(x+3)(x-3)(x-2)}$

54. $\dfrac{x-1}{x^2+2x-15}; \dfrac{x}{x^2+6x+5}$

$\dfrac{x^2-1}{(x-3)(x+5)(x+1)}; \dfrac{x^2-3x}{(x-3)(x+5)(x+1)}$

55. $\dfrac{x}{9-x^2}; \dfrac{x-1}{x^2-6x+9}$

$-\dfrac{x^2-3x}{(x-3)^2(x+3)}; \dfrac{x^2+2x-3}{(x-3)^2(x+3)}$

56. $\dfrac{2x}{10+3x-x^2}; \dfrac{x+2}{x^2-8x+15}$

$-\dfrac{2x^2-6x}{(x-5)(x+2)(x-3)}; \dfrac{x^2+4x+4}{(x-5)(x+2)(x-3)}$

57. $\dfrac{3x}{x-5}; \dfrac{x}{x+4}; \dfrac{3}{20+x-x^2}$

$\dfrac{3x^2+12x}{(x-5)(x+4)}; \dfrac{x^2-5x}{(x-5)(x+4)}; -\dfrac{3}{(x-5)(x+4)}$

58. $\dfrac{x+1}{x+5}; \dfrac{x+2}{x-7}; \dfrac{3}{35+2x-x^2}$

$\dfrac{x^2-6x-7}{(x+5)(x-7)}; \dfrac{x^2+7x+10}{(x+5)(x-7)}; -\dfrac{3}{(x+5)(x-7)}$

APPLYING CONCEPTS 9.2

Write each expression in terms of the LCM of the denominators.

59. $\dfrac{3}{10^2}; \dfrac{5}{10^4}$ $\dfrac{300}{10^4}; \dfrac{5}{10^4}$

60. $\dfrac{8}{10^3}; \dfrac{9}{10^5}$ $\dfrac{800}{10^5}; \dfrac{9}{10^5}$

61. $b; \dfrac{5}{b}$ $\dfrac{b^2}{b}; \dfrac{5}{b}$

62. $3; \dfrac{2}{n}$ $\dfrac{3n}{n}; \dfrac{2}{n}$

63. $1; \dfrac{y}{y-1}$ $\dfrac{y-1}{y-1}; \dfrac{y}{y-1}$

64. $x; \dfrac{x}{x^2-1}$ $\dfrac{x^3-x}{x^2-1}; \dfrac{x}{x^2-1}$

65. $\dfrac{x^2+1}{(x-1)^3}; \dfrac{x+1}{(x-1)^2}; \dfrac{1}{x-1}$

$\dfrac{x^2+1}{(x-1)^3}; \dfrac{x^2-1}{(x-1)^3}; \dfrac{x^2-2x+1}{(x-1)^3}$

66. $\dfrac{a^2+a}{(a+1)^3}; \dfrac{a+1}{(a+1)^2}; \dfrac{1}{a+1}$

$\dfrac{a^2+a}{(a+1)^3}; \dfrac{a^2+2a+1}{(a+1)^3}; \dfrac{a^2+2a+1}{(a+1)^3}$

[C] 67. $\dfrac{b}{4a^2-4b^2}; \dfrac{a}{8a-8b}$

$\dfrac{2b}{8(a+b)(a-b)}; \dfrac{a^2+ab}{8(a+b)(a-b)}$

[C] 68. $\dfrac{c}{6c^2+7cd+d^2}; \dfrac{d}{3c^2-3d^2}$

$\dfrac{3c^2-3cd}{3(6c+d)(c+d)(c-d)}; \dfrac{6cd+d^2}{3(6c+d)(c+d)(c-d)}$

[C] **69.** $\dfrac{1}{x^2 + 2x + xy + 2y}; \dfrac{1}{x^2 + xy - 2x - 2y}$

$\dfrac{x - 2}{(x + y)(x + 2)(x - 2)}; \dfrac{x + 2}{(x + y)(x + 2)(x - 2)}$

[C] **70.** $\dfrac{1}{ab + 3a - 3b - b^2}; \dfrac{1}{ab + 3a + 3b + b^2}$

$\dfrac{a + b}{(a + b)(a - b)(b + 3)}; \dfrac{a - b}{(a + b)(a - b)(b + 3)}$

71. When is the LCM of two expressions equal to their product?

S E C T I O N 9.3

Addition and Subtraction of Algebraic Fractions

1 Add and subtract algebraic fractions with the same denominator

When adding algebraic fractions in which the denominators are the same, add the numerators. The denominator of the sum is the common denominator.

$$\frac{a}{b} + \frac{c}{b} = \frac{a + c}{b}$$

$$\frac{5x}{18} + \frac{7x}{18} = \frac{12x}{18} = \frac{2x}{3}$$

$$\frac{x}{x^2 - 1} + \frac{1}{x^2 - 1} = \frac{x + 1}{x^2 - 1} = \frac{\overset{1}{\cancel{(x + 1)}}}{(x - 1)\cancel{(x + 1)}} = \frac{1}{x - 1}$$

Note that the sum is written in simplest form.

INSTRUCTOR NOTE

Some students are surprised that $\dfrac{2x}{x - 2} - \dfrac{4}{x - 2} = 2$, as shown at the right. Evaluate the expression for several values of x, and show students that the calculation always yields 2 (with the exception of $x = 2$).

When subtracting algebraic fractions in which the denominators are the same, subtract the numerators. The denominator of the difference is the common denominator. Write the answer in simplest form.

$$\frac{2x}{x - 2} - \frac{4}{x - 2} = \frac{2x - 4}{x - 2} = \frac{2\overset{1}{\cancel{(x - 2)}}}{\cancel{x - 2}} = 2$$

$$\frac{3x - 1}{x^2 - 5x + 4} - \frac{2x + 3}{x^2 - 5x + 4} = \frac{(3x - 1) - (2x + 3)}{x^2 - 5x + 4}$$

$$= \frac{x - 4}{x^2 - 5x + 4}$$

$$= \frac{\overset{1}{\cancel{(x - 4)}}}{\cancel{(x - 4)}(x - 1)}$$

$$= \frac{1}{x - 1}$$

LOOK CLOSELY

Be careful with signs when subtracting algebraic fractions. Note that we must subtract the *entire* numerator $2x + 3$.
$(3x - 1) - (2x + 3)$
$= 3x - 1 - 2x - 3$

Example 1   Add or subtract.   **A.** $\dfrac{7}{x^2} + \dfrac{9}{x^2}$ **B.** $\dfrac{3x^2}{x^2 - 1} - \dfrac{x + 4}{x^2 - 1}$

Solution   **A.** $\dfrac{7}{x^2} + \dfrac{9}{x^2} = \dfrac{7 + 9}{x^2}$ ▶ The denominators are the same. Add the numerators.

$= \dfrac{16}{x^2}$

B. $\dfrac{3x^2}{x^2 - 1} - \dfrac{x + 4}{x^2 - 1} = \dfrac{3x^2 - (x + 4)}{x^2 - 1}$ ▶ The denominators are the same. Subtract the numerators.

$= \dfrac{3x^2 - x - 4}{x^2 - 1}$

$= \dfrac{(3x - 4)\overset{1}{\cancel{(x + 1)}}}{(x - 1)\underset{1}{\cancel{(x + 1)}}}$ ▶ Write the answer in simplest form.

$= \dfrac{3x - 4}{x - 1}$

Problem 1   Add or subtract.   **A.** $\dfrac{3}{xy} + \dfrac{12}{xy}$ **B.** $\dfrac{2x^2}{x^2 - x - 12} - \dfrac{7x + 4}{x^2 - x - 12}$

Solution   See page S20.   **A.** $\dfrac{15}{xy}$ **B.** $\dfrac{2x + 1}{x + 3}$

2   ## Add and subtract algebraic fractions with different denominators

LOOK CLOSELY

This objective requires using the skills learned in the objective on writing two fractions in terms of the LCM of their denominators and the objective on adding and subtracting algebraic fractions with the same denominator.

INSTRUCTOR NOTE

Have students write down a list of the basic steps that are used to simplify sums or differences of rational expressions. Here is a suggested list.

• Find the LCM of the denominators.
• Write each fraction as a fraction with the LCM as a denominator.
• Add or subtract the fractions that have the same denominators.
• Write the answer in factored form, and express the answer in simplest form.

Before two fractions with different denominators can be added or subtracted, each fraction must be expressed in terms of a common denominator. This common denominator is the LCM of the denominators of the fractions.

▶ Add: $\dfrac{x - 3}{x^2 - 2x} + \dfrac{6}{x^2 - 4}$

Find the LCM of the denominators.

$x^2 - 2x = x(x - 2)$
$x^2 - 4 = (x - 2)(x + 2)$

The LCM is $x(x - 2)(x + 2)$.

$\dfrac{x - 3}{x^2 - 2x} + \dfrac{6}{x^2 - 4}$

Write each fraction in terms of the LCM of the denominators.

$= \dfrac{x - 3}{x(x - 2)} \cdot \dfrac{x + 2}{x + 2} + \dfrac{6}{(x - 2)(x + 2)} \cdot \dfrac{x}{x}$

Multiply the factors in the numerator.

$= \dfrac{x^2 - x - 6}{x(x - 2)(x + 2)} + \dfrac{6x}{x(x - 2)(x + 2)}$

Add the fractions.

$= \dfrac{x^2 - x - 6 + 6x}{x(x - 2)(x + 2)}$

$= \dfrac{x^2 + 5x - 6}{x(x - 2)(x + 2)}$

Factor the numerator to determine whether there are common factors in the numerator and denominator.

$= \dfrac{(x + 6)(x - 1)}{x(x - 2)(x + 2)}$

Example 2   Add or subtract.

A. $\dfrac{y}{x} - \dfrac{4y}{3x} + \dfrac{3y}{4x}$ B. $\dfrac{2x}{x-3} - \dfrac{5}{3-x}$ C. $x - \dfrac{3}{5x}$

Solution   A. The LCM of the de-   ▸ Find the LCM of the denomina-
nominators is $12x$.   tors.

$$\dfrac{y}{x} - \dfrac{4y}{3x} + \dfrac{3y}{4x}$$

$$= \dfrac{y}{x} \cdot \dfrac{12}{12} - \dfrac{4y}{3x} \cdot \dfrac{4}{4} + \dfrac{3y}{4x} \cdot \dfrac{3}{3}$$ ▸ Write each fraction in terms of the LCM.

$$= \dfrac{12y}{12x} - \dfrac{16y}{12x} + \dfrac{9y}{12x}$$

$$= \dfrac{12y - 16y + 9y}{12x}$$

$$= \dfrac{5y}{12x}$$

B. The LCM of $x - 3$ ▸ $3 - x = -(x - 3)$
and $3 - x$ is $x - 3$.

$$\dfrac{2x}{x-3} - \dfrac{5}{3-x}$$

$$= \dfrac{2x}{x-3} - \dfrac{5}{-(x-3)} \cdot \dfrac{-1}{-1}$$ ▸ Multiply $\dfrac{5}{-(x-3)}$ by $\dfrac{-1}{-1}$ so that the denominator will be $x - 3$.

$$= \dfrac{2x}{x-3} - \dfrac{-5}{x-3}$$

$$= \dfrac{2x - (-5)}{x-3}$$

$$= \dfrac{2x + 5}{x-3}$$

C. The LCM of the denominators is $5x$.

$$x - \dfrac{3}{5x} = \dfrac{x}{1} - \dfrac{3}{5x}$$

$$= \dfrac{x}{1} \cdot \dfrac{5x}{5x} - \dfrac{3}{5x}$$

$$= \dfrac{5x^2}{5x} - \dfrac{3}{5x}$$

$$= \dfrac{5x^2 - 3}{5x}$$

Problem 2   Add or subtract.

A. $\dfrac{z}{8y} - \dfrac{4z}{3y} + \dfrac{5z}{4y}$ B. $\dfrac{5x}{x-2} - \dfrac{3}{2-x}$ C. $y + \dfrac{5}{y-7}$

Solution   See page S20.   A. $\dfrac{z}{24y}$ B. $\dfrac{5x+3}{x-2}$ C. $\dfrac{y^2 - 7y + 5}{y-7}$

Example 3   Add or subtract.   A. $\dfrac{2x}{2x-3} - \dfrac{1}{x+1}$ B. $\dfrac{x+3}{x^2-2x-8} + \dfrac{3}{4-x}$

Solution   A. The LCM is $(2x-3)(x+1)$.

$$\dfrac{2x}{2x-3} - \dfrac{1}{x+1} = \dfrac{2x}{2x-3} \cdot \dfrac{x+1}{x+1} - \dfrac{1}{x+1} \cdot \dfrac{2x-3}{2x-3}$$

$$= \dfrac{2x^2+2x}{(2x-3)(x+1)} - \dfrac{2x-3}{(2x-3)(x+1)}$$

$$= \dfrac{(2x^2+2x)-(2x-3)}{(2x-3)(x+1)}$$

$$= \dfrac{2x^2+3}{(2x-3)(x+1)}$$

B. The LCM is $(x-4)(x+2)$.

$$\dfrac{x+3}{x^2-2x-8} + \dfrac{3}{4-x} = \dfrac{x+3}{(x-4)(x+2)} + \dfrac{3}{-(x-4)} \cdot \dfrac{-1 \cdot (x+2)}{-1 \cdot (x+2)}$$

$$= \dfrac{x+3}{(x-4)(x+2)} + \dfrac{-3(x+2)}{(x-4)(x+2)}$$

$$= \dfrac{(x+3)+(-3)(x+2)}{(x-4)(x+2)}$$

$$= \dfrac{x+3-3x-6}{(x-4)(x+2)}$$

$$= \dfrac{-2x-3}{(x-4)(x+2)}$$

Problem 3   Add or subtract.   A. $\dfrac{4x}{3x-1} - \dfrac{9}{x+4}$ B. $\dfrac{2x-1}{x^2-25} + \dfrac{2}{5-x}$

Solution   See page S20.   A. $\dfrac{4x^2-11x+9}{(3x-1)(x+4)}$ B. $-\dfrac{11}{(x+5)(x-5)}$

CONCEPT REVIEW 9.3

Determine whether the statement is always true, sometimes true, or never true.

1. To add two fractions, add the numerators and the denominators.   Never true

2. The procedure for subtracting two algebraic fractions is the same as that for subtracting two arithmetic fractions.   Always true

3. To add two algebraic fractions, first multiply both fractions by the LCM of their denominators.   Never true

4. If $x \neq -2$ and $x \neq 0$, then $\dfrac{x}{x+2} + \dfrac{3}{x+2} = \dfrac{x+3}{x+2} = \dfrac{3}{2}$.   Never true

5. If $y \neq 8$, then $\dfrac{y}{y-8} - \dfrac{8}{y-8} = \dfrac{y-8}{y-8} = 1$.   Always true

6. If $x \neq 0$, then $\dfrac{4x-3}{x} - \dfrac{3x+1}{x} = \dfrac{4x-3-3x+1}{x} = \dfrac{x-2}{x}$.   Never true

EXERCISES 9.3

1 Add or subtract.

1. $\dfrac{3}{y^2} + \dfrac{8}{y^2}$ $\dfrac{11}{y^2}$

2. $\dfrac{6}{ab} - \dfrac{2}{ab}$ $\dfrac{4}{ab}$

3. $\dfrac{3}{x+4} - \dfrac{10}{x+4}$ $-\dfrac{7}{x+4}$

4. $\dfrac{x}{x+6} - \dfrac{2}{x+6}$ $\dfrac{x-2}{x+6}$

5. $\dfrac{3x}{2x+3} + \dfrac{5x}{2x+3}$ $\dfrac{8x}{2x+3}$

6. $\dfrac{6y}{4y+1} - \dfrac{11y}{4y+1}$ $-\dfrac{5y}{4y+1}$

7. $\dfrac{2x+1}{x-3} + \dfrac{3x+6}{x-3}$ $\dfrac{5x+7}{x-3}$

8. $\dfrac{4x+3}{2x-7} + \dfrac{3x-8}{2x-7}$ $\dfrac{7x-5}{2x-7}$

9. $\dfrac{5x-1}{x+9} - \dfrac{3x+4}{x+9}$ $\dfrac{2x-5}{x+9}$

10. $\dfrac{6x-5}{x-10} - \dfrac{3x-4}{x-10}$ $\dfrac{3x-1}{x-10}$

11. $\dfrac{x-7}{2x+7} - \dfrac{4x-3}{2x+7}$ $\dfrac{-3x-4}{2x+7}$

12. $\dfrac{2n}{3n+4} - \dfrac{5n-3}{3n+4}$ $\dfrac{-3n+3}{3n+4}$

13. $\dfrac{x}{x^2+2x-15} - \dfrac{3}{x^2+2x-15}$ $\dfrac{1}{x+5}$

14. $\dfrac{3x}{x^2+3x-10} - \dfrac{6}{x^2+3x-10}$ $\dfrac{3}{x+5}$

15. $\dfrac{2x+3}{x^2-x-30} - \dfrac{x-2}{x^2-x-30}$ $\dfrac{1}{x-6}$

16. $\dfrac{3x-1}{x^2+5x-6} - \dfrac{2x-7}{x^2+5x-6}$ $\dfrac{1}{x-1}$

17. $\dfrac{4y+7}{2y^2+7y-4} - \dfrac{y-5}{2y^2+7y-4}$ $\dfrac{3}{2y-1}$

18. $\dfrac{x+1}{2x^2-5x-12} + \dfrac{x+2}{2x^2-5x-12}$ $\dfrac{1}{x-4}$

19. $\dfrac{2x^2+3x}{x^2-9x+20} + \dfrac{2x^2-3}{x^2-9x+20} - \dfrac{4x^2+2x+1}{x^2-9x+20}$ $\dfrac{1}{x-5}$

20. $\dfrac{2x^2+3x}{x^2-2x-63} - \dfrac{x^2-3x+21}{x^2-2x-63} - \dfrac{x-7}{x^2-2x-63}$ $\dfrac{x-2}{x-9}$

2 **21.** Why must two fractions have the same denominators before they can be added or subtracted?

22. Explain the procedure for adding algebraic fractions with different denominators.

Add or subtract.

23. $\dfrac{4}{x} + \dfrac{5}{y}$ $\dfrac{4y+5x}{xy}$

24. $\dfrac{7}{a} + \dfrac{5}{b}$ $\dfrac{7b+5a}{ab}$

25. $\dfrac{12}{x} - \dfrac{5}{2x}$ $\dfrac{19}{2x}$

26. $\dfrac{5}{3a} - \dfrac{3}{4a}$ $\dfrac{11}{12a}$

27. $\dfrac{1}{2x} - \dfrac{5}{4x} + \dfrac{7}{6x}$ $\dfrac{5}{12x}$

28. $\dfrac{7}{4y} + \dfrac{11}{6y} - \dfrac{8}{3y}$ $\dfrac{11}{12y}$

29. $\dfrac{5}{3x} - \dfrac{2}{x^2} + \dfrac{3}{2x}$ $\dfrac{19x-12}{6x^2}$

30. $\dfrac{6}{y^2} + \dfrac{3}{4y} - \dfrac{2}{5y}$ $\dfrac{120+7y}{20y^2}$

31. $\dfrac{2}{x} - \dfrac{3}{2y} + \dfrac{3}{5x} - \dfrac{1}{4y}$ $\dfrac{52y-35x}{20xy}$

32. $\dfrac{5}{2a} + \dfrac{7}{3b} - \dfrac{2}{b} - \dfrac{3}{4a}$ $\dfrac{21b+4a}{12ab}$

33. $\dfrac{2x+1}{3x} + \dfrac{x-1}{5x}$ $\dfrac{13x+2}{15x}$

34. $\dfrac{4x-3}{6x} + \dfrac{2x+3}{4x}$ $\dfrac{14x+3}{12x}$

35. $\dfrac{x-3}{6x} + \dfrac{x+4}{8x}$ $\dfrac{7}{24}$

36. $\dfrac{2x-3}{2x} + \dfrac{x+3}{3x}$ $\dfrac{8x-3}{6x}$

37. $\dfrac{2x+9}{9x} - \dfrac{x-5}{5x}$ $\dfrac{x+90}{45x}$

38. $\dfrac{3y-2}{12y} - \dfrac{y-3}{18y}$ $\dfrac{7}{36}$

39. $\dfrac{x+4}{2x} - \dfrac{x-1}{x^2}$ $\dfrac{x^2+2x+2}{2x^2}$

40. $\dfrac{x-2}{3x^2} - \dfrac{x+4}{x}$ $\dfrac{-3x^2-11x-2}{3x^2}$

41. $\dfrac{x-10}{4x^2} + \dfrac{x+1}{2x}$ $\dfrac{2x^2+3x-10}{4x^2}$

42. $\dfrac{x+5}{3x^2} + \dfrac{2x+1}{2x}$ $\dfrac{6x^2+5x+10}{6x^2}$

43. $y + \dfrac{8}{3y}$ $\dfrac{3y^2+8}{3y}$

44. $\dfrac{7}{2n} - n$ $\dfrac{7-2n^2}{2n}$

45. $\dfrac{4}{x+4} + x$ $\dfrac{x^2+4x+4}{x+4}$

46. $x + \dfrac{3}{x+2}$ $\dfrac{x^2+2x+3}{x+2}$

47. $5 - \dfrac{x-2}{x+1}$ $\dfrac{4x+7}{x+1}$

48. $3 + \dfrac{x-1}{x+1}$ $\dfrac{2(2x+1)}{x+1}$

49. $\dfrac{2x+1}{6x^2} - \dfrac{x-4}{4x}$ $\dfrac{-3x^2+16x+2}{12x^2}$

50. $\dfrac{x+3}{6x} - \dfrac{x-3}{8x^2}$ $\dfrac{4x^2+9x+9}{24x^2}$

51. $\dfrac{x+2}{xy} - \dfrac{3x-2}{x^2y}$ $\dfrac{x^2-x+2}{x^2y}$

52. $\dfrac{3x-1}{xy^2} - \dfrac{2x+3}{xy}$ $\dfrac{3x-1-2xy-3y}{xy^2}$

53. $\dfrac{4x-3}{3x^2y} + \dfrac{2x+1}{4xy^2}$ $\dfrac{16xy-12y+6x^2+3x}{12x^2y^2}$

54. $\dfrac{5x+7}{6xy^2} - \dfrac{4x-3}{8x^2y}$ $\dfrac{20x^2+28x-12xy+9y}{24x^2y^2}$

55. $\dfrac{x-2}{8x^2} - \dfrac{x+7}{12xy}$ $\dfrac{3xy-6y-2x^2-14x}{24x^2y}$

56. $\dfrac{3x-1}{6y^2} - \dfrac{x+5}{9xy}$ $\dfrac{9x^2-3x-2xy-10y}{18xy^2}$

57. $\dfrac{4}{x-2} + \dfrac{5}{x+3}$ $\dfrac{9x+2}{(x-2)(x+3)}$

58. $\dfrac{2}{x-3} + \dfrac{5}{x-4}$ $\dfrac{7x-23}{(x-3)(x-4)}$

59. $\dfrac{6}{x-7} - \dfrac{4}{x+3}$ $\dfrac{2(x+23)}{(x-7)(x+3)}$

60. $\dfrac{3}{y+6} - \dfrac{4}{y-3}$ $\dfrac{-y-33}{(y+6)(y-3)}$

61. $\dfrac{2x}{x+1} + \dfrac{1}{x-3}$ $\dfrac{2x^2-5x+1}{(x+1)(x-3)}$

62. $\dfrac{3x}{x-4} + \dfrac{2}{x+6}$ $\dfrac{3x^2+20x-8}{(x-4)(x+6)}$

63. $\dfrac{4x}{2x-1} - \dfrac{5}{x-6}$ $\dfrac{4x^2-34x+5}{(2x-1)(x-6)}$

64. $\dfrac{6x}{x+5} - \dfrac{3}{2x+3}$ $\dfrac{3(4x^2+5x-5)}{(x+5)(2x+3)}$

65. $\dfrac{2a}{a-7} + \dfrac{5}{7-a}$ $\dfrac{2a-5}{a-7}$

66. $\dfrac{4x}{6-x} + \dfrac{5}{x-6}$ $\dfrac{-4x+5}{x-6}$

67. $\dfrac{x}{x^2-9} + \dfrac{3}{x-3}$ $\dfrac{4x+9}{(x+3)(x-3)}$

68. $\dfrac{y}{y^2-16} + \dfrac{1}{y-4}$ $\dfrac{2(y+2)}{(y+4)(y-4)}$

69. $\dfrac{2x}{x^2-x-6} - \dfrac{3}{x+2}$ $\dfrac{-x+9}{(x-3)(x+2)}$

70. $\dfrac{5x}{x^2+2x-8} - \dfrac{2}{x+4}$ $\dfrac{3x+4}{(x+4)(x-2)}$

71. $\dfrac{3x-1}{x^2-10x+25} - \dfrac{3}{x-5}$ $\dfrac{14}{(x-5)^2}$

72. $\dfrac{2a+3}{a^2-7a+12} - \dfrac{2}{a-3}$ $\dfrac{11}{(a-3)(a-4)}$

73. $\dfrac{x+4}{x^2-x-42} + \dfrac{3}{7-x}$ $\dfrac{-2(x+7)}{(x-7)(x+6)}$

74. $\dfrac{x+3}{x^2-3x-10} + \dfrac{2}{5-x}$ $\dfrac{-x-1}{(x+2)(x-5)}$

75. $\dfrac{x}{2x+4} - \dfrac{2}{x^2+2x}$ $\dfrac{x-2}{2x}$

76. $\dfrac{x+2}{4x+16} - \dfrac{2}{x^2+4x}$ $\dfrac{x-2}{4x}$

77. $\dfrac{x-1}{x^2-x-2} + \dfrac{3}{x^2-3x+2}$ $\dfrac{x^2+x+4}{(x-1)(x+1)(x-2)}$

78. $\dfrac{a+2}{a^2+a-2} + \dfrac{3}{a^2+2a-3}$ $\dfrac{a+6}{(a+3)(a-1)}$

79. $\dfrac{1}{x+1} + \dfrac{x}{x-6} - \dfrac{5x-2}{x^2-5x-6}$ $\dfrac{x-4}{x-6}$

80. $\dfrac{x}{x-4} + \dfrac{5}{x+5} - \dfrac{11x-8}{x^2+x-20}$ $\dfrac{x+3}{x+5}$

81. $\dfrac{3x+1}{x-1} - \dfrac{x-1}{x-3} + \dfrac{x+1}{x^2-4x+3}$ $\dfrac{2x+1}{x-1}$

82. $\dfrac{4x+1}{x-8} - \dfrac{3x+2}{x+4} - \dfrac{49x+4}{x^2-4x-32}$ $\dfrac{x-2}{x+4}$

APPLYING CONCEPTS 9.3

Simplify.

83. $\dfrac{a}{a-b} + \dfrac{b}{b-a} + 1$ 2

84. $\dfrac{y}{x-y} + 2 - \dfrac{x}{y-x}$ $\dfrac{3x-y}{x-y}$

85. $b - 3 + \dfrac{5}{b+4}$ $\dfrac{b^2+b-7}{b+4}$

86. $2y - 1 + \dfrac{6}{y+5}$ $\dfrac{2y^2+9y+1}{y+5}$

87. $\dfrac{(n+1)^2}{(n-1)^2} - 1$ $\dfrac{4n}{(n-1)^2}$

88. $1 - \dfrac{(y-2)^2}{(y+2)^2}$ $\dfrac{8y}{(y+2)^2}$

89. $\dfrac{2x+9}{3-x} + \dfrac{x+5}{x+7} - \dfrac{2x^2+3x-3}{x^2+4x-21}$ $-\dfrac{3(x^2+8x+25)}{(x-3)(x+7)}$

90. $\dfrac{3x+5}{x+5} - \dfrac{x+1}{2-x} - \dfrac{4x^2-3x-1}{x^2+3x-10}$ $\dfrac{4(2x-1)}{(x+5)(x-2)}$

[C] 91. $\dfrac{x^2+x-6}{x^2+2x-8} \cdot \dfrac{x^2+5x+4}{x^2+2x-3} - \dfrac{2}{x-1}$ 1

[C] 92. $\dfrac{x^2+9x+20}{x^2+4x-5} \div \dfrac{x^2-49}{x^2+6x-7} - \dfrac{x}{x-7}$ $\dfrac{4}{x-7}$

[C] 93. $\dfrac{x^2-9}{x^2+6x+9} \div \dfrac{x^2+x-20}{x^2-x-12} + \dfrac{1}{x+1}$ $\dfrac{x^2-x+2}{(x+5)(x+1)}$

[C] 94. $\dfrac{x^2-25}{x^2+10x+25} \cdot \dfrac{x^2-7x+10}{x^2-x-2} + \dfrac{1}{x+1}$ $\dfrac{x^2-9x+30}{(x+5)(x+1)}$

95. Find the sum of the following: $\dfrac{1}{1 \cdot 2} + \dfrac{1}{2 \cdot 3}$ $\dfrac{2}{3}$

$$\dfrac{1}{1 \cdot 2} + \dfrac{1}{2 \cdot 3} + \dfrac{1}{3 \cdot 4} \quad \dfrac{3}{4}$$

$$\dfrac{1}{1 \cdot 2} + \dfrac{1}{2 \cdot 3} + \dfrac{1}{3 \cdot 4} + \dfrac{1}{4 \cdot 5} \quad \dfrac{4}{5}$$

Note the pattern in these sums, and then find the sum of 50 terms, of 100 terms, and of 1000 terms. $\dfrac{50}{51}, \dfrac{100}{101}, \dfrac{1000}{1001}$

Rewrite the expression as the sum of two fractions in simplest form.

96. $\dfrac{5b + 4a}{ab}$ $\dfrac{5}{a} + \dfrac{4}{b}$

97. $\dfrac{6x + 7y}{xy}$ $\dfrac{6}{y} + \dfrac{7}{x}$

98. $\dfrac{3x^2 + 4xy}{x^2y^2}$ $\dfrac{3}{y^2} + \dfrac{4}{xy}$

99. $\dfrac{2mn^2 + 8m^2n}{m^3n^3}$ $\dfrac{2}{m^2n} + \dfrac{8}{mn^2}$

SECTION 9.4
Complex Fractions

1 Simplify complex fractions

POINT OF INTEREST

There are many instances of complex fractions in application problems. The fraction $\dfrac{1}{\dfrac{1}{r_1} + \dfrac{1}{r_2}}$ is used to determine the total resistance in certain electric circuits.

A **complex fraction** is a fraction whose numerator or denominator contains one or more fractions. Examples of complex fractions are shown at the right.

$$\dfrac{3}{2 - \dfrac{1}{2}}, \qquad \dfrac{4 + \dfrac{1}{x}}{3 + \dfrac{2}{x}}, \qquad \dfrac{\dfrac{1}{x - 1} + x + 3}{x - 3 + \dfrac{1}{x + 4}}$$

➡ Simplify: $\dfrac{1 - \dfrac{4}{x^2}}{1 + \dfrac{2}{x}}$

LOOK CLOSELY

First, we are multiplying the complex fraction by $\dfrac{x^2}{x^2}$, which equals 1, so we are not changing the value of the fraction. Second, we are using the Distributive Property to multiply $\left(1 - \dfrac{4}{x^2}\right)x^2$ and $\left(1 + \dfrac{2}{x}\right)x^2$.

Find the LCM of the denominators of the fractions in the numerator and denominator.

The LCM of x^2 and x is x^2.

Multiply the numerator and denominator of the complex fraction by the LCM.

$$\dfrac{1 - \dfrac{4}{x^2}}{1 + \dfrac{2}{x}} = \dfrac{1 - \dfrac{4}{x^2}}{1 + \dfrac{2}{x}} \cdot \dfrac{x^2}{x^2}$$

$$= \dfrac{1 \cdot x^2 - \dfrac{4}{x^2} \cdot x^2}{1 \cdot x^2 + \dfrac{2}{x} \cdot x^2}$$

$$= \dfrac{x^2 - 4}{x^2 + 2x}$$

Simplify.

$$= \dfrac{\overset{1}{\cancel{(x - 2)}}\cancel{(x + 2)}}{x\cancel{(x + 2)}}$$

$$= \dfrac{x - 2}{x}$$

Example 1 Simplify. A. $\dfrac{\dfrac{1}{x}+\dfrac{1}{2}}{\dfrac{1}{x^2}-\dfrac{1}{4}}$ B. $\dfrac{1-\dfrac{2}{x}-\dfrac{15}{x^2}}{1-\dfrac{11}{x}+\dfrac{30}{x^2}}$

Solution A. The LCM of x, 2, x^2, and 4 is $4x^2$.

$$\frac{\dfrac{1}{x}+\dfrac{1}{2}}{\dfrac{1}{x^2}-\dfrac{1}{4}} = \frac{\dfrac{1}{x}+\dfrac{1}{2}}{\dfrac{1}{x^2}-\dfrac{1}{4}} \cdot \frac{4x^2}{4x^2}$$

$$= \frac{\dfrac{1}{x}\cdot 4x^2 + \dfrac{1}{2}\cdot 4x^2}{\dfrac{1}{x^2}\cdot 4x^2 - \dfrac{1}{4}\cdot 4x^2}$$

$$= \frac{4x + 2x^2}{4 - x^2}$$

$$= \frac{\overset{1}{2x\cancel{(2+x)}}}{(2-x)\underset{1}{\cancel{(2+x)}}}$$

$$= \frac{2x}{2-x}$$

B. The LCM of x and x^2 is x^2.

$$\frac{1-\dfrac{2}{x}-\dfrac{15}{x^2}}{1-\dfrac{11}{x}+\dfrac{30}{x^2}} = \frac{1-\dfrac{2}{x}-\dfrac{15}{x^2}}{1-\dfrac{11}{x}+\dfrac{30}{x^2}} \cdot \frac{x^2}{x^2}$$

$$= \frac{1\cdot x^2 - \dfrac{2}{x}\cdot x^2 - \dfrac{15}{x^2}\cdot x^2}{1\cdot x^2 - \dfrac{11}{x}\cdot x^2 + \dfrac{30}{x^2}\cdot x^2}$$

$$= \frac{x^2 - 2x - 15}{x^2 - 11x + 30}$$

$$= \frac{\overset{1}{\cancel{(x-5)}}(x+3)}{\underset{1}{\cancel{(x-5)}}(x-6)}$$

$$= \frac{x+3}{x-6}$$

Problem 1 Simplify. A. $\dfrac{\dfrac{1}{3}-\dfrac{1}{x}}{\dfrac{1}{9}-\dfrac{1}{x^2}}$ B. $\dfrac{1+\dfrac{4}{x}+\dfrac{3}{x^2}}{1+\dfrac{10}{x}+\dfrac{21}{x^2}}$

Solution See page S20. A. $\dfrac{3x}{x+3}$ B. $\dfrac{x+1}{x+7}$

CONCEPT REVIEW 9.4

Determine whether the statement is always true, sometimes true, or never true.

1. A complex fraction is a fraction that has fractions in the numerator and denominator.   Sometimes true

2. The first step in simplifying a complex fraction is to find the least common multiple of the denominators of the fractions in the numerator and denominator of the complex fraction.   Always true

3. To simplify a complex fraction, multiply the complex fraction by the LCM of the denominators of the fractions in the numerator and denominator of the complex fraction.   Never true

4. When we multiply the numerator and denominator of a complex fraction by the same expression, we are using the Multiplication Property of One.
   Always true

5. Our goal in simplifying a complex fraction is to rewrite it so that there are no fractions in the numerator or in the denominator. We then express the fraction in simplest form.   Always true

6. For the complex fraction $\dfrac{1 + \dfrac{4}{x} + \dfrac{3}{x^2}}{1 + \dfrac{10}{x} + \dfrac{21}{x^2}}$, x can be any real number except 0.
   Always true

EXERCISES 9.4

1 Simplify.

1. $\dfrac{1 + \dfrac{3}{x}}{1 - \dfrac{9}{x^2}}$ $\dfrac{x}{x-3}$

2. $\dfrac{1 + \dfrac{4}{x}}{1 - \dfrac{16}{x^2}}$ $\dfrac{x}{x-4}$

3. $\dfrac{2 - \dfrac{8}{x+4}}{3 - \dfrac{12}{x+4}}$ $\dfrac{2}{3}$

4. $\dfrac{5 - \dfrac{25}{x+5}}{1 - \dfrac{3}{x+5}}$ $\dfrac{5x}{x+2}$

5. $\dfrac{1 + \dfrac{5}{y-2}}{1 - \dfrac{2}{y-2}}$ $\dfrac{y+3}{y-4}$

6. $\dfrac{2 - \dfrac{11}{2x-1}}{3 - \dfrac{17}{2x-1}}$ $\dfrac{4x-13}{2(3x-10)}$

7. $\dfrac{4 - \dfrac{2}{x+7}}{5 + \dfrac{1}{x+7}}$ $\dfrac{2(2x+13)}{5x+36}$

8. $\dfrac{5 + \dfrac{3}{x-8}}{2 - \dfrac{1}{x-8}}$ $\dfrac{5x-37}{2x-17}$

9. $\dfrac{\dfrac{3}{x-2} + 3}{\dfrac{4}{x-2} + 4}$ $\dfrac{3}{4}$

10. $\dfrac{\dfrac{3}{2x+1} - 3}{2 - \dfrac{4x}{2x+1}}$ $-3x$

11. $\dfrac{2 - \dfrac{3}{x} - \dfrac{2}{x^2}}{2 + \dfrac{5}{x} + \dfrac{2}{x^2}}$ $\dfrac{x-2}{x+2}$

12. $\dfrac{2 + \dfrac{5}{x} - \dfrac{12}{x^2}}{4 - \dfrac{4}{x} - \dfrac{3}{x^2}}$ $\dfrac{x+4}{2x+1}$

13. $\dfrac{1 - \dfrac{1}{x} - \dfrac{6}{x^2}}{1 - \dfrac{9}{x^2}}$ $\dfrac{x+2}{x+3}$

14. $\dfrac{1 + \dfrac{4}{x} + \dfrac{4}{x^2}}{1 - \dfrac{2}{x} - \dfrac{8}{x^2}}$ $\dfrac{x+2}{x-4}$

15. $\dfrac{1 - \dfrac{5}{x} - \dfrac{6}{x^2}}{1 + \dfrac{6}{x} + \dfrac{5}{x^2}}$ $\dfrac{x-6}{x+5}$

16. $\dfrac{1 - \dfrac{7}{a} + \dfrac{12}{a^2}}{1 + \dfrac{1}{a} - \dfrac{20}{a^2}}$ $\dfrac{a-3}{a+5}$

17. $\dfrac{1 - \dfrac{6}{x} + \dfrac{8}{x^2}}{\dfrac{4}{x^2} + \dfrac{3}{x} - 1}$ $\dfrac{x-2}{x+1}$

18. $\dfrac{1 + \dfrac{3}{x} - \dfrac{18}{x^2}}{\dfrac{21}{x^2} - \dfrac{4}{x} - 1}$ $\dfrac{x+6}{x+7}$

19. $\dfrac{x - \dfrac{4}{x+3}}{1 + \dfrac{1}{x+3}}$ $x-1$

20. $\dfrac{y + \dfrac{1}{y-2}}{1 + \dfrac{1}{y-2}}$ $y-1$

21. $\dfrac{1 - \dfrac{x}{2x+1}}{x - \dfrac{1}{2x+1}}$ $\dfrac{1}{2x-1}$

22. $\dfrac{1 - \dfrac{2x-2}{3x-1}}{x - \dfrac{4}{3x-1}}$ $\dfrac{1}{3x-4}$

23. $\dfrac{x - 5 + \dfrac{14}{x+4}}{x + 3 - \dfrac{2}{x+4}}$ $\dfrac{x-3}{x+5}$

24. $\dfrac{a + 4 + \dfrac{5}{a-2}}{a + 6 + \dfrac{15}{a-2}}$ $\dfrac{a-1}{a+1}$

25. $\dfrac{x + 3 - \dfrac{10}{x-6}}{x + 2 - \dfrac{20}{x-6}}$ $\dfrac{x-7}{x-8}$

26. $\dfrac{x - 7 + \dfrac{5}{x-1}}{x - 3 + \dfrac{1}{x-1}}$ $\dfrac{x-6}{x-2}$

27. $\dfrac{y - 6 + \dfrac{22}{2y+3}}{y - 5 + \dfrac{11}{2y+3}}$ $\dfrac{2y-1}{2y+1}$

28. $\dfrac{x + 2 - \dfrac{12}{2x-1}}{x + 1 - \dfrac{9}{2x-1}}$ $\dfrac{2x+7}{2x+5}$

29. $\dfrac{x - \dfrac{2}{2x-3}}{2x - 1 - \dfrac{8}{2x-3}}$ $\dfrac{x-2}{2x-5}$

30. $\dfrac{x + 3 - \dfrac{18}{2x+1}}{x - \dfrac{6}{2x+1}}$ $\dfrac{x+5}{x+2}$

31. $\dfrac{1 - \dfrac{2}{x+1}}{1 + \dfrac{1}{x-2}}$ $\dfrac{x-2}{x+1}$

32. $\dfrac{1 - \dfrac{1}{x+2}}{1 + \dfrac{2}{x-1}}$ $\dfrac{x-1}{x+2}$

33. $\dfrac{1 - \dfrac{2}{x+4}}{1 + \dfrac{3}{x-1}}$ $\dfrac{x-1}{x+4}$

34. $\dfrac{1 + \dfrac{1}{x-2}}{1 - \dfrac{3}{x+2}}$ $\dfrac{x+2}{x-2}$

35. $\dfrac{\dfrac{1}{x} - \dfrac{2}{x-1}}{\dfrac{3}{x} + \dfrac{1}{x-1}}$ $\dfrac{-x-1}{4x-3}$

36. $\dfrac{\dfrac{3}{n+1} + \dfrac{1}{n}}{\dfrac{2}{n+1} + \dfrac{3}{n}}$ $\dfrac{4n+1}{5n+3}$

37. $\dfrac{\dfrac{3}{2x-1} - \dfrac{1}{x}}{\dfrac{4}{x} + \dfrac{2}{2x-1}}$ $\dfrac{x+1}{2(5x-2)}$

38. $\dfrac{\dfrac{4}{3x+1} + \dfrac{3}{x}}{\dfrac{6}{x} - \dfrac{2}{3x+1}}$ $\dfrac{13x+3}{2(8x+3)}$

39. $\dfrac{\dfrac{3}{b-4} - \dfrac{2}{b+1}}{\dfrac{5}{b+1} - \dfrac{1}{b-4}}$ $\dfrac{b+11}{4b-21}$

40. $\dfrac{\dfrac{5}{x-5} - \dfrac{3}{x-1}}{\dfrac{6}{x-1} + \dfrac{2}{x-5}}$ $\dfrac{x+5}{4(x-4)}$

APPLYING CONCEPTS 9.4

Simplify.

41. $1 + \dfrac{1}{1 + \dfrac{1}{2}}$ $\dfrac{5}{3}$

42. $1 + \dfrac{1}{1 + \dfrac{1}{1 + \dfrac{1}{2}}}$ $\dfrac{8}{5}$

[C] 43. $1 - \dfrac{1}{1 - \dfrac{1}{x}}$ $-\dfrac{1}{x-1}$

[C] 44. $1 - \dfrac{1}{1 - \dfrac{1}{y+1}}$ $-\dfrac{1}{y}$

[C] 45. $\dfrac{a^{-1} - b^{-1}}{a^{-2} - b^{-2}}$ $\dfrac{ab}{b+a}$

[C] 46. $\dfrac{x^{-2} - y^{-2}}{x^{-2}y^{-2}}$ $y^2 - x^2$

[C] 47. $\left(\dfrac{y}{4} - \dfrac{4}{y}\right) \div \left(\dfrac{4}{y} - 3 + \dfrac{y}{2}\right)$ $\dfrac{y+4}{2(y-2)}$

[C] 48. $\left(\dfrac{b}{8} - \dfrac{8}{b}\right) \div \left(\dfrac{8}{b} - 5 + \dfrac{b}{2}\right)$ $\dfrac{b+8}{4(b-2)}$

49. ✏ How would you explain to a classmate why we multiply the numerator and denominator of a complex fraction by the LCM of the denominators of the fractions in the numerator and denominator?

9.5

Equations Containing Fractions

1 Solve equations containing fractions

In the chapter on Solving Equations and Inequalities, equations containing fractions were solved by the method of clearing denominators. Recall that to **clear denominators**, we multiply each side of an equation by the LCM of the denominators. The result is an equation that contains no fractions. In this section, we will again solve equations containing fractions by multiplying each side of the equation by the LCM of the denominators. The difference between this section and the chapter on Solving Equations and Inequalities, is that the fractions in these equations contain variables in the denominators.

➡ Solve: $\dfrac{3x-1}{4x} + \dfrac{2}{3x} = \dfrac{7}{6x}$

LOOK CLOSELY

Note that we are now solving *equations*, not operating on *expressions*. We are not writing each fraction in terms of the LCM of the denominators; we are multiplying both sides of the equation by the LCM of the denominators.

Find the LCM of the denominators.

The LCM of $4x$, $3x$, and $6x$ is $12x$.

$$\frac{3x-1}{4x} + \frac{2}{3x} = \frac{7}{6x}$$

Multiply each side of the equation by the LCM of the denominators.

$$12x\left(\frac{3x-1}{4x} + \frac{2}{3x}\right) = 12x\left(\frac{7}{6x}\right)$$

Simplify using the Distributive Property.

$$12x\left(\frac{3x-1}{4x}\right) + 12x\left(\frac{2}{3x}\right) = 12x\left(\frac{7}{6x}\right)$$

$$\frac{12x}{1}\left(\frac{3x-1}{4x}\right) + \frac{12x}{1}\left(\frac{2}{3x}\right) = \frac{12x}{1}\left(\frac{7}{6x}\right)$$

$$3(3x-1) + 4(2) = 2(7)$$

Solve for x.

$$9x - 3 + 8 = 14$$
$$9x + 5 = 14$$
$$9x = 9$$
$$x = 1$$

1 checks as a solution.
The solution is 1.

Example 1   Solve: $\dfrac{4}{x} - \dfrac{x}{2} = \dfrac{7}{2}$

Solution

$$\frac{4}{x} - \frac{x}{2} = \frac{7}{2}$$ ▶ The LCM of x and 2 is $2x$.

$$2x\left(\frac{4}{x} - \frac{x}{2}\right) = 2x\left(\frac{7}{2}\right)$$

$$\frac{2x}{1}\cdot\frac{4}{x} - \frac{2x}{1}\cdot\frac{x}{2} = \frac{2x}{1}\cdot\frac{7}{2}$$

$$8 - x^2 = 7x$$ ▶ This is a quadratic equation.

$$0 = x^2 + 7x - 8$$
$$0 = (x+8)(x-1)$$

$$x + 8 = 0 \qquad\qquad x - 1 = 0$$
$$x = -8 \qquad\qquad x = 1$$

Both -8 and 1 check as solutions.
The solutions are -8 and 1.

Problem 1   Solve: $x + \frac{1}{3} = \frac{4}{3x}$

       Solution   See page S20. $-\frac{4}{3}$ and 1

Occasionally, a value of a variable in a fractional equation makes one of the denominators zero. In this case, that value of the variable is not a solution of the equation.

➡ Solve: $\dfrac{2x}{x-2} = 1 + \dfrac{4}{x-2}$

INSTRUCTOR NOTE

This example illustrates the importance of checking a solution of a rational equation when each side is multiplied by a variable expression.

   You might emphasize that the Multiplication Property of Equations states that each side can be multiplied by a *nonzero* number. If *x* were allowed to be 2, each side of the equation would be multiplied by zero.

Find the LCM of the denominators.

The LCM is $x - 2$.

$$\frac{2x}{x-2} = 1 + \frac{4}{x-2}$$

Multiply each side of the equation by the LCM of the denominators.

$$(x-2)\frac{2x}{x-2} = (x-2)\left(1 + \frac{4}{x-2}\right)$$

Simplify using the Distributive Property.

$$(x-2)\left(\frac{2x}{x-2}\right) = (x-2) \cdot 1 + (x-2) \cdot \frac{4}{x-2}$$

Solve for *x*.

$$2x = x - 2 + 4$$
$$2x = x + 2$$
$$x = 2$$

When x is replaced by 2, the denominators of $\dfrac{2x}{x-2}$ and $\dfrac{4}{x-2}$ are zero.

Therefore, 2 is not a solution of the equation. The equation has no solution.

◄

Example 2   Solve: $\dfrac{3x}{x-4} = 5 + \dfrac{12}{x-4}$

       Solution

$$\frac{3x}{x-4} = 5 + \frac{12}{x-4}$$ ▶ The LCM is $x - 4$.

$$(x-4) \cdot \frac{3x}{x-4} = (x-4)\left(5 + \frac{12}{x-4}\right)$$
$$3x = (x-4)5 + 12$$
$$3x = 5x - 20 + 12$$
$$3x = 5x - 8$$
$$-2x = -8$$
$$x = 4$$

4 does not check as a solution. The equation has no solution.

Problem 2   Solve: $\dfrac{5x}{x+2} = 3 - \dfrac{10}{x+2}$

       Solution   See page S21.   No solution

2   Solve proportions

Quantities such as 4 meters, 15 seconds, and 8 gallons are number quantities written with units. In these examples, the units are meters, seconds, and gallons.

A **ratio** is the quotient of two quantities that have the same unit.

The length of a living room is 16 ft, and the width is 12 ft. The ratio of the length to the width is written

$$\frac{16 \text{ ft}}{12 \text{ ft}} = \frac{16}{12} = \frac{4}{3}$$ A ratio is in simplest form when the two numbers do not have a common factor. Note that the units are not written.

A **rate** is the quotient of two quantities that have different units.

There are 2 lb of salt in 8 gal of water. The salt-to-water rate is

$$\frac{2 \text{ lb}}{8 \text{ gal}} = \frac{1 \text{ lb}}{4 \text{ gal}}$$ A rate is in simplest form when the two numbers do not have a common factor. The units are written as part of the rate.

A **proportion** is an equation that states the equality of two ratios or rates.

Examples of proportions are shown below.

$$\frac{30 \text{ mi}}{4 \text{ h}} = \frac{15 \text{ mi}}{2 \text{ h}} \qquad \frac{4}{6} = \frac{8}{12} \qquad \frac{3}{4} = \frac{x}{8}$$

Because a proportion is an equation containing fractions, the same method used to solve an equation containing fractions is used to solve a proportion. Multiply each side of the equation by the LCM of the denominators. Then solve for the variable.

⮕ Solve the proportion $\frac{4}{x} = \frac{2}{3}$.

$$\frac{4}{x} = \frac{2}{3}$$

Multiply each side of the proportion by the LCM of the denominators.

$$3x\left(\frac{4}{x}\right) = 3x\left(\frac{2}{3}\right)$$

$$12 = 2x$$

Solve the equation.

$$6 = x$$

The solution is 6. ⬅

Example 3   Solve.   A. $\dfrac{8}{x+3} = \dfrac{4}{x}$ B. $\dfrac{6}{x+4} = \dfrac{12}{5x-13}$

Solution   A.

$$\frac{8}{x+3} = \frac{4}{x}$$

$$x(x+3)\frac{8}{x+3} = x(x+3)\frac{4}{x}$$ ▶ Multiply each side of the proportion by the LCM of the denominators.

$$8x = (x+3)4$$

$$8x = 4x + 12$$

$$4x = 12$$

$$x = 3$$ ▶ Remember to check the solution because it is a fractional equation.

The solution is 3.

B.
$$\frac{6}{x+4} = \frac{12}{5x-13}$$

$$(5x-13)(x+4)\frac{6}{x+4} = (5x-13)(x+4)\frac{12}{5x-13}$$

$$(5x-13)6 = (x+4)12$$
$$30x - 78 = 12x + 48$$
$$18x - 78 = 48$$
$$18x = 126$$
$$x = 7$$

The solution is 7.

Problem 3   Solve.   A. $\dfrac{2}{x+3} = \dfrac{6}{5x+5}$ B. $\dfrac{5}{2x-3} = \dfrac{10}{x+3}$

Solution   See page S21.   A. 2   B. 3

---

3   # Applications of proportions

Example 4   The monthly loan payment for a car is $29.50 for each $1000 borrowed. At this rate, find the monthly payment for a $9000 car loan.

Strategy   To find the monthly payment, write and solve a proportion using P to represent the monthly car payment.

Solution
$$\frac{29.50}{1000} = \frac{P}{9000}$$
$$9000\left(\frac{29.50}{1000}\right) = 9000\left(\frac{P}{9000}\right)$$
$$265.50 = P$$

▶ The monthly payments are in the numerators. The loan amounts are in the denominators.

The monthly payment is $265.50.

LOOK CLOSELY

It is also correct to write the proportion with the loan amounts in the numerators and the monthly payments in the denominators. The solution will be the same.

Problem 4   Nine ceramic tiles are required to tile a 4 ft² area. At this rate, how many square feet can be tiled with 270 ceramic tiles?

4 square feet

Solution   See page S21.   120 ft²

Example 5   An investment of $1200 earns $96 each year. At the same rate, how much additional money must be invested to earn $128 each year?

Strategy   To find the additional amount of money that must be invested, write and solve a proportion using x to represent the additional money. Then $1200 + x$ is the total amount invested.

Solution $\dfrac{1200}{96} = \dfrac{1200 + x}{128}$ ▶ The amounts invested are in the numerators. The amounts earned are in the denominators.

$$\frac{25}{2} = \frac{1200 + x}{128}$$ ▶ Simplify $\dfrac{1200}{96}$.

$$128\left(\frac{25}{2}\right) = 128\left(\frac{1200 + x}{128}\right)$$

$$1600 = 1200 + x$$

$$400 = x$$

An additional $400 must be invested.

Problem 5 Three ounces of a medication are required for a 120-pound adult. At the same rate, how many additional ounces of the medication are required for a 180-pound adult?

Solution See page S21.   1.5 additional ounces

4 Problems involving similar triangles

Similar objects have the same shape but not necessarily the same size. A tennis ball is similar to a basketball. A model ship is similar to an actual ship.

Similar objects have corresponding parts; for example, the rudder on the model ship corresponds to the rudder on the actual ship. The relationship between the sizes of each of the corresponding parts can be written as a ratio, and each ratio will be the same. If the rudder on the model ship is $\dfrac{1}{100}$ the size of the rudder on the actual ship, then the model wheelhouse is $\dfrac{1}{100}$ the size of the actual wheelhouse, the width of the model is $\dfrac{1}{100}$ the width of the actual ship, and so on.

The two triangles *ABC* and *DEF* shown at the right are similar. Side *AB* corresponds to *DE*, side *BC* corresponds to *EF*, and side *AC* corresponds to *DF*. The height *CH* corresponds to the height *FK*. The ratios of corresponding parts are equal.

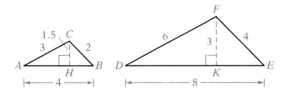

$$\frac{AB}{DE} = \frac{4}{8} = \frac{1}{2}, \qquad \frac{AC}{DF} = \frac{3}{6} = \frac{1}{2}, \qquad \frac{BC}{EF} = \frac{2}{4} = \frac{1}{2}, \qquad \text{and} \qquad \frac{CH}{FK} = \frac{1.5}{3} = \frac{1}{2}$$

Because the ratios of corresponding parts are equal, three proportions can be formed using the sides of the triangles.

$$\frac{AB}{DE} = \frac{AC}{DF}, \qquad \frac{AB}{DE} = \frac{BC}{EF}, \qquad \text{and} \qquad \frac{AC}{DF} = \frac{BC}{EF}$$

Three proportions can also be formed by using the sides and height of the triangles.

$$\frac{AB}{DE} = \frac{CH}{FK}, \qquad \frac{AC}{DF} = \frac{CH}{FK}, \qquad \text{and} \qquad \frac{BC}{EF} = \frac{CH}{FK}$$

The corresponding angles in similar triangles are equal. Therefore,

$$\angle A = \angle D, \qquad \angle B = \angle E, \qquad \text{and} \qquad \angle C = \angle F$$

➡ Triangles ABC and DEF at the right are similar. Find the area of triangle ABC.

Solve a proportion to find the height of triangle ABC.

$$\frac{AB}{DE} = \frac{CH}{FG}$$

$$\frac{5}{12} = \frac{CH}{3}$$

$$12 \cdot \frac{5}{12} = 12 \cdot \frac{CH}{3}$$

$$5 = 4(CH)$$

The height is 1.25 in. The base is 5 in.

$$1.25 = CH$$

Use the formula for the area of a triangle.

$$A = \frac{1}{2}bh = \frac{1}{2}(5)(1.25) = 3.125$$

The area of triangle ABC is 3.125 in².

It is also true that if the three angles of one triangle are equal, respectively, to the three angles of another triangle, then the two triangles are similar.

A line DE is drawn parallel to the base AB in the triangle at the right. $\angle x = \angle m$ and $\angle y = \angle n$ because corresponding angles are equal. Because $\angle C = \angle C$, the three angles of triangle DEC are equal respectively to the three angles of triangle ABC. Triangle DEC is similar to triangle ABC.

The sum of the three angles of a triangle is 180°. If two angles of one triangle are equal to two angles of another triangle, then the third angles must be equal. Thus we can say that if two angles of one triangle are equal to two angles of another triangle, then the two triangles are similar.

➡ The lines AB and CD intersect at point O in the figure at the right. Angles C and D are right angles. Find the length of DO.

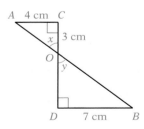

First determine whether triangle AOC is similar to triangle BOD.

Angle C = angle D because they are right angles. Angle x = angle y because they are vertical angles.

Therefore, triangle AOC is similar to triangle BOD because two angles of one triangle are equal to two angles of the other triangle.

Use a proportion to find the length of the unknown side.

$$\frac{AC}{DB} = \frac{CO}{DO}$$

$$\frac{4}{7} = \frac{3}{DO}$$

$$7(DO)\frac{4}{7} = 7(DO)\frac{3}{DO}$$

$$4(DO) = 7(3)$$

$$4(DO) = 21$$

$$DO = 5.25$$

The length of DO is 5.25 cm.

Example 6 In the figure at the right, AB is parallel to DC, angles B and D are right angles. $AB = 12$ m, $DC = 4$ m, and $AC = 18$ m. Find the length of CO.

Strategy Triangle AOB is similar to triangle DOC. Solve a proportion to find the length of CO. Let x represent the length of CO. Then $18 - x$ represents the length of AO.

Solution

$$\frac{DC}{AB} = \frac{CO}{AO}$$

$$\frac{4}{12} = \frac{x}{18 - x}$$

$$12(18 - x) \cdot \frac{4}{12} = 12(18 - x) \cdot \frac{x}{18 - x}$$

$$(18 - x)4 = 12x$$

$$72 - 4x = 12x$$

$$72 = 16x$$

$$4.5 = x$$

The length of CO is 45 m.

Problem 6 In the figure at the right, AB is parallel to DC and angles A and D are right angles. $AB = 10$ cm, $CD = 4$ cm, and $DO = 3$ cm. Find the area of triangle AOB.

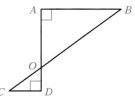

Solution See page S21.   37.5 cm²

CONCEPT REVIEW 9.5

Determine whether the statement is always true, sometimes true, or never true.

1. The process of clearing denominators in an equation containing fractions is an application of the Multiplication Property of Equations.   Always true

2. If the denominator of a fraction is $x + 3$, then $x \neq 3$ for that fraction.

    Never true

3. The first step in solving an equation containing fractions is to find the LCM of the denominators.   Always true

4. The solutions to an equation containing algebraic fractions must be checked because a solution might make one of the denominators equal to zero.
    Always true

5. Suppose, after the clearing of denominators, a fractional equation results in a quadratic equation. Then the equation has two solutions.   Sometimes true

6. Both sides of an equation containing fractions can be multiplied by the same number without changing the solution of the equation.   Sometimes true

7. To solve a proportion, multiply each side of the proportion by the LCM of the denominators.   Always true

EXERCISES 9.5

1 1. ✎ In solving an equation containing fractions, why do we first multiply each side of the equation by the LCM of the denominators?

2. ✎ After solving an equation containing fractions, why must we check the solution?

Solve.

3. $2 + \dfrac{5}{x} = 7$ 1

4. $3 + \dfrac{8}{n} = 5$ 4

5. $1 - \dfrac{9}{x} = 4$ -3

6. $3 - \dfrac{12}{x} = 7$ -3

7. $\dfrac{2}{y} + 5 = 9$ $\dfrac{1}{2}$

8. $\dfrac{6}{x} + 3 = 11$ $\dfrac{3}{4}$

9. $\dfrac{4x}{x-4} + 5 = \dfrac{5x}{x-4}$ 5

10. $\dfrac{2x}{x+2} - 5 = \dfrac{7x}{x+2}$ -1

11. $2 + \dfrac{3}{a-3} = \dfrac{a}{a-3}$ No solution

12. $\dfrac{x}{x+4} = 3 - \dfrac{4}{x+4}$ No solution

13. $\dfrac{x}{x-1} = \dfrac{8}{x+2}$ 2, 4

14. $\dfrac{x}{x+12} = \dfrac{1}{x+5}$ $-6, 2$

15. $\dfrac{2x}{x+4} = \dfrac{3}{x-1}$ $-\dfrac{3}{2}, 4$

16. $\dfrac{5}{3n-8} = \dfrac{n}{n+2}$ $-\dfrac{2}{3}, 5$

17. $x + \dfrac{6}{x-2} = \dfrac{3x}{x-2}$ 3

18. $x - \dfrac{6}{x-3} = \dfrac{2x}{x-3}$ $6, -1$

19. $\dfrac{x}{x+2} + \dfrac{2}{x-2} = \dfrac{x+6}{x^2-4}$ -1

20. $\dfrac{x}{x+4} = \dfrac{11}{x^2-16} + 2$ $-7, 3$

21. $\dfrac{8}{y} = \dfrac{2}{y-2} + 1$ 4

22. $\dfrac{8}{r} + \dfrac{3}{r-1} = 3$ $\dfrac{2}{3}, 4$

23. ✎ Are the solutions of the equations $2x = 9x$ and $\dfrac{1}{2x} = \dfrac{1}{9x}$ the same? Explain your answer.

2 Solve.

24. $\dfrac{x}{12} = \dfrac{3}{4}$ 9

25. $\dfrac{6}{x} = \dfrac{2}{3}$ 9

26. $\dfrac{4}{9} = \dfrac{x}{27}$ 12

27. $\dfrac{16}{9} = \dfrac{64}{x}$ 36

28. $\dfrac{x+3}{12} = \dfrac{5}{6}$ 7

29. $\dfrac{3}{5} = \dfrac{x-4}{10}$ 10

30. $\dfrac{18}{x+4} = \dfrac{9}{5}$ 6

31. $\dfrac{2}{11} = \dfrac{20}{x-3}$ 113

32. $\dfrac{2}{x} = \dfrac{4}{x+1}$ 1

33. $\dfrac{16}{x-2} = \dfrac{8}{x}$ -2

34. $\dfrac{x+3}{4} = \dfrac{x}{8}$ -6

35. $\dfrac{x-6}{3} = \dfrac{x}{5}$ 15

36. $\dfrac{2}{x-1} = \dfrac{6}{2x+1}$ 4

37. $\dfrac{9}{x+2} = \dfrac{3}{x-2}$ 4

38. $\dfrac{2x}{7} = \dfrac{x-2}{14}$ $-\dfrac{2}{3}$

39. *Elections*   An exit poll showed that 4 out of every 7 voters cast a ballot in favor of an amendment to a city charter. At this rate, how many people voted in favor of the amendment if 35,000 people voted?   20,000 people

40. *Business*   A quality control inspector found 3 defective transistors in a shipment of 500 transistors. At this rate, how many transistors would be defective in a shipment of 2000 transistors?   12 transistors

41. *Construction*   An air conditioning specialist recommends 2 air vents for every 300 ft² of floor space. At this rate, how many air vents are required for an office building of 21,000 ft²?   140 air vents

42. *Television*   In a city of 25,000 homes, a survey was taken to determine the number with cable television. Of the 300 homes surveyed, 210 had cable television. Estimate the number of homes in the city that have cable television.   17,500 homes

43. *Cooking*   A simple syrup is made by dissolving 2 c of sugar in $\dfrac{2}{3}$ c of boiling water. At this rate, how many cups of sugar are required for 2 c of boiling water?   6 c

44. *Energy*   The lighting for a billboard is provided by solar energy. If three energy panels generate 10 watts of power, how many panels are needed to provide 600 watts of power?   180 panels

45. *Conservation*   As part of a conservation effort for a lake, 40 fish were caught, tagged, and then released. Later, 80 fish were caught from the lake. Four of these 80 fish were found to have tags. Estimate the number of fish in the lake.   800 fish

46. *Conservation*   In a wildlife preserve, 10 elk were captured, tagged, and then released. Later, 15 elk were captured and 2 were found to have tags. Estimate the number of elk in the preserve.   75 elk

47. *Health*   A health department estimates that 8 vials of a malaria serum will treat 100 people. At this rate, how many vials are required to treat 175 people?   14 vials

48. *Business*   A company will accept a shipment of 10,000 computer disks if there are 2 or fewer defects in a sample of 100 randomly chosen disks. Assume that there are 300 defective disks in the shipment and that the rate of defective disks in the sample is the same as the rate in the shipment. Will the shipment be accepted?   No

49. *Business*   A company will accept a shipment of 20,000 precision bearings if there are 3 or fewer defects in a sample of 100 randomly chosen bearings. Assume that there are 400 defective bearings in the shipment and that the rate of defective bearings in the sample is the same as the rate in the shipment. Will the shipment be accepted?   Yes

50. *Cartography*   On a map, two cities are $2\frac{5}{8}$ in. apart. If $\frac{3}{8}$ in. on the map represents 25 mi, find the number of miles in the distance between the two cities.
    175 mi

51. *Cartography*   On a map, two cities are $5\frac{5}{8}$ in. apart. If $\frac{3}{4}$ in. on the map represents 100 mi, find the number of miles in the distance between the two cities.   750 mi

52. *Redecorating*   A painter estimates that 5 gal of paint will cover 1200 ft^2 of wall surface. How many additional gallons are required to cover 1680 ft^2?
    2 additional gallons

53. *Agriculture*   A 50-acre field yields 1100 bushels of wheat annually. How many additional acres must be planted so that the annual yield will be 1320 bushels?   10 additional acres

54. *Taxes*   The sales tax on a car that sold for $12,000 is $780. At the same rate, how much higher is the sales tax on a car that sells for $13,500? $97.50

55. *Construction*   To conserve energy and still allow for as much natural lighting as possible, an architect suggests that the ratio of the area of a window to the area of the total wall surface be 5 to 12. Using this ratio, determine the recommended area of a window to be installed in a wall that measures 8 ft by 12 ft.   40 ft^2

56. *Rocketry*   The engine of a small rocket burns 170,000 lb of fuel in 1 min. At this rate, how many pounds of fuel does the rocket burn in 45 s?   127,500 lb

57. *Catering*   A caterer estimates that 5 gal of coffee will serve 50 people. How much additional coffee is necessary to serve 70 people?   2 additional gallons

58. *Paint Mixtures*   A green paint is created by mixing 3 parts of yellow with every 5 parts of blue. How many gallons of yellow paint are needed to make 60 gal of this green paint?   22.5 gal

59. *The Food Industry*   A soft drink is made by mixing 4 parts of carbonated water with every 3 parts of syrup. How many milliliters of carbonated water are in 280 ml of soft drink?   160 ml

4 Solve. Triangles *ABC* and *DEF* in Exercises 60 to 67 are similar. Round answers to the nearest tenth.

60. Find side *AC*.

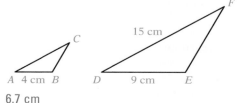

6.7 cm

61. Find side *DE*.

12.8 in.

62. Find the height of triangle *ABC*.

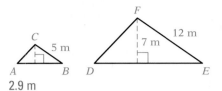

2.9 m

63. Find the height of triangle *DEF*.

4.7 ft

64. Find the perimeter of triangle *DEF*.

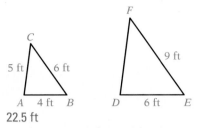

22.5 ft

65. Find the perimeter of triangle *ABC*.

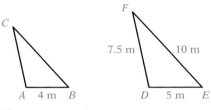

18 m

66. Find the area of triangle *ABC*.

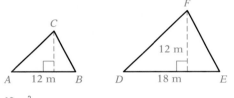

48 m²

67. Find the area of triangle *ABC*.

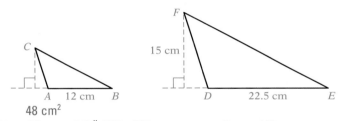

48 cm²

68. Given *BD* ∥ *AE*, *BD* measures 5 cm, *AE* measures 8 cm, and *AC* measures 10 cm, find the length of *BC*.

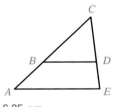

6.25 cm

69. Given *AC* ∥ *DE*, *BD* measures 8 m, *AD* measures 12 m, and *BE* measures 6 m, find the length of *BC*.

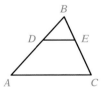

15 m

70. Given *DE* ∥ *AC*, *DE* measures 6 in., *AC* measures 10 in., and *AB* measures 15 in., find the length of *DA*.

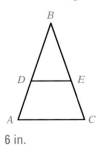

6 in.

71. Given *MP* and *NQ* intersect at *O*, *NO* measures 25 ft, *MO* measures 20 ft, and *PO* measures 8 ft, find the length of *QO*.

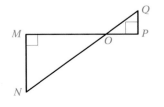

10 ft

72. Given *MP* and *NQ* intersect at *O*, *NO* measures 24 cm, *MN* measures 10 cm, *MP* measures 39 cm, and *QO* measures 12 cm, find the length of *OP*.

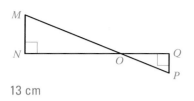

13 cm

73. Given *MQ* and *NP* intersect at *O*, *NO* measures 12 m, *MN* measures 9 m, *PQ* measures 3 m, and *MQ* measures 20 m, find the perimeter of triangle *OPQ*.

12 m

74. Similar triangles can be used as an indirect way to measure inaccessible distances. The diagram at the right represents a river of width *DC*. The triangles *AOB* and *DOC* are similar. The distances *AB*, *BO*, and *OC* can be measured. Find the width of the river.
35 m

75. The sun's rays cast a shadow as shown in the diagram at the right. Find the height of the flagpole. Write the answer in terms of feet.
14.375 ft

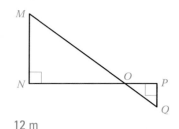

APPLYING CONCEPTS 9.5

Solve.

76. $\frac{2}{3}(x + 2) - \frac{x + 1}{6} = \frac{1}{2}$ $-\frac{4}{3}$

77. $\frac{3}{4}a = \frac{1}{2}(3 - a) + \frac{a - 2}{4}$ 1

78. $\frac{x}{2x^2 - x - 1} = \frac{3}{x^2 - 1} + \frac{3}{2x + 1}$ $0, -\frac{5}{2}$

79. $\frac{x + 1}{x^2 + x - 2} = \frac{x + 2}{x^2 - 1} + \frac{3}{x + 2}$ $0, -\frac{2}{3}$

80. *Number Problems* The sum of a number and its reciprocal is $\frac{26}{5}$. Find the number.   5 or $\frac{1}{5}$

81. *Number Problems* The sum of the multiplicative inverses of two consecutive integers is $-\frac{7}{12}$. Find the integers. -3 and -4

[C] **82.** *Number Problems*   The denominator of a fraction is 2 more than the numerator. If both the numerator and denominator of the fraction are increased by 3, the new fraction is $\frac{4}{5}$. Find the original fraction. $\frac{5}{7}$

[C] **83.** *Lotteries*   Three people put their money together to buy lottery tickets. The first person put in $25, the second person put in $30, and the third person put in $35. One of their tickets was a winning ticket. If they won $4.5 million, what was the first person's share of the winnings? $1.25 million

[C] **84.** *Sports*   A basketball player has made 5 out of every 6 foul shots attempted. If 42 foul shots were missed in the player's career, how many foul shots were made in the player's career?   210 foul shots

[C] **85.** *Photography*   The "sitting fee" for school pictures is $4. If 10 photos cost $10, including the sitting fee, what would 24 photos cost, including the sitting fee? $18.40

[C] **86.** *Fundraising*   No one belongs to both the Math Club and the Photography Club, but the two clubs join to hold a car wash. Ten members of the Math Club and 6 members of the Photography Club participate. The profits from the car wash are $120. If each club's profits are proportional to the number of members participating, what share of the profits does the Math Club receive? $75

87.   *Demography*   The number of Americans aged 65 and over is increasing dramatically. This demographic fact is a concern for the medical profession because the ratio of the population who are caregivers (ages 50 to 64) to the population needing care (ages 85 and older) will be shrinking. The ratios are shown on the chart below.

Ratios of Caregivers to Those Needing Care	
1990	🧍🧍🧍🧍🧍🧍🧍🧍🧍🧍🧍 to 🧍
2010	🧍🧍🧍🧍🧍🧍🧍🧍🧍🧍 to 🧍
2030	🧍🧍🧍🧍🧍🧍 to 🧍
2050	🧍🧍🧍🧍 to 🧍

Source: Copyright © 1996, *USA Today*. Reprinted with permission.

The "aging of America" is also a major concern for the Social Security Administration. Because the number of Americans aged 65 and over is increasing dramatically, the ratio of the number of workers contributing to Social Security to the number of beneficiaries will decrease dramatically during the next few decades.

Use a resource to find the present and predicted future ratios of the number of employees contributing to Social Security to the number of Social Security recipients. Write a paragraph describing a proposal for "fixing" the Social Security system.

88.   *Economics*   The table below shows, for each state and the District of Columbia, the average income of the 20% of families with children that have the highest incomes and the 20% of families with children that have the lowest incomes. Also shown is the ratio of these two averages.

State	Average income of bottom fifth of families with children	Average income of top fifth of families with children	Ratio
1. New York	$6,787	$132,390	19.5
2. Louisiana	$6,430	$102,339	15.9
3. New Mexico	$6,408	$91,741	14.3
4. Arizona	$7,273	$103,392	14.2
5. Connecticut	$10,415	$147,594	14.2
6. California	$9,033	$127,719	14.1
7. Florida	$7,705	$107,811	14.0
8. Kentucky	$7,364	$99,210	13.5
9. Alabama	$7,531	$99,062	13.2
10. West Virginia	$6,439	$84,479	13.1
11. Tennessee	$8,156	$106,966	13.1
12. Texas	$8,642	$113,149	13.1
13. Mississippi	$6,257	$80,980	12.9
14. Michigan	$9,257	$117,107	12.7
15. Oklahoma	$7,483	$94,380	12.6
16. Massachusetts	$10,694	$132,962	12.4
17. Georgia	$9,978	$123,837	12.4
18. Illinois	$10,002	$123,233	12.3
19. Ohio	$9,346	$111,894	12.0
20. South Carolina	$8,146	$96,712	11.9
21. Pennsylvania	$10,512	$124,537	11.8
22. North Carolina	$9,363	$107,490	11.5
23. Rhode Island	$9,914	$111,015	11.2
24. Washington	$10,116	$112,501	11.1
25. Maryland	$13,346	$147,971	11.1
26. Virginia	$10,816	$116,202	10.7
27. Kansas	$10,790	$110,341	10.2
28. Oregon	$9,627	$97,589	10.1
29. New Jersey	$14,211	$143,010	10.1
30. Indiana	$11,115	$110,876	10.0
31. Montana	$9,051	$89,902	9.9
32. South Dakota	$9,474	$93,822	9.9
33. Idaho	$10,721	$104,725	9.8
34. Delaware	$12,041	$116,965	9.7
35. Arkansas	$8,995	$83,434	9.3
36. Colorado	$14,326	$131,368	9.2
37. Hawaii	$12,735	$116,060	9.1
38. Missouri	$11,090	$100,837	9.1
39. Alaska	$14,868	$129,025	8.7
40. Wyoming	$11,174	$94,845	8.5
41. Minnesota	$14,655	$120,344	8.2
42. Nebraska	$12,546	$102,992	8.2
43. Maine	$11,275	$92,457	8.2
44. New Hampshire	$14,299	$116,018	8.1
45. Nevada	$12,276	$98,693	8.0
46. Iowa	$13,148	$104,253	7.9
47. Wisconsin	$13,398	$103,551	7.7
48. Vermont	$13,107	$97,898	7.5
49. North Dakota	$12,424	$91,041	7.3
50. Utah	$15,709	$110,938	7.1
Dist. of Columbia	$5,293	$149,508	28.2
Total U.S.	$9,254	$117,499	12.7

Source: Copyright © 1997, *USA Today.* Reprinted with permission.

How were the ratios calculated? What does the ratio of 13.1 for Texas mean? Use the ratios for New York and Utah to compare the income statistics in these two states.

In the 1970s, no state had a ratio greater than 10 to 1. Provide an explanation for the widening gap between the richest and the poorest. For example, you might consider increased technology, a low minimum wage, the decline in union membership, or the increase in international trade.

S E C T I O N **9.6**

Literal Equations

1 Solve a literal equation for one of the variables

A **literal equation** is an equation that contains more than one variable. Examples of literal equations are shown at the right.

$$2x + 3y = 6$$
$$4w - 2x + z = 0$$

Formulas are used to express a relationship among physical quantities. A **formula** is a literal equation that states rules about measurements. Examples of formulas are shown below.

$$\frac{1}{R_1} + \frac{1}{R_2} = \frac{1}{R} \qquad \text{(Physics)}$$

$$s = a + (n - 1)d \qquad \text{(Mathematics)}$$

$$A = P + Prt \qquad \text{(Business)}$$

The Addition and Multiplication Properties can be used to solve a literal equation for one of the variables. The goal is to rewrite the equation so that the letter being solved for is alone on one side of the equation and all numbers and other variables are on the other side.

➡ Solve $A = P(1 + i)$ for i.

The goal is to rewrite the equation so that i is on one side of the equation and all other variables are on the other side.

$$A = P(1 + i)$$

Use the Distributive Property to remove parentheses.

$$A = P + Pi$$

Subtract P from each side of the equation.

$$A - P = P - P + Pi$$
$$A - P = Pi$$

Divide each side of the equation by P.

$$\frac{A - P}{P} = \frac{Pi}{P}$$

$$\frac{A - P}{P} = i$$

Example 1 A. Solve $I = \dfrac{E}{R + r}$ for R.   B. Solve $L = a(1 + ct)$ for c.

Solution A.

$$I = \dfrac{E}{R + r}$$

$$(R + r)I = (R + r)\dfrac{E}{R + r}$$

$$RI + rI = E$$

$$RI + rI - rI = E - rI$$

$$RI = E - rI$$

$$\dfrac{RI}{I} = \dfrac{E - rI}{I}$$

$$R = \dfrac{E - rI}{I}$$

B.

$$L = a(1 + ct)$$
$$L = a + act$$
$$L - a = a - a + act$$
$$L - a = act$$
$$\dfrac{L - a}{at} = \dfrac{act}{at}$$
$$\dfrac{L - a}{at} = c$$

Problem 1 A. Solve $s = \dfrac{A + L}{2}$ for L.   B. Solve $S = a + (n - 1)d$ for n.

Solution See page S21.   A. $L = 2s - A$ B. $n = \dfrac{S - a + d}{d}$

Example 2 Solve $S = C - rC$ for C.

Solution

$$S = C - rC$$
$$S = C(1 - r)$$ ▸ Factor C from $C - rC$.
$$\dfrac{S}{1 - r} = \dfrac{C(1 - r)}{1 - r}$$ ▸ Divide each side of the equation by $1 - r$.
$$\dfrac{S}{1 - r} = C$$

Problem 2 Solve $S = C + rC$ for C.

Solution See page S22. $C = \dfrac{S}{1 + r}$

CONCEPT REVIEW 9.6

Determine whether the statement is always true, sometimes true, or never true.

1. An equation that contains more than one variable is a literal equation.
   Always true

2. The linear equation $y = 4x - 5$ is not a literal equation.   Never true

3. Literal equations are solved using the same properties of equations that are used to solve equations in one variable.   Always true

4. In solving a literal equation, the goal is to get the variable being solved for alone on one side of the equation and all numbers and other variables on the other side of the equation.   Always true

5. In solving $L = a(1 + ct)$ for c, you need to use the Distributive Property. In solving $S = C - rC$ for C, you need to factor.   Always true

6. We can divide both sides of a literal equation by the same nonzero expression. Always true

EXERCISES 9.6

1 Solve the formula for the variable given.

1. $A = \frac{1}{2}bh; h$ (Geometry) $h = \frac{2A}{b}$

2. $P = a + b + c; b$ (Geometry) $b = P - a - c$

3. $d = rt; t$ (Physics) $t = \frac{d}{r}$

4. $E = IR; R$ (Physics) $R = \frac{E}{I}$

5. $PV = nRT; T$ (Chemistry) $T = \frac{PV}{nR}$

6. $A = bh; h$ (Geometry) $h = \frac{A}{b}$

7. $P = 2L + 2W; L$ (Geometry) $L = \frac{P - 2W}{2}$

8. $F = \frac{9}{5}C + 32; C$ (Temperature conversion) $C = \frac{5F - 160}{9}$

9. $A = \frac{1}{2}h(b_1 + b_2); b_1$ (Geometry) $b_1 = \frac{2A - hb_2}{h}$

10. $C = \frac{5}{9}(F - 32); F$ (Temperature conversion) $F = \frac{9C + 160}{5}$

11. $V = \frac{1}{3}Ah; h$ (Geometry) $h = \frac{3V}{A}$

12. $P = R - C; C$ (Business) $C = R - P$

13. $R = \frac{C - S}{t}; S$ (Business) $S = C - Rt$

14. $P = \frac{R - C}{n}; R$ (Business) $R = Pn + C$

15. $A = P + Prt; P$ (Business) $P = \frac{A}{1 + rt}$

16. $T = fm - gm; m$ (Engineering) $m = \frac{T}{f - g}$

17. $A = Sw + w; w$ (Physics) $w = \frac{A}{S + 1}$

18. $a = S - Sr; S$ (Mathematics) $S = \frac{a}{1 - r}$

APPLYING CONCEPTS 9.6

Geometry   The surface area of a right circular cylinder is given by the formula $S = 2\pi rh + 2\pi r^2$, where r is the radius of the base and h is the height of the cylinder.

19. **a.** Solve the formula $S = 2\pi rh + 2\pi r^2$ for h. $h = \frac{S - 2\pi r^2}{2\pi r}$
   b. Use your answer to part (a) to find the height of a right circular cylinder when the surface area is 12π in^2 and the radius is 1 in.   5 in.
   c. Use your answer to part (a) to find the height of a right circular cylinder when the surface area is 24π in^2 and the radius is 2 in.   4 in.

1 in.

$S = 12\pi$ in^2

Business   Break-even analysis is a method used to determine the sales volume required for a company to break even, or experience neither a profit nor a loss, on the sale of its product. The break-even point represents the number of units that must be made and sold for income from sales to equal the cost of producing the product. The break-even point can be calculated using the formula $B = \dfrac{F}{S - V}$, where F is the fixed costs, S is the selling price per unit, and V is the variable costs per unit.

[C] **20.**   **a.** Solve the formula $B = \dfrac{F}{S - V}$ for S. $S = \dfrac{F + BV}{B}$

       b. Use your answer to part (a) to find the selling price per desk required for a company to break even. The fixed costs are $20,000, the variable costs per desk are $80, and the company plans to make and sell 200 desks. $180

       c. Use your answer to part (a) to find the selling price per camera required for a company to break even. The fixed costs are $15,000, the variable costs per camera are $50, and the company plans to make and sell 600 cameras. $75

Business   When markup is based on selling price, the selling price of a product is given by the formula $S = \dfrac{C}{1 - r}$, where C is the cost of the product and r is the markup rate.

[C] **21.**   **a.** Solve the formula $S = \dfrac{C}{1 - r}$ for r. $r = \dfrac{S - C}{S}$

       b. Use your answer to part (a) to find the markup rate on a tennis racket when the cost is $112 and the selling price is $140.   20%

       c. Use your answer to part (a) to find the markup rate on a radio when the cost is $50.40 and the selling price is $72.   30%

Electricity   Resistors are used to control the flow of current. The total resistance of two resistors in a circuit can be given by the formula $R = \dfrac{1}{\dfrac{1}{R_1} + \dfrac{1}{R_2}}$, where R_1 and R_2 are the resistances of the two resistors in the circuit. Resistance is measured in ohms.

[C] **22.**   **a.** Solve the formula $R = \dfrac{1}{\dfrac{1}{R_1} + \dfrac{1}{R_2}}$ for R_1. $R_1 = \dfrac{RR_2}{R_2 - R}$

       b. Use your answer to part (a) to find the resistance in R_1 if the resistance in R_2 is 30 ohms and the total resistance is 12 ohms.   20 ohms

       c. Use your answer to part (a) to find the resistance in R_1 if the resistance in R_2 is 15 ohms and the total resistance is 6 ohms.   10 ohms

Application Problems

1 Work problems

If a painter can paint a room in 4 h, then in 1 h the painter can paint $\frac{1}{4}$ of the room. The painter's rate of work is $\frac{1}{4}$ of the room each hour. The **rate of work** is that part of a task that is completed in 1 unit of time.

A pipe can fill a tank in 30 min. This pipe can fill $\frac{1}{30}$ of the tank in 1 min. The rate of work is $\frac{1}{30}$ of the tank each minute. If a second pipe can fill the tank in x min, the rate of work for the second pipe is $\frac{1}{x}$ of the tank each minute.

In solving a work problem, the goal is to determine the time it takes to complete a task. The basic equation that is used to solve work problems is

Rate of work · Time worked = Part of task completed

For example, if a faucet can fill a sink in 6 min, then in 5 min the faucet will fill $\frac{1}{6} \cdot 5 = \frac{5}{6}$ of the sink. In 5 min, the faucet completes $\frac{5}{6}$ of the task.

Solve: A painter can paint a ceiling in 60 min. The painter's apprentice can paint the same ceiling in 90 min. How long will it take to paint the ceiling if they work together?

STRATEGY for solving a work problem

■ For each person or machine, write a numerical or variable expression for the rate of work, the time worked, and the part of the task completed. The results can be recorded in a table.

Unknown time to paint the ceiling working together: t

	Rate of work	·	Time worked	=	Part of task completed
Painter	$\frac{1}{60}$	·	t	=	$\frac{t}{60}$
Apprentice	$\frac{1}{90}$	·	t	=	$\frac{t}{90}$

■ Determine how the parts of the task completed are related. Use the fact that the sum of the parts of the task completed must equal 1, the complete task.

$$\frac{t}{60} + \frac{t}{90} = 1$$

▶ The part of the task completed by the painter plus the part of the task completed by the apprentice must equal 1.

$$180\left(\frac{t}{60} + \frac{t}{90}\right) = 180 \cdot 1$$

▶ Multiply each side of the equation by the LCM of 60 and 90.

$$3t + 2t = 180$$
$$5t = 180$$
$$t = 36$$

Working together, they will paint the ceiling in 36 min.

Example 1   A small water pipe takes four times longer to fill a tank than does a large water pipe. With both pipes open, it takes 3 h to fill the tank. Find the time it would take the small pipe, working alone, to fill the tank.

Strategy   ■ Time for large pipe to fill the tank: t
■ Time for small pipe to fill the tank: $4t$

Fills tank in $4t$ hours

Fills tank in t hours

Fills $\frac{3}{4t}$ of the tank in 3 hours

Fills $\frac{3}{t}$ of the tank in 3 hours

	Rate	Time	Part
Small pipe	$\frac{1}{4t}$	3	$\frac{3}{4t}$
Large pipe	$\frac{1}{t}$	3	$\frac{3}{t}$

■ The sum of the parts of the task completed must equal 1.

Solution
$$\frac{3}{4t} + \frac{3}{t} = 1$$

▶ The part of the task completed by the small pipe plus the part of the task completed by the large pipe must equal 1.

$$4t\left(\frac{3}{4t} + \frac{3}{t}\right) = 4t \cdot 1$$
$$3 + 12 = 4t$$
$$15 = 4t$$
$$\frac{15}{4} = t$$

▶ t is the time for the large pipe to fill the tank.

$$4t = 4\left(\frac{15}{4}\right) = 15$$

▶ Substitute the value of t into the variable expression for the time for the small pipe to fill the tank.

The small pipe, working alone, takes 15 h to fill the tank.

Problem 1   Two computer printers that work at the same rate are working together to print the payroll checks for a corporation. After they work together for 3 h, one of the printers quits. The second requires 2 more hours to complete the checks. Find the time it would take one printer, working alone, to print the checks.

Solution   See page S22.   8 h

2   Uniform motion problems

A car that travels constantly in a straight line at 30 mph is in uniform motion. When an object is in **uniform motion,** its speed does not change.

The basic equation used to solve uniform motion problems is

Distance = Rate · Time

An alternative form of this equation is written by solving the equation for time:

$$\frac{\text{Distance}}{\text{Rate}} = \text{Time}$$

This form of the equation is useful when the total time of travel for two objects is known or the times of travel for two objects are equal.

Solve: The speed of a boat in still water is 20 mph. The boat traveled 120 mi down a river in the same amount of time it took the boat to travel 80 mi up the river. Find the rate of the river's current.

STRATEGY for solving a uniform motion problem

■ For each object, write a numerical or variable expression for the distance, rate, and time. The results can be recorded in a table.

The unknown rate of the river's current: r

	Distance	÷	Rate	=	Time
Down river	120	÷	$20 + r$	=	$\frac{120}{20 + r}$
Up river	80	÷	$20 - r$	=	$\frac{80}{20 - r}$

■ Determine how the times traveled by the two objects are related. For example, it may be known that the times are equal, or the total time may be known.

$$\frac{120}{20 + r} = \frac{80}{20 - r}$$

$$(20 + r)(20 - r)\frac{120}{20 + r} = (20 + r)(20 - r)\frac{80}{20 - r}$$

$$(20 - r)120 = (20 + r)80$$

$$2400 - 120r = 1600 + 80r$$

$$-200r = -800$$

$$r = 4$$

The rate of the river's current is 4 mph.

▶ The time spent traveling down the river is equal to the time spent traveling up the river.

Example 2   A cyclist rode the first 20 mi of a trip at a constant rate. For the next 16 mi, the cyclist reduced the speed by 2 mph. The total time for the 36 mi was 4 h. Find the rate of the cyclist for each leg of the trip.

20 mi   16 mi

36 mi in 4 h

Strategy   ■ Rate for the first 20 mi: r
■ Rate for the next 16 mi: $r - 2$

	Distance	Rate	Time
First 20 mi	20	r	$\dfrac{20}{r}$
Next 16 mi	16	$r - 2$	$\dfrac{16}{r - 2}$

■ The total time for the trip was 4 h.

Solution

$$\frac{20}{r} + \frac{16}{r - 2} = 4$$

$$r(r - 2)\left[\frac{20}{r} + \frac{16}{r - 2}\right] = r(r - 2) \cdot 4$$

$$(r - 2)20 + 16r = 4r^2 - 8r$$

$$20r - 40 + 16r = 4r^2 - 8r$$

$$36r - 40 = 4r^2 - 8r$$

$$0 = 4r^2 - 44r + 40$$

$$0 = 4(r^2 - 11r + 10)$$

$$0 = r^2 - 11r + 10$$

$$0 = (r - 10)(r - 1)$$

▶ The time spent riding the first 20 mi plus the time spent riding the next 16 mi is equal to 4 h.

▶ This is a quadratic equation.

▶ Divide each side by 4.
▶ Solve by factoring.

$$r - 10 = 0 \qquad\qquad r - 1 = 0$$
$$r = 10 \qquad\qquad\quad r = 1$$

$$r - 2 = 10 - 2 \qquad r - 2 = 1 - 2$$
$$= 8 \qquad\qquad\quad = -1$$

▶ Find the rate for the last 16 mi. The solution $r = 1$ mph is not possible, because the rate on the last 16 mi would be -1 mph.

10 mph was the rate for the first 20 mi.
8 mph was the rate for the next 16 mi.

Problem 2   The total time for a sailboat to sail back and forth across a lake 6 km wide was 3 h. The rate sailing back was twice the rate sailing across the lake. Find the rate of the sailboat going across the lake.

Solution   See page S22.   3 km/h

CONCEPT REVIEW 9.7

Determine whether the statement is always true, sometimes true, or never true.

1. The work problems in this section require use of the equation
   Rate of work · Time worked = 1.   Never true

2. If it takes a janitorial crew 5 hours to clean a company's offices, then in x hours the crew has completed $\frac{x}{5}$ of the job.   Always true

3. If it takes an automotive crew x min to service a car, then the rate of work is $\frac{1}{x}$ of the job each minute.   Always true

4. If only two people worked on a job and together they completed it, and one person completed $\frac{t}{30}$ of the job and the other person completed $\frac{t}{20}$ of the job, then $\frac{t}{30} + \frac{t}{20} = 1$.   Always true

5. Uniform motion problems are based on the equation Distance · Rate = Time.   Never true

6. If a plane flies 300 mph in calm air and the rate of the wind is r mph, then the rate of the plane flying with the wind can be represented as $300 - r$ and the rate of the plane flying against the wind can be represented as $300 + r$. Never true

---

EXERCISES 9.7

1 **Work Problems**

1. A park has two sprinklers that are used to fill a fountain. One sprinkler can fill the fountain in 3 h, whereas the second sprinkler can fill the fountain in 6 h. How long will it take to fill the fountain with both sprinklers operating? 2 h

2. One grocery clerk can stock a shelf in 20 min. A second clerk requires 30 min to stock the same shelf. How long would it take to stock the shelf if the two clerks worked together?   12 min

3. One person with a skiploader requires 12 h to remove a large quantity of earth. With a larger skiploader, the same amount of earth can be removed in 4 h. How long would it take to remove the earth if both skiploaders were operated together?   3 h

4. It takes Doug 6 days to reroof a house. If Doug's son helps him, the job can be completed in 4 days. How long would it take Doug's son, working alone, to do the job?   12 days

5. One computer can solve a complex prime factorization problem in 75 h. A second computer can solve the same problem in 50 h. How long would it take both computers, working together, to solve the problem?   30 h

6. A new machine makes 10,000 aluminum cans three times faster than an older machine. With both machines operating, it takes 9 h to make 10,000 cans. How long would it take the new machine, working alone, to make 10,000 cans?   12 h

7. A small air conditioner can cool a room 5°F in 60 min. A larger air conditioner can cool the room 5°F in 40 min. How long would it take to cool the room 5°F with both air conditioners working?   24 min

8. One printing press can print the first edition of a book in 55 min. A second printing press requires 66 min to print the same number of copies. How long would it take to print the first edition of the book with both presses operating? 30 min

9. Two welders working together can complete a job in 6 h. One of the welders, working alone, can complete the task in 10 h. How long would it take the second welder, working alone, to complete the task? 15 h

10. Working together, Pat and Chris can reseal a driveway in 6 h. Working alone, Pat can reseal the driveway in 15 h. How long would it take Chris, working alone, to reseal the driveway? 10 h

11. Two oil pipelines can fill a small tank in 30 min. Using one of the pipelines would require 45 min to fill the tank. How long would it take the second pipeline, working alone, to fill the tank? 90 min

12. A cement mason can construct a retaining wall in 8 h. A second mason requires 12 h to do the same job. After working alone for 4 h, the first mason quits. How long would it take the second mason to complete the wall? 6 h

13. With two reapers operating, a field can be harvested in 1 h. If only the newer reaper is used, the crop can be harvested in 1.5 h. How long would it take to harvest the field using only the older reaper? 3 h

14. A manufacturer of prefabricated homes has the company's employees work in teams. Team 1 can erect the Silvercrest model in 15 h. Team 2 can erect the same model in 10 h. How long would it take for Team 1 and Team 2, working together, to erect the Silvercrest model home? 6 h

15. One computer technician can wire a modem in 4 h. A second technician requires 6 h to do the same job. After working alone for 2 h, the first technician quits. How long will it take the second technician to complete the wiring? 3 h

16. A wallpaper hanger requires 2 h to hang the wallpaper on one wall of a room. A second wallpaper hanger requires 4 h to hang the same amount of wallpaper. The first wallpaper hanger works alone for 1 h and then quits. How long will it take the second hanger, working alone, to finish papering the wall? 2 h

17. A large heating unit and a small heating unit are being used to heat the water in a pool. The large unit, working alone, requires 8 h to heat the pool. After both units have been operating for 2 h, the large unit is turned off. The small unit requires 9 more hours to heat the pool. How long would it take the small unit, working alone, to heat the pool? $14\frac{2}{3}$ h

18. Two machines fill cereal boxes at the same rate. After the two machines work together for 7 h, one machine breaks down. The second machine requires 14 more hours to finish filling the boxes. How long would it have taken one of the machines, working alone, to fill the boxes? 28 h

19. Two welders who work at the same rate are riveting the girders of a building. After they work together for 10 h, one of the welders quits. The second welder requires 20 more hours to complete the welds. Find the time it would have taken one of the welders, working alone, to complete the welds.   40 h

20. A large drain and a small drain are opened to drain a pool. The large drain can empty the pool in 6 h. After both drains have been open 1 h, the large drain becomes clogged and is closed. The small drain remains open and requires 9 more hours to empty the pool. How long would it have taken the small drain, working alone, to empty the pool?   12 h

2 Uniform Motion Problems

21. A camper drove 90 mi to a recreational area and then hiked 5 mi into the woods. The rate of the camper while driving was nine times the rate while hiking. The time spent hiking and driving was 3 h. Find the rate at which the camper hiked.   5 mph

22. The president of a company traveled 1800 mi by jet and 300 mi on a prop plane. The rate of the jet was four times the rate of the prop plane. The entire trip took 5 h. Find the rate of the jet plane.   600 mph

23. To assess the damage done by a fire, a forest ranger traveled 1080 mi by jet and then an additional 180 mi by helicopter. The rate of the jet was four times the rate of the helicopter. The entire trip took 5 h. Find the rate of the jet.
360 mph

24. An engineer traveled 165 mi by car and then an additional 660 mi by plane. The rate of the plane was four times the rate of the car. The total trip took 6 h. Find the rate of the car.   55 mph

25. After sailing 15 mi, a sailor changed direction and increased the boat's speed by 2 mph. An additional 19 mi was sailed at the increased speed. The total sailing time was 4 h. Find the rate of the boat for the first 15 mi.   7.5 mph

26. On a recent trip, a trucker traveled 330 mi at a constant rate. Because of road conditions, the trucker then reduced the speed by 25 mph. An additional 30 mi was traveled at the reduced rate. The entire trip took 7 h. Find the rate of the trucker for the first 330 mi.   55 mph

27. In calm water, the rate of a small rental motorboat is 15 mph. The rate of the current on the river is 3 mph. How far down the river can a family travel and still return the boat in 3 h?   21.6 mi

28. The rate of a small aircraft in calm air is 125 mph. If the wind is currently blowing south at a rate of 15 mph, how far north can a pilot fly the plane and return it within 2 h?   123.2 mi

29. Commuting from work to home, a lab technician traveled 10 mi at a constant rate through congested traffic. Upon reaching the expressway, the technician increased the speed by 20 mph. An additional 20 mi was traveled at the increased speed. The total time for the trip was 1 h. How fast did the technician travel through the congested traffic?   20 mph

30. As part of a conditioning program, a jogger ran 8 mi in the same amount of time as it took a cyclist to ride 20 mi. The rate of the cyclist was 12 mph faster than the rate of the jogger. Find the rate of the jogger and the rate of the cyclist.   jogger: 8 mph; cyclist: 20 mph

31. The speed of a boat in still water is 20 mph. The Jacksons traveled 75 mi down the Woodset River in the same amount of time as it took them to return 45 mi up the river. Find the rate of the river's current.   5 mph

32. Crystal Lake is 6 mi wide. The total time it took Helena to kayak back and forth across the lake was 2 h. Her rate kayaking back was three times her rate going out across the lake. What was Helena's rate kayaking out across the lake?   4 mph

33. An express train traveled 600 mi in the same amount of time as it took a freight train to travel 360 mi. The rate of the express train was 20 mph greater than the rate of the freight train. Find the rate of each train.
    freight train: 30 mph; express train: 50 mph

34. A twin-engine plane flies 800 mi in the same amount of time as it takes a single-engine plane to fly 600 mi. The rate of the twin-engine plane is 50 mph greater than the rate of the single-engine plane. Find the rate of the twin-engine plane.   200 mph

35. A car is traveling at a rate that is 36 mph faster than the rate of a cyclist. The car travels 384 mi in the same time as it takes the cyclist to travel 96 mi. Find the rate of the car.   48 mph

36. A small motor on a fishing boat can move the boat at a rate of 6 mph in calm water. Traveling with the current, the boat can travel 24 mi in the same amount of time as it takes to travel 12 mi against the current. Find the rate of the current.   2 mph

37. A commercial jet can fly 550 mph in calm air. Traveling with the jet stream, the plane flew 2400 mi in the same amount of time as it takes to fly 2000 mi against the jet stream. Find the rate of the jet stream.   50 mph

38. A cruise ship can sail 28 mph in calm water. Sailing with the Gulf Stream, the ship can sail 170 mi in the same amount of time as it takes to sail 110 mi against the Gulf Stream. Find the rate of the Gulf Stream.   6 mph

39. Rowing with the current of a river, a rowing team can row 25 mi in the same amount of time as it takes to row 15 mi against the current. The rate of the rowing team in calm water is 20 mph. Find the rate of the current.   5 mph

40. A plane can fly 180 mph in calm air. Flying with the wind, the plane can fly 600 mi in the same amount of time as it takes to fly 480 mi against the wind. Find the rate of the wind.   20 mph

APPLYING CONCEPTS 9.7

41. *Work Problems* One pipe can fill a tank in 2 h, a second pipe can fill the tank in 4 h, and a third pipe can fill the tank in 5 h. How long would it take to fill the tank with all three pipes operating? $1\frac{1}{19}$ h

[C] **42.** *Work Problems* A mason can construct a retaining wall in 10 h. The mason's more experienced apprentice can do the same job in 15 h. How long would it take the mason's less experienced apprentice to do the job if, working together, all three can complete the wall in 5 h?   30 h

[C] **43.** *Uniform Motion Problems* An Outing Club traveled 32 mi by canoe and then hiked 4 mi. The rate by boat was four times the rate on foot. The time spent walking was 1 h less than the time spent canoeing. Find the amount of time spent traveling by canoe.   2 h

[C] **44.** *Uniform Motion Problems* A motorist drove 120 mi before running out of gas and walking 4 mi to a gas station. The rate of the motorist in the car was ten times the rate walking. The time spent walking was 2 h less than the time spent driving. How long did it take for the motorist to drive the 120 mi?   3 h

[C] **45.** *Uniform Motion Problems* Because of bad weather, a bus driver reduced the usual speed along a 150-mile bus route by 10 mph. The bus arrived only 30 min later than its usual arrival time. How fast does the bus usually travel?   60 mph

Focus on Problem Solving

Negations and *If . . . then . . .* Sentences

The sentence "George Washington was the first president of the United States" is a true sentence. The **negation** of that sentence is "George Washington was **not** the first president of the United States." That sentence is false. In general, the negation of a true sentence is a false sentence.

The negation of a false sentence is a true sentence. For instance, the sentence "The moon is made of green cheese" is a false sentence. The negation of that sentence, "The moon is **not** made of green cheese," is true.

The words *all*, *no* (or *none*) and *some* are called **quantifiers**. Writing the negation of a sentence that contains these words requires special attention. Consider the sentence "All pets are dogs." This sentence is not true because there are pets that are not dogs; cats, for example, are pets. Because the sentence is false, its negation must be true. You might be tempted to write "All pets are not dogs," but that sentence is not true because some pets are dogs. The correct negation of "All pets are dogs," is "Some pets are not dogs." Note the use of the word *some* in the negation.

Now consider the sentence "Some computers are portable." Because that sentence is true, its negation must be false. Writing "Some computers are not portable" as the negation is not correct, because that sentence is true. The negation of "Some computers are portable" is "No computers are portable."

The sentence "No flowers have red blooms" is false, because there is at least one flower (roses, for example) that has red blooms. Because the sentence is false, its negation must be true. The negation is "Some flowers have red blooms."

Statement	Negation
All *A* are *B*.	Some *A* are not *B*.
No *A* are *B*.	Some *A* are *B*.
Some *A* are *B*.	No *A* are *B*.
Some *A* are not *B*.	All *A* are *B*.

Write the negation of the sentence.

1. All cats like milk.

2. All computers need people.

3. Some trees are tall.

4. Some vegetables are good for you to eat.

5. No politicians are honest.

6. No houses have kitchens.

7. All police officers are tall.

8. All lakes are not polluted.

9. Some banks are not open on Sunday.

10. Some colleges do not offer night classes.

11. Some drivers are unsafe.

12. Some speeches are interesting.

13. All laws are good.

14. All Mark Twain books are funny.

15. All businesses are not profitable.

16. All motorcycles are not large.

A **premise** is a known or assumed fact. A premise can be stated using one of the quantifiers (*all, no, none,* or *some*) or can be stated using an *If . . . then . . .* sentence. For instance, the sentence "All triangles have three sides" can be written "If a figure is a triangle, *then* it has three sides."

We can write the sentence "No whole numbers are negative numbers" as an *If . . . then . . .* sentence: "If a number is a whole number, then it is not a negative number."

Write the sentence as an *If . . . then . . .* sentence.

17. All students at Barlock College must take a life science course.

18. All baseballs are round.

19. All computers need people.

20. All cats like milk.

21. No odd number is evenly divisible by 2.

22. No rectangles have five sides.

23. All roads lead to Rome.

24. All dogs have fleas.

25. No triangle has four angles.

26. No prime number greater than 2 is an even number.

Calculators

A calculator is an important tool for problem solving. It can be used as an aid to guessing or estimating a solution to a problem. Here are a few problems to solve with a calculator.

1. Choose any positive integer less than 9. Multiply the number by 1507. Now multiply the result by 7519. What is the answer? Choose another positive single-digit number and again multiply by 1507 and 7519. What is the answer? What pattern do you see? Why does this work?

2. Are there enough people in the United States so that if they held hands in a line, they would stretch around the world at the equator? To answer this question, begin by determining what information you need. What assumptions must you make?

3. Which of the reciprocals of the first 16 natural numbers have a terminating decimal representation and which have a repeating decimal representation?

4. What is the largest natural number n for which $4^n > 1 \cdot 2 \cdot 3 \cdot \;\cdots\; \cdot n$?

5. Calculate $15^2, 35^2, 65^2$, and 85^2. Study the results. Make a conjecture about a relationship between a number ending in 5 and its square. Use your conjecture to find 75^2 and 95^2. Does your conjecture work for 125^2?

6. Find the sum of the first 1000 natural numbers. (*Hint:* You could just start adding $1 + 2 + 3 + 4 + \cdots$, but even if you performed one operation each second, it would take over 15 minutes to find the sum. Instead, try pairing the numbers and then adding the numbers in each pair. Pair 1 and 1000, 2 and 999, 3 and 998, and so on. What is the sum of each pair? How many pairs are there? Use this information to answer the original question.)

7. For a borrower to qualify for a home loan, a bank requires that the monthly mortgage payment be less than 25% of the borrower's monthly take-home income. A laboratory technician has deductions for taxes, insurance, and retirement that amount to 25% of the technician's monthly gross income. What minimum gross monthly income must this technician earn to receive a bank loan that has a mortgage payment of $1200 per month?

Projects and Group Activities

Intensity of Illumination

You are already aware that the standard unit of length in the metric system is the meter (m) and that the standard unit of mass in the metric system is the kilogram (kg). You may not know that the standard unit of light intensity is the candela.

The rate at which light falls upon a one-square-unit area of surface is called the **intensity of illumination.** Intensity of illumination is measured in **lumens** (lm). A lumen is defined in the following illustration.

Picture a source of light equal to 1 candela positioned at the center of a hollow sphere that has a radius of 1 m. The rate at which light falls upon 1 m² of the inner surface of the sphere is equal to one lumen (1 lm). If a light source equal to 4 candelas is positioned at the center of the sphere, each square meter of the inner surface receives four times as much illumination, or 4 lm.

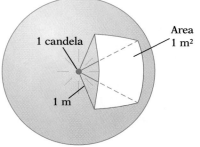

Light rays diverge as they leave a light source. The light that falls upon an area of 1 m² at a distance of 1 m from the source of light spreads out over an area of 4 m² when it is 2 m from the source. The same light spreads out over an area of 9 m² when it is 3 m from the light source and over an area of 16 m² when it is 4 m from the light source. Therefore, as a surface moves farther away from the source of light, the intensity of illumination on the surface decreases from its value at 1 m to $\left(\frac{1}{2}\right)^2$, or $\frac{1}{4}$, that value at 2 m; to $\left(\frac{1}{3}\right)^2$, or $\frac{1}{9}$, that value at 3 m; and to $\left(\frac{1}{4}\right)^2$, or $\frac{1}{16}$, that value at 4 m.

The formula for the intensity of illumination is

$$I = \frac{s}{r^2}$$

where I is the intensity of illumination in lumens, s is the strength of the light source in candelas, and r is the distance in meters between the light source and the illuminated surface.

A 30-candela lamp is 0.5 m above a desk. Find the illumination on the desk.

$$I = \frac{s}{r^2}$$

$$I = \frac{30}{(0.5)^2} = 120$$

The illumination on the desk is 120 lm.

Similar Triangles

Similar triangles have the same shape but not necessarily the same size. The ratios of corresponding sides of similar triangles are equal. The ratio of corresponding heights is equal to the ratio of corresponding sides.   (Objective 9.5.4)

Triangles *ABC* and *DEF* are similar triangles. The ratios of corresponding sides and corresponding heights is $\frac{1}{3}$.

Solving Literal Equations

Rewrite the equation so that the letter being solved for is alone on one side of the equation and all numbers and other variables are on the other side.   (Objective 9.6.1)

Solve $A = \frac{1}{2}bh$ for b.

$$2(A) = 2\left(\frac{1}{2}bh\right)$$
$$2A = bh$$
$$\frac{2A}{h} = \frac{bh}{h}$$
$$\frac{2A}{h} = b$$

Work Problems

Rate of work · Time worked = Part of task completed (Objective 9.7.1)

Pat can do a certain job in 3 h. Chris can do the same job in 5 h. How long would it take them, working together, to get the job done?

$$\frac{t}{3} + \frac{t}{5} = 1$$

Uniform Motion Problems

Distance ÷ Rate = Time   (Objective 9.7.2)

Train A's speed is 15 mph faster than Train B's speed. Train A travels 150 mi in the same amount of time as it takes Train B to travel 120 mi. Find the rate of Train B.

$$\frac{120}{r} = \frac{150}{r + 15}$$

Chapter Review Exercises

1. Multiply: $\dfrac{8ab^2}{15x^3y} \cdot \dfrac{5xy^4}{16a^2b}$ $\dfrac{by^3}{6ax^2}$

2. Add: $\dfrac{5}{3x - 4} + \dfrac{4}{2x + 3}$ $\dfrac{22x - 1}{(3x - 4)(2x + 3)}$

3. Solve $4x + 3y = 12$ for x. $x = -\dfrac{3}{4}y + 3$

4. Simplify: $\dfrac{16x^5y^3}{24xy^{10}}$ $\dfrac{2x^4}{3y^7}$

5. Divide: $\dfrac{20x^2 - 45x}{6x^3 + 4x^2} \div \dfrac{40x^3 -\cdot 90x^2}{12x^2 + 8x}$ $\dfrac{1}{x^2}$

6. Simplify: $\dfrac{x - \dfrac{16}{5x - 2}}{3x - 4 - \dfrac{88}{5x - 2}}$ $\dfrac{x - 2}{3x - 10}$

7. Find the LCM of $24a^2b^5$ and $36a^3b$. $72a^3b^5$

8. Subtract: $\dfrac{5x}{3x + 7} - \dfrac{x}{3x + 7}$ $\dfrac{4x}{3x + 7}$

9. Write each fraction in terms of the LCM of the denominators.
$\dfrac{3}{16x}, \dfrac{5}{8x^2}$ $\dfrac{3x}{16x^2}, \dfrac{10}{16x^2}$

10. Simplify: $\dfrac{2x^2 - 13x - 45}{2x^2 - x - 15}$ $\dfrac{x - 9}{x - 3}$

11. Divide: $\dfrac{x^2 - 5x - 14}{x^2 - 3x - 10} \div \dfrac{x^2 - 4x - 21}{x^2 - 9x + 20}$ $\dfrac{x - 4}{x + 3}$

12. Add: $\dfrac{2y}{5y - 7} + \dfrac{3}{7 - 5y}$ $\dfrac{2y - 3}{5y - 7}$

13. Multiply: $\dfrac{3x^3 + 10x^2}{10x - 2} \cdot \dfrac{20x - 4}{6x^4 + 20x^3}$ $\dfrac{1}{x}$

14. Subtract: $\dfrac{5x + 3}{2x^2 + 5x - 3} - \dfrac{3x + 4}{2x^2 + 5x - 3}$ $\dfrac{1}{x + 3}$

15. Find the LCM of $5x^4(x - 7)^2$ and $15x(x - 7)$. $15x^4(x - 7)^2$

16. Solve: $\dfrac{6}{x - 7} = \dfrac{8}{x - 6}$ 10

17. Solve: $\dfrac{x + 8}{x + 4} = 1 + \dfrac{5}{x + 4}$ No solution

18. Simplify: $\dfrac{12a^2b(4x - 7)}{15ab^2(7 - 4x)}$ $-\dfrac{4a}{5b}$

19. Simplify: $\dfrac{5x - 1}{x^2 - 9} + \dfrac{4x - 3}{x^2 - 9} - \dfrac{8x - 1}{x^2 - 9}$ $\dfrac{1}{x + 3}$

20. Triangles *ABC* and *DEF* at the right are similar. Find the perimeter of triangle *ABC*.   24 in.

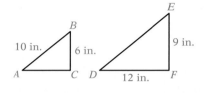

21. Solve: $\dfrac{20}{2x + 3} = \dfrac{17x}{2x + 3} - 5$ 5

22. Simplify: $\dfrac{\dfrac{5}{x - 1} - \dfrac{3}{x + 3}}{\dfrac{6}{x + 3} + \dfrac{2}{x - 1}}$ $\dfrac{x + 9}{4x}$

23. Add: $\dfrac{x - 1}{x + 2} + \dfrac{3x - 2}{5 - x} + \dfrac{5x^2 + 15x - 11}{x^2 - 3x - 10}$ $\dfrac{3x - 1}{x - 5}$

24. Divide: $\dfrac{18x^2 + 25x - 3}{9x^2 - 28x + 3} \div \dfrac{2x^2 + 9x + 9}{x^2 - 6x + 9}$ $\dfrac{x - 3}{x + 3}$

25. Simplify: $\dfrac{x^2 + x - 30}{15 + 2x - x^2}$ $-\dfrac{x + 6}{x + 3}$

26. Solve: $\dfrac{5}{7} + \dfrac{x}{2} = 2 - \dfrac{x}{7}$ 2

27. Simplify: $\dfrac{x + \dfrac{6}{x - 5}}{1 + \dfrac{2}{x - 5}}$ $x - 2$

28. Multiply: $\dfrac{3x^2 + 4x - 15}{x^2 - 11x + 28} \cdot \dfrac{x^2 - 5x - 14}{3x^2 + x - 10}$ $\dfrac{x + 3}{x - 4}$

29. Solve: $\dfrac{x}{5} = \dfrac{x + 12}{9}$ 15

30. Solve: $\dfrac{3}{20} = \dfrac{x}{80}$ 12

31. Simplify: $\dfrac{1 - \dfrac{1}{x}}{1 - \dfrac{8x - 7}{x^2}}$ $\dfrac{x}{x - 7}$

32. Solve $x - 2y = 15$ for x. $x = 2y + 15$

33. Add: $\dfrac{6}{a} + \dfrac{9}{b}$ $\dfrac{3(3a + 2b)}{ab}$

34. Find the LCM of $10x^2 - 11x + 3$ and $20x^2 - 17x + 3$. $(2x - 1)(4x - 1)(5x - 3)$

35. Solve $i = \dfrac{100m}{c}$ for c. $c = \dfrac{100m}{i}$

36. Solve: $\dfrac{15}{x} = \dfrac{3}{8}$ 40

37. Solve: $\dfrac{22}{2x + 5} = 2$ 3

38. Add: $\dfrac{x + 7}{15x} + \dfrac{x - 2}{20x}$ $\dfrac{7x + 22}{60x}$

39. Multiply: $\dfrac{16a^2 - 9}{16a^2 - 24a + 9} \cdot \dfrac{8a^2 - 13a - 6}{4a^2 - 5a - 6}$ $\dfrac{8a + 3}{4a - 3}$

40. Write each fraction in terms of the LCM of the denominators.

$\dfrac{x}{12x^2 + 16x - 3}, \dfrac{4x^2}{6x^2 + 7x - 3}$

$\dfrac{3x^2 - x}{(6x - 1)(2x + 3)(3x - 1)}, \dfrac{24x^3 - 4x^2}{(6x - 1)(2x + 3)(3x - 1)}$

41. Add: $\dfrac{3}{4ab} + \dfrac{5}{4ab}$ $\dfrac{2}{ab}$

42. Solve: $\dfrac{20}{x + 2} = \dfrac{5}{16}$ 62

43. Solve: $\dfrac{5x}{3} - \dfrac{2}{5} = \dfrac{8x}{5}$ 6

44. Divide: $\dfrac{6a^2b^7}{25x^3y} \div \dfrac{12a^3b^4}{5x^2y^2}$ $\dfrac{b^3y}{10ax}$

45. A brick mason can construct a patio in 3 h. If the mason works with an apprentice, they can construct the patio in 2 h. How long would it take the apprentice, working alone, to construct the patio?   6 h

46. A weight of 21 lb stretches a spring 14 in. At the same rate, how far would a weight of 12 lb stretch the spring?   8 in.

47. The rate of a jet is 400 mph in calm air. Traveling with the wind, the jet can fly 2100 mi in the same amount of time as it takes to fly 1900 mi against the wind. Find the rate of the wind.   20 mph

48. A gardener uses 4 oz of insecticide to make 2 gal of garden spray. At this rate, how much additional insecticide is necessary to make 10 gal of the garden spray?   16 additional ounces

49. One hose can fill a pool in 15 h. A second hose can fill the pool in 10 h. How long would it take to fill the pool using both hoses?   6 h

50. A car travels 315 mi in the same amount of time as it takes a bus to travel 245 mi. The rate of the car is 10 mph greater than that of the bus. Find the rate of the car.   45 mph

Chapter Test

1. Divide: $\dfrac{x^2 + 3x + 2}{x^2 + 5x + 4} \div \dfrac{x^2 - x - 6}{x^2 + 2x - 15}$ $\dfrac{x + 5}{x + 4}$

2. Subtract: $\dfrac{2x}{x^2 + 3x - 10} - \dfrac{4}{x^2 + 3x - 10}$ $\dfrac{2}{x + 5}$

3. Find the LCM of $6x - 3$ and $2x^2 + x - 1$.
$3(2x - 1)(x + 1)$

4. Solve: $\dfrac{3}{x + 4} = \dfrac{5}{x + 6}$ -1

5. Multiply: $\dfrac{x^3y^4}{x^2 - 4x + 4} \cdot \dfrac{x^2 - x - 2}{x^6y^4}$ $\dfrac{x + 1}{x^3(x - 2)}$

6. Simplify: $\dfrac{1 + \dfrac{1}{x} - \dfrac{12}{x^2}}{1 + \dfrac{2}{x} - \dfrac{8}{x^2}}$ $\dfrac{x - 3}{x - 2}$

7. Write each fraction in terms of the LCM of the denominators.

$\dfrac{3}{x^2 - 2x}, \dfrac{x}{x^2 - 4}$ $\dfrac{3x + 6}{x(x - 2)(x + 2)}, \dfrac{x^2}{x(x - 2)(x + 2)}$

8. Solve $3x + 5y + 15 = 0$ for x. $x = -\dfrac{5}{3}y - 5$

9. Solve: $\dfrac{6}{x} - 2 = 1$ 2

10. Subtract: $\dfrac{2}{2x - 1} - \dfrac{3}{3x + 1}$ $\dfrac{5}{(2x - 1)(3x + 1)}$

11. Divide: $\dfrac{x^2 - x - 56}{x^2 + 8x + 7} \div \dfrac{x^2 - 13x + 40}{x^2 - 4x - 5}$ 1

12. Subtract: $\dfrac{3x}{x^2 + 5x - 24} - \dfrac{9}{x^2 + 5x - 24}$ $\dfrac{3}{x + 8}$

13. Find the LCM of $3x^2 + 6x$ and $2x^2 + 8x + 8$. $6x(x + 2)^2$

14. Simplify: $\dfrac{x^2 - 7x + 10}{25 - x^2}$ $-\dfrac{x - 2}{x + 5}$

15. Solve: $\dfrac{3x}{x - 3} - 2 = \dfrac{10}{x - 3}$ 4

16. Solve $f = v + at$ for t. $t = \dfrac{f - v}{a}$

17. Simplify: $\dfrac{12x^4y^2}{18xy^7}$ $\dfrac{2x^3}{3y^5}$

18. Subtract: $\dfrac{2}{2x - 1} - \dfrac{1}{x + 1}$ $\dfrac{3}{(2x - 1)(x + 1)}$

19. Solve: $\dfrac{2}{x - 2} = \dfrac{12}{x + 3}$ 3

20. Multiply: $\dfrac{x^5y^3}{x^2 - x - 6} \cdot \dfrac{x^2 - 9}{x^2y^4}$ $\dfrac{x^3(x + 3)}{y(x + 2)}$

21. Write each fraction in terms of the LCM of the denominators.

$\dfrac{3y}{x(1 - x)}, \dfrac{x}{(x + 1)(x - 1)}$ $-\dfrac{3xy + 3y}{x(x + 1)(x - 1)}, \dfrac{x^2}{x(x + 1)(x - 1)}$

22. Simplify: $\dfrac{1 - \dfrac{2}{x} - \dfrac{15}{x^2}}{1 - \dfrac{25}{x^2}}$ $\dfrac{x + 3}{x + 5}$

23. A salt solution is formed by mixing 4 lb of salt with 10 gal of water. At this rate, how many additional pounds of salt are required for 15 gal of water?   2 lb

24. A small plane can fly at 110 mph in calm air. Flying with the wind, the plane can fly 260 mi in the same amount of time as it takes to fly 180 mi against the wind. Find the rate of the wind.   20 mph

25. One pipe can fill a tank in 9 min. A second pipe requires 18 min to fill the tank. How long would it take both pipes, working together, to fill the tank?   6 min

Cumulative Review Exercises

1. Evaluate: $-|-17|$ -17

2. Evaluate: $-\dfrac{3}{4} \cdot (2)^3$ -6

3. Simplify: $\left(\dfrac{2}{3}\right)^2 \div \left(\dfrac{3}{2} - \dfrac{2}{3}\right) + \dfrac{1}{2}$ $\dfrac{31}{30}$

4. Evaluate $-a^2 + (a - b)^2$ when $a = -2$ and $b = 3$.   21

5. Simplify: $-2x - (-3y) + 7x - 5y$ $5x - 2y$

6. Simplify: $2[3x - 7(x - 3) - 8]$ $-8x + 26$

7. Solve: $3 - \dfrac{1}{4}x = 8$ -20

8. Solve: $3[x - 2(x - 3)] = 2(3 - 2x)$ -12

9. Find $16\dfrac{2}{3}\%$ of 60.   10

10. Solve: $\dfrac{5}{9}x < 1$ $x < \dfrac{9}{5}$

11. Solve: $x - 2 \geq 4x - 47$ $x \leq 15$

12. Graph: $y = 2x - 1$

13. Graph: $f(x) = 3x + 2$

14. Graph: $x = 3$

15. Graph the solution set of $5x + 2y < 6$.

16. Find the range of the function given by the equation $f(x) = -2x + 11$ if the domain is $\{-8, -4, 0, 3, 7\}$. $\{-3, 5, 11, 19, 27\}$

17. Evaluate $f(x) = 4x - 3$ at $x = 10$.   37

18. Solve by substitution: $6x - y = 1$
$y = 3x + 1$ $\left(\frac{2}{3}, 3\right)$

19. Solve by the addition method: $2x - 3y = 4$
$4x + y = 1$
$\left(\frac{1}{2}, -1\right)$

20. Multiply: $(3xy^4)(-2x^3y)$ $-6x^4y^5$

21. Simplify: $(a^4b^3)^5$ $a^{20}b^{15}$

22. Simplify: $\dfrac{a^2b^{-5}}{a^{-1}b^{-3}}$ $\dfrac{a^3}{b^2}$

23. Multiply: $(a - 3b)(a + 4b)$ $a^2 + ab - 12b^2$

24. Divide: $\dfrac{15b^4 - 5b^2 + 10b}{5b}$ $3b^3 - b + 2$

25. Divide: $(x^3 - 8) \div (x - 2)$ $x^2 + 2x + 4$

26. Factor: $12x^2 - x - 1$ $(4x + 1)(3x - 1)$

27. Factor: $y^2 - 7y + 6$ $(y - 6)(y - 1)$

28. Factor: $2a^3 + 7a^2 - 15a$ $a(2a - 3)(a + 5)$

29. Factor: $4b^2 - 100$ $4(b + 5)(b - 5)$

30. Solve: $(x + 3)(2x - 5) = 0$ $-3, \frac{5}{2}$

31. Simplify: $\dfrac{x^2 + 3x - 28}{16 - x^2}$ $-\dfrac{x + 7}{x + 4}$

32. Divide: $\dfrac{x^2 - 3x - 10}{x^2 - 4x - 12} \div \dfrac{x^2 - x - 20}{x^2 - 2x - 24}$ 1

33. Subtract: $\dfrac{6}{3x-1} - \dfrac{2}{x+1}$ $\dfrac{8}{(3x-1)(x+1)}$

34. Solve: $\dfrac{4x}{x-3} - 2 = \dfrac{8}{x-3}$ 1

35. Solve $f = v + at$ for a. $a = \dfrac{f-v}{t}$

36. Translate "the difference between five times a number and eighteen is the opposite of three" into an equation and solve. $5x - 18 = -3;\ x = 3$

37. An investment of $5000 is made at an annual simple interest rate of 7%. How much additional money must be invested at an annual simple interest rate of 11% so that the total interest earned is 9% of the total investment? $5000

38. A silversmith mixes 60 g of an alloy that is 40% silver with 120 g of another silver alloy. The resulting alloy is 60% silver. Find the percent of silver in the 120-gram alloy.   70%

39. The length of the base of a triangle is 2 in. less than twice the height. The area of the triangle is 30 in². Find the base and height of the triangle.
Base: 10 in.; height: 6 in.

40. One water pipe can fill a tank in 12 min. A second pipe requires 24 min to fill the tank. How long would it take both pipes, working together, to fill the tank?   8 min

Drafters prepare detailed drawings from sketches and specifications made by architects, designers, engineers, and scientists. Usually drafters specialize in a particular field, such as architectural, civil, mechanical, electrical, or aeronautical drafting. The study of radical expressions is important for drafters because working with right triangles requires radicals. See Section 4 of this chapter.

10

Radical Expressions

OBJECTIVES

461

A Table of Square Roots

The practice of finding the square root of a number has existed for at least two thousand years. The process of finding a square root is tedious and time-consuming. Therefore, before the advent of the hand-held calculator, it was convenient to have tables of square roots.

The table shown at the left is part of an old Babylonian clay table that was written around 350 B.C. It is an incomplete table of square roots written in a style called *cuneiform*.

The number base of the Babylonians was 60 instead of the 10 we use today. The symbol $\vee$ was used for 1, and 10 was written as $\triangleleft$. Examples of numbers written using this system are given below.

A translation of the first two lines of the table is given below. The number in parentheses is the equivalent base-10 number that would be used today. You might try to translate the third line. The answer appears at the bottom of this page.

$40 \times 60 + 1$ (= 2401), which is the square of 49

$41 \times 60 + 40$ (= 2500), which is the square of 50

Answer: $43 \times 60 + 21$ (= 2601), which is the square of 51.

462

SECTION **10.1**

Introduction to Radical Expressions

1 Simplify numerical radical expressions   `29` `30` HM³

A **square root** of a positive number x is a number whose square is x.

A square root of 16 is 4 because $4^2 = 16$.

A square root of 16 is -4 because $(-4)^2 = 16$.

Every positive number has two square roots, one a positive number and one a negative number. The symbol $\sqrt{}$, called a **radical sign,** is used to indicate the positive or **principal square root** of a number. For example, $\sqrt{16} = 4$ and $\sqrt{25} = 5$. The number or variable expression under the radical sign is called the **radicand.**

When the negative square root of a number is to be found, a negative sign is placed in front of the radical. For example, $-\sqrt{16} = -4$ and $-\sqrt{25} = -5$.

The square of an integer is a **perfect square.** 49, 81, and 144 are examples of perfect squares.

$$7^2 = 49$$
$$9^2 = 81$$
$$12^2 = 144$$

An integer that is a perfect square can be written as the product of prime factors, each of which has an exponent that is an even number when expressed in exponential form.

$$49 = 7 \cdot 7 = 7^2$$
$$81 = 3 \cdot 3 \cdot 3 \cdot 3 = 3^4$$
$$144 = 2 \cdot 2 \cdot 2 \cdot 2 \cdot 3 \cdot 3 = 2^4 3^2$$

To find the square root of a perfect square written in exponential form, remove the radical sign, and divide each exponent by 2.

➡ Simplify: $\sqrt{625}$

Write the prime factorization of the radicand in exponential form.

$$\sqrt{625} = \sqrt{5^4}$$

Remove the radical sign, and divide the exponent by 2.

$$= 5^2$$

Simplify.

$$= 25 \quad \Longleftarrow$$

The square root of a negative number is not a real number because the square of a real number is always positive or zero.

$\sqrt{-4}$ is not a real number.

$\sqrt{-25}$ is not a real number.

If a number is not a perfect square, its square root can only be approximated. For example, 2 and 7 are not perfect squares. Thus their square roots can only be approximated. These numbers are **irrational numbers.** Their decimal representations never terminate or repeat.

$$\sqrt{2} \approx 1.4142135\ldots$$
$$\sqrt{7} \approx 2.6457513\ldots$$

The approximate square roots of numbers that are not perfect squares can be found using a calculator. The square roots can be rounded to any given place value.

A radical expression is in simplest form when the radicand contains no factor greater than 1 that is a perfect square. The Product Property of Square Roots is used to simplify radical expressions.

The Product Property of Square Roots

If a and b are positive real numbers, then $\sqrt{ab} = \sqrt{a} \cdot \sqrt{b}$.

➡ Simplify: $\sqrt{96}$

Write the prime factorization of the radicand in exponential form.	$\sqrt{96} = \sqrt{2^5 \cdot 3}$
Write the radicand as a product of a perfect square and factors that do not contain a perfect square. Remember that a perfect square has an even exponent when expressed in exponential form.	$= \sqrt{2^4(2 \cdot 3)}$
Use the Product Property of Square Roots. Write perfect squares under the first radical sign and all remaining factors under the second radical sign.	$= \sqrt{2^4}\sqrt{2 \cdot 3}$
Simplify.	$= 2^2\sqrt{2 \cdot 3}$
	$= 4\sqrt{6}$

The last example shows that $\sqrt{96} = 4\sqrt{6}$. The two expressions are different representations of the same number. Using a calculator to evaluate each expression, we find that $\sqrt{96} \approx 9.79796$ and $4\sqrt{6} \approx 4(2.44949) = 9.79796$.

Example 1   Simplify: $3\sqrt{90}$

    Solution $3\sqrt{90} = 3\sqrt{2 \cdot 3^2 \cdot 5}$ ▸ Write the prime factorization of the radicand in exponential form.

                 $= 3\sqrt{3^2(2 \cdot 5)}$ ▸ Write the radicand as a product of a perfect square and factors that do not contain a perfect square.

                 $= 3\sqrt{3^2}\sqrt{2 \cdot 5}$ ▸ Use the Product Property of Square Roots.

                 $= 3 \cdot 3\sqrt{10}$ ▸ Simplify.

                 $= 9\sqrt{10}$

Problem 1   Simplify: $-5\sqrt{32}$

    Solution   See page S22. $-20\sqrt{2}$

Example 2   Simplify: $\sqrt{252}$

    Solution $\sqrt{252} = \sqrt{2^2 \cdot 3^2 \cdot 7}$

                 $= \sqrt{2^2 \cdot 3^2}\sqrt{7}$

                 $= 2 \cdot 3\sqrt{7}$

                 $= 6\sqrt{7}$

> **Problem 2** Simplify: $\sqrt{216}$
>
> **Solution** See page S22. $6\sqrt{6}$

2 Simplify variable radical expressions

Variable expressions that contain radicals do not always represent real numbers.

The variable expression at the right does not represent a real number when x is a negative number, such as -4.

$$\sqrt{x^3}$$
$$\sqrt{(-4)^3} = \sqrt{-64} \leftarrow \text{Not a real number}$$

Now consider the expression $\sqrt{x^2}$ and evaluate this expression for $x = -2$ and $x = 2$.

$$\sqrt{x^2}$$
$$\sqrt{(-2)^2} = \sqrt{4} = 2 = |-2|$$
$$\sqrt{2^2}\quad = \sqrt{4} = 2 = |2|$$

This suggests the following.

The Square Root of a^2

> For any real number a, $\sqrt{a^2} = |a|$.
>
> If $a \geq 0$, then $\sqrt{a^2} = a$.

In order to avoid variable expressions that do not represent real numbers, and so that absolute value signs are not needed for certain expressions, the variables in this chapter will represent *positive* numbers unless otherwise stated.

A variable or a product of variables written in exponential form is a **perfect square** when each exponent is an even number.

To find the square root of a perfect square, remove the radical sign, and divide each exponent by 2.

⇨ Simplify: $\sqrt{a^6}$

Remove the radical sign, and divide the exponent by 2. $\sqrt{a^6} = a^3$ ⬅

A variable radical expression is in simplest form when the radicand contains no factor greater than 1 that is a perfect square.

⇨ Simplify: $\sqrt{x^7}$

Write x^7 as the product of x and a perfect square. $\sqrt{x^7} = \sqrt{x^6 \cdot x}$

Use the Product Property of Square Roots. $= \sqrt{x^6}\sqrt{x}$

Simplify the square root of the perfect square. $= x^3\sqrt{x}$ ⬅

> **Example 3** Simplify: $\sqrt{b^{15}}$
>
> **Solution** $\sqrt{b^{15}} = \sqrt{b^{14} \cdot b} = \sqrt{b^{14}} \cdot \sqrt{b} = b^7\sqrt{b}$
>
> **Problem 3** Simplify: $\sqrt{y^{19}}$
>
> **Solution** See page S22. $y^9\sqrt{y}$

➡ Simplify: $3x\sqrt{8x^3y^{13}}$

Write the prime factorization of the radi-
cand in exponential form. $3x\sqrt{8x^3y^{13}} = 3x\sqrt{2^3x^3y^{13}}$

Write the radicand as a product of a perfect square and factors that do not contain
a perfect square. $= 3x\sqrt{2^2x^2y^{12}(2xy)}$

Use the Product Property of Square Roots. $= 3x\sqrt{2^2x^2y^{12}}\,\sqrt{2xy}$

Simplify. $= 3x \cdot 2xy^6\sqrt{2xy}$
     $= 6x^2y^6\sqrt{2xy}$ ◀

Example 4   Simplify.   A. $\sqrt{24x^5}$ B. $2a\sqrt{18a^3b^{10}}$

    Solution   A. $\sqrt{24x^5} = \sqrt{2^3 \cdot 3 \cdot x^5}$ B. $2a\sqrt{18a^3b^{10}} = 2a\sqrt{2 \cdot 3^2 \cdot a^3b^{10}}$
           $= \sqrt{2^2x^4(2 \cdot 3x)}$ $= 2a\sqrt{3^2a^2b^{10}(2a)}$
           $= \sqrt{2^2x^4}\,\sqrt{2 \cdot 3x}$ $= 2a\sqrt{3^2a^2b^{10}}\,\sqrt{2a}$
           $= 2x^2\sqrt{6x}$ $= 2a \cdot 3ab^5\sqrt{2a}$
                                         $= 6a^2b^5\sqrt{2a}$

Problem 4   Simplify.   A. $\sqrt{45b^7}$ B. $3a\sqrt{28a^9b^{18}}$

    Solution   See page S22.   A. $3b^3\sqrt{5b}$ B. $6a^5b^9\sqrt{7a}$

INSTRUCTOR NOTE

As a class exercise, show students that $\sqrt{a^2 + b^2} \neq a + b$
by using $a = 3$ and $b = 4$.

➡ Simplify: $\sqrt{25(x + 2)^2}$

Write the prime factorization of the radi-
cand in exponential form. $\sqrt{25(x + 2)^2} = \sqrt{5^2(x + 2)^2}$

Simplify. $= 5(x + 2)$
     $= 5x + 10$ ◀

Example 5   Simplify: $\sqrt{16(x + 5)^2}$

    Solution $\sqrt{16(x + 5)^2} = \sqrt{2^4(x + 5)^2} = 2^2(x + 5) = 4(x + 5) = 4x + 20$

Problem 5   Simplify: $\sqrt{25(a + 3)^2}$

    Solution   See page S22. $5a + 15$

CONCEPT REVIEW 10.1

Determine whether the statement is always true, sometimes true, or never true.

1. The square root of a positive number is a positive number, and the square
   root of a negative number is a negative number.   Never true

2. Every positive number has two square roots, one of which is the additive
   inverse of the other.   Always true

3. The square root of a number that is not a perfect square is an irrational
   number.   Always true

4. If the radicand of a radical expression is evenly divisible by a perfect square greater than 1, then the radical expression is not in simplest form.   Always true

5. Suppose a and b are real numbers. Then $\sqrt{ab} = \sqrt{a} \cdot \sqrt{b}$.   Sometimes true

6. When a perfect square is written in exponential form, the exponents are multiples of 2.   Always true

EXERCISES 10.1

1 1. Show by example that a positive number has two square roots.

2. Why is the square root of a negative number not a real number?

Simplify.

3. $\sqrt{16}$ 4	4. $\sqrt{64}$ 8	5. $\sqrt{49}$ 7	6. $\sqrt{144}$ 12	7. $\sqrt{32}$ $4\sqrt{2}$	8. $\sqrt{50}$ $5\sqrt{2}$
9. $\sqrt{8}$ $2\sqrt{2}$	10. $\sqrt{12}$ $2\sqrt{3}$	11. $6\sqrt{18}$ $18\sqrt{2}$	12. $-3\sqrt{48}$ $-12\sqrt{3}$	13. $5\sqrt{40}$ $10\sqrt{10}$	14. $2\sqrt{28}$ $4\sqrt{7}$
15. $\sqrt{15}$ $\sqrt{15}$	16. $\sqrt{21}$ $\sqrt{21}$	17. $\sqrt{29}$ $\sqrt{29}$	18. $\sqrt{13}$ $\sqrt{13}$	19. $-9\sqrt{72}$ $-54\sqrt{2}$	20. $11\sqrt{80}$ $44\sqrt{5}$
21. $\sqrt{45}$ $3\sqrt{5}$	22. $\sqrt{225}$ 15	23. $\sqrt{0}$ 0	24. $\sqrt{210}$ $\sqrt{210}$	25. $6\sqrt{128}$ $48\sqrt{2}$	26. $9\sqrt{288}$ $108\sqrt{2}$
27. $\sqrt{105}$ $\sqrt{105}$	28. $\sqrt{55}$ $\sqrt{55}$	29. $\sqrt{900}$ 30	30. $\sqrt{300}$ $10\sqrt{3}$	31. $5\sqrt{180}$ $30\sqrt{5}$	32. $7\sqrt{98}$ $49\sqrt{2}$
33. $\sqrt{250}$ $5\sqrt{10}$	34. $\sqrt{120}$ $2\sqrt{30}$	35. $\sqrt{96}$ $4\sqrt{6}$	36. $\sqrt{160}$ $4\sqrt{10}$	37. $\sqrt{324}$ 18	38. $\sqrt{444}$ $2\sqrt{111}$

Find the decimal approximation to the nearest thousandth.

39. $\sqrt{240}$ 15.492	40. $\sqrt{300}$ 17.321	41. $\sqrt{288}$ 16.971	42. $\sqrt{600}$ 24.495
43. $\sqrt{245}$ 15.652	44. $\sqrt{525}$ 22.913	45. $\sqrt{352}$ 18.762	46. $\sqrt{363}$ 19.053

2 47. How can you tell whether a variable exponential expression is a perfect square?

48. When is a radical expression in simplest form?

Simplify.

49. $\sqrt{x^6}$ x^3	50. $\sqrt{x^{12}}$ x^6	51. $\sqrt{y^{15}}$ $y^7\sqrt{y}$	52. $\sqrt{y^{11}}$ $y^5\sqrt{y}$
53. $\sqrt{a^{20}}$ a^{10}	54. $\sqrt{a^{16}}$ a^8	55. $\sqrt{x^4y^4}$ x^2y^2	56. $\sqrt{x^{12}y^8}$ x^6y^4
57. $\sqrt{4x^4}$ $2x^2$	58. $\sqrt{25y^8}$ $5y^4$	59. $\sqrt{24x^2}$ $2x\sqrt{6}$	60. $\sqrt{x^3y^{15}}$ $xy^7\sqrt{xy}$
61. $\sqrt{x^3y^7}$ $xy^3\sqrt{xy}$	62. $\sqrt{a^{15}b^5}$ $a^7b^2\sqrt{ab}$	63. $\sqrt{a^3b^{11}}$ $ab^5\sqrt{ab}$	64. $\sqrt{24y^7}$ $2y^3\sqrt{6y}$
65. $\sqrt{60x^5}$ $2x^2\sqrt{15x}$	66. $\sqrt{72y^7}$ $6y^3\sqrt{2y}$	67. $\sqrt{49a^4b^8}$ $7a^2b^4$	68. $\sqrt{144x^2y^8}$ $12xy^4$

69. $\sqrt{18x^5y^7}$ $3x^2y^3\sqrt{2xy}$ **70.** $\sqrt{32a^5b^{15}}$ $4a^2b^7\sqrt{2ab}$ **71.** $\sqrt{40x^{11}y^7}$ $2x^5y^3\sqrt{10xy}$

72. $\sqrt{72x^9y^3}$ $6x^4y\sqrt{2xy}$ **73.** $\sqrt{80a^9b^{10}}$ $4a^4b^5\sqrt{5a}$ **74.** $\sqrt{96a^5b^7}$ $4a^2b^3\sqrt{6ab}$

75. $2\sqrt{16a^2b^3}$ $8ab\sqrt{b}$ **76.** $5\sqrt{25a^4b^7}$ $25a^2b^3\sqrt{b}$ **77.** $x\sqrt{x^4y^2}$ x^3y

78. $y\sqrt{x^3y^6}$ $xy^4\sqrt{x}$ **79.** $4\sqrt{20a^4b^7}$ $8a^2b^3\sqrt{5b}$ **80.** $5\sqrt{12a^3b^4}$ $10ab^2\sqrt{3a}$

81. $3x\sqrt{12x^2y^7}$ $6x^2y^3\sqrt{3y}$ **82.** $4y\sqrt{18x^5y^4}$ $12x^2y^3\sqrt{2x}$ **83.** $2x^2\sqrt{8x^2y^3}$ $4x^3y\sqrt{2y}$

84. $3y^2\sqrt{27x^4y^3}$ $9x^2y^3\sqrt{3y}$ **85.** $\sqrt{25(a+4)^2}$ $5a+20$ **86.** $\sqrt{81(x+y)^4}$ $9x^2+18xy+9y^2$

87. $\sqrt{4(x+2)^4}$ $2x^2+8x+8$ **88.** $\sqrt{9(x+2)^2}$ $3x+6$ **89.** $\sqrt{x^2+4x+4}$ $x+2$

90. $\sqrt{b^2+8b+16}$ $b+4$ **91.** $\sqrt{y^2+2y+1}$ $y+1$ **92.** $\sqrt{a^2+6a+9}$ $a+3$

APPLYING CONCEPTS 10.1

Simplify.

93. $\sqrt{0.0025a^3b^5}$ **94.** $-\dfrac{3y}{4}\sqrt{64x^4y^2}$ **95.** $\sqrt{x^2y^3+x^3y^2}$ **96.** $\sqrt{4a^5b^4-4a^4b^5}$

$0.05ab^2\sqrt{ab}$ $-6x^2y^2$ $xy\sqrt{y+x}$ $2a^2b^2\sqrt{a-b}$

97. Given $f(x) = \sqrt{2x-1}$, find each of the following. Write your answer in simplest form.
  a. $f(1)$ 1 **b.** $f(5)$ 3 **c.** $f(14)$ $3\sqrt{3}$

98. Use the roster method to list the whole numbers between $\sqrt{8}$ and $\sqrt{90}$.
$\{3, 4, 5, 6, 7, 8, 9\}$

99. *Geometry* The area of a square is 76 cm². Find the length of a side of the square. Round to the nearest tenth. 8.7 cm

$A = 76\ \text{cm}^2$
s

Assuming x can be any real number, for what values of x is the radical expression a real number? Write the answer as an inequality or write "all real numbers."

100. $\sqrt{x}$ $x \geq 0$ **101.** $\sqrt{4x}$ $x \geq 0$ **102.** $\sqrt{x-2}$ $x \geq 2$ **103.** $\sqrt{x+5}$ $x \geq -5$

[C] **104.** $\sqrt{6-4x}$ $x \leq \dfrac{3}{2}$ [C] **105.** $\sqrt{5-2x}$ $x \leq \dfrac{5}{2}$ [C] **106.** $\sqrt{x^2+7}$ [C] **107.** $\sqrt{x^2+1}$

All real numbers All real numbers

108. Describe in your own words how to simplify a radical expression.

109. Explain why $2\sqrt{2}$ is in simplest form and $\sqrt{8}$ is not in simplest form.

S E C T I O N **10.2**

Addition and Subtraction of Radical Expressions

1 Add and subtract radical expressions

INSTRUCTOR NOTE

Operations with radical expressions are similar to operations with variable expressions. Making this connection for students may help them with simplifying radical expressions.

The Distributive Property is used to simplify the sum or difference of radical expressions with the same radicand.

$$5\sqrt{2} + 3\sqrt{2} = (5 + 3)\sqrt{2} = 8\sqrt{2}$$
$$6\sqrt{2x} - 4\sqrt{2x} = (6 - 4)\sqrt{2x} = 2\sqrt{2x}$$

Radical expressions that are in simplest form and have different radicands cannot be simplified by the Distributive Property.

$2\sqrt{3} + 4\sqrt{2}$ cannot be simplified by the Distributive Property.

To simplify the sum or difference of radical expressions, simplify each term. Then use the Distributive Property.

▶ Subtract: $4\sqrt{8} - 10\sqrt{2}$

Simplify each term.

$$\begin{aligned}
4\sqrt{8} - 10\sqrt{2} &= 4\sqrt{2^3} - 10\sqrt{2} \\
&= 4\sqrt{2^2 \cdot 2} - 10\sqrt{2} \\
&= 4\sqrt{2^2}\,\sqrt{2} - 10\sqrt{2} \\
&= 4 \cdot 2\sqrt{2} - 10\sqrt{2} \\
&= 8\sqrt{2} - 10\sqrt{2}
\end{aligned}$$

Subtract by using the Distributive Property.

$$\begin{aligned}
&= (8 - 10)\sqrt{2} \\
&= -2\sqrt{2}
\end{aligned}$$

Example 1 Simplify.   A. $5\sqrt{2} - 3\sqrt{2} + 12\sqrt{2}$ B. $3\sqrt{12} - 5\sqrt{27}$

  Solution A. $5\sqrt{2} - 3\sqrt{2} + 12\sqrt{2}$
  $$= (5 - 3 + 12)\sqrt{2} \quad \text{▶ Use the Distributive Property.}$$
  $$= 14\sqrt{2}$$

  B. $3\sqrt{12} - 5\sqrt{27} = 3\sqrt{2^2 \cdot 3} - 5\sqrt{3^3}$
  $$\begin{aligned}
  &= 3\sqrt{2^2 \cdot 3} - 5\sqrt{3^2 \cdot 3} \\
  &= 3\sqrt{2^2}\,\sqrt{3} - 5\sqrt{3^2}\,\sqrt{3} \\
  &= 3 \cdot 2\sqrt{3} - 5 \cdot 3\sqrt{3} \\
  &= 6\sqrt{3} - 15\sqrt{3} \\
  &= -9\sqrt{3}
  \end{aligned}$$

Problem 1 Simplify.   A. $9\sqrt{3} + 3\sqrt{3} - 18\sqrt{3}$ B. $2\sqrt{50} - 5\sqrt{32}$

  Solution See page S22.   A. $-6\sqrt{3}$ B. $-10\sqrt{2}$

➡ Subtract: $8\sqrt{18x} - 2\sqrt{32x}$

Simplify each term.

$$8\sqrt{18x} - 2\sqrt{32x} = 8\sqrt{2 \cdot 3^2 x} - 2\sqrt{2^5 x}$$
$$= 8\sqrt{3^2}\sqrt{2x} - 2\sqrt{2^4}\sqrt{2x}$$
$$= 8 \cdot 3\sqrt{2x} - 2 \cdot 2^2\sqrt{2x}$$
$$= 24\sqrt{2x} - 8\sqrt{2x}$$

Subtract the radical expressions.
$$= 16\sqrt{2x}$$ ◀

Example 2 Simplify.

A. $3\sqrt{12x^3} - 2x\sqrt{3x}$ B. $2x\sqrt{8y} - 3\sqrt{2x^2 y} + 2\sqrt{32x^2 y}$

Solution A. $3\sqrt{12x^3} - 2x\sqrt{3x} = 3\sqrt{2^2 \cdot 3 \cdot x^3} - 2x\sqrt{3x}$
$$= 3\sqrt{2^2 \cdot x^2}\sqrt{3x} - 2x\sqrt{3x}$$
$$= 3 \cdot 2x\sqrt{3x} - 2x\sqrt{3x}$$
$$= 6x\sqrt{3x} - 2x\sqrt{3x}$$
$$= 4x\sqrt{3x}$$

B. $2x\sqrt{8y} - 3\sqrt{2x^2 y} + 2\sqrt{32x^2 y}$
$$= 2x\sqrt{2^3 y} - 3\sqrt{2x^2 y} + 2\sqrt{2^5 x^2 y}$$
$$= 2x\sqrt{2^2}\sqrt{2y} - 3\sqrt{x^2}\sqrt{2y} + 2\sqrt{2^4 x^2}\sqrt{2y}$$
$$= 2x \cdot 2\sqrt{2y} - 3 \cdot x\sqrt{2y} + 2 \cdot 2^2 x\sqrt{2y}$$
$$= 4x\sqrt{2y} - 3x\sqrt{2y} + 8x\sqrt{2y}$$
$$= 9x\sqrt{2y}$$

Problem 2 Simplify.

A. $y\sqrt{28y} + 7\sqrt{63y^3}$ B. $2\sqrt{27a^5} - 4a\sqrt{12a^3} + a^2\sqrt{75a}$

Solution See page S23.   A. $23y\sqrt{7y}$ B. $3a^2\sqrt{3a}$

CONCEPT REVIEW 10.2

Determine whether the statement is always true, sometimes true, or never true.

1. $5\sqrt{2} + 6\sqrt{3} = 11\sqrt{5}$ Never true

2. The Distributive Property is used to add or subtract radical expressions with the same radicand.   Always true

3. $4\sqrt{7}$ and $\sqrt{7}$ are examples of like radical expressions.   Always true

4. The expressions $3\sqrt{12}$ and $5\sqrt{3}$ cannot be subtracted until $3\sqrt{12}$ is rewritten in simplest form.   Always true

5. $5\sqrt{32x} + 4\sqrt{18x} = 5(4\sqrt{2x}) + 4(3\sqrt{2x}) = 20\sqrt{2x} + 12\sqrt{2x} = 32\sqrt{2x}$
    Always true

6. The expressions $9\sqrt{11}$ and $10\sqrt{13}$ can be added after each radical is written in simplest form.   Never true

EXERCISES 10.2

1 Simplify.

1. $2\sqrt{2} + \sqrt{2}$ $3\sqrt{2}$

2. $3\sqrt{5} + 8\sqrt{5}$ $11\sqrt{5}$

3. $-3\sqrt{7} + 2\sqrt{7}$ $-\sqrt{7}$

4. $4\sqrt{5} - 10\sqrt{5}$ $-6\sqrt{5}$

5. $-3\sqrt{11} - 8\sqrt{11}$ $-11\sqrt{11}$

6. $-3\sqrt{3} - 5\sqrt{3}$ $-8\sqrt{3}$

7. $2\sqrt{x} + 8\sqrt{x}$ $10\sqrt{x}$

8. $3\sqrt{y} + 2\sqrt{y}$ $5\sqrt{y}$

9. $8\sqrt{y} - 10\sqrt{y}$ $-2\sqrt{y}$

10. $-5\sqrt{2a} + 2\sqrt{2a}$ $-3\sqrt{2a}$

11. $-2\sqrt{3b} - 9\sqrt{3b}$ $-11\sqrt{3b}$

12. $-7\sqrt{5a} - 5\sqrt{5a}$ $-12\sqrt{5a}$

13. $3x\sqrt{2} - x\sqrt{2}$ $2x\sqrt{2}$

14. $2y\sqrt{3} - 9y\sqrt{3}$ $-7y\sqrt{3}$

15. $2a\sqrt{3a} - 5a\sqrt{3a}$ $-3a\sqrt{3a}$

16. $-5b\sqrt{3x} - 2b\sqrt{3x}$ $-7b\sqrt{3x}$

17. $3\sqrt{xy} - 8\sqrt{xy}$ $-5\sqrt{xy}$

18. $-4\sqrt{xy} + 6\sqrt{xy}$ $2\sqrt{xy}$

19. $\sqrt{45} + \sqrt{125}$ $8\sqrt{5}$

20. $\sqrt{32} - \sqrt{98}$ $-3\sqrt{2}$

21. $2\sqrt{2} + 3\sqrt{8}$ $8\sqrt{2}$

22. $4\sqrt{128} - 3\sqrt{32}$ $20\sqrt{2}$

23. $5\sqrt{18} - 2\sqrt{75}$ $15\sqrt{2} - 10\sqrt{3}$ **24.** $5\sqrt{75} - 2\sqrt{18}$ $25\sqrt{3} - 6\sqrt{2}$

25. $5\sqrt{4x} - 3\sqrt{9x}$ $\sqrt{x}$

26. $-3\sqrt{25y} + 8\sqrt{49y}$ $41\sqrt{y}$

27. $3\sqrt{3x^2} - 5\sqrt{27x^2}$ $-12x\sqrt{3}$

28. $-2\sqrt{8y^2} + 5\sqrt{32y^2}$ $16y\sqrt{2}$

29. $2x\sqrt{xy^2} - 3y\sqrt{x^2y}$ $2xy\sqrt{x} - 3xy\sqrt{y}$

30. $4a\sqrt{b^2a} - 3b\sqrt{a^2b}$ $4ab\sqrt{a} - 3ab\sqrt{b}$

31. $3x\sqrt{12x} - 5\sqrt{27x^3}$ $-9x\sqrt{3x}$

32. $2a\sqrt{50a} + 7\sqrt{32a^3}$ $38a\sqrt{2a}$

33. $4y\sqrt{8y^3} - 7\sqrt{18y^5}$ $-13y^2\sqrt{2y}$

34. $2a\sqrt{8ab^2} - 2b\sqrt{2a^3}$ $2ab\sqrt{2a}$

35. $b^2\sqrt{a^5b} + 3a^2\sqrt{ab^5}$ $4a^2b^2\sqrt{ab}$

36. $y^2\sqrt{x^5y} + x\sqrt{x^3y^5}$ $2x^2y^2\sqrt{xy}$

37. $4\sqrt{2} - 5\sqrt{2} + 8\sqrt{2}$ $7\sqrt{2}$

38. $3\sqrt{3} + 8\sqrt{3} - 16\sqrt{3}$ $-5\sqrt{3}$

39. $5\sqrt{x} - 8\sqrt{x} + 9\sqrt{x}$ $6\sqrt{x}$

40. $\sqrt{x} - 7\sqrt{x} + 6\sqrt{x}$ 0

41. $8\sqrt{2} - 3\sqrt{y} - 8\sqrt{2}$ $-3\sqrt{y}$

42. $8\sqrt{3} - 5\sqrt{2} - 5\sqrt{3}$ $3\sqrt{3} - 5\sqrt{2}$

43. $8\sqrt{8} - 4\sqrt{32} - 9\sqrt{50}$ $-45\sqrt{2}$

44. $2\sqrt{12} - 4\sqrt{27} + \sqrt{75}$ $-3\sqrt{3}$

45. $-2\sqrt{3} + 5\sqrt{27} - 4\sqrt{45}$ $13\sqrt{3} - 12\sqrt{5}$

46. $-2\sqrt{8} - 3\sqrt{27} + 3\sqrt{50}$ $11\sqrt{2} - 9\sqrt{3}$

47. $4\sqrt{75} + 3\sqrt{48} - \sqrt{99}$ $32\sqrt{3} - 3\sqrt{11}$

48. $2\sqrt{75} - 5\sqrt{20} + 2\sqrt{45}$ $10\sqrt{3} - 4\sqrt{5}$

49. $\sqrt{25x} - \sqrt{9x} + \sqrt{16x}$ $6\sqrt{x}$

50. $\sqrt{4x} - \sqrt{100x} - \sqrt{49x}$ $-15\sqrt{x}$

51. $3\sqrt{3x} + \sqrt{27x} - 8\sqrt{75x}$ $-34\sqrt{3x}$

52. $5\sqrt{5x} + 2\sqrt{45x} - 3\sqrt{80x}$ $-\sqrt{5x}$

53. $2a\sqrt{75b} - a\sqrt{20b} + 4a\sqrt{45b}$ $10a\sqrt{3b} + 10a\sqrt{5b}$

54. $2b\sqrt{75a} - 5b\sqrt{27a} + 2b\sqrt{20a}$
$-5b\sqrt{3a} + 4b\sqrt{5a}$

55. $x\sqrt{3y^2} - 2y\sqrt{12x^2} + xy\sqrt{3}$ $-2xy\sqrt{3}$

56. $a\sqrt{27b^2} + 3b\sqrt{147a^2} - ab\sqrt{3}$ $23ab\sqrt{3}$

57. $3\sqrt{ab^3} + 4a\sqrt{a^2b} - 5b\sqrt{4ab}$ $-7b\sqrt{ab} + 4a^2\sqrt{b}$

58. $5\sqrt{a^3b} + a\sqrt{4ab} - 3\sqrt{49a^3b}$ $-14a\sqrt{ab}$

59. $3a\sqrt{2ab^2} - \sqrt{a^2b^2} + 4b\sqrt{3a^2b}$
$3ab\sqrt{2a} - ab + 4ab\sqrt{3b}$

60. $2\sqrt{4a^2b^2} - 3a\sqrt{9ab^2} + 4b\sqrt{a^2b}$
$4ab - 9ab\sqrt{a} + 4ab\sqrt{b}$

APPLYING CONCEPTS 10.2

Add or subtract.

61. $5\sqrt{x+2} + 3\sqrt{x+2}$ $8\sqrt{x+2}$

62. $8\sqrt{a+5} - 4\sqrt{a+5}$ $4\sqrt{a+5}$

63. $\frac{1}{2}\sqrt{8x^2y} + \frac{1}{3}\sqrt{18x^2y}$
$2x\sqrt{2y}$

64. $\frac{1}{4}\sqrt{48ab^2} + \frac{1}{5}\sqrt{75ab^2}$ $2b\sqrt{3a}$

65. $\frac{a}{3}\sqrt{54ab^3} + \frac{b}{4}\sqrt{96a^3b}$ $2ab\sqrt{6ab}$

66. $\frac{x}{6}\sqrt{72xy^5} + \frac{y}{7}\sqrt{98x^3y^3}$
$2xy^2\sqrt{2xy}$

67. $2\sqrt{8x+4y} - 5\sqrt{18x+9y}$
$-11\sqrt{2x+y}$

68. $3\sqrt{a^3+a^2} + 5\sqrt{4a^3+4a^2}$ $13a\sqrt{a+1}$

69. *Geometry* The lengths of the sides of a triangle are $4\sqrt{3}$ cm, $2\sqrt{3}$ cm, and $2\sqrt{15}$ cm. Find the perimeter of the triangle.
$(6\sqrt{3} + 2\sqrt{15})$ cm

70. *Geometry* The length of a rectangle is $3\sqrt{2}$ cm. The width is $\sqrt{2}$ cm. Find the perimeter of the rectangle. $8\sqrt{2}$ cm

71. *Geometry* The length of a rectangle is $4\sqrt{5}$ cm. The width is $\sqrt{5}$ cm. Find the decimal approximation of the perimeter. Round to the nearest tenth.   22.4 cm

72. Given $G(x) = \sqrt{x+5} + \sqrt{5x+3}$, write $G(3)$ in simplest form. $5\sqrt{2}$

[C] 73. Is the equation $\sqrt{a^2+b^2} = \sqrt{a} + \sqrt{b}$ true for all real numbers a and b?   No

74. ✏ Use complete sentences to explain the steps in simplifying the radical expression $4\sqrt{2a^3b} + 5\sqrt{2a^3b}$.

S E C T I O N **10.3**

Multiplication and Division of Radical Expressions

■ 1 Multiply radical expressions

The Product Property of Square Roots is used to multiply variable radical expressions.

$\sqrt{2x}\,\sqrt{3y} = \sqrt{2x \cdot 3y}$
$\qquad = \sqrt{6xy}$

→ Multiply: $\sqrt{2x^2}\,\sqrt{32x^5}$

Use the Product Property of Square Roots. $\sqrt{2x^2}\,\sqrt{32x^5} = \sqrt{2x^2 \cdot 32x^5}$

Multiply the radicands. $= \sqrt{64x^7}$

Simplify. $= \sqrt{2^6 x^7}$
$= \sqrt{2^6 x^6}\,\sqrt{x}$
$= 2^3 x^3 \sqrt{x}$
$= 8x^3 \sqrt{x}$ ◀

Example 1   Multiply: $\sqrt{3x^4}\,\sqrt{2x^2 y}\,\sqrt{6xy^2}$

Solution $\sqrt{3x^4}\,\sqrt{2x^2 y}\,\sqrt{6xy^2} = \sqrt{3x^4 \cdot 2x^2 y \cdot 6xy^2}$
$= \sqrt{36x^7 y^3}$
$= \sqrt{2^2 3^2 x^7 y^3}$
$= \sqrt{2^2 3^2 x^6 y^2}\,\sqrt{xy}$
$= 2 \cdot 3x^3 y \sqrt{xy}$
$= 6x^3 y \sqrt{xy}$

Problem 1   Multiply: $\sqrt{5a}\,\sqrt{15a^3 b^4}\,\sqrt{3b^5}$

Solution   See page S23. $15a^2 b^4 \sqrt{b}$

When the expression $(\sqrt{x})^2$ is simplified by using the Product Property of Square Roots, the result is x.

$(\sqrt{x})^2 = \sqrt{x}\,\sqrt{x}$
$= \sqrt{x \cdot x}$
$= \sqrt{x^2}$
$= x$

For $a > 0$, $(\sqrt{a})^2 = \sqrt{a^2} = a$.

→ Multiply: $\sqrt{2x}(x + \sqrt{2x})$

Use the Distributive Property to remove parentheses. $\sqrt{2x}(x + \sqrt{2x}) = \sqrt{2x}(x) + \sqrt{2x}\,\sqrt{2x}$
$= x\sqrt{2x} + (\sqrt{2x})^2$
$= x\sqrt{2x} + 2x$ ◀

Example 2   Multiply: $\sqrt{3ab}(\sqrt{3a} + \sqrt{9b})$

Solution $\sqrt{3ab}(\sqrt{3a} + \sqrt{9b}) = \sqrt{3ab}(\sqrt{3a}) + \sqrt{3ab}(\sqrt{9b})$
$= \sqrt{9a^2 b} + \sqrt{27ab^2}$
$= \sqrt{3^2 a^2 b} + \sqrt{3^3 ab^2}$
$= \sqrt{3^2 a^2}\,\sqrt{b} + \sqrt{3^2 b^2}\,\sqrt{3a}$
$= 3a\sqrt{b} + 3b\sqrt{3a}$

Problem 2   Multiply: $\sqrt{5x}(\sqrt{5x} - \sqrt{25y})$

Solution   See page S23. $5x - 5\sqrt{5xy}$

To multiply $(\sqrt{2} - 3x)(\sqrt{2} + x)$, use the FOIL method.

$(\sqrt{2} - 3x)(\sqrt{2} + x) = (\sqrt{2})^2 + x\sqrt{2} - 3x\sqrt{2} - 3x^2$
$= 2 + (x - 3x)\sqrt{2} - 3x^2$
$= 2 - 2x\sqrt{2} - 3x^2$

Example 3   Multiply: $(2\sqrt{x} - \sqrt{y})(5\sqrt{x} - 2\sqrt{y})$

Solution $(2\sqrt{x} - \sqrt{y})(5\sqrt{x} - 2\sqrt{y})$
$= 10(\sqrt{x})^2 - 4\sqrt{xy} - 5\sqrt{xy} + 2(\sqrt{y})^2$
$= 10x - 9\sqrt{xy} + 2y$

Problem 3   Multiply: $(3\sqrt{x} - \sqrt{y})(5\sqrt{x} - 2\sqrt{y})$

Solution   See page S23. $15x - 11\sqrt{xy} + 2y$

The expressions $a + b$ and $a - b$, which are the sum and difference of two terms, are called **conjugates** of each other.

The product of conjugates is the difference of two squares.

$$(a + b)(a - b) = a^2 - b^2$$
$$(2 + \sqrt{7})(2 - \sqrt{7}) = 2^2 - (\sqrt{7})^2 = 4 - 7 = -3$$
$$(3 + \sqrt{y})(3 - \sqrt{y}) = 3^2 - (\sqrt{y})^2 = 9 - y$$

Example 4   Multiply: $(\sqrt{a} - \sqrt{b})(\sqrt{a} + \sqrt{b})$

Solution $(\sqrt{a} - \sqrt{b})(\sqrt{a} + \sqrt{b}) = (\sqrt{a})^2 - (\sqrt{b})^2 = a - b$

Problem 4   Multiply: $(2\sqrt{x} + 7)(2\sqrt{x} - 7)$

Solution   See page S23. $4x - 49$

2   Divide radical expressions

The square root of a quotient is equal to the quotient of the square roots.

The Quotient Property of Square Roots

If a and b are positive real numbers, then $\sqrt{\dfrac{a}{b}} = \dfrac{\sqrt{a}}{\sqrt{b}}$.

➡ Simplify: $\sqrt{\dfrac{4x^2}{z^6}}$

Rewrite the radical expression as the quotient of the square roots.

Take the square root of the perfect squares.

$\sqrt{\dfrac{4x^2}{z^6}} = \dfrac{\sqrt{4x^2}}{\sqrt{z^6}} = \dfrac{\sqrt{2^2x^2}}{\sqrt{z^6}}$

$= \dfrac{2x}{z^3}$ ⬅

➡ Simplify: $\sqrt{\dfrac{24x^3y^7}{3x^7y^2}}$

Simplify the radicand.

$\sqrt{\dfrac{24x^3y^7}{3x^7y^2}} = \sqrt{\dfrac{8y^5}{x^4}}$

Rewrite the radical expression as the quotient of the square roots.

$= \dfrac{\sqrt{8y^5}}{\sqrt{x^4}}$

Simplify.

$= \dfrac{\sqrt{2^3y^5}}{\sqrt{x^4}}$

$= \dfrac{\sqrt{2^2y^4}\sqrt{2y}}{\sqrt{x^4}}$

$= \dfrac{2y^2\sqrt{2y}}{x^2}$ ⬅

⇒ Simplify: $\dfrac{\sqrt{4x^2y}}{\sqrt{xy}}$

Use the Quotient Property of Square Roots.

$$\dfrac{\sqrt{4x^2y}}{\sqrt{xy}} = \sqrt{\dfrac{4x^2y}{xy}}$$

Simplify the radicand.

$$= \sqrt{4x}$$

Simplify the radical expression.

$$= \sqrt{2^2}\,\sqrt{x}$$
$$= 2\sqrt{x}\; ⬅$$

INSTRUCTOR NOTE

Rationalizing the denominator is another case where the Multiplication Property of One is used. Students do not always believe that $\dfrac{2}{\sqrt{3}}$ and $\dfrac{2\sqrt{3}}{3}$ are equal. Have these students use a calculator to verify, to the limits of the calculator, that the two expressions are equal.

A radical expression is not in simplest form if a radical remains in the denominator. The procedure used to remove a radical from the denominator is called **rationalizing the denominator.**

⇒ Simplify: $\dfrac{2}{\sqrt{3}}$

The expression $\dfrac{2}{\sqrt{3}}$ has a radical expression in the denominator. Multiply the expression by $\dfrac{\sqrt{3}}{\sqrt{3}}$, which equals 1.

$$\dfrac{2}{\sqrt{3}} = \dfrac{2}{\sqrt{3}} \cdot \dfrac{\sqrt{3}}{\sqrt{3}}$$

Simplify.

$$= \dfrac{2\sqrt{3}}{(\sqrt{3})^2}$$
$$= \dfrac{2\sqrt{3}}{3}\; ⬅$$

Thus $\dfrac{2}{\sqrt{3}} = \dfrac{2\sqrt{3}}{3}$, but $\dfrac{2}{\sqrt{3}}$ is not in simplest form. Because no radical remains in the denominator and the radical in the numerator contains no perfect-square factors other than 1, $\dfrac{2\sqrt{3}}{3}$ is in simplest form.

When the denominator contains a radical expression with two terms, simplify the radical expression by multiplying the numerator and denominator by the conjugate of the denominator.

⇒ Simplify: $\dfrac{\sqrt{2y}}{\sqrt{y} + 3}$

Multiply the numerator and denominator by $\sqrt{y} - 3$, the conjugate of $\sqrt{y} + 3$.

$$\dfrac{\sqrt{2y}}{\sqrt{y} + 3} = \dfrac{\sqrt{2y}}{\sqrt{y} + 3} \cdot \dfrac{\sqrt{y} - 3}{\sqrt{y} - 3}$$

Simplify.

$$= \dfrac{\sqrt{2y^2} - 3\sqrt{2y}}{(\sqrt{y})^2 - 3^2}$$
$$= \dfrac{y\sqrt{2} - 3\sqrt{2y}}{y - 9}\; ⬅$$

The following list summarizes the discussions about radical expressions in simplest form.

Radical Expressions in Simplest Form

A radical expression is in simplest form if:

1. The radicand contains no factor greater than 1 that is a perfect square.
2. There is no fraction under the radical sign.
3. There is no radical in the denominator of a fraction.

Example 5 Simplify. A. $\dfrac{\sqrt{4x^2y^5}}{\sqrt{3x^4y}}$ B. $\dfrac{\sqrt{2}}{\sqrt{2}-\sqrt{x}}$ C. $\dfrac{3-\sqrt{5}}{2+3\sqrt{5}}$

Solution A. $\dfrac{\sqrt{4x^2y^5}}{\sqrt{3x^4y}} = \sqrt{\dfrac{2^2x^2y^5}{3x^4y}} = \sqrt{\dfrac{2^2y^4}{3x^2}} = \dfrac{2y^2}{x\sqrt{3}} = \dfrac{2y^2}{x\sqrt{3}} \cdot \dfrac{\sqrt{3}}{\sqrt{3}} = \dfrac{2y^2\sqrt{3}}{3x}$

B. $\dfrac{\sqrt{2}}{\sqrt{2}-\sqrt{x}} = \dfrac{\sqrt{2}}{\sqrt{2}-\sqrt{x}} \cdot \dfrac{\sqrt{2}+\sqrt{x}}{\sqrt{2}+\sqrt{x}} = \dfrac{2+\sqrt{2x}}{2-x}$

C. $\dfrac{3-\sqrt{5}}{2+3\sqrt{5}} = \dfrac{3-\sqrt{5}}{2+3\sqrt{5}} \cdot \dfrac{2-3\sqrt{5}}{2-3\sqrt{5}}$

$= \dfrac{6 - 9\sqrt{5} - 2\sqrt{5} + 3 \cdot 5}{4 - 9 \cdot 5}$

$= \dfrac{21 - 11\sqrt{5}}{-41}$

$= -\dfrac{21 - 11\sqrt{5}}{41}$

Problem 5 Simplify. A. $\sqrt{\dfrac{15x^6y^7}{3x^7y^9}}$ B. $\dfrac{\sqrt{y}}{\sqrt{y}+3}$ C. $\dfrac{5+\sqrt{y}}{1-2\sqrt{y}}$

Solution See page S23. A. $\dfrac{\sqrt{5x}}{xy}$ B. $\dfrac{y-3\sqrt{y}}{y-9}$ C. $\dfrac{5+11\sqrt{y}+2y}{1-4y}$

CONCEPT REVIEW 10.3

Determine whether the statement is always true, sometimes true, or never true.

1. By the Product Property of Square Roots, if $a > 0$ and $b > 0$, then $\sqrt{a} \cdot \sqrt{b} = \sqrt{ab}$. Always true

2. When we square a square root, the result is the radicand. Always true

3. The procedure for rationalizing the denominator is used when a fraction has a radical expression in the denominator. Always true

4. The square root of a fraction is equal to the square root of the numerator over the square root of the denominator. Always true

5. A radical expression is in simplest form if the radicand contains no factor other than 1 that is a perfect square. Sometimes true

6. The conjugate of $5 - \sqrt{3}$ is $\sqrt{3} - 5$. Never true

---

EXERCISES 10.3

1 Multiply.

1. $\sqrt{5}\,\sqrt{5}$ 5

2. $\sqrt{11}\,\sqrt{11}$ 11

3. $\sqrt{3}\,\sqrt{12}$ 6

4. $\sqrt{2}\,\sqrt{8}$ 4

5. $\sqrt{x}\,\sqrt{x}$ x

6. $\sqrt{y}\,\sqrt{y}$ y

7. $\sqrt{xy^3}\,\sqrt{x^5y}$ x^3y^2

8. $\sqrt{a^3b^5}\,\sqrt{ab^5}$ a^2b^5

9. $\sqrt{3a^2b^5}\,\sqrt{6ab^7}$
$3ab^6\sqrt{2a}$

10. $\sqrt{5x^3y}\,\sqrt{10x^2y}$
$5x^2y\sqrt{2x}$

11. $\sqrt{6a^3b^2}\,\sqrt{24a^5b}$
$12a^4b\sqrt{b}$

12. $\sqrt{8ab^5}\,\sqrt{12a^7b}$
$4a^4b^3\sqrt{6}$

13. $\sqrt{2}(\sqrt{2}-\sqrt{3})$
$2-\sqrt{6}$

14. $3(\sqrt{12}-\sqrt{3})$
$3\sqrt{3}$

15. $\sqrt{x}(\sqrt{x}-\sqrt{y})$
$x-\sqrt{xy}$

16. $\sqrt{b}(\sqrt{a}-\sqrt{b})$
$\sqrt{ab}-b$

17. $\sqrt{5}(\sqrt{10}-\sqrt{x})$
$5\sqrt{2}-\sqrt{5x}$

18. $\sqrt{6}(\sqrt{y}-\sqrt{18})$
$\sqrt{6y}-6\sqrt{3}$

19. $\sqrt{8}(\sqrt{2}-\sqrt{5})$
$4-2\sqrt{10}$

20. $\sqrt{10}(\sqrt{20}-\sqrt{a})$
$10\sqrt{2}-\sqrt{10a}$

21. $(\sqrt{x}-3)^2$
$x-6\sqrt{x}+9$

22. $(2\sqrt{a}-y)^2$
$4a-4y\sqrt{a}+y^2$

23. $\sqrt{3a}(\sqrt{3a}-\sqrt{3b})$
$3a-3\sqrt{ab}$

24. $\sqrt{5x}(\sqrt{10x}-\sqrt{x})$
$5x\sqrt{2}-x\sqrt{5}$

25. $\sqrt{2ac}\,\sqrt{5ab}\,\sqrt{10cb}$
$10abc$

26. $\sqrt{3xy}\,\sqrt{6x^3y}\,\sqrt{2y^2}$
$6x^2y^2$

27. $(3\sqrt{x}-2y)(5\sqrt{x}-4y)$
$15x-22y\sqrt{x}+8y^2$

28. $(5\sqrt{x}+2\sqrt{y})(3\sqrt{x}-\sqrt{y})$
$15x+\sqrt{xy}-2y$

29. $(\sqrt{x}-\sqrt{y})(\sqrt{x}+\sqrt{y})$
$x-y$

30. $(\sqrt{3x}+y)(\sqrt{3x}-y)$
$3x-y^2$

31. $(2\sqrt{x}+\sqrt{y})(5\sqrt{x}+4\sqrt{y})$
$10x+13\sqrt{xy}+4y$

32. $(5\sqrt{x}-2\sqrt{y})(3\sqrt{x}-4\sqrt{y})$
$15x-26\sqrt{xy}+8y$

2 **33.** Explain why $\dfrac{\sqrt{5}}{5}$ is in simplest form and $\dfrac{1}{\sqrt{5}}$ is not in simplest form.

34. Why can we multiply $\dfrac{1}{\sqrt{3}}$ by $\dfrac{\sqrt{3}}{\sqrt{3}}$ without changing the value of $\dfrac{1}{\sqrt{3}}$?

Simplify.

35. $\dfrac{\sqrt{32}}{\sqrt{2}}$ 4

36. $\dfrac{\sqrt{45}}{\sqrt{5}}$ 3

37. $\dfrac{\sqrt{98}}{\sqrt{2}}$ 7

38. $\dfrac{\sqrt{48}}{\sqrt{3}}$ 4

39. $\dfrac{\sqrt{27a}}{\sqrt{3a}}$ 3

40. $\dfrac{\sqrt{72x^5}}{\sqrt{2x}}$ $6x^2$

41. $\dfrac{\sqrt{15x^3y}}{\sqrt{3xy}}$ $x\sqrt{5}$

42. $\dfrac{\sqrt{40x^5y^2}}{\sqrt{5xy}}$ $2x^2\sqrt{2y}$

43. $\dfrac{\sqrt{2a^5b^4}}{\sqrt{98ab^4}}$ $\dfrac{a^2}{7}$

44. $\dfrac{\sqrt{48x^5y^2}}{\sqrt{3x^3y}}$ $4x\sqrt{y}$

45. $\dfrac{1}{\sqrt{3}}$ $\dfrac{\sqrt{3}}{3}$

46. $\dfrac{1}{\sqrt{8}}$ $\dfrac{\sqrt{2}}{4}$

47. $\dfrac{15}{\sqrt{75}}$ $\sqrt{3}$

48. $\dfrac{6}{\sqrt{72}}$ $\dfrac{\sqrt{2}}{2}$

49. $\dfrac{6}{\sqrt{12x}}$ $\dfrac{\sqrt{3x}}{x}$

50. $\dfrac{14}{\sqrt{7y}}$ $\dfrac{2\sqrt{7y}}{y}$

51. $\dfrac{8}{\sqrt{32x}}$ $\dfrac{\sqrt{2x}}{x}$

52. $\dfrac{15}{\sqrt{50x}}$ $\dfrac{3\sqrt{2x}}{2x}$

53. $\dfrac{3}{\sqrt{x}}$ $\dfrac{3\sqrt{x}}{x}$

54. $\dfrac{4}{\sqrt{2x}}$ $\dfrac{2\sqrt{2x}}{x}$

55. $\dfrac{\sqrt{8x^2y}}{\sqrt{2x^4y^2}}$ $\dfrac{2\sqrt{y}}{xy}$

56. $\dfrac{\sqrt{4x^2}}{\sqrt{9y}}$ $\dfrac{2x\sqrt{y}}{3y}$

57. $\dfrac{\sqrt{16a}}{\sqrt{49ab}}$ $\dfrac{4\sqrt{b}}{7b}$

58. $\dfrac{5\sqrt{8}}{4\sqrt{50}}$ $\dfrac{1}{2}$

59. $\dfrac{5\sqrt{18}}{9\sqrt{27}}$ $\dfrac{5\sqrt{6}}{27}$

60. $\dfrac{\sqrt{12a^3b}}{\sqrt{24a^2b^2}}$ $\dfrac{\sqrt{2ab}}{2b}$

61. $\dfrac{\sqrt{3xy}}{\sqrt{27x^3y^2}}$ $\dfrac{\sqrt{y}}{3xy}$

62. $\dfrac{\sqrt{9xy^2}}{\sqrt{27x}}$ $\dfrac{y\sqrt{3}}{3}$

63. $\dfrac{\sqrt{4x^2y}}{\sqrt{3xy^3}}$ $\dfrac{2\sqrt{3x}}{3y}$

64. $\dfrac{\sqrt{16x^3y^2}}{\sqrt{8x^3y}}$ $\sqrt{2y}$

65. $\dfrac{1}{\sqrt{2}-3}$ $-\dfrac{\sqrt{2}+3}{7}$

66. $\dfrac{5}{\sqrt{7}-3}$ $-\dfrac{5\sqrt{7}+15}{2}$

67. $\dfrac{3}{5+\sqrt{5}}$ $\dfrac{15-3\sqrt{5}}{20}$

68. $\dfrac{7}{\sqrt{2}-7}$ $\dfrac{7\sqrt{2}+49}{47}$

69. $\dfrac{\sqrt{xy}}{\sqrt{x}-\sqrt{y}}$ $\dfrac{x\sqrt{y}+y\sqrt{x}}{x-y}$

70. $\dfrac{\sqrt{x}}{\sqrt{x}-\sqrt{y}}$ $\dfrac{x+\sqrt{xy}}{x-y}$

71. $\dfrac{5\sqrt{x^2y}}{\sqrt{75xy^2}}$ $\dfrac{\sqrt{3xy}}{3y}$

72. $\dfrac{3\sqrt{ab}}{a\sqrt{6b}}$ $\dfrac{\sqrt{6a}}{2a}$

73. $\dfrac{\sqrt{2}}{\sqrt{2}-\sqrt{3}}$ $-2-\sqrt{6}$

74. $\dfrac{1+\sqrt{2}}{1-\sqrt{2}}$ $-3-2\sqrt{2}$

75. $\dfrac{\sqrt{5}}{\sqrt{2}-\sqrt{5}}$ $-\dfrac{\sqrt{10}+5}{3}$

76. $\dfrac{\sqrt{6}}{\sqrt{3}-\sqrt{2}}$ $3\sqrt{2}+2\sqrt{3}$

77. $\dfrac{\sqrt{x}}{\sqrt{x}+3}$ $\dfrac{x-3\sqrt{x}}{x-9}$

78. $\dfrac{\sqrt{y}}{2-\sqrt{y}}$ $\dfrac{2\sqrt{y}+y}{4-y}$

79. $\dfrac{5\sqrt{3}-7\sqrt{3}}{4\sqrt{3}}$ $-\dfrac{1}{2}$

80. $\dfrac{10\sqrt{7}-2\sqrt{7}}{2\sqrt{7}}$ 4

81. $\dfrac{5\sqrt{8}-3\sqrt{2}}{\sqrt{2}}$ 7

82. $\dfrac{5\sqrt{12}-\sqrt{3}}{\sqrt{27}}$ 3

83. $\dfrac{3\sqrt{2}-8\sqrt{2}}{\sqrt{2}}$ -5

84. $\dfrac{5\sqrt{3}-2\sqrt{3}}{2\sqrt{3}}$ $\dfrac{3}{2}$

85. $\dfrac{2\sqrt{8}+3\sqrt{2}}{\sqrt{32}}$ $\dfrac{7}{4}$

86. $\dfrac{3 - \sqrt{6}}{5 - 2\sqrt{6}}$ $3 + \sqrt{6}$

87. $\dfrac{6 - 2\sqrt{3}}{4 + 3\sqrt{3}}$ $\dfrac{42 - 26\sqrt{3}}{11}$

88. $\dfrac{\sqrt{2} + 2\sqrt{6}}{2\sqrt{2} - 3\sqrt{6}}$ $\dfrac{20 + 7\sqrt{3}}{23}$

89. $\dfrac{2\sqrt{3} - \sqrt{6}}{5\sqrt{3} + 2\sqrt{6}}$ $\dfrac{14 - 9\sqrt{2}}{17}$

90. $\dfrac{3 + \sqrt{x}}{2 - \sqrt{x}}$ $\dfrac{6 + 5\sqrt{x} + x}{4 - x}$

91. $\dfrac{\sqrt{a} - 4}{2\sqrt{a} + 2}$ $\dfrac{a - 5\sqrt{a} + 4}{2a - 2}$

92. $\dfrac{3 + 2\sqrt{y}}{2 - \sqrt{y}}$ $\dfrac{6 + 7\sqrt{y} + 2y}{4 - y}$

93. $\dfrac{2 + \sqrt{y}}{\sqrt{y} - 3}$ $\dfrac{y + 5\sqrt{y} + 6}{y - 9}$

94. $\dfrac{\sqrt{x} + \sqrt{y}}{\sqrt{x} - \sqrt{y}}$ $\dfrac{x + 2\sqrt{xy} + y}{x - y}$

APPLYING CONCEPTS 10.3

Simplify.

95. $-\sqrt{1.3}\,\sqrt{1.3}$ -1.3

96. $\sqrt{\dfrac{5}{8}}\,\sqrt{\dfrac{5}{8}}$ $\dfrac{5}{8}$

97. $-\sqrt{\dfrac{16}{81}}$ $-\dfrac{4}{9}$

98. $\sqrt{1\dfrac{9}{16}}$ $\dfrac{5}{4}$

99. $\sqrt{2\dfrac{1}{4}}$ $\dfrac{3}{2}$

100. $-\sqrt{6\dfrac{1}{4}}$ $-\dfrac{5}{2}$

[C] **101.** Answer true or false. If the equation is false, correct the right side.
  a. $(\sqrt{y})^4 = y^2$ True   **b.** $(2\sqrt{x})^3 = 8x\sqrt{x}$ True

  c. $(\sqrt{x} + 1)^2 = x + 1$ **d.** $\dfrac{1}{2 - \sqrt{3}} = 2 + \sqrt{3}$ True
  False; $x + 2\sqrt{x} + 1$

102. Show that 2 is a solution of the equation $\sqrt{x + 2} + \sqrt{x - 1} = 3$.

103. Is 16 a solution of the equation $\sqrt{x} - \sqrt{x + 9} = 1$?   No

[C] **104.** Show that $(1 + \sqrt{6})$ and $(1 - \sqrt{6})$ are solutions of the equation $x^2 - 2x - 5 = 0$.

105. In your own words, describe the process of rationalizing the denominator.

106. The number $\dfrac{\sqrt{5} + 1}{2}$ is called the golden ratio. Research the golden ratio and write a few paragraphs about this number and its applications.

SECTION 10.4

Solving Equations Containing Radical Expressions

1 Solve equations containing one or more radical expressions

32   HM³

An equation that contains a variable expression in a radicand is a **radical equation**.

$\left.\begin{array}{l} \sqrt{x} = 4 \\[4pt] \sqrt{x + 2} = \sqrt{x - 7} \end{array}\right\}$ Radical equations

The following property of equality states that if two numbers are equal, then the squares of the numbers are equal. This property is used to solve radical equations.

Property of Squaring Both Sides of an Equation

If a and b are real numbers and $a = b$, then $a^2 = b^2$.

Solve: $\sqrt{x - 2} - 7 = 0$

Rewrite the equation with the radical on one side of the equation and the constant on the other side.

$$\sqrt{x - 2} - 7 = 0$$
$$\sqrt{x - 2} = 7$$

Square both sides of the equation.

$$(\sqrt{x - 2})^2 = 7^2$$

Solve the resulting equation.

$$x - 2 = 49$$
$$x = 51$$

Check the solution. When both sides of an equation are squared, the resulting equation may have a solution that is not a solution of the original equation.

Check:
$$\begin{array}{c|c} \sqrt{x - 2} - 7 = 0 & \\ \hline \sqrt{51 - 2} - 7 & 0 \\ \sqrt{49} - 7 & 0 \\ \sqrt{7^2} - 7 & 0 \\ 7 - 7 & 0 \\ 0 = 0 \end{array}$$

The solution is 51.

Example 1   Solve: $\sqrt{3x} + 2 = 5$

Solution $\sqrt{3x} + 2 = 5$
$\sqrt{3x} = 3$ ▶ Rewrite the equation so that the radical is alone on one side of the equation.

$(\sqrt{3x})^2 = 3^2$ ▶ Square both sides of the equation.
$3x = 9$ ▶ Solve for x.
$x = 3$

Check:
$$\begin{array}{c|c} \sqrt{3x} + 2 = 5 & \\ \hline \sqrt{3 \cdot 3} + 2 & 5 \\ \sqrt{3^2} + 2 & 5 \\ 3 + 2 & 5 \\ 5 = 5 \end{array}$$

▶ Both sides of the equation were squared. The solution must be checked.

▶ This is a true equation. The solution checks.

The solution is 3.

Problem 1   Solve: $\sqrt{4x} + 3 = 7$

Solution   See page S23.   4

Example 2   Solve.   A. $0 = 3 - \sqrt{2x - 3}$ B. $\sqrt{2x - 5} + 3 = 0$

Solution   A.
$$0 = 3 - \sqrt{2x - 3}$$
$$\sqrt{2x - 3} = 3$$

▶ Rewrite the equation so that the radical is alone on one side of the equation.

$$(\sqrt{2x - 3})^2 = 3^2$$
$$2x - 3 = 9$$
$$2x = 12$$
$$x = 6$$

▶ Square both sides of the equation.

Check

$$0 = 3 - \sqrt{2x - 3}$$

0	$3 - \sqrt{2 \cdot 6 - 3}$
0	$3 - \sqrt{12 - 3}$
0	$3 - \sqrt{9}$
0	$3 - \sqrt{3^2}$
0	$3 - 3$
$0 = 0$	

▶ This is a true equation. The solution checks.

The solution is 6.

B.
$$\sqrt{2x - 5} + 3 = 0$$
$$\sqrt{2x - 5} = -3$$

▶ Rewrite the equation so that the radical is alone on one side of the equation.

$$(\sqrt{2x - 5})^2 = (-3)^2$$
$$2x - 5 = 9$$
$$2x = 14$$
$$x = 7$$

▶ Square each side of the equation.
▶ Solve for x.

Check

$$\sqrt{2x - 5} + 3 = 0$$

$\sqrt{2 \cdot 7 - 5} + 3$	0
$\sqrt{14 - 5} + 3$	0
$\sqrt{9} + 3$	0
$3 + 3$	0
$6 \neq 0$	

▶ This is not a true equation. The solution does not check.

There is no solution.

Problem 2   Solve.   A. $\sqrt{3x - 2} - 5 = 0$ B. $\sqrt{4x - 7} + 5 = 0$

Solution   See page S23.   A. 9   B. No solution

The following example illustrates the procedure for solving a radical equation containing two radical expressions. Note that the process of squaring both sides of the equation is performed twice.

⟶ Solve: $\sqrt{5+x} + \sqrt{x} = 5$

Solve for one of the radical expressions.
Square each side.

Recall that $(a-b)^2 = a^2 - 2ab + b^2$.

Simplify.

This is still a radical equation.

Square each side.

$$\sqrt{5+x} + \sqrt{x} = 5$$
$$\sqrt{5+x} = 5 - \sqrt{x}$$
$$(\sqrt{5+x})^2 = (5 - \sqrt{x})^2$$
$$5 + x = 25 - 10\sqrt{x} + x$$
$$-20 = -10\sqrt{x}$$
$$2 = \sqrt{x}$$
$$2^2 = (\sqrt{x})^2$$
$$4 = x$$

4 checks as the solution.   The solution is 4.

Example 3   Solve: $\sqrt{x} - \sqrt{x-5} = 1$

Solution
$$\sqrt{x} - \sqrt{x-5} = 1$$
$$\sqrt{x} = 1 + \sqrt{x-5}$$
$$(\sqrt{x})^2 = (1 + \sqrt{x-5})^2$$
$$x = 1 + 2\sqrt{x-5} + (x-5)$$
$$4 = 2\sqrt{x-5}$$
$$2 = \sqrt{x-5}$$

$$2^2 = (\sqrt{x-5})^2$$
$$4 = x - 5$$
$$9 = x$$

▶ Solve for one of the radical expressions.
▶ Square each side.
▶ Simplify.

▶ This is a radical equation.
▶ Square each side.
▶ Simplify.

Check
$$\sqrt{x} - \sqrt{x-5} = 1$$

$\sqrt{9} - \sqrt{9-5}$	1
$3 - \sqrt{4}$	1
$3 - 2$	1
$1 = 1$	

The solution is 9.

Problem 3   Solve: $\sqrt{x} + \sqrt{x+9} = 9$

Solution   See page S23.   16

---

2   ## Application problems

A right triangle contains one 90° angle. The side opposite the 90° angle is called the **hypotenuse**. The other two sides are called **legs**.

The angles in a right triangle are usually labeled with the capital letters A, B, and C, with C reserved for the right angle. The side opposite angle A is side a, the side opposite angle B is side b, and c is the hypotenuse.

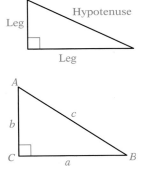

The Greek mathematician Pythagoras is generally credited with the discovery that the square of the hypotenuse of a right triangle is equal to the sum of the squares of the two legs. This is called the **Pythagorean Theorem.**

The figure at the right is a right triangle with legs measuring 3 units and 4 units and a hypotenuse measuring 5 units. Each side of the triangle is also the side of a square. The number of square units in the area of the largest square is equal to the sum of the numbers of square units in the areas of the smaller squares.

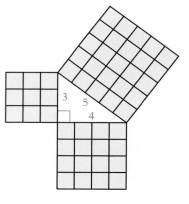

Square of the hypotenuse	=	Sum of the squares of the two legs

$$5^2 = 3^2 + 4^2$$
$$25 = 9 + 16$$
$$25 = 25$$

Pythagorean Theorem

If a and b are the lengths of the legs of a right triangle and c is the length of the hypotenuse, then $c^2 = a^2 + b^2$.

If the lengths of two sides of a right triangle are known, the Pythagorean Theorem can be used to find the length of the third side.

The Pythagorean Theorem is used to find the hypotenuse when the two legs are known.

$$\text{Hypotenuse} = \sqrt{(\text{leg})^2 + (\text{leg})^2}$$
$$c = \sqrt{a^2 + b^2}$$
$$c = \sqrt{(5)^2 + (12)^2}$$
$$c = \sqrt{25 + 144}$$
$$c = \sqrt{169}$$
$$c = 13$$

The Pythagorean Theorem is used to find the length of a leg when one leg and the hypotenuse are known.

$$\text{Leg} = \sqrt{(\text{hypotenuse})^2 - (\text{leg})^2}$$
$$a = \sqrt{c^2 - b^2}$$
$$a = \sqrt{(25)^2 - (20)^2}$$
$$a = \sqrt{625 - 400}$$
$$a = \sqrt{225}$$
$$a = 15$$

Example 4 and Problem 4 illustrate the use of the Pythagorean Theorem. Example 5 and Problem 5 illustrate other applications of radical equations.

Example 4   A guy wire is attached to a point 22 m above the ground on a telephone pole that is perpendicular to the ground. The wire is anchored to the ground at a point 9 m from the base of the pole. Find the length of the guy wire. Round to the nearest hundredth.

Strategy   To find the length of the guy wire, use the Pythagorean Theorem. One leg is the distance from the bottom of the wire to the base of the telephone pole. The other leg is the distance from the top of the wire to the base of the telephone pole. The guy wire is the hypotenuse. Solve the Pythagorean Theorem for the hypotenuse.

Solution $c = \sqrt{a^2 + b^2}$

$c = \sqrt{(22)^2 + (9)^2}$

$c = \sqrt{484 + 81}$

$c = \sqrt{565}$

$c \approx 23.77$

The guy wire has a length of 23.77 m.

Problem 4   A ladder 12 ft long is resting against a building. How high on the building will the ladder reach when the bottom of the ladder is 5 ft from the building? Round to the nearest hundredth.

Solution   See page S24.   10.91 ft

Example 5   How far would a submarine periscope have to be above the water for the lookout to locate a ship 5 mi away? The equation for the distance in miles that the lookout can see is $d = \sqrt{1.5h}$, where h is the height in feet above the surface of the water. Round to the nearest hundredth.

Strategy   To find the height above water, replace d in the equation with the given value. Then solve for h.

Solution $d = \sqrt{1.5h}$

$5 = \sqrt{1.5h}$

$5^2 = (\sqrt{1.5h})^2$

$25 = 1.5h$

$\dfrac{25}{1.5} = h$

$16.67 \approx h$

The periscope must be 16.67 ft above the water.

Problem 5   Find the length of a pendulum that makes one swing in 1.5 s. The equation for the time for one swing is $T = 2\pi\sqrt{\dfrac{L}{32}}$, where T is the time in seconds and L is the length in feet. Round to the nearest hundredth.

Solution   See page S24.   1.82 ft

CONCEPT REVIEW 10.4

Determine whether the statement is always true, sometimes true, or never true.

1. A radical equation is an equation that contains a radical.   Sometimes true

2. We can square both sides of an equation without changing the solutions of the equation.   Sometimes true

3. We use the Property of Squaring Both Sides of an Equation in order to eliminate a radical expression from an equation.   Always true

4. The first step in solving a radical equation is to square both sides of the equation.
   Sometimes true

5. Suppose $a^2 = b^2$. Then $a = b$.   Sometimes true

6. The Pythagorean Theorem is used to find the length of a side of a triangle.
   Sometimes true

EXERCISES 10.4

1 1. Which of the following equations are radical equations?
   a. $8 = \sqrt{5} + x$
   b. $\sqrt{x - 7} = 9$
   c. $\sqrt{x} + 4 = 6$
   d. $12 = \sqrt{3} x$
   b and c

2. What does the Property of Squaring Both Sides of an Equation state?

Solve and check.

3. $\sqrt{x} = 5$ 25

4. $\sqrt{y} = 7$ 49

5. $\sqrt{a} = 12$ 144

6. $\sqrt{a} = 9$ 81

7. $\sqrt{5x} = 5$ 5

8. $\sqrt{3x} = 4$ $\frac{16}{3}$

9. $\sqrt{4x} = 8$ 16

10. $\sqrt{6x} = 3$ $\frac{3}{2}$

11. $\sqrt{2x} - 4 = 0$ 8

12. $3 - \sqrt{5x} = 0$ $\frac{9}{5}$

13. $\sqrt{4x + 5} = 2$
    No solution

14. $\sqrt{3x + 9} = 4$
    No solution

15. $\sqrt{3x - 2} = 4$ 6

16. $\sqrt{5x + 6} = 1$ -1

17. $\sqrt{2x + 1} = 7$ 24

18. $\sqrt{5x + 4} = 3$ 1

19. $0 = 2 - \sqrt{3 - x}$
    -1

20. $0 = 5 - \sqrt{10 + x}$ 15

21. $\sqrt{5x + 2} = 0$ $-\frac{2}{5}$

22. $\sqrt{3x - 7} = 0$ $\frac{7}{3}$

23. $\sqrt{3x} - 6 = -4$ $\frac{4}{3}$

24. $\sqrt{5x + 8} = 23$ 45

25. $0 = \sqrt{3x - 9} - 6$
    15

26. $0 = \sqrt{2x + 7} - 3$ 1

27. $\sqrt{5x - 1} = \sqrt{3x + 9}$ 5

28. $\sqrt{3x + 4} = \sqrt{12x - 14}$ 2

29. $\sqrt{5x - 3} = \sqrt{4x - 2}$ 1

30. $\sqrt{5x - 9} = \sqrt{2x - 3}$ 2

31. $\sqrt{x^2 - 5x + 6} = \sqrt{x^2 - 8x + 9}$ 1

32. $\sqrt{x^2 - 2x + 4} = \sqrt{x^2 + 5x - 12}$ $\frac{16}{7}$

33. $\sqrt{x} = \sqrt{x + 3} - 1$ 1

34. $\sqrt{x + 5} = \sqrt{x} + 1$ 4

35. $\sqrt{2x + 5} = 5 - \sqrt{2x}$ 2

36. $\sqrt{2x} + \sqrt{2x + 9} = 9$ 8

37. $\sqrt{3x} - \sqrt{3x + 7} = 1$ No solution

38. $\sqrt{x} - \sqrt{x + 9} = 1$ No solution

2 Solve. Round to the nearest hundredth.

39. *Integer Problem*   Five added to the square root of the product of four and a number is equal to seven. Find the number.   1

40. *Integer Problem*   The product of a number and the square root of three is equal to the square root of twenty-seven. Find the number.   3

41. *Integer Problem*   Two added to the square root of the sum of a number and five is equal to six. Find the number.   11

42. *Integer Problem*   The product of a number and the square root of seven is equal to the square root of twenty-eight. Find the number.   2

43. What does the Pythagorean Theorem state?

44. Label the right triangle shown at the right. Include the right angle symbol, the three angles, the two legs, and the hypotenuse.

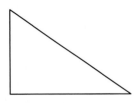

45. *Geometry*   The two legs of a right triangle measure 5 cm and 9 cm. Find the length of the hypotenuse.   10.30 cm

46. *Geometry*   The two legs of a right triangle measure 8 in. and 4 in. Find the length of the hypotenuse.   8.94 in.

47. *Geometry*   The hypotenuse of a right triangle measures 12 ft. One leg of the triangle measures 7 ft. Find the length of the other leg of the triangle.   9.75 ft

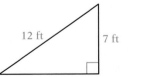

48. *Geometry*   The hypotenuse of a right triangle measures 20 cm. One leg of the triangle measures 16 cm. Find the length of the other leg of the triangle.   12 cm

49. *Geometry*   The diagonal of a rectangle is a line drawn from one vertex to the opposite vertex. Find the length of the diagonal in the rectangle shown at the right. Round to the nearest tenth.   12.1 mi

50. *Education*   One method used to "curve" the grades on an exam is to use the formula $R = 10\sqrt{O}$, where R is the revised score and O is the original score. Use this formula to find the original score on an exam that has a revised score of 75. Round to the nearest whole number.   56

51. *Physics*   A formula used in the study of shallow-water wave motion is $C = \sqrt{32H}$, where C is the wave velocity in feet per second and H is the depth in feet. Use this formula to find the depth of the water when the wave velocity is 20 ft/s.   12.5 ft

52. *Sports* The infield of a baseball diamond is a square. The distance between successive bases is 90 ft. The pitcher's mound is on the diagonal between home plate and second base at a distance of 60.5 ft from home plate. Is the pitcher's mound more or less than halfway between home plate and second base?   Less than halfway

53. *Sports* The infield of a softball diamond is a square. The distance between successive bases is 60 ft. The pitcher's mound is on the diagonal between home plate and second base at a distance of 46 ft from home plate. Is the pitcher's mound more or less than halfway between home plate and second base?   More than halfway

54. *Communications* Marta Lightfoot leaves a dock in her sailboat and sails 2.5 mi due east. She then tacks and sails 4 mi due north. The walkie-talkie Marta has on board has a range of 5 mi. Will she be able to call a friend on the dock from her location using the walkie-talkie?   Yes

55. *Navigation* How far would a submarine periscope have to be above the water for the lookout to locate a ship 4 mi away? The equation for the distance in miles that the lookout can see is $d = \sqrt{1.5h}$, where h is the height in feet above the surface of the water.   10.67 ft

56. *Navigation* How far would a submarine periscope have to be above the water for the lookout to locate a ship 7 mi away? The equation for the distance in miles that the lookout can see is $d = \sqrt{1.5h}$, where h is the height in feet above the surface of the water.   32.67 ft

57. *Home Maintenance* Rick Wyman needs to clean the gutters of his home. The gutters are 24 ft above the ground. For safety, the distance a ladder reaches up a wall should be four times the distance from the bottom of the ladder to the base of the side of the house. Therefore, the ladder must be 6 ft from the base of the house. Will a 25-foot ladder be long enough to reach the gutters?   Yes

58. *Physics* The speed of a child riding a merry-go-round at a carnival is given by the equation $v = \sqrt{12r}$, where v is the speed in feet per second and r is the distance in feet from the center of the merry-go-round to the rider. If a child is moving at 15 ft/s, how far is the child from the center of the merry-go-round?   18.75 ft

59. *Physics* Find the length of a pendulum that makes one swing in 3 s. The equation for the time of one swing is $T = 2\pi\sqrt{\dfrac{L}{32}}$, where T is the time in seconds and L is the length in feet.   7.30 ft

60. *Physics* Find the length of a pendulum that makes one swing in 2 s. The equation for the time of one swing is $T = 2\pi\sqrt{\dfrac{L}{32}}$, where T is the time in seconds and L is the length in feet.   3.24 ft

61. *Parks*   An L-shaped sidewalk from the parking lot to a memorial is shown in the figure at the right. The distance directly across the grass to the memorial is 650 ft. The distance to the corner is 600 ft. Find the distance from the corner to the memorial.   250 ft

62. *Aviation*   A commuter plane leaves an airport traveling due south at 400 mph. Another plane leaving at the same time travels due east at 300 mph. Find the distance between the two planes after 2 h.   1000 mi

63. *Physics*   A stone is dropped from a bridge and hits the water 2 s later. How high is the bridge? The equation for the distance an object falls in T seconds is $T = \sqrt{\dfrac{d}{16}}$, where d is the distance in feet.   64 ft

64. *Physics*   A stone is dropped into a mine shaft and hits the bottom 3.5 s later. How deep is the mine shaft? The equation for the distance an object falls in T seconds is $T = \sqrt{\dfrac{d}{16}}$, where d is the distance in feet.   196 ft

65. *Television*   The measure of a television screen is given by the length of a diagonal across the screen. A 36-inch television has a width of 28.8 in. Find the height of the screen.   21.6 in.

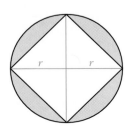

66. *Television*   The measure of a television screen is given by the length of a diagonal across the screen. A 33-inch big-screen television has a width of 26.4 in. Find the height of the screen.   19.8 in.

APPLYING CONCEPTS 10.4

Solve.

67. $\sqrt{\dfrac{5y + 2}{3}} = 3$ 5

68. $\sqrt{\dfrac{3y}{5}} - 1 = 2$ 15

69. $\sqrt{9x^2 + 49} + 1 = 3x + 2$ 8

[C] 70. *Geometry*   In the coordinate plane, a triangle is formed by drawing lines between the points (0, 0) and (5, 0), (5, 0) and (5, 12), and (5, 12) and (0, 0). Find the number of units in the perimeter of the triangle.   30 units

[C] 71. *Geometry*   The hypotenuse of a right triangle is $5\sqrt{2}$ cm, and one leg is $4\sqrt{2}$ cm.
   a. Find the perimeter of the triangle.   b. Find the area of the triangle.
      $12\sqrt{2}$ cm   12 cm²

[C] 72. *Geometry*   Write an expression in factored form for the shaded region in the diagram at the right. $r^2(\pi - 2)$

[C] **73.** *Geometry*   A circular fountain is being designed for a triangular plaza in a cultural center. The fountain is placed so that each side of the triangle touches the fountain as shown in the diagram at the right. Find the area of the fountain. The formula for the radius of the circle is given by

$$r = \sqrt{\frac{(s-a)(s-b)(s-c)}{s}}$$

where $s = \frac{1}{2}(a + b + c)$ and a, b, and c are the lengths of the sides of the tri-

angle. Round to the nearest hundredth.   244.78 ft²

74. Can the Pythagorean Theorem be used to find the length of side c of the triangle at the right? If so, determine c. If not, explain why the theorem cannot be used.

75. What is a Pythagorean triple? Provide at least three examples of Pythagorean triples.

76. Complete the statement using the symbol $<$, $=$, or $>$. Explain how you determined which symbol to use.

a. For an acute triangle with side c the longest side, $a^2 + b^2 \_\_ c^2$.

b. For a right triangle with side c the longest side, $a^2 + b^2 \_\_ c^2$.

c. For an obtuse triangle with side c the longest side, $a^2 + b^2 \_\_ c^2$.

Focus on Problem Solving

Deductive Reasoning

Deductive reasoning uses a rule or statement of fact to reach a conclusion. In the section Equations Containing Fractions in the "Algebraic Fractions" chapter, we established the rule that if two angles of one triangle are equal to two angles of another triangle, then the two triangles are similar. Thus any time we establish this fact about two triangles, we know that the triangles are similar. Below are two examples of deductive reasoning.

Given that △△△ = ◇◇◇◇ and ◇◇◇◇ = ÓÓ, then △△△△△△ is equivalent to how many Ós?

Because 3 △s = 4 ◇s and 4 ◇s = 2 Ós, 3 △s = 2 Ós.

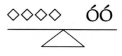

6 △s is twice 3 △s. We need to find twice 2 Ós, which is 4 Ós.

Therefore, △△△△△△ = ÓÓÓÓ.

Lomax, Parish, Thorpe, and Wong are neighbors. Each drives a different type of vehicle: a compact car, a sedan, a sports car, or a station wagon. From the following statements, determine which type of vehicle each of the neighbors drives.

1. Although the vehicle owned by Lomax has more mileage on it than does either the sedan or the sports car, it does not have the highest mileage of all four cars. (Use X1 in the chart below to eliminate whatever possibilities this statement enables you to rule out.)

2. Wong and the owner of the sports car live on one side of the street, and Thorpe and the owner of the compact car live on the other side of the street. (Use X2 to eliminate possibilities that this statement rules out.)

3. Thorpe owns the vehicle with the most mileage on it. (Use X3 to eliminate possibilities that this statement rules out.)

LOOK CLOSELY

To use the chart to solve this problem, write an X in a box to indicate that a possibility has been eliminated. Write a √ to show that a match has been found. When a row or column has 3 X's, a √ is written in the remaining open box in that row or column of the chart.

	Compact	Sedan	Sports Car	Wagon
Lomax	√	X1	X1	X2
Parish	X2	X2	√	X2
Thorpe	X2	X3	X2	√
Wong	X2		X2	

Lomax drives the compact car, Parish drives the sports car, Thorpe drives the station wagon, and Wong drives the sedan.

4. Given that ‡‡ = ••••• and ••••• = ΛΛ, then ‡‡‡‡‡ = how many Λs?

5. Given that □□□□□□ = ÓÓÓÓ and ÓÓÓÓ = ÎÎ, then □□□ = how many Îs?

6. Given that ◻◻◻◻ = ΩΩΩ and ΩΩΩ = ΔΔ, then ΔΔΔΔ = how many ◻s?

7. Given that ¥¥¥¥ = §§ and §§ = ÂÂÂ, then ÂÂÂÂÂÂ = how many ¥s?

8. Anna, Kay, Megan, and Nicole decide to travel together during spring break, but they need to find a destination where each of them will be able to participate in her favorite sport (golf, horseback riding, sailing, or tennis). From the following statements, determine the favorite sport of each student.

   a. Anna and the student whose favorite sport is sailing both like to swim, whereas Nicole and the student whose favorite sport is tennis would prefer to scuba dive.

   b. Megan and the student whose favorite sport is sailing are roommates. Nicole and the student whose favorite sport is golf both live in a single.

9. Chang, Nick, Pablo, and Saul all take different forms of transportation (bus, car, subway, or taxi) from the office to the airport. From the following statements, determine which form of transportation each takes.

   a. Chang spent more on transportation than the fellow who took the bus but less than the fellow who took the taxi.

   b. Pablo, who did not travel by bus and who spent the least on transportation, arrived at the airport after Nick but before the fellow who took the subway.

   c. Saul spent less on transportation than either Chang or Nick.

Projects and Group Activities

Mean and Standard Deviation

An automotive engineer tests the miles-per-gallon ratings of 15 cars and records the results as follows:

25   22   21   27   25   35   29   31   25   26   21   39   34   32   28

The **mean** of the data is the sum of the measurements divided by the number of measurements. The symbol for the mean is $\bar{x}$.

$$\text{Mean} = \bar{x} = \frac{\text{sum of all data values}}{\text{number of data values}}$$

To find the mean for the data above, add the numbers and then divide by 15.

$$\bar{x} = \frac{25 + 22 + 21 + 27 + 25 + 35 + 29 + 31 + 25 + 26 + 21 + 39 + 34 + 32 + 28}{15}$$

$$= \frac{420}{15} = 28$$

The mean number of miles per gallon for the 15 cars tested was 28 mi/gal.

The mean is one of the most frequently computed averages. It is the one that is commonly used to calculate a student's performance in a class.

➡ The scores for a history student on 5 tests were 78, 82, 91, 87, and 93. What was the mean score for this student?

To find the mean, add the numbers. Then divide by 5.

$$\bar{x} = \frac{78 + 82 + 91 + 87 + 93}{5}$$

$$= \frac{431}{5} = 86.2$$

The mean score for the history student was 86.2.   ⬅

Consider two students, each of whom has taken 5 exams.

Scores for Student A

84	86	83	85	87

Scores for Student B

90	75	94	68	98

$$\bar{x} = \frac{84 + 86 + 83 + 85 + 87}{5} = \frac{425}{5} = 85 \qquad \bar{x} = \frac{90 + 75 + 94 + 68 + 98}{5} = \frac{425}{5} = 85$$

The mean for Student A is 85.   The mean for Student B is 85.

For each of these students, the mean (average) for the 5 exams is 85. However, Student A has a more consistent record of scores than Student B. One way to measure the consistency, or "clustering" near the mean, of data is to use the **standard deviation.**

To calculate the standard deviation:

Step 1. Sum the squares of the differences between each value of the data and the mean.

Step 2. Divide the result in Step 1 by the number of items in the set of data.

Step 3. Take the square root of the result in Step 2.

The calculation for Student A is shown at the right.

Step 1:

x	$x - \bar{x}$	$(x - \bar{x})^2$
84	$84 - 85$	$(-1)^2 = 1$
86	$86 - 85$	$1^2 = 1$
83	$83 - 85$	$(-2)^2 = 4$
85	$85 - 85$	$0^2 = 0$
87	$87 - 85$	$2^2 = 4$
		Total $= 10$

Step 2: $\frac{10}{5} = 2$

The symbol for standard deviation is the lower case Greek letter *sigma*, σ.

Step 3: $\sigma = \sqrt{2} \approx 1.414$

The standard deviation for Student A's scores is approximately 1.414.

Following a similar procedure for Student B shows that the standard deviation for Student B's scores is approximately 11.524. Because the standard deviation of Student B's scores is greater than that of Student A's scores ($11.524 > 1.414$), Student B's scores are not as consistent as those of Student A.

1. The weights in ounces of 6 newborn infants were recorded by a hospital. The weights were 96, 105, 84, 90, 102, and 99. Find the standard deviation of the weights.

2. The numbers of rooms occupied in a hotel on 6 consecutive days were 234, 321, 222, 246, 312, and 396. Find the standard deviation of the numbers of rooms occupied.

3. Seven coins were tossed 100 times. The numbers of heads recorded for each coin were 56, 63, 49, 50, 48, 53, and 52. Find the standard deviation of the numbers of heads.

4. The temperatures for 11 consecutive days at a desert resort were 95°, 98°, 98°, 104°, 97°, 100°, 96°, 97°, 108°, 93°, and 104°. For the same days, temperatures in Antarctica were 27°, 28°, 28°, 30°, 28°, 27°, 30°, 25°, 24°, 26°, and 21°. Which location has the greater standard deviation of temperatures?

5. The scores for 5 college basketball games were 56, 68, 60, 72, and 64. The scores for 5 professional basketball games were 106, 118, 110, 122, and 114. Which scores have the greater standard deviation?

6. The weights in pounds of the 5-man front line of a college football team are 210, 245, 220, 230, and 225. Find the standard deviation of the weights.

7. One student received test scores of 85, 92, 86, and 89. A second student received scores of 90, 97, 91, and 94 (exactly 5 points more on each test). Are the means of the two students the same? If not, what is the relationship between the means of the two students? Are the standard deviations of the scores of the two students the same? If not, what is the relationship between the standard deviations of the scores of the two students?

8. Grade-point average (GPA) is a *weighted* mean. It is called a weighted mean because a grade in a 5-unit course has more influence on your GPA than a grade in a 2-unit course. GPA is calculated by multiplying the numerical equivalent of each grade by the number of units, adding those products, and then dividing by the total number of units. Calculate your GPA for the last quarter or semester.

9. If you average 40 mph for 1 h and then 50 mph for 1 h, is your average speed $\frac{40 + 50}{2} = 45$ mph? Why or why not?

10. A company is negotiating with its employees the terms of a raise in salary. One proposal would add $500 a year to each employee's salary. The second proposal would give each employee a 4% raise. Explain how each of these proposals would affect the current mean and standard deviation of salaries for the company.

Distance to the Horizon

In Section 4 of this chapter, we used the formula $d = \sqrt{1.5h}$ to calculate the approximate distance d (in miles) that a person could see who uses a periscope h feet above the water. That formula is derived by using the Pythagorean Theorem.

Consider the diagram (not to scale) at the right, which shows Earth as a sphere and the periscope extending h feet above the surface. From geometry, because AB is tangent to the circle and OA is a radius, triangle AOB is a right triangle. Therefore,

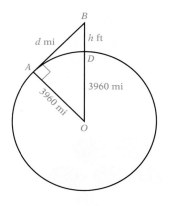

$$(OA)^2 + (AB)^2 = (OB)^2$$

Substituting into this formula, we have

$$3960^2 + d^2 = \left(3960 + \frac{h}{5280}\right)^2$$

▶ Because h is in feet, $\frac{h}{5280}$ is in miles.

$$3960^2 + d^2 = 3960^2 + \frac{2 \cdot 3960}{5280}h + \left(\frac{h}{5280}\right)^2$$

$$d^2 = \frac{3}{2}h + \left(\frac{h}{5280}\right)^2$$

$$d = \sqrt{\frac{3}{2}h + \left(\frac{h}{5280}\right)^2}$$

At this point, an assumption is made that $\sqrt{\frac{3}{2}h + \left(\frac{h}{5280}\right)^2} \approx \sqrt{1.5h}$, where we have written $\frac{3}{2}$ as 1.5. Thus $d \approx \sqrt{1.5h}$ is used to approximate the distance that can be seen using a periscope h feet above the water.

1. Write a paragraph that justifies the assumption that

$$\sqrt{\frac{3}{2}h + \left(\frac{h}{5280}\right)^2} \approx \sqrt{1.5h}$$

(*Suggestion:* Evaluate each expression for various values of h. Because h is the height of a periscope above water, it is unlikely that $h > 25$ ft.)

2. The distance d is the distance from the top of the periscope to A. The distance along the surface of the water is given by arc AD. This distance, D, can be approximated by the equation

$$D \approx \sqrt{1.5h} + 0.306186\left(\sqrt{\frac{h}{5280}}\right)^3$$

Using this formula, calculate D when $h = 10$.

Expressway On-Ramp Curves

Highway engineers design expressway on-ramps with both efficiency and safety in mind. An on-ramp cannot be built with too sharp a curve, or the speed at which drivers take the curve will cause them to skid off the road. However, an on-ramp built with too wide a curve requires more building material, takes longer to travel, and uses more land. The following formula states the relationship between the maximum speed at which a car can travel around a curve without skidding: $v = \sqrt{2.5r}$. In this formula, v is speed in miles per hour, and r is the radius, in feet, of an unbanked curve.

1. Use a graphing calculator to graph this equation. Use a window of Xmin = 0, Xmax = 2000, Ymin = 0, Ymax = 100. What do the values used for Xmin, Xmax, Ymin, and Ymax represent?

2. As the radius of the curve increases, does the maximum safe speed increase or decrease? Explain your answer on the basis of the graph of the equation.

3. Use the graph to approximate the maximum safe speed when the radius of the curve is 100 ft. Round to the nearest whole number.

4. Use the graph to approximate the radius of the curve for which the maximum safe speed is 40 mph. Round to the nearest whole number.

5. Arie Luyendyk won the Indianapolis 500 in 1997 driving at an average speed of 145.827 mph. At this speed, should the radius of an unbanked curve be more or less than 1 mi?

Chapter Summary

Key Words

A *square root* of a positive number x is a number whose square is x. The square root of a negative number is not a real number. (Objective 10.1.1)

A square root of 25 is 5 because $5^2 = 25$.

A square root of 25 is -5 because $(-5)^2 = 25$.

$\sqrt{-9}$ is not a real number.

The *principal square root* of a number is the positive square root. The symbol $\sqrt{}$ is called a *radical sign* and is used to indicate the principal square root of a number. The negative square root of a number is indicated by placing a negative sign in front of the radical. The *radicand* is the expression under the radical symbol. (Objective 10.1.1)

$\sqrt{25} = 5$

$-\sqrt{25} = -5$

In the expression $\sqrt{25}$, 25 is the radicand.

The square of an integer is a *perfect square*. If a number is not a perfect square, its square root can only be approximated. Such numbers are *irrational numbers*. Their decimal representations never terminate or repeat. (Objective 10.1.1)

$2^2 = 4$, $3^2 = 9$, $4^2 = 16$, $5^2 = 25$, $6^2 = 36$, . . .

4, 9, 16, 25, 36, . . . are perfect squares.

5 is not a perfect square. $\sqrt{5}$ is an irrational number.

Conjugates are expressions with two terms that differ only in the sign of the second term. The expressions $a + b$ and $a - b$ are conjugates. (Objective 10.3.1)

$3 + \sqrt{7}$ and $3 - \sqrt{7}$ are conjugates.

$\sqrt{x} + 2$ and $\sqrt{x} - 2$ are conjugates.

A *radical equation* is an equation that contains a variable expression in a radicand.   (Objective 10.4.1)

$\sqrt{2x} + 8 = 12$ is a radical equation.

$2x + \sqrt{8} = 12$ is not a radical equation.

Essential Rules and Procedures

The Product Property of Square Roots
If a and b are positive real numbers, then $\sqrt{ab} = \sqrt{a} \cdot \sqrt{b}$.
(Objective 10.1.1)

$\sqrt{12} = \sqrt{4 \cdot 3} = \sqrt{4}\,\sqrt{3} = 2\sqrt{3}$

Adding and Subtracting Radical Expressions
The Distributive Property is used to simplify the sum or difference of like radical expressions.   (Objective 10.2.1)

$16\sqrt{3x} - 4\sqrt{3x} = (16 - 4)\sqrt{3x} = 12\sqrt{3x}$

Multiplying Radical Expressions
The Product Property of Square Roots is used to multiply radical expressions.

$\sqrt{5x}\,\sqrt{7y} = \sqrt{5x \cdot 7y} = \sqrt{35xy}$

Use the Distributive Property to remove parentheses.

$\sqrt{y}(2 + \sqrt{3x}) = 2\sqrt{y} + \sqrt{3xy}$

Use the FOIL method to multiply radical expressions with two terms.   (Objective 10.3.1)

$(5 - \sqrt{x})(11 + \sqrt{x})$
$= 55 + 5\sqrt{x} - 11\sqrt{x} - (\sqrt{x})^2$
$= 55 - 6\sqrt{x} - x$

The Quotient Property of Square Roots
If a and b are positive real numbers, then $\sqrt{\dfrac{a}{b}} = \dfrac{\sqrt{a}}{\sqrt{b}}$.
(Objective 10.3.2)

$\sqrt{\dfrac{9x^2}{y^8}} = \dfrac{\sqrt{9x^2}}{\sqrt{y^8}} = \dfrac{3x}{y^4}$

Dividing Radical Expressions
The Quotient Property of Square Roots is used to divide radical expressions.   (Objective 10.3.2)

$\dfrac{\sqrt{3x^5y}}{\sqrt{75xy^3}} = \sqrt{\dfrac{3x^5y}{75xy^3}} = \sqrt{\dfrac{x^4}{25y^2}} = \dfrac{\sqrt{x^4}}{\sqrt{25y^2}} = \dfrac{x^2}{5y}$

Rationalizing the Denominator
A radical is not in simplest form if there is a radical in the denominator. The procedure used to remove a radical from the denominator is called rationalizing the denominator.
(Objective 10.3.2)

$\dfrac{5}{\sqrt{7}} = \dfrac{5}{\sqrt{7}} \cdot \dfrac{\sqrt{7}}{\sqrt{7}} = \dfrac{5\sqrt{7}}{7}$

Radical Expressions in Simplest Form
A radical expression is in simplest form if:
1. The radicand contains no factor greater than 1 that is a perfect square.
2. There is no fraction under the radical sign.
3. There is no radical in the denominator of a fraction.
(Objective 10.3.2)

$\sqrt{12}$, $\sqrt{\dfrac{3}{4}}$, and $\dfrac{1}{\sqrt{2}}$ are not in simplest form.

$2\sqrt{3}$, $\dfrac{\sqrt{3}}{2}$, and $\dfrac{\sqrt{2}}{2}$ are in simplest form.

Property of Squaring Both Sides of an Equation
If a and b are real numbers and $a = b$, then $a^2 = b^2$.
(Objective 10.4.1)

$\sqrt{x + 3} = 4$
$(\sqrt{x + 3})^2 = 4^2$
$x + 3 = 16$
$x = 13$

Solving Radical Equations

When an equation contains one radical expression, write the equation with the radical alone on one side of the equation. Square both sides of the equation. Solve for the variable. Whenever both sides of an equation are squared, the solutions must be checked.   (Objective 10.4.1)

$$\sqrt{2x} - 1 = 5$$
$$\sqrt{2x} = 6$$
$$(\sqrt{2x})^2 = 6^2$$
$$2x = 36$$
$$x = 18 \quad \text{The solution checks.}$$

Pythagorean Theorem

If a and b are the lengths of the legs of a right triangle and c is the hypotenuse, then $c^2 = a^2 + b^2$.   (Objective 10.4.2)

Two legs of a right triangle measure 4 cm and 7 cm. To find the length of the hypotenuse, use the equation

$$c = \sqrt{a^2 + b^2}$$
$$c = \sqrt{4^2 + 7^2} = \sqrt{16 + 49} = \sqrt{65}$$

The hypotenuse measures $\sqrt{65}$ cm.

Chapter Review Exercises

1. Subtract: $5\sqrt{3} - 16\sqrt{3}$ $-11\sqrt{3}$

2. Simplify: $\dfrac{2x}{\sqrt{3} - \sqrt{5}}$ $-x\sqrt{3} - x\sqrt{5}$

3. Simplify: $\sqrt{x^2 + 16x + 64}$ $x + 8$

4. Solve: $3 - \sqrt{7x} = 5$ No solution

5. Simplify: $\dfrac{5\sqrt{y} - 2\sqrt{y}}{3\sqrt{y}}$ 1

6. Add: $6\sqrt{7} + \sqrt{7}$ $7\sqrt{7}$

7. Multiply: $(6\sqrt{a} + 5\sqrt{b})(2\sqrt{a} + 3\sqrt{b})$ $12a + 28\sqrt{ab} + 15b$

8. Simplify: $\sqrt{49(x + 3)^4}$ $7x^2 + 42x + 63$

9. Simplify: $2\sqrt{36}$ 12

10. Solve: $\sqrt{b} = 4$ 16

11. Subtract: $9x\sqrt{5} - 5x\sqrt{5}$ $4x\sqrt{5}$

12. Multiply: $(\sqrt{5ab} - \sqrt{7})(\sqrt{5ab} + \sqrt{7})$ $5ab - 7$

13. Solve: $\sqrt{2x + 9} = \sqrt{8x - 9}$ 3

14. Simplify: $\sqrt{35}$ $\sqrt{35}$

15. Add: $2x\sqrt{60x^3y^3} + 3x^2y\sqrt{15xy}$ $7x^2y\sqrt{15xy}$

16. Simplify: $\dfrac{\sqrt{3x^3y}}{\sqrt{27xy^5}}$ $\dfrac{x}{3y^2}$

17. Simplify: $(3\sqrt{x} - \sqrt{y})^2$ $9x - 6\sqrt{xy} + y$

18. Simplify: $\sqrt{(a + 4)^2}$ $a + 4$

19. Simplify: $5\sqrt{48}$ $20\sqrt{3}$

20. Add: $3\sqrt{12x} + 5\sqrt{48x}$ $26\sqrt{3x}$

21. Simplify: $\dfrac{8}{\sqrt{x} - 3}$ $\dfrac{8\sqrt{x} + 24}{x - 9}$

22. Multiply: $\sqrt{6a}(\sqrt{3a} + \sqrt{2a})$ $3a\sqrt{2} + 2a\sqrt{3}$

23. Simplify: $3\sqrt{18a^5b}$ $9a^2\sqrt{2ab}$

24. Simplify: $-3\sqrt{120}$ $-6\sqrt{30}$

25. Subtract: $\sqrt{20a^5b^9} - 2ab^2\sqrt{45a^3b^5}$ $-4a^2b^4\sqrt{5ab}$

26. Simplify: $\dfrac{\sqrt{98x^7y^9}}{\sqrt{2x^3y}}$ $7x^2y^4$

27. Solve: $\sqrt{5x + 1} = \sqrt{20x - 8}$ $\dfrac{3}{5}$

28. Simplify: $\sqrt{c^{18}}$ c^9

29. Simplify: $\sqrt{450}$ $15\sqrt{2}$

30. Simplify: $6a\sqrt{80b} - \sqrt{180a^2b} + 5a\sqrt{b}$ $18a\sqrt{5b} + 5a\sqrt{b}$

31. Simplify: $\dfrac{16}{\sqrt{a}}$ $\dfrac{16\sqrt{a}}{a}$

32. Solve: $6 - \sqrt{2y} = 2$ 8

33. Multiply: $\sqrt{a^3 b^4 c} \ \sqrt{a^7 b^2 c^3}$ $a^5 b^3 c^2$

34. Simplify: $7\sqrt{630}$ $21\sqrt{70}$

35. Simplify: $y\sqrt{24y^6}$ $2y^4\sqrt{6}$

36. Simplify: $\dfrac{\sqrt{250}}{\sqrt{10}}$ 5

37. Solve: $\sqrt{x^2 + 5x + 4} = \sqrt{x^2 + 7x - 6}$ 5

38. Multiply: $(4\sqrt{y} - \sqrt{5})(2\sqrt{y} + 3\sqrt{5})$
$8y + 10\sqrt{5y} - 15$

39. Find the decimal approximation of $\sqrt{9900}$ to the nearest thousandth.   99.499

40. Multiply: $\sqrt{7} \ \sqrt{7}$ 7

41. Simplify: $5x\sqrt{150x^7}$ $25x^4\sqrt{6x}$

42. Simplify:
$2x^2\sqrt{18x^2 y^5} + 6y\sqrt{2x^6 y^3} - 9xy^2\sqrt{8x^4 y}$
$-6x^3 y^2 \sqrt{2y}$

43. Simplify: $\dfrac{\sqrt{54a^3}}{\sqrt{6a}}$ $3a$

44. Simplify: $4\sqrt{250}$ $20\sqrt{10}$

45. Solve: $\sqrt{5x} = 10$ 20

46. Simplify: $\dfrac{3a\sqrt{3} + 2\sqrt{12a^2}}{\sqrt{27}}$ $\dfrac{7a}{3}$

47. Multiply: $\sqrt{2} \ \sqrt{50}$ 10

48. Simplify: $\sqrt{36x^4 y^5}$ $6x^2 y^2 \sqrt{y}$

49. Simplify: $4y\sqrt{243x^{17} y^9}$ $36x^8 y^5 \sqrt{3xy}$

50. Solve: $\sqrt{x + 1} - \sqrt{x - 2} = 1$ 3

51. Simplify: $\sqrt{400}$ 20

52. Simplify: $-4\sqrt{8x} + 7\sqrt{18x} - 3\sqrt{50x}$ $-2\sqrt{2x}$

53. Solve: $0 = \sqrt{10x + 4} - 8$ 6

54. Multiply: $\sqrt{3}(\sqrt{12} - \sqrt{3})$ 3

55. The square root of the sum of two consecutive odd integers is equal to 10. Find the larger integer.   51

56. The weight of an object is related to the object's distance from the surface of the earth. An equation for this relationship is $d = 4000\sqrt{\dfrac{W_0}{W_a}}$, where W_0 is the object's weight on the surface of the earth and W_a is the object's weight at a distance of d miles above the earth's surface. A space explorer weighs 36 lb when 8000 mi above the earth's surface. Find the explorer's weight on the surface of the earth.   144 lb

57. The hypotenuse of a right triangle measures 18 cm. One leg of the triangle measures 11 cm. Find the length of the other leg of the triangle. Round to the nearest hundredth.   14.25 cm

58. A bicycle will overturn if it rounds a corner too sharply or too quickly. The equation for the maximum velocity at which a cyclist can turn a corner without tipping over is given by the equation $v = 4\sqrt{r}$, where v is the velocity of the bicycle in miles per hour and r is the radius of the corner in feet. Find the radius of the sharpest corner that a cyclist can safely turn when riding at a speed of 20 mph.   25 ft

59. A tsunami is a great sea wave produced by underwater earthquakes or volcanic eruption. The velocity of a tsunami as it approaches land is approximated by the equation $v = 3\sqrt{d}$, where v is the velocity in feet per second and d is the depth of the water in feet. Find the depth of the water when the velocity of a tsunami is 30 ft/s.   100 ft

60. A guy wire is attached to a point 25 ft above the ground on a telephone pole that is perpendicular to the ground. The wire is anchored to the ground at a point 8 ft from the base of the pole. Find the length of the guy wire. Round to the nearest hundredth.   26.25 ft

Chapter Test

1. Simplify: $\sqrt{121x^8y^2}$ $11x^4y$

2. Subtract: $5\sqrt{8} - 3\sqrt{50}$ $-5\sqrt{2}$

3. Multiply: $\sqrt{3x^2y}\,\sqrt{6x^2}\,\sqrt{2x}$ $6x^2\sqrt{xy}$

4. Simplify: $\sqrt{45}$ $3\sqrt{5}$

5. Simplify: $\sqrt{72x^7y^2}$ $6x^3y\sqrt{2x}$

6. Simplify: $3\sqrt{8y} - 2\sqrt{72x} + 5\sqrt{18x}$
$6\sqrt{2y} + 3\sqrt{2x}$

7. Multiply: $(\sqrt{y} + 3)(\sqrt{y} + 5)$ $y + 8\sqrt{y} + 15$

8. Simplify: $\dfrac{4}{\sqrt{8}}$ $\sqrt{2}$

9. Simplify: $\dfrac{\sqrt{162}}{\sqrt{2}}$ 9

10. Solve: $\sqrt{5x - 6} = 7$ 11

11. Find the decimal approximation of $\sqrt{500}$ to the nearest thousandth.   22.361

12. Simplify: $\sqrt{32a^5b^{11}}$ $4a^2b^5\sqrt{2ab}$

13. Multiply: $\sqrt{a}(\sqrt{a} - \sqrt{b})$ $a - \sqrt{ab}$

14. Multiply: $\sqrt{8x^3y}\,\sqrt{10xy^4}$ $4x^2y^2\sqrt{5y}$

15. Simplify: $\dfrac{\sqrt{98a^6b^4}}{\sqrt{2a^3b^2}}$ $7ab\sqrt{a}$

16. Solve: $\sqrt{9x} + 3 = 18$ 25

17. Simplify: $\sqrt{192x^{13}y^5}$ $8x^6y^2\sqrt{3xy}$

18. Simplify: $2a\sqrt{2ab^3} + b\sqrt{8a^3b} - 5ab\sqrt{ab}$
$4ab\sqrt{2ab} - 5ab\sqrt{ab}$

19. Multiply: $(\sqrt{a} - 2)(\sqrt{a} + 2)$ $a - 4$

20. Simplify: $\dfrac{3}{2 - \sqrt{5}}$ $-6 - 3\sqrt{5}$

21. Solve: $3 = 8 - \sqrt{5x}$ 5

22. Multiply: $\sqrt{3}(\sqrt{6} - \sqrt{x^2})$ $3\sqrt{2} - x\sqrt{3}$

23. Subtract: $3\sqrt{a} - 9\sqrt{a}$ $-6\sqrt{a}$

24. Simplify: $\sqrt{108}$ $6\sqrt{3}$

25. Find the decimal approximation of $\sqrt{63}$ to the nearest thousandth.   7.937

26. Simplify: $\dfrac{\sqrt{108a^7b^3}}{\sqrt{3a^4b}}$ $6ab\sqrt{a}$

27. Solve: $\sqrt{x} - \sqrt{x + 3} = 1$ No solution

28. The square root of the sum of two consecutive integers is equal to 9. Find the smaller integer.   40

29. Find the length of a pendulum that makes one swing in 2.5 s. The equation for the time of one swing of a pendulum is $T = 2\pi\sqrt{\dfrac{L}{32}}$, where T is the time in seconds and L is the length in feet. Round to the nearest hundredth.   5.07 ft

30. A ladder 10 ft long is resting against a building. How high on the building will the ladder reach when the bottom of the ladder is 2 ft from the building? Round to the nearest hundredth.   9.80 ft

Cumulative Review Exercises

1. Simplify: $\left(\dfrac{2}{3}\right)^2\left(\dfrac{3}{4} - \dfrac{3}{2}\right) + \left(\dfrac{1}{2}\right)^2$ $-\dfrac{1}{12}$

2. Simplify: $-3[x - 2(3 - 2x) - 5x] + 2x$ $2x + 18$

3. Solve: $2x - 4[3x - 2(1 - 3x)] = 2(3 - 4x)$ $\dfrac{1}{13}$

4. Solve: $3(x - 7) \geq 5x - 12$ $x \leq -\dfrac{9}{2}$

5. Find the slope of the line that contains the points whose coordinates are $(2, -5)$ and $(-4, 3)$. $-\dfrac{4}{3}$

6. Find the equation of the line that contains the point whose coordinates are $(-2, -3)$ and has slope $\dfrac{1}{2}$. $y = \dfrac{1}{2}x - 2$

7. Evaluate $f(x) = \dfrac{5}{2}x - 8$ at $x = -4$. -18

8. Graph: $f(x) = -4x + 2$

9. Graph the solution set of $2x + y < -2$.

10. Solve by graphing: $3x - 2y = 8$
$4x + 5y = 3$ $(2, -1)$

11. Solve by substitution: $4x - 3y = 1$
$2x + y = 3$ $(1, 1)$

12. Solve by the addition method: $5x + 4y = 7$
$3x - 2y = 13$ $(3, -2)$

13. Simplify: $(-3x^2y)(-2x^3y^{-4})$ $\dfrac{6x^5}{y^3}$

14. Simplify: $\dfrac{12b^4 - 6b^2 + 2}{-6b^2}$ $-2b^2 + 1 - \dfrac{1}{3b^2}$

15. Factor: $12x^3y^2 - 9x^2y^3$ $3x^2y^2(4x - 3y)$

16. Factor: $9b^2 + 3b - 20$ $(3b + 5)(3b - 4)$

17. Factor: $2a^3 - 16a^2 + 30a$ $2a(a - 3)(a - 5)$

18. Multiply: $\dfrac{3x^3 - 6x^2}{4x^2 + 4x} \cdot \dfrac{3x - 9}{9x^3 - 45x^2 + 54x}$ $\dfrac{1}{4(x + 1)}$

19. Simplify: $\dfrac{1 - \dfrac{2}{x} - \dfrac{15}{x^2}}{1 - \dfrac{9}{x^2}}$ $\dfrac{x - 5}{x - 3}$

20. Subtract: $\dfrac{x + 2}{x - 4} - \dfrac{6}{(x - 4)(x - 3)}$ $\dfrac{x + 3}{x - 3}$

21. Solve: $\dfrac{x}{2x - 5} - 2 = \dfrac{3x}{2x - 5}$ $\dfrac{5}{3}$

22. Simplify: $2\sqrt{27a} - 5\sqrt{49a} + 8\sqrt{48a}$ $38\sqrt{3a} - 35\sqrt{a}$

23. Simplify: $\dfrac{\sqrt{320}}{\sqrt{5}}$ 8

24. Solve: $\sqrt{2x - 3} - 5 = 0$ 14

25. Three-eighths of a number is less than negative twelve. Find the largest integer that satisfies the inequality. -33

26. The selling price of a book is $29.40. The markup rate used by the bookstore is 20% of the cost. Find the cost of the book. $24.50

27. How many ounces of pure water must be added to 40 oz of a 12% salt solution to make a salt solution that is 5% salt? 56 oz

28. The sum of two numbers is twenty-one. Three more than twice the smaller number is equal to the larger. Find the two numbers. 6 and 15

29. A small water pipe takes twice as long to fill a tank as does a larger water pipe. With both pipes open, it takes 16 h to fill the tank. Find the time it would take the small pipe, working alone, to fill the tank.   48 h

30. The square root of the sum of two consecutive integers is equal to 7. Find the smaller integer.   24

A forensic scientist assists police in the investigation of crimes. Chemistry, biology, and mathematics are critical tools for the forensic scientist when analyzing evidence, such as matching the DNA of a suspect to the DNA found at a crime scene.

11

Quadratic Equations

OBJECTIVES

Algebraic Symbolism

The way in which an algebraic expression or equation is written has gone through several stages of development. First there was the *rhetoric*, which was in vogue until the late 13th century. In this method, an expression would be written out in sentences. The word *res* was used to represent an unknown.

Rhetoric: From the additive *res* in the additive *res* results in a square *res*. From the three in an additive *res* comes three additive *res*, and from the subtractive four in the additive *res* comes subtractive four *res*. From three in subtractive four comes subtractive twelve.

Modern: $(x + 3)(x - 4) = x^2 - x - 12$

The second stage was the *syncoptic*, which was a shorthand in which abbreviations were used for words.

Syncoptic: *a* 6 in *b* quad − *c* plano 4 in *b* + *b* cub

Modern: $6ab^2 - 4cb + b^3$

The current modern stage, called the *symbolic* stage, began with the use of exponents rather than words to symbolize exponential expressions. This occurred near the beginning of the 17th century with the publication of the book *La Géométrie* by René Descartes. Modern notation is still evolving as mathematicians continue to search for convenient methods to symbolize concepts.

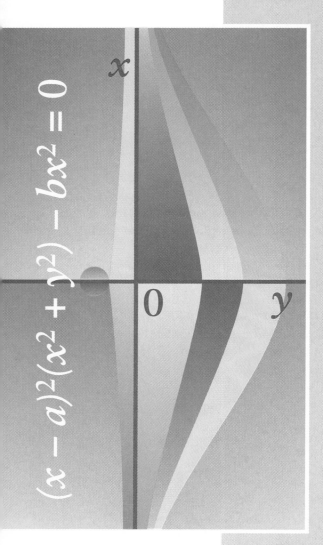

$$(x - a)^2(x^2 + y^2) - bx^2 = 0$$

Solving Quadratic Equations by Factoring or by Taking Square Roots

1   Solve quadratic equations by factoring

In Section 5 of the chapter on Factoring, we solved quadratic equations by factoring. In this section, we will review that material and then solve quadratic equations by taking square roots.

INSTRUCTOR NOTE

As a class discussion, ask students why the condition $a \neq 0$ is placed on the quadratic equation.

An equation of the form $ax^2 + bx + c = 0$, $a \neq 0$, is a **quadratic equation.**

$$4x^2 - 3x + 1 = 0, \qquad a = 4, b = -3, c = 1$$

$$3x^2 - 4 = 0, \qquad a = 3, b = 0, \quad c = -4$$

A quadratic equation is also called a **second-degree equation.**

A quadratic equation is in **standard form** when the polynomial is in descending order and equal to zero.

Recall that the Principle of Zero Products states that if the product of two factors is zero, then at least one of the factors must be zero.

If $a \cdot b = 0$, then $a = 0$ or $b = 0$.

The Principle of Zero Products can be used in solving quadratic equations.

⇒Solve by factoring: $2x^2 - x = 1$

$$2x^2 - x = 1$$

Write the equation in standard form. $2x^2 - x - 1 = 0$

Factor the left side of the equation. $(2x + 1)(x - 1) = 0$

If $(2x + 1)(x - 1) = 0$, then either $2x + 1 = 0$ or $x - 1 = 0$. $\qquad 2x + 1 = 0 \qquad\qquad x - 1 = 0$

Solve each equation for x. $\qquad 2x = -1 \qquad\qquad\quad x = 1$

$$x = -\frac{1}{2}$$

The solutions are $-\frac{1}{2}$ and 1. ◀

A graphing calculator can be used to check the solutions of a quadratic equation. Consider the example above. The solutions appear to be $-\frac{1}{2}$ and 1. To check these solutions, store one value of x, $-\frac{1}{2}$, in the calculator. Note that after you store $-\frac{1}{2}$ in the calculator's memory, your calculator rewrites the fraction as the decimal -0.5. Evaluate the expression on the left side of the original equation: $2(-0.5)^2 - (-0.5)$. The result is 1, which is the number on the right side of the original equation. The solution -0.5 checks. Now store the other value of x, 1, in the calculator. Evaluate the expression on the left side of the original equation: $2(1)^2 - 1$. The result is 1, which is the number on the right side of the equation. The solution 1 checks.

➡ Solve by factoring: $x^2 = 10x - 25$

	$x^2 = 10x - 25$
Write the equation in standard form.	$x^2 - 10x + 25 = 0$
Factor the left side of the equation.	$(x - 5)(x - 5) = 0$
Let each factor equal 0.	$x - 5 = 0 \qquad x - 5 = 0$
Solve each equation for x.	$x = 5 \qquad\qquad x = 5$

The factorization in this example produced two identical factors. Because $x - 5$ occurs twice in the factored form of the equation, 5 is a **double root** of the equation.   ◀

Example 1   Solve by factoring: $\frac{z^2}{2} + \frac{z}{3} - \frac{1}{6} = 0$

Solution $\frac{z^2}{2} + \frac{z}{3} - \frac{1}{6} = 0$

$6\left(\frac{z^2}{2} + \frac{z}{3} - \frac{1}{6}\right) = 6(0)$ ▶ To eliminate the fractions, multiply each side of the fraction by 6.

$3z^2 + 2z - 1 = 0$ ▶ The quadratic equation is in standard form.

$(3z - 1)(z + 1) = 0$ ▶ Factor the left side of the equation.

$3z - 1 = 0 \qquad z + 1 = 0$ ▶ Let each factor equal zero.
$3z = 1 \qquad\qquad z = -1$ ▶ Solve each equation for z.
$z = \frac{1}{3}$

The solutions are $\frac{1}{3}$ and -1.   ▶ $\frac{1}{3}$ and -1 check as solutions

Problem 1   Solve by factoring: $\frac{3y^2}{2} + y - \frac{1}{2} = 0$

Solution   See page S24. $\frac{1}{3}$ and -1

2   Solve quadratic equations by taking square roots

Consider a quadratic equation of the form $x^2 = a$. This equation can be solved by factoring.

$$x^2 = 25$$
$$x^2 - 25 = 0$$
$$(x + 5)(x - 5) = 0$$

$$x + 5 = 0 \qquad x - 5 = 0$$
$$x = -5 \qquad x = 5$$

The solutions are -5 and 5.

Solutions that are plus or minus the same number are frequently written using $\pm$. For the example above, this would be written: "The solutions are ± 5." Because the solutions ± 5 can be written as $\pm\sqrt{25}$, an alternative method of solving this equation is suggested.

Principle of Taking the Square Root of Each Side of an Equation

If $x^2 = a$, then $x = \pm\sqrt{a}$.

LOOK CLOSELY

Recall that the solution of the equation $|x| = 5$ is ± 5. This principle is used when solving an equation by taking square roots. Remember that $\sqrt{x^2} = |x|$.   Therefore,

$$x^2 = 25$$
$$\sqrt{x^2} = \sqrt{25}$$
$$|x| = 5 \qquad \blacktriangleright \sqrt{x^2} = |x|$$
$$x = \pm 5 \qquad \blacktriangleright \text{If } |x| = 5,$$
$$\text{then } x = \pm 5.$$

➡ Solve by taking square roots: $x^2 = 25$

Take the square root of each side of the equation.

Simplify.

Write the solutions.

$$x^2 = 25$$
$$\sqrt{x^2} = \sqrt{25}$$

$$x = \pm\sqrt{25} = \pm 5$$

The solutions are 5 and -5.   ◀

➡ Solve by taking square roots: $3x^2 = 36$

Solve for x^2.

$$3x^2 = 36$$
$$x^2 = 12$$

Take the square root of each side of the equation.

$$\sqrt{x^2} = \sqrt{12}$$

Simplify.

$$x = \pm\sqrt{12} = \pm 2\sqrt{3}$$

LOOK CLOSELY

You should always check your solutions by substituting the proposed solutions back into the *original* equation.

Check:

$$\begin{array}{c|c} 3x^2 = 36 & 3x^2 = 36 \\ \hline 3(2\sqrt{3})^2 \mid 36 & 3(-2\sqrt{3})^2 \mid 36 \\ 3(12) \mid 36 & 3(12) \mid 36 \\ 36 = 36 & 36 = 36 \end{array}$$

These are true equations. The solutions check.

Write the solutions.

The solutions are $2\sqrt{3}$ and $-2\sqrt{3}$.   ◀

A graphing calculator can be used to check irrational solutions of a quadratic equation. Consider the example above; the solutions $2\sqrt{3}$ and $-2\sqrt{3}$ checked. To check these solutions on a calculator, store one value of x, $2\sqrt{3}$, in the calculator. Note that after you store this number in the calculator's memory, your calculator rewrites the expression as the decimal 3.464101615, which is an approximation of $2\sqrt{3}$. Evaluate the expression on the left side of the original equation. The result is 36, which is the number on the right side of the original equation. The solution $2\sqrt{3}$ checks. Now store the other value of x, $-2\sqrt{3}$, in the calculator. Note that after you store this number in the calculator's memory, your calculator rewrites the expression as the decimal -3.464101615, which is an approximation of $-2\sqrt{3}$. Evaluate the expression on the left side of the original equation. The result is 36, which is the number on the right side of the equation. The solution $-2\sqrt{3}$ checks.

Example 2   Solve by taking square roots.

A. $2x^2 - 72 = 0$ B. $x^2 + 16 = 0$

Solution   A. $2x^2 - 72 = 0$

$$2x^2 = 72$$ ▶ Solve for x^2.
$$x^2 = 36$$
$$\sqrt{x^2} = \sqrt{36}$$ ▶ Take the square root of each side of the
$$x = \pm\sqrt{36}$$ equation.
$$x = \pm 6$$

The solutions are 6 and -6.

B. $x^2 + 16 = 0$
$$x^2 = -16$$
$$\sqrt{x^2} = \sqrt{-16}$$ ▶ $\sqrt{-16}$ is not a real number.

The equation has no real number solution.

Problem 2   Solve by taking square roots.

A. $4x^2 - 96 = 0$ B. $x^2 + 81 = 0$

Solution   See page S24.   A. $\pm 2\sqrt{6}$ B. No real number solution

An equation containing the square of a binomial can be solved by taking square roots.

▶ Solve by taking square roots: $2(x - 1)^2 - 36 = 0$

$$2(x - 1)^2 - 36 = 0$$

Solve for $(x - 1)^2$.
$$2(x - 1)^2 = 36$$
$$(x - 1)^2 = 18$$

Take the square root of each side of the equation.
$$\sqrt{(x - 1)^2} = \sqrt{18}$$

Simplify.
$$x - 1 = \pm\sqrt{18}$$
$$x - 1 = \pm 3\sqrt{2}$$

Solve for x.

$$x - 1 = 3\sqrt{2} \qquad\qquad x - 1 = -3\sqrt{2}$$
$$x = 1 + 3\sqrt{2} \qquad\qquad x = 1 - 3\sqrt{2}$$

Check:

$$2(x - 1)^2 - 36 = 0$$

$2(1 + 3\sqrt{2} - 1)^2 - 36$	0
$2(3\sqrt{2})^2 - 36$	0
$2(18) - 36$	0
$36 - 36$	0
	$0 = 0$

$$2(x - 1)^2 - 36 = 0$$

$2(1 - 3\sqrt{2} - 1)^2 - 36$	0
$2(-3\sqrt{2})^2 - 36$	0
$2(18) - 36$	0
$36 - 36$	0
	$0 = 0$

Write the solutions.

The solutions are $1 + 3\sqrt{2}$ and $1 - 3\sqrt{2}$. ◀

Example 3 Solve by taking square roots: $(x - 6)^2 = 12$

Solution
$$(x - 6)^2 = 12$$
$$\sqrt{(x - 6)^2} = \sqrt{12}$$
$$x - 6 = \pm\sqrt{12}$$
$$x - 6 = \pm 2\sqrt{3}$$

▶ Take the square root of each side of the equation.

$$x - 6 = 2\sqrt{3} \qquad\qquad x - 6 = -2\sqrt{3}$$
$$x = 6 + 2\sqrt{3} \qquad\qquad x = 6 - 2\sqrt{3}$$

▶ Solve for x.

The solutions are $6 + 2\sqrt{3}$ and $6 - 2\sqrt{3}$.

Problem 3 Solve by taking square roots: $(x + 5)^2 = 20$

Solution See page S24. $-5 \pm 2\sqrt{5}$

CONCEPT REVIEW 11.1

Determine whether the statement is always true, sometimes true, or never true.

1. $2x^2 - 3x + 9$ is a quadratic equation.   Never true

2. By the Principle of Zero Products, if $(3x + 4)(x - 7) = 0$, then $3x + 4 = 0$ or $x - 7 = 0$.   Always true

3. A quadratic equation has two distinct solutions.   Sometimes true

4. To solve the equation $3x^2 - 26x = 9$ by factoring, first write the equation in standard form.   Always true

5. To say that the solutions are ± 6 means that the solutions are 6 and -6.   Always true

6. If we take the square root of the square of a binomial, the result is the binomial.   Always true

EXERCISES 11.1

1 For the given quadratic equation, find the values of a, b, and c.

1. $3x^2 - 4x + 1 = 0$
$a = 3, b = -4, c = 1$

2. $x^2 + 2x - 5 = 0$
$a = 1, b = 2, c = -5$

3. $2x^2 - 5 = 0$
$a = 2, b = 0, c = -5$

4. $4x^2 + 1 = 0$
$a = 4, b = 0, c = 1$

5. $6x^2 - 3x = 0$
$a = 6, b = -3, c = 0$

6. $-x^2 + 7x = 0$
$a = -1, b = 7, c = 0$

Write the quadratic equation in standard form.

7. $x^2 - 8 = 3x$
$x^2 - 3x - 8 = 0$

8. $2x^2 = 4x - 1$
$2x^2 - 4x + 1 = 0$

9. $x^2 = 16$
$x^2 - 16 = 0$

10. $x + 5 = x(x - 3)$
$x^2 - 4x - 5 = 0$

11. $2(x + 3)^2 = 5$
$2x^2 + 12x + 13 = 0$

12. $4(x - 1)^2 = 3$
$4x^2 - 8x + 1 = 0$

13. How does a quadratic equation differ from a linear equation?

14. What does the Principle of Zero Products state?

15. Explain why the equation $x(x + 5) = 12$ cannot be solved by saying $x = 12$ or $x + 5 = 12$.

16. What is a double root of a quadratic equation?

Solve by factoring.

17. $x^2 + 2x - 15 = 0$ $\quad -5, 3$

18. $t^2 + 3t - 10 = 0$ $\quad -5, 2$

19. $z^2 - 4z + 3 = 0$ $\quad 1, 3$

20. $s^2 - 5s + 4 = 0$ $\quad 4, 1$

21. $p^2 + 3p + 2 = 0$ $\quad -1, -2$

22. $v^2 + 6v + 5 = 0$ $\quad -5, -1$

23. $x^2 - 6x + 9 = 0$ $\quad 3$

24. $y^2 - 8y + 16 = 0$ $\quad 4$

25. $6x^2 - 9x = 0$ $\quad 0, \frac{3}{2}$

26. $12y^2 + 8y = 0$ $\quad 0, -\frac{2}{3}$

27. $r^2 - 10 = 3r$ $\quad 5, -2$

28. $t^2 - 12 = 4t$ $\quad -2, 6$

29. $3v^2 - 5v + 2 = 0$ $\quad \frac{2}{3}, 1$

30. $2p^2 - 3p - 2 = 0$ $\quad -\frac{1}{2}, 2$

31. $3s^2 + 8s = 3$ $\quad \frac{1}{3}, -3$

32. $3x^2 + 5x = 12$ $\quad \frac{4}{3}, -3$

33. $6r^2 = 12 - r$ $\quad -\frac{3}{2}, \frac{4}{3}$

34. $4t^2 = 4t + 3$ $\quad -\frac{1}{2}, \frac{3}{2}$

35. $5y^2 + 11y = 12$ $\quad -3, \frac{4}{5}$

36. $4v^2 - 4v + 1 = 0$ $\quad \frac{1}{2}$

37. $9s^2 - 6s + 1 = 0$ $\quad \frac{1}{3}$

38. $x^2 - 9 = 0$ $\quad 3, -3$

39. $t^2 - 16 = 0$ $\quad -4, 4$

40. $4y^2 - 1 = 0$ $\quad \frac{1}{2}, -\frac{1}{2}$

41. $9z^2 - 4 = 0$ $\quad -\frac{2}{3}, \frac{2}{3}$

42. $x + 15 = x(x - 1)$ $\quad 5, -3$

43. $\frac{3x^2}{2} = 4x - 2$ $\quad \frac{2}{3}, 2$

44. $\frac{2x^2}{5} = 3x - 5$ $\quad -\frac{5}{2}, 5$

45. $\frac{2x^2}{9} + x = 2$ $\quad \frac{3}{2}, -6$

46. $\frac{3x^2}{8} - x = 2$ $\quad -\frac{4}{3}, 4$

47. $\frac{3}{4}z^2 - z = -\frac{1}{3}$ $\quad \frac{2}{3}$

48. $\frac{r^2}{2} = 1 - \frac{r}{12}$ $\quad -\frac{3}{2}, \frac{4}{3}$

49. $p + 18 = p(p - 2)$ $\quad -3, 6$

50. $r^2 - r - 2 = (2r - 1)(r - 3)$ $\quad 5, 1$

51. $s^2 + 5s - 4 = (2s + 1)(s - 4)$ $\quad 0, 12$

52. $x^2 + x + 5 = (3x + 2)(x - 4)$ $\quad -1, \frac{13}{2}$

2 Solve by taking square roots.

53. $x^2 = 36$ ± 6

54. $y^2 = 49$ ± 7

55. $v^2 - 1 = 0$ ± 1

56. $z^2 - 64 = 0$ ± 8

57. $4x^2 - 49 = 0$ $\pm\frac{7}{2}$

58. $9w^2 - 64 = 0$ $\pm\frac{8}{3}$

59. $9y^2 = 4$ $\pm\frac{2}{3}$

60. $4z^2 = 25$ $\pm\frac{5}{2}$

61. $16v^2 - 9 = 0$ $\pm\frac{3}{4}$

62. $25x^2 - 64 = 0$ $\pm\frac{8}{5}$

63. $y^2 + 81 = 0$ No real number solution

64. $z^2 + 49 = 0$ No real number solution

65. $w^2 - 24 = 0$ $\pm 2\sqrt{6}$

66. $v^2 - 48 = 0$ $\pm 4\sqrt{3}$

67. $(x - 1)^2 = 36$ $-5, 7$

68. $(y + 2)^2 = 49$ $-9, 5$

69. $2(x + 5)^2 = 8$ $-3, -7$

70. $4(z - 3)^2 = 100$ $8, -2$

71. $2(x + 1)^2 = 50$ $4, -6$

72. $3(x - 4)^2 = 27$ $7, 1$

73. $4(x + 5)^2 = 64$ $-1, -9$

74. $9(x - 3)^2 = 81$ $6, 0$

75. $2(x - 9)^2 = 98$ $16, 2$

76. $5(x + 5)^2 = 125$ $-10, 0$

77. $12(x + 3)^2 = 27$ $-\frac{3}{2}, -\frac{9}{2}$

78. $8(x - 4)^2 = 50$ $\frac{13}{2}, \frac{3}{2}$

79. $9(x - 1)^2 - 16 = 0$ $-\frac{1}{3}, \frac{7}{3}$

80. $4(y + 3)^2 - 81 = 0$ $\frac{3}{2}, -\frac{15}{2}$

81. $49(v + 1)^2 - 25 = 0$ $-\frac{2}{7}, -\frac{12}{7}$

82. $81(y - 2)^2 - 64 = 0$ $\frac{26}{9}, \frac{10}{9}$

83. $(x - 4)^2 - 20 = 0$ $4 \pm 2\sqrt{5}$

84. $(y + 5)^2 - 50 = 0$ $-5 \pm 5\sqrt{2}$

85. $(x + 1)^2 + 36 = 0$ No real number solution

86. $(y - 7)^2 + 49 = 0$ No real number solution

87. $2\left(z - \frac{1}{2}\right)^2 = 12$ $\frac{1}{2} \pm \sqrt{6}$

88. $3\left(v + \frac{3}{4}\right)^2 = 36$ $-\frac{3}{4} \pm 2\sqrt{3}$

89. $4\left(x - \frac{2}{3}\right)^2 = 16$ $\frac{8}{3}, -\frac{4}{3}$

APPLYING CONCEPTS 11.1

Solve for x.

[C] **90.** $(x^2 - 1)^2 = 9$ ± 2

[C] **91.** $(x^2 + 3)^2 = 25$ $\pm\sqrt{2}$

[C] **92.** $(6x^2 - 5)^2 = 1$ $\pm 1, \pm\frac{\sqrt{6}}{3}$

[C] **93.** $x^2 = x$ $0, 1$

[C] **94.** $ax^2 - bx = 0, a > 0$ and $b > 0$ $0, \frac{b}{a}$

[C] **95.** $ax^2 - b = 0, a > 0$ and $b > 0$ $\pm\frac{\sqrt{ab}}{a}$

96. *Investments*   The value P of an initial investment of A dollars after 2 years is given by $P = A(1 + r)^2$, where r is the annual percentage rate earned by the investment. If an initial investment of \$1500 grew to a value of \$1782.15 in 2 years, what was the annual percentage rate?   9%

97. *Energy*   The kinetic energy of a moving body is given by $E = \frac{1}{2}mv^2$, where E is the kinetic energy in newton-meters, m is the mass in kilograms, and v is the speed in meters per second. What is the speed of a moving body whose mass is 5 kg and whose kinetic energy is 250 newton-meters?   10 m/s

98.   *Automobiles*   On a certain type of street surface, the equation $d = 0.055v^2$ can be used to approximate the distance d a car traveling v miles per hour will slide when its brakes are applied. After applying the brakes, the owner of a car involved in an accident skidded 40 ft. Did the traffic officer investigating the accident issue the car owner a ticket for speeding if the speed limit was 30 mph?   No ($v \approx 27.0$ mph)

SECTION **11.2**

Solving Quadratic Equations by Completing the Square

1   Solve quadratic equations by completing the square

Recall that a perfect-square trinomial is the square of a binomial.

Perfect-square Trinomial		Square of a Binomial
$x^2 + 6x + 9$	$=$	$(x + 3)^2$
$x^2 - 10x + 25$	$=$	$(x - 5)^2$
$x^2 + 8x + 16$	$=$	$(x + 4)^2$

For each perfect-square trinomial, the square of $\frac{1}{2}$ of the coefficient of x equals the constant term.

$$x^2 + 6x + 9, \qquad \left(\frac{1}{2} \cdot 6\right)^2 = 9$$

$$x^2 - 10x + 25, \qquad \left[\frac{1}{2}(-10)\right]^2 = 25 \qquad \left(\frac{1}{2} \text{ coefficient of } x\right)^2 = \text{Constant term}$$

$$x^2 + 8x + 16, \qquad \left(\frac{1}{2} \cdot 8\right)^2 = 16$$

This relationship can be used to write the constant term for a perfect-square trinomial. Adding to a binomial the constant term that makes it a perfect-square trinomial is called **completing the square.**

➡ Complete the square of $x^2 - 8x$. Write the resulting perfect-square trinomial as the square of a binomial.

$$x^2 - 8x$$

Find the constant term.

$$\left[\frac{1}{2}(-8)\right]^2 = 16$$

Complete the square of $x^2 - 8x$ by adding the constant term.

$$x^2 - 8x + 16$$

Write the resulting perfect-square trinomial as the square of a binomial.

$$x^2 - 8x + 16 = (x - 4)^2$$

⇒Complete the square of $y^2 + 5y$. Write the resulting perfect-square trinomial as the square of a binomial.

$$y^2 + 5y$$

Find the constant term.

$$\left(\frac{1}{2} \cdot 5\right)^2 = \left(\frac{5}{2}\right)^2 = \frac{25}{4}$$

Complete the square of $y^2 + 5y$ by adding the constant term.

$$y + 5y + \frac{25}{4}$$

Write the resulting perfect-square trinomial as the square of a binomial.

$$y^2 + 5y + \frac{25}{4} = \left(y + \frac{5}{2}\right)^2$$ ◀

A quadratic equation that cannot be solved by factoring can be solved by completing the square. The procedure is:

1. Write the equation in the form $x^2 + bx = c$.
2. Add to each side of the equation the term that completes the square on $x^2 + bx$.
3. Factor the perfect-square trinomial. Write it as the square of a binomial.
4. Take the square root of each side of the equation.
5. Solve for x.

⇒Solve by completing the square: $x^2 - 6x - 3 = 0$

Add the opposite of the constant term to each side of the equation.

$$x^2 - 6x - 3 = 0$$
$$x^2 - 6x = 3$$

Find the constant term that completes the square of $x^2 - 6x$.

$$\left[\frac{1}{2}(-6)\right]^2 = 9$$

Add this term to each side of the equation.

$$x^2 - 6x + 9 = 3 + 9$$

Factor the perfect-square trinomial.

$$(x - 3)^2 = 12$$

Take the square root of each side of the equation.

$$\sqrt{(x - 3)^2} = \sqrt{12}$$

Simplify.

$$x - 3 = \pm\sqrt{12}$$
$$x - 3 = \pm 2\sqrt{3}$$

Solve for x.

$$x - 3 = 2\sqrt{3} \qquad\qquad x - 3 = -2\sqrt{3}$$
$$x = 3 + 2\sqrt{3} \qquad\qquad x = 3 - 2\sqrt{3}$$

Check:

$$x^2 - 6x - 3 = 0$$
$$\frac{(3 + 2\sqrt{3})^2 - 6(3 + 2\sqrt{3}) - 3 \;\big|\; 0}{9 + 12\sqrt{3} + 12 - 18 - 12\sqrt{3} - 3 \;\big|\; 0}$$
$$0 = 0$$

$$x^2 - 6x - 3 = 0$$
$$\frac{(3 - 2\sqrt{3})^2 - 6(3 - 2\sqrt{3}) - 3 \;\big|\; 0}{9 - 12\sqrt{3} + 12 - 18 + 12\sqrt{3} - 3 \;\big|\; 0}$$
$$0 = 0$$

Write the solutions.

The solutions are $3 + 2\sqrt{3}$ and $3 - 2\sqrt{3}$. ◀

For the method of completing the square to be used, the coefficient of the x^2 term must be 1. If it is not 1, we must multiply each side of the equation by the reciprocal of the coefficient of x^2. This is illustrated in the example below.

▶ Solve by completing the square: $2x^2 - x - 1 = 0$

Add the opposite of the constant term to each side of the equation.

$$2x^2 - x - 1 = 0$$
$$2x^2 - x = 1$$

The coefficient of the x^2 term must be 1. Multiply each side by the reciprocal of the coefficient of x^2.

$$\frac{1}{2}(2x^2 - x) = \frac{1}{2} \cdot 1$$
$$x^2 - \frac{1}{2}x = \frac{1}{2}$$

Find the constant term that completes the square of $x^2 - \frac{1}{2}x$.

$$\left[\frac{1}{2}\left(-\frac{1}{2}\right)\right]^2 = \left(-\frac{1}{4}\right)^2 = \frac{1}{16}$$

Add this term to each side of the equation.

$$x^2 - \frac{1}{2}x + \frac{1}{16} = \frac{1}{2} + \frac{1}{16}$$

Factor the perfect-square trinomial.

$$\left(x - \frac{1}{4}\right)^2 = \frac{9}{16}$$

Take the square root of each side of the equation.

$$\sqrt{\left(x - \frac{1}{4}\right)^2} = \sqrt{\frac{9}{16}}$$

Simplify.

$$x - \frac{1}{4} = \pm\sqrt{\frac{9}{16}}$$

$$x - \frac{1}{4} = \pm\frac{3}{4}$$

Solve for x.

$$x - \frac{1}{4} = \frac{3}{4} \qquad x - \frac{1}{4} = -\frac{3}{4}$$
$$x = 1 \qquad x = -\frac{1}{2}$$

Check:

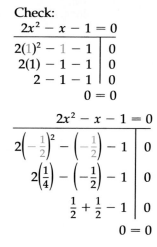

$$\begin{array}{c|c} 2x^2 - x - 1 = 0 & \\ \hline 2(1)^2 - 1 - 1 & 0 \\ 2(1) - 1 - 1 & 0 \\ 2 - 1 - 1 & 0 \\ 0 = 0 & \end{array}$$

$$\begin{array}{c|c} 2x^2 - x - 1 = 0 & \\ \hline 2\left(-\frac{1}{2}\right)^2 - \left(-\frac{1}{2}\right) - 1 & 0 \\ 2\left(\frac{1}{4}\right) - \left(-\frac{1}{2}\right) - 1 & 0 \\ \frac{1}{2} + \frac{1}{2} - 1 & 0 \\ 0 = 0 & \end{array}$$

Write the solutions.

The solutions are 1 and $-\frac{1}{2}$. ◀

Example 1   Solve by completing the square.

A. $2x^2 - 4x - 1 = 0$ B. $p^2 - 4p + 6 = 0$

Solution   A. $2x^2 - 4x - 1 = 0$

$2x^2 - 4x = 1$ ▶ Add the opposite of -1 to each side of the equation.

$\frac{1}{2}(2x^2 - 4x) = \frac{1}{2} \cdot 1$ ▶ The coefficient of the x^2 term must be 1.

$x^2 - 2x = \frac{1}{2}$

$x^2 - 2x + 1 = \frac{1}{2} + 1$ ▶ Complete the square of $x^2 - 2x$. Add 1 to each side of the equation.

$(x - 1)^2 = \frac{3}{2}$ ▶ Factor the perfect-square trinomial.

$\sqrt{(x - 1)^2} = \sqrt{\frac{3}{2}}$ ▶ Take the square root of each side of the equation.

$x - 1 = \pm \sqrt{\frac{3}{2}}$

$x - 1 = \pm \frac{\sqrt{3}}{\sqrt{2}}$

$x - 1 = \pm \frac{\sqrt{6}}{2}$ ▶ Rationalize the denominator.
$\frac{\sqrt{3}}{\sqrt{2}} = \frac{\sqrt{3}}{\sqrt{2}} \cdot \frac{\sqrt{2}}{\sqrt{2}} = \frac{\sqrt{6}}{2}$

$x - 1 = \frac{\sqrt{6}}{2}$ $x - 1 = -\frac{\sqrt{6}}{2}$

$x = 1 + \frac{\sqrt{6}}{2}$ $x = 1 - \frac{\sqrt{6}}{2}$

$= \frac{2}{2} + \frac{\sqrt{6}}{2}$ $= \frac{2}{2} - \frac{\sqrt{6}}{2}$

$= \frac{2 + \sqrt{6}}{2}$ $= \frac{2 - \sqrt{6}}{2}$

The solutions are $\frac{2 + \sqrt{6}}{2}$ and $\frac{2 - \sqrt{6}}{2}$.

B. $p^2 - 4p + 6 = 0$

$p^2 - 4p = -6$ ▶ Add the opposite of the constant term to each side of the equation.

$p^2 - 4p + 4 = -6 + 4$ ▶ Complete the square of $p^2 - 4p$. Add 4 to each side of the equation.

$(p - 2)^2 = -2$ ▶ Factor the perfect-square trinomial.

$\sqrt{(p - 2)^2} = \sqrt{-2}$ ▶ Take the square root of each side of the equation.

$\sqrt{-2}$ is not a real number.
The equation has no real number solution.

Problem 1   Solve by completing the square.

A. $3x^2 - 6x - 2 = 0$ B. $y^2 - 6y + 10 = 0$

Solution   See page S24.   A. $\frac{3 \pm \sqrt{15}}{3}$ B. No real number solution

Example 2 Solve by completing the square: $x^2 + 6x + 4 = 0$
Approximate the solutions to the nearest thousandth.

Solution $x^2 + 6x + 4 = 0$

$x^2 + 6x = -4$

$x^2 + 6x + 9 = -4 + 9$ ▶ Complete the square of $x^2 + 6x$. Add 9 to

$(x + 3)^2 = 5$ each side of the equation.

$\sqrt{(x + 3)^2} = \sqrt{5}$

$x + 3 = \pm\sqrt{5}$

$x + 3 \approx \pm 2.2361$

$x + 3 \approx 2.2361$ $x + 3 \approx -2.2361$

$x \approx -3 + 2.2361$ $x \approx -3 - 2.2361$

≈ -0.764 ≈ -5.236

The solutions are approximately -0.764 and -5.236.

Problem 2 Solve by completing the square: $x^2 + 8x + 8 = 0$
Approximate the solutions to the nearest thousandth.

Solution See page S25. -1.172 and -6.828

CONCEPT REVIEW 11.2

Determine whether the statement is always true, sometimes true, or never true.

1. When we square a binomial, the result is a perfect-square trinomial.   Always true

2. The constant term in a perfect-square trinomial is equal to the square of one-half the coefficient of x.   Always true

3. To "complete the square" means to add to $x^2 + bx$ the constant term that will make it a perfect-square trinomial.   Always true

4. To complete the square of $x^2 + 4x$, add 16 to it.   Never true

5. To complete the square of $3x^2 + 6x$, add 9 to it.   Never true

6. In solving a quadratic equation by completing the square, the next step after writing the equation in the form $(x + a)^2 = b$ is to take the square root of each side of the equation.   Always true

EXERCISES 11.2

1 Complete the square. Write the resulting perfect-square trinomial as the square of a binomial.

1. $x^2 + 12x$
$x^2 + 12x + 36; (x + 6)^2$

2. $x^2 - 4x$
$x^2 - 4x + 4; (x - 2)^2$

3. $x^2 + 10x$
$x^2 + 10x + 25; (x + 5)^2$

4. $x^2 + 3x$
$x^2 + 3x + \frac{9}{4}; \left(x + \frac{3}{2}\right)^2$

5. $x^2 - x$
$x^2 - x + \frac{1}{4}; \left(x - \frac{1}{2}\right)^2$

6. $x^2 + 5x$
$x^2 + 5x + \frac{25}{4}; \left(x + \frac{5}{2}\right)^2$

Solve by completing the square.

7. $x^2 + 2x - 3 = 0$
$-3, 1$

8. $y^2 + 4y - 5 = 0$
$-5, 1$

9. $v^2 + 4v + 1 = 0$
$-2 \pm \sqrt{3}$

10. $y^2 - 2y - 5 = 0$
$1 \pm \sqrt{6}$

11. $v^2 - 6v + 13 = 0$
No real number solution

12. $x^2 + 4x + 13 = 0$
No real number solution

13. $x^2 + 6x = 5$
$-3 \pm \sqrt{14}$

14. $w^2 - 8w = 3$
$4 \pm \sqrt{19}$

15. $x^2 = 4x - 4$ 2

16. $z^2 = 8z - 16$ 4

17. $z^2 = 2z + 1$
$1 \pm \sqrt{2}$

18. $y^2 = 10y - 20$
$5 \pm \sqrt{5}$

Solve. First try to solve the equation by factoring. If you are unable to solve the equation by factoring, solve the equation by completing the square.

19. $p^2 + 3p = 1$ $\dfrac{-3 \pm \sqrt{13}}{2}$

20. $r^2 + 5r = 2$ $\dfrac{-5 \pm \sqrt{33}}{2}$

21. $w^2 + 7w = 8$ $-8, 1$

22. $y^2 + 5y = -4$ $-1, -4$

23. $x^2 + 6x + 4 = 0$ $-3 \pm \sqrt{5}$

24. $y^2 - 8y - 1 = 0$ $4 \pm \sqrt{17}$

25. $r^2 - 8r = -2$ $4 \pm \sqrt{14}$

26. $s^2 + 6s = 5$ $-3 \pm \sqrt{14}$

27. $t^2 - 3t = -2$ $1, 2$

28. $y^2 = 4y + 12$ $6, -2$

29. $w^2 = 3w + 5$ $\dfrac{3 \pm \sqrt{29}}{2}$

30. $x^2 = 1 - 3x$ $\dfrac{-3 \pm \sqrt{13}}{2}$

31. $x^2 - x - 1 = 0$ $\dfrac{1 \pm \sqrt{5}}{2}$

32. $x^2 - 7x = -3$ $\dfrac{7 \pm \sqrt{37}}{2}$

33. $y^2 - 5y + 3 = 0$ $\dfrac{5 \pm \sqrt{13}}{2}$

34. $z^2 - 5z = -2$ $\dfrac{5 \pm \sqrt{17}}{2}$

35. $v^2 + v - 3 = 0$ $\dfrac{-1 \pm \sqrt{13}}{2}$

36. $x^2 - x = 1$ $\dfrac{1 \pm \sqrt{5}}{2}$

37. $y^2 = 7 - 10y$ $-5 \pm 4\sqrt{2}$

38. $v^2 = 14 + 16v$ $8 \pm \sqrt{78}$

39. $s^2 + 3s = -1$ $\dfrac{-3 \pm \sqrt{5}}{2}$

40. $r^2 - 3r = 5$ $\dfrac{3 \pm \sqrt{29}}{2}$

41. $t^2 - t = 4$ $\dfrac{1 \pm \sqrt{17}}{2}$

42. $y^2 + y - 4 = 0$ $\dfrac{-1 \pm \sqrt{17}}{2}$

43. $x^2 - 3x + 5 = 0$
No real number solution

44. $z^2 + 5z + 7 = 0$
No real number solution

45. $2t^2 - 3t + 1 = 0$ $1, \dfrac{1}{2}$

46. $2x^2 - 7x + 3 = 0$ $3, \dfrac{1}{2}$

47. $2r^2 + 5r = 3$ $-3, \dfrac{1}{2}$

48. $2y^2 - 3y = 9$ $3, -\dfrac{3}{2}$

49. $4v^2 - 4v - 1 = 0$ $\dfrac{1 \pm \sqrt{2}}{2}$

50. $2s^2 - 4s - 1 = 0$ $\dfrac{2 \pm \sqrt{6}}{2}$

51. $4z^2 - 8z = 1$ $\dfrac{2 \pm \sqrt{5}}{2}$

52. $3r^2 - 2r = 2$ $\dfrac{1 \pm \sqrt{7}}{3}$

53. $3y - 5 = (y - 1)(y - 2)$
$3 \pm \sqrt{2}$

54. $4p + 2 = (p - 1)(p + 3)$
$1 \pm \sqrt{6}$

55. $\dfrac{x^2}{4} - \dfrac{x}{2} = 3$ $1 \pm \sqrt{13}$

56. $\dfrac{x^2}{6} - \dfrac{x}{3} = 1$ $1 \pm \sqrt{7}$

57. $\dfrac{2x^2}{3} = 2x + 3$ $\dfrac{3 \pm 3\sqrt{3}}{2}$

58. $\dfrac{3x^2}{2} = 3x + 2$ $\dfrac{3 \pm \sqrt{21}}{3}$

59. $\dfrac{x}{3} + \dfrac{3}{x} = \dfrac{8}{3}$ $4 \pm \sqrt{7}$

60. $\dfrac{x}{4} - \dfrac{2}{x} = \dfrac{3}{4}$ $\dfrac{3 \pm \sqrt{41}}{2}$

Solve by completing the square. Approximate the solutions to the nearest thousandth.

61. $y^2 + 3y = 5$ 1.193, -4.193 **62.** $w^2 + 5w = 2$ 0.372, -5.372 **63.** $2z^2 - 3z = 7$ 2.766, -1.266

64. $2x^2 + 3x = 11$ 1.712, -3.212 **65.** $4x^2 + 6x - 1 = 0$ **66.** $4x^2 + 2x - 3 = 0$
  0.151, -1.651 0.651, -1.151

APPLYING CONCEPTS 11.2

Solve.

67. $\sqrt{2x + 7} - 4 = x$ -3 [C] **68.** $\dfrac{x + 1}{2} + \dfrac{3}{x - 1} = 4$ $4 \pm \sqrt{3}$ [C] **69.** $\dfrac{x - 2}{3} + \dfrac{2}{x + 2} = 4$ $6 \pm \sqrt{58}$

70. Explain why the equation $(x - 2)^2 = -4$ does not have a real number solution.

SECTION **11.3**

Solving Quadratic Equations by Using the Quadratic Formula

1   Solve quadratic equations by using the quadratic formula

Any quadratic equation can be solved by completing the square. Applying this method to the standard form of a quadratic equation produces a formula that can be used to solve any quadratic equation.

INSTRUCTOR NOTE
Students wonder why we discuss the different ways in which a quadratic equation can be solved. Explain to students that factoring, when it is easy to determine the factors, is the quickest way. Completing the square has other uses besides being used to derive the quadratic formula. It is rarely used to solve an equation. The quadratic formula is used for those equations that do not factor.

To solve $ax^2 + bx + c = 0$, $a \neq 0$, by completing the square, subtract the constant term from each side of the equation.

$$ax^2 + bx + c = 0$$
$$ax^2 + bx + c - c = 0 - c$$
$$ax^2 + bx = -c$$

Multiply each side of the equation by the reciprocal of a, the coefficient of x^2.

$$\frac{1}{a}(ax^2 + bx) = \frac{1}{a}(-c)$$
$$x^2 + \frac{b}{a}x = -\frac{c}{a}$$

Complete the square by adding $\left(\frac{1}{2} \cdot \frac{b}{a}\right)^2$ to each side of the equation.

$$x^2 + \frac{b}{a}x + \left(\frac{1}{2} \cdot \frac{b}{a}\right)^2 = \left(\frac{1}{2} \cdot \frac{b}{a}\right)^2 - \frac{c}{a}$$
$$x^2 + \frac{b}{a}x + \frac{b^2}{4a^2} = \frac{b^2}{4a^2} - \frac{c}{a}$$

Simplify the right side of the equation.

$$x^2 + \frac{b}{a}x + \frac{b^2}{4a^2} = \frac{b^2}{4a^2} - \left(\frac{c}{a} \cdot \frac{4a}{4a}\right)$$

$$x^2 + \frac{b}{a}x + \frac{b^2}{4a^2} = \frac{b^2}{4a^2} - \frac{4ac}{4a^2}$$

$$x^2 + \frac{b}{a}x + \frac{b^2}{4a^2} = \frac{b^2 - 4ac}{4a^2}$$

Factor the perfect-square trinomial on the left side of the equation.

$$\left(x + \frac{b}{2a}\right)^2 = \frac{b^2 - 4ac}{4a^2}$$

Take the square root of each side of the equation.

$$\sqrt{\left(x + \frac{b}{2a}\right)^2} = \sqrt{\frac{b^2 - 4ac}{4a^2}}$$

$$x + \frac{b}{2a} = \pm\frac{\sqrt{b^2 - 4ac}}{2a}$$

Solve for x.

$$x + \frac{b}{2a} = \frac{\sqrt{b^2 - 4ac}}{2a} \qquad\qquad x + \frac{b}{2a} = -\frac{\sqrt{b^2 - 4ac}}{2a}$$

$$x = -\frac{b}{2a} + \frac{\sqrt{b^2 - 4ac}}{2a} \qquad\qquad x = -\frac{b}{2a} - \frac{\sqrt{b^2 - 4ac}}{2a}$$

$$x = \frac{-b + \sqrt{b^2 - 4ac}}{2a} \qquad\qquad x = \frac{-b - \sqrt{b^2 - 4ac}}{2a}$$

The Quadratic Formula

The solution of $ax^2 + bx + c = 0, a \neq 0$, is

$$x = \frac{-b + \sqrt{b^2 - 4ac}}{2a} \quad \text{or} \quad x = \frac{-b - \sqrt{b^2 - 4ac}}{2a}$$

The quadratic formula is frequently written in the form

$$x = \frac{-b \pm \sqrt{b^2 - 4ac}}{2a}$$

INSTRUCTOR NOTE

It may help to give examples of just determining a, b, and c for different equations. Here are some suggestions.

$$2x = x^2 - 3$$
$$4x - 3x^2 + 3 = 0$$
$$2x^2 - x = 0$$

Students will ask whether it matters on which side of the equation a term is moved. To convince these students that it does not matter, have them solve $3x = x^2 - 4$ by rewriting it as

$$x^2 - 3x - 4 = 0$$

and as

$$-x^2 + 3x + 4 = 0$$

➡ Solve by using the quadratic formula: $2x^2 = 4x - 1$

Write the equation in standard form.
$a = 2, b = -4$, and $c = 1$.

$$2x^2 = 4x - 1$$
$$2x^2 - 4x + 1 = 0$$

Replace a, b, and c in the quadratic formula by their values.

$$x = \frac{-b \pm \sqrt{b^2 - 4ac}}{2a}$$

Simplify.

$$= \frac{-(-4) \pm \sqrt{(-4)^2 - 4 \cdot 2 \cdot 1}}{2 \cdot 2}$$

$$= \frac{4 \pm \sqrt{16 - 8}}{4}$$

$$= \frac{4 \pm \sqrt{8}}{4}$$

$$= \frac{4 \pm 2\sqrt{2}}{4} = \frac{2(2 \pm \sqrt{2})}{2 \cdot 2} = \frac{2 \pm \sqrt{2}}{2}$$

Check:

$$2x^2 = 4x - 1$$

$$2\left(\frac{2+\sqrt{2}}{2}\right)^2 \quad \bigg| \quad 4\left(\frac{2+\sqrt{2}}{2}\right) - 1$$

$$2\left(\frac{4+4\sqrt{2}+2}{4}\right) \quad \bigg| \quad 2(2+\sqrt{2}) - 1$$

$$2\left(\frac{6+4\sqrt{2}}{4}\right) \quad \bigg| \quad 4 + 2\sqrt{2} - 1$$

$$\frac{6+4\sqrt{2}}{2} \quad \bigg| \quad 3 + 2\sqrt{2}$$

$$3 + 2\sqrt{2} = 3 + 2\sqrt{2}$$

$$2x^2 = 4x - 1$$

$$2\left(\frac{2-\sqrt{2}}{2}\right)^2 \quad \bigg| \quad 4\left(\frac{2-\sqrt{2}}{2}\right) - 1$$

$$2\left(\frac{4-4\sqrt{2}+2}{4}\right) \quad \bigg| \quad 2(2-\sqrt{2}) - 1$$

$$2\left(\frac{6-4\sqrt{2}}{4}\right) \quad \bigg| \quad 4 - 2\sqrt{2} - 1$$

$$\frac{6-4\sqrt{2}}{2} \quad \bigg| \quad 3 - 2\sqrt{2}$$

$$3 - 2\sqrt{2} = 3 - 2\sqrt{2}$$

Write the solutions.   The solutions are $\frac{2+\sqrt{2}}{2}$ and $\frac{2-\sqrt{2}}{2}$. ◀

Example 1 Solve by using the quadratic formula.

A. $2x^2 - 3x + 1 = 0$ B. $2x^2 = 8x - 5$

C. $t^2 - 3t + 7 = 0$

Solution A. $2x^2 - 3x + 1 = 0$ ▶ $a = 2, b = -3, c = 1$

$$x = \frac{-(-3) \pm \sqrt{(-3)^2 - 4(2)(1)}}{2 \cdot 2}$$

$$= \frac{3 \pm \sqrt{9 - 8}}{4} = \frac{3 \pm \sqrt{1}}{4} = \frac{3 \pm 1}{4}$$

$$x = \frac{3 + 1}{4} \qquad x = \frac{3 - 1}{4}$$

$$= \frac{4}{4} = 1 \qquad = \frac{2}{4} = \frac{1}{2}$$

The solutions are 1 and $\frac{1}{2}$.

B. $$2x^2 = 8x - 5$$
$$2x^2 - 8x + 5 = 0$$ ▶ Write the equation in standard form. $a = 2, b = -8, c = 5$

$$x = \frac{-(-8) \pm \sqrt{(-8)^2 - 4(2)(5)}}{2 \cdot 2}$$

$$= \frac{8 \pm \sqrt{64 - 40}}{4}$$

$$= \frac{8 \pm \sqrt{24}}{4}$$

$$= \frac{8 \pm 2\sqrt{6}}{4}$$

$$= \frac{2(4 \pm \sqrt{6})}{2 \cdot 2} = \frac{4 \pm \sqrt{6}}{2}$$

The solutions are $\frac{4 + \sqrt{6}}{2}$ and $\frac{4 - \sqrt{6}}{2}$.

C. $t^2 - 3t + 7 = 0$ ▶ $a = 1, b = -3, c = 7$

$$t = \frac{-(-3) \pm \sqrt{(-3)^2 - 4(1)(7)}}{2(1)}$$

$$= \frac{3 \pm \sqrt{9 - 28}}{2} = \frac{3 \pm \sqrt{-19}}{2}$$

$\sqrt{-19}$ **is not a real number.**

The equation has no real number solution.

> **Problem 1** Solve by using the quadratic formula.
> A. $3x^2 + 4x - 4 = 0$ B. $x^2 + 2x = 1$
> C. $z^2 + 2z + 6 = 0$
>
> **Solution** See page S25.   A. $\frac{2}{3}, -2$ B. $-1 \pm \sqrt{2}$
> C. No real number solution

CONCEPT REVIEW 11.3

Determine whether the statement is always true, sometimes true, or never true.

1. Any quadratic equation can be solved by using the quadratic formula.
    Always true
2. The solutions of a quadratic equation can be written as $x = \dfrac{-b + \sqrt{b^2 - 4ac}}{2a}$
    and $x = \dfrac{-b - \sqrt{b^2 - 4ac}}{2a}$.   Always true

3. The equation $4x^2 - 3x = 9$ is a quadratic equation in standard form.   Never true

4. In the quadratic formula $x = \dfrac{-b \pm \sqrt{b^2 - 4ac}}{2a}$, b is the coefficient of x^2.   Never true

5. $\dfrac{6 \pm 2\sqrt{3}}{2}$ simplifies to $3 \pm 2\sqrt{3}$.   Never true

EXERCISES 11.3

1

1. ✎ Write the quadratic formula. Explain what each variable in the formula represents.

2. ✎ Explain what the quadratic formula is used for.

Solve by using the quadratic formula.

3. $z^2 + 6z - 7 = 0$
    $-7, 1$
4. $s^2 + 3s - 10 = 0$
    $-5, 2$
5. $w^2 = 3w + 18$
    $6, -3$
6. $r^2 = 5 - 4r$
    $-5, 1$

7. $t^2 - 2t = 5$
    $1 \pm \sqrt{6}$
8. $y^2 - 4y = 6$
    $2 \pm \sqrt{10}$
9. $t^2 + 6t - 1 = 0$
    $-3 \pm \sqrt{10}$
10. $z^2 + 4z + 1 = 0$
    $-2 \pm \sqrt{3}$

11. $w^2 + 3w + 5 = 0$
    No real number solution
12. $x^2 - 2x + 6 = 0$
    No real number solution
13. $w^2 = 4w + 9$
    $2 \pm \sqrt{13}$
14. $y^2 = 8y + 3$
    $4 \pm \sqrt{19}$

Solve. First try to solve the equation by factoring. If you are unable to solve the equation by factoring, solve the equation by using the quadratic formula.

15. $p^2 - p = 0$ $0, 1$

16. $2v^2 + v = 0$ $0, -\frac{1}{2}$

17. $4t^2 - 4t - 1 = 0$ $\frac{1 \pm \sqrt{2}}{2}$

18. $4x^2 - 8x - 1 = 0$ $\frac{2 \pm \sqrt{5}}{2}$

19. $4t^2 - 9 = 0$ $\pm\frac{3}{2}$

20. $4s^2 - 25 = 0$ $\pm\frac{5}{2}$

21. $3x^2 - 6x + 2 = 0$ $\frac{3 \pm \sqrt{3}}{3}$

22. $5x^2 - 6x = 3$ $\frac{3 \pm 2\sqrt{6}}{5}$

23. $3t^2 = 2t + 3$ $\frac{1 \pm \sqrt{10}}{3}$

24. $4n^2 = 7n - 2$ $\frac{7 \pm \sqrt{17}}{8}$

25. $2x^2 + x + 1 = 0$
    No real number solution

26. $3r^2 - r + 2 = 0$
    No real number solution

27. $2y^2 + 3 = 8y$ $\dfrac{4 \pm \sqrt{10}}{2}$

28. $5x^2 - 1 = x$ $\dfrac{1 \pm \sqrt{21}}{10}$

29. $3t^2 = 7t + 6$ $-\dfrac{2}{3}, 3$

30. $3x^2 = 10x + 8$ $-\dfrac{2}{3}, 4$

31. $3y^2 - 4 = 5y$ $\dfrac{5 \pm \sqrt{73}}{6}$

32. $6x^2 - 5 = 3x$ $\dfrac{3 \pm \sqrt{129}}{12}$

33. $3x^2 = x + 3$ $\dfrac{1 \pm \sqrt{37}}{6}$

34. $2n^2 = 7 - 3n$ $\dfrac{-3 \pm \sqrt{65}}{4}$

35. $5d^2 - 2d - 8 = 0$ $\dfrac{1 \pm \sqrt{41}}{5}$

36. $x^2 - 7x - 10 = 0$ $\dfrac{7 \pm \sqrt{89}}{2}$

37. $5z^2 + 11z = 12$ $\dfrac{4}{5}, -3$

38. $4v^2 = v + 3$ $1, -\dfrac{3}{4}$

39. $v^2 + 6v + 1 = 0$ $-3 \pm 2\sqrt{2}$

40. $s^2 + 4s - 8 = 0$ $-2 \pm 2\sqrt{3}$

41. $4t^2 - 12t - 15 = 0$ $\dfrac{3 \pm 2\sqrt{6}}{2}$

42. $4w^2 - 20w + 5 = 0$ $\dfrac{5 \pm 2\sqrt{5}}{2}$

43. $2x^2 = 4x - 5$
No real number solution

44. $3r^2 = 5r - 6$
No real number solution

45. $9y^2 + 6y - 1 = 0$ $\dfrac{-1 \pm \sqrt{2}}{3}$

46. $9s^2 - 6s - 2 = 0$ $\dfrac{1 \pm \sqrt{3}}{3}$

47. $6s^2 - s - 2 = 0$ $-\dfrac{1}{2}, \dfrac{2}{3}$

48. $6y^2 + 5y - 4 = 0$ $\dfrac{1}{2}, -\dfrac{4}{3}$

49. $4p^2 + 16p = -11$ $\dfrac{-4 \pm \sqrt{5}}{2}$

50. $4y^2 - 12y = -1$ $\dfrac{3 \pm 2\sqrt{2}}{2}$

51. $4x^2 = 4x + 11$ $\dfrac{1 \pm 2\sqrt{3}}{2}$

52. $4s^2 + 12s = 3$ $\dfrac{-3 \pm 2\sqrt{3}}{2}$

53. $4p^2 = -12p - 9$ $-\dfrac{3}{2}$

54. $3y^2 + 6y = -3$ -1

55. $9v^2 = -30v - 23$ $\dfrac{-5 \pm \sqrt{2}}{3}$

56. $9t^2 = 30t + 17$ $\dfrac{5 \pm \sqrt{42}}{3}$

57. $\dfrac{x^2}{2} - \dfrac{x}{3} = 1$ $\dfrac{1 \pm \sqrt{19}}{3}$

58. $\dfrac{x^2}{4} - \dfrac{x}{2} = 5$ $1 \pm \sqrt{21}$

59. $\dfrac{2x^2}{5} = x + 1$ $\dfrac{5 \pm \sqrt{65}}{4}$

60. $\dfrac{3x^2}{2} + 2x = 1$ $\dfrac{-2 \pm \sqrt{10}}{3}$

61. $\dfrac{x}{5} + \dfrac{5}{x} = \dfrac{12}{5}$ $6 \pm \sqrt{11}$

62. $\dfrac{x}{4} + \dfrac{3}{x} = \dfrac{5}{2}$ $5 \pm \sqrt{13}$

Solve by using the quadratic formula. Approximate the solutions to the nearest thousandth.

63. $x^2 - 2x - 21 = 0$
5.690, −3.690

64. $y^2 + 4y - 11 = 0$
1.873, −5.873

65. $s^2 - 6s - 13 = 0$
7.690, −1.690

66. $w^2 + 8w - 15 = 0$
1.568, −9.568

67. $2p^2 - 7p - 10 = 0$
4.589, −1.089

68. $3t^2 - 8t - 1 = 0$
2.786, −0.120

69. $4z^2 + 8z - 1 = 0$
0.118, −2.118

70. $4x^2 + 7x + 1 = 0$
−0.157, −1.593

71. $5v^2 - v - 5 = 0$
1.105, −0.905

APPLYING CONCEPTS 11.3

Solve.

72. $\sqrt{x^2 + 2x + 1} = x - 1$
No solution

[C] **73.** $\dfrac{x + 2}{3} - \dfrac{4}{x - 2} = 2$ $3 \pm \sqrt{13}$

[C] **74.** $\dfrac{x + 1}{5} - \dfrac{3}{x - 1} = 2$ $5 \pm \sqrt{31}$

75. True or false?
  a. The equations $x = \sqrt{12 - x}$ and $x^2 = 12 - x$ have the same solution.   False
  b. If $\sqrt{a} + \sqrt{b} = c$, then $a + b = c^2$.   False
  c. $\sqrt{9} = \pm 3$ False
  d. $\sqrt{x^2} = |x|$ True

76. Factoring, completing the square, and using the quadratic formula are three methods of solving quadratic equations. Describe each method, and cite the advantages and disadvantages of using each.

77. Explain why the equation $0x^2 + 3x + 4 = 0$ cannot be solved by the quadratic formula.

SECTION **11.4**

Graphing Quadratic Equations in Two Variables

1 Graph a quadratic equation of the form $y = ax^2 + bx + c$

An equation of the form $y = ax^2 + bx + c$, $a \neq 0$, is a **quadratic equation in two variables.** Examples of quadratic equations in two variables are shown at the right.

$$y = 3x^2 - x + 1$$
$$y = -x^2 - 3$$
$$y = 2x^2 - 5x$$

For these equations, y is a function of x, and we can write $f(x) = ax^2 + bx + c$. This represents a **quadratic function.**

The graph of a quadratic equation in two variables is a **parabola.** The graph is "cup-shaped" and opens either up or down. The graphs of two parabolas are shown below.

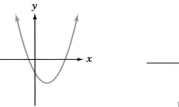

Parabola that opens up   Parabola that opens down

➡ Graph: $y = x^2 - 2x - 3$

Find several solutions of the equation. Because the graph is not a straight line, several solutions must be found in order to determine the cup shape.

Display the ordered-pair solutions in a table.

x	y
0	-3
1	-4
-1	0
2	-3
3	0

Graph the ordered-pair solutions on a rectangular coordinate system.

Draw a parabola through the points.

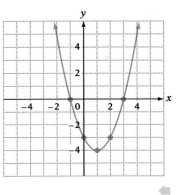

> ⊠ Using a graphing utility, enter the equation $y = x^2 - 2x - 3$ and verify the graph shown above. (Refer to the Appendix for instructions on using a graphing calculator to graph a quadratic equation.) Trace along the graph and verify that $(0, -3)$, $(1, -4)$, $(-1, 0)$, $(2, -3)$, and $(3, 0)$ are coordinates of points on the graph.

The graph of $y = -2x^2 + 1$ is shown below.

x	y
0	1
1	-1
-1	-1
2	-7
-2	-7

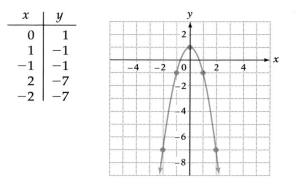

> ⊠ Use a graphing utility to verify the graph of $y = -2x^2 + 1$ shown above.

Note that the graph of $y = x^2 - 2x - 3$, shown on the previous page, opens up and that the coefficient of x^2 is positive. The graph of $y = -2x^2 + 1$ opens down, and the coefficient of x^2 is negative. For any quadratic equation in two variables, the coefficient of x^2 determines whether the parabola opens up or down. **When a is positive, the parabola opens up. When a is negative, the parabola opens down.**

POINT OF INTEREST

Mirrors in some telescopes are ground into the shape of a parabola. The mirror at the Mount Palomar Observatory is 2 ft thick at the ends and weighs 14.75 tons. The mirror has been ground to a true paraboloid (the three-dimensional version of a parabola) to within 0.0000015 in. An equation of the mirror is $y = 2640x^2$.

Every parabola has an axis of symmetry and a **vertex** that is on the axis of symmetry. If the parabola opens up, the vertex is the lowest point on the graph. If the parabola opens down, the vertex is the highest point on the graph.

To understand the axis of symmetry, think of folding the paper along that axis. The two halves of the graph will match up.

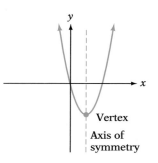

When graphing a quadratic equation in two variables, use the value of a to determine whether the parabola opens up or down. After graphing ordered-pair solutions of the equation, use symmetry to help you draw the parabola.

Example 1   Graph.   A. $y = x^2 - 2x$ B. $y = -x^2 + 4x - 4$

Solution   A. $a = 1$. a is positive
The parabola opens up.

x	y
0	0
1	−1
−1	3
2	0
3	3

B. $a = -1$. a is negative.
The parabola opens down.

x	y
0	−4
1	−1
2	0
3	−1
4	−4

Problem 1   Graph.   A. $y = x^2 + 2$ B. $y = -x^2 - 2x + 3$

Solution   See page S26.   A.   B.

CONCEPT REVIEW 11.4

Determine whether the statement is always true, sometimes true, or never true.

1. The equation $y = 3x^2 - 2x + 1$ is an example of a quadratic equation in two variables.   Always true

2. The graph of an equation of the form $y = ax^2 + bx + c$, $a \neq 0$, is a parabola. Always true

3. The graph of an equation of the form $y = ax^2 + c$, $a \neq 0$, is a straight line. Never true

4. For the equation $y = -x^2 + 2x - 1$, when $x = 1$, $y = 2$.   Never true

5. The graph of the equation $y = -\frac{1}{2}x^2 + 5x$ is a parabola opening up.   Never true

6. If a parabola opens down, then the vertex is the highest point on the graph. Always true

EXERCISES 11.4

1. ▮ What is a parabola?

2. Explain how you know whether the graph of the equation $y = -2x^2 + 3x + 4$ opens up or down.

3. ✏ Explain the axis of symmetry of a parabola.

4. ✏ What is the vertex of a parabola?

Determine whether the graph of the equation opens up or down.

5. $y = x^2 - 3$ Up

6. $y = -x^2 + 4$ Down

7. $y = \frac{1}{2}x^2 - 2$ Up

8. $y = -\frac{1}{3}x^2 + 5$ Down

9. $y = x^2 - 2x + 3$ Up

10. $y = -x^2 + 4x - 1$ Down

Graph.

11. $y = x^2$

12. $y = -x^2$

13. $y = -x^2 + 1$

14. $y = x^2 - 1$

15. $y = 2x^2$

16. $y = \frac{1}{2}x^2$

17. $y = -\frac{1}{2}x^2 + 1$

18. $y = 2x^2 - 1$

19. $y = x^2 - 4x$

20. $y = x^2 + 4x$

21. $y = x^2 - 2x + 3$

22. $y = x^2 - 4x + 2$

23. $y = -x^2 + 2x + 3$

24. $y = x^2 + 2x + 1$

25. $y = -x^2 + 3x - 4$

26. $y = -x^2 + 6x - 9$

27. $y = 2x^2 + x - 3$

28. $y = -2x^2 - 3x + 3$

Graph using a graphing utility. Verify that the graph is a graph of a parabola opening up if a is positive or opening down if a is negative.

29. $y = x^2 - 2$

30. $y = -x^2 + 3$

31. $y = x^2 + 2x$

32. $y = -2x^2 + 4x$

33. $y = \frac{1}{2}x^2 - x$

34. $y = -\frac{1}{2}x^2 + 2$

35. $y = x^2 - x - 2$

36. $y = x^2 - 3x + 2$

37. $y = 2x^2 - x - 5$

38. $y = -2x^2 - 3x + 2$

39. $y = -x^2 - 2x - 1$

40. $y = \frac{1}{2}x^2 - 2x - 1$

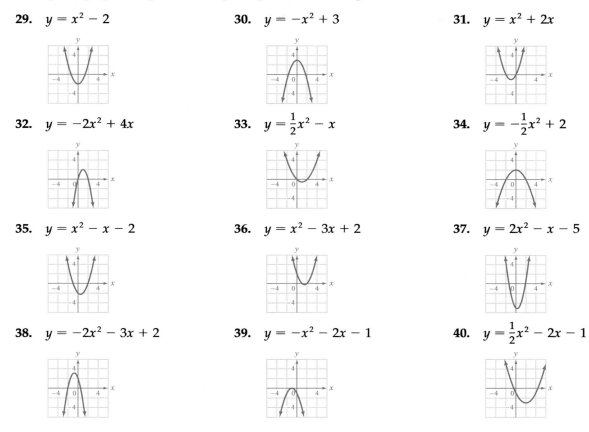

APPLYING CONCEPTS 11.4

Show that the equation is a quadratic equation in two variables by writing it in the form $y = ax^2 + bx + c$.

41. $y + 1 = (x - 4)^2$
$y = x^2 - 8x + 15$

42. $y - 2 = 3(x + 1)^2$
$y = 3x^2 + 6x + 5$

43. $y - 4 = 2(x - 3)^2$
$y = 2x^2 - 12x + 22$

The x-intercepts of a parabola are the points at which the graph crosses the x-axis. Because any point on the x-axis has y-coordinate 0, the x-intercepts of a parabola occur when $y = 0$. Therefore, the x-coordinate of an x-intercept is a solution of the equation $ax^2 + bx + c = 0$. For example, the solutions of the equation $x^2 - 1 = 0$ are 1 and -1, and the graph of the equation $y = x^2 - 1$ crosses the x-axis at $(1, 0)$ and $(-1, 0)$. Determine the x-intercepts of the graphs of the following equations.

44. $y = x^2 - 4$ $(2, 0), (-2, 0)$

45. $y = -x^2 + 4$ $(2, 0), (-2, 0)$

46. $y = x^2 - x$ $(0, 0), (1, 0)$

47. $y = x^2 - 4x$ $(0, 0), (4, 0)$

48. $y = x^2 - 4x + 3$ $(1, 0), (3, 0)$

49. $y = 2x^2 - x - 1$
$\left(-\frac{1}{2}, 0\right), (1, 0)$

Evaluate the function.

50. Find $f(3)$ when $f(x) = x^2 + 3$.   12

51. Find $g(2)$ when $g(x) = x^2 - 2x - 3$. -3

52. Find $S(-2)$ when $S(t) = 2t^2 - 3t - 1$.   13

53. Find $P(-3)$ when $P(x) = 3x^2 - 6x - 7$.   38

Graph.

54. $f(x) = 2x^2 - 3$

55. $f(x) = \dfrac{1}{3}x^2$

56. $f(x) = x^2 + 2x - 4$

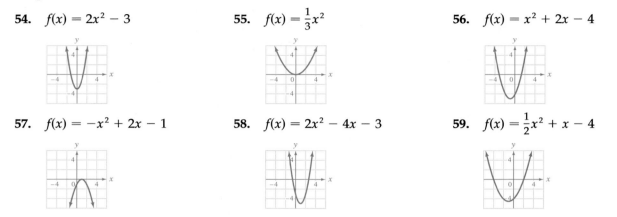

57. $f(x) = -x^2 + 2x - 1$

58. $f(x) = 2x^2 - 4x - 3$

59. $f(x) = \dfrac{1}{2}x^2 + x - 4$

60. *The Postal Service*   The graph below shows the cost of a first-class postage stamp from the 1950s to 1999. A quadratic function that approximately models these data is $y = 0.01147x^2 - 0.98960x + 21.39750$, where $x \geq 55$ and $x = 55$ for the year 1955, and y is the cost in cents of a first-class stamp. Using the model equation, determine what the model predicts the cost of a first-class stamp will be in the year 2010. Round to the nearest cent.   51¢

Cost of a First-Class Postage Stamp

[C] **61.** The point whose coordinates are (x_1, y_1) lies in quadrant I and is a point on the graph of the equation $y = 2x^2 - 2x + 1$. Given $y_1 = 13$, find x_1.   3

[C] **62.** The point whose coordinates are (x_1, y_1) lies in quadrant II and is a point on the graph of the equation $y = 2x^2 - 3x - 2$. Given $y_1 = 12$, find x_1. -2

[C] **63.** Graph $y = x^2 + 4x + 5$. By examining the graph, determine whether the solutions of the equation $x^2 + 4x + 5 = 0$ are real numbers.   No

[C] **64.** Graph $y = -2x^2 - 4x + 5$. By examining the graph, determine whether the solutions of the equation $-2x^2 - 4x + 5 = 0$ are real numbers.   Yes

S E C T I O N **11.5**

Application Problems

1 Application problems

The application problems in this section are varieties of those problems solved earlier in the text. Each of the strategies for the problems in this section results in a quadratic equation.

Solve: It took a motorboat a total of 7 h to travel 48 mi down a river and then 48 mi back again. The rate of the current was 2 mph. Find the rate of the motorboat in calm water.

STRATEGY for solving an application problem

▪ Determine the type of problem. For example, is it a uniform motion problem, a geometry problem, a work problem, or an age problem?

The problem is a uniform motion problem.

▪ Choose a variable to represent the unknown quantity. Write numerical or variable expressions for all the remaining quantities. These results can be recorded in a table.

The unknown rate of the motorboat: r

	Distance	÷	Rate	=	Time
Down river	48	÷	$r + 2$	=	$\dfrac{48}{r + 2}$
Up river	48	÷	$r - 2$	=	$\dfrac{48}{r - 2}$

▪ Determine how the quantities are related. If necessary, review the strategies presented in the chapter on Solving Equations and Inequalities: Applications.

The total time of the trip was 7 h.

$$\frac{48}{r + 2} + \frac{48}{r - 2} = 7$$

$$(r + 2)(r - 2)\left(\frac{48}{r + 2} + \frac{48}{r - 2}\right) = (r + 2)(r - 2)7$$

$$(r - 2)48 + (r + 2)48 = 7r^2 - 28$$

$$48r - 96 + 48r + 96 = 7r^2 - 28$$

$$96r = 7r^2 - 28$$

$$0 = 7r^2 - 96r - 28$$

$$0 = (7r + 2)(r - 14)$$

$$7r + 2 = 0 \qquad\qquad r - 14 = 0$$
$$7r = -2 \qquad\qquad\quad r = 14$$
$$r = -\frac{2}{7}$$

The solution $-\dfrac{2}{7}$ is not possible, because the rate cannot be negative.

The rate of the motorboat in calm water is 14 mph.

Example 1   Working together, a painter and the painter's apprentice can paint a room in 4 h. Working alone, the apprentice requires 6 more hours to paint the room than the painter requires working alone. How long does it take the painter, working alone, to paint the room?

Strategy   ▪ This is a work problem.
   ▪ Time for the painter to paint the room: t
   Time for the apprentice to paint the room: $t + 6$

	Rate	Time	Part
Painter	$\dfrac{1}{t}$	4	$\dfrac{4}{t}$
Apprentice	$\dfrac{1}{t+6}$	4	$\dfrac{4}{t+6}$

   ▪ The sum of the parts of the task completed must equal 1.

Solution
$$\frac{4}{t} + \frac{4}{t+6} = 1$$

$$t(t+6)\left(\frac{4}{t} + \frac{4}{t+6}\right) = t(t+6) \cdot 1$$

$$(t+6)4 + t(4) = t(t+6)$$

$$4t + 24 + 4t = t^2 + 6t$$

$$0 = t^2 - 2t - 24$$

$$0 = (t-6)(t+4)$$

$$t - 6 = 0 \qquad t + 4 = 0$$
$$t = 6 \qquad\qquad t = -4 \quad \blacktriangleright \text{ The solution } t = -4 \text{ is not possible.}$$

Working alone, the painter requires 6 h to paint the room.

Problem 1   The length of a rectangle is 3 m more than the width. The area is 40 m². Find the width.

Solution   See page S26.   5 m

CONCEPT REVIEW 11.5

Determine whether the statement is always true, sometimes true, or never true.

1. If the length of a rectangle is three more than twice the width and the width is represented by W, then the length is represented by $3W + 2$.   Never true

2. The sum of the squares of two consecutive odd integers can be represented as $n^2 + (n+1)^2$.   Never true

3. If it takes one pipe 15 min longer to fill a tank than it does a second pipe, then the rate of work for the second pipe can be represented by $\frac{1}{t}$ and the rate of work for the first pipe can be represented by $\frac{1}{t+15}$.   Always true

4. If a plane's rate of speed is r and the rate of the wind is 30 mph, then the plane's rate of speed flying with the wind is $30 + r$ and the plane's rate of speed flying against the wind is $30 - r$.   Never true

5. The graph of the equation $h = 48t - 16t^2$ is the graph of a parabola opening down.   Always true

6. A number that is a solution to a quadratic equation may not be a possible answer to the application problem it models. Such a solution is disregarded. Always true

EXERCISES 11.5

1   1. *Sports*   The area of the batter's box on a major-league baseball field is 24 ft². The length of the batter's box is 2 ft more than the width. Find the length and width of the rectangular batter's box.   Length: 6 ft; width: 4 ft

2. *Sports*   The length of the batter's box on a softball field is 1 ft more than twice the width. The area of the batter's box is 21 ft². Find the length and width of the rectangular batter's box.   Length: 7 ft; width: 3 ft

3. *Recreation*   The length of a children's playground is twice the width. The area is 5000 ft². Find the length and width of the rectangular playground. Length: 100 ft; width: 50 ft

4. *Sports*   The length of a singles tennis court is 24 ft more than twice the width. The area is 2106 ft². Find the length and width of the singles tennis court.   Length: 78 ft; width: 27 ft

5. *Integer Problem*   The sum of the squares of two positive consecutive odd integers is 130. Find the two integers.   7 and 9

6. *Integer Problem*   The sum of two integers is 12. The product of the two integers is 35. Find the two integers.   5 and 7

7. *Integer Problem*   The difference between two integers is 4. The product of the two integers is 60. Find the integers.   6 and 10, or -10 and -6

8. *Integer Problem*   Twice an integer equals the square of the integer. Find the integer.   0 or 2

9. *Work Problem*   One computer takes 21 min longer to calculate the value of a complex equation than a second computer. Working together, these computers can complete the calculation in 10 min. How long would it take each computer, working alone, to calculate the value?   First computer: 35 min; second computer: 14 min

10. *Work Problem*   A tank has two drains. One drain takes 16 min longer to empty the tank than does the second drain. With both drains open, the tank is emptied in 6 min. How long would it take each drain, working alone, to empty the tank?   First drain: 24 min; second drain: 8 min

11. *Uniform Motion Problem*   It takes 6 h longer to cross a channel in a ferry-boat when one engine of the boat is used alone than when a second engine is used alone. Using both engines, the ferryboat can make the crossing in 4 h. How long would it take each engine, working alone, to power the ferryboat across the channel?   First engine: 12 h; second engine: 6 h

12. *Work Problem*   An apprentice mason takes 8 h longer than an experienced mason to build a small fireplace. Working together, they can build the fireplace in 3 h. How long would it take the experienced mason, working alone, to build the fireplace?   4 h

13. *Uniform Motion Problem*   It took a small plane 2 h more to fly 375 mi against the wind than it took the plane to fly the same distance with the wind. The rate of the wind was 25 mph. Find the rate of the plane in calm air. 100 mph

14. *Uniform Motion Problem*   It took a motorboat 1 h longer to travel 36 mi against the current than it took the boat to travel 36 mi with the current. The rate of the current was 3 mph. Find the rate of the boat in calm water. 15 mph

15. *Uniform Motion Problem*   A motorcycle traveled 150 mi at a constant rate before decreasing the speed by 15 mph. Another 35 mi was driven at the decreased speed. The total time for the 185-mile trip was 4 h. Find the cyclist's rate during the first 150 mi.   50 mph

16. *Uniform Motion Problem*   A cruise ship sailed through a 20-mile inland passageway at a constant rate before increasing its speed by 15 mph. Another 75 mi was traveled at the increased rate. The total time for the 95-mile trip was 5 h. Find the rate of the ship during the last 75 mi.   25 mph

17. *Physics*   An arrow is projected into the air with an initial velocity of 48 ft/s. At what times will the arrow be 32 ft above the ground? Use the equation $h = 48t - 16t^2$, where h is the height, in feet, above the ground after t seconds. 1 s, 2 s

18. *Physics*   A model rocket is launched with an initial velocity of 200 feet per second. The height, h, of the rocket t seconds after launch is given by $h = -16t^2 + 200t$. How many seconds after the launch will the rocket be 300 ft above the ground? Round to the nearest hundredth.   1.74 s, 10.76 s

19. *Travel*   In Germany there are no speed limits on some portions of the autobahn (highway). Other portions have a speed limit of 180 km/h (approximately 112 mph). The distance, d (in meters), required to stop a car traveling at v kilometers per hour is $d = 0.0056v^2 + 0.14v$. What is the maximum speed a driver can be traveling and still be able to stop within 150 m? Round to the nearest tenth.   151.6 km/h

20. *Sports*   In a slow-pitch softball game, the height of the ball thrown by a pitcher can be modeled by the equation $h = -16t^2 + 24t + 4$, where h is the height of the ball and t is the time since it was released by the pitcher. If the batter hits the ball when it is 2 ft off the ground, how many seconds has the ball been in the air? Round to the nearest hundredth.   1.58 s

21. *Safety*   The path of water from a hose on a fire tugboat can be modeled by the equation $y = -0.005x^2 + 1.2x + 10$, where y is the height in feet of the water above the ocean when it is x feet from the tugboat. At what distance from the tugboat is the water from the hose when the water from the hose is 5 ft above the ocean? Round to the nearest tenth.   244.1 ft

22. *Sports*   A baseball player hits a ball. The height of the ball above the ground at time t can be approximated by the equation $h = -16t^2 + 76t + 5$. When will the ball hit the ground? Round to the nearest hundredth. (*Hint:* The ball strikes the ground when $h = 0$ ft.)   4.81 s

5 ft

23. *Sports*   A basketball player shoots at a basket 25 ft away. The height h of the ball above the ground at time t is given by $h = -16t^2 + 32t + 6.5$. How many seconds after the ball is released does it hit the basket? Round to the nearest hundredth. (*Hint:* When it hits the basket, $h = 10$ ft.)   1.88 s

24. *Sports*   The hang time of a football that is kicked on the opening kickoff is given by $s = -16t^2 + 88t + 1$, where s is the height, in feet, of the football t seconds after leaving the kicker's foot. What is the hang time of a kickoff that hits the ground without being caught? Round to the nearest tenth.   5.5 s

APPLYING CONCEPTS 11.5

25. *Geometry*   A tin can has a volume of 1500 cm³ and a height of 15 cm. Find the radius of the base of the tin can. Round to the nearest hundredth.   5.64 cm

15 cm

26. *Geometry*   The hypotenuse of a right triangle is $\sqrt{13}$ cm. One leg is 1 cm shorter than twice the length of the other leg. Find the lengths of the legs of the right triangle.   2 cm and 3 cm

27. *Integer Problem*   The sum of the squares of four consecutive integers is 86. Find the four integers.   −6, −5, −4, and −3, or 3, 4, 5, and 6

28. *Geometry*   Find the radius of a right circular cone that has a volume of 800 cm³ and a height of 12 cm. Round to the nearest hundredth.   7.98 cm

12 cm

[C] 29. *The Food Industry*   The radius of a large pizza is 1 in. less than twice the radius of a small pizza. The difference between the areas of the two pizzas is 33π in². Find the radius of the large pizza.   7 in.

[C] 30. *Gardening*   The perimeter of a rectangular garden is 54 ft. The area of the garden is 180 ft². Find the length and width of the garden.   Length: 15 ft; width: 12 ft

[C] 31. *The Food Industry*   A square piece of cardboard is to be formed into a box to transport pizzas. The box is formed by cutting 2-inch square corners from the cardboard and folding them up as shown in the figure at the right. If the volume of the box is 512 in³, what are the dimensions of the cardboard? 20 in. by 20 in.

[C] **32.** *Metalwork*   A wire 8 ft long is cut into two pieces. A circle is formed from one piece and a square is formed from the other. The total area of both figures is given by $A = \frac{1}{16}(8 - x)^2 + \frac{x^2}{4\pi}$. What is the length of each piece of wire if the total area is 4.5 ft²? Round to the nearest thousandth.   7.507 ft, 0.493 ft

Focus on Problem Solving

Algebraic Manipulation and Graphing Techniques

Problem solving is often easier when we have both algebraic manipulation and graphing techniques at our disposal. Solving quadratic equations and graphing quadratic equations in two variables are used here to solve problems involving profit.

A company's revenue, R, is the total amount of money the company earned by sellings its products. The cost, C, is the total amount of money the company spent to manufacture and sell its products. A company's profit, P, is the difference between the revenue and cost: $P = R - C$. A company's revenue and cost may be represented by equations.

A company manufactures and sells woodstoves. The total monthly cost, in dollars, to produce n woodstoves is $C = 30n + 2000$. Write a variable expression for the company's monthly profit if the revenue, in dollars, obtained from selling all n woodstoves is $R = 150n - 0.4n^2$.

$$P = R - C$$
$$P = 150n - 0.4n^2 - (30n + 2000) \quad \blacktriangleright \text{ Replace } R \text{ by } 150n - 0.4n^2 \text{ and}$$
$$P = -0.4n^2 + 120n - 2000 \qquad\qquad C \text{ by } 30n + 2000. \text{ Then simplify.}$$

The company's monthly profit is $P = -0.4n^2 + 120n - 2000$.

How many woodstoves must the company manufacture and sell in order to make a profit of $6000 a month?

$$P = -0.4n^2 + 120n - 2000$$
$$6000 = -0.4n^2 + 120n - 2000 \quad \blacktriangleright \text{ Substitute 6000 for } P.$$
$$0 = -0.4n^2 + 120n - 8000 \quad \blacktriangleright \text{ Write the equation in}$$
$$\qquad\qquad\qquad\qquad\qquad\qquad\qquad \text{standard form.}$$
$$0 = n^2 - 300n + 20{,}000 \quad \blacktriangleright \text{ Divide each side of the}$$
$$\qquad\qquad\qquad\qquad\qquad\qquad\qquad \text{equation by } -0.4.$$
$$0 = (n - 100)(n - 200) \quad \blacktriangleright \text{ Factor.}$$

$$n - 100 = 0 \qquad\quad n - 200 = 0 \quad \blacktriangleright \text{ Solve for } n.$$
$$n = 100 \qquad\qquad n = 200$$

The company will make a monthly profit of $6000 if either 100 or 200 woodstoves are manufactured and sold.

The graph of $P = -0.4n^2 + 120n - 2000$ is shown at the right. Note that when $P = 6000$, the values of n are 100 and 200.

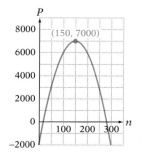

Also note that the coordinates of the highest point on the graph are (150, 7000). This means that the company makes a *maximum* profit of $7000 per month when 150 woodstoves are manufactured and sold.

1. The total cost, in dollars, for a company to produce and sell n guitars per month is $C = 240n + 1200$. The company's revenue, in dollars, from selling all n guitars is $R = 400n - 2n^2$.

    a. How many guitars must the company produce and sell each month in order to make a monthly profit of $1200?

    b. Graph the profit equation. What is the maximum monthly profit the company can make?

2. A company's total monthly cost, in dollars, for manufacturing and selling n videotapes per month is $C = 35n + 2000$. The company's revenue, in dollars, from selling all n videotapes is $R = 175n - 0.2n^2$.

    a. How many videotapes must be produced and sold each month in order for the company to make a monthly profit of $18,000?

    b. Graph the profit equation. How many videotapes must the company produce and sell in order to make the maximum monthly profit?

Projects and Group Activities

Graphical Solutions of Quadratic Equations

The *real* number solutions of quadratic equations can be approximated by graphing. Recall that to find an x-intercept for a graph, we replace y by 0 and solve for x. For instance, to find the x-intercepts of $y = x^2 - 3x - 5$, first replace y by zero. That produces the quadratic equation $0 = x^2 - 3x - 5$. The solutions of this equation can be found by using the quadratic formula or by graphing $y = x^2 - 3x - 5$ and approximating the x-intercepts.

The approximate solutions are -1.192582 and 4.1925824.

1. Graphically approximate the solutions of $2x^2 - 3x - 7 = 0$.

2. Graphically approximate the solutions of $x^2 + 5x = 1$. *Suggestion:* First write the equation in standard form.

3. Graphically approximate the solution of $\pi x^2 - \sqrt{17}x - \dfrac{1}{\sqrt{3}} = 0$.

4. The solution of $0.5x^2 - 2x + 2 = 0$ is a double root. Graphically approximate the solution and explain how the graph of $y = 0.5x^2 - 2x + 2$ confirms that statement.

5. There are no real number solutions of $x^2 + 4x + 5 = 0$. Explain how the graph of $y = x^2 + 4x + 5$ confirms that statement.

Iterative Calculations

Consider the following three expressions:

$$p + 3p(1 - p) \qquad p(4 - 3p) \qquad 4p - 3p^2$$

When these expressions are written in simplest form, each becomes $4p - 3p^2$. It would seem that if you used a graphing calculator to evaluate these expressions, each one should give the same result. However, that is not the case, as we show in this project.

We begin with $p = 0.05$. Evaluating each of the expressions gives the same result, 0.1925. Now replace p in each expression with the current value in the display, 0.1925 in this case. This is called *feedback* because we are feeding our outputs back into each expression as inputs. Each new evaluation is called an *iteration*. The table below shows the results of performing the calculations on a *TI-83* calculator.

Iteration	$p + 3p(1 - p)$	$p(4 - 3p)$	$4p - 3p^2$
1	0.1925	0.1925	0.1925
2	0.65883125	0.65883125	0.65883125
3	1.333149152	1.333149152	1.333149152
4	7.366232839E-4	7.366232839E-4	7.366232838E-4
5	0.0029448653	0.0029448653	0.0029448653
6	0.0117534445	0.0117534445	0.0117534445
7	0.0465993476	0.0465993476	0.0465993475
20	1.121356187	1.121356207	1.121356084
30	0.9471633048	0.9471899467	0.9470331284
40	0.5648166575	0.5352103994	0.7113151932

Note that for the 40th iteration the values are approximately 0.03 different between columns 2 and 3, and 0.15 different between columns 2 and 4.

1. Use a calculator to find the first 40 iterations for $p = 0.025$ for $4p - 3p^2$ and $p + 3p(1 - p)$.

2. Use a calculator to find the first 40 iterations for $p = 0.5$ for $4p - 3p^2$ and $p + 3p(1 - p)$.

3. Expressions of the form $p + rp(1 - p)$ [which is the form of $p + 3p(1 - p)$ with $r = 3$] are called Verhulst population models. Make up your own expression of this form, choosing some other value of r and a value of p.

4. Write a short paragraph on Verhulst population models.

Geometric Construction of Completing the Square

Completing the square as a method of solving a quadratic equation has been known for centuries. The Persian mathematician Al-Khwarismi used this method in a textbook written around 825 A.D. The method was very geometric. That is, Al-Khwarismi literally completed a square. To understand how this method works, consider the following geometric shapes: a square whose area is x^2, a rectangle whose area is x, and another square whose area is 1.

Now consider the expression $x^2 + 6x$. From our discussion in this chapter, to complete the square, we added $\left(\frac{1}{2} \cdot 6\right)^2 = 3^2 = 9$ to the expression. Here is the geometric construction that Al-Khwarismi used.

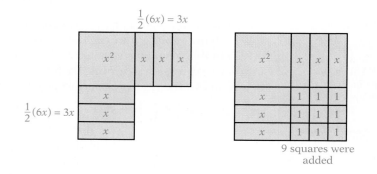

9 squares were added

Note that it is necessary to add 9 squares to the figure to "complete the square." One of the difficulties of using a geometric method such as this is that it cannot easily be extended to $x^2 - 6x$. There is no way to draw an area of $-6x$! That really did not bother Al-Khwarismi much. Negative numbers were not a significant part of mathematics until well into the 13th century.

1. Show how Al-Khwarismi would have completed the square for $x^2 + 4x$.

2. Show how Al-Khwarismi would have completed the square for $x^2 + 10x$.

3. Do the geometric constructions for Exercises 1 and 2 correspond to the algebraic method shown in this chapter?

Chapter Summary

Key Words

A *quadratic equation* is an equation that can be written in the form $ax^2 + bx + c = 0$, $a \neq 0$. A quadratic equation is also called a *second-degree equation.* (Objective 11.1.1)

The equation $4x^2 - 3x + 6 = 0$ is a quadratic equation. In this equation, $a = 4$, $b = -3$, and $c = 6$.

A quadratic equation is in *standard form* when the polynomial is in descending order and equal to zero.   (Objective 11.1.1)

The quadratic equation $5x^2 + 3x - 1 = 0$ is in standard form.

Adding to a binomial the constant term that makes it a perfect-square trinomial is called *completing the square.* (Objective 11.2.1)

Adding to $x^2 - 6x$ the constant term 9 results in a perfect-square trinomial:

$$x^2 - 6x + 9 = (x - 3)(x - 3) = (x - 3)^2$$

The graph of an equation of the form $y = ax^2 + bx + c$ is a *parabola*. The *vertex* is the lowest point on a parabola that opens up or the highest point on a parabola that opens down. (Objective 11.4.1)

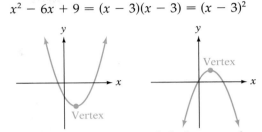

Parabola that opens up   Parabola that opens down

Essential Rules and Procedures

Solving a Quadratic Equation by Factoring
Write the equation in standard form, factor the left side of the equation, apply the Principle of Zero Products, and solve for the variable.   (Objective 11.1.1)

$$x^2 + 2x = 15$$
$$x^2 + 2x - 15 = 0$$
$$(x - 3)(x + 5) = 0$$

$$x - 3 = 0 \qquad x + 5 = 0$$
$$x = 3 \qquad x = -5$$

Principle of Taking the Square Root of Each Side of an Equation
If $x^2 = a$, then $x = \pm\sqrt{a}$.

This principle is used to solve quadratic equations by taking square roots.   (Objective 11.1.2)

$$3x^2 - 48 = 0$$
$$3x^2 = 48$$
$$x^2 = 16$$
$$\sqrt{x^2} = \sqrt{16}$$
$$x = \pm\sqrt{16}$$
$$x = \pm 4$$

Solving a Quadratic Equation by Completing the Square
When the quadratic equation is in the form $x^2 + bx = c$, add to each side of the equation the term that completes the square on $x^2 + bx$. Factor the perfect-square trinomial, and write it as the square of a binomial. Take the square root of each side of the equation and solve for x.   (Objective 11.2.1)

$$x^2 + 6x = 5$$
$$x^2 + 6x + 9 = 5 + 9$$
$$(x + 3)^2 = 14$$
$$\sqrt{(x + 3)^2} = \sqrt{14}$$
$$x + 3 = \pm\sqrt{14}$$
$$x = -3 \pm\sqrt{14}$$

The Quadratic Formula
The solutions of $ax^2 + bx + c = 0$, $a \neq 0$, are
$$x = \frac{-b \pm \sqrt{b^2 - 4ac}}{2a}.$$
(Objective 11.3.1)

$$3x^2 = x + 5$$
$$3x^2 - x - 5 = 0$$
$$x = \frac{-b \pm \sqrt{b^2 - 4ac}}{2a}$$
$$= \frac{-(-1) \pm \sqrt{(-1)^2 - 4(3)(-5)}}{2(3)}$$
$$= \frac{1 \pm \sqrt{1 + 60}}{6} = \frac{1 \pm \sqrt{61}}{6}$$

Graphing a Quadratic Equation in Two Variables
Find several solutions of the equation. Graph the ordered-pair solutions on a rectangular coordinate system. Draw a parabola through the points. (Objective 11.4.1)

$y = x^2 - x - 2$

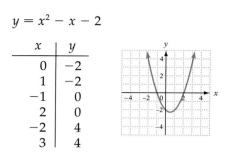

x	y
0	-2
1	-2
-1	0
2	0
-2	4
3	4

Chapter Review Exercises

1. Solve: $b^2 - 16 = 0$ $4, -4$

2. Solve: $x^2 - x - 3 = 0$ $\dfrac{1 \pm \sqrt{13}}{2}$

3. Solve: $x^2 - 3x - 5 = 0$ $\dfrac{3 \pm \sqrt{29}}{2}$

4. Solve: $49x^2 = 25$ $\pm\dfrac{5}{7}$

5. Graph: $y = -\dfrac{1}{4}x^2$

6. Graph: $y = -3x^2$

7. Solve: $x^2 = 10x - 2$ $5 \pm \sqrt{23}$

8. Solve: $6x(x + 1) = x - 1$ $-\dfrac{1}{2}, -\dfrac{1}{3}$

9. Solve: $4y^2 + 9 = 0$ No real number solution

10. Solve: $5x^2 + 20x + 12 = 0$ $\dfrac{-10 \pm 2\sqrt{10}}{5}$

11. Solve: $x^2 - 4x + 1 = 0$ $2 \pm \sqrt{3}$

12. Solve: $x^2 - x = 30$ $6, -5$

13. Solve: $6x^2 + 13x - 28 = 0$ $\dfrac{4}{3}, -\dfrac{7}{2}$

14. Solve: $x^2 = 40$ $\pm 2\sqrt{10}$

15. Solve: $3x^2 - 4x = 1$ $\dfrac{2 \pm \sqrt{7}}{3}$

16. Solve: $x^2 - 2x - 10 = 0$ $1 \pm \sqrt{11}$

17. Solve: $x^2 - 12x + 27 = 0$ $3, 9$

18. Solve: $(x - 7)^2 = 81$ $16, -2$

19. Graph: $y = 2x^2 + 1$

20. Graph: $y = \dfrac{1}{2}x^2 - 1$

21. Solve: $(y + 4)^2 - 25 = 0$ $1, -9$

22. Solve: $4x^2 + 16x = 7$ $\dfrac{-4 \pm \sqrt{23}}{2}$

23. Solve: $24x^2 + 34x + 5 = 0$ $-\dfrac{1}{6}, -\dfrac{5}{4}$

24. Solve: $x^2 = 4x - 8$ No real number solution

25. Solve: $x^2 - 5 = 8x$ $4 \pm \sqrt{21}$

26. Solve: $25(2x^2 - 2x + 1) = (x + 3)^2$ $\dfrac{4}{7}$

27. Solve: $\left(x - \dfrac{1}{2}\right)^2 = \dfrac{9}{4}$ $2, -1$

28. Solve: $16x^2 = 30x - 9$ $\dfrac{3}{8}, \dfrac{3}{2}$

29. Solve: $x^2 + 7x = 3$ $\dfrac{-7 \pm \sqrt{61}}{2}$

30. Solve: $12x^2 + 10 = 29x$ $2, \dfrac{5}{12}$

31. Solve: $4(x - 3)^2 = 20$ $3 \pm \sqrt{5}$

32. Solve: $x^2 + 8x - 3 = 0$ $-4 \pm \sqrt{19}$

33. Graph: $y = x^2 - 3x$

34. Graph: $y = x^2 - 4x + 3$

35. Solve: $(x + 9)^2 = x + 11$ $-7, -10$

36. Solve: $(x - 2)^2 - 24 = 0$ $2 \pm 2\sqrt{6}$

37. Solve: $x^2 + 6x + 12 = 0$ No real number solution

38. Solve: $x^2 + 6x - 2 = 0$ $-3 \pm \sqrt{11}$

39. Solve: $18x^2 - 52x = 6$ $3, -\dfrac{1}{9}$

40. Solve: $2x^2 + 5x = 1$ $\dfrac{-5 \pm \sqrt{33}}{4}$

41. Graph: $y = -x^2 + 4x - 5$

42. Solve: $x^2 + 3 = 9x$ $\dfrac{9 \pm \sqrt{69}}{2}$

43. Solve: $2x^2 + 5 = 7x$ $1, \dfrac{5}{2}$

44. Graph: $y = 4 - x^2$

45. It took an air balloon 1 h more to fly 60 mi against the wind than it took to fly 60 mi with the wind. The rate of the wind was 5 mph. Find the rate of the air balloon in calm air.   25 mph

46. The height of a triangle is 2 m more than twice the length of the base. The area of the triangle is 20 m². Find the height of the triangle and the length of the base.   Height: 10 m; base: 4 m

47. The sum of the squares of two consecutive positive odd integers is thirty-four. Find the two integers.   3, 5

48. In 5 h, two campers rowed 12 mi down a stream and then rowed back to their campsite. The rate of the stream's current was 1 mph. Find the rate of the boat in still water.   5 mph

49. An object is thrown into the air with an initial velocity of 32 ft/s. At what times will the object be 12 ft above the ground? Use the equation $h = 32t - 16t^2$, where h is the height, in feet, above the ground after t seconds. $\dfrac{1}{2}$ s, $1\dfrac{1}{2}$ s

50. A smaller drain takes 8 h longer to empty a tank than does a larger drain. Working together, the drains can empty the tank in 3 h. How long would it take each drain, working alone, to empty the tank?   Smaller drain: 12 h; larger drain: 4 h

Chapter Test

1. Solve: $3(x + 4)^2 - 60 = 0$ $-4 \pm 2\sqrt{5}$

2. Solve: $2x^2 + 8x = 3$ $\dfrac{-4 \pm \sqrt{22}}{2}$

3. Solve: $3x^2 + 7x = 20$ $-4, \dfrac{5}{3}$

4. Solve: $x^2 - 3x = 6$ $\dfrac{3 \pm \sqrt{33}}{2}$

5. Solve: $x^2 + 4x - 16 = 0$ $-2 \pm 2\sqrt{5}$

6. Graph: $y = x^2 + 2x - 4$

7. Solve: $x^2 + 4x + 2 = 0$ $-2 \pm \sqrt{2}$

8. Solve: $x^2 + 3x = 8$ $\dfrac{-3 \pm \sqrt{41}}{2}$

9. Solve: $2x^2 - 5x - 3 = 0$ $-\dfrac{1}{2}, 3$

10. Solve: $2x^2 - 6x + 1 = 0$ $\dfrac{3 \pm \sqrt{7}}{2}$

11. Solve: $3x^2 - x = 1$ $\dfrac{1 \pm \sqrt{13}}{6}$

12. Solve: $2(x - 5)^2 = 36$ $5 \pm 3\sqrt{2}$

13. Solve: $x^2 - 6x - 5 = 0$ $3 \pm \sqrt{14}$

14. Solve: $x^2 - 5x = 1$ $\dfrac{5 \pm \sqrt{29}}{2}$

15. Solve: $x^2 - 5x = 2$ $\dfrac{5 \pm \sqrt{33}}{2}$

16. Solve: $6x^2 - 17x = -5$ $\dfrac{5}{2}, \dfrac{1}{3}$

17. Solve: $x^2 + 3x - 7 = 0$ $\dfrac{-3 \pm \sqrt{37}}{2}$

18. Solve: $2x^2 - 4x - 5 = 0$ $\dfrac{2 \pm \sqrt{14}}{2}$

19. Solve: $2x^2 - 3x - 2 = 0$ $-\dfrac{1}{2}, 2$

20. Graph: $y = x^2 - 2x - 3$

21. Solve: $3x^2 - 2x = 3$ $\dfrac{1 \pm \sqrt{10}}{3}$

22. The length of a rectangle is 2 ft less than twice the width. The area of the rectangle is 40 ft². Find the length and width of the rectangle.   Length: 8 ft; width: 5 ft

23. It took a motorboat 1 h more to travel 60 mi against the current than it took to go 60 mi with the current. The rate of the current was 1 mph. Find the rate of the boat in calm water.   11 mph

24. The sum of the squares of three consecutive odd integers is 83. Find the middle odd integer.   5 or −5

25. A jogger ran 7 mi at a constant rate and then reduced the rate by 3 mph. An additional 8 mi was run at the reduced rate. The total time spent jogging the 15 mi was 3 h. Find the rate for the last 8 mi.   4 mph

Cumulative Review Exercises

1. Simplify: $2x - 3[2x - 4(3 - 2x) + 2] - 3$
   $-28x + 27$

2. Solve: $-\dfrac{3}{5}x = -\dfrac{9}{10}$ $\dfrac{3}{2}$

3. Solve: $2x - 3(4x - 5) = -3x - 6$ 3

4. Solve: $2x - 3(2 - 3x) > 2x - 5$ $x > \dfrac{1}{9}$

5. Find the x- and y-intercepts of the line
$4x - 3y = 12$.   (3, 0) and (0, −4)

6. Find the equation of the line that contains the point whose coordinates are $(-3, 2)$ and has slope $-\frac{4}{3}$. $y = -\frac{4}{3}x - 2$

7. Find the domain and range of the relation $\{(-2, -8), (-1, -1), (0, 0), (1, 1), (2, 8)\}$. Is the relation a function?
D: $\{-2, -1, 0, 1, 2\}$; R: $\{-8, -1, 0, 1, 8\}$; yes

8. Evaluate $f(x) = -3x + 10$ at $x = -9$.   37

9. Graph: $y = \frac{1}{4}x - 2$

10. Graph the solution set of $2x - 3y > 6$.

11. Solve by substitution: $3x - y = 5$
$y = 2x - 3$
(2, 1)

12. Solve by the addition method: $3x + 2y = 2$
$5x - 2y = 14$
(2, −2)

13. Simplify: $\dfrac{(2a^{-2}b)^2}{-3a^{-5}b^4}$ $-\dfrac{4a}{3b^2}$

14. Divide: $(x^2 - 8) \div (x - 2)$ $x + 2 - \dfrac{4}{x - 2}$

15. Factor: $4y(x - 4) - 3(x - 4)$ $(x - 4)(4y - 3)$

16. Factor: $3x^3 + 2x^2 - 8x$ $x(3x - 4)(x + 2)$

17. Divide: $\dfrac{3x^2 - 6x}{4x - 6} \div \dfrac{2x^2 + x - 6}{6x^2 - 24x}$ $\dfrac{9x^2(x - 2)(x - 4)}{(2x - 3)^2(x + 2)}$

18. Subtract: $\dfrac{x}{2(x - 1)} - \dfrac{1}{(x - 1)(x + 1)}$ $\dfrac{x + 2}{2(x + 1)}$

19. Simplify: $\dfrac{1 - \dfrac{7}{x} + \dfrac{12}{x^2}}{2 - \dfrac{1}{x} - \dfrac{15}{x^2}}$ $\dfrac{x - 4}{2x + 5}$

20. Solve: $\dfrac{x}{x + 6} = \dfrac{3}{x}$ −3, 6

21. Multiply: $(\sqrt{a} - \sqrt{2})(\sqrt{a} + \sqrt{2})$ $a - 2$

22. Solve: $3 = 8 - \sqrt{5x}$ 5

23. Solve: $2x^2 - 7x = -3$ $\frac{1}{2}, 3$

24. Solve: $3(x - 2)^2 = 36$ $2 \pm 2\sqrt{3}$

25. Solve: $3x^2 - 4x - 5 = 0$ $\frac{2 \pm \sqrt{19}}{3}$

26. Graph: $y = x^2 - 3x - 2$

27. In a certain state, the sales tax is $7\frac{1}{4}\%$. The sales tax on a chemistry textbook is $2.61. Find the cost of the textbook before the tax is added. $36

28. Find the cost per pound of a mixture made from 20 lb of cashews that cost $3.50 per pound and 50 lb of peanuts that cost $1.75 per pound. $2.25

29. A stock investment of 100 shares paid a dividend of $215. At this rate, how many additional shares are required to earn a dividend of $752.50?
250 additional shares

30. A 720-mile trip from one city to another takes 3 h when a plane is flying with the wind. The return trip, against the wind, takes 4.5 h. Find the rate of the plane in calm air and the rate of the wind.   Plane: 200 mph; wind: 40 mph

31. A student received a 70, a 91, an 85, and a 77 on four tests in a math class. What scores on the fifth test will enable the student to receive a minimum of 400 points?   77 or better

32. A guy wire is attached to a point 30 m above the ground on a telephone pole that is perpendicular to the ground. The wire is anchored to the ground at a point 10 m from the base of the pole. Find the length of the guy wire. Round to the nearest hundredth.   31.62 m

33. The sum of the squares of three consecutive odd integers is 155. Find the middle odd integer.   −7 or 7

FINAL EXAM

1. Evaluate: $-|-3|$ -3

2. Subtract: $-15 - (-12) - 3$ -6

3. Write $\frac{1}{8}$ as a percent. 12.5%

4. Simplify: $-2^4 \cdot (-2)^4$ -256

5. Simplify: $-7 - \dfrac{12 - 15}{2 - (-1)} \cdot (-4)$ -11

6. Evaluate $\dfrac{a^2 - 3b}{2a - 2b^2}$ when $a = 3$ and $b = -2$. $-\dfrac{15}{2}$

7. Simplify: $6x - (-4y) - (-3x) + 2y$ $9x + 6y$

8. Multiply: $(-15z)\left(-\dfrac{2}{5}\right)$ $6z$

9. Simplify: $-2[5 - 3(2x - 7) - 2x]$ $16x - 52$

10. Solve: $20 = -\dfrac{2}{5}x$ -50

11. Solve: $4 - 2(3x + 1) = 3(2 - x) + 5$ -3

12. Find 19% of 80. 15.2

13. Solve: $4 - x \geq 7$ $x \leq -3$

14. Solve: $2 - 2(y - 1) \leq 2y - 6$ $y \geq \dfrac{5}{2}$

15. Find the slope of the line that contains the points whose coordinates are $(-1, -3)$ and $(2, -1)$. $\dfrac{2}{3}$

16. Find the equation of the line that contains the point whose coordinates are $(3, -4)$ and has slope $-\dfrac{2}{3}$. $y = -\dfrac{2}{3}x - 2$

17. Graph the line with slope $-\frac{1}{2}$ and y-intercept $(0, -3)$.

18. Graph: $f(x) = \frac{2}{3}x - 4$

19. Find the range of the function given by the equation $f(x) = -x + 5$ if the domain is $\{-6, -3, 0, 3, 6\}$. $\{-1, 2, 5, 8, 11\}$

20. Graph the solution set of $3x - 2y \geq 6$.

21. Solve by substitution: $y = 4x - 7$
$y = 2x + 5$ $(6, 17)$

22. Solve by the addition method: $4x - 3y = 11$
$(2, -1)$ $2x + 5y = -1$

23. Subtract: $(2x^2 - 5x + 1) - (5x^2 - 2x - 7)$
$-3x^2 - 3x + 8$

24. Simplify: $(-3xy^3)^4$ $81x^4y^{12}$

25. Multiply: $(3x^2 - x - 2)(2x + 3)$
$6x^3 + 7x^2 - 7x - 6$

26. Simplify: $\dfrac{(-2x^2y^3)^3}{(-4x^{-1}y^4)^2}$ $-\dfrac{x^8y}{2}$

27. Simplify: $(4x^{-2}y)^3(2xy^{-2})^{-2}$ $\dfrac{16y^7}{x^8}$

28. Divide: $\dfrac{12x^3y^2 - 16x^2y^2 - 20y^2}{4xy^2}$ $3x^2 - 4x - \dfrac{5}{x}$

29. Divide: $(5x^2 - 2x - 1) \div (x + 2)$
$5x - 12 + \dfrac{23}{x + 2}$

30. Write 0.000000039 in scientific notation.
$3.9 \cdot 10^{-8}$

31. Factor: $2a(4 - x) - 6(x - 4)$ $2(4 - x)(a + 3)$

32. Factor: $x^2 - 5x - 6$ $(x - 6)(x + 1)$

33. Factor: $2x^2 - x - 3$ $(2x - 3)(x + 1)$

34. Factor: $6x^2 - 5x - 6$ $(3x + 2)(2x - 3)$

35. Factor: $8x^3 - 28x^2 + 12x$ $4x(2x - 1)(x - 3)$

36. Factor: $25x^2 - 16$ $(5x + 4)(5x - 4)$

37. Factor: $75y - 12x^2y$ $3y(5 + 2x)(5 - 2x)$

38. Solve: $2x^2 = 7x - 3$ $\frac{1}{2}, 3$

39. Multiply: $\dfrac{2x^2 - 3x + 1}{4x^2 - 2x} \cdot \dfrac{4x^2 + 4x}{x^2 - 2x + 1}$ $\dfrac{2(x + 1)}{x - 1}$

40. Subtract: $\dfrac{5}{x + 3} - \dfrac{3x}{2x - 5}$ $\dfrac{-3x^2 + x - 25}{(2x - 5)(x + 3)}$

41. Simplify: $\dfrac{x - \dfrac{3}{2x - 1}}{1 - \dfrac{2}{2x - 1}}$ $x + 1$

42. Solve: $\dfrac{5x}{3x - 5} - 3 = \dfrac{7}{3x - 5}$ 2

43. Solve $a = 3a - 2b$ for a. $a = b$

44. Simplify: $\sqrt{49x^6}$ $7x^3$

45. Add: $2\sqrt{27a} + 8\sqrt{48a}$ $38\sqrt{3a}$

46. Simplify: $\dfrac{\sqrt{3}}{\sqrt{5} - 2}$ $\sqrt{15} + 2\sqrt{3}$

47. Solve: $\sqrt{x + 4} - \sqrt{x - 1} = 1$ 5

48. Solve: $(x - 3)^2 = 7$ $3 \pm \sqrt{7}$

49. Solve: $4x^2 - 2x - 1 = 0$ $\dfrac{1 \pm \sqrt{5}}{4}$

50. Graph: $y = x^2 - 4x + 3$

51. Translate and simplify "the sum of twice a number and three times the difference between the number and two." $2x + 3(x - 2); 5x - 6$

52. Because of depreciation, the value of an office machine is now $2400. This is 80% of its original value. Find the original value of the machine. $3000

53. A coin bank contains quarters and dimes. There are three times as many dimes as quarters. The total value of the coins in the bank is $11. Find the number of dimes in the bank.   60 dimes

54. One angle of a triangle is 10° more than the measure of the second angle. The third angle is 10° more than the measure of the first angle. Find the measure of each angle of the triangle.   60°, 50°, 70°

55. The manufacturer's cost for a laser printer is $900. The manufacturer sells the printer for $1485. Find the markup rate.   65%

56. An investment of $3000 is made at an annual simple interest rate of 8%. How much additional money must be invested at 11% so that the total interest earned is 10% of the total investment? $6000

57. A grocer mixes 4 lb of peanuts that cost $2 per pound with 2 lb of walnuts that cost $5 per pound. What is the cost per pound of the resulting mixture? $3

58. A pharmacist mixes 20 L of a solution that is 60% acid with 30 L of a solution that is 20% acid. What is the percent concentration of acid in the resulting mixture?   36%

59. A small plane flew at a constant rate for 1 h. The pilot then doubled the plane's speed. An additional 1.5 h was flown at the increased speed. If the entire flight was 860 km, how far did the plane travel during the first hour?   215 km

60. With the current, a motorboat travels 50 mi in 2.5 h. Against the current, it takes twice as long to travel 50 mi. Find the rate of the boat in calm water and the rate of the current.   Boat: 15 mph; current: 5 mph

61. The length of a rectangle is 5 m more than the width. The area of the rectangle is 50 m². Find the dimensions of the rectangle.   Length: 10 m; width: 5 m

62. A paint formula requires 2 oz of dye for every 15 oz of base paint. How many ounces of dye are required for 120 oz of base paint?   16 oz

63. It takes a chef 1 h to prepare a dinner. The chef's apprentice can prepare the same dinner in 1.5 h. How long would it take the chef and the apprentice, working together, to prepare the dinner?   0.6 h

64. The hypotenuse of a right triangle measures 14 cm. One leg of the triangle measures 8 cm. Find the length of the other leg of the triangle. Round to the nearest tenth.   11.5 cm

65. It took a plane $\frac{1}{2}$ h more to fly 500 mi against the wind than it took to fly the same distance with the wind. The rate of the plane in calm air is 225 mph. Find the rate of the wind.   25 mph

APPENDIX

Guidelines for Using Graphing Calculators

Texas Instruments TI-83

To evaluate an expression

a. Press the $\boxed{\text{Y=}}$ key. A menu showing $\backslash Y_1 =$ through $\backslash Y_7 =$ will be displayed vertically with a blinking cursor to the right of $\backslash Y_1 =$. Press $\boxed{\text{CLEAR}}$, if necessary, to delete an unwanted expression.

b. Input the expression to be evaluated. For example, to input the expression $-3a^2b - 4c$, use the following keystrokes:

$\boxed{\text{(−)}}$ 3 $\boxed{\text{ALPHA}}$ A $\boxed{\wedge}$ 2 $\boxed{\text{ALPHA}}$ B $\boxed{\text{−}}$ 4 $\boxed{\text{ALPHA}}$ C $\boxed{\text{2nd}}$ QUIT

Note the difference between the key for a negative sign $\boxed{\text{(−)}}$ and the key for a *minus* sign $\boxed{\text{−}}$.

c. Store the value of each variable that will be used in the expression. For example, to evaluate the expression above when $a = 3$, $b = -2$, and $c = -4$, use the following keystrokes:

3 $\boxed{\text{STO▷}}$ $\boxed{\text{ALPHA}}$ A $\boxed{\text{ENTER}}$ $\boxed{\text{(−)}}$ 2 $\boxed{\text{STO▷}}$ $\boxed{\text{ALPHA}}$ B $\boxed{\text{ENTER}}$
$\boxed{\text{(−)}}$ 4 $\boxed{\text{STO▷}}$ $\boxed{\text{ALPHA}}$ C $\boxed{\text{ENTER}}$

These steps store the value of each variable.

d. Press $\boxed{\text{2nd}}$ $\boxed{\text{VARS}}$ $\boxed{\triangleright}$ $\boxed{1}$ $\boxed{1}$ $\boxed{\text{ENTER}}$. The value for the expression, Y_1, for the given values is displayed; in this case, $Y_1 = 70$.

To graph a function

a. Press the $\boxed{\text{Y=}}$ key. A menu showing $\backslash Y_1 =$ through $\backslash Y_7 =$ will be displayed vertically with a blinking cursor to the right of $\backslash Y_1 =$. Press $\boxed{\text{CLEAR}}$, if necessary, to delete an unwanted expression.

b. Input the expression for each function that is to be graphed. Press $\boxed{\text{X,T,θ,}n}$ to input x. For example, to input $y = x^3 + 2x^2 - 5x - 6$, use the following keystrokes:

$\boxed{\text{X,T,θ,}n}$ $\boxed{\wedge}$ 3 $\boxed{+}$ 2 $\boxed{\text{X,T,θ,}n}$ $\boxed{\wedge}$ 2 $\boxed{\text{−}}$ 5 $\boxed{\text{X,T,θ,}n}$ $\boxed{\text{−}}$ 6

c. Set the domain and range by pressing $\boxed{\text{WINDOW}}$. Enter the values for the minimum x value (Xmin), the maximum x value (Xmax), the distance between tick marks on the x-axis (Xscl), the minimum y value (Ymin), the maximum y value (Ymax), and the distance between tick marks on the y-axis (Yscl). Now press $\boxed{\text{GRAPH}}$. For the graph shown at the left, Xmin $= -10$, Xmax $= 10$, Xscl $= 1$, Ymin $= -10$, Ymax $= 10$, and Yscl $= 1$. This is called the standard viewing rectangle. Pressing $\boxed{\text{ZOOM}}$ $\boxed{6}$ is a quick way to set the calculator to the standard viewing rectangle. *Note:* This will also immediately graph the function in that window.

d. Press the $\boxed{\text{Y=}}$ key. The equals sign has a black rectangle around it. This indicates that the function is active and will be graphed when the $\boxed{\text{GRAPH}}$ key is pressed. A function is deactivated by using the arrow keys. Move the cursor over the equals sign and press ENTER . When the cursor is moved to the right, the black rectangle will not be present, and that equation will not be active.

e. Graphing some radical equations requires special care. To graph the function $y = \sqrt{2x + 3}$, enter the following keystrokes:

The graph is shown below.

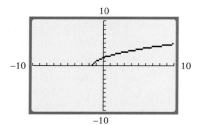

To display the x-coordinates of rectangular coordinates as integers

a. Set the viewing window as follows: Xmin $= -47$, Xmax $= 47$, Xscl $= 10$, Ymin $= -31$, Ymax $= 31$, Yscl $= 10$.

b. Graph the function and use the TRACE feature. Press TRACE and then move the cursor with the ◁ and ▷ keys. The values of x and $y = f(x)$ displayed on the bottom of the screen are the coordinates of a point on the graph.

To display the x-coordinates of rectangular coordinates in tenths

a. Set the viewing window as follows: ZOOM   4

b. Graph the function and use the TRACE feature. Press TRACE and then move the cursor with the ◁ and ▷ keys. The values of x and $y = f(x)$ displayed on the bottom of the screen are the coordinates of a point on the graph.

To evaluate a function for a given value of x, or to produce ordered pairs of a function

a. Input the equation; for example, input Y₁ $= 2x^3 - 3x + 2$.

b. Press 2nd QUIT.

c. Input a value for x; for example, to input 3, press 3 STO▷   X,T,θ,n   ENTER .

d. Press VARS   ▷   1   1   ENTER . The value for the expression, Y₁, for the given x value is displayed, in this case, Y₁ $= 47$. An ordered pair of the function is (3, 47).

e. Repeat steps **c.** and **d.** to produce as many pairs as desired. The TABLE feature of the *TI-83* can also be used to determine pairs.

Zoom Features

To zoom in or out on a graph

a. Here are two methods of using ZOOM. The first method uses the built-in features of the calculator. Move the cursor to a point on the graph that is of interest. Press ⬚ZOOM⬚. The ZOOM menu will appear. Press ⬚2⬚ ⬚ENTER⬚ to zoom in on the graph by the amount shown under the SET FACTORS menu. The center of the new graph is the location at which you placed the cursor. Press ⬚ZOOM⬚ ⬚3⬚ ⬚ENTER⬚ to zoom out on the graph by the amount under the SET FACTORS menu. (The SET FACTORS menu is accessed by pressing ⬚ZOOM⬚ ⬚▷⬚ ⬚4⬚.)

b. The second method uses the ZBOX option under the ZOOM menu. To use this method, press ⬚ZOOM⬚ ⬚1⬚. A cursor will appear on the graph. Use the arrow keys to move the cursor to a portion of the graph that is of interest. Press ⬚ENTER⬚. Now use the arrow keys to draw a box around the portion of the graph you wish to see. Press ⬚ENTER⬚. The portion of the graph defined by the box will be drawn.

c. Pressing ⬚ZOOM⬚ ⬚6⬚ resets the window to the standard 10×10 viewing window.

Solving Equations

This discussion is based on the fact that the solution of an equation can be related to the x-intercepts of a graph. For instance, the real solutions of the equation $x^2 = x + 1$ are the x-intercepts of the graph of $f(x) = x^2 - x - 1$, which are the zeros of f.

To solve $x^2 = x + 1$, rewrite the equation with all terms on one side. The equation is now $x^2 - x - 1 = 0$. Think of this equation as $Y_1 = x^2 - x - 1$. The x-intercepts of the graph of Y_1 are the solutions of the equation $x^2 = x + 1$.

a. Enter $x^2 - x - 1$ into Y_1.

b. Graph the equation. You may need to adjust the viewing window so that the x-intercepts are visible.

c. Press ⬚2nd⬚ CALC ⬚2⬚.

d. Move the cursor to a point on the curve that is to the left of an x-intercept. Press ⬚ENTER⬚.

e. Move the cursor to a point on the curve that is to the right of an x-intercept. Press ⬚ENTER⬚.

f. Press ⬚ENTER⬚.

g. The root is shown as the x-coordinate on the bottom of the screen; in this case, the root is approximately -0.618034. To find the next intercept, repeat steps **c.** through **f.** The SOLVER feature under the MATH menu can also be used to find solutions of equations.

Solving Systems of Equations in Two Variables

To solve a system of equations

The system of equations $\begin{array}{l} y = x^2 - 1 \\ \frac{1}{2}x + y = 1 \end{array}$ will be solved.

a. Solve each equation for y.

3.1

−4.7   4.7

Intersection
X=-1.686141   Y=1.8430703

−3.1

b. Enter the first equation as Y₁. For instance, $Y_1 = x^2 - 1$.

c. Enter the second equation as Y₂. For instance, $Y_2 = 1 - \frac{1}{2}x$.

d. Graph both equations. (*Note:* The point(s) of intersection must appear on the screen. It may be necessary to adjust the viewing window so that the point(s) of intersection are displayed.)

e. Press [2nd] CALC [5].

f. Move the cursor to the left of the first point of intersection. Press [ENTER].

g. Move the cursor to the right of the first point of intersection. Press [ENTER].

h. Press [ENTER].

i. The first point of intersection is $(-1.686141, 1.8430703)$.

j. Repeat steps **e.** through **h.** for each point of intersection.

Finding the Minimum or Maximum Value of a Function

a. Enter the function into Y₁. The equation $y = x^2 - x - 1$ is used here.

b. Graph the equation. You may need to adjust the viewing window so that the maximum or minimum point is visible.

c. Press [2nd] CALC [3] to determine a minimum value or press [2nd] CALC [4] to determine a maximum value.

d. Move the cursor to a point on the curve that is to the left of the minimum (maximum). Press [ENTER].

e. Move the cursor to a point on the curve that is to the right of the minimum (maximum). Press [ENTER].

f. Press [ENTER].

g. The minimum (maximum) is shown as the y-coordinate on the bottom of the screen; in this case, the minimum value is -1.25.

Sharp EL-9600

To evaluate an expression

a. The SOLVER mode of the calculator is used to evaluate expressions. To enter SOLVER mode, press [2ndF] SOLVER [CL]. The expression $-3a^2b - 4c$ must be entered as the equation $-3a^2b - 4c = t$. The letter t can be any letter other than one used in the expression. Use the following keystrokes to input $-3a^2b - 4c = t$:

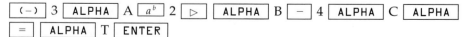

[(−)] 3 [ALPHA] A [aᵇ] 2 [▷] [ALPHA] B [−] 4 [ALPHA] C [ALPHA]
[=] [ALPHA] T [ENTER]

Note the difference between the key for a *negative* sign [(−)] and the key for a *minus* sign [−].

b. After you press [ENTER], variables used in the equation will be displayed on the screen. To evaluate the expression for $a = 3$, $b = -2$, and $c = -4$, input each value, pressing [ENTER] after each number. When the cursor moves to T, press ⌐2ndF⌐ EXE. T = 70 will appear on the screen. This is the value of the expression. To evaluate the expression again for different values of a, b, and c, press ⌐2ndF⌐ QUIT and then ⌐2ndF⌐ SOLVER.

c. Press 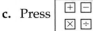 to return to normal operation.

To graph a function

a. Press the ⌐Y=⌐ key. The screen will show Y₁ through Y₈.

b. Input the expression for a function that is to be graphed. Press ⌐X/θ/T/n⌐ to enter an x. For example, to input $y = \frac{1}{2}x - 3$, use the following keystrokes:

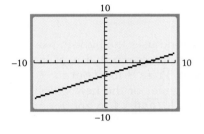

⌐Y=⌐ ⌐CL⌐ ⌐(⌐ 1 ⌐÷⌐ 2 ⌐)⌐ ⌐X/θ/T/n⌐ ⌐−⌐ 3 ⌐ENTER⌐

c. Set the viewing window by pressing ⌐WINDOW⌐. Enter the values for the minimum x value (Xmin), the maximum x value (Xmax), the distance between tick marks on the x-axis (Xscl), the minimum y value (Ymin), the maximum y value (Ymax), and the distance between tick marks on the y-axis (Yscl). Press ⌐ENTER⌐ after each entry. Press ⌐GRAPH⌐. For the graph shown at the left, enter Xmin = −10, Xmax = 10, Xscl = 1, Ymin = −10, Ymax = 10, and Yscl = 1. Press ⌐GRAPH⌐.

d. Press ⌐Y=⌐ to return to the equation. The equals sign has a black rectangle around it. This indicates that the function is active and will be graphed when the ⌐GRAPH⌐ key is pressed. A function is deactivated by using the arrow keys. Move the cursor over the equals sign and press ⌐ENTER⌐. When the cursor is moved to the right, the black rectangle will not be present, and that equation will not be active.

e. Graphing some radical equations requires special care. To graph the function $y = \sqrt{2x + 3}$, enter the following keystrokes:

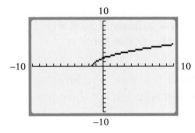

⌐Y=⌐ ⌐CL⌐ ⌐2ndF⌐ ⌐√⌐ 2 ⌐X/θ/T/n⌐ ⌐+⌐ 3 ⌐▷⌐ ⌐GRAPH⌐

The graph is shown at the left.

To display the *xy*-coordinates as integers

a. Press ⌐ZOOM⌐ ⌐▷⌐ 8.

b. Graph the function. Press ⌐TRACE⌐. Use the left arrow and right arrow keys to trace along the graph of the function. The x- and y-coordinates of the function are shown on the bottom of the screen.

To display the *xy*-coordinates in tenths

a. Press ⌐ZOOM⌐ ⌐▷⌐ 7.

b. Graph the function. Press ⌐TRACE⌐. Use the left arrow and right arrow keys to trace along the graph of the function. The x- and y-coordinates of the function are shown on the bottom of the screen.

To evaluate a function for a given value of x, or to produce ordered pairs of the function

a. Press ⌐Y=⌐. Input the expression. For instance, input

⌐Y=⌐ ⌐CL⌐ 2 ⌐X/θ/T/n⌐ ⌐∧⌐ 3 ⌐−⌐ 3 ⌐X/θ/T/n⌐ ⌐+⌐ 2. Press ⌐ENTER⌐.

b. Press $\boxed{\begin{smallmatrix} + & - \\ \times & \div \end{smallmatrix}}$. Store the x-coordinate of the ordered pair you want in $\boxed{\text{X}/\theta/\text{T}/n}$. For instance, enter 3 $\boxed{\text{STO}}$ $\boxed{\text{X}/\theta/\text{T}/n}$ $\boxed{\text{ENTER}}$.

c. Press $\boxed{\text{VARS}}$ $\boxed{\text{ENTER}}$ 1 $\boxed{\text{ENTER}}$. The value of y, 47, will be displayed on the screen. The ordered pair is (3, 47). The TABLE feature of the calculator can also be used to find many ordered pairs for a function.

Zoom Features

To zoom in or out on a graph

a. Here are two methods of using ZOOM. The first method uses the built-in features of the calculator. Move the cursor to a point on the graph that is of interest. Press $\boxed{\text{ZOOM}}$. The ZOOM menu will appear. Press 3 to zoom in on the graph by the amount shown by FACTOR. The center of the new graph is the location at which you placed the cursor. Press $\boxed{\text{ZOOM}}$ 4 to zoom out on the graph by the amount shown in FACTOR.

b. The second method uses the BOX option under the ZOOM menu. To use this method, press $\boxed{\text{ZOOM}}$ 2. A cursor will appear on the screen. Use the arrow keys to move the cursor to a portion of the graph that is of interest. Press $\boxed{\text{ENTER}}$. Use the arrow keys to draw a box around the portion of the graph you wish to see. Press $\boxed{\text{ENTER}}$.

Solving Equations

This discussion is based on the fact that the real solutions of an equation can be related to the x-intercepts of a graph. For instance, the real solutions of $x^2 = x + 1$ are the x-intercepts of the graph of $f(x) = x^2 - x - 1$, which are the zeros of f.

To solve $x^2 = x + 1$, rewrite the equation with all terms on one side of the equation. The equation is now $x^2 - x - 1 = 0$. Think of this equation as $Y_1 = x^2 - x - 1$. The x-intercepts of the graph of Y_1 are the solutions of the equation $x^2 = x + 1$.

a. Enter $x^2 - x - 1$ into Y_1.

b. Graph the equation. You may need to adjust the viewing window so that the x-intercepts are visible.

c. Press $\boxed{\text{2ndF}}$ CALC 5.

d. A solution is shown as the x-coordinate at the bottom of the screen. To find another intercept, move the cursor to the right of the next x-intercept. Then press $\boxed{\text{2ndF}}$ CALC 5.

Solving Systems of Equations in Two Variables

To solve a system of equations

a. Solve each equation for y.

b. Press $\boxed{\text{Y=}}$ and then enter both equations.

c. Graph the equations. You may need to adjust the viewing window so that the point of intersection is visible.

d. Press $\boxed{\text{2ndF}}$ CALC 2 to find the point of intersection. Press $\boxed{\text{2ndF}}$ CALC 2 again to find another point of intersection.

e. The x- and y-coordinates at the bottom of the screen are the coordinates for the point of intersection.

Finding Maximum and Minimum Values of a Function

a. Press $\boxed{\text{Y=}}$ and then enter the function.

b. Graph the equation. You may need to adjust the viewing window so that the maximum (minimum) is visible.

c. Press $\boxed{\text{2ndF}}$ CALC 3 for the minimum value of the function or $\boxed{\text{2ndF}}$ CALC 4 for the maximum value of the function.

d. The y-coordinate at the bottom of the screen is the maximum (minimum).

Casio *CFX-9850G*

To evaluate an expression

a. Press $\boxed{\text{MENU}}$ $\boxed{\text{5}}$. Use the arrow keys to highlight Y1.

b. Input the expression to be evaluated. For example, to input the expression $-3A^2B - 4C$, use the following keystrokes:

$\boxed{\text{(-)}}$ 3 $\boxed{\text{ALPHA}}$ A $\boxed{x^2}$ $\boxed{\text{ALPHA}}$ B $\boxed{-}$ 4 $\boxed{\text{ALPHA}}$ C $\boxed{\text{EXE}}$

Note the difference between the key for a *negative* sign $\boxed{\text{(-)}}$ and the key for a *minus* sign $\boxed{-}$.

c. Press $\boxed{\text{MENU}}$ 1. Store the value of each variable that will be used in the expression. For example, to evaluate the expression above when $A = 3$, $B = -2$, and $C = -4$, use the following keystrokes:

3 → $\boxed{\text{ALPHA}}$ A $\boxed{\text{EXE}}$ $\boxed{\text{(-)}}$ 2 → $\boxed{\text{ALPHA}}$ B $\boxed{\text{EXE}}$ $\boxed{\text{(-)}}$ 4 → $\boxed{\text{ALPHA}}$ C $\boxed{\text{EXE}}$

These steps store the value of each variable.

d. Press $\boxed{\text{VARS}}$ $\boxed{\text{F4}}$ $\boxed{\text{F1}}$ 1 $\boxed{\text{EXE}}$.

The value of the expression, Y1, for the given values is displayed; in this case, Y1 = 70.

To graph a function

a. Press Menu $\boxed{\text{5}}$ to obtain the GRAPH FUNCTION Menu.

b. Input the function that you want to graph. Press $\boxed{\text{X,}\theta\text{,T}}$ to input the variable x. For example, to input Y1 = $x^3 + 2x^2 - 5x - 6$, use the following keystrokes:

$\boxed{\text{X,}\theta\text{,T}}$ $\boxed{\wedge}$ 3 $\boxed{+}$ 2 $\boxed{\text{X,}\theta\text{,T}}$ $\boxed{x^2}$ $\boxed{-}$ 5 $\boxed{\text{X,}\theta\text{,T}}$ $\boxed{-}$ 6 $\boxed{\text{EXE}}$

c. Set the viewing window by pressing $\boxed{\text{SHIFT}}$ $\boxed{\text{F3}}$ and the Range Parameter Menu will appear. Enter the values for the minimum x value (Xmin), maximum x value (Xmax), the units between tick marks on the x-axis (Xscl), minimum y value (Ymin), maximum y value (Ymax), and the units between tick marks on the y-axis (Yscl). Press $\boxed{\text{EXE}}$ after each of these six entries.

Press EXIT , or SHIFT QUIT , to leave the Range Parameter Menu.

d. Press F6 to draw the graph. For the graph shown at the left, Xmin = −10, Xmax = 10, Xscl = 1, Ymin = −10, Ymax = 10, and Yscl = 1.

e. In the equation for Y1, there is a rectangle around the equals sign. This indicates that this function is *active* and will be graphed when the F6 key is pressed. A function is deactivated by using the F1 key. After this key is used once, the rectangle around the equals sign will not be present, and that function will not be graphed.

To display the x-coordinates of rectangular coordinates as integers

a. Set the Range as follows: Xmin = −63, Xmax = 63, Xscl = 10, Ymin = −32, Ymax = 32, and Yscl = 10.

b. Graph a function and use the Trace feature. Press F1 and then move the cursor with the ◁ and the ▷ keys. The values of x and y = f(x) displayed on the bottom of the screen are the coordinates of a point on the graph. Observe that the x value is given as an integer.

To display the x-coordinates of rectangular coordinates in tenths

a. Set the Range as follows: Xmin = −6.3 and Xmax = 6.3. A quick way to choose these range parameter settings is to press F1 from the V-Window Menu.

b. Graph a function and use the Trace feature. Press F1 and then move the cursor with the ◁ and the ▷ keys. The values of x and y = f(x) displayed on the bottom of the screen are the coordinates of a point on the graph. Observe that the x value is given in tenths.

To evaluate a function for a given value of x, or to produce ordered pairs of the function

a. Press MENU 5 .

b. Input the function to be evaluated. For example, input $2x^3 - 3x + 2$ into Y1.

c. Press MENU 1.

d. Input a value for x; for example, to input 3, press
3 → X,θ,T EXE

e. Press VARS F4 F1 1 EXE .
The value of Y1 for the given value x = 3 is displayed. In this case, Y1 = 47.

Zoom Features

To zoom in or out on a graph

a. After drawing a graph, press SHIFT Zoom to display the Zoom/Auto Range menu. To zoom in on a graph by a factor of 2 on the x-axis and a factor of 1.5 on the y-axis:
Press F2 to display the Factor Input Screen. Input the zoom factors for each axis: 2 EXE 1 · 5 EXE EXIT . Press F3 to redraw the graph according to the factors specified above. To specify the center point of the

enlarged (reduced) display after pressing [SHIFT] Zoom, use the arrow keys to move the pointer to the position you wish to become the center of the next display. You can repeat the zoom procedures as needed. If you wish to see the original graph, press [F6] [F1]. This procedure resets the range parameters to their original values and redraws the graph.

b. A second method of zooming makes use of the Box Zoom Function. To use this method, first draw a graph. Then press [SHIFT] Zoom [F1]. Now use the arrow (cursor) keys to move the pointer. Once the pointer is located at a portion of the graph that is of interest, press [EXE]. Now use the arrow keys to draw a box around the portion of the graph you wish to see. Press [EXE]. The portion of the graph defined by the box will be drawn.

Solving Equations

This discussion is based on the fact that the real solutions of an equation can be related to the x-intercepts of a graph. For instance, the real solutions of $x^2 = x + 1$ are the x-intercepts of the graph of $f(x) = x^2 - x - 1$, which are the zeros of f.

To solve $x^2 = x + 1$, rewrite the equation with all terms on one side. The equation is now $x^2 - x - 1 = 0$. Think of this equation as $Y_1 = x^2 - x - 1$. The x-intercepts of the graph of Y_1 are the solutions of the equation $x^2 = x + 1$.

a. Enter $x^2 - x - 1$ into Y_1.

b. Graph the equation. You may need to adjust the viewing window so that the x-intercept is visible.

c. Press [SHIFT] G-SOLV [F1].

d. The root is shown as the x-coordinate on the bottom of the screen; in this case, the root is approximately -0.618034. To find another x-intercept, press the right arrow key.

The EQUA Mode (Press [MENU] [ALPHA] A) can also be used to find solutions of linear, quadratic, and cubic equations.

Solving Systems of Two Equations in Two Variables

The following discussion is based on the concept that the solutions of a system of two equations are represented by the point(s) of intersection of the graphs.

The system of equations $\begin{aligned} y &= x^2 - 1 \\ \tfrac{1}{2}x + y &= 1 \end{aligned}$ will be solved.

a. Solve each equation for y.

b. Enter the first equation in the Graph Menu as Y_1. For instance, let $Y_1 = x^2 - 1$.

c. Enter the second equation as Y_2. For instance, let $Y_2 = 1 - \dfrac{1}{2}x$.

d. Graph both equations. (*Note:* The point of intersection must appear on the screen. It may be necessary to adjust the viewing window so that the point of intersection that is of interest is the only intersection point that is displayed.)

e. Press ⎡ SHIFT ⎤ G-SOL ⎡ F5 ⎤ ⎡ EXE ⎤.

f. The display will show that the graphs intersect at $(-1.686141, 1.8430703)$. To find another point of intersection, repeat step **e.**

Finding the Minimum or Maximum Value of a Function

a. Enter the function into the graphing menu. For this example we have used $y = x^2 - x - 1$.

b. Graph the function. Adjust the viewing window so that the maximum or minimum is visible.

c. Press ⎡ SHIFT ⎤ G-SOL ⎡ F2 ⎤ ⎡ EXE ⎤ for a maximum and ⎡ F3 ⎤ ⎡ EXE ⎤ for a minimum.

d. The local maximum (minimum) is shown as the y-coordinate on the bottom of the screen; in this case, the minimum value is -1.25.

SOLUTIONS to Chapter 1 Problems

SECTION 1.1

Problem 1 $A = \{1, 2, 3, 4\}$

Problem 2 $-5 < -1$
$-1 = -1$
$5 > -1$
The element 5 is greater than -1.

Problem 3 **A.** 9   **B.** -62

Problem 4 **A.** $|-5| = 5$ **B.** $-|-9| = -9$

SECTION 1.2

Problem 1 **A.** $-162 + 98 = -64$

B. $-154 + (-37) = -191$

C. $-36 + 17 + (-21) = -19 + (-21)$
$= -40$

Problem 2 $-8 - 14 = -8 + (-14)$
$= -22$

Problem 3 $4 - (-3) - 12 - (-7) - 20$
$= 4 + 3 + (-12) + 7 + (-20)$
$= 7 + (-12) + 7 + (-20)$
$= -5 + 7 + (-20)$
$= 2 + (-20)$
$= -18$

Problem 4 **A.** $-38 \cdot 51 = -1938$

B. $-7(-8)(9)(-2) = 56(9)(-2)$
$= 504(-2)$
$= -1008$

Problem 5 **A.** $(-135) \div (-9) = 15$

B. $\dfrac{84}{-6} = -14$

C. $-\dfrac{36}{-12} = -(-3) = 3$

Problem 6

Strategy To find the average daily high temperature:
- Add the seven temperature readings.
- Divide the sum by 7.

Solution $-5 + (-6) + 3 + 0 + (-4) + (-7) + (-2)$
$= -11 + 3 + 0 + (-4) + (-7) + (-2)$
$= -8 + 0 + (-4) + (-7) + (-2)$
$= -8 + (-4) + (-7) + (-2)$
$= -12 + (-7) + (-2)$
$= -19 + (-2)$
$= -21$

$-21 \div 7 = -3$

The average daily high temperature was $-3°C$.

SECTION 1.3

Problem 1

$$\begin{array}{r} 0.16 \\ 25\overline{)4.00} \\ \underline{-25} \\ 1\,50 \\ \underline{-1\,50} \\ 0 \end{array}$$

$\dfrac{4}{25} = 0.16$

Problem 2

$$\begin{array}{r} 0.444 \\ 9\overline{)4.000} \\ \underline{-3\,6} \\ 40 \\ \underline{-36} \\ 40 \\ \underline{-36} \\ 4 \end{array}$$

$\dfrac{4}{9} = 0.\overline{4}$

Problem 3 $125\% = 125\left(\dfrac{1}{100}\right) = \dfrac{125}{100} = 1\dfrac{1}{4}$
$125\% = 125(0.01) = 1.25$

Problem 4 $16\dfrac{2}{3}\% = 16\dfrac{2}{3}\left(\dfrac{1}{100}\right) = \dfrac{50}{3}\left(\dfrac{1}{100}\right) = \dfrac{1}{6}$

Problem 5 $6.08\% = 6.08(0.01) = 0.0608$

Problem 6 **A.** $0.043 = 0.043(100\%) = 4.3\%$

B. $2.57 = 2.57(100\%) = 257\%$

Problem 7 $\dfrac{5}{9} = \dfrac{5}{9}(100\%) = \dfrac{500}{9}\% \approx 55.6\%$

Problem 8 $\dfrac{9}{16} = \dfrac{9}{16}(100\%) = \dfrac{900}{16}\% = 56\dfrac{1}{4}\%$

Problem 9 Prime factorization of 9 and 12:
$9 = 3 \cdot 3 \qquad 12 = 2 \cdot 2 \cdot 3$
$\text{LCM} = 2 \cdot 2 \cdot 3 \cdot 3 = 36$
$\dfrac{5}{9} - \dfrac{11}{12} = \dfrac{20}{36} - \dfrac{33}{36} = \dfrac{20}{36} + \dfrac{-33}{36}$
$\qquad = \dfrac{20 + (-33)}{36} = \dfrac{-13}{36} = -\dfrac{13}{36}$

Problem 10
$$-\frac{7}{8} - \frac{5}{6} + \frac{1}{2} = -\frac{21}{24} - \frac{20}{24} + \frac{12}{24}$$
$$= \frac{-21}{24} + \frac{-20}{24} + \frac{12}{24}$$
$$= \frac{-21 + (-20) + 12}{24} = \frac{-29}{24} = -\frac{29}{24}$$

Problem 11
$$\begin{array}{r} 3.097 \\ 4.9 \\ + \ 3.09 \\ \hline 11.087 \end{array}$$

Problem 12
$$\begin{array}{r} 67.910 \\ -16.127 \\ \hline 51.783 \end{array}$$
$$16.127 - 67.91 = -51.783$$

Problem 13
$$-\frac{7}{12} \cdot \frac{9}{14} = -\frac{7 \cdot 9}{12 \cdot 14} = -\frac{\overset{1}{7} \cdot \overset{1}{3} \cdot 3}{2 \cdot 2 \cdot \underset{1}{3} \cdot 2 \cdot \underset{1}{7}}$$
$$= -\frac{3}{8}$$

Problem 14
$$-\frac{3}{8} \div \left(-\frac{5}{12}\right) = \frac{3}{8} \cdot \frac{12}{5}$$
$$= \frac{3 \cdot 12}{8 \cdot 5} = \frac{3 \cdot \overset{1}{2} \cdot \overset{1}{2} \cdot 3}{2 \cdot 2 \cdot 2 \cdot 5} = \frac{9}{10}$$

Problem 15
$$\begin{array}{r} 5.44 \\ \times \quad 3.8 \\ \hline 4352 \\ 1632 \\ \hline 20.672 \end{array}$$
$$(-5.44)(3.8) = -20.672$$

Problem 16
$$\begin{array}{r} 0.231 \\ 1.7\overline{)0.3.940} \\ -3\ 4 \\ \hline 54 \\ -51 \\ \hline 30 \\ -17 \\ \hline 13 \end{array}$$
$$-0.394 \div 1.7 \approx -0.23$$

SECTION 1.4

Problem 1
$(-5)^3 = (-5)(-5)(-5) = 25(-5) = -125$
$-5^3 = -(5 \cdot 5 \cdot 5) = -(25 \cdot 5) = -125$

Problem 2
$(-3)^3 = (-3)(-3)(-3) = 9(-3) = -27$
$(-3)^4 = (-3)(-3)(-3)(-3)$
$\quad\quad = 9(-3)(-3) = -27(-3) = 81$

Problem 3
$(3^3)(-2)^3 = (3)(3)(3) \cdot (-2)(-2)(-2)$
$\quad\quad = 27 \cdot (-8) = -216$
$\left(-\frac{2}{5}\right)^2 = \left(-\frac{2}{5}\right)\left(-\frac{2}{5}\right) = \frac{2 \cdot 2}{5 \cdot 5} = \frac{4}{25}$

Problem 4
$36 \div (8 - 5)^2 - (-3)^2 \cdot 2$
$\quad = 36 \div (3)^2 - (-3)^2 \cdot 2$
$\quad = 36 \div 9 - 9 \cdot 2$
$\quad = 4 - 9 \cdot 2$
$\quad = 4 - 18$
$\quad = -14$

Problem 5
$27 \div 3^2 + (-3)^2 \cdot 4$
$\quad = 27 \div 9 + 9 \cdot 4$
$\quad = 3 + 9 \cdot 4$
$\quad = 3 + 36$
$\quad = 39$

Problem 6
$4 - 3[4 - 2(6 - 3)] \div 2$
$\quad = 4 - 3[4 - 2(3)] \div 2$
$\quad = 4 - 3[4 - 6] \div 2$
$\quad = 4 - 3(-2) \div 2$
$\quad = 4 - (-6) \div 2$
$\quad = 4 - (-3)$
$\quad = 7$

SOLUTIONS to Chapter 2 Problems

SECTION 2.1

Problem 1 -4

Problem 2 $2xy + y^2$
$2(-4)(2) + (2)^2 = 2(-4)(2) + 4$
$\quad\quad\quad\quad\quad = -8(2) + 4$
$\quad\quad\quad\quad\quad = -16 + 4$
$\quad\quad\quad\quad\quad = -12$

Problem 3 $\dfrac{a^2 + b^2}{a + b}$

$$\dfrac{(5)^2 + (-3)^2}{5 + (-3)} = \dfrac{25 + 9}{5 + (-3)}$$

$$= \dfrac{34}{2}$$

$$= 17$$

Problem 4 $x^3 - 2(x + y) + z^2$
$(2)^3 - 2[2 + (-4)] + (-3)^2$
$= (2)^3 - 2(-2) + (-3)^2$
$= 8 - 2(-2) + 9$
$= 8 + 4 + 9$
$= 12 + 9$
$= 21$

Problem 5 $V = \dfrac{1}{3}\pi r^2 h$

$$V = \dfrac{1}{3}\pi (4.5)^2(9.5) \qquad \blacktriangleright\ r = \dfrac{1}{2}d = \dfrac{1}{2}(9) = 4.5$$

$$V = \dfrac{1}{3}\pi (20.25)(9.5)$$

$$V \approx 201.5$$

The volume is approximately 201.5 cm³.

SECTION 2.2

Problem 1 $7 + (-7) = 0$

Problem 2 The Associative Property of Addition

Problem 3 **A.** $9x + 6x = (9 + 6)x = 15x$

  B. $-4y - 7y = [-4 + (-7)]y = -11y$

Problem 4 **A.** $3a - 2b + 5a = 3a + 5a - 2b$
$= (3a + 5a) - 2b$
$= 8a - 2b$

  B. $x^2 - 7 + 9x^2 - 14$
$= x^2 + 9x^2 - 7 - 14$
$= (x^2 + 9x^2) + (-7 - 14)$
$= 10x^2 - 21$

Problem 5 **A.** $-7(-2a) = [-7(-2)]a$
$= 14a$

  B. $-\dfrac{5}{6}(-30y^2) = \left[-\dfrac{5}{6}(-30)\right]y^2$
$= 25y^2$

  C. $(-5x)(-2) = (-2)(-5x)$
$= [-2(-5)]x$
$= 10x$

Problem 6 **A.** $7(4 + 2y) = 7(4) + 7(2y)$
$= 28 + 14y$

  B. $-(5x - 12) = -1(5x - 12)$
$= -1(5x) - (-1)(12)$
$= -5x + 12$

  C. $(3a - 1)5 = (3a)(5) - (1)(5)$
$= 15a - 5$

  D. $-3(6a^2 - 8a + 9)$
$= -3(6a^2) - (-3)(8a) + (-3)(9)$
$= -18a^2 + 24a - 27$

Problem 7 $7(x - 2y) - 3(-x - 2y)$
$= 7x - 14y + 3x + 6y$
$= 10x - 8y$

Problem 8 $3y - 2[x - 4(2 - 3y)]$
$= 3y - 2[x - 8 + 12y]$
$= 3y - 2x + 16 - 24y$
$= -2x - 21y + 16$

SECTION 2.3

Problem 1 **A.** eighteen <u>less than</u> the <u>cube</u> of x
$x^3 - 18$

  B. y <u>decreased by</u> the <u>sum</u> of z and nine
$y - (z + 9)$

  C. the <u>difference between</u> the <u>square</u> of q
and the <u>sum</u> of r and t
$q^2 - (r + t)$

Problem 2 the unknown number: n
the square of the number: n^2
the product of five and the square of the
number: $5n^2$

$5n^2 + n$

Problem 3 the unknown number: n
twice the number: $2n$
the sum of seven and twice the number:
$7 + 2n$

$3(7 + 2n)$

Problem 4 the unknown number: n
the difference between twice the number
and 17: $2n - 17$

$n - (2n - 17) = n - 2n + 17$
$= -n + 17$

Problem 5   the unknown number: n

three-fourths of the number: $\frac{3}{4}n$

one-fifth of the number: $\frac{1}{5}n$

$$\frac{3}{4}n + \frac{1}{5}n = \frac{15}{20}n + \frac{4}{20}n$$
$$= \frac{19}{20}n$$

Problem 6   the time required by the newer model: t

the time required by the older model is twice the time required for the newer model: $2t$

Problem 7   the length of one piece: L

the length of the second piece: $6 - L$

SOLUTIONS to Chapter 3 Problems

SECTION 3.1

Problem 1

$$5 - 4x = 8x + 2$$

$$\begin{array}{c|c} 5 - 4\left(\frac{1}{4}\right) & 8\left(\frac{1}{4}\right) + 2 \\ 5 - 1 & 2 + 2 \\ 4 = 4 \end{array}$$

Yes, $\frac{1}{4}$ is a solution.

Problem 2

$$10x - x^2 = 3x - 10$$

$$\begin{array}{c|c} 10(5) - (5)^2 & 3(5) - 10 \\ 50 - 25 & 15 - 10 \\ 25 \neq 5 \end{array}$$

No, 5 is not a solution.

Problem 3

$$x - \frac{1}{3} = -\frac{3}{4}$$

$$x - \frac{1}{3} + \frac{1}{3} = -\frac{3}{4} + \frac{1}{3}$$

$$x + 0 = -\frac{9}{12} + \frac{4}{12}$$

$$x = -\frac{5}{12}$$

Check: $x - \frac{1}{3} = -\frac{3}{4}$

$$\begin{array}{c|c} -\frac{5}{12} - \frac{1}{3} & -\frac{3}{4} \\ -\frac{3}{4} = -\frac{3}{4} \end{array}$$

The solution is $-\frac{5}{12}$.

Problem 4

$$-8 = 5 + x$$
$$-8 - 5 = 5 - 5 + x$$
$$-13 = x$$

The solution is -13.

Problem 5

$$-\frac{2x}{5} = 6$$

$$\left(-\frac{5}{2}\right)\left(-\frac{2}{5}x\right) = \left(-\frac{5}{2}\right)(6)$$
$$1x = -15$$
$$x = -15$$

The solution is -15.

Problem 6 $6x = 10$

$$\frac{6x}{6} = \frac{10}{6}$$
$$x = \frac{5}{3}$$

Check: $6x = 10$

$$\begin{array}{c|c} 6\left(\frac{5}{3}\right) & 10 \\ 10 = 10 \end{array}$$

The solution is $\frac{5}{3}$.

Problem 7 $4x - 8x = 16$

$$-4x = 16$$
$$\frac{-4x}{-4} = \frac{16}{-4}$$
$$x = -4$$

The solution is -4.

Problem 8

$$PB = A$$
$$P(60) = 27$$
$$60P = 27$$
$$\frac{60P}{60} = \frac{27}{60}$$
$$P = 0.45$$

27 is 45% of 60.

Problem 9

Strategy   To find the percent of the questions answered correctly, solve the basic percent equation using $B = 80$ and $A = 72$. The percent is unknown.

Solution
$$PB = A$$
$$P(80) = 72$$
$$80P = 72$$
$$\frac{80P}{80} = \frac{72}{80}$$
$$P = 0.9$$

90% of the questions were answered correctly.

Problem 10

Strategy   To determine the tax on the King Size Value Meal, solve the basic percent equation using $B = 5.18$ and $P = 5\% = 0.05$. The amount is unknown.

Solution
$$PB = A$$
$$0.05(5.18) = A$$
$$0.26 \approx A$$

The tax was $.26.

SECTION 3.2

Problem 1
$$5x + 7 = 10$$
$$5x + 7 - 7 = 10 - 7$$
$$5x = 3$$
$$\frac{5x}{5} = \frac{3}{5}$$
$$x = \frac{3}{5}$$

The solution is $\frac{3}{5}$.

Problem 2
$$11 = 11 + 3x$$
$$11 - 11 = 11 - 11 + 3x$$
$$0 = 3x$$
$$\frac{0}{3} = \frac{3x}{3}$$
$$0 = x$$

The solution is 0.

Problem 3

$$\frac{5}{2} - \frac{2}{3}x = \frac{1}{2}$$
$$6\left(\frac{5}{2} - \frac{2}{3}x\right) = 6\left(\frac{1}{2}\right)$$
$$6\left(\frac{5}{2}\right) - 6\left(\frac{2}{3}x\right) = 3$$
$$15 - 4x = 3$$
$$15 - 15 - 4x = 3 - 15$$
$$-4x = -12$$
$$\frac{-4x}{-4} = \frac{-12}{-4}$$
$$x = 3$$

The solution is 3.

Problem 4
$$5x + 4 = 6 + 10x$$
$$5x - 10x + 4 = 6 + 10x - 10x$$
$$-5x + 4 = 6$$
$$-5x + 4 - 4 = 6 - 4$$
$$-5x = 2$$
$$\frac{-5x}{-5} = \frac{2}{-5}$$
$$x = -\frac{2}{5}$$

The solution is $-\frac{2}{5}$.

Problem 5
$$5x - 4(3 - 2x) = 2(3x - 2) + 6$$
$$5x - 12 + 8x = 6x - 4 + 6$$
$$13x - 12 = 6x + 2$$
$$13x - 6x - 12 = 6x - 6x + 2$$
$$7x - 12 = 2$$
$$7x - 12 + 12 = 2 + 12$$
$$7x = 14$$
$$\frac{7x}{7} = \frac{14}{7}$$
$$x = 2$$

The solution is 2.

Problem 6
$$-2[3x - 5(2x - 3)] = 3x - 8$$
$$-2[3x - 10x + 15] = 3x - 8$$
$$-2[-7x + 15] = 3x - 8$$
$$14x - 30 = 3x - 8$$
$$14x - 3x - 30 = 3x - 3x - 8$$
$$11x - 30 = -8$$
$$11x - 30 + 30 = -8 + 30$$
$$11x = 22$$
$$\frac{11x}{11} = \frac{22}{11}$$
$$x = 2$$

The solution is 2.

Problem 7

Strategy   To find the number of years, replace V with 10,200 in the given equation and solve for t.

Solution
$$V = 450t + 7500$$
$$10,200 = 450t + 7500$$
$$10,200 - 7500 = 450t + 7500 - 7500$$
$$2700 = 450t$$
$$\frac{2700}{450} = \frac{450t}{450}$$
$$6 = t$$

The value of the investment will be $10,200 in 6 years.

Problem 8

Strategy   The lever is 14 ft long, so $d = 14$. One force is 6 ft from the fulcrum, so $x = 6$. The one force is 40 lb, so $F_1 = 40$. To find the other force when the system balances, replace the variables F_1, x, and d in the lever system equation with the given values, and solve for F_2.

Solution

$$F_1 x = F_2(d - x)$$
$$40(6) = F_2(14 - 6)$$
$$240 = F_2(8)$$
$$240 = 8F_2$$
$$\frac{240}{8} = \frac{8F_2}{8}$$
$$30 = F_2$$

A 30-pound force must be applied to the other end.

SECTION 3.3

Problem 1   The solution set is the numbers greater than -2.

Problem 2

$$x + 2 < -2$$
$$x + 2 - 2 < -2 - 2$$
$$x < -4$$

Problem 3

$$5x + 3 > 4x + 5$$
$$5x - 4x + 3 > 4x - 4x + 5$$
$$x + 3 > 5$$
$$x + 3 - 3 > 5 - 3$$
$$x > 2$$

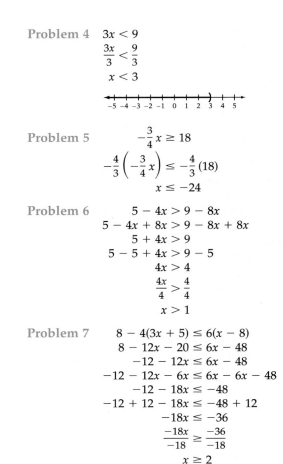

Problem 4 $3x < 9$

$$\frac{3x}{3} < \frac{9}{3}$$
$$x < 3$$

Problem 5 $-\dfrac{3}{4}x \geq 18$

$$-\frac{4}{3}\left(-\frac{3}{4}x\right) \leq -\frac{4}{3}(18)$$
$$x \leq -24$$

Problem 6

$$5 - 4x > 9 - 8x$$
$$5 - 4x + 8x > 9 - 8x + 8x$$
$$5 + 4x > 9$$
$$5 - 5 + 4x > 9 - 5$$
$$4x > 4$$
$$\frac{4x}{4} > \frac{4}{4}$$
$$x > 1$$

Problem 7

$$8 - 4(3x + 5) \leq 6(x - 8)$$
$$8 - 12x - 20 \leq 6x - 48$$
$$-12 - 12x \leq 6x - 48$$
$$-12 - 12x - 6x \leq 6x - 6x - 48$$
$$-12 - 18x \leq -48$$
$$-12 + 12 - 18x \leq -48 + 12$$
$$-18x \leq -36$$
$$\frac{-18x}{-18} \geq \frac{-36}{-18}$$
$$x \geq 2$$

SOLUTIONS to Chapter 4 Problems

SECTION 4.1

Problem 1   the unknown number: n

nine less than twice a number	is	five times the sum of the number and twelve

$$2n - 9 = 5(n + 12)$$
$$2n - 9 = 5n + 60$$
$$2n - 5n - 9 = 5n - 5n + 60$$
$$-3n - 9 = 60$$
$$-3n - 9 + 9 = 60 + 9$$
$$-3n = 69$$
$$\frac{-3n}{-3} = \frac{69}{-3}$$
$$n = -23$$

The number is -23.

Problem 2

Strategy To find the number of carbon atoms, write and solve an equation using n to represent the number of carbon atoms.

Solution

eight	represents	twice the number of carbon atoms

$$8 = 2n$$
$$\frac{8}{2} = \frac{2n}{2}$$
$$4 = n$$

There are 4 carbon atoms in a butane molecule.

Problem 3

Strategy To find the number of 10-speed bicycles made, write and solve an equation using n to represent the number of 10-speed bicycles and $160 - n$ to represent the number of 3-speed bicycles.

Solution

four times the number of 3-speed bicycles made	equals	30 less than the number of 10-speed bicycles made

$$4(160 - n) = n - 30$$
$$640 - 4n = n - 30$$
$$640 - 4n - n = n - n - 30$$
$$640 - 5n = -30$$
$$640 - 640 - 5n = -30 - 640$$
$$-5n = -670$$
$$\frac{-5n}{-5} = \frac{-670}{-5}$$
$$n = 134$$

There are 134 10-speed bicycles made each day.

SECTION 4.2

Problem 1

Strategy
- First consecutive integer: n
  Second consecutive integer: $n + 1$
  Third consecutive integer: $n + 2$
- The sum of the three integers is -12.

Solution
$$n + (n + 1) + (n + 2) = -12$$
$$3n + 3 = -12$$
$$3n = -15$$
$$n = -5$$

$$n + 1 = -5 + 1 = -4$$
$$n + 2 = -5 + 2 = -3$$

The three consecutive integers are -5, -4, and -3.

Problem 2

Strategy
- Number of dimes: x
  Number of nickels: $5x$
  Number of quarters: $x + 6$

Coin	Number	Value	Total value
Dime	x	10	$10x$
Nickel	$5x$	5	$5(5x)$
Quarter	$x + 6$	25	$25(x + 6)$

- The sum of the total values of the individual denominations of coins equals the total value of all the coins (630 cents).

Solution
$$10x + 5(5x) + 25(x + 6) = 630$$
$$10x + 25x + 25x + 150 = 630$$
$$60x + 150 = 630$$
$$60x = 480$$
$$x = 8$$

$$5x = 5(8) = 40$$
$$x + 6 = 8 + 6 = 14$$

The bank contains 8 dimes, 40 nickels, and 14 quarters.

SECTION 4.3

Problem 1

Strategy
- Each equal side: s
- Use the equation for the perimeter of a square.

Solution
$$P = 4s$$
$$52 = 4s$$
$$13 = s$$

The length of each side is 13 ft.

Problem 2

Strategy To find the supplement, let x represent the supplement of a 107° angle. Use the fact that supplementary angles are two angles whose sum is 180° to write an equation. Solve for x.

Solution
$$107° + x = 180°$$
$$x = 73°$$

The supplement of a 107° degree angle is a 73° angle.

Problem 3

Strategy The angles labeled are adjacent angles of intersecting lines and are therefore supplementary angles. To find x, write an equation and solve for x.

Solution
$$x + (3x + 20°) = 180°$$
$$4x + 20° = 180°$$
$$4x = 160°$$
$$x = 40°$$

Problem 4

Strategy $2x = y$ because alternate exterior angles have the same measure.

$y + (x + 15°) = 180°$ because adjacent angles of intersecting lines are supplementary angles. Substitute $2x$ for y and solve for x.

Solution
$$y + (x + 15°) = 180°$$
$$2x + (x + 15°) = 180°$$
$$3x + 15° = 180°$$
$$3x = 165°$$
$$x = 55°$$

Problem 5

Strategy
- To find the measure of $\angle a$, use the fact that $\angle a$ and $\angle y$ are vertical angles.
- To find the measure of $\angle b$, use the fact that the sum of the interior angles of a triangle is 180°.
- To find the measure of $\angle d$, use the fact that $\angle b$ and $\angle d$ are supplementary angles.

Solution $\angle a = \angle y = 55°$

$$\angle a + \angle b + 90° = 180°$$
$$55° + \angle b + 90° = 180°$$
$$145° + \angle b = 180°$$
$$\angle b = 35°$$

$$\angle b + \angle d = 180°$$
$$35° + \angle d = 180°$$
$$\angle d = 145°$$

Problem 6

Strategy To find the measure of the third angle, use the fact that the sum of the measures of the interior angles of a triangle is 180°. Write an equation using x to represent the measure of the third angle. Solve the equation for x.

Solution
$$x + 90° + 27° = 180°$$
$$x + 117° = 180°$$
$$x = 63°$$

The measure of the third angle is 63°.

SECTION 4.4

Problem 1

Strategy Given: $C = \$60$
$S = \$90$
Unknown markup rate: r
Use the equation $S = C + rC$.

Solution
$$S = C + rC$$
$$90 = 60 + 60r$$
$$30 = 60r$$
$$0.5 = r$$

The markup rate is 50%.

Problem 2

Strategy Given: $r = 40\% = 0.40$
$S = \$133$
Unknown cost: C
Use the equation $S = C + rC$.

Solution
$$S = C + rC$$
$$133 = C + 0.4C$$
$$133 = 1.40C$$
$$95 = C$$

The cost is $95.

Problem 3

Strategy Given: $R = \$29.80$
$S = \$22.35$
Unknown discount rate: r
Use the equation $S = R - rR$.

Solution
$$S = R - rR$$
$$22.35 = 29.80 - 29.80r$$
$$-7.45 = -29.80r$$
$$0.25 = r$$

The discount rate is 25%.

Problem 4

Strategy Given: $S = \$43.50$
$r = 25\% = 0.25$
Unknown regular price: R
Use the equation $S = R - rR$.

Solution
$S = R - rR$
$43.50 = R - 0.25R$
$43.50 = 0.75R$
$58 = R$

The regular price is $58.

SECTION 4.5

Problem 1

Strategy ▪ Additional amount: x

	Principal	·	Rate	=	Interest
Amount at 7%	2500	·	0.07	=	0.07(2500)
Amount of 10%	x	·	0.10	=	0.10x
Amount of 9%	$2500 + x$	·	0.09	=	0.09(2500 + x)

▪ The sum of the interest earned by the two investments equals the interest earned on the total investment.

Solution $0.07(2500) + 0.10x = 0.09(2500 + x)$
$175 + 0.10x = 225 + 0.09x$
$175 + 0.01x = 225$
$0.01x = 50$
$x = 5000$

$5000 more must be invested at 10%.

SECTION 4.6

Problem 1

Strategy ▪ Pounds of $.75 fertilizer: x

	Amount	Cost	Value
$.90 fertilizer	20	$.90	0.90(20)
$.75 fertilizer	x	$.75	0.75x
$.85 fertilizer	$20 + x$	$.85	0.85(20 + x)

▪ The sum of the values before mixing equals the value after mixing.

Solution $0.90(20) + 0.75x = 0.85(20 + x)$
$18 + 0.75x = 17 + 0.85x$
$18 - 0.10x = 17$
$-0.10x = -1$
$x = 10$

10 lb of the $.75 fertilizer must be added.

Problem 2

Strategy ▪ Pure orange juice is 100% orange juice.
$100\% = 1.00$
Amount of pure orange juice: x

	Amount	Percent	Quantity
Pure orange juice	x	1.00	1.00x
Fruit drink	5	0.10	0.10(5)
Orange drink	$x + 5$	0.25	0.25($x + 5$)

▪ The sum of the quantities before mixing is equal to the quantity after mixing.

Solution $1.00x + 0.10(5) = 0.25(x + 5)$
$1.00x + 0.5 = 0.25x + 1.25$
$0.75x + 0.5 = 1.25$
$0.75x = 0.75$
$x = 1$

To make the orange drink, 1 qt of pure orange juice is added to the fruit drink.

SECTION 4.7

Problem 1

Strategy ▪ Rate of the first train: r
Rate of the second train: $2r$

	Rate	Time	Distance
First train	r	3	$3r$
Second train	$2r$	3	$3(2r)$

▪ The sum of the distances traveled by each train equals 306 mi.

Solution $3r + 3(2r) = 306$
$3r + 6r = 306$
$9r = 306$
$r = 34$

$2r = 2(34) = 68$

The first train is traveling at 34 mph.
The second train is traveling at 68 mph.

Problem 2

Strategy ▪ Time spent flying out: t
Time spent flying back: $7 - t$

	Rate	Time	Distance
Out	120	t	120t
Back	90	$7 - t$	$90(7 - t)$

▪ The distance out equals the distance back.

Solution $120t = 90(7 - t)$
$120t = 630 - 90t$
$210t = 630$
$\quad t = 3$ (The time out was 3 h.)

The distance $= 120t = 120(3) = 360$ mi.

The parcel of land was 360 mi away.

SECTION 4.8

Problem 1

Strategy   To find the minimum selling price, write and solve an inequality using S to represent the selling price.

Solution $340 < 0.70S$

$$\frac{340}{0.70} < \frac{0.70S}{0.70}$$

$485.71429 < S$

The minimum selling price is $485.72.

Problem 2

Strategy   To find the maximum number of miles:
- Write an expression for the cost of each car, using x to represent the number of miles driven during the week.
- Write and solve an inequality.

Solution

cost of a Company A car	is less than	cost of a Company B car

$$9(7) + 0.10x < 12(7) + 0.08x$$
$$63 + 0.10x < 84 + 0.08x$$
$$63 + 0.10x - 0.08x < 84 + 0.08x - 0.08x$$
$$63 + 0.02x < 84$$
$$63 - 63 + 0.02x < 84 - 63$$
$$0.02x < 21$$
$$\frac{0.02x}{0.02} < \frac{21}{0.02}$$
$$x < 1050$$

The maximum number of miles is 1049.

SOLUTIONS to Chapter 5 Problems

SECTION 5.1

Problem 1

Problem 2 $A(4, 2), B(-3, 4), C(-3, 0), D(0, 0)$

Problem 3

SECTION 5.2

Problem 1 $y = -\frac{1}{2}x - 3$

-4	$-\frac{1}{2}(2) - 3$
	$-1 - 3$
	-4
$-4 = -4$	

Yes, $(2, -4)$ is a solution of $y = -\frac{1}{2}x - 3$.

Problem 2 $y = -\frac{1}{4}x + 1$

$$= -\frac{1}{4}(4) + 1$$
$$= -1 + 1$$
$$= 0$$

The ordered-pair solution is $(4, 0)$.

Problem 3

Problem 4

Problem 5 $5x - 2y = 10$

$$5x - 5x - 2y = -5x + 10$$
$$-2y = -5x + 10$$
$$\frac{-2y}{-2} = \frac{-5x + 10}{-2}$$
$$y = \frac{-5x}{-2} + \frac{10}{-2}$$
$$y = \frac{5}{2}x - 5$$

Problem 6 **A.** $5x - 2y = 10$

$$-2y = -5x + 10$$

$$y = \frac{5}{2}x - 5$$

B. $x - 3y = 9$

$$-3y = -x + 9$$

$$y = \frac{1}{3}x - 3$$

Problem 7 x-intercept: $4x - y = 4$

$$4x - 0 = 4$$

$$4x = 4$$

$$x = 1$$

The x-intercept is $(1, 0)$.

y-intercept: $4x - y = 4$

$$4(0) - y = 4$$

$$-y = 4$$

$$y = -4$$

The y-intercept is $(0, -4)$.

Problem 8 **A.**   **B.**

SECTION 5.3

Problem 1 **A.** $m = \dfrac{y_2 - y_1}{x_2 - x_1} = \dfrac{3 - 2}{1 - (-1)} = \dfrac{1}{2}$

The slope is $\dfrac{1}{2}$.

B. $m = \dfrac{y_2 - y_1}{x_2 - x_1} = \dfrac{-5 - 2}{4 - 1} = \dfrac{-7}{3}$

The slope is $-\dfrac{7}{3}$.

C. $m = \dfrac{y_2 - y_1}{x_2 - x_1} = \dfrac{7 - 3}{2 - 2} = \dfrac{4}{0}$

The slope is undefined.

D. $m = \dfrac{y_2 - y_1}{x_2 - x_1} = \dfrac{-3 - (-3)}{-5 - 1} = \dfrac{0}{-6} = 0$

The slope is 0.

Problem 2 $m = \dfrac{8650 - 6100}{1 - 4} = \dfrac{2550}{-3} = -850$

A slope of -850 means that the value of the car is decreasing at a rate of $850 per year.

Problem 3 y-intercept $= (0, b) = (0, -1)$

$$m = -\frac{1}{4}$$

Problem 4 Solve the equation for y.

$$x - 2y = 4$$

$$-2y = -x + 4$$

$$y = \frac{1}{2}x - 2$$

y-intercept $= (0, b) = (0, -2)$

$$m = \frac{1}{2}$$

SECTION 5.4

Problem 1 $y = \dfrac{3}{2}x + b$

$$-2 = \frac{3}{2}(4) + b$$

$$-2 = 6 + b$$

$$-8 = b$$

$$y = \frac{3}{2}x - 8$$

Problem 2 $m = \dfrac{2}{5}$ $(x_1, y_1) = (5, 4)$

$$y - y_1 = m(x - x_1)$$

$$y - 4 = \frac{2}{5}(x - 5)$$

$$y - 4 = \frac{2}{5}x - 2$$

$$y = \frac{2}{5}x + 2$$

SECTION 5.5

Problem 1   The domain is {1}.
The range is {0, 1, 2, 3, 4}.
There are ordered pairs with the same first coordinate and different second coordinates. The relation is not a function.

Problem 2 $f(x) = -5x + 1$
$f(2) = -5(2) + 1$
$f(2) = -10 + 1$
$f(2) = -9$

The ordered pair $(2, -9)$ is an element of the function.

Problem 3 $f(x) = 4x - 3$
$f(-5) = 4(-5) - 3 = -20 - 3 = -23$
$f(-3) = 4(-3) - 3 = -12 - 3 = -15$
$f(-1) = 4(-1) - 3 = -4 - 3 = -7$
$f(1) = 4(1) - 3 = 4 - 3 = 1$

The range is $\{-23, -15, -7, 1\}$.
The ordered pairs $(-5, -23)$, $(-3, -15)$, $(-1, -7)$, and $(1, 1)$ belong to the function.

Problem 4 $f(x) = -\dfrac{1}{2}x - 3$

$y = -\dfrac{1}{2}x - 3$

Problem 5   **A.** $d = 40t$
$f(t) = 40t$

B.

C.   The ordered pair $(3, 120)$ means that in 3 h, the car travels a distance of 120 mi.

SECTION 5.6

Problem 1 $x - 3y < 2$
$x - x - 3y < -x + 2$
$-3y < -x + 2$
$\dfrac{-3y}{-3} > \dfrac{-x + 2}{-3}$

$y > \dfrac{1}{3}x - \dfrac{2}{3}$

Problem 2 $x < 3$

SOLUTIONS to Chapter 6 Problems

SECTION 6.1

Problem 1

$2x - 5y = 8$	$-x + 3y = -5$
$2(-1) - 5(-2) \mid 8$	$-(-1) + 3(-2) \mid -5$
$-2 + 10 \mid 8$	$1 + (-6) \mid -5$
$8 = 8$	$-5 = -5$

Yes, $(-1, -2)$ is a solution of the system of equations.

Problem 2   **A.**

     B.

The solution is $(-3, 2)$.

The lines are parallel and therefore do not intersect. The system of equations is inconsistent and has no solution.

SECTION 6.2

Problem 1   (1) $7x - y = 4$
             (2) $3x + 2y = 9$

$$7x - y = 4$$ ▶ Solve equation (1) for y.
$$-y = -7x + 4$$
$$y = 7x - 4$$

$$3x + 2y = 9$$ ▶ Substitute $7x - 4$ for y in equation (2).
$$3x + 2(7x - 4) = 9$$
$$3x + 14x - 8 = 9$$
$$17x - 8 = 9$$
$$17x = 17$$
$$x = 1$$

$$7x - y = 4$$ ▶ Substitute the value of x in equation (1).
$$7(1) - y = 4$$
$$7 - y = 4$$
$$-y = -3$$
$$y = 3$$

The solution is (1, 3).

Problem 2 $3x - y = 4$
             $y = 3x + 2$

$$3x - y = 4$$
$$3x - (3x + 2) = 4$$
$$3x - 3x - 2 = 4$$
$$-2 = 4$$

The system of equations is inconsistent and has no solution.

Problem 3 $y = -2x + 1$
             $6x + 3y = 3$

$$6x + 3y = 3$$
$$6x + 3(-2x + 1) = 3$$
$$6x - 6x + 3 = 3$$
$$3 = 3$$

The system of equations is dependent. The solutions are the ordered pairs that satisfy the equation $y = -2x + 1$.

SECTION 6.3

Problem 1   (1) $x - 2y = 1$
             (2) $2x + 4y = 0$

$$2(x - 2y) = 2 \cdot 1$$ ▶ Eliminate y.
$$2x + 4y = 0$$

$$2x - 4y = 2$$
$$2x + 4y = 0$$
$$4x = 2$$ ▶ Add the equations.
$$x = \frac{2}{4} = \frac{1}{2}$$

$$2x + 4y = 0$$ ▶ Replace x in equation (2).
$$2\left(\frac{1}{2}\right) + 4y = 0$$
$$1 + 4y = 0$$
$$4y = -1$$
$$y = -\frac{1}{4}$$

The solution is $\left(\frac{1}{2}, -\frac{1}{4}\right)$.

Problem 2   (1) $2x - 3y = 4$
            (2) $-4x + 6y = -8$

$$2(2x - 3y) = 2 \cdot 4 \qquad \blacktriangleright \text{Eliminate } y.$$
$$-4x + 6y = -8$$

$$4x - 6y = 8$$
$$-4x + 6y = -8$$
$$0 + 0 = 0 \qquad \blacktriangleright \text{Add the equations.}$$
$$0 = 0$$

The system of equations is dependent. The solutions are the ordered pairs that satisfy the equation $2x - 3y = 4$.

SECTION 6.4

Problem 1

Strategy   ▪ Rate of the current: c
           Rate of the canoeist in calm water: r

	Rate	Time	Distance
With current	$r + c$	3	$3(r + c)$
Against current	$r - c$	4	$4(r - c)$

           ▪ The distance traveled with the current is 24 mi.
            The distance traveled against the current is 24 mi.

Solution $3(r + c) = 24 \qquad \dfrac{3(r + c)}{3} = \dfrac{24}{3} \qquad r + c = 8$

            $4(r - c) = 24 \qquad \dfrac{4(r - c)}{4} = \dfrac{24}{4} \qquad r - c = 6$
$$2r = 14$$
$$r = 7$$

$$r + c = 8$$
$$7 + c = 8$$
$$c = 1$$

The rate of the current is 1 mph.
The rate of the canoeist in calm water is 7 mph.

Problem 2

Strategy   ▪ The number of dimes in the first bank: d
           The number of quarters in the first bank: q

First bank

	Number	Value	Total value
Dimes	d	10	$10d$
Quarters	q	25	$25q$

Second bank

	Number	Value	Total value
Dimes	$2d$	10	$20d$
Quarters	$\dfrac{1}{2}q$	25	$\dfrac{25}{2}q$

           ▪ The total value of the coins in the first bank is $3.90.
            The total value of the coins in the second bank is $3.30.

Solution

$$10d + 25q = 390$$
$$20d + \frac{25}{2}q = 330$$

$$10d + 25q = 390$$
$$-2\left(20d + \frac{25}{2}q\right) = -2(330)$$

$$10d + 25q = 390$$
$$-40d - 25q = -660$$
$$-30d = -270$$
$$d = 9$$

$$10d + 25q = 390$$
$$10(9) + 25q = 390$$
$$90 + 25q = 390$$
$$25q = 300$$
$$q = 12$$

There are 9 dimes and 12 quarters in the first bank.

SOLUTIONS to Chapter 7 Problems

SECTION 7.1

Problem 1

$$2x^2 + 4x - 3$$
$$5x^2 - 6x$$
$$\overline{7x^2 - 2x - 3}$$

Problem 2

$$(-4x^2 - 3xy + 2y^2) + (3x^2 - 4y^2)$$
$$= (-4x^2 + 3x^2) - 3xy + (2y^2 - 4y^2)$$
$$= -x^2 - 3xy - 2y^2$$

Problem 3

The opposite of $2y^2 - xy + 5x^2$ is
$-2y^2 + xy - 5x^2$.

$$8y^2 - 4xy + x^2$$
$$-2y^2 + xy - 5x^2$$
$$\overline{6y^2 - 3xy - 4x^2}$$

Problem 4

$$(-3a^2 - 4a + 2) - (5a^3 + 2a - 6)$$
$$= (-3a^2 - 4a + 2) + (-5a^3 - 2a + 6)$$
$$= -5a^3 - 3a^2 + (-4a - 2a) + (2 + 6)$$
$$= -5a^3 - 3a^2 - 6a + 8$$

SECTION 7.2

Problem 1 $(3x^2)(6x^3) = (3 \cdot 6)(x^2 \cdot x^3) = 18x^5$

Problem 2 $(-3xy^2)(-4x^2y^3)$
$$= [(-3)(-4)](x \cdot x^2)(y^2 \cdot y^3)$$
$$= 12x^3y^5$$

Problem 3 $(3x)(2x^2y)^3 = (3x)(2^3x^6y^3) = (3x)(8x^6y^3)$
$$= (3 \cdot 8)(x \cdot x^6)y^3 = 24x^7y^3$$

SECTION 7.3

Problem 1   **A.** $(-2y + 3)(-4y) = 8y^2 - 12y$

B. $-a^2(3a^2 + 2a - 7) = -3a^4 - 2a^3 + 7a^2$

Problem 2

$$2y^3 + 2y^2 - 3$$
$$3y - 1$$
$$\overline{- 2y^3 - 2y^2 \quad\; + 3}$$
$$6y^4 + 6y^3 \quad\;\;\; - 9y$$
$$\overline{6y^4 + 4y^3 - 2y^2 - 9y + 3}$$

Problem 3

$$3x^3 - 2x^2 + x - 3$$
$$2x + 5$$
$$\overline{15x^3 - 10x^2 + 5x - 15}$$
$$6x^4 - 4x^3 + 2x^2 - 6x$$
$$\overline{6x^4 + 11x^3 - 8x^2 - x - 15}$$

Problem 4 $(4y - 5)(3y - 3)$
$$= 12y^2 - 12y - 15y + 15$$
$$= 12y^2 - 27y + 15$$

Problem 5 $(3a + 2b)(3a - 5b)$
$$= 9a^2 - 15ab + 6ab - 10b^2$$
$$= 9a^2 - 9ab - 10b^2$$

Problem 6 $(2a + 5c)(2a - 5c) = (2a)^2 - (5c)^2$
$$= 4a^2 - 25c^2$$

Problem 7 $(3x + 2y)^2 = (3x)^2 + 2(3x)(2y) + (2y)^2$
$$= 9x^2 + 12xy + 4y^2$$

Problem 8 $(6x - y)^2 = (6x)^2 + 2(6x)(-y) + (-y)^2$
$$= 36x^2 - 12xy + y^2$$

Problem 9

Strategy   To find the area in terms of x, replace the variables L and W in the equation $A = LW$ with the given values, and solve for A.

Solution $A = LW$
$$A = (x + 7)(x - 4)$$
$$A = x^2 - 4x + 7x - 28$$
$$A = x^2 + 3x - 28$$

The area is $(x^2 + 3x - 28)$ m^2.

Problem 10

Strategy To find the area of the triangle in terms of x, replace the variables b and h in the equation $A = \frac{1}{2}bh$ with the given values, and solve for A.

Solution $A = \frac{1}{2}bh$

$A = \frac{1}{2}(x + 3)(4x - 6)$

$A = \frac{1}{2}(4x^2 + 6x - 18)$

$A = 2x^2 + 3x - 9$

The area is $(2x^2 + 3x - 9)$ cm².

SECTION 7.4

Problem 1 $\dfrac{2^{-2}}{2^3} = 2^{-2-3} = 2^{-5} = \dfrac{1}{2^5} = \dfrac{1}{32}$

Problem 2 $\dfrac{b^8}{a^{-5}b^6} = a^5 b^{8-6} = a^5 b^2$

Problem 3 **A.** $\dfrac{12x^{-8}y^4}{-16xy^{-3}} = -\dfrac{3x^{-9}y^7}{4} = -\dfrac{3y^7}{4x^9}$

B. $(-3ab)(2a^3b^{-2})^{-3} = (-3ab)(2^{-3}a^{-9}b^6)$

$= -\dfrac{3a^{-8}b^7}{2^3} = -\dfrac{3b^7}{8a^8}$

Problem 4 **A.** $57{,}000{,}000{,}000 = 5.7 \cdot 10^{10}$

B. $0.000000017 = 1.7 \cdot 10^{-8}$

Problem 5 **A.** $5 \cdot 10^{12} = 5{,}000{,}000{,}000{,}000$

B. $4.0162 \cdot 10^{-9} = 0.0000000040162$

Problem 6 **A.** $(2.4 \cdot 10^{-9})(1.6 \cdot 10^3) = 3.84 \cdot 10^{-6}$

B. $\dfrac{5.4 \cdot 10^{-2}}{1.8 \cdot 10^{-4}} = 3 \cdot 10^2$

Problem 7 $\dfrac{4x^3y + 8x^2y^2 - 4xy^3}{2xy} = \dfrac{4x^3y}{2xy} + \dfrac{8x^2y^2}{2xy} - \dfrac{4xy^3}{2xy}$

$= 2x^2 + 4xy - 2y^2$

Problem 8 $\dfrac{24x^2y^2 - 18xy + 6y}{6xy} = \dfrac{24x^2y^2}{6xy} - \dfrac{18xy}{6xy} + \dfrac{6y}{6xy}$

$= 4xy - 3 + \dfrac{1}{x}$

Problem 9

$$
\begin{array}{r}
x^2 + 2x + 2 \\
x - 2{\overline{\smash{)}\,x^3 + 0x^2 - 2x - 4}} \\
\underline{x^3 - 2x^2} \\
2x^2 - 2x \\
\underline{2x^2 - 4x} \\
2x - 4 \\
\underline{2x - 4} \\
0
\end{array}
$$

$(x^3 - 2x - 4) \div (x - 2) = x^2 + 2x + 2$

SOLUTIONS to Chapter 8 Problems

SECTION 8.1

Problem 1 $4x^6y = 2 \cdot 2 \cdot x^6 \cdot y$
$18x^2y^6 = 2 \cdot 3 \cdot 3 \cdot x^2 \cdot y^6$
$GCF = 2 \cdot x^2 \cdot y = 2x^2y$

Problem 2 **A.** $14a^2 = 2 \cdot 7 \cdot a^2$
$21a^4b = 3 \cdot 7 \cdot a^4 \cdot b$
The GCF is $7a^2$.

$14a^2 - 21a^4b = 7a^2(2) + 7a^2(-3a^2b)$
$= 7a^2(2 - 3a^2b)$

B. $6x^4y^2 = 2 \cdot 3 \cdot x^4 \cdot y^2$
$9x^3y^2 = 3 \cdot 3 \cdot x^3 \cdot y^2$
$12x^2y^4 = 2 \cdot 2 \cdot 3 \cdot x^2 \cdot y^4$
The GCF is $3x^2y^2$.

$6x^4y^2 - 9x^3y^2 + 12x^2y^4$
$= 3x^2y^2(2x^2) + 3x^2y^2(-3x) + 3x^2y^2(4y^2)$
$= 3x^2y^2(2x^2 - 3x + 4y^2)$

Problem 3 $a(b - 7) + b(b - 7) = (b - 7)(a + b)$

Problem 4 $3y(5x - 2) - 4(2 - 5x)$
$= 3y(5x - 2) + 4(5x - 2)$
$= (5x - 2)(3y + 4)$

Problem 5 $y^5 - 5y^3 + 4y^2 - 20$
$= (y^5 - 5y^3) + (4y^2 - 20)$
$= y^3(y^2 - 5) + 4(y^2 - 5)$
$= (y^2 - 5)(y^3 + 4)$

SECTION 8.2

Problem 1

Factors of 15	Sum
$-1, -15$	-16
$-3, -5$	-8

$x^2 - 8x + 15 = (x - 3)(x - 5)$

Problem 2

Factors of -18	Sum
1, -18	-17
-1, 18	17
2, -9	-7
-2, 9	7
3, -6	-3
-3, 6	3

$x^2 + 3x - 18 = (x + 6)(x - 3)$

Problem 3 The GCF is $3b$.

$3a^2b - 18ab - 81b = 3b(a^2 - 6a - 27)$

Factors of -27	Sum
1, -27	-26
-1, 27	26
3, -9	-6
-3, 9	6

$3a^2b - 18ab - 81b = 3b(a + 3)(a - 9)$

Problem 4 The GCF is 4.

$4x^2 - 40xy + 84y^2$
$= 4(x^2 - 10xy + 21y^2)$

Factors of 21	Sum
-1, -21	-22
-3, -7	-10

$4x^2 - 40xy + 84y^2 = 4(x - 3y)(x - 7y)$

SECTION 8.3

Problem 1

Factors of 6	Factors of 5
1, 6	-1, -5
2, 3	

Trial Factors	Middle Term
$(x - 1)(6x - 5)$	$-5x - 6x = -11x$

$6x^2 - 11x + 5 = (x - 1)(6x - 5)$

Problem 2

Factors of 8	Factors of -15
1, 8	1, -15
2, 4	-1, 15
	3, -5
	-3, 5

Trial Factors	Middle Term
$(x + 1)(8x - 15)$	$-15x + 8x = -7x$
$(x - 1)(8x + 15)$	$15x - 8x = 7x$
$(x + 3)(8x - 5)$	$-5x + 24x = 19x$
$(x - 3)(8x + 5)$	$5x - 24x = -19x$
$(2x + 1)(4x - 15)$	$-30x + 4x = -26x$
$(2x - 1)(4x + 15)$	$30x - 4x = 26x$
$(2x + 3)(4x - 5)$	$-10x + 12x = 2x$
$(2x - 3)(4x + 5)$	$10x - 12x = -2x$
$(8x + 1)(x - 15)$	$-120x + x = -119x$
$(8x - 1)(x + 15)$	$120x - x = 119x$
$(8x + 3)(x - 5)$	$-40x + 3x = -37x$
$(8x - 3)(x + 5)$	$40x - 3x = 37x$
$(4x + 1)(2x - 15)$	$-60x + 2x = -58x$
$(4x - 1)(2x + 15)$	$60x - 2x = 58x$
$(4x + 3)(2x - 5)$	$-20x + 6x = -14x$
$(4x - 3)(2x + 5)$	$20x - 6x = 14x$

$8x^2 + 14x - 15 = (4x - 3)(2x + 5)$

Problem 3

Factors of 24	Factors of -1
1, 24	1, -1
2, 12	
3, 8	
4, 6	

Trial Factors	Middle Term
$(1 - y)(24 + y)$	$y - 24y = -23y$
$(2 - y)(12 + y)$	$2y - 12y = -10y$
$(3 - y)(8 + y)$	$3y - 8y = -5y$
$(4 - y)(6 + y)$	$4y - 6y = -2y$

$24 - 2y - y^2 = (4 - y)(6 + y)$

Problem 4 The GCF is $2a^2$.

$4a^2b^2 - 30a^2b + 14a^2$
$= 2a^2(2b^2 - 15b + 7)$

Factors of 2	Factors of 7
1, 2	-1, -7

Trial Factors	Middle Term
$(b - 1)(2b - 7)$	$-7b - 2b = -9b$
$(b - 7)(2b - 1)$	$-b - 14b = -15b$

$4a^2b^2 - 30a^2b + 14a^2$
$= 2a^2(b - 7)(2b - 1)$

Problem 5 $a \cdot c = -14$
$-1(14) = -14, \; -1 + 14 = 13$

$2a^2 + 13a - 7$
$= 2a^2 - a + 14a - 7$
$= (2a^2 - a) + (14a - 7)$
$= a(2a - 1) + 7(2a - 1)$
$= (2a - 1)(a + 7)$

Problem 6 $a \cdot c = -12$
$1(-12) = -12, \; 1 - 12 = -11$

$4a^2 - 11a - 3$
$= 4a^2 + a - 12a - 3$
$= (4a^2 + a) - (12a + 3)$
$= a(4a + 1) - 3(4a + 1)$
$= (4a + 1)(a - 3)$

Problem 7   The GCF is $5x$.

$15x^3 + 40x^2 - 80x = 5x(3x^2 + 8x - 16)$
$3(-16) = -48$
$-4(12) = -48, \; -4 + 12 = 8$

$3x^2 + 8x - 16$
$= 3x^2 - 4x + 12x - 16$
$= (3x^2 - 4x) + (12x - 16)$
$= x(3x - 4) + 4(3x - 4)$
$= (3x - 4)(x + 4)$

$15x^3 + 40x^2 - 80x = 5x(3x^2 + 8x - 16)$
$\qquad\qquad\qquad\qquad = 5x(3x - 4)(x + 4)$

SECTION 8.4

Problem 1   **A.** $25a^2 - b^2 = (5a)^2 - b^2$
$\qquad\qquad\quad = (5a + b)(5a - b)$

B. $6x^2 - 1$ is nonfactorable over the integers.

C. $n^8 - 36 = (n^4)^2 - 6^2$
$\qquad\qquad = (n^4 + 6)(n^4 - 6)$

Problem 2 $n^4 - 81 = (n^2 + 9)(n^2 - 9)$
$\qquad\qquad = (n^2 + 9)(n + 3)(n - 3)$

Problem 3   **A.** $16y^2 = (4y)^2, \; 1 = 1^2$

$(4y + 1)^2 = (4y)^2 + 2(4y)(1) + (1)^2$
$\qquad\qquad = 16y^2 + 8y + 1$

$16y^2 + 8y + 1 = (4y + 1)^2$

B. $x^2 = (x)^2, \; 36 = 6^2$

$(x + 6)^2 = x^2 + 2(x)(6) + 6^2$
$\qquad\qquad = x^2 + 12x + 36$

The polynomial is not a perfect square.

$x^2 + 14x + 36$ is nonfactorable over the integers.

Problem 4   **A.** $12x^3 - 75x = 3x(4x^2 - 25)$
$\qquad\qquad\qquad = 3x(2x + 5)(2x - 5)$

B. $a^2 b - 7a^2 - b + 7$
$\qquad = (a^2 b - 7a^2) - (b - 7)$
$\qquad = a^2(b - 7) - (b - 7)$
$\qquad = (b - 7)(a^2 - 1)$
$\qquad = (b - 7)(a + 1)(a - 1)$

C. $4x^3 + 28x^2 - 120x = 4x(x^2 + 7x - 30)$
$\qquad\qquad\qquad\qquad = 4x(x + 10)(x - 3)$

SECTION 8.5

Problem 1 $2x^2 - 50 = 0$
$\qquad\quad 2(x^2 - 25) = 0$
$\qquad\qquad\; x^2 - 25 = 0$
$\qquad (x + 5)(x - 5) = 0$

$x + 5 = 0 \qquad\quad x - 5 = 0$
$\qquad x = -5 \qquad\qquad x = 5$

The solutions are -5 and 5.

Problem 2 $(x + 2)(x - 7) = 52$
$\qquad\quad x^2 - 5x - 14 = 52$
$\qquad\quad x^2 - 5x - 66 = 0$
$\qquad (x - 11)(x + 6) = 0$

$x - 11 = 0 \qquad\quad x + 6 = 0$
$\qquad x = 11 \qquad\qquad x = -6$

The solutions are -6 and 11.

Problem 3

Strategy   First positive integer: n
Second positive integer: $n + 1$
Square of the first positive integer: n^2
Square of the second positive integer: $(n + 1)^2$

The sum of the squares of the two integers is 85.

Solution $n^2 + (n + 1)^2 = 85$
$\quad n^2 + n^2 + 2n + 1 = 85$
$\qquad\quad 2n^2 + 2n - 84 = 0$
$\qquad\quad 2(n^2 + n - 42) = 0$
$\qquad\qquad n^2 + n - 42 = 0$
$\qquad\quad (n + 7)(n - 6) = 0$

$n + 7 = 0 \qquad\quad n - 6 = 0$
$\quad n = -7 \qquad\qquad n = 6$

-7 is not a positive integer.

$n + 1 = 6 + 1 = 7$

The two integers are 6 and 7.

Problem 4

Strategy Width $= x$
Length $= 2x + 3$

The area of the rectangle is 90 m².
Use the equation $A = LW$.

Solution $A = LW$
$90 = (2x + 3)x$
$90 = 2x^2 + 3x$
$0 = 2x^2 + 3x - 90$
$0 = (2x + 15)(x - 6)$

$2x + 15 = 0 \qquad\qquad x - 6 = 0$
$2x = -15 \qquad\qquad x = 6$
$x = -\dfrac{15}{2}$

The width cannot be a negative number.

$2x + 3 = 2(6) + 3 = 12 + 3 = 15$

The width is 6 m. The length is 15 m.

SOLUTIONS to Chapter 9 Problems

SECTION 9.1

Problem 1 **A.** $\dfrac{6x^5y}{12x^2y^3} = \dfrac{\overset{1}{\cancel{2}} \cdot \overset{1}{\cancel{3}} \cdot x^5 y}{\underset{1}{\cancel{2}} \cdot 2 \cdot \underset{1}{\cancel{3}} \cdot x^2 y^3} = \dfrac{x^3}{2y^2}$

B. $\dfrac{x^2 + 2x - 24}{16 - x^2} = \dfrac{\overset{-1}{\cancel{(x - 4)}}(x + 6)}{\underset{1}{\cancel{(4 - x)}}(4 + x)} = -\dfrac{x + 6}{x + 4}$

Problem 2 **A.** $\dfrac{12x^2 + 3x}{10x - 15} \cdot \dfrac{8x - 12}{9x + 18}$

$= \dfrac{3x(4x + 1)}{5(2x - 3)} \cdot \dfrac{4(2x - 3)}{9(x + 2)}$

$= \dfrac{3x(4x + 1) \cdot \overset{1}{\cancel{2}} \cdot 2\overset{1}{\cancel{(2x - 3)}}}{5\underset{1}{\cancel{(2x - 3)}} \cdot \underset{1}{\cancel{3}} \cdot 3(x + 2)}$

$= \dfrac{4x(4x + 1)}{15(x + 2)}$

B. $\dfrac{x^2 + 2x - 15}{9 - x^2} \cdot \dfrac{x^2 - 3x - 18}{x^2 - 7x + 6}$

$= \dfrac{(x - 3)(x + 5)}{(3 - x)(3 + x)} \cdot \dfrac{(x + 3)(x - 6)}{(x - 1)(x - 6)}$

$= \dfrac{\overset{-1}{\cancel{(x - 3)}}(x + 5) \cdot \overset{1}{\cancel{(x + 3)}}\overset{1}{\cancel{(x - 6)}}}{\underset{1}{\cancel{(3 - x)}}\underset{1}{\cancel{(3 + x)}} \cdot (x - 1)\underset{1}{\cancel{(x - 6)}}}$

$= -\dfrac{x + 5}{x - 1}$

Problem 3 **A.** $\dfrac{a^2}{4bc^2 - 2b^2c} \div \dfrac{a}{6bc - 3b^2}$

$= \dfrac{a^2}{4bc^2 - 2b^2c} \cdot \dfrac{6bc - 3b^2}{a}$

$= \dfrac{a^2 \cdot 3b\overset{1}{\cancel{(2c - b)}}}{2bc\underset{1}{\cancel{(2c - b)}} \cdot a} = \dfrac{3a}{2c}$

B. $\dfrac{3x^2 + 26x + 16}{3x^2 - 7x - 6} \div \dfrac{2x^2 + 9x - 5}{x^2 + 2x - 15}$

$= \dfrac{3x^2 + 26x + 16}{3x^2 - 7x - 6} \cdot \dfrac{x^2 + 2x - 15}{2x^2 + 9x - 5}$

$= \dfrac{\overset{1}{\cancel{(3x + 2)}}(x + 8)}{\underset{1}{\cancel{(3x + 2)}}\overset{1}{\cancel{(x - 3)}}} \cdot \dfrac{\overset{1}{\cancel{(x + 5)}}\overset{1}{\cancel{(x - 3)}}}{(2x - 1)\underset{1}{\cancel{(x + 5)}}}$

$= \dfrac{x + 8}{2x - 1}$

SECTION 9.2

Problem 1 $8uv^2 = 2 \cdot 2 \cdot 2 \cdot u \cdot v \cdot v$
$12uw = 2 \cdot 2 \cdot 3 \cdot u \cdot w$

$\text{LCM} = 2 \cdot 2 \cdot 2 \cdot 3 \cdot u \cdot v \cdot v \cdot w$
$= 24uv^2w$

Problem 2 $m^2 - 6m + 9 = (m - 3)(m - 3)$
$m^2 - 2m - 3 = (m + 1)(m - 3)$

$\text{LCM} = (m - 3)(m - 3)(m + 1)$

Problem 3 The LCM is $36xy^2z$.

$\dfrac{x - 3}{4xy^2} = \dfrac{x - 3}{4xy^2} \cdot \dfrac{9z}{9z} = \dfrac{9xz - 27z}{36xy^2z}$

$\dfrac{2x + 1}{9y^2z} = \dfrac{2x + 1}{9y^2z} \cdot \dfrac{4x}{4x} = \dfrac{8x^2 + 4x}{36xy^2z}$

Problem 4 $\dfrac{2x}{25 - x^2} = \dfrac{2x}{-(x^2 - 25)} = -\dfrac{2x}{x^2 - 25}$

The LCM is $(x + 2)(x - 5)(x + 5)$.

$\dfrac{x + 4}{x^2 - 3x - 10} = \dfrac{x + 4}{(x + 2)(x - 5)} \cdot \dfrac{x + 5}{x + 5} = \dfrac{x^2 + 9x + 20}{(x + 2)(x - 5)(x + 5)}$

$\dfrac{2x}{25 - x^2} = -\dfrac{2x}{(x - 5)(x + 5)} \cdot \dfrac{x + 2}{x + 2} = -\dfrac{2x^2 + 4x}{(x + 2)(x - 5)(x + 5)}$

SECTION 9.3

Problem 1 **A.** $\dfrac{3}{xy} + \dfrac{12}{xy} = \dfrac{3 + 12}{xy} = \dfrac{15}{xy}$

B. $\dfrac{2x^2}{x^2 - x - 12} - \dfrac{7x + 4}{x^2 - x - 12} = \dfrac{2x^2 - (7x + 4)}{x^2 - x - 12}$

$= \dfrac{2x^2 - 7x - 4}{x^2 - x - 12} = \dfrac{(2x + 1)(x - 4)}{(x + 3)(x - 4)} = \dfrac{2x + 1}{x + 3}$

Problem 2 **A.** The LCM of the denominators is $24y$.

$\dfrac{z}{8y} - \dfrac{4z}{3y} + \dfrac{5z}{4y} = \dfrac{z}{8y} \cdot \dfrac{3}{3} - \dfrac{4z}{3y} \cdot \dfrac{8}{8} + \dfrac{5z}{4y} \cdot \dfrac{6}{6}$

$= \dfrac{3z}{24y} - \dfrac{32z}{24y} + \dfrac{30z}{24y} = \dfrac{3z - 32z + 30z}{24y} = \dfrac{z}{24y}$

B. The LCM is $x - 2$.

$\dfrac{5x}{x - 2} - \dfrac{3}{2 - x} = \dfrac{5x}{x - 2} - \dfrac{3}{-(x - 2)} \cdot \dfrac{-1}{-1}$

$= \dfrac{5x}{x - 2} - \dfrac{-3}{x - 2} = \dfrac{5x - (-3)}{x - 2} = \dfrac{5x + 3}{x - 2}$

C. The LCM is $y - 7$.

$y + \dfrac{5}{y - 7} = \dfrac{y}{1} + \dfrac{5}{y - 7} = \dfrac{y}{1} \cdot \dfrac{y - 7}{y - 7} + \dfrac{5}{y - 7}$

$= \dfrac{y^2 - 7y}{y - 7} + \dfrac{5}{y - 7} = \dfrac{y^2 - 7y + 5}{y - 7}$

Problem 3 **A.** The LCM is $(3x - 1)(x + 4)$.

$\dfrac{4x}{3x - 1} - \dfrac{9}{x + 4}$

$= \dfrac{4x}{3x - 1} \cdot \dfrac{x + 4}{x + 4} - \dfrac{9}{x + 4} \cdot \dfrac{3x - 1}{3x - 1}$

$= \dfrac{4x^2 + 16x}{(3x - 1)(x + 4)} - \dfrac{27x - 9}{(3x - 1)(x + 4)}$

$= \dfrac{(4x^2 + 16x) - (27x - 9)}{(3x - 1)(x + 4)}$

$= \dfrac{4x^2 + 16x - 27x + 9}{(3x - 1)(x + 4)} = \dfrac{4x^2 - 11x + 9}{(3x - 1)(x + 4)}$

B. The LCM is $(x + 5)(x - 5)$.

$\dfrac{2x - 1}{x^2 - 25} + \dfrac{2}{5 - x}$

$= \dfrac{2x - 1}{(x + 5)(x - 5)} + \dfrac{2}{-(x - 5)} \cdot \dfrac{-1(x + 5)}{-1(x + 5)}$

$= \dfrac{2x - 1}{(x + 5)(x - 5)} + \dfrac{-2(x + 5)}{(x + 5)(x - 5)}$

$= \dfrac{(2x - 1) + (-2)(x + 5)}{(x + 5)(x - 5)}$

$= \dfrac{2x - 1 - 2x - 10}{(x + 5)(x - 5)}$

$= \dfrac{-11}{(x + 5)(x - 5)} = -\dfrac{11}{(x + 5)(x - 5)}$

SECTION 9.4

Problem 1 **A.** The LCM of 3, x, 9, and x^2 is $9x^2$.

$\dfrac{\frac{1}{3} - \frac{1}{x}}{\frac{1}{9} - \frac{1}{x^2}} = \dfrac{\frac{1}{3} - \frac{1}{x}}{\frac{1}{9} - \frac{1}{x^2}} \cdot \dfrac{9x^2}{9x^2} = \dfrac{\frac{1}{3} \cdot 9x^2 - \frac{1}{x} \cdot 9x^2}{\frac{1}{9} \cdot 9x^2 - \frac{1}{x^2} \cdot 9x^2}$

$= \dfrac{3x^2 - 9x}{x^2 - 9} = \dfrac{3x(x - 3)}{(x - 3)(x + 3)} = \dfrac{3x}{x + 3}$

B. The LCM of x and x^2 is x^2.

$\dfrac{1 + \frac{4}{x} + \frac{3}{x^2}}{1 + \frac{10}{x} + \frac{21}{x^2}} = \dfrac{1 + \frac{4}{x} + \frac{3}{x^2}}{1 + \frac{10}{x} + \frac{21}{x^2}} \cdot \dfrac{x^2}{x^2}$

$= \dfrac{1 \cdot x^2 + \frac{4}{x} \cdot x^2 + \frac{3}{x^2} \cdot x^2}{1 \cdot x^2 + \frac{10}{x} \cdot x^2 + \frac{21}{x^2} \cdot x^2}$

$= \dfrac{x^2 + 4x + 3}{x^2 + 10x + 21}$

$= \dfrac{(x + 1)(x + 3)}{(x + 3)(x + 7)} = \dfrac{x + 1}{x + 7}$

SECTION 9.5

Problem 1 The LCM of 3 and $3x$ is $3x$.

$x + \dfrac{1}{3} = \dfrac{4}{3x}$

$3x\left(x + \dfrac{1}{3}\right) = 3x\left(\dfrac{4}{3x}\right)$

$3x \cdot x + \dfrac{3x}{1} \cdot \dfrac{1}{3} = \dfrac{3x}{1} \cdot \dfrac{4}{3x}$

$3x^2 + x = 4$

$3x^2 + x - 4 = 0$

$(3x + 4)(x - 1) = 0$

$3x + 4 = 0 \qquad x - 1 = 0$

$3x = -4 \qquad\qquad x = 1$

$x = -\dfrac{4}{3}$

Both $-\dfrac{4}{3}$ and 1 check as solutions.

The solutions are $-\dfrac{4}{3}$ and 1.

Problem 2   The LCM is $x + 2$.

$$\frac{5x}{x + 2} = 3 - \frac{10}{x + 2}$$

$$\frac{(x + 2)}{1} \cdot \frac{5x}{x + 2} = \frac{(x + 2)}{1}\left(3 - \frac{10}{x + 2}\right)$$

$$5x = (x + 2)3 - 10$$

$$5x = 3x + 6 - 10$$

$$5x = 3x - 4$$

$$2x = -4$$

$$x = -2$$

-2 does not check as a solution.
The equation has no solution.

Problem 3

A.

$$\frac{2}{x + 3} = \frac{6}{5x + 5}$$

$$(x + 3)(5x + 5)\frac{2}{x + 3} = (x + 3)(5x + 5)\frac{6}{5x + 5}$$

$$(5x + 5)2 = (x + 3)6$$

$$10x + 10 = 6x + 18$$

$$4x + 10 = 18$$

$$4x = 8$$

$$x = 2$$

The solution is 2.

B.

$$\frac{5}{2x - 3} = \frac{10}{x + 3}$$

$$(x + 3)(2x - 3)\frac{5}{2x - 3} = (x + 3)(2x - 3)\frac{10}{x + 3}$$

$$(x + 3)5 = (2x - 3)10$$

$$5x + 15 = 20x - 30$$

$$-15x + 15 = -30$$

$$-15x = -45$$

$$x = 3$$

The solution is 3.

Problem 4

Strategy   To find the total area that 270 ceramic tiles will cover, write and solve a proportion using x to represent the number of square feet that 270 tiles will cover.

Solution

$$\frac{4}{9} = \frac{x}{270}$$

$$270\left(\frac{4}{9}\right) = 270\left(\frac{x}{270}\right)$$

$$120 = x$$

A 120 ft^2 area can be tiled using 270 ceramic tiles.

Problem 5

Strategy   To find the additional amount of medication required for a 180-pound adult, write and solve a proportion using x to represent the additional medication. Then $3 + x$ is the total amount required for a 180-pound adult.

Solution

$$\frac{120}{3} = \frac{180}{3 + x}$$

$$\frac{40}{1} = \frac{180}{3 + x}$$

$$(3 + x) \cdot 40 = (3 + x) \cdot \frac{180}{3 + x}$$

$$120 + 40x = 180$$

$$40x = 60$$

$$x = 1.5$$

1.5 additional ounces are required for a 180-pound adult.

Problem 6

Strategy   Triangle AOB is similar to triangle DOC. Solve a proportion to find the length of AO. Then use the formula for the area of a triangle to find the area of triangle AOB.

Solution

$$\frac{CD}{AB} = \frac{DO}{AO}$$

$$\frac{4}{10} = \frac{3}{x}$$

$$10x\left(\frac{4}{10}\right) = 10x\left(\frac{3}{x}\right)$$

$$4x = 30$$

$$x = 7.5$$

$$A = \frac{1}{2}bh$$

$$A = \frac{1}{2}(10)(7.5)$$

$$A = 37.5$$

The area of triangle AOD is 37.5 cm^2.

SECTION 9.6

Problem 1   **A.**

$$s = \frac{A + L}{2}$$

$$2 \cdot s = 2\left(\frac{A + L}{2}\right)$$

$$2s = A + L$$

$$2s - A = A - A + L$$

$$2s - A = L$$

B.
$$S = a + (n - 1)d$$
$$S = a + nd - d$$
$$S - a = a - a + nd - d$$
$$S - a = nd - d$$
$$S - a + d = nd - d + d$$
$$S - a + d = nd$$
$$\frac{S - a + d}{d} = \frac{nd}{d}$$
$$\frac{S - a + d}{d} = n$$

Problem 2
$$S = C + rC$$
$$S = (1 + r)C$$
$$\frac{S}{1 + r} = \frac{(1 + r)C}{1 + r}$$
$$\frac{S}{1 + r} = C$$

SECTION 9.7

Problem 1

Strategy ▪ Time for one printer to complete the job: t

	Rate	Time	Part
1st printer	$\frac{1}{t}$	3	$\frac{3}{t}$
2nd printer	$\frac{1}{t}$	5	$\frac{5}{t}$

▪ The sum of the parts of the task completed must equal 1.

Solution
$$\frac{3}{t} + \frac{5}{t} = 1$$
$$t\left(\frac{3}{t} + \frac{5}{t}\right) = t \cdot 1$$
$$3 + 5 = t$$
$$8 = t$$

Working alone, one printer takes 8 h to print the payroll.

Problem 2

Strategy ▪ Rate sailing across the lake: r
Rate sailing back: $2r$

	Distance	Rate	Time
Across	6	r	$\frac{6}{r}$
Back	6	$2r$	$\frac{6}{2r}$

▪ The total time for the trip was 3 h.

Solution
$$\frac{6}{r} + \frac{6}{2r} = 3$$
$$2r\left(\frac{6}{r} + \frac{6}{2r}\right) = 2r(3)$$
$$2r \cdot \frac{6}{r} + 2r \cdot \frac{6}{2r} = 6r$$
$$12 + 6 = 6r$$
$$18 = 6r$$
$$3 = r$$

The rate across the lake was 3 km/h.

SOLUTIONS to Chapter 10 Problems

SECTION 10.1

Problem 1 $-5\sqrt{32} = -5\sqrt{2^5} = -5\sqrt{2^4 \cdot 2}$
$= -5\sqrt{2^4}\sqrt{2} = -5 \cdot 2^2\sqrt{2} = -20\sqrt{2}$

Problem 2 $\sqrt{216} = \sqrt{2^3 \cdot 3^3} = \sqrt{2^2 \cdot 3^2(2 \cdot 3)}$
$= \sqrt{2^2 \cdot 3^2}\sqrt{2 \cdot 3} = 2 \cdot 3\sqrt{2 \cdot 3} = 6\sqrt{6}$

Problem 3 $\sqrt{y^{19}} = \sqrt{y^{18} \cdot y} = \sqrt{y^{18}}\sqrt{y} = y^9\sqrt{y}$

Problem 4   **A.** $\sqrt{45b^7} = \sqrt{3^2 \cdot 5 \cdot b^7} = \sqrt{3^2b^6(5 \cdot b)}$
$= \sqrt{3^2b^6}\sqrt{5b} = 3b^3\sqrt{5b}$

B. $3a\sqrt{28a^9b^{18}} = 3a\sqrt{2^2 \cdot 7 \cdot a^9b^{18}}$
$= 3a\sqrt{2^2a^8b^{18}(7a)} = 3a\sqrt{2^2a^8b^{18}}\sqrt{7a}$
$= 3a \cdot 2a^4b^9\sqrt{7a} = 6a^5b^9\sqrt{7a}$

Problem 5 $\sqrt{25(a + 3)^2} = \sqrt{5^2(a + 3)^2}$
$= 5(a + 3) = 5a + 15$

SECTION 10.2

Problem 1   **A.** $9\sqrt{3} + 3\sqrt{3} - 18\sqrt{3}$
$= (9 + 3 - 18)\sqrt{3} = -6\sqrt{3}$

B. $2\sqrt{50} - 5\sqrt{32} = 2\sqrt{2 \cdot 5^2} - 5\sqrt{2^5}$
$= 2\sqrt{5^2}\sqrt{2} - 5\sqrt{2^4}\sqrt{2}$
$= 2 \cdot 5\sqrt{2} - 5 \cdot 2^2\sqrt{2}$
$= 10\sqrt{2} - 20\sqrt{2} = -10\sqrt{2}$

Problem 2 **A.** $y\sqrt{28y} + 7\sqrt{63y^3}$
$= y\sqrt{2^2 \cdot 7y} + 7\sqrt{3^2 \cdot 7 \cdot y^3}$
$= y\sqrt{2^2}\sqrt{7y} + 7\sqrt{3^2 \cdot y^2}\sqrt{7y}$
$= y \cdot 2\sqrt{7y} + 7 \cdot 3y\sqrt{7y}$
$= 2y\sqrt{7y} + 21y\sqrt{7y} = 23y\sqrt{7y}$

B. $2\sqrt{27a^5} - 4a\sqrt{12a^3} + a^2\sqrt{75a}$
$= 2\sqrt{3^3 \cdot a^5} - 4a\sqrt{2^2 \cdot 3 \cdot a^3} + a^2\sqrt{3 \cdot 5^2 \cdot a}$
$= 2\sqrt{3^2 \cdot a^4}\sqrt{3a} - 4a\sqrt{2^2 \cdot a^2}\sqrt{3a} + a^2\sqrt{5^2}\sqrt{3a}$
$= 2 \cdot 3a^2\sqrt{3a} - 4a \cdot 2a\sqrt{3a} + a^2 \cdot 5\sqrt{3a}$
$= 6a^2\sqrt{3a} - 8a^2\sqrt{3a} + 5a^2\sqrt{3a} = 3a^2\sqrt{3a}$

SECTION 10.3

Problem 1 $\sqrt{5a}\,\sqrt{15a^3b^4}\,\sqrt{3b^5} = \sqrt{225a^4b^9}$
$= \sqrt{3^25^2a^4b^9} = \sqrt{3^25^2a^4b^8}\sqrt{b}$
$= 3 \cdot 5a^2b^4\sqrt{b} = 15a^2b^4\sqrt{b}$

Problem 2 $\sqrt{5x}(\sqrt{5x} - \sqrt{25y}) = \sqrt{5^2x^2} - \sqrt{5^3xy}$
$= \sqrt{5^2x^2} - \sqrt{5^2}\sqrt{5xy} = 5x - 5\sqrt{5xy}$

Problem 3 $(3\sqrt{x} - \sqrt{y})(5\sqrt{x} - 2\sqrt{y})$
$= 15(\sqrt{x})^2 - 6\sqrt{xy} - 5\sqrt{xy} + 2(\sqrt{y})^2$
$= 15x - 11\sqrt{xy} + 2y$

Problem 4 $(2\sqrt{x} + 7)(2\sqrt{x} - 7)$
$= (2\sqrt{x})^2 - 7^2 = 4x - 49$

Problem 5 **A.** $\dfrac{\sqrt{15x^6y^7}}{\sqrt{3x^7y^9}} = \sqrt{\dfrac{15x^6y^7}{3x^7y^9}} = \sqrt{\dfrac{5}{xy^2}} = \dfrac{\sqrt{5}}{\sqrt{xy^2}}$
$= \dfrac{\sqrt{5}}{y\sqrt{x}} = \dfrac{\sqrt{5}}{y\sqrt{x}} \cdot \dfrac{\sqrt{x}}{\sqrt{x}} = \dfrac{\sqrt{5x}}{xy}$

B. $\dfrac{\sqrt{y}}{\sqrt{y} + 3} = \dfrac{\sqrt{y}}{\sqrt{y} + 3} \cdot \dfrac{\sqrt{y} - 3}{\sqrt{y} - 3} = \dfrac{y - 3\sqrt{y}}{y - 9}$

C. $\dfrac{5 + \sqrt{y}}{1 - 2\sqrt{y}} = \dfrac{5 + \sqrt{y}}{1 - 2\sqrt{y}} \cdot \dfrac{1 + 2\sqrt{y}}{1 + 2\sqrt{y}}$
$= \dfrac{5 + 10\sqrt{y} + \sqrt{y} + 2y}{1 - 4y}$
$= \dfrac{5 + 11\sqrt{y} + 2y}{1 - 4y}$

SECTION 10.4

Problem 1 $\sqrt{4x} + 3 = 7$
$\sqrt{4x} = 4$
$(\sqrt{4x})^2 = 4^2$
$4x = 16$
$x = 4$

Check: $\sqrt{4x} + 3 = 7$

$$\begin{array}{c|c} \sqrt{4 \cdot 4} + 3 & 7 \\ \sqrt{4^2} + 3 & 7 \\ 4 + 3 & 7 \\ & 7 = 7 \end{array}$$

The solution is 4.

Problem 2 **A.** $\sqrt{3x - 2} - 5 = 0$
$\sqrt{3x - 2} = 5$
$(\sqrt{3x - 2})^2 = 5^2$
$3x - 2 = 25$
$3x = 27$
$x = 9$

Check: $\sqrt{3x - 2} - 5 = 0$

$$\begin{array}{c|c} \sqrt{3 \cdot 9 - 2} - 5 & 0 \\ \sqrt{27 - 2} - 5 & 0 \\ \sqrt{25} - 5 & 0 \\ \sqrt{5^2} - 5 & 0 \\ 5 - 5 & 0 \\ & 0 = 0 \end{array}$$

The solution is 9.

B. $\sqrt{4x - 7} + 5 = 0$
$\sqrt{4x - 7} = -5$
$(\sqrt{4x - 7})^2 = (-5)^2$
$4x - 7 = 25$
$4x = 32$
$x = 8$

Check: $\sqrt{4x - 7} + 5 = 0$

$$\begin{array}{c|c} \sqrt{4 \cdot 8 - 7} + 5 & 0 \\ \sqrt{32 - 7} + 5 & 0 \\ \sqrt{25} + 5 & 0 \\ 5 + 5 & 0 \\ & 10 \neq 0 \end{array}$$

There is no solution.

Problem 3

$\sqrt{x} + \sqrt{x + 9} = 9$
$\sqrt{x} = 9 - \sqrt{x + 9}$
$(\sqrt{x})^2 = (9 - \sqrt{x + 9})^2$
$x = 81 - 18\sqrt{x + 9} + (x + 9)$
$18\sqrt{x + 9} = 90$
$\sqrt{x + 9} = 5$
$(\sqrt{x + 9})^2 = 5^2$
$x + 9 = 25$
$x = 16$

Check: $\sqrt{x} + \sqrt{x + 9} = 9$

$$\begin{array}{c|c} \sqrt{16} + \sqrt{16 + 9} & 9 \\ 4 + \sqrt{25} & 9 \\ 4 + 5 & 9 \\ & 9 = 9 \end{array}$$

The solution is 16.

Problem 4

Strategy   To find the distance, use the Pythagorean Theorem. The hypotenuse is the length of the ladder. One leg is the distance from the bottom of the ladder to the base of the building. The distance along the building from the ground to the top of the ladder is the unknown leg.

Solution $a = \sqrt{c^2 - b^2}$
$a = \sqrt{(12)^2 - (5)^2}$
$a = \sqrt{144 - 25}$
$a = \sqrt{119}$
$a \approx 10.91$

The distance is 10.91 ft.

Problem 5

Strategy   To find the length of the pendulum, replace T in the equation with the given value and solve for L.

Solution

$$T = 2\pi\sqrt{\frac{L}{32}}$$

$$1.5 = 2\pi\sqrt{\frac{L}{32}}$$

$$\frac{1.5}{2\pi} = \sqrt{\frac{L}{32}}$$

$$\left(\frac{1.5}{2\pi}\right)^2 = \left(\sqrt{\frac{L}{32}}\right)^2$$

$$\left(\frac{1.5}{2\pi}\right)^2 = \frac{L}{32}$$

$$32\left(\frac{1.5}{2\pi}\right)^2 = L \qquad \blacktriangleright \text{ Use the } \pi \text{ key on your calculator.}$$

$$1.82 \approx L$$

The length of the pendulum is 1.82 ft.

SOLUTIONS to Chapter 11 Problems

SECTION 11.1

Problem 1 $\dfrac{3y^2}{2} + y - \dfrac{1}{2} = 0$

$2\left(\dfrac{3y^2}{2} + y - \dfrac{1}{2}\right) = 2(0)$

$3y^2 + 2y - 1 = 0$

$(3y - 1)(y + 1) = 0$

$3y - 1 = 0 \qquad y + 1 = 0$
$3y = 1 \qquad\qquad y = -1$

$y = \dfrac{1}{3}$

The solutions are $\dfrac{1}{3}$ and -1.

Problem 2   **A.** $4x^2 - 96 = 0$
$4x^2 = 96$
$x^2 = 24$
$\sqrt{x^2} = \sqrt{24}$
$x = \pm\sqrt{24}$
$x = \pm 2\sqrt{6}$

The solutions are $2\sqrt{6}$ and $-2\sqrt{6}$.

B. $x^2 + 81 = 0$
$x^2 = -81$
$\sqrt{x^2} = \sqrt{-81}$ (not a real number)

The equation has no real number solution.

Problem 3 $(x + 5)^2 = 20$
$\sqrt{(x + 5)^2} = \sqrt{20}$
$x + 5 = \pm\sqrt{20}$
$x + 5 = \pm 2\sqrt{5}$

$x + 5 = 2\sqrt{5} \qquad\qquad x + 5 = -2\sqrt{5}$
$x = -5 + 2\sqrt{5} \qquad\quad x = -5 - 2\sqrt{5}$

The solutions are $-5 + 2\sqrt{5}$ and $-5 - 2\sqrt{5}$.

SECTION 11.2

Problem 1   **A.** $3x^2 - 6x - 2 = 0$
$3x^2 - 6x = 2$
$\dfrac{1}{3}(3x^2 - 6x) = \dfrac{1}{3} \cdot 2$
$x^2 - 2x = \dfrac{2}{3}$

Complete the square.

$$x^2 - 2x + 1 = \frac{2}{3} + 1$$

$$(x - 1)^2 = \frac{5}{3}$$

$$\sqrt{(x - 1)^2} = \sqrt{\frac{5}{3}}$$

$$x - 1 = \pm\sqrt{\frac{5}{3}}$$

$$x - 1 = \pm\frac{\sqrt{15}}{3}$$

$$x - 1 = \frac{\sqrt{15}}{3} \qquad x - 1 = -\frac{\sqrt{15}}{3}$$

$$x = 1 + \frac{\sqrt{15}}{3} \qquad x = 1 - \frac{\sqrt{15}}{3}$$

$$= \frac{3 + \sqrt{15}}{3} \qquad = \frac{3 - \sqrt{15}}{3}$$

The solutions are $\dfrac{3 + \sqrt{15}}{3}$ and $\dfrac{3 - \sqrt{15}}{3}$.

B. $y^2 - 6y + 10 = 0$

$$y^2 - 6y = -10$$

Complete the square.

$$y^2 - 6y + 9 = -10 + 9$$

$$(y - 3)^2 = -1$$

$$\sqrt{(y - 3)^2} = \sqrt{-1}$$

$\sqrt{-1}$ is not a real number.
The equation has no real number solution.

Problem 2 $x^2 + 8x + 8 = 0$

$$x^2 + 8x = -8$$

$$x^2 + 8x + 16 = -8 + 16$$

$$(x + 4)^2 = 8$$

$$\sqrt{(x + 4)^2} = \sqrt{8}$$

$$x + 4 = \pm\sqrt{8}$$

$$x + 4 = \pm 2.828$$

$$x + 4 \approx 2.828 \qquad\qquad x + 4 \approx -2.828$$

$$x \approx -4 + 2.828 \qquad x \approx -4 - 2.828$$

$$\approx -1.172 \qquad\qquad \approx -6.828$$

The solutions are approximately -1.172 and -6.828.

SECTION 11.3

Problem 1   **A.** $3x^2 + 4x - 4 = 0$

$$a = 3, b = 4, c = -4$$

$$x = \frac{-(4) \pm \sqrt{(4)^2 - 4(3)(-4)}}{2 \cdot 3}$$

$$= \frac{-4 \pm \sqrt{16 + 48}}{6}$$

$$= \frac{-4 \pm \sqrt{64}}{6} = \frac{-4 \pm 8}{6}$$

$$x = \frac{-4 + 8}{6} \qquad x = \frac{-4 - 8}{6}$$

$$= \frac{4}{6} = \frac{2}{3} \qquad = \frac{-12}{6} = -2$$

The solutions are $\dfrac{2}{3}$ and -2.

B. $x^2 + 2x = 1$

$$x^2 + 2x - 1 = 0$$

$$a = 1, b = 2, c = -1$$

$$x = \frac{-(2) \pm \sqrt{(2)^2 - 4(1)(-1)}}{2 \cdot 1}$$

$$= \frac{-2 \pm \sqrt{4 + 4}}{2}$$

$$= \frac{-2 \pm \sqrt{8}}{2}$$

$$= \frac{-2 \pm 2\sqrt{2}}{2}$$

$$= \frac{2(-1 \pm \sqrt{2})}{2} = -1 \pm \sqrt{2}$$

The solutions are $-1 + \sqrt{2}$ and $-1 - \sqrt{2}$.

C. $z^2 + 2z + 6 = 0$

$$a = 1, b = 2, c = 6$$

$$z = \frac{-(2) \pm \sqrt{2^2 - 4(1)(6)}}{2(1)}$$

$$= \frac{-2 \pm \sqrt{4 - 24}}{2} = \frac{-2 \pm \sqrt{-20}}{2}$$

$\sqrt{-20}$ is not a real number.
The equation has no real number solution.

SECTION 11.4

Problem 1   **A.** $y = x^2 + 2$

$a = 1$. a is positive.

The parabola opens up.

x	y
0	2
1	3
−1	3
2	6
−2	6

B. $y = -x^2 - 2x + 3$

$a = -1$. a is negative.

The parabola opens down.

x	y
0	3
1	0
−1	4
2	−5
−2	3
−3	0
−4	−5

SECTION 11.5

Problem 1

Strategy
- This is a geometry problem.
- Width of the rectangle: W
  Length of the rectangle: $W + 3$
- Use the equation $A = LW$.

Solution

$A = LW$

$40 = (W + 3)W$

$40 = W^2 + 3W$

$0 = W^2 + 3W - 40$

$0 = (W + 8)(W - 5)$

$$W + 8 = 0 \qquad W - 5 = 0$$
$$W = -8 \qquad W = 5$$

The solution -8 is not possible.
The width is 5 m.

CONCEPT REVIEW 1.1

1. Sometimes true **3.** Never true **5.** Sometimes true **7.** Always true **9.** Always true

SECTION 1.1

3. $>$ **5.** $<$ **7.** $>$ **9.** $>$ **11.** $<$ **13.** $>$ **15.** $>$ **17.** $<$ **19.** $\{1, 2, 3, 4, 5, 6, 7, 8\}$
21. $\{1, 2, 3, 4, 5, 6, 7, 8\}$ **23.** $\{-6, -5, -4, -3, -2, -1\}$ **25.** 5 **27.** $-23, -18$ **29.** 21, 37
31. $-52, -46, 0$ **33.** $-17, 0, 4, 29$ **35.** $5, 6, 7, 8, 9$ **37.** $-10, -9, -8, -7, -6, -5$ **41.** -22
43. 31 **45.** 168 **47.** -630 **49.** 18 **51.** -49 **53.** 16 **55.** 12 **57.** -29 **59.** -14 **61.** 0
63. -34 **65. a.** $8, 5, 2, -1, -3$ **b.** $8, 5, 2, 1, 3$ **67.** $>$ **69.** $<$ **71.** $>$ **73.** $<$
75. $-19, -|-8|, |-5|, 6$ **77.** $-22, -(-3), |-14|, |-25|$ **79. a.** 5°F with a 20 mph wind feels colder.
b. -15°F with a 20 mph wind feels colder. **81.** $-4, 4$ **83.** $-3, 11$ **85.** Negative **87.** 0 **89.** True

CONCEPT REVIEW 1.2

1. Sometimes true **3.** Always true **5.** Always true **7.** Never true **9.** Never true

SECTION 1.2

3. -11 **5.** -9 **7.** -3 **9.** 1 **11.** -5 **13.** -30 **15.** 9 **17.** 1 **19.** -10 **21.** -28
23. -392 **27.** 8 **29.** -7 **31.** 7 **33.** -2 **35.** -28 **37.** -13 **39.** 6 **41.** -9 **43.** 2
45. -138 **47.** -8 **51.** 42 **53.** -20 **55.** -16 **57.** 25 **59.** 0 **61.** -72 **63.** -102
65. 140 **67.** -70 **69.** 162 **71.** 120 **73.** 36 **75.** 192 **77.** -108 **79.** 0 **81.** -2
83. 8 **85.** 0 **87.** -9 **89.** -9 **91.** 9 **93.** -24 **95.** -12 **97.** -13 **99.** -18 **101.** 19
103. 26 **105.** 11 **107.** -13 **109.** 13 **111.** The temperature is 3°C. **113.** The difference is 14°C.
115. The difference is 399°C. **117.** The difference in elevation is 5662 m.
119. The difference in elevation is 6028 m. **121.** The difference in elevation is 9248 m.
123. The average daily high temperature is -3°C. **125.** The temperature dropped 100°F.
127. The difference between the net income or loss in 1993 and that in 1994 is $292 million.
129. The difference is greatest for the years 1997 and 1992. That difference is $2,254 million.
131. The student's score is 93. **133.** The 5-day moving average for the Disney stock is $-84, -150, -68, -62, -32, 10$.
135. 17 **137.** 3 **139.** $-4, -9, -14$ **141.** $-16, 4, -1$ **143.** 5436 **145.** b **147.** a
149. No. $10 - (-8) = 18$

CONCEPT REVIEW 1.3

1. Never true **3.** Sometimes true **5.** Always true **7.** Never true **9.** Always true

SECTION 1.3

1. $0.\overline{3}$ **3.** 0.25 **5.** $0.\overline{4}$ **7.** $0.1\overline{6}$ **9.** 0.125 **11.** $0.\overline{2}$ **13.** $0.\overline{45}$ **15.** $0.58\overline{3}$ **17.** $0.2\overline{6}$

19. 0.5625 **21.** $0.\overline{24}$ **23.** 0.225 **25.** $0.68\overline{1}$ **27.** $0.458\overline{3}$ **29.** $0.1\overline{5}$ **31.** $0.08\overline{1}$ **35.** $\frac{3}{4}$, 0.75

37. $\frac{1}{2}$, 0.5 **39.** $\frac{16}{25}$, 0.64 **41.** $1\frac{3}{4}$, 1.75 **43.** $\frac{19}{100}$, 0.19 **45.** $\frac{1}{20}$, 0.05 **47.** $4\frac{1}{2}$, 4.5 **49.** $\frac{2}{25}$, 0.08

51. $\frac{1}{9}$ **53.** $\frac{5}{16}$ **55.** $\frac{1}{200}$ **57.** $\frac{1}{16}$ **59.** 0.073 **61.** 0.158 **63.** 0.0915 **65.** 0.1823 **67.** 15%

69. 5% **71.** 17.5% **73.** 115% **75.** 0.8% **77.** 6.5% **79.** 54% **81.** 33.3% **83.** 44.4%

85. 250%   **87.** $37\frac{1}{2}$%   **89.** $35\frac{5}{7}$%   **91.** 125%   **93.** $155\frac{5}{9}$%   **95.** $\frac{13}{12}$ **97.** $-\frac{5}{24}$ **99.** $-\frac{19}{24}$

101. $\frac{5}{26}$ **103.** $\frac{7}{24}$ **105.** 0   **107.** $-\frac{7}{16}$ **109.** $\frac{11}{24}$ **111.** 1   **113.** $\frac{11}{8}$ **115.** $\frac{169}{315}$ **117.** -38.8

119. -6.192 **121.** 13.355   **123.** 4.676   **125.** -10.03 **127.** -37.19 **129.** -17.5 **131.** 853.2594

133. $-\frac{3}{8}$ **135.** $\frac{1}{10}$ **137.** $\frac{15}{64}$ **139.** $\frac{3}{2}$ **141.** $-\frac{8}{9}$ **143.** $\frac{2}{3}$ **145.** 4.164   **147.** 4.347

149. -4.028 **151.** -2.22 **153.** 12.26448   **155.** 0.75   **157.** -2060.55 **159.** 0.09

161. Natural number, integer, positive integer, rational number, real number   **163.** Rational number, real number

165. Irrational number, real number   **167.** The cost is \$1.21.   **169.** The difference is greatest for the years 1993 and 1994. That difference is \$6.264 billion.   **171.** The new fraction is greater than $\frac{2}{5}$.   **173.** $1.06x$ **175.** 53¢

177. Yes. For example, $c = \frac{a+b}{2}$.

CONCEPT REVIEW 1.4

1. Never true   **3.** Never true   **5.** Always true   **7.** Never true   **9.** Never true

SECTION 1.4

1. 36   **3.** -49 **5.** 9   **7.** 81   **9.** $\frac{1}{4}$ **11.** 0.09   **13.** 12   **15.** 0.216   **17.** -12 **19.** 16

21. -864 **23.** -1008 **25.** 3   **27.** $-77{,}760$ **31.** 9   **33.** 12   **35.** 1   **37.** 7   **39.** -36

41. 13   **43.** 4   **45.** 15   **47.** -1 **49.** 4   **51.** 0.51   **53.** 1.7   **55.** $\frac{17}{48}$ **57.** $<$ **59.** $>$

61. 100   **63.** 120   **65.** It will take the computer 17 s.   **67.** 6   **69.** 9

CHAPTER REVIEW EXERCISES

1. $\{1, 2, 3, 4, 5, 6\}$ (Obj. 1.1.1)   **2.** 62.5% (Obj. 1.3.2)   **3.** -4 (Obj. 1.1.2)   **4.** 4 (Obj. 1.2.2)

5. 17 (Obj. 1.2.4)   **6.** $0.\overline{7}$ (Obj. 1.3.1)   **7.** -5.3578 (Obj. 1.3.4)   **8.** 8 (Obj. 1.4.2)   **9.** 4 (Obj. 1.1.2)

10. -14 (Obj. 1.2.2)   **11.** 67.2% (Obj. 1.3.2)   **12.** $\frac{159}{200}$ (Obj. 1.3.2)   **13.** -9 (Obj. 1.2.4)

14. 0.85 (Obj. 1.3.1)   **15.** $-\frac{1}{2}$ (Obj. 1.3.4)   **16.** 9 (Obj. 1.4.2)   **17.** $<$ (Obj. 1.1.1)

18. -16 (Obj. 1.2.1)   **19.** 90 (Obj. 1.2.3)   **20.** -6.881 (Obj. 1.3.3)   **21.** $-5, -3$ (Obj. 1.1.1)

22. 0.07 (Obj. 1.3.2)   **23.** 12 (Obj. 1.4.1)   **24.** $>$ (Obj. 1.1.1)   **25.** -3 (Obj. 1.2.1)

26. -48 (Obj. 1.2.3)   **27.** $\frac{1}{15}$ (Obj. 1.3.3)   **28.** -108 (Obj. 1.4.1)   **29.** 277.8% (Obj. 1.3.2)

30. 2.4 (Obj. 1.3.2)   **31.** 2 (Obj. 1.1.2)   **32.** -14 (Obj. 1.2.2)   **33.** -8 (Obj. 1.2.4)

34. 0.35 (Obj. 1.3.1)   **35.** $-\frac{7}{6}$ (Obj. 1.3.4)   **36.** 12 (Obj. 1.4.2)   **37.** 3 (Obj. 1.1.2)   **38.** 18 (Obj. 1.2.2)

39. $288\frac{8}{9}$% (Obj. 1.3.2)   **40. a.** $12, 8, 1, -7$ **b.** $12, 8, 1, 7$ (Obj. 1.1.2)   **41.** 12 (Obj. 1.2.4)

42. $0.\overline{63}$ (Obj. 1.3.1)   **43.** -11.5 (Obj. 1.3.4)   **44.** 8 (Obj. 1.4.2)   **45.** $>$ (Obj. 1.1.1)

46. -8 (Obj. 1.2.1)   **47.** 72 (Obj. 1.2.3)   **48.** $-\frac{11}{24}$ (Obj. 1.3.3)   **49.** $-17, -9, 0, 4$ (Obj. 1.1.1)

50. 0.2% (Obj. 1.3.2)   **51.** -4 (Obj. 1.4.1)   **52.** 3.561 (Obj. 1.3.3)   **53.** -17 (Obj. 1.1.2)

54. -27 (Obj. 1.2.2)   **55.** $-\frac{1}{10}$ (Obj. 1.3.4)   **56.** $<$ (Obj. 1.1.1)   **57.** 0.72 (Obj. 1.3.1)

58. -128 (Obj. 1.4.1)   **59.** 7.5% (Obj. 1.3.2)   **60.** $54\frac{2}{7}$% (Obj. 1.3.2)   **61.** -18 (Obj. 1.2.1)

62. 0 (Obj. 1.2.3)   **63.** 9 (Obj. 1.4.2)   **64.** $\frac{7}{8}$ (Obj. 1.3.3)   **65.** 16 (Obj. 1.2.4)   **66.** $<$ (Obj. 1.1.1)

67. -3 (Obj. 1.4.1)   **68.** -6 (Obj. 1.2.1)   **69.** 300 (Obj. 1.2.3)   **70.** $\{-3, -2, -1\}$ (Obj. 1.1.1)

71. The temperature is 8°C. (Obj. 1.2.5)   **72.** The average low temperature was -2°C. (Obj. 1.2.5)

73. The difference was 13°C. (Obj. 1.2.5)   **74.** The temperature is -6°C. (Obj. 1.2.5)

75. The difference is 714°C. (Obj. 1.2.5)

CHAPTER TEST

1. $\frac{11}{20}$ (Obj. 1.3.2)   **2.** $-6, -8$ (Obj. 1.1.1)   **3.** -3 (Obj. 1.2.2)   **4.** 0.85 (Obj. 1.3.1)

5. $-\frac{1}{14}$ (Obj. 1.3.4)   **6.** -15 (Obj. 1.2.4)   **7.** $-\frac{8}{3}$ (Obj. 1.4.1)   **8.** 2 (Obj. 1.2.1)

9. $\{1, 2, 3, 4, 5, 6\}$ (Obj. 1.1.1)   **10.** 159% (Obj. 1.3.2)   **11.** 29 (Obj. 1.1.2)   **12.** $>$ (Obj. 1.1.1)

13. $-\frac{23}{18}$ (Obj. 1.3.3)   **14.** 258 (Obj. 1.2.3)   **15.** 3 (Obj. 1.4.2)   **16.** $\frac{5}{6}$ (Obj. 1.3.4)

17. 23.1% (Obj. 1.3.2)   **18.** 0.062 (Obj. 1.3.2)   **19.** 14 (Obj. 1.2.2)   **20.** $0.4\overline{3}$ (Obj. 1.3.1)

21. -2.43 (Obj. 1.3.4)   **22.** 15 (Obj. 1.2.4)   **23.** 640 (Obj. 1.4.1)   **24.** -12 (Obj. 1.2.1)

25. -34 (Obj. 1.1.2)   **26.** $>$ (Obj. 1.1.1)   **27.** **a.** $17, 6, -5, -9$ **b.** $17, 6, 5, 9$ (Obj. 1.1.1)

28. $69\frac{13}{23}\%$ (Obj. 1.3.2)   **29.** -11.384 (Obj. 1.3.3)   **30.** 160 (Obj. 1.2.3)   **31.** -2 (Obj. 1.4.2)

32. The temperature is 4°C. (Obj. 1.2.5)   **33.** The average high temperature was -4°C. (Obj. 1.2.5)

ANSWERS to Chapter 2 Odd-Numbered Exercises

CONCEPT REVIEW 2.1

1. Always true   **3.** Sometimes true   **5.** Always true

SECTION 2.1

1. $2x^2, 5x, -8$ **3.** $-a^4, 6$ **5.** $7x^2y, 6xy^2$ **7.** $1, -9$ **9.** $1, -4, -1$ **13.** 10 **15.** 32 **17.** 21
19. 16 **21.** -9 **23.** 3 **25.** -7 **27.** 13 **29.** -15 **31.** 41 **33.** 1 **35.** 5 **37.** 1
39. 57 **41.** 5 **43.** 12 **45.** 6 **47.** 10 **49.** 8 **51.** -3 **53.** -2 **55.** -22 **57.** 4
59. 20 **61.** 24 **63.** 4.96 **65.** -5.68 **67.** The volume is 25.8 in³.   **69.** The area is 93.7 cm².

71. The volume is 484.9 m³.   **73.** 24 **75.** $\frac{1}{2}$ **77.** 13 **79.** -1 **81.** 4 **83.** 81

CONCEPT REVIEW 2.2

1. Never true   **3.** Always true   **5.** Always true   **7.** Never true

SECTION 2.2

1. 2 **3.** 5 **5.** 6 **7.** -8 **9.** -4 **11.** The Inverse Property of Addition   **13.** The Commutative
Property of Addition   **15.** The Associative Property of Addition   **17.** The Commutative Property of Multiplication
19. The Associative Property of Multiplication   **21.** $14x$ **23.** $5a$ **25.** $-6y$ **27.** $-3b - 7$ **29.** $5a$

31. $-2ab$ **33.** $5xy$ **35.** 0 **37.** $-\frac{5}{6}x$ **39.** $-\frac{1}{24}x^2$ **41.** $11x$ **43.** $7a$ **45.** $-14x^2$

47. $-x + 3y$ **49.** $17x - 3y$ **51.** $-2a - 6b$ **53.** $-3x - 8y$ **55.** $-4x^2 - 2x$ **57.** $12x$ **59.** $-21a$
61. $6y$ **63.** $8x$ **65.** $-6a$ **67.** $12b$ **69.** $-15x^2$ **71.** x^2 **73.** x **75.** n **77.** x **79.** n
81. $2x$ **83.** $-2x$ **85.** $-15a^2$ **87.** $6y$ **89.** $3y$ **91.** $-2x$ **93.** $-x - 2$ **95.** $8x - 6$
97. $-2a - 14$ **99.** $-6y + 24$ **101.** $35 - 21b$ **103.** $-9 + 15x$ **105.** $15x^2 + 6x$ **107.** $2y - 18$
109. $-15x - 30$ **111.** $-6x^2 - 28$ **113.** $-6y^2 + 21$ **115.** $-6a^2 + 7b^2$ **117.** $4x^2 - 12x + 20$

119. $-3y^2 + 9y + 21$ **121.** $-12a^2 - 20a + 28$ **123.** $12x^2 - 9x + 12$ **125.** $10x^2 - 20xy - 5y^2$
127. $-8b^2 + 6b - 9$ **129.** $a - 7$ **131.** $-11x + 13$ **133.** $-4y - 4$ **135.** $-2x - 16$ **137.** $18y - 51$
139. $a + 7b$ **141.** $6x + 28$ **143.** $5x - 75$ **145.** $4x - 4$ **147.** $38x - 63$ **149.** b **151.** $20x + y$
153. $-3x + y$ **155.** 0 **157.** $-a + b$ **159. a.** Yes **b.** No

CONCEPT REVIEW 2.3

1. Never true   **3.** Never true   **5.** Always true   **7.** Never true

SECTION 2.3

1. $19 - d$ **3.** $r - 12$ **5.** $28a$ **7.** $5(n - 7)$ **9.** $y - 3y$ **11.** $-6b$ **13.** $\dfrac{4}{p - 6}$ **15.** $\dfrac{x - 9}{2x}$

17. $-4s - 21$ **19.** $\dfrac{d + 8}{d}$ **21.** $\dfrac{3}{8}(t + 15)$ **23.** $w + \dfrac{7}{w}$ **25.** $d + (16d - 3)$ **27.** $\dfrac{n}{19}$ **29.** $n + 40$

31. $(n - 90)^2$ **33.** $\dfrac{4}{9}n + 20$ **35.** $n(n + 10)$ **37.** $7n + 14$ **39.** $\dfrac{12}{n + 2}$ **41.** $\dfrac{2}{n + 1}$ **43.** $60 - \dfrac{n}{50}$

45. $n^2 + 3n$ **47.** $(n + 3) + n^3$ **49.** $n^2 - \dfrac{1}{4}n$ **51.** $2n - \dfrac{7}{n}$ **53.** $n^3 - 12n$ **55.** $n + (n + 10); 2n + 10$

57. $n - (9 - n); 2n - 9$ **59.** $\dfrac{1}{5}n - \dfrac{3}{8}n; -\dfrac{7}{40}n$ **61.** $(n + 9) + 4; n + 13$ **63.** $2(3n + 40); 6n + 80$

65. $7(5n); 35n$ **67.** $17n + 2n; 19n$ **69.** $n + 12n; 13n$ **71.** $3(n^2 + 4); 3n^2 + 12$ **73.** $\dfrac{3}{4}(16n + 4); 12n + 3$

75. $16 - (n + 9); -n + 7$ **77.** $\dfrac{4n}{2} + 5; 2n + 5$ **79.** $6(n + 8); 6n + 48$ **81.** $7 - (n + 2); -n + 5$

83. $\dfrac{1}{3}(n + 6n); \dfrac{7n}{3}$ **85.** $(8 + n^3) + 2n^3; 3n^3 + 8$ **87.** $(n + 12) + (n - 6); 2n + 6$

89. $(n + 9) + (n - 20); 2n - 11$ **91.** $14 + (n - 3)10; 10n - 16$ **93.** $P + 7650$ **95.** $3s$ **97.** $\dfrac{1}{2}L$

99. $2p$ **101.** $\dfrac{1}{2}L - 3$ **103.** $0.33 + 0.22(w - 1), w \geq 1$ **105.** n and $35 - n$ **107.** $200 - x$

109. $92 + 25h$ **111.** $\dfrac{1}{4}x$

CHAPTER REVIEW EXERCISES

1. y^2 (Obj. 2.2.2)   **2.** $3x$ (Obj. 2.2.3)   **3.** $-10a$ (Obj. 2.2.3)   **4.** $-4x + 8$ (Obj. 2.2.4)   **5.** $7x + 38$
(Obj. 2.2.5)   **6.** 16 (Obj. 2.1.1)   **7.** 9 (Obj. 2.2.1)   **8.** $36y$ (Obj. 2.2.3)   **9.** $6y - 18$ (Obj. 2.2.4)
10. $-3x + 21y$ (Obj. 2.2.5)   **11.** $-8x^2 + 12y^2$ (Obj. 2.2.4)   **12.** $5x$ (Obj. 2.2.2)   **13.** 22 (Obj. 2.1.1)
14. $2x$ (Obj. 2.2.3)   **15.** $15 - 35b$ (Obj. 2.2.4)   **16.** $-7x + 33$ (Obj. 2.2.5)   **17.** The Commutative Property
of Multiplication (Obj. 2.2.1)   **18.** $24 - 6x$ (Obj. 2.2.4)   **19.** $5x^2$ (Obj. 2.2.2)   **20.** $-7x + 14$ (Obj. 2.2.5)
21. $-9y^2 + 9y + 21$ (Obj. 2.2.4)   **22.** $2x + y$ (Obj. 2.2.5)   **23.** 3 (Obj. 2.1.1)   **24.** $36y$ (Obj. 2.2.3)
25. $5x - 43$ (Obj. 2.2.5)   **26.** $2x$ (Obj. 2.2.3)   **27.** $-6x^2 + 21y^2$ (Obj. 2.2.4)   **28.** 6 (Obj. 2.1.1)
29. $-x + 6$ (Obj. 2.2.5)   **30.** $-5a - 2b$ (Obj. 2.2.2)   **31.** $-10x^2 + 15x - 30$ (Obj. 2.2.4)
32. $-9x - 7y$ (Obj. 2.2.2)   **33.** $6a$ (Obj. 2.2.3)   **34.** $17x - 24$ (Obj. 2.2.5)   **35.** $-2x - 5y$ (Obj. 2.2.2)
36. $30b$ (Obj. 2.2.3)   **37.** 21 (Obj. 2.2.1)   **38.** $-2x^2 + 4x$ (Obj. 2.2.2)   **39.** $-6x^2$ (Obj. 2.2.3)
40. $15x - 27$ (Obj. 2.2.5)   **41.** $-8a^2 + 3b^2$ (Obj. 2.2.4)   **42.** The Multiplication Property of Zero (Obj. 2.2.1)

43. $b - 7b$ (Obj. 2.3.1)   **44.** $n + 2n^2$ (Obj. 2.3.2)   **45.** $\dfrac{6}{n} - 3$ (Obj. 2.3.2)   **46.** $\dfrac{10}{y - 2}$ (Obj. 2.3.1)

47. $8\left(\dfrac{2n}{16}\right); n$ (Obj. 2.3.3)   **48.** $4(2 + 5n); 8 + 20n$ (Obj. 2.3.3)   **49.** $s + 15$ (Obj. 2.3.4)

50. b and $20 - b$ (Obj. 2.3.4)

CHAPTER TEST

1. $36y$ (Obj. 2.2.3) **2.** $4x - 3y$ (Obj. 2.2.2) **3.** $10n - 6$ (Obj. 2.2.5) **4.** 2 (Obj. 2.1.1)

5. The Multiplication Property of One (Obj. 2.2.1) **6.** $4x - 40$ (Obj. 2.2.4) **7.** $\frac{1}{12}x^2$ (Obj. 2.2.2)

8. $4x$ (Obj. 2.2.3) **9.** $-24y^2 + 48$ (Obj. 2.2.4) **10.** 19 (Obj. 2.2.1) **11.** 6 (Obj. 2.1.1)

12. $-3x + 13y$ (Obj. 2.2.5) **13.** b (Obj. 2.2.2) **14.** $78a$ (Obj. 2.2.3) **15.** $3x^2 - 15x + 12$ (Obj. 2.2.4)

16. -32 (Obj. 2.1.1) **17.** $37x - 5y$ (Obj. 2.2.5) **18.** $\frac{n+8}{17}$ (Obj. 2.3.1) **19.** $(a + b) - b^2$ (Obj. 2.3.1)

20. $n^2 + 11n$ (Obj. 2.3.2) **21.** $20(n + 9); 20n + 180$ (Obj. 2.3.3) **22.** $(n + 2) + (n - 3); 2n - 1$ (Obj. 2.3.3)

23. $n - \frac{1}{4}(2n); \frac{1}{2}n$ (Obj. 2.3.3) **24.** $30d$ (Obj. 2.3.4) **25.** L and $9 - L$ (Obj. 2.3.4)

CUMULATIVE REVIEW EXERCISES

1. -7 (Obj. 1.2.1) **2.** 5 (Obj. 1.2.2) **3.** 24 (Obj. 1.2.3) **4.** -5 (Obj. 1.2.4) **5.** 1.25 (Obj. 1.3.1)

6. $\frac{3}{5}, 0.60$ (Obj. 1.3.2) **7.** $\{-4, -3, -2, -1\}$ (Obj. 1.1.1) **8.** 8% (Obj. 1.3.2) **9.** $\frac{11}{48}$ (Obj. 1.3.3)

10. $\frac{5}{18}$ (Obj. 1.3.4) **11.** $\frac{1}{4}$ (Obj. 1.3.4) **12.** $\frac{8}{3}$ (Obj. 1.4.1) **13.** -5 (Obj. 1.4.2) **14.** $\frac{53}{48}$ (Obj. 1.4.2)

15. -8 (Obj. 2.1.1) **16.** $5x^2$ (Obj. 2.2.2) **17.** $-a - 12b$ (Obj. 2.2.2) **18.** $3a$ (Obj. 2.2.3)

19. $20b$ (Obj. 2.2.3) **20.** $20 - 10x$ (Obj. 2.2.4) **21.** $6y - 21$ (Obj. 2.2.4) **22.** $-6x^2 + 8y^2$ (Obj. 2.2.4)

23. $-8y^2 + 20y + 32$ (Obj. 2.2.4) **24.** $-10x + 15$ (Obj. 2.2.5) **25.** $5x - 17$ (Obj. 2.2.5)

26. $13x - 16$ (Obj. 2.2.5) **27.** $6x + 29y$ (Obj. 2.2.5) **28.** $6 - 12n$ (Obj. 2.3.2)

29. $5 + (n - 7); n - 2$ (Obj. 2.3.3) **30.** $\frac{1}{2}s$ (Obj. 2.3.4)

ANSWERS to Chapter 3 Odd-Numbered Exercises

CONCEPT REVIEW 3.1

1. Sometimes true **3.** Always true **5.** Always true **7.** Always true

SECTION 3.1

3. Yes **5.** No **7.** No **9.** Yes **11.** Yes **13.** Yes **15.** No **17.** No **19.** No **21.** Yes
23. No **25.** No **29.** 2 **31.** 15 **33.** 6 **35.** -6 **37.** 3 **39.** 0 **41.** -2 **43.** -7

45. -7 **47.** -12 **49.** 2 **51.** -5 **53.** 15 **55.** 9 **57.** 14 **59.** -1 **61.** 1 **63.** $-\frac{1}{2}$

65. $-\frac{3}{4}$ **67.** $\frac{1}{12}$ **69.** $-\frac{7}{12}$ **71.** $-\frac{5}{7}$ **73.** $-\frac{1}{3}$ **75.** 1.869 **77.** 0.884 **81.** 7 **83.** -7

85. -4 **87.** 5 **89.** 9 **91.** -8 **93.** 0 **95.** -7 **97.** 8 **99.** 12 **101.** 12 **103.** -18

105. -18 **107.** 6 **109.** -12 **111.** 3 **113.** -24 **115.** 9 **117.** $\frac{1}{3}$ **119.** $\frac{15}{7}$ **121.** 4

123. 3 **125.** 4.48 **127.** 2.06 **129.** -2.1 **133.** 24% **135.** 7.2 **137.** 400 **139.** 9
141. 25% **143.** 5 **145.** 200% **147.** 400 **149.** 7.7 **151.** 200 **153.** 400 **155.** 20
157. 80% **159.** 250 seats are reserved for wheelchair accessibility.
161. 140 more people voted for Robin Williams than for Jerry Seinfeld.
163. 51% of a typical traveler's vacation bill is paid in cash.

165. A student must answer $83\frac{1}{3}$% of the questions correctly in order to receive a B grade.

167. 12% of the deaths were not attributed to motor vehicle accidents.
169. There is insufficient information.
171. A minimum of 67 votes are needed to override a veto.
173. The price of the less expensive model is $1423.41.
175. -21 **177.** -27 **179.** 21   **181.** 22°   **183.** The cost of dinner was $45.
185. The new value is two times the original value.   **187.** One possible answer is $5x = -10$.

CONCEPT REVIEW 3.2

1. Always true   **3.** Never true   **5.** Never true   **7.** Always true

SECTION 3.2

1. 3   **3.** 6   **5.** -1 **7.** 1   **9.** -9 **11.** 3   **13.** 3   **15.** 3   **17.** 2   **19.** 2   **21.** 4
23. $\frac{6}{7}$ **25.** $\frac{2}{3}$ **27.** -1 **29.** $\frac{3}{4}$ **31.** $\frac{1}{3}$ **33.** $-\frac{3}{4}$ **35.** $\frac{1}{3}$ **37.** $-\frac{1}{6}$ **39.** 1   **41.** 0
43. $\frac{2}{5}$ **45.** $-\frac{3}{2}$ **47.** 18   **49.** 8   **51.** -16 **53.** 25   **55.** 21   **57.** 15   **59.** -16 **61.** $\frac{7}{6}$
63. $\frac{1}{8}$ **65.** $\frac{15}{2}$ **67.** $-\frac{18}{5}$ **69.** 2   **71.** 3   **73.** 1   **75.** 2   **77.** 3.95   **79.** -0.8 **81.** -11
83. 0   **85.** 3   **87.** 8   **89.** 2   **91.** -2 **93.** -3 **95.** 2   **97.** -2 **99.** -2 **101.** -7
103. 0   **105.** -2 **107.** -2 **109.** 4   **111.** 10   **113.** 3   **115.** $\frac{3}{4}$ **117.** $\frac{2}{7}$ **119.** $-\frac{3}{4}$
121. 3   **123.** 10   **125.** $\frac{4}{3}$ **127.** 3   **129.** -14 **131.** 7   **133.** 3   **135.** 4   **137.** 2   **139.** 2
141. 2   **143.** -7 **145.** $\frac{4}{7}$ **147.** $\frac{1}{2}$ **149.** $-\frac{1}{3}$ **151.** $\frac{10}{3}$ **153.** $-\frac{1}{4}$ **155.** 0.5   **157.** 0
159. -1 **161.** The initial velocity is 8 ft/s.   **163.** The depth of the diver is 40 ft.   **165.** The car will slide 168 ft.   **167.** The length of the humerus is approximately 31.8 in.   **169.** The passenger was driven 6 mi.
171. He made 8 errors.   **173.** The population is approximately 51,000 people.   **175.** The break-even point is 350 television sets.   **179.** No, the see-saw is not balanced.   **181.** A force of 25 lb must be applied to the other end of the lever.   **183.** The fulcrum must be placed 10 ft from the 128-pound acrobat.   **185.** No solution   **187.** $-\frac{11}{4}$
189. 62   **191.** One possible answer is $3x - 6 = 2x - 2$.

CONCEPT REVIEW 3.3

1. Always true   **3.** Sometimes true   **5.** Never true   **7.** Always true   **9.** Sometimes true

SECTION 3.3

1.   **3.**   **5.** $x < 2$
7. $x > 3$ **9.** $n \geq 3$
11. $x \leq -4$ **13.** $x \geq -1$ **15.** $y \geq -9$ **17.** $x < 12$
19. $x \geq 5$ **21.** $x < -11$ **23.** $x \leq 10$ **25.** $x \geq -6$ **27.** $x > 2$ **29.** $d < -\frac{1}{6}$ **31.** $x \geq -\frac{31}{24}$

33. $x < \dfrac{5}{4}$ **35.** $x > \dfrac{5}{24}$ **37.** $x \le -1.2$ **39.** $x \le 0.70$ **41.** $x < -7.3$

43. $x \le -3$ **45.** $x > -2$

47. $x > 0$ **49.** $n \ge 4$

51. $x > -2$ **53.** $x < \dfrac{5}{3}$ **55.** $x \ge 5$ **57.** $x > -\dfrac{5}{2}$ **59.** $x \le -\dfrac{2}{3}$

61. $x < -18$ **63.** $x > -16$ **65.** $y \ge 6$ **67.** $x \ge -6$ **69.** $b \le 33$ **71.** $n < \dfrac{3}{4}$ **73.** $x \le -\dfrac{6}{7}$

75. $y \le \dfrac{5}{6}$ **77.** $x \le \dfrac{27}{28}$ **79.** $y > -\dfrac{3}{2}$ **81.** $x > -0.5$ **83.** $y \ge -0.8$ **85.** $x \le 4.2$ **87.** $x \le 5$

89. $x < -5.4$ **93.** $x < 4$ **95.** $x < -4$ **97.** $x \ge 1$ **99.** $x \le 5$ **101.** $x < 0$ **103.** $x < 20$

105. $x > 500$ **107.** $x > 2$ **109.** $x \le -5$ **111.** $y \le \dfrac{5}{2}$ **113.** $x < \dfrac{25}{11}$ **115.** $x > 11$ **117.** $n \le \dfrac{11}{18}$

119. $x \ge 6$ **121.** $x \le \dfrac{2}{5}$ **123.** $t < 1$ **125.** $n > \dfrac{7}{10}$ **127.** $\{1, 2\}$ **129.** $\{1, 2, 3\}$ **131.** $\{3, 4, 5\}$

133. $\{10, 11, 12, 13\}$ **135.**   **137.**

CHAPTER REVIEW EXERCISES

1. No (Obj. 3.1.1)   **2.** 20 (Obj. 3.1.2)   **3.** -7 (Obj. 3.1.3)   **4.** 7 (Obj. 3.2.1)   **5.** 4 (Obj. 3.2.2)

6. $-\dfrac{1}{5}$ (Obj. 3.2.3)   **7.** 405 (Obj. 3.1.4)   **8.** 25 (Obj. 3.1.4)   **9.** 67.5% (Obj. 3.1.4)

10. (Obj. 3.3.1)   **11.** $x > 2$ (Obj. 3.3.1)

12. $x > -4$ (Obj. 3.3.2)   **13.** $x \ge -4$ (Obj. 3.3.3)   **14.** $x \ge 4$ (Obj. 3.3.3)

15. Yes (Obj. 3.1.1)   **16.** 2.5 (Obj. 3.1.2)   **17.** -49 (Obj. 3.1.3)   **18.** $\dfrac{1}{2}$ (Obj. 3.2.1)   **19.** $\dfrac{1}{3}$ (Obj. 3.2.2)

20. 10 (Obj. 3.2.3)   **21.** 16 (Obj. 3.1.4)   **22.** 125 (Obj. 3.1.4)   **23.** $16\dfrac{2}{3}\%$ (Obj. 3.1.4)

24. $x < -4$ (Obj. 3.3.1)   **25.** $x \le -2$ (Obj. 3.3.2)

26. -2 (Obj. 3.2.3)   **27.** $\dfrac{5}{6}$ (Obj. 3.1.2)   **28.** 20 (Obj. 3.1.3)   **29.** 6 (Obj. 3.2.1)   **30.** 0 (Obj. 3.2.3)

31. $x < 12$ (Obj. 3.3.3)   **32.** 15 (Obj. 3.1.4)   **33.** 5 (Obj. 3.2.1)   **34.** $x > 5$ (Obj. 3.3.3)

35. 4% (Obj. 3.1.4)   **36.** $x > -18$ (Obj. 3.3.3)   **37.** $x < \dfrac{1}{2}$ (Obj. 3.3.3)   **38.** The measure of the third angle is 110°. (Obj. 3.2.4)   **39.** A force of 24 lb must be applied to the other end of the lever. (Obj. 3.2.4)
40. The width is 6 ft. (Obj. 3.2.4)   **41.** The discount is $31.99. (Obj. 3.2.4)
42. The number of bankruptcy filings increased 19% from 1996 to 1997. (Obj. 3.1.4)
43. The depth is 80 ft. (Obj. 3.2.4)   **44.** The fulcrum is 3 ft from the 25 lb force. (Obj. 3.2.4)
45. The length of the rectangle is 24 ft. (Obj. 3.2.4)

CHAPTER TEST

1. -12 (Obj. 3.1.3)   **2.** $-\dfrac{1}{2}$ (Obj. 3.2.2)   **3.** -3 (Obj. 3.2.1)   **4.** No (Obj. 3.1.1)   **5.** $\dfrac{1}{8}$ (Obj. 3.1.2)

6. $-\dfrac{1}{3}$ (Obj. 3.2.3)   **7.** 5 (Obj. 3.2.1)   **8.** $\dfrac{1}{2}$ (Obj. 3.2.2)   **9.** -5 (Obj. 3.1.2)   **10.** -5 (Obj. 3.2.2)

11. $-\dfrac{40}{3}$ (Obj. 3.1.3)   **12.** $-\dfrac{22}{7}$ (Obj. 3.2.3)   **13.** 2 (Obj. 3.2.3)   **14.** $\dfrac{12}{11}$ (Obj. 3.2.3)

15. -3 (Obj. 3.2.3)   **16.** 125% (Obj. 3.1.4)   **17.** 40 (Obj. 3.1.4)   **18.** (Obj. 3.3.1)

19. $x \le -1$ (Obj. 3.3.1)   **20.** $x > -2$ (Obj. 3.3.2)

21. $x > \dfrac{1}{2}$ (Obj. 3.3.1)   **22.** $x \le -\dfrac{9}{2}$ (Obj. 3.3.3)   **23.** $x \ge -16$ (Obj. 3.3.2)   **24.** $x \le 2$ (Obj. 3.3.3)

25. $x \le -3$ (Obj. 3.3.3)   **26.** $x > 2$ (Obj. 3.3.3)   **27.** 4 (Obj. 3.2.2)   **28.** 24 (Obj. 3.1.4)

29. $x \ge 3$ (Obj. 3.3.2)   **30.** Yes (Obj. 3.1.1)   **31.** The astronaut would weigh 30 lb on the moon. (Obj. 3.1.4)   **32.** The final temperature of the water after mixing is 60°C. (Obj. 3.2.4)   **33.** The number of calculators produced was 200. (Obj. 3.2.4)

CUMULATIVE REVIEW EXERCISES

1. 6 (Obj. 1.2.2)   **2.** -48 (Obj. 1.2.3)   **3.** $-\dfrac{19}{48}$ (Obj. 1.3.3)   **4.** -2 (Obj. 1.3.4)   **5.** 54 (Obj. 1.4.1)

6. 24 (Obj. 1.4.2)   **7.** 6 (Obj. 2.1.1)   **8.** $-17x$ (Obj. 2.2.2)   **9.** $-5a - 2b$ (Obj. 2.2.2)

10. $2x$ (Obj. 2.2.3)   **11.** $36y$ (Obj. 2.2.3)   **12.** $2x^2 + 6x - 4$ (Obj. 2.2.4)   **13.** $-4x + 14$ (Obj. 2.2.5)

14. $6x - 34$ (Obj. 2.2.5)   **15.** $\{-7, -6, -5, -4, -3, -2, -1\}$ (Obj. 1.1.1)   **16.** $87\dfrac{1}{2}\%$ (Obj. 1.3.2)

17. 3.42 (Obj. 1.3.2)   **18.** $\dfrac{5}{8}$ (Obj. 1.3.2)   **19.** Yes (Obj. 3.1.1)   **20.** -5 (Obj. 3.1.2)

21. -25 (Obj. 3.1.3)   **22.** 3 (Obj. 3.2.1)   **23.** -3 (Obj. 3.2.2)   **24.** 13 (Obj. 3.2.3)

25. $x < -\dfrac{8}{9}$ (Obj. 3.3.2)   **26.** $x \ge 12$ (Obj. 3.3.3)   **27.** $x > 9$ (Obj. 3.3.3)   **28.** $8 - \dfrac{n}{12}$ (Obj. 2.3.2)

29. $n + (n + 2); 2n + 2$ (Obj. 2.3.3)   **30.** b and $35 - b$ (Obj. 2.3.4)

31. The length of the shorter piece: s; the length of the longer piece is 4 in. less than three times the length of the shorter piece: $3s - 4$ (Obj. 2.3.4)   **32.** 17% of the computer programmer's salary is deducted for income tax. (Obj. 3.1.4)

33. The equation predicts that the first 4-minute mile was run in 1952. (Obj. 3.2.4)   **34.** The final temperature of the water after mixing is 60°C. (Obj. 3.2.4)   **35.** A force of 24 lb must be applied to the other end of the lever. (Obj. 3.2.4)

ANSWERS to Chapter 4 Odd-Numbered Exercises

CONCEPT REVIEW 4.1

1. Always true   **3.** Always true   **5.** Never true

SECTION 4.1

1. $n - 15 = 7; n = 22$ **3.** $7n = -21; n = -3$ **5.** $3n - 4 = 5; n = 3$ **7.** $4(2n + 3) = 12; n = 0$

9. $12 = 6(n - 3); n = 5$ **11.** $22 = 6n - 2; n = 4$ **13.** $4n + 7 = 2n + 3; n = -2$ **15.** $5n - 8 = 8n + 4; n = -4$

17. $2(n - 25) = 3n; n = -50$ **19.** $3n = 2(20 - n); 8$ and 12   **21.** $3n + 2(18 - n) = 44; 8$ and 10

23. The original value was $16,000.   **25.** The storage capacity is 2 gigabytes.   **27.** The intensity of the sound is 140 decibels.   **29.** The amount of mulch is 15 lb.   **31.** The monthly payment is $117.75.   **33.** To replace the water pump, 5 h of labor were required.   **35.** You are purchasing 9 tickets.   **37.** The length is 80 ft. The width is 50 ft.   **39.** The union member worked 168 h during the month of March.   **41.** The customer used the service for

11 min. **43.** The width is 3 ft. **45.** One-third of the container is filled at 3:39 P.M. **47.** The phone call lasted 15 min. **49.** There are 60 coins in the bank.

CONCEPT REVIEW 4.2

1. Always true   **3.** Always true   **5.** Never true

SECTION 4.2

3. The integers are 17, 18, and 19.   **5.** The integers are 26, 28, and 30.   **7.** The integers are 17, 19, and 21.
9. The integers are 8 and 10.   **11.** The integers are 7 and 9.   **13.** The integers are −9, −8, and −7.   **15.** The integers are 10, 12, and 14.   **17.** No solution   **21.** There are 12 dimes and 15 quarters in the bank.   **23.** The executive bought eight 23¢ stamps and thirty-two 33¢ stamps.   **25.** There are five 29¢ stamps in the drawer.
27. There are 28 quarters in the bank.   **29.** There are 20 one-dollar bills and 6 five-dollar bills in the cash box.
31. There are 11 pennies in the bank.   **33.** There are twenty-seven 22¢ stamps in the collection.   **35.** There are thirteen 3¢ stamps, eighteen 7¢ stamps, and nine 12¢ stamps in the collection.   **37.** There are eighteen 6¢ stamps, six 8¢ stamps, and twenty-four 15¢ stamps.   **39.** The integers are −12, −10, −8, and −6.   **41.** There is $6.70 in the bank.
43. For any three consecutive odd integers, the sum of the first and third integers is twice the second integer.

CONCEPT REVIEW 4.3

1. Always true   **3.** Always true   **5.** Never true

SECTION 4.3

1. The sides measure 50 ft, 50 ft, and 25 ft.   **3.** The length is 13 m. The width is 8 m.   **5.** The length is 40 ft. The width is 20 ft.   **7.** The sides measure 40 cm, 20 cm, and 50 cm.   **9.** The length is 130 ft. The width is 39 ft.
11. The width is 12 ft.   **13.** Each side measures 12 in.   **15.** The complement of a 28° angle is 62°.   **17.** The supplement of a 73° angle is 107°.   **19.** 35°   **21.** 20°   **23.** 53°   **25.** 121°   **27.** 15°   **29.** 18°
31. 45°   **33.** 49°   **35.** 12°   **37.** $\angle a = 122°; \angle b = 58°$ **39.** $\angle a = 44°; \angle b = 136°$ **41.** 20°   **43.** 40°
45. 128°   **47.** $\angle x = 160°, \angle y = 145°$ **49.** $\angle a = 40°, \angle b = 140°$ **51.** $75° - x$ **53.** The measure of the third angle is 45°.   **55.** The measure of the third angle is 73°.   **57.** The measure of the third angle is 43°.
59. The angles measure 38°, 38°, and 104°.   **61.** The angles measure 60°, 30°, and 90°.   **63.** The length is 9 cm. The width is 4 cm.

CONCEPT REVIEW 4.4

1. Always true   **3.** Never true   **5.** Always true

SECTION 4.4

3. The selling price is $56.   **5.** The price is $565.64.   **7.** The markup rate is 75%.   **9.** The markup rate is 44.4%.
11. The markup rate is 60%.   **13.** The cost of the compact disc player is $120.   **15.** The cost of the basketball is $59.   **17.** The cost of the computer is $1750.   **21.** The sale price is $71.25.   **23.** The discount price is $218.50.
25. The discount rate is 25%.   **27.** The discount rate is 23.2%.   **29.** The markdown rate is 38%.   **31.** The regular price is $310.   **33.** The regular price is $300.   **35.** The regular price is $275.   **37.** The markup is $18.
39. The markup rate is 40%.   **41.** The cost of the camera is $230.   **43.** The regular price is $80.
45. No. The single discount that would give the same sale price is 28%.

CONCEPT REVIEW 4.5

1. Always true   **3.** Always true   **5.** Never true

SECTION 4.5

1. $9000 was invested at 7%, and $6000 was invested at 6.5%.   **3.** $1500 was invested in the mutual fund.
5. $200,000 was deposited at 10%, and $100,000 was deposited at 8.5%.   **7.** Teresa has $3000 invested in bonds that earn 8% annual simple interest.   **9.** She has $2500 invested at 11%.   **11.** $40,500 was invested at 8%, and $13,500 was invested at 12%.   **13.** The total amount invested was $650,000.   **15.** The total amount invested was $500,000.
17. The amount of the research consultant's investment is $45,000.   **19.** The total annual interest received was $3040.
21. The value of the investment in three years is $3831.87.   **23a.** By age 55, the couple should have $170,000 saved for retirement.

CONCEPT REVIEW 4.6

1. Always true   **3.** Always true   **5.** Never true   **7.** Always true

SECTION 4.6

3. The clinic should use 2 lb of dog food and 3 lb of vitamin supplement.   **5.** The mixture costs $6.98 per pound.
7. 56 oz of the $4.30 alloy and 144 oz of the $1.80 alloy were used.   **9.** You can add 1 lb of blueberries.   **11.** 10 kg of hard candy must be mixed with the jelly beans.   **13.** To make the mixture, 3 lb of caramel are needed.   **15.** To make the mixture, 300 lb of the $.80 meal are needed.   **17.** 37 lb of almonds and 63 lb of walnuts were used.
19. The cost per pound is $.70.   **21.** The cost per ounce is $3.   **25.** The percent concentration is 24%.
27. 20 gal of the 15% solution must be mixed with 5 gal of the 20% solution.   **29.** 30 lb of 25% wool yarn is used.
31. 6.25 gal of the plant food that is 9% nitrogen are combined with the plant food that is 25% nitrogen.   **33.** The percent concentration is 19%.   **35.** 30 oz of the potpourri that is 60% lavender are used.   **37.** To make the solution, 100 ml of the 7% solution and 200 ml of the 4% solution are used.   **39.** 150 oz of pure chocolate are added.
41. The percent concentration is 12%.   **43.** 1.2 oz of dried apricots must be added.   **45.** The cost is $3.65 per ounce.   **47.** 10 oz of water evaporated from the solution.   **49.** 75 g of pure water must be added.
51. 85 adults and 35 children attended the performance.

CONCEPT REVIEW 4.7

1. Never true   **3.** Never true   **5.** Always true

SECTION 4.7

1. The speed of the first plane is 105 mph. The speed of the second plane is 130 mph.   **3.** They will be 3000 km apart at 11 A.M.   **5.** Michael's boat will be alongside the tour boat in 2 h.   **7.** The airport is 120 mi from the corporate offices.   **9.** The sailboat traveled 36 mi in the first 3 h.   **11.** The passenger train is traveling at 50 mph. The freight train is traveling at 30 mph.   **13.** It takes the second ship 1 h to catch up to the first ship.   **15.** The two trains will pass each other in 4 h.   **17.** The average speed on the winding road was 34 mph.   **19.** The car overtakes the cyclist 48 mi from the starting point.   **21.** The rate of the cyclist is 13 mph.   **23.** The rate of the car is 60 mph.
25. The joggers will meet at 7:48 A.M.   **27.** The cyclist's average speed is $13\frac{1}{3}$ mph.

CONCEPT REVIEW 4.8

1. Never true   **3.** Always true   **5.** Never true

SECTION 4.8

1. The smallest integer is 2. **3.** The amount of income tax to be paid is $3150 or more. **5.** The organization must collect more than 440 lb. **7.** The student must score 78 or better. **9.** The dollar amount in sales must be more than $5714. **11.** The dollar amount the agent expects to sell is $20,000 or less. **13.** A person must use this service for more than 60 min. **15.** 8 ounces or less must be added. **17.** The ski area is more than 38 mi away. **19.** The maximum number of miles you can drive is 166. **21.** The integers are 1, 3, and 5; or 3, 5, and 7.
23. The crew can prepare 8 to 12 aircraft in this period of time. **25.** The minimum number is 467 calendars.

CHAPTER REVIEW EXERCISES

1. $2x - 7 = x; 7$ (Obj. 4.1.1) **2.** The length of the shorter piece is 14 in. (Obj. 4.1.2) **3.** The two numbers are 8 and 13. (Obj. 4.1.2) **4.** $2x + 6 = 4(x - 2); 7$ (Obj. 4.1.1) **5.** The discount rate is $33\frac{1}{3}\%$. (Obj. 4.4.2)
6. $8000 is invested at 6%, and $7000 is invested at 7%. (Obj. 4.5.1) **7.** The angles measure 65°, 65°, and 50°. (Obj. 4.3.3) **8.** The rate of the motorcyclist is 45 mph. (Obj. 4.7.1) **9.** The measures of the three angles are 16°, 82°, and 82°. (Obj. 4.3.3) **10.** The markup rate is 80%. (Obj. 4.4.1) **11.** The concentration of butterfat is 14%. (Obj. 4.6.2) **12.** The length is 80 ft. The width is 20 ft. (Obj. 4.3.1) **13.** A minimum of 1150 copies can be ordered. (Obj. 4.6.1) **14.** The regular price is $32. (Obj. 4.4.2) **15.** 7 qt of cranberry juice and 3 qt of apple juice were used. (Obj. 4.6.1) **16.** The cost is $12.27. (Obj. 4.4.1) **17.** The two numbers are 6 and 30. (Obj. 4.1.2) **18.** $5600 is deposited in the 12% account. (Obj. 4.5.1) **19.** The cards are the 7 and 8 of hearts. (Obj. 4.2.1) **20.** One liter of pure water should be added. (Obj. 4.6.2) **21.** The lowest score the student can receive is 72. (Obj. 4.8.1) **22.** $-7 = \frac{1}{2}x - 10; 6$ (Obj. 4.1.1) **23.** The height is 993 ft. (Obj. 4.1.2) **24.** The measures of the three angles are 75°, 60°, and 45°. (Obj. 4.3.3) **25.** There are 128 one-dollar bills. (Obj. 4.2.2) **26.** The length of the longer piece is 7 ft. (Obj. 4.1.2) **27.** The number of hours of consultation was 8. (Obj. 4.1.2) **28.** There are 77 12¢ stamps and 37 17¢ stamps. (Obj. 4.2.2) **29.** The cost is $671.25. (Obj. 4.4.1) **30.** They will meet after 4 min. (Obj. 4.7.1) **31.** The measures of the three sides are 8 in., 12 in., and 15 in. (Obj. 4.3.1) **32.** The integers are -17, -15, and -13. (Obj. 4.2.1) **33.** The maximum width is 11 ft. (Obj. 4.8.1) **34.** $\angle a = 138°, \angle b = 42°$ (Obj. 4.3.2)

CHAPTER TEST

1. $6n + 13 = 3n - 5; n = -6$ (Obj. 4.1.1) **2.** $3n - 15 = 27; n = 14$ (Obj. 4.1.1) **3.** The numbers are 8 and 10. (Obj. 4.1.2) **4.** The lengths are 6 ft and 12 ft. (Obj. 4.1.2) **5.** The cost is $200. (Obj. 4.4.1) **6.** The discount rate is 20%. (Obj. 4.4.2) **7.** 20 gal of the 15% solution must be added. (Obj. 4.6.2) **8.** The length is 14 m. The width is 5 m. (Obj. 4.3.1) **9.** The integers are 5, 7, and 9. (Obj. 4.2.1) **10.** Five or more residents are in the nursing home. (Obj. 4.8.1) **11.** $5000 is invested at 10%, and $2000 is invested at 15%. (Obj. 4.5.1) **12.** 8 lb of the $7 coffee and 4 lb of the $4 coffee should be used. (Obj. 4.6.1) **13.** The rate of the first plane is 225 mph. The rate of the second plane is 125 mph. (Obj. 4.7.1) **14.** The measures of the three angles are 48°, 33°, and 99°. (Obj. 4.3.3) **15.** There are 15 nickels and 35 quarters in the bank. (Obj. 4.2.2) **16.** The amounts to be deposited are $1400 at 6.75% and $1000 at 9.45%. (Obj. 4.5.1) **17.** The minimum length is 24 ft. (Obj. 4.8.1) **18.** The sale price is $79.20. (Obj. 4.4.2)

CUMULATIVE REVIEW EXERCISES

1. $-12, -6$ (Obj. 1.1.1) **2.** 6 (Obj. 1.2.2) **3.** $-\frac{1}{6}$ (Obj. 1.4.1) **4.** $-\frac{11}{6}$ (Obj. 1.4.2)
5. -18 (Obj. 1.1.2) **6.** -24 (Obj. 2.1.1) **7.** $9x + 4y$ (Obj. 2.2.2) **8.** $-12 + 8x + 20x^3$ (Obj. 2.2.4)
9. $4x + 4$ (Obj. 2.2.5) **10.** $6x^2$ (Obj. 2.2.2) **11.** No (Obj. 3.1.1) **12.** -3 (Obj. 3.2.1)
13. -15 (Obj. 3.1.3) **14.** 3 (Obj. 3.2.1) **15.** -10 (Obj. 3.2.3) **16.** $\frac{2}{5}$ (Obj. 1.3.2)

17. $x \geq 4$ 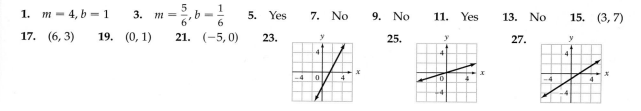   (Obj. 3.3.2)   **18.** $x \geq -3$ (Obj. 3.3.2)   **19.** $x > 18$ (Obj. 3.3.3)

20. $x \geq 4$ (Obj. 3.3.3)   **21.** 2.5%   (Obj. 1.3.2)   **22.** 12%   (Obj. 1.3.2)   **23.** 3   (Obj. 3.1.4)

24. 45   (Obj. 3.1.4)   **25.** $8n + 12 = 4n; n = -3$ (Obj. 4.1.1)   **26.** The area of the garage is 600 ft².   (Obj. 4.1.2)

27. The number of hours of labor is 5.   (Obj. 4.1.2)   **28.** 20% of the libraries had the reference book.   (Obj. 3.1.4)

29. The amount of money deposited is $2000.   (Obj. 4.5.1)   **30.** The markup rate is 75%.   (Obj. 4.4.1)   **31.** 60 g of the gold alloy must be used.   (Obj. 4.6.1)   **32.** 30 oz of pure water must be added.   (Obj. 4.6.2)   **33.** The measure of one of the equal angles is 47°.   (Obj. 4.3.3)   **34.** The middle even integer is 14.   (Obj. 4.2.1)   **35.** There are 7 dimes in the bank.   (Obj. 4.2.2)

ANSWERS to Chapter 5 Odd-Numbered Exercises

CONCEPT REVIEW 5.1

1. Always true   **3.** Never true   **5.** Never true   **7.** Always true

SECTION 5.1

3.   **5.**   **7.**   **9.** $A(2, 3), B(4, 0), C(-4, 1), D(-2, -2)$

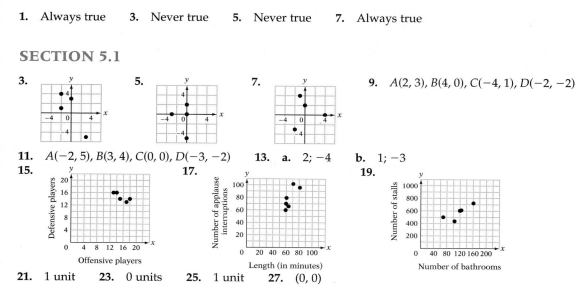

11. $A(-2, 5), B(3, 4), C(0, 0), D(-3, -2)$ **13. a.** $2; -4$ **b.** $1; -3$

15.   **17.**   **19.**

21. 1 unit   **23.** 0 units   **25.** 1 unit   **27.** $(0, 0)$

CONCEPT REVIEW 5.2

1. Never true   **3.** Always true   **5.** Never true   **7.** Never true   **9.** Always true

SECTION 5.2

1. $m = 4, b = 1$ **3.** $m = \dfrac{5}{6}, b = \dfrac{1}{6}$ **5.** Yes   **7.** No   **9.** No   **11.** Yes   **13.** No   **15.** $(3, 7)$

17. $(6, 3)$ **19.** $(0, 1)$ **21.** $(-5, 0)$ **23.**   **25.**   **27.**

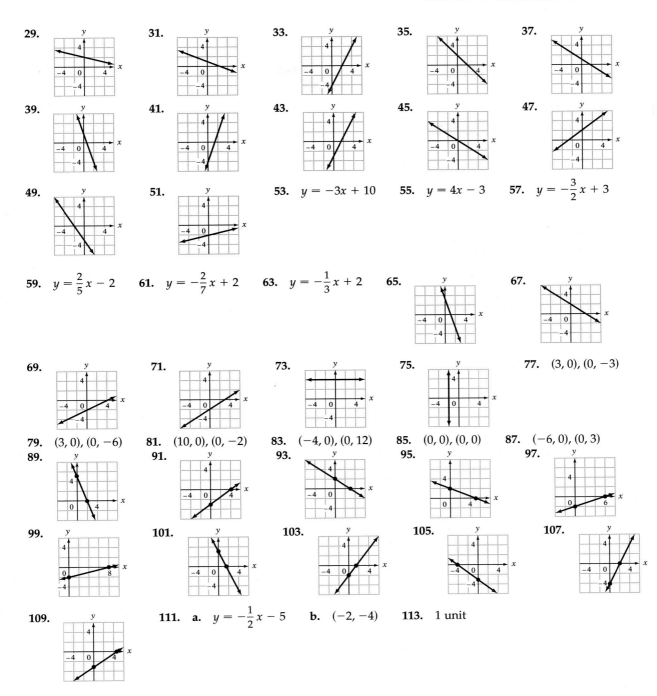

29.

31.

33.

35.

37.

39.

41.

43.

45.

47.

49.

51.

53. $y = -3x + 10$ **55.** $y = 4x - 3$ **57.** $y = -\dfrac{3}{2}x + 3$

59. $y = \dfrac{2}{5}x - 2$ **61.** $y = -\dfrac{2}{7}x + 2$ **63.** $y = -\dfrac{1}{3}x + 2$ **65.**

67.

69.

71.

73.

75.

77. $(3, 0), (0, -3)$

79. $(3, 0), (0, -6)$ **81.** $(10, 0), (0, -2)$ **83.** $(-4, 0), (0, 12)$ **85.** $(0, 0), (0, 0)$ **87.** $(-6, 0), (0, 3)$

89.

91.

93.

95.

97.

99.

101.

103.

105.

107.

109.

111. **a.** $y = -\dfrac{1}{2}x - 5$ **b.** $(-2, -4)$ **113.** 1 unit

CONCEPT REVIEW 5.3

1. Always true   **3.** Never true   **5.** Never true

SECTION 5.3

3. -2 **5.** $\dfrac{1}{3}$ **7.** $-\dfrac{5}{2}$ **9.** $-\dfrac{1}{2}$ **11.** -1 **13.** Undefined **15.** 0 **17.** $-\dfrac{1}{3}$ **19.** 0 **21.** -5

23. Undefined **25.** $-\dfrac{2}{3}$ **27.** $m = 200{,}000{,}000$. A slope of 200,000,000 means that sales of sunglasses have been increasing at a rate of 200,000,000 per year. **29.** $m = -64{,}600$. A slope of $-64{,}600$ means that the population of London is decreasing at a rate of 64,600 people per year.

33. **35.** **37.** **39.** **41.**

43. **45.** **47.** **49.**

51. Increasing the coefficient of x increases the slope. **53.** Increasing the constant term increases the y-intercept.
55. No, not all graphs of straight lines have a y-intercept. In general, vertical lines do not have a y-intercept. For example, $x = 2$ does not have a y-intercept.

CONCEPT REVIEW 5.4

1. Always true **3.** Sometimes true **5.** Always true

SECTION 5.4

1. $y = 2x + 2$ **3.** $y = -3x - 1$ **5.** $y = \dfrac{1}{3}x$ **7.** $y = \dfrac{3}{4}x - 5$ **9.** $y = -\dfrac{3}{5}x$ **11.** $y = \dfrac{1}{4}x + \dfrac{5}{2}$

13. $y = -\dfrac{2}{3}x - 7$ **17.** $y = 2x - 3$ **19.** $y = -2x - 3$ **21.** $y = \dfrac{2}{3}x$ **23.** $y = \dfrac{1}{2}x + 2$

25. $y = -\dfrac{3}{4}x - 2$ **27.** $y = \dfrac{3}{4}x + \dfrac{5}{2}$ **29.** $y = -\dfrac{4}{3}x - 9$ **31.** Yes; $y = -x + 6$ **33.** No **35.** 7

37. -1 **39.** $F = \dfrac{9}{5}C + 32$ **41.** $y = -\dfrac{2}{3}x + \dfrac{5}{3}$

CONCEPT REVIEW 5.5

1. Always true **3.** Never true **5.** Always true **7.** Always true

SECTION 5.5

3. {(37, 44), (6, 3), (16, 16), (6, 13), (8, 15), (33, 20)}; no **5.** {(197, 125), (205, 122), (257, 498), (226, 108), (205, 150)}; no
7. {(55, 273), (65, 355), (75, 447), (85, 549)}; yes **9.** Domain: {0, 2, 4, 6}; range: {0}; yes **11.** Domain: {2};
range: {2, 4, 6, 8}; no **13.** Domain: {0, 1, 2, 3}; range: {0, 1, 2, 3}; yes **15.** Domain: $\{-3, -2, -1, 1, 2, 3\}$;
range: $\{-3, 2, 3, 4\}$; yes **17.** 40; (10, 40) **19.** -11; $(-6, -11)$ **21.** 12; $(-2, 12)$ **23.** $\dfrac{7}{2}$; $\left(\dfrac{1}{2}, \dfrac{7}{2}\right)$

25. 2; $(-5, 2)$ **27.** 32; $(-4, 32)$ **29.** Range: $\{-19, -13, -7, -1, 5\}$; the ordered pairs $(-5, -19)$, $(-3, -13)$, $(-1, -7)$, $(1, -1)$, and $(3, 5)$ belong to the function. **31.** Range: {1, 2, 3, 4, 5}; the ordered pairs $(-4, 1)$, $(-2, 2)$,

(0, 3), (2, 4), and (4, 5) belong to the function. **33.** Range: {6, 7, 15}; the ordered pairs (−3, 15), (−1, 7), (0, 6),
(1, 7), and (3, 15) belong to the function. **35.** (1, 7), and (3, 15) belong to the function. **37.** **39.**

41. **43.** **45.** **47.** **49.**

51. **53.** **55.**

57. **a.** $f(x) = 30,000 − 5000x$ **b.** **c.** The value of the computer after 1 year is $25,000.

59. **a.** $f(m) = 0.18m + 50$ **b.** **c.** The cost to drive this car 500 mi is $140.

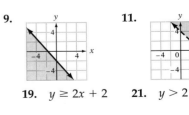

CONCEPT REVIEW 5.6

1. Never true **3.** Always true **5.** Always true

SECTION 5.6

3. **5.** **7.** **9.** **11.**

13. **15.** **17.** **19.** $y \geq 2x + 2$ **21.** $y > 2$

23. **25.**

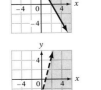

CHAPTER REVIEW EXERCISES

1. (3, 0)   (Obj. 5.2.1)   **2.** $y = 3x - 1$ (Obj. 5.4.1/5.4.2)   **3.** 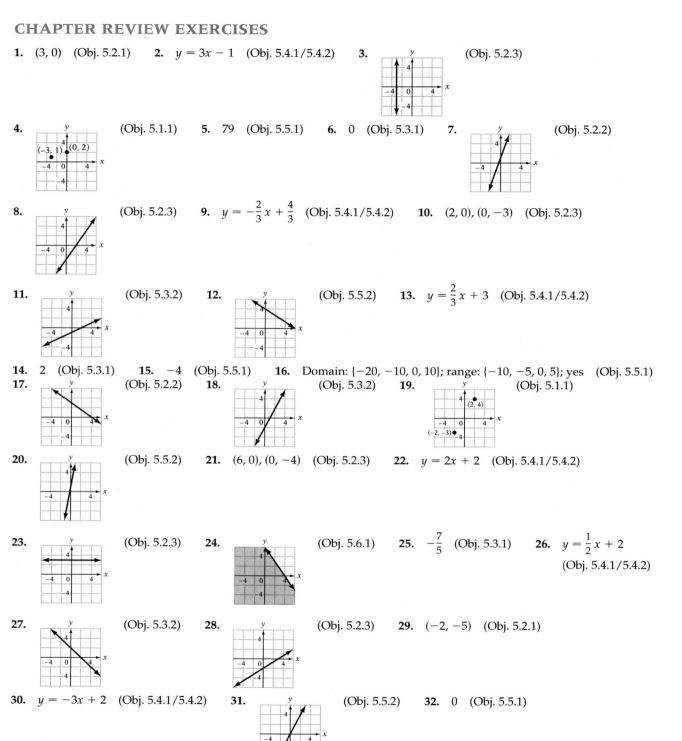   (Obj. 5.2.3)

4.   (Obj. 5.1.1)   **5.** 79   (Obj. 5.5.1)   **6.** 0   (Obj. 5.3.1)   **7.**   (Obj. 5.2.2)

8.   (Obj. 5.2.3)   **9.** $y = -\dfrac{2}{3}x + \dfrac{4}{3}$ (Obj. 5.4.1/5.4.2)   **10.** (2, 0), (0, −3)   (Obj. 5.2.3)

11.   (Obj. 5.3.2)   **12.**   (Obj. 5.5.2)   **13.** $y = \dfrac{2}{3}x + 3$ (Obj. 5.4.1/5.4.2)

14. 2   (Obj. 5.3.1)   **15.** −4   (Obj. 5.5.1)   **16.** Domain: {−20, −10, 0, 10}; range: {−10, −5, 0, 5}; yes   (Obj. 5.5.1)

17.   (Obj. 5.2.2)   **18.**   (Obj. 5.3.2)   **19.**   (Obj. 5.1.1)

20.   (Obj. 5.5.2)   **21.** (6, 0), (0, −4)   (Obj. 5.2.3)   **22.** $y = 2x + 2$ (Obj. 5.4.1/5.4.2)

23.   (Obj. 5.2.3)   **24.**   (Obj. 5.6.1)   **25.** $-\dfrac{7}{5}$ (Obj. 5.3.1)   **26.** $y = \dfrac{1}{2}x + 2$

(Obj. 5.4.1/5.4.2)

27.   (Obj. 5.3.2)   **28.**   (Obj. 5.2.3)   **29.** (−2, −5)   (Obj. 5.2.1)

30. $y = -3x + 2$ (Obj. 5.4.1/5.4.2)   **31.**   (Obj. 5.5.2)   **32.** 0   (Obj. 5.5.1)

33. Undefined (Obj. 5.3.1)   **34.** $y = \frac{1}{2}x - 2$ (Obj. 5.4.1/5.4.2)   **35.** Yes (Obj. 5.2.1)   **36.** $(2, -1)$

(Obj. 5.2.1)   **37.** $(0, 0)$; $(0, 0)$ (Obj. 5.2.3)   **38.** $y = 3$ (Obj. 5.4.1/5.4.2)   **39.**   (Obj. 5.6.1)

40.   (Obj. 5.3.2)   **41.** $y = 3x - 4$ (Obj. 5.4.1/5.4.2)   **42.**   (Obj. 5.2.3)

43. Domain: $\{-10, -5, 5\}$; range $\{-5, 0\}$; no (Obj. 5.5.1)   **44.** Range: $\{-53, -23, 7, 37, 67\}$ (Obj. 5.5.1)
45. Range: $\{2, 3, 4, 5, 6\}$ (Obj. 5.5.1)   **46.**   (Obj. 5.1.2)

47.   (Obj. 5.1.2)   **48.** $\{(25, 4.8), (35, 3.5), (40, 2.1), (20, 5.5), (45, 1.0)\}$; yes (Obj. 5.5.1)

49. a. $f(s) = 70s + 40,000$ **b.**   **c.** The contractor's cost to build a house of 1500 ft^2 is $145,000. (Obj. 5.5.2)

50. The slope is 58.5. The number of heart surgeries performed is increasing at a rate of 58.5 per year. (Obj. 5.3.1)

CHAPTER TEST

1. $y = -\frac{1}{3}x$ (Obj. 5.4.1/5.4.2)   **2.** $\frac{7}{11}$ (Obj. 5.3.1)   **3.** $(8, 0)$; $(0, -12)$ (Obj. 5.2.3)   **4.** $(9, -13)$ (Obj. 5.2.1)

5.   (Obj. 5.2.3)   **6.**   (Obj. 5.2.2)   **7.** 10 (Obj. 5.5.1)   **8.** No (Obj. 5.2.1)

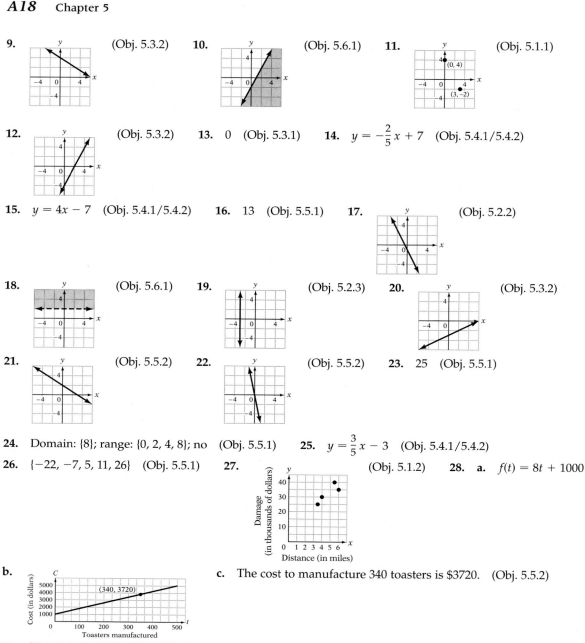

9. (Obj. 5.3.2) **10.** (Obj. 5.6.1) **11.** (Obj. 5.1.1)

12. (Obj. 5.3.2) **13.** 0 (Obj. 5.3.1) **14.** $y = -\dfrac{2}{5}x + 7$ (Obj. 5.4.1/5.4.2)

15. $y = 4x - 7$ (Obj. 5.4.1/5.4.2) **16.** 13 (Obj. 5.5.1) **17.** (Obj. 5.2.2)

18. (Obj. 5.6.1) **19.** (Obj. 5.2.3) **20.** (Obj. 5.3.2)

21. (Obj. 5.5.2) **22.** (Obj. 5.5.2) **23.** 25 (Obj. 5.5.1)

24. Domain: {8}; range: {0, 2, 4, 8}; no (Obj. 5.5.1) **25.** $y = \dfrac{3}{5}x - 3$ (Obj. 5.4.1/5.4.2)

26. {−22, −7, 5, 11, 26} (Obj. 5.5.1) **27.** (Obj. 5.1.2) **28.** **a.** $f(t) = 8t + 1000$

b.   **c.** The cost to manufacture 340 toasters is $3720.   (Obj. 5.5.2)

29. {(8.5, 64), (9.4, 68), (10.1, 76), (11.4, 87), (12.0, 92)}; yes (Obj. 5.5.1) **30.** The slope is 36. The cost of lumber has been increasing by $36 per month. (Obj. 5.3.1)

CUMULATIVE REVIEW EXERCISES

1. −12 (Obj. 1.4.2) **2.** $-\dfrac{5}{8}$ (Obj. 2.1.1) **3.** $-17x + 28$ (Obj. 2.2.5) **4.** $\dfrac{3}{2}$ (Obj. 3.2.1) **5.** 1

(Obj. 3.2.3) **6.** $\dfrac{1}{15}$ (Obj. 1.3.2) **7.** {1, 2, 3, 4, 5, 6, 7, 8} (Obj. 1.1.1) **8.** −4, 0, 5 (Obj. 1.1.1)

9. $a \geq -1$ (Obj. 3.3.3) **10.** $y = \dfrac{4}{5}x - 3$ (Obj. 5.2.3) **11.** (−2, −7) (Obj. 5.2.1) **12.** 0 (Obj. 5.3.1)

13. (4, 0); (0, 10) (Obj. 5.2.3)   **14.** $y = -x + 5$ (Obj. 5.4.1/5.4.2)   **15.** (Obj. 5.2.2)

16. (Obj. 5.2.3)   **17.** (Obj. 5.5.2)   **18.** (Obj. 5.6.1)

19. Domain: {0, 1, 2, 3, 4}; range: {0, 1, 2, 3, 4}; yes (Obj. 5.5.1)   **20.** -11 (Obj. 5.5.1)   **21.** {−7, −2, 3, 8, 13, 18}
(Obj. 5.5.1)   **22.** 7 and 17 (Obj. 4.1.2)   **23.** The fulcrum is 7 ft from the 80-pound force. (Obj. 3.2.4)
24. The length of the first side is 22 ft. (Obj. 4.3.1)   **25.** The sale price is $62.30. (Obj. 4.4.2)

ANSWERS to Chapter 6 Odd-Numbered Exercises

CONCEPT REVIEW 6.1

1. Always true   **3.** Sometimes true   **5.** Sometimes true

SECTION 6.1

3. Yes   **5.** Yes   **7.** No   **9.** No   **11.** No   **13.** Yes   **15.** Yes   **19.** (4, 1)   **21.** (4, 1)
23. (4, 3)   **25.** (3, −2)   **27.** (2, −2)   **29.** The system of equations is inconsistent and has no solution.
31. The system of equations is dependent. The solutions are the ordered pairs that satisfy the equation $y = 2x - 2$.
33. (1, −4)   **35.** (0, 0)   **37.** The system of equations is inconsistent and has no solution.   **39.** (0, −2)
41. (1, −1)   **43.** (2, 0)   **45.** (−3, −2)   **47.** The system of equations is inconsistent and has no solution.
49. $y = 2$ **51.** $y = x$ **53. a.** Always true   **b.** Never true   **c.** Always true
  $y = x + 4$ $y = -x + 2$

CONCEPT REVIEW 6.2

1. Always true   **3.** Never true   **5.** Never true

SECTION 6.2

1. (2, 1)   **3.** (4, 1)   **5.** (−1, 1)   **7.** (3, 1)   **9.** (1, 1)   **11.** (−1, 1)   **13.** The system of equations is
inconsistent and has no solution.   **15.** The system of equations is inconsistent and has no solution.
17. $\left(-\dfrac{3}{4}, -\dfrac{3}{4}\right)$ **19.** $\left(\dfrac{9}{5}, \dfrac{6}{5}\right)$ **21.** (−7, −23)   **23.** (1, 1)   **25.** (2, 0)   **27.** (2, 1)   **29.** $\left(\dfrac{9}{19}, -\dfrac{13}{19}\right)$
31. (5, 7)   **33.** (1, 7)   **35.** $\left(\dfrac{17}{5}, -\dfrac{7}{5}\right)$ **37.** $\left(-\dfrac{6}{11}, \dfrac{31}{11}\right)$ **39.** (2, 3)   **41.** (0, 0)   **43.** The system of
equations is dependent. The solutions are the ordered pairs that satisfy the equation $3x + y = 4$.   **45.** $\left(\dfrac{20}{17}, -\dfrac{15}{17}\right)$
47. (5, 2)   **49.** (−17, −8)   **51.** $\left(-\dfrac{5}{7}, \dfrac{13}{7}\right)$ **53.** (3, −2)   **55.** $\left(-\dfrac{11}{20}, \dfrac{23}{40}\right)$ **57.** (3, −2)   **59.** (1, 7)
61. 2   **63.** 2

CONCEPT REVIEW 6.3

1. Always true   **3.** Never true   **5.** Never true

SECTION 6.3

1. $(5, -1)$ **3.** $(1, 3)$ **5.** $(1, 1)$ **7.** $(3, -2)$ **9.** The system of equations is dependent. The solutions are the ordered pairs that satisfy the equation $2x - y = 1$.   **11.** $(3, 1)$ **13.** The system of equations is inconsistent and has no solution.   **15.** $\left(-\dfrac{13}{17}, -\dfrac{24}{17}\right)$ **17.** $(2, 0)$ **19.** $(0, 0)$ **21.** $(5, -2)$ **23.** $\left(\dfrac{32}{19}, -\dfrac{9}{19}\right)$ **25.** $(3, 4)$ **27.** $(1, -1)$ **29.** The system of equations is dependent. The solutions are the ordered pairs that satisfy the equation $x + 3y = 4$.   **31.** $(3, 1)$ **33.** $(-1, 2)$ **35.** $(1, 1)$ **37.** $\left(\dfrac{1}{2}, -\dfrac{1}{2}\right)$ **39.** $\left(\dfrac{2}{3}, \dfrac{1}{9}\right)$ **41.** $\left(\dfrac{7}{25}, -\dfrac{1}{25}\right)$ **43.** $(5, 2)$ **45.** $(1, 4)$ **47.** $(1, 2)$ **49.** $A = 3, B = -1$ **51.** $A = 2$ **53. a.** $k \neq 1$ **b.** $k \neq \dfrac{3}{2}$ **c.** $k \neq 4$

CONCEPT REVIEW 6.4

1. Always true   **3.** Never true   **5.** Never true

SECTION 6.4

1. The speed of the whale in calm water is 35 mph. The rate of the current is 5 mph.   **3.** The team's rowing rate in calm water was 14 km/h. The rate of the current was 6 km/h.   **5.** The rate of the boat in calm water was 7 mph. The rate of the current was 3 mph.   **7.** The speed of the jet in calm air was 525 mph. The rate of the wind was 35 mph.   **9.** The rate of the plane in calm air was 100 mph. The rate of the wind was 20 mph.   **11.** The speed of the helicopter in calm air was 225 mph. The rate of the wind was 45 mph.   **13.** The cost is $245.   **15.** The cost of the wheat is $.65 per pound. The cost of the rye is $.70 per pound.   **17.** The daytime rate is $7 per hour. The nighttime rate is $9 per hour.   **19.** The team scored 21 two-point baskets and 15 three-point baskets.   **21.** There are 8 nickels and 10 quarters in the first bank.   **23.** There are 8 dimes and 10 quarters in the bank.   **25.** The two angles measure 55° and 125°.   **27.** $6000 was invested in the 9% account, and $4000 was invested in the 8% account.   **29.** There are 0 dimes and 5 nickels, or 1 dime and 3 nickels, or 2 dimes and 1 nickel in the bank.

CHAPTER REVIEW EXERCISES

1. $(-1, 1)$ (Obj. 6.2.1)   **2.** $(2, -3)$ (Obj. 6.1.1)   **3.** $(-3, 1)$ (Obj. 6.3.1)   **4.** $(1, 6)$ (Obj. 6.2.1)   **5.** $(1, 1)$ (Obj. 6.1.1)   **6.** $(1, -5)$ (Obj. 6.3.1)   **7.** $(3, 2)$ (Obj. 6.2.1)   **8.** The system of equations is dependent. The solutions are the ordered pairs that satisfy the equation $8x - y = 25$. (Obj. 6.3.1)   **9.** $(3, -1)$ (Obj. 6.3.1)   **10.** $(1, -3)$ (Obj. 6.1.1)   **11.** $(-2, -7)$ (Obj. 6.3.1)   **12.** $(4, 0)$ (Obj. 6.2.1)   **13.** Yes (Obj. 6.1.1)   **14.** $\left(-\dfrac{5}{6}, \dfrac{1}{2}\right)$ (Obj. 6.3.1)   **15.** $(-1, -2)$ (Obj. 6.3.1)   **16.** $(3, -3)$ (Obj. 6.1.1)   **17.** The system of equations is inconsistent and has no solution. (Obj. 6.3.1)   **18.** $\left(-\dfrac{1}{3}, \dfrac{1}{6}\right)$ (Obj. 6.2.1)   **19.** The system of equations is dependent. The solutions are the ordered pairs that satisfy the equation $y = 2x - 4$. (Obj. 6.1.1)   **20.** The system of equations is dependent. The solutions are the ordered pairs that satisfy the equation $3x + y = -2$. (Obj. 6.3.1)   **21.** $(-2, -13)$ (Obj. 6.3.1)   **22.** The system of equations is dependent. The solutions are the ordered pairs that satisfy the equation $4x + 3y = 12$. (Obj. 6.2.1)   **23.** $(4, 2)$ (Obj. 6.1.1)   **24.** The system of equations is inconsistent and has no solution. (Obj. 6.3.1)   **25.** $\left(\dfrac{1}{2}, -1\right)$ (Obj. 6.2.1)   **26.** No (Obj. 6.1.1)   **27.** $\left(\dfrac{2}{3}, -\dfrac{1}{6}\right)$ (Obj. 6.3.1)   **28.** The system of equations is inconsistent and has no solution. (Obj. 6.2.1)   **29.** $\left(\dfrac{1}{3}, 6\right)$ (Obj. 6.2.1)   **30.** The system of equations is inconsistent and has no solution. (Obj. 6.1.1)   **31.** $(0, -1)$ (Obj. 6.3.1)   **32.** $(-1, -3)$

(Obj. 6.2.1)   **33.** (0, −2) (Obj. 6.2.1)   **34.** (2, 0) (Obj. 6.3.1)   **35.** (−4, 2) (Obj. 6.3.1)   **36.** (1, 6)
(Obj. 6.2.1)   **37.** The rate of the plane in calm air is 180 mph. The rate of the wind is 20 mph.   (Obj. 6.4.1)
38. There were 60 adults' tickets and 140 children's tickets sold.   (Obj. 6.4.2)   **39.** The rate of the canoeist in calm water was 8 mph. The rate of the current was 2 mph.   (Obj. 6.4.1)   **40.** There were 130 mailings requiring 33¢ in postage.   (Obj. 6.4.2)   **41.** The rate of the boat in calm water was 14 km/h. The rate of the current was 2 km/h.   (Obj. 6.4.1)   **42.** The customer purchased 4 compact discs at $15 each and 6 at $10 each.   (Obj. 6.4.2)   **43.** The rate of the plane in calm air was 125 km/h. The rate of the wind was 15 km/h.   (Obj. 6.4.1)   **44.** The rate of the paddle boat in calm water was 3 mph. The rate of the current was 1 mph.   (Obj. 6.4.1)   **45.** There are 350 bushels of lentils and 200 bushels of corn in the silo.   (Obj. 6.4.2)   **46.** The rate of the plane in calm air was 105 mph. The rate of the wind was 15 mph.   (Obj. 6.4.1)   **47.** There are 4 dimes in the coin purse.   (Obj. 6.4.2)   **48.** The rate of the plane in calm air was 325 mph. The rate of the wind was 25 mph.   (Obj. 6.4.1)   **49.** The investor bought 1300 of the $6 shares and 200 of the $25 shares.   (Obj. 6.4.2)   **50.** The rate of the sculling team in calm water was 9 mph. The rate of the current was 3 mph.   (Obj. 6.4.1)

CHAPTER TEST

1. (3, 1) (Obj. 6.2.1)   **2.** (2, 1) (Obj. 6.3.1)   **3.** Yes (Obj. 6.1.1)   **4.** (1, −1) (Obj. 6.2.1)   **5.** $\left(\frac{1}{2}, -1\right)$
(Obj. 6.3.1)   **6.** (−2, 6) (Obj. 6.1.1)   **7.** The system of equations is inconsistent and has no solution.   (Obj. 6.2.1)
8. (2, −1) (Obj. 6.2.1)   **9.** (2, −1) (Obj. 6.3.1)   **10.** $\left(\frac{22}{7}, -\frac{5}{7}\right)$ (Obj. 6.2.1)   **11.** (1, −2) (Obj. 6.3.1)
12. No (Obj. 6.1.1)   **13.** (2, 1) (Obj. 6.2.1)   **14.** (2, −2) (Obj. 6.3.1)   **15.** (2, 0) (Obj. 6.1.1)   **16.** (4, 1)
(Obj. 6.2.1)   **17.** (3, −2) (Obj. 6.3.1)   **18.** The system of equations is dependent. The solutions are the ordered pairs that satisfy the equation $3x + 6y = 2$.   (Obj. 6.1.1)   **19.** (1, 1) (Obj. 6.2.1)   **20.** (4, −3) (Obj. 6.3.1)
21. (−6, 1) (Obj. 6.2.1)   **22.** (1, −4) (Obj. 6.3.1)   **23.** The rate of the plane in calm air is 100 mph. The rate of the wind is 20 mph.   (Obj. 6.4.1)   **24.** The rate of the boat in calm water is 14 mph. The rate of the current is 2 mph.
(Obj. 6.4.1)   **25.** There are 40 dimes and 30 nickels in the first bank.   (Obj. 6.4.2)

CUMULATIVE REVIEW EXERCISES

1. −8, −4 (Obj. 1.1.1)   **2.** {1, 2, 3, 4, 5, 6, 7, 8, 9, 10} (Obj. 1.1.1)   **3.** 10 (Obj. 1.4.2)   **4.** $40a - 28$
(Obj. 2.2.5)   **5.** $\frac{3}{2}$ (Obj. 2.1.1)   **6.** $-\frac{3}{2}$ (Obj. 3.1.3)   **7.** $-\frac{7}{2}$ (Obj. 3.2.3)   **8.** $-\frac{2}{9}$ (Obj. 3.2.3)
9. $x < -5$ (Obj. 3.3.3)   **10.** $x \leq 3$ (Obj. 3.3.3)   **11.** 24% (Obj. 3.1.4)   **12.** (4, 0), (0, −2) (Obj. 5.2.3)
13. $-\frac{7}{5}$ (Obj. 5.3.1)   **14.** $y = -\frac{3}{2}x$ (Obj. 5.4.1/5.4.2)   **15.**   (Obj. 5.2.3)

16.   (Obj. 5.2.2)   **17.**   (Obj. 5.6.1)   **18.**   (Obj. 5.5.2)

19. Domain: {−5, 0, 1, 5}; range: {5}; yes (Obj. 5.5.1)   **20.** 3 (Obj. 5.5.1)   **21.** Yes (Obj. 6.1.1)
22. (−2, 1) (Obj. 6.2.1)   **23.** (0, 2) (Obj. 6.1.1)   **24.** (2, 1) (Obj. 6.3.1)   **25.** {−22, −12, −2, 8, 18} (Obj. 5.5.1)
26. 200 cameras were produced during the month.   (Obj. 3.2.4)   **27.** $3750 should be invested at 9.6%, and $5000 should be invested at 7.2%.   (Obj. 4.5.1)   **28.** The rate of the plane is 160 mph. The rate of the wind is 30 mph.
(Obj. 6.4.1)   **29.** The rate of the boat in calm water is 10 mph.   (Obj. 6.4.1)   **30.** There are 40 dimes in the first bank.   (Obj. 6.4.2)

ANSWERS to Chapter 7 Odd-Numbered Exercises

CONCEPT REVIEW 7.1

1. Always true **3.** Never true **5.** Always true

SECTION 7.1

1. Binomial **3.** Monomial **5.** No **7.** Yes **9.** Yes **11.** $-2x^2 + 3x$ **13.** $y^2 - 8$
15. $5x^2 + 7x + 20$ **17.** $x^3 + 2x^2 - 6x - 6$ **19.** $2a^3 - 3a^2 - 11a + 2$ **21.** $5x^2 + 8x$ **23.** $7x^2 + xy - 4y^2$
25. $3a^2 - 3a + 17$ **27.** $5x^3 + 10x^2 - x - 4$ **29.** $3r^3 + 2r^2 - 11r + 7$ **31.** $-2x^3 + 3x^2 + 10x + 11$
33. $4x$ **35.** $3y^2 - 4y - 2$ **37.** $-7x - 7$ **39.** $4x^3 + 3x^2 + 3x + 1$ **41.** $y^3 - y^2 + 6y - 6$
43. $-y^2 - 13xy$ **45.** $2x^2 - 3x - 1$ **47.** $-2x^3 + x^2 + 2$ **49.** $3a^3 - 2$ **51.** $4y^3 - 2y^2 + 2y - 4$
53. $-a^2 - 1$ **55.** $-4x^2 + 6x + 3$ **57.** $4x^2 - 6x + 3$
59. Yes. For example, $(3x^3 - 2x^2 + 3x - 4) - (3x^3 + 4x^2 - 6x + 5) = -6x^2 + 9x - 9$

CONCEPT REVIEW 7.2

1. Never true **3.** Always true **5.** Never true

SECTION 7.2

3. $2x^2$ **5.** $12x^2$ **7.** $6a^7$ **9.** x^3y^5 **11.** $-10x^9y$ **13.** x^7y^8 **15.** $-6x^3y^5$ **17.** x^4y^5z **19.** $a^3b^5c^4$
21. $-a^5b^8$ **23.** $-6a^5b$ **25.** $40y^{10}z^6$ **27.** $-20a^2b^3$ **29.** $x^3y^5z^3$ **31.** $-12a^{10}b^7$ **33.** 64 **35.** 4
37. -64 **39.** x^9 **41.** x^{14} **43.** x^4 **45.** $4x^2$ **47.** $-8x^6$ **49.** x^4y^6 **51.** $9x^4y^2$ **53.** $27a^8$
55. $-8x^7$ **57.** x^8y^4 **59.** a^4b^6 **61.** $16x^{10}y^3$ **63.** $-18x^3y^4$ **65.** $-8a^7b^5$ **67.** $-54a^9b^3$ **69.** $-72a^5b^5$
71. $32x^3$ **73.** $-3a^3b^3$ **75.** $13x^5y^5$ **77.** $27a^5b^3$ **79.** $-5x^7y^4$ **81.** a^{2n} **83.** a^{2n} **85.** True
87. False; $x^{2 \cdot 5} = x^{10}$ **89.** No; $2^{(3^2)}$ is larger. $(2^3)^2 = 8^2 = 64$, whereas $2^{(3^2)} = 2^9 = 512$. **91.** $x = y$ when n is odd.

CONCEPT REVIEW 7.3

1. Always true **3.** Sometimes true **5.** Always true **7.** Sometimes true

SECTION 7.3

1. $x^2 - 2x$ **3.** $-x^2 - 7x$ **5.** $3a^3 - 6a^2$ **7.** $-5x^4 + 5x^3$ **9.** $-3x^5 + 7x^3$ **11.** $12x^3 - 6x^2$
13. $6x^2 - 12x$ **15.** $-x^3y + xy^3$ **17.** $2x^4 - 3x^2 + 2x$ **19.** $2a^3 + 3a^2 + 2a$ **21.** $3x^6 - 3x^4 - 2x^2$
23. $-6y^4 - 12y^3 + 14y^2$ **25.** $-2a^3 - 6a^2 + 8a$ **27.** $6y^4 - 3y^3 + 6y^2$ **29.** $x^3y - 3x^2y^2 + xy^3$
31. $x^3 + 4x^2 + 5x + 2$ **33.** $a^3 - 6a^2 + 13a - 12$ **35.** $-2b^3 + 7b^2 + 19b - 20$ **37.** $-6x^3 + 31x^2 - 41x + 10$
39. $x^4 - 4x^3 - 3x^2 + 14x - 8$ **41.** $15y^3 - 16y^2 - 70y + 16$ **43.** $5a^4 - 20a^3 - 15a^2 + 62a - 8$
45. $y^4 + 4y^3 + y^2 - 5y + 2$ **47.** $x^2 + 4x + 3$ **49.** $a^2 + a - 12$ **51.** $y^2 - 5y - 24$ **53.** $y^2 - 10y + 21$
55. $2x^2 + 15x + 7$ **57.** $3x^2 + 11x - 4$ **59.** $4x^2 - 31x + 21$ **61.** $3y^2 - 2y - 16$ **63.** $9x^2 + 54x + 77$
65. $21a^2 - 83a + 80$ **67.** $15b^2 + 47b - 78$ **69.** $2a^2 + 7ab + 3b^2$ **71.** $6a^2 + ab - 2b^2$
73. $2x^2 - 3xy - 2y^2$ **75.** $10x^2 + 29xy + 21y^2$ **77.** $6a^2 - 25ab + 14b^2$ **79.** $2a^2 - 11ab - 63b^2$
81. $100a^2 - 100ab + 21b^2$ **83.** $15x^2 + 56xy + 48y^2$ **85.** $14x^2 - 97xy - 60y^2$ **87.** $56x^2 - 61xy + 15y^2$
89. $y^2 - 25$ **91.** $4x^2 - 9$ **93.** $x^2 + 2x + 1$ **95.** $9a^2 - 30a + 25$ **97.** $9x^2 - 49$ **99.** $4a^2 + 4ab + b^2$
101. $x^2 - 4xy + 4y^2$ **103.** $16 - 9y^2$ **105.** $25x^2 + 20xy + 4y^2$ **107.** The area is $(10x^2 - 35x)$ ft^2.
109. The area is $(18x^2 + 12x + 2)$ in^2. **111.** The area is $(4x^2 + 4x + 1)$ km^2. **113.** The area is $(4x^2 + 10x)$ m^2.
115. The area is $(\pi x^2 + 8\pi x + 16\pi)$ cm^2. **117.** The area is $(90x + 2025)$ ft^2. **119.** $4ab$
121. $9a^4 - 24a^3 + 28a^2 - 16a + 4$ **123.** $24x^3 - 3x^2$ **125.** $x^{2n} + x^n$ **127.** $x^{2n} + 2x^n + 1$ **129.** $x^2 - 1$
131. $x^4 - 1$ **133.** $x^6 - 1$ **135.** 1024 **137.** $12x^2 - x - 20$ **139.** $7x^2 - 11x - 8$

CONCEPT REVIEW 7.4

1. Never true   **3.** Always true   **5.** Never true   **7.** Never true

SECTION 7.4

1. $\dfrac{1}{25}$ **3.** 64 **5.** $\dfrac{1}{27}$ **7.** 1 **11.** y^4 **13.** a^3 **15.** p^4 **17.** $2x^3$ **19.** $2k$ **21.** m^5n^2 **23.** $\dfrac{3r^2}{2}$

25. $-\dfrac{2a}{3}$ **27.** $\dfrac{1}{x^2}$ **29.** a^6 **31.** $\dfrac{4}{x^7}$ **33.** $5b^8$ **35.** $\dfrac{x^2}{3}$ **37.** 1 **39.** $\dfrac{1}{y^5}$ **41.** $\dfrac{1}{a^6}$ **43.** $\dfrac{1}{3x^3}$

45. $\dfrac{2}{3x^5}$ **47.** $\dfrac{y^4}{x^2}$ **49.** $\dfrac{2}{5m^3n^8}$ **51.** $\dfrac{1}{p^3q}$ **53.** $\dfrac{1}{2y^3}$ **55.** $\dfrac{7xz}{8y^3}$ **57.** $\dfrac{p^2}{2m^3}$ **59.** $-\dfrac{8x^3}{y^6}$ **61.** $\dfrac{9}{x^2y^4}$

63. $\dfrac{2}{x^4}$ **65.** $-\dfrac{5}{a^8}$ **67.** $-\dfrac{a^5}{8b^4}$ **69.** $\dfrac{10y^3}{x^4}$ **71.** $\dfrac{1}{2x^3}$ **73.** $\dfrac{3}{x^3}$ **75.** $\dfrac{1}{2x^2y^6}$ **77.** $-\dfrac{1}{6x^3}$ **81.** $2.37 \cdot 10^6$

83. $4.5 \cdot 10^{-4}$ **85.** $3.09 \cdot 10^5$ **87.** $6.01 \cdot 10^{-7}$ **89.** 710,000 **91.** 0.000043 **93.** 671,000,000
95. 0.00000713 **97.** $1.6 \cdot 10^{10}$ **99.** $5.98 \cdot 10^{24}$ **101.** $1.6 \cdot 10^{-19}$ **103.** $1 \cdot 10^{-12}$ **105.** $6.65 \cdot 10^{19}$
107. $3.22 \cdot 10^{-14}$ **109.** $3.6 \cdot 10^5$ **111.** $1.8 \cdot 10^{-18}$ **113.** $x + 1$ **115.** $2a - 5$ **117.** $3a + 2$
119. $4b^2 - 3$ **121.** $x - 2$ **123.** $-x + 2$ **125.** $x^2 + 3x - 5$ **127.** $x^4 - 3x^2 - 1$ **129.** $xy + 2$

131. $-3y^3 + 5$ **133.** $3x - 2 + \dfrac{1}{x}$ **135.** $-3x + 7 - \dfrac{6}{x}$ **137.** $4a - 5 + 6b$ **139.** $9x + 6 - 3y$

141. $x + 2$ **143.** $2x + 1$ **145.** $2x - 4$ **147.** $x + 1 + \dfrac{2}{x - 1}$ **149.** $2x - 1 - \dfrac{2}{3x - 2}$

151. $5x + 12 + \dfrac{12}{x - 1}$ **153.** $a + 3 + \dfrac{4}{a + 2}$ **155.** $y - 6 + \dfrac{26}{2y + 3}$ **157.** $2x + 5 + \dfrac{8}{2x - 1}$

159. $5a - 6 + \dfrac{4}{3a + 2}$ **161.** $3x - 5$ **163.** $x^2 + 2x + 3$ **165.** $x^2 - 3$ **167.** $\dfrac{3}{64}$

169. For 2^x: $\dfrac{1}{4}, \dfrac{1}{2}, 1, 2, 4$. For 2^{-x}: $4, 2, 1, \dfrac{1}{2}, \dfrac{1}{4}$. **171.** 0.0625 **173.** xy^2 **175.** $\dfrac{x^6z^6}{4y^5}$ **177.** 1 **179.** 0

181. False; $(2a)^{-3} = \dfrac{1}{8a^3}$ **183.** False; $(2 + 3)^{-1} = 5^{-1} = \dfrac{1}{5}$ **185.** $3a^2$ **187.** $4x^2 - 6x + 3$

CHAPTER REVIEW EXERCISES

1. $21y^2 + 4y - 1$ (Obj. 7.1.1)   **2.** $-20x^3y^5$ (Obj. 7.2.1)   **3.** $-8x^3 - 14x^2 + 18x$ (Obj. 7.3.1)
4. $10a^2 + 31a - 63$ (Obj. 7.3.3)   **5.** $6x^2 - 7x + 10$ (Obj. 7.4.3)   **6.** $2x^2 + 3x - 8$ (Obj. 7.1.2)
7. -729 (Obj. 7.2.2)   **8.** $x^3 - 6x^2 + 7x - 2$ (Obj. 7.3.2)   **9.** $a^2 - 49$ (Obj. 7.3.4)   **10.** 1296 (Obj. 7.4.1)
11. $x - 6$ (Obj. 7.4.4)   **12.** $2x^3 + 9x^2 - 3x - 12$ (Obj. 7.1.1)   **13.** $18a^8b^6$ (Obj. 7.2.1)
14. $3x^4y - 2x^3y + 12x^2y$ (Obj. 7.3.1)   **15.** $8b^2 - 2b - 15$ (Obj. 7.3.3)   **16.** $-4y + 8$ (Obj. 7.4.3)
17. $13y^3 - 12y^2 - 5y - 1$ (Obj. 7.1.2)   **18.** 64 (Obj. 7.2.2)   **19.** $6y^3 + 17y^2 - 2y - 21$ (Obj. 7.3.2)

20. $4b^2 - 81$ (Obj. 7.3.4)   **21.** $\dfrac{b^6c^2}{a^4}$ (Obj. 7.4.1)   **22.** $2y - 9$ (Obj. 7.4.4)   **23.** $3.97 \cdot 10^{-6}$ (Obj. 7.4.2)

24. $x^4y^8z^4$ (Obj. 7.2.1)   **25.** $-12y^5 + 4y^4 - 18y^3$ (Obj. 7.3.1)   **26.** $18x^2 - 48x + 24$ (Obj. 7.3.3)
27. 0.0000623 (Obj. 7.4.2)   **28.** $-7a^2 - a + 4$ (Obj. 7.1.2)   **29.** $9x^4y^6$ (Obj. 7.2.2)

30. $12a^3 - 8a^2 - 9a + 6$ (Obj. 7.3.3)   **31.** $25y^2 - 70y + 49$ (Obj. 7.3.4)   **32.** $\dfrac{x^4y^6}{9}$ (Obj. 7.4.1)

33. $x + 5 + \dfrac{4}{x + 12}$ (Obj. 7.4.4)   **34.** 240,000 (Obj. 7.4.2)   **35.** $a^6b^{11}c^9$ (Obj. 7.2.1)

36. $8a^3b^3 - 4a^2b^4 + 6ab^5$ (Obj. 7.3.1)   **37.** $6x^2 - 7xy - 20y^2$ (Obj. 7.3.3)   **38.** $4b^4 + 12b^2 - 1$ (Obj. 7.4.3)
39. $-4b^2 - 13b + 28$ (Obj. 7.1.2)   **40.** $100a^{15}b^{13}$ (Obj. 7.2.2)   **41.** $12b^5 - 4b^4 - 6b^3 - 8b^2 + 5$ (Obj. 7.3.2)

42. $36 - 25x^2$ (Obj. 7.3.4)   **43.** $\dfrac{2y^3}{x^3}$ (Obj. 7.4.1)   **44.** $a^2 - 2a + 6$ (Obj. 7.4.4)   **45.** $4b^3 - 5b^2 - 9b + 7$

(Obj. 7.1.1)   **46.** $-54a^{13}b^5c^7$ (Obj. 7.2.1)   **47.** $-18x^4 - 27x^3 + 63x^2$ (Obj. 7.3.1)   **48.** $30y^2 - 109y + 30$
(Obj. 7.3.3)   **49.** $9.176 \cdot 10^{12}$ (Obj. 7.4.2)   **50.** $-2y^2 + y - 5$ (Obj. 7.1.2)   **51.** $144x^{14}y^{18}z^{16}$ (Obj. 7.2.2)

52. $-12x^4 - 17x^3 - 2x^2 - 33x - 27$ (Obj. 7.3.2)   **53.** $64a^2 + 16a + 1$ (Obj. 7.3.4)   **54.** $\dfrac{2}{ab^6}$ (Obj. 7.4.1)

55. $b^2 + 5b + 2 + \dfrac{7}{b-7}$ (Obj. 7.4.4)   **56.** The area is $(20x^2 - 35x)$ m². (Obj. 7.3.5)   **57.** The area is $(25x^2 + 40x + 16)$ in². (Obj. 7.3.5)   **58.** The area is $(9x^2 - 4)$ ft². (Obj. 7.3.5)   **59.** The area is $(\pi x^2 - 12\pi x + 36\pi)$ cm². (Obj. 7.3.5)   **60.** The area is $(15x^2 - 28x - 32)$ mi². (Obj. 7.3.5)

CHAPTER TEST

1. $3x^3 + 6x^2 - 8x + 3$ (Obj. 7.1.1)   **2.** $-4x^4 + 8x^3 - 3x^2 - 14x + 21$ (Obj. 7.3.2)   **3.** $4x^3 - 6x^2$ (Obj. 7.3.1)
4. $-8a^6b^3$ (Obj. 7.2.2)   **5.** $-4x^6$ (Obj. 7.4.1)   **6.** $\dfrac{6b}{a}$ (Obj. 7.4.1)   **7.** $-5a^3 + 3a^2 - 4a + 3$ (Obj. 7.1.2)

8. $a^2 + 3ab - 10b^2$ (Obj. 7.3.3)   **9.** $4x^4 - 2x^2 + 5$ (Obj. 7.4.3)   **10.** $2x + 3 + \dfrac{2}{2x-3}$ (Obj. 7.4.4)

11. $-6x^3y^6$ (Obj. 7.2.1)   **12.** $6y^4 - 9y^3 + 18y^2$ (Obj. 7.3.1)   **13.** $\dfrac{9}{x^3}$ (Obj. 7.4.1)   **14.** $4x^2 - 20x + 25$

(Obj. 7.3.4)   **15.** $10x^2 - 43xy + 28y^2$ (Obj. 7.3.3)   **16.** $x^3 - 7x^2 + 17x - 15$ (Obj. 7.3.2)   **17.** $\dfrac{a^4}{b^6}$ (Obj. 7.4.1)
18. $2.9 \cdot 10^{-5}$ (Obj. 7.4.2)   **19.** $16y^2 - 9$ (Obj. 7.3.4)   **20.** $3y^3 + 2y^2 - 10y$ (Obj. 7.1.2)   **21.** $9a^6b^4$

(Obj. 7.2.2)   **22.** $10a^3 - 39a^2 + 20a - 21$ (Obj. 7.3.2)   **23.** $9b^2 + 12b + 4$ (Obj. 7.3.4)   **24.** $-\dfrac{1}{4a^2b^5}$

(Obj. 7.4.1)   **25.** $4x + 8 + \dfrac{21}{2x-3}$ (Obj. 7.4.4)   **26.** a^3b^7 (Obj. 7.2.1)   **27.** $a^2 + ab - 12b^2$ (Obj. 7.3.3)
28. 0.000000035 (Obj. 7.4.2)   **29.** The area is $(4x^2 + 12x + 9)$ m². (Obj. 7.3.5)   **30.** The area is $(\pi x^2 - 10\pi x + 25\pi)$ in². (Obj. 7.3.5)

CUMULATIVE REVIEW EXERCISES

1. $\dfrac{1}{144}$ (Obj. 1.3.3)   **2.** $\dfrac{25}{9}$ (Obj. 1.4.1)   **3.** $\dfrac{4}{5}$ (Obj. 1.4.2)   **4.** 87 (Obj. 1.1.2)   **5.** 0.775 (Obj. 1.3.1)

6. $-\dfrac{27}{4}$ (Obj. 2.1.1)   **7.** $-x - 4xy$ (Obj. 2.2.2)   **8.** $-12x$ (Obj. 2.2.3)   **9.** $-22x + 20$ (Obj. 2.2.5)
10. 8 (Obj. 2.2.1)   **11.** -18 (Obj. 3.1.3)   **12.** 16 (Obj. 3.2.2)   **13.** 12 (Obj. 3.2.3)   **14.** 80 (Obj. 3.2.2)
15. 24% (Obj. 3.1.4)   **16.** $x \geq -3$ (Obj. 3.3.3)   **17.** $-\dfrac{9}{5}$ (Obj. 5.3.1)   **18.** $y = -\dfrac{3}{2}x - \dfrac{3}{2}$

(Obj. 5.4.1/5.4.2)   **19.**   (Obj. 5.2.3)   **20.**   (Obj. 5.6.1)

21. Domain: $\{-8, -6, -4, -2\}$; range: $\{-7, -5, -2, 0\}$; yes (Obj. 5.5.1)   **22.** -2 (Obj. 5.5.1)
23. $(4, 1)$ (Obj. 6.2.1)   **24.** $(1, -4)$ (Obj. 6.3.1)   **25.** $5b^3 - 7b^2 + 8b - 10$ (Obj. 7.1.2)
26. $15x^3 - 26x^2 + 11x - 4$ (Obj. 7.3.2)   **27.** $20b^2 - 47b + 24$ (Obj. 7.3.3)   **28.** $25b^2 + 30b + 9$ (Obj. 7.3.4)
29. $-\dfrac{b^4}{4a}$ (Obj. 7.4.1)   **30.** $5y - 4 + \dfrac{1}{y}$ (Obj. 7.4.3)   **31.** $a - 7$ (Obj. 7.4.4)   **32.** $\dfrac{9y^2}{x^6}$ (Obj. 7.4.1)
33. $\{1, 9, 17, 21, 25\}$ (Obj. 5.5.1)   **34.** $5(n - 12); 5n - 60$ (Obj. 2.3.3)   **35.** $8n - 2n = 18; n = 3$ (Obj. 4.1.1)
36. The length is 15 m. The width is 6 m. (Obj. 4.3.1)   **37.** The selling price is $43.20. (Obj. 4.4.1)
38. The concentration of orange juice is 28%. (Obj. 4.6.2)   **39.** The car overtakes the cyclist 25 mi from the starting point. (Obj. 4.7.1)   **40.** The area is $(9x^2 + 12x + 4)$ ft². (Obj. 7.3.5)

ANSWERS to Chapter 8 Odd-Numbered Exercises

CONCEPT REVIEW 8.1

1. Always true   **3.** Always true   **5.** Never true   **7.** Never true

SECTION 8.1

3. x^3 **5.** xy^4 **7.** xy^4z^2 **9.** $7a^3$ **11.** 1   **13.** $3a^2b^2$ **15.** ab **17.** $2x$ **19.** $3x$ **21.** $5(a+1)$
23. $8(2-a^2)$ **25.** $4(2x+3)$ **27.** $6(5a-1)$ **29.** $x(7x-3)$ **31.** $a^2(3+5a^3)$ **33.** $y(14y+11)$
35. $2x(x^3-2)$ **37.** $2x^2(5x^2-6)$ **39.** $xy(x-y^2)$ **41.** $2a^2b+3xy^3$ **43.** $6b^2(a^2b-2)$ **45.** $2abc(3a+2b)$
47. $9(2x^2y^2-a^2b^2)$ **49.** $6x^3y^3(1-2x^3y^3)$ **51.** $x(x^2-3x-1)$ **53.** $2(x^2+4x-6)$ **55.** $b(b^2-5b-7)$
57. $4(2y^2-3y+8)$ **59.** $5y(y^2-4y+2)$ **61.** $3y^2(y^2-3y-2)$ **63.** $3y(y^2-3y+8)$ **65.** $a^2(6a^3-3a-2)$
67. $x^2(8y^2-4y+1)$ **69.** $x^3y^3(4x^2y^2-8xy+1)$ **71.** $(a+b)(x+2)$ **73.** $(b+2)(x-y)$ **75.** $(x-2)(a-5)$
77. $(y-3)(b-3)$ **79.** $(x-y)(a+2)$ **81.** $(x+4)(x^2+3)$ **83.** $(y+2)(2y^2+3)$ **85.** $(a+3)(b-2)$
87. $(a-2)(x^2-3)$ **89.** $(a-b)(3x-2y)$ **91.** $(x-3)(x+4a)$ **93.** $(x-5)(y-2)$ **95.** $(7x+2y)(3x-7)$
97. $(2r+a)(a-1)$ **99.** $(4x+3y)(x-4)$ **101.** $(2y-3)(5xy+3)$ **103. a.** $(x+3)(2x+5)$
b. $(2x+5)(x+3)$ **105. a.** $(a-b)(2a-3b)$ **b.** $(2a-3b)(a-b)$ **107.** 28   **109.** P doubles

CONCEPT REVIEW 8.2

1. Never true   **3.** Always true   **5.** Never true

SECTION 8.2

1. $(x+1)(x+2)$ **3.** $(x+1)(x-2)$ **5.** $(a+4)(a-3)$ **7.** $(a-1)(a-2)$ **9.** $(a+2)(a-1)$
11. $(b-3)(b-3)$ **13.** $(b+8)(b-1)$ **15.** $(y+11)(y-5)$ **17.** $(y-2)(y-3)$ **19.** $(z-5)(z-9)$
21. $(z+8)(z-20)$ **23.** $(p+3)(p+9)$ **25.** $(x+10)(x+10)$ **27.** $(b+4)(b+5)$ **29.** $(x+3)(x-14)$
31. $(b+4)(b-5)$ **33.** $(y+3)(y-17)$ **35.** $(p+3)(p-7)$ **37.** Nonfactorable over the integers
39. $(x-5)(x-15)$ **41.** $(x-7)(x-8)$ **43.** $(x+8)(x-7)$ **45.** $(a+3)(a-24)$ **47.** $(a-3)(a-12)$
49. $(z+8)(z-17)$ **51.** $(c+9)(c-10)$ **53.** $2(x+1)(x+2)$ **55.** $3(a+3)(a-2)$ **57.** $a(b+5)(b-3)$
59. $x(y-2)(y-3)$ **61.** $z(z-3)(z-4)$ **63.** $3y(y-2)(y-3)$ **65.** $3(x+4)(x-3)$ **67.** $5(z+4)(z-7)$
69. $2a(a+8)(a-4)$ **71.** $(x-2y)(x-3y)$ **73.** $(a-4b)(a-5b)$ **75.** $(x+4y)(x-7y)$
77. Nonfactorable over the integers   **79.** $z^2(z-5)(z-7)$ **81.** $b^2(b-10)(b-12)$ **83.** $2y^2(y+3)(y-16)$
85. $x^2(x+8)(x-1)$ **87.** $4y(x+7)(x-2)$ **89.** $8(y-1)(y-3)$ **91.** $c(c+3)(c+10)$ **93.** $3x(x-3)(x-9)$
95. $(x-3y)(x-5y)$ **97.** $(a-6b)(a-7b)$ **99.** $(y+z)(y+7z)$ **101.** $3y(x+21)(x-1)$
103. $3x(x+4)(x-3)$ **105.** $4z(z+11)(z-3)$ **107.** $(c+4)(c+5)$ **109.** $a^2(b-5)(b-9)$
111. $36, 12, -12, -36$ **113.** $22, 10, -10, -22$ **115.** $3, 4$ **117.** $5, 8, 9$ **119.** 2

CONCEPT REVIEW 8.3

1. Never true   **3.** Sometimes true   **5.** Always true

SECTION 8.3

1. $(x+1)(2x+1)$ **3.** $(y+3)(2y+1)$ **5.** $(a-1)(2a-1)$ **7.** $(b-5)(2b-1)$ **9.** $(x+1)(2x-1)$
11. $(x-3)(2x+1)$ **13.** Nonfactorable over the integers   **15.** $(2t-1)(3t-4)$ **17.** $(x+4)(8x+1)$
19. $(b-4)(3b-4)$ **21.** $(z-14)(2z+1)$ **23.** $(p+8)(3p-2)$ **25.** $(2x-3)(3x-4)$
27. $(b+7)(5b-2)$ **29.** $(2a-3)(3a+8)$ **31.** $(3t+1)(6t-5)$ **33.** $(3a+7)(5a-3)$

35. $(2y - 5)(4y - 3)$ **37.** $(2z + 3)(4z - 5)$ **39.** $(x + 5)(3x - 1)$ **41.** $(3x + 4)(4x + 3)$
43. Nonfactorable over the integers   **45.** $(x + y)(3x - 2y)$ **47.** $(4 + z)(7 - z)$ **49.** $(1 - x)(8 + x)$
51. $3(x + 5)(3x - 4)$ **53.** $4(2x - 3)(3x - 2)$ **55.** $a^2(5a + 2)(7a - 1)$ **57.** $5(b - 7)(3b - 2)$
59. $2x(x + 1)(5x + 1)$ **61.** $2y(y - 4)(5y - 2)$ **63.** $yz(z + 2)(4z - 3)$ **65.** $b^2(4b + 5)(5b + 4)$
67. $xy(3x + 2)(3x + 2)$ **69.** $(t + 2)(2t - 5)$ **71.** $(p - 5)(3p - 1)$ **73.** $(3y - 1)(4y - 1)$
75. Nonfactorable over the integers   **77.** $(3y + 1)(4y + 5)$ **79.** $(a + 7)(7a - 2)$ **81.** $(z + 2)(4z + 3)$
83. $(2p + 5)(11p - 2)$ **85.** $(y + 1)(8y + 9)$ **87.** $(2b - 3)(3b - 2)$ **89.** $(3b + 5)(11b - 7)$
91. $(3y - 4)(6y - 5)$ **93.** Nonfactorable over the integers   **95.** $(2z - 5)(5z - 2)$ **97.** $(6z + 5)(6z + 7)$
99. $(2y - 3)(7y - 4)$ **101.** $(x + 6)(6x - 1)$ **103.** $3(x + 3)(4x - 1)$ **105.** $10(y + 1)(3y - 2)$
107. $x(x + 1)(2x - 5)$ **109.** $(a - 3b)(2a - 3b)$ **111.** $(y + z)(2y + 5z)$ **113.** $(1 + x)(18 - x)$
115. $4(9y + 1)(10y - 1)$ **117.** $8(t + 4)(2t - 3)$ **119.** $p(2p + 1)(3p + 1)$ **121.** $3(2z - 5)(5z - 2)$
123. $3a(2a + 3)(7a - 3)$ **125.** $y(3x - 5y)(3x - 5y)$ **127.** $xy(3x - 4y)(3x - 4y)$ **129.** $2y(y - 3)(4y - 1)$
131. $ab(a + 4)(a - 6)$ **133.** $5t(3 + 2t)(4 - t)$ **135.** $(y + 3)(2y + 1)$ **137.** $(2x - 1)(5x + 7)$
139. $7, 5, -7, -5$ **141.** $7, -7, 5, -5$ **143.** $11, -11, 7, -7$ **145.** $(x + 2)(x - 3)(x - 1)$

CONCEPT REVIEW 8.4

1. Never true   **3.** Sometimes true   **5.** Always true   **7.** Never true

SECTION 8.4

3. $(x + 2)(x - 2)$ **5.** $(a + 9)(a - 9)$ **7.** $(2x + 1)(2x - 1)$ **9.** $(y + 1)^2$ **11.** $(a - 1)^2$ **13.** Nonfactorable over the integers   **15.** $(x^3 + 3)(x^3 - 3)$ **17.** $(5x + 1)(5x - 1)$ **19.** $(1 + 7x)(1 - 7x)$ **21.** $(x + y)^2$
23. $(2a + 1)^2$ **25.** $(8a - 1)^2$ **27.** Nonfactorable over the integers   **29.** $(x^2 + y)(x^2 - y)$
31. $(3x + 4y)(3x - 4y)$ **33.** $(4b + 1)^2$ **35.** $(2b + 7)^2$ **37.** $(5a + 3b)^2$ **39.** $(xy + 2)(xy - 2)$
41. $(4 + xy)(4 - xy)$ **43.** $(2y - 9z)^2$ **45.** $(3ab - 1)^2$ **47.** $(m^2 + 16)(m + 4)(m - 4)$ **49.** $(x + 1)(9x + 4)$
51. $(y^4 + 9)(y^2 + 3)(y^2 - 3)$ **53.** $2(x + 3)(x - 3)$ **55.** $x^2(x + 7)(x - 5)$ **57.** $5(b + 3)(b + 12)$
59. Nonfactorable over the integers   **61.** $2y(x + 11)(x - 3)$ **63.** $x(x^2 - 6x - 5)$ **65.** $3(y^2 - 12)$
67. $(2a + 1)(10a + 1)$ **69.** $y^2(x + 1)(x - 8)$ **71.** $5(a + b)(2a - 3b)$ **73.** $2(5 + x)(5 - x)$
75. $ab(3a - b)(4a + b)$ **77.** $2(x - 1)(a + b)$ **79.** $3a(2a - 1)^2$ **81.** $3(81 + a^2)$ **83.** $2a(2a - 5)(3a - 4)$
85. $(x - 2)(x + 1)(x - 1)$ **87.** $a(2a + 5)^2$ **89.** $3b(3a - 1)^2$ **91.** $6(4 + x)(2 - x)$ **93.** $(x + 2)(x - 2)(a + b)$
95. $x^2(x + y)(x - y)$ **97.** $2a(3a + 2)^2$ **99.** $b(2 - 3a)(1 + 2a)$ **101.** $(x - 5)(2 + x)(2 - x)$ **103.** $8x(3y + 1)^2$
105. $y^2(5 + x)(3 - x)$ **107.** $y(y + 3)(y - 3)$ **109.** $2x^2y^2(x + 1)(x - 1)$ **111.** $x^5(x^2 + 1)(x + 1)(x - 1)$
113. $2xy(3x - 2)(4x + 5)$ **115.** $x^2y^2(2x - 5)^2$ **117.** $(x - 2)^2(x + 2)$ **119.** $4xy^2(1 - x)(2 - 3x)$
121. $2ab(2a - 3b)(9a - 2b)$ **123.** $x^2y^2(1 - 3x)(5 + 4x)$ **125.** $(4x - 3 + y)(4x - 3 - y)$
127. $(x - 2 + y)(x - 2 - y)$ **129.** $12, -12$ **131.** $12, -12$ **133.** 9   **135.** 1   **137.** 4   **139.** 3
141. $(x + 2)(x^2 - 2x + 4)$ **143.** $(y - 3)(y^2 + 3y + 9)$ **145.** $(y + 4)(y^2 - 4y + 16)$ **147.** $(2x - 1)(4x^2 + 2x + 1)$

CONCEPT REVIEW 8.5

1. Always true   **3.** Always true   **5.** Never true

SECTION 8.5

3. $-3, -2$ **5.** $7, 3$ **7.** $0, 5$ **9.** $0, 9$ **11.** $0, -\dfrac{3}{2}$ **13.** $0, \dfrac{2}{3}$ **15.** $-2, 5$ **17.** $9, -9$ **19.** $\dfrac{7}{4}, -\dfrac{7}{4}$

21. $3, 5$ **23.** $8, -9$ **25.** $-\dfrac{1}{2}, 1$ **27.** $-\dfrac{2}{3}, -4$ **29.** $-7, 3$ **31.** $0, 7$ **33.** $-1, -4$ **35.** $2, 3$

37. $\dfrac{1}{2}, -4$ **39.** $\dfrac{1}{3}, 4$ **41.** $3, 9$ **43.** $9, -2$ **45.** $-1, -2$ **47.** $5, -9$ **49.** $4, -7$ **51.** $-2, -3$

53. $-8, -5$ **55.** $1, 3$ **57.** $-12, 5$ **59.** $3, 4$ **61.** $-\dfrac{1}{2}, -4$ **63.** The number is 6.   **65.** The numbers are 2 and 4.   **67.**   The integers are 4 and 5.   **69.**   The integers are 15 and 16.   **71.**   The base is 18 ft. The height is 6 ft.   **73.**   The length is 18 ft. The width is 8 ft.   **75.**   The length of a side of the original square is 4 m.   **77.**   The radius of the original circle is 3.81 in.   **79.**   The dimensions are 4 in. by 7 in.   **81.**   The object will hit the ground 10 s later.   **83.**   12 consecutive natural numbers beginning with 1 will give a sum of 78.   **85.**   There are 8 teams in the league.   **87.**   The ball will be 64 ft above the ground 2 s after it hits home plate.   **89.** $-\frac{3}{2}, -5$

91. $9, -3$ **93.** $0, 9$ **95.** $-6, 3$ **97.** 48 or 3   **99.** The length is 10 cm. The width is 7 cm.

CHAPTER REVIEW EXERCISES

1. $7y^3(2y^6 - 7y^3 + 1)$ (Obj. 8.1.1)   **2.** $(a - 4)(3a + b)$ (Obj. 8.1.2)   **3.** $(c + 2)(c + 6)$ (Obj. 8.2.1)
4. $a(a - 2)(a - 3)$ (Obj. 8.2.2)   **5.** $(2x - 7)(3x - 4)$ (Obj. 8.3.1/8.3.2)   **6.** $(y + 6)(3y - 2)$ (Obj. 8.3.1/8.3.2)
7. $(3a + 2)(6a - 5)$ (Obj. 8.3.1/8.3.2)   **8.** $(ab + 1)(ab - 1)$ (Obj. 8.4.1)   **9.** $4(y - 2)^2$ (Obj. 8.4.2)

10. $0, -\frac{1}{5}$ (Obj. 8.5.1)   **11.** $3ab(4a + b)$ (Obj. 8.1.1)   **12.** $(b - 3)(b - 10)$ (Obj. 8.2.1)

13. $(2x + 5)(5x + 2y)$ (Obj. 8.1.2)   **14.** $3(a + 2)(a - 7)$ (Obj. 8.2.2)   **15.** $n^2(n + 1)(n - 3)$ (Obj. 8.2.2)
16. Nonfactorable over the integers (Obj. 8.3.1/8.3.2)   **17.** $(2x - 1)(3x - 2)$ (Obj. 8.3.1/8.3.2)

18. Nonfactorable over the integers (Obj. 8.4.1)   **19.** $2, \frac{3}{2}$ (Obj. 8.5.1)   **20.** $7(x + 1)(x - 1)$ (Obj. 8.4.2)

21. $x^3(3x^2 - 9x - 4)$ (Obj. 8.1.1)   **22.** $(x - 3)(4x + 5)$ (Obj. 8.1.2)   **23.** $(a + 7)(a - 2)$ (Obj. 8.2.1)
24. $(y + 9)(y - 4)$ (Obj. 8.2.1)   **25.** $5(x - 12)(x + 2)$ (Obj. 8.2.2)   **26.** $-3, 7$ (Obj. 8.5.1)
27. $(a + 2)(7a + 3)$ (Obj. 8.3.1/8.3.2)   **28.** $(x + 20)(4x + 3)$ (Obj. 8.3.1/8.3.2)   **29.** $(3y^2 + 5z)(3y^2 - 5z)$

(Obj. 8.4.1)   **30.** $5(x + 2)(x - 3)$ (Obj. 8.2.2)   **31.** $-\frac{3}{2}, \frac{2}{3}$ (Obj. 8.5.1)   **32.** $2b(2b - 7)(3b - 4)$ (Obj. 8.3.1/8.3.2)

33. $5x(x^2 + 2x + 7)$ (Obj. 8.1.1)   **34.** $(x - 2)(x - 21)$ (Obj. 8.2.1)   **35.** $(3a + 2)(a - 7)$ (Obj. 8.1.2)
36. $(2x - 5)(4x - 9)$ (Obj. 8.3.1/8.3.2)   **37.** $10x(a - 4)(a - 9)$ (Obj. 8.2.2)   **38.** $(a - 12)(2a + 5)$
(Obj. 8.3.1/8.3.2)   **39.** $(3a - 5b)(7x + 2y)$ (Obj. 8.1.2)   **40.** $(a^3 + 10)(a^3 - 10)$ (Obj. 8.4.1)

41. $(4a + 1)^2$ (Obj. 8.4.1)   **42.** $\frac{1}{4}, -7$ (Obj. 8.5.1)   **43.** $10(a + 4)(2a - 7)$ (Obj. 8.3.1/8.3.2)

44. $6(x - 3)$ (Obj. 8.1.1)   **45.** $x^2y(3x^2 + 2x + 6)$ (Obj. 8.1.1)   **46.** $(d - 5)(d + 8)$ (Obj. 8.2.1)
47. $2(2x - y)(6x - 5)$ (Obj. 8.1.2)   **48.** $4x(x + 1)(x - 6)$ (Obj. 8.2.2)   **49.** $-2, 10$ (Obj. 8.5.1)
50. $(x - 5)(3x - 2)$ (Obj. 8.3.1/8.3.2)   **51.** $(2x - 11)(8x - 3)$ (Obj. 8.3.1/8.3.2)   **52.** $(3x - 5)^2$ (Obj. 8.4.1)
53. $(2y + 3)(6y - 1)$ (Obj. 8.3.1/8.3.2)   **54.** $3(x + 6)^2$ (Obj. 8.4.2)   **55.** The length is 100 yd. The width is
50 yd. (Obj. 8.5.2)   **56.** The length is 100 yd. The width is 60 yd. (Obj. 8.5.2)   **57.** The two integers are 4 and 5.
(Obj. 8.5.2)   **58.** The distance is 20 ft. (Obj. 8.5.2)   **59.** The width of the larger rectangle is 15 ft. (Obj. 8.5.2)
60. The length of a side of the original square was 20 ft. (Obj. 8.5.2)

CHAPTER TEST

1. $3y^2(2x^2 + 3x + 4)$ (Obj. 8.1.1)   **2.** $2x(3x^2 - 4x + 5)$ (Obj. 8.1.1)   **3.** $(p + 2)(p + 3)$ (Obj. 8.2.1)

4. $(x - 2)(a - b)$ (Obj. 8.1.2)   **5.** $\frac{3}{2}, -7$ (Obj. 8.5.1)   **6.** $(a - 3)(a - 16)$ (Obj. 8.2.1)   **7.** $x(x + 5)(x - 3)$

(Obj. 8.2.2)   **8.** $4(x + 4)(2x - 3)$ (Obj. 8.3.1/8.3.2)   **9.** $(b + 6)(a - 3)$ (Obj. 8.1.2)   **10.** $\frac{1}{2}, -\frac{1}{2}$ (Obj. 8.5.1)

11. $(2x + 1)(3x + 8)$ (Obj. 8.3.1/8.3.2)   **12.** $(x + 3)(x - 12)$ (Obj. 8.2.1)   **13.** $2(b + 4)(b - 4)$ (Obj. 8.4.2)
14. $(2a - 3b)^2$ (Obj. 8.4.1)   **15.** $(p + 1)(x - 1)$ (Obj. 8.1.2)   **16.** $5(x^2 - 9x - 3)$ (Obj. 8.1.1)
17. Nonfactorable over the integers. (Obj. 8.3.1/8.3.2)   **18.** $(2x + 7y)(2x - 7y)$ (Obj. 8.4.1)   **19.** $3, 5$
(Obj. 8.5.1)   **20.** $(p + 6)^2$ (Obj. 8.4.1)   **21.** $2(3x - 4y)^2$ (Obj. 8.4.2)   **22.** $2y^2(y + 1)(y - 8)$ (Obj. 8.2.2)
23. The length is 15 cm. The width is 6 cm. (Obj. 8.5.2)   **24.** The length of the base is 12 in. (Obj. 8.5.2)
25. The two integers are -13 and -12. (Obj. 8.5.2)

CUMULATIVE REVIEW EXERCISES

1. -8 (Obj. 1.2.2) **2.** -8.1 (Obj. 1.3.4) **3.** 4 (Obj. 1.4.2) **4.** -7 (Obj. 2.1.1) **5.** The Associative

Property of Addition (Obj. 2.2.1) **6.** $18x^2$ (Obj. 2.2.3) **7.** $-6x + 24$ (Obj. 2.2.5) **8.** $\dfrac{2}{3}$ (Obj. 3.1.3)

9. 5 (Obj. 3.2.3) **10.** $\dfrac{7}{4}$ (Obj. 3.2.2) **11.** 3 (Obj. 3.2.3) **12.** 35 (Obj. 3.1.4) **13.** $x \le -3$ (Obj. 3.3.3)

14. $x < \dfrac{1}{5}$ (Obj. 3.3.3) **15.** (Obj. 5.2.2) **16.** (Obj. 5.5.2)

17. Domain: $\{-5, -3, -1, 1, 3\}$; range: $\{-4, -2, 0, 2, 4\}$; yes (Obj. 5.5.1) **18.** 61 (Obj. 5.5.1)
19. (Obj. 5.6.1) **20.** $(2, -5)$ (Obj. 6.2.1) **21.** $(1, 2)$ (Obj. 6.3.1)

22. $3y^3 - 3y^2 - 8y - 5$ (Obj. 7.1.1) **23.** $-27a^{12}b^6$ (Obj. 7.2.2) **24.** $x^3 - 3x^2 - 6x + 8$ (Obj. 7.3.2)
25. $4x + 8 + \dfrac{21}{2x - 3}$ (Obj. 7.4.4) **26.** $\dfrac{y^6}{x^{12}}$ (Obj. 7.4.1) **27.** $(a - b)(3 - x)$ (Obj. 8.1.2)
28. $(x + 5y)(x - 2y)$ (Obj. 8.2.2) **29.** $2a^2(3a + 2)(a + 3)$ (Obj. 8.3.1/8.3.2) **30.** $(5a + 6b)(5a - 6b)$ (Obj. 8.4.1)
31. $3(2x - 3y)^2$ (Obj. 8.4.2) **32.** $\dfrac{4}{3}, -5$ (Obj. 8.5.1) **33.** $\{-11, -7, -3, 1, 5\}$ (Obj. 5.5.1) **34.** The average
daily high temperature was $-3°C$. (Obj. 1.2.5) **35.** The length is 15 cm. The width is 6 cm. (Obj. 4.3.1)
36. The pieces measure 4 ft and 6 ft. (Obj. 4.1.2) **37.** The maximum distance you can drive a Company A car
is 359 mi. (Obj. 4.8.1) **38.** $6500 must be invested at an annual simple interest rate of 11%. (Obj. 4.5.1)
39. The discount rate is 40%. (Obj. 4.4.2) **40.** The three integers are 10, 12, and 14. (Obj. 4.2.1)

ANSWERS to Chapter 9 Odd-Numbered Exercises

CONCEPT REVIEW 9.1

1. Always true **3.** Never true **5.** Always true **7.** Never true

SECTION 9.1

5. $\dfrac{3}{4x}$ **7.** $\dfrac{1}{x + 3}$ **9.** -1 **11.** $\dfrac{2}{3y}$ **13.** $-\dfrac{3}{4x}$ **15.** $\dfrac{a}{b}$ **17.** $-\dfrac{2}{x}$ **19.** $\dfrac{y - 2}{y - 3}$ **21.** $\dfrac{x + 5}{x + 4}$

23. $\dfrac{x + 4}{x - 3}$ **25.** $-\dfrac{x + 2}{x + 5}$ **27.** $\dfrac{2(x + 2)}{x + 3}$ **29.** $\dfrac{2x - 1}{2x + 3}$ **31.** $\dfrac{2}{3xy}$ **33.** $\dfrac{8xy^2ab}{3}$ **35.** $\dfrac{2}{9}$ **37.** $\dfrac{y^2}{x}$

39. $\dfrac{y(x + 4)}{x(x + 1)}$ **41.** $\dfrac{x^3(x - 7)}{y^2(x - 4)}$ **43.** $-\dfrac{y}{x}$ **45.** $\dfrac{x + 3}{x + 1}$ **47.** $\dfrac{x - 5}{x + 3}$ **49.** $-\dfrac{x + 3}{x + 5}$ **51.** $\dfrac{12x^4}{(x + 1)(2x + 1)}$

53. $-\dfrac{x + 3}{x - 12}$ **55.** $\dfrac{x + 2}{x + 4}$ **57.** $\dfrac{2x - 5}{2x - 1}$ **59.** $\dfrac{3x - 4}{2x + 3}$ **63.** $\dfrac{2xy^2ab^2}{9}$ **65.** $\dfrac{5}{12}$ **67.** $3x$ **69.** $\dfrac{y(x + 3)}{x(x + 1)}$

71. $\dfrac{x + 7}{x - 7}$ **73.** $-\dfrac{4ac}{y}$ **75.** $\dfrac{x - 5}{x - 6}$ **77.** 1 **79.** $-\dfrac{x + 6}{x + 5}$ **81.** $\dfrac{2x + 3}{2x - 6}$ **83.** $\dfrac{4x + 3}{2x - 1}$ **85.** $\dfrac{(2x + 5)(4x - 1)}{(2x - 1)(4x + 5)}$

87. $-6, 1$ **89.** $-1, 1$ **91.** $3, -2$ **93.** -3 **95.** $\dfrac{4}{3}, -\dfrac{1}{2}$ **97.** $\dfrac{4a}{3b}$ **99.** $\dfrac{8}{9}$ **101.** $\dfrac{x - 4}{y^4}$

103. $\dfrac{(x - 2)(x - 2)}{(x - 4)(x + 4)}$

CONCEPT REVIEW 9.2

1. Always true   **3.** Never true   **5.** Always true

SECTION 9.2

1. $24x^3y^2$ **3.** $30x^4y^2$ **5.** $8x^2(x + 2)$ **7.** $6x^2y(x + 4)$ **9.** $40x^3(x - 1)^2$ **11.** $4(x - 3)^2$
13. $(2x - 1)(2x + 1)(x + 4)$ **15.** $(x - 7)^2(x + 2)$ **17.** $(x + 4)(x - 3)$ **19.** $(x + 5)(x - 2)(x + 7)$
21. $(x - 7)(x - 3)(x - 5)$ **23.** $(x + 2)(x + 5)(x - 5)$ **25.** $(2x - 1)(x - 3)(x + 1)$

27. $(2x - 5)(x - 2)(x + 3)$ **29.** $(x + 3)(x - 5)$ **31.** $(x + 6)(x - 3)$ **33.** $\dfrac{4x}{x^2}; \dfrac{3}{x^2}$ **35.** $\dfrac{4x}{12y^2}; \dfrac{3yz}{12y^2}$

37. $\dfrac{xy}{x^2(x - 3)}; \dfrac{6x - 18}{x^2(x - 3)}$ **39.** $\dfrac{9x}{x(x - 1)^2}; \dfrac{6x - 6}{x(x - 1)^2}$ **41.** $\dfrac{3x}{x(x - 3)}; \dfrac{5}{x(x - 3)}$ **43.** $\dfrac{3}{(x - 5)^2}; -\dfrac{2x - 10}{(x - 5)^2}$

45. $\dfrac{3x}{x^2(x + 2)}; \dfrac{4x + 8}{x^2(x + 2)}$ **47.** $\dfrac{x^2 - 6x + 8}{(x + 3)(x - 4)}; \dfrac{x^2 + 3x}{(x + 3)(x - 4)}$ **49.** $\dfrac{3}{(x + 2)(x - 1)}; \dfrac{x^2 - x}{(x + 2)(x - 1)}$

51. $\dfrac{5}{(2x - 5)(x - 2)}; \dfrac{x^2 - 3x + 2}{(2x - 5)(x - 2)}$ **53.** $\dfrac{x^2 - 3x}{(x + 3)(x - 3)(x - 2)}; \dfrac{2x^2 - 4x}{(x + 3)(x - 3)(x - 2)}$ **55.** $-\dfrac{x^2 - 3x}{(x - 3)^2(x + 3)};$

$\dfrac{x^2 + 2x - 3}{(x - 3)^2(x + 3)}$ **57.** $\dfrac{3x^2 + 12x}{(x - 5)(x + 4)}; \dfrac{x^2 - 5x}{(x - 5)(x + 4)}; -\dfrac{3}{(x - 5)(x + 4)}$ **59.** $\dfrac{300}{10^4}; \dfrac{5}{10^4}$ **61.** $\dfrac{b^2}{b}; \dfrac{5}{b}$ **63.** $\dfrac{y - 1}{y - 1}; \dfrac{y}{y - 1}$

65. $\dfrac{x^2 + 1}{(x - 1)^3}; \dfrac{x^2 - 1}{(x - 1)^3}; \dfrac{x^2 - 2x + 1}{(x - 1)^3}$ **67.** $\dfrac{2b}{8(a + b)(a - b)}; \dfrac{a^2 + ab}{8(a + b)(a - b)}$ **69.** $\dfrac{x - 2}{(x + y)(x + 2)(x - 2)}; \dfrac{x + 2}{(x + y)(x + 2)(x - 2)}$

CONCEPT REVIEW 9.3

1. Never true   **3.** Never true   **5.** Always true

SECTION 9.3

1. $\dfrac{11}{y^2}$ **3.** $-\dfrac{7}{x + 4}$ **5.** $\dfrac{8x}{2x + 3}$ **7.** $\dfrac{5x + 7}{x - 3}$ **9.** $\dfrac{2x - 5}{x + 9}$ **11.** $\dfrac{-3x - 4}{2x + 7}$ **13.** $\dfrac{1}{x + 5}$ **15.** $\dfrac{1}{x - 6}$

17. $\dfrac{3}{2y - 1}$ **19.** $\dfrac{1}{x - 5}$ **23.** $\dfrac{4y + 5x}{xy}$ **25.** $\dfrac{19}{2x}$ **27.** $\dfrac{5}{12x}$ **29.** $\dfrac{19x - 12}{6x^2}$ **31.** $\dfrac{52y - 35x}{20xy}$

33. $\dfrac{13x + 2}{15x}$ **35.** $\dfrac{7}{24}$ **37.** $\dfrac{x + 90}{45x}$ **39.** $\dfrac{x^2 + 2x + 2}{2x^2}$ **41.** $\dfrac{2x^2 + 3x - 10}{4x^2}$ **43.** $\dfrac{3y^2 + 8}{3y}$ **45.** $\dfrac{x^2 + 4x + 4}{x + 4}$

47. $\dfrac{4x + 7}{x + 1}$ **49.** $\dfrac{-3x^2 + 16x + 2}{12x^2}$ **51.** $\dfrac{x^2 - x + 2}{x^2y}$ **53.** $\dfrac{16xy - 12y + 6x^2 + 3x}{12x^2y^2}$ **55.** $\dfrac{3xy - 6y - 2x^2 - 14x}{24x^2y}$

57. $\dfrac{9x + 2}{(x - 2)(x + 3)}$ **59.** $\dfrac{2(x + 23)}{(x - 7)(x + 3)}$ **61.** $\dfrac{2x^2 - 5x + 1}{(x + 1)(x - 3)}$ **63.** $\dfrac{4x^2 - 34x + 5}{(2x - 1)(x - 6)}$ **65.** $\dfrac{2a - 5}{a - 7}$

67. $\dfrac{4x + 9}{(x + 3)(x - 3)}$ **69.** $\dfrac{-x + 9}{(x + 2)(x - 3)}$ **71.** $\dfrac{14}{(x - 5)^2}$ **73.** $\dfrac{-2(x + 7)}{(x + 6)(x - 7)}$ **75.** $\dfrac{x - 2}{2x}$ **77.** $\dfrac{x^2 + x + 4}{(x - 2)(x + 1)(x - 1)}$

79. $\dfrac{x - 4}{x - 6}$ **81.** $\dfrac{2x + 1}{x - 1}$ **83.** 2   **85.** $\dfrac{b^2 + b - 7}{b + 4}$ **87.** $\dfrac{4n}{(n - 1)^2}$ **89.** $-\dfrac{3(x^2 + 8x + 25)}{(x - 3)(x + 7)}$ **91.** 1

93. $\dfrac{x^2 - x + 2}{(x + 5)(x + 1)}$ **95.** $\dfrac{2}{3}; \dfrac{3}{4}; \dfrac{4}{5}; \dfrac{50}{51}; \dfrac{100}{101}; \dfrac{1000}{1001}$ **97.** $\dfrac{6}{y} + \dfrac{7}{x}$ **99.** $\dfrac{2}{m^2n} + \dfrac{8}{mn^2}$

CONCEPT REVIEW 9.4

1. Sometimes true   **3.** Never true   **5.** Always true

SECTION 9.4

1. $\dfrac{x}{x-3}$ **3.** $\dfrac{2}{3}$ **5.** $\dfrac{y+3}{y-4}$ **7.** $\dfrac{2(2x+13)}{5x+36}$ **9.** $\dfrac{3}{4}$ **11.** $\dfrac{x-2}{x+2}$ **13.** $\dfrac{x+2}{x+3}$ **15.** $\dfrac{x-6}{x+5}$ **17.** $-\dfrac{x-2}{x+1}$

19. $x-1$ **21.** $\dfrac{1}{2x-1}$ **23.** $\dfrac{x-3}{x+5}$ **25.** $\dfrac{x-7}{x-8}$ **27.** $\dfrac{2y-1}{2y+1}$ **29.** $\dfrac{x-2}{2x-5}$ **31.** $\dfrac{x-2}{x+1}$ **33.** $\dfrac{x-1}{x+4}$

35. $\dfrac{-x-1}{4x-3}$ **37.** $\dfrac{x+1}{2(5x-2)}$ **39.** $\dfrac{b+11}{4b-21}$ **41.** $\dfrac{5}{3}$ **43.** $-\dfrac{1}{x-1}$ **45.** $\dfrac{ab}{b+a}$ **47.** $\dfrac{y+4}{2(y-2)}$

CONCEPT REVIEW 9.5

1. Always true   **3.** Always true   **5.** Sometimes true   **7.** Always true

SECTION 9.5

3. 1   **5.** -3 **7.** $\dfrac{1}{2}$ **9.** 5   **11.** No solution   **13.** 2, 4   **15.** $-\dfrac{3}{2}$, 4   **17.** 3   **19.** -1 **21.** 4
25. 9   **27.** 36   **29.** 10   **31.** 113   **33.** -2 **35.** 15   **37.** 4   **39.** 20,000 people voted in favor of the amendment.   **41.** The office building requires 140 air vents.   **43.** For 2 c of boiling water, 6 c of sugar are required.   **45.** There are about 800 fish in the lake.   **47.** 14 vials are required to treat 175 people.   **49.** Yes, the shipment will be accepted.   **51.** The distance between the two cities is 750 mi.   **53.** For an annual yield of 1320 bushels, 10 additional acres must be planted.   **55.** The recommended area of a window is 40 ft². **57.** To serve 70 people, 2 additional gallons are necessary.   **59.** There are 160 ml of carbonated water in 280 ml of soft drink.
61. The measure of side *DE* is 12.8 in.   **63.** The height of triangle *DEF* is 4.7 ft.   **65.** The perimeter of triangle *ABC* is 18 m.   **67.** The area of triangle *ABC* is 48 cm².   **69.** The length of *BC* is 15 m.   **71.** The length of *QO* is 10 ft.   **73.** The perimeter of triangle *OPQ* is 12 m.   **75.** The height of the flagpole is 14.375 ft.   **77.** 1

79. $0, -\dfrac{2}{3}$ **81.** -3 and -4 **83.** The first person's share of the winnings was $1.25 million.   **85.** The cost would be $18.40.

CONCEPT REVIEW 9.6

1. Always true   **3.** Always true   **5.** Always true

SECTION 9.6

1. $h = \dfrac{2A}{b}$ **3.** $t = \dfrac{d}{r}$ **5.** $T = \dfrac{PV}{nR}$ **7.** $L = \dfrac{P-2W}{2}$ **9.** $b_1 = \dfrac{2A-hb_2}{h}$ **11.** $h = \dfrac{3V}{A}$ **13.** $S = C - Rt$

15. $P = \dfrac{A}{1+rt}$ **17.** $w = \dfrac{A}{S+1}$ **19. a.** $h = \dfrac{S-2\pi r^2}{2\pi r}$ **b.** 5 in.   **c.** 4 in.   **21. a.** $r = \dfrac{S-C}{S}$

b. 20%   **c.** 30%

CONCEPT REVIEW 9.7

1. Never true   **3.** Always true   **5.** Never true

SECTION 9.7

1. It will take 2 h to fill the fountain with both sprinklers operating.   **3.** It would take 3 h to remove the earth.
5. It would take the computers 30 h.   **7.** It would take 24 min to cool the room 5°F.   **9.** It would take the second welder 15 h.   **11.** It would take the second pipeline 90 min to fill the tank.   **13.** It would take 3 h to harvest the field using only the older reaper.   **15.** It will take the second technician 3 h.   **17.** It would take the

small unit $14\frac{2}{3}$ h. **19.** It would have taken one of the welders 40 h. **21.** The camper hiked at a rate of 5 mph. **23.** The rate of the jet was 360 mph. **25.** The rate of the boat for the first 15 mi was 7.5 mph. **27.** The family can travel 21.6 mi down the river. **29.** The technician traveled at a rate of 20 mph through the congested traffic. **31.** The rate of the river's current was 5 mph. **33.** The rate of the freight train was 30 mph. The rate of the express train was 50 mph. **35.** The rate of the car is 48 mph. **37.** The rate of the jet stream was 50 mph. **39.** The rate of the current is 5 mph. **41.** It would take $1\frac{1}{19}$ h to fill the tank. **43.** The amount of time spent traveling by canoe was 2 h. **45.** The bus usually travels at a rate of 60 mph.

CHAPTER REVIEW EXERCISES

1. $\dfrac{by^3}{6ax^2}$ (Obj. 9.1.2) **2.** $\dfrac{22x-1}{(3x-4)(2x+3)}$ (Obj. 9.3.2) **3.** $x=-\dfrac{3}{4}y+3$ (Obj. 9.6.1) **4.** $\dfrac{2x^4}{3y^7}$ (Obj. 9.1.1)

5. $\dfrac{1}{x^2}$ (Obj. 9.1.3) **6.** $\dfrac{x-2}{3x-10}$ (Obj. 9.4.1) **7.** $72a^3b^5$ (Obj. 9.2.1) **8.** $\dfrac{4x}{3x+7}$ (Obj. 9.3.1) **9.** $\dfrac{3x}{16x^2}$;

$\dfrac{10}{16x^2}$ (Obj. 9.2.2) **10.** $\dfrac{x-9}{x-3}$ (Obj. 9.1.1) **11.** $\dfrac{x-4}{x+3}$ (Obj. 9.1.3) **12.** $\dfrac{2y-3}{5y-7}$ (Obj. 9.3.2) **13.** $\dfrac{1}{x}$

(Obj. 9.1.2) **14.** $\dfrac{1}{x+3}$ (Obj. 9.3.1) **15.** $15x^4(x-7)^2$ (Obj. 9.2.1) **16.** 10 (Obj. 9.5.2) **17.** No solution

(Obj. 9.5.1) **18.** $-\dfrac{4a}{5b}$ (Obj. 9.1.1) **19.** $\dfrac{1}{x+3}$ (Obj. 9.3.1) **20.** 24 in. (Obj. 9.5.4) **21.** 5 (Obj. 9.5.1)

22. $\dfrac{x+9}{4x}$ (Obj. 9.4.1) **23.** $\dfrac{3x-1}{x-5}$ (Obj. 9.3.2) **24.** $\dfrac{x-3}{x+3}$ (Obj. 9.1.3) **25.** $-\dfrac{x+6}{x+3}$ (Obj. 9.1.1)

26. 2 (Obj. 9.5.1) **27.** $x-2$ (Obj. 9.4.1) **28.** $\dfrac{x+3}{x-4}$ (Obj. 9.1.2) **29.** 15 (Obj. 9.5.2) **30.** 12

(Obj. 9.5.2) **31.** $\dfrac{x}{x-7}$ (Obj. 9.4.1) **32.** $x=2y+15$ (Obj. 9.6.1) **33.** $\dfrac{3(3a+2b)}{ab}$ (Obj. 9.3.2)

34. $(5x-3)(2x-1)(4x-1)$ (Obj. 9.2.1) **35.** $c=\dfrac{100m}{i}$ (Obj. 9.6.1) **36.** 40 (Obj. 9.5.2) **37.** 3 (Obj. 9.5.1)

38. $\dfrac{7x+22}{60x}$ (Obj. 9.3.2) **39.** $\dfrac{8a+3}{4a-3}$ (Obj. 9.1.2) **40.** $\dfrac{3x^2-x}{(6x-1)(2x+3)(3x-1)}$; $\dfrac{24x^3-4x^2}{(6x-1)(2x+3)(3x-1)}$ (Obj. 9.2.2)

41. $\dfrac{2}{ab}$ (Obj. 9.3.1) **42.** 62 (Obj. 9.5.1) **43.** 6 (Obj. 9.5.1) **44.** $\dfrac{b^3y}{10ax}$ (Obj. 9.1.3) **45.** It would take the apprentice 6 h. (Obj. 9.7.1) **46.** The spring would stretch 8 in. (Obj. 9.5.3) **47.** The rate of the wind is 20 mph. (Obj. 9.7.2) **48.** To make 10 gal of the garden spray will require 16 additional ounces. (Obj. 9.5.3) **49.** Using both hoses, it would take 6 h to fill the pool. (Obj. 9.7.1) **50.** The rate of the car is 45 mph. (Obj. 9.7.2)

CHAPTER TEST

1. $\dfrac{x+5}{x+4}$ (Obj. 9.1.3) **2.** $\dfrac{2}{x+5}$ (Obj. 9.3.1) **3.** $3(2x-1)(x+1)$ (Obj. 9.2.1) **4.** -1 (Obj. 9.5.2)

5. $\dfrac{x+1}{x^3(x-2)}$ (Obj. 9.1.2) **6.** $\dfrac{x-3}{x-2}$ (Obj. 9.4.1) **7.** $\dfrac{3x+6}{x(x-2)(x+2)}$; $\dfrac{x^2}{x(x-2)(x+2)}$ (Obj. 9.2.2)

8. $x=-\dfrac{5}{3}y-5$ (Obj. 9.6.1) **9.** 2 (Obj. 9.5.1) **10.** $\dfrac{5}{(2x-1)(3x+1)}$ (Obj. 9.3.2) **11.** 1 (Obj. 9.1.3)

12. $\dfrac{3}{x+8}$ (Obj. 9.3.1) **13.** $6x(x+2)^2$ (Obj. 9.2.1) **14.** $-\dfrac{x-2}{x+5}$ (Obj. 9.1.1) **15.** 4 (Obj. 9.5.1)

16. $t=\dfrac{f-v}{a}$ (Obj. 9.6.1) **17.** $\dfrac{2x^3}{3y^5}$ (Obj. 9.1.1) **18.** $\dfrac{3}{(2x-1)(x+1)}$ (Obj. 9.3.2) **19.** 3 (Obj. 9.5.2)

20. $\dfrac{x^3(x+3)}{y(x+2)}$ (Obj. 9.1.2) **21.** $-\dfrac{3xy+3y}{x(x+1)(x-1)}$; $\dfrac{x^2}{x(x+1)(x-1)}$ (Obj. 9.2.2) **22.** $\dfrac{x+3}{x+5}$ (Obj. 9.4.1) **23.** For 15 gal of water, 2 lb of additional salt will be required. (Obj. 9.5.3) **24.** The rate of the wind is 20 mph. (Obj. 9.7.2) **25.** It would take both pipes 6 min to fill the tank. (Obj. 9.7.1)

CUMULATIVE REVIEW EXERCISES

1. -17 (Obj. 1.1.2)   **2.** -6 (Obj. 1.4.1)   **3.** $\frac{31}{30}$ (Obj. 1.4.2)   **4.** 21 (Obj. 2.1.1)   **5.** $5x - 2y$
(Obj. 2.2.2)   **6.** $-8x + 26$ (Obj. 2.2.4)   **7.** -20 (Obj. 3.2.1)   **8.** -12 (Obj. 3.2.3)   **9.** 10 (Obj. 3.1.4)
10. $x < \frac{9}{5}$ (Obj. 3.3.2)   **11.** $x \le 15$ (Obj. 3.3.3)   **12.**   (Obj. 5.2.2)

13.   (Obj. 5.5.2)   **14.**   (Obj. 5.2.3)   **15.**   (Obj. 5.6.1)

16. $\{-3, 5, 11, 19, 27\}$ (Obj. 5.5.1)   **17.** 37 (Obj. 5.5.1)   **18.** $\left(\frac{2}{3}, 3\right)$ (Obj. 6.2.1)   **19.** $\left(\frac{1}{2}, -1\right)$ (Obj. 6.3.1)
20. $-6x^4y^5$ (Obj. 7.2.1)   **21.** $a^{20}b^{15}$ (Obj. 7.2.2)   **22.** $\frac{a^3}{b^2}$ (Obj. 7.4.1)   **23.** $a^2 + ab - 12b^2$ (Obj. 7.3.3)
24. $3b^3 - b + 2$ (Obj. 7.4.3)   **25.** $x^2 + 2x + 4$ (Obj. 7.4.4)   **26.** $(4x + 1)(3x - 1)$ (Obj. 8.3.1/8.3.2)
27. $(y - 6)(y - 1)$ (Obj. 8.2.1)   **28.** $a(2a - 3)(a + 5)$ (Obj. 8.3.1/8.3.2)   **29.** $4(b + 5)(b - 5)$ (Obj. 8.4.2)
30. -3 and $\frac{5}{2}$ (Obj. 8.5.1)   **31.** $-\frac{x + 7}{x + 4}$ (Obj. 9.1.1)   **32.** 1 (Obj. 9.1.3)   **33.** $\frac{8}{(3x - 1)(x + 1)}$ (Obj. 9.3.2)
34. 1 (Obj. 9.5.1)   **35.** $a = \frac{f - v}{t}$ (Obj. 9.6.1)   **36.** $5x - 18 = -3; x = 3$ (Obj. 4.1.1)   **37.** $5000 must be
invested at an annual simple interest rate of 11%. (Obj. 4.5.1)   **38.** There is 70% silver in the 120-gram alloy.
(Obj. 4.6.2)   **39.** The base is 10 in. The height is 6 in. (Obj. 8.5.2)   **40.** It would take both pipes 8 min to fill
the tank. (Obj. 9.7.1)

ANSWERS to Chapter 10 Odd-Numbered Exercises

CONCEPT REVIEW 10.1

1. Never true   **3.** Always true   **5.** Sometimes true

SECTION 10.1

3. 4   **5.** 7   **7.** $4\sqrt{2}$ **9.** $2\sqrt{2}$ **11.** $18\sqrt{2}$ **13.** $10\sqrt{10}$ **15.** $\sqrt{15}$ **17.** $\sqrt{29}$ **19.** $-54\sqrt{2}$
21. $3\sqrt{5}$ **23.** 0   **25.** $48\sqrt{2}$ **27.** $\sqrt{105}$ **29.** 30   **31.** $30\sqrt{5}$ **33.** $5\sqrt{10}$ **35.** $4\sqrt{6}$ **37.** 18
39. 15.492   **41.** 16.971   **43.** 15.652   **45.** 18.762   **49.** x^3 **51.** $y^7\sqrt{y}$ **53.** a^{10} **55.** x^2y^2
57. $2x^2$ **59.** $2x\sqrt{6}$ **61.** $xy^3\sqrt{xy}$ **63.** $ab^5\sqrt{ab}$ **65.** $2x^2\sqrt{15x}$ **67.** $7a^2b^4$ **69.** $3x^2y^3\sqrt{2xy}$
71. $2x^5y^3\sqrt{10xy}$ **73.** $4a^4b^5\sqrt{5a}$ **75.** $8ab\sqrt{b}$ **77.** x^3y **79.** $8a^2b^3\sqrt{5b}$ **81.** $6x^2y^3\sqrt{3y}$ **83.** $4x^3y\sqrt{2y}$
85. $5a + 20$ **87.** $2x^2 + 8x + 8$ **89.** $x + 2$ **91.** $y + 1$ **93.** $0.05ab^2\sqrt{ab}$ **95.** $xy\sqrt{y + x}$
97. **a.** 1   **b.** 3   **c.** $3\sqrt{3}$ **99.** The length of a side of the square is 8.7 cm.   **101.** $x \ge 0$ **103.** $x \ge -5$
105. $x \le \frac{5}{2}$ **107.** All real numbers

CONCEPT REVIEW 10.2

1. Never true   **3.** Always true   **5.** Always true

SECTION 10.2

1. $3\sqrt{2}$ **3.** $-\sqrt{7}$ **5.** $-11\sqrt{11}$ **7.** $10\sqrt{x}$ **9.** $-2\sqrt{y}$ **11.** $-11\sqrt{3b}$ **13.** $2x\sqrt{2}$ **15.** $-3a\sqrt{3a}$
17. $-5\sqrt{xy}$ **19.** $8\sqrt{5}$ **21.** $8\sqrt{2}$ **23.** $15\sqrt{2} - 10\sqrt{3}$ **25.** $\sqrt{x}$ **27.** $-12x\sqrt{3}$ **29.** $2xy\sqrt{x} - 3xy\sqrt{y}$
31. $-9x\sqrt{3x}$ **33.** $-13y^2\sqrt{2y}$ **35.** $4a^2b^2\sqrt{ab}$ **37.** $7\sqrt{2}$ **39.** $6\sqrt{x}$ **41.** $-3\sqrt{y}$ **43.** $-45\sqrt{2}$
45. $13\sqrt{3} - 12\sqrt{5}$ **47.** $32\sqrt{3} - 3\sqrt{11}$ **49.** $6\sqrt{x}$ **51.** $-34\sqrt{3x}$ **53.** $10a\sqrt{3b} + 10a\sqrt{5b}$
55. $-2xy\sqrt{3}$ **57.** $-7b\sqrt{ab} + 4a^2\sqrt{b}$ **59.** $3ab\sqrt{2a} - ab + 4ab\sqrt{3b}$ **61.** $8\sqrt{x+2}$ **63.** $2x\sqrt{2y}$
65. $2ab\sqrt{6ab}$ **67.** $-11\sqrt{2x+y}$ **69.** The perimeter is $(6\sqrt{3} + 2\sqrt{15})$ cm.   **71.** The perimeter is 22.4 cm.
73. No

CONCEPT REVIEW 10.3

1. Always true   **3.** Always true   **5.** Sometimes true

SECTION 10.3

1. 5   **3.** 6   **5.** x **7.** x^3y^2 **9.** $3ab^6\sqrt{2a}$ **11.** $12a^4b\sqrt{b}$ **13.** $2 - \sqrt{6}$ **15.** $x - \sqrt{xy}$
17. $5\sqrt{2} - \sqrt{5x}$ **19.** $4 - 2\sqrt{10}$ **21.** $x - 6\sqrt{x} + 9$ **23.** $3a - 3\sqrt{ab}$ **25.** $10abc$
27. $15x - 22y\sqrt{x} + 8y^2$ **29.** $x - y$ **31.** $10x + 13\sqrt{xy} + 4y$ **35.** 4   **37.** 7   **39.** 3   **41.** $x\sqrt{5}$
43. $\dfrac{a^2}{7}$ **45.** $\dfrac{\sqrt{3}}{3}$ **47.** $\sqrt{3}$ **49.** $\dfrac{\sqrt{3x}}{x}$ **51.** $\dfrac{\sqrt{2x}}{x}$ **53.** $\dfrac{3\sqrt{x}}{x}$ **55.** $\dfrac{2\sqrt{y}}{xy}$ **57.** $\dfrac{4\sqrt{b}}{7b}$ **59.** $\dfrac{5\sqrt{6}}{27}$
61. $\dfrac{\sqrt{y}}{3xy}$ **63.** $\dfrac{2\sqrt{3x}}{3y}$ **65.** $-\dfrac{\sqrt{2}+3}{7}$ **67.** $\dfrac{15 - 3\sqrt{5}}{20}$ **69.** $\dfrac{x\sqrt{y} + y\sqrt{x}}{x - y}$ **71.** $\dfrac{\sqrt{3xy}}{3y}$ **73.** $-2 - \sqrt{6}$
75. $-\dfrac{\sqrt{10}+5}{3}$ **77.** $\dfrac{x - 3\sqrt{x}}{x - 9}$ **79.** $-\dfrac{1}{2}$ **81.** 7   **83.** -5 **85.** $\dfrac{7}{4}$ **87.** $-\dfrac{42 - 26\sqrt{3}}{11}$
89. $\dfrac{14 - 9\sqrt{2}}{17}$ **91.** $\dfrac{a - 5\sqrt{a} + 4}{2a - 2}$ **93.** $\dfrac{y + 5\sqrt{y} + 6}{y - 9}$ **95.** -1.3 **97.** $-\dfrac{4}{9}$ **99.** $\dfrac{3}{2}$ **101.** **a.** True
b. True   **c.** False; $x + 2\sqrt{x} + 1$ **d.** True   **103.** No

CONCEPT REVIEW 10.4

1. Sometimes true   **3.** Always true   **5.** Sometimes true

SECTION 10.4

3. 25   **5.** 144   **7.** 5   **9.** 16   **11.** 8   **13.** No solution   **15.** 6   **17.** 24   **19.** -1 **21.** $-\dfrac{2}{5}$
23. $\dfrac{4}{3}$ **25.** 15   **27.** 5   **29.** 1   **31.** 1   **33.** 1   **35.** 2   **37.** No solution   **39.** The number is 1.
41. The number is 11.   **45.** The length of the hypotenuse is 10.30 cm.   **47.** The length of the other leg of the triangle is 9.75 ft.   **49.** The length of the diagonal is 12.1 mi.   **51.** The depth of the water is 12.5 ft.   **53.** The pitcher's mound is more than halfway between homeplate and second base.   **55.** The periscope has to be 10.67 ft above the water.   **57.** Yes, the ladder will be long enough to reach the gutters.   **59.** The length of the pendulum is 7.30 ft.   **61.** The distance to the memorial is 250 ft.   **63.** The bridge is 64 ft high.   **65.** The height of the screen is 21.6 in.   **67.** 5   **69.** 8   **71.** **a.** The perimeter is $12\sqrt{2}$ cm.   **b.** The area is 12 cm^2.   **73.** The area is 244.78 ft^2.

CHAPTER REVIEW EXERCISES

1. $-11\sqrt{3}$ (Obj. 10.2.1)   **2.** $-x\sqrt{3} - x\sqrt{5}$ (Obj. 10.3.2)   **3.** $x + 8$ (Obj. 10.1.2)   **4.** No solution
(Obj. 10.4.1)   **5.** 1 (Obj. 10.3.2)   **6.** $7\sqrt{7}$ (Obj. 10.2.1)   **7.** $12a + 28\sqrt{ab} + 15b$ (Obj. 10.3.1)
8. $7x^2 + 42x + 63$ (Obj. 10.1.2)   **9.** 12 (Obj. 10.1.1)   **10.** 16 (Obj. 10.4.1)   **11.** $4x\sqrt{5}$ (Obj. 10.2.1)

12. $5ab - 7$ (Obj. 10.3.1)   **13.** 3   (Obj. 10.4.1)   **14.** $\sqrt{35}$ (Obj. 10.1.1)   **15.** $7x^2y\sqrt{15xy}$ (Obj. 10.2.1)

16. $\dfrac{x}{3y^2}$ (Obj. 10.3.2)   **17.** $9x - 6\sqrt{xy} + y$ (Obj. 10.3.1)   **18.** $a + 4$ (Obj. 10.1.2)   **19.** $20\sqrt{3}$ (Obj. 10.1.1)

20. $26\sqrt{3x}$ (Obj. 10.2.1)   **21.** $\dfrac{8\sqrt{x} + 24}{x - 9}$ (Obj. 10.3.2)   **22.** $3a\sqrt{2} + 2a\sqrt{3}$ (Obj. 10.3.1)   **23.** $9a^2\sqrt{2ab}$

(Obj. 10.1.2)   **24.** $-6\sqrt{30}$ (Obj. 10.1.1)   **25.** $-4a^2b^4\sqrt{5ab}$ (Obj. 10.2.1)   **26.** $7x^2y^4$ (Obj. 10.3.2)

27. $\dfrac{3}{5}$ (Obj. 10.4.1)   **28.** c^9 (Obj. 10.1.2)   **29.** $15\sqrt{2}$ (Obj. 10.1.1)   **30.** $18a\sqrt{5b} + 5a\sqrt{b}$ (Obj. 10.2.1)

31. $\dfrac{16\sqrt{a}}{a}$ (Obj. 10.3.2)   **32.** 8   (Obj. 10.4.1)   **33.** $a^5b^3c^2$ (Obj. 10.3.1)   **34.** $21\sqrt{70}$ (Obj. 10.1.1)

35. $2y^4\sqrt{6}$ (Obj. 10.1.2)   **36.** 5   (Obj. 10.3.2)   **37.** 5   (Obj. 10.4.1)   **38.** $8y + 10\sqrt{5y} - 15$ (Obj. 10.3.1)
39. 99.499   (Obj. 10.1.1)   **40.** 7   (Obj. 10.3.1)   **41.** $25x^4\sqrt{6x}$ (Obj. 10.1.2)   **42.** $-6x^3y^2\sqrt{2y}$ (Obj. 10.2.1)

43. $3a$ (Obj. 10.3.2)   **44.** $20\sqrt{10}$ (Obj. 10.1.1)   **45.** 20   (Obj. 10.4.1)   **46.** $\dfrac{7a}{3}$ (Obj. 10.3.2)

47. 10   (Obj. 10.3.1)   **48.** $6x^2y^2\sqrt{y}$ (Obj. 10.1.2)   **49.** $36x^8y^5\sqrt{3xy}$ (Obj. 10.1.2)   **50.** 3   (Obj. 10.4.1)
51. 20   (Obj. 10.1.1)   **52.** $-2\sqrt{2x}$ (Obj. 10.2.1)   **53.** 6   (Obj. 10.4.1)   **54.** 3   (Obj. 10.3.1)   **55.** The
larger integer is 51.   (Obj. 10.4.2)   **56.** The explorer's weight on the surface of the earth is 144 lb.   (Obj. 10.4.2)
57. The length of the other leg is 14.25 cm.   (Obj. 10.4.2)   **58.** The radius of the sharpest corner is 25 ft.
(Obj. 10.4.2)   **59.** The depth is 100 ft.   (Obj. 10.4.2)   **60.** The length of the guy wire is 26.25 ft.   (Obj. 10.4.2)

CHAPTER TEST

1. $11x^4y$ (Obj. 10.1.2)   **2.** $-5\sqrt{2}$ (Obj. 10.2.1)   **3.** $6x^2\sqrt{xy}$ (Obj. 10.3.1)   **4.** $3\sqrt{5}$ (Obj. 10.1.1)
5. $6x^3y\sqrt{2x}$ (Obj. 10.1.2)   **6.** $6\sqrt{2y} + 3\sqrt{2x}$ (Obj. 10.2.1)   **7.** $y + 8\sqrt{y} + 15$ (Obj. 10.3.1)   **8.** $\sqrt{2}$
(Obj. 10.3.2)   **9.** 9   (Obj. 10.3.2)   **10.** 11   (Obj. 10.4.1)   **11.** 22.361   (Obj. 10.1.1)   **12.** $4a^2b^5\sqrt{2ab}$
(Obj. 10.1.2)   **13.** $a - \sqrt{ab}$ (Obj. 10.3.1)   **14.** $4x^2y^2\sqrt{5y}$ (Obj. 10.3.1)   **15.** $7ab\sqrt{a}$ (Obj. 10.3.2)
16. 25   (Obj. 10.4.1)   **17.** $8x^6y^2\sqrt{3xy}$ (Obj. 10.1.2)   **18.** $4ab\sqrt{2ab} - 5ab\sqrt{ab}$ (Obj. 10.2.1)   **19.** $a - 4$
(Obj. 10.3.1)   **20.** $-6 - 3\sqrt{5}$ (Obj. 10.3.2)   **21.** 5   (Obj. 10.4.1)   **22.** $3\sqrt{2} - x\sqrt{3}$ (Obj. 10.3.1)
23. $-6\sqrt{a}$ (Obj. 10.2.1)   **24.** $6\sqrt{3}$ (Obj. 10.1.1)   **25.** 7.937   (Obj. 10.1.1)   **26.** $6ab\sqrt{a}$ (Obj. 10.3.2)
27. No solution   (Obj. 10.4.1)   **28.** The smaller integer is 40.   (Obj. 10.4.2)   **29.** The length of the pendulum
is 5.07 ft.   (Obj. 10.4.2)   **30.** The ladder is 9.80 ft high on the building.   (Obj. 10.4.2)

CUMULATIVE REVIEW EXERCISES

1. $-\dfrac{1}{12}$ (Obj. 1.4.2)   **2.** $2x + 18$ (Obj. 2.2.5)   **3.** $\dfrac{1}{13}$ (Obj. 3.2.3)   **4.** $x \le -\dfrac{9}{2}$ (Obj. 3.3.3)

5. $-\dfrac{4}{3}$ (Obj. 5.3.1)   **6.** $y = \dfrac{1}{2}x - 2$ (Obj. 5.4.1/5.4.2)   **7.** -18 (Obj. 5.5.1)

8.   (Obj. 5.5.2)   **9.**   (Obj. 5.6.1)   **10.** $(2, -1)$ (Obj. 6.1.1)

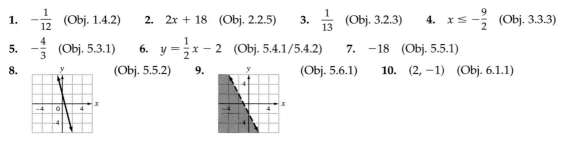

11. $(1, 1)$ (Obj. 6.2.1)   **12.** $(3, -2)$ (Obj. 6.3.1)   **13.** $\dfrac{6x^5}{y^3}$ (Obj. 7.4.1)   **14.** $-2b^2 + 1 - \dfrac{1}{3b^2}$ (Obj. 7.4.3)

15. $3x^2y^2(4x - 3y)$ (Obj. 8.1.1)   **16.** $(3b + 5)(3b - 4)$ (Obj. 8.3.1/8.3.2)   **17.** $2a(a - 3)(a - 5)$

(Obj. 8.2.2)   **18.** $\dfrac{1}{4(x + 1)}$ (Obj. 9.1.2)   **19.** $\dfrac{x - 5}{x - 3}$ (Obj. 9.4.1)   **20.** $\dfrac{x + 3}{x - 3}$ (Obj. 9.3.2)   **21.** $\dfrac{5}{3}$ (Obj. 9.5.1)

22. $38\sqrt{3a} - 35\sqrt{a}$ (Obj. 10.2.1)   **23.** 8   (Obj. 10.3.2)   **24.** 14   (Obj. 10.4.1)   **25.** The largest integer that
satisfies the inequality is -33.   (Obj. 4.8.1)   **26.** The cost is $24.50.   (Obj. 4.4.1)   **27.** 56 oz of pure water must be
added.   (Obj. 4.6.2)   **28.** The two numbers are 6 and 15.   (Obj. 4.1.2)   **29.** It would take the small pipe 48 h to fill
the tank.   (Obj. 9.7.1)   **30.** The smaller integer is 24.   (Obj. 10.4.2)

ANSWERS to Chapter 11 Odd-Numbered Exercises

CONCEPT REVIEW 11.1

1. Never true   **3.** Sometimes true   **5.** Always true

SECTION 11.1

1. $a = 3, b = -4, c = 1$ **3.** $a = 2, b = 0, c = -5$ **5.** $a = 6, b = -3, c = 0$ **7.** $x^2 - 3x - 8 = 0$
9. $x^2 - 16 = 0$ **11.** $2x^2 + 12x + 13 = 0$ **17.** -5 and 3 **19.** 1 and 3 **21.** -1 and -2 **23.** 3
25. 0 and $\frac{3}{2}$ **27.** -2 and 5 **29.** $\frac{2}{3}$ and 1 **31.** -3 and $\frac{1}{3}$ **33.** $-\frac{3}{2}$ and $\frac{4}{3}$ **35.** -3 and $\frac{4}{5}$ **37.** $\frac{1}{3}$
39. -4 and 4 **41.** $-\frac{2}{3}$ and $\frac{2}{3}$ **43.** $\frac{2}{3}$ and 2 **45.** -6 and $\frac{3}{2}$ **47.** $\frac{2}{3}$ **49.** -3 and 6 **51.** 0 and 12
53. -6 and 6 **55.** -1 and 1 **57.** $-\frac{7}{2}$ and $\frac{7}{2}$ **59.** $-\frac{2}{3}$ and $\frac{2}{3}$ **61.** $-\frac{3}{4}$ and $\frac{3}{4}$ **63.** There is no real
number solution.   **65.** $2\sqrt{6}$ and $-2\sqrt{6}$ **67.** -5 and 7 **69.** -7 and -3 **71.** -6 and 4 **73.** -9 and -1
75. 2 and 16 **77.** $-\frac{9}{2}$ and $-\frac{3}{2}$ **79.** $-\frac{1}{3}$ and $\frac{7}{3}$ **81.** $-\frac{12}{7}$ and $-\frac{2}{7}$ **83.** $4 + 2\sqrt{5}$ and $4 - 2\sqrt{5}$
85. There is no real number solution.   **87.** $\frac{1}{2} + \sqrt{6}$ and $\frac{1}{2} - \sqrt{6}$ **89.** $-\frac{4}{3}$ and $\frac{8}{3}$ **91.** $\sqrt{2}$ and $-\sqrt{2}$
93. 0 and 1 **95.** $\frac{\sqrt{ab}}{a}$ and $-\frac{\sqrt{ab}}{a}$ **97.** The speed is 10 m/s.

CONCEPT REVIEW 11.2

1. Always true   **3.** Always true   **5.** Never true

SECTION 11.2

1. $x^2 + 12x + 36; (x + 6)^2$ **3.** $x^2 + 10x + 25; (x + 5)^2$ **5.** $x^2 - x + \frac{1}{4}; \left(x - \frac{1}{2}\right)^2$ **7.** -3 and 1
9. $-2 + \sqrt{3}$ and $-2 - \sqrt{3}$ **11.** There is no real number solution.   **13.** $-3 + \sqrt{14}$ and $-3 - \sqrt{14}$ **15.** 2
17. $1 + \sqrt{2}$ and $1 - \sqrt{2}$ **19.** $\frac{-3 + \sqrt{13}}{2}$ and $\frac{-3 - \sqrt{13}}{2}$ **21.** -8 and 1 **23.** $-3 + \sqrt{5}$ and $-3 - \sqrt{5}$
25. $4 + \sqrt{14}$ and $4 - \sqrt{14}$ **27.** 1 and 2 **29.** $\frac{3 + \sqrt{29}}{2}$ and $\frac{3 - \sqrt{29}}{2}$ **31.** $\frac{1 + \sqrt{5}}{2}$ and $\frac{1 - \sqrt{5}}{2}$
33. $\frac{5 + \sqrt{13}}{2}$ and $\frac{5 - \sqrt{13}}{2}$ **35.** $\frac{-1 + \sqrt{13}}{2}$ and $\frac{-1 - \sqrt{13}}{2}$ **37.** $-5 + 4\sqrt{2}$ and $-5 - 4\sqrt{2}$ **39.** $\frac{-3 + \sqrt{5}}{2}$ and
$\frac{-3 - \sqrt{5}}{2}$ **41.** $\frac{1 + \sqrt{17}}{2}$ and $\frac{1 - \sqrt{17}}{2}$ **43.** There is no real number solution.   **45.** $\frac{1}{2}$ and 1 **47.** -3 and $\frac{1}{2}$
49. $\frac{1 + \sqrt{2}}{2}$ and $\frac{1 - \sqrt{2}}{2}$ **51.** $\frac{2 + \sqrt{5}}{2}$ and $\frac{2 - \sqrt{5}}{2}$ **53.** $3 + \sqrt{2}$ and $3 - \sqrt{2}$ **55.** $1 + \sqrt{13}$ and $1 - \sqrt{13}$
57. $\frac{3 + 3\sqrt{3}}{2}$ and $\frac{3 - 3\sqrt{3}}{2}$ **59.** $4 + \sqrt{7}$ and $4 - \sqrt{7}$ **61.** 1.193 and -4.193 **63.** 2.766 and -1.266
65. 0.151 and -1.651 **67.** -3 **69.** $6 + \sqrt{58}$ and $6 - \sqrt{58}$

CONCEPT REVIEW 11.3

1. Always true   **3.** Never true   **5.** Never true

SECTION 11.3

3. −7 and 1   **5.** −3 and 6   **7.** $1 + \sqrt{6}$ and $1 - \sqrt{6}$ **9.** $-3 + \sqrt{10}$ and $-3 - \sqrt{10}$ **11.** There is no real number solution.   **13.** $2 + \sqrt{13}$ and $2 - \sqrt{13}$ **15.** 0 and 1   **17.** $\dfrac{1 + \sqrt{2}}{2}$ and $\dfrac{1 - \sqrt{2}}{2}$ **19.** $-\dfrac{3}{2}$ and $\dfrac{3}{2}$

21. $\dfrac{3 + \sqrt{3}}{3}$ and $\dfrac{3 - \sqrt{3}}{3}$ **23.** $\dfrac{1 + \sqrt{10}}{3}$ and $\dfrac{1 - \sqrt{10}}{3}$ **25.** There is no real number solution.   **27.** $\dfrac{4 + \sqrt{10}}{2}$ and $\dfrac{4 - \sqrt{10}}{2}$ **29.** $-\dfrac{2}{3}$ and 3   **31.** $\dfrac{5 + \sqrt{73}}{6}$ and $\dfrac{5 - \sqrt{73}}{6}$ **33.** $\dfrac{1 + \sqrt{37}}{6}$ and $\dfrac{1 - \sqrt{37}}{6}$ **35.** $\dfrac{1 + \sqrt{41}}{5}$ and $\dfrac{1 - \sqrt{41}}{5}$

37. −3 and $\dfrac{4}{5}$ **39.** $-3 + 2\sqrt{2}$ and $-3 - 2\sqrt{2}$ **41.** $\dfrac{3 + 2\sqrt{6}}{2}$ and $\dfrac{3 - 2\sqrt{6}}{2}$ **43.** There is no real number solution.   **45.** $\dfrac{-1 + \sqrt{2}}{3}$ and $\dfrac{-1 - \sqrt{2}}{3}$ **47.** $-\dfrac{1}{2}$ and $\dfrac{2}{3}$ **49.** $\dfrac{-4 + \sqrt{5}}{2}$ and $\dfrac{-4 - \sqrt{5}}{2}$ **51.** $\dfrac{1 + 2\sqrt{3}}{2}$ and $\dfrac{1 - 2\sqrt{3}}{2}$

53. $-\dfrac{3}{2}$ **55.** $\dfrac{-5 + \sqrt{2}}{3}$ and $\dfrac{-5 - \sqrt{2}}{3}$ **57.** $\dfrac{1 + \sqrt{19}}{3}$ and $\dfrac{1 - \sqrt{19}}{3}$ **59.** $\dfrac{5 + \sqrt{65}}{4}$ and $\dfrac{5 - \sqrt{65}}{4}$

61. $6 + \sqrt{11}$ and $6 - \sqrt{11}$ **63.** 5.690 and −3.690   **65.** 7.690 and −1.690   **67.** 4.589 and −1.089
69. 0.118 and −2.118   **71.** 1.105 and −0.905   **73.** $3 + \sqrt{13}$ and $3 - \sqrt{13}$ **75. a.** False   **b.** False
c. False   **d.** True

CONCEPT REVIEW 11.4

1. Always true   **3.** Never true   **5.** Never true

SECTION 11.4

5. Up   **7.** Up   **9.** Up   **11.**   **13.**   **15.**   **17.**

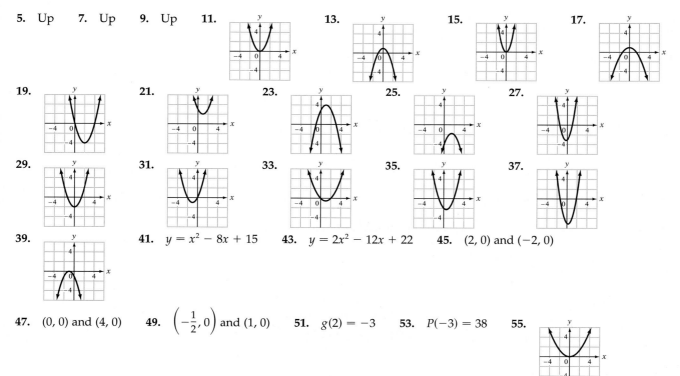

19.   **21.**   **23.**   **25.**   **27.**

29.   **31.**   **33.**   **35.**   **37.**

39.   **41.** $y = x^2 - 8x + 15$ **43.** $y = 2x^2 - 12x + 22$ **45.** $(2, 0)$ and $(-2, 0)$

47. $(0, 0)$ and $(4, 0)$ **49.** $\left(-\dfrac{1}{2}, 0\right)$ and $(1, 0)$ **51.** $g(2) = -3$ **53.** $P(-3) = 38$ **55.**

57.   **59.**   **61.** 3   **63.** No

CONCEPT REVIEW 11.5

1. Never true   **3.** Always true   **5.** Always true

SECTION 11.5

1. The length is 6 ft. The width is 4 ft.   **3.** The length is 100 ft. The width is 50 ft.   **5.** The two integers are 7 and 9.
7. The integers are 6 and 10, or −10 and −6.   **9.** It would take the first computer 35 min and the second computer
14 min.   **11.** It would take the first engine 12 h and the second engine 6 h.   **13.** The rate of the plane in calm air
was 100 mph.   **15.** The cyclist's rate during the first 150 mi was 50 mph.   **17.** The arrow will be 32 ft above the
ground at 1 s and at 2 s.   **19.** The maximum speed is 151.6 km/h.   **21.** The water from the hose is 244.1 ft from the
tugboat.   **23.** The ball hits the basket 1.88 s after it is released.   **25.** The radius of the base is 5.64 cm.   **27.** The
integers are −6, −5, −4 and −3, or 3, 4, 5, and 6.   **29.** The radius of the large pizza is 7 in.   **31.** The dimensions of
the cardboard are 20 in. by 20 in.

CHAPTER REVIEW EXERCISES

1. 4 and −4 (Obj. 11.1.2)   **2.** $\dfrac{1 + \sqrt{13}}{2}$ and $\dfrac{1 - \sqrt{13}}{2}$ (Obj. 11.2.1/11.3.1)   **3.** $\dfrac{3 + \sqrt{29}}{2}$ and $\dfrac{3 - \sqrt{29}}{2}$

(Obj. 11.2.1/11.3.1)   **4.** $\dfrac{5}{7}$ and $-\dfrac{5}{7}$ (Obj. 11.1.2)   **5.** (Obj. 11.4.1)   **6.** (Obj. 11.4.1)

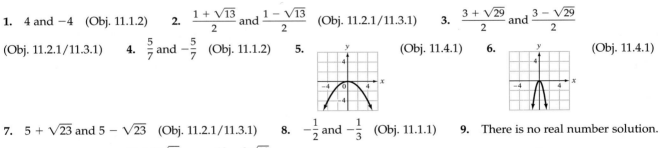

7. $5 + \sqrt{23}$ and $5 - \sqrt{23}$ (Obj. 11.2.1/11.3.1)   **8.** $-\dfrac{1}{2}$ and $-\dfrac{1}{3}$ (Obj. 11.1.1)   **9.** There is no real number solution.

(Obj. 11.1.2)   **10.** $\dfrac{-10 + 2\sqrt{10}}{5}$ and $\dfrac{-10 - 2\sqrt{10}}{5}$ (Obj. 11.2.1/11.3.1)   **11.** $2 + \sqrt{3}$ and $2 - \sqrt{3}$ (Obj. 11.2.1/11.3.1)

12. 6 and −5 (Obj. 11.1.1)   **13.** $\dfrac{4}{3}$ and $-\dfrac{7}{2}$ (Obj. 11.1.1)   **14.** $2\sqrt{10}$ and $2 - \sqrt{10}$ (Obj. 11.1.2)

15. $\dfrac{2 + \sqrt{7}}{3}$ and $\dfrac{2 - \sqrt{7}}{3}$ (Obj. 11.2.1/11.3.1)   **16.** $1 + \sqrt{11}$ and $1 - \sqrt{11}$ (Obj. 11.2.1/11.3.1)   **17.** 3 and 9

(Obj. 11.1.1)   **18.** 16 and −2 (Obj. 11.1.2)   **19.** (Obj. 11.4.1)   **20.** (Obj. 11.4.1)

21. 1 and −9 (Obj. 11.1.2)   **22.** $\dfrac{-4 + \sqrt{23}}{2}$ and $\dfrac{-4 - \sqrt{23}}{2}$ (Obj. 11.2.1/11.3.1)   **23.** $-\dfrac{1}{6}$ and $-\dfrac{5}{4}$ (Obj. 11.1.1)

24. There is no real number solution. (Obj. 11.2.1/11.3.1)   **25.** $4 + \sqrt{21}$ and $4 - \sqrt{21}$ (Obj. 11.2.1/11.3.1)

26. $\dfrac{4}{7}$ (Obj. 11.1.1)   **27.** 2 and −1 (Obj. 11.1.2)   **28.** $\dfrac{3}{8}$ and $\dfrac{3}{2}$ (Obj. 11.1.1)   **29.** $\dfrac{-7 + \sqrt{61}}{2}$ and $\dfrac{-7 - \sqrt{61}}{2}$

(Obj. 11.2.1/11.3.1)   **30.** 2 and $\dfrac{5}{12}$ (Obj. 11.1.1)   **31.** $3 + \sqrt{5}$ and $3 - \sqrt{5}$ (Obj. 11.1.2)   **32.** $-4 + \sqrt{19}$ and

$-4 - \sqrt{19}$ (Obj. 11.2.1/11.3.1)   **33.**   (Obj. 11.4.1)   **34.**   (Obj. 11.4.1)

35. -7 and -10 (Obj. 11.1.1)   **36.** $2 + 2\sqrt{6}$ and $2 - 2\sqrt{6}$ (Obj. 11.1.2)   **37.**   There is no real number solution.
(Obj. 11.2.1/11.3.1)   **38.** $-3 + \sqrt{11}$ and $-3 - \sqrt{11}$ (Obj. 11.2.1/11.3.1)   **39.** 3 and $-\dfrac{1}{9}$ (Obj. 11.1.1)

40. $\dfrac{-5 + \sqrt{33}}{4}$ and $\dfrac{-5 - \sqrt{33}}{4}$ (Obj. 11.2.1/11.3.1)   **41.**   (Obj. 11.4.1)   **42.** $\dfrac{9 + \sqrt{69}}{2}$ and $\dfrac{9 - \sqrt{69}}{2}$

(Obj. 11.2.1/11.3.1)   **43.** 1 and $\dfrac{5}{2}$ (Obj. 11.1.1)   **44.**   (Obj. 11.4.1)   **45.**   The rate of the air balloon

is 25 mph.   (Obj. 11.5.1)   **46.**   The height is 10 m. The base is 4 m.   (Obj. 11.5.1)   **47.**   The two integers are 3 and 5.
(Obj. 11.5.1)   **48.**   The rate of the boat in still water is 5 mph.   (Obj. 11.5.1)   **49.**   The object will be 12 ft above the
ground at $\dfrac{1}{2}$ s and $1\dfrac{1}{2}$ s.   (Obj. 11.5.1)   **50.**   It would take the smaller drain 12 h and the larger drain 4 h.   (Obj. 11.5.1)

CHAPTER TEST

1. $-4 + 2\sqrt{5}$ and $-4 - 2\sqrt{5}$ (Obj. 11.1.2)   **2.** $\dfrac{-4 + \sqrt{22}}{2}$ and $\dfrac{-4 - \sqrt{22}}{2}$ (Obj. 11.2.1/11.3.1)   **3.** -4 and $\dfrac{5}{3}$

(Obj. 11.1.1)   **4.** $\dfrac{3 + \sqrt{33}}{2}$ and $\dfrac{3 - \sqrt{33}}{2}$ (Obj. 11.2.1/11.3.1)   **5.** $-2 + 2\sqrt{5}$ and $-2 - 2\sqrt{5}$ (Obj. 11.2.1/11.3.1)

6.   (Obj. 11.4.1)   **7.** $-2 + \sqrt{2}$ and $-2 - \sqrt{2}$ (Obj. 11.2.1/11.3.1)

8. $\dfrac{-3 + \sqrt{41}}{2}$ and $\dfrac{-3 - \sqrt{41}}{2}$ (Obj. 11.2.1/11.3.1)   **9.** $-\dfrac{1}{2}$ and 3 (Obj. 11.1.1)   **10.** $\dfrac{3 + \sqrt{7}}{2}$ and $\dfrac{3 - \sqrt{7}}{2}$

(Obj. 11.2.1/11.3.1)   **11.** $\dfrac{1 + \sqrt{13}}{6}$ and $\dfrac{1 - \sqrt{13}}{6}$ (Obj. 11.2.1/11.3.1)   **12.** $5 + 3\sqrt{2}$ and $5 - 3\sqrt{2}$ (Obj. 11.1.2)

13. $3 + \sqrt{14}$ and $3 - \sqrt{14}$ (Obj. 11.2.1/11.3.1)   **14.** $\dfrac{5 + \sqrt{29}}{2}$ and $\dfrac{5 - \sqrt{29}}{2}$ (Obj. 11.2.1/11.3.1)   **15.** $\dfrac{5 + \sqrt{33}}{2}$ and

$\dfrac{5 - \sqrt{33}}{2}$ (Obj. 11.2.1/11.3.1)   **16.** $\dfrac{5}{2}$ and $\dfrac{1}{3}$ (Obj. 11.1.1)   **17.** $\dfrac{-3 + \sqrt{37}}{2}$ and $\dfrac{-3 - \sqrt{37}}{2}$ (Obj. 11.2.1/11.3.1)

18. $\dfrac{2 + \sqrt{14}}{2}$ and $\dfrac{2 - \sqrt{14}}{2}$ (Obj. 11.2.1/11.3.1)   **19.** $-\dfrac{1}{2}$ and 2 (Obj. 11.1.1)   **20.**   (Obj. 11.4.1)

21. $\dfrac{1 + \sqrt{10}}{3}$ and $\dfrac{1 - \sqrt{10}}{3}$ (Obj. 11.2.1/11.3.1)   **22.**   The length is 8 ft. The width is 5 ft.   (Obj. 11.5.1)

23. The rate of the boat in calm water is 11 mph.   (Obj. 11.5.1)   **24.** The middle odd integer is 5 or −5   (Obj. 11.5.1)
25. The rate for the last 8 mi was 4 mph.   (Obj. 11.5.1)

CUMULATIVE REVIEW EXERCISES

1. $-28x + 27$ (Obj. 2.2.5)   **2.** $\frac{3}{2}$ (Obj. 3.1.3)   **3.** 3   (Obj. 3.2.3)   **4.** $x > \frac{1}{9}$ (Obj. 3.3.3)

5. $(3, 0)$ and $(0, -4)$ (Obj. 5.2.3)   **6.** $y = -\frac{4}{3}x - 2$ (Obj. 5.4.1/5.4.2)   **7.** Domain: $\{-2, -1, 0, 1, 2\}$;

range: $\{-8, -1, 0, 1, 8\}$; yes   (Obj. 5.5.1)   **8.** 37   (Obj. 5.5.1)   **9.**   (Obj. 5.2.2)

10.   (Obj. 5.6.1)   **11.** $(2, 1)$ (Obj. 6.2.1)   **12.** $(2, -2)$ (Obj. 6.3.1)   **13.** $-\frac{4a}{3b^2}$ (Obj. 7.4.1)

14. $x + 2 - \frac{4}{x - 2}$ (Obj. 7.4.4)   **15.** $(x - 4)(4y - 3)$ (Obj. 8.1.2)   **16.** $x(3x - 4)(x + 2)$ (Obj. 8.3.1/8.3.2)

17. $\frac{9x^2(x - 2)(x - 4)}{(2x - 3)^2(x + 2)}$ (Obj. 9.1.3)   **18.** $\frac{x + 2}{2(x + 1)}$ (Obj. 9.3.2)   **19.** $\frac{x - 4}{2x + 5}$ (Obj. 9.4.1)   **20.** −3 and 6

(Obj. 9.5.1)   **21.** $a - 2$ (Obj. 10.3.1)   **22.** 5   (Obj. 10.4.1)   **23.** $\frac{1}{2}$ and 3   (Obj. 11.1.1)   **24.** $2 + 2\sqrt{3}$ and

$2 - 2\sqrt{3}$ (Obj. 11.1.2)   **25.** $\frac{2 + \sqrt{19}}{3}$ and $\frac{2 - \sqrt{19}}{3}$ (Obj. 11.2.1/11.3.1)   **26.**   (Obj. 11.4.1)

27. The cost is $36.   (Obj. 3.1.4)   **28.** The cost is $2.25 per pound.   (Obj. 4.6.1)   **29.** To earn a dividend of
$752.50, 250 additional shares are required.   (Obj. 9.5.2)   **30.** The rate of the plane in calm air is 200 mph. The rate of
the wind is 40 mph.   (Obj. 6.4.1)   **31.** The student must receive a score of 77 or better.   (Obj. 4.8.1)
32. The length of the guy wire is 31.62 m.   (Obj. 10.4.2)   **33.** The middle odd integer is −7 or 7.   (Obj. 11.5.1)

FINAL EXAM

1. −3   (Obj. 1.1.2)   **2.** −6   (Obj. 1.2.2)   **3.** 12.5%   (Obj. 1.3.2)   **4.** −256   (Obj. 1.4.1)

5. −11   (Obj. 1.4.2)   **6.** $-\frac{15}{2}$ (Obj. 2.1.1)   **7.** $9x + 6y$ (Obj. 2.2.2)   **8.** $6z$ (Obj. 2.2.3)

9. $16x - 52$ (Obj. 2.2.5)   **10.** −50   (Obj. 3.1.3)   **11.** −3   (Obj. 3.2.3)   **12.** 15.2   (Obj. 3.1.4)

13. $x \le -3$ (Obj. 3.3.3)   **14.** $y \ge \frac{5}{2}$ (Obj. 3.3.3)   **15.** $\frac{2}{3}$ (Obj. 5.3.1)   **16.** $y = -\frac{2}{3}x - 2$ (Obj. 5.4.1/5.4.2)

17.   (Obj. 5.3.2)   **18.**   (Obj. 5.5.2)   **19.** $\{-1, 2, 5, 8, 11\}$ (Obj. 5.5.1)

20.   (Obj. 5.6.1)   **21.** (6, 17) (Obj. 6.2.1)   **22.** (2, −1) (Obj. 6.3.1)

23. $-3x^2 - 3x + 8$ (Obj. 7.1.2)   **24.** $81x^4y^{12}$ (Obj. 7.2.2)   **25.** $6x^3 + 7x^2 - 7x - 6$ (Obj. 7.3.2)

26. $-\dfrac{x^8y}{2}$ (Obj. 7.4.1)   **27.** $\dfrac{16y^7}{x^8}$ (Obj. 7.4.1)   **28.** $3x^2 - 4x - \dfrac{5}{x}$ (Obj. 7.4.3)   **29.** $5x - 12 + \dfrac{23}{x + 2}$

(Obj. 7.4.4)   **30.** $3.9 \cdot 10^{-8}$ (Obj. 7.4.2)   **31.** $2(4 - x)(a + 3)$ (Obj. 8.1.2)   **32.** $(x - 6)(x + 1)$ (Obj. 8.2.1)

33. $(2x - 3)(x + 1)$ (Obj. 8.3.1/8.3.2)   **34.** $(3x + 2)(2x - 3)$ (Obj. 8.3.1/8.3.2)   **35.** $4x(2x - 1)(x - 3)$

(Obj. 8.3.1/8.3.2)   **36.** $(5x + 4)(5x - 4)$ (Obj. 8.4.1)   **37.** $3y(5 + 2x)(5 - 2x)$ (Obj. 8.4.2)   **38.** $\dfrac{1}{2}$ and 3

(Obj. 8.5.1/11.1.1)   **39.** $\dfrac{2(x + 1)}{x - 1}$ (Obj. 9.1.2)   **40.** $\dfrac{-3x^2 + x - 25}{(2x - 5)(x + 3)}$ (Obj. 9.3.2)   **41.** $x + 1$ (Obj. 9.4.1)

42. 2 (Obj. 9.5.1)   **43.** $a = b$ (Obj. 9.6.1)   **44.** $7x^3$ (Obj. 10.1.2)   **45.** $38\sqrt{3a}$ (Obj. 10.2.1)

46. $\sqrt{15} + 2\sqrt{3}$ (Obj. 10.3.2)   **47.** 5 (Obj. 10.4.1)   **48.** $3 + \sqrt{7}$ and $3 - \sqrt{7}$ (Obj. 11.1.2)   **49.** $\dfrac{1 + \sqrt{5}}{4}$ and

$\dfrac{1 - \sqrt{5}}{4}$ (Obj. 11.2.1/11.3.1)   **50.** (Obj. 11.4.1)   **51.** $2x + 3(x - 2); 5x - 6$ (Obj. 2.3.3)

52. The original value of the machine was $3000. (Obj. 3.1.4)   **53.** There are 60 dimes in the bank. (Obj. 4.2.2) **54.** The angles measure 60°, 50°, and 70°. (Obj. 4.3.3)   **55.** The markup rate is 65%. (Obj. 4.41)   **56.** $6000 must be invested at 11%. (Obj. 4.5.1)   **57.** The cost is $3 per pound. (Obj. 4.6.1)   **58.** The percent concentration is 36%. (Obj. 4.6.2)   **59.** The plane traveled 215 km during the first hour. (Obj. 4.7.1)   **60.** The rate of the boat is 15 mph. The rate of the current is 5 mph. (Obj. 6.4.1)   **61.** The length is 10 m. The width is 5 m. (Obj. 8.5.2)   **62.** 16 oz of dye are required. (Obj. 9.5.3)   **63.** It would take them 0.6 h to prepare the dinner. (Obj. 9.7.1)   **64.** The length of the other leg is 11.5 cm. (Obj. 10.4.2)   **65.** The rate of the wind is 25 mph. (Obj. 11.5.1)

GLOSSARY

abscissa   The first number in an ordered pair. It measures a horizontal distance and is also called the first coordinate. (Sec. 5.1)

absolute value of a number   The distance of the number from zero on the number line. (Sec. 1.1)

acute angle   An angle whose measure is between 0° and 90°. (Sec. 4.3)

addend   In addition, a number being added. (Sec. 1.2)

addition   The process of finding the total of two numbers. (Sec. 1.2)

addition method   An algebraic method of finding an exact solution of a system of linear equations. (Sec. 6.3)

additive inverses   Numbers that are the same distance from zero on the number line, but on opposite sides; also called opposites. (Sec. 1.1, 2.2)

adjacent angles   Two angles that share a common side. (Sec. 4.3)

algebraic fraction   A fraction in which the numerator and denominator are polynomials. (Sec. 9.1)

alternate exterior angles   Two angles that are on opposite sides of the transversal and outside the parallel lines. (Sec. 4.3)

alternate interior angles   Two angles that are on opposite sides of the transversal and between the parallel lines. (Sec. 4.3)

analytic geometry   Geometry in which a coordinate system is used to study the relationships between variables. (Sec. 5.1)

arithmetic mean of values   Average determined by calculating the sum of the values and then dividing that result by the number of values. (Sec. 1.2)

axes   The two number lines that form a rectangular coordinate system; also called coordinate axes. (Sec. 5.1)

base   In exponential notation, the factor that is multiplied the number of times shown by the exponent. (Sec. 1.4)

basic percent equation   Percent times base equals amount. (Sec. 3.1)

binomial   A polynomial of two terms. (Sec. 7.1)

clearing denominators   Removing denominators from an equation that contains fractions by multiplying each side of the equation by the LCM of the denominators. (Sec. 3.2, 9.5)

coefficient   The number part of a variable term. (Sec. 2.1)

combining like terms   Using the Distributive Property to add the coefficients of like variable terms; adding like terms of a variable expression. (Sec. 2.2)

complementary angles   Two angles whose sum is 90°. (Sec. 4.3)

completing the square   Adding to a binomial the constant term that makes it a perfect-square trinomial. (Sec. 11.2)

complex fraction   A fraction whose numerator or denominator contains one or more fractions. (Sec. 9.4)

conjugates   Binomial expressions that differ only in the sign of a term. The expressions $a + b$ and $a - b$ are conjugates. (Sec. 10.3)

consecutive even integers   Even integers that follow one another in order. (Sec. 4.2)

consecutive integers   Integers that follow one another in order. (Sec. 4.2)

consecutive odd integers   Odd integers that follow one another in order. (Sec. 4.2)

constant term   A term that includes no variable part; also called a constant. (Sec. 2.1)

coordinate axes   The two number lines that form a rectangular coordinate system; also simply called axes. (Sec. 5.1)

coordinates of a point   The numbers in an ordered pair that is associated with a point. (Sec. 5.1)

corresponding angles   Two angles that are on the same side of the transversal and are both acute angles or are both obtuse angles. (Sec. 4.3)

cost   The price that a business pays for a product. (Sec. 4.4)

decimal notation   Notation in which a number consists of a whole-number part, a decimal point, and a decimal part. (Sec. 1.3)

degree   A unit used to measure angles. (Sec. 4.3)

degree of a polynomial in one variable   The largest exponent that appears on the variable. (Sec. 7.1)

dependent system of equations   A system of equations that has an infinite number of solutions. (Sec. 6.1)

dependent variable   In a function, the variable whose value depends on the value of another variable known as the independent variable. (Sec. 5.5)

descending order   The terms of a polynomial in one variable arranged so that the exponents on the variable decrease from left to right. The polynomial $9x^5 - 2x^4 + 7x^3 + x^2 - 8x + 1$ is in descending order. (Sec. 7.1)

discount   The amount by which a retailer reduces the regular price of a product for a promotional sale. (Sec. 4.4)

discount rate   The percent of the regular price that the discount represents. (Sec. 4.4)

domain   The set of first coordinates of the ordered pairs in a relation. (Sec. 5.5)

element of a set   One of the objects in a set. (Sec. 1.1)

equation   A statement of the equality of two mathematical expressions. (Sec. 3.1)

equilateral triangle   A triangle in which all three sides are of equal length. (Sec. 4.3)

evaluating a function   Replacing x in $f(x)$ with some value and then simplifying the numerical expression that results. (Sec. 5.5)

evaluating a variable expression   Replacing each variable by its value and then simplifying the resulting numerical expression. (Sec. 2.1)

even integer   An integer that is divisible by 2. (Sec. 4.2)

exponent   In exponential notation, the elevated number that indicates how many times the base occurs in the multiplication. (Sec. 1.4)

exponential form   The expression 2^5 is in exponential form. Compare *factored form*. (Sec. 1.4)

factor   In multiplication, a number being multiplied. (Sec. 1.2)

factor a polynomial   To write the polynomial as a product of other polynomials. (Sec. 8.1)

factor a trinomial of the form $ax^2 + bx + c$ To express the trinomial as the product of two binomials. (Sec. 8.3)

factored form   The expression $2 \cdot 2 \cdot 2 \cdot 2 \cdot 2$ is in factored form. Compare *exponential form*. (Sec. 1.4)

FOIL   A method of finding the product of two binomials; the letters stand for First, Outer, Inner, and Last. (Sec. 7.3)

formula   A literal equation that states rules about measurements. (Sec. 9.6)

function   A relation in which no two ordered pairs that have the same first coordinate have different second coordinates. (Sec. 5.5)

functional notation   A function designated by $f(x)$, which is the value of the function at x. (Sec. 5.5)

graph of a function   A graph of the ordered pairs (x, y) of the function. (Sec. 5.5)

graph of a relation   The graph of the ordered pairs that belong to the relation. (Sec. 5.5)

graph of an equation in two variables   A graph of the ordered-pair solutions of the equation. (Sec. 5.2)

graph of an integer   A heavy dot directly above that number on the number line. (Sec. 1.1)

graph of an ordered pair   The dot drawn at the coordinates of the point in the plane. (Sec. 5.1)

graphing a point in the plane   Placing a dot at the location given by the ordered pair; also called plotting a point in the plane. (Sec. 5.1)

greater than   A number a is greater than another number b, written $a > b$, if a is to the right of b on the number line. (Sec. 1.1)

greater than or equal to   The symbol $\geq$ means "is greater than or equal to." (Sec. 1.1)

greatest common factor   The greatest common factor (GCF) of two or more integers is the greatest integer that is a factor of all the integers. The greatest common factor of two or more monomials is the product of the GCF of the coefficients and the common variable factors. (Sec. 8.1)

half-plane   The solution set of an inequality in two variables. (Sec. 5.6)

hypotenuse   In a right triangle, the side opposite the 90° angle. (Sec. 10.4)

inconsistent system of equations   A system of equations that has no solution. (Sec. 6.1)

independent system of equations   A system of equations that has one solution. (Sec. 6.1)

independent variable   In a function, the variable that varies independently and whose value determines the value of the dependent variable. (Sec. 5.5)

inequality   An expression that contains the symbol $>$, $<$, $\geq$ (is greater than or equal to), or $\leq$ (is less than or equal to). (Sec. 3.3)

integers   The numbers $\ldots, -3, -2, -1, 0, 1, 2, 3, \ldots$. (Sec. 1.1)

irrational number   The decimal representation of an irrational number never repeats or terminates and can only be approximated. (Sec. 1.3, 10.1)

isosceles triangle   A triangle that has two equal angles and two equal sides. (Sec. 4.3)

least common denominator   The smallest number that is a multiple of each denominator in question. (Sec. 1.3)

least common multiple (LCM)   The LCM of two or more numbers is the smallest number that contains the prime factorization of each number. The LCM of two or more polynomials is the polynomial of least degree that contains the factors of each polynomial. (Sec. 1.3, 9.2)

legs   In a right triangle, the sides opposite the acute angles, or the two shortest sides of the triangle. (Sec. 10.4)

less than   A number a is less than another number b, written $a < b$, if a is to the left of b on the number line. (Sec. 1.1)

less than or equal to   The symbol $\leq$ means "is less than or equal to." (Sec. 1.1)

like terms Terms of a variable expression that have the same variable part. (Sec. 2.2)

linear equation in two variables An equation of the form $y = mx + b$, where m and b are constants; also called a linear function. (Sec. 5.2)

linear function An equation of the form $y = mx + b$, where m and b are constants; also called a linear equation in two variables. (Sec. 5.5)

literal equation An equation that contains more than one variable. (Sec. 9.6)

markup The difference between selling price and cost. (Sec. 4.4)

markup rate The percent of a retailer's cost that the markup represents. (Sec. 4.4)

monomial A number, a variable, or a product of numbers and variables; a polynomial of one term. (Sec. 7.1)

multiplication The process of finding the product of two numbers. (Sec. 1.2)

multiplicative inverse of a number The reciprocal of a number. (Sec. 2.2)

natural numbers The numbers 1, 2, 3, . . . (Sec. 1.1)

negative integers The numbers . . . , $-4, -3, -2, -1$. (Sec. 1.1)

negative slope A property of a line that slants downward to the right. (Sec. 5.3)

nonfactorable over the integers A polynomial that does not factor when only integers are used. (Sec. 8.1)

numerical coefficient The number part of a variable term. When the numerical coefficient is 1 or -1, the 1 is usually not written. (Sec. 2.1)

obtuse angle An angle whose measure is between 90° and 180°. (Sec. 4.3)

odd integer An integer that is not divisible by 2. (Sec. 4.2)

opposite of a polynomial The polynomial created when the sign of each term of the original polynomial is changed. (Sec. 7.1)

opposites Numbers that are the same distance from zero on the number line, but on opposite sides; also called additive inverses. (Sec. 1.1)

ordered pair A pair of numbers, such as (a, b) that can be used to identify a point in the plane determined by the axes of a rectangular coordinate system. (Sec. 5.1)

Order of Operations Agreement A set of rules that tells us in what order to perform the operations that occur in a numerical expression. (Sec. 1.4)

ordinate The second number in an ordered pair. It measures a vertical distance and is also called the second coordinate. (Sec. 5.1)

origin The point of intersection of the two coordinate axes that form a rectangular coordinate system. (Sec. 5.1)

parabola The graph of a quadratic equation in two variables. (Sec. 11.4)

parallel lines Lines that never meet; the distance between them is always the same. (Sec. 4.3)

percent Parts of 100. (Sec. 1.3)

perfect cube The cube of an integer. (Sec. 8.4)

perfect square The square of an integer. (Sec. 10.1)

perfect-square trinomial A trinomial that is a product of a binomial and itself. (Sec. 8.4)

perimeter The distance around a plane geometric figure. (Sec. 4.3)

perpendicular lines Intersecting lines that form right angles. (Sec. 4.3)

plane Flat surface determined by the intersection of two lines. (Sec. 5.1)

plotting a point in the plane Placing a dot at the location given by the ordered pair; also called graphing a point in the plane. (Sec. 5.1)

point-slope formula If (x_1, y_1) is a point on a line with slope m, then $y - y_1 = m(x - x_1)$. (Sec. 5.4)

polynomial A variable expression in which the terms are monomials. (Sec. 7.1)

positive integers The integers, 1, 2, 3, 4, ... (Sec. 1.1)

positive slope A property of a line that slants upward to the right. (Sec. 5.3)

principal square root The positive square root of a number. (Sec. 10.1)

product In multiplication, the result of multiplying two numbers. (Sec. 1.2)

proportion An equation that states the equality of two ratios or rates. (Sec. 9.5)

Pythagorean Theorem The square of the hypotenuse of a right triangle is equal to the sum of the squares of the two legs. (Sec. 10.4)

quadrant One of the four regions into which the two axes of a rectangular coordinate system divide the plane. (Sec. 5.1)

quadratic equation An equation of the form $ax^2 + bx + c = 0$, where a, b, and c are constants and a is not equal to zero; also called a second-degree equation. (Sec. 8.5, 11.1)

quadratic equation in two variables An equation of the form $y = ax^2 + bx + c$, where a is not equal to zero. (Sec. 11.4)

quadratic function A quadratic function is given by $f(x) = ax^2 + bx + c$, where a is not equal to zero. (Sec. 11.4)

radical equation An equation that contains a variable expression in a radicand. (Sec. 10.4)

radical sign The symbol $\sqrt{\ }$, which is used to indicate the positive, or principal, square root of a number. (Sec. 10.1)

radicand In a radical expression, the expression under the radical sign. (Sec. 10.1)

range The set of second coordinates of the ordered pairs in a relation. (Sec. 5.5)

rate The quotient of two quantities that have different units. (Sec. 9.5)

rate of work That part of a task that is completed in one unit of time. (Sec. 9.7)

ratio The quotient of two quantities that have the same unit. (Sec. 9.5)

rational number A number that can be written in the form a/b, where a and b are integers and b is not equal to zero. (Sec. 1.3)

rationalizing the denominator The procedure used to remove a radical from the denominator of a fraction. (Sec. 10.3)

real numbers The rational numbers and the irrational numbers. (Sec. 1.3)

reciprocal Interchanging the numerator and denominator of a rational number yields that number's reciprocal. (Sec. 2.2, 9.1)

rectangular coordinate system System formed by two number lines, one horizontal and one vertical, that intersect at the zero point of each line. (Sec. 5.1)

relation Any set of ordered pairs. (Sec. 5.5)

repeating decimal Decimal that is formed when dividing the numerator of its fractional counterpart by the denominator results in a decimal part wherein a block of digits repeats infinitely. (Sec. 1.3)

right angle An angle whose measure is 90°. (Sec. 4.3)

roster method Method of writing a set by enclosing a list of the elements in braces. (Sec. 1.1)

scatter diagram A graph of collected data as points in a coordinate system. (Sec. 5.1)

scientific notation Notation in which each number is expressed as the product of two factors, one a number between 1 and 10 and the other a power of ten. (Sec. 7.4)

second-degree equation An equation of the form $ax^2 + bx + c = 0$, where a, b, and c are constants and a is not equal to zero; also called a quadratic equation. (Sec. 11.1)

selling price The price for which a business sells a product to a customer. (Sec. 4.4)

set A collection of objects. (Sec. 1.1)

similar objects Similar objects have the same shape but not necessarily the same size. (Sec. 9.5)

simplest form of a fraction A fraction is in simplest form when there are no common factors in the numerator and the denominator. (Sec. 9.1)

slope The measure of the slant of a line. The symbol for slope is m. (Sec. 5.3)

slope-intercept form The slope-intercept form of an equation of a straight line is $y = mx + b$. (Sec. 5.3)

solution of a system of equations in two variables An ordered pair that is a solution of each equation of the system. (Sec. 6.1)

solution of an equation A number that, when substituted for the variable, results in a true equation. (Sec. 3.1)

solution of an equation in two variables An ordered pair whose coordinates make the equation a true statement. (Sec. 5.2)

solution set of an inequality A set of numbers, each element of which, when substituted for the variable, results in a true inequality. (Sec. 3.3)

solving an equation Finding a solution of the equation. (Sec. 3.1)

square root A square root of a positive number x is a number a for which $a^2 = x$. (Sec. 10.1)

standard form A quadratic equation is in standard form when the polynomial is in descending order and equal to zero. $ax^2 + bx + c = 0$ is in standard form. (Sec. 8.5, 11.1)

straight angle An angle whose measure is 180°. (Sec. 4.3)

substitution method An algebraic method of finding an exact solution of a system of equations. (Sec. 6.2)

subtraction The process of finding the difference between two numbers. (Sec. 1.2)

sum In addition, the total of two or more numbers. (Sec. 1.2)

supplementary angles Two angles whose sum is 180°. (Sec. 4.3)

system of equations Equations that are considered together. (Sec. 6.1)

terminating decimal A decimal that is formed when dividing the numerator of its fractional counterpart by the denominator results in a remainder of zero. (Sec. 1.3)

terms of a variable expression The addends of the expression. (Sec. 2.1)

transversal A line intersecting two other lines at two different points. (Sec. 4.3)

triangle A three-sided closed figure. (Sec. 4.3)

trinomial A polynomial of three terms. (Sec. 7.1)

undefined slope A property of a vertical line. (Sec. 5.3)

uniform motion   The motion of a moving object whose speed and direction do not change. (Sec. 4.7, 9.7)

variable   A letter of the alphabet used to stand for a number that is unknown or that can change. (Sec. 2.1)

variable expression   An expression that contains one or more variables. (Sec. 2.1)

variable part   In a variable term, the variable or variables and their exponents. (Sec. 2.1)

variable term   A term composed of a numerical coefficient and a variable part. (Sec. 2.1)

vertex of a parabola   The lowest point on the graph of a parabola if the parabola opens up. The highest point on the graph of a parabola if the parabola opens down. (Sec. 11.4)

vertical angles   Two angles that are on opposite sides of the intersection of two lines. (Sec. 4.3)

whole numbers   The whole numbers are 0, 1, 2, 3, ... (Sec. 1.1)

x-coordinate   The abscissa in an xy-coordinate system. (Sec. 5.1)

x-intercept   The point at which a graph crosses the x-axis. (Sec. 5.2)

y-coordinate   The ordinate in an xy-coordinate system. (Sec. 5.1)

y-intercept   The point at which a graph crosses the y-axis. (Sec. 5.2)

zero slope   A property of a horizontal line. (Sec. 5.3)

INDEX